Ninth Edition

LITERATURE
and the
WRITING PROCESS

Elizabeth McMahan
Illinois State University

Susan X Day
University of Houston

Robert Funk
Eastern Illinois University

Linda S. Coleman
Eastern Illinois University

Longman
Boston Columbus Indianapolis New York San Francisco
Upper Saddle River Amsterdam Cape Town Dubai London Madrid
Milan Munich Paris Montreal Toronto Delhi Mexico City
São Paulo Sydney Hong Kong Seoul Singapore Taipei Tokyo

Senior Editor: Vivian Garcia
Senior Supplements Editor: Donna Campion
Executive Marketing Manager: Joyce Nilsen
Production Manager: Jacqueline A. Martin
Project Coordination and Electronic Page Makeup: Elm Street Publishing Services
Cover Design Manager: Wendy Ann Fredericks
Cover Designer: Nancy Saks
Cover Image: Lake Moraine, Banff, Alberta, Canada © AlphaDoug/Alamy
Photo Researcher: Pearson Image Resource Center/Kathy Ringrose
Image Permission Coordinator: Joanne Dippel
Senior Manufacturing Buyer: Alfred C. Dorsey
Printer and Binder: Courier Corporation/Westford
Cover Printer: Phoenix Color Corporation/Hagerstown

Library of Congress Cataloging-in-Publication Data
McMahan, Elizabeth.
Literature and the writing process / Elizabeth McMahan . . . [et al.].—9th ed.
p. cm.
Previous ed.: Literature and the writing process / by Elizabeth McMahan, Susan X Day, Robert Funk. 8th ed. Pearson/Prentice, 2007.
Includes bibliographical references and index.
ISBN-13: 978-0-205-74505-0
ISBN-10: 0-205-74505-9
1. College readers. 2. English language—Rhetoric—Problems, exercises, etc. 3. Report writing—Problems, exercises, etc. 4. Literature—Collections. I. Title.
PE1417.M45 2009
808'.0427—dc22

2009021105

1 2 3 4 5 6 7 8 9 10—CEW—12 11 10 09

Longman
is an imprint of

www.pearsonhighered.com

ISBN-13: 978-0-205-74505-0
ISBN-10: 0-205-74505-9

Contents

The Art of Poetry

Anthology of Poetry 563

CASEBOOK *FENCES: Interpreting Troy Maxson* 822

Contents by Genre

Short Fiction

Poetry

Drama

Drama

Thematic Table of Contents

Rebellion and Conformity

Illusion and Reality

Drama

Love and Loss

Short Fiction

Poetry

Drama

Nature and Technology

Short Fiction

Poetry

Male and Female

Short Fiction

Poetry

Poetry

Drama

Power and Powerlessness

Short Fiction

Poetry

Drama

Comedy and Satire

Short Fiction

Poetry

Drama

Immigration and Exclusion

Short Fiction

Poetry

Drama

Preface

This book grew out of our long-standing interest in the possibilities of integrating the study of literature with the practice of composition. Many of our students have learned to write perceptively and well using literature as their subject matter. Great literature is always thought-provoking, always new. Why not utilize it to sharpen critical thinking and improve writing skills? Toward that end, we have combined an introduction to literature anthology with detailed instruction in the writing process.

Our Purpose

Literature and the Writing Process, Ninth Edition, presents literary selections as materials for students to read, analyze, and write about. Designed to guide students through the allied processes of analytical reading and argumentative writing, the text carefully integrates rhetorical instruction with the critical study of literature by showing students how to write essays about the elements involved in interpreting short stories, poems, and plays.

Our Organization

The book is divided into four main parts:

- **Part I, Composing: An Overview**, provides a thorough introduction to the composing process as it applies to writing about literature. This part contains individual chapters on prewriting, writing (drafting), writing convincing arguments, and rewriting. Part I also includes a chapter on researched writing, which offers instruction in planning, researching, and documenting a paper with secondary sources, along with an updated description of the MLA Style for citing and crediting these sources.
- **Part II, Writing About Short Fiction,** begins with a brief introduction on how to read short stories, followed by five chapters on writing about the individual elements of fiction: structure, imagery and symbolism, point of view, setting and atmosphere, and theme. Each chapter focuses on a story that clearly illustrates the literary technique to be studied. This part also contains a critical casebook on the story "Where Are You Going, Where Have You Been?" by Joyce Carol Oates, an anthology of 27 short stories, and a portfolio of six humorous and satirical stories.
- **Part III, Writing About Poetry,** begins with a brief chapter on reading poetry, followed by three chapters on writing about key elements in poetry: persona and tone, poetic language, and poetic form. These chapters focus on poems that illustrate the literary concepts under discussion. This part also contains a casebook on the prose and poetry of Langston Hughes; a color insert that contains reproductions of six

paintings with corresponding poems that respond to and comment on the art; an anthology of 160 poems; a group of twelve paired poems for comparison; a thematic portfolio of nine poems about war; and a portfolio of ten humorous and satirical poems.

- **Part IV, Writing About Drama,** begins with an introductory chapter on how to read a play, followed by three chapters on writing about structure, character, and cultural issues in drama. Each chapter focuses on a particular play, and the chapter on character is followed by a critical casebook about the protagonist of August Wilson's *Fences*. This part also contains an anthology of four classic plays and a portfolio of four humorous and satirical plays.

These four parts are supplemented by a Handbook for Correcting Errors, a concise discussion of Critical Approaches for Interpreting Literature, and a Glossary of Literary and Rhetorical Terms. We also include a Thematic Table of Contents for instructors who favor a thematic approach to literary study.

Student and Professional Writing Samples

These eleven examples of critical writing model how to analyze and argue about literature:

- The complete composing protocol that a student followed in developing her interpretation of James Joyce's "Eveline," including samples of prewriting, drafting, post-draft outlining, revising, editing, and the final draft (Chapters 1, 2, and 4).
- A new student paper illustrating the use of claims, evidence, and reasoning in arguing an interpretation of Dagoberto Gilb's "Love in L. A." (Chapter 3).
- An expanded and documented version of the student paper on "Eveline" (Chapter 5).
- A documented published article on Kate Chopin's depiction of marriage in "Désireé's Baby" (Chapter 5).
- The second and final drafts of a student paper on symbolism in Shirley Jackson's "The Lottery" (Chapter 8).
- A student response paper on persona and tone in A. E. Housman's "To an Athlete Dying Young" (Chapter 13).
- The second and final drafts of a student paper on imagery in John Donne's "A Valediction: Forbidding Mourning" (Chapter 14).
- A new student paper on form and meaning in Robert Frost's "The Silken Tent" (Chapter 15).
- A published article on the elements of poetic form in Robert Hayden's "Those Winter Sundays" (Chapter 15).
- A student paper on the gender conflict in Sophocles's *Antigone* (Chapter 17).
- A documented student paper on cultural issues in David Henry Hwang's *M. Butterfly* (Chapter 19).

New to This Edition

As always, we have been guided by the advice of our reviewers in revising this edition. In addition to updating the material in the three anthologies, we have added a new chapter on arguing an interpretation. We have also added three new thematic groupings of humorous and satiric readings. Here is a list of the major additions and changes in the ninth edition:

- "Writing a Convincing Argument" (Chapter 3), which extends the coverage of argumentative writing in Chapters 1 and 2, providing detailed instruction and numerous examples on the most effective ways to argue an interpretation of a literary selection.
- New and revised writing assignments throughout the book, which stress the importance of using argument in writing about literature.
- Three new portfolios of humorous and satiric selections, one for each literary genre.
- Improved and updated biographical headnotes for most of the authors.
- Eighteen new photographs and images chosen to provide context and background for the literary selections.
- Two additional art reproductions in the "Art of Poetry" insert.
- Questions for discussing and writing about the poems and art works in the "Art of Poetry" section.
- Two new sample student papers and a new documented published article.
- *A Raisin in the Sun* restored to the Anthology of Drama.
- New short stories by Margaret Atwood, Chinua Achebe, Rosario Morales, Daniel Orozco, and David Sedaris.
- New poems by Billy Collins, Lucille Clifton, Sharon Olds, Martín Espada, Marge Piercy, Robert Frost, George Bilgere, Edward Hirsch, Dudley Randall, Dwight Okita, W. D. Snodgrass, Craig Raine, Essex Hemphill, Jan Beatty, Jeanne Marie Beaumont, Peg Lauber, Jay Leeming, Nancy A. Henry, Ron Koertge, Peter Pereira, and U. A. Fanthorpe.
- New plays by Fernando Arrabal and Jane Martin.

Our Appreciation

We are grateful to the reviewers whose comments and suggestions helped us craft this ninth edition: Marsha Anderson, Wharton County Junior College; Abigail Bardi, Prince George's Community College; Denice Delgado, Arizona Western College; Lisa Dresdner, Norwalk Community College; Janet Henderson, Bergen County Community College; Ethan Joella, Albright College; Shannon Lawson, Pikes Peak Community College; Bill Nedrow, Triton College; Sharon Prince, Wharton County Junior College; Tracey Sherard, College of the Canyons; Jon Marc Smith, Texas State University–San Marcos; and Meri Weiss, College of New Rochelle.

Thanks also to the Pearson staff who assisted us in producing the new edition: our editor, Vivian Garcia; her editorial assistant, Heather Vomero;

and Jacqueline A. Martin, production manager. We would also like to thank Susan Nodine, project editor at Elm Street Publishing Services.

To Dan LeSeure, Brian Carter, Bill Weber, and Casey Sutherland: our undying appreciation for their inspiration, support, and comfort.

Elizabeth McMahan
Susan X Day
Robert Funk
Linda S. Coleman

LITERATURE
and the
WRITING PROCESS

Part I

Composing: An Overview

This text serves a dual purpose: to enable you to enjoy, understand, and learn from imaginative literature; and to help you to write clearly, intelligently, and correctly about what you have learned. Our instruction is designed to guide you through the interrelated processes of analytical reading and critical writing. Part I begins with the prewriting process and then shows you how to follow through to the completion of a finished essay about a literary work. In this section we also offer a separate chapter on how to use the elements of argument in writing about literature, and we conclude with detailed instruction on how to incorporate secondary sources into your writing.

The Prewriting Process

Your study of writing, as we approach it in this book, will focus on the composing process: prewriting, writing, rewriting, and editing. The first part of the text takes you through each stage, explaining one way of putting together a paper on James Joyce's "Eveline." The following parts, which include more short stories, plus poems and plays, offer further advice for understanding and writing about these various kinds of literature.

We realize, of course, that our chronological, linear (step-by-step) explanations of the writing process are not entirely true to experience; most of us juggle at least two of the steps at a time when we write. We put down half a sentence, go back and revise it, make notes of some details to include later in the essay, and then finish the sentence, perhaps crossing out and correcting a misspelled word—a combination of prewriting, writing, rewriting, and editing. We have adopted the linear, step-by-step presentation because it allows us to explain this complicated process.

Reading for Writing

To prepare for your study of the stages of writing an essay about a literary topic, find a comfortable spot and read the following short story.

James Joyce 1882–1941

James Joyce rejected his Irish Catholic heritage and left his homeland at age twenty. Though an expatriate most of his adult life, Joyce wrote almost exclusively about his native Dublin. His first book, *Dubliners* (1914), was a series of sharply drawn vignettes based on his experiences in Ireland, the homeland he later described as "a sow that eats its own farrow." His novel *Ulysses* (1933) was banned for a time in the United States because of its coarse language and frank treatment of sexuality; it is now often ranked as the greatest novel of the twentieth century.

Eveline

She sat at the window watching the evening invade the avenue. Her head was leaned against the window curtains and in her nostrils was the odour of dusty cretonne. She was tired.

Few people passed. The man out of the last house passed on his way home; she heard his footsteps clacking along the concrete pavement and afterwards crunching on the cinder path before the new red houses. One time there used to be a field there in which they used to play every evening with other people's children. Then a man from Belfast bought the field and built houses in it—not like their little brown houses but bright brick houses with shining roofs. The children of the avenue used to play together in that field—the Devines, the Waters, the Dunns, little Keogh the cripple, she and her brothers and sisters. Ernest, however, never played: he was too grown up. Her father used often to hunt them in out of the field with his blackthorn stick; but usually little Keogh used to keep nix and call out when he saw her father coming. Still they seemed to have been rather happy then. Her father was not so bad then; and besides, her mother was alive. That was a long time ago; she and her brothers and sisters were all grown up; her mother was dead. Tizzie Dunn was dead, too, and the Waters had gone back to England. Everything changes. Now she was going to go away like the others, to leave her home.

Home! She looked round the room, reviewing all its familiar objects which she had dusted once a week for so many years, wondering where on earth all the dust came from. Perhaps she would never see again those familiar objects from which she had never dreamed of being divided. And yet during all those years she had never found out the name of the priest whose yellowing photograph hung on the wall above the broken harmonium beside the coloured print of the promises made to Blessed Margaret Mary Alacoque. He had been a school friend of her father. Whenever he showed the photograph to a visitor her father used to pass it with a casual word:

"He is in Melbourne now."

5 She had consented to go away, to leave her home. Was that wise? She tried to weigh each side of the question. In her home anyway she had shelter and food; she had those whom she had known all her life about her. Of course she had to work hard, both in the house and at business. What would they say of her in the Stores when they found out that she had run away with a fellow? Say she was a fool, perhaps; and her place would be filled up by advertisement. Miss Gavan would be glad. She had always had an edge on her, especially whenever there were people listening.

"Miss Hill, don't you see these ladies are waiting?"

"Look lively, Miss Hill, please."

She would not cry many tears at leaving the Stores.

But in her new home, in a distant unknown country, it would not be like that. Then she would be married—she, Eveline. People would treat her with respect then. She would not be treated as her mother had been. Even now, though she was over nineteen, she sometimes felt herself in danger of her father's violence. She knew it was that that had given her the palpitations. When they were growing up he had never gone for her, like he used to go for Harry and Ernest, because she was a girl; but latterly he had begun to threaten her and say what he would do to her only for her dead mother's sake. And now she had nobody to

A late nineteenth-century photo of Fade Street in Dublin, which conveys a sense of the neighborhood where Eveline grew up.

protect her. Ernest was dead and Harry, who was in the church decorating business, was nearly always down somewhere in the country. Besides, the invariable squabble for money on Saturday nights had begun to weary her unspeakably. She always gave her entire wages—seven shillings—and Harry always sent up what he could but the trouble was to get any money from her father. He said she used to squander the money, that she had no head, that he wasn't going to give her his hard-earned money to throw about the streets, and much more, for he was usually fairly bad on Saturday night. In the end he would give her the money and ask her had she any intention of buying Sunday's dinner. Then she had to rush out as quickly as she could and do her marketing, holding her black leather purse tightly in her hand as she elbowed her way through the crowds and returning home late under her load of provisions. She had hard work to keep the house together and to see that the two young children who had been left to her charge went to school regularly and got their meals regularly. It was hard work— a hard life—but now that she was about to leave it she did not find it a wholly undesirable life.

She was about to explore another life with Frank. Frank was very kind, manly, 10
open-hearted. She was to go away with him by the night-boat to be his wife and to live with him in Buenos Ayres where he had a home waiting for her. How well she remembered the first time she had seen him; he was lodging in a house on the main road where she used to visit. It seemed a few weeks ago. He was standing at the gate, his peaked cap pushed back on his head and his hair tumbled forward over a face of bronze. Then they had come to know each other. He used to

meet her outside the Stores every evening and see her home. He took her to see *The Bohemian Girl* and she felt elated as she sat in an unaccustomed part of the theatre with him. He was awfully fond of music and sang a little. People knew that they were courting and, when he sang about the lass that loves a sailor, she always felt pleasantly confused. He used to call her Poppens out of fun. First of all it had been an excitement for her to have a fellow and then she had begun to like him. He had tales of distant countries. He had started as a deck boy at a pound a month on a ship of the Allan Line going out to Canada. He told her the names of the ships he had been on and the names of the different services. He had sailed through the Straits of Magellan and he told her stories of the terrible Patagonians. He had fallen on his feet in Buenos Ayres, he said, and had come over to the old country just for a holiday. Of course, her father had found out the affair and had forbidden her to have anything to say to him.

"I know these sailor chaps," he said.

One day he had quarrelled with Frank and after that she had to meet her lover secretly.

The evening deepened in the avenue. The white of two letters in her lap grew indistinct. One was to Harry; the other was to her father. Ernest had been her favourite but she liked Harry too. Her father was becoming old lately, she noticed; he would miss her. Sometimes he could be very nice. Not long before, when she had been laid up for a day, he had read her out a ghost story and made toast for her at the fire. Another day, when their mother was alive, they had all gone for a picnic to the Hill of Howth. She remembered her father putting on her mother's bonnet to make the children laugh.

Her time was running out but she continued to sit by the window, leaning her head against the window curtain, inhaling the odour of dusty cretonne. Down far in the avenue she could hear a street organ playing. She knew the air. Strange that it should come that very night to remind her of the promise to her mother, her promise to keep the home together as long as she could. She remembered the last night of her mother's illness; she was again in the close dark room at the other side of the hall and outside she heard a melancholy air of Italy. The organ-player had been ordered to go away and given sixpence. She remembered her father strutting back into the sickroom saying:

"Damned Italians! coming over here!"

As she mused the pitiful vision of her mother's life laid its spell on the very quick of her being—that life of commonplace sacrifices closing in final craziness. She trembled as she heard again her mother's voice saying constantly with foolish insistence:

"Derevaun Seraun! Derevaun Seraun!"[1]

She stood up in a sudden impulse of terror. Escape! She must escape! Frank would save her. He would give her life, perhaps love, too. But she wanted to live. Why should she be unhappy? She had a right to happiness. Frank would take her in his arms, fold her in his arms. He would save her.

She stood among the swaying crowd in the station at the North Wall. He held her hand and she knew that he was speaking to her, saying something about the passage over and over again. The station was full of soldiers with brown baggages. Through the wide doors of the sheds she caught a glimpse of the black

[1]"The end of pleasure is pain!"

mass of the boat, lying in beside the quay wall, with illumined portholes. She answered nothing. She felt her cheek pale and cold and, out of a maze of distress, she prayed to God to direct her, to show her what was her duty. The boat blew a long mournful whistle into the mist. If she went, tomorrow she would be on the sea with Frank, steaming towards Buenos Ayres. This passage had been booked. Could she still draw back after all he had done for her? Her distress awoke a nausea in her body and she kept moving her lips in silent fervent prayer.

A bell clanged upon her heart. She felt him seize her hand:

"Come!"

All the seas of the world tumbled about her heart. He was drawing her into them: he would drown her. She gripped with both hands at the iron railing.

"Come!"

No! No! No! It was impossible. Her hands clutched the iron in frenzy. Amid the seas she sent a cry of anguish.

"Eveline! Evvy!"

He rushed beyond the barrier and called to her to follow. He was shouted at to go on but he still called to her. She set her white face to him, passive, like a helpless animal. Her eyes gave him no sign of love or farewell or recognition.

(1914)

Now that your reading of Joyce's story has given you material to mull over, you should consider some questions that good writers think about as they prepare to write. Granted, experienced writers might go over some of these ***prewriting*** matters almost unconsciously—and perhaps *as* they write instead of before. But in order to explain how to get the process going for you, we will present these considerations one by one.

Who Are My Readers?

Unless you are writing a journal or a diary for your own satisfaction, your writing always has an ***audience***—the person or group of people who will read it. You need to keep this audience in mind as you plan what to say and as you choose the best way to express your ideas.

Analyze the Audience

No doubt you already have considerable audience awareness. You would never write a job application letter using the latest in-group slang, nor would you normally correspond with your dear Aunt Minnie in impersonal formal English. Writing for diverse groups about whom you know little is more difficult than writing for a specific audience whom you know well. In this class, for instance, you will be writing for your fellow students and for your instructor, a mixed group sorted together by a computer registration system. Although they are diverse, they do share some characteristics. For one thing, when you begin to write a paper about "Eveline," you know that your audience has read the story; thus, you need not summarize the plot. Also, the people in your audience are college-educated (or becoming so); therefore, you need not avoid difficult words like *epitome*, *eclectic*, or *protean* if they are the appropriate choices. Other shared qualities will become apparent as you get to know your classmates and your instructor.

Prewriting Exercise

Compose a brief letter persuading Eveline that she should (or should not) leave Frank. Your argumentative tactics, your attitude, and even your word choice must be affected by what you know about Eveline from reading the story—her essential timidity, her insecurity, her self-doubt, her capacity for self-deception. Take all this into account as you present your argument for or against leaving Frank.

Then, write briefly to her bullying father explaining to him why his dutiful daughter has deserted him (assuming she has gone).

Finally, write Frank a short letter explaining why Eveline will not be going away with him (assuming she stays in Dublin).

Be prepared to discuss with the class specific ways in which your letters are different when you change your audience. Read at least one other student's letters to see how another writer handled the tasks.

Why Am I Writing?

Every kind of writing, even a grocery list, has a purpose. You seldom sit down to write without some aim in mind, and this purpose affects your whole approach to writing. The immediate response to the question "Why am I writing?" may be that your teacher or your employer asked you to. But that answer will not help you understand the reasons that make writing worth doing—and worth reading.

Reasons for Writing

Sometimes you may write in order *to express* your own feelings, as in a diary or a love letter. More frequently, though, you will be writing for several other people, and the response you want from these prospective readers will determine your purpose. If, for instance, you want your audience to be amused by your writing (as in an informal essay or friendly letter), your purpose is *to entertain*. If you want your readers to gain some knowledge from your writing (say, how to get to your house from the airport), then you are writing *to inform*. If you want your readers to agree with an opinion or to accept an idea (as in a letter to the editor or an advertisement), then you are writing *to persuade*. Of course, these aims overlap—as do most things in the writing process—but usually one purpose predominates.

Most of your writing in this course, as in real life, will be an argument one way or another. Your purpose is often to convince your reader to agree with the points you are making. Logical ideas set down in clear, interesting writing should prove convincing and keep your readers reading.

Prewriting Exercise

In writing the three letters to various characters, you have already noticed how audience and purpose can change the way you think and write about "Eveline." After studying the four writing suggestions that follow, reread the story. You may discover that you have more ideas and feelings about it than you first imagined. Thinking about prospective readers and determining your purpose will help you understand your own views and reactions better.

1. If your purpose is *to express* your personal response:
   Write down your feelings about Eveline in a journal entry or in a brief note to a close friend. Do you sympathize with Eveline? Pity her? Does she irritate you or make you angry? Be as forthright as you can.
2. If your purpose is *to inform* someone else:
   Write a brief summary (less than one hundred words) of "Eveline" for a fellow student who wants to know if the story is worth reading.
   Write a slightly longer summary for your instructor (or someone else who has read the story) who wants to know if you have grasped its important points.
   Which summary was easier to write? What purposes besides providing information were involved in each summary?
3. If your purpose is *to entertain* yourself or your readers:
   How would you rewrite the ending of "Eveline" to make it more positive or romantic—to make it appeal to a wider audience? Would such an ending be consistent with the earlier parts of the story? Would it be true to human experience?
4. If your purpose is *to persuade* your readers:
   The author tells us that Eveline held two letters in her lap, but we do not know their contents. Write your version of one of them. Try to construe from evidence in the story what Eveline would have said to convince her father or her brother that she had good reasons for going away with Frank. How would she persuade them to forgive her? Consider also what other purposes Eveline would try to achieve in each of these letters.

What Ideas Should I Use?

Understanding literature involves learning what questions to ask yourself as you read. To deepen your comprehension and develop ideas for writing, you need to examine the work carefully and think critically about its component parts.

Reading and Thinking Critically

Critical reading and thinking involves several overlapping procedures: analysis, inference, synthesis, and evaluation. The word *critical* does not mean "disapproving" or "faultfinding" in this context; it means thorough, thoughtful, inquisitive, and logically demanding. As a critical reader you want to discover meanings and relationships that you might otherwise miss in uncritical, superficial reading.

- *Analysis* involves examining the parts or elements of a work, the better to understand it.
- *Inference* entails drawing conclusions about a work based on your analysis. When you infer, you explore the implications of various elements (such as plot, characterization, structure, tone) and interpret their meaning.
- *Synthesis* is the process of putting your analysis and inferences together into a new, more informed understanding of the work. You create this new understanding by making connections, identifying patterns, and drawing conclusions.
- *Evaluation* means defending the judgments you have made about a work's meaning, significance, or quality.

Chapters 6, 12, and 16—"How Do I Read Short Fiction?" "How Do I Read Poetry?" and "How Do I Read a Play?"—provide specific suggestions and questions to guide you in analyzing, making inferences, synthesizing, and evaluating literary works. Here are some suggestions and questions from those chapters, along with their critical reading basis.

Example of Questions Inviting Analysis
What is the central conflict of the play? Does the play contain any secondary conflicts (subplots)? How do they relate to the main conflict?

Example of Questions That Require Inferences
Who is the main character? Does this person's character change during the course of the story? Do you feel sympathetic toward the main character? What sort of person is she or he?

Example of Questions Involving Synthesis
What is the theme (the central idea) of this poem? Can you state it in a single sentence?

Example of Evaluation Questions
Which of the poems conveys the horrors of war most effectively? Why?

Discovering and Developing Ideas

You read critically to derive meaning from a work, and you continue to think critically as you go about discovering ideas to write about. This discovery process, called ***invention***, is more effective if you employ one of the following techniques designed to help you analyze literary works and generate ideas about them.

Self-Questioning

These are the kinds of questions you might ask yourself when studying a work of literature: questions about characters, their circumstances, their motives and conflicts, their fears and expectations, their relations with other characters; questions about the setting in which the story takes place; questions about any repeated details that seem significant; questions about the meaning and value of actions and events. Write out your responses to these questions about "Eveline" and keep them handy as you formulate your essay.

1. What is Eveline's home life like?
2. How does she expect her new life to be different?
3. Do you think this expectation is realistic?
4. Why is the word *dust* mentioned so often?
5. List all the concrete details you can find that describe Eveline's home.
6. How old is Eveline? Is her age important for any reason?
7. What sort of person is her father? What kind of "bad way" is he in on Saturday nights?
8. How does Eveline feel about her father?
9. What sort of person was Eveline's mother? What happened to her? Does Eveline identify with her mother in any way?
10. How does Eveline feel about her dead mother?
11. What do you think her mother meant when she kept repeating "the end of pleasure is pain"? Why would she say this? Was she really crazy—or only worn down?
12. What does Eveline's father mean when he tells her, "I know these sailor chaps"? What possible reasons could he have for trying to break up Eveline's romance?
13. What sort of person is Frank? What does Eveline actually know about him?
14. Has Eveline romanticized Frank in any way? Is her father's objection to him perhaps justified?
15. What is Eveline's duty to her father? What promise did she make to her dying mother?
16. What is her duty to herself? Does she really believe she has a "right to happiness"? Why or why not?
17. How does Eveline feel about leaving her brother?
18. In what ways is Eveline "like a helpless animal"? What is she afraid of?
19. Why do you think her eyes give Frank "no sign of love or farewell or recognition"?
20. Do you think Eveline made the right decision? Why or why not?

During the invention stage, you want to turn up as many ideas as possible. Later, after choosing a focus for your paper, such as characterization or theme, you will select those story details that you will be discussing when developing your argument. Even though you narrow your focus, you still need to consider other elements of the story—imagery, symbolism, setting, point of view—as these elements serve to reveal character or theme.

Directed Freewriting

Many people find that they can best bring ideas to the surface by writing freely, with no restrictions about correctness. When you engage in ***freewriting*** in order to "free" ideas from your subconscious mind, you should think of a pertinent question and just start writing.

Consider this question: "Why does Eveline stay with her abusive father?" As you think, start writing. Set down everything that comes to mind; do not concern yourself with spelling, word choice, or punctuation. You are writing for your own benefit, attempting to discover everything about Eveline's decision that you have in mind after reading and thinking about the story.

After writing for ten minutes (or after you run out of ideas), stop and read over what you have said. Underline any idea that might serve as the focus for a paper. Put stars or asterisks in the margin beside any ideas that sound useful as support for your interpretation. Figure 1-1 provides an example of freewriting turned out by a student on this same question.

If you find freewriting a good method for generating ideas, you may want to go through the process again. This time write down a statement that you underlined in your first freewriting as a possible approach for your paper. Let's say you decide to focus (as our student did) on the idea that Eveline's sense of insecurity causes her to remain with her father. Put that sentence at the top of a fresh sheet of paper and begin writing. Continue recording your thoughts until you either run out of ideas or run out of time (fifteen minutes is usually enough). Then read over your freewriting, underlining or putting stars by any ideas that you think would be good support to include in your paper.

Problem Solving

Another method of generating material for a paper involves *problem solving*. Consider some part of the work that you feel you need to understand better and pose yourself a problem, like the following:

> Explain the ending of the story so that it is understandable and believable.

As you seek a solution, ask yourself more questions.

- Why does Eveline refuse to leave her pinched, narrow life with her father and the younger children?
- Is there anything about the way she was brought up that makes this action seem reasonable, perhaps inevitable?
- Would her life have been different if she had been born male instead of female? What happened to her brothers, for instance?
- Does her religion have any bearing on her decision?

Write down all the reasons you can find to help explain why Eveline does not leave home. Do any of these reasons shed light on the overall meaning of the story? Do you now perhaps see a meaningful point you could develop into an essay?

Clustering

Another useful way of getting ideas out of your head and down on paper involves *clustering*. Begin with a blank sheet of paper. In the center, write a crucial question about the story that you want to investigate, and circle the words. Then, draw a line out from that circle, write an idea or a question related to the central idea, and circle that.

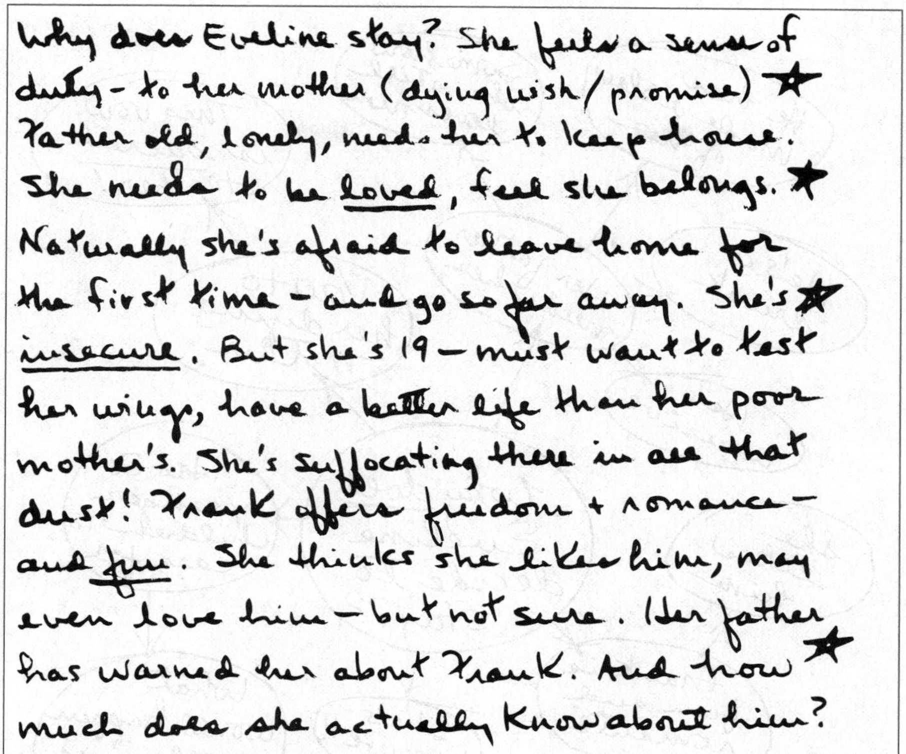

Why does Eveline stay? She feels a sense of
duty – to her mother (dying wish/promise) ★
Father old, lonely, needs her to keep house.
She needs to be <u>loved</u>, feel she belongs. ★
Naturally she's afraid to leave home for
the first time – and go so far away. She's ★
<u>insecure</u>. But she's 19 — must want to test
her wings, have a better life than her poor
mother's. She's suffocating there in all that
dust! Frank offers freedom + romance –
and <u>fun</u>. She thinks she likes him, may
even love him – but not sure. Her father
has warned her about Frank. And how ★
much does she actually know about him?
What if he's all promises, promises — and
then deserts her halfway around the world?
Maybe her father's right! How does she ★
feel about her parents? She knows her
mother's life was miserable + she died a
pitiful death. She fears her father (who ★
must have caused a lot of her mom's misery
+ hardship) But E. <u>has a strong sense of duty</u>.
And does love her father, despite his faults.

Figure 1-1 Directed Freewriting

Spiraling out from that circle, add and circle any further associations that you can make. Continue drawing lines from the center, like spokes radiating from a wheel, and record any other ideas or questions that are related. When you finish, you will have a cluster of related

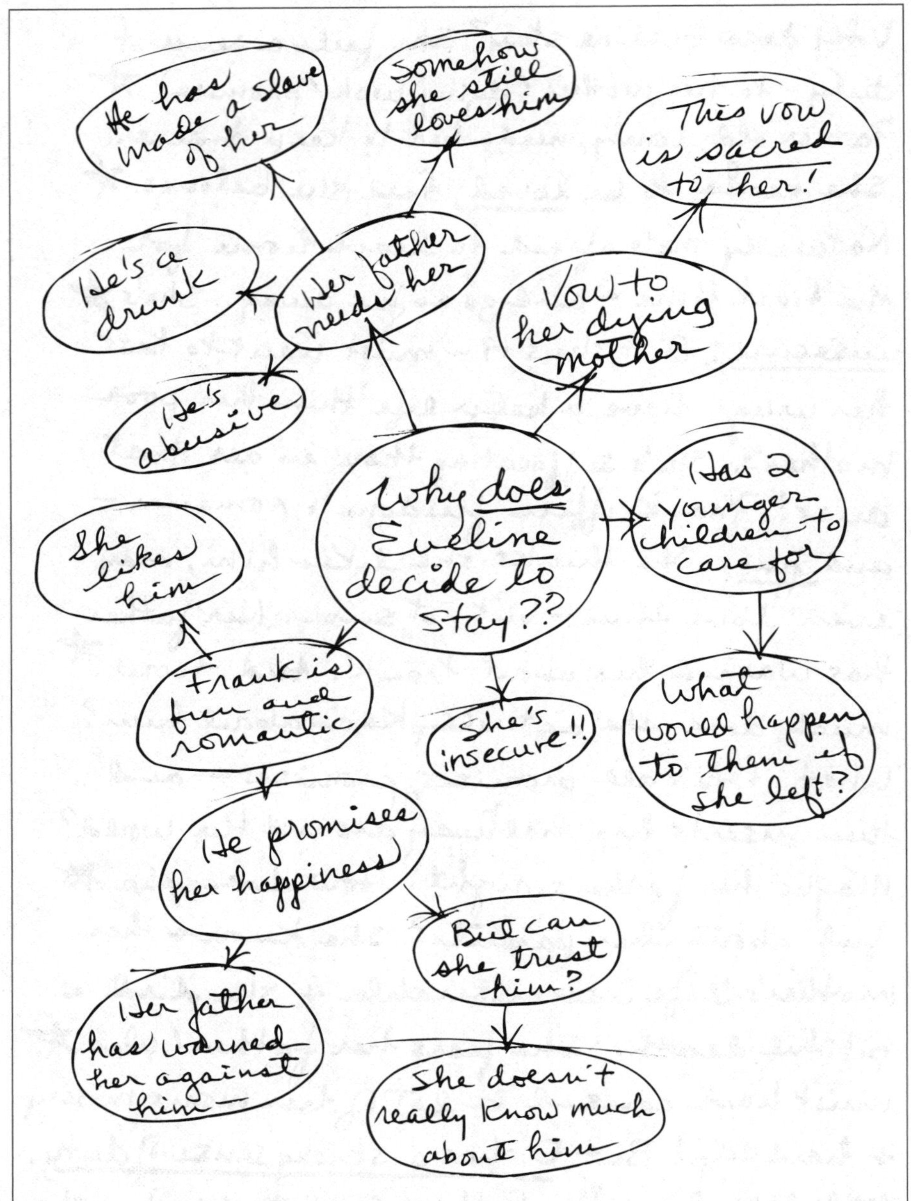

Figure 1-2 Clustering

ideas resembling Figure 1-2, which explores the question "Why does Eveline decide to stay with her father?"

Clustering works just fine with statements, as well as with questions. If you think you might want to write a paper focusing on the characterization of Eveline, you could just write her name in the center of the page and begin recording all that you know about her. Your first ring of circles might include father, mother, siblings, house, church, job, Frank, lifestyle, personality—and spiral out from there.

You can see that this technique works well for exploring any aspect of a work. As you progress through this course, you may decide to write in the middle of the page *point of view*, *setting*, *imagery*, or whatever element you think might serve as a meaningful focus for your paper.

What Point Should I Make?

Besides providing a thorough understanding of the story, these prewriting activities serve to stir up ideas for a *thesis*—the controlling idea for your paper—and to help you discover evidence to support convincingly the observations you will make in developing that thesis.

Relate a Part to the Whole

One bit of advice that will help you write meaningful literary papers is the following:

> Devise a thesis that makes its point by relating some aspect of the work to the meaning of the whole—that is, to its theme.

Our questions so far have led you to approach Joyce's story by analyzing character and plot. But writing a simple character sketch (in which you discuss what sort of person Eveline is) would not produce a satisfactory critical paper. You need to go beyond that one-dimensional approach and make your essay say something about the story itself. In short, you must argue that your analysis of her character relates to the theme.

How Do I Find the Theme?

You may have learned that the ***theme*** of a work is the moral. In a sense that is true, but a moral suggests a neatly stated, preachy comment on some vice or virtue, whereas a literary theme will seldom be so pat and should never sound preachy. In order to discover theme you need to decide what you have learned from reading the story. What did the author reveal about the behavior of human beings, about the conduct of society? Rather than looking for a moral, look for some insight into the human condition.

Sometimes you may have a theme in mind but be unable to express it except in a cliché. You could, for instance, see the theme of "Eveline" as an acceptance of the old adage "Better the devil you know than the devil you don't." Although this idea is acceptable as a theme, a clearer statement would relate the concept more closely to the story, as follows:

> In "Eveline," Joyce focuses on the painful choices a young woman faces concerning her desire for a better life, her duty to her family, and her fear of leaving home.

Certainly her character—the kind of person she is—relates directly to this theme. If, for instance, Eveline had been a willful, disobedient child who grew up into a rebellious, irresponsible young woman, the outcome of the story would surely be different.

The problem is thus to find a thesis that will allow you to argue that Eveline's upbringing has conditioned her for the inevitable failure of nerve, the return to servitude and security, the relinquishing of hopes and dreams.

Stating the Thesis

A good thesis statement should be a *complete sentence* that clearly conveys the point you plan to support in your argument. Notice the difference between a *topic*, which is not a complete sentence, and a ***thesis***, which is.

Topic A characterization of Eveline

Thesis Joyce's characterization of Eveline as a dutiful daughter enables us to discover why she makes her strange decision at the end.

Topic The role of the church in "Eveline"

Thesis The role of the Catholic church is crucial in shaping Eveline's personality and in helping us understand why she sacrifices herself for her family.

Topic Dust as a symbol in "Eveline"

Thesis Joyce's use of dust as a controlling symbol in "Eveline" reinforces our understanding of this young woman's dreary, suffocating, arid life.

Your thesis sentence should be broad enough to include all the ideas that are necessary as evidence but narrow enough to make a precise statement of your main point and focus your thoughts. If your thesis is too broad—as, for example, "Joyce's characterization of Eveline is extremely well drawn"—you may end up skimming the surface, never providing a meaningful interpretation of the work. A thesis evaluating the excellence of Joyce's character development needs to connect this point with the whole story. Notice that the previous overly broad thesis is unsatisfactory for another reason: it fails to make a real point.

A better thesis for a paper on "Eveline" might be stated in any of the following ways:

Eveline's Catholic upbringing as a dutiful daughter makes impossible her hopes for a happier life.

If Eveline had been born male instead of female, she might have escaped her unhappy home life, as her brother did.

Eveline, "trapped like a helpless animal" by her promise to her dying mother, is morally unable to break her vow and flee her miserable home to seek a new life for herself.

Having been thoroughly beaten down by her brutal, domineering father, Eveline lacks the self-confidence to flee in search of her own life.

Most of the ideas and details you need to support any of these thesis statements will appear in the freewriting or clustering that you have already completed. In the next chapter, we will suggest some ways in which you might arrange this material in the paper itself.

2

The Writing Process

Now that you have examined your reactions to "Eveline," collected your ideas, and formulated a thesis sentence, you are ready to organize this material into a workable arrangement for writing.

How Should I Organize My Ideas?

A traditional but effective format includes three parts: the beginning (the introduction), the middle (the body), and the end (the conclusion). This simple plan will serve for almost any piece of writing.

The *beginning* of the paper has two main functions: to engage your readers' interest and to let them know what point you expect to make. The *middle* portion of your paper develops and supports the main point with details, examples, reasons, and explanations that make the general thesis more specific and more understandable. The *end* of the paper returns your readers to the main point by spotlighting the general idea you want them to accept after reading your essay. Later in the chapter, we will offer you more specific suggestions about how to begin and end a paper effectively. For now, we want to wrestle with the problem of organizing the body—or the middle part—of your paper about "Eveline."

Arguing Your Interpretation

If you want your readers to accept your interpretation of "Eveline," you have to convince them that your point of view is valid. In other words, an interpretation is an argument, and you can organize your essay according to the standard features of argumentative writing.

The Elements of Good Argument

Claims, evidence, reasoning, and *refutation* are the building blocks of effective ***argument***; you need to understand and use them in order to write persuasively. Knowing how these elements work together will also help you organize your thoughts more effectively.

Claims The "engine" that propels any argument is its *claim*. In various kinds of writing, claims are also called propositions, premises, conclusions, hypotheses, or recommendations. In literary criticism, a claim is usually called a *thesis*, the term we use in this book. The sample thesis "Eveline lacks courage to flee from her domineering father and to seek her own happiness" makes a claim about the title character; it also implies that explaining her behavior is a meaningful way to interpret the story as a whole. The primary claim is usually broken down into several secondary claims, or *topic sentences*, that justify and explain the main thesis.

Evidence Evidence tells your readers how you arrived at your interpretation and shows them what your claims are based on. Most of the evidence in literary argument will come from within the reading—details and examples from the work itself. In some cases, evidence can come from your own experience; for example, your observation that people often fear the unknown might support an analysis of Eveline's motivation. Some of your evidence may also come from outside the text; for example, you might use information about the situation of Catholic working-class women in Ireland in the early 1900s and connect it to Eveline's decisions.

Reasoning The thinking process you use to connect the evidence to your claims is called *reasoning*. Sometimes the point or validity of the evidence is obvious, but more often than not you need to explain how you arrived at your interpretation. For example, you can identify words and phrases from the story that indicate Eveline is afraid of her father, but you probably should explain how you arrived at that conclusion and why you think this fear could extend to all men, including Frank. This way, your reader can share your line of reasoning.

Refutation Arguments always assume that other points of view are possible. In literary criticism, the case for your interpretation will be strengthened if you treat other possible readings with respect and understanding. Acknowledging and responding to these other views is called *refutation*. There is no best place to refute opposing opinions. Sometimes you will want to bring up other interpretations early and deal with them right away. Another approach is to anticipate objections as you argue your own interpretation point by point. Many writers add a refutation section after they have presented the evidence and reasoning on their own side. Wherever you include the refutation, your goal is to show why other interpretations are faulty or inaccurate or limited. Often, you will be able to present contrasting evidence or alternate reasoning to reveal both the weakness of another view and the strength of your own position.

Building an Effective Argument

Presenting a conventional argument involves five tasks.

1. Introduce the subject you are going to write about—for example, Eveline's decision not to go with Frank—and supply some context for your approach.
2. State your main point or thesis. This is your *claim.*
3. Provide *evidence* and *reasoning* to support your claims. This will be the longest part of your argument; each secondary claim will probably take a paragraph or more to develop.
4. Respond to opposing viewpoints. This is called the *refutation.*
5. Sum up your argument by reminding your readers of your thesis and the strength of your evidence.

Writers often alter this conventional order of tasks, especially steps 3 and 4. For example, in the sample student essay at the end of Chapter 4, the author considers several possible answers to her thesis question before presenting her main claim in the last two paragraphs. In other words, the writer rejects, or refutes, other interpretations before advancing her own.

Following are two brief plans for a literary argument based on one of our sample thesis statements. The first plan states the thesis, or claim, and indicates the subpoints that will become topic sentences for several paragraphs of development and support.

1. *Beginning:* Eveline lacks courage to flee from her domineering father and to seek her own happiness.
2. *Middle:* Evidence of Eveline's lack of courage can be seen in the following:
   —her passivity as a female who lacks the resources and imagination to challenge her traditional role
   —her physical fear of her father, perhaps generalized to all men
   —her reverence for her mother's memory and the promise she made to keep the family together
3. *End:* Eveline exemplifies how a woman may be trapped by passivity, fear, and obligations.

The second plan organizes the middle of an argument on the same thesis by stating the topic sentences as fears that contribute to Eveline's lack of courage. These topic sentences act as secondary claims that support and explain the main interpretation.

2. *Middle:* Eveline's lack of courage is illustrated in these ways:
   —She is afraid to go against her religious beliefs.
   —She is afraid something will happen to her father if she leaves him.
   —She is afraid her mother's memory will continue to haunt her.
   —She is afraid Frank will treat her as her father treated her mother.

By writing out the subpoints, you provide yourself with a plan to follow in writing the paragraphs that will make up the main part (the body) of your essay. Chart 2-1 offers a checklist for arguing an interpretation.

Arranging the Ideas

As you write the middle section of your argument, you will have to decide which point to take up first and which ones to use later in the development of your main claim. Ordinarily, you can arrange your secondary claims in two ways: logical order or chronological order.

Logical order involves arranging ideas in a way that will appeal to your readers' intelligence and good sense. Many writers begin with a less crucial idea and work up to their most important one. The logic behind this arrangement is based on the assumption that since your final point is the one your readers are most likely to remember, it should also be your strongest point.

In the second plan for writing just presented to you for a paper on "Eveline," the topic sentences about fears are arranged according to the increasing strength of Eveline's feelings. The plan starts with a general point about religion, moves to more specific fears about leaving her father and remembering her mother, and concludes with an insight into what could happen in her life with Frank. The last idea is particularly appropriate, because it sums up the previous two points by relating Eveline's anxiety about Frank to her feelings about her parents' relationship.

Chronological order, which is based on time, involves writing about events in the order in which they occur. Most narratives, such as short stories and novels, use a chronological approach. Because you will be

Chart 2-1 Checklist for Arguing an Interpretation

1. Make sure your interpretation is reasonable and consistent.
2. Express your interpretation in a clear thesis statement.
3. Write an introduction that states your thesis and indicates briefly how you intend to support it.
4. Place the key claims of your argument in topic sentences.
5. Present your claims in a clearly defined, logical order.
6. Provide plenty of specific evidence to back up your interpretive claims.
7. Make explicit the links between your interpretation and the evidence you provide.
8. Avoid getting bogged down in mere summary.
9. Anticipate objections to your interpretation and address them in your paper.
10. Write a conclusion that recaps your argument and highlights the significance of your interpretation.

writing about literature, your organization for a paper could simply follow the chronology of the work under consideration. If you do this, be sure that your essay clearly reflects a critical thinking process, or your paper will seem like a mere plot summary.

Developing with Details

The balance between your interpretive points and the details you use to support them is critical. If your argument goes too far in the interpretive direction, it sounds too abstract, personal, and unconvincing. If it goes too far in listing details, it seems as though you are summarizing the work rather than analyzing it. Let us look further into maintaining an effective balance.

Within your argument, you will make several critical generalizations relating to your main point. These are the topic sentences that bolster the thesis. Remember to state each generalization clearly and to support each one with enough specific references to the story to be convincing. Sort through the observations that you made in your prewriting, and select those that relate to the topic sentences in your plan. The following example shows how a writer uses specific details and brief quotations from the story to develop the idea stated in the topic sentence:

> Eveline lacks courage to seek a life of her own because she fears that her father will not be able to cope if she leaves him. Her anxiety is heightened as she recalls that she and her brothers and sisters are grown up and that her mother is dead. If she leaves, her father will be all alone. She realizes that he is "usually fairly bad on a Saturday night" and recognizes that his drinking problem will not get any better after she leaves. Also she has noticed that "Her father was becoming old lately" and she assumes that "he would miss her." As a dutiful daughter, Eveline seems to feel that going away with Frank means abandoning her aging father, and that may be why she has written a letter to him—to ease the blow of her departure and to soothe her own conscience.

Questions for Consideration

In the preceding example, is there adequate support for the topic sentence? What story details has the writer cited to develop the main point? What other details could be used? Where does the writer bring in personal opinion or interpretation? Do you think the interpretation is reasonable?

Maintaining a Critical Focus

The placement of your analytical content affects how a reader perceives your argument. Even with a solid interpretation, your paper could still sound like a plot summary if you imbed your critical insights in the middle of paragraphs. In order to achieve a sharp critical focus, the topic sentences (usually the first one of each paragraph in the body of the paper) should be critical observations supporting or relating to your thesis. In academic writing, placing the topic sentences at the beginnings of paragraphs helps your instructor to follow your thinking. You should, in each paragraph, use the plot details to support or prove the critical generalization in the topic sentence.

Distinguishing Critical Comments from Plot Details

The difference between a critical comment and a plot detail or poetry detail is illustrated in these sample sentences:

Plot detail	Jackson's story opens on a balmy summer day.
Critical comment	By setting her story on a balmy summer day, Jackson creates a false sense of well-being.
Plot detail	"Seventeen Syllables" begins with a communication problem between the teenager Rosie and her mother.
Critical comment	The first scene, a communication breakdown between the teenager Rosie and her mother, introduces the conflict between first- and second-generation immigrants to the United States.
Poetry detail	In Brooks's poem "Sadie and Maud," Sadie's life is described more fully than Maud's.
Critical comment	Brooks describes Sadie's life more fully than Maud's, suggesting that Sadie lived more fully.

(Notice that authors can be referred to by their last names: "Jackson" is Shirley Jackson and "Brooks" is Gwendolyn Brooks.)

Plot detail	Larry eventually identifies with his father in "My Oedipus Complex."
Critical comment	Larry provides a humorous model of Freud's developmental theory.
Combined	Larry's final identification with his father resolves his Oedipus complex in a humorous rendering of Freud's developmental theory.

How Should I Begin?

Your introduction is crucial to the effectiveness of your essay—and often proves to be the most difficult to write. Try to think of this part as challenging (rather than merely hard to do), and you may find yourself rising to new heights of accomplishment.

Postpone If Nothing Comes

Remember that you do not have to write your introduction first just because it appears first in the finished essay. As long as you have your thesis clearly in mind (or clearly written out on your planning sheet), you can start right in on the body of the paper. Once you begin generating material, you may suddenly perceive an idea that will serve nicely as a beginning. Or if you postpone your introduction until the next day, your subconscious mind may provide you with the perfect opening. You may find that some of your best ideas come to you in the shower.

Write an Appealing Opening

Work especially hard on your opening sentence. You want to engage the interest of your readers immediately. If you begin like this,

> "Eveline" is a very interesting short story by James Joyce.

no one other than your loving mother is likely to read any further unless paid to. You should mention the author and title somewhere in your introduction (even though both may appear in your title). But try also to incorporate something specific in that first sentence. You might want to focus your readers' attention on an incident that you consider significant.

> In his short story "Eveline," James Joyce portrays a young woman paralyzed by the need to make a decision that will change the course of her life.

Or you could start this way:

> In James Joyce's "Eveline," we see a tired young woman accustomed to the "odour of dusty cretonne" trying to muster courage to exchange her dreary existence for the unknown excitements of life with a "sailor chap" in exotic Buenos Ayres.

Or you might try this:

> In the closing lines of James Joyce's "Eveline," the young woman of the title stands "passive, like a helpless animal," watching her dreams of romance and excitement fade into the mist.

State the Thesis

Even more important than an arresting opening sentence is the need to let your readers know somewhere in the introductory paragraph what the paper is going to be about. But try to avoid stating your main point too bluntly.

> I am going to show that Eveline stays home with her domineering father because she lacks courage to go with Frank.

Beginning the thesis with "I am going to show" is stylistically ineffective because that part is understood—any thesis at all could begin with those words. They waste the first few words of the sentence, words that should be full of meaning. Instead, describe the direction of your thought, the case that you will present within your essay, using vivid language. Your thesis should sound more like this:

> Having been thoroughly beaten down by her brutal, domineering father, Eveline lacks the courage to go with Frank in search of her own happiness.

That sentence includes some psychologically powerful words—*beaten down*, *brutal*, *domineering*, *courage*, and *happiness*—which invite a reader to continue.

If you combine your thesis with a general statement about the story, you should produce a worthwhile introduction for a short paper.

> In James Joyce's "Eveline," we see a tired young woman accustomed to the "odour of dusty cretonne" trying to muster courage to exchange her dreary existence for the unknown excitements of life with a "sailor chap" in exotic Buenos Ayres. But having been thoroughly beaten down by her brutal father, Eveline lacks the courage to go with Frank in search of her own happiness.

How Should I End?

Your conclusion is just as important as your introduction—perhaps even more so. You want to leave your readers feeling satisfied that you have written something worth reading, that their time has not been wasted. Do not give them a chance to ask, "Well, so what?" at the end.

Relate the Discussion to Theme

Impress your readers with the value of your discussion by reinforcing in the conclusion how your analysis illuminates the theme, or meaning, of the work. This process may involve echoing your thesis statement from the introduction. But take care to avoid simply repeating what you said at the beginning. Your conclusion should offer a clear expression of how your discussion relates to the theme of the story.

Postpone or Write Ahead

Conclusions, like introductions, do not necessarily have to be written when you come to them. If you should get some additional insight concerning the theme as you work on composing the main part of the paper, take a minute to jot down the idea so that you can later incorporate this insight into your ending. Or you could stop right then, write the final paragraph, and put it aside until you come to it. Chances are that you may change this conclusion later, but having something to work with is an enormous help—especially if you are getting tired.

Write an Emphatic Final Sentence

No matter how exhausted you are when you compose your final paragraph, do not risk ruining the effect of your entire essay by letting your conclusion trail off at the end with a limp last sentence. Regardless of the brilliance of your argument, your readers are going to feel let down if you end like this:

> All in all, I think "Eveline" was a fine story, and I think anyone would enjoy reading it and maybe even learn something from it.

One student's final paper on "Eveline" (which you will read in its entirety later) closes briefly, yet effectively:

> Afraid of failing on her own, Eveline retreats into the familiar, telling herself that life with father cannot be as frightening as a risky, unknown life with Frank. So strong is her fear of failure that it overrides her fear of her father. She seems to decide that a predictable—if dreary and abused—life is better than a life without security or pattern.

Composing the First Draft

At this point you should be ready to compose the first draft of your essay on "Eveline." You have completed the prewriting activities, devised a working thesis statement, arranged your main supporting points, and selected plenty of details to use for development. You may even have written some of your introduction and conclusion. Now is the time to move beyond these preliminary stages and write a complete draft of your paper.

Pausing to Rescan

You may have been told to get your first draft down on paper as quickly as possible and then, once it is completed, to revise it. This is probably not bad advice if you suffer from writer's block, but recent studies show that most skilled writers go about it in a different way. Experienced writers tend to pause frequently as they compose—to scan and perhaps reword what they have just written; to think about what to say next; to make additions, substitutions, or deletions; to be sure a sentence says what they want it to say.

If you tend to write headlong without pausing once you begin, perhaps you should try to slow down. Mina Shaughnessy, a noted composition expert, speaks of "the messy process that leads to clarity" in writing. This messy process involves pausing and thinking and reviewing in order to write well.

Quoting from Your Sources

The Modern Language Association (MLA) has set a standard way to credit a source when you quote material in an essay. If you are using only a single *primary* source—the work of literature under discussion—you cite in parentheses after the quotation the page (or pages) on which you found that material.

> Eveline admits that hers is "a hard life," yet decides "now that she was about to leave it she did not find it a wholly undesirable life" (5).

If you are using more than one primary source, you need to include the author's last name in the parentheses—with only a single blank space separating it from the page number—unless you mention the author's name in the text of your paper.

> At the end of the story Eveline is "like a helpless animal" (Joyce 7), and Hulga at the end is similarly helpless, "left sitting on the straw in the dusty sunlight" (O'Connor 130).

(*Note:* If you are using library sources, the situation becomes more complicated. Consult Chapter 5 for complete instruction in writing researched papers.)

The Source Citation Even if you are citing only your primary source, let your readers know what it is. If you use direct quotations, you will include page numbers in your paper, and readers need to know which book those page numbers come from. On a separate page at the end of your essay, center the title (Work Cited or Works Cited) at the top. Using double spacing, provide complete publication information for your source or sources. The Work Cited entry for a paper on "Eveline" using the current edition of this text would look like this:

> Joyce, James. "Eveline." *Literature and the Writing Process.* Ed. Elizabeth McMahan et al. 9th ed. Upper Saddle River: Pearson, 2010. 3–7. Print.

Notice the *hanging* indention. Indent all lines after the first line five spaces. Use an abbreviated form of the publisher's name—just *Pearson,* not *Pearson Education, Inc.* If you are using more than one source, alphabetize the entries by their authors' last names.

Sample Student Paper: First Draft

The paper that follows is the first draft of an essay on "Eveline" written by Wendy Dennison, a student at Illinois State University. The directed freewriting for this paper appears in Figure 1-1. The comments, suggestions, and questions in the margin were made by Wendy's instructor.

Sample Student Paper: First Draft

1

Wendy Dennison

English 102

January 23, 2005

Are there too many rhetorical questions?

For Fear of Failing Alone

Eveline, the title character of Joyce's short story, is given that once-in-a-lifetime chance—to leave her old life to begin a new one. But she rejects the offer Fate—or God—makes, preferring instead to settle back down into the dusty, abusive life she has led. Why does she not go away with Frank? The obvious responses—duty to her mother's dying wish, the love of her father, the love of her home—do not quite ring true, for Eveline owes little or nothing to her parents or her home. In fact, leaving seems a much more logical choice. So why does Eveline really stay behind? She is afraid of failure.

Mention title of story here (arrow pointing to "old life")

Isn't it Frank? (beside underlined "Fate—or God")

Do you want to give away your conclusion? (arrow pointing to "She is afraid of failure.")

What does Eveline really owe her mother? Her "promise . . . that she keep the home together as long as she could" (6) was unfairly given. It was unfair of her mother to ask such a thing of her, as it prevents her from having a life of her own. It is very likely that Eveline will never marry and leave her father as long as he is alive, for she will always recall that promise. Why stay for this?

Does this ¶ need more details?

Why should we be surprised that Eveline might wish to leave her father? An abusive drunk, he has taken advantage of her promise to her mother. She is forced to keep house for him, yet must beg from him money with which to do so. He practically accuses her of stealing, claiming, "she used to squander the money, that she had no head, that he wasn't going to give her

good intro of quotation

Dennison 2

his hard-earned money to throw about the streets . . ." (5). A bully, he has scared her with threats of beatings, giving her "palpitations" (4). Eveline realizes that with her brothers gone, there is "nobody to protect her" (4) from her father's rage. Why would she ever want to stay with a man of whom she is terribly afraid? She did remember happy moments with him when the family went on picnics and he was jolly and played with the children.

Does this detail fit?

Eveline's home life is so unhealthy that she would be wise to leave it all behind. For all that she does, she still does not feel quite a part of everything. For example, she knows nothing about the picture of the priest, not even his name. The dustiness of the house, of which Joyce reminds us periodically, is suggestive of the pervading dirtiness and squalor of her daily life. It is significant also that she often thinks about her unpleasant, unhappy job. Her home is clearly not conducive to happiness. So why does she stay there?

Why is this important?

best word?

Does this fit?

Combine sentences?

The only real reason why Eveline would stay in Irelnad is the fact that she is desperately afraid of failing on her own. If she leaves the familiar, no matter how unpleasant, she risks failure. "She was about to explore another life with Frank" (5). The word "explore" is significant here, as it brings to mind uncertainty and risk, two factors that Eveline is not prepared to deal with. She admits that hers "was a hard life," yet thinks, "now that she was about to leave it she did not find it a wholly undesirable life" (5). When she sits in the growing darkness—the threat of her father returning from work—with the letters in her lap, Eveline calls up a couple of good memories to calm her fears, effectively helping to convince herself to stay home.

Check whole paper for typos

good!

tense shift?

sentence OK?

Dennison 3

Afraid of failing on her own, Eveline retreats into the familiar, convincing herself that life with father cannot be as frightening as a risky life with Frank. "Why should she be unhappy? She had a right to happiness" (6) Indeed, Eveline decides that a predictable—if abusive and unhealthy—life is better than one without direction or pattern.

Is this a good detail to use here?

Well done, Wendy! But please outline this draft to be sure the material is tightly unified.

Dennison 4

Not accurate! Check the MLA style!

Work Cited

Joyce, James. "Eveline," in Literature and the Writing Process. By Elizabeth McMahan, Susan X Day, and Robert Funk. NJ: Prentice Hall, 2005. Pages 3–7.

3

Writing a Convincing Argument

You can write about literary works in several ways. You can record your reactions and explore how the work affects you personally; you can describe the work for others who might want to read it; you can evaluate the work and tell why you liked or disliked it. But the customary way to write about a literary work is to *interpret* it. Interpreting is also one of the most challenging ways to write about literature. The goal of this chapter is to show you how to develop your opinions about literature and shape them into clear, convincing essays that explain what a literary work means.

Interpreting and Arguing

When you interpret a story or poem or play, you say to other readers, "This is how I read this work; this is what I think it means." Because literary texts are often complex and seldom obvious, you can assume that other readers will not necessarily interpret a work in the same way you do. So, in addition to explaining the meaning, you will also have to convince your audience that your reading is reasonable and well founded. In other words, you will be *arguing* for your interpretation.

Presenting your interpretation as an argument will focus your writing and require you to look more carefully and closely at the literary selection. An effective way to mount an argument for your interpretation is to begin with these two steps:

- Identify an ***issue*** about the work that you want to discuss.
- Formulate a ***claim*** that takes a position on the issue.

Identifying Issues

An issue is a subject or problem that people argue about. Many issues about a literary work relate to its *theme*. When you interpret a story or play or poem, you are actually explaining its theme—and arguing for your understanding of that theme. You'll remember in Chapter 1 we offered this advice: "Devise a thesis that makes its point by relating some aspect of the work to the meaning of the whole—that is, to its theme." This strategy of identifying an issue and making a claim about it will help you to write a meaningful literary paper.

A good way to identify an issue is to see it as a question with no obvious or clear answer. In Chapter 1, we recommended that you ask yourself questions as you are reading. This self-questioning will not only generate material to consider using as evidence, but it will also help you to locate the issues in a literary work. For her essay on "Fear of Failure in Joyce's 'Eveline'" (pages 67–70), Wendy Dennison identified this key issue:

> Why does Eveline not go away with Frank when the opportunity seems so attractive?

The issue that Wendy identified is a *major issue*, a question asked by most readers of the story and one that has a number of answers.

There are, of course, other questions that readers ask about "Eveline." Several came out in our prewriting exercises in Chapter 1:

- What is the significance of Eveline's promise to her mother?
- Would Eveline's life have been different if she had been born male?
- What role does religion play in Eveline's decision?
- How realistic is Eveline's romance with Frank?
- Why does the author mention "dust" so often in the story?

These issues are interesting and important, but individually they are *minor issues* that relate to just one part of the story. Identifying a broader issue, however, would make it possible to include some of them as part of a more complete interpretation of the story's themes:

> How did social custom and her religious upbringing condition Eveline to abandon her hopes and dreams for a better life?

The specific issues of gender, religion, and Eveline's promise to her mother could then be used to answer this larger question.

The issues, of course, are quite different in various works of literature, but in working toward a claim, the process remains the same. In preparing to write about Dagoberto Gilb's short story "Love in L. A.," for instance, Brian Carter used the self-questioning approach to identify a couple of issues that he thought would direct him to a convincing interpretation:

- What is the nature of the "love" referred to in the title?
- Who is fooled by Jake's lies?
- What purpose does fantasy serve for Jake?

Making Claims

Once you have identified the issue that will be the center of your interpretation, you are ready to make a claim about that issue. If you stated the issue as a question, then your claim will be an answer to that question. Wendy Dennison answered her issue question with this claim:

> Afraid of failing on her own, Eveline retreats into the familiar, telling herself that life with her father cannot be as frightening as a risky, unknown life with Frank.

Working out an answer to your issue question may require several drafts, and you will probably refine and revise your claim as you are putting your interpretation together.

An effective claim will make a clear, significant assertion about the way you interpret the work's theme. It can also provide a concise preview of the way you are going to develop your case. For example, the issue question about the influence of custom and religion might be answered with this claim:

> Religious and social traditions have trapped Eveline: her Catholic upbringing, her responsibilities as a dutiful daughter, and her promise to her dying mother make it impossible for her to imagine leaving home and seeking a new life for herself.

The answers to issue questions about "Love in L. A." might produce these claims:

> The "love" that exists in L. A., according to this story, is superficial, materialistic, and self-centered.
>
> Jake consciously adapts his performance to fool and manipulate his audience, but he doesn't succeed with Mariana.
>
> Jake's fantasies allow him to avoid the truth: he isn't going anywhere.

If you think a claim is the same as a thesis statement, you're right. The term *claim* makes it clear that you are taking a stand about the meaning of a work and that you will back up your interpretation with ***evidence*** and ***reasoning***.

Using Evidence

As we pointed out in Chapter 2, the evidence in a literary argument tells your audience where you got the ideas for your interpretation. The most important evidence will come from the literary work itself: facts, details, descriptions, incidents, key terms, and phrases. Direct quotations provide clear evidence that your claims are grounded in the text, but you'll want to be smart about quoting from the literary work.

Presumably, your audience has already read the story or poem or play; you need only remind them of passages that support your interpretation. You also have to think about when to summarize and how to use a brief summary to advance your claims. You can summarize an incident or scene to help establish a point or observation—and then explain or interpret that point—but long summaries will detract from your argument. The following example uses material from the story to support a claim that religion plays a role in Eveline's decision. The supporting evidence is highlighted and labeled:

> Eveline's Catholic upbringing is established early in the story. As **she looks around the room, surveying the "familiar objects from which she had never dreamed of being divided" (4),** Eveline takes special note of two items: **an old photograph of the priest who had been a friend of her father's** and **a colored print of the promises made to Blessed Margaret Mary Alacoque**. Then, in the story's final scene, as **she stands in the station, waiting to board the boat**, Eveline**"prayed to God to direct her, to show her what was her duty"** and **"kept moving her lips in silent fervent prayer" (7).**

summary and quotation

specific details

summary

quotations

Brian Carter supported his claim about the "web of falsehoods" Jake weaves for Mariana by listing examples:

> His car has **fake license plates;** he has **no insurance**; he has no intention of paying for his mistake. He claims to have **glamorous occupations,** despite driving **a decrepit '58 Buick**.

specific details

You may also be asked to use evidence from outside the literary work. You might wonder, for instance, why James Joyce mentioned the promises made to Blessed Margaret Mary Alacoque. Information about those promises might be useful in developing and supporting a claim about Eveline's religious upbringing. The process of finding and using evidence in sources outside a literary work is covered in detail in Chapter 5.

Obviously, the more evidence you have, the more convincing your interpretation will be. But facts, details, and quotations by themselves do not make an argument. You have to explain how you are using this evidence to support your interpretation.

Using Reasoning

As we pointed out in Chapter 2, "the thinking process you use to connect the evidence to your claims is called *reasoning*." You'll want to give the *reasons* for drawing your conclusions about a work's meaning. In this excerpt from her essay, Wendy Dennison explained the reasoning behind her claim that Eveline's main problem is fear of the unknown (the explanations are highlighted in bold type):

> **If she leaves the familiar, no matter how unpleasant, she risks failure.** "She was about to explore another life with Frank" (5), we are told, in faraway Beunos Ayres. **The word *explore* is significant, as it brings to mind uncertainty and risk, two factors that Eveline is not prepared to deal with.** She admits that hers is "a hard life," yet she thinks that "now that she was about to leave it she did not find it a wholly undesirable life" (5). When she sits in the growing darkness with the letters in her lap, Eveline calls up a couple of good memories—of her father being jolly once on a picnic, of his kindness once when she was sick. **We see her trying to calm her fears, trying to convince herself that her home life is more bearable than it is.**

You can see a clear pattern in the six sentences of this paragraph:

—Make a claim (sentence 1).
—Quote some evidence from the story (sentence 2).
—Interpret the meaning of the evidence (sentence 3).
—Bring up some more evidence (sentences 4 and 5).
—Explain how the evidence supports the claim in the first sentence (sentence 6).

This pattern of stating claims, citing evidence, explaining the evidence, making another (related) claim, and citing more evidence is used time and again in developing an interpretation.

Here's another example that combines evidence and interpretive explanations to support a claim about Eveline's decision. The explanations are highlighted in bold type:

> **Religion plays an important role in shaping Eveline's decision not to leave with Frank.** As she sits by the window, looking at the "familiar objects" that she "had dusted once a week for so many years" (4), she notices a faded photograph of a priest who had once been a school friend of her father. But the priest is in Melbourne now, **having left Eveline's father just as she is planning to do.** Next to the photo is "a coloured print of the promises made to Blessed Margaret Mary Alacoque," **a symbol of devotion to home and family in the Catholic Church.** Margaret Mary Alacoque had a vision in which Jesus promised to bless any home where Alacoque's picture is exhibited, **a promise that parallels the one that Eveline made to her dying mother to "keep the home together as long as she could" (6). The photo and the print indicate how Eveline is tied to her parents; they also remind her of the traditional obligations of a good Catholic daughter. Their religious associations only increase the guilt she feels about trying to make a life for herself.**

In his final paragraph, Brian Carter used reasoning to explain why Jake's character is so transparently foolish:

> We all laugh at such a clown, and it makes us comfortable to know that *we* aren't like Jake. Perhaps, though, while we are off guard, Gilb intends to plant a nagging thought that we *are*—just a little.

Answering Opposing Views

As we explained in Chapter 2, your interpretation will be strengthened if you anticipate and respond to other readings of the work, a process sometimes referred to as *refutation* or *rebuttal*. By definition, your claims are arguable, so you can expect that other readers will not always agree with the way you interpret the evidence. As you plan and draft your interpretation, make a list of all the opposing views you can think of. You can get help from friends and classmates who have also read the literary work. Anticipating other possible readings should cause you to reexamine why and how you arrived at your own point of view. Such a reconsideration will almost certainly help you to refine and deepen your interpretation.

Some writers answer opposing views in a separate section, sometimes immediately after the introduction as a bridge to rest of the essay. Other writers save their refutations until after they have presented their own case. A particularly effective strategy is to handle opposing views point by point as you argue at the same time for your claims, as Wendy Dennison did when weighing the importance of Eveline's promise to her dying mother:

> But surely her promise to "keep the home together as long as she could" (6) was given under extreme circumstances. It was unjust of her mother to ask such a sacrifice of her, and Eveline is aware of the unfairness. . . . Surely that promise cannot be the only reason she stays.

Brian Carter led into his main claim by including an opposing interpretation of Jake:

> Some readers might find Jake too obvious and predictable to be interesting. But his character is drawn large and clueless to make a point.

Wherever you place your response to different readings, your goal is to explain why these views are faulty or incomplete. At the very least you want to show that your reading is just as valid and compelling.

Organizing Your Argument

The conventional structure for arguing your interpretation should include five elements, usually presented in this order:

1. The issue (subject)
2. Your claim about the issue (thesis)
3. The evidence that supports your claim (facts, details, quotations)
4. The reasoning that connects the evidence to your claim (explanations)
5. Your refutation of opposing views (explanations and counterevidence)

As you saw in the examples in this chapter, writers frequently combine elements 3, 4, and 5 (evidence, reasoning, and refutation).

In Chapter 2, we showed you how to arrange the steps for arguing the claim that "Eveline lacks courage to flee from her domineering father and to seek her own happiness" (see page 20). The approach we illustrated in Chapter 2 is called ***inductive reasoning***. It is perhaps the most common way of arguing an interpretation. But you can also arrange your arguments in other ways; two common ones are the ***counterargument*** and the ***comparative argument***.

Using the Inductive Approach

An inductive argument moves from specific examples and observations to a general conclusion. It parallels the process you go through when reading a piece of literature: you notice details and points, words and phrases, comments and actions, which add up to your understanding of what the work means. When you reread in order to write about the work, you look even more closely for specifics to confirm your initial reactions, raise possible questions, and build an interpretation. With this accumulation of specific evidence, you can then identify the issues you want to write about and the claims you want to make about those issues.

In planning an inductive argument, you start with your major claim (thesis) and then list the minor claims that support your interpretation. You can see a sample outline for this method on page 20. Here is another example:

> **Major claim:** Eveline doesn't leave with Frank because she subconsciously suspects that he will not really "save her" and "give her life."
>
> **Minor claims:**
>
> 1. Eveline doesn't really know much about Frank.
> 2. She may recognize that what he has told her is more fiction than fact.
> 3. She has firsthand knowledge of the duplicity men are capable of.
> 4. The ending seems to confirm her suspicions.

If you were to flesh out these claims with specific details and explanations, you would be prepared to write a draft.

Major claim: Eveline doesn't leave with Frank because she subconsciously suspects that he will not really "save her" and "give her life." Her doubts and suspicions make it impossible for her to overcome the power of family and religion.

Minor claims:

1. Eveline doesn't really know much about Frank.
   —met only "a few weeks ago"
   —"They had come to know each other"—vague and unclear
   —no last name
2. She may recognize that what he has told her is more fiction than fact, too good to be true.
   —exotic "tales of distant countries" and "terrible Patagonians"
   —why the "pleasantly confused" feeling when he sang "about the lass that loves a sailor"?
   —claims he "had fallen on his feet" in Buenos Aries: vague and without specific content
   —romantic promise of a "home he has waiting for her"
   —father's suspicions: "I know these sailor chaps"
3. She has firsthand knowledge of the duplicity of men.
   —father sometimes nice and thoughtful
   —but also a violent drunk who abused his wife and threatens Eveline
   —would Frank treat her the same way?
4. The ending seems to confirm her suspicions.
   —thought he "would take her in his arms, fold her in his arms"
   —instead he "seize[ed]" her hand and called to her
   —he "rushed beyond the barrier and called to her to follow"—but he did not come back

The inductive plan of Brian Carter's essay would look like this:

Major claim: Through presenting a clownishly self-glorifying character, "Love in L. A." leads the reader to think about the illusions of personal glory in his or her own life.

Minor claims:

1. The metaphor of the cars going nowhere is central: Jake is stuck, with no destination in life, though the situation might appear otherwise.
2. Jake tells plenty of lies about the quality of his life, but doesn't fool Mariana.
3. Jake's failure with Mariana gives him only the slightest self-doubt, and then he returns to his fantasy world.
4. While we are amused at the situation and ridiculing Jake's excesses, our defenses are down, and we remember our own self-inflating fantasies.

Making a Counterargument

You can anticipate how other readers might interpret a work and organize your own interpretation as a point-by-point refutation of those other possible views. This approach is effective for tackling especially complex or controversial selections and for clearing up common misunderstandings. Wendy Dennison, for example, defines her major claim by suggesting how other people might answer the issue (Why does Eveline fail to leave with Frank?) and by talking back to them. After dealing with several other readings of Eveline's motives, Wendy is ready to make the case for her own interpretation.

Arguing through Comparison

Another way to argue an interpretation is to use comparisons. Setting two works or two interpretations side-by-side permits you to use one of them to throw light on the other. Comparison involves looking at similarities; contrast directs attention to differences. But you can combine the two by showing how things that seem to be alike are really different, or vice versa.

The comparison/contrast method follows the notion that we can find out what something *is* by discovering what it is *not*. You can begin by establishing the basis for the comparison (the similarities) and then move on to the features that set the two works apart (the differences). For example, in comparing Dagoberto Gilb's "Love in L. A." (page 45) with John Updike's "A & P" (page 440), you might start by noting that both stories feature a brash, disaffected young man who unsuccessfully tries to impress an attractive young woman. You could then argue that the endings reveal a significant contrast: Jake remains pretty much unenlightened and unchanged, while Sammy realizes he has perhaps made a life-altering decision.

You could also develop an interpretation that shows how two seemingly different characters are alike in several key ways. For example, you could contrast Eveline with Elisa, the main character in John Steinbeck's "The Chrysanthemums" (page 298), pointing out the differences in their age, marital status, personality, attitude toward work, and interaction with the men in their families. After describing their differences, you could then point out two surprising and significant similarities: each woman gets a glimpse of an attractive new life from a charming stranger, but neither one has the courage to break away from her domestic trap.

Organizing a Comparison/Contrast There are two standard ways of arranging the material in a comparison/contrast. One way is to make all your points about one work first and then to do the same for the second work. You could group all the pertinent details about Eveline in one block, followed by the contrasting points about Elisa in a second block.

This method is relatively easy to handle and works perfectly for showing how things have changed—or, in the case of Eveline and Elisa, have *not* changed. The two stories were written twenty-five years apart and deal with women of very different means and temperament, yet both end up defeated in their effort to find happiness and fulfillment. Eveline is paralyzed "like a helpless animal," and Elisa is "crying weakly—like an old woman."

A second approach involves subdividing your major claim into specific points and explaining how each point relates to one work (or character) and then to the other. The method allows you to emphasize the primary points of comparison (or contrast). But the point-by-point organization can disintegrate into little more than a list of similarities and differences if you fail to relate the points to a unifying claim. Here is a sample plan for an interlocking comparison of the stories "A & P" and "Love in L. A.," focusing on the main characters, Jake and Sammy. The comparison supports the claim that both young men are slackers but that only Sammy appears ready to grow up and move on.

1. Life/work situation
   —Jake: unemployed; main accomplishment is keeping his old car clean and running
   —Sammy: stuck in a dead-end job, taking orders from a boss he doesn't like and being careful not to upset his parents
2. Character and personality
   —Jake: fantasizes mainly about cars; concerned only with showiness and appearances, not with honesty and ethics
   —Sammy: lively, frustrated, judgmental; builds up his low self-esteem by denigrating and stereotyping customers and co-workers
3. Interaction with women
   —Jake: tries to charm and impress Mariana, who is way out of his league; gets her phone number (which may be phony), but can tell that she really doesn't buy his act
   —Sammy: critical and sexist, but very taken with Queenie, mainly because she's aloof and clearly unattainable; quits his job to impress her, but she takes no notice
4. Final realization
   —Jake: unfazed and carefree; resumes driving and fantasizing about his dream car
   —Sammy: sticks to his decision to quit, but realizes "how hard the world was going to be to me hereafter"

Sample Student Essay

In the following essay, student Brian Carter argues for his interpretation of the story "Love in L. A." by Dagoberto Gilb. You can read the story at the end of this chapter on pages 45–47. The main character, Jake, dominates the story and provides the focus for Brian's major claim, which argues for a carefully designed effect on the story's readers. The marginal notes identify key features and strategies in building this argument.

Carter 1

Brian Carter

Professor Day

English 102A

14 October 2008

Lying in L. A.

Dagoberto Gilb's misleading title "Love in L. A." sets the stage for this short, humorous story involving a fender bender on a crowded Los Angeles freeway. This story is not about love, certainly not in the traditional sense of the word, nor is it about a minor car accident; it is about something more profound: our highly prized illusion of personal good fortune and the fantasies and lies we use to maintain that illusion. The story establishes its central metaphor in the first sentence with the phrase "motionless traffic" (432). The automobile is supposed to be one of our main keys to personal freedom, providing the means to a destination—but not in this case. We are introduced to the main character, Jake, while he is mentally creating a detailed fantasy about his quest for the ultimate lifestyle, achieved through upgrading his automobile. An FM radio, a velvet interior, heating and cooling systems—such luxuries would, of course, lead him to the promised land of "necklaced ladies in satin gowns, misty and sexy like a tequila ad" (432).

Major claim

Minor claim

Evidence: details, quotation

Reality snaps Jake out of his fantasy world when he hits the car in front of him. Unfortunately, Jake's capacity for self-delusion thrusts him into another equally ridiculous fantasyland, this time played out in the real world. In his interactions with Mariana, the victim of his carelessness, we learn that Jake's self-concept is built on lies, presumably distilled from endless practice at imagining what his life should be

Minor claim

Carter 2

at this stage of development. He clumsily tries to woo Mariana with a web of falsehoods. His car has fake license plates; he has no insurance; he has no intention of paying for his mistake. He claims to have glamorous occupations, despite driving a decrepit '58 Buick. Mariana is young, lives with her immigrant parents, drives the car her dad bought her, but nonetheless is more worldly-wise than Jake and views him with suspicion. Although Jake interprets her polite smiles as promising, Mariana isn't buying any of his lines, clearly wanting to get the whole accident information exchange over with as soon as possible. Her skepticism about Jake is revealed when she pulls up behind him and writes down the license plate numbers on his car before leaving (434).

Evidence: details

Evidence: reasoning

Gilb draws the character of Jake quite broadly as a self-deluded fool, although Jake does seem to have a fleeting moment of awareness when he takes "a moment or two to feel both proud and sad" about his interaction with Mariana (434). Perhaps his repeatedly failing efforts to set up a date crack his fantasy shell. However, he immediately repairs it: "His sense of freedom swelled as he drove into the now moving street traffic" (434). Some readers might find Jake too obvious and predictable to be interesting. But his character is drawn large and clueless to make a point. We all laugh at such a clown, and it makes us comfortable to know that *we* aren't like Jake. Perhaps, though, while we are off guard, Gilb intends to plant a nagging thought that we *are*—just a little. Haven't most of us been stuck in a traffic jam, imagining some unearned luxuries that would change our lives, oblivious to the fact that we aren't going anywhere?

Minor claim

Evidence: quotation

Refutation

Major claim: conclusion

Carter 3

Work Cited

Gilb, Dagoberto. "Love in L. A." *Literature and the Writing Process*. Ed. Elizabeth McMahan, Susan X Day, and Robert Funk. 8th ed. Upper Saddle River: Prentice, 2007. 432-34. Print.

Dagoberto Gilb 1950–

Dagoberto Gilb was born in Los Angeles, the son of an undocumented immigrant Mexican mother and a Spanish-speaking Anglo father from East Los Angeles. He put himself through college, earning a B.A. and an M.A. in philosophy. He then spent sixteen years as a construction worker, taking time off every few months to write. His collection of stories, *The Magic of Blood* (1993), made him, according to one critic, "the voice of labor and unionism, once even as a headliner alongside legendary folk singer Pete Seegar." He now lives in Austin, Texas, and is a professor in the creative writing program at Southwest Texas State University, in San Marcos.

Love in L. A.

Jake slouched in a clot of near motionless traffic, in the peculiar gray of concrete, smog, and early morning beneath the overpass of the Hollywood Freeway on Alvarado Street. He didn't really mind because he knew how much worse it could be trying to make a left onto the onramp. He certainly didn't do that every day of his life, and he'd assure anyone who'd ask that he never would either. A steady occupation had its advantages and he couldn't deny thinking about that too. He needed an FM radio in something better than this '58 Buick he drove. It would have crushed velvet interior with electric controls for the L. A. summer, a nice warm heater and defroster for the winter drives at the beach, a cruise control for those longer trips, mellow speakers front and rear of course, windows that hum closed, snuffing out that nasty exterior noise of freeways. The fact was that he'd probably have to change his whole style. Exotic colognes, plush, dark nightclubs, mai tais and daiquiris, necklaced ladies in satin gowns, misty and sexy like in a tequila ad. Jake could imagine lots of possibilities when he let himself, but none that ended up with him pressed onto a stalled freeway.

Jake was thinking about this freedom of his so much that when he glimpsed its green light he just went ahead and stared bye-bye to the steadily employed. When he turned his head the same direction his windshield faced, it was maybe one second too late. He pounced the brake pedal and steered the front wheels away from the tiny brake lights but the smack was unavoidable. Just one second sooner and it would only have been close. One second more and he'd be crawling up the Toyota's trunk. As it was, it seemed like only a harmless smack, much less solid than the one against his back bumper.

Jake considered driving past the Toyota but was afraid the traffic ahead would make it too difficult. As he pulled up against the curb a few car lengths ahead, it occurred to him that the traffic might have helped him get away too. He slammed the car door twice to make sure it was closed fully and to give himself another second more, then toured front and rear of his Buick for damage on or near the bumpers. Not an impressionable scratch even in the chrome. He perked up. Though the car's beauty was secondary to its ability to start and move, the body and paint were clean except for a few minor dings. This stood out as one of his few clearcut accomplishments over the years.

Before he spoke to the driver of the Toyota, whose looks he could see might present him with an added complication, he signaled to the driver of the car that hit him, still in his car and stopped behind the Toyota, and waved his hands and shook his head to let the man know there was no problem as far as he was concerned. The driver waved back and started his engine.

"It didn't even scratch my paint," Jake told her in that way of his. "So how you doin'? Any damage to the car? I'm kinda hoping so, just so it takes a little more time and we can talk some. Or else you can give me your phone number now and I won't have to lay my regular b. s. on you to get it later."

He took her smile as a good sign and relaxed. He inhaled her scent like it was clean air and straightened out his less than new but not unhip clothes.

"You've got Florida plates. You look like you must be Cuban."

"My parents are from Venezuela."

"My name's Jake." He held out his hand.

"Mariana."

They shook hands like she'd never done it before in her life.

"I really am sorry about hitting you like that." He sounded genuine. He fondled the wide dimple near the cracked taillight. "It's amazing how easy it is to put a dent in these new cars. They're so soft they might replace waterbeds soon." Jake was confused about how to proceed with this. So much seemed so unlikely, but there was always possibility. "So maybe we should go out to breakfast somewhere and talk it over."

"I don't eat breakfast."

"Some coffee then."

"Thanks, but I really can't."

"You're not married, are you? Not that that would matter that much to me. I'm an open-minded kinda guy."

She was smiling. "I have to get to work."

"That sounds boring."

"I better get your driver's license," she said.

Jake nodded, disappointed. "One little problem," he said. "I didn't bring it. I just forgot it this morning. I'm a musician," he exaggerated greatly, "and, well, I dunno, I left my wallet in the pants I was wearing last night. If you have some paper and a pen I'll give you my address and all that."

He followed her to the glove compartment side of her car.

"What if we don't report it to the insurance companies? I'll just get it fixed for you."

"I don't think my dad would let me do that."

"Your dad? It's not your car?"

"He bought it for me. And I live at home."

"Right." She was slipping away from him. He went back around to the back of her new Toyota and looked over the damage again. There was the trunk lid, the bumper, a rear panel, a taillight.

"You do have insurance?" she asked, suspicious, as she came around the back of the car.

"Oh yeah," he lied.

"I guess you better write the name of that down too."

He made up a last name and address and wrote down the name of an insurance company an old girlfriend once belonged to. He considered giving a real phone number but went against that idea and made one up.

"I act too," he lied to enhance the effect more. "Been in a couple of movies."

She smiled like a fan.

"So how about your phone number?" He was rebounding maturely.

She gave it to him.

"Mariana, you are beautiful," he said in his most sincere voice.

"Call me," she said timidly.

Jake beamed. "We'll see you, Mariana," he said holding out his hand. Her hand felt so warm and soft he felt like he'd been kissed.

Back in his car he took a moment or two to feel both proud and sad about his performance. Then he watched the rear view mirror as Mariana pulled up behind him. She was writing down the license plate numbers on his Buick, ones that he'd taken off a junk because the ones that belonged to his had expired so long ago. He turned the ignition key and revved the big engine and clicked into drive. His sense of freedom swelled as he drove into the now moving street traffic, though he couldn't stop the thought about that FM stereo radio and crushed velvet interior and the new car smell that would even make it better.

(1993)

The Rewriting Process

You are probably relieved and pleased that you have completed the first draft of your essay. A large portion of your work is finished. But do not be in a rush to print out the final version yet. You need first to do a careful revision of your paper.

What Is Revision?

Revision involves more than just tidying your prose. The process of correcting your spelling, punctuation, and mechanics is called *editing*, but your paper is not ready for that yet. First you need *re-vision*, seeing again, to discover ways to make your writing better. Schedule your time so that you are able to lay the rough draft aside at least overnight before attempting to revise. While a draft is still warm from the writing, you cannot look at it objectively. And looking at it objectively is the basis of revision.

As you examine your cooled-down essay, you may even see that while you were writing, your main claim shifted somewhat. Sometimes writers discover what they actually want to say while trying to write something different. For example, one student argued the point in the first draft of a paper on Flannery O'Connor's short story "Good Country People" that the main characters are all self-deceived. As she reread her draft, she noticed that she had focused almost entirely on Hulga Joy and her mother but had said almost nothing about the young Bible salesman. After some reflection—and another reading of the story—she decided to change her claim to emphasize the point that the Bible salesman, who makes his living through willful deception, is the only character who is not self-deceived. By shifting her focus to a consideration of this insight, the student discovered a number of related ideas that she had previously overlooked and thus was able to strengthen the content of her interpretation.

That student was able to get some distance from her own writing, to look at it as another reader might. In revising, *look at your paper from the reader's point of view.* What questions might a reader want to ask you? These must be anticipated in the paper, because you will not be around to answer them. One of the best ways to get another reader's perspective is to enlist the help of peer reviewers.

Getting Feedback: Peer Review

Writers routinely seek the help of potential readers to find out what is working and what is not working in their drafts. Even professional writers ask for suggestions from editors, reviewers, teachers, and friends. Someone else can often see places where you *thought* you were being clear but were actually filling in details only in your head, not on the page.

The ideal people to help you evaluate your first draft are the members of your own writing class. They will be familiar with the assignment and will understand why you are writing the paper and for whom. Here are some guidelines to follow when asking for help with your revision.

1. *Specify the kind of help you want.* If you already know that the spelling needs to be checked, ask your readers to ignore those errors and focus on other elements in the draft. If you want suggestions about the thesis or the introduction or the tone or the organization or the examples, then ask questions about those features.
2. *Ask productive questions.* Be sure to pose questions that require more than a yes or no answer. Ask readers to tell you in detail what *they* see. You can use the questions in the Peer Evaluation Checklist (Chart 4-1, page 50) to help you solicit feedback.
3. *Don't get defensive.* Listen carefully to what your reviewers say; don't argue with them. If something confused them, it confused them. You want to see the writing through their eyes, not browbeat them into seeing it the way you do.
4. *Make your own decisions.* Remember that this is your paper; you are responsible for accepting or rejecting the feedback you get. If you don't agree with the suggestions, then don't follow them. But also keep in mind that your peer reviewers are likely to be more objective about your writing than you are.

Revising in Peer Groups

In many writing classes, students work together on their papers. Meeting in small groups, they read photocopies of each other's drafts and respond to them. Sometimes, students post their drafts on a classroom management system or by e-mail. If your instructor doesn't arrange for peer review, try to get several readers' reactions to your drafts. You can meet together outside of class or use Internet communication.

Working in peer review groups gives you a chance to write for readers other than the teacher. You increase your audience awareness, get immediate feedback on your drafts, and have a chance to discuss them with someone who doesn't have the power of a grade over you.

Chart 4-1 Peer Evaluation Checklist for Revision

The following questions are designed to address the typical concerns in arguing a literary interpretation. They will help you evaluate your own or another student's first draft.

1. Does the paper meet the assignment? What is the major claim? Does the whole paper relate to this claim? Is the claim interesting or too predictable?
2. Is the interpretation argued clearly and consistently? Make a note of any sentences or paragraphs that you had to reread. Make a note of any words or phrases that you found confusing.
3. Is the argument well organized? Is it logical? Is there perhaps a better order for the major points of the argument? Are there any paragraphs or points that do not seem to belong?
4. Is there enough material to make the interpretation clear and convincing? Does it need further details or examples? Make a note of places you would like to see more details or examples. Write questions to help the writer add details. For example, if the essay says, "Eveline did not much like her father," you could ask, "Exactly how did she feel about him?"
5. Are all the quotations from the story accurate? Do they appear within quotation marks?
6. Does the opening capture the reader's attention and make the major claim of the paper clear? Does the conclusion provide an intelligent, satisfactory ending for the argument?

But it takes skill to be an honest and critical reader of someone else's writing. When giving feedback, whether in groups or one-on-one, you should observe certain ground rules to ensure that your responses are productive and helpful.

- Remember that drafts are works in progress which writers intend to develop and improve. You are acting as an informed, interested reader who has questions and suggestions for improvement.
- Pay attention to *what* the other writers are saying, just as you hope they'll pay attention to what you are saying. In other words, focus on content first.
- Avoid the extremes of saying that everything is wonderful or finding fault with every detail. Instead, give thoughtful, sympathetic responses—the kind of feedback that you would like to receive.
- Talk about the writing, not about the writer. If you notice errors, feel free to mention them, but concentrate on responding and suggesting rather than correcting the writer.

Once you have gathered reactions and suggestions from your peer reviewers—and perhaps from your instructor, too—you are ready to begin rewriting. The rest of this chapter will guide you through the specifics of revising and editing.

What Should I Add or Take Out?

Revising is hard work, and you may wonder just where and how to start. If you have not been following a plan carefully worked out before you began writing, you should begin the revising process by outlining your first draft.

Outlining After the First Draft

To be sure that your discussion is unified and complete—that is, to discover whether anything needs to be taken out or added—you should briefly outline your rough draft. It may seem odd to make an outline *after* you have written the paper, but listing your main ideas and supporting details will enable you to review your essay quickly and easily. You can examine its skeleton and decide whether everything fits together properly. This step in the revising process is *essential* if you have written the first draft without an outline or a detailed plan.

Making the Outline

An outline, whether done before or after the first draft, allows you to check for sufficient and logical development of ideas as well as for unity throughout the essay. Your introductory paragraph should contain your thesis, perhaps stated in a general way but stated clearly enough to let your readers know what your focus is. Here is one way to construct an after-writing outline:

1. Take a separate sheet of paper and write your thesis statement at the top.
2. Add the topic sentences stating the main ideas of your paragraphs, along with the supporting points in each one.

Your final paragraph should draw a conclusion concerning the thesis—a conclusion that relates the material in the body of the paper to the theme or purpose of the literary work.

Checking the Outline

Check your outline this way:

1. Make sure that the idea in every topic sentence is a significant critical observation relating directly to your thesis.
2. If not, revise the topic sentence until it clearly supports your thesis—or else delete the whole paragraph.

Just as the topic sentence of each paragraph should relate to the thesis of the paper, every piece of supporting evidence in the paragraph should relate to its topic sentence. So, next check the organization within each paragraph this way:

3. In each body paragraph, examine your supporting details to be sure that each relates directly to the topic sentence.
4. Make sure that none of your points repeats an idea included elsewhere (unless you are repeating for emphasis). Eliminate any careless repetition.
5. Decide whether your support is adequate. Think about whether you have included the most convincing details and whether you have enough of them.
6. If you decide you do not have sufficient support for a topic sentence, you need to rethink the point in order to expand it, or consider omitting the paragraph if the ideas are not essential. Sometimes you can combine the material from two paragraphs into a single new one having a broader topic sentence.

Sample After-Writing Outline

Because one peer reader of Wendy Dennison's paper on "Eveline" noticed that a couple of examples might be out of place, Wendy outlined her first draft. Here is her after-writing outline. (Her draft appeared in Chapter 2.)

1. Introduction
   —Eveline refuses to leave with Frank because she fears failure (thesis)
2. Her deathbed promise to her mother was unfair.
   —unfair to ask Eveline to give up her own life
3. She has good reasons to want to leave her father.
   —he's a drunk, takes advantage of the promise
   —he's stingy
   —he abuses her verbally
   —he's a bully, might actually beat her
   —he was sometimes fun in past, played at picnics
4. Her home life is so unhealthy she should leave.
   —doesn't feel a part of everything (picture of priest)
   —dust in house = dirtiness, squalor of her life
   —thinks of leaving and remembers her dreary job
5. Her only reason for staying is that she's afraid.
   —leaving the familiar could mean failure
   —quotation: "about to explore" suggests uncertainty
   —life is hard, so she thinks of good memories to convince herself to stay

6. She retreats into the familiar to avoid risk.
   —feels she has a right to happiness
   —decides a predictable life is better than one without direction and pattern (conclusion)

Examining the Sample Outline

If you examine Wendy's outline carefully, you can see a few problems.

Paragraph 2 Wendy needs more material about why the promise to her dying mother was unfair.

Paragraph 3 The last point, about "fun in past," does not relate to the topic sentence for the paragraph, which focuses on "good reasons to want to leave."

Paragraph 4 The last point, about Eveline's job, does not relate to the topic sentence for the paragraph, which focuses on Eveline's "unhealthy" home life.

Paragraph 5 The last point, about Eveline's "good memories," provides a good place to move the example about "fun in past" from paragraph 3.

Paragraph 6 The first point, about Eveline's "right to happiness," does not relate to the topic sentence, which focuses on Eveline's retreat "into the familiar," but could well be moved to paragraph 2 to support the topic sentence idea that her death bed promise was unfair.

In the final draft of Wendy's paper, which appears on pages 67–70, you will see how she took care of the problems revealed by her outline.

Outlining Exercise

For practice in checking the relevance and organization of ideas, outline the following paragraph in the way we just described, putting the topic sentence at the top of the page, and then listing each supporting idea.

> Eveline lacks courage to seek a life of her own because she fears that her father will not be able to cope if she leaves him. Her anxiety is heightened as she recalls that she and her brothers and sisters are grown up and that her mother is dead. If she leaves, her father will soon be all alone. She realizes that he is "usually fairly bad on a Saturday night" (5) and recognizes that his drinking problem will not get any better after she leaves. Also she has noticed that "Her father was becoming old lately" and assumes that "he would miss her" (6). As a dutiful daughter, Eveline seems to feel that going away with Frank means abandoning her aging father, and that may be why she has written a letter to him—to ease the blow of her departure and to soothe her own conscience.

Next, examine your outline. Do you see any irrelevant points? Can you think of any important ideas or details that have been omitted from the paragraph? Are the points arranged in an effective order? Would another arrangement be better?

Now look at the following outline and see whether it matches yours.

Topic sentence: Eveline fears her father will not be able to manage if she leaves him.

1. Eveline thinks about his loneliness—children grown, wife dead.
2. She fears his drinking problem worsening.
3. She worries that he is becoming old lately.
4. She assumes "he would miss her."
5. She writes letter to ease the blow.

Your outline may not come out exactly like this one, but the main idea is to be sure you have included all of the supporting details.

Here are some observations to consider for a revision of the sample paragraph, based on the outline of its major points:

1. Point 1 could be expanded to include details about the neighbors who have died (Tizzie Dunn) and moved away (the Waters family).
2. An earlier draft of the paragraph included the point about Eveline's promise to her mother, but it was dropped as being irrelevant to the topic sentence. Do you agree?
3. The paragraph's supporting points appear in the same order as they do in the story. Is this chronological organization effective? Would some logical order be better?

What Should I Rearrange?

A crucial part of revision involves giving some thought to the order of your paragraphs and the order of the supporting details within them. The order in which they came to your mind is not necessarily the best. Luckily, rearranging is fairly easy once you have an after-writing outline.

Many writers use cutting and pasting on the computer to experiment with various arrangements of their ideas, reading different versions and deciding which order is most effective. They rearrange paragraphs and even sentences. For instance, sometimes the last sentence you write in a paragraph turns out to be a good topic sentence and should be moved to the beginning. Sometimes the paragraph you write at the essay's end would work better as the introduction to the paper.

If you experiment this way, save each version under a different file name (eve1, eve2, eve3, for example), so that your computer retains all the choices you have created. Otherwise, each new version may overwrite the old one, and you will lose pieces you may want later.

The two principles you need to use in considering how well your points are arranged are *logic* and *emphasis.* Both principles allow you to arrange ideas in a certain sequence. The following questions will help you devise an appropriate arrangement.

1. Should I arrange the paragraphs and details in my essay in the same order in which they appear in the work I am analyzing?

If you are writing a paragraph supporting the topic that Eveline is timid, you might collect details from throughout the story. You could then put those details in the same order as they appear in the story.

2. Should I organize the descriptions in terms of space?

In a paper examining the significance of the objects in Eveline's home, you might take up these objects as though presented in a tour around the room. Other descriptions may be arranged from near to far, from outside to inside, from small to large.

3. Should I arrange my main points along a scale of value, of power, of weight, or of forcefulness? Could I use an arrangement of
   —negative to positive?
   —universal to individual?
   —most influential to least influential?
   —general to specific?
   —least impressive to most impressive?

You can arrange your ideas in either direction along any of these scales—negative to positive or positive to negative, for instance. It is usually effective to place the most emphatic point last in any essay. If you are writing about several of Eveline's reasons for not going with Frank, and you believe that the most influential reason is her promise to her dying mother, you would include that idea in the last paragraph of the body of your paper, opening with a transition like this:

> Though her timidity in general and her fear of her father in particular affect Eveline's final decision, her promise to her mother is the most powerful influence.

The strongest-point rule is just a guideline, of course. Try to arrange your ideas in a way your readers will find effective.

Does It Flow?

The best way to examine the flow (the ***coherence***) of your prose is to read it aloud. Recording your essays on tape and playing them back enables you to hear with some objectivity how your writing sounds. You might also entice a friend to read your paper aloud to you. Whatever method you use, listen for choppiness or abruptness. Your ideas should be arranged in a clear sequence that is easy to follow. Will your readers experience any confusion when a new idea comes up? If so, you need stronger connections between sentences or between paragraphs—*transitions* that indicate how one idea is related to the next.

For example, when you see the words *for example*, you know what to expect. When you see *furthermore* opening a paragraph, your mind gets ready for some addition to the previous point. By contrast, when you see phrases like *on the other hand* or *by contrast*, you are prepared for something different from the previous point.

These clearly transitional phrases can be supplemented by more subtle echo transitions (in this paragraph, the words *transitional phrases* echo the main idea of the preceding paragraph), and by pronoun reference (in this paragraph, the word *these* refers to the examples in the preceding paragraph). Another technique that increases coherence in writing is the repetition of key terms and structures. In the paragraph you are reading, the key terms are forms of the words *transition*, *echo*, *refer*, and *repeat.* In the paragraph preceding this one, notice the repetition of the phrase *when you see* and, in this paragraph, the repetition of *in this paragraph* and *the word(s).* Parallel ideas are presented in parallel ways.

In short, here are the techniques for achieving coherence.

1. A clearly sequenced flow of ideas
2. Transitional terms (see Chart 4-2 on page 57 for a handy list)
3. Echo transitions (see the "Handbook for Correcting Errors" for further explanation)
4. Repetition of key terms
5. Repetition of parallel sentence structures

A Revising Checklist to help you review all the important aspects of the revising process appears in Chart 4-3 on page 57.

What Is Editing?

During revision, you focused on making your paper organized, well developed, and coherent. In the editing stage, you should concentrate on improving your sentences and refining your use of language.

Which Sentences Should I Combine?

Once you are satisfied that your ideas proceed smoothly, consider the possibility of combining sentences to avoid needless repetition of words and to eliminate choppiness. You may also decide to combine sentences to achieve emphasis and variety. Probably you can discover many ways to improve your sentences.

Chart 4-2 Transitional Terms for All Occasions

To Continue to a New Point

next, second, third, besides, further, finally

To Make an Addition to a Point

too, moreover, in addition, for example, such as, that is, as an illustration, for instance, furthermore

To Show Cause and Effect

therefore, consequently, as a result, accordingly, then, thus, so, hence

To Show Contrast

but, still, on the other hand, nevertheless, however, conversely, notwithstanding, yet

To Show Similarity

too, similarly, in the same way, likewise, also

To Emphasize or Restate

again, namely, in other words, finally, especially, without doubt, indeed, in short, in brief, primarily, chiefly, as a matter of fact, no doubt

To Conclude a Point

finally, in conclusion, to summarize, to sum up, in sum

Chart 4-3 Revising Checklist

1. Is my thesis idea intelligent and clearly stated?
2. Is my argument logically and effectively organized? Does the main idea of every paragraph relate directly to the thesis?
3. Are the paragraphs fully developed, with plenty of specific examples or illustrations to support the topic sentences?
4. Do the ideas flow coherently? Are the transitions easy to follow?
5. Have I accomplished my purpose? Does the paper make the point I set out to prove?

Combining for Conciseness

If you find that you are sometimes repeating the same word without meaning to, you may eliminate the problem by combining sentences. For instance, you might have written something like this:

> Twain savagely attacks conformity in the scene where the villagers stone the woman. The woman is suspected of being a witch.

Because the repetition of *the woman* serves no useful purpose, the two statements can be more effectively phrased in a single sentence.

> In a scene showing the villagers stoning a woman suspected of being a witch, Twain savagely attacks conformity.

When you combine sentences in this way, you take the main idea from one sentence and tuck it, usually as a modifier of some sort, within another sentence. We can illustrate the process in reverse to help you see more clearly what the technique involves. Notice that the following sentence contains two simple statements:

> Theodore, who did not wish to throw a stone, was horrified by the cruelty.

The two main ideas in that sentence are these:

> Theodore was horrified by the cruelty.
> Theodore did not wish to throw a stone.

You can recombine those sentences in various ways, depending on which idea you choose to emphasize.

> Horrified by the cruelty, Theodore did not wish to throw a stone.
> Not wishing to throw a stone, Theodore was horrified by the cruelty.

Sentence combining not only eliminates wordiness but also adds variety and focus. The various combinations provide numerous stylistic choices.

Sentence-Combining Exercise

The following sentences, all written by students, include needless repetition and wordiness that can be eliminated by sentence combining. Decide which idea in each pair of sentences should be emphasized, and put that idea in the main (independent) clause. You will, of course, need to change, add, or omit words as you work to improve these sentences, but try not to leave out any significant ideas.

1. The second common stereotype is the dark lady. Usually the dark lady stereotype symbolizes sexual temptation.
2. Kate Chopin wrote a short story called "The Storm." As the title of the story suggests, it is about a rainstorm and shows how people respond to the storm.
3. Emily Dickinson's poetry is sometimes elliptical. It is thus sometimes difficult for readers to get even the literal meaning of her poems.
4. There are three major things to consider in understanding Goodman Brown's character. These things include what the author tells us about

Brown, what Brown himself says and does, and how other people respond to him.

5. Most of the incidents that inspire Walter Mitty's fantasies have humorous connotations associated with them. These can be broken down into basically two groups, the first one being his desire to be in charge of a situation.

Rearranging for Emphasis and Variety

When you rewrite to gain emphasis and variety, you will probably restructure sentences as well as combine them. In fact, you may find yourself occasionally dividing a sentence for easier reading or to produce a short, emphatic sentence. The following are some techniques to help you in polishing your sentence structure.

Varying the Pattern

The usual way of forming sentences in English is to begin with the subject, follow with the verb, and add a complement (something that completes the verb), like this:

> Walter Mitty is not a brave person.

Any time you depart from this expected pattern, you gain variety and some degree of emphasis. Notice the difference.

> A brave person Walter Mitty is not.

Here are other variations that you may want to try.

> **A Dash at the End:** Twain found constant fault with humanity—with what he called "the damned human race."

> **An Interrupter Set Off by Dashes or Commas:** Twain considered humanity in general—"the damned human race"—inferior to the so-called lower animals.

> **A Modifier at the Beginning:** Although he loved individual human beings, Twain professed to loathe what he called "the damned human race."

A Short-Short Sentence Because most of the sentences you will write are moderately long, you gain considerable emphasis when you follow a sentence of normal length with an extremely short one.

> Plagiarizing, which means borrowing the words or ideas of another writer without giving proper credit, is a serious infraction. Do not do it.

Deliberate Repetition Just a few pages ago, we cautioned you to combine sentences rather than to repeat words needlessly. That caution still holds. But repeating words for emphasis is a different matter. Purposeful repetition can produce effective and emphatic sentences.

> Twain believed that organized religion was folly, a folly to be ridiculed discreetly.
>
> One cannot talk well, study well, or write well if one cannot think well.

That last sentence (modeled after one written by Virginia Woolf) repeats the same grammatical structure as well as the same words to achieve a powerful effect.

Exercise on Style

Rewrite the following ordinary sentences to achieve greater emphasis, variety, and conciseness.

1. Edith Wharton was born into a rich, upper-class family, but she was not even allowed to have paper on which to write when she was a child.
2. Her governesses never taught her how to organize ideas in writing, so when she decided to write a book on the decoration of houses, she had to ask her friend Walter Berry to help her write it.
3. She married Teddy Wharton when she was twenty-three years old, and he always carried a one-thousand-dollar bill in case she wanted anything.
4. Her good friend Henry James gave her advice to help her improve her novels, yet her novels invariably sold far more copies than James's did.
5. She was awarded the Legion of Honor, which is the highest award given by the French government, following World War I for her refugee relief activities.

Which Words Should I Change?

You may have a good thesis and convincing, detailed support for it—but your writing ***style*** can make the difference between a dull, boring presentation and a rich, engaging one.

Check Your Verbs

After examining the construction of your sentences, look at the specific language you have used. Read through the rough draft and underline the verbs. Look for forms of these useful but well-worn words:

is (are, was, were, etc.)	go	has
get	come	move
do	make	use

Consider substituting a different verb, one that presents a type of image—visual or otherwise—to your readers. For example, this sentence is grammatically correct but dull:

> Eveline does her work with reluctance.

Searching for a more precise verb than *does*, you might write

> Eveline reluctantly plods through her work.

Plods suggests a picture of poor Eveline with slumped shoulders and slow steps, dragging through the day.

Occasionally you can pick up a lively word from somewhere else in a limp sentence and convert it into the main verb.

> Eveline is unable to leave her home because she is trapped by a promise to her dead mother.

Trapped is an arresting word in that sentence, and you could shift it to an earlier position to good effect.

> A promise to her dead mother traps Eveline in her miserable home.

This revision also cuts unnecessary words out of the first version.

Use Active Voice Most of the Time

Although the passive voice sometimes offers the best way to construct a sentence, the habitual use of the passive sprinkles your prose with colorless helping verbs, like *is* and *was.* If a sentence is in passive voice, the subject does *not* perform the action implied by the verb.

> The paper was written by Janet, Jo's roommate.
>
> The assignment was given poorly.
>
> Her roommate's efforts were hindered by a lack of understanding.

The paper, the assignment, and the roommate's efforts did *not* carry out the writing, the giving, or the hindering. In active voice, the subjects of the sentences are the doers or the causes of the action.

> Jo's roommate, Janet, wrote the paper.
>
> The teacher gave the assignment poorly.
>
> Lack of understanding hindered her roommate's efforts.

Use Passive Voice If Appropriate

Sometimes, of course, you may have a good reason for writing in the passive voice. For example, you may want to give a certain word the important position of subject even though it is not the agent of the action. In the sentence

> Sensory details are emphasized in this paragraph.

the *details* are the key point. The writer of the paragraph (the agent of the action) is not important enough even to be included. In active voice, the key term would be pushed to the middle of the sentence, a much weaker position.

> The writer emphasizes sensory details in this paragraph.

Clearly, you need not shun the passive, but if any of your sentences sound stilted or awkward, check to see if the passive voice may be the culprit.

Exercise on Passive Voice

Change passive voice to active in the following sentences. Feel free to add, delete, or change words.

1. Antigone is treated brutally by Creon because of her struggle to achieve justice.
2. Creon was not convinced by her tirade against his unbending authority.
3. Conflict between male and female was portrayed in the play by the author.
4. If even a small point is won against a tyrant by society, considerable benefit may be experienced.
5. The tragedy is caused by the ironbound authority exercised by Creon.

Feel the Words

Words have emotional meanings (***connotations***) as well as direct dictionary meanings (***denotations***). You may be invited to a get-together, a soiree, a social gathering, a blowout, a blast, a reception, a bash, or a do, and although all are words for parties, the connotations tell you whether to wear jeans or feathers, whether to bring a case of cheap beer or a bottle of expensive wine.

In writing, take into account the emotional content of the words you use. One of our favorite essays, "The Discus Thrower," opens with this sentence:

> I spy on my patients.

The word *spy* immediately captures the imagination with its connotations of intrigue and mystery and its slight flavor of deception. "I watch my patients when they don't know it" is still an interesting sentence because of its denotative content, but essayist Richard Selzer's version commands emotional as well as intellectual engagement.

We are not encouraging you to puff up your prose with strings of adverbs and adjectives; indeed, a single emotionally charged word in a simple sentence can be quite powerful.

Exercise on Word Choice

Rewrite the following sentences using livelier words and cutting unnecessary words.

1. The first sentence of "A Good Man Is Hard to Find" is a foreshadowing of what happens to the grandmother at the end of the story.
2. The conversations between members of the family show that they are not the idealized American family on vacation but are self-absorbed and ignorant.
3. There are many instances of lying, untruths, and self-deception in the story.
4. Three men come up to the family after their car accident, but they are strange in their clothing and actions, and they are not there to help.
5. Each character has his or her own way of saying things, a manner of speech which is often amusing in a dark kind of way.

Attend to Tone

Tone—the reflection of a writer's attitude—is usually described in terms of emotion: serious, solemn, satirical, humorous, sly, mournful, expectant, and so on. Although most writing about literature calls for a plain, direct tone, other attitudes can be conveyed. Negative book reviews, for instance, sometimes have a sarcastic tone. A writer unsympathetic to Eveline might describe her as "a spineless drudge who enjoys her oppression," whereas a sympathetic reader might state that Eveline is "a pitiful victim of a brutal home life." Someone who wants to remain neutral could describe Eveline as "a young woman trapped by duty and her own fears." These variations in tone, conveyed by word choice, reflect the writers' differing attitudes toward what is being discussed.

Once you establish a tone, you should stick with it. A humorous or sarcastic section set unexpectedly in a straightforward, direct essay will distract or disconcert your readers. Be sure to set your tone in the first paragraph; then your readers will unconsciously adjust their expectations about the rest of the paper.

Use Formal Language

The nature of your audience will also determine the level of usage for your writing. Essays for college classes usually require *formal language*, a style that takes a serious or neutral tone and avoids such ***informal usage*** as most contractions, slang, and sentence fragments, even intentional ones. (See the "Handbook for Correcting Errors" at the end of this book for information about fragments.)

Even one shift from formal usage to informal usage can distract your readers:

> Eveline fully intends to leave with Frank, but she gets hung up at the point of departure.

The words *hung up* are surprisingly slangy in the context of a literary essay. An alternative that stays at the same usage level might read this way:

> Eveline fully intends to leave with Frank, but she becomes paralyzed at the point of departure

Formal writing often involves a third-person approach.

> One can sympathize with Eveline, at the same time regretting her weakness.
>
> The reader sympathizes with Eveline,...

Most people today consider the use of first-person plural (*we*, *us*, *our*, *ours*) quite acceptable in formal papers.

> We sympathize with Eveline,...
>
> Eveline gains our sympathy,...

A growing number of people think the use of the first-person singular (*I*, *me*, *my*, *mine*) is also acceptable in formal writing.

> I sympathize with Eveline,...
>
> Eveline gains my sympathy,...

But avoid the informal second person, *you.* Do *not* write, "You can see that Eveline is caught in a terrible bind."

What Is Proofreading?

Proofreading is the last step in preparing your final draft. After you have improved your sentences and refined your word choices, you must force yourself to read the paper one last time to pick up any careless mistakes or typographical errors. Jessica Mitford rightly says that "failure to proofread is like preparing a magnificent dinner and forgetting to set the table."

Try Reading It Backward

To avoid getting so interested in what you have written that you don't see your errors, read your sentences from the last one on the page to the first, that is, from the bottom to the top. Because your ideas will lack continuity in reverse order, you stand a better chance of keeping your attention focused on each sentence *as* a sentence. Be sure that every word is correctly spelled, that each sentence is complete and correctly punctuated. Be sure to run your spelling checker and to think over its suggestions, which may be imperfect. Don't automatically accept whatever appears, or you may end up using *slyly* when you meant *slightly*!

Look for Your Typical Errors

If you know that you often have problems with certain elements of punctuation or ***diction***, be on guard for these particular errors as you examine each sentence.

1. Make sure that each sentence really is a sentence, not some fragment—especially those beginning with *because, since, which, that, although, as, when*, or *what*, and those beginning with words ending in *ing*.
2. Make sure that independent clauses joined by *indeed, moreover, however, nevertheless, thus*, and *hence* have a semicolon before those words, not just a comma.
3. Make sure that every modifying phrase or clause is close to the word it modifies.
4. If you know you have a problem with spelling, check every word and look up all questionable ones. Run your spelling checker, and verify that its suggestions are really the words you want.
5. Be alert for words that you know you consistently get wrong. If you are aware that you sometimes confuse words that sound alike (*it's/its, your/you're, there/their/they're, effect/affect*), check the accuracy of your usage. Remember that your spelling checker will not help you here.

If you are not sure how to correct the errors just mentioned, you will find advice in the "Handbook for Correcting Errors" at the end of this book. You will also find a handy Proofreading Checklist in Chart 4-4 on page 66.

Read the Paper Aloud

In an earlier section, we recommended reading your paper aloud as a means of checking coherence. It's a good idea to read it aloud again to catch words left out or carelessly repeated.

Find a Friend to Help

If you have a literate friend who will help you proofread your paper, you are in luck. Ask this kind person to point out errors and to let you know whether your thesis is made plain at the beginning, whether every

Chart 4-4 Proofreading Checklist

1. Have I mixed up any of these easily confused words?

its/it's	their/they're/there	lie/lay
effect/affect	suppose/supposed	our/are
your/you're	woman/women	use/used
to/too/two	prejudice/prejudiced	then/than
who's/whose	accept/except	cite/site

2. Have I put an apostrophe appropriately in each of my possessive nouns?
3. Have I carelessly repeated any word?
4. Have I carelessly left any words out?
5. Have I omitted the first or final letter from any words?
6. Have I used the proper punctuation at the end of every sentence?
7. Have I spelled every word correctly?

sentence is clear, and whether the paper as a whole makes sense. You risk having to do further revising if any of your friend's responses prove negative, but try to be grateful for the help. You want to turn in a paper you can be proud of.

Relying on someone else to do your proofreading, though, is unwise. There will be writing situations in college that preclude your bringing a friend to help (e.g., essay examinations and in-class essays). Learn to find and correct your own errors so you will not risk failure when you go it alone.

Sample Student Paper: Final Draft

The following is the final draft of Wendy Dennison's paper on "Eveline." This finished version reflects the changes she made in organization to correct the problems revealed by her after-writing outline. The paper also includes editing changes she made to achieve precision in word choice and to increase the effectiveness of each individual sentence.

Sample Student Paper: Final Draft

Wendy Dennison
Professor McMahan
English 102
6 February 2005

Fear of Failure in Joyce's "Eveline"

In his short story "Eveline," James Joyce gives the protagonist an exciting chance to leave her old life and begin a new one. But she rejects this offer that Frank—or Fate—makes, preferring instead to settle back into the dreary life she has known all along. Why does she not go away with Frank when the opportunity seems so attractive? We need to examine Eveline's timid personality in order to discover the answer.

Since Eveline has been raised a Catholic, we know she would not take her promise to her dying mother lightly. But surely her promise to "keep the home together as long as she could" (6) was given under extreme circumstances. It was unjust of her mother to ask such a sacrifice of her, and Eveline is aware of the unfairness: "Why should she be unhappy? She had a right to happiness" (6). We know that Eveline will always be haunted by that promise, but we do not expect her to give up her chance for a life of her own in order to be a dutiful daughter. Surely that promise cannot be the only reason she stays.

We certainly should not be surprised that Eveline might wish to leave her abusive father. A hot-tempered heavy drinker, he has taken advantage of his daughter's promise to her mother. She is forced to keep house for him, yet must beg for money to feed the family.

He practically accuses her of stealing, claiming that "she used to squander the money, that she had no head, that he wasn't going to give her his hard-earned money to throw about the streets" (4-5). He has so frightened her with threats of beatings that she has "palpitations" (4). Eveline realizes that with her brothers gone, there is "nobody to protect her" (4) from her father's rage. Her father has treated Eveline badly and may abuse her even worse in the future. To leave him would obviously be in her best interest, yet something keeps her there.

Eveline's home life is so unhealthy that we feel she would be wise to leave. Despite all the chores she performs, she still does not feel entirely at home in her father's house. For example, she knows nothing about the picture of the priest (4), not even his name, yet the portrait seems quite important to her father. The dustiness of the house, of which Joyce reminds us periodically, suggests the pervasive dreariness of her daily life as she looks around "wondering where on earth all the dust came from" (4). Since her home is clearly not conducive to happiness, why does she stay there?

The main reason Eveline would remain in Ireland is that she is desperately afraid of the unknown. If she leaves the familiar, no matter how unpleasant, she risks failure. "She was about to explore another life with Frank" (5), we are told, in faraway Buenos Ayres. The word *explore* is significant, as it brings to mind uncertainty and risk, two factors that Eveline is not prepared to deal with. She admits that hers is "a hard life," yet thinks that "now that she was about to leave it she did not find it a wholly undesirable life"

Dennison 3

(5). When she sits in the growing darkness with the letters in her lap, Eveline calls up a couple of good memories—of her father being jolly once on a picnic, of his kindness once when she was sick. We see her trying to calm her fears, trying to convince herself that her home life is more bearable than it is.

Afraid of failing on her own, Eveline retreats into the familiar, telling herself that life with father cannot be as frightening as a risky, unknown life with Frank. So strong is her fear of failure that it overrides her fear of her father. She seems to decide that a predictable—if dreary and abused—life is better than a life without security or pattern.

Dennison 4

Work Cited

Joyce, James. "Eveline." *Literature and the Writing Process.* Ed. Elizabeth McMahan, Susan X Day, and Robert Funk. 7th ed. Upper Saddle River: Prentice, 2005. 3–7. Print.

5

Researched Writing

At some point you may be asked to write a literary paper that doesn't draw entirely on your own understanding and judgments. In other words, you will have to do some *research*. When writing a researched paper about literature, you begin, as always, with a ***primary source***—the story, poem, or play the paper is about—but you expand the range of your coverage to include ***secondary sources***—critical, biographical, historical, and cultural documents that support your interpretation of the primary work (or works).

Using Library Sources in Your Writing

Most student writers consult secondary sources to help them explain, develop, and strengthen their ideas and opinions. That's what Wendy Dennison did with her essay "Fear of Failure in Joyce's 'Eveline'" (see pages 67–70 in the previous chapter). Although Wendy had worked out her own arguments for why Eveline did not go away with Frank, she and her instructor thought it would be enlightening to see what other readers thought. So Wendy went to the library to find material by critics who had published their interpretations of "Eveline," especially about the ending of the story. After reading and taking notes from a number of books and articles, Wendy revised her paper by incorporating comments from several critics into her discussion. The revised, documented version of her essay appears on pages 88–92.

Although not everyone produces a finished paper before doing research, some writers do prepare a first draft before looking at secondary sources. Others consult secondary materials to help them decide on a topic. Another common strategy is to use the ideas of others as a platform for an interpretation, first summarizing several views and then presenting a different interpretation, a synthesizing conclusion, or an analysis of their conflicting points of view.

Secondary sources can help you in a number of different ways to develop an essay about literature:

- *Analyzing the features of a single work.* Why does E. E. Cummings disregard traditional form and punctuation in his poetry? How does the chorus function in *Antigone*?
- *Exploring connections between a work and the author's life.* How might Dorothy Parker's attitudes toward romance in her life illuminate her poem "One Perfect Rose"? How autobiographical is Anne Sexton's "You All Know the Story of the Other Woman"?
- *Assessing the impact of social, historical, or cultural backgrounds on a work.* How do attitudes toward homosexuality in China affect your understanding of "The Bridegroom" by Ha Jin? What is the role of the blues tradition in *Fences* by August Wilson? How do psychological theories of family systems illuminate "The Rocking-Horse Winner"?
- *Understanding the political or artistic objectives of a work.* In what ways can Luis Valdez's play *Los Vendidos* be seen as a drama of social protest? How well does "The Cask of Amontillado" illustrate Poe's theory about achieving "a certain unique or single effect" in a short story?
- *Comparing themes or characters in several works.* How do the mother-daughter relationships in stories by Tillie Olsen, Hisaye Yamamoto, Flannery O'Connor, and Joyce Carol Oates illustrate different kinds of maternal-filial bonding? What attitudes toward sports are expressed in Housman's "To an Athlete Dying Young," Updike's "Ex-Basketball Player," and Hirsch's "Execution"?

You will find ideas for researched writing in the questions that follow most of the literary selections in this book.

Conducting Your Research

The prewriting you do for a documented paper is similar to the prewriting you would do for any literary essay. You still need to consider your audience, determine your purpose, discover and develop your ideas, and decide what point you want to make. The techniques and advice presented in Chapter 1 will help you with these tasks. But the next steps will be different, perhaps even new to you. First and foremost, you have to track down relevant secondary sources, a challenging procedure that involves libraries, computer terminals, and stacks of papers and index cards. The following sections will guide you through this process.

Locating Sources

More than likely you will conduct your search for sources on a computer. Most college libraries offer workshops to help students locate materials, conduct computer searches, use online databases, and navigate the Internet. If these courses are not required, take them anyway—you could save yourself hours of aimless wandering. Your library's information desk will provide you with schedules of these valuable sessions.

Using the Online Catalog

Most libraries today list their holdings in a computerized *online public access catalog* (OPAC). The opening screen of the OPAC at the library Wendy Dennison used shows that she can search for books, journals and magazines, and other items owned by her library and by other libraries in the state. In electronic databases, such as InfoTrac and EBSCO, you can usually search for sources by author, title, and publication year and also by subject or *keywords*.

Subject searches focus only on the source's contents and yield more limited, precise results. They work best when the *descriptors* (subject headings) conform to a database's directory of terms. For your library's catalog, the directory is the *Library of Congress Subject Headings (LCSH)*, which is available in printed form in the reference room. *Keyword searches* look through the entire database and are not dependent on preset subject headings. If you know your exact subject, you will want to begin with a subject search. A keyword search, on the other hand, is a good place to limit and refine your subject and discover specific descriptors. Remember that computers are unforgiving about spelling and typing errors. When your results are not what you expected, check the accuracy of the search terms you used.

To begin her search of the online catalog, Wendy typed in the LSCH heading "Joyce, James, 1882–1941" and selected "subject" in the "search by" menu. The results showed more than seventy entries, most of which contained sublistings for specific titles. In other words, her library owns hundreds of books and other materials about James Joyce. Wendy refined her search by adding "Dubliners" (the title of the collection that contains "Eveline") to her descriptor; she found that her library had eight books on this topic. She saw which ones were available and where they were located in the library. Wendy also browsed a number of items under the subheading "criticism and interpretation" and took down information about books that appeared to deal with Joyce's early works. She felt she had plenty of material to begin her review of critical opinions about the motivations of Eveline.

Using Indexes and Databases

Even though you might find valuable material in books to use in documenting your ideas and critical judgments, your paper will not be well researched unless you also find articles and reviews relevant to your topic. These sources are now available electronically through online databases and text archives that your library subscribes to. The library homepage that Wendy was using allowed her to move from the online catalog to a list of more than a hundred searchable indexes, bibliographies, and other electronic reference tools.

The reference librarian recommended that Wendy look first at two computerized indexes to find publication information on articles about "Eveline": the *MLA International Bibliography* and the *Humanities International Index*. Other databases, like *Academic Search Elite* and *Expanded Academic Index ASAP*, also provide citations for journal articles, but they cover a wide range of academic subjects. These may be suitable for gathering background information, but the *MLA International Bibliography* is the best choice for finding authoritative, scholarly sources about literature. Journals, like magazines and newspapers, are published periodically, but are written by and for academics or expert scholars. Journals rarely have advertising, eye-catching artistic touches, or slick covers. Each journal is devoted to a specific academic subject, often a very narrow one.

When Wendy typed "Eveline" in the "find" box of the MLA search screen, she got 132 hits. The display also prompted her to narrow her results by subject and gave her several words and phrases to add to her search term. Wendy selected "Joyce, James," which reduced the list to forty-one entries. She could view these entries one at a time or print out the entire list. Each citation included the article title, the name of the periodical, and the volume, date, and page number; it also supplied the call number for any publications in her library. Many of the entries contained a brief summary of the article's content, and several included the full text of the article for her to read or print. She could also send the data to her home computer by e-mail.

Wendy browsed through these findings and printed the citations for several articles that looked promising. Because the library did not own several of the periodicals, the librarian suggested requesting copies of the articles through an interlibrary loan, but that would take several days. Another option was to consult a full-text database, such as *JSTOR (Journal Storage Project)* or *ProjectMUSE*, to see if the articles were available there. Wendy discovered two promising articles in *JSTOR* and printed them out.

These were just some of the electronic tools that Wendy used to search for possible sources. Other generally available indexes and abstracts for researching literary topics include *Gale's Literary Index*, *Humanities International Index*, *Periodical Abstracts*, and *Readers' Guide to Periodical Literature*. Popular and relevant full-text databases include *Annual Bibliography of English Language and Literature*, *EBSCO Academic Search Premier*, *Humanities Full Text*, *InfoTrac Expanded Academic Index ASAP*, *LexisNexis Academic Universe*, *WilsonSelect Plus*, *Book Review Digest Plus*, *Literature Online*, and *Literature Resource Center.*

Your library may subscribe to many of the same indexes and databases, but you need to find out what's available and how to use them. You may also be able to access these resources from your home or other location through a proxy service that verifies your status as a library card holder.

Using the Internet

A number of useful online databases and text archives are accessible over the Internet. Chart 5-1 presents selected Internet sources for doing literary research; this listing focuses on well-established popular and scholarly sites that feature useful links and other resources that may be valuable during the initial stages of your research. You can locate additional resources using any one of several different search engines—such as Netscape, Safari, Firefox, Google, Yahoo!, Ask.com, and Microsoft Explorer—that catalog Web sites in directories and allow you to conduct keyword searches.

You can also join electronic communities called *newsgroups*, through which members exchange information about a common interest or affiliation by posting questions and answers to online sites. Or you can

Chart 5-1 Internet Sources for Literature

Directories for Finding Sites

Voice of the Shuttle http://vos.ucsb.edu
An annotated guide to literary resources online, with more than seventy pages of links.

Literary Resources on the Net http://andromeda.rutgers.edu/~jlynch/Lit
A collection of links dealing primarily with English and American literature.

IPL Literary Criticism Collection http://www.ipl.org/div/litcrit
From the Internet Public Library, a collection of critical and biographical Web sites about authors and their works.

Virtual Reference Works

Bartleby.com http://www.bartleby.com
Bills itself as the "preeminent Internet publisher of literature, reference, and verse, providing students, researchers, and the intellectually curious with unlimited access to books and information on the Web, free of charge."

Encyclopedia Mythica http://www.pantheon.org
Online encyclopedia covering mythology, folklore, and legends.

Reviews and Criticism

Arts & Letters Daily http://aldaily.com
A service of the *Chronicle of Higher Education;* includes daily links to essays, book reviews, interviews, and news in a wide range of online publications; coverage of literary topics is substantial.

become a member of an Internet discussion group, frequently called a *listserv*, whose subscribers use e-mail to converse on a particular subject. You will find e-mail discussion groups to join at Google Groups (http://groups.google.com), Yahoo! Groups (http://groups.yahoo.com), and Tile.net (www.tile.net/lists).

If you need additional information, you can visit one of these helpful reference sites:

Librarians' Internet Index	http://lii.org/search/file/netsearch
Matisse's Glossary of Internet Terms	http://www.matisse.net/files/glossary.html

Evaluating Online Sources

Although many online sources are informative and valuable, determining their credibility can be challenging. With scholarly books and journal articles, you can consider the information credible because it has been reviewed and edited; the authors are often recognized authorities, and their claims are documented. But anyone can create and publish a Web site or join a newsgroup. So when you use information from an electronic source, you want to be confident that it is reliable and that it comes from someone with the appropriate authority. Here are some guidelines for evaluating online materials:

- *Look for credentials.* What do you know about the people supplying the information? What's the basis of their expertise? Is the source also available in an established, conventional printed form?
- *Track down affiliations.* Who sponsors the online site? Is it a reputable group that you can easily identify? Is the information influenced by commercial or political sponsorship? Does the site include links to other resources?
- *Analyze motives.* What purpose does the site serve? Many online postings are trying to buy or sell something; others are promoting a favorite cause. These don't usually make good sources for research.
- *Consider currency and stability.* Is the material updated regularly? Is there an archive for older information?
- *Confirm your information.* Can you find other sources to verify what you've found online? Ideally, you want to have several different kinds of sources to achieve a credible balance of research material.

For more details about evaluating online sources, you can visit one of these sites:

- *Evaluating Web Sites*, a comprehensive and instructive guide to judging information resources for reliability and accuracy, at http://www.lesley.edu/library/guides/research/evaluating_web.html

- *Evaluating Web Pages: Techniques to Apply & Questions to Ask*, an online tutorial from the UC Berkeley Library, at http://www.lib.berkeley.edu/TeachingLib/Guides/Internet/Evaluate.html

Finally, check with your instructor to determine the types of resources considered appropriate for your specific assignment.

Using Reference Works in Print

As you can see, the library's computers provide an overwhelming number of sources and service options. You will have to spend some time with these data systems to find out how they work and how useful they are for your research. Most libraries still hold much of this and additional useful reference material in print. The *MLA International Bibliography*, for example, continues to be issued in book form. Your library probably has print versions of many indexes and guides to articles on literature. So if the computer terminals are crowded or not working, or if you simply want some peace and quiet while researching, the reference librarian can tell you where on the shelves these books are kept. You are likely to run across valuable material on shelves near the books you seek, an advantage to this often neglected ambulatory research system.

Working with Sources

Once you have located the books and articles you want to read and assimilate, you can begin reading, taking notes, and synthesizing the material.

Taking Notes

Many researchers use note cards for keeping track of the facts and opinions they find. If you decide to use cards, work out some system for recording information. Here are some suggestions:

1. Fill out a bibliography card every time you consult a new source, and record all the details necessary for citing this source in your paper, including where to find the source again. Then put the author's last name, an abbreviated title, and the page number or numbers on all the note cards you use for this source.
2. Write only one idea or point on each card. This allows you to shuffle the cards as you figure out the precise organization of your paper.
3. Put subject headings on the cards—one or two words in the upper right-hand corner to tell you what each note is about.
4. Summarize the ideas in your own words. If you think you might want to quote directly from the source, copy the author's exact words and enclose them in quotation marks.

Computers now come with a note card program, or you can purchase software for a note card system. You can use the computer note cards just as you would use index cards: title each card by topic, and then type your notes onto the card provided by the computer.

Using a Research Notebook

Another option is a double-entry research notebook where you summarize and analyze readings all in one location.

1. Divide a notebook or computer page vertically down the middle.
2. On the left side of the page, summarize your reading of the source material, and write down the complete bibliographic data and any URLs. Any exact words or phrases need to be placed within quotation marks.
3. On the right side of the page, comment on your sources, noting their importance to your topic and their relationship to other sources.

The response side of the divided notebook shows the evolution of your thinking, lets you articulate questions that arise as you read and process information, and guides you toward a thesis for your paper. The system also helps you to avoid the cut-and-paste style of research writing because it encourages synthesis and analysis throughout the process. Finally, this record of your thoughts helps to identify which ideas are your own and which you picked up along the way—a key distinction that safeguards against inadvertent plagiarism and allows you to claim your own thoughts with confidence.

Figure 5-1 provides an example of a student's notes on the article "Eveline and the Blessed Margaret Mary Alacoque" by Donald Torchiana. In the left column, the student summarizes the key points in his own words and includes a couple of direct quotations from the article. In the right column, the student records his thoughts and reactions to the article.

Using the Printout/Photocopy Option

If the time you can spend in the library is limited, you might want to print out an online article or photocopy portions of books in order to have these materials available to study at your convenience. In fact, you might find it easier to take notes from a printout than from a computer screen. You can underline or highlight key ideas, even color-coding these highlighted passages to fit different subtopics in your paper. You can also write comments or cross-references to other sources in the margins. It's a good idea to put the information from printouts and photocopies on note cards or into your research notebook. This procedure forces you to summarize the material in your own words and makes it much easier to sort the separate items into categories.

Notes	Responses
Source: Torchiana, p. 70	
Torchiana says about Margaret Mary Alacoque that: —as a child she lost a parent and was treated like a servant by relatives who raised her. —at age 10, refused an offer of marriage	Parallels with Eveline seem clear, but what do they mean? What's Joyce suggesting? The influence of Eveline's Catholic upbringing, for sure. Her destiny to be some kind of martyr?
—entered convent at age 24 —met hostility from the rest of sisters —performed menial tasks, took care of young children —Quotation: "Virtually addicted to suffering, she was corrected more than once for her singular notions or her clumsiness and slowness." —had a vision of Christ at age 26	The first vision could be like her first glimpse of Frank. How old was Eveline when she met Frank? If he's her savior, then why not go with him? Or does she think she needs to stay and be a "sacrificial victim"? To whom? Surely not her father.
p. 71 —told she had been chosen to be the instrument by which Christ's love would be made known —The Lord took her heart and put it within His own, then returned it to her breast	Is Eveline "addicted to suffering"? Could be. Is she comfortable with this role? This idea seems similar to Brandabur's view of Eveline.
—had a number of visions; in one she was told she would be a "sacrificial victim for the lack of charity among her sister communicants."	Her promise to her dying mother seems related to this role. But it's a warning to Eveline, one she seems to recognize.
—but her vision of the Sacred Heart spread	Do the critics read too much into this? Margaret Mary is mentioned only once in the story.

Figure 5-1 Sample Entry from a Divided-Page Research Notebook

Summarizing, Paraphrasing, and Quoting

In most of your notes, you will be summarizing or paraphrasing your source materials, rather than quoting the author's exact words. In a ***summary*** you condense the main point of an argument or passage in your own words. A summary is useful when you want to capture the gist of an idea without including the background or supporting details. Compare these sentences from an article about "Eveline" with the summary that follows it.

> **Original** "Joyce indicates why Eveline will not, in fact, be able to escape. Paralysis will win because she is not worthy to defeat it. Her inertia is revealed by the excessive value she places on the routine satisfactions of her present existence, and on the pathetically small indications of affection which her father has been prepared to give" (Hart 50).
>
> **Summary** Eveline won't be able to leave because she's too attached to her father and to the familiarity of her everyday life, according to Clive Hart (50).

In a ***paraphrase*** you restate comments and ideas from a source, using approximately the same number of words as the original. Although written in your own words and style, a good paraphrase will reflect the author's idea, tone, and point of view more clearly than a summary does. Here's a paraphrase of the passage from Clive Hart's article:

> Hart argues that Joyce shows us that Eveline is incapable of leaving home. That she doesn't have the strength of character to break away can be seen in her desperate attachment to the comforts of a familiar life, as well as to her father's meager expressions of love (50).

You will also find comments and observations that are so well expressed that you want to use the original wording rather than summarize or paraphrase it. Be sure to record the exact words of the original quotation, as well as the numbers of the pages on which they appear. Here is an example:

> Critic Clive Hart observes that Eveline's father "used to hunt Eveline and her companions in from their play" by "wielding his blackthorn stick like an angry god" (49).

Devising a Working Outline

As you are reading and taking notes, you should also be thinking about the organization of your points and ideas. Chances are the best arrangement won't emerge until you are fairly well along with your research—possibly not until you have finished it. But as you collect more and more notes, leaf through your cards or printouts occasionally to see if you can arrange them into three or four main categories to form the major claims in your argument or analysis. The sooner you can get a plan worked out, the more efficient your research becomes. You can see exactly what you are looking for and avoid wasting time on sources that would prove irrelevant or redundant.

Writing a First Draft

As we pointed out at the beginning of this chapter, some people write a preliminary draft before beginning their research, especially if they are eager to get their arguments written down before they forget them. If you use this method, you should devise a thesis, assemble your evidence from the primary source, order your ideas, and write a first draft, following the procedures discussed in Chapter 2. Then you can go to the library, as Wendy did, to locate and read a number of pertinent secondary sources and incorporate ideas from this reading into your paper at appropriate places.

On the other hand, if you are not sure about your topic or your approach, you can go to the library, locate some relevant secondary sources, and study them carefully. Then return to the primary source and begin the discovery process again, using freewriting or questioning or problem solving to refine your topic, devise a major claim, and generate ideas. You may have to do further research as you work through your interpretation, but that's all part of the recursive nature of writing.

Organizing Your Notes

Once you have a clearly focused thesis, go back and read through your note cards. Using the headings that you put on the cards, group the ones with similar ideas together in stacks. If you photocopied most or all of your sources, write headings on the first page of each photocopy and sort the articles that way. Then consult your working plan or rough outline, and arrange the stacks in the order that the headings appear there. As you write, the necessary information will be in front of you, ready to be incorporated into the first draft of your paper.

If your stacks of cards don't follow the outline but lie there in a confused, overlapping mess, all is not lost. You can still bring order out of chaos. Here are a few methods:

1. *Tinker with your outline.* It may seem like a step backward, but now that you have new information from your research, the whole topic may look different. Look at the main headings and change any that don't seem to fit; add others that you have good material for but overlooked when you made the working outline.
2. *Put your note cards into different groupings.* This process may suggest an organizing strategy that you wouldn't think of any other way.
3. *Set your notes aside and begin writing*—even if you begin in the middle of a thought. Force yourself, as in freewriting, to keep going, even if

your paper seems repetitive, disorganized, and sketchy. Eventually, the writing will begin to take shape, giving you an idea about where to start your first draft.

4. *Find a key article on the topic, and examine its structure.* You may be able to find an organizational scheme that will work for your paper.
5. *Explain your ideas to a friend who agrees to ask questions along the way.* Tape-record your discussion, and see whether it suggests a sensible order of exposition.

Using Quotations and Paraphrases

You want to be judicious in using the material you have gathered from secondary sources. In general, depend most upon your own interpretations of the primary material, use paraphrasing to introduce ideas gleaned through research, and turn to direct quotations of secondary sources only when the wording is especially original or powerful, saving that technique for special effect. Your main goal is to argue *your* thesis or advance *your* interpretation, not simply to paste together other people's thoughts and words. Don't just sprinkle your discussion with quotations and paraphrases; work them into your analysis and explain how they support your claims. Take a look at this example from a paper about "The Lottery":

> The author reveals the savagery that is hidden just beneath the surface of seemingly civilized exteriors. This duality of human nature is exhibited through the characterization and actions of the villagers. As Cleanth Brooks and Robert Penn Warren point out, "The cruel stoning is carried out by 'decent' citizens who in many other respects show themselves kind and thoughtful" (130). When it was time for the scapegoat to be murdered, Mrs. Delacroix, who earlier had made neighborly conversation with the victim, was one of the first to pick up a stone.

As you can see, the student writer backed up her observation about the duality of human nature with a direct quotation from a secondary source. She then used a detail from the primary source to nail down the point.

Integrating Sources

Whether you are quoting directly or simply paraphrasing someone else's ideas and observations, you should always give credit in the text of your paper to the person from whom you are borrowing. The MLA documentation style requires you to cite all sources *within* the paper. These in-text citations contain three important parts:

1. an introduction of the source, telling your reader that material from some authority is coming up, who or what the source is, and what the person's credentials are, if you know them;
2. the material from the source, quoted or paraphrased; and

3. the parenthetical documentation, which tells your reader that your use of the source is over and gives the page number for the source of that particular material.

More details about in-text citations are given in the explanation of the MLA documentation style at the end of this chapter (pages 98–99).

If you want your paper to read smoothly, pay particular attention to the way you introduce quotations and paraphrases. You need a ready supply of introductory phrases to slide the source material in gracefully—phrases like "As LeSeure discovered," "Professor Weber notes," and "According to Dr. Carter." These attributions help your readers to evaluate the source material as they read it and to distinguish source material from your remarks about it. Here are some more models for you to go by:

> As critic Lawrence Stone explains, daughters in Shakespeare's England were "often unwanted and might be regarded as no more than a tiresome drain on the economic resources of the family" (112).
>
> According to biographer Joan Givner, the failure of Porter's personal relationship with Josephson caused a temporary inability to write (221).
>
> D. G. Gillham remarks that the "male 'worm' " and "female 'rose' " in "The Sick Rose" have Freudian significance and "give rise in the speaker to half-hidden feelings of indecency, guilt, and fear so easily associated with sexual experience" (11).
>
> Prospero's suite in "The Masque of the Red Death" has been described by Kermit Vanderbilt as "a metaphor of nature and mortality" (382).
>
> "A beautiful virgin walled off from an imperfect world," Rachel Brownstein points out, "is the central figure in romance" (35).

Quoting from Primary Sources

The advice for handling quotations from secondary sources also applies to quoted material from primary sources: keep quoted passages brief; use them as support for your own observations, and don't rely on a quotation to make a point for you; integrate quotations smoothly and grammatically into your own sentences; vary the way you introduce the quotations. In her essay on "Eveline," Wendy Dennison provided these models:

> Eveline realizes that with her brothers gone, there is "nobody to protect her" (5).
>
> "She was about to explore another life with Frank" (Joyce 4), we are told, in faraway Buenos Ayres.

You will also need to cite the work you are quoting from so that your readers know exactly which passage you are referring to and where it is located. For short stories and novels, give the author's last name and the page number in the parenthetical citation. The author's name may be omitted if you mention it in your paper or if authorship is clear from context.

> We are told that Jake "took a moment or two to feel both proud and sad about his performance" (Gilb 56).
>
> The narrator of Gilb's story tells us that Jake "took a moment or two to feel both proud and sad about his performance" (56).

For poems, line numbers alone are usually sufficient to identify the source—provided that the author and title are given in your essay.

> The speaker's assertion that "Something there is that doesn't love a wall, / That wants it down" (35–36) represents one side of Frost's theme.

You do not need to include the word *line* or *lines* or its abbreviation in the parenthetical citation. When citing a play, give the act and scene numbers (without abbreviations), plus the line numbers if the work is in verse.

> In *Othello*, Iago's striking comment, "What you know, you know. / From this time forth I will never speak a word" (5.2.299–300), serves as a philosophic closure.

The numbers separated by periods mean "act 5, scene 2, lines 299 through 300." In plays that are not written in verse, you may simply cite page numbers, as you would with a quotation from a short story.

> Bono, Troy's friend and coworker, understands why Rose keeps after her husband to build a fence around their yard. "Some people build fences to keep people out," says Bono, "and other people build fences to keep people in. Rose wants to hold on to you all" (816).

You can get additional guidance for quoting primary sources on pages 26–27 (short stories), pages 477–79 (poetry), and pages 760–61 (drama). You will also find details about punctuating quoted material on pages 1151–53 in the "Handbook for Correcting Errors."

Avoiding Plagiarism

Research is a kind of conversation among writers, their sources, and others interested in the topic. One of the challenges for writers, then, is to clearly define their part in this broader conversation both accurately and ethically. The core principle here is *respect*: for the person whose ideas you are employing, for your own voice and credibility, and for your readers.

The failure to give proper credit to your sources is called ***plagiarism.*** It usually involves carelessly—or, far worse, deliberately—presenting the words or ideas of another writer as your own. Most universities have strict policies on academic dishonesty that require sanctions ranging from failing a paper, to assigning a failing grade for the course, to dismissal from the university.

You can avoid this dishonesty by using a moderate amount of care in taking notes. Put quotation marks around any passages, even brief phrases, that you copy word for word. Circle the quotation marks in red or highlight the quoted material in some way, as a reminder to give credit to the source.

You must also avoid the original wording if you decide to ***paraphrase*** your sources, rather than quoting directly. Changing a few words or rearranging the phrases is not enough: such close paraphrasing is still considered plagiarism. The following examples may help you to see the difference between plagiarism and paraphrasing:

> **Original Passage:** "The interest of the story lies not in the events, but in the reasons for Eveline's failure to accept the offer of salvation" (Hart 48).
>
> **Plagiarism:** One critic notes that the story's main interest is not in its events but in the reasons why Eveline fails to accept Frank's offer of salvation.
>
> **Plagiarism:** Most readers are interested not in the events of "Eveline" but in the reasons for the protagonist's failure to accept her salvation.
>
> **Paraphrase:** As Clive Hart notes, we are interested not in what happens in the story but in why Eveline doesn't take the chance to save herself (48).
>
> **Combined Paraphrase and Direct Quotation:** Hart notes that the main interest for the reader "lies not in the events" but in "Eveline's failure to accept the offer of salvation" (48).
>
> **Direct Quotation:** "The interest of the story lies not in the events," critic Clive Hart claims, "but in the reasons for Eveline's failure to accept the offer of salvation" (48).

As you use your secondary sources, remember that no one wants to do the hard work of creating ideas and shaping an appropriate language only to have someone else take credit for it.

Rewriting and Editing

Many people who do researched writing make no attempt to work in direct quotations or provide complete citations in the first draft because pausing to do so interrupts the flow of their ideas. They just jot down the name of the person who has provided the information or idea; they go back later to fill in page numbers and integrate exact quotations as they revise their first draft. Putting self-stick notes on pages of sources you intend to use will help you find the precise material later.

Documenting Your Sources

Various academic disciplines use different documentation styles. Because you are writing about literature, the appropriate one for you to follow is the Modern Language Association style. Sample entries illustrating the MLA format appear at the end of this chapter. You may also use as a model the documentation included in the sample research papers that follow on pages 88–97 or the one at the end of Chapter 19 (pages 881–88).

Revising the Draft

Because a research paper entails the extra demands of incorporating other people's ideas and acknowledging these sources, you will want to take special care in rewriting your early drafts. The checklist for revising and editing researched writing, Chart 5-2 (page 87), will help you to turn your draft into a successful essay.

Formatting Your Paper

The document format recommended by the *MLA Handbook* is fairly simple. But individual course requirements may vary from the MLA design, so check with your instructor before you begin preparing your final copy. Here are some features to examine:

Margins. Provide margins of at least one inch at the top, bottom, and both sides of the page.

Spacing and indentions. Double-space throughout, including quotations and the Works Cited page. Indent paragraphs one-half inch or five spaces. Long prose quotations (five or more typed lines) and quotations of more than three lines of poetry should be double-spaced and indented one inch or ten spaces from the left margin.

Page numbers. Number all pages, beginning on the first page. Put the numbers in the upper-right-hand corner about one-half inch from the top. Place your last name before the page number in case the pages later become separated. Note the correct page numbering on the sample student paper, which follows.

Heading. The MLA does not require a separate title page. If your instructor asks you to use one, follow the format he or she provides. Otherwise, give your name and the date, plus any other information requested by your instructor (such as the title and number of the course), on the first page of your text. Place this heading an inch from the top of the page, aligned with the left margin. Note the heading on the sample student paper.

Title. Double-space after the heading and center the title of your paper. Do *not* underline or place your title in quotation marks, and do not set it in large type or capitalize all the letters. Do capitalize the first and last

Chart 5-2 Checklist for Revising and Editing Researched Writing

Check the Usual Things

1. Be sure the introduction states your thesis (see pages 15–17, 24–25).
2. Be sure each paragraph is unified, coherent, and directly related to your thesis (see pages 51–52, 55–56).
3. Be sure that the transitions between paragraphs are clear and effective (see page 57).
4. Be sure your conclusion reinforces your main argument (see page 26).

Check the Special Things

1. Be sure that you have introduced direct quotations gracefully, using the name and, if appropriate, the title or occupation of the person quoted.
2. Be sure each citation is accurate.
3. Be sure that paraphrases are in your own words and that sources are clearly acknowledged.
4. Be sure that you have not relied too heavily on a single source.
5. Be sure that you have written most of the paper yourself; you need to examine, analyze, or explain the material, not just splice together a lot of quotations and paraphrases.
6. Be sure to separate quotations with some comment of your own.
7. Be sure to underline or italicize the titles of books and magazines; put quotation marks around the titles of articles, stories, poems, and chapters in books.

words and all other words *except* articles (*a*, *an*, *the*), prepositions, coordinating conjunctions, and the *to* in infinitives. Double-space between your title and the first line of text.

Textual headings. If you use headings within your paper to guide readers through the discussion, keep them as short as possible and make them specific to the material that follows. Do not boldface, italicize, or use bigger type or all capitals for these headings.

Sample Documented Student Paper

The following is the documented version of the essay that Wendy Dennison wrote about "Eveline." See pages 67–70 for the undocumented version.

Dennison 1

Wendy Dennison

Professor McMahan

English 102

11 March 2005

Fear of Failure in Joyce's "Eveline"

In his short story "Eveline," James Joyce gives the protagonist an exciting chance to leave her old life and begin a new one. But she rejects this offer that Frank—or Fate—makes, preferring instead to settle back into the dreary life she has known all along. Why does she not go away with Frank when the opportunity seems so attractive? One critic, Magda de Tolentino, says "Nothing but family bonds hold her back" (74). Another critic thinks Eveline is "imprisoned" in her passive, feminine role of housekeeper (Ingersoll 4), while another calls her "a meaningless sacrificial victim for a religious community lacking charity" (Torchiana 75). Some commentators think she's afraid of marrying Frank. Professor Edward Brandabur, for example, claims Eveline "is ever conscious of the effects on her mother of a brutal marriage" (63), and Professor Thomas Dilworth maintains that "her mother's marriage to her father must subconsciously condition her anticipation of married life" (458).

Obviously many factors affect Eveline and influence her decision not to go with Frank. But in the last analysis, I think, we need to examine Eveline's own character, especially her timid personality, to discover the answer to our question. For, as Professor Warren Beck, has pointed out, "Eveline is not simply timid; she is racked by inner conflict, finally to the point of distraction" (113).

Since Eveline has been raised a Catholic, we know she would not take her promise to her dying mother lightly. But surely her promise to "keep the home together as long as she could" (Joyce 6) was given under extreme circumstances. It was unjust of her mother to ask such a sacrifice of her, and Eveline is aware of the unfairness: "Why should she be unhappy? She had a right to happiness" (6). We know that Eveline will always be haunted by that promise, but we do not expect her to give up her chance for a life of her own in order to be a dutiful daughter. Surely that promise cannot be the only reason she stays.

We certainly should not be surprised that Eveline might wish to leave her abusive father. A hot-tempered heavy drinker, he has taken advantage of his daughter's promise to her mother. She is forced to keep house for him, yet must beg for money to feed the family. He practically accuses her of stealing, claiming that "she used to squander the money, that she had no head, that he wasn't going to give her his hard-earned money to throw about the streets" (5). He has so frightened her with threats of beatings that she has "palpitations" (4). Eveline realizes that with her brothers gone, there is "nobody to protect her" (5) from her father's rage. Her father has treated Eveline badly and may abuse her even worse in the future. On the other hand, as Professor Ingersoll points out, Eveline's father offers "the comfort and security of the familiar" and as he grows older will probably be "less likely to have the strength to abuse her, as he did her mother" (3). Yes, getting away from her father would be in her best interests, but something keeps her there.

Dennison 3

Eveline's home life is so unhealthy that we feel she would be wise to leave. Despite all the chores she performs, she still does not feel entirely at home in her father's house. For example, she knows nothing about the picture of the priest (Joyce 4), not even his name, yet the portrait seems quite important to her father. The dustiness of the house, of which Joyce reminds us periodically, suggests the pervasive dreariness of her daily life as she looks around "wondering where on earth all the dust came from" (4). Critic Clive Hart sums up her condition this way:

> Eveline has memories of a happier, freer past which contrasts both with the tedium of the present and with the uncertainty of the future.... The evenings, which used to be a time for play, are now one of drudgery, and even in childhood it was evident that happiness was something transient. (49).

Since her home is clearly not conducive to happiness, why does she stay there?

The main reason Eveline would remain in Ireland is that she is desperately afraid of the unknown. If she leaves the familiar, no matter how unpleasant, she risks failure. "She was about to explore another life with Frank" (Joyce 5), we are told, in faraway Buenos Ayres. The word *explore* is significant, as it brings to mind uncertainty and risk, two factors that Eveline is not prepared to deal with. She admits that hers is "a hard life," yet thinks that "now that she was about to leave it she did not find it a wholly undesirable life" (5). According to Professor Hart, Eveline is psychologically incapable

Dennison 4

of breaking away, and it shows in "the excessive value she places on the routine satisfactions of her present existence, and on the pathetically small indications of affection which her father has been prepared to give" (50). When she sits in the growing darkness with the letters in her lap, Eveline calls up a couple of good memories—of her father being jolly once on a picnic, of his kindness once when she was sick (Joyce 6). We see her trying to calm her fears, trying to convince herself that her home life is more bearable than it is. But, as Martin Dolch points out, "Change is already beyond her capacity and fills her with a crazy fear which mistakes salvation for destruction" (99).

Afraid of failing on her own, Eveline retreats into the familiar, telling herself that life with father cannot be as frightening as a risky, unknown life with Frank. In Professor Warren Beck's view, Eveline doesn't doubt Frank: "What she doubts is herself" (116). Eveline's doubts and her fear of failure override her fear of her father. She seems to decide that a predictable—if dreary and abused—life is better than a life without security or pattern. As William York Tindall puts it, "The end [of this story] is not a coming of awareness but an animal experience of inability" (15).

Dennison 5

Works Cited

Beck, Warren. *Joyce's* Dubliners: *Substance, Vision, and Art*. Durham: Duke UP, 1969. Print.

Brandabur, Edward. *A Scrupulous Meanness: A Study of Joyce's Early Work*. Urbana: U of Illinois P, 1971. Print.

de Tolentino, Magda. "Family Bonds and Bondage within the Family: A Study of Family Ties in Clarice Lipsector and James Joyce." *Modern Language Studies* 18.2 (1988): 73–78. *JSTOR*. Web. 28 Feb. 2005.

Dilworth, Thomas. "The Numina of Joyce's 'Eveline.'" *Studies in Short Fiction* 15.4 (1978): 456–58. *Academic Search Premier*. Web. 28 Feb. 2005.

Dolch, Martin. "Eveline." *James Joyce's* Dubliners: *A Critical Handbook*. Ed. James R. Baker and Thomas F. Staley. Belmont: Wadsworth, 1969. 96–101. Print.

Hart, Clive. "Eveline." *James Joyce's* Dubliners: *Critical Essays*. Ed. Clive Hart. New York: Viking, 1969. 48–52. Print.

Ingersoll, Earl G. "The Stigma of Femininity in James Joyce's 'Eveline' and 'The Boarding House.' " *Studies in Short Fiction* 30.4 (1993): 501–10. *Academic Search Premier*. Web. 29 Feb. 2005.

Joyce, James. "Eveline." *Literature and the Writing Process*. Ed. Elizabeth McMahan, Susan X Day, and Robert Funk. 8th ed. Upper Saddle River: Prentice, 2007. 3–7. Print.

Tindall, William York. *A Reader's Guide to James Joyce*. New York: Noonday, 1959. Print.

Torchiana, Donald T. *Backgrounds for Joyce's* Dubliners. Boston: Allen, 1986. Print.

Sample Published Article

The following is an edited version of "Nature's Decoy: Kate Chopin's Presentation of Women and Marriage in Her Short Fiction" by Professor Elizabeth McMahan. It originally appeared in *Turn-of-the-Century Women* in 1985. You can use this article as a model for introducing and documenting direct quotations from the primary source (Chopin's story) as well as from secondary sources (published works about Chopin and the story) following the MLA style. The story appears in this textbook on pages 241–45.

Kate Chopin's Presentation of Marriage in "Désirée's Baby"

Written before the turn of the twentieth century, Kate Chopin's short works convey attitudes toward marriage and its effects upon women. Chopin depicts marriage almost always as restricting the female's individuality. Seldom does she show males suffering in the toils of an unfortunate union. She is most often concerned with the devastating effect of marriage on the woman's sense of self. We learn much about how late nineteenth-century patriarchal society encouraged the sweet submissiveness of women in marriage.

The tragic heroine of "Désirée's Baby" has married for love. Yet Chopin suggests in this story that such total devotion to a mate can prove disastrous for a woman. Désirée's love is so selfless that when her husband "frowned she trembled, but loved him. When he smiled, she asked no greater blessing of God" (175). For a time Désirée basks in her husband's love, but after their child is born, she notices "a strange, an awful change in [his] manner, which she dared not ask him to explain" (175). Everyone on the plantation except Désirée has already perceived that the child has Negro blood. Since Désirée was a foundling, adopted as a toddler by her aristocratic parents, her husband Armand concludes that Désirée is "not white."

Like Browning's Duke who faults his last duchess for ranking his "gift of a nine-hundred-years-old name / With anybody's gift," Armand Aubigny cares greatly about his family name, "one of the oldest and proudest in Louisiana" (174). Before anyone suspected that the baby was of mixed race, Désirée had told her adopted mother, "Oh, Armand is the proudest father in the parish, I believe, chiefly because it is a boy to bear his name . . ." (175). Armand, after rejecting both Désirée and the baby, ceases to love her "because of the unconscious injury she has brought upon his home and his name" (177). In a typically ironic surprise ending, Chopin reveals that it is not Désirée but Armand who "belongs to the race that is cursed with the brand of slavery" (178).

The knowledge comes too late to save "the gentle Désirée." Since she has no concept of herself as a person apart from her husband, she considers her life not worth living after he shuns her. Although her mother begs, "Come home to Valmondé; back to your mother who loves you. Come with your child" (177), Désirée cannot. As Professor Cynthia Griffin Wolff observes, "When Armand's love slips into cruelty . . . , Désirée loses her own tenuous grasp on the balance of life" (83). She takes the little one in her arms and walks "across a deserted field, where the stubble bruised her tender feet so delicately shod, and tore her thin gown to shreds" (177).

The scene in the deserted field focuses on two powerful images. First, the imagery suggests death—"It was an October afternoon; the sun was just sinking" (177). October brings the end of summer's living vegetation, here coupled with the literal dying of the light as the sun sinks beneath the horizon. Second, the imagery suggests Désirée's innocence—her gown is white; the setting sun brings a "golden gleam" to her brown hair. White is, of course, an archetypal symbol of innocence, and the gold in her hair suggests her Caucasian heritage. Like *Hamlet*'s Ophelia, she vanishes "among the reeds and willows that grew thick along the banks of the deep, sluggish bayou; and she did not come back again" (177).

Kate Chopin's view of marriage for women is considerably jaundiced. Yet she herself appears to have been quite happily married. Her earliest biographer, Daniel Rankin, reports that she and her husband enjoyed a felicitous union (107). Even Per Seyersted, in his thorough appraisal of Chopin's life and work, could find no evidence to contradict this report. When Oscar Chopin succumbed to swamp fever, Kate, at age thirty, was left a widow with six children. Only after Oscar's death did she begin to write. We can only speculate, of course, but something—perhaps the influence of Ibsen whom we know she read—enabled her to perceive that women as well as men can have a genuine need for self-determination.

Today a woman who is lucky in her choice of a husband can have both—marriage and self-direction. But in Chopin's fictional world that option does not exist. As Barbara Solomon says, Kate Chopin was indeed "a woman much ahead of her time" (xxvii).

Works Cited

Chopin, Kate. "Désirée's Baby." Solomon 173–178. Print.

Rankin, Daniel. *Kate Chopin and Her Creole Stories.* Philadelphia: U of Pennsylvania P, 1932. Print.

Seyersted, Per. *Kate Chopin: A Critical Biography.* Baton Rouge: Louisiana State UP, 1969. Print.

Solomon, Barbara H. Introduction. The Awakening *and Selected Stories of Kate Chopin.* Ed. Barbara H. Solomon. New York: Signet, 1976. vii–xxvii. Print.

Wolff, Cynthia Griffin. "Kate Chopin and the Fiction of Limits: 'Désirée's Baby.' " *Southern Literary Journal* 10.2 (1978): 123–33. Print.

EXPLANATION OF THE MLA DOCUMENTATION STYLE

The documentation style of the Modern Language Association (MLA)—used in English, foreign languages and some other humanities—requires that source citations be given in the text of the paper rather than in footnotes or endnotes. This in-text style of documentation involves parenthetical references.

Throughout this section, all titles of independently published works—books, plays, magazines, journals, Web sites, online databases, television and radio programs, films, and works of art—are italicized. Titles of stories, articles, songs, and other shorter works included in larger publications are punctuated with quotation marks and not italicized.

In-Text Citations

A. You will usually introduce the cited material, whether quoted or paraphrased, by mentioning the name of the author in your lead-in and giving the page number (or numbers) in parentheses. Put the parenthetical reference near the cited material, but preserve the flow of your writing by placing the citation where a pause would naturally occur, preferably at the end of the sentence, as in this example:

   Edmund Wilson tells us that the author of *Uncle Tom's Cabin* felt "the book had been written by God" (5).

B. Your readers can identify this source by consulting your Works Cited at the end of your paper. The entry for the source cited above would appear like this one:

   Wilson, Edmund. *Patriotic Gore: Studies in the Literature of the American Civil War.* New York: Oxford UP, 1966. Print.

C. If you do not mention the author in your lead-in, include his or her last name in parentheses along with the page number, without an intervening comma, like this:

   One of the great all-time best-sellers, *Uncle Tom's Cabin* sold over 300,000 copies in America and more than 2 million copies world wide (Wilson 3).

D. If you refer to one of two or more works by the same author, put a comma after the author's last name and include a shortened title in the parenthetical reference.

   (Pinker, *Stuff* 95).

E. If you are using a source written or edited by more than three people, use only the name of the first person listed, followed by "et al." (meaning "and others") in your lead-in.

> Blair et al. observe that the fine arts were almost ignored by colonial writers (21).

Because *et* means "and," it isn't an abbreviation and therefore doesn't need a period.

F. If you have to quote indirectly—something from another source not available to you—use "qtd. in" (for "quoted in") in your parenthetical reference. This example refers to a book written by Donald Johanson and Maitland Edey:

> Richard Leakey's wife, Maeve, told the paleoanthropologist David Johanson, "We heard all about your bones on the radio last night" (qtd. in Johanson and Edey 162).

Note: It is always best to track down the original source, in case it has not been quoted precisely. You may also find even better material for your purposes in the original.

Preparing the List of Works Cited

On a separate page at the end of the paper, alphabetize your Works Cited list for all sources mentioned in your paper. Format the list according to the these rules:

- Center Works Cited at the top of the page.
- Arrange your sources in alphabetical order by the last name of the author. If the author is not given in the source, alphabetize the source by the first main word in the title (excluding *A*, *An*, or *The*).
- Double-space the entire list, both within and between entries.
- Use hanging indention: put the first line of each entry flush with the left margin, and indent any subsequent lines in the entry one-half inch.
- In both titles and subtitles, capitalize the first and last words and all other words *except* articles (*a, an, the*), prepositions, coordinating conjunctions, and the *to* in infinitives.
- Omit any use of the words *page* or *pages* or *line* or *lines.* Do not even include abbreviations for these terms. Use numbers alone:

  Kinsley, Michael. "Continental Divide" *Time* 7 July 1997: 89–91.

- Shorten publishers' names: for example, use Pearson instead of Pearson Education or Norton instead of W. W. Norton and Co. or Oxford UP instead of Oxford University Press or U of Illinois P instead of University of Illinois Press. See sample entries 1 through 12.
- For books, include the city of publication, usually given on the title page of the work cited. If you find two or more cities, use only the first. It is not necessary to identify a state, province, or country after the city name.
- Use lowercase roman numerals (ii, xiv) for citing page numbers from a preface, introduction, or table of contents; use uppercase roman numerals in names of monarchs (Elizabeth II).

- Abbreviate months and titles of magazines as shown in the sample entries.
- Leave one space after all concluding punctuation marks.

Sample Entries for a List of Works Cited

The following models will help you write Works Cited entries for most of the sources you will use. If you use a source not illustrated in these examples, consult the more extensive list of sample entries found in the *MLA Style Manual and Guide to Scholarly Publishing*, 3rd ed. or the *MLA Handbook for Writers of Research Papers*, 7th ed., or ask your instructor for guidance.

The MLA now recommends including the medium of publication for all entries. Sources are divided into three categories: print, Web, and other common sources. Use *Print* for books, periodicals (magazine, journals, newspapers), and other printed materials. Use *Web* for any material you retrieved online. Other common sources include *Film*, *CD*, *DVD*, and *Radio* or *Television program*. The medium of publication will usually be the last item in the citation. But when *Web* is the medium, the last item should be the date of access. The sample entries on the following pages provide plenty of examples.

Citing Print Publications

Books

1. Book by one author

Mizejewski, Linda. *Divine Decadence: Fascism, Female Spectacle, and the Makings of Sally Bowles.* Princeton: Princeton UP, 1992. Print.

2. Two or more books by the same author

Pinker, Steven. *The Language Instinct: How the Mind Creates Language.* New York: Morrow, 1994. Print.

---. *The Stuff of Thought: Language as a Window into Human Nature.* New York: Viking, 2007. Print.

[Give the author's name in the first entry only. Thereafter, use three hyphens in place of the author's name, followed by a period and the title.]

3. Book by two or three authors

Anderson, Terry, and Donald Leal. *Free Market Environmentalism.* Boulder: Westview, 1991. Print.

McCrum, William, William Cran, and Robert MacNeil. *The Story of English.* New York: Viking, 1986. Print.

[Notice that only the first author's name is in reversed order.]

4. Book by more than three authors

Medhurst, Martin J., et al. *Cold War Rhetoric: Strategy, Metaphor, and Ideology.* New York: Greenwood, 1990. Print.

[The phrase *et al.* is an abbreviation for *et alii*, meaning "and others." Because *et* is the whole Latin word for *and*, don't put a period after it.]

5. Book with an editor

Gallegos, Bee, ed. *English: Our Official Language?* New York: Wilson, 1994. Print.

[When the entry begins with the editor's name, put a comma and the abbreviation "ed." for "editor" after the person's name. For a book with two or more editors, use "eds."]

6. Book with an author and an editor

Vidal, Gore. *The Selected Essays of Gore Vidal.* Ed. Jay Parini. New York: Doubleday, 2008. Print.

["Ed." in front of a name means "Edited by."]

7. Essay or article in a collection, casebook, or critical edition.

Geist, Stanley. "Portraits from a Family Album: *Daisy Miller.*" *Hudson Review* 5 (Summer 1952): 203–6. Rpt. in *James's* Daisy Miller. Ed. William T. Stafford. New York: Scribner's, 1963. 131–33. Print.

[If an italicized title contains another title that should be italicized, leave the inner title without italics.]

Matthews, James H. "Frank O'Connor." Lewisburg: Bucknell UP, 1976. Rpt. in *Contemporary Literary Criticism.* Ed. Dedria Bryfonski and Laurie Harris. Vol. 14. Detroit: Gale, 1983. 399–402. Print.

["Rpt." means "reprinted."]

8. Introduction, preface, or forward

Alexie, Sherman. Introduction. *Smoke Signals: A Screenplay.* By Sherman Alexie. New York: Hyperion, 1998. vii–xi. Print.

9. Work in an anthology

Butler, Octavia. "Bloodchild." *The Norton Anthology of African American Literature.* Ed. Henry Louis Gates Jr. and Nellie Y. McKay. New York: Norton, 1997. 2480–94. Print.

10. Article in a reference book (unsigned and signed)

"Vietnam War." *The Columbia Encyclopedia.* 6th ed. 2007. Print.

Van Doren, Carl. "Samuel Langhorne Clemens." *The Dictionary of American Biography.* 1958 ed. Print.

[For widely used reference books, do not give full publication information. List only the edition, the year of publication, and the medium of publication.]

11. Later (second or subsequent) edition

Harmon, William, and Hugh Holman. *A Handbook to Literature.* 11th ed. Upper Saddle River: Prentice, 2008. Print.

12. A translated book

Cirlot, J. E. *A Dictionary of Symbols.* Trans. Jack Sage. 2nd ed. New York: Philosophical Lib., 1976. Print.

Periodicals

13. Article in a scholarly journal

Mason, John B. "Whitman's Catalogues: Rhetorical Means for Two Journeys in 'Song of Myself.'" *American Literature* 45 (1973): 34–49. Print.

Treuer, David. "Smartberries: Interpreting Erdrich's *Love Medicine.*" *American Indian Culture & Research Journal* 29.1 (2005): 21–36. Print.

[Give the volume number and the issue number, when available, for all journals. Add a period and the issue number directly after the volume number: 29.1 means volume 29, issue 1.]

14. Article from a monthly or bimonthly magazine

Tocalino, Rob. "The 20-Century American Short Story: Three Authors, Three Generations." *Bookmarks* May/June 2006: 26–31. Print.

15. Article from a weekly or biweekly magazine

Lahr, John. "Land of Lost Souls: David Rabe's America." *New Yorker* 24 Nov. 2008: 114–20. Print.

16. Newspaper article

Weiner, Jon. "Vendetta: The Government's Secret War against John Lennon." *Chicago Tribune* 5 Aug. 1984, sec 3:1. Print.

17. Review of a book or movie

Grice, Helena. Rev. of *Image and Power: Women in Fiction in the Twentieth Century,* ed. Sarah Sceats and Gail Cunningham. *English* 46 (1997): 175–78. Print.

Stack, Peter. "'Smoke' Causes Tears of Sadness, Joy." Rev. of *Smoke Signals,* dir. Chris Eyre. *San Francisco Chronicle* 3 July 1998:C7. Print.

Citing Online Publications

You are no longer required to include uniform resource locators (URLs, also called Web addresses) when citing online sources—unless you think your readers will not be able to locate the source without the URL. Conclude all entries with *Web* as the medium of publication, followed by the date of access.

Online Periodicals

18. Articles from online databases

If you retrieve source material from a full-text database, you need to indicate that you read it in electronic form. You will probably use a service to which your library subscribes, such as Academic Search Premier, JSTOR, Expanded Academic ASAP, ProQuest, Project Muse, Galenet, LexisNexis. Most of the items in these databases were previously published in print. Give the print information first. If possible, give the inclusive page numbers or, when pagination is not continuous, the first page number and a plus sign; if page numbers are not available, use *n. pag*. Do *not* include the database URL or information about the library. Complete the citation by giving the name of the database (italicized), medium of publication (Web), and the date of access. Here are examples of entries for periodical publications retrieved from online databases:

Hammer, Langdon. "Confluences of Sound and Sense: Kay Ryan's Idiosyncratic Approach to the Commonplace." *American Scholar* 77.2 (Summer 2008): 58–59. *Academic Search Premier.* Web. 14 Dec. 2008.

Kennedy, J. Gerald, and Robert Beuka. "Imperilled Communities in Edward P. Jones's *Lost in the City* and Dagoberto Gilb's *The Magic of Blood.*" *The Yearbook of English Studies* 31 (2001): 10–23. *JSTOR.* Web. 6 Oct. 2008.

Parascandola, Louis J. "Love and Sex in a Totalitarian Society: An Exploration of Ha Jin and George Orwell." *Studies in the Humanities* 33.1 (June 2005): 38+. *Expanded Academic ASAP.* Web. 22 Nov. 2008.

Welty, Eudora. Rev. of *Pilgrim at Tinker Creek* by Annie Dillard. *New York Times Book Review* 24 Mar. 1974: 36–37. *ProQuest.* Web. 14 Sept. 2007.

19. Articles published independently on the Web

For articles that are available on independent Web sites—as opposed to articles accessed from an aggregate database—cite the author, title, and publication data for the printed version as usual; then give the number of pages, paragraphs, or other sections of the electronic version, if provided on the site. Conclude with the medium of publication (*Web*) and the date of access. Here are sample entries for articles on the Web:

Borroff, Marie. "Another Look at Robert Frost's 'Birches.'" *Literary Imagination Online* 7 (2005): 69–80. Web. 8 Jan. 2009.

Yeoman, Barry. "Into the Closet: Can Therapy Make Gay People Straight?" *Salon.com* 22 May 2000: n. pag. Web. 23 May 2000.

"Vietnam War Memorial." *Encyclopaedia Britannica Online.* Encyclopaedia Britannica, 2008. Web. 14 June 2008.

Keller, Julia. "New Hope for Do-Nothing Nobodies: A Guy Named Sam Johnson." *ChicagoTribune.com.* Chicago Tribune, 19 Oct. 2008. Web. 23 Nov. 2008.

Other Web Sources

20. An entire Web site

Celestial TimePiece: A Joyce Carol Oates Home Page. Ed. Randy Souther. Gleeson Library, U of San Francisco, 1995. Web. 27 Nov. 2008.

21. Part of a Web site

Nelson, Cary. "Japanese American Concentration Camp Haiku." *Modern American Poetry.* Dept. of English, U of Illinois, Urbana-Champaign, 2002. Web. 18 Nov. 2008.

Citing Other Common Sources

For other sources, include enough information to permit an interested reader to locate your original source. Be sure to arrange this information in a logical fashion, following as much as possible the order and punctuation of the entries provided earlier. To be safe, consult your instructor for suggestions about documenting unusual material.

23. A television or radio broadcast

Sedaris, David. Interview by Terry Gross. *Fresh Air.* NPR. WHYY, Philadelphia. 9 June 2008. Radio.

24. Sound recording

Welty, Eudora. "Why I Live at the P. O." Read by the author. *Essential Welty.* Rec. 1956. Dir. Ward Botsford. Caedmon, 2006. CD.

25. Film or video recording

Brokeback Mountain. Dir. Ang Lee. Perf. Heath Ledger, Jake Gyllenhaal, Michelle Williams. Screenplay by Larry McMurtry and Diana Ossana. Universal, 2005. Focus Features, 2006. DVD.

[Begin with the title (italicized) and include the director, distributor, and year of release. Include any other details that seem pertinent—names of performers, screenwriters, and producer—between the title and the distributor. For video recordings, include the release date and the medium.]

Part II

Writing About Short Fiction

This section, focusing on the short story, covers the literary and rhetorical elements that you need to understand in order to write effectively about short fiction.

6

How Do I Read Short Fiction?

As noted author Joyce Carol Oates has observed, short fiction can be difficult to understand "because it demands compression; each sentence must contribute to the effect of the whole. Its strategy is not to include an excess of detail but to exclude, to select, to focus as sharply as possible." In order to grasp the full meaning of a story, you need to read it at least twice. Preferably, let some time elapse between readings so that you can mull the story over in your mind. Your initial reading can be purely for pleasure, but the second reading should involve careful and deliberate study of all the elements that combine to produce a unified whole. You should gain both pleasure and knowledge from reading short fiction. The knowledge frequently stems from understanding the *theme*, which usually provides some insight into the human condition, although sometimes contemporary short stories simply raise moral or ethical questions and make no pretense of providing answers.

Notice the Structure

During the second reading, notice the way the story is structured. The action (that is, what happens) is called the ***plot*** and is usually spurred by some ***conflict*** involving the main character (the ***protagonist***). Except in some modern works, most short stories have a clear beginning, middle, and end during which the conflict producing the action becomes increasingly intense, building to a ***climax*** that sometimes resolves the conflict and sometimes simply concludes it—often in catastrophe. Do not expect many happy endings in serious fiction. A somber conclusion is more likely.

Usually stories proceed in regular chronological order following a time sequence similar to that in real life. But occasionally an author employs ***flashbacks***—stopping the forward action to recount an episode that happened in the past—in order to supply necessary background material or to maintain suspense. By closely following the shifts in time in Louise Erdrich's "The Red Convertible," readers discover what the narrator means when he says, "Now Henry owns the whole car, and…Lyman walks everywhere he goes." And if William Faulkner had written "A Rose for Emily" chronologically, without the distorted time sequence, the stunning impact of the conclusion would have been lost.

Consider Point of View and Setting

Sometimes the ***point of view***—the position from which an author chooses to relate a story—can be crucial to the effectiveness, even to the understanding, of short fiction. In Alice Walker's "Everyday Use," we are given the mother's views and feelings about her two quite different daughters. In other stories, the point of view provides access to the thoughts and feelings of more than one character. In Nathaniel Hawthorne's "Birthmark," for example, an all-seeing, all-knowing or *omniscient* narrator provides access to the thoughts and feelings of all the major characters in the story. Ernest Hemingway, in "Hills like White Elephants," chooses to let his characters tell the story themselves through conversation. This *objective* (sometimes called *dramatic*) point of view is revealed by a glance at the pages, which consist primarily of dialogue. Some authors select one character to tell the story firsthand, but these first-person narrators can play quite different roles. In "I Stand Here Ironing," Tillie Olsen creates a strong sense of believability by presenting the reflections running through a mother's mind as she recalls her difficulties in raising a daughter with too little money and no husband to help. In Raymond Carver's "What We Talk About When We Talk About Love," the first-person narrator is essentially an observer, a peripheral character who reports the conversation between Mel and Terry but is not himself the focus of it. The narrator of "The Lesson" by Toni Cade Bambara acts as a "hostile witness" to the scenes and events she encounters, resisting the hard truths about class and oppression that she, and the reader, must finally acknowledge.

The ***setting*** of a story, like the point of view, is sometimes important, sometimes not. In many of the stories included in this anthology, setting plays a role of some consequence. For instance, John Steinbeck opens "The Chrysanthemums" with this description:

> The high gray-flannel fog of winter closed off the Salinas Valley from the sky and from all the rest of the world. On every side it sat like a lid on the mountains and made of the great valley a closed pot.

The isolation of the valley by the fog suggests the isolation of Elisa Allen, whose energies and experiences are restricted by her living on the ranch. As you study a short story, give some thought to the setting. Could the events just as well take place somewhere else? Or does the setting seem to play an integral part? How does its time period affect the story? Does the setting in some way add to the meaning of the work?

Study the Characters

Focusing on *characterization* often proves a fruitful approach to analyzing and writing about a short story or a play. Wendy Dennison adopts this strategy in her paper on "Eveline" (pp. 67–70). You'll notice, if you look again at Wendy's paper, that she examines several other key elements to gain a thorough understanding of the title character. She discusses the setting because Eveline's dreary life is influenced by the drabness of her surroundings. She considers the plot and finds Eveline's paralysis at the end tied directly to her characterization as a timid, duty-bound daughter. She examines the imagery and finds that the religious images underscore Eveline's devout nature while, at the same time, the pervasive dust shrouds her barren existence. All of these elements combine to reveal Joyce's theme of a young woman's life sadly circumscribed by her submission to duty, family, and church.

As you reread a story, pay special attention to those passages in quotation marks that characters speak to each other. You can begin to determine characterization from these exchanges, just as you come to know real people partly by what they say. As you form an understanding of a character, notice what other people in the story say about that person and how they respond to that person, as well as what the author reveals of that person's thoughts and past behavior. Because fiction often allows us access to what the characters are thinking (as well as doing), we can sometimes know fictional persons better than we do our closest friends and family members. Sometimes, we can be certain of a character's motivation for behaving in a certain way; at other times, motivation becomes one of the elements to be determined before we can fully appreciate the work.

In Hawthorne's "The Birthmark," in order to understand why Dr. Aylmer is willing to risk his young wife's life, we need to examine his motives and behavior. In doing so, we discover that his faith in science leads to his overweening desire to create perfection—to establish (without success, of course) that science can control and improve on nature. And in Tim O'Brien's "The Things They Carried," we see that the author uses the details of what the men carried with them to take us into their minds—to reveal their motivations and define their personalities.

Foils

A ***foil*** is a minor character whose role sharpens our understanding of a major character by providing a contrast. Although far more common in drama than in the short story, foils can also prove useful in the analysis of works of fiction.

In Flannery O'Connor's "Good Country People," Mrs. Freeman's placid, uncultivated, but contented daughters serve to point up the discontent of the well-educated but neurotic main character, Joy/Hulga. In

"A & P," John Updike uses two minor characters to highlight why the story's narrator, Sammy, decides to quit his job. Stoksie, the fellow checker, prefigures what Sammy might become if he stays at the A & P; and Lengel, the store manager, represents the authority figure Sammy is rebelling against.

After you have read a fictional work, ask yourself why the author included the minor characters. What role do they serve in the work as a whole? Often the role of a minor character will provide an appropriate focus for writing an analysis of a short story, a novel, or a play.

Look for Specialized Literary Techniques

As you study a story on second reading, you may notice irony and foreshadowing that you missed the first time through. Since ***irony*** involves an upsetting of expectations—having the opposite happen from what would be usual—you sometimes need to know the outcome of an action in order to detect the full extent of the irony. ***Foreshadowing*** works the same way: you may not be aware of these hints of future happenings until the happenings finally occur. But when you go through a story again, both irony and foreshadowing become easily apparent and contribute to the meaning and effectiveness.

Be alert also for ***images***—for words and phrases that put a picture in your mind. These images increase the enjoyment of reading fiction and, if deliberately repeated, can become ***motifs*** that emphasize some important element in the story and thus convey meaning. The numerous images of the protagonist's active hands and fluttering fingers in Sherwood Anderson's "Hands" establish an impression of Wing Biddlebaum's fragile, panicky nature. If a repeated image gathers significant meaning, it then becomes a ***symbol***—to be clearly related to the theme or central argument of the story. Biddlebaum's nervous hands symbolize the fear and repression that restrict his existence, just as the repeated images of dust and decay in Faulkner's "A Rose for Emily" symbolize the deterioration of Miss Emily's mind and the fortunes of her once revered family.

Examine the Title

The title may in some way point toward or be related to the meaning. Richard Wright's title "The Man Who Was Almost a Man" evokes his theme: the difficulty that black males encounter in achieving manhood in America. Sometimes, the title identifies the controlling symbol, as in John Steinbeck's "The Chrysanthemums" and Sherwood Anderson's "Hands." Joseph Conrad's title "Heart of Darkness" directs us straight to his subject: the evil that lurks at the core of human nature.

Investigate the Author's Life and Times

Sometimes biographical and background information can be illuminating. For instance, knowing Hawthorne's attitude toward original sin enriches a reading of "The Birthmark," just as some knowledge of the Catholic faith can explain the circumstances that influence the young woman's decision in Joyce's "Eveline." Knowing what life was like for poor Americans during the Great Depression of the 1930s helps to clarify the forces that drive the protagonists in Wright's "The Man Who Was Almost a Man" and Olsen's "I Stand Here Ironing."

Continue Questioning to Discover Theme

Your entire study of these various elements of fiction should lead to an understanding of the meaning, or *theme*, of the story. You need to ponder everything about a short story in order to discover its theme. Keep asking yourself questions until you come up with some meaningful observation about human behavior or the conduct of society. The questions in Chart 6-1 on page 114 will guide you in exploring any story and perhaps spark that essential insight that leads to understanding.

Chart 6-1 Critical Questions for Reading the Short Story

Before planning an analysis of any of the selections in the anthology of short stories, write out the answers to the following questions to be sure you understand the piece and to help you generate material for your paper.

1. Who is the main character? Does this person's character change during the course of the story? Do you feel sympathetic toward the main character? What sort of person is she or he? Does this character have a foil?
2. What pattern or structure is there to the development of the plot? Can you describe the way the events are organized? Is the structure significant to the meaning?
3. Does surprise play an important role in the plot? Is there foreshadowing? Does the author use flashbacks?
4. Is anything about the story ironic?
5. Is there any symbolism in the story? How does the author make you aware of symbolic actions, people, or objects?
6. What is the setting—the time and location? How important are these elements in the story? Could it be set in another time or place just as well? Is the setting significant to the meaning?
7. Describe the atmosphere of the story, if it is important. How does the author create this atmosphere?
8. Who narrates the story? Is the narrator reliable? What effect does the point of view have on your understanding of the story? What would be gained or lost if the story were told from a different point of view (for example, by another character)?
9. How does the title relate to the other elements in the story and to the overall meaning?
10. What is the theme of the story? Can you state it in a single sentence? How is this theme carried out?
11. Does the author's style of writing affect your interpretation of the story? If so, how would you describe the style? For example, is it conversational or formal? Familiar or unfamiliar? Simple or ornate? Ironic or satiric?

7

Writing About Structure

When you focus on structure in discussing a literary work, you are examining the way the parts fit together to form a unified whole. Examining the structure often proves an excellent means of understanding a short story, novel, poem, or play and also provides a good way to approach a written literary analysis.

What Is Structure?

Most works of literature have an underlying pattern that serves as a framework or ***structure***. You are familiar with the way plays are divided into acts and scenes, identified with numerals in the script, and marked in a stage production by the opening and closing of the curtain. The structure of television drama is often marked by commercial breaks. (For a discussion of dramatic structure, see Chapter 17, "Writing About Dramatic Structure.") Poems also have a visible structure, being divided into lines and stanzas. Sometimes poetic structure is complex and arbitrary, involving a certain number of lines, an established meter, and a fixed rhyme scheme. (See Chapter 15, "Writing About Poetic Form.") Novels, as you know, are divided into chapters, usually numbered and often titled, but sometimes not. Some short stories have no visible structure at all, but many do: they have space breaks indicating the divisions. Occasionally in stories (like Faulkner's "A Rose for Emily") and often in novellas, these sections are numbered.

In ***narrative*** works like novels and short stories, the plot itself is the main structural element, but these works also contain underlying structural features. Although not visible like chapter divisions or space breaks, the underlying structure serves an integral function just as a skeleton does in providing support for the body. Discovering, examining, and understanding these underlying structures will involve delving beneath the surface to discover the meaning of the work.

How Do I Discover Structure?

First, consider the ***plot.*** What is the central conflict and how is it resolved? Do the events in the story move in a straight line from the beginning of the conflict to its resolution? Or are there interruptions and digressions? Are there flashbacks? Is time manipulated in any other way? If so, why? For instance, without the time shifts in the plot of Faulkner's "A Rose for Emily," there would be no suspense, and we would lose the impact of the final revelation.

If the story has any visible structural features, such as space between sections, try to figure out why they are there. Do they divide scenes? Do they indicate time shifts?

Look next for patterns, especially for contrasts and for repetitions. In "The Things They Carried," the story included in this chapter, Tim O'Brien alternates descriptions of the physical burdens of the soldiers with descriptions of the inner, psychological burdens they carry with them. The story also involves repetitions of key events told from different vantage points and with different amounts of detail.

Look always at beginnings and endings. "The Things They Carried" begins with the romantic fantasies of the main character, Jimmy Cross, which contrast sharply with the same character's fantasies of leadership at the end of the story. How did this change in character happen?

When analyzing any work of literature, don't forget to consider the title. Does it have any relationship to the plot? Sometimes the title touches on the central conflict or an important idea, thus focusing our attention on the structure of the story and reinforcing our understanding of the theme.

Looking at Structure

With our discussion of structure in mind, read Tim O'Brien's "The Things They Carried," which follows, and try to determine how the parts work together to convey the meaning of the story.

Tim O'Brien 1946–

Tim O'Brien was born in Austin, Minnesota. After graduating *summa cum laude* from Macalester College and doing graduate work at Harvard, he was drafted into the army and served in Vietnam, where he was promoted to sergeant and received the Purple Heart. "Good stories," he told an interviewer, "deal with our moral struggles, our uncertainties, our dreams, our blunders, our contradictions, our endless quest for understanding. Good stories do not resolve the mysteries of the human spirit but rather describe and expand upon those mysteries."

The Things They Carried

First Lieutenant Jimmy Cross carried letters from a girl named Martha, a junior at Mount Sebastian College in New Jersey. They were not love letters, but Lieutenant Cross was hoping, so he kept them folded in plastic at the bottom of his rucksack. In the late afternoon, after a day's march, he would dig his foxhole, wash his hands under a canteen, unwrap the letters, hold them with the tips of his fingers, and spend the last hour of light pretending. He would imagine romantic camping trips into the White Mountains in New Hampshire. He would sometimes taste the envelope flaps, knowing her tongue had been there. More than anything, he wanted Martha to love him as he loved her, but the letters were mostly chatty, elusive on the matter of love. She was a virgin, he was almost sure. She was an English major at Mount Sebastian, and she wrote beautifully about her professors and roommates and midterm exams, about her respect for Chaucer and her great affection for Virginia Woolf. She often quoted lines of poetry; she never mentioned the war, except to say, Jimmy, take care of yourself. The letters weighed ten ounces. They were signed "Love, Martha," but Lieutenant Cross understood that "Love" was only a way of signing and did not mean what he sometimes pretended it meant. At dusk, he would carefully return the letters to his rucksack. Slowly, a bit distracted, he would get up and move among his men, checking the perimeter, then at full dark he would return to his hole and watch the night and wonder if Martha was a virgin.

The things they carried were largely determined by necessity. Among the necessities or near necessities were P-38 can openers, pocket knives, heat tabs, wrist watches, dog tags, mosquito repellant, chewing gum, candy, cigarettes, salt tablets, packets of Kool-Aid, lighters, matches, sewing kits, Military Payment Certificates, C rations, and two or three canteens of water. Together, these items weighed between fifteen and twenty pounds, depending upon a man's habits or rate of metabolism. Henry Dobbins, who was a big man, carried extra rations; he was especially fond of canned peaches in heavy syrup over pound cake. Dave Jensen, who practiced field hygiene, carried a toothbrush, dental floss, and several hotel-size bars of soap he'd stolen on R & R in Sydney, Australia. Ted Lavender, who was scared, carried tranquilizers until he was shot in the head outside the village of Than Khe in mid-April. By necessity, and because it was SOP,[1] they all carried steel helmets that weighed five pounds including the liner and camouflage cover. They carried the standard fatigue jackets and trousers. Very few carried underwear. On their feet they carried jungle boots—2.1 pounds—and Dave Jensen carried three pairs of socks and a can of Dr. Scholl's foot powder as a precaution against trench foot. Until he was shot, Ted Lavender carried six or seven ounces of premium dope, which for him was a necessity. Mitchell Sanders, the RTO,[2] carried condoms. Norman Bowker carried a diary. Rat Kiley carried comic books. Kiowa, a devout Baptist, carried an illustrated New Testament that had been presented to him by his father, who taught Sunday school in Oklahoma City, Oklahoma. As a hedge against bad times, however, Kiowa also carried his grandmother's distrust of the white man, his grandfather's old hunting hatchet. Necessity dictated. Because the land was mined and booby-trapped, it was SOP

[1]Standard operating procedure.
[2]Radiotelephone operator.

for each man to carry a steel-centered, nylon-covered flak jacket, which weighed 6.7 pounds, but which on hot days seemed much heavier. Because you could die so quickly, each man carried at least one large compress bandage, usually in the helmet band for easy access. Because the nights were cold, and because the monsoons were wet, each carried a green plastic poncho that could be used as a raincoat or ground sheet or makeshift tent. With its quilted liner, the poncho weighed almost two pounds, but it was worth every ounce. In April, for instance, when Ted Lavender was shot, they used his poncho to wrap him up, then to carry him across the paddy, then to lift him into the chopper that took him away.

They were called legs or grunts.

To carry something was to "hump" it, as when Lieutenant Jimmy Cross humped his love for Martha up the hills and through the swamps. In its intransitive form, "to hump" meant "to walk," or "to march," but it implied burdens far beyond the intransitive.

5 Almost everyone humped photographs. In his wallet, Lieutenant Cross carried two photographs of Martha. The first was a Kodachrome snapshot signed "Love," though he knew better. She stood against a brick wall. Her eyes were gray and neutral, her lips slightly open as she stared straight-on at the camera. At night, sometimes, Lieutenant Cross wondered who had taken the picture, because he knew she had boyfriends, because he loved her so much, and because he could see the shadow of the picture taker spreading out against the brick wall. The second photograph had been clipped from the 1968 Mount Sebastian yearbook. It was an action shot—women's volleyball—and Martha was bent horizontal to the floor, reaching, the palms of her hands in sharp focus, the tongue taut, the expression frank and competitive. There was no visible sweat. She wore white gym shorts. Her legs, he thought, were almost certainly the legs of a virgin, dry and without hair, the left knee cocked and carrying her entire weight, which was just over one hundred pounds. Lieutenant Cross remembered touching that left knee. A dark theater, he remembered, and the movie was *Bonnie and Clyde*, and Martha wore a tweed skirt, and during the final scene, when he touched her knee, she turned and looked at him in a sad, sober way that made him pull his hand back, but he would always remember the feel of the tweed skirt and the knee beneath it and the sound of the gunfire that killed Bonnie and Clyde, how embarrassing it was, how slow and oppressive. He remembered kissing her good night at the dorm door. Right then, he thought, he should've done something brave. He should've carried her up the stairs to her room and tied her to the bed and touched that left knee all night long. He should've risked it. Whenever he looked at the photographs, he thought of new things he should've done.

What they carried was partly a function of rank, partly of field specialty.

As a first lieutenant and platoon leader, Jimmy Cross carried a compass, maps, code books, binoculars, and a .45-caliber pistol that weighed 2.9 pounds fully loaded. He carried a strobe light and the responsibility for the lives of his men.

As an RTO, Mitchell Sanders carried the PRC-25 radio, a killer, twenty-six pounds with its battery.

As a medic, Rat Kiley carried a canvas satchel filled with morphine and plasma and malaria tablets and surgical tape and comic books and all the things a medic must carry, including M & M's for especially bad wounds, for a total weight of nearly twenty pounds.

As a big man, therefore a machine gunner, Henry Dobbins carried the M-60, 10
which weighed twenty-three pounds unloaded, but which was almost always loaded. In addition, Dobbins carried between ten and fifteen pounds of ammunition draped in belts across his chest and shoulders.

As PFCs or Spec 4s, most of them were common grunts and carried the standard M-16 gas-operated assault rifle. The weapon weighed 7.5 pounds unloaded, 8.2 pounds with its full twenty-round magazine. Depending on numerous factors, such as topography and psychology, the rifleman carried anywhere from twelve to twenty magazines, usually in cloth bandoliers, adding on another 8.4 pounds at minimum, fourteen pounds at maximum. When it was available, they also carried M-16 maintenance gear—rods and steel brushes and swabs and tubes of LSA oil—all of which weighed about a pound. Among the grunts, some carried the M-79 grenade launcher, 5.9 pounds unloaded, a reasonably light weapon except for the ammunition, which was heavy. A single round weighed ten ounces. The typical load was twenty-five rounds. But Ted Lavender, who was scared, carried thirty-four rounds when he was shot and killed outside Than Khe, and he went down under an exceptional burden, more than twenty pounds of ammunition, plus the flak jacket and helmet and rations and water and toilet paper and tranquilizers and all the rest, plus the unweighed fear. He was dead weight. There was no twitching or flopping. Kiowa, who saw it happen, said it was like watching a rock fall, or a big sandbag or something—just boom, then down—not like the movies where the dead guy rolls around and does fancy spins and goes ass over teakettle—not like that, Kiowa said, the poor bastard just flat-fuck fell. Boom. Down. Nothing else. It was a bright morning in mid-April. Lieutenant Cross felt the pain. He blamed himself. They stripped off Lavender's canteens and ammo, all the heavy things, and Rat Kiley said the obvious, the guy's dead, and Mitchell Sanders used his radio to report one U.S. KIA[3] and to request a chopper. Then they wrapped Lavender in his poncho. They carried him out to a dry paddy, established security, and sat smoking the dead man's dope until the chopper came. Lieutenant Cross kept to himself. He pictured Martha's smooth young face, thinking he loved her more than anything, more than his men, and now Ted Lavender was dead because he loved her so much and could not stop thinking about her. When the dust-off[4] arrived, they carried Lavender aboard. Afterward they burned Than Khe. They marched until dusk, then dug their holes, and that night Kiowa kept explaining how you had to be there, how fast it was, how the poor guy just dropped like so much concrete. Boom-down, he said. Like cement.

In addition to the three standard weapons—the M-60, M-16, and M-79—they carried whatever presented itself, or whatever seemed appropriate as a means of killing or staying alive. They carried catch-as-catch-can. At various times, in various situations, they carried M-14s and CAR-15s and Swedish Ks and grease guns and captured AK-47s and Chi-Coms and RPGs and Simonov carbines and black-market Uzis and .38-caliber Smith & Wesson handguns and 66 mm LAWs

[3]Killed in action.

[4]Helicopter.

and shotguns and silencers and blackjacks and bayonets and C-4 plastic explosives. Lee Strunk carried a slingshot; a weapon of last resort, he called it. Mitchell Sanders carried brass knuckles. Kiowa carried his grandfather's feathered hatchet. Every third or fourth man carried a Claymore antipersonnel mine—3.5 pounds with its firing device. They all carried fragmentation grenades—fourteen ounces each. They all carried at least one M-18 colored smoke grenade—twenty-four ounces. Some carried CS or tear-gas grenades. Some carried white-phosphorus grenades. They carried all they could bear, and then some, including a silent awe for the terrible power of the things they carried.

In the first week of April, before Lavender died, Lieutenant Jimmy Cross received a good-luck charm from Martha. It was a simple pebble, an ounce at most. Smooth to the touch, it was a milky-white color with flecks of orange and violet, oval-shaped, like a miniature egg. In the accompanying letter, Martha wrote that she had found the pebble on the Jersey shoreline, precisely where the land touched water at high tide, where things came together but also separated. It was this separate-but-together quality, she wrote, that had inspired her to pick up the pebble and to carry it in her breast pocket for several days, where it seemed weightless, and then to send it through the mail, by air, as a token of her truest feelings for him. Lieutenant Cross found this romantic. But he wondered what her truest feelings were, exactly, and what she meant by separate-but-together. He wondered how the tides and waves had come into play on that afternoon along the Jersey shoreline when Martha saw the pebble and bent down to rescue it from geology. He imagined bare feet. Martha was a poet, with the poet's sensibilities, and her feet would be brown and bare, the toenails unpainted, the eyes chilly and somber like the ocean in March, and though it was painful, he wondered who had been with her that afternoon. He imagined a pair of shadows moving along the strip of sand where things came together but also separated. It was phantom jealousy, he knew, but he couldn't help himself. He loved her so much. On the march, through the hot days of early April, he carried the pebble in his mouth, turning it with his tongue, tasting sea salts and moisture. His mind wandered. He had difficulty keeping his attention on the war. On occasion he would yell at his men to spread out the column, to keep their eyes open, but then he would slip away into daydreams, just pretending, walking barefoot along the Jersey shore, with Martha, carrying nothing. He would feel himself rising. Sun and waves and gentle winds, all love and lightness.

What they carried varied by mission.

When a mission took them to the mountains, they carried mosquito netting, 15
machetes, canvas tarps, and extra bug juice.

If a mission seemed especially hazardous, or if it involved a place they knew to be bad, they carried everything they could. In certain heavily mined AOs,[5] where the land was dense with Toe Poppers and Bouncing Betties, they took turns humping a twenty-eight-pound mine detector. With its headphones and big sensing plate, the equipment was a stress on the lower back and shoulders, awkward to handle, often useless because of the shrapnel in the earth, but they carried it anyway, partly for safety, partly for the illusion of safety.

---

[5]Areas of operations.

On ambush, or other night missions, they carried peculiar little odds and ends. Kiowa always took along his New Testament and a pair of moccasins for silence. Dave Jensen carried night-sight vitamins high in carotin. Lee Strunk carried his slingshot; ammo, he claimed, would never be a problem. Rat Kiley carried brandy and M & M's. Until he was shot, Ted Lavender carried the star-light scope, which weighed 6.3 pounds with its aluminum carrying case. Henry Dobbins carried his girlfriend's pantyhose wrapped around his neck as a comforter. They all carried ghosts. When dark came, they would move out single file across the meadows and paddies to their ambush coordinates, where they would quietly set up the Claymores and lie down and spend the night waiting.

Other missions were more complicated and required special equipment. In mid-April, it was their mission to search out and destroy the elaborate tunnel complexes in the Than Khe area south of Chu Lai. To blow the tunnels, they carried one-pound blocks of pentrite high explosives, four blocks to a man, sixty-eight pounds in all. They carried wiring, detonators, and battery-powered clackers. Dave Jensen carried earplugs. Most often, before blowing the tunnels, they were ordered by higher command to search them, which was considered bad news, but by and large they just shrugged and carried out orders. Because he was a big man, Henry Dobbins was excused from tunnel duty. The others would draw numbers. Before Lavender died there were seventeen men in the platoon, and whoever drew the number seventeen would strip off his gear and crawl in head first with a flashlight and Lieutenant Cross's .45-caliber pistol. The rest of them would fan out as security. They would sit down or kneel, not facing the hole, listening to the ground beneath them, imagining cobwebs and ghosts, whatever was down there—the tunnel walls squeezing in—how the flashlight seemed impossibly heavy in the hand and how it was tunnel vision in the very strictest sense, compression in all ways, even time, and how you had to wiggle in—ass and elbows—a swallowed-up feeling—and how you found yourself worrying about odd things—will your flashlight go dead? Do rats carry rabies? If you screamed, how far would the sound carry? Would your buddies hear it? Would they have the courage to drag you out? In some respects, though not many, the waiting was worse than the tunnel itself. Imagination was a killer.

On April 16, when Lee Strunk drew the number seventeen, he laughed and muttered something and went down quickly. The morning was hot and very still. Not good, Kiowa said. He looked at the tunnel opening, then out across a dry paddy toward the village of Than Khe. Nothing moved. No clouds or birds or people. As they waited, the men smoked and drank Kool-Aid, not talking much, feeling sympathy for Lee Strunk but also feeling the luck of the draw. You win some, you lose some, said Mitchell Sanders, and sometimes you settle for a rain check. It was a tired line and no one laughed.

Henry Dobbins ate a tropical chocolate bar. Ted Lavender popped a tran- 20
quilizer and went off to pee.

After five minutes, Lieutenant Jimmy Cross moved to the tunnel, leaned down, and examined the darkness. Trouble, he thought—a cave-in maybe. And then suddenly, without willing it, he was thinking about Martha. The stresses and fractures, the quick collapse, the two of them buried alive under all that weight. Dense, crushing love. Kneeling, watching the hole, he tried to concentrate on Lee Strunk and the war, all the dangers, but his love was too much for him, he felt paralyzed, he wanted to sleep inside her lungs and breathe her blood and be smothered. He wanted her to be a virgin and not a virgin, all at once. He wanted to know her. Intimate secrets—why poetry? Why so sad? Why the grayness in her eyes? Why so alone? Not lonely, just alone—riding her bike across campus or sitting off by herself in the cafeteria. Even dancing, she danced alone—and it was the aloneness that filled him with love. He remembered telling her that one evening. How she nodded and looked away. And how, later, when he kissed her, she received the kiss without returning it, her eyes wide open, not afraid, not a virgin's eyes, just flat and uninvolved.

Lieutenant Cross gazed at the tunnel. But he was not there. He was buried with Martha under the white sand at the Jersey shore. They were pressed together, and the pebble in his mouth was her tongue. He was smiling. Vaguely, he was aware of how quiet the day was, the sullen paddies, yet he could not bring himself to worry about matters of security. He was beyond that. He was just a kid at war, in love. He was twenty-two years old. He couldn't help it.

A few moments later Lee Strunk crawled out of the tunnel. He came up grinning, filthy but alive. Lieutenant Cross nodded and closed his eyes while the others clapped Strunk on the back and made jokes about rising from the dead.

Worms, Rat Kiley said. Right out of the grave. Fuckin' zombie.

The men laughed. They all felt great relief.

Spook City, said Mitchell Sanders.

Lee Strunk made a funny ghost sound, a kind of moaning, yet very happy and right then, when Strunk made that high happy moaning sound, when he went *Ahhooooo*, right then Ted Lavender was shot in the head on his way back from peeing. He lay with his mouth open. The teeth were broken. There was a swollen black bruise under his left eye. The cheekbone was gone. Oh shit, Rat Kiley said, the guy's dead. The guy's dead, he kept saying, which seemed profound—the guy's dead. I mean really.

The things they carried were determined to some extent by superstition. Lieutenant Cross carried his good-luck pebble. Dave Jensen carried a rabbit's foot. Norman Bowker, otherwise a very gentle person, carried a thumb that had been presented to him as a gift by Mitchell Sanders. The thumb was dark brown, rubbery to the touch, and weighed four ounces at most. It had been cut from a VC[6] corpse, a boy of fifteen or sixteen. They'd found him at the bottom of an irrigation ditch, badly burned, flies in his mouth and eyes. The boy wore black shorts and sandals. At the time of his death he had been carrying a pouch of rice, a rifle, and three magazines of ammunition.

You want my opinion, Mitchell Sanders said, there's a definite moral here.

He put his hand on the dead boy's wrist. He was quiet for a time, as if counting a pulse, then he patted the stomach, almost affectionately, and used Kiowa's hunting hatchet to remove the thumb.

Henry Dobbins asked what the moral was.

Moral?

You know. *Moral.*

Sanders wrapped the thumb in toilet paper and handed it across to Norman Bowker. There was no blood. Smiling, he kicked the boy's head, watched the flies scatter, and said, It's like with that old TV show—Paladin. Have gun, will travel.

---

[6]Vietcong, the North Vietnam army.

Soldiers in Vietnam on patrol.

Henry Dobbins thought about it. 35

Yeah, well, he finally said. I don't see no moral.

There it *is*, man.

Fuck off.

They carried USO stationery and pencils and pens. They carried Sterno, safety pins, trip flares, signal flares, spools of wire, razor blades, chewing tobacco, liberated joss sticks and statuettes of the smiling Buddha, candles, grease pencils, *The Stars and Stripes*,[7] fingernail clippers, Psy Ops[8] leaflets, bush hats, bolos, and much more. Twice a week, when the resupply choppers came in, they carried hot chow in green Mermite cans and large canvas bags filled with iced beer and soda pop. They carried plastic water containers, each with a two-gallon capacity. Mitchell Sanders carried a set of starched tiger fatigues for special occasions. Henry Dobbins carried Black Flag insecticide. Dave Jensen carried empty sandbags that could be filled at night for added protection. Lee Strunk carried tanning lotion. Some things they carried in common. Taking turns, they carried the big PRC-77 scrambler radio, which weighed thirty pounds with its battery. They shared the weight of memory. They took up what others could no longer bear. Often, they carried each other, the wounded or weak. They carried infections. They carried chess sets, basketballs, Vietnamese-English dictionaries, insignia of rank, Bronze Stars and Purple Hearts, plastic cards imprinted with the Code of Conduct. They carried diseases, among them malaria and dysentery. They carried lice and ringworm and leeches and paddy algae and various rots and molds. They carried the land itself—Vietnam, the place, the soil—a powdery orange-red dust that covered their boots and fatigues and faces.

---

[7]Official overseas military newspaper.

[8]Psychological operations.

They carried the sky. The whole atmosphere, they carried it, the humidity, the monsoons, the stink of fungus and decay, all of it, they carried gravity. They moved like mules. By daylight they took sniper fire, at night they were mortared, but it was not battle, it was just the endless march, village to village, without purpose, nothing won or lost. They marched for the sake of the march. They plodded along slowly, dumbly, leaning forward against the heat, unthinking, all blood and bone, simple grunts, soldiering with their legs, toiling up the hills and down into the paddies and across the rivers and up again and down, just humping, one step and then the next and then another, but no volition, no will, because it was automatic, it was anatomy, and the war was entirely a matter of posture and carriage, the hump was everything, a kind of inertia, a kind of emptiness, a dullness of desire and intellect and conscience and hope and human sensibility. Their principles were in their feet. Their calculations were biological. They had no sense of strategy or mission. They searched the villages without knowing what to look for, not caring, kicking over jars of rice, frisking children and old men, blowing tunnels, sometimes setting fires and sometimes not, then forming up and moving on to the next village, then other villages, where it would always be the same. They carried their own lives. The pressures were enormous. In the heat of early afternoon, they would remove their helmets and flak jackets, walking bare, which was dangerous but which helped ease the strain. They would often discard things along the route of march. Purely for comfort, they would throw away rations, blow their Claymores and grenades, no matter, because by nightfall the resupply choppers would arrive with more of the same, then a day or two later still more, fresh watermelons and crates of ammunition and sunglasses and woolen sweaters—the resources were stunning—sparklers for the Fourth of July, colored eggs for Easter. It was the great American war chest—the fruits of science, the smokestacks, the canneries, the arsenals at Hartford, the Minnesota forests, the machine shops, the vast fields of corn and wheat—they carried like freight trains; they carried it on their backs and shoulders—and for all the ambiguities of Vietnam, all the mysteries and unknowns, there was at least the single abiding certainty that they would never be at a loss for things to carry.

After the chopper took Lavender away, Lieutenant Jimmy Cross led his men 40
into the village of Than Khe. They burned everything. They shot chickens and dogs, they trashed the village well, they called in artillery and watched the wreckage, then they marched for several hours through the hot afternoon, and then at dusk, while Kiowa explained how Lavender died, Lieutenant Cross found himself trembling.

He tried not to cry. With his entrenching tool, which weighed five pounds, he began digging a hole in the earth.

He felt shame. He hated himself. He had loved Martha more than his men, and as a consequence Lavender was now dead, and this was something he would have to carry like a stone in his stomach for the rest of the war.

All he could do was dig. He used his entrenching tool like an ax, slashing, feeling both love and hate, and then later, when it was full dark, he sat at the bottom of his foxhole and wept. It went on for a long while. In part, he was grieving for Ted Lavender, but mostly it was for Martha, and for himself, because she belonged to another world, which was not quite real, and because she was a junior at Mount Sebastian College in New Jersey, a poet and a virgin and uninvolved, and because he realized she did not love him and never would.

Like cement, Kiowa whispered in the dark. I swear to God—boom-down. Not a word.

I've heard this, said Norman Bowker.

A pisser, you know? Still zipping himself up. Zapped while zipping.

All right, fine. That's enough.

Yeah, but you had to see it, the guy just—

I *heard*, man. Cement. So why not shut the fuck *up*?

Kiowa shook his head sadly and glanced over at the hole where Lieutenant Jimmy Cross sat watching the night. The air was thick and wet. A warm, dense fog had settled over the paddies and there was the stillness that precedes rain.

After a time Kiowa sighed.

One thing for sure, he said. The Lieutenant's in some deep hurt. I mean that crying jag—the way he was carrying on—it wasn't fake or anything, it was real heavy-duty hurt. The man cares.

Sure, Norman Bowker said.

Say what you want, the man does care.

We all got problems.

Not Lavender.

No, I guess not, Bowker said. Do me a favor, though.

Shut up?

That's a smart Indian. Shut up.

Shrugging, Kiowa pulled off his boots. He wanted to say more, just to lighten up his sleep, but instead he opened his New Testament and arranged it beneath his head as a pillow. The fog made things seem hollow and unattached. He tried not to think about Ted Lavender, but then he was thinking how fast it was, no drama, down and dead, and how it was hard to feel anything except surprise. It seemed un-Christian. He wished he could find some great sadness, or even anger, but the emotion wasn't there and he couldn't make it happen. Mostly he felt pleased to be alive. He liked the smell of the New Testament under his cheek, the leather and ink and paper and glue, whatever the chemicals were. He liked hearing the sounds of night. Even his fatigue, it felt fine, the stiff muscles and the prickly awareness of his own body, a floating feeling. He enjoyed not being dead. Lying there, Kiowa admired Lieutenant Jimmy Cross's capacity for grief. He wanted to share the man's pain, he wanted to care as Jimmy Cross cared. And yet when he closed his eyes, all he could think was Boom-down, and all he could feel was the pleasure of having his boots off and the fog curling in around him and the damp soil and the Bible smells and the plush comfort of night.

After a moment Norman Bowker sat up in the dark.

What the hell, he said. You want to talk, *talk*. Tell it to me.

Forget it.

No, man, go on. One thing I hate, it's a silent Indian.

For the most part they carried themselves with poise, a kind of dignity. Now and then, however, there were times of panic, when they squealed or wanted to squeal but couldn't, when they twitched and made moaning sounds and covered their heads and said Dear Jesus and flopped around on the earth and fired their weapons blindly and cringed and sobbed and begged for the noise to stop and went wild and made stupid promises to themselves and to God and to their mothers and fathers, hoping not to die. In different ways, it happened to all of them. Afterward, when the firing ended, they would blink and peek up. They would touch their bodies, feeling shame, then quickly hiding it. They would force themselves to stand. As if in slow motion, frame by frame, the world would take on the old logic—absolute silence, then the wind, then sunlight, then voices. It was the burden of being alive. Awkwardly, the men would reassemble themselves, first in private, then in groups, becoming soldiers again. They would repair the leaks in their eyes. They would check for casualties, call in dust-offs, light cigarettes, try to smile, clear their throats and spit and begin cleaning their weapons. After a time someone would shake his head and say, No lie, I almost shit my pants, and someone else would laugh, which meant it was bad, yes, but the guy had obviously not shit his pants, it wasn't that bad, and in any case nobody would ever do such a thing and then go ahead and talk about it. They would squint into the dense, oppressive sunlight. For a few moments, perhaps, they would fall silent, lighting a joint and tracking its passage from man to man, inhaling, holding in the humiliation. Scary stuff, one of them might say. But then someone else would grin or flick his eyebrows and say, Roger-dodger, almost cut me a new asshole, *almost.*

There were numerous such poses. Some carried themselves with a sort of wistful resignation, others with pride or stiff soldierly discipline or good humor or macho zeal. They were afraid of dying but they were even more afraid to show it.

They found jokes to tell.

They used a hard vocabulary to contain the terrible softness. *Greased*, they'd say. *Offed, lit up, zapped while zipping.* It wasn't cruelty, just stage presence. They were actors and the war came at them in 3-D. When someone died, it wasn't quite dying, because in a curious way it seemed scripted, and because they had their lines mostly memorized, irony mixed with tragedy, and because they called it by other names, as if to encyst and destroy the reality of death itself. They kicked corpses. They cut off thumbs. They talked grunt lingo. They told stories about Ted Lavender's supply of tranquilizers, how the poor guy didn't feel a thing, how incredibly tranquil he was.

There's a moral here, said Mitchell Sanders.

They were waiting for Lavender's chopper, smoking the dead man's dope.

The moral's pretty obvious, Sanders said, and winked. Stay away from drugs. No joke, they'll ruin your day every time.

Cute, said Henry Dobbins.

Mind-blower, get it? Talk about wiggy—nothing left, just blood and brains.

They made themselves laugh.

There it is, they'd say, over and over, as if the repetition itself were an act of poise, a balance between crazy and almost crazy, knowing without going. There it is, which meant be cool, let it ride, because oh yeah, man, you can't change what can't be changed, there it is, there it absolutely and positively and fucking well *is.*

They were tough.

They carried all the emotional baggage of men who might die. Grief, terror, love, longing—these were intangibles, but the intangibles had their own mass and specific gravity, they had tangible weight. They carried shameful memories. They carried the common secret of cowardice barely restrained, the instinct to run or freeze or hide, and in many respects this was the heaviest burden of all, for it could never be put down, it required perfect balance and perfect posture. They carried their reputations. They carried the soldier's greatest fear, which was the fear of blushing. Men killed, and died, because they were embarrassed not to. It was what had brought them to the war in the first place, nothing positive, no dreams of glory or honor, just to avoid the blush of dishonor. They died so as not to die of embarrassment. They crawled into tunnels and walked point and advanced under fire. Each morning, despite the unknowns, they made their legs move. They endured. They kept humping. They did not submit to the obvious alternative, which was simply to close the eyes and fall. So easy, really. Go limp and tumble to the ground and let the muscles unwind and not speak and not budge until your buddies picked you up and lifted you into the chopper that would roar and dip its nose and carry you off to the world. A mere matter of falling, yet no one ever fell. It was not courage, exactly; the object was not valor. Rather, they were too frightened to be cowards.

By and large they carried these things inside, maintaining the masks of composure. They sneered at sick call. They spoke bitterly about guys who had found release by shooting off their own toes or fingers. Pussies, they'd say. Candyasses. It was fierce, mocking talk, with only a trace of envy or awe, but even so, the image played itself out behind their eyes.

They imagined the muzzle against flesh. They imagined the quick, sweet pain, then the evacuation to Japan, then a hospital with warm beds and cute geisha nurses.

They dreamed of freedom birds. 80

At night, on guard, staring into the dark, they were carried away by jumbo jets. They felt the rush of takeoff. *Gone!* they yelled. And then velocity, wings and engines, a smiling stewardess—but it was more than a plane, it was a real bird, a big sleek silver bird with feathers and talons and high screeching. They were flying. The weights fell off, there was nothing to bear. They laughed and held on tight, feeling the cold slap of wind and altitude, soaring, thinking *It's over, I'm gone!*—they were naked, they were light and free—it was all lightness, bright and fast and buoyant, light as light, a helium buzz in the brain, a giddy bubbling in the lungs as they were taken up over the clouds and the war, beyond duty, beyond gravity and mortification and global entanglements—*Sin loi!*[9] they yelled, *I'm sorry, motherfuckers, but I'm out of it, I'm goofed, I'm on a space cruise, I'm gone!*—and it was a restful, disencumbered sensation, just riding the light waves, sailing that big silver freedom bird over the mountains and oceans, over America, over the farms and great sleeping cities and cemeteries and highways and the golden arches of McDonald's. It was flight, a kind of fleeing, a kind of falling, falling higher and higher, spinning off the edge of the earth and beyond the sun and through the vast, silent vacuum where there were no burdens and where everything weighed exactly nothing. *Gone!* they screamed, *I'm sorry but I'm gone!* And so at night, not quite dreaming, they gave themselves over to lightness, they were carried, they were purely borne.

On the morning after Ted Lavender died, First Lieutenant Jimmy Cross crouched at the bottom of his foxhole and burned Martha's letters. Then he burned the two photographs. There was a steady rain falling, which made it difficult, but he used heat tabs and Sterno to build a small fire, screening it with his body, holding the photographs over the tight blue flame with the tips of his fingers.

---

[9] "Sorry about that!"

He realized it was only a gesture. Stupid, he thought. Sentimental, too, but mostly just stupid.

Lavender was dead. You couldn't burn the blame.

Besides, the letters were in his head. And even now, without photographs, 85
Lieutenant Cross could see Martha playing volleyball in her white gym shorts and yellow T-shirt. He could see her moving in the rain.

When the fire died out, Lieutenant Cross pulled his poncho over his shoulders and ate breakfast from a can.

There was no great mystery, he decided.

In those burned letters Martha had never mentioned the war, except to say, Jimmy, take care of yourself. She wasn't involved. She signed the letters "Love," but it wasn't love, and all the fine lines and technicalities did not matter.

The morning came up wet and blurry. Everything seemed part of everything else, the fog and Martha and the deepening rain.

It was a war, after all. 90

Half smiling, Lieutenant Jimmy Cross took out his maps. He shook his head hard, as if to clear it, then bent forward and began planning the day's march. In ten minutes, or maybe twenty, he would rouse the men and they would pack up and head west, where the maps showed the country to be green and inviting. They would do what they had always done. The rain might add some weight, but otherwise it would be one more day layered upon all the other days.

He was realistic about it. There was that new hardness in his stomach.

No more fantasies, he told himself.

Henceforth, when he thought about Martha, it would be only to think that she belonged elsewhere. He would shut down the daydreams. This was not Mount Sebastian, it was another world, where there were no pretty poems or midterm exams, a place where men died because of carelessness and gross stupidity. Kiowa was right. Boom-down, and you were dead, never partly dead.

Briefly, in the rain, Lieutenant Cross saw Martha's gray eyes gazing back at him. 95

He understood.

It was very sad, he thought. The things men carried inside. The things men did or felt they had to do.

He almost nodded at her, but didn't.

Instead he went back to his maps. He was now determined to perform his duties firmly and without negligence. It wouldn't help Lavender, he knew that, but from this point on he would comport himself as a soldier. He would dispose of his good-luck pebble. Swallow it, maybe, or use Lee Strunk's sling-shot, or just drop it along the trail. On the march he would impose strict field discipline. He would be careful to send out flank security, to prevent straggling or bunching up, to keep his troops moving at the proper pace and at the proper interval. He would insist on clean weapons. He would confiscate the remainder of Lavender's dope. Later in the day, perhaps, he would call the men together and speak to them plainly. He would accept the blame for what had happened to Ted Lavender. He would be a man about it. He would look them in the eyes, keeping his chin level, and he would issue the new SOPs in a calm, impersonal tone of voice, an officer's voice, leaving no room for argument or discussion. Commencing immediately, he'd tell them, they would no longer abandon equipment along the route of march. They would police up their acts. They would get their shit together, and keep it together, and maintain it neatly and in good working order.

He would not tolerate laxity. He would show strength, distancing himself.

Among the men there would be grumbling, of course, and maybe worse, because their days would seem longer and their loads heavier, but Lieutenant Cross reminded himself that his obligation was not to be loved but to lead. He would dispense with love; it was not now a factor. And if anyone quarreled or complained, he would simply tighten his lips and arrange his shoulders in the correct command posture. He might give a curt little nod. Or he might not. He might just shrug and say Carry on, then they would saddle up and form into a column and move out toward the villages of Than Khe.

(1986)

PREWRITING

Before you can begin to write about structure, you must first determine the underlying patterns that serve as a framework for the story.

Finding Patterns

Read the following questions; then carefully reread the story. Write down your answers to the questions.

1. How does each part of the story relate to the title, "The Things They Carried"?
2. What visible structure is evident, separating the parts of the story? Give each part a title that fits it. If possible, compare your titles with a classmate's and discuss your choices. If you want, create a diagram or chart that illustrates the story's structure.
3. How many different time periods are described in the story? Make a list of the main events that are described. Then organize the list according to time order.
4. Trace the Martha story line that is woven through the tale. What is the reality of the relationship between Jimmy Cross and Martha? What evidence are you looking at when you guess at this reality?
5. What do we know about each soldier in the story? How do we accumulate knowledge about each one? On the other hand, what is left out of our knowledge about each soldier, information that you might have expected? If O'Brien had written some scenes from each soldier's past as a civilian, how would that change the story? Why do you think he generally avoids these scenes?
6. Why is the death of Ted Lavender important to your understanding of the story? How many times is Lavender's death retold? How is it different in the various retellings?

WRITING

Once you understand some of the structural elements of the story, you need to choose a framework within which you can effectively present your observations—that is, a structure for your own paper.

Grouping Details

Write a sentence that explains something about the author's selection of scenes, themes, or events to include repeatedly through the story. Next, discuss which details in the story support your explanations. For example, if you mentioned that the scenes involving Martha relate to the crucial change undergone by Jimmy Cross, supporting details would include the following:

- the content of the letters from Martha
- the photographs of Martha
- the lucky pebble
- descriptions of his encounters with Martha at home
- his fantasies of what might have happened or what might happen in the future with Martha
- episodes of daydreaming about Martha
- the burning of the letters and photographs

Relating Details to Theme

An accurate description of a pattern in the story and a convincing list of supporting details will be crucial to any essay about structure. But you also need to work out a thesis—a major claim that relates the structure to the overall impact or meaning of the work. For example, an essay about the structure of "The Things They Carried" might make this claim:

> Jimmy Cross's recurring thoughts about Martha throughout the story create a picture of him as a romantic, self-deceiving, sensitive young man, a character he himself rejects in the end with the symbolic burning of her letters and photographs.

IDEAS FOR WRITING

Ideas for Responsive Writing

1. In "The Things They Carried," physical objects take on extra significance as part of each soldier's kit. Are there any items in your life that

have extra significance because they are associated with a certain period of time? What do you carry with you almost every day? What could we tell about you by looking through your backpack, handbag, wallet, or pockets? Write about how certain objects in your life could be interpreted.

2. In this story, Jimmy Cross builds an elaborate fantasy surrounding Martha, and sometimes he is quite aware that it's a fantasy. Have you ever built a fantasy on a small amount of evidence or information? How aware were you that you were out of touch with reality? Write about a daydream or fantasy that you have created with some small grounding in real life.

Ideas for Critical Writing

The following claims relate structure to meaning. Adopt one of them, revise one, or create your own for arguing an interpretation of "The Things They Carried."

1. The soldiers' situation is illuminated in "The Things They Carried" by words and details referring to different kinds of weight and lightness.
2. CRITICAL APPROACHES: For this topic, review the summary of "formalism" in the appendix on Critical Approaches for Interpreting Literature, and use a close-reading approach. Once an event or topic is introduced in "The Things They Carried," it accumulates more meaning each time it reoccurs. This process involves the reader in the construction of a coherent story about each event.
3. "The Things They Carried" is organized to mirror how people think as they go about their business in daily life, giving readers the feeling that they have entered the minds of the characters.
4. The narrator of "The Things They Carried" continually slips out of his concrete cataloguing of physical objects and wanders into the realm of psychological burdens, suggesting that Jimmy Cross will not be able to live up to his resolves at the end of the story.

Ideas for Researched Writing

1. "The Things They Carried" is the first story in a collection by Tim O'Brien, also titled *The Things They Carried.* Find out more about the whole book and how the story you have read fits into it. What is interesting about the structure of this collection of Vietnam stories? You can enter the title into your Internet search engine or start from O'Brien's home page at www.illyria.com/tobhp.html.
2. What kind of critical reception did O'Brien's story receive? Find a number of reviews and analyses of the story, and write an essay summarizing the reactions and interpretations.

REWRITING

Our advice in this section focuses on problems involved in quoting when writing about a literary work.

Integrating Quotations Gracefully

In any literary essay you will need quotations from the text of the work you are examining. In fact, when you revise your essay, always consider adding more specific evidence straight from the text. This evidence will help your readers understand the general points you make and will show what inspired your thoughts. Quoting directly also serves as a self-check; by finding specific support in the work, you confirm that your ideas are, indeed, grounded in the text and not in your fancy.

Be sure that you enclose these borrowings in quotation marks as you gracefully introduce them into your own sentences. And be sure that your own language leads grammatically into the language you are quoting. For example:

> O'Brien describes the soldiers' inner experience as "a dullness of desire and intellect and conscience and hope and human sensibility."
>
> At the close of the story, Cross imagines himself giving "a curt little nod" in his new role as a man in command.
>
> Although the narrator claims that "the things they [the soldiers] carried were largely determined by necessity," for some men these necessities included such items as a diary, comic books, and marijuana.

That last example shows how you may add your own words to explain a possibly confusing word in a quotation: use brackets. Most of the time, however, you can devise a way to avoid this awkwardness by rewriting the sentence.

> The soldiers carried objects "largely determined by necessity," according to the narrator, but for some these necessities included such items as a diary, comic books, and marijuana.

Exercise on Integrating Quotations

Here, we reprint a passage from "The Things They Carried." To practice integrating quotations, try your hand at using parts of the passage in sentences of your own.

1. Write a sentence that uses a phrase you quote directly as an example of a general point you make about the characters, events, or setting of the story.

2. Write a sentence that relates a detail to a theme of the story, using some exact quotation from the passage.

They used a hard vocabulary to contain the terrible softness. *Greased,* they'd say. *Offed, lit up, zapped while zipping.* It wasn't cruelty, just stage presence. They were actors and the war came at them in 3-D. When someone died, it wasn't quite dying, because in a curious way it seemed scripted, and because they had their lines mostly memorized, irony mixed with tragedy, and because they called it by other names, as if to encyst and destroy the reality of death itself.

8

Writing About Imagery and Symbolism

Imagery and symbolism, two of the most important elements of serious imaginative literature, provide rich sources of insight. The interpretive skill necessary to detect and understand them can be developed with practice. Because the meaning or theme of a literary work is often reinforced through imagery and symbolism, you can effectively devote an entire paper to an examination of a key symbol or a pattern of imagery.

What Are Images?

Images are words, sometimes phrases, that appeal to the senses and often put a picture in your mind. Literary critics classify images roughly into several categories.

Visual	images of sight ("future days strung together like pearls in a rosary"—Mary E. Wilkins Freeman)
Auditory	images of sound ("the loud, iron clanking of the lift machinery"—John Cheever)
Gustatory	images of taste ("the acrid, metallic taste of gunfire"—Alberto Moravia)
Kinetic	images of motion (a thought "bumping like a helium balloon at the ceiling of the brain"—Sandra Cisneros)
Thermal	images of temperature ("the blueblack cold" of early morning—Robert Hayden)
Tactile	images of feeling ("the ache of marriage throbs in the teeth"—Denise Levertov)

Such images enrich our pleasure in reading and, if deliberately repeated, can become ***motifs***, or patterns of imagery, that illuminate some element of the story. The images of clothing in Katherine Anne Porter's "The Grave" form a significant motif, one that shows how the main character, Miranda, is beginning to mature, that she's tired of being a tomboy and wants to try on the trappings of traditional female attire. In Chopin's "Désirée's Baby," the repeated images of whiteness serve to reinforce the innocence and purity of the unjustly accused Désirée.

What Are Symbols?

If a repeated image gathers significant meaning and seems to stand for something more than itself, it then becomes a ***symbol***. In Louise Erdrich's "The Red Convertible," the old Oldsmobile symbolizes the changing relationship between the narrator and his brother. The repeated mention of dust in Joyce's "Eveline" settles into our consciousness as symbolizing the dreariness of the title character's daily life, just as dust settles on all surfaces in an unkempt house. In Kate Chopin's "The Story of an Hour," Mrs. Mallard gazes out her window at "the tops of trees that were all aquiver with the new spring life. The delicious breath of rain was in the air." Those images of spring and rain represent the prospect of a vibrant new life that is awakening in Mrs. Mallard's subconscious mind.

Because spring rains literally bring renewed life to the earth, water is used in the baptismal service in church to signify rebirth. Thus, in literature, we associate water with a vigorous, living spirit and its opposite—dryness, dust, aridity—with the death of the human spirit or the decay of moral values.

Archetypal Symbols

Some symbols, like the water and dust, are considered ***archetypal*** or universal—supposedly conveying a similar meaning in all cultures from the time of earliest civilizations. The circle, for instance, is an ancient symbol of wholeness or perfection; the sea has for centuries symbolized the voyage through life. Colors are often symbolic, like the crimson of the mark on Georgiana's cheek in Hawthorne's "The Birthmark." Occasionally a symbol can convey diametrically opposing meanings, depending on its context. For instance, white in our culture often stands for purity, as in bridal gowns; but Herman Melville makes the white whale in *Moby Dick* a symbol of evil incarnate, as Frost does with the "dimpled spider, fat and white" in his poem "Design." Both of those images also convey the often hidden, deceptive nature of evil. And black, frequently linked with death and evil, has many positive associations, such as a Black Belt in Judo; a cup of strong coffee; or the robes of a priest, judge, or graduate.

Phallic and Yonic Symbols

Two important and commonly employed symbols are associated with human sexuality. A ***phallic symbol*** suggests the potency of the male (as does the gun in Richard Wright's "The Man Who Was Almost a Man") or the force of male dominance in a patriarchal society (as do the stone pillar in Chopin's "Désirée's Baby" and the rolling pin in Bharati Mukherjee's "A Father").

A ***yonic symbol*** suggests the fecundity of the female and the allure of female sexuality. Common yonic symbols are caves, pots, rooms, full-blown roses—round or concave objects resembling the shape of the primary sex organs of women. If you think fruit, then bananas are phallic and apples are yonic. Remember, though, that these objects will not always be charged with sexual significance. You must be sure that context supports a reasonable association with sexuality. Even Freud supposedly said that sometimes a cigar is just a cigar.

How Will I Recognize Symbols?

"How am I supposed to know the significance of all these things?" you may well ask. Many symbols you already understand through knowledge gathered from experience and observation. You just have to make the association. Spring signifying rebirth, for example, is a connection anyone can make who has seen the earth come alive at winter's end. Pay attention to the way objects and colors gather associations: white for brides, black for funerals, blue for sadness, red for passion or anger. Just keep making associations until you come up with a meaning that seems to fit the symbol in its context.

Reference Works on Symbols

If you draw an absolute blank, you can consult several handy volumes that allow you to look up words to discover their symbolic implications. Your library should have copies of the following works in the humanities reference section:

- Cirlot, J. E. *A Dictionary of Symbols*
- Cooper, J. C. *An Illustrated Encyclopaedia of Traditional Symbols*
- Frazer, Sir James. *The Golden Bough*
- Olderr, Stephen. *Symbolism: A Comprehensive Dictionary*
- Walker, Barbara. *The Woman's Encyclopedia of Myths and Secrets*

Looking at Images and Symbols

Recognizing images and symbols and responding to them sensitively are requirements for an informed reading of serious fiction. Read the following story by Shirley Jackson and see if you are aware, on first reading, of her use of symbolic imagery.

Shirley Jackson 1919–1965

Shirley Jackson did not receive attention as a writer until 1948, when the *New Yorker* published "The Lottery," a story that she wrote in just two hours. The magazine was flooded with letters, almost all of them wanting to know what the story meant. While Jackson is best known for her tales of supernatural terror, she also wrote about "the perpetual pandemonium and the constant crises" of her family life. "I can't persuade myself that writing is honest work," she once remarked. "It's great fun and I love it. For one thing, it's the only way I can get to sit down."

The Lottery

The morning of June 27th was clear and sunny, with the fresh warmth of a full-summer day; the flowers were blossoming profusely and the grass was richly green. The people of the village began to gather in the square, between the post office and the bank, around ten o'clock; in some towns there were so many people that the lottery took two days and had to be started on June 26th, but in this village, where there were only about three hundred people, the whole lottery took less than two hours, so it could begin at ten o'clock in the morning and still be through in time to allow the villagers to get home for noon dinner.

The children assembled first, of course. School was recently over for the summer, and the feeling of liberty sat uneasily on most of them; they tended to gather together quietly for a while before they broke into boisterous play, and their talk was still of the classroom and the teacher, of books and reprimands. Bobby Martin had already stuffed his pockets full of stones, and the other boys soon followed his example, selecting the smoothest and roundest stones; Bobby and Harry Jones and Dickie Delacroix—the villagers pronounced his name "Dellacroy"—eventually made a great pile of stones in one corner of the square and guarded it against the raids of the other boys. The girls stood aside, talking among themselves, looking over their shoulders at the boys, and the very small children rolled in the dust or clung to the hands of their older brothers or sisters.

Soon the men began to gather, surveying their own children, speaking of planting and rain, tractors and taxes. They stood together, away from the pile of stones in the corner, and their jokes were quiet and they smiled rather than laughed. The women, wearing faded house dresses and sweaters, came shortly after their menfolk. They greeted one another and exchanged bits of gossip as they went to join their husbands. Soon the women, standing by their husbands, began to call to their children, and the children came reluctantly, having to be called four or five times. Bobby Martin ducked under his mother's grasping hand and ran, laughing, back to the pile of stones. His father spoke up sharply, and Bobby came quickly and took his place between his father and his oldest brother.

The lottery was conducted—as were the square dances, the teen-age club, the Halloween program—by Mr. Summers, who had time and energy to devote to civic activities. He was a round-faced, jovial man and he ran the coal business, and people were sorry for him, because he had no children and his wife was a scold. When he arrived in the square, carrying the black wooden box, there was a murmur of conversation among the villagers, and he waved and called, "Little late today, folks." The postmaster, Mr. Graves, followed him, carrying a three-legged stool, and the stool was put in the center of the square and Mr. Summers set the black box down on it. The villagers kept their distance, leaving a space between themselves and the stool, and when Mr. Summers said, "Some of you fellows want to give me a hand?" there was a hesitation before two men, Mr. Martin and his oldest son, Baxter, came forward to hold the box steady on the stool while Mr. Summers stirred up the paper inside it.

The original paraphernalia for the lottery had been lost long ago, and the 5
black box now resting on the stool had been put into use even before Old Man Warner, the oldest man in town, was born. Mr. Summers spoke frequently to the villagers about making a new box, but no one liked to upset even as much tradition as was represented by the black box. There was a story that the present box had been made with some pieces of the box that had preceded it, the one that had been constructed when the first people settled down to make a village here. Every year, after the lottery, Mr. Summers began talking again about a new box, but every year the subject was allowed to fade off without anything's being done. The black box grew shabbier each year; by now it was no longer completely black but splintered badly along one side to show the original wood color, and in some places faded or stained.

Mr. Martin and his oldest son, Baxter, held the black box securely on the stool until Mr. Summers had stirred the papers thoroughly with his hand. Because so much of the ritual had been forgotten or discarded, Mr. Summers had been successful in having slips of paper substituted for the chips of wood that had been used for generations. Chips of wood, Mr. Summers had argued, had been all very well when the village was tiny, but now that the population was more than three hundred and likely to keep on growing, it was necessary to use something that would fit more easily into the black box. The night before the lottery, Mr. Summers and Mr. Graves made up the slips of paper and put them in the box, and it was then taken to the safe of Mr. Summers's coal company and locked up until Mr. Summers was ready to take it to the square next morning. The rest of the year, the box was put away, sometimes one place, sometimes another; it had spent one year in Mr. Graves's barn and another year underfoot in the post office, and sometimes it was set on a shelf in the Martin grocery and left there.

There was a great deal of fussing to be done before Mr. Summers declared the lottery open. There were the lists to make up—of heads of families, heads of households in each family, members of each household in each family. There was the proper swearing-in of Mr. Summers by the postmaster, as the official of the lottery; at one time, some people remembered, there had been a recital of some sort, performed by the official of the lottery, a perfunctory, tuneless chant that had been rattled off duly each year; some people believed that the official of the lottery used to stand just so when he said or sang it, others believed that he was supposed to walk among the people, but years and years ago this part of the ritual had been allowed to lapse. There had been, also, a ritual salute, which the official of the lottery had had to use in addressing each person who came up to draw from the box, but this also had changed with time, until now it was felt necessary only for the official to speak to each person approaching. Mr. Summers was very good at all this; in his clean white shirt and blue jeans, with one hand resting carelessly on the black box, he seemed very proper and important as he talked interminably to Mr. Graves and the Martins.

Just as Mr. Summers finally left off talking and turned to the assembled villagers, Mrs. Hutchinson came hurriedly along the path to the square, her sweater thrown over her shoulders, and slid into place in the back of the crowd. "Clean forgot what day it was," she said to Mrs. Delacroix, who stood next to her, and they both laughed softly. "Thought my old man was out back stacking wood," Mrs. Hutchinson went on, "and then I looked out the window and the kids were gone, and then I remembered it was the twenty-seventh and came a-running." She dried her hands on her apron, and Mrs. Delacroix said, "You're in time, though. They're still talking away up there."

Mrs. Hutchinson craned her neck to see through the crowd and found her husband and children standing near the front. She tapped Mrs. Delacroix on the arm as a farewell and began to make her way through the crowd. The people separated good-humoredly to let her through; two or three people said, in voices just loud enough to be heard across the crowd, "Here comes your Missus, Hutchinson," and "Bill, she made it after all." Mrs. Hutchinson reached her husband, and Mr. Summers, who had been waiting, said cheerfully, "Thought we were going to have to get on without you, Tessie." Mrs. Hutchinson said, grinning, "Wouldn't have me leave m'dishes in the sink, now, would you, Joe?," and soft laughter ran through the crowd as the people stirred back into position after Mrs. Hutchinson's arrival.

"Well, now," Mr. Summers said soberly, "guess we better get started, get this 10
over with, so's we can go back to work. Anybody ain't here?"

"Dunbar," several people said. "Dunbar, Dunbar."

Mr. Summers consulted his list. "Clyde Dunbar," he said. "That's right. He's broke his leg, hasn't he? Who's drawing for him?"

"Me, I guess," a woman said, and Mr. Summers turned to look at her. "Wife draws for her husband," Mr. Summers said. "Don't you have a grown boy to do it for you, Janey?" Although Mr. Summers and everyone else in the village knew the answer perfectly well, it was the business of the official of the lottery to ask such questions formally. Mr. Summers waited with an expression of polite interest while Mrs. Dunbar answered.

"Horace's not but sixteen yet," Mrs. Dunbar said regretfully. "Guess I gotta fill in for the old man this year."

"Right," Mr. Summers said. He made a note on the list he was holding. Then 15
he asked, "Watson boy drawing this year?"

A tall boy in the crowd raised his hand. "Here," he said. "I'm drawing for m' mother and me." He blinked his eyes nervously and ducked his head as several voices in the crowd said things like "Good fellow, Jack," and "Glad to see your mother's got a man to do it."

"Well," Mr. Summers said, "guess that's everyone. Old Man Warner make it?"

"Here," a voice said, and Mr. Summers nodded.

A sudden hush fell on the crowd as Mr. Summers cleared his throat and looked at the list. "All ready?" he called. "Now, I'll read the names—heads of families first—and the men come up and take a paper out of the box. Keep the paper folded in your hand without looking at it until everyone has had a turn. Everything clear?"

The people had done it so many times that they only half listened to the direc- 20
tions; most of them were quiet, wetting their lips, not looking around. Then

Mr. Summers raised one hand high and said, "Adams." A man disengaged himself from the crowd and came forward. "Hi, Steve," Mr. Summers said, and Mr. Adams said, "Hi, Joe." They grinned at one another humorlessly and nervously. Then Mr. Adams reached into the black box and took out a folded paper. He held it firmly by one corner as he turned and went hastily back to his place in the crowd, where he stood a little apart from his family, not looking down at his hand.

"Allen." Mr. Summers said. "Anderson.... Bentham."

"Seems like there's no time at all between lotteries any more," Mrs. Delacroix said to Mrs. Graves in the back row. "Seems like we got through with the last one only last week."

"Time sure goes fast," Mrs. Graves said.

"Clark.... Delacroix."

"There goes my old man," Mrs. Delacroix said. She held her breath while 25
her husband went forward.

"Dunbar," Mr. Summers said, and Mrs. Dunbar went steadily to the box while one of the women said, "Go on, Janey," and another said, "There she goes."

"We're next," Mrs. Graves said. She watched while Mr. Graves came around from the side of the box, greeted Mr. Summers gravely, and selected a slip of paper from the box. By now, all through the crowd there were men holding the small folded papers in their large hands, turning them over and over nervously. Mrs. Dunbar and her two sons stood together, Mrs. Dunbar holding the slip of paper.

"Harburt.... Hutchinson."

"Get up there, Bill," Mrs. Hutchinson said, and the people near her laughed.

"Jones." 30

"They do say," Mr. Adams said to Old Man Warner, who stood next to him, "that over in the north village they're talking of giving up the lottery."

Old Man Warner snorted. "Pack of crazy fools," he said. "Listening to the young folks, nothing's good enough for *them.* Next thing you know, they'll be wanting to go back to living in caves, nobody work any more, live *that* way for a while. Used to be a saying about 'Lottery in June, corn be heavy soon.' First thing you know, we'd all be eating stewed chickweed and acorns. There's *always* been a lottery," he added petulantly. "Bad enough to see young Joe Summers up there joking with everybody."

"Some places have already quit lotteries," Mrs. Adams said.

"Nothing but trouble in *that,*" Old Man Warner said stoutly. "Pack of young fools."

"Martin." And Bobby Martin watched his father go forward. "Overdyke.... 35
Percy."

"I wish they'd hurry," Mrs. Dunbar said to her oldest son. "I wish they'd hurry."

"They're almost through," her son said.

"You get ready to run tell Dad," Mrs. Dunbar said.

Mr. Summers called his own name and then stepped forward precisely and selected a slip from the box. Then he called, "Warner."

"Seventy-seventh year I been in the lottery," Old Man Warner said as he 40
went through the crowd. "Seventy-seventh time."

"Watson." The tall boy came awkwardly through the crowd. Someone said, "Don't be nervous, Jack," and Mr. Summers said, "Take your time, son."

"Zanini."

After that, there was a long pause, a breathless pause, until Mr. Summers, holding his slip of paper in the air, said, "All right, fellows." For a minute, no one moved, and then all the slips of paper were opened. Suddenly, all the women began to speak at once, saying, "Who is it?," "Who's got it?," "Is it the Dunbars?," "Is it the Watsons?" Then the voices began to say, "It's Hutchinson. It's Bill," "Bill Hutchinson's got it."

"Go tell your father," Mrs. Dunbar said to her older son.

45 People began to look around to see the Hutchinsons. Bill Hutchinson was standing quiet, staring down at the paper in his hand. Suddenly, Tessie Hutchinson shouted to Mr. Summers, "You didn't give him time enough to take any paper he wanted. I saw you. It wasn't fair!"

"Be a good sport, Tessie," Mrs. Delacroix called, and Mrs. Graves said, "All of us took the same chance."

"Shut up, Tessie," Bill Hutchinson said.

"Well, everyone," Mr. Summers said, "that was done pretty fast, and now we've got to be hurrying a little more to get it done in time." He consulted his next list. "Bill," he said, "you draw for the Hutchinson family. You got any other households in the Hutchinsons?"

"There's Don and Eva," Mrs. Hutchinson yelled. "Make *them* take their chance!"

50 "Daughters draw with their husbands' families, Tessie," Mr. Summers said gently. "You know that as well as anyone else."

"It wasn't *fair*," Tessie said.

"I guess not, Joe," Bill Hutchinson said regretfully. "My daughter draws with her husband's family, that's only fair. And I've got no other family except the kids."

"Then, as far as drawing for families is concerned, it's you," Mr. Summers said in explanation, "and as far as drawing for households is concerned, that's you, too. Right?"

"Right," Bill Hutchinson said.

55 "How many kids, Bill?" Mr. Summers asked formally.

"Three," Bill Hutchinson said. "There's Bill, Jr., and Nancy, and little Dave. And Tessie and me."

"All right, then," Mr. Summers said. "Harry, you got their tickets back?"

Mr. Graves nodded and held up the slips of paper. "Put them in the box, then," Mr. Summers directed. "Take Bill's and put it in."

"I think we ought to start over," Mrs. Hutchinson said, as quietly as she could. "I tell you it wasn't *fair*. You didn't give him time enough to choose. *Every*body saw that."

60 Mr. Graves had selected the five slips and put them in the box, and he dropped all the papers but those onto the ground, where the breeze caught them and lifted them off.

"Listen, everybody," Mrs. Hutchinson was saying to the people around her.

"Ready, Bill?" Mr. Summers asked, and Bill Hutchinson, with one quick glance around at his wife and children, nodded.

"Remember," Mr. Summers said, "take the slips and keep them folded until each person has taken one. Harry, you help little Dave." Mr. Graves took the hand of the little boy, who came willingly with him up to the box. "Take a paper out of the box, Davy," Mr. Summers said. Davy put his hand into the box and laughed. "Take just *one* paper," Mr. Summers said. "Harry, you hold it for him." Mr. Graves took the child's hand and removed the folded paper from the tight fist and held it while little Dave stood next to him and looked up at him wonderingly.

"Nancy, next," Mr. Summers said. Nancy was twelve, and her school friends breathed heavily as she went forward, switching her skirt, and took a slip daintily from the box. "Bill, Jr.," Mr. Summers said, and Billy, his face red and his feet overlarge, nearly knocked the box over as he got a paper out. "Tessie," Mr. Summers said. She hesitated for a minute, looking around defiantly, and then set her lips and went up to the box. She snatched a paper out and held it behind her.

"Bill," Mr. Summers said, and Bill Hutchinson reached into the box and felt 65
around, bringing his hand out at last with the slip of paper in it.

The crowd was quiet. A girl whispered, "I hope it's not Nancy," and the sound of the whisper reached the edges of the crowd.

"It's not the way it used to be," Old Man Warner said clearly. "People ain't the way they used to be."

"All right," Mr. Summers said. "Open the papers. Harry, you open little Dave's."

Mr. Graves opened the slip of paper and there was a general sigh through the crowd as he held it up and everyone could see that it was blank. Nancy and Bill, Jr., opened theirs at the same time, and both beamed and laughed, turning around to the crowd and holding their slips of paper above their heads.

"Tessie," Mr. Summers said. There was a pause, and then Mr. Summers looked 70
at Bill Hutchinson, and Bill unfolded his paper and showed it. It was blank.

"It's Tessie," Mr. Summers said, and his voice was hushed. "Show us her paper, Bill."

Bill Hutchinson went over to his wife and forced the slip of paper out of her hand. It had a black spot on it, the black spot Mr. Summers had made the night before with the heavy pencil in the coal-company office. Bill Hutchinson held it up, and there was a stir in the crowd.

"All right, folks," Mr. Summers said. "Let's finish quickly."

Although the villagers had forgotten the ritual and lost the original black box, they still remembered to use stones. The pile of stones the boys had made earlier was ready; there were stones on the ground with the blowing scraps of paper that had come out of the box. Mrs. Delacroix selected a stone so large she had to pick it up with both hands and turned to Mrs. Dunbar. "Come on," she said. "Hurry up."

Mrs. Dunbar had small stones in both hands, and she said, gasping for 75
breath, "I can't run at all. You'll have to go ahead and I'll catch up with you."

The children had stones already, and someone gave little Davy Hutchinson a few pebbles.

Tessie Hutchinson was in the center of a cleared space by now, and she held her hands out desperately as the villagers moved in on her. "It isn't fair," she said. A stone hit her on the side of the head.

Old Man Warner was saying, "Come on, come on, everyone." Steve Adams was in the front of the crowd of villagers, with Mrs. Graves beside him.

"It isn't fair, it isn't right," Mrs. Hutchinson screamed, and then they were upon her.

(1948)

PREWRITING

Since much of the imagery in "The Lottery" carries symbolic significance, we will focus on symbolism as the topic for writing here. Symbols in fiction are not difficult to recognize. Usually an author will give a symbol particular emphasis by mentioning it repeatedly (like the dust in "Eveline"). A crucial symbol will sometimes be placed in the story's opening or ending.

Interpreting Symbols

Shirley Jackson directs our attention to the lottery by making it the title of her story. She also gives us abundant detail about this traditional ritual. We know the exact date and time, how the lottery is conducted, who draws and in what order, what the box and the slips of paper look like, and so forth. Clearly the lottery is the story's central symbol as well as its title. The meaning of the lottery is the meaning of "The Lottery."

Here are some points and questions to consider as you read the story a second time and try to work out your interpretation of its symbolism. Write out your answers, and if possible, share your responses with a small group of classmates.

1. Social psychologists observe that every group develops its own outcast or misfit, who is blamed for all sorts of group malfunctions and woes. Have you observed this dynamic in your own work, school, church, or family groups?
2. We are told a lot about the lottery, but not its exact purpose. Do the townspeople know? Is this omission significant? Intentional?
3. Why is much of the history of the lottery and the black box uncertain and vague? Why does Mr. Summers have to ask a question that he and everybody else already know the answer to?
4. The box used in the lottery is mentioned almost thirty times in the story—more than ten times in the phrase *the black box.* Why does the author emphasize this object and its color so strongly?
5. The stones are mentioned five times near the beginning of the story and then five or six times more at the end. Why is their presence so important? What are the historical/biblical associations of a "stoning"? Do they apply in this situation?
6. Which characters seem to stand for particular ideas or views? What about Old Man Warner? Look at his speeches and comments throughout the story. Tessie Hutchinson also gets a lot of attention, of course. What is ironic about her being the chosen

victim? Does her last name have any significance for you? If not, look up *Hutchinson* in a good encyclopedia.

WRITING

The key to a successful essay is a good ***thesis***—the *claim* (or *premise* or *hypothesis* or *recommendation*) that you will argue in your interpretation. Before you get too far in your writing, try to state your thesis in a single sentence.

Producing a Workable Thesis

A useful thesis should narrow the topic to an idea you can cover within your word limit. It should indicate the direction of your thinking—what you intend to say about that idea. Be sure to state your thesis in a complete sentence that indicates how you will successfully argue your claim. The following exercise provides examples.

Exercise on Thesis Statements

The numbered thesis statements lack a clear claim. Figure out how each one can be revised to include an argument for an interpretation of the story; then write an improved version. Here is an example of the kind of revisions we hope you will produce.

No claim Shirley Jackson's "The Lottery" contains a number of significant symbols.

Improved In "The Lottery" Shirley Jackson uses simple objects—a box, some stones, some slips of paper—to symbolize the narrow-mindedness and brutality that result from superstitious thinking.

1. Shirley Jackson's "The Lottery" is a compelling story about scapegoats.
2. The ritual of the lottery itself serves as a symbol in Shirley Jackson's story.
3. The setting of Shirley Jackson's "The Lottery" is an important element in contributing to the effectiveness of the story.
4. The characters function symbolically in Shirley Jackson's "The Lottery."
5. Shirley Jackson's "The Lottery" reveals a great deal about society and human nature.

IDEAS FOR WRITING

Ideas for Responsive Writing

1. What is Shirley Jackson saying about traditional rituals in "The Lottery"? Think of some ritual in our present society that you think ought to be dropped—or at least reconsidered and modified—and write an essay arguing your viewpoint. Consider, for example, proms, weddings, Christmas gift exchanges, dating conventions, beauty pageants, boxing matches, funeral services, graduation ceremonies, or fraternity/sorority pledging.
2. Many readers have remarked on the hypnotic power and emotional impact of this story. Did you experience a similar reaction? Do you think the author manipulated your feelings in any way?

Ideas for Critical Writing

1. Look up the word *scapegoat* in a desk-sized or online dictionary; then look at the entry in the print or online version of *Encyclopaedia Britannica*, which will give you some historical examples of the use of scapegoats. Formulate a claim that relates the symbolism of "The Lottery" to the practice of scapegoating.
2. Write an essay focusing on the symbolism of the characters in "The Lottery," especially Tessie Hutchinson, Old Man Warner, Bill Hutchinson, Mr. Graves, and Mr. Summers. Or consider the role of the children in the story. What do they symbolize? Conclude your argument by relating your observations to the story's theme.
3. CRITICAL APPROACHES: Review the reader response approach to literary interpretation (page 1161). Write an essay arguing that the symbolism in "The Lottery" can be interpreted in several different ways. Before you begin, you might ask several people to read the story and tell you what the symbols mean to them. Also read the student paper on "The Lottery" starting on page 148 as you gather material for your essay.

Ideas for Researched Writing

1. When "The Lottery" first appeared in the *New Yorker* on June 28, 1948, it was greeted with great consternation. So many subscribers wrote in seeking enlightenment or expressing outrage that Jackson responded to the deluge of mail with an essay entitled "Biography of a Story." Find out more about the initial reactions to "The Lottery," and read Jackson's response. Then write an essay arguing why you think the story generated such anger and was so widely misinterpreted.
2. Do some research on scapegoats. Write an essay claiming that scapegoats play a useful role in society, using examples from history, current events, novels, films, and your own experience. Or, if you prefer, argue the opposite—that scapegoating is so cruel and senseless that it must be condemned and eliminated.

REWRITING

As you revise your first draft, try to improve it in every way possible. Our advice at this point involves ideas for improving your introduction.

Sharpening the Introduction

Look at your introductory paragraph. Does it give your readers a clear idea of the topic and purpose? Will it arouse curiosity and interest, as well as lead into your subject?

One strategy for catching the attention of your readers involves using a pertinent quotation.

> "The less there is to justify a traditional custom," wrote Mark Twain, "the harder it is to get rid of it." This comment accurately describes the situation that Shirley Jackson presents in "The Lottery." Her story illustrates how ignorance and superstition become instilled in human society and lead to unnecessary violence.

Another relevant quotation for this introduction might be Gathorne Cranbrook's observation that "The tradition of preserving traditions became a tradition." Useful quotations like these are available in library and online sources such as *Bartlett's Familiar Quotations.*

You can also take an arresting or tantalizing quotation from the story itself. Tessie Hutchinson's final scream, "It isn't fair, it isn't right," or Old Man Warner's "There's *always* been a lottery" might serve as an effective opening for an essay on this story.

Another strategy is to pose a startling question, like this:

> Why would the people in a quiet, peaceful village publicly murder one of their neighbors every summer? This is the shocking question that Shirley Jackson forces us to consider in her symbolic story "The Lottery."

Or you can combine some suspense with a *brief* overview of the story.

> The weather is sunny and clear. The residents of a peaceful village have gathered for an important annual event. They smile and chat with one another, while the children scurry about in play. Then someone brings out a black box, and the ordinary people of this ordinary town begin the process of choosing which one of their neighbors they are going to stone to death this summer. This shocking turn of events is the premise for Shirley Jackson's story about the fear and violence that lie beneath the placid surface of human societies. The story is called "The Lottery."

Another way to introduce a critical essay is to use interesting details about the author or the story's background that relate to the focus of your essay.

> In June 1948 the *New Yorker* magazine published "The Lottery," a story by Shirley Jackson. Within days the magazine began to receive a flood of telephone calls and letters, more than for any other piece of fiction it had ever published. Almost all of those who wrote were outraged or bewildered—sometimes both. Why did this story prompt such reactions? Why does it still shock readers? The answer may lie in the story's strong symbolic representation of the pointless violence and casual inhumanity that exist in all our lives.

Whatever approach you choose, keep the reader in mind. Think about reading an essay yourself. What do you expect from the introduction? Remember that the reader forms an important first impression from your opening paragraph.

Sample Student Paper on Symbolism: Second and Final Drafts

On the following left-hand pages appears the uncorrected second draft of an essay written by Todd Hageman, a student at Eastern Illinois University. On the right-hand pages you will see Todd's finished version. The questions in the margins of the final version ask you to consider the changes Todd made when he revised the paper.

Sample Student Paper: Second Draft

Hageman 1

Todd Hageman

English 102

March 2, 2005

Symbollism in The Lottery

Shirley Jackson's "The Lottery" uses subtle symbollism along with inconngruities to exemplify the loss of significance of some rituals & traditions, and supersitions and flaws of human nature. The first incongruity used is the day the story takes place, June 27th. Jackson paints a picture of a nice, sunny summer day in a small "Anytown, USA." While Jackson paints this picture, though, the reader feels an uneasy mood and senses something is going to happen. Jackson does this by using the words "hesitant" and "reluctant" to describe the crowd while they "smile at jokes instead of laugh" (78).

The next, and one of the biggest symbols used in the story, is the box—the black box to be more exact. The box is mentioned repeatedly to bring significance to it, although the reader isn't sure why until toward the end of the story. As the lottery symbolizes tradition, the box symbolizes the lottery.

Mr. Summers, the lottery official, tells about getting a new box every year, but the talk seems to "fade off." The box was described as "faded," "splintered," and "grew shabbyier each year" (79).

Sample Student Paper: Final Draft

Hageman 1

Todd Hageman

Professor Funk

English102

9 March 2005

Symbolism in "The Lottery"

Why did Todd make the changes that he did in this opening sentence?

In "The Lottery" Shirley Jackson uses subtle symbolism to exemplify the emptiness of some rituals and traditions, as well as to illustrate several flaws of human nature. She begins with an incongruity in the setting on the day the story takes place, June 27. Jackson paints a picture of a sunny summer day in a small "Anytown, USA." While Jackson introduces this pleasant setting, though, the reader feels uneasy and senses that something bad is going to happen. Jackson creates this tension by using the words "hesitant" and "reluctant" to describe the crowd and by mentioning that they "smiled rather than laughed" at jokes (78).

Why did Todd delete the second part of his thesis statement (regarding "incongruities")?

Why did he change "Jackson does this…" to "Jackson creates this tension…"?

Why did he change the quotation?

How did he improve the opening sentence of this paragraph?

The controlling symbol in the story is the box—the black box suggestive of death. The box is mentioned repeatedly to increase its significance, although the reader is not sure why the author stresses its importance until toward the end of the story. As the lottery symbolizes empty tradition, the box symbolizes the lottery itself.

Why did Todd change this quotation from "grew shabbier each year"?

Mr. Summers, the lottery official, speaks about getting a new box every year, but his talk seems to "fade off." The box is described as "faded," "splintered," and growing "shabbier

Second Draft

Hageman 2

The condition of the box symbolize the tradition of the lottery, and the need for a new box symbolizes the need for a new tradition.

There is a need for a new tradition because the lottery itself had lost its significance. Parts of the original lottery ritual had been allowed to lapse, and other parts, such as the salute of the official had "changed with the times" (79). The lottery had lapsed and changed so much from the original lottery that the people really didn't know why they were going through it any more. Probably the only reason they were going through it was the intellectual argument used by Old Man Warner, who said, "There's always been a lottery" (81). When Mr. Warner is informed that some places have stopped the lottery, he comes back with such wit as "Nothing but trouble in that," and "pack of young fools." (81). The latter idea expressed brings out the idea that all change is bad and the young are the ones who make changes.

It is generally aknowledged that the preceeding statement is false, leaving Mr. Warner on thin ice from which to argue. I think the author shows the uselessness of the lottery through Mr. Warner's ignorance.

Human nature is shown very clearliy through Tessie in the story. Tessie shows up late at the lottery very lackadaisical and in a joking mood before she was picked. She even gave her husband an extra

Final Draft

Hageman 2

each year" (79). The worn-out condition of the box symbolizes the tradition of the lottery, while the need for a new box symbolizes the need for a new tradition, but the townspeople fail to see the need for change.

Why did Todd add this last comment?

There is a need for a new tradition because the lottery itself has lost its significance. Parts of the original lottery ritual have been allowed to lapse, and other parts, such as the salute of the official, have "changed with time" (79). The lottery has lapsed and changed so much from the original that the people really do not know why they are going through it anymore. Probably the only reason they continue is solemnly stated by Old Man Warner: "There's *always* been a lottery" (81). When Mr. Warner is informed that some places have stopped the lottery, he comes back with such meaningless arguments as "Nothing but trouble in *that*" and "Pack of young fools" (81). He simply believes that all change is bad and that the young are the ones who make changes.

Why did he eliminate the sarcasm directed at Old Man Warner?

Can you think of another way to revise the stilted, wordy language of Todd's original statement, "It is generally acknowledged that the preceding statement is false..."?

Most people would disagree, for Mr. Warner has little evidence to support his ideas. I think the author emphasizes the uselessness of the lottery through Mr. Warner's ignorant defense of it.

The selfishness in human nature is shown clearly in the story through Tessie. She shows up late at the lottery, lackadaisically joking with her neighbors before she is picked. She even

How does the addition of the word "selfishness" in the opening sentence improve this whole paragraph?

Second Draft

Hageman 3

nudge as he went to draw. When Tessie found out one of her family would be chosen, her mood changed rather quickly, screaming "unfair!" She even wanted her two daughters to take their chances; which she knew was wrong. Her "friends" around her showed their flaws by saying, "Be a good sport," and "We all took the same chance," and not showing a bit of pity (82). Tessie's kids also showed no pity, as they opened their blank pieces of paper, they were described as "beaming and laughing" (83) with the crowd, even though they knew it was going to be Mom or Dad picked. The final part of human nature exemplified was when Tessie drew the black dot. Every time she said, "It isn't fair," the following sentence was always her getting hit with a stone, almost as punishment for saying it. The stones seem to be saying, "You thought it was fair until you were picked; now take your medicine."

The story has one key sentence which puts the whole theme in a nutshell: "Although the villagers had forgotten the ritual and lost the original box, they still remembered to use stones"(83). Through the symbolism being used, the sentence can be translated into a theme for the story. The ritual had changed with the times and lost the original purpose, but people still remember to look out for themselves. Every time a villager threw a stone, he was probably thinking, "Better you than me."

A final thought could be about the slips of paper and what they symbolized. Jackson mentioned

Final Draft

Hageman 3

gives her husband an encouraging nudge as he goes to draw. When Tessie finds out one of her family will be chosen, her mood changes quickly, and she screams, "It wasn't fair!" (82). She even wants her married daughter and son-in-law to take their chances along with her, which hardly suggests mother love. Her "friends" around her show their lack of pity by saying, "Be a good sport" and "All of us took the same chance!" (82). Tessie's children also show no sympathy. As they open their blank pieces of paper, they are described as beaming and laughing with the crowd, even though they know one of their parents is going to be picked. Human cruelty is also exemplified after Tessie draws the black dot. Both times she cries, "It isn't fair" (83), she gets hit with a stone, almost as punishment for objecting.

Would you have used a period in revising the comma splice, as he did? Or would you have used a semicolon? Why or why not?

Why did Todd move his final paragraph to this position?

The slips of paper also serve a symbolic purpose. Jackson mentions that the unused papers dropped to the ground "where the breeze caught them and lifted them off" (82). The papers could symbolize the people who have been sacrificed through the lottery. The village people make use of both the papers and the sacrificed people, then discard them as trash.

The story has one key sentence which captures the whole theme: "Although the villagers had forgotten the ritual and lost the original black box, they still remembered to use stones" (83).

Why did Todd replace the phrase "in a nutshell"?

Second Draft

Hageman 4

that the unused papers were dropped to the ground "where the breeze caught them and lifted them off" (82). The papers could be meant to symbolize the people who had been sacrificed through the lottery. The village people had used both the papers and the sacrificed people and had discarded them as trash.

Final Draft

Hageman 4

Considering the symbolism in the story, the sentence can be translated into a theme. Although the ritual had changed with the times and lost the original purpose, people still remember to look out for themselves. Every time the villagers threw a stone, they were probably thinking, "Better you than me." Jackson dramatizes for us the harm done by ignorance which causes people to cling to outworn rituals. She also shows the selfishness and cruelty that lie just beneath the civilized surface of human behavior.

How do these last two sentences that he added improve the paper?

Second Draft

Hageman 5

Work Cited

Shirley Jackson, "The Lottery," in Literature and the Writing Process, New Jersey: Prentice Hall, Inc.: 2005. 78–83.

Final Draft

Hageman 5

Work Cited

Jackson, Shirley. "The Lottery." *Literature and the Writing Process*. Ed. Elizabeth McMahan, Susan X Day, and Robert Funk. 7th ed. Upper Saddle River: Prentice, 2005. 83–89. Print.

What corrections did Todd make in his Work Cited entry?

9

Writing About Point of View

Learning about point of view in fiction will help you to understand how the author has shaped what you know and how you feel about the events in a story. When the point of view is unusual, you may want to focus your written analysis on the narrator or on the significance of the writer's choice of narrative focus.

What Is Point of View?

In identifying ***point of view***, you decide who tells the story—that is, whose thoughts and feelings the reader has access to. The storyteller, called the ***narrator***, is a creation of the author and should not be confused with the author. In the following passage from "Everyday Use," Alice Walker takes the reader into the private world of her narrator's fantasy:

> Sometimes I dream a dream in which Dee and I are suddenly brought together on a TV program of this sort. Out of a dark and soft-seated limousine I am ushered into a bright room filled with many people.

In John Updike's story "A & P," the narrator's distinctive voice is established in the opening lines:

> In walks these three girls in nothing but bathing suits. I'm in the third checkout slot, with my back to the door, so I don't see them until they're over by the bread.

But in the opening of "The Lottery," we are not conscious of a narrator at all:

> The morning of June 27th was clear and sunny, with the fresh warmth of a full-summer day; the flowers were blossoming profusely and the grass was richly green.

Describing Point of View

There are several systems for labeling the point of view in a work of literature. They classify the stance and the identity of the person who reports the action—that is, the person whose eyes and mind become ours as we read the story.

In actuality, a great many points of view are possible, and you may find some overlapping among the categories we provide here, but the following should allow you to describe all of the works included in this text.

- *Omniscient:* An all-knowing narrator, who is not a character in the story or involved in the action, freely relates many or all of the character's thoughts, feelings, and actions. In this example from Sherwood Anderson's "Hands," the omniscient narrator gives us considerable information about the main character's life and personality in a single sentence:

  > Wing Biddlebaum, forever frightened and beset by a ghostly band of doubts, did not think of himself as in any way a part of the life of the town where he had lived for twenty years.

- *Limited omniscience:* The narration is limited to the thoughts and observations of a single character. In detective fiction, for instance, we often see the plot unfold strictly from the main character's (the detective's) point of view. Sometimes our perceptions are limited to those of a minor character. In the Sherlock Holmes stories, for instance, the events are reported from the point of view of Dr. Watson, the great detective's sidekick, whose admiration and awe for Holmes's skills become ours. Raymond Carver's "What We Talk About When We Talk About Love" is another example of limited omniscience in which a minor character narrates the entire story.
- *First-Person:* The narrator recounts events in which he or she has been involved as a major participant. The narrator, identified as "I" in the story, speaks directly to us. First-person narrators often present only their side of the story. Sammy, the first-person narrator in John Updike's "A & P," gives an obviously subjective account of why he quit his job. The narrator of Tillie Olsen's "I Stand Here Ironing" appears to tell her story quite honestly and with little self-deception:

  > We were poor and could not afford for her the soil of easy growth. I was a young mother, I was a distracted mother. There were other children pushing, demanding.

- *Unreliable:* If the storyteller misrepresents the facts, the narrator is considered unreliable. An emotionally disturbed person like the murderous narrator of "The Cask of Amontillado," for instance, is not interested in giving a truthful account of his motives and actions. Poe intensifies the shock and horror of the story by letting us see into the inner workings of a sinister mind.

Writers often use an unreliable narrator to emphasize the subjectivity of experience or to reveal the shallowness or self-absorption of the main character. In Eudora Welty's "Why I Live at the P.O.," the narrator, Sister, gives us her perception of the conflicts in the household—colored by her hurt feelings, her desire to be loved by everyone, and her need to be always in the right. As the narrator, however, Sister inadvertently reveals that others in the household see matters quite differently, leaving us to sort out what's really going on in the story.

- *Objective:* Here the narrator disappears and the story seems to tell itself through action and dialogue. An objective narrative does not get into the minds of the characters; it gives us only what could be recorded by a camera and a microphone.

  In reading this kind of story, we have to make judgments and draw conclusions on our own. The objective narrator may edit the tape and direct the camera, but we have to figure out why the characters behave as they do. Shirley Jackson's "The Lottery" illustrates an objective point of view: the narrator presents the events without comment; we have to determine why the actions occur and what they mean.

  Sometimes a story with an objective point of view is easily identified because it consists largely of conversation, like Hemingway's "Hills Like White Elephants." In this story no author comments appear, only a few actions and brief scenic details. Our understanding of the characters is based entirely on the conclusions we are able to infer from reading their conversation. Because of its similarity to the script of a play, this type of story can also be called a *dramatic* point of view.

Looking at Point of View

As you read Alice Walker's "Everyday Use," think about the implications of our getting only Mama's perception of the events surrounding her daughter Dee's visit.

Alice Walker 1944–

Alice Walker was born in Eatonton, Georgia, the daughter of poor sharecroppers. When playing with her brothers at age eight, she was blinded in her right eye by a BB gun pellet. After attending Spellman and Sarah Lawrence colleges, she became a civil rights activist. In 1965, she married Mel Leventhal, a Jewish civil rights lawyer; they became the first legally married interracial couple in Mississippi. She later coined the term "womanist," meaning a feminist of color. Her novel *The Color Purple* won the 1983 Pulitzer Prize and was made into a popular film.

Everyday Use

For Your Grandmama

I will wait for her in the yard that Maggie and I made so clean and wavy yesterday afternoon. A yard like this is more comfortable than most people know. It is not just a yard. It is like an extended living room. When the hard clay is swept clean as a floor and the fine sand around the edges lined with tiny, irregular grooves, anyone can come and sit and look up into the elm tree and wait for the breezes that never come inside the house.

Maggie will be nervous until after her sister goes: she will stand hopelessly in corners, homely and ashamed of the burn scars down her arms and legs, eying her sister with a mixture of envy and awe. She thinks her sister has held life always in the palm of one hand, that "no" is a word the world never learned to say to her.

You've no doubt seen those TV shows where the child who has "made it" is confronted, as a surprise, by her own mother and father, tottering in weakly from backstage. (A pleasant surprise, of course: What would they do if parent and child came on the show only to curse out and insult each other?) On TV mother and child embrace and smile into each other's faces. Sometimes the mother and father weep, the child wraps them in her arms and leans across the table to tell how she would not have made it without their help. I have seen these programs.

Sometimes I dream a dream in which Dee and I are suddenly brought together on a TV program of this sort. Out of a dark and soft-seated limousine I am ushered into a bright room filled with many people. There I meet a smiling, gray, sporty man like Johnny Carson who shakes my hand and tells me what a fine girl I have. Then we are on the stage and Dee is embracing me with tears in her eyes. She pins on my dress a large orchid, even though she has told me once that she thinks orchids are tacky flowers.

In real life I am a large, big-boned woman with rough, man-working hands. 5
In the winter I wear flannel nightgowns to bed and overalls during the day. I can kill and clean a hog as mercilessly as a man. My fat keeps me hot in zero weather. I can work outside all day, breaking ice to get water for washing; I can eat pork liver cooked over the open fire minutes after it comes steaming from the hog. One winter I knocked a bull calf straight in the brain between the eyes with a sledge hammer and had the meat hung up to chill before nightfall. But of course all this does not show on television. I am the way my daughter would want me to be: a hundred pounds lighter, my skin like an uncooked barley pancake. My hair glistens in the hot bright lights. Johnny Carson has much to do to keep up with my quick and witty tongue.

But that is a mistake. I know even before I wake up. Who ever knew a Johnson with a quick tongue? Who can even imagine me looking a strange white man in the eye? It seems to me I have talked to them always with one foot raised in flight, with my head turned in whichever way is farthest from them. Dee, though. She would always look anyone in the eye. Hesitation was no part of her nature.

"How do I look, Mama?" Maggie says, showing just enough of her thin body enveloped in pink skirt and red blouse for me to know she's there, almost hidden by the door.

"Come out into the yard," I say.

Have you ever seen a lame animal, perhaps a dog run over by some careless person rich enough to own a car, sidle up to someone who is ignorant enough to be kind to him? That is the way my Maggie walks. She has been like this, chin on chest, eyes on ground, feet in shuffle, ever since the fire that burned the other house to the ground.

Dee is lighter than Maggie, with nicer hair and a fuller figure. She's a woman 10
now, though sometimes I forget. How long ago was it that the other house burned? Ten, twelve years? Sometimes I can still hear the flames and feel Maggie's arms sticking to me, her hair smoking and her dress falling off her in little black papery flakes. Her eyes seemed stretched open, blazed open by the flames reflected in them. And Dee. I see her standing off under the sweet gum tree she used to dig gum out of; a look of concentration on her face as she watched the last dingy gray board of the house fall in toward the red-hot brick chimney. Why don't you do a dance around the ashes? I'd wanted to ask her. She had hated the house that much.

I used to think she hated Maggie, too. But that was before we raised the money, the church and me, to send her to Augusta to school. She used to read to us without pity; forcing words, lies, other folks' habits, whole lives upon us two, sitting trapped and ignorant underneath her voice. She washed us in a river of make-believe, burned us with a lot of knowledge we didn't necessarily need to know. Pressed us to her with the serious way she read, to shove us away at just the moment, like dimwits, we seemed about to understand.

A quilt in the traditional Lone Star pattern (The Newark Museum/Art Resource, NY)

Dee wanted nice things. A yellow organdy dress to wear to her graduation from high school; black pumps to match a green suit she'd made from an old suit somebody gave me. She was determined to stare down any disaster in her efforts. Her eyelids would not flicker for minutes at a time. Often I fought off the temptation to shake her. At sixteen she had a style of her own: and knew what style was.

I never had an education myself. After second grade the school was closed down. Don't ask me why: in 1927 colored asked fewer questions than they do now. Sometimes Maggie reads to me. She stumbles along good-naturedly but can't see well. She knows she is not bright. Like good looks and money, quickness passed her by. She will marry John Thomas (who has mossy teeth in an earnest face) and then I'll be free to sit here and I guess just sing church songs to myself. Although I never was a good singer. Never could carry a tune. I was always better at a man's job. I used to love to milk till I was hooked in the side in '49. Cows are soothing and slow and don't bother you, unless you try to milk them the wrong way.

I have deliberately turned my back on the house. It is three rooms, just like the one that burned, except the roof is tin; they don't make shingle roofs any more. There are no real windows, just some holes cut in the sides, like the portholes in a ship, but not round and not square, with rawhide holding the shutters up on the outside. This house is in a pasture, too, like the other one. No doubt when Dee sees it she will want to tear it down. She wrote me once that no matter where we "choose" to live, she will manage to come see us. But she will never bring her friends. Maggie and I thought about this and Maggie asked me, "Mama, when did Dee ever *have* any friends?"

She had a few. Furtive boys in pink shirts hanging about on washday after 15
school. Nervous girls who never laughed. Impressed with her they worshipped the well-turned phrase, the cute shape, the scalding humor that erupted like bubbles in lye. She read to them.

When she was courting Jimmy T she didn't have much time to pay to us, but turned all her faultfinding power on him. He *flew* to marry a cheap city girl from a family of ignorant flashy people. She hardly had time to recompose herself.

When she comes I will meet—but there they are!

Maggie attempts to make a dash for the house, in her shuffling way, but I stay her with my hand. "Come back here," I say. And she stops and tries to dig a well in the sand with her toe.

It is hard to see them clearly through the strong sun. But even the first glimpse of leg out of the car tells me it is Dee. Her feet were always neat-looking, as if God himself had shaped them with a certain style. From the other side of the car comes a short, stocky man. Hair is all over his head a foot long and hanging from his chin like a kinky mule tail. I hear Maggie suck in her breath. "Uhnnnh," is what it sounds like. Like when you see the wriggling end of a snake just in front of your foot on the road. "Uhnnnh."

Dee next. A dress down to the ground, in this hot weather. A dress so loud it 20
hurts my eyes. There are yellows and oranges enough to throw back the light of the sun. I feel my whole face warming from the heat waves it throws out. Earrings gold, too, and hanging down to her shoulders. Bracelets dangling and making noises when she moves her arm up to shake the folds of the dress out of her armpits. The dress is loose and flows, and as she walks closer, I like it. I hear

Maggie go "Uhnnnh" again. It is her sister's hair. It stands straight up like the wool on a sheep. It is black as night and around the edges are two long pigtails that rope about like small lizards disappearing behind her ears.

"Wa-su-zo-Tean-o!" she says, coming on in that gliding way the dress makes her move. The short stocky fellow with the hair to his navel is all grinning and he follows up with "Asalamalakim, my mother and sister!" He moves to hug Maggie but she falls back, right up against the back of my chair. I feel her trembling there and when I look up I see the perspiration falling off her chin.

"Don't get up," says Dee. Since I am stout it takes something of a push. You can see me trying to move a second or two before I make it. She turns, showing white heels through her sandals, and goes back to the car. Out she peeks next with a Polaroid. She stoops down quickly and lines up picture after picture of me sitting there in front of the house with Maggie cowering behind me. She never takes a shot without making sure the house is included. When a cow comes nibbling around the edge of the yard she snaps it and me and Maggie *and* the house. Then she puts the Polaroid in the back seat of the car, and comes up and kisses me on the forehead.

Meanwhile Asalamalakim is going through motions with Maggie's hand. Maggie's hand is as limp as a fish, and probably as cold, despite the sweat, and she keeps trying to pull it back. It looks like Asalamalakim wants to shake hands but wants to do it fancy. Or maybe he don't know how people shake hands. Anyhow, he soon gives up on Maggie.

"Well," I say. "Dee."

"No, Mama," she says. "Not 'Dee,' Wangero Leewanika Kemanjo!" 25

"What happened to 'Dee'?" I wanted to know.

"She's dead," Wangero said. "I couldn't bear it any longer, being named after the people who oppress me."

"You know as well as me you was named after your aunt Dicie," I said. Dicie is my sister. She named Dee. We called her "Big Dee" after Dee was born.

"But who was *she* named after?" asked Wangero.

"I guess after Grandma Dee," I said. 30

"And who was she named after?" asked Wangero.

"Her mother," I said, and saw Wangero was getting tired. "That's about as far back as I can trace it," I said. Though, in fact, I probably could have carried it back beyond the Civil War through the branches.

"Well," said Asalamalakim, "there you are."

"Uhnnnh," I heard Maggie say.

"There I was not," I said, "before 'Dicie' cropped up in our family, so why should I try to trace it that far back?" 35

He just stood there grinning, looking down on me like somebody inspecting a Model A car. Every once in a while he and Wangero sent eye signals over my head.

"How do you pronounce this name?" I asked.

"You don't have to call me by it if you don't want to," said Wangero.

"Why shouldn't I?" I asked. "If that's what you want us to call you, we'll call you."

"I know it might sound awkward at first," said Wangero. 40

"I'll get used to it," I said. "Ream it out again."

Well, soon we got the name out of the way. Asalamalakim had a name twice as long and three times as hard. After I tripped over it two or three times he told me to just call him Hakim-a-barber. I wanted to ask him was he a barber, but I didn't really think he was, so I didn't ask.

"You must belong to those beef-cattle peoples down the road," I said. They said "Asalamalakim" when they met you, too, but they didn't shake hands. Always too busy: feeding the cattle, fixing the fences, putting up salt-lick shelters, throwing down hay. When the white folks poisoned some of the herd the men stayed up all night with rifles in their hands. I walked a mile and a half just to see the sight.

Hakim-a-barber said, "I accept some of their doctrines, but farming and raising cattle is not my style." (They didn't tell me, and I didn't ask, whether Wangero (Dee) had really gone and married him.)

We sat down to eat and right away he said he didn't eat collards and pork was 45
unclean. Wangero, though, went on through the chitlins and corn bread, the greens and everything else. She talked a blue streak over the sweet potatoes. Everything delighted her. Even the fact that we still used the benches her daddy made for the table when we couldn't afford to buy chairs.

"Oh, Mama!" she cried. Then turned to Hakim-a-barber. "I never knew how lovely these benches are. You can feel the rump prints," she said, running her hands underneath her and along the bench. Then she gave a sigh and her hand closed over Grandma Dee's butter dish. "That's it!" she said. "I knew there was something I wanted to ask you if I could have." She jumped up from the table and went over in the corner where the churn stood, the milk in it clabber by now. She looked at the churn and looked at it.

"This churn top is what I need," she said. "Didn't Uncle Buddy whittle it out of a tree you all used to have?"

"Yes," I said.

"Uh huh," she said happily. "And I want the dasher, too."

"Uncle Buddy whittle that, too?" asked the barber. 50

Dee (Wangero) looked up at me.

"Aunt Dee's first husband whittled the dash," said Maggie so low you almost couldn't hear her. "His name was Henry, but they called him Stash."

"Maggie's brain is like an elephant's," Wangero said, laughing. "I can use the churn top as a centerpiece for the alcove table," she said, sliding a plate over the churn, "and I'll think of something artistic to do with the dasher."

When she finished wrapping the dasher the handle stuck out. I took it for a moment in my hands. You didn't even have to look close to see where hands pushing the dasher up and down to make butter had left a kind of sink in the wood. In fact, there were a lot of small sinks; you could see where thumbs and fingers had sunk into the wood. It was beautiful light yellow wood, from a tree that grew in the yard where Big Dee and Stash had lived.

After dinner Dee (Wangero) went to the trunk at the foot of my bed and 55
started rifling through it. Maggie hung back in the kitchen over the dishpan. Out came Wangero with two quilts. They had been pieced by Grandma Dee and then Big Dee and me had hung them on the quilt frames on the front porch and quilted them. One was in the Lone Star pattern. The other was Walk Around the Mountain. In both of them were scraps of dresses Grandma Dee had worn fifty and more years ago. Bits and pieces of Grandpa Jarrell's Paisley shirts. And one teeny faded blue piece, about the size of a penny matchbox, that was from Great Grandpa Ezra's uniform that he wore in the Civil War.

"Mama," Wangero said sweet as a bird. "Can I have these old quilts?"

I heard something fall in the kitchen, and a minute later the kitchen door slammed.

"Why don't you take one or two of the others?" I asked. "These old things was just done by me and Big Dee from some tops your grandma pieced before she died."

"No," said Wangero. "I don't want those. They are stitched around the borders by machine."

"That'll make them last better," I said. 60

"That's not the point," said Wangero. "These are all pieces of dresses Grandma used to wear. She did all this stitching by hand. Imagine!" She held the quilts securely in her arms, stroking them.

"Some of the pieces, like those lavender ones, come from old clothes her mother handed down to her," I said, moving up to touch the quilts. Dee (Wangero) moved back just enough so that I couldn't reach the quilts. They already belonged to her.

"Imagine!" she breathed again, clutching them closely to her bosom.

"The truth is," I said, "I promised to give them quilts to Maggie, for when she marries John Thomas."

She gasped like a bee had stung her. 65

"Maggie can't appreciate these quilts!" she said. "She'd probably be backward enough to put them to everyday use."

"I reckon she would," I said. "God knows I been saving 'em for long enough with nobody using 'em. I hope she will!" I didn't want to bring up how I had offered Dee (Wangero) a quilt when she went away to college. Then she had told me they were old-fashioned, out of style.

"But they're *priceless*!" she was saying now, furiously; for she has a temper. "Maggie would put them on the bed and in five years they'd be in rags. Less than that!"

"She can always make some more," I said. "Maggie knows how to quilt."

Dee (Wangero) looked at me with hatred. "You just will not understand. The 70
point is these quilts, *these* quilts!"

"Well," I said, stumped. "What would *you* do with them?"

"Hang them," she said. As if that was the only thing you *could* do with quilts.

Maggie by now was standing in the door. I could almost hear the sound her feet made as they scraped over each other.

"She can have them, Mama," she said, like somebody used to never winning anything, or having anything reserved for her. "I can 'member Grandma Dee without the quilts."

I looked at her hard. She had filled her bottom lip with checkerberry snuff 75
and it gave her face a kind of dopey, hangdog look. It was Grandma Dee and Big Dee who taught her how to quilt herself. She stood there with her scarred hands hidden in the folds of her skirt. She looked at her sister with something like fear but she wasn't mad at her. This was Maggie's portion. This was the way she knew God to work.

When I looked at her like that something hit me in the top of my head and ran down to the soles of my feet. Just like when I'm in church and the spirit of God touches me and I get happy and shout. I did something I never had done before: hugged Maggie to me, then dragged her on into the room, snatched the quilts out of Miss Wangero's hands and dumped them into Maggie's lap. Maggie just sat there on my bed with her mouth open.

"Take one or two of the others," I said to Dee.

But she turned without a word and went out to Hakim-a-barber.

"You just don't understand," she said, as Maggie and I came out to the car.

"What don't I understand?" I wanted to know. 80

"Your heritage," she said. And then she turned to Maggie, kissed her, and said, "You ought to try to make something of yourself, too, Maggie. It's really a new day for us. But from the way you and Mama still live you'd never know it."

She put on some sunglasses that hid everything above the tip of her nose and her chin.

Maggie smiled; maybe at the sunglasses. But a real smile, not scared. After we watched the car dust settle I asked Maggie to bring me a dip of snuff. And then the two of us sat there just enjoying, until it was time to go in the house and go to bed.

(1973)

PREWRITING

To help you examine the point of view of "Everyday Use" and see how it affects other elements of the story, write out answers to the following questions.

Analyzing Point of View

1. Who is telling this story? What kind of person is she? Describe her character traits, her strengths and weaknesses, and explain how you feel about her. Is it significant that she is not given a first name but is called only Mama throughout?
2. Why do you think Walker chose Mama as the narrator instead of Maggie or Dee/Wangero? How would the story be different if told from the point of view of one of the daughters?
3. Describe the character traits of Maggie and Dee/Wangero. How do you respond to them? Do you admire them, feel sorry for them, dislike them? Explain why.
4. Why does Mama include the account of the fire in her narration? Do we know how the house caught fire? Is it important to know? Does this past tragedy shed light on the characters' actions in the story?
5. What is the significance of the African names, dress, and hair styles? Why do you think Asalamalakim appears in the story?
6. Why does Dee/Wangero want the quilts? Why does Mama give them to Maggie?
7. What is the major conflict in the story? Who best understands the family's heritage? How do you know this?
8. Imagine the conversation that Maggie and Mama have after Dee/Wangero has left. Write a page or two of dialogue in which Maggie and Mama talk to each other about Dee.

WRITING

Before you decide to focus your paper on point of view, you need to determine its importance in the story. An analysis of point of view may not always merit a full-length paper. For instance, an omniscient point of view, while a conventional and often effective choice for narrating a story, may not prove a fruitful subject for an essay. But an analysis of point of view will sometimes, as in "Everyday Use," reveal rich insights into the meaning of the story.

Relating Point of View to Theme

After analyzing a story from the vantage of point of view, you need to think about how all your discoveries relate to its theme—its main point, its impact, its insight into human behavior. Your essay will explain why this particular point of view is effective for this particular story.

IDEAS FOR WRITING

Ideas for Responsive Writing

1. Write a description of Mama from the point of view of either Maggie or Dee/Wangero.
2. Have you ever known someone like Mama? Write a character sketch of this person, pointing out similarities to Mama.
3. In "Everyday Use," objects take on more importance than their simple functions—the quilts and the churn, for example. Are there any items like this in your life? Which of your belongings do you think your grandchildren will value? Why? Write about how objects acquire special significance.
4. Have you ever changed your name? Have you asked people to call you by a new name—for example, changing from Billy to Bill? Do you know anyone who has? Why do people change their names? Write an essay about what our names mean to us.

Ideas for Critical Writing

Here are some possible major claims that focus on point of view. Choose one of these claims, revise one, or make up your own to develop an interpretation of "Everyday Use."

1. Each memory recorded in "Everyday Use" serves to strengthen the foil relationship between Dee/Wangero and the narrator, a contrast that flares into a clash between two notions of heritage.

2. Alice Walker uses explanatory flashbacks to Dee/Wangero's early life but excludes any depiction of her current life (even such details as whether she is married or where she lives); this character appears from nowhere, ironically suggesting her own lack of heritage or cultural tradition, a lack she is quick to perceive in others.
3. By telling the story through the eyes of Mama, Walker subtly encourages us to agree with Mama's side of the underlying argument about cultural heritage.
4. Because we as readers have access to Mama's unspoken thoughts about her daughters and Hakim-a-barber, we realize that, despite the seriousness of the story, she is a great comic narrator.

Ideas for Researched Writing

1. Look up and study the topic "black nationalism" in a reference work, such as *The African-American Encyclopedia* or *Encyclopedia of African-American Culture* (the latter is available online). Then write an essay explaining how you think this social movement from the 1960s has influenced the appearance, behavior, and attitudes of Dee/Wangero.
2. "Everyday Use" is a story about many different themes and issues. Research the various critical readings of this story, and prepare a report for your classmates that summarizes and evaluates the interpretations you found.

REWRITING

When you revise, do not neglect your conclusion just because it comes last. It has a psychologically important place in your paper. Ask yourself, "Does my closing restate the main idea in an obvious, repetitive way? Will readers feel let down, dropped off, cut short?" If so, consider these ways to make your ending more lively.

Sharpening the Conclusion

1. *Description.* In concluding a discussion of the conflicts between Mama and her distasteful daughter, you might write the following:

   Thus Dee/Wangero, with her new name, her African dress, her dangling bracelets, and her braided hair, rejects the rural simplicity of her childhood culture. Sliding on her fashionable sunglasses, she leaves Mama and Maggie sitting on their porch "just enjoying" their dip of snuff, the pleasant evening, and the comfortable everydayness of their lives.

2. *A quotation from the story.* Remember that a quotation must be integrated into your own sentence, perhaps like this:

   When Maggie says, quietly, "I can 'member Grandma Dee without the quilts," we see that heritage can have a deeper meaning than co-opting churn tops as centerpieces and hand-stitched quilts as wall hangings.

3. *An echo from your introduction.* If you wrote in your opening of the clash between two black cultures in the story, you could conclude with this echo:

   Mama, pushed too far, finally proves herself a match for her sophisticated daughter, who ignores her own family heritage as she shows off her newly adopted African roots.

4. *A thought-provoking question, suggestion, or statement.*

   Were Mama and Maggie right in rejecting the unfamiliar African heritage that Dee/Wangero introduces?

   Perhaps society would generate fewer conflicts if people paid less attention to their individual ethnic and cultural background.

10

Writing About Setting and Atmosphere

Setting and atmosphere contribute to the effectiveness of short stories in various ways. Sometimes these elements assume enough importance to become the focus of a literary analysis.

What Are Setting and Atmosphere?

You know, of course, the meaning of ***setting*** in reference to a work of literature: the setting includes the location and time of the action in a story, novel, play, or poem. Sometimes setting conveys an ***atmosphere***—the emotional effect of the setting and events—that contributes to the impact or to the meaning of the work. Atmosphere (or ***mood***) is that feeling of chill foreboding that Poe creates by setting his tale of "The Fall of the House of Usher" in a remote, moldering mansion on the edge of a black, stagnant pool and then having eerie things happen. Atmosphere can also serve to increase irony, as Shirley Jackson does in "The Lottery" by conveying the deceptive feeling of carefree summer festivity just before turning her tale abruptly toward ritual murder. Usually, though, setting and atmosphere reflect the dominant tone and theme of a work.

In deciding whether to focus on setting or atmosphere in writing a literary paper, you need to ask yourself not only how much the effect of the work would be changed if these elements were different, but also how much you have to say about them—especially what they contribute to the power of the narrative. For instance, the stalled freeway where Dagoberto Gilb's "Love in L.A." takes place seems the perfect setting for that story. We can scarcely imagine its being set as effectively anywhere else. Los Angeles, the home of Hollywood and all the fantasies of movieland, clearly molded the main character's imaginative life and inspired the false surfaces of his identity. Sweaty, noisy traffic jams pervade this L.A. dweller's life, shape his aspirations, and stick him with plenty of downtime in which to embellish his daydreams. A freeway collision is a completely believable site for Jake to bump into his version of love. Concerning any story, if you ask yourself, "In what other surroundings and time could this story happen?" and find it difficult to imagine an answer, probably the setting is a worthwhile focus for a paper.

Looking at Setting and Atmosphere

As you read the following story by Tobias Wolff, consider how crucial setting and atmosphere are in contributing to the story's effect.

Tobias Wolff 1945–

Tobias Wolff, a Stanford University graduate, served four years as an army paratrooper, including a year in Vietnam, and now teaches creative writing at Stanford. "The disaster of television," he says, "has created a tremendous vacuum in our culture. I really regard it as a catastrophe. The monster in our house devours the imagination; it's a completely passive entertainment. And reading has been the first casualty, because reading is active, demanding." His memoir, *This Boy's Life* (1989), a painful reminiscence of growing up in his stepfather's home, was made into a popular film starring Robert De Niro and Leonardo DiCaprio.

Hunters in the Snow

Tub had been waiting for an hour in the falling snow. He paced the sidewalk to keep warm and stuck his head out over the curb whenever he saw lights approaching. One driver stopped for him but before Tub could wave the man on he saw the rifle on Tub's back and hit the gas. The tires spun on the ice.

The fall of snow thickened. Tub stood below the overhang of a building. Across the road the clouds whitened just above the rooftops, and the street lights went out. He shifted the rifle strap to his other shoulder. The whiteness seeped up the sky.

A truck slid around the corner, horn blaring, rear end sashaying. Tub moved to the sidewalk and held up his hand. The truck jumped the curb and kept coming, half on the street and half on the sidewalk. It wasn't slowing down at all. Tub stood for a moment, still holding up his hand, then jumped back. His rifle slipped off his shoulder and clattered on the ice, a sandwich fell out of his pocket. He ran for the steps of the building. Another sandwich and a package of cookies tumbled onto the new snow. He made the steps and looked back.

The truck had stopped several feet beyond where Tub had been standing. He picked up his sandwiches and his cookies and slung the rifle and went up to the driver's window. The driver was bent against the steering wheel, slapping his knees and drumming his feet on the floorboards. He looked like a cartoon of a person laughing, except that his eyes watched the man on the seat beside him.

"You ought to see yourself," the driver said. "He looks just like a beach ball with a hat on, doesn't he? Doesn't he, Frank?"

The man beside him smiled and looked off. 5

"You almost ran me down," Tub said. "You could've killed me."

"Come on, Tub," said the man beside the driver. "Be mellow. Kenny was just messing around." He opened the door and slid over to the middle of the seat.

Tub took the bolt out of his rifle and climbed in beside him. "I waited an hour," he said. "If you meant ten o'clock why didn't you say ten o'clock?"

"Tub, you haven't done anything but complain since we got here," said the man in the middle. "If you want to piss and moan all day you might as well go home and bitch at your kids. Take your pick." When Tub didn't say anything he turned to the driver. "Okay, Kenny, let's hit the road."

Some juvenile delinquents had heaved a brick through the windshield on the driver's side, so the cold and snow tunneled right into the cab. The heater didn't work. They covered themselves with a couple of blankets Kenny had brought along and pulled down the muffs on their caps. Tub tried to keep his hands warm by rubbing them under the blanket but Frank made him stop. 10

They left Spokane and drove deep into the country, running along black lines of fences. The snow let up, but still there was no edge to the land where it met the sky. Nothing moved in the chalky fields. The cold bleached their faces and made the stubble stand out on their cheeks and along their upper lips. They stopped twice for coffee before they got to the woods where Kenny wanted to hunt.

Tub was for trying someplace different; two years in a row they'd been up and down this land and hadn't seen a thing. Frank didn't care one way or the other, he just wanted to get out of the goddamned truck. "Feel that," Frank said, slamming the door. He spread his feet and closed his eyes and leaned his head way back and breathed deeply. "Tune in on that energy."

"Another thing," Kenny said. "This is open land. Most of the land around here is posted."

"I'm cold," Tub said.

Frank breathed out. "Stop bitching, Tub. Get centered." 15

"I wasn't bitching."

"Centered," Kenny said. "Next thing you'll be wearing a nightgown, Frank. Selling flowers out at the airport."

"Kenny," Frank said, "you talk too much."

"Okay," Kenny said. "I won't say a word. Like I won't say anything about a certain babysitter."

"What babysitter?" Tub asked. 20

"That's between us," Frank said, looking at Kenny. "That's confidential. You keep your mouth shut."

Kenny laughed.

"You're asking for it," Frank said.

"Asking for what?"

"You'll see." 25

"Hey," Tub said, "are we hunting or what?"

They started off across the field. Tub had trouble getting through the fences. Frank and Kenny could have helped him; they could have lifted up on the top wire and stepped on the bottom wire, but they didn't. They stood and watched him. There were a lot of fences and Tub was puffing when they reached the woods.

They hunted for over two hours and saw no deer, no tracks, no sign. Finally they stopped by the creek to eat. Kenny had several slices of pizza and a couple of candy bars; Frank had a sandwich, an apple, two carrots, and a square of chocolate; Tub ate one hard-boiled egg and a stick of celery.

"You ask me how I want to die today," Kenny said, "I'll tell you burn me at the stake." He turned to Tub. "You still on that diet?" He winked at Frank.

"What do you think? You think I like hard-boiled eggs?" 30

"All I can say is, it's the first diet I ever heard of where you gained weight from it."

"Who said I gained weight?"

"Oh, pardon me. I take it back. You're just wasting away before my very eyes. Isn't he, Frank?"

Frank had his fingers fanned out, tips against the bark of the stump where he'd laid his food. His knuckles were hairy. He wore a heavy wedding band and on his right pinky another gold ring with a flat face and an "F" in what looked like diamonds. He turned the ring this way and that. "Tub," he said, "you haven't seen your own balls in ten years."

Kenny doubled over laughing. He took off his hat and slapped his leg with it. 35

"What am I supposed to do?" Tub said. "It's my glands."

They left the woods and hunted along the creek. Frank and Kenny worked one bank and Tub worked the other, moving upstream. The snow was light but the drifts were deep and hard to move through. Wherever Tub looked the surface was smooth, undisturbed, and after a time he lost interest. He stopped looking for tracks and just tried to keep up with Frank and Kenny on the other side. A moment came when he realized he hadn't seen them in a long time. The breeze was moving from him to them; when it stilled he could sometimes hear Kenny laughing but that was all. He quickened his pace, breasting hard into the drifts, fighting away the snow with his knees and elbows. He heard his heart and felt the flush on his face but he never once stopped.

Tub caught up with Frank and Kenny at a bend of the creek. They were standing on a log that stretched from their bank to his. Ice had backed up behind the log. Frozen reeds stuck out, barely nodding when the air moved.

"See anything?" Frank asked.

Tub shook his head. 40

There wasn't much daylight left and they decided to head back toward the road. Frank and Kenny crossed the log and they started downstream, using the trail Tub had broken. Before they had gone very far Kenny stopped. "Look at that," he said, and pointed to some tracks going from the creek back into the woods. Tub's footprints crossed right over them. There on the bank, plain as day, were several mounds of deer sign. "What do you think that is, Tub?" Kenny kicked at it. "Walnuts on vanilla icing?"

"I guess I didn't notice."

Kenny looked at Frank.

"I was lost."

"You were lost. Big deal." 45

They followed the tracks into the woods. The deer had gone over a fence half buried in drifting snow. A no hunting sign was nailed to the top of one of the posts. Frank laughed and said the son of a bitch could read. Kenny wanted to go after him but Frank said no way, the people out here didn't mess around. He thought maybe the farmer who owned the land would let them use it if they asked. Kenny wasn't so sure. Anyway, he figured that by the time they walked to the truck and drove up the road and doubled back it would be almost dark.

"Relax," Frank said. "You can't hurry nature. If we're meant to get that deer, we'll get it. If we're not, we won't."

They started back toward the truck. This part of the woods was mainly pine. The snow was shaded and had a glaze on it. It held up Kenny and Frank but Tub kept falling through. As he kicked forward, the edge of the crust bruised his shins. Kenny and Frank pulled ahead of him, to where he couldn't even hear their voices any more. He sat down on a stump and wiped his face. He ate both the sandwiches and half the cookies, taking his own sweet time. It was dead quiet.

When Tub crossed the last fence into the road the truck started moving. Tub had to run for it and just managed to grab hold of the tailgate and hoist himself into the bed. He lay there, panting. Kenny looked out the rear window and grinned. Tub crawled into the lee of the cab to get out of the freezing wind. He pulled his earflaps low and pushed his chin into the collar of his coat. Someone rapped on the window but Tub would not turn around.

He and Frank waited outside while Kenny went into the farmhouse to ask permission. The house was old and paint was curling off the sides. The smoke streamed westward off the top of the chimney, fanning away into a thin gray plume. Above the ridge of the hills another ridge of blue clouds was rising.

"You've got a short memory," Tub said.

"What?" Frank said. He had been staring off.

"I used to stick up for you."

"Okay, so you used to stick up for me. What's eating you?"

"You shouldn't have just left me back there like that."

"You're a grown-up, Tub. You can take care of yourself. Anyway, if you think you're the only person with problems I can tell you that you're not."

"Is something bothering you, Frank?"

Frank kicked at a branch poking out of the snow. "Never mind," he said.

"What did Kenny mean about the babysitter?"

"Kenny talks too much," Frank said. "You just mind your own business."

Kenny came out of the farmhouse and gave the thumbs-up and they began walking back toward the woods. As they passed the barn a large black hound with a grizzled snout ran out and barked at them. Every time he barked he slid backwards a bit, like a cannon recoiling. Kenny got down on all fours and snarled and barked back at him, and the dog slunk away into the barn, looking over his shoulder and peeing a little as he went.

"That's an old-timer," Frank said. "A real graybeard. Fifteen years if he's a day."

"Too old," Kenny said.

Past the barn they cut off through the fields. The land was unfenced and the crust was freezing up thick and they made good time. They kept to the edge of the field until they picked up the tracks again and followed them into the woods, farther and farther back toward the hills. The trees started to blur with the shadows and the wind rose and needled their faces with the crystals it swept off the glaze. Finally they lost the tracks.

65 Kenny swore and threw down his hat. "This is the worst day of hunting I ever had, bar none." He picked up his hat and brushed off the snow. "This will be the first season since I was fifteen I haven't got my deer."

"It isn't the deer," Frank said. "It's the hunting. There are all these forces out here and you just have to go with them."

"You go with them," Kenny said. "I came out here to get me a deer, not listen to a bunch of hippie bullshit. And if it hadn't been for dimples here I would have, too."

"That's enough," Frank said.

"And you—you're so busy thinking about that little jailbait of yours you wouldn't know a deer if you saw one."

70 "Drop dead," Frank said, and turned away.

Kenny and Tub followed him back across the fields. When they were coming up to the barn Kenny stopped and pointed. "I hate that post," he said. He raised his rifle and fired. It sounded like a dry branch cracking. The post splintered along its right side, up towards the top. "There," Kenny said. "It's dead."

"Knock it off," Frank said, walking ahead.

Kenny looked at Tub. He smiled. "I hate that tree," he said, and fired again. Tub hurried to catch up with Frank. He started to speak but just then the dog ran out of the barn and barked at them. "Easy, boy," Frank said.

"I hate that dog." Kenny was behind them.

75 "That's enough," Frank said. "You put that gun down."

Kenny fired. The bullet went in between the dog's eyes. He sank right down into the snow, his legs splayed out on each side, his yellow eyes open and staring. Except for the blood he looked like a small bearskin rug. The blood ran down the dog's muzzle into the snow.

They all looked at the dog lying there.

"What did he ever do to you?" Tub asked. "He was just barking."

Kenny turned to Tub. "I hate you."

80 Tub shot from the waist. Kenny jerked backward against the fence and buckled to his knees. He folded his hands across his stomach. "Look," he said. His hands were covered with blood. In the dusk his blood was more blue than red. It seemed to belong to the shadows. It didn't seem out of place. Kenny eased himself onto his back. He sighed several times, deeply. "You shot me," he said.

"I had to," Tub said. He knelt beside Kenny. "Oh God," he said. "Frank. Frank."

Frank hadn't moved since Kenny killed the dog.

"Frank!" Tub shouted.

"I was just kidding around," Kenny said. "It was a joke. Oh!" he said, and arched his back suddenly. "Oh!" he said again, and dug his heels into the snow and pushed himself along on his head for several feet. Then he stopped and lay there, rocking back and forth on his heels and head like a wrestler doing warm-up exercises.

85 Frank roused himself. "Kenny," he said. He bent down and put his gloved hand on Kenny's brow. "You shot him," he said to Tub.

"He made me," Tub said.

"No no no," Kenny said.

Tub was weeping from the eyes and nostrils. His whole face was wet. Frank closed his eyes, then looked down at Kenny again. "Where does it hurt?"

"Everywhere," Kenny said, "just everywhere."

"Oh God," Tub said.

"I mean where did it go in?" Frank said.

"Here." Kenny pointed at the wound in his stomach. It was welling slowly with blood.

"You're lucky," Frank said. "It's on the left side. It missed your appendix. If it had hit your appendix you'd really be in the soup." He turned and threw up onto the snow, holding his sides as if to keep warm.

"Are you all right?" Tub said.

"There's some aspirin in the truck," Kenny said.

"I'm all right," Frank said.

"We'd better call an ambulance," Tub said.

"Jesus," Frank said. "What are we going to say?"

"Exactly what happened," Tub said. "He was going to shoot me but I shot him first."

"No sir!" Kenny said. "I wasn't either!"

Frank patted Kenny on the arm. "Easy does it, partner." He stood. "Let's go."

Tub picked up Kenny's rifle as they walked down toward the farmhouse. "No sense leaving this around," he said. "Kenny might get ideas."

"I can tell you one thing," Frank said. "You've really done it this time. This definitely takes the cake."

They had to knock on the door twice before it was opened by a thin man with lank hair. The room behind him was filled with smoke. He squinted at them. "You get anything?" he asked.

"No," Frank said.

"I knew you wouldn't. That's what I told the other fellow."

"We've had an accident."

The man looked past Frank and Tub into the gloom. "Shoot your friend, did you?"

Frank nodded.

"I did," Tub said.

"I suppose you want to use the phone."

"If it's okay."

The man in the door looked behind him, then stepped back. Frank and Tub followed him into the house. There was a woman sitting by the stove in the middle of the room. The stove was smoking badly. She looked up and then down again at the child asleep in her lap. Her face was white and damp; strands of hair were pasted across her forehead. Tub warmed his hands over the stove while Frank went into the kitchen to call. The man who had let them in stood at the window, his hands in his pockets.

"My friend shot your dog," Tub said.

The man nodded without turning around. "I should have done it myself. I just couldn't."

"He loved that dog so much," the woman said. The child squirmed and she rocked it.

"You asked him to?" Tub said. "You asked him to shoot your dog?"

"He was old and sick. Couldn't chew his food any more. I would have done it myself but I don't have a gun."

"You couldn't have anyway," the woman said. "Never in a million years."

The man shrugged.

Frank came out of the kitchen. "We'll have to take him ourselves. The nearest hospital is fifty miles from here and all their ambulances are out anyway."

The woman knew a shortcut but the directions were complicated and Tub had to write them down. The man told them where they could find some boards to carry Kenny on. He didn't have a flashlight but he said he would leave the porch light on.

It was dark outside. The clouds were low and heavy-looking and the wind blew in shrill gusts. There was a screen loose on the house and it banged slowly and then quickly as the wind rose again. They could hear it all the way to the barn. Frank went for the boards while Tub looked for Kenny, who was not where they had left him. Tub found him farther up the drive, lying on his stomach. "You okay?" Tub said.

"It hurts."

"Frank says it missed your appendix." 125

"I already had my appendix out."

"All right," Frank said, coming up to them. "We'll have you in a nice warm bed before you can say Jack Robinson." He put the two boards on Kenny's right side.

"Just as long as I don't have one of those male nurses," Kenny said.

"Ha ha," Frank said. "That's the spirit. Get ready, set, *over you go*," and he rolled Kenny onto the boards. Kenny screamed and kicked his legs in the air. When he quieted down Frank and Tub lifted the boards and carried him down the drive. Tub had the back end, and with the snow blowing into his face he had trouble with his footing. Also he was tired and the man inside had forgotten to turn the porch light on. Just past the house Tub slipped and threw out his hands to catch himself. The boards fell and Kenny tumbled out and rolled to the bottom of the drive, yelling all the way. He came to rest against the right front wheel of the truck.

"You fat moron," Frank said. "You aren't good for diddly." 130

Tub grabbed Frank by the collar and backed him hard up against the fence. Frank tried to pull his hands away but Tub shook him and snapped his head back and forth and finally Frank gave up.

"What do you know about fat," Tub said. "What do you know about glands." As he spoke he kept shaking Frank. "What do you know about me."

"All right," Frank said.

"No more," Tub said.

"All right." 135

"No more talking to me like that. No more watching. No more laughing."

"Okay, Tub. I promise."

Tub let go of Frank and leaned his forehead against the fence. His arms hung straight at his sides.

"I'm sorry, Tub." Frank touched him on the shoulder. "I'll be down at the truck."

Tub stood by the fence for a while and then got the rifles off the porch. Frank 140 had rolled Kenny back onto the boards and they lifted him into the bed of the truck. Frank spread the seat blankets over him. "Warm enough?" he asked.

Kenny nodded.

"Okay. Now how does reverse work on this thing?"

"All the way to the left and up." Kenny sat up as Frank started forward to the cab. "Frank!"

"What?"

"If it sticks don't force it."

The truck started right away. "One thing," Frank said, "you've got to hand it to the Japanese. A very ancient, very spiritual culture and they can still make a hell of a truck." He glanced over at Tub. "Look, I'm sorry. I didn't know you felt that way, honest to God I didn't. You should have said something."

"I did."

"When? Name one time."

"A couple of hours ago."

"I guess I wasn't paying attention."

"That's true, Frank," Tub said. "You don't pay attention very much."

"Tub," Frank said, "what happened back there, I should have been more sympathetic. I realize that. You were going through a lot. I just want you to know it wasn't your fault. He was asking for it."

"You think so?"

"Absolutely. It was him or you. I would have done the same thing in your shoes, no question."

The wind was blowing into their faces. The snow was a moving white wall in front of their lights; it swirled into the cab through the hole in the windshield and settled on them. Tub clapped his hands and shifted around to stay warm, but it didn't work.

"I'm going to have to stop," Frank said. "I can't feel my fingers."

Up ahead they saw some lights off the road. It was a tavern. Outside in the parking lot there were several jeeps and trucks. A couple of them had deer strapped across their hoods. Frank parked and they went back to Kenny. "How you doing, partner," Frank said.

"I'm cold."

"Well, don't feel like the Lone Ranger. It's worse inside, take my word for it. You should get that windshield fixed."

"Look," Tub said, "he threw the blankets off." They were lying in a heap against the tailgate.

"Now look, Kenny," Frank said, "it's no use whining about being cold if you're not going to try and keep warm. You've got to do your share." He spread the blankets over Kenny and tucked them in at the corners.

"They blew off."

"Hold on to them then."

"Why are we stopping, Frank?"

"Because if me and Tub don't get warmed up we're going to freeze solid and then where will you be?" He punched Kenny lightly in the arm. "So just hold your horses."

The bar was full of men in colored jackets, mostly orange. The waitress brought coffee. "Just what the doctor ordered," Frank said, cradling the steaming cup in his hand. His skin was bone white. "Tub, I've been thinking. What you said about me not paying attention, that's true."

"It's okay."

"No. I really had that coming. I guess I've just been a little too interested in old number one. I've had a lot on my mind. Not that that's any excuse."

"Forget it, Frank. I sort of lost my temper back there. I guess we're all a little on edge."

Frank shook his head. "It isn't just that."

"You want to talk about it?"

"Just between us, Tub?"

"Sure, Frank. Just between us."

"Tub, I think I'm going to be leaving Nancy."

"Oh, Frank. Oh, Frank." Tub sat back and shook his head. 175

Frank reached out and laid his hand on Tub's arm. "Tub, have you ever been really in love?"

"Well—"

"I mean *really* in love." He squeezed Tub's wrist. "With your whole being."

"I don't know. When you put it like that, I don't know."

"You haven't then. Nothing against you, but you'd know it if you had." Frank 180
let go of Tub's arm. "This isn't just some bit of fluff I'm talking about."

"Who is she, Frank?"

Frank paused. He looked into his empty cup. "Roxanne Brewer."

"Cliff Brewer's kid? The babysitter?"

"You can't just put people into categories like that, Tub. That's why the whole system is wrong. And that's why this country is going to hell in a rowboat."

"But she can't be more than—" Tub shook his head. 185

"Fifteen. She'll be sixteen in May." Frank smiled. "May fourth, three twenty-seven p.m. Hell, Tub, a hundred years ago she'd have been an old maid by that age. Juliet was only thirteen."

"Juliet? Juliet Miller? Jesus, Frank, she doesn't even have breasts. She doesn't even wear a top to her bathing suit. She's still collecting frogs."

"Not Juliet Miller. The real Juliet. Tub, don't you see how you're dividing people up into categories? He's an executive, she's a secretary, he's a truck driver, she's fifteen years old. Tub, this so-called babysitter, this so-called fifteen-year-old has more in her little finger than most of us have in our entire bodies. I can tell you this little lady is something special."

Tub nodded. "I know the kids like her."

"She's opened up whole worlds to me that I never knew were there." 190

"What does Nancy think about all of this?"

"She doesn't know."

"You haven't told her?"

"Not yet. It's not so easy. She's been damned good to me all these years. Then there's the kids to consider." The brightness in Frank's eyes trembled and he wiped quickly at them with the back of his hand. "I guess you think I'm a complete bastard."

"No, Frank. I don't think that." 195

"Well, you *ought* to."

"Frank, when you've got a friend it means you've always got someone on your side, no matter what. That's the way I feel about it, anyway."

"You mean that, Tub?"

"Sure I do."

Frank smiled. "You don't know how good it feels to hear you say that." 200

Kenny had tried to get out of the truck but he hadn't made it. He was jackknifed over the tailgate, his head hanging above the bumper. They lifted him back into the bed and covered him again. He was sweating and his teeth chattered. "It hurts, Frank."

"It wouldn't hurt so much if you just stayed put. Now we're going to the hospital. Got that? Say it—I'm going to the hospital."

"I'm going to the hospital."

"Again."

"I'm going to the hospital."

"Now just keep saying that to yourself and before you know it we'll be there."

After they had gone a few miles Tub turned to Frank. "I just pulled a real boner," he said.

"What's that?"

"I left the directions on the table back there."

"That's okay. I remember them pretty well."

The snowfall lightened and the clouds began to roll back off the fields, but it was no warmer and after a time both Frank and Tub were bitten through and shaking. Frank almost didn't make it around a curve, and they decided to stop at the next roadhouse.

There was an automatic hand-dryer in the bathroom and they took turns standing in front of it, opening their jackets and shirts and letting the jet of hot air breathe across their faces and chests.

"You know," Tub said, "what you told me back there, I appreciate it. Trusting me."

Frank opened and closed his fingers in front of the nozzle. "The way I look at it, Tub, no man is an island. You've got to trust someone."

"Frank—"

Frank waited.

"When I said that about my glands, that wasn't true. The truth is I just shovel it in."

"Well, Tub—"

"Day and night, Frank. In the shower. On the freeway." He turned and let the air play over his back. "I've even got stuff in the paper towel machine at work."

"There's nothing wrong with your glands at all?" Frank had taken his boots and socks off. He held first his right, then his left foot up to the nozzle.

"No. There never was."

"Does Alice know?" The machine went off and Frank started lacing up his boots.

"Nobody knows. That's the worst of it, Frank. Not the being fat, I never got any big kick out of being thin, but the lying. Having to lead a double life like a spy or a hit man. This sounds strange but I feel sorry for those guys, I really do. I know what they go through. Always having to think about what you say and do. Always feeling like people are watching you, trying to catch you at something. Never able to just be yourself. Like when I make a big deal about only having an orange for breakfast and then scarf all the way to work. Oreos, Mars Bars, Twinkies. Sugar Babies. Snickers." Tub glanced at Frank and looked quickly away. "Pretty disgusting, isn't it?"

"Tub. Tub." Frank shook his head. "Come on." He took Tub's arm and led him into the restaurant half of the bar. "My friend is hungry," he told the waitress. "Bring four orders of pancakes, plenty of butter and syrup."

"Frank—"

"Sit down."

When the dishes came Frank carved out slabs of butter and just laid them on the pancakes. Then he emptied the bottle of syrup, moving it back and forth over the plates. He leaned forward on his elbows and rested his chin in one hand. "Go on, Tub."

Tub ate several mouthfuls, then started to wipe his lips. Frank took the napkin away from him. "No wiping," he said. Tub kept at it. The syrup covered his chin; it dripped to a point like a goatee. "Weigh in, Tub," Frank said, pushing another fork across the table. "Get down to business." Tub took the fork in his left hand and lowered his head and started really chowing down. "Clean your plate," Frank said when the pancakes were gone, and Tub lifted each of the four plates and licked it clean. He sat back, trying to catch his breath.

"Beautiful," Frank said. "Are you full?"

"I'm full," Tub said. "I've never been so full."

Kenny's blankets were bunched up against the tailgate again.

"They must have blown off," Tub said.

"They're not doing him any good," Frank said. "We might as well get some use out of them."

Kenny mumbled. Tub bent over him. "What? Speak up."

"I'm going to the hospital," Kenny said.

"Attaboy," Frank said.

The blankets helped. The wind still got their faces and Frank's hands but it was much better. The fresh snow on the road and the trees sparkled under the beam of the headlight. Squares of light from farmhouse windows fell onto the blue snow in the fields.

"Frank," Tub said after a time, "you know that farmer? He told Kenny to kill the dog."

"You're kidding!" Frank leaned forward, considering. "That Kenny. What a card." He laughed and so did Tub. Tub smiled out the back window. Kenny lay with his arms folded over his stomach, moving his lips at the stars. Right overhead was the Big Dipper, and behind, hanging between Kenny's toes in the direction of the hospital, was the North Star, Pole Star, Help to Sailors. As the truck twisted through the gentle hills the star went back and forth between Kenny's boots, staying always in his sight. "I'm going to the hospital," Kenny said. But he was wrong. They had taken a different turn a long way back.

(1980)

PREWRITING

As you read the story carefully a second time, pay particular attention to the descriptive passages that appeal to the senses—especially, in this story, images of snow, cold, and ice. Underline any specific words or phrases that you think contribute to the atmosphere.

Prewriting Exercise

1. Write one or two paragraphs that describe Frank, Kenny, and Tub going fishing on a hundred-degree summer day. What elements of "Hunters in the Snow" would stay the same, and what would change in this altered setting?
2. Examine the first ten paragraphs of the story, when Frank and Kenny come to pick up Tub to go hunting. What do these paragraphs reveal about the three men? What can you say about their relationship after reading only the opening of the tale?

3. What features of the setting seem essential to the way "Hunters in the Snow" unfolds? In other words, how do the snow and cold determine what happens in important ways?
4. Before planning your paper, write your responses to the following questions:
   a. When you think of men going on a hunting trip, what associations come forth? Are any of these associations reflected in the story? Are any of them contradicted or undermined?
   b. How soon in the story can you distinguish among the three characters? What are some of the ways they are distinct from one another?
   c. List the indoor scenes in this basically outdoor story. What critical events or revelations happen in each of the indoor scenes?
   d. What do you make of Frank's ordering the pancakes for Tub at the roadhouse? Is it an act of acceptance, friendship, cruelty, humor, vicarious satisfaction, or what?
   e. Although women are generally off the scene, in what ways do they influence the characters?
   f. At several points in the story, you may have been shocked by what happens. What are some of these points? Why were they shocking?

WRITING

Now that you have become familiar with the story, ask yourself still more questions: How can I make a statement about the function of setting in relation to theme? What, indeed, does the setting contribute to the overall effectiveness of the story? What does the atmosphere contribute? How do both relate to the meaning of the story? Do they *heighten* the theme, do they provide a unique opportunity for the events, or do they help the reader to understand what the story is about? Would a different setting change the story in important ways? As you think about answers to these questions, review your prewriting material and continue consulting the story for clues.

Discovering an Organization

As you are trying to solve the problems posed by the questions in the preceding paragraph, write down all the likely ideas that strike you. Do not trust your memory, or some of your best inspirations may slip away. Then try to think of some point you can make about the story that will allow you to use this information. Such a point will usually make a link between the setting and something else about the story: the characters, action, plot, motivation, meaning, or emotional impact. Once you have discovered an interesting point to pursue, write out this idea in a single, clear sentence. This idea will be your thesis. Then sort through the details related to setting in the story and ask yourself: How can I organize these details in support of my thesis? You might, for instance, group your material chronologically, arranging details according to the episodes in the story as they occur from morning till night. Or you might consider a logical arrangement, emphasizing each of the main characters in turn or focusing first on everything that happens outdoors and then on everything that happens indoors.

IDEAS FOR WRITING

Ideas for Responsive Writing

1. "Hunters in the Snow" takes place in a traditionally all-male setting, a hunting trip. In your experience, do people in small same-sex groups behave differently than they would in mixed-sex groups? If so, do they behave better or worse? Outside of hunting trips, what other occasions usually bring together small same-sex groups? Write a description of a same-sex occasion you have encountered. Emphasize the influence of the setting on people's behavior.
2. It would appear that Kenny, Frank, and Tub are a group of friends. What is the evidence? On the other hand, how do they behave as though they are not friends? What philosophies of friendship are spoken out loud? What philosophies are acted out among the three characters? Do you think that these philosophies are unusual or common?

Ideas for Critical Writing

1. Examine each reference to the snow and cold. What attitude toward nature is suggested by the way it is described? How is this attitude related to the view of human nature suggested by the story?
2. The weather conditions in "Hunters in the Snow" are portrayed as obscuring the true state of things and blurring perceptions such as vision and hearing. Relate this feature of the setting to the blurring and obscuring of truth in the human arena. What lie is pivotal to each character?
3. What effect does being cold for long periods have on people? Argue for an interpretation of the story that explains how the freezing cold drives much of the action of the story.

Ideas for Researched Writing

1. CRITICAL APPROACHES: Review the historical approaches to literary interpretation (pages 1158–59). Do some research on Tobias Wolff's life, and use a biographical approach to explain his choice of setting, character, and theme in "Hunters in the Snow."

2. Using the PsychLIT database or your Internet search engine, investigate contemporary thought about male friendships. Find two or three sources that give theoretical or experimental support to the depiction of male friendship in "Hunters in the Snow." How are such friendships described and explained by experts in human behavior? Write a paper that makes a claim about the characters' relationships.

REWRITING

Once you have written out your ideas, you will try to improve every element of that draft—from the overall organization to the individual sentences.

Checking Your Organization

Each paragraph should have a topic, a main point that you can summarize in a sentence. On a separate sheet of paper, list the topics of your paragraphs. When you see the bare bones of your essay this way, you can ask yourself questions about your organization.

1. Do any of the topics repeat each other? If so, think about combining them or placing them close together. If there is a fine distinction between them, go back to the essay and express the distinction clearly.
2. Is each topic fully supported? Compare the topic as stated on your outline with the paragraph in your essay. Make sure that you can see how each sentence in the paragraph relates to the topic. Weed out sentences that only repeat the topic. Add specific details from the literary work instead.
3. Does the order of topics make sense? You might have originally written your paragraphs in the order the topics occurred to you, but that may not be the most reasonable organization for the final essay. Group similar topics together—for example, all the topics that relate setting to character should be close to each other, and so should all the topics that relate setting to theme. At the beginning of each paragraph, write a word, phrase, clause, or sentence that shows that paragraph's relationship to the paragraph before it. These transitions will help your readers know what to expect and prepare them for what comes next.

Improving the Style: Balanced Sentences

Sound organization is vital to the success of your essay; graceful style is an added gift to your reader. One stylistic plus is the balanced or parallel sentence, which puts similar ideas into similar grammatical structures, like this:

> Wolff's stories are known for their *sudden*, *profound*, and *powerful* endings.
>
> Good writers acknowledge the necessity of *thinking*, *planning*, *writing*, *revising*, *resting*, and then *thinking* and *revising* still further.

In the following sentence, though, the third item in the italicized series does not match. Compare it to the corrected version.

Unbalanced The main character would not willingly give up the *carefree*, *extravagant*, and *drinking and staying out late* as he did when a bachelor.

Balanced The main character would not willingly give up the *carefree*, *extravagant*, *carousing* ways of his bachelorhood.

Probably you can already handle such balancing in ordinary sentences. But pay attention during revising to make sure that all items in series are indeed balanced.

If you need an emphatic sentence for your introduction or conclusion, a good way to learn to write impressive balanced sentences is through *sentence modeling*. Many expert writers—Robert Louis Stevenson, Abraham Lincoln, Winston Churchill, Somerset Maugham—attest that they perfected their writing by studiously copying and imitating the sentences of stylists whom they admired.

Sentence Modeling Exercise

Examine the model sentence shown below to discover its structure. How is it formed? Does it use balanced phrases, clauses, or single words? Does it include any deliberate repetition of words as well as structures? Does it build to a climax at the end? If so, how? By adding ideas of increasing importance? By establishing a pattern that gathers momentum?

Once you have discovered the structure of the model sentence, write one as nearly like it as possible *using your own words and subject matter*. Then repeat this process of imitation four more times, changing your ideas with each new sentence, like this:

Model Until the young are informed as much about the courage of pacifists as about the obedience of soldiers, they aren't educated.

—*Coleman McCarthy*

Imitation Until Americans become as interested in the speeches of candidates as in the performance of athletes, they aren't ideal citizens.

Imitation Until men are interested as much by the minds of women as by the bodies of women, they will be seen as sexist.

First copy each of the numbered sentences carefully—including the exact punctuation. Then imitate each one at least five times.

1. He sees no seams or joints or points of intersection—only irrevocable wholes.

   —*Mina Shaughnessy*

2. We made meals and changed diapers and took out the garbage and paid bills—while other people died.

   —*Ellen Goodman*

3. The refrigerator was full of sulfurous scraps, dark crusts, furry oddments.

   —*Alice Munro*

4. It is sober without being dull; massive without being oppressive.

   —*Sir Kenneth Clark*

5. Joint by joint, line by line, pill by pill, the use of illegal drugs has become a crisis for American business.

   —*Newsweek*

11

Writing About Theme

A story's theme or meaning grows out of all the elements of imaginative fiction: character, structure, symbolism, point of view, and setting. The theme is usually not an obvious moral or message, and it may be difficult to sum up succinctly. But thinking about the theme of a story and trying to state it in your own words will help you to focus your scattered reactions and to make your understanding of the author's purpose more certain. One of the pleasures of reading a good story comes from deciding what it means and why it captures your interest.

What Is Theme?

Theme has been defined in many ways: the central idea or thesis; the central thought; the underlying meaning, either implied or directly stated; the general insight revealed by the entire story; the central truth; the dominating idea; the abstract concept that is made concrete through representation in person, action, and image.

Because the theme involves ideas and insights, we usually state it in general terms. "Eveline," for instance, concerns the conflicts of a specific character, but the story's main idea—its theme—relates to abstract qualities like *duty* and *fear*. If someone asks what "Eveline" is *about*, we might respond with a summary of the plot, with details about the title character's encounter with Frank and her failure to go away with him. But if someone asks for the story's *theme*, we would answer with a general statement of ideas or values: "Eveline" shows how people can be trapped by fear and obligation.

It is easy to confuse *subject* with *theme*. The subject is the topic or material the story examines—love, death, war, identity, prejudice, power, human relations, growing up, and so forth. The theme is the direct or implied statement that the story makes *about* the subject. For example, the *subject* of "Everyday Use" is mother–daughter relationships, but the *theme* emerges from what the story says about Mama, Maggie, and Dee—and from an understanding of why these characters behave and interact as they do. The theme, then, is the insight that we gain from thinking about what we have read.

Looking at Theme

As you read "Good Country People" by Flannery O'Connor, think about how this story of a mother and a daughter and their encounter with a Bible salesman relates to other areas of human experience.

Flannery O'Connor 1925–1964

Afflicted with lupus, Flannery O'Connor spent most of her short life in Milledgeville, Georgia. After earning an M.F.A. from the University of Iowa, she returned to the family farm to raise peacocks and write about contemporary Southern life. She once observed, "Anything that comes out of the South is going to be called grotesque by the northern reader, unless it is grotesque, in which case it is going to be called realistic." A deeply religious person, O'Connor often explored the violence symbolized by physical deformity and produced by spiritual malaise.

Good Country People

Besides the neutral expression that she wore when she was alone, Mrs. Freeman had two others, forward and reverse, that she used for all her human dealings. Her forward expression was steady and driving like the advance of a heavy truck. Her eyes never swerved to left or right but turned as the story turned as if they followed a yellow line down the center of it. She seldom used the other expression because it was not often necessary for her to retract a statement, but when she did, her face came to a complete stop, there was an almost imperceptible movement of her black eyes, during which they seemed to be receding, and then the observer would see that Mrs. Freeman, though she might stand there as real as several grain sacks thrown on top of each other, was no longer there in spirit. As for getting anything across to her when this was the case, Mrs. Hopewell had given it up. She might talk her head off. Mrs. Freeman could never be brought to admit herself wrong on any point. She would stand there and if she could be brought to say anything, it was something like, "Well, I wouldn't of said it was and I wouldn't of said it wasn't," or letting her gaze range over the top kitchen shelf where there was an assortment of dusty bottles, she might remark, "I see you ain't ate many of them figs you put up last summer."

They carried on their most important business in the kitchen at breakfast. Every morning Mrs. Hopewell got up at seven o'clock and lit her gas heater and Joy's. Joy was her daughter, a large blonde girl who had an artificial leg. Mrs. Hopewell thought of her as a child though she was thirty-two years old and highly educated. Joy would get up while her mother was eating and lumber into the bathroom and slam the door, and before long, Mrs. Freeman would arrive at the back door. Joy would hear her mother call, "Come on in," and then they would talk for a while in low voices that were indistinguishable in the bathroom. By the time Joy came in, they had usually finished the weather report and were on one or the other of Mrs. Freeman's daughters, Glynese or Carramae. Joy called them Glycerin and Caramel. Glynese, a redhead, was eighteen and had many admirers; Carramae, a blonde, was only fifteen but already married and pregnant. She could not keep anything on her stomach. Every morning Mrs. Freeman told Mrs. Hopewell how many times she had vomited since the last report.

Mrs. Hopewell liked to tell people that Glynese and Carramae were two of the finest girls she knew and that Mrs. Freeman was a *lady* and that she was never ashamed to take her anywhere or introduce her to anybody they might meet. Then she would tell how she had happened to hire the Freemans in the first place and how they were a godsend to her and how she had had them four years. The reason for her keeping them so long was that they were not trash. They were good country people. She had telephoned the man whose name they had given as reference and he had told her that Mr. Freeman was a good farmer but that his wife was the nosiest woman ever to walk the earth. "She's got to be into everything," the man said. "If she don't get there before the dust settles, you can bet she's dead, that's all. She'll want to know all your business. I can stand him real good," he had said, "but me nor my wife neither could have stood that woman one more minute on this place." That had put Mrs. Hopewell off for a few days.

She had hired them in the end because there were no other applicants but she had made up her mind beforehand exactly how she would handle the woman. Since she was the type who had to be into everything, then, Mrs. Hopewell had decided, she would not only let her be into everything, she would *see to it* that she was into everything—she would give her the responsibility of everything, she would put her in charge. Mrs. Hopewell had no bad qualities of her own but she was able to use other people's in such a constructive way that she never felt the lack. She had hired the Freemans and she had kept them four years.

Nothing is perfect. This was one of Mrs. Hopewell's favorite sayings. 5
Another was: that is life! And still another, the most important, was: well, other people have their opinions too. She would make these statements, usually at the table, in a tone of gentle insistence as if no one held them but her, and the large hulking Joy, whose constant outrage had obliterated every expression from her face, would stare just a little to the side of her, her eyes icy blue, with the look of someone who had achieved blindness by an act of will and means to keep it.

When Mrs. Hopewell said to Mrs. Freeman that life was like that, Mrs. Freeman would say, "I always said so myself." Nothing had been arrived at by anyone that had not first been arrived at by her. She was quicker than Mr. Freeman. When Mrs. Hopewell said to her after they had been on the place for a while, "You know, you're the wheel behind the wheel," and winked, Mrs. Freeman had said, "I know it. I've always been quick. It's some that are quicker than others."

"Everybody is different," Mrs. Hopewell said.

"Yes, most people is," Mrs. Freeman said.

"It takes all kinds to make the world."

"I always said it did myself." 10

The girl was used to this kind of dialogue for breakfast and more of it for dinner; sometimes they had it for supper too. When they had no guest they ate in the kitchen because that was easier. Mrs. Freeman always managed to arrive at some point during the meal and to watch them finish it. She would stand in the doorway if it were summer but in the winter she would stand with one elbow on top of the refrigerator and look down at them, or she would stand by the gas heater, lifting the back of her skirt slightly. Occasionally she would stand against the wall and roll her head from side to side. At no time was she in any hurry to leave. All this was very trying on Mrs. Hopewell but she was a woman of great patience. She realized that nothing is perfect and that in the Freemans she had good country people and that if, in this day and age, you get good country people, you had better hang onto them.

She had had plenty of experience with trash. Before the Freemans she had averaged one tenant family a year. The wives of these farmers were not the kind you would want to be around you for very long. Mrs. Hopewell, who had divorced her husband long ago, needed someone to walk over the fields with her; and when Joy had to be impressed for these services, her remarks were usually so ugly and her face so glum that Mrs. Hopewell would say, "If you can't come pleasantly, I don't want you at all," to which the girl, standing square and rigid-shouldered with her neck thrust slightly forward, would reply, "If you want me, here I am—LIKE I AM."

Mrs. Hopewell excused this attitude because of the leg (which had been shot off in a hunting accident when Joy was ten). It was hard for Mrs. Hopewell to realize that her child was thirty-two now and that for more than twenty years she had had only one leg. She thought of her still as a child because it tore her heart to think instead of the poor stout girl in her thirties who had never danced a step or had any *normal* good times. Her name was really Joy but as soon as she was twenty-one and away from home, she had had it legally changed. Mrs. Hopewell was certain that she had thought and thought until she had hit upon the ugliest name in any language. Then she had gone and had the beautiful name, Joy, changed without telling her mother until after she had done it. Her legal name was Hulga.

When Mrs. Hopewell thought the name, Hulga, she thought of the broad blank hull of a battleship. She would not use it. She continued to call her Joy to which the girl responded but in a purely mechanical way.

Hulga had learned to tolerate Mrs. Freeman who saved her from taking walks 15
with her mother. Even Glynese and Carramae were useful when they occupied attention that might otherwise have been directed at her. At first she had thought she could not stand Mrs. Freeman for she had found it was not possible to be rude to her. Mrs. Freeman would take on strange resentments and for days together she would be sullen but the source of her displeasure was always obscure; a direct attack, a positive leer, blatant ugliness to her face—these never touched her. And without warning one day, she began calling her Hulga.

She did not call her that in front of Mrs. Hopewell who would have been incensed but when she and the girl happened to be out of the house together, she would say something and add the name Hulga to the end of it, and the big spectacled Joy-Hulga would scowl and redden as if her privacy had been intruded upon. She considered the name her personal affair. She had arrived at it first purely on the basis of its ugly sound and then the full genius of its fitness had struck her. She had a vision of the name working like the ugly sweating Vulcan who stayed in the furnace and to whom, presumably, the goddess had to come when called. She saw it as the name of her highest creative act. One of her major triumphs was that her mother had not been able to turn her dust into Joy, but the greater one was that she had been able to turn it herself into Hulga. However, Mrs. Freeman's relish for using the name only irritated her. It was as if Mrs. Freeman's beady steel-pointed eyes had penetrated far enough behind her face to reach some secret fact.

Something about her seemed to fascinate Mrs. Freeman and then one day Hulga realized that it was the artificial leg. Mrs. Freeman had a special fondness for the details of secret infections, hidden deformities, assaults upon children. Of diseases, she preferred the lingering or incurable. Hulga had heard Mrs. Hopewell give her the details of the hunting accident, how the leg had been literally blasted off, how she had never lost consciousness. Mrs. Freeman could listen to it any time as if it had happened an hour ago.

When Hulga stumped into the kitchen in the morning (she could walk without making the awful noise but she made it—Mrs. Hopewell was certain—because it was ugly-sounding), she glanced at them and did not speak. Mrs. Hopewell would be in her red kimono with her hair tied around her head in rags. She would be sitting at the table, finishing her breakfast and Mrs. Freeman would be hanging by her elbow outward from the refrigerator, looking down at the table. Hulga always put her eggs on the stove to boil and then stood over them with her arms folded, and Mrs. Hopewell would look at her—a kind of indirect gaze divided between her and Mrs. Freeman—and would think that if she would only keep herself up a little, she wouldn't be so bad looking. There was nothing wrong with her face that a pleasant expression wouldn't help. Mrs. Hopewell said that people who looked on the bright side of things would be beautiful even if they were not.

Whenever she looked at Joy this way, she could not help but feel that it would have been better if the child had not taken the Ph.D. It had certainly not brought her out any and now that she had it, there was no more excuse for her to go to school again. Mrs. Hopewell thought it was nice for girls to go to school to have a good time but Joy had "gone through." Anyhow, she would not have been strong enough to go again. The doctors had told Mrs. Hopewell that with the best of care, Joy might see forty-five. She had a weak heart. Joy had made it plain that if it had not been for this condition, she would be far from these red hills and good country people. She would be in a university lecturing to people who knew what she was talking about. And Mrs. Hopewell could very well picture her there, looking like a scarecrow and lecturing to more of the same. Here she went about all day in a six-year-old skirt and a yellow sweat shirt with a faded cowboy on a horse embossed on it. She thought this was funny; Mrs. Hopewell thought it was idiotic and showed simply that she was still a child. She was brilliant but she didn't have a grain of sense. It seemed to Mrs. Hopewell that every year she grew less like other people and more like herself—bloated, rude, and squint-eyed. And she said such strange things! To her own mother she had said—without warning, without excuse, standing up in the middle of a meal with her face purple and her mouth half full—"Woman! do you ever look inside? Do you ever look inside and see what you are *not*? God!" she had cried sinking down again and staring at her plate, "Malebranche[1] was right: we are not our own light. We are not our own light!" Mrs. Hopewell had no idea to this day what brought that on. She had only made the remark, hoping Joy would take it in, that a smile never hurt anyone.

The girl had taken the Ph.D. in philosophy and this left Mrs. Hopewell at a complete loss. You could say, "My daughter is a nurse," or "My daughter is a school teacher," or even, "My daughter is a chemical engineer." You could not say, "My daughter is a philosopher." That was something that had ended with the Greeks

[1]Nicolas Malebranche (1638–1715), French philosopher.

and Romans. All day Joy sat on her neck in a deep chair, reading. Sometimes she went for walks but she didn't like dogs or cats or birds or flowers or nature or nice young men. She looked at nice young men as if she could smell their stupidity.

One day Mrs. Hopewell had picked up one of the books the girl had just put 20
down and opening it at random, she read, "Science, on the other hand, has to assert its soberness and seriousness afresh and declare that it is concerned solely with what-is. Nothing—how can it be for science anything but a horror and a phantasm? If science is right, then one thing stands firm: science wishes to know nothing of nothing. Such is after all the strictly scientific approach to Nothing. We know it by wishing to know nothing of Nothing." These words had been underlined with a blue pencil and they worked on Mrs. Hopewell like some evil incantation in gibberish. She shut the book quickly and went out of the room as if she were having a chill.

This morning when the girl came in, Mrs. Freeman was on Carramae. "She thrown up four times after supper," she said, "and was up twict in the night after three o'clock. Yesterday she didn't do nothing but ramble in the bureau drawer. All she did. Stand up there and see what she could run up on."

"She's got to eat," Mrs. Hopewell muttered, sipping her coffee, while she watched Joy's back at the stove. She was wondering what the child had said to the Bible salesman. She could not imagine what kind of a conversation she could possibly have had with him.

He was a tall gaunt hatless youth who had called yesterday to sell them a Bible. He had appeared at the door, carrying a large black suitcase that weighted him so heavily on one side that he had to brace himself against the door facing. He seemed on the point of collapse but he said in a cheerful voice, "Good morning, Mrs. Cedars!" and set the suitcase down on the mat. He was not a bad-looking young man though he had on a bright blue suit and yellow socks that were not pulled up far enough. He had prominent face bones and a streak of sticky-looking brown hair falling across his forehead.

"I'm Mrs. Hopewell," she said.

"Oh!" he said, pretending to look puzzled but with his eyes sparkling, "I saw it 25
said 'The Cedars' on the mailbox so I thought you was Mrs. Cedars!" and he burst out in a pleasant laugh. He picked up the satchel and under cover of a pant, he fell forward into her hall. It was rather as if the suitcase had moved first, jerking him after it. "Mrs. Hopewell!" he said and grabbed her hand. "I hope you are well!" and he laughed again and then all at once his face sobered completely. He paused and gave her a straight earnest look and said, "Lady, I've come to speak of serious things."

"Well, come in," she muttered, none too pleased because her dinner was almost ready. He came into the parlor and sat down on the edge of a straight chair and put the suitcase between his feet and glanced around the room as if he were sizing her up by it. Her silver gleamed on the two sideboards; she decided he had never been in a room as elegant as this.

"Mrs. Hopewell," he began, using her name in a way that sounded almost intimate, "I know you believe in Chrustian service."

"Well, yes," she murmured.

"I know," he said and paused, looking very wise with his head cocked on one side, "that you're a good woman. Friends have told me."

Mrs. Hopewell never liked to be taken for a fool. "What are you selling?" she 30
asked.

"Bibles," the young man said and his eye raced around the room before he added, "I see you have no family Bible in your parlor, I see that is the one lack you got!"

Mrs. Hopewell could not say, "My daughter is an atheist and won't let me keep the Bible in the parlor." She said, stiffening slightly, "I keep my Bible by my bedside." This was not the truth. It was in the attic somewhere.

"Lady," he said, "the word of God ought to be in the parlor."

"Well, I think that's a matter of taste," she began, "I think..."

"Lady," he said, "for a Chrustian, the word of God ought to be in every room 35
in the house besides in his heart. I know you're a Chrustian because I can see it in every line of your face."

She stood up and said, "Well, young man, I don't want to buy a Bible and I smell my dinner burning."

He didn't get up. He began to twist his hands and looking down at them, he said softly, "Well lady, I'll tell you the truth—not many people want to buy one nowadays and besides, I know I'm real simple. I don't know how to say a thing but to say it. I'm just a country boy." He glanced up into her unfriendly face. "People like you don't like to fool with country people like me!"

"Why!" she cried, "good country people are the salt of the earth! Besides, we all have different ways of doing, it takes all kinds to make the world go 'round. That's life!"

"You said a mouthful," he said.

"Why, I think there aren't enough good country people in the world!" she 40
said, stirred. "I think that's what's wrong with it!"

His face had brightened. "I didn't inraduce myself," he said. "I'm Manley Pointer from out in the country around Willohobie, not even from a place, just from near a place."

"You wait a minute," she said. "I have to see about my dinner." She went out to the kitchen and found Joy standing near the door where she had been listening.

"Get rid of the salt of the earth," she said, "and let's eat."

Mrs. Hopewell gave her a pained look and turned the heat down under the vegetables. "*I* can't be rude to anybody," she murmured and went back into the parlor.

He had opened the suitcase and was sitting with a Bible on each knee. 45

"You might as well put those up," she told him. "I don't want one."

"I appreciate your honesty," he said. "You don't see any more real honest people unless you go way out in the country."

"I know," she said, "real genuine folks!" Through the crack in the door she heard a groan.

"I guess a lot of boys come telling you they're working their way through college," he said, "but I'm not going to tell you that. Somehow," he said, "I don't want to go to college. I want to devote my life to Chrustian service. See," he said, lowering his voice, "I got this heart condition. I may not live long. When you know it's something wrong with you and you may not live long, well then, lady..." He paused, with his mouth open, and stared at her.

He and Joy had the same condition! She knew that her eyes were filling 50
with tears but she collected herself quickly and murmured, "Won't you stay for dinner? We'd love to have you!" and was sorry the instant she heard herself say it.

"Yes mam," he said in an abashed voice, "I would sher love to do that!"

Joy had given him one look on being introduced to him and then throughout the meal had not glanced at him again. He had addressed several remarks to her, which she had pretended not to hear. Mrs. Hopewell could not understand deliberate rudeness, although she lived with it, and she felt she had always to overflow with hospitality to make up for Joy's lack of courtesy. She urged him to talk about himself and he did. He said he was the seventh child of twelve and that his father had been crushed under a tree when he himself was eight years old. He had been crushed very badly, in fact, almost cut in two and was practically not recognizable. His mother had got along the best she could by hard working and she had always seen that her children went to Sunday School and that they read the Bible every evening. He was now nineteen years old and he had been selling Bibles for four months. In that time he had sold seventy-seven Bibles and had the promise of two more sales. He wanted to become a missionary because he thought that was the way you could do most for people. "He who losest his life shall find it," he said simply and he was so sincere, so genuine and earnest that Mrs. Hopewell would not for the world have smiled. He prevented his peas from sliding onto the table by blocking them with a piece of bread which he later cleaned his plate with. She could see Joy observing sidewise how he handled his knife and fork and she saw too that every few minutes, the boy would dart a keen appraising glance at the girl as if he were trying to attract her attention.

After dinner Joy cleared the dishes off the table and disappeared and Mrs. Hopewell was left to talk with him. He told her again about his childhood and his father's accident and about various things that had happened to him. Every five minutes or so she would stifle a yawn. He sat for two hours until finally she told him she must go because she had an appointment in town. He packed his Bibles and thanked her and prepared to leave, but in the doorway he stopped and wrung her hand and said that not on any of his trips had he met a lady as nice as her and he asked if he could come again. She had said she would always be happy to see him.

Joy had been standing in the road, apparently looking at something in the distance, when he came down the steps toward her, bent to the side with his heavy valise. He stopped where she was standing and confronted her directly. Mrs. Hopewell could not hear what he said but she trembled to think what Joy would say to him. She could see that after a minute Joy said something and that then the boy began to speak again, making an excited gesture with his free hand. After a minute Joy said something else at which the boy began to speak once more. Then to her amazement, Mrs. Hopewell saw the two of them walk off together, toward the gate. Joy had walked all the way to the gate with him and Mrs. Hopewell could not imagine what they had said to each other, and she had not yet dared to ask.

Mrs. Freeman was insisting upon her attention. She had moved from the refrigerator to the heater so that Mrs. Hopewell had to turn and face her in order to seem to be listening. "Glynese gone out with Harvey Hill again last night," she said. "She had this sty."

"Hill," Mrs. Hopewell said absently, "is that the one who works in the garage?"

"Nome, he's the one that goes to chiropracter school," Mrs. Freeman said. "She had this sty. Been had it two days. So she says when he brought her in the other night he says, 'Lemme get rid of that sty for you,' and she says, 'How?' and he says, 'You just lay yourself down acrost the seat of that car and I'll show you.' So she done it and he popped her neck. Kept on a-popping it several times until she made him quit. This morning," Mrs. Freeman said, "she ain't got no sty. She ain't got no traces of a sty."

"I never heard of that before," Mrs. Hopewell said.

"He ast her to marry him before the Ordinary,"[2] Mrs. Freeman went on, "and she told him she wasn't going to be married in no *office*."

"Well, Glynese is a fine girl," Mrs. Hopewell said. "Glynese and Carramae are both fine girls."

"Carramae said when her and Lyman was married Lyman said it sure felt sacred to him. She said he said he wouldn't take five hundred dollars for being married by a preacher."

"How much would he take?" the girl asked from the stove.

"He said he wouldn't take five hundred dollars," Mrs. Freeman repeated.

"Well we all have work to do," Mrs. Hopewell said.

"Lyman said it just felt more sacred to him," Mrs. Freeman said. "The doctor wants Carramae to eat prunes. Says instead of medicine. Says them cramps is coming from pressure. You know where I think it is?"

"She'll be better in a few weeks," Mrs. Hopewell said.

"In the tube," Mrs. Freeman said. "Else she wouldn't be as sick as she is."

Hulga had cracked her two eggs into a saucer and was bringing them to the table along with a cup of coffee that she had filled too full. She sat down carefully and began to eat, meaning to keep Mrs. Freeman there by questions if for any reason she showed an inclination to leave. She could perceive her mother's eye on her. The first round-about question would be about the Bible salesman and she did not wish to bring it on. "How did he pop her neck?" she asked.

Mrs. Freeman went into a description of how he had popped her neck. She said he owned a '55 Mercury but that Glynese said she would rather marry a man with only a '36 Plymouth who would be married by a preacher. The girl asked what if he had a '32 Plymouth and Mrs. Freeman said what Glynese had said was a '36 Plymouth.

Mrs. Hopewell said there were not many girls with Glynese's common sense. She said what she admired in those girls was their common sense. She said that reminded her that they had had a nice visitor yesterday, a young man selling Bibles. "Lord," she said, "he bored me to death but he was so sincere and genuine I couldn't be rude to him. He was just good country people, you know," she said, "—just the salt of the earth."

"I seen him walk up," Mrs. Freeman said, "and then later—I seen him walk off," and Hulga could feel the slight shift in her voice, the slight insinuation, that he had not walked off alone, had he? Her face remained expressionless but the color rose into her neck and she seemed to swallow it down with the next spoonful of egg. Mrs. Freeman was looking at her as if they had a secret together.

"Well, it takes all kinds of people to make the world go 'round," Mrs. Hopewell said. "It's very good we aren't all alike."

"Some people are more alike than others," Mrs. Freeman said.

Hulga got up and stumped, with about twice the noise that was necessary, into her room and locked the door. She was to meet the Bible salesman at ten o'clock at the gate. She had thought about it half the night. She had started

[2]Judge of probate court.

thinking of it as a great joke and then she had begun to see profound implications in it. She had lain in bed imagining dialogues for them that were insane on the surface but that reached below to depths that no Bible salesman would be aware of. Their conversation yesterday had been of this kind.

He had stopped in front of her and had simply stood there. His face was bony 75
and sweaty and bright, with a little pointed nose in the center of it, and his look was different from what it had been at the dinner table. He was gazing at her with open curiosity, with fascination, like a child watching a new fantastic animal at the zoo, and he was breathing as if he had run a great distance to reach her. His gaze seemed somehow familiar but she could not think where she had been regarded with it before. For almost a minute he didn't say anything. Then on what seemed an insuck of breath, he whispered, "You ever ate a chicken that was two days old?"

The girl looked at him stonily. He might have just put this question up for consideration at the meeting of a philosophical association. "Yes," she presently replied as if she had considered it from all angles.

"It must have been mighty small!" he said triumphantly and shook all over with little nervous giggles, getting very red in the face, and subsiding finally into his gaze of complete admiration, while the girl's expression remained exactly the same.

"How old are you?" he asked softly.

She waited some time before she answered. Then in a flat voice she said, "Seventeen."

His smiles came in succession like waves breaking on the surface of a little 80
lake. "I see you got a wooden leg," he said. "I think you're brave. I think you're real sweet."

The girl stood blank and solid and silent.

"Walk to the gate with me," he said. "You're a brave sweet little thing and I liked you the minute I seen you walk in the door."

Hulga began to move forward.

"What's your name?" he asked, smiling down on the top of her head.

"Hulga," she said. 85

"Hulga," he murmured, "Hulga. Hulga. I never heard of anybody name Hulga before. You're shy, aren't you, Hulga?" he asked.

She nodded, watching his large red hand on the handle of the giant valise.

"I like girls that wear glasses," he said. "I think a lot. I'm not like these people that a serious thought don't ever enter their heads. It's because I may die."

"I may die too," she said suddenly and looked up at him. His eyes were very small and brown, glittering feverishly.

"Listen," he said, "don't you think some people was meant to meet on account 90
of what all they got in common and all? Like they both think serious thoughts and all?" He shifted the valise to his other hand so that the hand nearest her was free. He caught hold of her elbow and shook it a little. "I don't work on Saturday," he said. "I like to walk in the woods and see what Mother Nature is wearing. O'er the hills and far away. Picnics and things. Couldn't we go on a picnic tomorrow? Say yes, Hulga," he said and gave her a dying look as if he felt his insides about to drop out of him. He had even seemed to sway slightly toward her.

During the night she had imagined that she seduced him. She imagined that the two of them walked on the place until they came to the storage barn beyond the two back fields and there, she imagined, that things came to such a pass that she very easily seduced him and that then, of course, she had to reckon with his remorse. True genius can get an idea across even to an inferior mind. She imagined that she took his remorse in hand and changed it into a deeper understanding of life. She took all his shame away and turned it into something useful.

She set off for the gate at exactly ten o'clock, escaping without drawing Mrs. Hopewell's attention. She didn't take anything to eat, forgetting that food is usually taken on a picnic. She wore a pair of slacks and a dirty white shirt, and as an afterthought, she had put some Vapex[3] on the collar of it since she did not own any perfume. When she reached the gate no one was there.

She looked up and down the empty highway and had the furious feeling that she had been tricked, that he had only meant to make her walk to the gate after the idea of him. Then suddenly he stood up, very tall, from behind a bush on the opposite embankment. Smiling, he lifted his hat which was new and wide-brimmed. He had not worn it yesterday and she wondered if he had bought it for the occasion. It was toast-colored with a red and white band around it and was slightly too large for him. He stepped from behind the bush still carrying the black valise. He had on the same suit and the same yellow socks sucked down in his shoes from walking. He crossed the highway and said, "I knew you'd come!"

The girl wondered acidly how he had known this. She pointed to the valise and asked, "Why did you bring your Bibles?"

He took her elbow, smiling down on her as if he could not stop. "You can 95
never tell when you'll need the word of God, Hulga," he said. She had a moment in which she doubted that this was actually happening and then they began to climb the embankment. They went down into the pasture toward the woods. The boy walked lightly by her side, bouncing on his toes. The valise did not seem to be heavy today; he even swung it. They crossed half the pasture without saying anything and then, putting his hand easily on the small of her back, he asked softly, "Where does your wooden leg join on?"

She turned an ugly red and glared at him and for an instant the boy looked abashed. "I didn't mean you no harm," he said. "I only meant you're so brave and all. I guess God takes care of you."

"No," she said, looking forward and walking fast, "I don't even believe in God."

At this he stopped and whistled. "No!" he exclaimed as if he were too astonished to say anything else.

She walked on and in a second he was bouncing at her side, fanning with his hat. "That's very unusual for a girl," he remarked, watching her out of the corner of his eye. When they reached the edge of the wood, he put his hand on her back again and drew her against him without a word and kissed her heavily.

The kiss, which had more pressure than feeling behind it, produced that extra 100
surge of adrenalin in the girl that enables one to carry a packed trunk out of a burning house, but in her, the power went at once to the brain. Even before he released her, her mind, clear and detached and ironic anyway, was regarding him from a great distance, with amusement but with pity. She had never been kissed before and she was pleased to discover that it was an unexceptional experience and all a matter of the mind's control. Some people might enjoy drain water if they were told it was vodka. When the boy, looking expectant but uncertain, pushed her gently away, she turned and walked on, saying nothing as if such business, for her, were common enough.

---

[3]Brand name for nasal spray.

He came along panting at her side, trying to help her when he saw a root that she might trip over. He caught and held back the long swaying blades of thorn vine until she had passed beyond them. She led the way and he came breathing heavily behind her. Then they came out on a sunlit hillside, sloping softly into another one a little smaller. Beyond, they could see the rusted top of the old barn where the extra hay was stored.

The hill was sprinkled with small pink weeds. "Then you ain't saved?" he asked suddenly, stopping.

The girl smiled. It was the first time she had smiled at him at all. "In my economy," she said, "I'm saved and you are damned but I told you I didn't believe in God."

Nothing seemed to destroy the boy's look of admiration. He gazed at her now as if the fantastic animal at the zoo had put its paw through the bars and given him a loving poke. She thought he looked as if he wanted to kiss her again and she walked on before he had the chance.

"Ain't there somewheres we can sit down sometime?" he murmured, his voice softening toward the end of the sentence.

"In that barn," she said.

They made for it rapidly as if it might slide away like a train. It was a large two-story barn, cool and dark inside. The boy pointed up the ladder that led into the loft and said, "It's too bad we can't go up there."

"Why can't we?" she asked.

"Yer leg," he said reverently.

The girl gave him a contemptuous look and putting both hands on the ladder, she climbed it while he stood below, apparently awestruck. She pulled herself expertly through the opening and then looked down at him and said, "Well, come on if you're coming," and he began to climb the ladder, awkwardly bringing the suitcase with him.

"We won't need the Bible," she observed.

"You never can tell," he said, panting. After he had got into the loft, he was a few seconds catching his breath. She had sat down in a pile of straw. A wide sheath of sunlight, filled with dust particles, slanted over her. She lay back against a bale, her face turned away, looking out the front opening of the barn where hay was thrown from a wagon into the loft. The two pink-speckled hillsides lay back against a dark ridge of woods. The sky was cloudless and cold blue. The boy dropped down by her side and put one arm under her and the other over her and began methodically kissing her face, making little noises like a fish. He did not remove his hat but it was pushed far enough back not to interfere. When her glasses got in his way, he took them off of her and slipped them into his pocket.

The girl at first did not return any of the kisses but presently she began to and after she had put several on his cheek, she reached his lips and remained there, kissing him again and again as if she were trying to draw all the breath out of him. His breath was clear and sweet like a child's and the kisses were sticky like a child's. He mumbled about loving her and about knowing when he first seen her that he loved her, but the mumbling was like the sleepy fretting of a child being put to sleep by his mother. Her mind, throughout this, never stopped or lost itself for a second to her feelings. "You ain't said you loved me none," he whispered finally, pulling back from her. "You got to say that."

She looked away from him off into the hollow sky and then down at a black ridge and then down farther into what appeared to be two green swelling lakes.

She didn't realize he had taken her glasses but this landscape could not seem exceptional to her for she seldom paid any close attention to her surroundings.

115 "You got to say it," he repeated. "You got to say you love me."

She was always careful how she committed herself. "In a sense," she began, "if you use the word loosely, you might say that. But it's not a word I use. I don't have illusions. I'm one of those people who see *through* to nothing."

The boy was frowning. "You got to say it. I said it and you got to say it," he said.

The girl looked at him almost tenderly. "You poor baby," she murmured. "It's just as well you don't understand," and she pulled him by the neck, face-down, against her. "We are all damned," she said, "but some of us have taken off our blindfolds and see that there's nothing to see. It's a kind of salvation."

The boy's astonished eyes looked blankly through the ends of her hair. "Okay," he almost whined, "but do you love me or don'tcher?"

120 "Yes," she said and added, "in a sense. But I must tell you something. There mustn't be anything dishonest between us." She lifted his head and looked him in the eye. "I am thirty years old," she said. "I have a number of degrees."

The boy's look was irritated but dogged. "I don't care," he said. "I don't care a thing about what all you done. I just want to know if you love me or don'tcher?" and he caught her to him and wildly planted her face with kisses until she said, "Yes, yes."

"Okay then," he said, letting her go. "Prove it."

She smiled, looking dreamily out on the shifty landscape. She had seduced him without even making up her mind to try. "How?" she asked, feeling that he should be delayed a little.

He leaned over and put his lips to her ear. "Show me where your wooden leg joins on," he whispered.

125 The girl uttered a sharp little cry and her face instantly drained of color. The obscenity of the suggestion was not what shocked her. As a child she had sometimes been subject to feelings of shame but education had removed the last traces of that as a good surgeon scrapes for cancer; she would no more have felt it over what he was asking than she would have believed in his Bible. But she was as sensitive about the artificial leg as a peacock about his tail. No one ever touched it but her. She took care of it as someone else would his soul, in private and almost with her own eyes turned away. "No," she said.

"I known it," he muttered, sitting up. "You're just playing me for a sucker."

"Oh no no!" she cried. "It joins on at the knee. Only at the knee. Why do you want to see it?"

The boy gave her a long penetrating look. "Because," he said, "it's what makes you different. You ain't like anybody else."

She sat staring at him. There was nothing about her face or her round freezing-blue eyes to indicate that this had moved her; but she felt as if her heart had stopped and left her mind to pump her blood. She decided that for the first time in her life she was face to face with real innocence. This boy, with an instinct that came from beyond wisdom, had touched the truth about her. When after a minute, she said in a hoarse high voice, "All right," it was like surrendering to him completely. It was like losing her own life and finding it again, miraculously, in his.

130 Very gently, he began to roll the slack leg up. The artificial limb, in a white sock and brown flat shoe, was bound in a heavy material like canvas and ended in an ugly jointure where it was attached to the stump. The boy's face and his

voice were entirely reverent as he uncovered it and said, "Now show me how to take it off and on."

She took it off for him and put it back on again and then he took it off himself, handling it as tenderly as if it were a real one. "See!" he said with a delighted child's face. "Now I can do it myself!"

"Put it back on," she said. She was thinking that she would run away with him and that every night he would take the leg off and every morning put it back on again. "Put it back on," she said.

"Not yet," he murmured, setting it on its foot out of her reach. "Leave it off for awhile. You got me instead."

She gave a little cry of alarm but he pushed her down and began to kiss her again. Without the leg she felt entirely dependent on him. Her brain seemed to have stopped thinking altogether and to be about some other function that it was not very good at. Different expressions raced back and forth over her face. Every now and then the boy, his eyes like two steel spikes, would glance behind him where the leg stood. Finally she pushed him off and said, "Put it back on me now."

"Wait," he said. He leaned the other way and pulled the valise toward him and 135
opened it. It had a pale blue spotted lining and there were only two Bibles in it. He took one of these out and opened the cover of it. It was hollow and contained a pocket flask of whiskey, a pack of cards, and a small blue box with printing on it. He laid these out in front of her one at a time in an evenly-spaced row, like one presenting offerings at the shrine of a goddess. He put the blue box in her hand. THIS PRODUCT TO BE USED ONLY FOR THE PREVENTION OF DISEASE, she read, and dropped it. The boy was unscrewing the top of the flask. He stopped and pointed, with a smile, to the deck of cards. It was not an ordinary deck but one with an obscene picture on the back of each card. "Take a swig," he said, offering her the bottle first. He held it in front of her, but like one mesmerized, she did not move.

Her voice when she spoke had an almost pleading sound. "Aren't you," she murmured, "aren't you just good country people?"

The boy cocked his head. He looked as if he were just beginning to understand that she might be trying to insult him. "Yeah," he said, curling his lip slightly, "but it ain't held me back none. I'm as good as you any day in the week."

"Give me my leg," she said.

He pushed it farther away with his foot. "Come on now, let's begin to have us a good time," he said coaxingly. "We ain't got to know one another good yet."

"Give me my leg!" she screamed and tried to lunge for it but he pushed her 140
down easily.

"What's the matter with you all of a sudden?" he asked, frowning as he screwed the top on the flask and put it quickly back inside the Bible. "You just a while ago said you didn't believe in nothing. I thought you was some girl!"

Her face was almost purple. "You're a Christian!" she hissed. "You're a fine Christian! You're just like them all—say one thing and do another. You're a perfect Christian, you're..."

The boy's mouth was set angrily. "I hope you don't think," he said in a lofty indignant tone, "that I believe in that crap! I may sell Bibles but I know which end is up and I wasn't born yesterday and I know where I'm going!"

"Give me my leg!" she screeched. He jumped up so quickly that she barely saw him sweep the cards and the blue box back into the Bible and throw the Bible into the valise. She saw him grab the leg and then she saw it for an instant slanted forlornly across the inside of the suitcase with a Bible at either side of its opposite ends. He slammed the lid shut and snatched up the valise and swung it down the hole and then stepped through himself.

When all of him had passed but his head, he turned and regarded her with a 145
look that no longer had any admiration in it. "I've gotten a lot of interesting things," he said. "One time I got a woman's glass eye this way. And you needn't to think you'll catch me because Pointer ain't really my name. I use a different name at every house I call at and don't stay nowhere long. And I'll tell you another thing, Hulga," he said, using the name as if he didn't think much of it, "you ain't so smart. I been believing in nothing ever since I was born!" and then the toast-colored hat disappeared down the hole and the girl was left, sitting on the straw in the dusty sunlight. When she turned her churning face toward the opening, she saw his blue figure struggling successfully over the green speckled lake.

Mrs. Hopewell and Mrs. Freeman, who were in the back pasture, digging up onions, saw him emerge a little later from the woods and head across the meadow toward the highway. "Why, that looks like that nice dull young man that tried to sell me a Bible yesterday," Mrs. Hopewell said, squinting. "He must have been selling them to the Negroes back in there. He was so simple," she said, "but I guess the world would be better off if we were all that simple."

Mrs. Freeman's gaze drove forward and just touched him before he disappeared under the hill. Then she returned her attention to the evil-smelling onion shoot she was lifting from the ground. "Some can't be that simple," she said. "I know I never could."

(1955)

PREWRITING

Understanding the theme of a piece of literature involves figuring out what the whole work means. Your prewriting task here is, as usual, to ask yourself questions that will lead to the meaning of the story you just read.

Figuring Out the Theme

Reread "Good Country People" and formulate specific leading questions about the following elements of the story. For example, you might ask yourself, "How does the title apply to the characters in the story?" or "Do the characters' names seem appropriate? Do they describe the characters in any way? Are they straightforward or satiric?" Consider the following:

1. The title.
2. The setting, especially the descriptions of the Hopewells' house and their living situation.
3. The characters in the story, especially their names, their physical descriptions, and their relationships with one another.
4. Any significant objects, such as Hulga's artificial leg and Manley's Bible, as well as repeated uses of language like the platitudes that Mrs. Hopewell strings together and Hulga's academic comments and references.

5. Any changes that you notice in the characters and their feelings toward themselves or one another.
6. Any reversals or surprises that occur.
7. Any comments or observations the narrator makes about the characters and their actions.
8. The ending.

Stating the Theme

After writing out the answers to the questions you have set for yourself, try to sum up the theme in a complete sentence. You may need to rewrite the sentence several times until you can express the theme satisfactorily. Then state the theme in another way, using other words. Are both statements valid? Are there any secondary themes that enrich the story and add to the primary theme? Write those down, too.

Take one of the statements of theme that you have formulated, and write it at the top of a blank sheet of paper. Fill the page with freewriting about this idea, expressing as quickly as you can your thoughts and feelings about O'Connor's view of human nature.

WRITING

We have emphasized that your essays should be filled with supporting details from your source. Without specific references to the literary work that you are writing about, your judgments and conclusions will be vague and unconvincing.

Choosing Supporting Details

During a close second reading of a story, pay special attention to details that have potential for symbolic meaning. Thoughtful consideration of the names, places, objects, incidents, and minor characters can guide you to a deeper understanding of the work's theme. In "Good Country People," for example, you may notice how often Hulga's artificial limb is mentioned. Go through the story one more time, and put a check mark next to each mention of the wooden leg. During this third examination, you may also note other references to the human body, such as Hulga's weak heart and short-sighted eyes, the Bible salesman's heart condition, and Mrs. Freeman's intense interest in Carramae's vomit and Glynese's sty. Then try to come up with an insight that expresses the meaning of these details—perhaps something like "All the characters seem preoccupied in one way or another with the physical side of being human." You now have a useful thesis for your paper or a topic sentence for a section of it.

A list of specific examples from the story could support your thesis statement, but a simple list would probably sound mechanical and unrevealing. So, if possible, classify the details. In this case, some of the characters seem fascinated with physical details and others try to ignore them. Quote one or two examples of each kind, and then—most important—explain their significance. In this story, the fascination with the physical seems perverse and superficial, while the avoidance is pretentious and hypocritical. Both attitudes suggest a lack of spiritual awareness.

Approach the following writing ideas by rereading the story with your topic in mind. Jot down any details that seem relevant. Review all your notes on the story and see what general observations you can make; then select appropriate supporting details from your list and show how they support your critical generalizations.

IDEAS FOR WRITING

Ideas for Responsive Writing

1. Do you agree with Mrs. Hopewell that "good country people are the salt of the earth" and that "there aren't enough good country people in the world"? Evaluate the validity of these assertions, especially as they relate to the country people you know and the ones you read about in the story.
2. Have you ever met anyone like Manley Pointer? Do such people really exist? Write a character sketch (an extended description) of Pointer, comparing him to people you have known or met.
3. Rewrite the story from Hulga's point of view. You might put your rewrite in the form of a letter from Hulga to her mother.

Ideas for Critical Writing

1. In the essay "Writing Short Stories," O'Connor wrote that "there is a wooden part of [Hulga's] soul that corresponds to her wooden leg." Write an essay using O'Connor's statement as your major claim.
2. The last two paragraphs of the story, concerning Mrs. Hopewell and Mrs. Freeman, were added at the suggestion of O'Connor's editor. What is the purpose of these paragraphs? Analyze this ending, and explain what it contributes to the story's themes.
3. What does "Good Country People" say about uniqueness ("everybody is different") and imperfection? Write an essay examining the story's messages about one or both of these subjects.
4. CRITICAL APPROACHES: All the characters in "Good Country People" except Manley Pointer are female. Review literary interpretations based on gender (pages 1160–61). How is the daily life of the main characters affected by an all-female setting? What would be different if men were in the picture? Why are they mainly absent? Write an essay that argues for or against the importance of gender in this story.

Ideas for Researched Writing

1. When Hulga tells the Bible salesman, "Some of us have taken off our blindfolds and see that there's nothing to see," and he later responds, "I have been believing in nothing since I was born," they are expressing the philosophy of *nihilism*. Look up *nihilism* in a reference work like the *Encyclopedia of Philosophy* or the *Oxford Companion to Philosophy*. With this information, write an essay that demonstrates how Hulga's nihilism, her "spiritual affliction," serves to reveal the story's theme.
2. The theme of "Good Country People" has been defined in a number of ways. Find critical commentaries that offer at least three distinct interpretations of the story and its theme. Write your own essay that evaluates, reconciles, or argues against these differing interpretations.

REWRITING

When you revise, you should make sure that your paper *flows*—that your readers can follow your ideas easily.

Achieving Coherence

The best way to make your writing *coherent*—to make it easy to follow—is to have a clear thesis and to make sure that all your subpoints pertain to that thesis. If you organize the development of your ideas carefully, your paragraphs should unfold in a logical, connected way. Continuity also evolves from thinking through your ideas completely and developing them adequately. Leaps in thought and shifts in meaning often result from too much generalization and too little development.

Checking for Coherence

Type up or print out a clean copy of the latest draft of your essay. In the margins, write a word or phrase that labels the point or describes the function of every group of related sentences. These words and phrases are called *glosses*. (You can even use short sentences.) To help write glosses for your sentences and paragraphs, ask yourself these questions: What have I said here? How many ideas are in this passage? What does this sentence/paragraph do?

When you have finished putting glosses in the margins of your essay, go back and review the glosses. Can you see a clear sequence of points? Are there any sentences or passages that you could not write a gloss for? Is there any place where you digress or introduce an unrelated idea? Using the glosses as a guide, make revisions that will improve the coherence of your essay: fill in gaps, combine repetitive sentences, cut out irrelevant material, add transitions. (See Chart 4–2, "Transitional Terms for All Occasions," page 57, and "Writing Smooth Transitions" in the "Handbook for Correcting Errors," pages 1154–55.)

EDITING

Here are some other ways to help you strengthen the flow and coherence of your sentences.

Repeat Words and Synonyms

Repeat key words for coherence as well as for emphasis:

> I do not want to *read another gothic romance. I especially do not want to read another long gothic romance.*

If repetition is tiresome or you want more variety, use a synonym:

> It was a rare *caper*, planned to the last second. Such elaborate *heists* seem to come right from a detective novel.

Take care when using repetition. Repeated words should be important or emphatic. Do not repeat a common, limp term because you are too tired to find a synonym. Be aware, however, that synonyms are not always interchangeable; check the meaning of any word you are not sure of. The following introduction to a student paper suffers because the writer needlessly repeats the same uninteresting verb (which we have italicized):

> Shirley Jackson's "The Lottery" is a complex story that deals with a fundamental part of human psychology, the *using* of scapegoats. Scapegoats have been *used* throughout history to justify actions. Many times scapegoats are *used* to conceal human errors or prejudices. Scapegoats are, in fact, still *used* today.

Notice that the repetition of the key word *scapegoats* emphasizes the main idea of the paper. But the ineffective repetition should be revised (our substituted verbs are italicized in the following revision):

> Shirley Jackson's "The Lottery" is a complex story that deals with a fundamental element of human psychology—using scapegoats. Scapegoats have been *created* throughout history to justify actions. Many times they are *employed* to conceal human errors or prejudices. In fact, scapegoats still *exist* today.

Try Parallel Structure

Repeat a grammatical pattern to tie points and details together:

> In the morning Emma Bovary ate breakfast with her husband; in the afternoon she picnicked with her paramour.

> The play was about to end: the villain stalked off, the lovers kissed, the curtain fell, and the audience applauded wildly.

Be sure that your grammatical patterns actually are parallel. If your phrases or clauses do not follow the same structure, you will lose the good effect.

Not parallel	In "The Lottery" these characteristics include *unwillingness to change, sticking to tradition, fear of peer pressure,* and *just plain being afraid.*
Parallel	In "The Lottery" these characteristics include *unwillingness to change, enslavement to tradition, fear of peer pressure,* and *fear of the unknown.*
Not parallel	Many times scapegoats are invoked to conceal *human errors* or *the way people unfairly judge one another.*
Parallel	Many times scapegoats are used to conceal *human errors* and *prejudices.*

CASEBOOK

Joyce Carol Oates's *"Where Are You Going, Where Have You Been?"*

Of the more than four hundred stories that Joyce Carol Oates has published, "Where Are You Going, Where Have You Been?" continues to be the most anthologized and the most discussed. Inspired by a magazine article about a young killer in Arizona, the story was first published in 1966. Oates has described the story as "psychological realism" and a "realistic allegory," but the exact nature of its form and meaning remains a matter for debate and discussion among literary critics and general readers alike. This casebook presents the text of the story, some information about the story's origin, and excerpts from five critical interpretations.

Joyce Carol Oates 1938–

Joyce Carol Oates grew up during the depression on a farm in upstate New York. She won a scholarship to Syracuse University, where she became valedictorian of her graduating class. Oates has achieved a prodigious literary output, publishing more than eighty books of fiction, poetry, drama, essays, and literary criticism. Wryly, she once suggested that her epitaph could read, "She certainly tried." Oates has said she writes about "real people in a real society," but her fiction frequently centers on the connection between violence and sexual obsession.

Where Are You Going, Where Have You Been?

For Bob Dylan[1]

Her name was Connie. She was fifteen and she had a quick, nervous giggling habit of craning her neck to glance into mirrors or checking other people's faces to make sure her own was all right. Her mother, who noticed everything and knew everything and who hadn't much reason any longer to look at her own face, always scolded Connie about it. "Stop gawking at yourself. Who are you? You think you're so pretty?" she would say. Connie would raise her eyebrows at these familiar complaints and look right through her mother, into a shadowy vision of

[1]Bob Dylan (b. 1941), the composer, author, and singer who devised and popularized folk rock during the 1960s.

herself as she was right at that moment: she knew she was pretty and that was everything. Her mother had been pretty once too, if you could believe those old snapshots in the album, but now her looks were gone and that was why she was always after Connie.

"Why don't you keep your room clean like your sister? How've you got your hair fixed—what the hell stinks? Hair spray? You don't see your sister using that junk."

Her sister June was twenty-four and still lived at home. She was a secretary in the high school Connie attended, and if that wasn't bad enough—with her in the same building—she was so plain and chunky and steady that Connie had to hear her praised all the time by her mother and her mother's sisters. June did this, June did that, she saved money and helped clean the house and cooked and Connie couldn't do a thing, her mind was all filled with trashy daydreams. Their father was away at work most of the time and when he came home he wanted supper and he read the newspaper at supper and after supper he went to bed. He didn't bother talking much to them, but around his bent head Connie's mother kept picking at her until Connie wished her mother was dead and she herself was dead and it was all over. "She makes me want to throw up sometimes," she complained to her friends. She had a high, breathless, amused voice that made everything she said sound a little forced, whether it was sincere or not.

There was one good thing: June went places with girl friends of hers, girls who were just as plain and steady as she, and so when Connie wanted to do that her mother had no objections. The father of Connie's best girl friend drove the girls the three miles to town and left them off at a shopping plaza so they could walk through the stores or go to a movie, and when he came to pick them up again at eleven he never bothered to ask what they had done.

They must have been familiar sights, walking around the shopping plaza in 5
their shorts and flat ballerina slippers that always scuffed the sidewalk, with charm bracelets jingling on their thin wrists; they would lean together to whisper and laugh secretly if someone passed who amused or interested them. Connie had long dark blond hair that drew anyone's eye to it, and she wore part of it pulled up on her head and puffed out and the rest of it she let fall down her back. She wore a pull-over jersey blouse that looked one way when she was at home and another way when she was away from home. Everything about her had two sides to it, one for home and one for anywhere that was not home: her walk, which could be childlike and bobbing, or languid enough to make anyone think she was hearing music in her head; her mouth, which was pale and smirking most of the time, but bright and pink on these evenings out; her laugh, which was cynical and drawling at home—"Ha, ha, very funny"—but high-pitched and nervous anywhere else, like the jingling of the charms on her bracelet.

Sometimes they did go shopping or to a movie, but sometimes they went across the highway, ducking fast across the busy road, to a drive-in restaurant where older kids hung out. The restaurant was shaped like a big bottle, though squatter than a real bottle, and on its cap was a revolving figure of a grinning boy who held a hamburger aloft. One night in mid-summer they ran across, breathless with daring, and right away someone leaned out a car window and invited them over, but it was just a boy from high school they didn't like. It made them feel good to be able to ignore him. They went up through the maze of parked and cruising cars to the bright-lit, fly-infested restaurant, their faces pleased and expectant as if they were entering a sacred building that loomed up out of the night to give them what haven and blessing they yearned for. They sat at the counter and crossed their legs at the ankles, their thin shoulders rigid with excitement, and listened to the music that made everything so good: the music was always in the background, like music at a church service; it was something to depend upon.

A boy named Eddie came in to talk with them. He sat backwards on his stool, turning himself jerkily around in semi-circles and then stopping and turning again, and after a while he asked Connie if she would like something to eat. She said she would and so she tapped her friend's arm on her way out—her friend pulled her face up into a brave, droll look—and Connie said she would meet her at eleven, across the way. "I just hate to leave her like that," Connie said earnestly, but the boy said that she wouldn't be alone for long. So they went out to his car, and on the way Connie couldn't help but let her eyes wander over the windshields and faces all around her, her face gleaming with a joy that had nothing to do with Eddie or even this place; it might have been the music. She drew her shoulders up and sucked in her breath with the pure pleasure of being alive, and just at that moment she happened to glance at a face just a few feet from hers. It was a boy with shaggy black hair, in a convertible jalopy painted gold. He stared at her and then his lips widened into a grin. Connie slit her eyes at him and turned away, but she couldn't help glancing back and there he was still watching her. He wagged a finger and laughed and said, "Gonna get you, baby," and Connie turned away again without Eddie noticing anything.

She spent three hours with him, at the restaurant where they ate hamburgers and drank Cokes in wax cups that were always sweating, and then down an alley a mile or so away, and when he left her off at five to eleven only the movie house was still open at the plaza. Her girl friend was there, talking with a boy. When Connie came up, the two girls smiled at each other and Connie said, "How was the movie?" and the girl said, "*You* should know." They rode off with the girl's father, sleepy and pleased, and Connie couldn't help but look back at the darkened shopping plaza with its big empty parking lot and its signs that were faded and ghostly now, and over at the drive-in restaurant where cars were still circling tirelessly. She couldn't hear the music at this distance.

Next morning June asked her how the movie was and Connie said, "So-so."

She and that girl and occasionally another girl went out several times a 10
week, and the rest of the time Connie spent around the house—it was summer vacation—getting in her mother's way and thinking, dreaming about the boys she met. But all the boys fell back and dissolved into a single face that was not even a face, but an idea, a feeling, mixed up with the urgent insistent pounding of the music and the humid night air of July. Connie's mother kept dragging her back to the daylight by finding things for her to do or saying, suddenly, "What's this about the Pettinger girl?"

And Connie would say nervously, "Oh, her. That dope." She always drew thick clear lines between herself and such girls, and her mother was simple and kind enough to believe her. Her mother was so simple, Connie thought, that it was maybe cruel to fool her so much. Her mother went scuffling around the house in old bedroom slippers and complained over the telephone to one sister about the other, then the other called up and the two of them complained about the third one. If June's name was mentioned her mother's tone was approving, and if Connie's name was mentioned it was disapproving. This did not really mean she disliked Connie, and actually Connie thought that her mother preferred her to June just because she was prettier, but the two of them kept up a pretense of exasperation, a sense that they were tugging and struggling over something of little value to either of them. Sometimes, over coffee, they were almost friends, but something would come up—some vexation that was like a fly buzzing suddenly around their heads—and their faces went hard with contempt.

One Sunday Connie got up at eleven—none of them bothered with church—and washed her hair so that it could dry all day long in the sun. Her parents and sister were going to a barbecue at an aunt's house and Connie said no, she wasn't interested, rolling her eyes to let her mother know just what she thought of it. "Stay home alone then," her mother said sharply. Connie sat out back in a lawn chair and watched them drive away, her father quiet and bald, hunched around so that he could back the car out, her mother with a look that was still angry and not at all softened through the windshield, and in the back seat poor old June, all dressed up as if she didn't know what a barbecue was, with all the running yelling kids and the flies. Connie sat with her eyes closed in the sun, dreaming and dazed with the warmth about her as if this were a kind of love, the caresses of love, and her mind slipped over onto thoughts of the boy she had been with the night before and how nice he had been, how sweet it always was, not the way someone like June would suppose but sweet, gentle, the way it was in movies and promised in songs; and when she opened her eyes she hardly knew where she was, the back yard ran off into weeds and a fence-like line of trees and behind it the sky was perfectly blue and still. The asbestos "ranch house" that was now three years old startled her—it looked small. She shook her head as if to get awake.

It was too hot. She went inside the house and turned on the radio to drown out the quiet. She sat on the edge of her bed, barefoot, and listened for an hour and a half to a program called XYZ Sunday Jamboree, record after record of hard, fast, shrieking songs she sang along with, interspersed by exclamations from "Bobby King": "An' look here, you girls at Napoleon's—Son and Charley want you to pay real close attention to this song coming up!"

And Connie paid close attention herself, bathed in a glow of slow-pulsed joy that seemed to rise mysteriously out of the music itself and lay languidly about the airless little room, breathed in and breathed out with each gentle rise and fall of her chest.

After a while she heard a car coming up the drive. She sat up at once, startled, 15
because it couldn't be her father so soon. The gravel kept crunching all the way in from the road—the driveway was long—and Connie ran to the window. It was a car she didn't know. It was an open jalopy, painted a bright gold that caught the sunlight opaquely. Her heart began to pound and her fingers snatched at her hair, checking it, and she whispered, "Christ. Christ," wondering how bad she looked. The car came to a stop at the side door and the horn sounded four short taps, as if this were a signal Connie knew.

She went into the kitchen and approached the door slowly, then hung out the screen door, her bare toes curling down off the step. There were two boys in the car and now she recognized the driver: he had shaggy, shabby black hair that looked crazy as a wig and he was grinning at her.

"I ain't late, am I?" he said.

"Who the hell do you think you are?" Connie said.

"Toldja I'd be out, didn't I?"

"I don't even know who you are." 20

She spoke sullenly, careful to show no interest or pleasure, and he spoke in a fast, bright monotone. Connie looked past him to the other boy, taking her time. He had fair brown hair, with a lock that fell onto his forehead. His sideburns gave him a fierce, embarrassed look, but so far he hadn't even bothered to glance at her. Both boys wore sunglasses. The driver's glasses were metallic and mirrored everything in miniature.

"You wanta come for a ride?" he said.

Connie smirked and let her hair fall loose over one shoulder.

"Don'tcha like my car? New paint job," he said. "Hey."

"What?" 25

"You're cute."

She pretended to fidget, chasing flies away from the door.

"Don'tcha believe me, or what?" he said.

"Look, I don't even know who you are," Connie said in disgust.

"Hey, Ellie's got a radio, see. Mine's broke down." He lifted his friend's arm and 30
showed her the little transistor radio the boy was holding, and now Connie began to hear the music. It was the same program that was playing inside the house.

"Bobby King?" she said.

"I listen to him all the time. I think he's great."

"He's kind of great," Connie said reluctantly.

"Listen, that guy's *great*. He knows where the action is."

Connie blushed a little, because the glasses made it impossible for her to see 35
just what this boy was looking at. She couldn't decide if she liked him or if he was just a jerk, and so she dawdled in the doorway and wouldn't come down or go back inside. She said, "What's all that stuff painted on your car?"

"Can'tcha read it?" He opened the door very carefully, as if he were afraid it might fall off. He slid out just as carefully, planting his feet firmly on the ground, the tiny metallic world in his glasses slowing down like gelatine hardening and in the midst of it Connie's bright green blouse. "This here is my name to begin with," he said. ARNOLD FRIEND was written in tarlike black letters on the side, with a drawing of a round, grinning face that reminded Connie of a pumpkin, except it wore sunglasses. "I wanta introduce myself. I'm Arnold Friend and that's my real name and I'm gonna be your friend, honey, and inside the car's Ellie Oscar, he's kinda shy." Ellie brought his transistor radio up to his shoulder and balanced it there. "Now these numbers are a secret code, honey," Arnold Friend explained. He read off the numbers 33, 19, 17 and raised his eyebrows at her to see what she thought of that, but she didn't think much of it. The left rear fender had been smashed and around it was written, on the gleaming gold background: DONE BY CRAZY WOMAN DRIVER. Connie had to laugh at that. Arnold Friend was pleased at her laughter and looked up at her. "Around the other side's a lot more—you wanta come and see them?"

"No."

"Why not?"

"Why should I?"

"Don'tcha wanta see what's on the car? Don'tcha wanta go for a ride?" 40

"I don't know."

"Why not?"

"I got things to do."

"Like what?"

"Things." 45

He laughed as if she had said something funny. He slapped his thigh. He was standing in a strange way, leaning back against the car as if he were balancing himself. He wasn't tall, only an inch or so taller than she would be if she came down to him. Connie liked the way he was dressed, which was the way all of them dressed: tight faded jeans stuffed into black, scuffed boots, a belt that pulled his waist in and showed how lean he was, and a white pull-over shirt that was a little soiled and showed the hard small muscles of his arms and shoulders. He looked as if he probably did hard work, lifting and carrying things. Even his neck looked muscular. And his face was a familiar face, somehow: the jaw and chin and cheeks slightly darkened because he hadn't shaved for a day or two, and the nose long and hawklike, sniffing as if she were a treat he was going to gobble up and it was all a joke.

"Connie, you ain't telling the truth. This is your day set aside for a ride with me and you know it," he said, still laughing. The way he straightened and recovered from his fit of laughing showed that it had been all fake.

"How do you know what my name is?" she said suspiciously.

"It's Connie."

"Maybe and maybe not." 50

"I know my Connie," he said, wagging his finger. Now she remembered him even better, back at the restaurant, and her cheeks warmed at the thought of how she had sucked in her breath just at the moment she passed him—how she must have looked to him. And he had remembered her. "Ellie and I come out here especially for you," he said. "Ellie can sit in back. How about it?"

"Where?"

"Where what?"

"Where're we going?"

He looked at her. He took off the sunglasses and she saw how pale the skin 55
around his eyes was, like holes that were not in shadow but instead in light. His eyes were chips of broken glass that catch the light in an amiable way. He smiled. It was as if the idea of going for a ride somewhere, to some place, was a new idea to him.

"Just for a ride, Connie sweetheart."

"I never said my name was Connie," she said.

"But I know what it is. I know your name and all about you, lots of things," Arnold Friend said. He had not moved yet but stood still leaning back against the side of his jalopy. "I took a special interest in you, such a pretty girl, and found out all about you—like I know your parents and sister are gone somewheres and I know where and how long they're going to be gone, and I know who you were with last night, and your best girl friend's name is Betty. Right?"

He spoke in a simple lilting voice, exactly as if he were reciting the words to a song. His smile assured her that everything was fine. In the car Ellie turned up the volume on his radio and did not bother to look around at them.

"Ellie can sit in the back seat," Arnold Friend said. He indicated his friend with a 60
casual jerk of his chin, as if Ellie did not count and she should not bother with him.

"How'd you find out all that stuff?" Connie said.

"Listen: Betty Schultz and Tony Fitch and Jimmy Pettinger and Nancy Pettinger," he said in a chant. "Raymond Stanley and Bob Hutter—"

"Do you know all those kids?"

"I know everybody."

"Look, you're kidding. You're not from around here." 65

"Sure."

"But—how come we never saw you before?"

"Sure you saw me before," he said. He looked down at his boots, as if he were a little offended. "You just don't remember."

"I guess I'd remember you," Connie said.

"Yeah?" He looked up at this, beaming. He was pleased. He began to mark time 70 with the music from Ellie's radio, tapping his fists lightly together. Connie looked away from his smile to the car, which was painted so bright it almost hurt her eyes to look at it. She looked at that name, ARNOLD FRIEND. And up at the front fender was an expression that was familiar—MAN THE FLYING SAUCERS. It was an expression kids had used the year before but didn't use this year. She looked at it for a while as if the words meant something to her that she did not yet know.

"What're you thinking about? Huh?" Arnold Friend demanded. "Not worried about your hair blowing around in the car, are you?"

"No."

"Think I maybe can't drive good?"

"How do I know?"

"You're a hard girl to handle. How come?" he said. "Don't you know I'm your 75 friend? Didn't you see me put my sign in the air when you walked by?"

"What sign?"

"My sign." And he drew an X in the air, leaning out toward her. They were maybe ten feet apart. After his hand fell back to his side the X was still in the air, almost visible. Connie let the screen door close and stood perfectly still inside it, listening to the music from her radio and the boy's blend together. She stared at Arnold Friend. He stood there so stiffly relaxed, pretending to be relaxed, with one hand idly on the door handle as if he were keeping himself up that way and had no intention of ever moving again. She recognized most things about him, the tight jeans that showed his thighs and buttocks and the greasy leather boots and the tight shirt, and even that slippery friendly smile of his, that sleepy dreamy smile that all the boys used to get across ideas they didn't want to put into words. She recognized all this and also the singsong way he talked, slightly mocking, kidding, but serious and a little melancholy, and she recognized the way he tapped one fist against the other in homage to the perpetual music behind him. But all these things did not come together.

She said suddenly, "Hey, how old are you?"

His smile faded. She could see then that he wasn't a kid, he was much older—thirty, maybe more. At this knowledge her heart began to pound faster.

"That's a crazy thing to ask. Can'tcha see I'm your own age?" 80

"Like hell you are."

"Or maybe a coupla years older. I'm eighteen."

"Eighteen?" she said doubtfully.

He grinned to reassure her and lines appeared at the corners of his mouth. His teeth were big and white. He grinned so broadly his eyes became slits and she saw how thick the lashes were, thick and black as if painted with a black tar-like material. Then, abruptly, he seemed to become embarrassed and looked over his shoulder at Ellie. "*Him*, he's crazy," he said. "Ain't he a riot? He's a nut, a real character." Ellie was still listening to the music. His sunglasses told nothing about what he was thinking. He wore a bright orange shirt unbuttoned halfway to show his chest, which was a pale, bluish chest and not muscular like Arnold Friend's. His shirt collar was turned up all around and the very tips of the collar pointed out past his chin as if they were protecting him. He was pressing the transistor radio up against his ear and sat there in a kind of daze, right in the sun.

"He's kinda strange," Connie said. 85

"Hey, she says you're kinda strange! Kinda strange!" Arnold Friend cried. He pounded on the car to get Ellie's attention. Ellie turned for the first time and Connie saw with shock that he wasn't a kid either—he had a fair, hairless face, cheeks reddened slightly as if the veins grew too close to the surface of his skin, the face of a forty-year-old baby. Connie felt a wave of dizziness rise in her at this sight and she stared at him as if waiting for something to change the shock of the moment, make it all right again. Ellie's lips kept shaping words, mumbling along with the words blasting in his ear.

"Maybe you two better go away," Connie said faintly.

"What? How come?" Arnold Friend cried. "We come out here to take you for a ride. It's Sunday." He had the voice of the man on the radio now. It was the same voice, Connie thought. "Don'tcha know it's Sunday all day? And honey, no matter who you were with last night, today you're with Arnold Friend and don't you forget it! Maybe you better step out here," he said, and this last was in a different voice. It was a little flatter, as if the heat was finally getting to him.

"No. I got things to do."

"Hey." 90

"You two better leave."

"We ain't leaving until you come with us."

"Like hell I am—"

"Connie, don't fool around with me. I mean—I mean, don't fool *around*," he said, shaking his head. He laughed incredulously. He placed his sunglasses on top of his head, carefully, as if he were indeed wearing a wig, and brought the stems down behind his ears. Connie stared at him, another wave of dizziness and fear rising in her so that for a moment he wasn't even in focus but was just a blur standing there against his gold car, and she had the idea that he had driven up the driveway all right but had come from nowhere before that and belonged nowhere and that everything about him and even about the music that was so familiar to her was only half real.

"If my father comes and sees you—" 95

"He ain't coming. He's at a barbecue."

"How do you know that?"

"Aunt Tillie's. Right now they're—uh—they're drinking. Sitting around," he said vaguely, squinting as if he were staring all the way to town and over to Aunt Tillie's back yard. Then the vision seemed to get clear and he nodded energetically. "Yeah. Sitting around. There's your sister in a blue dress, huh? And high heels, the poor sad bitch—nothing like you, sweetheart! And your mother's helping some fat woman with the corn, they're cleaning the corn—husking the corn—"

"What fat woman?" Connie cried.

"How do I know what fat woman. I don't know every goddamn fat woman in the world!" Arnold Friend laughed. 100

"Oh, that's Mrs. Hornsby. . . . Who invited her?" Connie said. She felt a little light-headed. Her breath was coming quickly.

"She's too fat. I don't like them fat. I like them the way you are, honey," he said, smiling sleepily at her. They stared at each other for a while through the screen door. He said softly, "Now, what you're going to do is this: you're going to come out that door. You're going to sit up front with me and Ellie's going to sit in the back, the hell with Ellie, right? This isn't Ellie's date. You're my date. I'm your lover, honey."

"What? You're crazy—"

"Yes, I'm your lover. You don't know what that is but you will," he said. "I know that too. I know all about you. But look: it's real nice and you couldn't ask for nobody better than me, or more polite. I always keep my word. I'll tell you how it is, I'm always nice at first, the first time. I'll hold you so tight you won't think you have to try to get away or pretend anything because you'll know you can't. And I'll come inside you where it's all secret and you'll give in to me and you'll love me—"

105 "Shut up! You're crazy!" Connie said. She backed away from the door. She put her hands up against her ears as if she'd heard something terrible, something not meant for her. "People don't talk like that, you're crazy," she muttered. Her heart was almost too big now for her chest and its pumping made sweat break out all over her. She looked out to see Arnold Friend pause and then take a step toward the porch, lurching. He almost fell. But, like a clever drunken man, he managed to catch his balance. He wobbled in his high boots and grabbed hold of one of the porch posts.

"Honey?" he said. "You still listening?"

"Get the hell out of here!"

"Be nice, honey. Listen."

"I'm going to call the police—"

110 He wobbled again and out of the side of his mouth came a fast spat curse, an aside not meant for her to hear. But even this "Christ!" sounded forced. Then he began to smile again. She watched this smile come, awkward as if he were smiling from inside a mask. His whole face was a mask, she thought wildly, tanned down to his throat but then running out as if he had plastered makeup on his face but had forgotten about his throat.

"Honey—? Listen, here's how it is. I always tell the truth and I promise you this: I ain't coming in that house after you."

"You better not! I'm going to call the police if you—if you don't—"

"Honey," he said, talking right through her voice, "honey, I'm not coming in there but you are coming out here. You know why?"

She was panting. The kitchen looked like a place she had never seen before, some room she had run inside but that wasn't good enough, wasn't going to help her. The kitchen window had never had a curtain, after three years, and there were dishes in the sink for her to do—probably—and if you ran your hand across the table you'd probably feel something sticky there.

115 "You listening honey? Hey?"

"—going to call the police—"

"Soon as you touch the phone I don't need to keep my promise and can come inside. You won't want that."

She rushed forward and tried to lock the door. Her fingers were shaking. "But why lock it," Arnold Friend said gently, talking right into her face. "It's just a screen door. It's just nothing." One of his boots was at a strange angle, as if his foot wasn't in it. It pointed out to the left, bent at the ankle. "I mean, anybody can break through a screen door and glass and wood and iron or anything else if he needs to, anybody at all, and specially Arnold Friend. If the place got lit up with a fire, honey, you'd come runnin' out into my arms, right into my arms an' safe at home—like you knew I was your lover and'd stopped fooling around. I don't mind a nice shy girl but I don't like no fooling around." Part of those words were spoken with a slight rhythmic lilt, and Connie somehow recognized them—the echo of a song from last year, about a girl rushing into her boy friend's arms and coming home again—

Connie stood barefoot on the linoleum floor, staring at him. "What do you want?" she whispered.

"I want you," he said. 120

"What?"

"Seen you that night and thought, that's the one, yes sir. I never needed to look anymore."

"But my father's coming back. He's coming to get me. I had to wash my hair first—" She spoke in a dry, rapid voice, hardly raising it for him to hear.

"No, your daddy is not coming and yes, you had to wash your hair and you washed it for me. It's nice and shining and all for me. I thank you sweetheart," he said with a mock bow, but again he almost lost his balance. He had to bend and adjust his boots. Evidently his feet did not go all the way down; the boots must have been stuffed with something so that he would seem taller. Connie stared out at him and behind him at Ellie in the car, who seemed to be looking off toward Connie's right, into nothing. This Ellie said, pulling the words out of the air one after another as if he were just discovering them, "You want me to pull out the phone?"

"Shut your mouth and keep it shut," Arnold Friend said, his face red from 125
bending over or maybe from embarrassment because Connie had seen his boots. "This ain't none of your business."

"What—what are you doing? What do you want?" Connie said. "If I call the police they'll get you, they'll arrest you—"

"Promise was not to come in unless you touch that phone, and I'll keep that promise," he said. He resumed his erect position and tried to force his shoulders back. He sounded like a hero in a movie, declaring something important. But he spoke too loudly and it was as if he were speaking to someone behind Connie. "I ain't made plans for coming in that house where I don't belong but just for you to come out to me, the way you should. Don't you know who I am?"

"You're crazy," she whispered. She backed away from the door but did not want to go into another part of the house, as if this would give him permission to come through the door. "What do you... you're crazy, you...."

"Huh? What're you saying, honey?"

Her eyes darted everywhere in the kitchen. She could not remember what it 130
was, this room.

"This is how it is, honey: you come out and we'll drive away, have a nice ride. But if you don't come out we're gonna wait till your people come home and then they're all going to get it."

"You want that telephone pulled out?" Ellie said. He held the radio away from his ear and grimaced, as if without the radio the air was too much for him.

"I toldja shut up, Ellie," Arnold Friend said, "you're deaf, get a hearing aid, right? Fix yourself up. This little girl's no trouble and's gonna be nice to me, so Ellie keep to yourself, this ain't your date—right? Don't hem in on me, don't hog, don't crush, don't bird dog, don't trail me," he said in a rapid, meaningless voice, as if he were running through all the expressions he'd learned but was no longer sure which of them was in style, then rushing on to new ones, making them up with his eyes closed. "Don't crawl under my fence, don't squeeze in my chipmunk hole, don't sniff my glue, suck my popsicle, keep your own greasy fingers on yourself!" He shaded his eyes and peered in at Connie, who was backed against the kitchen table. "Don't mind him, honey, he's just a creep. He's a dope. Right? I'm the boy for you and like I said, you come out here nice like a lady and give me your hand, and nobody else gets hurt, I mean, your nice old bald-headed daddy and your mummy and your sister in her high heels. Because listen: why bring them in this?"

"Leave me alone," Connie whispered.

"Hey, you know that old woman down the road, the one with the chickens 135
and stuff—you know her?"

"She's dead!"

"Dead? What? You know her?" Arnold Friend said.

"She's dead—"

"Don't you like her?"

"She's dead—she's—she isn't here any more—"? 140

"But don't you like her, I mean, you got something against her? Some grudge or something?" Then his voice dipped as if he were conscious of a rudeness. He touched the sunglasses perched up on top of his head as if to make sure they were still there. "Now, you be a good girl."

"What are you going to do?"

"Just two things, or maybe three," Arnold Friend said. "But I promise it won't last long and you'll like me that way you get to like people you're close to. You will. It's all over for you here, so come on out. You don't want your people in any trouble, do you?"

She turned and bumped against a chair or something, hurting her leg, but she ran into the back room and picked up the telephone. Something roared in her ear, a tiny roaring, and she was so sick with fear that she could do nothing but listen to it—the telephone was clammy and very heavy and her fingers groped down to the dial but were too weak to touch it. She began to scream into the phone, into the roaring. She cried out, she cried for her mother, she felt her breath start jerking back and forth in her lungs as if it were something Arnold Friend was stabbing her with again and again with no tenderness. A noisy sorrowful wailing rose all about her and she was locked inside it the way she was locked inside this house.

After a while she could hear again. She was sitting on the floor with her wet 145
back against the wall.

Arnold Friend was saying from the door, "That's a good girl. Put the phone back."

She kicked the phone away from her.

"No, honey. Pick it up. Put it back right."

She picked it up and put it back. The dial tone stopped.

"That's a good girl. Now, you come outside." 150

She was hollow with what had been fear but what was now just an emptiness. All that screaming had blasted it out of her. She sat, one leg cramped under her, and deep inside her brain was something like a pinpoint of light that kept going and would not let her relax. She thought, I'm not going to see my mother again. She thought, I'm not going to sleep in my bed again. Her bright green blouse was all wet.

Arnold Friend said, in a gentle-loud voice that was like a stage voice, "The place where you came from ain't there any more, and where you had in mind to go is cancelled out. This place you are now—inside your daddy's house—is nothing but a cardboard box I can knock down any time. You know that and always did know it. You hear me?"

She thought, I have got to think. I have to know what to do.

"We'll go out to a nice field, out in the country here where it smells so nice and it's sunny," Arnold Friend said. "I'll have my arms tight around you so you won't need to try to get away and I'll show you what love is like, what it does. The hell with this house! It looks solid all right," he said. He ran a fingernail down the screen and the noise did not make Connie shiver, as it would have the day before. "Now, put your hand on your heart, honey. Feel that? That feels solid too but we know better. Be nice to me, be sweet like you can because what else is there for a girl like you but to be sweet and pretty and give in?—and get away before her people come back?"

She felt her pounding heart. Her hand seemed to enclose it. She thought for 155
the first time in her life that it was nothing that was hers, that belonged to her, but just a pounding, living thing inside this body that wasn't really hers either.

"You don't want them to get hurt," Arnold Friend went on. "Now, get up, honey. Get up all by yourself."

She stood.

"Now, turn this way. That's right. Come over here to me—Ellie, put that away, didn't I tell you? You dope. You miserable creepy dope," Arnold Friend said. His words were not angry but only part of an incantation. The incantation was kindly. "Now, come out through the kitchen to me, honey, and let's see a smile, try it, you're a brave, sweet little girl and now they're eating corn and hot dogs cooked to bursting over an outdoor fire, and they don't know one thing about you and never did and honey, you're better than them because not a one of them would have done this for you."

Connie felt the linoleum under her feet; it was cool. She brushed her hair back out of her eyes. Arnold Friend let go of the post tentatively and opened his arms for her, his elbows pointing in toward each other and his wrists limp, to show that this was an embarrassed embrace and a little mocking, he didn't want to make her self-conscious.

She put out her hand against the screen. She watched herself push the door 160
slowly open as if she were back safe somewhere in the other doorway, watching this body and this head of long hair moving out into the sunlight where Arnold Friend waited.

"My sweet little blue-eyed girl," he said in a half-sung sigh that had nothing to do with her brown eyes but was taken up just the same by the vast sunlit reaches of the land behind him and on all sides of him—so much land that Connie had never seen before and did not recognize except to know that she was going to it.

(1966)

The Story's Origins

Oates has acknowledged that she often bases stories on newspaper headlines: "It is the very skeletal nature of the newspaper, I think, that attracts me to it, the need it inspires in me to give flesh to such neatly and thinly-told tales." The inspiration for "Where Are You Going" was the tale of Charles Schmid, a twenty-three-year-old from Tucson who cruised teenage hangouts, picking up girls for rides in his gold convertible. Eventually, he murdered three of them, while other teenagers served as accomplices. He was convicted of murder in 1966; his story was written up in *Life*, as well as other newsmagazines, during the winter of

1965–66. Here are the opening paragraphs of the *Life* magazine article by Don Moser, which Oates read:

> At dusk in Tucson, as the stark, yellow-flared mountains begin to blur against the sky, the golden car slowly cruises Speedway. Smoothly it rolls down the long, divided avenue, past the supermarkets, the gas stations and the motels; past the twist joints, the sprawling drive-in restaurants. The car slows for an intersection, stops, then pulls away again. The exhaust mutters against the pavement as the young man driving takes the machine swiftly, expertly through the gears. A car pulls even with him; the teenage girls in the front seat laugh, wave and call his name. The young man glances toward the rearview mirror, turned always so that he can look at his own reflection, and he appraises himself.
>
> The face is his own creation: the hair dyed a raven black, the skin darkened to a deep tan with pancake make-up, the lips whitened, the whole effect heightened by a mole he has painted on one cheek. But the deep-set blue eyes are all his own. Beautiful eyes, the girls say.
>
> Approaching the Hi-Ho, the teenagers' nightclub, he backs off on the accelerator, then slowly cruises on past Johnie's Drive-in. There the cars are beginning to orbit and accumulate in the parking lot—neat sharp cars with deep-throated mufflers and Maltese-cross decals on the windows. But it's early yet. Not much going on. The driver shifts up again through the gears, and the golden car slides away along the glitter and gimcrack of Speedway. Smitty keeps looking for the action.
>
> "The Pied Piper of Tucson," *Life*, March 4, 1966: 19–24, 80c–90

Biographer Greg Johnson describes how Oates dealt with this source material.

> In early March, Joyce had picked up a copy of *Life* magazine and begun reading an article about Charles Schmid, an Arizona serial killer of teenage girls whom the article dubbed "The Pied Piper of Tucson." Joyce immediately saw material for fiction in Schmid's story, which included many grotesque elements: only five three, Schmid stuffed rags and tin cans in the bottoms of his boots to make himself appear taller. Yet Joyce had read only part of the article, not wanting "to be distracted by too much detail." With her usual impulse toward blending realism and allegory, she connected Schmid's exploits to mythic legends and folk songs about "Death and the Maiden," and "the story came to me more or less in a piece." Focusing on Connie, an ordinary teenage girl who succumbs to the demonic Arnold Friend, the story was originally titled "Death and the Maiden," but Joyce decided the title was "too pompous, too literary." After the story's first appearance, in the fall 1966 issue of *Epoch*, Joyce dedicated the story to Bob Dylan. While writing "Where Are You Going, Where Have You Been?" she had been listening to Dylan's song "It's All Over Now, Baby Blue," which struck Joyce as "hauntingly elegiac," similar in tone to the story she had written.
>
> *Invisible Writer: A Biography of Joyce Carol Oates*, 1998: 135

Four Critical Interpretations

Greg Johnson interprets the story as a "feminist allegory."

When the ironically named Arnold Friend first arrives at Connie's house, driving his sleazy gold jalopy and accompanied by a strange, ominously silent male sidekick, Connie deflects him with her usual pert sarcasms and practiced indifference. Throughout the long scene that follows, Connie's terror slowly builds. The fast-talking Arnold Friend insinuates himself into her thinking, attempting to persuade her that he's her "lover," his smooth-talking seductiveness finally giving way to threats of violence against Connie's family if she doesn't surrender to his desires. Oates places Connie inside the kitchen and Arnold Friend outside with only a locked screen door between them. While Friend could enter by force at any time, Oates emphasizes the seduction, the sinister singsong of Friend's voice: a demonic outsider, he has arrived to wrest Connie from the protective confines of her family, her home, and her own innocence. Oates makes clear that Friend represents Connie's initiation not into sex itself—she is already sexually experienced—but into sexual bondage: "I promise it won't last long," he tells her, "and you will like me the way you get to like people you're close to. You will. It's all over for you here." As feminist allegory, then, the story describes the beginning of a young and sexually attractive girl's enslavement within a conventional, male-dominated sexual relationship....

While in realistic terms, especially considering the story's source, Connie may be approaching her actual death, in allegorical terms she is dying spiritually, surrendering her autonomous selfhood to male desire and domination. Her characterization as a typical girl reaching sexual maturity suggests that her fate represents that suffered by most young women—unwillingly and in secret terror—even in America in the 1960s. As a feminist allegory, then, "Where Are You Going, Where Have You Been?" is a cautionary tale, suggesting that young women are "going" exactly where their mothers and grandmothers have already "been": into sexual bondage at the hands of a male "Friend."

Understanding Joyce Carol Oates, 1987: 101–02

Larry Rubin argues that Connie has fallen asleep in the sun and has a dream about a composite figure that symbolizes her fear of the adult world. He discusses the references to sleep that frame the Arnold Friend episode and the nightmare quality of her inability to control the situation.

The fact that Connie recognizes the sensual music being broadcast on Arnold's car radio as being the same as that emanating from her own in the house provides another strong clue to his real nature—that of a dream-like projection of her erotic fantasies. His music and hers, Oates tells us, blend perfectly, and indeed Arnold's voice is perceived by Connie as being the same as that of the disc jockey on the radio. Thus the protagonist's inner state of consciousness is being given physical form by her imagination....Connie's initial response to her first view of Arnold the night before, in the shopping center, was one of intense sexual excitement; now she discovers how dangerous that excitement can be to her survival as a person. Instinctively, she recoils; but the conflict between excitement and desire, on the one hand, and fear, on the other, leaves her will paralyzed, and she cannot even dial the phone for help. Such physical paralysis in the face of oncoming danger is a phenomenon familiar to all dreamers, like being unable to run from the monster because your legs won't respond to your will.

Finally, the rather un-devil-like tribute that Arnold pays Connie as she finally succumbs to his threats against her family and goes out of the house to him—"you're better than them [her family] because not a one of them would have done this for you"—is exactly what poor, unappreciated Connie wants to hear. She is making a noble sacrifice, and in her dream she gives herself full credit for it.

Explicator 42 (1984): 57–59

Joyce M. Wegs contends that "Arnold is clearly a symbolic Satan."

As is usual with Satan, he is in disguise; the distortions in his appearance and behavior suggest not only that his identity is faked but also hint at his real self.... When he introduces himself, his name too hints at his identity, for "friend" is uncomfortably close to "fiend"; his initials could well stand for Arch Fiend. The frightened Connie sees Arnold as "only half real": he "had driven up the driveway all right but had come from nowhere before that and belonged nowhere." Especially supernatural is his mysterious knowledge about her, her family, and her friends. At one point, he even seems to be able to see all the way to the barbecue which Connie's family is attending and to get a clear vision of what all the guests are doing.

Journal of Narrative Technique 5 (1975): 69–70

But Mike Tierce and John Micheal Crafton argue for an opposite interpretation: they see Arnold as a savior or messiah figure and base their case on identifying Arnold with Bob Dylan, the popular singer to whom Oates dedicated the story.

In the mid-sixties Bob Dylan's followers perceived him to be a messiah. According to his biographer [Anthony Scaduto], Dylan was a "rock-and-roll king." It is no wonder then that Arnold speaks with "the voice of the man on the radio," the disc jockey whose name, Bobby King, is a reference to "Bobby" Dylan, the "king" of rock-and-roll. Dylan was more than a "friend" to his listeners; he was "Christ revisited," "the prophet leading [his followers] into [a new] Consciousness." In fact, "people were making him an idol;...thousands of men and women, young and old, felt their lives entwined with his because they saw him as a mystic, a messiah who would lead them to salvation."

That Oates consciously associates Arnold Friend with Bob Dylan is clearly suggested by the similarities of their physical descriptions. Arnold's "shaggy, shabby black hair that looked crazy as a wig," his "long and hawk-like" nose, his unshaven face, his "big and white" teeth, his lashes, "thick and black as if painted with a black tarlike material," and his size ("only an inch or so taller than Connie") are all characteristic of Bob Dylan....

Arnold is the personification of popular music, particularly Bob Dylan's music; and as such, Connie's interaction with him is a musically induced fantasy, a kind of "magic carpet ride" in a "convertible jalopy painted gold." Rising out of Connie's radio, Arnold Friend/Bob Dylan is a magical, musical messiah; he persuades Connie to abandon her father's house. As a manifestation of her own desires, he frees her from the limitations of a fifteen-year-old girl, assisting her maturation by stripping her of her childlike vision.

Studies in Short Fiction 22 (1985): 220, 223

Topics for Discussion and Writing

1. Explain the title. Why is it in the form of a question, and why are there two parts to the question? Who does "you" refer to?
2. Who is the story's main character, Connie or Arnold Friend?
3. How do you interpret Arnold? Do you agree with what the critics say about him?
4. What do you think of the various members of Connie's family? Why has Oates limited their roles in the story?
5. Where does Arnold take Connie, and what happens to her? Write your own continuation of the story.
6. Write a comparison between Connie and Eveline (see pages 4–7). Argue that these seemingly different protagonists are similar in several significant ways.

Laura Dern as Connie and Treat Williams as Arnold Friend in *Smooth Talk*, the 1985 film version of "Where Are You Going, Where Have You Been?"

Ideas for Researched Writing

1. In 1986, Oates's story was made into a movie called *Smooth Talk*. Watch the film on video or DVD and read several reviews of it, including the one Oates wrote for the *New York Times* (March 23, 1986). You can run down reviews of *Smooth Talk* on the Internet Movie Database and the Movie Review Query Engine. Oates's review has been reprinted in her collection of essays *(Woman) Writer: Occasions and Opportunities* (1988). Write a paper comparing the movie to the story. Does the film do justice to the story? Respond to Oates's claim that the film's different ending is justified.
2. Oates wrote this story more than forty years ago. How much of the story is a product of its time? Is its picture of teenage culture still accurate and relevant? Are the story's themes and ideas still relevant and meaningful? Write an essay arguing that this story is (or is not) relevant to present-day readers.

Anthology of Short Fiction

Nathaniel Hawthorne 1804–1864

Nathaniel Hawthorne ranks with the great writers of fiction in English. He wrote richly symbolic novels and tales, often involving the supernatural, yet he once declared, "I am not quite sure that I entirely comprehend my own meaning in some of these blasted allegories." The appearance of his masterpiece of hidden guilt and redemption, *The Scarlet Letter* (1850), secured his position as America's foremost romancer. His last years were troubled by the outbreak of the Civil War, and he vehemently declared himself "a man of peace."

The Birthmark

In the latter part of the last century, there lived a man of science—an eminent proficient in every branch of natural philosophy—who, not long before our story opens, had made experience of a spiritual affinity, more attractive than any chemical one. He had left his laboratory to the care of an assistant, cleared his fine countenance from the furnace-smoke, washed the stain of acids from his fingers, and persuaded a beautiful woman to become his wife. In those days, when the comparatively recent discovery of electricity, and other kindred mysteries of nature, seemed to open paths into the region of miracle, it was not unusual for the love of science to rival the love of woman, in its depth and absorbing energy. The higher intellect, the imagination, the spirit, and even the heart, might all find their congenial aliment in pursuits which, as some of their ardent votaries believed, would ascend from one step of powerful intelligence to another, until the philosopher should lay his hand on the secret of creative force, and perhaps make new worlds for himself. We know not whether Aylmer possessed this degree of faith in man's ultimate control over nature. He had devoted himself, however, too unreservedly to scientific studies, ever to be weaned from them by any second passion. His love for his young wife might prove the stronger of the two; but it could only be by intertwining itself with his love of science, and uniting the strength of the latter to its own.

Such a union accordingly took place, and was attended with truly remarkable consequences, and a deeply impressive moral. One day, very soon after their marriage, Aylmer sat gazing at his wife, with a trouble in his countenance that grew stronger, until he spoke.

"Georgiana," said he, "has it never occurred to you that the mark upon your cheek might be removed?"

"No, indeed," said she, smiling; but perceiving the seriousness of his manner, she blushed deeply. "To tell you the truth, it has been so often called a charm, that I was simple enough to imagine it might be so."

5 "Ah, upon another face, perhaps it might," replied her husband. "But never on yours! No, dearest Georgiana, you came so nearly perfectly from the hand of Nature, that this slightest possible defect—which we hesitate whether to term a defect or a beauty—shocks me, as being the visible mark of earthly imperfection."

"Shocks you, my husband!" cried Georgiana, deeply hurt; at first reddening with momentary anger, but then bursting into tears. "Then why did you take me from my mother's side? You cannot love what shocks you!"

To explain this conversation, it must be mentioned, that, in the centre of Georgiana's left cheek, there was a singular mark, deeply interwoven, as it were, with the texture and substance of her face. In the usual state of her complexion—a healthy, though delicate bloom—the mark wore a tint of deeper crimson, which imperfectly defined its shape amid the surrounding rosiness. When she blushed, it gradually became more indistinct, and finally vanished amid the triumphant rush of blood, that bathed the whole cheek with its brilliant glow. But, if any shifting emotion caused her to turn pale, there was the mark again, a crimson stain upon the snow, in what Aylmer sometimes deemed an almost fearful distinctness. Its shape bore not a little similarity to the human hand, though of the smallest pigmy size. Georgiana's lovers were wont to say, that some fairy, at her birth-hour, had laid her tiny hand upon the infant's cheek, and left this impress there, in token of the magic endowments that were to give her such sway over all hearts. Many a desperate swain would have risked life for the privilege of pressing his lips to the mysterious hand. It must not be concealed, however, that the impression wrought by this fairy sign-manual varied exceedingly, according to the difference of temperament in the beholders. Some fastidious persons—but they were exclusively of her own sex—affirmed that the Bloody Hand, as they chose to call it, quite destroyed the effect of Georgiana's beauty, and rendered her countenance even hideous. But it would be as reasonable to say, that one of those small blue stains, which sometimes occur in the purest statuary marble, would convert the Eve of Powers to a monster. Masculine observers, if the birthmark did not heighten their admiration, contented themselves with wishing it away, that the world might possess one living specimen of ideal loveliness, without the semblance of a flaw. After his marriage—for he thought little or nothing of the matter before—Aylmer discovered that this was the case with himself.

Had she been less beautiful—if Envy's self could have found aught else to sneer at—he might have felt his affection heightened by the prettiness of this mimic hand, now vaguely portrayed, now lost, now stealing forth again, and glimmering to-and-fro with every pulse of emotion that throbbed within her heart. But, seeing her otherwise so perfect, he found this one defect grow more and more intolerable, with every moment of their united lives. It was the fatal flaw of humanity, which Nature, in one shape or another, stamps ineffaceably on all her productions, either to imply that they are temporary and finite, or that their perfection must be wrought by toil and pain. The Crimson Hand expressed the ineludible gripe, in which mortality clutches the highest and purest of earthly mould, degrading them into kindred with the lowest, and even with the very brutes, like whom their visible frames return to dust. In this manner, selecting it as the symbol of his wife's liability to sin, sorrow, decay, and death, Alymer's sombre imagination was not long in rendering the birthmark a frightful object, causing him more trouble and horror than ever Georgiana's beauty, whether of soul or sense, had given him delight.

At all the seasons which should have been their happiest, he invariably, and without intending it—nay, in spite of a purpose to the contrary—reverted to this one disastrous topic. Trifling as it at first appeared, it so connected itself with innumerable trains of thought, and modes of feeling, that it became the central point of all. With the morning twilight, Aylmer opened his eyes upon his wife's face, and recognized the symbol of imperfection; and when they sat together at the evening hearth, his eyes wandered stealthily to her cheek, and beheld, flickering with the blaze of the wood fire, the spectral Hand that wrote mortality, where he would fain have worshipped. Georgiana soon learned to shudder at his gaze. It needed but a glance, with the peculiar expression that his face often wore, to change the roses of her cheek into a deathlike paleness, amid which the Crimson Hand was brought strongly out, like a bas-relief of ruby on the whitest marble.

Late, one night, when the lights were growing dim, so as hardly to betray the 10
stain on the poor wife's cheek, she herself, for the first time, voluntarily took up the subject.

"Do you remember, my dear Aylmer," said she, with a feeble attempt at a smile—"have you any recollection of a dream, last night, about this odious Hand?"

"None!—none whatever!" replied Aylmer, starting; but then he added in a dry, cold tone, affected for the sake of concealing the real depth of his emotion:—"I might well dream of it; for before I fell asleep, it had taken a pretty firm hold of my fancy."

"And you did dream of it," continued Georgiana, hastily; for she dreaded lest a gush of tears should interrupt what she had to say—"A terrible dream! I wonder that you can forget it. Is it possible to forget this one expression?—'It is in her heart now—we must have it out!'—Reflect, my husband; for by all means I would have you recall that dream."

The mind is in a sad note, when Sleep, the all-involving, cannot confine her spectres within the dim region of her sway, but suffers them to break forth, affrighting this actual life with secrets that perchance belong to a deeper one. Aylmer now remembered his dream. He had fancied himself with his servant Aminadab, attempting an operation for the removal of the birthmark. But the deeper went the knife, the deeper sank the Hand, until at length its tiny grasp appeared to have caught hold of Georgiana's heart; whence, however, her husband was inexorably resolved to cut or wrench it away.

When the dream had shaped itself perfectly in his memory, Aylmer sat in his 15
wife's presence with a guilty feeling. Truth often finds its way to the mind close-muffled in robes of sleep, and then speaks with uncompromising directness of matters in regard to which we practise an unconscious self-deception, during our waking moments. Until now, he had not been aware of the tyrannizing influence acquired by one idea over his mind, and of the lengths which he might find in his heart to go, for the sake of giving himself peace.

"Aylmer," resumed Georgiana, solemnly, "I know not what may be the cost to both of us, to rid me of this fatal birthmark. Perhaps its removal may cause cureless deformity. Or, it may be, the stain goes as deep as life itself. Again, do we know that there is a possibility, on any terms, of unclasping the firm gripe of this little Hand, which was laid upon me before I came into the world?"

"Dearest Georgiana, I have spent much thought upon the subject," hastily interrupted Aylmer—"I am convinced of the perfect practicability of its removal."

"If there be the remotest possibility of it," continued Georgiana, "let the attempt be made, at whatever risk. Danger is nothing to me; for life—while this hateful mark makes me the object of your horror and disgust—life is a burthen which I would fling down with joy. Either remove this dreadful Hand, or take my wretched life! You have deep science! All the world bears witness of it. You have achieved great wonders! Cannot you remove this little, little mark, which I cover with the tips of two small fingers? Is this beyond your power, for the sake of your own peace, and to save your poor wife from madness?"

"Noblest—dearest—tenderest wife!" cried Aylmer, rapturously. "Doubt not my power. I have already given this matter the deepest thought—thought which might almost have enlightened me to create a being less perfect than yourself. Georgiana, you have led me deeper than ever into the heart of science. I feel myself fully competent to render this dear cheek as faultless as its fellow; and then, most beloved, what will be my triumph, when I shall have corrected what Nature left imperfect, in her fairest work! Even Pygmalion, when his sculptured woman assumed life, felt not greater ecstasy than mine will be."

"It is resolved, then," said Georgiana, faintly smiling,—"And, Aylmer, spare 20
me not, though you should find the birthmark take refuge in my heart at last."

Her husband tenderly kissed her cheek—her right cheek—not that which bore the impress of the Crimson Hand.

The next day, Aylmer apprized his wife of a plan that he had formed, whereby he might have opportunity for the intense thought and constant watchfulness, which the proposed operation would require; while Georgiana, likewise, would enjoy the perfect repose essential to its success. They were to seclude themselves in the extensive apartments occupied by Aylmer as a laboratory, and where, during his toilsome youth, he had made discoveries in the elemental powers of nature that had roused the admiration of all the learned societies in Europe. Seated calmly in this laboratory, the pale philosopher had investigated the secrets of the highest cloud-region, and of the profoundest mines; he had satisfied himself of the causes that kindled and kept alive the fires of the volcano; and had explained the mystery of fountains, and how it is that they gush forth, some so bright and pure, and others with such rich medicinal virtues, from the dark bosom of the earth. Here, too, at an earlier period, he had studied the wonders of the human frame, and attempted to fathom the very process by which Nature assimilates all her precious influences from earth and air, and from the spiritual world, to create and foster Man, her masterpiece. The latter pursuit, however, Aylmer had long laid aside, in unwilling recognition of the truth, against which all seekers sooner or later stumble, that our great creative Mother, while she amuses us with apparently working in the broadest sunshine, is yet severely careful to keep her own secrets, and, in spite of her pretended openness, shows us nothing but results. She permits us indeed, to mar, but seldom to mend, and, like a jealous patentee, on no account to make. Now, however, Aylmer resumed these half-forgotten investigations; not, of course, with such hopes or wishes as first suggested them; but because they involved much physiological truth, and lay in the path of his proposed scheme for the treatment of Georgiana.

As he led her over the threshold of the laboratory, Georgiana was cold and tremulous. Aylmer looked cheerfully into her face, with intent to reassure her, but was so startled with the intense glow of the birthmark upon the whiteness of her cheek, that he could not restrain a strong convulsive shudder. His wife fainted.

"Aminadab! Aminadab!" shouted Aylmer, stamping violently on the floor.

Forthwith, there issued from an inner apartment a man of low stature, but bulky frame, with shaggy hair hanging about his visage, which was grimed with the vapors of the furnace. This personage had been Aylmer's under-worker during his whole scientific career, and was admirably fitted for that office by his great mechanical readiness, and the skill with which, while incapable of comprehending a single principle, he executed all the practical details of his master's experiments. With his vast strength, his shaggy hair, his smoky aspect, and the indescribable earthiness that incrusted him, he seemed to represent man's physical nature; while Aylmer's slender figure, and pale, intellectual face, were no less apt a type of the spiritual element.

"Throw open the door of the boudoir, Aminadab," said Aylmer, "and burn a pastille."

"Yes, master," answered Aminadab, looking intently at the lifeless form of Georgiana; and then he muttered to himself:—"If she were my wife, I'd never part with that birthmark."

When Georgiana recovered consciousness, she found herself breathing an atmosphere of penetrating fragrance, the gentle potency of which had recalled her from her deathlike faintness. The scene around her looked like enchantment. Aylmer had converted those smoky, dingy, sombre rooms, where he had spent his brightest years in recondite pursuits, into a series of beautiful apartments, not unfit to be the secluded abode of a lovely woman. The walls were hung with gorgeous curtains, which imparted the combination of grandeur and grace, that no other species of adornment can achieve; and as they fell from the ceiling to the floor, their rich and ponderous folds, concealing all angles and straight lines, appeared to shut in the scene from infinite space. For aught Georgiana knew, it might be a pavilion among the clouds. And Aylmer, excluding the sunshine, which would have interfered with his chemical processes, had supplied its place with perfumed lamps, emitting flames of various hue, but all uniting in a soft, empurpled radiance. He now knelt by his wife's side, watching her earnestly, but without alarm; for he was confident in his science, and felt that he could draw a magic circle round her, within which no evil might intrude.

"Where am I?—Ah, I remember!" said Georgiana, faintly; and she placed her hand over her cheek, to hide the terrible mark from her husband's eyes.

"Fear not, dearest!" exclaimed he. "Do not shrink from me! Believe me, Georgiana, I even rejoice in this single imperfection, since it will be such rapture to remove it."

"Oh, spare me!" sadly replied his wife—"Pray do not look at it again. I never can forget that convulsive shudder."

In order to soothe Georgiana, and, as it were, to release her mind from the burthen of actual things, Aylmer now put in practice some of the light and playful secrets, which science had taught him among its profounder lore. Airy figures, absolutely bodiless ideas, and forms of unsubstantial beauty came and danced before her, imprinting their momentary footsteps on beams of light. Though she had some indistinct idea of the method of these optical phenomena, still the illusion was almost perfect enough to warrant the belief, that her husband possessed sway over the spiritual world. Then again, when she felt a wish to look forth from her seclusion, immediately, as if her thoughts were answered, the procession of external existence flitted across a screen. The scenery and the figures of actual life were perfectly represented, but with that bewitching, yet indescribable difference, which always makes a picture, an image, or a shadow, so much more attractive than the original. When wearied of this, Aylmer bade her cast her eyes upon a vessel, containing a quantity of earth. She did so, with little interest at first, but was soon startled to perceive the germ of a plant, shooting upward from the soil. Then came the slender stalk—the leaves gradually unfolded themselves—and amid them was a perfect and lovely flower.

"It is magical!" cried Georgiana, "I dare not touch it."

"Nay, pluck it," answered Aylmer, "pluck it, and inhale its brief perfume while you may. The flower will wither in a few moments, and leave nothing save its brown seed-vessels—but thence may be perpetuated a race as ephemeral as itself."

But Georgiana had no sooner touched the flower than the whole plant suf- 35
fered a blight, its leaves turning coal-black, as if by the agency of fire.

"There was too powerful a stimulus," said Aylmer thoughtfully.

To make up for this abortive experiment, he proposed to take her portrait by a scientific process of his own invention. It was to be effected by rays of light striking upon a polished plate of metal. Georgiana assented—but, on looking at the result, was affrighted to find the features of the portrait blurred and indefinable; while the minute figure of a hand appeared where the cheek should have been. Aylmer snatched the metallic plate, and threw it into a jar of corrosive acid.

Soon, however, he forgot these mortifying failures. In the intervals of study and chemical experiment, he came to her, flushed and exhausted, but seemed invigorated by her presence, and spoke in glowing language of the resources of his art. He gave a history of the long dynasty of the Alchemists, who spent so many ages in quest of the universal solvent, by which the Golden Principle might be elicted from all things vile and base. Aylmer appeared to believe that, by the plainest scientific logic, it was altogether within the limits of possibility to discover this long-sought medium; but, he added, a philosopher who should go deep enough to acquire the power, would attain too lofty a wisdom to stoop to the exercise of it. Not less singular were his opinions in regard to the Elixir Vitæ. He more than intimated, that it was his option to concoct a liquid that should prolong life for years—perhaps interminably—but that it would produce a discord in nature, which all the world, and chiefly the quaffer of the immortal nostrum, would find cause to curse.

"Aylmer, are you in earnest?" asked Georgiana, looking at him with amazement and fear; "it is terrible to possess such power, or even to dream of possessing it!"

"Oh, do not tremble, my love!" said her husband, "I would not wrong either 40
you or myself by working such inharmonious effects upon our lives. But I would have you consider how trifling, in comparison, is the skill requisite to remove this little Hand."

At the mention of the birthmark, Georgiana, as usual, shrank, as if a red-hot iron had touched her cheek.

Again Aylmer applied himself to his labors. She could hear his voice in the distant furnace-room, giving directions to Aminadab, whose harsh, uncouth, misshapen tones were audible in response, more like the grunt or growl of a brute than human speech. After hours of absence, Aylmer reappeared, and proposed that she should now examine his cabinet of chemical products, and natural treasures of the earth. Among the former he showed her a small vial, in which, he remarked, was contained a gentle yet most powerful fragrance, capable of impregnating all the breezes that blow across a kingdom. They were of inestimable value, the contents of that little vial; and, as he said so, he threw some of the perfume into the air, and filled the room with piercing and invigorating delight.

"And what is this?" asked Georgiana, pointing to a small crystal globe, containing a gold-colored liquid. "It is so beautiful to the eye, that I could imagine it the Elixir of Life."

"In one sense it is," replied Aylmer, "or rather the Elixir of Immortality. It is the most precious poison that ever was concocted in this world. By its aid, I could apportion the lifetime of any mortal at whom you might point your finger. The strength of the dose would determine whether he were to linger out years, or drop dead in the midst of a breath. No king, on his guarded throne, could keep his life, if I, in my private station, should deem that the welfare of millions justified me in depriving him of it."

"Why do you keep such a terrific drug?" inquired Georgiana in horror. 45

"Do not mistrust me, dearest!" said her husband, smiling; "its virtuous potency is yet greater than its harmful one. But, see! here is a powerful cosmetic. With a few drops of this, in a vase of water, freckles may be washed away as easily as the hands are cleansed. A stronger infusion would take the blood out of the cheek, and leave the rosiest beauty a pale ghost."

"Is it with this lotion that you intend to bathe my cheek?" asked Georgiana anxiously.

"Oh, no!" hastily replied her husband—"this is merely superficial. Your case demands a remedy that shall go deeper."

In his interviews with Georgiana, Aylmer generally made minute inquiries as to her sensations, and whether the confinement of the rooms, and the temperature of the atmosphere, agreed with her. These questions had such a particular drift, that Georgiana began to conjecture that she was already subjected to certain physical influences, either breathed in with the fragrant air, or taken with her food. She fancied, likewise—but it might be altogether fancy—that there was a stirring up of her system—a strange indefinite sensation creeping through her veins, and tingling, half painfully, half pleasurably, at her heart. Still, whenever she dared to look into the mirror, there she beheld herself, pale as a white rose, and with the crimson birthmark stamped upon her cheek. Not even Aylmer now hated it so much as she.

To dispel the tedium of the hours which her husband found it necessary to 50
devote to the processes of combination and analysis, Georgiana turned over the volumes of his scientific library. In many dark old tomes, she met with chapters full of romance and poetry. They were the works of the philosophers of the middle ages, such as Albertus Magnus, Cornelius Agrippa, Paracelsus, and the famous friar who created the prophetic Brazen Head. All these antique naturalists stood in advance of their centuries, yet were imbued with some of their credulity, and therefore were believed, and perhaps imagined themselves, to have acquired from the investigation of nature a power above nature, and from physics a sway over the spiritual world. Hardly less curious and imaginative were the early volumes of the Transactions of the Royal Society, in which the members, knowing little of the limits of natural possibility, were continually recording wonders, or proposing methods whereby wonders might be wrought.

But, to Georgiana, the most engrossing volume was a large folio from her husband's own hand, in which he had recorded every experiment of his scientific career, with its original aim, the methods adopted for its development, and its final success or failure, with the circumstances to which either event was attributable. The book, in truth, was both the history and emblem of his ardent, ambitious, imaginative, yet practical and laborious, life. He handled physical details, as if there were nothing beyond them; yet spiritualized them all, and redeemed himself from materialism, by his strong and eager aspiration towards the infinite. In his grasp, the veriest clod of earth assumed a soul. Georgiana, as she read, reverenced Aylmer, and loved him more profoundly than ever, but with a less entire dependence on his judgment than heretofore. Much as he had accomplished, she could not but observe that his most splendid successes were almost invariably failures, if compared with the ideal at which he aimed. His brightest diamonds were the merest pebbles, and felt to be so by himself, in comparison with the inestimable gems which lay hidden beyond his reach. The volume, rich with achievements that had won renown for its author, was yet as melancholy a record as ever mortal hand had penned. It was the sad confession, and continual exemplification, of the short-comings of the composite man—the spirit burthened with clay and working in matter—and of the despair that assails the higher nature, at finding itself so miserably thwarted by the earthly part. Perhaps every man of genius, in whatever sphere, might recognize the image of his own experience in Aylmer's journal.

So deeply did these reflections affect Georgiana, that she laid her face upon the open volume, and burst into tears. In this situation she was found by her husband.

"It is dangerous to read in a sorcerer's books," said he, with a smile, though his countenance was uneasy and displeased. "Georgiana, there are pages in that volume, which I can scarcely glance over and keep my senses. Take heed lest it prove as detrimental to you!"

"It has made me worship you more than ever," said she.

"Ah! wait for this one success," rejoined he, "then worship me if you will. I shall deem myself hardly unworthy of it. But, come! I have sought you for the luxury of your voice. Sing to me, dearest!"

So she poured out the liquid music of her voice to quench the thirst of his spirit. He then took his leave, with a boyish exuberance of gaiety, assuring her that her seclusion would endure but a little longer, and that the result was already certain. Scarcely had he departed, when Georgiana felt irresistibly impelled to follow him. She had forgotten to inform Aylmer of a symptom, which, for two or three hours past, had begun to excite her attention. It was a sensation in the fatal birthmark, not painful, but which induced a restlessness throughout her system. Hastening after her husband, she intruded, for the first time, into the laboratory.

The first thing that struck her eye was the furnace, that hot and feverish worker, with the intense glow of its fire, which, by the quantities of soot clustered above it, seemed to have been burning for ages. There was a distilling apparatus in full operation. Around the room were retorts, tubes, cylinders, crucibles, and other apparatus of chemical research. An electrical machine stood ready for immediate use. The atmosphere felt oppressively close, and was tainted with gaseous odors, which had been tormented forth by the processes of science. The severe and homely simplicity of the apartment, with its naked walls and brick pavement, looked strange, accustomed as Georgiana had become to the fantastic elegance of her boudoir. But what chiefly, indeed almost solely, drew her attention, was the aspect of Aylmer himself.

He was pale as death, anxious, and absorbed, and hung over the furnace as if it depended upon his utmost watchfulness whether the liquid, which it was distilling, should be the draught of immortal happiness or misery. How different from the sanguine and joyous mien that he had assumed for Georgiana's encouragement!

"Carefully now, Aminadab! Carefully, thou human machine! Carefully, thou man of clay!" muttered Aylmer, more to himself than his assistant. "Now, if there be a thought too much or too little, it is all over!"

"Hoh! hoh!" mumbled Aminadab—"look, master, look!"

Aylmer raised his eyes hastily, and at first reddened, then grew paler than ever, on beholding Georgiana. He rushed towards her, and seized her arm with a gripe that left the print of his fingers upon it.

"Why do you come hither? Have you no trust in your husband?" cried he impetuously. "Would you throw the blight of that fatal birthmark over my labors? It is not well done. Go, prying woman, go!"

"Nay, Aylmer," said Georgiana, with the firmness of which she possessed no stinted endowment, "it is not you that have a right to complain. You mistrust your wife! You have concealed the anxiety with which you watch the development of this experiment. Think not so unworthily of me, my husband! Tell me all the risk we run; and fear not that I shall shrink, for my share in it is far less than your own!"

"No, no, Georgiana!" said Aylmer impatiently, "it must not be."

"I submit," replied she calmly. "And, Aylmer, I shall quaff whatever draught you bring me; but it will be on the same principle that would induce me to take a dose of poison, if offered by your hand."

"My noble wife," said Aylmer, deeply moved, "I knew not the height and depth of your nature, until now. Nothing shall be concealed. Know, then, that this Crimson Hand, superficial as it seems, has clutched its grasp into your being, with a strength of which I had no previous conception. I have already administered agents powerful enough to do aught except to change your entire physical system. Only one thing remains to be tried. If that fail us, we are ruined!"

"Why did you hesitate to tell me this?" asked she.

"Because, Georgiana," said Aylmer, in a low voice, "there is danger!"

"Danger? There is but one danger—that this horrible stigma shall be left upon my cheek!" cried Georgiana. "Remove it! remove it!—whatever be the cost—or we shall both go mad!"

"Heaven knows, your words are too true," said Aylmer, sadly. "And now, dearest, return to your boudoir. In a little while, all will be tested."

He conducted her back, and took leave of her with a solemn tenderness, which spoke far more than his words how much was now at stake. After his departure, Georgiana became wrapt in musings. She considered the character of Aylmer, and did it completer justice than at any previous moment. Her heart exulted, while it trembled, at his honorable love, so pure and lofty that it would accept nothing less than perfection, nor miserably make itself contented with an earthlier nature than he had dreamed of. She felt how much more precious was such a sentiment, than that meaner kind which would have borne with the imperfection for her sake, and have been guilty of treason to holy love, by degrading its perfect idea to the level of the actual. And, with her whole spirit, she prayed, that, for a single moment, she might satisfy his highest and deepest conception. Longer than one moment, she well knew, it could not be; for his spirit was ever on the march—ever ascending—and each instant required something that was beyond the scope of the instant before.

The sound of her husband's footsteps aroused her. He bore a crystal goblet, containing a liquor colorless as water, but bright enough to be the draught of immortality. Aylmer was pale; but it seemed rather the consequence of a highly wrought state of mind, and tension of spirit, than of fear or doubt.

"The concoction of the draught has been perfect," said he, in answer to Georgiana's look. "Unless all my science have deceived me, it cannot fail."

"Save on your account, my dearest Aylmer," observed his wife, "I might wish to put off this birthmark of mortality by relinquishing mortality itself, in preference to any other mode. Life is but a sad possession to those who have attained precisely the degree of moral advancement at which I stand. Were I weaker and blinder, it might be happiness. Were I stronger, it might be endured hopefully. But, being what I find myself, methinks I am of all mortals the most fit to die."

"You are fit for heaven without tasting death!" replied her husband. "But why 75
do we speak of dying? The draught cannot fail. Behold its effect upon this plant!"

On the window-seat there stood a geranium, diseased with yellow blotches, which had overspread all its leaves. Aylmer poured a small quantity of the liquid upon the soil in which it grew. In a little time, when the roots of the plant had taken up the moisture, the unsightly blotches began to be extinguished in a living verdure.

"There needed no proof," said Georgiana, quietly. "Give me the goblet. I joyfully stake all upon your word."

"Drink, then, thou lofty creature!" exclaimed Aylmer, with fervid admiration. "There is no taint of imperfection on thy spirit. Thy sensible frame, too, shall soon be all perfect!"

She quaffed the liquid, and returned the goblet to his hand.

"It is grateful," said she, with a placid smile. "Methinks it is like water from a 80
heavenly fountain; for it contains I know not what of unobtrusive fragrance and deliciousness. It allays feverish thirst, that had parched me for many days. Now, dearest, let me sleep. My earthly senses are closing over my spirit, like the leaves round the heart of a rose, at sunset."

She spoke the last words with a gentle reluctance, as if it required almost more energy than she could command to pronounce the faint and lingering syllables. Scarcely had they loitered through her lips, ere she was lost in slumber. Aylmer sat by her side, watching her aspect with the emotions proper to a man, the whole value of whose existence was involved in the process now to be tested. Mingled with this mood, however, was the philosophic investigation, characteristic of the man of science. Not the minutest symptom escaped him. A heightened flush of the cheek—a slight irregularity of breath—a quiver of the eyelid—a hardly perceptible tremor through the frame—such were the details which, as the moments passed, he wrote down in his folio volume. Intense thought had set its stamp upon every previous page of that volume; but the thoughts of years were all concentrated upon the last.

While thus employed, he failed not to gaze often at the fatal Hand, and not without a shudder. Yet once, by a strange and unaccountable impulse, he pressed it with his lips. His spirit recoiled, however, in the very act, and Georgiana, out of the midst of her deep sleep, moved uneasily and murmured, as if in remonstrance. Again, Aylmer resumed his watch. Nor was it without avail. The Crimson Hand, which at first had been strongly visible upon the marble paleness of Georgiana's cheek now grew more faintly outlined. She remained not less pale than ever; but the birthmark, with every breath that came and went, lost somewhat of its former distinctness. Its presence had been awful; its departure was more awful still. Watch the stain of the rainbow fading out of the sky; and you will know how that mysterious symbol passed away.

"By Heaven, it is well nigh gone!" said Aylmer to himself, in almost irrepressible ecstasy. "I can scarcely trace it now. Success! Success! And now it is like the faintest rose-color. The slightest flush of blood across her cheek would overcome it. But she is so pale!"

He drew aside the window-curtain, and suffered the light of natural day to fall into the room, and rest upon her cheek. At the same time, he heard a gross, hoarse chuckle, which he had long known as his servant Aminadab's expression of delight.

"Ah, clod! Ah, earthly mass!" cried Aylmer, laughing in a sort of frenzy. 85
"You have served me well! Matter and Spirit—Earth and Heaven—have both done their part in this! Laugh, thing of senses! You have earned the right to laugh."

These exclamations broke Georgiana's sleep. She slowly unclosed her eyes, and gazed into the mirror, which her husband had arranged for that purpose. A faint smile flitted over her lips, when she recognized how barely perceptible was now that Crimson Hand, which had once blazed forth with such disastrous brilliancy as to scare away all their happiness. But then her eyes sought Aylmer's face, with a trouble and anxiety that he could by no means account for.

"My poor Aylmer!" murmured she.

"Poor? Nay, richest! Happiest! Most favored!" exclaimed he. "My peerless bride, it is successful! You are perfect!"

"My poor Aylmer!" she repeated, with a more than human tenderness. "You have aimed loftily!—you have done nobly! Do not repent, that, with so high and pure a feeling, you have rejected the best that earth could offer. Aylmer—dearest Aylmer—I am dying!"

Alas, it was too true! The fatal Hand had grappled with the mystery of life, 90
and was the bond by which an angelic spirit kept itself in union with a mortal frame. As the last crimson tint of the birthmark—that sole token of human imperfection—faded from her cheek, the parting breath of the now perfect woman passed into the atmosphere, and her soul, lingering a moment near her husband, took its heavenward flight. Then a hoarse, chuckling laugh was heard again! Thus ever does the gross Fatality of Earth exult in its invariable triumph over the immortal essence, which, in this dim sphere of half-development, demands the completeness of a higher state. Yet, had Aylmer reached a profounder wisdom, he need not thus have flung away the happiness, which would have woven his mortal life of the self-same texture with the celestial. The momentary circumstance was too strong for him; he failed to look beyond the shadowy scope of Time, and living once for all in Eternity to find the perfect Future in the present.

(1843)

Questions for Discussion and Writing

1. This story is often seen as a partial allegory. What concepts does each of the three characters stand for? In what way is each one flawed?
2. Is it significant that the birthmark is in the shape of a hand?
3. How would you state the conflict in the story?
4. What is the meaning of the allegory? In other words, what is Hawthorne's theme? Is it still relevant today?
5. Write an essay arguing that Georgiana is complicit in her own fate by encouraging Aylmer's folly.

Edgar Allan Poe 1809–1849

Edgar Allan Poe was born in Boston to parents who were actors. His father abandoned the family, and his mother died when Poe was only two. Taken in by a wealthy tobacco merchant, he enjoyed a happy childhood in Richmond. After a brief stay at the University of Virginia, Poe married and moved to Boston, where he began publishing poetry. His foster father sent him to West Point, but he was expelled for gambling and not attending class. Divorced and working as a journalist in New York and Baltimore, he married his thirteen-year-old cousin in 1835. It was during this time that Poe began writing the tales of horror and the supernatural for which he is best known. In 1845, he published his poem "The Raven" to great success. He died four years later in Baltimore after a drinking binge.

The Cask of Amontillado

The thousand injuries of Fortunato I had borne as I best could, but when he ventured upon insult I vowed revenge. You, who so well know the nature of my soul, will not suppose, however, that I gave utterance to a threat. *At length* I would be avenged; this was a point definitely settled—but the very definitiveness with which it was resolved precluded the idea of risk. I must not only punish but punish with impunity. A wrong is unredressed when retribution overtakes its redresser. It is equally unredressed when the avenger fails to make himself felt as such to him who has done the wrong.

It must be understood that neither by word nor by deed had I given Fortunato cause to doubt my good will. I continued, as was my wont, to smile in his face, and he did not perceive that my smile *now* was at the thought of his immolation.

He had a weak point—this Fortunato—although in other regards he was a man to be respected and even feared. He prided himself on his connoisseurship in wine. Few Italians have the true virtuoso spirit. For the most part their enthusiasm is adopted to suit the time and opportunity, to practise imposture upon the British and Austrian *millionaires*. In painting and gemmary, Fortunato, like his countrymen, was a quack, but in the matter of old wines he was sincere.

In this respect I did not differ from him materially;—I was skillful in the Italian vintages myself, and bought largely whenever I could.

It was about dusk, one evening during the supreme madness of the carnival season, that I encountered my friend. He accosted me with excessive warmth, for he had been drinking much. The man wore motley.[1] He had on a tight-fitting parti-striped dress, and his head was surmounted by the conical cap and bells. I was so pleased to see him that I thought I should never have done wringing his hand.

I said to him—"My dear Fortunato, you are luckily met. How remarkably well you are looking to-day. But I have received a pipe[2] of what passes for Amontillado,[3] and I have my doubts."

"How?" said he. "Amontillado? A pipe? Impossible! And in the middle of the carnival!"

"I have my doubts," I replied; "and I was silly enough to pay the full Amontillado price without consulting you in the matter. You were not to be found, and I was fearful of losing a bargain."

"Amontillado!"

"I have my doubts."

"Amontillado!"

"And I must satisfy them."

"Amontillado!"

"As you are engaged, I am on my way to Luchesi. If any one has a critical turn it is he. He will tell me—"

"Luchesi cannot tell Amontillado from Sherry."

"And yet some fools will have it that his taste is a match for your own."

"Come, let us go."

"Whither?"

"To your vaults."

"My friend, no; I will not impose upon your good nature. I perceive you have an engagement. Luchesi—"

"I have no engagement;—come."

"My friend, no. It is not the engagement, but the severe cold with which I perceive you are afflicted. The vaults are insufferably damp. They are encrusted with nitre."[4]

"Let us go, nevertheless. The cold is merely nothing. Amontillado! You have been imposed upon. And as for Luchesi, he cannot distinguish Sherry from Amontillado."

Thus speaking, Fortunato possessed himself of my arm; and putting on a mask of black silk and drawing a *roquelaire*[5] closely about my person, I suffered him to hurry me to my palazzo.

There were no attendants at home; they had absconded to make merry in honor of the time. I had told them that I should not return until the morning, and had given them explicit orders not to stir from the house. These orders were sufficient, I well knew, to insure their immediate disappearance, one and all, as soon as my back was turned.

---

[1]A clown costume.
[2]A large wine cask.
[3]An expensive pale, dry wine.
[4]Potassium nitrate, a preservative.
[5]A heavy, silk-lined cloak.

25 I took from their sconces two flambeaux, and giving one to Fortunato, bowed him through several suites of rooms to the archway that led into the vaults. I passed down a long and winding staircase, requesting him to be cautious as he followed. We came at length to the foot of the descent, and stood together upon the damp ground of the catacombs of the Montresors.

The gait of my friend was unsteady, and the bells upon his cap jingled as he strode.

"The pipe?" he said.

"It is farther on," said I; "but observe the white web-work which gleams from these cavern walls."

He turned towards me, and looked into my eyes with two filmy orbs that distilled the rheum of intoxication.

30 "Nitre?" he asked at length.

"Nitre," I replied. "How long have you had that cough?"

"Ugh! ugh! ugh!—ugh! ugh! ugh!—ugh! ugh! ugh!—ugh! ugh! ugh!—ugh! ugh! ugh!"

My poor friend found it impossible to reply for many minutes.

"It is nothing," he said at last.

35 "Come," I said, with decision, "we will go back; your health is precious. You are rich, respected, admired, beloved; you are happy, as once I was. You are a man to be missed. For me it is no matter. We will go back; you will be ill, and I cannot be responsible. Besides, there is Luchesi—"

"Enough," he said; "the cough is a mere nothing; it will not kill me. I shall not die of a cough."

"True—true," I replied; "and, indeed, I had no intention of alarming you unnecessarily—but you should use all proper caution. A draught of this Medoc will defend us from the damps."

Here I knocked off the neck of a bottle which I drew from a long row of its fellows that lay upon the mould.

"Drink," I said, presenting him the wine.

40 He raised it to his lips with a leer. He paused and nodded to me familiarly, while his bells jingled.

"I drink," he said, "to the buried that repose around us."

"And I to your long life."

He again took my arm, and we proceeded.

"These vaults," he said, "are extensive."

45 "The Montresors," I replied, "were a great and numerous family."

"I forget your arms."

"A huge human foot d'or,[6] in a field azure; the foot crushes a serpent rampant whose fangs are imbedded in the heel."

"And the motto?"

"*Nemo me impune lacessit.*"[7]

50 "Good!" he said.

The wine sparkled in his eyes and the bells jingled. My own fancy grew warm with the Medoc. We had passed through walls of piled bones, with casks and puncheons intermingling, into the inmost recesses of the catacombs. I paused again, and this time I made bold to seize Fortunato by an arm above the elbow.

---

[6] Of gold.

[7] "No one attacks me without paying dearly."

"The nitre!" I said; "see, it increases. It hangs like moss upon the vaults. We are below the river's bed. The drops of moisture trickle among the bones. Come, we will go back ere it is too late. Your cough—"

"It is nothing," he said; "let us go on. But first, another draught of the Medoc."

I broke and reached him a flagon of De Grâve. He emptied it at a breath. His eyes flashed with a fierce light. He laughed and threw the bottle upwards with a gesticulation I did not understand.

I looked at him in surprise. He repeated the movement—a grotesque one.

"You do not comprehend?" he said.

"Not I," I replied.

"Then you are not of the brotherhood."

"How?"

"You are not of the masons."

"Yes, yes," I said; "yes, yes."

"You? Impossible! A mason?"

"A mason," I replied.

"A sign," he said.

"It is this," I answered, producing a trowel from beneath the folds of my *roquelaire*.

"You jest," he exclaimed, recoiling a few paces. "But let us proceed to the Amontillado."

"Be it so," I said, replacing the tool beneath the cloak and again offering him my arm. He leaned upon it heavily. We continued our route in search of the Amontillado. We passed through a range of low arches, descended, passed on, and descending again, arrived at a deep crypt, in which the foulness of the air caused our flambeaux rather to glow than flame.

At the most remote end of the crypt there appeared another less spacious. Its walls had been lined with human remains, piled to the vault overhead, in the fashion of the great catacombs of Paris. Three sides of this interior crypt were still ornamented in this manner. From the fourth side the bones had been thrown down, and lay promiscuously[8] upon the earth, forming at one point a mound of some size. Within the wall thus exposed by the displacing of the bones, we perceived a still interior crypt or recess, in depth about four feet, in width three, in height six or seven. It seemed to have been constructed for no especial use within itself, but formed merely the interval between two of the colossal supports of the roof of the catacombs, and was backed by one of their circumscribing walls of solid granite.

It was in vain that Fortunato, uplifting his dull torch, endeavored to pry into the depths of the recess. Its termination the feeble light did not enable us to see.

"Proceed," I said; "herein is the Amontillado. As for Luchesi—"

"He is an ignoramus," interrupted my friend, as he stepped unsteadily forward, while I followed immediately at his heels. In an instant he had reached the extremity of the niche, and finding his progress arrested by the rock, stood stupidly bewildered. A moment more and I had fettered him to the granite. In its surface were two iron staples, distant from each other about two feet, horizontally. From one of these depended a short chain, from the other a padlock. Throwing the links about his waist, it was but the work of a few seconds to secure it. He was too much astounded to resist. Withdrawing the key I stepped back from the recess.

---

[8]Mixed together.

"Pass your hand," I said, "over the wall; you cannot help feeling the nitre. Indeed, it is *very* damp. Once more let me *implore* you to return. No? Then I must positively leave you. But I must first render you all the little attentions in my power."

"The Amontillado!" ejaculated my friend, not yet recovered from his astonishment.

"True," I replied; "the Amontillado."

As I said these words I busied myself among the pile of bones of which I have 75
before spoken. Throwing them aside, I soon uncovered a quantity of building stone and mortar. With these materials and with the aid of my trowel, I began vigorously to wall up the entrance of the niche.

I had scarcely laid the first tier of the masonry when I discovered that the intoxication of Fortunato had in a great measure worn off. The earliest indication I had of this was a low moaning cry from the depth of the recess. It was *not* the cry of a drunken man. There was a long and obstinate silence. I laid the second tier, and the third, and the fourth; and then I heard the furious vibrations of the chain. The noise lasted for several minutes, during which, that I might hearken to it with the more satisfaction, I ceased my labors and sat down upon the bones. When at last the clanking subsided, I resumed the trowel, and finished without interruption the fifth, the sixth, and the seventh tier. The wall was now nearly upon a level with my breast. I again paused, and holding the flambeaux over the mason-work, threw a few feeble rays upon the figure within.

A succession of loud and shrill screams, bursting suddenly from the throat of the chained form, seemed to thrust me violently back. For a brief moment I hesitated, I trembled. Unsheathing my rapier, I began to grope with it about the recess; but the thought of an instant reassured me. I placed my hand upon the solid fabric of the catacombs, and felt satisfied. I reapproached the wall; I replied to the yells of him who clamoured. I re-echoed, I aided, I surpassed them in volume and in strength. I did this, and the clamourer grew still.

It was now midnight, and my task was drawing to a close. I had completed the eighth, the ninth, and the tenth tier. I had finished a portion of the last and the eleventh; there remained but a single stone to be fitted and plastered in. I struggled with its weight; I placed it partially in its destined position. But now there came from out the niche a low laugh that erected the hairs upon my head. It was succeeded by a sad voice, which I had difficulty in recognizing as that of the noble Fortunato. The voice said—

"Ha! ha! ha!—he! he! he!—a very good joke, indeed—an excellent jest. We will have many a rich laugh about it at the palazzo—he! he! he!—over our wine—he! he! he!"

"The Amontillado!" I said. 80

"He! he! he!—he! he! he!—yes, the Amontillado. But is it not getting late? Will not they be awaiting us at the palazzo, the Lady Fortunato and the rest? Let us be gone."

"Yes," I said, "let us be gone."

"*For the love of God, Montresor!*"

"Yes," I said, "for the love of God."

But to these words I hearkened in vain for a reply. I grew impatient. I called 85
aloud—

"Fortunato!"

No answer. I called again—

"Fortunato!"

No answer still. I thrust a torch through the remaining aperture and let it fall within. There came forth in return only a jingling of the bells. My heart grew sick; it was the dampness of the catacombs that made it so. I hastened to make an end of my labor. I forced the last stone into its position; I plastered it up. Against the new masonry I re-erected the old rampart of bones. For the half of a century no mortal has disturbed them. *In pace requiescat!*[9]

(1846)

Questions for Discussion and Writing

1. Why is the first-person point of view particularly well chosen?
2. Why does Poe not tell us the nature of the insult or describe any of the "thousand injuries" that the narrator suffered?
3. How does the setting contribute to the effectiveness of the story?
4. Why is Luchesi mentioned? What other examples of reverse psychology does the narrator employ?
5. Write an interpretation that makes a major claim about Montresor's character.

Kate Chopin 1851–1904

Kate Chopin was born Kate O'Flaherty in St. Louis. After her father died in a train accident when she was four, she was raised by her mother, grandmother, and great-grandmother—all widows. In 1870 she married Oscar Chopin, the son of a wealthy cotton-growing family. After their marriage, they lived in New Orleans, where she had five boys and two girls, all before she was twenty-eight. When Oscar died of swamp fever in 1882, Kate returned to St. Louis, and to support her young family, began to write stories about people she had known in Louisiana. Her explorations of female sexuality and her championing of women's self-worth in her fiction were so shocking that she was denied membership in the St. Louis Literary Society.

Désirée's Baby

As the day was pleasant, Madame Valmondé drove over to L'Abri to see Désirée and the baby.

It made her laugh to think of Désirée with a baby. Why, it seemed but yesterday that Désirée was little more than a baby herself; when Monsieur in

[9]Let him rest in peace!

riding through the gateway of Valmondé had found her lying asleep in the shadow of the big stone pillar.

The little one awoke in his arms and began to cry for "Dada." That was as much as she could do or say. Some people thought she might have strayed there of her own accord, for she was of the toddling age. The prevailing belief was that she had been purposely left by a party of Texans, whose canvas-covered wagon, late in the day, had crossed the ferry that Coton Maïs kept, just below the plantation. In time Madame Valmondé abandoned every speculation but the one that Désirée had been sent to her by a beneficent Providence to be the child of her affection, seeing that she was without child of the flesh. For the girl grew to be beautiful and gentle, affectionate and sincere,—the idol of Valmondé.

It was no wonder, when she stood one day against the stone pillar in whose shadow she had lain asleep, eighteen years before, that Armand Aubigny riding by and seeing her there, had fallen in love with her. That was the way all the Aubignys fell in love, as if struck by a pistol shot. The wonder was that he had not loved her before; for he had known her since his father brought him home from Paris, a boy of eight, after his mother died there. The passion that awoke in him that day, when he saw her at the gate, swept along like an avalanche, or like a prairie fire, or like anything that drives headlong over all obstacles.

5 Monsieur Valmondé grew practical and wanted things well considered; that is, the girl's obscure origin. Armand looked into her eyes and did not care. He was reminded that she was nameless. What did it matter about a name when he could give her one of the oldest and proudest in Louisiana? He ordered the *corbeille*[1] from Paris, and contained himself with what patience he could until it arrived; then they were married.

Madame Valmondé had not seen Désirée and the baby for four weeks. When she reached L'Abri she shuddered at the first sight of it, as she always did. It was a sad looking place, which for many years had not known the gentle presence of a mistress, old Monsieur Aubigny having married and buried his wife in France, and she having loved her own land too well ever to leave it. The roof came down steep and black like a cowl, reaching out beyond the wide galleries that encircled the yellow stuccoed house. Big, solemn oaks grew close to it, and their thick-leaved, far-reaching branches shadowed it like a pall. Young Aubigny's rule was a strict one, too, and under it his negroes had forgotten how to be gay, as they had been during the old master's easy-going and indulgent lifetime.

The young mother was recovering slowly, and lay full length, in her soft white muslins and laces, upon a couch. The baby was beside her, upon her arm, where he had fallen asleep, at her breast. The yellow nurse woman sat beside a window fanning herself.

Madame Valmondé bent her portly figure over Désirée and kissed her, holding her an instant tenderly in her arms. Then she turned to the child.

"This is not the baby!" she exclaimed, in startled tones. French was the language spoken at Valmondé in those days.

10 "I knew you would be astonished," laughed Désirée, "at the way he has grown. The little *cochon de lait!*[2] Look at his legs, mamma, and his hands and

[1]Wedding presents given by the groom.
[2]Suckling pig.

finger-nails,—real finger-nails. Zandrine had to cut them this morning. Isn't it true, Zandrine?"

The woman bowed her turbaned head majestically, "Mais si, Madame."

"And the way he cries," went on Désirée, "is deafening. Armand heard him the other day as far away as La Blanche's cabin."

Madame Valmondé had never removed her eyes from the child. She lifted it and walked with it over to the window that was lightest. She scanned the baby narrowly, then looked as searchingly at Zandrine, whose face was turned to gaze across the fields.

"Yes, the child has grown, has changed," said Madame Valmondé, slowly, as she replaced it beside its mother. "What does Armand say?"

Désirée's face became suffused with a glow that was happiness itself. 15

"Oh, Armand is the proudest father in the parish, I believe, chiefly because it is a boy, to bear his name; though he says not,—that he would have loved a girl as well. But I know it isn't true. I know he says that to please me. And mamma," she added, drawing Madame Valmondé's head down to her, and speaking in a whisper, "he hasn't punished one of them—not one of them—since baby is born. Even Négrillon, who pretended to have burnt his leg that he might rest from work—he only laughed, and said Négrillon was a great scamp. Oh, mamma, I'm so happy; it frightens me."

What Désirée said was true. Marriage, and later the birth of his son, had softened Armand Aubigny's imperious and exacting nature greatly. This was what made the gentle Désirée so happy, for she loved him desperately. When he frowned she trembled, but loved him. When he smiled, she asked no greater blessing of God. But Armand's dark, handsome face had not often been disfigured by frowns since the day he fell in love with her.

When the baby was about three months old, Désirée awoke one day to the conviction that there was something in the air menacing her peace. It was at first too subtle to grasp. It had only been a disquieting suggestion; an air of mystery among the blacks; unexpected visits from far-off neighbors who could hardly account for their coming. Then a strange, an awful change in her husband's manner, which she dared not ask him to explain. When he spoke to her, it was with averted eyes, from which the old love-light seemed to have gone out. He absented himself from home; and when there, avoided her presence and that of her child, without excuse. And the very spirit of Satan seemed suddenly to take hold of him in his dealings with the slaves. Désirée was miserable enough to die.

She sat in her room, one hot afternoon, in her *peignoir*,[3] listlessly drawing through her fingers the strands of her long, silky brown hair that hung about her shoulders. The baby, half naked, lay asleep upon her own great mahogany bed, that was like a sumptuous throne, with its satin-lined half-canopy. One of La Blanche's little quadroon boys—half naked too—stood fanning the child slowly with a fan of peacock feathers. Désirée's eyes had been fixed absently and sadly upon the baby, while she was striving to penetrate the threatening mist that she felt closing about her. She looked from her child to the boy who stood beside him, and back again; over and over. "Ah!" It was a cry that she could not help; which she was not conscious of having uttered. The blood turned like ice in her veins, and a clammy moisture gathered upon her face.

---

[3]Dressing gown.

She tried to speak to the little quadroon boy; but no sound would come, at first. When he heard his name uttered, he looked up, and his mistress was pointing to the door. He laid aside the great, soft fan, and obediently stole away, over the polished floor, on his bare tiptoes.

She stayed motionless, with gaze riveted upon her child, and her face the picture of fright.

Presently her husband entered the room, and without noticing her, went to a table and began to search among some papers which covered it.

"Armand," she called to him, in a voice which must have stabbed him, if he was human. But he did not notice. "Armand," she said again. Then she rose and tottered towards him. "Armand," she panted once more, clutching his arm, "look at our child. What does it mean? Tell me."

He coldly but gently loosened her fingers from about his arm and thrust the hand away from him. "Tell me what it means!" she cried despairingly.

"It means," he answered lightly, "that the child is not white; it means that you are not white."

A quick conception of all that this accusation meant for her nerved her with unwonted courage to deny it. "It is a lie; it is not true, I am white! Look at my hair, it is brown; and my eyes are gray, Armand, you know they are gray. And my skin is fair," seizing his wrist. "Look at my hand; whiter than yours, Armand," she laughed hysterically.

"As white as La Blanche's," he returned cruelly; and went away leaving her alone with their child.

When she could hold a pen in her hand, she sent a despairing letter to Madame Valmondé.

"My mother, they tell me I am not white. Armand has told me I am not white. For God's sake tell them it is not true. You must know it is not true. I shall die. I must die. I cannot be so unhappy and live."

The answer that came was as brief:

"My own Désirée: Come home to Valmondé; back to your mother who loves you. Come with your child."

When the letter reached Désirée she went with it to her husband's study, and laid it open upon the desk before which he sat. She was like a stone image: silent, white, motionless after she placed it there.

In silence he ran his cold eyes over the written words. He said nothing. "Shall I go, Armand?" she asked in tones sharp with agonized suspense.

"Yes, go."

"Do you want me to go?"

"Yes, I want you to go."

He thought Almighty God had dealt cruelly and unjustly with him; and felt, somehow, that he was paying Him back in kind when he stabbed thus into his wife's soul. Moreover, he no longer loved her, because of the unconscious injury she had brought upon his home and his name.

She turned away like one stunned by a blow, and walked slowly towards the door, hoping he would call her back.

"Good-by, Armand," she moaned.

He did not answer her. That was his last blow at fate.

Désirée went in search of her child. Zandrine was pacing the sombre gallery with it. She took the little one from the nurse's arms with no word of explanation, and descending the steps, walked away, under the live-oak branches.

It was an October afternoon; the sun was just sinking. Out in the still fields the negroes were picking cotton.

Désirée had not changed the thin white garment nor the slippers she wore. Her hair was uncovered and the sun's rays brought a golden gleam from its brown meshes. She did not take the broad, beaten road which led to the far-off plantation of Valmondé. She walked across a deserted field, where the stubble bruised her tender feet, so delicately shod, and tore her thin gown to shreds.

She disappeared among the reeds and willows that grew thick along the banks of the deep, sluggish bayou; and she did not come back again.

Some weeks later there was a curious scene at L'Abri. In the centre of the 45
smoothly swept back yard was a great bonfire. Armand Aubigny sat in the wide hallway that commanded a view of the spectacle; and it was he who dealt out to a half dozen negroes the material which kept this fire ablaze.

A graceful cradle of willow, with all its dainty furbishings, was laid upon the pyre, which had already been fed with the richness of a priceless *layette*.[4] Then there were silk gowns, and velvet and satin ones added to these; laces, too, and embroideries; bonnets and gloves; for the *corbeille* had been of rare quality.

The last thing to go was a tiny bundle of letters; innocent little scribblings that Désirée had sent to him during the days of their espousal. There was the remnant of one back in the drawer from which he took them. But it was not Désirée's; it was part of an old letter from his mother to his father. He read it. She was thanking God for the blessing of her husband's love:—

"But, above all," she wrote, "night and day, I thank God for having so arranged our lives that our dear Armand will never know that his mother, who adores him, belongs to the race that is cursed with the brand of slavery."

(1893)

Questions for Discussion and Writing

1. What sort of wife is Désirée? What sort of person is Armand? Cite examples from the text to support your judgments.
2. Why is it important to Armand that his family is "one of the oldest and proudest in Louisiana"? How does this patriarchal pride relate symbolically to the shadow cast over Désirée by the stone pillar? (Remember that phallic symbols can be associated with male potency and male privilege as well as with male sexuality.)
3. What themes does this story convey?
4. What do you think happens to Désirée and the baby? What evidence is there to support your conclusion?
5. How do you think Armand reacted to the letter from his mother?
6. Write an essay focusing on the role of Désirée as slave in the story.

[4]Baby clothes.

The Story of an Hour

Knowing that Mrs. Mallard was afflicted with a heart trouble, great care was taken to break to her as gently as possible the news of her husband's death.

It was her sister Josephine who told her, in broken sentences; veiled hints that revealed in half concealing. Her husband's friend Richards was there, too, near her. It was he who had been in the newspaper office when intelligence of the railroad disaster was received, with Brently Mallard's name leading the list of "killed." He had only taken the time to assure himself of its truth by a second telegram, and had hastened to forestall any less careful, less tender friend in bearing the sad message.

She did not hear the story as many women have heard the same, with a paralyzed inability to accept its significance. She wept at once, with sudden, wild abandonment, in her sister's arms. When the storm of grief had spent itself she went away to her room alone. She would have no one follow her.

There stood, facing the open window, a comfortable, roomy armchair. Into this she sank, pressed down by a physical exhaustion that haunted her body and seemed to reach into her soul.

5 She could see in the open square before her house the tops of trees that were all aquiver with the new spring life. The delicious breath of rain was in the air. In the street below a peddler was crying his wares. The notes of a distant song which some one was singing reached her faintly, and countless sparrows were twittering in the eaves.

There were patches of blue sky showing here and there through the clouds that had met and piled one above the other in the west facing her window.

She sat with her head thrown back upon the cushion of the chair, quite motionless, except when a sob came up into her throat and shook her, as a child who has cried itself to sleep continues to sob in its dreams.

She was young, with a fair, calm face, whose lines bespoke repression and even a certain strength. But now there was a dull stare in her eyes, whose gaze was fixed away off yonder on one of those patches of blue sky. It was not a glance of reflection, but rather indicated a suspension of intelligent thought.

There was something coming to her and she was waiting for it, fearfully. What was it? She did not know; it was too subtle and elusive to name. But she felt it, creeping out of the sky, reaching toward her through the sounds, the scents, the color that filled the air.

10 Now her bosom rose and fell tumultuously. She was beginning to recognize this thing that was approaching to possess her, and she was striving to beat it back with her will—as powerless as her two white slender hands would have been.

When she abandoned herself a little whispered word escaped her slightly parted lips. She said it over and over under her breath: "free, free, free!" The vacant stare and the look of terror that had followed it went from her eyes. They stayed keen and bright. Her pulses beat fast, and the coursing blood warmed and relaxed every inch of her body.

She did not stop to ask if it were or were not a monstrous joy that held her. A clear and exalted perception enabled her to dismiss the suggestion as trivial.

She knew that she would weep again when she saw the kind, tender hands folded in death; the face that had never looked save with love upon her, fixed and gray and dead. But she saw beyond that bitter moment a long procession of years to come that would belong to her absolutely. And she opened and spread her arms out to them in welcome.

There would be no one to live for her during those coming years; she would live for herself. There would be no powerful will bending hers in that blind persistence with which men and women believe they have a right to impose a private will upon a fellow-creature. A kind intention or a cruel intention made the act seem no less a crime as she looked upon it in that brief moment of illumination.

And yet she had loved him—sometimes. Often she had not. What did it mat- 15
ter! What could love, the unsolved mystery, count for in face of this possession of self-assertion which she suddenly recognized as the strongest impulse of her being!

"Free! Body and soul free!" she kept whispering.

Josephine was kneeling before the closed door with her lips to the keyhole, imploring for admission. "Louise, open the door! I beg; open the door—you will make yourself ill. What are you doing, Louise? For heaven's sake open the door."

"Go away. I am not making myself ill." No; she was drinking in a very elixir of life through that open window.

Her fancy was running riot along those days ahead of her. Spring days, and summer days, and all sorts of days that would be her own. She breathed a quick prayer that life might be long. It was only yesterday she had thought with a shudder that life might be long.

She arose at length and opened the door to her sister's importunities. There 20
was a feverish triumph in her eyes, and she carried herself unwittingly like a goddess of Victory. She clasped her sister's waist, and together they descended the stairs. Richards stood waiting for them at the bottom.

Some one was opening the front door with a latchkey. It was Brently Mallard who entered, a little travel-stained, composedly carrying his grip-sack and umbrella. He had been far from the scene of accident, and did not even know there had been one. He stood amazed at Josephine's piercing cry; at Richards' quick motion to screen him from the view of his wife.

But Richards was too late.

When the doctors came they said she had died of heart disease—of joy that kills.

(1894)

Questions for Discussion and Writing

1. What is the double meaning of Mrs. Mallard's "heart trouble," mentioned in the first line of the story?
2. Discuss the function of the imagery in paragraphs 4, 5, and 6.
3. Discuss the dual irony of the final line.
4. Does this exceedingly short story have a theme? If so, can you state one?
5. Write an essay arguing that Mrs. Mallard is (or is not) a sympathetic character.

Sherwood Anderson 1876–1941

Sherwood Anderson, who grew up poor in Clyde, Ohio, delved into the dark side of small-town American life, exposing the psychological deformity and frustration beneath the placid surface. At age thirty-six, he just walked out on his thriving paint business, abandoning his wife and three children, and went to Chicago to become a writer. After the 1919 publication of *Winesburg, Ohio*, a collection of twenty-three linked stories, Anderson became financially comfortable, but he did not achieve a happy marriage until his third try in 1933. While traveling to South America in 1941, he died from peritonitis after swallowing a toothpick in an hors d'oeuvre. His writing influenced Faulkner, Hemingway, and Steinbeck.

Hands

Upon the half decayed veranda of a small frame house that stood near the edge of a ravine near the town of Winesburg, Ohio, a fat little old man walked nervously up and down. Across a long field that had been seeded for clover but that had produced only a dense crop of yellow mustard weeds, he could see the public highway along which went a wagon filled with berry pickers returning from the fields. The berry pickers, youths and maidens, laughed and shouted boisterously. A boy, clad in a blue shirt, leaped from the wagon and attempted to drag after him one of the maidens who screamed and protested shrilly. The feet of the boy in the road kicked up a cloud of dust that floated across the face of the departing sun. Over the long field came a thin girlish voice. "Oh, you Wing Biddlebaum, comb your hair, it's falling into your eyes," commanded the voice to the man, who was bald and whose nervous little hands fiddled about the bare white forehead as though arranging a mass of tangled locks.

Wing Biddlebaum, forever frightened and beset by a ghostly band of doubts, did not think of himself as in any way a part of the life of the town where he had lived for twenty years. Among all the people of Winesburg but one had come close to him. With George Willard, son of Tom Willard, the proprietor of the New Willard House, he had formed something like a friendship. George Willard was the reporter on the *Winesburg Eagle* and sometimes in the evening he walked out along the highway to Wing Biddlebaum's house. Now, as the old man walked up and down on the veranda, his hands moving nervously about, he was hoping that George Willard would come and spend the evening with him. After the wagon containing the berry pickers had passed, he went across the field through the tall mustard weeds and climbing a rail fence peered anxiously along the road to the town. For a moment he stood thus, rubbing his hands together and looking up and down the road, and then, fear overcoming him, ran back to walk again upon the porch of his own house.

In the presence of George Willard, Wing Biddlebaum, who for twenty years had been the town mystery, lost something of his timidity, and his shadowy personality, submerged in a sea of doubts, came forth to look at the world.

With the young reporter at his side, he ventured in the light of day into Main Street or strode up and down on the rickety front porch of his own house talking excitedly. The voice that had been low and trembling became shrill and loud. The bent figure straightened. With a kind of wriggle, like a fish returned to the brook by the fisherman, Biddlebaum the silent began to talk, striving to put into words the ideas that had been accumulated by his mind during long years of silence.

Wing Biddlebaum talked much with his hands. The slender expressive fingers, forever active, forever striving to conceal themselves in his pockets or behind his back, came forth and became the piston rods of his machinery of expression.

The story of Wing Biddlebaum is a story of hands. Their restless activity, like 5
unto the beating of the wings of an imprisoned bird, had given him his name. Some obscure "poet" of the town had thought of it. The hands alarmed their owner. He wanted to keep them hidden away and looked with amazement at the quiet inexpressive hands of other men who worked beside him in the fields, or passed driving sleepy teams on country roads.

When he talked to George Willard, Wing Biddlebaum closed his fists and beat with them upon a table or on the walls of his house. The action made him more comfortable. If the desire to talk came to him when the two were walking in the fields, he sought out a stump or the top board of a fence and with his hands pounding busily talked with renewed ease.

The story of Wing Biddlebaum's hands is worth a book in itself. Sympathetically set forth it would tap many strange, beautiful qualities in obscure men. It is a job for a poet. In Winesburg the hands had attracted attention merely because of their activity. With them Wing Biddlebaum had picked as high as a hundred and forty quarts of strawberries in a day. They became his distinguishing feature, the source of his fame. Also they made more grotesque an already grotesque and elusive individuality. Winesburg was proud of the hands of Wing Biddlebaum in the same spirit in which it was proud of Banker White's new stone house and Wesley Moyer's bay stallion, Tony Tip, that had won the two-fifteen trot at the fall races in Cleveland.

As for George Willard, he had many times wanted to ask about the hands. At times an almost overwhelming curiosity had taken hold of him. He felt that there must be a reason for their strange activity and their inclination to keep hidden away and only a growing respect for Wing Biddlebaum kept him from blurting out the questions that were often in his mind.

Once he had been on the point of asking. The two were walking in the fields on a summer afternoon and had stopped to sit upon a grassy bank. All afternoon Wing Biddlebaum had talked as one inspired. By a fence he had stopped and beating like a giant woodpecker upon the top board had shouted at George Willard, condemning his tendency to be too much influenced by the people about him. "You are destroying yourself," he cried. "You have the inclination to be alone and to dream and you are afraid of dreams. You want to be like others in town here. You hear them talk and you try to imitate them."

On the grassy bank Wing Biddlebaum had tried again to drive his point home. 10
His voice became soft and reminiscent, and with a sigh of contentment he launched into a long rambling talk, speaking as one lost in a dream.

Out of the dream Wing Biddlebaum made a picture for George Willard. In the picture men lived again in a kind of pastoral golden age. Across a green open country came clean-limbed young men, some afoot, some mounted upon horses.

In crowds the young men came to gather about the feet of an old man who sat beneath a tree in a tiny garden and who talked to them.

Wing Biddlebaum became wholly inspired. For once he forgot the hands. Slowly they stole forth and lay upon George Willard's shoulders. Something new and bold came into the voice that talked. "You must try to forget all you have learned," said the old man. "You must begin to dream. From this time on you must shut your ears to the roaring of the voices."

Pausing in his speech, Wing Biddlebaum looked long and earnestly at George Willard. His eyes glowed. Again he raised the hands to caress the boy and then a look of horror swept over his face.

With a convulsive movement of his body Wing Biddlebaum sprang to his feet and thrust his hands deep into his trousers pockets. Tears came to his eyes. "I must be getting along home. I can talk no more with you," he said nervously.

15 Without looking back, the old man had hurried down the hillside and across a meadow, leaving George Willard perplexed and frightened upon the grassy slope. With a shiver of dread the boy arose and went along the road toward town. "I'll not ask him about his hands," he thought, touched by the memory of the terror he had seen in the man's eyes. "There's something wrong, but I don't want to know what it is. His hands have something to do with his fear of me and of everyone."

And George Willard was right. Let us look briefly into the story of the hands. Perhaps our talking of them will arouse the poet who will tell the hidden wonder story of the influence for which the hands were but fluttering pennants of promise.

In his youth Wing Biddlebaum had been a school teacher in a town in Pennsylvania. He was not then known as Wing Biddlebaum but went by the less euphonic name of Adolph Myers. As Adolph Myers he was much loved by the boys of his school.

Adolph Myers was meant by nature to be a teacher of youth. He was one of those rare little-understood men who rule by a power so gentle that it passes as a lovable weakness. In their feeling for the boys under their charge such men are not unlike the finer sort of women in their love of men.

And yet that is but crudely stated. It needs the poet there. With the boys of his school, Adolph Myers had walked in the evening or had sat talking until dusk upon the school house steps, lost in a kind of dream. Here and there went his hands, caressing the shoulders of the boys, playing about the tousled heads. As he talked his voice became soft and musical. There was a caress in that also. In a way the voice and the hands, the stroking of the shoulders and the touching of the hair were a part of the school master's effort to carry a dream into the young minds. By the caress that was in his fingers he expressed himself. He was one of those men in whom the force that creates life is diffused, not centralized. Under the caress of his hands doubt and disbelief went out of the minds of the boys and they began also to dream.

20 And then the tragedy. A halfwitted boy of the school became enamored of the young master. In his bed at night he imagined unspeakable things and in the morning went forth to tell his dreams as facts. Strange hideous accusations fell from his loose-hung lips. Through the Pennsylvania town went a shiver. Hidden shadowy doubts that had been in men's minds concerning Adolph Myers were galvanized into beliefs.

The tragedy did not linger. Trembling lads were jerked out of bed and questioned. "He put his arms about me," said one. "His fingers were always playing in my hair," said another.

One afternoon a man of the town, Henry Bradford, who kept a saloon, came to the school house door. Calling Adolph Myers into the school yard he began to beat him with his fists. As his hard knuckles beat down into the frightened face of the schoolmaster, his wrath became more and more terrible. Screaming with dismay, the children ran here and there like disturbed insects. "I'll teach you to put your hands on my boy, you beast," roared the saloon keeper, who, tired of beating the master, had begun to kick him about the yard.

Adolph Myers was driven from the Pennsylvania town in the night. With lanterns in their hands a dozen men came to the door of the house where he lived alone and commanded that he dress and come forth. It was raining and one of the men had a rope in his hands. They had intended to hang the school master, but something in his figure, so small, white, and pitiful, touched their hearts and they let him escape. As he ran away into the darkness they repented of their weakness and ran after him, swearing and throwing sticks and great balls of soft mud at the figure that screamed and ran faster and faster into the darkness.

For twenty years Adolph Myers had lived alone in Winesburg. He was but forty but looked sixty-five. The name of Biddlebaum he got from a box of goods seen at a freight station as he hurried through an eastern Ohio town. He had an aunt in Winesburg, a black-toothed old woman who raised chickens, and with her he lived until she died. He had been ill for a year after the experience in Pennsylvania, and after his recovery worked as a day laborer in the fields, going timidly about and striving to conceal his hands. Although he did not understand what had happened he felt that the hands must be to blame. Again and again the fathers of the boys talked of the hands. "Keep your hands to yourself," the saloon keeper had roared, dancing with fury in the school house yard.

Upon the veranda of his house by the ravine, Wing Biddlebaum continued to 25
walk up and down until the sun had disappeared and the road beyond the field was lost in the grey shadows. Going into his house he cut slices of bread and spread honey upon them. When the rumble of the evening train that took away the express cars loaded with the day's harvest of berries had passed and restored the silence of the summer night, he went again to walk upon the veranda. In the darkness he could not see the hands and they became quiet. Although he still hungered for the presence of the boy, who was the medium through which he expressed his love of man, the hunger became again a part of his loneliness and his waiting. Lighting a lamp Wing Biddlebaum washed the few dishes soiled by his simple meal and, setting up a folding cot by the screen door that led to the porch, prepared to undress for the night. A few stray white bread crumbs lay on the cleanly washed floor by the table; putting the lamp upon a low stool he began to pick up the crumbs, carrying them to his mouth one by one with unbelievable rapidity. In the dense blotch of light beneath the table, the kneeling figure looked like a priest engaged in some service of his church. The nervous expressive fingers, flashing in and out of the light, might well have been mistaken for the fingers of the devotee going swiftly through decade after decade of his rosary.

(1919)

Questions for Discussion and Writing

1. Reread the first paragraph of the story closely. How does the imagery of the scene forecast themes developed later?
2. Why does the author say more than once that the story of Wing's hands is material for a poet? In what ways do you think a poem is different from a story?
3. What did the men of the Pennsylvania town decide about Adolph Myers? Why did they have such a rabid reaction? What is the significance of the source of the rumors? Why do you think the first confrontation came from the saloon keeper? Have you ever witnessed a situation like this?
4. What is Wing trying to tell George in their talks? What does he mean by "You must begin to dream"? Why do you think the content of Wing's teachings is left vague?
5. How do you reconcile the final image of Wing with the rest of the story? What emotional tone does it convey to you?

Susan Glaspell 1882–1948

See page 1027 for a biographical note about this author.

A Jury of Her Peers

When Martha Hale opened the storm-door and got a cut of the north wind, she ran back for her big woolen scarf. As she hurriedly wound that round her head her eye made a scandalized sweep of her kitchen. It was no ordinary thing that called her away—it was probably farther from ordinary than anything that had ever happened in Dickson County. But what her eye took in was that her kitchen was in no shape for leaving: her bread all ready for mixing, half the flour sifted and half unsifted.

She hated to see things half done; but she had been at that when the team from town stopped to get Mr. Hale, and then the sheriff came running in to say his wife wished Mrs. Hale would come too—adding, with a grin, that he guessed she was getting scary and wanted another woman along. So she had dropped everything right where it was.

"Martha!" now came her husband's impatient voice. "Don't keep folks waiting out here in the cold."

She again opened the storm-door, and this time joined the three men and the one woman waiting for her in the big two-seated buggy.

After she had the robes tucked around her she took another look at the 5
woman who sat beside her on the back seat. She had met Mrs. Peters the year before at the county fair, and the thing she remembered about her was that she

didn't seem like a sheriff's wife. She was small and thin and didn't have a strong voice. Mrs. Gorman, sheriff's wife before Gorman went out and Peters came in, had a voice that somehow seemed to be backing up the law with every word. But if Mrs. Peters didn't look like a sheriff's wife, Peters made it up in looking like a sheriff. He was to a dot the kind of man who could get himself elected sheriff—a heavy man with a big voice, who was particularly genial with the law-abiding, as if to make it plain that he knew the difference between criminals and non-criminals. And right there it came into Mrs. Hale's mind, with a stab, that this man who was so pleasant and lively with all of them was going to the Wrights' now as a sheriff.

"The country's not very pleasant this time of year," Mrs. Peters at last ventured, as if she felt they ought to be talking as well as the men.

Mrs. Hale scarcely finished her reply, for they had gone up a little hill and could see the Wright place now, and seeing it did not make her feel like talking. It looked very lonesome this cold March morning. It had always been a lonesome-looking place. It was down in a hollow, and the poplar trees around it were lonesome-looking trees. The men were looking at it and talking about what had happened. The country attorney was bending to one side of the buggy, and kept looking steadily at the place as they drew up to it.

"I'm glad you came with me," Mrs. Peters said nervously, as the two women were about to follow the men in through the kitchen door.

Even after she had her foot on the door-step, her hand on the knob, Martha Hale had a moment of feeling she could not cross that threshold. And the reason it seemed she couldn't cross it now was simply because she hadn't crossed it before. Time and time again it had been in her mind, "I ought to go over and see Minnie Foster"—she still thought of her as Minnie Foster, though for twenty years she had been Mrs. Wright. And then there was always something to do and Minnie Foster would go from her mind. But *now* she could come.

10 The men went over to the stove. The women stood close together by the door. Young Henderson, the county attorney, turned around and said, "Come up to the fire, ladies."

Mrs. Peters took a step forward, then stopped. "I'm, not—cold," she said.

And so the two women stood by the door, at first not even so much as looking around the kitchen.

The men talked for a minute about what a good thing it was the sheriff had sent his deputy out that morning to make a fire for them, and then Sheriff Peters stepped back from the stove, unbuttoned his outer coat, and leaned his hands on the kitchen table in a way that seemed to mark the beginning of official business. "Now, Mr. Hale," he said in a sort of semi-official voice, "before we move things about, you tell Mr. Henderson just what it was you saw when you came here yesterday morning."

The county attorney was looking around the kitchen.

15 "By the way," he said, "has anything been moved?" He turned to the sheriff. "Are things just as you left them yesterday?"

Peters looked from cupboard to sink; from that to a small worn rocker a little to one side of the kitchen table.

"It's just the same."

"Somebody should have been left here yesterday," said the county attorney.

"Oh—yesterday," returned the sheriff, with a little gesture as of yesterday having been more than he could bear to think of. "When I had to send Frank to

Morris Center for that man who went crazy—let me tell you, I had my hands full *yesterday*. I knew you could get back from Omaha by to-day, George, and as long as I went over everything here myself—"

"Well, Mr. Hale," said the county attorney, in a way of letting what was past 20 and gone go, "tell just what happened when you came here yesterday morning."

Mrs. Hale, still leaning against the door, had that sinking feeling of the mother whose child is about to speak a piece. Lewis often wandered along and got things mixed up in a story. She hoped he would tell this straight and plain, and not say unnecessary things that would just make things harder for Minnie Foster. He didn't begin at once, and she noticed that he looked queer—as if standing in that kitchen and having to tell what he had seen there yesterday morning made him almost sick.

"Yes, Mr. Hale?" the county attorney reminded.

"Harry and I had started to town with a load of potatoes," Mrs. Hale's husband began.

Harry was Mrs. Hale's oldest boy. He wasn't with them now, for the very good reason that those potatoes never got to town yesterday and he was taking them this morning, so he hadn't been home when the sheriff stopped to say he wanted Mr. Hale to come over to the Wright place and tell the county attorney his story there, where he could point it all out. With all Mrs. Hale's other emotions came the fear that maybe Harry wasn't dressed warm enough—they hadn't any of them realized how that north wind did bite.

"We come along this road," Hale was going on, with a motion of his hand to 25 the road over which they had just come, "and as we got in sight of the house I says to Harry, 'I'm goin' to see if I can't get John Wright to take a telephone.' You see," he explained to Henderson, "unless I can get somebody to go in with me they won't come out this branch road except for a price *I* can't pay. I'd spoke to Wright about it once before; but he put me off, saying folks talked too much anyway, and all he asked was peace and quiet—guess you know about how much he talked himself. But I thought maybe if I went to the house and talked about it before his wife, and said all the women-folks liked the telephones, and that in this lonesome stretch of road it would be a good thing—well, I said to Harry that that was what I was going to say—though I said at the same time that I didn't know as what his wife wanted made much difference to John—"

Now, there he was!—saying things he didn't need to say. Mrs. Hale tried to catch her husband's eye, but fortunately the county attorney interrupted with:

"Let's talk about that a little later, Mr. Hale. I do want to talk about that, but I'm anxious now to get along to just what happened when you got here."

When he began this time, it was very deliberately and carefully:

"I didn't see or hear anything. I knocked at the door. And still it was all quiet inside. I knew they must be up—it was past eight o'clock. So I knocked again, louder, and I thought I heard somebody say 'Come in.' I wasn't sure—I'm not sure yet. But I opened the door—this door," jerking a hand toward the door by which the two women stood, "and there, in that rocker"—pointing to it—"sat Mrs. Wright."

Everyone in the kitchen looked at the rocker. It came into Mrs. Hale's mind 30 that that rocker didn't look in the least like Minnie Foster—the Minnie Foster of twenty years before. It was a dingy red, with wooden rungs up the back, and the middle rung was gone, and the chair sagged to one side.

"How did she—look?" the county attorney was inquiring.

"Well," said Hale, "she looked—queer."

"How do you mean—queer?"

As he asked it he took out a note-book and pencil. Mrs. Hale did not like the sight of that pencil. She kept her eye fixed on her husband, as if to keep him from saying unnecessary things that would go into that note-book and make trouble.

Hale did speak guardedly, as if the pencil had affected him too.

"Well, as if she didn't know what she was going to do next. And kind of—done up."

"How did she seem to feel about your coming?"

"Why, I don't think she minded—one way or other. She didn't pay much attention. I said, 'Ho' do, Mrs. Wright? It's cold, ain't it?' And she said, 'Is it?'—and went on pleatin' at her apron.

"Well, I was surprised. She didn't ask me to come up to the stove, or to sit down, but just set there, not even lookin' at me. And so I said: 'I want to see John.'

"And then she—laughed. I guess you would call it a laugh.

"I thought of Harry and the team outside, so I said, a little sharp, 'Can I see John?' 'No,' says she—kind of dull like. 'Ain't he home?' says I. Then she looked at me. 'Yes,' says she, 'he's home.' 'Then why can't I see him?' I asked her, out of patience with her now. ''Cause he's dead,' says she, just as quiet and dull—and fell to pleatin' her apron. 'Dead?' says I, like you do when you can't take in what you've heard.

"She just nodded her head, not getting a bit excited, but rockin' back and forth.

"'Why—where is he?' says I, not knowing *what* to say.

"She just pointed upstairs—like this"—pointing to the room above.

"I got up, with the idea of going up there myself. By this time I—didn't know what to do. I walked from there to here; then I says: 'Why, what did he die of?'

"'He died of a rope around his neck,' says she; and just went on pleatin' at her apron."

Hale stopped speaking, and stood staring at the rocker, as if he were still seeing the woman who had sat there the morning before. Nobody spoke; it was as if every one were seeing the woman who had sat there the morning before.

"And what did you do then?" the county attorney at last broke the silence.

"I went out and called Harry. I thought I might—need help. I got Harry in, and we went upstairs." His voice fell almost to a whisper. "There he was—lying over the—"

"I think I'd rather have you go into that upstairs," the county attorney interrupted, "where you can point it all out. Just go on now with the rest of the story."

"Well, my first thought was to get that rope off. It looked—"

He stopped, his face twitching.

"But Harry, he went up to him, and he said, 'No, he's dead all right, and we'd better not touch anything.' So we went downstairs.

"She was still sitting that same way. 'Has anybody been notified?' I asked. 'No,' says she, unconcerned.

"'Who did this, Mrs. Wright?' said Harry. He said it business-like, and she stopped pleatin' at her apron. 'I don't know,' she says. 'You don't *know*?' says Harry. 'Weren't you sleepin' in the bed with him?' 'Yes,' says she, 'but I was on the inside.' 'Somebody slipped a rope round his neck and strangled him, and you didn't wake up?' says Harry. 'I didn't wake up,' she said after him.

"We may have looked as if we didn't see how that could be, for after a minute she said, 'I sleep sound.'

"Harry was going to ask her more questions, but I said maybe that weren't our business; maybe we ought to let her tell her story first to the coroner or the sheriff. So Harry went fast as he could over to High Road—the Rivers' place, where there's a telephone."

"And what did she do when she knew you had gone for the coroner?" The attorney got his pencil in his hand all ready for writing.

"She moved from that chair to this one over here"—Hale pointed to a small chair in the corner—"and just sat there with her hands held together and looking down. I got a feeling that I ought to make some conversation, so I said I had come in to see if John wanted to put in a telephone; and at that she started to laugh, and then she stopped and looked at me—scared."

At the sound of a moving pencil the man who was telling the story looked up.

"I dunno—maybe it wasn't scared," he hastened; "I wouldn't like to say it was. Soon Harry got back, and then Dr. Lloyd came, and you, Mr. Peters, and so I guess that's all I know that you don't."

He said that last with relief, and moved a little, as if relaxing. Every one moved a little. The county attorney walked toward the stair door.

"I guess we'll go upstairs first—then out to the barn and around there."

He paused and looked around the kitchen.

"You're convinced there was nothing important here?" he asked the sheriff. "Nothing that would—point to any motive?"

The sheriff too looked all around, as if to re-convince himself.

"Nothing here but kitchen things," he said, with a little laugh for the insignificance of kitchen things.

The county attorney was looking at the cupboard—a peculiar, ungainly structure, half closet and half cupboard, the upper part of it being built in the wall, and the lower part just the old-fashioned kitchen cupboard. As if its queerness attracted him, he got a chair and opened the upper part and looked in. After a moment he drew his hand away sticky.

"Here's a nice mess," he said resentfully.

The two women had drawn nearer, and now the sheriff's wife spoke.

"Oh—her fruit," she said, looking to Mrs. Hale for sympathetic understanding. She turned back to the county attorney and explained: "She worried about that when it turned so cold last night. She said the fire would go out and her jars might burst."

Mrs. Peters' husband broke into a laugh.

"Well, can you beat the woman! Held for murder, and worrying about her preserves!"

The young attorney set his lips.

"I guess before we're through with her she may have something more serious than preserves to worry about."

"Oh, well," said Mrs. Hale's husband, with good-natured superiority, "women are used to worrying over trifles."

The two women moved a little closer together. Neither of them spoke. The county attorney seemed suddenly to remember his manners—and think of his future.

"And yet," said he, with the gallantry of a young politician, "for all their worries, what would we do without the ladies?"

The women did not speak, did not unbend. He went to the sink and began washing his hands. He turned to wipe them on the roller towel—whirled it for a cleaner place.

"Dirty towels! Not much of a housekeeper, would you say, ladies?"

He kicked his foot against some dirty pans under the sink.

"There's a great deal of work to be done on a farm," said Mrs. Hale stiffly.

"To be sure. And yet"—with a little bow to her—"I know there are some Dickson County farm-houses that do not have such roller towels." He gave it a pull to expose its full length again.

"Those towels get dirty awful quick. Men's hands aren't always as clean as they might be."

"Ah, loyal to your sex, I see," he laughed. He stopped and gave her a keen look. "But you and Mrs. Wright were neighbors. I suppose you were friends, too."

Martha Hale shook her head.

"I've seen little enough of her of late years. I've not been in this house—it's more than a year."

"And why was that? You didn't like her?"

"I liked her well enough," she replied with spirit. "Farmers' wives have their hands full, Mr. Henderson. And then—" She looked around the kitchen.

"Yes?" he encouraged.

"It never seemed a very cheerful place," said she, more to herself than to him.

"No," he agreed; "I don't think any one would call it cheerful. I shouldn't say she had the home-making instinct."

"Well, I don't know as Wright had, either," she muttered.

"You mean they didn't get on very well?" he was quick to ask.

"No; I don't mean anything," she answered, with decision. As she turned a little away from him, she added: "But I don't think a place would be any the cheerfuler for John Wright's bein' in it."

"I'd like to talk to you about that a little later, Mrs. Hale," he said. "I'm anxious to get the lay of things upstairs now."

He moved toward the stair door, followed by the two men.

"I suppose anything Mrs. Peters does'll be all right?" the sheriff inquired. "She was to take in some clothes for her, you know—and a few little things. We left in such a hurry yesterday."

The county attorney looked at the two women whom they were leaving alone there among the kitchen things.

"Yes—Mrs. Peters," he said, his glance resting on the woman who was not Mrs. Peters, the big farmer woman who stood behind the sheriff's wife. "Of course Mrs. Peters is one of us," he said, in a manner of entrusting responsibility. "And keep your eye out, Mrs. Peters, for anything that might be of use. No telling; you women might come upon a clue to the motive—and that's the thing we need."

Mr. Hale rubbed his face after the fashion of a show man getting ready for a pleasantry.

"But would the women know a clue if they did come upon it?" he said; and, having delivered himself of this, he followed the others through the stair door.

The women stood motionless and silent, listening to the footsteps, first upon the stairs, then in the room above them.

Then, as if releasing herself from something strange, Mrs. Hale began to arrange the dirty pans under the sink, which the county attorney's disdainful push of the foot had deranged.

"I'd hate to have men comin' into my kitchen," she said testily—"snoopin' round and criticizin'." 105

"Of course it's no more than their duty," said the sheriff's wife, in her manner of timid acquiescence.

"Duty's all right," replied Mrs. Hale bluffly; "but I guess that deputy sheriff that come out to make the fire might have got a little of this on." She gave the roller towel a pull. "Wish I'd thought of that sooner! Seems mean to talk about her for not having things slicked up, when she had to come away in such a hurry."

She looked around the kitchen. Certainly it was not "slicked up." Her eye was held by a bucket of sugar on a low shelf. The cover was off the wooden bucket, and beside it was a paper bag—half full.

Mrs. Hale moved toward it.

"She was putting this in there," she said to herself—slowly. 110

She thought of the flour in her kitchen at home—half sifted, half not sifted. She had been interrupted, and had left things half done. What had interrupted Minnie Foster? Why had that work been left half done? She made a move as if to finish it—unfinished things always bothered her—and then she glanced around and saw that Mrs. Peters was watching her—and she didn't want Mrs. Peters to get that feeling she had got of work begun and then—for some reason—not finished.

"It's a shame about her fruit," she said, and walked toward the cupboard that the county attorney had opened, and got on the chair, murmuring: "I wonder if it's all gone."

It was a sorry enough looking sight, but "Here's one that's all right," she said at last. She held it toward the light. "This is cherries, too." She looked again. "I declare I believe that's the only one."

With a sigh, she got down from the chair, went to the sink, and wiped off the bottle.

"She'll feel awful bad, after all her hard work in the hot weather. I remember the afternoon I put up my cherries last summer." 115

She set the bottle on the table, and, with another sigh, started to sit down in the rocker. But she did not sit down. Something kept her from sitting down in that chair. She straightened—stepped back, and, half turned away, stood looking at it, seeing the woman who sat there "pleatin' at her apron."

The thin voice of the sheriff's wife broke in upon her: "I must be getting those things from the front room closet." She opened the door into the other room, started in, stepped back. "You coming with me, Mrs. Hale?" she asked nervously. "You—you could help me get them."

They were soon back—the stark coldness of that shut-up room was not a thing to linger in.

"My!" said Mrs. Peters, dropping the things on the table and hurrying to the stove.

Mrs. Hale stood examining the clothes the woman who was being detained in town had said she wanted. 120

"Wright was close!" she exclaimed, holding up a shabby black skirt that bore the marks of much making over. "I think maybe that's why she kept so much to herself. I s'pose she felt she couldn't do her part; and then, you don't enjoy things when you feel shabby. She used to wear pretty clothes and be lively—when she was Minnie Foster, one of the town girls, singing in the choir. But that—oh, that was twenty years ago."

With a carefulness in which there was something tender, she folded the shabby clothes and piled them at one corner of the table. She looked at Mrs. Peters, and there was something in the other woman's look that irritated her.

"She don't care," she said to herself. "Much difference it makes to her whether Minnie Foster had pretty clothes when she was a girl."

Then she looked again, and she wasn't so sure; in fact, she hadn't at any time been perfectly sure about Mrs. Peters. She had that shrinking manner, and yet her eyes looked as if they could see a long way into things.

"This all you was to take in?" asked Mrs. Hale.

"No," said the sheriff's wife; "she said she wanted an apron. Funny thing to want," she ventured in her nervous little way, "for there's not much to get you dirty in jail, goodness knows. But I suppose just to make her feel more natural. If you're used to wearing an apron—. She said they were in the bottom drawer of this cupboard. Yes—here they are. And then her little shawl that always hung on the stair door."

She took the small gray shawl from behind the door leading upstairs, and stood a minute looking at it.

Suddenly Mrs. Hale took a quick step toward the other woman.

"Mrs. Peters!"

"Yes, Mrs. Hale?"

"Do you think she—did it?"

A frightened look blurred the other things in Mrs. Peters' eyes.

"Oh, I don't know," she said, in a voice that seemed to shrink away from the subject.

"Well, I don't think she did," affirmed Mrs. Hale stoutly. "Asking for an apron, and her little shawl. Worryin' about her fruit."

"Mr. Peters says—." Footsteps were heard in the room above; she stopped, looked up, then went on in a lowered voice: "Mr. Peters says—it looks bad for her. Mr. Henderson is awful sarcastic in a speech, and he's going to make fun of her saying she didn't—wake up."

For a moment Mrs. Hale had no answer. Then, "Well, I guess John Wright didn't wake up—when they was slippin' that rope under his neck," she muttered.

"No, it's *strange*," breathed Mrs. Peters. "They think it was such a—funny way to kill a man."

She began to laugh; at the sound of the laugh, abruptly stopped.

"That's just what Mr. Hale said," said Mrs. Hale, in a resolutely natural voice. "There was a gun in the house. He says that's what he can't understand."

"Mr. Henderson said, coming out, that what was needed for the case was a motive. Something to show anger—or sudden feeling."

"Well, I don't see any signs of anger around here," said Mrs. Hale. "I don't—"

She stopped. It was as if her mind tripped on something. Her eye was caught by a dish-towel in the middle of the kitchen table. Slowly she moved toward the table. One half of it was wiped clean, the other half messy. Her eyes made a slow, almost unwilling turn to the bucket of sugar and the half empty bag beside it. Things begun—and not finished.

After a moment she stepped back, and said, in that manner of releasing herself:

"Wonder how they're finding things upstairs? I hope she had it a little more red up[1] up there. You know,"—she paused, and feeling gathered,— "it seems kind of *sneaking*; locking her up in town and coming out here to get her own house to turn against her!"

---

[1]Tidy

"But, Mrs. Hale," said the sheriff's wife, "the law is the law." 145

"I s'pose 'tis," answered Mrs. Hale shortly.

She turned to the stove, saying something about that fire not being much to brag of. She worked with it a minute, and when she straightened up she said aggresively:

"The law is the law—and a bad stove is a bad stove. How'd you like to cook on this?"—pointing with the poker to the broken lining. She opened the oven door and started to express her opinion of the oven; but she was swept into her own thoughts, thinking of what it would mean, year after year, to have that stove to wrestle with. The thought of Minnie Foster trying to bake in that oven—and the thought of her never going over to see Minnie Foster—.

She was startled by hearing Mrs. Peters say: "A person gets discouraged—and loses heart."

The sheriff's wife had looked from the stove to the sink—to the pail of water 150
which had been carried in from outside. The two women stood there silent, above them the footsteps of the men who were looking for evidence against the woman who had worked in that kitchen. That look of seeing into things, of seeing through a thing to something else, was in the eyes of the sheriff's wife now. When Mrs. Hale next spoke to her, it was gently:

"Better loosen up your things, Mrs. Peters. We'll not feel them when we go out."

Mrs. Peters went to the back of the room to hang up the fur tippet[2] she was wearing. A moment later she exclaimed, "Why, she was piecing a quilt," and held up a large sewing basket piled high with quilt pieces.

Mrs. Hale spread some of the blocks on the table.

"It's log-cabin pattern," she said, putting several of them together. "Pretty, isn't it?"

They were so engaged with the quilt that they did not hear the footsteps on 155
the stairs. Just as the stair door opened Mrs. Hale was saying:

"Do you suppose she was going to quilt it or just knot it?"[3]

The sheriff threw up his hands.

"They wonder whether she was going to quilt it or just knot it!"

There was a laugh for the ways of women, a warming of hands over the stove, and then the county attorney said briskly:

"Well, let's go right out to the barn and get that cleared up." 160

"I don't see as there's anything so strange," Mrs. Hale said resentfully, after the outside door had closed on the three men—"our taking up our time with little things while we're waiting for them to get the evidence. I don't see as it's anything to laugh about."

"Of course they've got awful important things on their minds," said the sheriff's wife apologetically.

They returned to an inspection of the blocks for the quilt. Mrs. Hale was looking at the fine, even sewing, and preoccupied with thoughts of the woman who had done that sewing, when she heard the sheriff's wife say, in a queer tone:

"Why, look at this one."

She turned to take the block held out to her. 165

[2]A short wrap covering the shoulders.

[3]*Quilting* holds the layers of a quilt together with multiple rows of stitching; *knotting* involves only a single stitch at regular intervals with the threads tied on top.

"The sewing," said Mrs. Peters, in a troubled way. "All the rest of them have been so nice and even—but—this one. Why, it looks as if she didn't know what she was about!"

Their eyes met—something flashed to life, passed between them; then, as if with an effort, they seemed to pull away from each other. A moment Mrs. Hale sat there, her hands folded over that sewing which was so unlike all the rest of the sewing. Then she had pulled a knot and drawn the threads.

"Oh, what are you doing, Mrs. Hale?" asked the sheriff's wife, startled.

"Just pulling out a stitch or two that's not sewed very good," said Mrs. Hale mildly.

"I don't think we ought to touch things," Mrs. Peters said, a little helplessly.

"I'll just finish up this end," answered Mrs. Hale, still in that mild, matter-of-fact fashion.

She threaded a needle and started to replace bad sewing with good. For a little while she sewed in silence. Then, in that thin, timid voice, she heard:

"Mrs. Hale!"

"Yes, Mrs. Peters?"

"What do you suppose she was so—nervous about?"

"Oh, *I* don't know," said Mrs. Hale, as if dismissing a thing not important enough to spend much time on. "I don't know as she was—nervous. I sew awful queer sometimes when I'm just tired."

She cut a thread, and out of the corner of her eye looked up at Mrs. Peters. The small, lean face of the sheriff's wife seemed to have tightened up. Her eyes had that look of peering into something. But the next moment she moved, and said in her thin, indecisive way:

"Well, I must get those clothes wrapped. They may be through sooner than we think. I wonder where I could find a piece of paper—and string."

"In that cupboard, maybe," suggested Mrs. Hale, after a glance around.

One piece of the crazy sewing remained unripped. Mrs. Peters' back turned, Martha Hale now scrutinized that piece, compared it with the dainty, accurate sewing of the other blocks. The difference was startling. Holding this block made her feel queer, as if the distracted thoughts of the woman who had perhaps turned to it to try and quiet herself were communicating themselves to her.

Mrs. Peters' voice roused her.

"Here's a bird-cage," she said. "Did she have a bird, Mrs. Hale?"

"Why, I don't know whether she did or not." She turned to look at the cage Mrs. Peters was holding up. "I've not been here in so long." She sighed. "There was a man round last year selling canaries cheap—but I don't know as she took one. Maybe she did. She used to sing real pretty herself."

Mrs. Peters looked around the kitchen.

"Seems kind of funny to think of a bird here." She half-laughed—an attempt to put up a barrier. "But she must have had one—or why would she have a cage? I wonder that happened to it."

"I suppose maybe the cat got it," suggested Mrs. Hale, resuming her sewing.

"No; she didn't have a cat. She's got that feeling some people have about cats—being afraid of them. When they brought her to our house yesterday, my cat got in the room, and she was real upset and asked me to take it out."

"My sister Bessie was like that," laughed Mrs. Hale.

The sheriff's wife did not reply. The silence made Mrs. Hale turn around. Mrs. Peters was examining the bird-cage.

"Look at this door," she said slowly. "It's broke. One hinge has been pulled 190
apart."

Mrs. Hale came nearer.

"Looks as if some one must have been—rough with it."

Again their eyes met—startled, questioning, apprehensive. For a moment neither spoke nor stirred. Then Mrs. Hale, turning away, said brusquely:

"If they're going to find any evidence, I wish they'd be about it. I don't like this place."

"But I'm awful glad you came with me, Mrs. Hale." Mrs. Peters put the bird- 195
cage on the table and sat down. "It would be lonesome for me—sitting here alone."

"Yes, it would, wouldn't it?" agreed Mrs. Hale, a certain determined naturalness in her voice. She picked up the sewing, but now it dropped in her lap, and she murmured in a different voice: "But I tell you what I *do* wish, Mrs. Peters. I wish I had come over sometimes when she was here. I wish—I had."

"But of course you were awful busy, Mrs. Hale. Your house—and your children."

"I could've come," retorted Mrs. Hale shortly. "I stayed away because it weren't cheerful—and that's why I ought to have come. I"—she looked around—"I've never liked this place. Maybe because it's down in a hollow and you don't see the road. I don't know what it is, but it's a lonesome place, and always was. I wish I had come over to see Minnie Foster sometimes. I can see now—" She did not put it into words.

"Well, you mustn't reproach yourself," counseled Mrs. Peters. "Somehow, we just don't see how it is with other folks till—something comes up."

"Not having children makes less work," mused Mrs. Hale, after a silence, 200
"but it makes a quiet house—and Wright out to work all day—and no company when he did come in. Did you know John Wright, Mrs. Peters?"

"Not to know him. I've seen him in town. They say he was a good man."

"Yes—good," conceded John Wright's neighbor grimly. "He didn't drink, and kept his word as well as most, I guess, and paid his debts. But he was a hard man, Mrs. Peters. Just to pass the time of day with him—." She stopped, shivered a little. "Like a raw wind that gets to the bone." Her eye fell upon the cage on the table before her, and she added, almost bitterly: "I should think she would've wanted a bird!"

Suddenly she leaned forward, looking intently at the cage. "But what do you s'pose went wrong with it?"

"I don't know," returned Mrs. Peters; "unless it got sick and died."

But after she said it she reached over and swung the broken door. Both 205
women watched it as if somehow held by it.

"You didn't know—her?" Mrs. Hale asked, a gentler note in her voice.

"Not till they brought her yesterday," said the sheriff's wife.

"She—come to think of it, she was kind of like a bird herself. Real sweet and pretty, but kind of timid and—fluttery. How—she—did—change."

That held her for a long time. Finally, as if struck with a happy thought and relieved to get back to everyday things, she exclaimed:

"Tell you what, Mrs. Peters, why don't you take the quilt in with you? It 210
might take up her mind."

"Why, I think that's a real nice idea, Mrs. Hale," agreed the sheriff's wife, as if she too were glad to come into the atmosphere of a simple kindness. "There couldn't possibly be any objection to that, could there? Now, just what will I take? I wonder if her patches are in here—and her things."

They turned to the sewing basket.

"Here's some red," said Mrs. Hale, bringing out a roll of cloth. Underneath that was a box. "Here, maybe her scissors are in here—and her things." She held it up. "What a pretty box! I'll warrant that was something she had a long time ago—when she was a girl."

She held it in her hand a moment; then, with a little sigh, opened it.

Instantly her hand went to her nose.

"Why—!"

Mrs. Peters drew nearer—then turned away.

"There's something wrapped up in this piece of silk," faltered Mrs. Hale.

"This isn't her scissors," said Mrs. Peters in a shrinking voice.

Her hand not steady, Mrs. Hale raised the piece of silk. "Oh, Mrs Peters!" she cried. "It's—"

Mrs. Peters bent closer.

"It's the bird," she whispered.

"But, Mrs. Peters!" cried Mrs. Hale. "*Look* at it! Its neck—look at its neck! It's all—other side *to*."

She held the box away from her.

The sheriff's wife again bent closer.

"Somebody wrung its neck," said she, in a voice that was slow and deep.

And then again the eyes of the two women met—this time clung together in a look of dawning comprehension, of growing horror. Mrs. Peters looked from the dead bird to the broken door of the cage. Again their eyes met. And just then there was a sound at the outside door.

Mrs. Hale slipped the box under the quilt pieces in the basket, and sank into the chair before it. Mrs. Peters stood holding to the table. The county attorney and the sheriff came in from outside.

"Well, ladies," said the county attorney, as one turning from serious things to little pleasantries, "have you decided whether she was going to quilt it or knot it?"

"We think," began the sheriff's wife in a flurried voice, "that she was going to—knot it."

He was too preoccupied to notice the change that came in her voice on that last.

"Well, that's very interesting, I'm sure," he said tolerantly. He caught sight of the bird-cage. "Has the bird flown?"

"We think the cat got it," said Mrs. Hale in a voice curiously even.

He was walking up and down, as if thinking something out.

"Is there a cat?" he asked absently.

Mrs. Hale shot a look up at the sheriff's wife.

"Well, not *now*," said Mrs. Peters. "They're superstitious, you know; they leave."

She sank into her chair.

The county attorney did not heed her. "No sign at all of any one having come in from the outside," he said to Peters, in the manner of continuing an interrupted conversation. "Their own rope. Now let's go upstairs again and go over it, piece by piece. It would have to have been some one who knew just the—"

The stair door closed behind them and their voices were lost.

The two women sat motionless, not looking at each other, but as if peering into something and at the same time holding back. When they spoke now it was as if they were afraid of what they were saying, but as if they could not help saying it.

"She liked the bird," said Martha Hale, low and slowly. "She was going to bury it in that pretty box."

"When I was a girl," said Mrs. Peters, under her breath, "my kitten—there was a boy took a hatchet, and before my eyes—before I could get there—" She covered her face an instant. "If they hadn't held me back I would have—" she caught herself, looked upstairs where footsteps were heard, and finished weakly—"hurt him."

Then they sat without speaking or moving.

"I wonder how it would seem," Mrs. Hale at last began, as if feeling her way over strange ground—"never to have had any children around?" Her eyes made a slow sweep of the kitchen, as if seeing what that kitchen had meant through all the years. "No, Wright wouldn't like the bird," she said after that—"a thing that sang. She used to sing. He killed that too." Her voice tightened.

Mrs. Peters moved uneasily.

"Of course we don't know who killed the bird."

"I knew John Wright," was Mrs. Hale's answer.

"It was an awful thing was done in this house that night, Mrs. Hale," said the sheriff's wife. "Killing a man while he slept—slipping a thing round his neck that choked the life out of him."

Mrs. Hale's hand went out to the bird-cage.

"His neck. Choked the life out of him."

"We don't *know* who killed him," whispered Mrs. Peters wildly. "We don't *know*."

Mrs. Hale had not moved. "If there had been years and years of—nothing, then a bird to sing to you, it would be awful—still—after the bird was still."

It was as if something within her not herself had spoken, and it found in Mrs. Peters something she did not know as herself.

"I know what stillness is," she said, in a queer, monotonous voice. "When we homesteaded in Dakota, and my first baby died—after he was two years old—and me with no other then—"

Mrs. Hale stirred.

"How soon do you suppose they'll be through looking for evidence?"

"I know what stillness is," repeated Mrs. Peters, in just that same way. Then she too pulled back. "The law has got to punish crime, Mrs. Hale," she said in her tight little way.

"I wish you'd seen Minnie Foster," was the answer, "when she wore a white dress with blue ribbons, and stood up there in the choir and sang."

The picture of that girl, the fact that she had lived neighbor to that girl for twenty years, and had let her die for lack of life, was suddenly more than she could bear.

"Oh, I *wish* I'd come over here once in a while!" she cried. "That was a crime! That was a crime! Who's going to punish that?"

"We mustn't take on," said Mrs. Peters, with a frightened look toward the stairs.

"I might 'a' *known* she needed help! I tell you, it's *queer*, Mrs. Peters. We live close together, and we live far apart. We all go through the same things—it's all just a different kind of the same thing! If it weren't—why do you and I *understand*? Why do we *know*—what we know this minute?"

She dashed her hand across her eyes. Then, seeing the jar of fruit on the table, she reached for it and choked out:

"If I was you I wouldn't *tell* her her fruit was gone! Tell her it *ain't*. Tell her 265
it's all right—all of it. Here—take this in to prove it to her! She—she may never know whether it was broke or not."

She turned away.

Mrs. Peters reached out for the bottle of fruit as if she were glad to take it—as if touching a familiar thing, having something to do, could keep her from something else. She got up, looked about for something to wrap the fruit in, took a petticoat from the pile of clothes she had brought from the front room, and nervously started winding that round the bottle.

"My!" she began, in a high, false voice, "it's a good thing the men couldn't hear us! Getting all stirred up over a little thing like a—dead canary." She hurried over that. "As if that could have anything to do with—with—My, wouldn't they *laugh*?"

Footsteps were heard on the stairs.

"Maybe they would," muttered Mrs. Hale—"maybe they wouldn't." 270

"No, Peters," said the county attorney incisively; "it's all perfectly clear, except the reason for doing it. But you know juries when it comes to women. If there was some definite thing—something to show. Something to make a story about. A thing that would connect up with this clumsy way of doing it."

In a covert way Mrs. Hale looked at Mrs. Peters. Mrs. Peters was looking at her. Quickly they looked away from each other. The outer door opened and Mr. Hale came in.

"I've got the team round now," he said. "Pretty cold out there."

"I'm going to stay here awhile by myself," the county attorney suddenly announced. "You can send Frank out for me, can't you?" he asked the sheriff. "I want to go over everything. I'm not satisfied we can't do better."

Again, for one brief moment, the two women's eyes found one another. 275

The sheriff came up to the table.

"Did you want to see what Mrs. Peters was going to take in?"

The county attorney picked up the apron. He laughed.

"Oh, I guess they're not very dangerous things the ladies have picked out."

Mrs. Hale's hand was on the sewing basket in which the box was concealed. 280
She felt that she ought to take her hand off the basket. She did not seem able to. He picked up one of the quilt blocks which she had piled on to cover the box. Her eyes felt like fire. She had a feeling that if he took up the basket she would snatch it from him.

But he did not take it up. With another little laugh, he turned away, saying:

"No; Mrs. Peters doesn't need supervising. For that matter, a sheriff's wife is married to the law. Ever think of it that way, Mrs. Peters?"

Mrs. Peters was standing beside the table. Mrs. Hale shot a look up at her; but she could not see her face. Mrs. Peters had turned away. When she spoke, her voice was muffled.

"Not—just that way," she said.

"Married to the law!" chuckled Mrs. Peters' husband. He moved toward the 285
door into the front room, and said to the county attorney:

"I just want you to come in here a minute, George. We ought to take a look at these windows."

"Oh—windows," said the county attorney scoffingly.

"We'll be right out, Mr. Hale," said the sheriff to the farmer, who was still waiting by the door.

Hale went to look after the horses. The sheriff followed the county attorney into the other room. Again—for one moment—the two women were alone in that kitchen.

Martha Hale sprang up, her hands tight together, looking at that other 290
woman, with whom it rested. At first she could not see her eyes, for the sheriff's wife had not turned back since she turned away at the suggestion of being married to the law. But now Mrs. Hale made her turn back. Her eyes made her turn back. Slowly, unwillingly, Mrs. Peters turned her head until her eyes met the eyes of the other woman. There was a moment when they held each other in a steady, burning look in which there was no evasion nor flinching. Then Martha Hale's eyes pointed the way to the basket in which was hidden the thing that would make certain the conviction of the other woman—that woman who was not there and yet who had been there with them all through the hour.

For a moment Mrs. Peters did not move. And then she did it. With a rush forward, she threw back the quilt pieces, got the box, tried to put it in her handbag. It was too big. Desperately she opened it, started to take the bird out. But there she broke—she could not touch the bird. She stood helpless, foolish.

There was the sound of a knob turning in the inner door. Martha Hale snatched the box from the sheriff's wife, and got it in the pocket of her big coat just as the sheriff and the county attorney came back into the kitchen.

"Well, Henry," said the county attorney facetiously, "at least we found out that she was not going to quilt it. She was going to—what is it you call it, ladies?"

Mrs. Hale's hand was against the pocket of her coat. 295

"We call it—knot it, Mr. Henderson."

(1917)

Questions for Discussion and Writing

1. What do Mrs. Hale and Mrs. Peters surmise about Minnie Wright's life and her motives for killing her husband? Why are they able to grasp the truth of the situation when the men cannot?
2. Why do Mrs. Hale and Mrs. Peters decide to conceal the evidence of the strangled bird? What do you think of that decision?
3. What does it mean that Mrs. Peters is "married to the law"? What is significant and ironic about that description?
4. In what ways do Mrs. Hale and Mrs. Peters act as a "jury" in this case? Whom do they convict and whom do they exonerate?
5. Glaspell wrote an earlier version of this story—in a play entitled *Trifles* (pages 1028–38 in the Anthology of Drama). Write an essay comparing the two versions, considering differences in tone and emphasis. Present an argument for the form—fiction or drama—that you think is the more effective vehicle for telling this story.

D. H. Lawrence 1885–1930

D[avid] H[erbert] Lawrence, son of a coal miner, was raised in poverty and said of his parents, "Their marriage life has been one carnal, bloody fight. I was born hating my father: as early as ever I can remember, I shivered with horror when he touched me." In 1912, he fell in love with a married woman who abandoned her husband and three children to live with Lawrence in exile. He never ceased to rebel against Puritanism and social conventions, a rebellion that led to some of the most famous censorship trials of the twentieth century. His controversial novel *Lady Chatterley's Lover* (1928), for example, was banned as pornographic in both Britain and the United States until 1960.

The Rocking-Horse Winner

There was a woman who was beautiful, who started with all the advantages, yet she had no luck. She married for love, and the love turned to dust. She had bonny children, yet she felt they had been thrust upon her, and she could not love them. They looked at her coldly, as if they were finding fault with her. And hurriedly she felt she must cover up some fault in herself. Yet what it was that she must cover up she never knew. Nevertheless, when her children were present, she always felt the centre of her heart go hard. This troubled her, and in her manner she was all the more gentle and anxious for her children, as if she loved them very much. Only she herself knew that at the centre of her heart was a hard little place that could not feel love, no, not for anybody. Everybody else said of her: "She is such a good mother. She adores her children." Only she herself, and her children themselves, knew it was not so. They read it in each other's eyes.

There were a boy and two little girls. They lived in a pleasant house, with a garden, and they had discreet servants, and felt themselves superior to anyone in the neighbourhood.

Although they lived in style, they felt always an anxiety in the house. There was never enough money. The mother had a small income, and the father had a small income, but not nearly enough for the social position which they had to keep up. The father went into town to some office. But though he had good prospects, these prospects never materialised. There was always the grinding sense of the shortage of money, though the style was always kept up.

At last the mother said: "I will see if *I* can't make something." But she did not know where to begin. She racked her brains, and tried this thing and the other, but could not find anything successful. The failure made deep lines come into her face. Her children were growing up, they would have to go to school. There must be more money, there must be more money. The father, who was always very handsome and expensive in his tastes, seemed as if he never *would* be able to do anything worth doing. And the mother, who had a great belief in herself, did not succeed any better, and her tastes were just as expensive.

And so the house came to be haunted by the unspoken phrase: *There must be* 5
more money! There must be more money! The children could hear it all the time, though nobody said it aloud. They heard it at Christmas, when the expensive

and splendid toys filled the nursery. Behind the shining modern rocking-horse, behind the smart doll's house, a voice would start whispering: "There *must* be more money! There *must* be more money!" And the children would stop playing, to listen for a moment. They would look into each other's eyes, to see if they had all heard. And each one saw in the eyes of the other two that they too had heard. "There *must* be more money! There *must* be more money!"

It came whispering from the springs of the still-swaying rocking-horse, and even the horse, bending his wooden, champing head, heard it. The big doll, sitting so pink and smirking in her new pram,[1] could hear it quite plainly, and seemed to be smirking all the more self-consciously because of it. The foolish puppy, too, that took the place of the teddybear, he was looking so extraordinarily foolish for no other reason but that he heard the secret whisper all over the house: "There *must* be more money!"

Yet nobody ever said it aloud. The whisper was everywhere, and therefore no one spoke it. Just as no one ever says: "We are breathing!" in spite of the fact that breath is coming and going all the time.

"Mother," said the boy Paul one day, "why don't we keep a car of our own? Why do we always use uncle's, or else a taxi?"

"Because we're the poor members of the family," said the mother.

"But why *are* we, mother?"

"Well—I suppose," she said slowly and bitterly, "it's because your father has no luck."

The boy was silent for some time.

"Is luck money, mother?" he asked, rather timidly.

"No, Paul. Not quite. It's what causes you to have money."

"Oh!" said Paul vaguely. "I thought when Uncle Oscar said *filthy lucker*, it meant money."

"*Filthy lucre* does mean money," said the mother. "But it's lucre, not luck."

"Oh!" said the boy. "Then what *is* luck, mother?"

"It's what causes you to have money. If you're lucky you have money. That's why it's better to be born lucky than rich. If you're rich, you may lose your money. But if you're lucky, you will always get more money."

"Oh! Will you? And is father not lucky?"

"Very unlucky, I should say," she said bitterly.

The boy watched her with unsure eyes.

"Why?" he asked.

"I don't know. Nobody ever knows why one person is lucky and another unlucky."

"Don't they? Nobody at all? Does *nobody* know?"

"Perhaps God. But He never tells."

"He ought to, then. And aren't you lucky either, mother?"

"I can't be, if I married an unlucky husband."

"But by yourself, aren't you?"

"I used to think I was, before I married. Now I think I am very unlucky indeed."

"Why?"

"Well—never mind! Perhaps I'm not really," she said.

---

[1] Baby carriage.

The child looked at her to see if she meant it. But he saw, by the lines of her mouth, that she was only trying to hide something from him.

"Well, anyhow," he said stoutly, "I'm a lucky person."

"Why?" said his mother, with a sudden laugh.

He stared at her. He didn't even know why he had said it.

"God told me," he asserted, brazening it out.

"I hope He did, dear!" she said, again with a laugh, but rather bitter.

"He did, mother!"

"Excellent!" said the mother, using one of her husband's exclamations.

The boy saw she did not believe him; or rather, that she paid no attention to his assertion. This angered him somewhat, and made him want to compel her attention.

He went off by himself, vaguely, in a childish way, seeking for the clue to "luck." Absorbed, taking no heed of other people, he went about with a sort of stealth, seeking inwardly for luck. He wanted luck, he wanted it, he wanted it. When the two girls were playing dolls in the nursery, he would sit on his big rocking-horse, charging madly into space, with a frenzy that made the little girls peer at him uneasily. Wildly the horse careered, the waving dark hair of the boy tossed, his eyes had a strange glare in them. The little girls dared not speak to him.

When he had ridden to the end of his mad little journey, he climbed down and stood in front of his rocking-horse, staring fixedly into its lowered face. Its red mouth was slightly open, its big eye was wide and glassy-bright.

"Now!" he would silently command the snorting steed. "Now, take me to where there is luck! Now take me!"

And he would slash the horse on the neck with the little whip he had asked Uncle Oscar for. He *knew* the horse could take him to where there was luck, if only he forced it. So he would mount again and start on his furious ride, hoping at last to get there. He knew he could get there.

"You'll break your horse, Paul!" said the nurse.

"He's always riding like that! I wish he'd leave off!" said his elder sister Joan.

But he only glared down on them in silence. Nurse gave him up. She could make nothing of him. Anyhow, he was growing beyond her.

One day his mother and his Uncle Oscar came in when he was on one of his furious rides. He did not speak to them.

"Hallo, you young jockey! Riding a winner?" said his uncle.

"Aren't you growing too big for a rocking-horse? You're not a very little boy any longer, you know," said his mother.

But Paul only gave a blue glare from his big, rather close-set eyes. He would speak to nobody when he was in full tilt. His mother watched him with an anxious expression on her face.

At last he suddenly stopped forcing his horse into the mechanical gallop and slid down.

"Well, I got there!" he announced fiercely, his blue eyes still flaring, and his sturdy long legs straddling apart.

"Where did you get to?" asked his mother.

"Where I wanted to go," he flared back at her.

"That's right, son!" said Uncle Oscar. "Don't you stop till you get there. What's the horse's name?"

"He doesn't have a name," said the boy.

"Gets on without all right?" asked the uncle.

"Well, he has different names. He was called Sansovino last week."

"Sansovino, eh? Won the Ascot.[2] How did you know this name?"

"He always talks about horse-races with Bassett," said Joan.

The uncle was delighted to find that his small nephew was posted with all the racing news. Bassett, the young gardener, who had been wounded in the left foot in the war and had got his present job through Oscar Cresswell, whose batman[3] he had been, was a perfect blade of the "turf." He lived in the racing events, and the small boy lived with him.

Oscar Cresswell got it all from Bassett.

"Master Paul comes and asks me, so I can't do more than tell him, sir," said Bassett, his face terribly serious, as if he were speaking of religious matters.

"And does he ever put anything on a horse he fancies?"

"Well—I don't want to give him away—he's a young sport, a fine sport, sir. Would you mind asking him himself? He sort of takes a pleasure in it, and perhaps he'd feel I was giving him away, sir, if you don't mind."

Bassett was serious as a church.

The uncle went back to his nephew and took him off for a ride in the car.

"Say, Paul, old man, do you ever put anything on a horse?" the uncle asked.

The boy watched the handsome man closely.

"Why, do you think I oughtn't to?" he parried.

"Not a bit of it! I thought perhaps you might give me a tip for the Lincoln."[4]

The car sped on into the country, going down to Uncle Oscar's place in Hampshire.

"Honour bright?" said the nephew.

"Honour bright, son!" said the uncle.

"Well, then, Daffodil."

"Daffodil! I doubt it, sonny. What about Mirza?"

"I only know the winner," said the boy. "That's Daffodil."

"Daffodil, eh?"

There was a pause. Daffodil was an obscure horse comparatively.

"Uncle!"

"Yes, son?"

"You won't let it go any further, will you? I promised Bassett."

"Bassett be damned, old man! What's he got to do with it?"

"We're partners. We've been partners from the first. Uncle, he lent me my first five shillings, which I lost. I promised him, honour bright, it was only between me and him; only you gave me that ten shilling note I started winning with, so I thought you were lucky. You won't let it go any further, will you?"

The boy gazed at his uncle from those big, hot, blue eyes, set rather close together. The uncle stirred and laughed uneasily.

"Right you are, son! I'll keep your tip private. Daffodil, eh? How much are you putting on him?"

"All except twenty pounds," said the boy. "I keep that in reserve."

The uncle thought it a good joke.

---

[2]A famous horse race run near Ascot in England.

[3]A military officer's orderly or assistant.

[4]A horse race run at Lincoln Downs.

“You keep twenty pounds in reserve, do you, you young romancer! What are 90
you betting, then?”

“I’m betting three hundred,” said the boy gravely. “But it’s between you and me, Uncle Oscar! Honour bright?”

The uncle burst into a roar of laughter.

“It’s between you and me all right, you young Nat Gould,”[5] he said, laughing. “But where’s your three hundred?”

“Bassett keeps it for me. We’re partners.”

“You are, are you! And what is Bassett putting on Daffodil?” 95

“He won’t go quite as high as I do, I expect. Perhaps he’ll go a hundred and fifty.”

“What, pennies?” laughed the uncle.

“Pounds,” said the child, with a surprised look at his uncle. “Bassett keeps a bigger reserve than I do.”

Between wonder and amusement Uncle Oscar was silent. He pursued the matter no further, but he determined to take his nephew with him to the Lincoln races.

“Now, son,” he said, “I’m putting twenty on Mirza, and I’ll put five on for 100
you on any horse you fancy. What’s your pick?”

“Daffodil, uncle.”

“No, not the fiver on Daffodil!”

“I should if it was my own fiver,” said the child.

“Good! Good! Right you are! A fiver for me and a fiver for you on Daffodil.”

The child had never been to a race-meeting before, and his eyes were blue 105
fire. He pursed his mouth tight and watched. A Frenchman just in front had put his money on Lancelot. Wild with excitement, he flayed his arms up and down, yelling, “*Lancelot! Lancelot!*” in his French accent.

Daffodil came in first, Lancelot second, Mirza third. The child, flushed and with eyes blazing, was curiously serene. His uncle brought him four five-pound notes, four to one.

“What am I to do with these?” he cried, waving them before the boy’s eyes.

“I suppose we’ll talk to Bassett,” said the boy. “I expect I have fifteen hundred now; and twenty in reserve; and this twenty.”

His uncle studied him for some moments.

“Look here, son!” he said. “You’re not serious about Bassett and that fifteen 110
hundred, are you?”

“Yes, I am. But it’s between you and me, uncle. Honour bright?”

“Honour bright all right, son! But I must talk to Bassett.”

“If you’d like to be a partner, uncle, with Bassett and me, we could all be partners. Only, you’d have to promise, honour bright, uncle, not to let it go beyond us three. Bassett and I are lucky, and you must be lucky, because it was your ten shillings I started winning with…”

Uncle Oscar took both Bassett and Paul into Richmond Park for an afternoon, and there they talked.

“It’s like this, you see, sir,” Bassett said. “Master Paul would get me talking 115
about racing events, spinning yarns, you know, sir. And he was always keen on knowing if I’d made or if I’d lost. It’s about a year since, now, that I put five

[5]Nathaniel Gould, a popular writer who specialized in fiction and articles about horse racing.

shillings on Blush of Dawn for him: and we lost. Then the luck turned, with that ten shillings he had from you: that we put on Singhalese. And since that time, it's been pretty steady, all things considering. What do you say, Master Paul?"

"We're all right when we're sure," said Paul. "It's when we're not quite sure that we go down."

"Oh, but we're careful then," said Bassett.

"But when are you *sure?*" smiled Uncle Oscar.

"It's Master Paul, sir," said Bassett in a secret, religious voice. "It's as if he had it from heaven. Like Daffodil, now, for the Lincoln. That was as sure as eggs."

"Did you put anything on Daffodil?" asked Oscar Cresswell.

"Yes, sir. I made my bit."

"And my nephew?"

Bassett was obstinately silent, looking at Paul.

"I made twelve hundred, didn't I, Bassett? I told uncle I was putting three hundred on Daffodil."

"That's right," said Bassett, nodding.

"But where's the money?" asked the uncle.

"I keep it safe locked up, sir. Master Paul he can have it any minute he likes to ask for it."

"What, fifteen hundred pounds?"

"And twenty! And *forty*, that is, with the twenty he made on the course."

"It's amazing!" said the uncle.

"If Master Paul offers you to be partners, sir, I would, if I were you: if you'll excuse me," said Bassett.

Oscar Cresswell thought about it.

"I'll see the money," he said.

They drove home again, and, sure enough, Bassett came round to the garden-house with fifteen hundred pounds in notes. The twenty pounds reserve was left with Joe Glee, in the Turf Commission deposit.

"You see, it's all right, uncle, when I'm *sure!* Then we go strong, for all we're worth. Don't we, Bassett?"

"We do that, Master Paul."

"And when are you sure?" said the uncle, laughing.

"Oh, well, sometimes I'm *absolutely* sure, like about Daffodil," said the boy; "and sometimes I have an idea; and sometimes I haven't even an idea, have I, Bassett? Then we're careful, because we mostly go down."

"You do, do you! And when you're sure, like about Daffodil, what makes you sure, sonny?"

"Oh, well, I don't know," said the boy uneasily. "I'm sure, you know, uncle; that's all."

"It's as if he had it from heaven, sir," Bassett reiterated.

"I should say so!" said the uncle.

But he became a partner. And when the Leger[6] was coming on Paul was "sure" about Lively Spark, which was a quite inconsiderable horse. The boy insisted on putting a thousand on the horse, Bassett went for five hundred, and Oscar Cresswell two hundred. Lively Spark came in first, and the betting had been ten to one against him. Paul had made ten thousand.

---

[6]The St. Leger Stakes race.

"You see," he said, "I was absolutely sure of him."

Even Oscar Cresswell had cleared two thousand. 145

"Look here, son," he said, "this sort of thing makes me nervous."

"It needn't, uncle! Perhaps I shan't be sure again for a long time."

"But what are you going to do with your money?" asked the uncle.

"Of course," said the boy, "I started it for mother. She said she had no luck, because father is unlucky, so I thought if *I* was lucky, it might stop whispering."

"What might stop whispering?" 150

"Our house. I *hate* our house for whispering."

"What does it whisper?"

"Why—why"—the boy fidgeted—"why, I don't know. But it's always short of money, you know, uncle."

"I know it, son, I know it."

"You know people send mother writs,[7] don't you, uncle?" 155

"I'm afraid I do," said the uncle.

"And then the house whispers, like people laughing at you behind your back. It's awful, that is! I thought if I was lucky—"

"You might stop it," added the uncle.

The boy watched him with big blue eyes, that had an uncanny cold fire in them, and he said never a word.

"Well, then!" said the uncle. "What are we doing?" 160

"I shouldn't like mother to know I was lucky," said the boy.

"Why not, son?"

"She'd stop me."

"I don't think she would."

"Oh"—and the boy writhed in an odd way—"I *don't* want her to know, uncle." 165

"All right, son! We'll manage it without her knowing."

They managed it very easily. Paul, at the other's suggestion, handed over five thousand pounds to his uncle, who deposited it with the family lawyer, who was then to inform Paul's mother that a relative had put five thousand pounds into his hands, which sum was to be paid out a thousand pounds at a time, on the mother's birthday, for the next five years.

"So she'll have a birthday present of a thousand pounds for five successive years," said Uncle Oscar. "I hope it won't make it all the harder for her later."

Paul's mother had her birthday in November. The house had been "whispering" worse than ever lately, and, even in spite of his luck, Paul could not bear up against it. He was very anxious to see the effect of the birthday letter, telling his mother about the thousand pounds.

When there were no visitors, Paul now took his meals with his parents, as he was beyond the nursery control. His mother went into town nearly every day. She had discovered that she had an odd knack of sketching furs and dress materials, so she worked secretly in the studio of a friend who was the chief "artist" for the leading drapers. She drew the figures of ladies in furs and ladies in silk and sequins for the newspaper advertisements. This young woman artist earned several thousand pounds a year, but Paul's mother only made several hundreds, 170

[7]Requests for payment from creditors.

and she was again dissatisfied. She so wanted to be first in something, and she did not succeed, even in making sketches for drapery advertisements.

She was down to breakfast on the morning of her birthday. Paul watched her face as she read her letters. He knew the lawyer's letter. As his mother read it, her face hardened and became more expressionless. Then a cold, determined look came on her mouth. She hid the letter under the pile of others, and said not a word about it.

"Didn't you have anything nice in the post for your birthday, mother?" said Paul.

"Quite moderately nice," she said, her voice cold and absent.

She went away to town without saying more.

But in the afternoon Uncle Oscar appeared. He said Paul's mother had had a long interview with the lawyer, asking if the whole five thousand could not be advanced at once, as she was in debt.

"What do you think, uncle?" asked the boy.

"I leave it to you, son."

"Oh, let her have it, then! We can get some more with the other," said the boy.

"A bird in the hand is worth two in the bush, laddie!" said Uncle Oscar.

"But I'm sure to *know* for the Grand National; or the Lincolnshire; or else the Derby.[8] I'm sure to know for *one* of them," said Paul.

So Uncle Oscar signed the agreement, and Paul's mother touched the whole five thousand. Then something very curious happened. The voices in the house suddenly went mad, like a chorus of frogs on a spring evening. There were certain new furnishings, and Paul had a tutor. He was *really* going to Eton, his father's school, in the following autumn. There were flowers in the winter, and a blossoming of the luxury Paul's mother had been used to. And yet the voices in the house, behind the sprays of mimosa and almond-blossom, and from under the piles of iridescent cushions, simply trilled and screamed in a sort of ecstasy: "There *must* be more money! Oh-h-h; there *must* be more money. Oh, now, now-w! Now-w-w—there *must* be more money!—more than ever! More than ever!"

It frightened Paul terribly. He studied away at his Latin and Greek with his tutor. But his intense hours were spent with Bassett. The Grand National had gone by: he had not "known," and had lost a hundred pounds. Summer was at hand. He was in agony for the Lincoln. But even for the Lincoln he didn't "know," and he lost fifty pounds. He became wild-eyed and strange, as if something were going to explode in him.

"Let it alone, son! Don't you bother about it!" urged Uncle Oscar. But it was as if the boy couldn't really hear what his uncle was saying.

"I've got to know for the Derby! I've got to know for the Derby!" the child reiterated, his big blue eyes blazing with a sort of madness.

His mother noticed how overwrought he was.

"You'd better go to the seaside. Wouldn't you like to go now to the seaside, instead of waiting? I think you'd better," she said, looking down at him anxiously, her heart curiously heavy because of him.

But the child lifted his uncanny blue eyes.

"I couldn't possibly go before the Derby, mother!" he said. "I couldn't possibly!"

[8]All important horse races.

"Why not?" she said, her voice becoming heavy when she was opposed. "Why not? You can still go from the seaside to see the Derby with your Uncle Oscar, if that's what you wish. No need for you to wait here. Besides, I think you care too much about these races. It's a bad sign. My family has been a gambling family, and you won't know till you grow up how much damage it has done. But it has done damage. I shall have to send Bassett away, and ask Uncle Oscar not to talk racing to you, unless you promise to be reasonable about it: go away to the seaside and forget it. You're all nerves!"

"I'll do what you like, mother, so long as you don't send me away till after the Derby," the boy said.

"Send you away from where? Just from this house?"

"Yes," he said, gazing at her.

"Why, you curious child, what makes you care about this house so much, suddenly? I never knew you loved it."

He gazed at her without speaking. He had a secret within a secret, something he had not divulged, even to Bassett or to his Uncle Oscar.

But his mother, after standing undecided and a little bit sullen for some moments, said:

"Very well, then! Don't go to the seaside till after the Derby, if you don't wish it. But promise me you won't let your nerves go to pieces. Promise you won't think so much about horse-racing and *events*, as you call them!"

"Oh no," said the boy casually. "I won't think much about them, mother. You needn't worry. I wouldn't worry, mother, if I were you."

"If you were me and I were you," said his mother, "I wonder what we *should* do!"

"But you know you needn't worry, mother, don't you?" the boy repeated.

"I should be awfully glad to know it," she said wearily.

"Oh, well, you *can*, you know. I mean, you *ought* to know you needn't worry," he insisted.

"Ought I? Then I'll see about it," she said.

Paul's secret of secrets was his wooden horse, that which had no name. Since he was emancipated from a nurse and a nursery-governess, he had had his rocking-horse removed to his own bedroom at the top of the house.

"Surely you're too big for a rocking-horse!" his mother had remonstrated.

"Well, you see, mother, till I can have a *real* horse, I like to have *some* sort of animal about," had been his quaint answer.

"Do you feel he keeps you company?" she laughed.

"Oh yes! He's very good, he always keeps me company, when I'm there," said Paul.

So the horse, rather shabby, stood in an arrested prance in the boy's bedroom.

The Derby was drawing near, and the boy grew more and more tense. He hardly heard what was spoken to him, he was very frail, and his eyes were really uncanny. His mother had sudden strange seizures of uneasiness about him. Sometimes, for half an hour, she would feel a sudden anxiety about him that was almost anguish. She wanted to rush to him at once, and know he was safe.

Two nights before the Derby, she was at a big party in town, when one of her rushes of anxiety about her boy, her first born, gripped her heart till she could hardly speak. She fought with the feeling, might and main, for she believed in common sense. But it was too strong. She had to leave the dance and go downstairs to telephone to the country. The children's nursery-governess was terribly surprised and startled at being rung up in the night.

"Are the children all right, Miss Wilmot?"

"Oh yes, they are quite all right."

"Master Paul? Is he all right?"

"He went to bed as right as a trivet. Shall I run up and look at him?"

"No," said Paul's mother reluctantly. "No! Don't trouble. It's all right. Don't sit up. We shall be home fairly soon." She did not want her son's privacy intruded upon.

"Very good," said the governess.

It was about one o'clock when Paul's mother and father drove up to their house. All was still. Paul's mother went to her room and slipped off her white fur cloak. She had told her maid not to wait up for her. She heard her husband downstairs, mixing a whisky and soda.

And then, because of the strange anxiety at her heart, she stole upstairs to her son's room. Noiselessly she went along the upper corridor. Was there a faint noise? What was it?

She stood, with arrested muscles, outside his door, listening. There was a strange, heavy, and yet not loud noise. Her heart stood still. It was a soundless noise, yet rushing and powerful. Something huge, in violent, hushed motion. What was it? What in God's name was it? She ought to know. She felt that she knew the noise. She knew what it was.

Yet she could not place it. She couldn't say what it was. And on and on it went, like a madness.

Softly, frozen with anxiety and fear, she turned the door-handle.

The room was dark. Yet in the space near the window, she heard and saw something plunging to and fro. She gazed in fear and amazement.

Then suddenly she switched on the light, and saw her son, in his green pyjamas, madly surging on the rocking-horse. The blaze of light suddenly lit him up, as he urged the wooden horse, and lit her up, as she stood, blonde, in her dress of pale green and crystal, in the doorway.

"Paul!" she cried. "Whatever are you doing?"

"It's Malabar!" he screamed in a powerful, strange voice. "It's Malabar!"

His eyes blazed at her for one strange and senseless second, as he ceased urging his wooden horse. Then he fell with a crash to the ground, and she, all her tormented motherhood flooding upon her, rushed to gather him up.

But he was unconscious, and unconscious he remained, with some brain-fever. He talked and tossed, and his mother sat stonily by his side.

"Malabar! Malabar! Bassett, Bassett, I *know*! It's Malabar!"

So the child cried, trying to get up and urge the rocking-horse that gave him his inspiration.

"What does he mean by Malabar?" asked the heart-frozen mother.

"I don't know," said the father stonily.

"What does he mean by Malabar?" she asked her brother Oscar.

"It's one of the horses running for the Derby," was the answer.

And, in spite of himself, Oscar Cresswell spoke to Bassett, and himself put a thousand on Malabar: at fourteen to one.

The third day of the illness was critical: they were waiting for a change. The boy, with his rather long, curly hair, was tossing ceaselessly on the pillow. He neither slept nor regained consciousness, and his eyes were like blue stones. His mother sat, feeling her heart had gone, turned actually into a stone.

In the evening, Oscar Cresswell did not come, but Bassett sent a message, saying could he come up for one moment, just one moment? Paul's mother was very angry at the intrusion, but on second thoughts she agreed. The boy was the same. Perhaps Bassett might bring him to consciousness.

The gardener, a shortish fellow with a little brown mustache and sharp little brown eyes, tiptoed into the room, touched his imaginary cap to Paul's mother, and stole to the bedside, staring with glittering, smallish eyes at the tossing, dying child.

"Master Paul!" he whispered. "Master Paul! Malabar came in first all right, a clean win. I did as you told me. You've made over seventy thousand pounds, you have; you've got over eighty thousand. Malabar came in all right, Master Paul."

"Malabar! Malabar! Did I say Malabar, mother? Did I say Malabar? Do you think I'm lucky, mother? I knew Malabar, didn't I? Over eighty thousand pounds! I call that lucky, don't you, mother? Over eighty thousand pounds! I knew, didn't I know I knew? Malabar came in all right. If I ride my horse till I'm sure, then I tell you, Bassett, you can go as high as you like. Did you go for all you were worth, Bassett?

"I went a thousand on it, Master Paul." 240

"I never told you, mother, that if I can ride my horse, and *get there*, then I'm absolutely sure—oh, absolutely! Mother, did I ever tell you? I *am* lucky!"

"No, you never did," said his mother.

But the boy died in the night.

And even as he lay dead, his mother heard her brother's voice saying to her: "My God, Hester, you're eighty thousand to the good, and a poor devil of a son to the bad. But, poor devil, poor devil, he's best gone out of a life where he rides his rocking-horse to find a winner."

(1932)

Questions for Discussion and Writing

1. How did you respond to the supernatural elements of "The Rocking-Horse Winner"? If you were able to suspend your disbelief as you read the story, what do you think allowed you to do so? If the unbelievable elements impaired your acceptance of the story, why? Why do you think the supernatural elements are used in the story?
2. What happens when Paul manages to present some money to his mother? Why do the voices become louder, rather than softer, over the course of the story? What does money represent to Paul and to his mother?
3. The story seems to criticize both people who think that success and failure are purely a matter of luck and those who pursue control zealously, as Paul does. How can these two criticisms be reconciled?
4. Why must Paul die in the end?
5. Most readers see the cold-hearted mother as the villain of the story. However, Oscar and Bassett take meaningful roles, too. Present a reading of the story in which you argue that the unfit mother is not the source of all evil.

Katherine Anne Porter 1890–1980

Katherine Anne Porter, reared on a hard-scrabble ranch in Texas by her father and her strict grandmother, finished only one year of high school because, at age sixteen, she ran away from her convent school and got married. This early marriage, like the three that followed, did not last long; she never had children. In 1918 she very nearly died during the Spanish influenza pandemic and, after her recovery, traveled widely, living for periods in Mexico and Europe. She became an agnostic during the 1930s but finally re-embraced Catholicism in the last decade of her life. During those final years, she kept her coffin upright on display as a decoration in her living room.

The Grave

The grandfather, dead for more than thirty years, had been twice disturbed in his long repose by the constancy and possessiveness of his widow. She removed his bones first to Louisiana and then to Texas as if she had set out to find her own burial place, knowing well she would never return to the places she had left. In Texas she set up a small cemetery in a corner of her first farm, and, as the family connection grew, and oddments of relations came over from Kentucky to settle, it contained at last about twenty graves. After the grandmother's death, part of her land was to be sold for the benefit of certain of her children, and the cemetery happened to lie in the part set aside for sale. It was necessary to take up the bodies and bury them again in the family plot in the big new public cemetery, where the grandmother had been buried. At last her husband was to lie beside her for eternity, as she had planned.

The family cemetery had been a pleasant small neglected garden of tangled rose bushes and ragged cedar trees and cypress, the simple flat stones rising out of uncropped sweet-smelling wild grass. The graves were lying open and empty one burning day when Miranda and her brother Paul, who often went together to hunt rabbits and doves, propped their twenty-two Winchester rifles carefully against the rail fence, climbed over and explored among the graves. She was nine years old and he was twelve.

They peered into the pits all shaped alike with such purposeful accuracy, and looking at each other with pleased adventurous eyes, they said in solemn tones: "These were graves!" trying by words to shape a special, suitable emotion in their minds, but they felt nothing except an agreeable thrill of wonder: they were seeing a new sight, doing something they had not done before. In them both there was also a small disappointment at the entire commonplaceness of the actual spectacle. Even if it had once contained a coffin for years upon years, when the coffin was gone a grave was just a hole in the ground. Miranda leaped into the pit that had held her grandfather's bones. Scratching around aimlessly and pleasurably as any young animal, she scooped up a lump of earth and weighed it in her palm. It had a pleasantly sweet, corrupt smell, being mixed with cedar needles and small leaves, and as the crumbs fell apart, she saw a silver dove no larger than a hazel nut, with spread wings and a neat fan-shaped tail. The breast had a deep round hollow in it. Turning it up to the fierce sunlight, she saw that the inside of the hollow was cut in little whorls. She scrambled out, over the pile of loose earth that had fallen back into one end of the grave, calling to Paul that she had found something, he must guess what.... His head appeared smiling over the rim of another grave. He waved a closed hand at her. "I've got something too!" They ran to compare treasures, making a game of it, so many guesses each, all wrong, and a final show-down with opened palms. Paul had found a thin wide gold ring carved with intricate flowers and leaves. Miranda was smitten at sight of the ring and wished to have it. Paul seemed more impressed by the dove. They made a trade, with some little bickering. After he had got the dove in his hand, Paul said, "Don't you know what this is? This is a screw head for a *coffin*!...I'll bet nobody else in the world has one like this!"

Miranda glanced at it without covetousness. She had the gold ring on her thumb; it fitted perfectly. "Maybe we ought to go now," she said, "maybe one of the niggers 'll see us and tell somebody." They knew the land had been sold, the cemetery was no longer theirs, and they felt like trespassers. They climbed back over the fence, slung their rifles loosely under their arms—they had been shooting at targets with various kinds of firearms since they were seven years old—and set out to look for the rabbits and doves or whatever small game might happen along. On these expeditions Miranda always followed at Paul's heels along the path, obeying instructions about handling her gun when going through fences, learning how to stand it up properly so it would not slip and fire unexpectedly; how to wait her time for a shot and not just bang away in the air without looking, spoiling shots for Paul, who really could hit things if given a chance. Now and then, in her excitement at seeing birds whizz up suddenly before her face, or a rabbit leap across her very toes, she lost her head, and almost without sighting she flung her rifle up and pulled the trigger. She hardly ever hit any sort of mark. She had no proper sense of hunting at all. Her brother would be often completely disgusted with her. "You don't care whether you get your bird or not," he said. "That's no way to hunt." Miranda could not understand his indignation. She had seen him smash his hat and yell with fury when he had missed his aim. "What I like about shooting," said Miranda, with exasperating inconsequence, "is pulling the trigger and hearing the noise."

5 "Then, by golly," said Paul, "whyn't you go back to the range and shoot at bulls-eyes?"

"I'd just as soon," said Miranda, "only like this, we walk around more."

"Well, you just stay behind and stop spoiling my shots," said Paul, who, when he made a kill, wanted to be certain he had made it. Miranda, who alone brought down a bird once in twenty rounds, always claimed as her own any game they got when they fired at the same moment. It was tiresome and unfair and her brother was sick of it.

"Now, the first dove we see, or the first rabbit, is mine," he told her. "And the next will be yours. Remember that and don't get smarty."

"What about snakes?" asked Miranda idly. "Can I have the first snake?"

10 Waving her thumb gently and watching her gold ring glitter, Miranda lost interest in shooting. She was wearing her summer roughing outfit: dark blue overalls, a light blue shirt, a hired-man's straw hat, and thick brown sandals. Her brother had the same outfit except his was a sober hickory-nut color. Ordinarily Miranda preferred her overalls to any other dress, though it was making rather a scandal in the countryside, for the year was 1903, and in the back country the law

of female decorum had teeth in it. Her father had been criticized for letting his girls dress like boys and go careering around astride barebacked horses. Big sister Maria, the really independent and fearless one, in spite of her rather affected ways, rode at a dead run with only a rope knotted around her horse's nose. It was said the motherless family was running down, with the grandmother no longer there to hold it together. It was known that she had discriminated against her son Harry in her will, and that he was in straits about money. Some of his old neighbors reflected with vicious satisfaction that now he would probably not be so stiff-necked, nor have any more high-stepping horses either. Miranda knew this, though she could not say how. She had met along the road old women of the kind who smoked corn-cob pipes, who had treated her grandmother with most sincere respect. They slanted their gummy old eyes side-ways at the granddaughter and said, "Ain't you ashamed of yoself, Missy? It's against the Scriptures to dress like that. What yo Pappy thinkin about?" Miranda, with her powerful social sense, which was like a fine set of antennae radiating from every pore of her skin, would feel ashamed because she knew well it was rude and ill-bred to shock anybody, even bad-tempered old crones, though she had faith in her father's judgment and was perfectly comfortable in the clothes. Her father had said, "They're just what you need, and they'll save your dresses for school. . . ." This sounded quite simple and natural to her. She had been brought up in rigorous economy. Wastefulness was vulgar. It was also a sin. These were truths; she had heard them repeated many times and never once disputed.

Now the ring, shining with the serene purity of fine gold on her rather grubby thumb, turned her feelings against her overalls and sockless feet, toes sticking through the thick brown leather straps. She wanted to go back to the farmhouse, take a good cold bath, dust herself with plenty of Maria's violet talcum powder—provided Maria was not present to object, of course—put on the thinnest, most becoming dress she owned, with a big sash; and sit in a wicker chair under the trees. . . . These things were not all she wanted, of course; she had vague stirrings of desire for luxury and a grand way of living which could not take precise form in her imagination but were founded on family legend of past wealth and leisure. These immediate comforts were what she could have, and she wanted them at once. She lagged rather far behind Paul, and once she thought of just turning back without a word and going home. She stopped, thinking that Paul would never do that to her, and so she would have to tell him. When a rabbit leaped, she let Paul have it without dispute. He killed it with one shot.

When she came up with him, he was already kneeling, examining the wound, the rabbit trailing from his hands. "Right through the head," he said complacently, as if he had aimed for it. He took out his sharp, competent bowie knife and started to skin the body. He did it very cleanly and quickly. Uncle Jimbilly knew how to prepare the skins so that Miranda always had fur coats for her dolls, for though she never cared much for her dolls she liked seeing them in fur coats. The children knelt facing each other over the dead animal. Miranda watched admiringly while her brother stripped the skin away as if he were taking off a glove. The flayed flesh emerged dark scarlet, sleek, firm; Miranda with thumb and finger felt the long fine muscles with the silvery flat strips binding them to the joints. Brother lifted the oddly bloated belly. "Look," he said, in a low amazed voice. "It was going to have young ones."

Very carefully he slit the thin flesh from the center ribs to the flanks, and a scarlet bag appeared. He slit again and pulled the bag open, and there lay a bundle of tiny rabbits, each wrapped in a thin scarlet veil. The brother pulled these off and there they were, dark gray, their sleek wet down lying in minute even ripples, like a baby's head just washed, their unbelievably small delicate ears folded close, their little blind faces almost featureless.

Miranda said, "Oh, I want to *see*," under her breath. She looked and looked—excited but not frightened, for she was accustomed to the sight of animals killed in hunting—filled with pity and astonishment and a kind of shocked delight in the wonderful little creatures for their own sakes, they were so pretty. She touched one of them ever so carefully, "Ah, there's blood running over them," she said and began to tremble without knowing why. Yet she wanted most deeply to see and to know. Having seen, she felt at once as if she had known all along. The very memory of her former ignorance faded, she had always known just this. No one had ever told her anything outright, she had been rather unobservant of the animal life around her because she was so accustomed to animals. They seemed simply disorderly and unaccountably rude in their habits, but altogether natural and not very interesting. Her brother had spoken as if he had known about everything all along. He may have seen all this before. He had never said a word to her, but she knew now a part at least of what he knew. She understood a little of the secret, formless intuitions in her own mind and body, which had been clearing up, taking form, so gradually and so steadily she had not realized that she was learning what she had to know. Paul said cautiously, as if he were talking about something forbidden: "They were just about ready to be born." His voice dropped on the last word. "I know," said Miranda, "like kittens. I know, like babies." She was quietly and terribly agitated, standing again with her rifle under her arm, looking down at the bloody heap. "I don't want the skin," she said, "I won't have it." Paul buried the young rabbits again in their mother's body, wrapped the skin around her, carried her to a clump of sage bushes, and hid her away. He came out again at once and said to Miranda, with an eager friendliness, a confidential tone quite unusual in him, as if he were taking her into an important secret on equal terms: "Listen now. Now you listen to me, and don't ever forget. Don't you ever tell a living soul that you saw this. Don't tell a soul: Don't tell Dad because I'll get into trouble. He'll say I'm leading you into things you ought not to do. He's always saying that. So now don't you go and forget and blab out sometime the way you're always doing.... Now, that's a secret. Don't you tell."

Miranda never told, she did not even wish to tell anybody. She thought about 15
the whole worrisome affair with confused unhappiness for a few days. Then it sank quietly into her mind and was heaped over by accumulated thousands of impressions, for nearly twenty years. One day she was picking her path among the puddles and crushed refuse of a market street in a strange city of a strange country, when without warning, plain and clear in its true colors as if she looked through a frame upon a scene that had not stirred nor changed since the moment it happened, the episode of that far-off day leaped from its burial place before her mind's eye. She was so reasonlessly horrified she halted suddenly staring, the scene before her eyes dimmed by the vision back of them. An Indian vendor had held up before her a tray of dyed sugar sweets, in the shapes of all kinds of small creatures: birds, baby chicks, baby rabbits, lambs, baby pigs. They were in gay colors and smelled of vanilla, maybe.... It was a very hot day and the smell in the market, with its piles of raw flesh and wilting flowers, was like the mingled sweetness and corruption she had smelled that other day in the empty cemetery at home: the day she had remembered always until now vaguely as the time she and her brother had found

treasure in the opened graves. Instantly upon this thought the dreadful vision faded, and she saw clearly her brother, whose childhood face she had forgotten, standing again in the blazing sunshine, again twelve years old, a pleased sober smile in his eyes, turning the silver dove over and over in his hands.

(1935)

Questions for Discussion and Writing

1. One critic observes that the two children are like Adam and Eve. What similarities do you see?
2. What associations can you make with Porter's symbols of the grave, the dove, the ring, and the stillborn rabbits?
3. Why is Miranda so shaken by seeing the dead babies? Can you explain the nature of the "secret formless intuitions" being revealed to her in paragraph 14?
4. What theme or themes can you discover in this story?
5. Write an interpretation that makes a claim about the central image of the grave and its associations with several types of burial.

Zora Neale Hurston 1891–1960

Zora Neale Hurston grew up in Eatonville, Florida, the first incorporated all-black community in America. Her father, a Baptist preacher, was the mayor, but the family was poor. "Mama," she said, "exhorted her children at every opportunity to 'jump at de sun.' We might not land on the sun, but at least we would get off the ground." She won a scholarship to Barnard College, studied anthropology, and became a prominent member of the black cultural revival known as the Harlem Renaissance. Although a noted author and folklorist, she alienated so many people by her opposition to the civil rights movement that she died in 1960 in proverty and obscurity.

Spunk

I

A giant of a brown-skinned man sauntered up the one street of the village and out into the palmetto thickets with a small pretty woman clinging lovingly to his arm.

"Looka theah, folkses!" cried Elijah Mosley, slapping his leg gleefully. "Theah they go, big as life an' brassy as tacks."

All the loungers in the store tried to walk to the door with an air of nonchalance but with small success.

"Now pee-eople!" Walter Thomas gasped. "Will you look at 'em!"

"But that's one thing Ah likes about Spunk Banks—he ain't skeered of nothin' 5
on God's green footstool—*nothin'*! He rides that log down at saw-mill jus' like he struts 'round wid another man's wife—jus' don't give a kitty. When Tes' Miller got cut to giblets on that circle-saw, Spunk steps right up and starts ridin'. The rest of us was skeered to go near it."

A round-shouldered figure in overalls much too large came nervously in the door and the talking ceased. The men looked at each other and winked.

"Gimme some soda-water. Sass'prilla. Ah reckon," the newcomer ordered, and stood far down the counter near the open pickled pig-feet tub to drink it.

Elijah nudged Walter and turned with mock gravity to the newcomer.

"Say, Joe, how's everything up yo' way? How's yo' wife?"

Joe started and all but dropped the bottle he was holding. He swallowed several 10
times painfully and his lips trembled.

"Aw 'Lige, you oughtn't to do nothin' like that," Walter grumbled. Elijah ignored him.

"She jus' passed heah a few minutes ago goin' thata way," with a wave of his hand in the direction of the woods.

Now Joe knew his wife had passed that way. He knew that the men lounging in the general store had seen her; moreover, he knew that the men knew *he* knew. He stood there silent for a long moment staring blankly, with his Adam's apple twitching nervously up and down his throat. One could actually *see* the pain he was suffering, his eyes, his face, his hands, and even the dejected slump of his shoulders. He set the bottle down upon the counter. He didn't bang it, just eased it out of his hand silently and fiddled with his suspender buckle.

"Well, Ah'm goin' after her to-day. Ah'm goin' an' fetch her back, Spunk's done gone too fur."

He reached deep down into his trouser pocket and drew out a hollow 15
ground razor, large and shiny, and passed his moistened thumb back and forth over the edge.

"Talkin' like a man, Joe. 'Course that's yo' fambly affairs, but Ah like to see grit in anybody."

Joe Kanty laid down a nickel and stumbled out into the street.

Dusk crept in from the woods. Ike Clarke lit the swinging oil lamp that was almost immediately surrounded by candle-flies. The men laughed boisterously behind Joe's back as they watched him shamble woodward.

"You oughtn't to said whut you said to him, 'Lige—look how it worked him up," Walter chided.

"And Ah hope it did work him up. Tain't even decent for a man to take and 20
take like he do."

"Spunk will sho' kill him."

"Aw, Ah doan know. You never kin tell. He might turn him up an' spank him fur gettin' in the way, but Spunk wouldn't shoot no unarmed man. Dat razor he carried outa heah ain't gonna run Spunk down an' cut him, an' Joe ain't got the nerve to go to Spunk with it knowin' he totes that Army .45. He makes that break outa heah to bluff us. He's gonna hide that razor behind the first palmetto root and sneak back home to bed. Don't tell me nothin' 'bout that rabbit-foot colored man. Didn't he meet Spunk an' Lena face to face one day las' week an' mumble sumthin' to Spunk 'bout lettin' his wife alone?"

"What did Spunk say?" Walter broke in. "Ah like him fine but tain't right the way he carries on wid Lena Kanty, jus' 'cause Joe's timid 'bout fightin'."

"You wrong theah, Walter. Tain't 'cause Joe's timid at all, it's 'cause Spunk wants Lena. If Joe was a passle of wile cats Spunk would tackle the job just the same. He'd go after *anything* he wanted the same way. As Ah wuz sayin' a minute ago, he tole Joe right to his face that Lena was his. 'Call her and see if she'll come. A woman knows her boss an' she answers when he calls.' 'Lena, ain't I yo' husband?' Joe sorter whines out. Lena looked at him real disgusted but she don't answer and she don't move outa her tracks. Then Spunk reaches out an' takes hold of her arm an' says: 'Lena, youse mine. From now on Ah works for you an' fights for you an' Ah never wants you to look to nobody for a crumb of bread, a stitch of close or a shingle to go over yo' head, but me long as Ah live. Ah'll git the lumber foh owah house to-morrow. Go home an' git yo' things together!'

" 'Thass mah house,' Lena speaks up. 'Papa gimme that.'

" 'Well,' says Spunk, 'doan give up whut's yours, but when youse inside doan forgit youse mine, an' let no other man git outa his place wid you!'

"Lena looked up at him with her eyes so full of love that they wuz runnin' over, an' Spunk seen it an' Joe seen it too, and his lip started to tremblin' and his Adam's apple was galloping up and down his neck like a race horse. Ah bet he's wore out half a dozen Adam's apples since Spunk's been on the job with Lena. That's all he'll do. He'll be back heah after while swallowin' an' workin' his lips like he wants to say somethin' an' can't."

"But didn't he do nothin' to stop 'em?"

"Nope, not a frazzlin' thing—jus' stood there. Spunk took Lena's arm and walked off jus' like nothin' ain't happened and he stood there gazin' after them till they was outa sight. Now you know a woman don't want no man like that. I'm jus' waitin' to see whut he's goin' to say when he gits back."

II

But Joe Kanty never came back, never. The men in the store heard the sharp report of a pistol somewhere distant in the palmetto thicket and soon Spunk came walking leisurely, with his big black Stetson set at the same rakish angle and Lena clinging to his arm, came walking right into the general store. Lena wept in a frightened manner.

"Well," Spunk announced calmly, "Joe came out there wid a meat axe an' made me kill him."

He sent Lena home and led the men back to Joe—crumpled and limp with his right hand still clutching his razor.

"See mah back? Mah close cut clear through. He sneaked up an' tried to kill me from the back, but Ah got him, an' got him good, first shot," Spunk said.

The men glared at Elijah, accusingly.

"Take him up an' plant him in Stony Lonesome," Spunk said in a careless voice. "Ah didn't wanna shoot him but he made me do it. He's a dirty coward, jumpin' on a man from behind."

Spunk turned on his heel and sauntered away to where he knew his love wept in fear for him and no man stopped him. At the general store later on, they all talked of locking him up until the sheriff should come from Orlando, but no one did anything but talk.

A clear case of self-defense, the trial was a short one, and Spunk walked out of the court house to freedom again. He could work again, ride the dangerous log-carriage that fed the singing, snarling, biting circle-saw; he could stroll the soft dark lanes with his guitar. He was free to roam the woods again; he was free to return to Lena. He did all these things.

III

"Whut you reckon, Walt?" Elijah asked one night later, "Spunk's gittin' ready to marry Lena!"

"Naw! Why, Joe ain't had time to git cold yit. Nohow Ah didn't figger Spunk was the marryin' kind."

"Well, he is," rejoined Elijah. "He done moved most of Lena's things—and her along wid 'em—over to the Bradley house. He's buying it. Jus' like Ah told yo' all right in heah the night Joe was kilt. Spunk's crazy 'bout Lena. He don't want folks to keep on talkin' 'bout her—thass reason he's rushin' so. Funny thing 'bout that bob-cat, wan't it?"

"What bob-cat, 'Lige? Ah ain't heered 'bout none."

"Ain't cher? Well, night befo' las' as they was goin' to bed, a big black bob-cat, black all over, you hear me, *black*, walked round and round that house and howled like forty, an' when Spunk got his gun an' went to the winder to shoot it, he says it stood right still an' looked him in the eye, an' howled right at him. The thing got Spunk so nervoused up he couldn't shoot. But Spunk says twan't no bob-cat nohow. He says it was Joe done sneaked back from Hell!"

"Humph!" sniffed Walter, "he oughter be nervous after what he done: Ah reckon Joe come back to dare him to marry Lena, or to come out an' fight. Ah bet he'll be back time and again, too. Known what Ah think? Joe wuz a braver man than Spunk."

There was a general shout of derision from the group.

"Thass a fact," went on Walter. "Lookit whut he done; took a razor an' went out to fight a man he knowed toted a gun an' wuz a crack shot, too; 'nother thing he wuz skeered of Spunk, skeered plumb stiff! But he went jes' the same. It took him a long time to get his nerve up. Tain't nothin' for Spunk to fight when he ain't skeered of nothin'. Now, Joe's done come back to have it out wid the man that's got all he ever had. Y'all know Joe ain't never had nothin' nor wanted nothin' besides Lena. It musta been a h'ant 'cause ain't nobody never seen no black bob-cat."

"'Nother thing," cut in one of the men, "Spunk was cussin' a blue streak to-day 'cause he 'lowed dat saw wuz wobblin'—almos' got 'im once. The machinist come, looked it over an' said it wuz alright. Spunk musta been leanin' t'wards it some. Den he claimed somebody pushed 'im but twan't nobody close to 'im. Ah wuz glad when knockin' off time came. I'm skeered of dat man when he gits hot. He'd beat you full of button holes as quick as he'd look atcher."

IV

The men gathered the next evening in a different mood, no laughter. No badinage this time.

"Look, 'Lige, you goin' to set up wid Spunk?"

"Naw, Ah reckon not, Walter. Tell yuh the truth, Ah'm a li'l bit skittish. Spunk died too wicket—died cussin' he did. You know he thought he was done outa life."

"Good Lawd, who'd he think done it?"

"Joe."

"Joe Kanty? How come?"

"Walter, Ah b'leeve Ah will walk up thata way an' set. Lena would like it Ah reckon."

"But whut did he say, 'Lige?"

Elijah did not answer until they had left the lighted store and were strolling down the dark street.

"Ah wuz loadin' a wagon wid scantlin' right near the saw when Spunk fell on the carriage but 'fore Ah could git to him the saw got him in the body—awful sight. Me an' Skint Miller got him off but it was too late. Anybody could see that. The fust thing he said wuz: 'He pushed me, 'Lige—the dirty hound pushed me in the back!'—he was spittin' blood at ev'ry breath. We laid him on the sawdust pile with his face to the East so's he could die easy. He helt mah han' till the last, Walter, and said: 'It was Joe, 'Lige... the dirty sneak shoved me... he didn't dare come to mah face... but Ah'll git the son-of-a-wood louse soon's Ah get there an' make hell too hot for him... Ah felt him shove me...!' Thass how he died."

"If spirits kin fight, there's a powerful tussle goin' on somewhere ovah Jordan,[1] cause Ah b'leeve Joe's ready for Spunk an' ain't skeered any more—yas, Ah b'leeve Joe pushed 'im mahself."

They had arrived at the house. Lena's lamentations were deep and loud. She had filled the room with magnolia blossoms that gave off a heavy sweet odor. The keepers of the wake tipped about whispering in frightened tones. Everyone in the village was there, even old Jeff Kanty, Joe's father, who a few hours before would have been afraid to come within ten feet of him, stood leering triumphantly down upon the fallen giant as if his fingers had been the teeth of steel that laid him low.

The cooling board consisted of three sixteen-inch boards on saw horses, a dingy sheet was his shroud.

The women ate heartily of the funeral baked meats and wondered who would be Lena's next. The men whispered coarse conjectures between guzzles of whiskey.

(1925)

Questions for Discussion and Writing

1. What is the significance of the title? Does it perhaps have a double meaning?
2. How does the southern black dialect in the characters' conversation contribute to the effectiveness of the story?
3. How are gender roles important in the plot?
4. How does the tone of the story change in the last two paragraphs?
5. Write an essay making a claim about the reactions of the nosy community to Spunk's behavior before and after Joe Kanty's death.

[1]Crossing the River Jordan means passing into the Promised Land, here seen as the hereafter.

William Faulkner 1897–1962

William Faulker lived most of his life in Oxford, Mississippi. He never graduated from high school or college and was rejected by the U.S. army during World War I for being too short. He worked briefly at the local post office but quit, saying he refused to be "at the beck and call of every son of a bitch with two cents in his pocket." In an interview he once observed, "The writer's only responsibility is to his art. He will be completely ruthless if he is a good one.... If a writer has to rob his mother, he wil not hesitate; the 'Ode on a Grecian Urn' is worth any number of old ladies." He won two Pulitzer Prizes, and in 1949 he was awarded the Nobel Prize for Literature.

A Rose for Emily

I

When Miss Emily Grierson died, our whole town went to her funeral: the men through a sort of respectful affection for a fallen monument, the women mostly out of curiosity to see the inside of her house, which no one save an old manservant—a combined gardener and cook—had seen in at least ten years.

It was a big, squarish frame house that had once been white, decorated with cupolas[1] and spires and scrolled balconies in the heavily lightsome style of the seventies, set on what had once been our most select street. But garages and cotton gins had encroached and obliterated even the august names of that neighborhood; only Miss Emily's house was left, lifting its stubborn and coquettish decay above the cotton wagons and the gasoline pumps—an eyesore among eyesores. And now Miss Emily had gone to join the representatives of those august names where they lay in the cedar-bemused cemetery among the ranked and anonymous graves of Union and Confederate soldiers who fell at the battle of Jefferson.

Alive, Miss Emily had been a tradition, a duty, and a care; a sort of hereditary obligation upon the town, dating from that day in 1894 when Colonel Sartoris, the mayor—he who fathered the edict that no Negro woman should appear on the streets without an apron—remitted her taxes, the dispensation dating from the death of her father on into perpetuity. Not that Miss Emily would have accepted charity. Colonel Sartoris invented an involved tale to the effect that Miss Emily's father had loaned money to the town, which the town, as a matter of business, preferred this way of repaying. Only a man of Colonel Sartoris' generation and thought could have invented it, and only a woman could have believed it.

When the next generation, with its more modern ideas, became mayors and aldermen, this arrangement created some little dissatisfaction. On the first of the year they mailed her a tax notice. February came, and there was no reply. They wrote her a formal letter, asking her to call at the sheriff's office at her

[1]Ornamental turrets on a roof.

convenience. A week later the mayor wrote her himself, offering to call or to send his car for her, and received in reply a note on paper of an archaic shape, in a thin, flowing calligraphy in faded ink, to the effect that she no longer went out at all. The tax notice was also enclosed, without comment.

They called a special meeting of the Board of Aldermen. A deputation waited 5
upon her, knocked at the door through which no visitor had passed since she ceased giving china-painting lessons eight or ten years earlier. They were admitted by the old Negro into a dim hall from which a stairway mounted into still more shadow. It smelled of dust and disuse—a close, dank smell. The Negro led them into the parlor. It was furnished in heavy, leather-covered furniture. When the Negro opened the blinds of one window, they could see that the leather was cracked; and when they sat down, a faint dust rose sluggishly about their thighs, spinning with slow motes in the single sun-ray. On a tarnished gilt easel before the fireplace stood a crayon portrait of Miss Emily's father.

They rose when she entered—a small, fat woman in black, with a thin gold chain descending to her waist and vanishing into her belt, leaning on an ebony cane with a tarnished gold head. Her skeleton was small and spare; perhaps that was why what would have been merely plumpness in another was obesity in her. She looked bloated, like a body long submerged in motionless water, and of that pallid hue. Her eyes, lost in the fatty ridges of her face, looked like two small pieces of coal pressed into a lump of dough as they moved from one face to another while the visitors stated their errand.

She did not ask them to sit. She just stood in the door and listened quietly until the spokesman came to a stumbling halt. Then they could hear the invisible watch ticking at the end of the gold chain.

Her voice was dry and cold. "I have no taxes in Jefferson. Colonel Sartoris explained it to me. Perhaps one of you can gain access to the city records and satisfy yourselves."

"But we have. We are the city authorities, Miss Emily. Didn't you get a notice from the sheriff, signed by him?"

"I received a paper, yes," Miss Emily said. "Perhaps he considers himself the 10
sheriff. . . . I have no taxes in Jefferson."

"But there is nothing on the books to show that, you see. We must go by the—"

"See Colonel Sartoris. I have no taxes in Jefferson."

"But, Miss Emily—"

"See Colonel Sartoris." (Colonel Sartoris had been dead almost ten years.) "I have no taxes in Jefferson. Tobe!" The Negro appeared. "Show these gentlemen out."

II

So she vanquished them, horse and foot, just as she had vanquished their 15
fathers thirty years before about the smell. That was two years after her father's death and a short time after her sweetheart—the one we believed would marry her—had deserted her. After her father's death she went out very little; after her sweetheart went away, people hardly saw her at all. A few of the ladies had the temerity to call, but were not received, and the only sign of life about the place was the Negro man—a young man then—going in and out with a market basket.

“Just as if a man—any man—could keep a kitchen properly,” the ladies said; so they were not surprised when the smell developed. It was another link between the gross, teeming world and the high and mighty Griersons.

A neighbor, a woman, complained to the mayor, Judge Stevens, eighty years old.

“But what will you have me do about it, madam?” he said.

“Why, send her word to stop it,” the woman said. “Isn't there a law?”

“I'm sure that won't be necessary,” Judge Stevens said. “It's probably just a 20
snake or a rat that nigger of hers killed in the yard. I'll speak to him about it.”

The next day he received two more complaints, one from a man who came in diffident deprecation. “We really must do something about it, Judge. I'd be the last one in the world to bother Miss Emily, but we've got to do something.” That night the Board of Aldermen met—three graybeards and one younger man, a member of the rising generation.

“It's simple enough,” he said. “Send her word to have her place cleaned up. Give her a certain time to do it in, and if she don't....”

“Dammit, sir,” Judge Stevens said, “will you accuse a lady to her face of smelling bad?”

So the next night, after midnight, four men crossed Miss Emily's lawn and slunk about the house like burglars, sniffing along the base of the brickwork and at the cellar openings while one of them performed a regular sowing motion with his hand out of a sack slung from his shoulder. They broke open the cellar door and sprinkled lime there, and in all the outbuildings. As they recrossed the lawn, a window that had been dark was lighted and Miss Emily sat in it, the light behind her, and her upright torso motionless as that of an idol. They crept quietly across the lawn and into the shadow of the locusts that lined the street. After a week or two the smell went away.

That was when people had begun to feel really sorry for her. People in our 25
town, remembering how old lady Wyatt, her great-aunt, had gone completely crazy at last, believed that the Griersons held themselves a little too high for what they really were. None of the young men were quite good enough for Miss Emily and such. We had long thought of them as a tableau,[2] Miss Emily a slender figure in white in the background, her father a spraddled silhouette in the foreground, his back to her and clutching a horsewhip, the two of them framed by the back-flung front door. So when she got to be thirty and was still single, we were not pleased exactly, but vindicated; even with insanity in the family she wouldn't have turned down all of her chances if they had really materialized.

When her father died, it got about that the house was all that was left to her; and in a way, people were glad. At last they could pity Miss Emily. Being left alone, and a pauper, she had become humanized. Now she too would know the old thrill and the old despair of a penny more or less.

The day after his death all the ladies prepared to call at the house and offer condolence and aid, as is our custom. Miss Emily met them at the door, dressed as usual and with no trace of grief on her face. She told them that her father was not dead. She did that for three days, with the ministers calling on her, and the doctors, trying to persuade her to let them dispose of the body. Just as they were about to resort to law and force, she broke down, and they buried her father quickly.

---

[2]A living picture created by silent, motionless actors.

We did not say she was crazy then. We believed she had to do that. We remembered all the young men her father had driven away, and we knew that with nothing left, she would have to cling to that which had robbed her, as people will.

III

She was sick for a long time. When we saw her again, her hair was cut short, making her look like a girl, with a vague resemblance to those angels in colored church windows—sort of tragic and serene.

The town had just let the contracts for paving the sidewalks, and in the 30
summer after her father's death they began the work. The construction company came with niggers and mules and machinery, and a foreman named Homer Barron, a Yankee—a big, dark, ready man, with a big voice and eyes lighter than his face. The little boys would follow in groups to hear him cuss the niggers, and the niggers singing in time to the rise and fall of picks. Pretty soon he knew everybody in town. Whenever you heard a lot of laughing anywhere about the square, Homer Barron would be in the center of the group. Presently, we began to see him and Miss Emily on Sunday afternoons driving in the yellow-wheeled buggy and the matched team of bays from the livery stable.

At first we were glad that Miss Emily would have an interest, because the ladies all said, "Of course a Grierson would not think seriously of a Northerner, a day laborer." But there were still others, older people, who said that even grief could not cause a real lady to forget *noblesse oblige*[3]—without calling it *noblesse oblige*. They just said, "Poor Emily. Her kinsfolk should come to her." She had some kin in Alabama; but years ago her father had fallen out with them over the estate of old lady Wyatt, the crazy woman, and there was no communication between the two families. They had not even been represented at the funeral.

And as soon as the old people said, "Poor Emily," the whispering began. "Do you suppose it's really so?" they said to one another. "Of course it is. What else could…" This behind their hands; rustling of craned silk and satin behind jalousies[4] closed upon the sun of Sunday afternoon as the thin, swift clop-clop-clop of the matched team passed: "Poor Emily."

She carried her head high enough—even when we believed that she was fallen. It was as if she demanded more than ever the recognition of her dignity as the last Grierson; as if it had wanted that touch of earthiness to reaffirm her imperviousness. Like when she bought the rat poison, the arsenic. That was over a year after they had begun to say "Poor Emily," and while the two female cousins were visiting her.

"I want some poison," she said to the druggist. She was over thirty then, still a slight woman, though thinner than usual, with cold, haughty black eyes in a face the flesh of which was strained across the temples and about the eye-sockets as you imagine a lighthouse-keeper's face ought to look. "I want some poison," she said.

"Yes, Miss Emily. What kind? For rats and such? I'd recom—" 35

"I want the best you have. I don't care what kind."

---

[3]The obligation of those of noble birth to behave honorably.

[4]Window blinds with slats that open and close.

The druggist named several. "They'll kill anything up to an elephant. But what you want is—"

"Arsenic," Miss Emily said. "Is that a good one?"

"Is . . . arsenic? Yes, ma'am. But what you want—"

"I want arsenic." 40

The druggist looked down at her. She looked back at him, erect, her face like a strained flag. "Why, of course," the druggist said. "If that's what you want. But the law requires you to tell what you are going to use it for."

Miss Emily just stared at him, her head tilted back in order to look him eye for eye, until he looked away and went and got the arsenic and wrapped it up. The Negro delivery boy brought her the package; the druggist didn't come back. When she opened the package at home there was written on the box, under the skull and bones: "For rats."

IV

So the next day we all said, "She will kill herself"; and we said it would be the best thing. When she had first begun to be seen with Homer Barron, we had said, "She will marry him." Then we said, "She will persuade him yet," because Homer himself had remarked—he liked men, and it was known that he drank with the younger men in the Elks' Club—that he was not a marrying man. Later we said, "Poor Emily" behind the jalousies as they passed on Sunday afternoon in the glittering buggy, Miss Emily with her head high and Homer Barron with his hat cocked and a cigar in his teeth, reins and whip in a yellow glove.

Then some of the ladies began to say that it was a disgrace to the town and a bad example to the young people. The men did not want to interfere, but at last the ladies forced the Baptist minister—Miss Emily's people were Episcopal—to call upon her. He would never divulge what happened during that interview, but he refused to go back again. The next Sunday they again drove about the streets, and the following day the minister's wife wrote to Miss Emily's relations in Alabama.

So she had blood-kin under her roof again and we sat back to watch devel- 45
opments. At first nothing happened. Then we were sure that they were to be married. We learned that Miss Emily had been to the jeweler's and ordered a man's toilet set in silver, with the letters H.B. on each piece. Two days later we learned that she had bought a complete outfit of men's clothing, including a nightshirt, and we said, "They are married." We were really glad. We were glad because the two female cousins were even more Grierson than Miss Emily had ever been.

So we were not surprised when Homer Barron—the streets had been finished some time since—was gone. We were a little disappointed that there was not a public blowing-off, but we believed that he had gone on to prepare for Miss Emily's coming, or to give her a chance to get rid of the cousins. (By that time it was a cabal, and we were all Miss Emily's allies to help circumvent the cousins.) Sure enough, after another week they departed. And, as we had expected all along, within three days Homer Barron was back in town. A neighbor saw the Negro man admit him at the kitchen door at dusk one evening.

And that was the last we saw of Homer Barron. And of Miss Emily for some time. The Negro man went in and out with the market basket, but the front door remained closed. Now and then we would see her at the window for a moment, as the men did that night when they sprinkled the lime, but for almost six months she did not appear on the streets. Then we knew that this was to be expected too; as if that quality of her father which had thwarted her woman's life so many times had been too virulent and too furious to die.

When we next saw Miss Emily, she had grown fat and her hair was turning gray. During the next few years it grew grayer and grayer until it attained an even pepper-and-salt iron-gray, when it ceased turning. Up to the day of her death at seventy-four it was still that vigorous iron-gray, like the hair of an active man.

From that time on her front door remained closed, save during a period of six or seven years, when she was about forty, during which she gave lessons in china-painting. She fitted up a studio in one of the downstairs rooms, where the daughters and granddaughters of Colonel Sartoris' contemporaries were sent to her with the same regularity and in the same spirit that they were sent to church on Sundays with a twenty-five-cent piece for the collection plate. Meanwhile her taxes had been remitted.

Then the newer generation became the backbone and the spirit of the town, 50
and the painting pupils grew up and fell away and did not send their children to her with boxes of color and tedious brushes and pictures cut from the ladies' magazines. The front door closed upon the last one and remained closed for good. When the town got free postal delivery, Miss Emily alone refused to let them fasten the metal numbers above her door and attach a mailbox to it. She would not listen to them.

Daily, monthly, yearly we watched the Negro grow grayer and more stooped, going in and out with the market basket. Each December we sent her a tax notice, which would be returned by the post office a week later, unclaimed. Now and then we would see her in one of the downstairs windows—she had evidently shut up the top floor of the house—like the carven torso of an idol in a niche, looking or not looking at us, we could never tell which. Thus she passed from generation to generation—dear, inescapable, impervious, tranquil, and perverse.

And so she died. Fell ill in the house filled with dust and shadows, with only a doddering Negro man to wait on her. We did not even know she was sick; we had long since given up trying to get any information from the Negro. He talked to no one, probably not even to her, for his voice had grown harsh and rusty, as if from disuse.

She died in one of the downstairs rooms, in a heavy walnut bed with a curtain, her gray head propped on a pillow yellow and moldy with age and lack of sunlight.

V

The Negro met the first of the ladies at the front door and let them in, with their hushed, sibilant voices and their quick, curious glances, and then he disappeared. He walked right through the house and out the back and was not seen again.

The two female cousins came at once. They held the funeral on the second 55
day, with the town coming to look at Miss Emily beneath a mass of bought flowers, with the crayon face of her father musing profoundly above the bier and the ladies sibilant and macabre; and the very old men—some in their brushed Confederate uniforms—on the porch and the lawn, talking of Miss Emily as if she had been a contemporary of theirs, believing that they had danced with her and courted her perhaps, confusing time with its mathematical progression, as

the old do, to whom all the past is not a diminishing road but, instead, a huge meadow which no winter ever quite touches, divided from them now by the narrow bottle-neck of the most recent decade of years.

Already we knew that there was one room in that region above stairs which no one had seen in forty years, and which would have to be forced. They waited until Miss Emily was decently in the ground before they opened it.

The violence of breaking down the door seemed to fill this room with pervading dust. A thin, acrid pall as of the tomb seemed to lie everywhere upon this room decked and furnished as for a bridal: upon the valance curtains of faded rose color, upon the rose-shaded lights, upon the dressing table, upon the delicate array of crystal and the man's toilet things backed with tarnished silver, silver so tarnished that the monogram was obscured. Among them lay a collar and tie, as if they had just been removed, which, lifted, left upon the surface a pale crescent in the dust. Upon a chair hung the suit, carefully folded; beneath it the two mute shoes and the discarded socks.

The man himself lay in the bed.

For a long while we just stood there, looking down at the profound and fleshless grin. The body had apparently once lain in the attitude of an embrace, but now the long sleep that outlasts love, that conquers even the grimace of love, had cuckolded him. What was left of him, rotted beneath what was left of the nightshirt, had become inextricable from the bed in which he lay; and upon him and upon the pillow beside him lay that even coating of the patient and biding dust.

Then we noticed that in the second pillow was the indentation of a head. 60
One of us lifted something from it, and leaning forward, that faint and invisible dust dry and acrid in the nostrils, we saw a long strand of iron-gray hair.

(1931)

Questions for Discussion and Writing

1. What does Faulkner achieve by disrupting the chronology of Miss Emily's story?
2. How would you describe the point of view here? Do you find it effective? Why or why not?
3. What kind of person is Emily Grierson? Why does she live in the past? How do the townspeople feel about her? How do you feel about her?
4. What kind of person is Homer Barron? Why do the townspeople consider him not good enough for Miss Emily?
5. Write an essay arguing that Emily Grierson's relationship with her father contributed to her tragedy.

Ernest Hemingway 1899–1961

Ernest Hemingway was born in Oak Park, a Chicago suburb he described as a "town of wide lawns and narrow minds." Rather than attend college, he became a newspaper reporter, a job that helped develop his spare, forceful writing style. As a volunteer ambulance driver in World War I, Hemingway was seriously wounded. He married the first of his four wives in

1921 and took her to Paris, where he worked as a foreign correspondent, wrote fiction, and became a voice of the "Lost Generation" of American expatriates. In 1954 he won the Nobel Prize for Literature. When he was sixty-two and terminally ill with cancer, he committed suicide by shooting himself with a shotgun.

Hills Like White Elephants*

The hills across the valley of the Ebro[1] were long and white. On this side there was no shade and no trees and the station was between two lines of rails in the sun. Close against the side of the station there was the warm shadow of the building and a curtain, made of strings of bamboo beads, hung across the open door into the bar, to keep out flies. The American and the girl with him sat at a table in the shade, outside the building. It was very hot and the express from Barcelona would come in forty minutes. It stopped at this junction for two minutes and went on to Madrid.

"What should we drink?" the girl asked. She had taken off her hat and put it on the table.

"It's pretty hot," the man said.

"Let's drink beer."

"Dos cervezas," the man said into the curtain. 5

"Big ones?" a woman asked from the doorway.

"Yes. Two big ones."

The woman brought two glasses of beer and two felt pads. She put the felt pads and the beer glasses on the table and looked at the man and the girl. The girl was looking off at the line of hills. They were white in the sun and the country was brown and dry.

"They look like white elephants," she said.

"I've never seen one," the man drank his beer. 10

"No, you wouldn't have."

"I might have," the man said. "Just because you say I wouldn't have doesn't prove anything."

The girl looked at the bead curtain. "They've painted something on it," she said. "What does it say?"

"Anis del Toro. It's a drink."

"Could we try it?" 15

The man called "Listen" through the curtain. The woman came out from the bar.

"Four reales."[2]

"We want two Anis del Toro."

"With water?"

"Do you want it with water?" 20

"I don't know," the girl said. "Is it good with water?"

---

*Ernest Hemingway, "Hills Like White Elephants." Reprinted with the permission of Scribner, a Division of Simon & Schuster, Inc., from *Men Without Women* by Ernest Hemingway. Copyright 1927 by Charles Scribner's Sons. Copyright renewed 1955 by Ernest Hemingway.

[1]A river in Spain.

[2]Spanish coins.

"It's all right."

"You want them with water?" asked the woman.

"Yes, with water."

"It tastes like licorice," the girl said and put the glass down.

"That's the way with everything."

"Yes," said the girl. "Everything tastes of licorice. Especially all the things you've waited so long for, like absinthe."

"Oh, cut it out."

"You started it," the girl said. "I was being amused. I was having a fine time."

"Well, let's try and have a fine time."

"All right. I was trying. I said the mountains looked like white elephants. Wasn't that bright?"

"That was bright."

"I wanted to try this new drink. That's all we do, isn't it—look at things and try new drinks?"

"I guess so."

The girl looked across at the hills.

"They're lovely hills," she said. "They don't really look like white elephants. I just meant the coloring of their skin through the trees."

"Should we have another drink?"

"All right."

The warm wind blew the bead curtain against the table.

"The beer's nice and cool," the man said.

"It's lovely," the girl said.

"It's really an awfully simple operation, Jig," the man said. "It's not really an operation at all."

The girl looked at the ground the table legs rested on.

"I know you wouldn't mind it, Jig. It's really not anything. It's just to let the air in."

The girl did not say anything.

"I'll go with you and I'll stay with you all the time. They just let the air in and then it's all perfectly natural."

"Then what will we do afterward?"

"We'll be fine afterward. Just like we were before."

"What makes you think so?"

"That's the only thing that bothers us. It's the only thing that's made us unhappy."

The girl looked at the bead curtain, put her hand out and took hold of two of the strings of beads.

"And you think then we'll be all right and be happy."

"I know we will. You don't have to be afraid. I've known lots of people that have done it."

"So have I," said the girl. "And afterward they were all so happy."

"Well," the man said, "if you don't want to you don't have to. I wouldn't have you do it if you didn't want to. But I know it's perfectly simple."

"And you really want to?"

"I think it's the best thing to do. But I don't want you to do it if you don't really want to."

"And if I do it you'll be happy and things will be like they were and you'll love me?"

"I love you now. You know I love you."

"I know. But if I do it, then it will be nice again if I say things are like white elephants, and you'll like it?"

"I'll love it. I love it now but I just can't think about it. You know how I get when I worry."

"If I do it you won't ever worry?"

"I won't worry about that because it's perfectly simple."

"Then I'll do it. Because I don't care about me."

"What do you mean?"

"I don't care about me."

"Well, I care about you."

"Oh, yes. But I don't care about me. And I'll do it and then everything will be fine."

"I don't want you to do it if you feel that way."

The girl stood up and walked to the end of the station. Across, on the other side, were fields of grain and trees along the banks of the Ebro. Far away, beyond the river, were mountains. The shadow of a cloud moved across the field of grain and she saw the river through the trees.

"And we could have all this," she said. "And we could have everything and every day we make it more impossible."

"What did you say?"

"I said we could have everything."

"We can have everything."

"No, we can't."

"We can have the whole world."

"No, we can't."

"We can go everywhere."

"No, we can't. It isn't ours any more."

"It's ours."

"No, it isn't. And once they take it away, you never get it back."

"But they haven't taken it away."

"We'll wait and see."

"Come on back in the shade," he said. "You mustn't feel that way."

"I don't feel any way," the girl said. "I just know things."

"I don't want you to do anything that you don't want to do—"

"Nor that isn't good for me," she said. "I know. Could we have another beer?"

"All right. But you've got to realize—"

"I realize," the girl said. "Can't we maybe stop talking?"

They sat down at the table and the girl looked across at the hills on the dry side of the valley and the man looked at her and at the table.

"You've got to realize," he said, "that I don't want you to do it if you don't want to. I'm perfectly willing to go through with it if it means anything to you."

"Doesn't it mean anything to you? We could get along."

"Of course it does. But I don't want anybody but you. I don't want anyone else. And I know it's perfectly simple."

"Yes, you know it's perfectly simple."

"It's all right for you to say that, but I do know it."

"Would you do something for me now?"

"I'd do anything for you."

"Would you please please please please please please please stop talking?"

He did not say anything but looked at the bags against the wall of the station. There were labels on them from all the hotels where they had spent nights.

"But I don't want you to," he said. "I don't care anything about it." 100

"I'll scream," the girl said.

The woman came out through the curtains with two glasses of beer and put them down on the damp felt pads. "The train comes in five minutes," she said.

"What did she say?" asked the girl.

"That the train is coming in five minutes."

The girl smiled brightly at the woman, to thank her. 105

"I'd better take the bags over to the other side of the station," the man said. She smiled at him.

"All right. Then come back and we'll finish the beer."

He picked up the two heavy bags and carried them around the station to the other tracks. He looked up the tracks but could not see the train. Coming back, he walked through the barroom, where people waiting for the train were drinking. He drank an Anis at the bar and looked at the people. They were all waiting reasonably for the train. He went out through the bead curtain. She was sitting at the table and smiled at him.

"Do you feel better?" he asked.

"I feel fine," she said. "There's nothing wrong with me. I feel fine." 110

(1927)

Questions for Discussion and Writing

1. How would you describe the point of view in this story?
2. The number *two* is used ten times in the story. What is the significance of this repetition? (Note especially the two parallel train tracks and the two strings of beads that do not intersect: Do they suggest anything about the characters' lives?)
3. What is the main point or theme of the story? What is the central issue between the lovers?
4. What is a "white elephant"? Explain the story's title.
5. Write an essay in which you argue that Jig will (or will not) do what her lover wants.

John Steinbeck 1902–1968

John Steinbeck was born in Salinas, California, where he worked as a fruit-picker, hod carrier, and ranch hand. After high school graduation, he continued working at menial jobs while taking classes in marine biology at Stanford University. In 1925, he went to New York City to become a writer. He got a job as a laborer on the building of Madison Square Garden but could not get published, so he moved back to California. His early works met with little success, but *Tortilla Flat* (1935) became a best seller and received the California Commonwealth Club's Gold Medal for best novel by a California author. Steinbeck went on to write a number of highly successful novels and stories. In 1962 he was awarded the Nobel Prize for Literature.

The Chrysanthemums

The high gray-flannel fog of winter closed off the Salinas Valley from the sky and from all the rest of the world. On every side it sat like a lid on the mountains and made of the great valley a closed pot. On the broad, level land floor the gang plows bit deep and left the black earth shining like metal where the shares had cut. On the foothill ranches across the Salinas River, the yellow stubble fields seemed to be bathed in pale cold sunshine, but there was no sunshine in the valley now in December. The thick willow scrub along the river flamed with sharp and positive yellow leaves.

It was a time of quiet and of waiting. The air was cold and tender. A light wind blew up from the southwest so that the farmers were mildly hopeful of a good rain before long; but fog and rain do not go together.

Across the river, on Henry Allen's foothill ranch there was little work to be done, for the hay was cut and stored and the orchards were plowed up to receive the rain deeply when it should come. The cattle on the higher slopes were becoming shaggy and rough-coated.

Elisa Allen, working in her flower garden, looked down across the yard and saw Henry, her husband, talking to two men in business suits. The three of them stood by the tractor shed, each man with one foot on the side of the little Fordson. They smoked cigarettes and studied the machine as they talked.

Elisa watched them for a moment and then went back to her work. She 5
was thirty-five. Her face was lean and strong and her eyes were as clear as water. Her figure looked blocked and heavy in her gardening costume, a man's black hat pulled down over her eyes, clodhopper shoes, a figured print dress almost completely covered by a big corduroy apron with four big pockets to hold the snips, the trowel and scratcher, the seeds and the knife she worked with. She wore heavy leather gloves to protect her hands while she worked.

She was cutting down the old year's chrysanthemum stalks with a pair of short and powerful scissors. She looked down toward the men by the tractor shed now and then. Her face was eager and mature and handsome; even her work with the scissors was over-eager, over-powerful. The chrysanthemum stems seemed too small and easy for her energy.

She brushed a cloud of hair out of her eyes with the back of her glove, and left a smudge of earth on her cheek in doing it. Behind her stood the neat white farm house with red geraniums close-banked around it as high as the windows. It was a hard-swept looking little house, with hard-polished windows, and a clean mud-mat on the front steps.

Elisa cast another glance toward the tractor shed. The strangers were getting into their Ford coupe. She took off a glove and put her strong fingers down into the forest of new green chrysanthemum sprouts that were growing around the old roots. She spread the leaves and looked down among the close-growing stems. No aphids were there, no sowbugs or snails or cutworms. Her terrier fingers destroyed such pests before they could get started.

Elisa started at the sound of her husband's voice. He had come near quietly, and he leaned over the wire fence that protected her flower garden from cattle and dogs and chickens.

"At it again," he said. "You've got a strong new crop coming."

Elisa straightened her back and pulled on the gardening glove again. "Yes. They'll be strong this coming year." In her tone and on her face there was a little smugness.

"You've got a gift with things," Henry observed. "Some of those yellow chrysanthemums you had this year were ten inches across. I wish you'd work out in the orchard and raise some apples that big."

Her eyes sharpened. "Maybe I could do it, too. I've a gift with things, all right. My mother had it. She could stick anything in the ground and make it grow. She said it was having planters' hands that knew how to do it."

"Well, it sure works with flowers," he said.

"Henry, who were those men you were talking to?"

"Why, sure, that's what I came to tell you. They were from the Western Meat Company. I sold them those thirty head of three-year-old steers. Got nearly my own price, too."

"Good," she said. "Good for you."

"And I thought," he continued, "I thought how it's Saturday afternoon, and we might go into Salinas for dinner at a restaurant, and then to a picture show—to celebrate, you see."

"Good," she repeated. "Oh, yes. That will be good."

Henry put on his joking tone. "There's fights tonight. How'd you like to go to the fights?"

"Oh, no," she said breathlessly. "No, I wouldn't like fights."

"Just fooling, Elisa. We'll go to a movie. Let's see. It's two now. I'm going to take Scotty and bring down those steers from the hill. It'll take us maybe two hours. We'll go in town about five and have dinner at the Cominos Hotel. Like that?"

"Of course I'll like it. It's good to eat away from home."

"All right, then. I'll go get up a couple of horses."

She said, "I'll have plenty of time to transplant some of these sets, I guess."

She heard her husband calling Scotty down by the barn. And a little later she saw the two men ride up the pale yellow hillside in search of the steers.

There was a little square sandy bed kept for rooting the chrysanthemums. With her trowel she turned the soil over and over, and smoothed it and patted it firm. Then she dug ten parallel trenches to receive the sets. Back at the chrysanthemum bed she pulled out the little crisp shoots, trimmed off the leaves of each one with her scissors and laid it on a small orderly pile.

A squeak of wheels and plod of hoofs came from the road. Elisa looked up. The country road ran along the dense bank of willows and cottonwoods that bordered the river, and up this road came a curious vehicle, curiously drawn. It was an old spring-wagon, with a round canvas top on it like the cover of a prairie schooner. It was drawn by an old bay horse and a little gray-and-white burro. A big stubble-bearded man sat between the cover flaps and drove the crawling team. Underneath the wagon, between the hind wheels, a lean and rangy mongrel dog walked sedately. Words were painted on the canvas, in clumsy, crooked letters. "Pots, pans, knives, sisors, lawn mores, Fixed." Two rows of articles, and the triumphantly definitive "Fixed" below. The black paint had run down in little sharp points beneath each letter.

Elisa, squatting on the ground, watched to see the crazy, loose-jointed wagon pass by. But it didn't pass. It turned into the farm road in front of her house, crooked old wheels skirling and squeaking. The rangy dog darted from between the wheels and ran ahead. Instantly the two ranch shepherds flew out at him. Then all three stopped, and with stiff and quivering tails, with taut straight legs, with ambassadorial dignity, they slowly circled, sniffing daintily. The caravan pulled up to Elisa's wire fence and stopped. Now the newcomer dog, feeling out-numbered, lowered his tail and retired under the wagon with raised hackles and bared teeth.

The man on the wagon seat called out, "That's a bad dog in a fight when he gets started."

Elisa laughed. "I see he is. How soon does he generally get started?"

The man caught up her laughter and echoed it heartily. "Sometimes not for weeks and weeks," he said. He climbed stiffly down, over the wheel. The horse and the donkey drooped like unwatered flowers.

Elisa saw that he was a very big man. Although his hair and beard were graying, he did not look old. His worn black suit was wrinkled and spotted with grease. The laughter had disappeared from his face and eyes the moment his laughing voice ceased. His eyes were dark, and they were full of the brooding that gets in the eyes of teamsters and of sailors. The calloused hands he rested on the wire fence were cracked, and every crack was a black line. He took off his battered hat.

"I'm off my general road, ma'am," he said. "Does this dirt road cut over across the river to the Los Angeles highway?"

Elisa stood up and shoved the thick scissors in her apron pocket. "Well, yes, it does, but it winds around and then fords the river. I don't think your team could pull through the sand."

He replied with some asperity, "It might surprise you what them beasts can pull through."

"When they get started?" she asked.

He smiled for a second. "Yes. When they get started."

"Well," said Elisa, "I think you'll save time if you go back to the Salinas road and pick up the highway there."

He drew a big finger down the chicken wire and made it sing. "I ain't in any hurry, ma'am. I go from Seattle to San Diego and back every year. Takes all my time. About six months each way. I aim to follow nice weather."

Elisa took off her gloves and stuffed them in the apron pocket with the scissors. She touched the under edge of her man's hat, searching for fugitive hairs. "That sounds like a nice kind of way to live," she said.

He leaned confidentially over the fence. "Maybe you noticed the writing on my wagon. I mend pots and sharpen knives and scissors. You got any of them things to do?"

"Oh, no," she said quickly. "Nothing like that." Her eyes hardened with resistance.

"Scissors is the worst thing," he explained. "Most people just ruin scissors trying to sharpen 'em, but I know how. I got a special tool. It's a little bobbit kind of thing, and patented. But it sure does the trick."

"No. My scissors are all sharp."

"All right, then. Take a pot," he continued earnestly, "a bent pot, or a pot with a hole. I can make it like new so you don't have to buy no new ones. That's a saving for you."

"No," she said shortly. "I tell you I have nothing like that for you to do."

His face fell to an exaggerated sadness. His voice took on a whining undertone. "I ain't had a thing to do today. Maybe I won't have no supper tonight. You see I'm off my regular road. I know folks on the highway clear from Seattle to San Diego. They save their things for me to sharpen up because they know I do it so good and save them money."

"I'm sorry," Elisa said irritably. "I haven't anything for you to do."

His eyes left her face and fell to searching the ground. They roamed about 50
until they came to the chrysanthemum bed where she had been working. "What's them plants, ma'am?"

The irritation and resistance melted from Elisa's face. "Oh, those are chrysanthemums, giant whites and yellows. I raise them every year, bigger than anybody around here."

"Kind of a long-stemmed flower? Looks like a quick puff of colored smoke?" he asked.

"That's it. What a nice way to describe them."

"They smell kind of nasty till you get used to them," he said.

"It's a good bitter smell," she retorted, "not nasty at all." 55

He changed his tone quickly. "I like the smell myself."

"I had ten-inch blooms this year," she said.

The man leaned farther over the fence. "Look. I know a lady down the road a piece, has got the nicest garden you ever seen. Got nearly every kind of flower but no chrysanthemums. Last time I was mending a copper-bottom washtub for her (that's a hard job but I do it good), she said to me, 'If you ever run acrost some nice chrysanthemums I wish you'd try to get me a few seeds.' That's what she told me."

Elisa's eyes grew alert and eager. "She couldn't have known much about chrysanthemums. You *can* raise them from seed, but it's much easier to root the little sprouts you see there."

"Oh," he said. "I s'pose I can't take none to her, then." 60

"Why yes you can," Elisa cried. "I can put some in damp sand, and you can carry them right along with you. They'll take root in the pot if you keep them damp. And then she can transplant them."

"She'd sure like to have some, ma'am. You say they're nice ones?"

"Beautiful," she said. "Oh, beautiful." Her eyes shone. She tore off the battered hat and shook out her dark pretty hair. "I'll put them in a flower pot, and you can take them right with you. Come into the yard."

While the man came through the picket gate Elisa ran excitedly along the geranium-bordered path to the back of the house. And she returned carrying a big red flower pot. The gloves were forgotten now. She kneeled on the ground by the starting bed and dug up the sandy soil with her fingers and scooped it into the bright new flower pot. Then she picked up the little pile of shoots she had prepared. With her strong fingers she pressed them into the sand and tamped around them with her knuckles. The man stood over her. "I'll tell you what to do," she said. "You remember so you can tell the lady."

"Yes, I'll try to remember." 65

"Well, look. These will take root in about a month. Then she must set them out, about a foot apart in good rich earth like this, see?" She lifted a handful of dark soil for him to look at. "They'll grow fast and tall. Now remember this: In July tell her to cut them down, about eight inches from the ground."

"Before they bloom?" he asked.

"Yes, before they bloom." Her face was tight with eagerness. "They'll grow right up again. About the last of September the buds will start."

She stopped and seemed perplexed. "It's the budding that takes the most care," she said hesitantly. "I don't know how to tell you." She looked deep into his eyes, searchingly. Her mouth opened a little, and she seemed to be listening. "I'll try to tell you," she said. "Did you ever hear of planting hands?"

"Can't say I have, ma'am." 70

"Well, I can only tell you what it feels like. It's when you're picking off the buds you don't want. Everything goes right down into your fingertips. You watch your fingers work. They do it themselves. You can feel how it is. They pick and pick the buds. They never make a mistake. They're with the plant. Do you see? Your fingers and the plant. You can feel that, right up your arm. They know. They never make a mistake. You can feel it. When you're like that you can't do anything wrong. Do you see that? Can you understand that?"

She was kneeling on the ground looking up at him. Her breast swelled passionately.

The man's eyes narrowed. He looked away self-consciously. "Maybe I know," he said. "Sometimes in the night in the wagon there—"

Elisa's voice grew husky. She broke in on him, "I've never lived as you do, but I know what you mean. When the night is dark—why, the stars are sharp-pointed, and there's quiet. Why, you rise up and up! Every pointed star gets driven into your body. It's like that. Hot and sharp and—lovely."

Kneeling there, her hand went out toward his legs in the greasy black 75
trousers. Her hesitant fingers almost touched the cloth. Then her hand dropped to the ground. She crouched low like a fawning dog.

He said, "It's nice, just like you say. Only when you don't have no dinner, it ain't."

She stood up then, very straight, and her face was ashamed. She held the flower pot out to him and placed it gently in his arms. "Here. Put it in your wagon, on the seat, where you can watch it. Maybe I can find something for you to do."

At the back of the house she dug in the can pile and found two old and battered aluminum saucepans. She carried them back and gave them to him. "Here, maybe you can fix these."

His manner changed. He became professional. "Good as new I can fix them." At the back of his wagon he set a little anvil, and out of an oily tool box dug a small machine hammer. Elisa came through the gate to watch him while he pounded out the dents in the kettles. His mouth grew sure and knowing. At a difficult part of the work he sucked his underlip.

"You sleep right in the wagon?" Elisa asked. 80

"Right in the wagon, ma'am. Rain or shine I'm dry as a cow in there."

"It must be nice," she said. "It must be very nice. I wish women could do such things."

"It ain't the right kind of life for a woman."

Her upper lip raised a little, showing her teeth. "How do you know? How can you tell?" she said.

"I don't know, ma'am," he protested. "Of course I don't know. Now here's 85
your kettles, done. You don't have to buy no new ones."

"How much?"

"Oh, fifty cents'll do. I keep my prices down and my work good. That's why I have all them satisfied customers up and down the highway."

Elisa brought him a fifty-cent piece from the house and dropped it in his hand. "You might be surprised to have a rival some time. I can sharpen scissors, too. And I can beat the dents out of little pots. I could show you what a woman might do."

He put his hammer back in the oily box and shoved the little anvil out of sight. "It would be a lonely life for a woman, ma'am, and a scary life, too, with animals creeping under the wagon all night." He climbed over the singletree, steadying himself with a hand on the burro's white rump. He settled himself in the seat, picked up the lines. "Thank you kindly, ma'am," he said. "I'll do like you told me; I'll go back and catch the Salinas road."

"Mind," she called, "if you're long in getting there, keep the sand damp." 90

"Sand, ma'am? . . . Sand? Oh, sure. You mean around the chrysanthemums. Sure I will." He clucked his tongue. The beasts leaned luxuriously into their collars. The mongrel dog took his place between the back wheels. The wagon turned and crawled out the entrance road and back the way it had come, along the river.

Elisa stood in front of her wire fence watching the slow progress of the caravan. Her shoulders were straight, her head thrown back, her eyes half-closed, so that the scene came vaguely into them. Her lips moved silently, forming the words "Good-bye—good-bye." Then she whispered, "That's a bright direction. There's a glowing there." The sound of her whisper startled her. She shook herself free and looked about to see whether anyone had been listening. Only the dogs had heard. They lifted their heads toward her from their sleeping in the dust, and then stretched out their chins and settled asleep again. Elisa turned and ran hurriedly into the house.

In the kitchen she reached behind the stove and felt the water tank. It was full of hot water from the noonday cooking. In the bathroom she tore off her soiled clothes and flung them into the corner. And then she scrubbed herself with a little block of pumice, legs and thighs, loins and chest and arms, until her skin was scratched and red. When she had dried herself she stood in front of a mirror in her bedroom and looked at her body. She tightened her stomach and threw out her chest. She turned and looked over her shoulder at her back.

After a while she began to dress slowly. She put on her newest underclothing and her nicest stockings and the dress which was the symbol of her prettiness. She worked carefully on her hair, penciled her eyebrows and rouged her lips.

Before she was finished she heard the little thunder of hoofs and the shouts of 95
Henry and his helper as they drove the red steers into the corral. She heard the gate bang shut and set herself for Henry's arrival.

His steps sounded on the porch. He entered the house calling, "Elisa, where are you?"

"In my room, dressing. I'm not ready. There's hot water for your bath. Hurry up. It's getting late."

When she heard him splashing in the tub, Elisa laid his dark suit on the bed, and shirt and socks and tie beside it. She stood his polished shoes on the floor beside the bed. Then she went to the porch and sat primly and stiffly down. She looked toward the river road where the willow-line was still yellow with frosted leaves so that under the high gray fog they seemed a thin band of sunshine. This was the only color in the gray afternoon. She sat unmoving for a long time. Her eyes blinked rarely.

Henry came banging out of the door, shoving his tie inside his vest as he came. Elisa stiffened and her face grew tight. Henry stopped short and looked at her. "Why—why, Elisa. You look so nice!"

"Nice? You think I look nice? What do you mean by 'nice'?" 100

Henry blundered on. "I don't know. I mean you look different, strong and happy."

"I am strong? Yes, strong. What do you mean 'strong'?"

He looked bewildered. "You're playing some kind of a game," he said helplessly. "It's a kind of a play. You look strong enough to break a calf over your knee, happy enough to eat it like a watermelon."

For a second she lost her rigidity. "Henry! Don't talk like that. You didn't know what you said." She grew complete again. "I'm strong," she boasted. "I never knew before how strong."

Henry looked down toward the tractor shed, and when he brought his eyes 105
back to her, they were his own again. "I'll get out the car. You can put on your coat while I'm starting."

Elisa went into the house. She heard him drive to the gate and idle down his motor, and then she took a long time to put on her hat. She pulled it here and pressed it there. When Henry turned the motor off she slipped into her coat and went out.

The little roadster bounced along on the dirt road by the river, raising the birds and driving the rabbits into the brush. Two cranes flapped heavily over the willow-line and dropped into the riverbed.

Far ahead on the road Elisa saw a dark speck. She knew.

She tried not to look as they passed it, but her eyes would not obey. She whispered to herself sadly, "He might have thrown them off the road. That wouldn't have been much trouble, not very much. But he kept the pot," she explained. "He had to keep the pot. That's why he couldn't get them off the road."

The roadster turned a bend and she saw the caravan ahead. She swung full 110
around toward her husband so she could not see the little covered wagon and the mismatched team as the car passed them.

In a moment it was over. The thing was done. She did not look back.

She said loudly, to be heard above the motor, "It will be good, tonight, a good dinner."

"Now you're changed again," Henry complained. He took one hand from the wheel and patted her knee. "I ought to take you in to dinner oftener. It would be good for both of us. We get so heavy out on the ranch."

"Henry," she asked, "could we have wine at dinner?"

"Sure we could. Say! That will be fine." 115

She was silent for a while; then she said, "Henry, at those prize fights, do the men hurt each other very much?"

"Sometimes a little, not often. Why?"

"Well, I've read how they break noses, and blood runs down their chests. I've read how the fighting gloves get heavy and soggy with blood."

He looked around at her. "What's the matter, Elisa? I didn't know you read things like that." He brought the car to a stop, then turned to the right over the Salinas River bridge.

"Do any women ever go to the fights?" she asked. 120

"Oh, sure, some. What's the matter, Elisa? Do you want to go? I don't think you'd like it, but I'll take you if you really want to go."

MARITAL RATING SCALE
WIFE'S CHART
George W. Crane, Ph.D., M.D.
(copyright 1939)

In computing the score, check the various items under DEMERITS which fit the wife, and add the total. Each item counts as one point unless specifically weighted as in parentheses. Then check the items under MERITS which apply; now subtract the DEMERIT score from the MERIT score. The result is the wife's raw score. Interpret it according to this table:

RAW SCORES	INTERPRETATION
0–24	Very Poor (Failures)
25–41	Poor
42–58	Average
59–75	Superior
76 and up	Very Superior

DEMERITS		MERITS	
1. Slow in coming to bed—delays til husband is almost asleep.		1. A good hostess—even to unexpected guests.	
2. Doesn't like children. (5)		2. Has supper on time.	
3. Fails to sew on buttons or clean socks regularly.		3. Can carry on interesting conversation.	
4. Wears soiled or ragged dresses and aprons around the house.		4. Can play a musical instrument, as piano, violin, etc.	
5. Wears red nail polish.		5. Dresses for breakfast.	
6. Often late for appointments. (5)		6. Neat housekeeper—tidy and clean.	
7. Seams in hose often crooked.		7. Personally puts children to bed.	
8. Goes to bed with curlers on her hair or much face cream.		8. Never goes to bed angry, always makes up first . (5)	
9. Puts her cold feet on husband at night to warm them.		9. Asks husband's opinion regarding important decisions and purchases.	
10. Is a back seat driver.		10. Good sense of humor—jolly and gay.	
11. Flirts with other men at parties or in restaurants. (5)		11. Religious—sends children to church or Sunday school and goes herself. (10)	
12. Is suspicious and jealous. (5)		12. Lets husband sleep late on Sunday and holidays.	

During the period of this story, women were often asked in popular magazines to review their performance as wives using scales like this one.

She relaxed limply in the seat. "Oh, no. No. I don't want to go. I'm sure I don't." Her face was turned away from him. "It will be enough if we can have wine. It will be plenty." She turned up her coat collar so he could not see that she was crying weakly—like an old woman.

(1938)

Questions for Discussion and Writing

1. The chrysanthemums are clearly a symbol. What do they represent? Write an essay that makes a claim about the symbolism of the chrysanthemums.
2. How does the description of the setting at the beginning relate to the condition of Elisa's life?
3. Discuss the interactions between Elisa and the two males in the story. How do the men manipulate her? How does she try to manipulate them?
4. Why is Elisa interested in the prize fights? Why does she ask, "Do the men hurt each other very much?"
5. How do you think Elisa would respond to the "Wife's Chart" on page 305? In what ways does Steinbeck's characterization of Elisa act as a rebuttal to the values articulated in the chart?

Richard Wright 1908–1960

Richard Wright was born poor near Natchez, Mississippi, and conditions worsened after his father deserted the family. As a child he collected coal along the railroad tracks to heat their house. Although the family moved often, he did well in school while working at menial jobs to help pay the bills. After making it to Chicago, he landed a job with the postal service and joined the Federal Writers' Project. Like many writers of the time, he joined the Communist Party but quit after several years and rejected the party line. In 1946, alienated by the racism in the United States, he moved to Paris where he spent the last fourteen years of his life. His first novel, *Native Son* (1940), dramatizes the brutality of racial conflict and has become an American classic.

The Man Who Was Almost a Man

Dave struck out across the fields, looking homeward through paling light. Whut's the use of talkin wid em niggers in the field? Anyhow, his mother was putting supper on the table. Them niggers can't understan nothing. One of these days he was going to get a gun and practice shooting, then they couldn't talk to him as though he were a little boy. He slowed, looking at the ground. Shucks, Ah ain scareda them even ef they are biggern me! Aw, Ah know whut Ahma do. Ahm going by ol Joe's sto n git that Sears Roebuck catlog n look at them guns. Mebbe Ma will lemme buy one when she gits mah pay from ol man Hawkins. Ahma beg her t gimme some money. Ahm ol ernough to hava gun. Ahm seventeen. Almost a man. He strode, feeling his long loose-jointed limbs. Shucks, a man oughta hava little gun aftah he done worked hard all day.

He came in sight of Joe's store. A yellow lantern glowed on the front porch. He mounted the steps and went through the screen door, hearing it bang behind him. There was a strong smell of coal oil and mackerel fish. He felt very confident until he saw fat Joe walk in through the rear door, then his courage began to ooze.

"Howdy, Dave! Whutcha want?"

"How yuh, Mistah Joe? Aw, Ah don wanna buy nothing. Ah jus wanted t see ef yuhd lemme look at tha catlog erwhile."

"Sure! You wanna see it here?"

"Nawsuh. Ah wans t take it home wid me. Ah'll bring it back termorrow when Ah come in from the fiels."

"You plannin on buying something?"

"Yessuh."

"Your ma lettin you have your own money now?"

"Shucks. Mistah Joe, Ahm gittin t be a man like anybody else!"

Joe laughed and wiped his greasy white face with a red bandanna.

"Whut you plannin on buyin?"

Dave looked at the floor, scratched his head, scratched his thigh, and smiled. Then he looked up shyly.

"Ah'll tell yuh, Mistah Joe, ef yuh promise yuh won't tell."

"I promise."

"Waal, Ahma buy a gun."

"A gun? Whut you want with a gun?"

"Ah wanna keep it."

"You ain't nothing but a boy. You don't need a gun."

"Aw, lemme have the catlog, Mistah Joe. Ah'll bring it back."

Joe walked through the rear door. Dave was elated. He looked around at barrels of sugar and flour. He heard Joe coming back. He craned his neck to see if he were bringing the book. Yeah, he's got it. Gawddog, he's got it!

"Here, but be sure you bring it back. It's the only one I got."

"Sho, Mistah Joe."

"Say, if you wanna buy a gun, why don't you buy one from me? I gotta gun to sell."

"Will it shoot?"

"Sure it'll shoot."

"Whut kind is it?"

"Oh, it's kinda old ... a left-hand Wheeler. A pistol. A big one."

"Is it got bullets in it?"

"It's loaded."

"Kin Ah see it?"

"Where's your money?"

"Whut yuh wan fer it?"

"I'll let you have it for two dollars."

"Just two dollahs? Shucks, Ah could buy tha when Ah git mah pay."

"I'll have it here when you want it."

"Awright, suh. Ah be in fer it."

He went through the door, hearing it slam again behind him. Ahma git some money from Ma n buy me a gun! Only two dollahs! He tucked the thick catalogue under his arm and hurried.

"Where yuh been, boy?" His mother held a steaming dish of black-eyed peas.

"Aw, Ma, Ah jus stopped down the road t talk wid the boys."

"Yuh know bettah t keep suppah waitin."

He sat down, resting the catalogue on the edge of the table.

"Yuh git up from there and git to the well n wash yoself! Ah ain feedin no hogs in mah house!"

She grabbed his shoulder and pushed him. He stumbled out of the room, then came back to get the catalogue.

"Whut this?"

"Aw, Ma, it's jusa catlog."

"Who yuh git it from?"

"From Joe, down at the sto."

"Waal, thas good. We kin use it in the outhouse."

"Naw, Ma." He grabbed for it. "Gimme ma catlog, Ma."

She held onto it and glared at him.

"Quit hollerin at me! Whut's wrong wid yuh? Yuh crazy?"

"But Ma, please. It ain mine! It's Joe's! He tol me t bring it back t im termorrow."

She gave up the book. He stumbled down the back steps, hugging the thick book under his arm. When he had splashed water on his face and hands, he groped back to the kitchen and fumbled in a corner for the towel. He bumped into a chair; it clattered to the floor. The catalogue sprawled at his feet. When he had dried his eyes he snatched up the book and held it again under his arm. His mother stood watching him.

"Now, ef yuh gonna act a fool over that ol book, Ah'll take it n burn it up."

"Naw, Ma, please."

"Waal, set down n be still!"

He sat down and drew the oil lamp close. He thumbed page after page, unaware of the food his mother set on the table. His father came in. Then his small brother.

"Whutcha got there, Dave?" his father asked.

"Jusa catlog," he answered, not looking up.

"Yeah, here they is!" His eyes glowed at blue-and-black revolvers. He glanced up, feeling sudden guilt. His father was watching him. He eased the book under the table and rested it on his knees. After the blessing was asked, he ate. He scooped up peas and swallowed fat meat without chewing. Buttermilk helped to wash it down. He did not want to mention money before his father. He would do much better by cornering his mother when she was alone. He looked at his father uneasily out of the edge of his eye.

"Boy, how come yuh don quit foolin wid tha book n eat yo suppah?"

"Yessuh."

"How you n ol man Hawkins gitten erlong?"

"Suh?"

"Can't yuh hear? Why don yuh lissen? Ah ast yu how wuz yuh n ol man Hawkins gittin erlong?"

"Oh, swell, Pa. Ah plows mo lan than anybody over there."

"Waal, yuh oughta keep yo mind on whut yuh doin."

"Yessuh."

He poured his plate full of molasses and sopped it up slowly with a chunk of 70
cornbread. When his father and brother had left the kitchen, he still sat and looked again at the guns in the catalogue, longing to muster courage enough to present his case to his mother. Lawd, ef Ah only had tha pretty one! He could almost feel the slickness of the weapon with his fingers. If he had a gun like that he would polish it and keep it shining so it would never rust. N Ah'd keep it loaded, by Gawd!

"Ma?" His voice was hesitant.

"Hunh?"

"Ol man Hawkins give yuh mah money yit?"

"Yeah, but ain no usa yuh thinking bout throwin nona it erway. Ahm keepin tha money sos yuh kin have cloes t go to school this winter."

He rose and went to her side with the open catalogue in his palms. She was 75
washing dishes, her head bent low over a pan. Shyly he raised the book. When he spoke, his voice was husky, faint.

"Ma, Gawd knows Ah wans one of these."

"One of whut?" she asked, not raising her eyes.

"One of these," he said again, not daring even to point. She glanced up at the page, then at him with wide eyes.

"Nigger, is yuh gone plumb crazy?"

"Aw, Ma—" 80

"Git outta here! Don yuh talk t me bout no gun! Yuh a fool!"

"Ma, Ah kin buy one fer two dollahs."

"Not ef Ah knows it, yuh ain!"

"But yuh promised me one—"

"Ah don care whut Ah promised! Yuh ain nothing but a boy yit!" 85

"Ma, ef yuh lemme buy one Ah'll *never* ast yuh fer nothing no mo."

"Ah tol yuh t git outta here! Yuh ain gonna toucha penny of tha money fer no gun! Thas how come Ah has Mistah Hawkins t pay yo wages t me, cause Ah knows yuh ain got no sense."

"But, Ma, we needa gun. Pa ain got no gun. We needa gun in the house. Yuh kin never tell whut might happen."

"Now don yuh try to maka fool outta me, boy! Ef we did hava gun, yuh wouldn't have it!"

He laid the catalogue down and slipped his arm around her waist. 90

"Aw, Ma, Ah done worked hard alla summer n ain ast yuh fer nothin, is Ah, now?"

"Thas whut yuh spose t do!"

"But Ma, Ah wans a gun. Yuh kin lemme have two dollahs outta mah money. Please, Ma. I kin give it to Pa.... Please, Ma! Ah loves yuh, Ma."

When she spoke her voice came soft and low.

"Whut yu wan wida gun, Dave? Yuh don need no gun. Yuh'll git in trouble. 95
N ef yo pa jus thought Ah let yuh have money t buy a gun he'd hava fit."

"Ah'll hide it, Ma. It ain but two dollahs."

"Lawd, chil, whut's wrong wid yuh?"

"Ain nothin wrong, Ma. Ahm almos a man now. Ah wans a gun."

"Who gonna sell yuh a gun?"

"Ol Joe at the sto." 100

"N it don cos but two dollahs?"

"Thas all, Ma. Jus two dollahs. Please, Ma."

She was stacking the plates away; her hands moved slowly, reflectively. Dave kept an anxious silence. Finally, she turned to him.

"Ah'll let yuh git tha gun ef yuh promise me one thing."

"Whut's tha, Ma?" 105

"Yuh bring it straight back t me, yuh hear? It be fer Pa."

"Yessum! Lemme go now, Ma."

She stopped, turned slightly to one side, raised the hem of her dress, rolled down the top of her stocking, and came up with a slender wad of bills.

"Here," she said. "Lawd knows yuh don need no gun. But yer pa does. Yuh bring it right back t me, yuh hear? Ahma put it up. Now ef yuh don, Ahma have yuh pa lick yuh so hard yuh won fergit it."

"Yessum." 110

He took the money, ran down the steps, and across the yard.

"Dave! Yuuuuuh Daaaaave!"

He heard, but he was not going to stop now. "Naw, Lawd!"

The first movement he made the following morning was to reach under his pillow for the gun. In the gray light of dawn he held it loosely, feeling a sense of power. Could kill a man with a gun like this. Kill anybody, black or white. And if he were holding his gun in his hand, nobody could run over him; they would have to respect him. It was a big gun, with a long barrel and a heavy handle. He raised and lowered it in his hand, marveling at its weight.

He had not come straight home with it as his mother had asked; instead he had stayed out in the fields, holding the weapon in his hand, aiming it now and then at some imaginary foe. But he had not fired it; he had been afraid that his father might hear. Also he was not sure he knew how to fire it. 115

To avoid surrendering the pistol he had not come into the house until he knew that they were all asleep. When his mother had tiptoed to his bedside late that night and demanded the gun, he had first played possum; then he had told her that the gun was hidden outdoors, that he would bring it to her in the morning. Now he lay turning it slowly in his hands. He broke it, took out the cartridges, felt them, and then put them back.

He slid out of bed, got a long strip of old flannel from a trunk, wrapped the gun in it, and tied it to his naked thigh while it was still loaded. He did not go in to breakfast. Even though it was not yet daylight, he started for Jim Hawkins' plantation. Just as the sun was rising he reached the barns where the mules and plows were kept.

"Hey! That you, Dave?"

He turned. Jim Hawkins stood eying him suspiciously.

"What're yuh doing here so early?" 120

"Ah didn't know Ah wuz gittin up so early, Mistah Hawkins. Ah wuz fixin t hitch up ol Jenny n take her t the fiels."

"Good. Since you're so early, how about plowing that stretch down by the woods?"

"Suits me, Mistah Hawkins."

"O.K. Go to it!"

He hitched Jenny to a plow and started across the fields. Hot dog! This was just what he wanted. If he could get down by the woods, he could shoot his gun 125 and nobody would hear. He walked behind the plow, hearing the traces creaking, feeling the gun tied tight to his thigh.

When he reached the woods, he plowed two whole rows before he decided to take out the gun. Finally, he stopped, looked in all directions, then untied the gun and held it in his hand. He turned to the mule and smiled.

"Know whut this is, Jenny? Naw, yuh wouldn know! Yuhs jusa ol mule! Anyhow, this is a gun, n it kin shoot, by Gawd!"

He held the gun at arm's length. Whut t hell, Ahma shoot this thing! He looked at Jenny again.

"Lissen here, Jenny! When Ah pull this ol trigger, Ah don wan yuh t run n acka fool now!"

Jenny stood with head down, her short ears pricked straight. Dave walked off 130
about twenty feet, held the gun far out from him at arm's length, and turned his head. Hell, he told himself, Ah ain afraid. The gun felt loose in his fingers; he waved it wildly for a moment. Then he shut his eyes and tightened his forefinger. Bloom! A report half deafened him and he thought his right hand was torn from his arm. He heard Jenny whinnying and galloping over the field, and he found himself on his knees, squeezing his fingers hard between his legs. His hand was numb; he jammed it into his mouth, trying to warm it, trying to stop the pain. The gun lay at his feet. He did not quite know what had happened. He stood up and stared at the gun as though it were a living thing. He gritted his teeth and kicked the gun. Yuh almos broke mah arm! He turned to look for Jenny; she was far over the fields, tossing her head and kicking wildly.

"Hol on there, ol mule!"

When he caught up with her she stood trembling, walling her big white eyes at him. The plow was far away; the traces had broken. Then Dave stopped short, looking, not believing. Jenny was bleeding. Her left side was red and wet with blood. He went closer. Lawd, have mercy! Wondah did Ah shoot this mule? He grabbed for Jenny's mane. She flinched, snorted, whirled, tossing her head.

"Hol on now! Hol on."

Then he saw the hole in Jenny's side, right between the ribs. It was round, wet, red. A crimson stream streaked down the front leg, flowing fast. Good Gawd! Ah wuzn't shootin at tha mule. He felt panic. He knew he had to stop that blood, or Jenny would bleed to death. He had never seen so much blood in all his life. He chased the mule for half a mile, trying to catch her. Finally she stopped, breathing hard, stumpy tail half arched. He caught her mane and led her back to where the plow and gun lay. Then he stooped and grabbed handfuls of damp black earth and tried to plug the bullet hole. Jenny shuddered, whinnied, and broke from him.

"Hol on! Hol on now!" 135

He tried to plug it again, but blood came anyhow. His fingers were hot and sticky. He rubbed dirt into his palms, trying to dry them. Then again he attempted to plug the bullet hole, but Jenny shied away, kicking her heels high. He stood helpless. He had to do something. He ran at Jenny; she dodged him. He watched a red stream of blood flow down Jenny's leg and form a bright pool at her feet.

"Jenny...Jenny," he called weakly.

His lips trembled. She's bleeding t death! He looked in the direction of home, wanting to go back, wanting to get help. But he saw the pistol lying in the damp black clay. He had a queer feeling that if he only did something, this would not be; Jenny would not be there bleeding to death.

When he went to her this time, she did not move. She stood with sleepy, dreamy eyes; and when he touched her she gave a low-pitched whinny and knelt to the ground, her front knees slopping in blood.

"Jenny…Jenny…" he whispered. 140

For a long time she held her neck erect; then her head sank, slowly. Her ribs swelled with a mighty heave and she went over.

Dave's stomach felt empty, very empty. He picked up the gun and held it gingerly between his thumb and forefinger. He buried it at the foot of a tree. He took a stick and tried to cover the pool of blood with dirt—but what was the use? There was Jenny lying with her mouth open and her eyes walled and glassy. He could not tell Jim Hawkins he had shot his mule. But he had to tell something. Yeah, Ah'll tell em Jenny started gittin wil n fell on the joint of the plow.…But that would hardly happen to a mule. He walked across the field slowly, head down.

It was sunset. Two of Jim Hawkins' men were over near the edge of the woods digging a hole in which to bury Jenny. Dave was surrounded by a knot of people, all of whom were looking down at the dead mule.

"I don't see how in the world it happened," said Jim Hawkins for the tenth time.

The crowd parted and Dave's mother, father, and small brother pushed into 145
the center.

"Where Dave?" his mother called.

"There he is," said Jim Hawkins.

His mother grabbed him.

"Whut happened, Dave? Whut yuh done?"

"Nothin." 150

"C'mon, boy, talk," his father said.

Dave took a deep breath and told the story he knew nobody believed.

"Waal," he drawled. "Ah brung ol Jenny down here sos Ah could do mah plowin. Ah plowed bout two rows, just like yuh see." He stopped and pointed at the long rows of upturned earth. "Then somethin musta been wrong wid ol Jenny. She wouldn ack right a-tall. She started snortin n kickin her heels. Ah tried t hol her, but she pulled erway, rearin n goin in. Then when the point of the plow was stickin up in the air, she swung erroun n twisted herself back on it.…She stuck herself n started t bleed. N fo Ah could do anything, she wuz dead."

"Did you ever hear of anything like that in all your life?" asked Jim Hawkins.

There were white and black standing in the crowd. They murmured. Dave's 155
mother came close to him and looked hard into his face. "Tell the truth, Dave," she said.

"Looks like a bullet hole to me," said one man.

"Dave, whut yuh do wid tha gun?" his mother asked.

The crowd surged in, looking at him. He jammed his hands into his pockets, shook his head slowly from left to right, and backed away. His eyes were wide and painful.

"Did he hava gun?" asked Jim Hawkins.

"By Gawd, Ah tol yuh tha wuz a gun wound," said a man, slapping his thigh. 160

His father caught his shoulders and shook him till his teeth rattled.

"Tell whut happened, yuh rascal! Tell whut..."

Dave looked at Jenny's stiff legs and began to cry.

"Whut yuh do wid tha gun?" his mother asked.

"Whut wuz he doin wida gun?" his father asked.

"Come on and tell the truth," said Hawkins. "Ain't nobody going to hurt you...."

His mother crowded close to him.

"Did yuh shoot tha mule, Dave?"

Dave cried, seeing blurred white and black faces.

"Ahh ddinn gggo tt sshooot hher....Ah ssswear ffo Gawd Ahh ddin....Ah wuz a-tryin t sssee ef the old gggun would sshoot—"

"Where yuh git the gun from?" his father asked.

"Ah got it from Joe, at the sto."

"Where yuh git the money?"

"Ma give it t me."

"He kept worryin me, Bob. Ah had t. Ah tol im t bring the gun right back t me....It was fer yuh, the gun."

"But how yuh happen to shoot that mule?" asked Jim Hawkins.

"Ah wuzn shootin at the mule, Mistah Hawkins. The gun jumped when Ah pulled the trigger....N fo Ah knowed anythin Jenny was there a-bleedin."

Somebody in the crowd laughed. Jim Hawkins walked close to Dave and looked into his face.

"Well, looks like you have bought you a mule, Dave."

"Ah swear fo Gawd, Ah didn go t kill the mule, Mistah Hawkins!"

"But you killed her!"

All the crowd was laughing now. They stood on tiptoe and poked heads over one another's shoulders.

"Well, boy, looks like yuh done bought a dead mule! Hahaha!"

"Ain tha ershame."

"Hohohohoho."

Dave stood, head down, twisting his feet in the dirt.

"Well, you needn't worry about it, Bob," said Jim Hawkins to Dave's father. "Just let the boy keep on working and pay me two dollars a month."

"Whut yuh wan fer yo mule, Mistah Hawkins?"

Jim Hawkins screwed up his eyes.

"Fifty dollars."

"Whut yuh do wid tha gun?" Dave's father demanded.

Dave said nothing.

"Yuh wan me t take a tree n beat yuh till yuh talk!"

"Nawsuh!"

"Whut yuh do wid it?"

"Ah throwed it erway."

"Where?"

"Ah...Ah throwed it in the creek."

"Waal, c'mon home. N firs thing in the mawnin git to tha creek n fin tha gun."

"Yessuh."

"Whut yuh pay fer it?"

"Two dollahs."

"Take tha gun n git yo money back n carry it t Mistah Hawkins, yuh hear? N don fergit Ahma lam you black bottom good fer this! Now march yosef on home, suh!"

Dave turned and walked slowly. He heard people laughing. Dave glared, his eyes welling with tears. Hot anger bubbled in him. Then he swallowed and stumbled on.

That night Dave did not sleep. He was glad that he had gotten out of killing the mule so easily, but he was hurt. Something hot seemed to turn over inside him each time he remembered how they had laughed. He tossed on his bed, feeling his hard pillow. N Pa says he's gonna beat me.... He remembered other beatings, and his back quivered. Naw, naw, Ah sho don wan im t beat me tha way no mo. Dam em all! Nobody ever gave him anything. All he did was work. They treat me like a mule, n then they beat me. He gritted his teeth. N Ma had t tell on me.

Well, if he had to, he would take old man Hawkins that two dollars. But 205
that meant selling the gun. And he wanted to keep that gun. Fifty dollars for a dead mule.

He turned over, thinking how he had fired the gun. He had an itch to fire it again. Ef other men kin shoota gun, by Gawd, Ah kin! He was still, listening. Mebbe they all sleepin now. The house was still. He heard the soft breathing of his brother. Yes, now! He would go down and get that gun and see if he could fire it! He eased out of bed and slipped into overalls.

The moon was bright. He ran almost all the way to the edge of the woods. He stumbled over the ground, looking for the spot where he had buried the gun. Yeah, here it is. Like a hungry dog scratching for a bone, he pawed it up. He puffed his black cheeks and blew dirt from the trigger and barrel. He broke it and found four cartridges unshot. He looked around; the fields were filled with silence and moonlight. He clutched the gun stiff and hard in his fingers. But, as soon as he wanted to pull the trigger, he shut his eyes and turned his head. Naw, Ah can't shoot wid mah eyes closed n mah head turned. With effort he held his eyes open; then he squeezed. *Blooooom*! He was stiff, not breathing. The gun was still in his hands. Dammit, he'd done it! He fired again. *Blooooom*! He smiled. *Blooooom*! *Blooooom*! *Click*, *click*. There! It was empty. If anybody could shoot a gun, he could. He put the gun into his hip pocket and started across the fields.

When he reached the top of a ridge he stood straight and proud in the moonlight, looking at Jim Hawkins' big white house, feeling the gun sagging in his pocket. Lawd, ef Ah had just one mo bullet Ah'd taka shot at tha house. Ah'd like t scare ol man Hawkins jusa little....Jusa enough t let im know Dave Saunders is a man.

To his left the road curved, running to the tracks of the Illinois Central. He jerked his head, listening. From far off came a faint *hoooof-hoooof*; *hoooof-hoooof*; *hoooof-hoooof*.... He stood rigid. Two dollahs a mont. Les see now.... Tha means it'll take bout two years. Shucks! Ah'll be dam!

He started down the road, toward the tracks. Yeah, here she comes! He stood 210
beside the track and held himself stiffly. Here she comes, erroun the ben.... C mon, yuh slow poke! C mon! He had his hand on his gun; something quivered in his stomach. Then the train thundered past, the gray and brown box cars rumbling and clinking. He gripped the gun tightly; then he jerked his hand out of his pocket. Ah betcha Bill wouldn't do it! Ah betcha.... The cars slid past, steel grinding upon steel. Ahm ridin yuh ternight, so hep me Gawd! He was hot all over. He hesitated just a moment; then he grabbed, pulled atop of a car, and lay flat. He felt his pocket; the gun was still there. Ahead the long rails were

glinting in the moonlight, stretching away, away to somewhere, somewhere where he could be a man....

(1940)

Questions for Discussion and Writing

1. What needs does Dave hope to satisfy by owning a gun? What are the sources of Dave's needs?
2. What does the accidental shooting of Jenny reveal about Dave? In what ways could this "accident" be seen as a subconscious act of rebellion against exploitation and shame? Is there any other evidence of Dave's rebelliousness or hostility?
3. What do the descriptions of the field, the store, and the house suggest about Dave's environment? How much do these living and working conditions affect Dave's attitudes and behavior?
4. What do you think of the story's ending?
5. Compare Dave's decision to leave town to Sammy's decision to quit his job (in the story "A & P"—pages 440–45).

Tillie Olsen 1913–2007

Tillie Olsen was born in Omaha, Nebraska, the daughter of political refugees from the repression of Czarist Russia. In her book *Silences* (1978), Olsen explains how gender, race, and class can render people inarticulate. Her own life illustrates the problem. She began working on a novel before she was twenty, but then she married, had four children, worked, participated in union activities, and did not resume writing until the 1950s, when her youngest daughter started school. The completed novel, *Yonnondio*, was finally published in 1974. Her long story "Tell Me a Riddle" won the O. Henry Prize in 1961. Olsen has said that she felt no personal guilt as a working parent because "guilt is a word used far too sloppily, to cover up harmful situations in society that must be changed."

I Stand Here Ironing

I stand here ironing, and what you asked me moves tormented back and forth with the iron.

"I wish you would manage the time to come in and talk with me about your daughter. I'm sure you can help me understand her. She's a youngster who needs help and whom I'm deeply interested in helping."

"Who needs help?" Even if I came what good would it do? You think because I am her mother I have a key, or that in some way you could use me as a key? She has lived for nineteen years. There is all that life that has happened outside of me, beyond me.

And when is there time to remember, to sift, to weigh, to estimate, to total? I will start and there will be an interruption and I will have to gather it all together again. Or I will become engulfed with all I did or did not do, with what should have been and what cannot be helped.

She was a beautiful baby. The first and only one of our five that was beautiful at 5
birth. You do not guess how new and uneasy her tenancy in her now-loveliness. You did not know her all those years she was thought homely, or see her poring over her baby pictures, making me tell her over and over how beautiful she had been—and would be, I would tell her—and was now, to the seeing eye. But the seeing eyes were few or nonexistent. Including mine.

I nursed her. They feel that's important nowadays. I nursed all the children, but with her, with all the fierce rigidity of first motherhood, I did like the books then said. Though her cries battered me to trembling and my breasts ached with swollenness, I waited till the clock decreed.

Why do I put that first? I do not even know if it matters, or if it explains anything.

She was a beautiful baby. She blew shining bubbles of sound. She loved motion, loved light, loved color and music and textures. She would lie on the floor in her blue overalls patting the surface so hard in ecstasy her hands and feet would blur. She was a miracle to me, but when she was eight months old I had to leave her daytimes with the woman downstairs to whom she was no miracle at all, for I worked or looked for work and for Emily's father, who "could no longer endure" (he wrote in his good-by note) "sharing want with us."

I was nineteen. It was the pre-relief, pre-WPA world of the depression. I would start running as soon as I got off the streetcar, running up the stairs, the place smelling sour, and awake or asleep to startle awake, when she saw me she would break into a clogged weeping that could not be comforted, a weeping I can yet hear.

After a while I found a job hashing at night so I could be with her days, and it 10
was better. But it came to where I had to bring her to his family and leave her.

It took a long time to raise the money for her fare back. Then she got chicken pox and I had to wait longer. When she finally came, I hardly knew her, walking quick and nervous like her father, looking like her father, thin, and dressed in a shoddy red that yellowed her skin and glared at the pockmarks. All the baby loveliness gone.

She was two. Old enough for nursery school they said, and I did not know then what I know now—the fatigue of the long day, and the lacerations of group life in the kinds of nurseries that are only parking places for children.

Except that it would have made no difference if I had known. It was the only place there was. It was the only way we could be together, the only way I could hold a job.

And even without knowing, I knew. I knew the teacher that was evil because all these years it has curdled into my memory, the little boy hunched in the corner, her rasp, "why aren't you outside, because Alvin hits you? that's no reason, go out, scaredy." I knew Emily hated it even if she did not clutch and implore "don't go Mommy" like the other children, mornings.

She always had a reason why we should stay home. Momma, you look sick. 15
Momma, I feel sick. Momma, the teachers aren't there today, they're sick. Momma, we can't go, there was a fire there last night. Momma, it's a holiday today, no school, they told me.

But never a direct protest, never rebellion. I think of our others in their three-, four-year-oldness—the explosions, the tempers, the denunciations, the demands—and I feel suddenly ill. I put the iron down. What in me demanded that goodness in her? And what was the cost, the cost to her of such goodness?

The old man living in the back once said in his gentle way: "You should smile at Emily more when you look at her." What *was* in my face when I looked at her? I loved her. There were all the acts of love.

It was only with the others I remembered what he said, so that it was the face of joy, and not of care or tightness or worry I turned to them—too late for Emily. She does not smile easily, let alone almost always as her brothers and sisters do. Her face is closed and somber, but when she wants, how fluid. You must have seen it in her pantomimes, you spoke of her rare gift for comedy on the stage that rouses a laughter out of the audience so dear they applaud and applaud and do not want to let her go.

Where does it come from, that comedy? There was none of it in her when she came back to me that second time, after I had had to send her away again. She had a new daddy now to learn to love, and I think perhaps it was a better time.

Except when we left her alone nights, telling ourselves she was old enough.

"Can't you go some other time, Mommy, like tomorrow?" she would ask. "Will it be just a little while you'll be gone? Do you promise?"

The time we came back, the front door open, the clock on the floor in the hall. She rigid awake. "It wasn't just a little while. I didn't cry. Three times I called you, just three times, and then I ran downstairs to open the door so you could come faster. The clock talked loud, I threw it away, it scared me when it talked."

She said the clock talked loud that night I went to the hospital to have Susan. She was delirious with the fever that comes before red measles, but she was fully conscious all the week I was gone and the week after we were home when she could not come near the new baby or me.

She did not get well. She stayed skeleton thin, not wanting to eat, and night after night she had nightmares. She would call for me, and I would sleepily call back, "you're all right, darling, go to sleep, it's just a dream," and if she still called, in a sterner voice, "now go to sleep, Emily, there's nothing to hurt you." Twice, only twice, when I had to get up for Susan anyway, I went in to sit with her.

Now when it is too late (as if she would let me hold and comfort her like I do the others) I get up and go to her at her moan or restless stirring. "Are you awake? Can I get you something?" And the answer is always the same: "No, I'm all right, go back to sleep, Mother."

They persuaded me at the clinic to send her away to a convalescent home in the country where "she can have the kind of food and care you can't manage for her, and you'll be free to concentrate on the new baby." They still send children to that place. I see pictures on the society page of sleek young women planning affairs to raise money for it, or dancing at the affairs, or decorating Easter eggs or filling Christmas stockings for children.

They never have a picture of the children so I do not know if they still wear those gigantic red bows and the ravaged looks on the every other Sunday when parents can come to visit "unless otherwise notified"—as we were notified the first six weeks.

Oh it is a handsome place, green lawns and tall trees and fluted flower beds. High up on the balconies of each cottage the children stand, the girls in their red bows and white dresses, the boys in white suits and giant red ties. The parents stand below shrieking up to be heard and the children shriek down to be heard, and between them the invisible wall "Not To Be Contaminated by Parental Germs or Physical Affection."

There was a tiny girl who always stood hand in hand with Emily. Her parents never came. One visit she was gone. "They moved her to Rose Cottage," Emily shouted in explanation. "They don't like you to love anybody here."

She wrote once a week, the labored writing of a seven-year-old. "I am fine. How 30
is the baby. If I write my leter nicly I will have a star. Love." There was never a star. We wrote every other day, letters she could never hold or keep but only hear read—once. "We simply do not have room for children to keep any personal possessions," they patiently explained when we pieced one Sunday's shrieking together to plead how much it would mean to Emily to keep her letters and cards.

Each visit she looked frailer. "She isn't eating," they told us.

(They had runny eggs for breakfast or mush with lumps, Emily said later, I'd hold it in my mouth and not swallow. Nothing ever tasted good, just when they had chicken.)

It took us eight months to get her released home, and only the fact that she gained back so little of her seven lost pounds convinced the social worker.

I used to try to hold and love her after she came back, but her body would stay stiff, and after a while she'd push away. She ate little. Food sickened her, and I think much of life too. Oh she had physical lightness and brightness, twinkling by on skates, bouncing like a ball up and down up and down over the jump rope, skimming over the hill; but these were momentary.

She fretted about her appearance, thin and dark and foreign-looking at a 35
time when every little girl was supposed to look or thought she should look a chubby blond replica of Shirley Temple. The doorbell sometimes rang for her, but no one seemed to come and play in the house or be a best friend. Maybe because we moved so much.

There was a boy she loved painfully through two school semesters. Months later she told me how she had taken pennies from my purse to buy him candy. "Licorice was his favorite and I bought him some every day, but he still liked Jennifer better'n me. Why, Mommy?" The kind of question for which there is no answer.

School was a worry to her. She was not glib or quick in a world where glibness and quickness were easily confused with ability to learn. To her over-worked and exasperated teachers she was an over-conscientious "slow learner" who kept trying to catch up and was absent entirely too often.

I let her be absent, though sometimes the illness was imaginary. How different from my now-strictness about attendance with the others. I wasn't working. We had a new baby, I was home anyhow. Sometimes, after Susan grew old enough, I would keep her home from school, too, to have them all together.

Mostly Emily had asthma, and her breathing, harsh and labored, would fill the house with a curiously tranquil sound. I would bring the two old dresser mirrors and her boxes of collections to her bed. She would select beads and single earrings, bottle tops and shells, dried flowers and pebbles, old postcards and scraps, all sorts of oddments; then she and Susan would play Kingdom, setting up landscapes and furniture, peopling them with action.

Those were the only times of peaceful companionship between her and 40
Susan. I have edged away from it, that poisonous feeling between them, that terrible balancing of hurts and needs I had to do between the two, and did so badly, those earlier years.

Oh there are conflicts between the others too, each one human, needing, demanding, hurting, taking—but only between Emily and Susan, no, Emily toward Susan that corroding resentment. It seems so obvious on the surface, yet it is not obvious. Susan, the second child, Susan, golden and curly haired and chubby, quick and articulate and assured, everything in appearance and manner Emily was not; Susan, not able to resist Emily's precious things, losing or sometimes clumsily breaking them; Susan telling jokes and riddles to company for applause while Emily sat silent (to say to me later: that was *my* riddle, Mother, I told it to Susan); Susan, who for all the five years' difference in age was just a year behind Emily in developing physically.

I am glad for that slow physical development that widened the difference between her and her contemporaries, though she suffered over it. She was too vulnerable for that terrible world of youthful competition, of preening and parading, of constant measuring of yourself against every other, of envy: "If I had that copper hair," or "If I had that skin...." She tormented herself enough about not looking like the others, there was enough of the unsureness, the having to be conscious of words before you speak, the constant caring—what are they thinking of me? what kind of an impression am I making?—without having it all magnified unendurably by the merciless physical drives.

Ronnie is calling. He is wet and I change him. It is rare there is such a cry now. That time of motherhood is almost behind me when the ear is not one's own but must always be racked and listening for the child cry, the child call. We sit for a while and I hold him, looking out over the city spread in charcoal with its soft aisles of light. "*Shoogily*," he breathes and curls closer. I carry him back to bed, asleep. *Shoogily*. A funny word, a family word, inherited from Emily, invented by her to say: *comfort*.

In this and other ways she leaves her seal, I say aloud. And startle at my saying it. What do I mean? What did I start to gather together, to try and make coherent? I was at the terrible, growing years. War years. I do not remember them well. I was working again, there were four smaller ones now, there was no time for her. She had to help be a mother, and housekeeper, and shopper. She had to set her seal. Mornings of crisis and near hysteria trying to get lunches packed, hair combed, coats and shoes found, everyone to school or Child Care on time, the baby ready for transportation. And always the paper scribbled on by a smaller one, the book looked at by Susan then mislaid, the homework not done. Running out to that huge school where she was one, she was lost, she was a drop; suffering over her unpreparedness, stammering and unsure in her classes.

There was so little left at night after the kids were bedded down. She would 45
struggle over her books, always eating (it was in those years she developed her enormous appetite that is legendary in our family) and I would be ironing, or preparing food for the next day, or writing V-mail[1] to Bill, or tending the baby. Sometimes, to make me laugh, or out of her despair, she would imitate happenings or types at school.

---

[1]Victory mail; letter written to personnel in the armed forces overseas during World War II.

I think I said once: "Why don't you do something like this in the school amateur show?" One morning she phoned me at work, hardly understandable through the weeping: "Mother, I did it. I won, I won; they gave me first prize; they clapped and clapped and wouldn't let me go."

Now suddenly she was Somebody, and as imprisoned in her difference as she had been in her anonymity.

She began to be asked to perform at other high schools, even in colleges, then at city and state-wide affairs. The first one we went to, I only recognized her that first moment when thin, shy, she almost drowned herself into the curtains. Then: Was this Emily? The control, the command, the convulsing and deadly clowning, the spell, then the roaring, stamping audience, unwilling to let this rare and precious laughter out of their lives.

Afterwards: You ought to do something about her with a gift like that—but without money or knowing how, what does one do? We have left it all to her, and the gift has as often eddied inside, clogged and clotted, as been used and growing.

She is coming. She runs up the stairs two at a time with her light graceful step, and I know she is happy tonight. Whatever it was that occasioned your call did not happen today.

"Aren't you ever going to finish the ironing, Mother? Whistler painted his mother in a rocker. I'd have to paint mine standing over an ironing board." This is one of the communicative nights and she tells me everything and nothing as she fixes herself a plate of food out of the icebox.

She is so lovely. Why did you want me to come in at all? Why were you concerned? She will find her way.

She starts up the stairs to bed. "Don't get *me* up with the rest in the morning." "But I thought you were having midterms." "Oh, those," she comes back in, kisses me, and says quite lightly, "in a couple of years when we'll all be atom-dead they won't matter a bit."

She has said it before. She *believes* it. But because I have been dredging the past, and all that compounds a human being is so heavy and meaningful in me, I cannot endure it tonight.

I will never total it all. I will never come in to say: She was a child seldom smiled at. Her father left me before she was a year old. I had to work away from her her first six years when there was work, or I sent her home and to his relatives. There were years she had care she hated. She was dark and thin and foreign-looking in a world where the prestige went to blondness and curly hair and dimples, she was slow where glibness was prized. She was a child of anxious, not proud, love. We were poor and could not afford for her the soil of easy growth. I was a young mother, I was a distracted mother. There were the other children pushing up, demanding. Her younger sister seemed all that she was not. There were years she did not want me to touch her. She kept too much in herself, her life was such she had to keep too much in herself. My wisdom came too late. She has much to her and probably little will come of it. She is a child of her age, of depression, of war, of fear.

Let her be. So all that is in her will not bloom—but in how many does it? There is still enough left to live by. Only help her to know—help make it so there is cause for her to know—that she is more than this dress on the ironing board, helpless before the iron.

(1961)

Questions for Discussion and Writing

1. The story is a monologue. What is the speaker's situation? Where is she and to whom is she talking?
2. Identify some of the conflicts in the story. Are any of them resolved?
3. How is personal responsibility portrayed in this story? To what extent is the speaker responsible for Emily's character and success in life? To what extent are circumstances responsible? To what extent is Emily herself responsible?
4. Write an essay in which you argue that this story reflects the common experiences of millions of people.
5. Rewrite the story from Emily's point of view.

Hisaye Yamamoto 1921–

Hisaye Yamamoto was born in Redondo Beach, California, the daughter of Japanese immigrants. She loved to read as a child and majored in foreign languages when she attended community college. During World War II, she and her family were forcibly interned in a relocation center in Arizona. While the family was confined, her brother Johnny, a soldier in the U.S. army, was killed in action in Italy. After returning to California, she became a housewife and mother, too busy to write much. "Most of the time I am cleaning house, or cooking or doing yard work," she once explained. "Very little time is spent writing. But if somebody told me I couldn't write, it would probably grieve me very much."

Seventeen Syllables

The first Rosie knew that her mother had taken to writing poems was one evening when she finished one and read it aloud for her daughter's approval. It was about cats, and Rosie pretended to understand it thoroughly and appreciate it no end, partly because she hesitated to disillusion her mother about the quantity and quality of Japanese she had learned in all the years now that she had been going to Japanese school every Saturday (and Wednesday, too, in the summer). Even so, her mother must have been skeptical about the depth of Rosie's understanding, because she explained afterwards about the kind of poem she was trying to write.

See, Rosie, she said, it was a *haiku*, a poem in which she must pack all her meaning into seventeen syllables only, which were divided into three lines of five, seven, and five syllables. In the one she had just read, she had tried to capture the charm of a kitten, as well as comment on the superstition that owning a cat of three colors meant good luck.

"Yes, yes, I understand. How utterly lovely," Rosie said, and her mother, either satisfied or seeing through the deception and resigned, went back to composing.

The truth was that Rosie was lazy; English lay ready on the tongue but Japanese had to be searched for and examined, and even then put forth tentatively (probably to meet with laughter). It was so much easier to say yes, yes, even when one meant no, no. Besides, this was what was in her mind to say: I was looking through one of your magazines from Japan last night, Mother, and towards the back I found some *haiku* in English that delighted me. There was one that made me giggle off and on until I fell asleep—

> It is morning, and lo!
> I lie awake, comme il faut,[1]
> sighing for some dough.

Now, how to reach her mother, how to communicate the melancholy song? 5
Rosie knew formal Japanese by fits and starts, her mother had even less English, no French. It was much more possible to say yes, yes.

It developed that her mother was writing the *haiku* for a daily newspaper, the *Mainichi Shimbun*, that was published in San Francisco. Los Angeles, to be sure, was closer to the farming community in which the Hayashi family lived and several Japanese vernaculars were printed there, but Rosie's parents said they preferred the tone of the northern paper. Once a week, the *Mainichi* would have a section devoted to *haiku*, and her mother became an extravagant contributor, taking for herself the blossoming pen name, Ume Hanazono.

So Rosie and her father lived for awhile with two women, her mother and Ume Hanazono. Her mother (Tome Hayashi by name) kept house, cooked, washed, and, along with her husband and the Carrascos, the Mexican family hired for the harvest, did her ample share of picking tomatoes out in the sweltering fields and boxing them in tidy strata in the cool packing shed. Ume Hanazono, who came to life after the dinner dishes were done, was an earnest, muttering stranger who often neglected speaking when spoken to and stayed busy at the parlor table as late as midnight scribbling with pencil on scratch paper or carefully copying characters on good paper with her fat, pale green Parker.

The new interest had some repercussions on the household routine. Before, Rosie had been accustomed to her parents and herself taking their hot baths early and going to bed almost immediately afterwards, unless her parents challenged each other to a game of flower cards or unless company dropped in. Now if her father wanted to play cards, he had to resort to solitaire (at which he always cheated fearlessly), and if a group of friends came over, it was bound to contain someone who was also writing *haiku*, and the small assemblage would be split in two, her father entertaining the non-literary members and her mother comparing ecstatic notes with the visiting poet.

If they went out, it was more of the same thing. But Ume Hanazono's life span, even for a poet's, was very brief—perhaps three months at most.

One night they went over to see the Hayano family in the neighboring town 10
to the west, an adventure both painful and attractive to Rosie. It was attractive

---

[1]In good form; proper. Pronounced *come il* fō.

Migrant workers harvesting a field in central California.

because there were four Hayano girls, all lovely and each one named after a season of the year (Haru, Natsu, Aki, Fuyu), painful because something had been wrong with Mrs. Hayano ever since the birth of her first child. Rosie would sometimes watch Mrs. Hayano, reputed to have been the belle of her native village, making her way about a room, stooped, slowly shuffling, violently trembling (*always* trembling), and she would be reminded that this woman, in this same condition, had carried and given issue to three babies. She would look wonderingly at Mr. Hayano, handsome, tall, and strong, and she would look at her four pretty friends. But it was not a matter she could come to any decision about.

On this visit, however, Mrs. Hayano sat all evening in the rocker, as motionless and unobtrusive as it was possible for her to be, and Rosie found the greater part of the evening practically anaesthetic. Too, Rosie spent most of it in the girls' room, because Haru, the garrulous one, said almost as soon as the bows and other greetings were over, "Oh, you must see my new coat!"

It was a pale plaid of grey, sand, and blue, with an enormous collar, and Rosie, seeing nothing special in it, said, "Gee, how nice."

"Nice?" said Haru, indignantly. "Is that all you can say about it? It's gorgeous! And so cheap, too. Only seventeen-ninety-eight, because it was a sale. The saleslady said it was twenty-five dollars regular."

"Gee," said Rosie. Natsu, who never said much and when she said anything said it shyly, fingered the coat covetously and Haru pulled it away.

"Mine," she said, putting it on. She minced in the aisle between the two large 15
beds and smiled happily. "Let's see how your mother likes it."

She broke into the front room and the adult conversation and went to stand in front of Rosie's mother, while the rest watched from the door. Rosie's mother was properly envious. "May I inherit it when you're through with it?"

Haru, pleased, giggled and said yes, she could, but Natsu reminded gravely from the door, "You promised me, Haru."

Everyone laughed but Natsu, who shamefacedly retreated into the bedroom. Haru came in laughing, taking off the coat. "We were only kidding, Natsu," she said. "Here, you try it on now."

After Natsu buttoned herself into the coat, inspected herself solemnly in the bureau mirror, and reluctantly shed it, Rosie, Aki, and Fuyu got their turns, and Fuyu, who was eight, drowned in it while her sisters and Rosie doubled up in amusement. They all went into the front room later, because Haru's mother quaveringly called to her to fix the tea and rice cakes and open a can of sliced peaches for everybody. Rosie noticed that her mother and Mr. Hayano were talking together at the little table—they were discussing a *haiku* that Mr. Hayano was planning to send to the *Mainichi*, while her father was sitting at one end of the sofa looking through a copy of *Life*, the new picture magazine. Occasionally, her father would comment on a photograph, holding it toward Mrs. Hayano and speaking to her as he always did—loudly, as though he thought someone such as she must surely be at least a trifle deaf also.

The five girls had their refreshments at the kitchen table, and it was while Rosie was showing the sisters her trick of swallowing peach slices without chewing (she chased each slippery crescent down with a swig of tea) that her father brought his empty teacup and untouched saucer to the sink and said, "Come on, Rosie, we're going home now."

"Already?" asked Rosie.

"Work tomorrow," he said.

He sounded irritated, and Rosie, puzzled, gulped one last yellow slice and stood up to go, while the sisters began protesting, as was their wont.

"We have to get up at five-thirty," he told them, going into the front room quickly, so that they did not have their usual chance to hang onto his hands and plead for an extension of time.

Rosie, following, saw that her mother and Mr. Hayano were sipping tea and still talking together, while Mrs. Hayano concentrated, quivering, on raising the handleless Japanese cup to her lips with both her hands and lowering it back to her lap. Her father, saying nothing, went out the door, onto the bright porch, and down the steps. Her mother looked up and asked, "Where is he going?"

"Where is he going?" Rosie said. "He said we were going home now."

"Going home?" Her mother looked with embarrassment at Mr. Hayano and his absorbed wife and then forced a smile. "He must be tired," she said.

Haru was not giving up yet. "May Rosie stay overnight?" she asked, and Natsu, Aki, and Fuyu came to reinforce their sister's plea by helping her make a circle around Rosie's mother. Rosie, for once having no desire to stay, was relieved when her mother, apologizing to the perturbed Mr. and Mrs. Hayano for her father's abruptness at the same time, managed to shake her head no at the quartet, kindly but adamant, so that they broke their circle and let her go.

Rosie's father looked ahead into the windshield as the two joined him. "I'm sorry," her mother said. "You must be tired." Her father, stepping on the starter, said nothing. "You know how I get when it's *haiku*," she continued, "I forget what time it is." He only grunted.

30 As they rode homeward silently, Rosie, sitting between, felt a rush of hate for both—for her mother for begging, for her father for denying her mother. I wish this old Ford would crash, right now, she thought, then immediately, no, no, I wish my father would laugh, but it was too late: already the vision had passed through her mind of the green pick-up crumpled in the dark against one of the mighty eucalyptus trees they were just riding past, of the three contorted, bleeding bodies, one of them hers.

Rosie ran between two patches of tomatoes, her heart working more rambunctiously than she had ever known it to. How lucky it was that Aunt Taka and Uncle Gimpachi had come tonight, though, how very lucky. Otherwise she might not have really kept her half-promise to meet Jesus Carrasco. Jesus was going to be a senior in September at the same school she went to, and his parents were the ones helping with the tomatoes this year. She and Jesus, who hardly remembered seeing each other at Cleveland High where there were so many other people and two whole grades between them, had become great friends this summer—he always had a joke for her when he periodically drove the loaded pick-up up from the fields to the shed where she was usually sorting while her mother and father did the packing, and they laughed a great deal together over infinitesimal repartee during the afternoon break for chilled watermelon or ice cream in the shade of the shed.

What she enjoyed most was racing him to see which could finish picking a double row first. He, who could work faster, would tease her by slowing down until she thought she would surely pass him this time, then speeding up furiously to leave her several sprawling vines behind. Once he had made her screech hideously by crossing over, while her back was turned, to place atop the tomatoes in her green-stained bucket a truly monstrous, pale green worm (it had looked more like an infant snake). And it was when they had finished a contest this morning, after she had pantingly pointed a green finger at the immature tomatoes evident in the lugs at the end of his row and he had returned the accusation (with justice), that he had startlingly brought up the matter of their possibly meeting outside the range of both their parents' dubious eyes.

"What for?" she had asked.

"I've got a secret I want to tell you," he said.

35 "Tell me now," she demanded.

"It won't be ready till tonight," he said.

She laughed. "Tell me tomorrow then."

"It'll be gone tomorrow," he threatened.

"Well, for seven hakes, what is it?" she had asked, more than twice, and when he had suggested that the packing shed would be an appropriate place to find out, she had cautiously answered maybe. She had not been certain she was going to keep the appointment until the arrival of mother's sister and her husband. Their coming seemed a sort of signal of permission, of grace, and she had definitely made up her mind to lie and leave as she was bowing them welcome.

40 So as soon as everyone appeared settled back for the evening, she announced loudly that she was going to the privy outside. "I'm going to the *benjo*!" and slipped out the door. And now that she was actually on her way, her heart pumped in such an undisciplined way that she could hear it with her ears. It's because I'm running, she told herself, slowing to a walk. The shed was up ahead, one more

patch away, in the middle of the fields. Its bulk, looming in the dimness, took on a sinisterness that was funny when Rosie reminded herself that it was only a wooden frame with a canvas roof and three canvas walls that made a slapping noise on breezy days.

Jesus was sitting on the narrow plank that was the sorting platform and she went around to the other side and jumped backwards to seat herself on the rim of a packing stand. "Well, tell me," she said without greeting, thinking her voice sounded reassuringly familiar.

"I saw you coming out the door," Jesus said. "I heard you running part of the way, too."

"Uh-huh," Rosie said. "Now tell me the secret."

"I was afraid you wouldn't come," he said.

Rosie delved around on the chicken-wire bottom of the stall for number two 45
tomatoes, ripe, which she was sitting beside, and came up with a left-over that felt edible. She bit into it and began sucking out the pulp and seeds. "I'm here," she pointed out.

"Rosie, are you sorry you came?"

"Sorry? What for?" she said. "You said you were going to tell me something."

"I will, I will," Jesus said, but his voice contained disappointment, and Rosie fleetingly felt the older of the two, realizing a brand-new power which vanished without category under her recognition.

"I have to go back in a minute," she said. "My aunt and uncle are here from Wintersburg. I told them I was going to the privy."

Jesus laughed. "You funny thing," he said. "You slay me!" 50

"Just because you have a bathroom *inside*," Rosie said. "Come on, tell me."

Chuckling, Jesus came around to lean on the stand facing her. They still could not see each other very clearly, but Rosie noticed that Jesus became very sober again as he took the hollow tomato from her hand and dropped it back into the stall. When he took hold of her empty hand, she could find no words to protest; her vocabulary had become distressingly constricted and she thought desperately that all that remained intact now was yes and no and oh, and even these few sounds would not easily out. Thus, kissed by Jesus, Rosie fell for the first time entirely victim to a helplessness delectable beyond speech. But the terrible, beautiful sensation lasted no more than a second, and the reality of Jesus' lips and tongue and teeth and hands made her pull away with such strength that she nearly tumbled.

Rosie stopped running as she approached the lights from the windows of home. How long since she had left? She could not guess, but gasping yet, she went to the privy in back and locked herself in. Her own breathing deafened her in the dark, close space, and she sat and waited until she could hear at last the nightly calling of the frogs and crickets. Even then, all she could think to say was oh, my, and the pressure of Jesus' face against her face would not leave.

No one had missed her in the parlor, however, and Rosie walked in and through quickly, announcing that she was next going to take a bath. "Your father's in the bathhouse," her mother said, and Rosie, in her room, recalled that she had not seen him when she entered. There had been only Aunt Taka and Uncle Gimpachi with her mother at the table, drinking tea. She got her robe and straw sandals and crossed the parlor again to go outside. Her mother was telling them about the *haiku* competition in the *Mainichi* and the poem she had entered.

Rosie met her father coming out of the bathhouse. "Are you through, 55
Father?" she asked. "I was going to ask you to scrub my back."

"Scrub your own back," he said shortly, going toward the main house.

"What have I done now?" she yelled after him. She suddenly felt like doing a lot of yelling. But he did not answer, and she went into the bathhouse. Turning on the dangling light, she removed her denims and T-shirt and threw them in the big carton for dirty clothes standing next to the washing machine. Her other things she took with her into the bath compartment to wash after her bath. After she had scooped a basin of hot water from the square wooden tub, she sat on the grey cement of the floor and soaped herself at exaggerated leisure, singing "Red Sails in the Sunset" at the top of her voice and using da-da-da where she suspected her words. Then, standing up, still singing, for she was possessed by the notion that any attempt now to analyze would result in spoilage and she believed that the larger her volume the less she would be able to hear herself think, she obtained more hot water and poured it on until she was free of lather. Only then did she allow herself to step into the steaming vat, one leg first, then the remainder of her body inch by inch until the water no longer stung and she could move around at will.

She took a long time soaking, afterwards remembering to go around outside to stoke the embers of the tin-lined fireplace beneath the tub and to throw on a few more sticks so that the water might keep its heat for her mother, and when she finally returned to the parlor, she found her mother still talking *haiku* with her aunt and uncle, the three of them on another round of tea. Her father was nowhere in sight.

At Japanese school the next day (Wednesday, it was), Rosie was grave and giddy by turns. Preoccupied at her desk in the row for students on Book Eight, she made up for it at recess by performing wild mimicry for the benefit of her friend Chizuko. She held her nose and whined a witticism or two in what she considered was the manner of Fred Allen; she assumed intoxication and a British accent to go over the climax of the Rudy Vallee recording of the pub conversation about William Ewart Gladstone; she was the child Shirley Temple piping, "On the Good Ship Lollipop"; she was the gentleman soprano of the Four Inkspots trilling, "If I Didn't Care." And she felt reasonably satisfied when Chizuko wept and gasped, "Oh, Rosie, you ought to be in the movies!"

Her father came after her at noon, bringing her sandwiches of minced ham 60
and two nectarines to eat while she rode, so that she could pitch right into the sorting when they got home. The lugs were piling up, he said, and the ripe tomatoes in them would probably have to be taken to the cannery tomorrow if they were not ready for the produce haulers tonight. "This heat's not doing them any good. And we've got no time for a break today."

It *was* hot, probably the hottest day of the year, and Rosie's blouse stuck damply to her back even under the protection of the canvas. But she worked as efficiently as a flawless machine and kept the stalls heaped, with one part of her mind listening in to the parental murmuring about the heat and the tomatoes and with another part planning the exact words she would say to Jesus when he drove up with the first load of the afternoon. But when at last she saw that the pick-up was coming, her hands went berserk and the tomatoes started falling in the wrong stalls, and her father said, "Hey, hey! Rosie, watch what you're doing!"

"Well, I have to go to the *benjo*," she said, hiding panic.

"Go in the weeds over there," he said, only half-joking.

"Oh, Father!" she protested.

"Oh, go on home," her mother said. "We'll make out for awhile." 65

In the privy Rosie peered through a knothole toward the fields, watching as much as she could of Jesus. Happily she thought she saw him look in the direction of the house from time to time before he finished unloading and went back toward the patch where his mother and father worked. As she was heading for the shed, a very presentable black car purred up the dirt driveway to the house and its driver motioned to her. Was this the Hayashi home, he wanted to know. She nodded. Was she a Hayashi? Yes, she said, thinking that he was a good-looking man. He got out of the car with a huge, flat package and she saw that he warmly wore a business suit. "I have something here for your mother then," he said, in a more elegant Japanese than she was used to.

She told him where her mother was and he came along with her, patting his face with an immaculate white handkerchief and saying something about the coolness of San Francisco. To her surprised mother and father, he bowed and introduced himself as, among other things, the *haiku* editor of the *Mainichi Shimbun*, saying that since he had been coming as far as Los Angeles anyway, he had decided to bring her the first prize she had won in the recent contest.

"First prize?" her mother echoed, believing and not believing, pleased and overwhelmed. Handed the package with a bow, she bobbed her head up and down numerous times to express her utter gratitude.

"It is nothing much," he added, "but I hope it will serve as a token of our great appreciation for your contributions and our great admiration of your considerable talent."

"I am not worthy," she said, falling easily into his style. "It is I who should 70
make some sign of my humble thanks for being permitted to contribute."

"No, no, to the contrary," he said, bowing again.

But Rosie's mother insisted, and then saying that she knew she was being unorthodox, she asked if she might open the package because her curiosity was so great. Certainly she might. In fact, he would like her reaction to it, for personally, it was one of his favorite *Hiroshiges*.

Rosie thought it was a pleasant picture, which looked to have been sketched with delicate quickness. There were pink clouds, containing some graceful calligraphy, and a sea that was a pale blue except at the edges, containing four sampans with indications of people in them. Pines edged the water and on the far-off beach there was a cluster of thatched huts towered over by pine-dotted mountains of grey and blue. The frame was scalloped and gilt.

After Rosie's mother pronounced it without peer and somewhat prodded her father into nodding agreement, she said Mr. Kuroda must at least have a cup of tea after coming all this way, and although Mr. Kuroda did not want to impose, he soon agreed that a cup of tea would be refreshing and went along with her to the house, carrying the picture for her.

"Ha, your mother's crazy!" Rosie's father said, and Rosie laughed uneasily as 75
she resumed judgment on the tomatoes. She had emptied six lugs when he broke into an imaginary conversation with Jesus to tell her to go and remind her mother of the tomatoes, and she went slowly.

Mr. Kuroda was in his shirtsleeves expounding some *haiku* theory as he munched a rice cake, and her mother was rapt. Abashed in the great man's presence, Rosie stood next to her mother's chair until her mother looked up inquiringly, and then she started to whisper the message, but her mother pushed her gently away and reproached, "You are not being very polite to our guest."

"Father says the tomatoes..." Rosie said aloud, smiling foolishly.

"Tell him I shall only be a minute," her mother said, speaking the language of Mr. Kuroda.

When Rosie carried the reply to her father, he did not seem to hear and she said again, "Mother says she'll be back in a minute."

80 "All right, all right," he nodded, and they worked again in silence. But suddenly, her father uttered an incredible noise, exactly like the cork of a bottle popping, and the next Rosie knew, he was stalking angrily toward the house, almost running in fact, and she chased after him crying, "Father! Father! What are you going to do?"

He stopped long enough to order her back to the shed. "Never mind!" he shouted. "Get on with the sorting!"

And from the place in the fields where she stood, frightened and vacillating, Rosie saw her father enter the house. Soon Mr. Kuroda came out alone, putting on his coat. Mr. Kuroda got into his car and backed out down the driveway onto the highway. Next her father emerged, also alone, something in his arms (it was the picture, she realized), and, going over to the bathhouse woodpile, he threw the picture on the ground and picked up the axe. Smashing the picture, glass and all (she heard the explosion faintly), he reached over for the kerosene that was used to encourage the bath fire and poured it over the wreckage. I am dreaming, Rosie said to herself, I am dreaming, but her father, having made sure that his act of cremation was irrevocable, was even then returning to the fields.

Rosie ran past him and toward the house. What had become of her mother? She burst into the parlor and found her mother at the back window watching the dying fire. They watched together until there remained only a feeble smoke under the blazing sun. Her mother was very calm.

"Do you know why I married your father?" she said without turning.

85 "No," said Rosie. It was the most frightening question she had ever been called upon to answer. Don't tell me now, she wanted to say, tell me tomorrow, tell me next week, don't tell me today. But she knew she would be told now, that the telling would combine with the other violence of the hot afternoon to level her life, her world to the very ground.

It was like a story out of the magazines illustrated in sepia, which she had consumed so greedily for a period until the information had somehow reached her that those wretchedly unhappy autobiographies, offered to her as the testimonials of living men and women, were largely inventions: Her mother, at nineteen, had come to America and married her father as an alternative to suicide.

At eighteen she had been in love with the first son of one of the well-to-do families in her village. The two had met whenever and wherever they could, secretly, because it would not have done for his family to see him favor her—her father had no money; he was a drunkard and a gambler besides. She had learned she was with child; an excellent match had already been arranged for her lover. Despised by her family, she had given premature birth to a stillborn son, who would be seventeen now. Her family did not turn her out, but she could no longer project herself in any direction without refreshing in them the memory of her indiscretion. She wrote to Aunt Taka, her favorite sister in America, threatening to kill herself if Aunt Taka would not send for her. Aunt Taka hastily arranged a marriage with a young man of whom she knew, but lately arrived from Japan, a young man of simple mind, it was said, but of kindly heart. The young man was never told why his unseen betrothed was so eager to hasten the day of meeting.

The story was told perfectly, with neither groping for words nor untoward passion. It was as though her mother had memorized it by heart, reciting it to herself so many times over that its nagging vileness had long since gone.

"I had a brother then?" Rosie asked, for this was what seemed to matter now; she would think about the other later, she assured herself, pushing back the illumination which threatened all that darkness that had hitherto been merely mysterious or even glamorous. "A half-brother?"

"Yes."

"I would have liked a brother," she said.

Suddenly, her mother knelt on the floor and took her by the wrists. "Rosie," she said urgently, "Promise me you will never marry!" Shocked more by the request than the revelation, Rosie stared at her mother's face. Jesus, Jesus, she called silently, not certain whether she was invoking the help of the son of the Carrascos or of God, until there returned sweetly the memory of Jesus' hand, how it had touched her and where. Still her mother waited for an answer, holding her wrists so tightly that her hands were going numb. She tried to pull free. Promise, her mother whispered fiercely, promise. Yes, yes, I promise, Rosie said. But for an instant she turned away, and her mother, hearing the familiar glib agreement, released her. Oh, you, you, you, her eyes and twisted mouth said, you fool. Rosie, covering her face, began at last to cry, and the embrace and consoling hand came much later than she expected.

(1949)

Questions for Discussion and Writing

1. What conflicts between the mother and teenaged daughter are set up in the opening section of the story? Why are these conflicts and Rosie's way of dealing with them important to the story as a whole?
2. How does Ume's talent affect her husband? How does he express his feelings about it? How does he finally end her career as a poet?
3. What does Rosie feel for Jesus? List the various feelings she has and how she deals with them. Why are these feelings important when Tome finally tells Rosie the story of her marriage?
4. What are the connections between the episodes in the story about Rosie and those about her mother?
5. What does the visit to the Hayanos contribute to your understanding of Rosie, her mother, and her father?
6. Why does Rosie find that "the embrace and consoling hand came much later than she expected" at the end of the story?

Flannery O'Connor 1925–1964

See page 189 for a biographical note about this author.

A Good Man Is Hard to Find

The dragon is by the side of the road, watching those who pass. Beware lest he devour you. We go to the Father of Souls, but it is necessary to pass by the dragon.

—*St. Cyril of Jerusalem*

The grandmother didn't want to go to Florida. She wanted to visit some of her connections in east Tennessee and she was seizing at every chance to change Bailey's mind. Bailey was the son she lived with, her only boy. He was sitting on the edge of his chair at the table, bent over the orange sports section of the *Journal*. "Now look here, Bailey," she said, "see here, read this," and she stood with one hand on her thin hip and the other rattling the newspaper at his bald head. "Here this fellow that calls himself The Misfit is aloose from the Federal Pen and headed toward Florida and you read here what it says he did to these people. Just you read it. I wouldn't take my children in any direction with a criminal like that aloose in it. I couldn't answer to my conscience if I did."

Bailey didn't look up from his reading so she wheeled around then and faced the children's mother, a young woman in slacks, whose face was as broad and innocent as a cabbage and was tied around with a green headkerchief that had two points on the top like a rabbit's ears. She was sitting on the sofa, feeding the baby his apricots out of a jar. "The children have been to Florida before," the old lady said. "You all ought to take them somewhere else for a change so they would see different parts of the world and be broad. They never have been to east Tennessee."

The children's mother didn't seem to hear her but the eight-year-old boy, John Wesley, a stocky child with glasses, said, "If you don't want to go to Florida, why dontcha stay at home?" He and the little girl, June Star, were reading the funny papers on the floor.

"She wouldn't stay at home to be queen for a day," June Star said without raising her yellow head.

"Yes and what would you do if this fellow, The Misfit, caught you?" the 5
grandmother asked.

"I'd smack his face," John Wesley said.

"She wouldn't stay at home for a million bucks," June Star said. "Afraid she'd miss something. She has to go everywhere we go."

"All right, Miss," the grandmother said. "Just remember that the next time you want me to curl your hair."

June Star said her hair was naturally curly.

The next morning the grandmother was the first one in the car, ready to go. 10
She had her big black valise that looked like the head of a hippopotamus in one corner, and underneath it she was hiding a basket with Pitty Sing, the cat, in it. She didn't intend for the cat to be left alone in the house for three days because

he would miss her too much and she was afraid he might brush against one of the gas burners and accidentally asphyxiate himself. Her son, Bailey, didn't like to arrive at a motel with a cat.

She sat in the middle of the back seat with John Wesley and June Star on either side of her. Bailey and the children's mother and the baby sat in front and they left Atlanta at eight forty-five with the mileage on the car at 55890. The grandmother wrote this down because she thought it would be interesting to say how many miles they had been when they got back. It took them twenty minutes to reach the outskirts of the city.

The old lady settled herself comfortably, removing her white cotton gloves and putting them up with her purse on the shelf in front of the back window. The children's mother still had on slacks and still had her head tied up in a green kerchief, but the grandmother had on a navy blue straw sailor hat with a bunch of white violets on the brim and a navy blue dress with a small white dot in the print. Her collars and cuffs were white organdy trimmed with lace and at her neckline she had pinned a purple spray of cloth violets containing a sachet. In case of an accident, anyone seeing her dead on the highway would know at once that she was a lady.

She said she thought it was going to be a good day for driving, neither too hot nor too cold, and she cautioned Bailey that the speed limit was fifty-five miles an hour and that the patrolmen hid themselves behind billboards and small clumps of trees and sped out after you before you had a chance to slow down. She pointed out interesting details of the scenery: Stone Mountain; the blue granite that in some places came up to both sides of the highway; the brilliant red clay banks slightly streaked with purple; and the various crops that made rows of green lace-work on the ground. The trees were full of silver-white sunlight and the meanest of them sparkled. The children were reading comic magazines and their mother had gone back to sleep.

"Let's go through Georgia fast so we won't have to look at it much," John Wesley said.

"If I were a little boy," said the grandmother, "I wouldn't talk about my native 15
state that way. Tennessee has the mountains and Georgia has the hills."

"Tennessee is just a hillbilly dumping ground," John Wesley said, "and Georgia is a lousy state too."

"You said it," June Star said.

"In my time," said the grandmother, folding her thin veined fingers, "children were more respectful of their native states and their parents and everything else. People did right then. Oh look at the cute little pickaninny!" she said and pointed to a Negro child standing in the door of a shack. "Wouldn't that make a picture, now?" she asked and they all turned and looked at the little Negro out of the back window. He waved.

"He didn't have any britches on," June Star said.

"He probably didn't have any," the grandmother explained. "Little niggers in 20
the country don't have things like we do. If I could paint, I'd paint that picture," she said.

The children exchanged comic books.

The grandmother offered to hold the baby and the children's mother passed him over the front seat to her. She set him on her knee and bounced him and told him about the things they were passing. She rolled her eyes and screwed up her mouth and stuck her leathery thin face into his smooth bland one. Occasionally he gave her a faraway smile. They passed a large cotton field with five or six graves fenced in the middle of it, like a small island. "Look at the graveyard!" the grandmother said, pointing it out. "That was the old family burying ground. That belonged to the plantation."

"Where's the plantation?" John Wesley asked.

"Gone with the Wind," said the grandmother. "Ha. Ha."

When the children finished all the comic books they had brought, they opened the lunch and ate it. The grandmother ate a peanut butter sandwich and an olive and would not let the children throw the box and the paper napkins out the window. When there was nothing else to do they played a game by choosing a cloud and making the other two guess what shape it suggested. John Wesley took one the shape of a cow and June Star guessed a cow and John Wesley said, no, an automobile, and June Star said he didn't play fair, and they began to slap each other over the grandmother.

The grandmother said she would tell them a story if they would keep quiet. When she told a story, she rolled her eyes and waved her head and was very dramatic. She said once when she was a maiden lady she had been courted by a Mr. Edgar Atkins Teagarden from Jasper, Georgia. She said he was a very good-looking man and a gentleman and that he brought her a watermelon every Saturday afternoon with his initials cut in it, E. A. T. Well, one Saturday, she said, Mr. Teagarden brought the watermelon and there was nobody at home and he left it on the front porch and returned in his buggy to Jasper, but she never got the watermelon, she said, because a nigger boy ate it when he saw the initials, E. A. T.! This story tickled John Wesley's funny bone and he giggled and giggled but June Star didn't think it was any good. She said she wouldn't marry a man that just brought her a watermelon on Saturday. The grandmother said she would have done well to marry Mr. Teagarden because he was a gentleman and had bought Coca-Cola stock when it first came out and that he had died only a few years ago, a very wealthy man.

They stopped at The Tower for barbecued sandwiches. The Tower was a part stucco and part wood filling station and dance hall set in a clearing outside of Timothy. A fat man named Red Sammy Butts ran it and there were signs stuck here and there on the building and for miles up and down the highway saying, TRY RED SAMMY'S FAMOUS BARBECUE. NONE LIKE FAMOUS RED SAMMY'S! RED SAM! THE FAT BOY WITH THE HAPPY LAUGH! A VETERAN!RED SAMMY'S YOUR MAN!

Red Sammy was lying on the bare ground outside The Tower with his head under a truck while a gray monkey about a foot high, chained to a small chinaberry tree, chattered nearby. The monkey sprang back into the tree and got on the highest limb as soon as he saw the children jump out of the car and run toward him.

Inside, The Tower was a long dark room with a counter at one end and tables at the other and dancing space in the middle. They all sat down at a board table next to the nickelodeon and Red Sam's wife, a tall burnt-brown woman with hair and eyes lighter than her skin, came and took their order. The children's mother put a dime in the machine and played "The Tennessee Waltz," and the grandmother said that tune always made her want to dance. She asked Bailey if he would like to dance but he only glared at her. He didn't have a naturally sunny disposition like she did and trips made him nervous. The grandmother's brown eyes were very bright. She swayed her head from side to side and pretended she was dancing in her chair. June Star said play something she could tap to so the children's mother put in another dime and played a fast number and June Star stepped out onto the dance floor and did her tap routine.

30 "Ain't she cute?" Red Sam's wife said, leaning over the counter. "Would you like to come be my little girl?"

"No I certainly wouldn't," June Star said. "I wouldn't live in a broken-down place like this for a million bucks!" and she ran back to the table.

"Ain't she cute?" the woman repeated, stretching her mouth politely.

"Aren't you ashamed?" hissed the grandmother.

Red Sam came in and told his wife to quit lounging on the counter and hurry up with these people's order. His khaki trousers reached just to his hip bones and his stomach hung over them like a sack of meal swaying under his shirt. He came over and sat down at a table nearby and let out a combination sigh and yodel. "You can't win," he said. "You can't win," and he wiped his sweating red face off with a gray handkerchief. "These days you don't know who to trust," he said. "Ain't that the truth?"

35 "People are certainly not nice like they used to be," said the grandmother.

"Two fellers come in here last week," Red Sammy said, "driving a Chrysler. It was a old beat-up car but it was a good one and these boys looked all right to me. Said they worked at the mill and you know I let them fellers charge the gas they bought? Now why did I do that?"

"Because you're a good man!" the grandmother said at once.

"Yes'm, I suppose so," Red Sam said as if he were struck with this answer.

His wife brought the orders, carrying the five plates all at once without a tray, two in each hand and one balanced on her arm. "It isn't a soul in this green world of God's that you can trust," she said. "And I don't count nobody out of that, not nobody," she repeated, looking at Red Sammy.

40 "Did you read about that criminal, The Misfit, that's escaped?" asked the grandmother.

"I wouldn't be a bit surprised if he didn't attack this place right here," said the woman. "If he hears about it being here, I wouldn't be none surprised to see him. If he hears it's two cent in the cash register, I wouldn't be a tall surprised if he. . . ."

"That'll do," Red Sam said. "Go bring these people their Co'-Colas," and the woman went off to get the rest of the order.

"A good man is hard to find," Red Sammy said. "Everything is getting terrible. I remember the day you could go off and leave your screen door unlatched. Not no more."

He and the grandmother discussed better times. The old lady said that in her opinion Europe was entirely to blame for the way things were now. She said the way Europe acted you would think we were made of money and Red Sam said it was no use talking about it, she was exactly right. The children ran outside into the white sunlight and looked at the monkey in the lacy chinaberry tree. He was busy catching fleas on himself and biting each one carefully between his teeth as if it were a delicacy.

45 They drove off again into the hot afternoon. The grandmother took cat naps and woke up every few minutes with her own snoring. Outside of Toombsboro she woke up and recalled an old plantation that she had visited in this neighborhood once when she was a young lady. She said the house had six white columns across the front and that there was an avenue of oaks leading

up to it and two little wooden trellis arbors on either side in front where you sat down with your suitor after a stroll in the garden. She recalled exactly which road to turn off to get to it. She knew that Bailey would not be willing to lose any time looking at an old house, but the more she talked about it, the more she wanted to see it once again and find out if the little twin arbors were still standing. "There was a secret panel in this house," she said craftily, not telling the truth but wishing that she were, "and the story went that all the family silver was hidden in it when Sherman came through but it was never found. . . ."

"Hey!" John Wesley said. "Let's go see it! We'll find it! We'll poke all the woodwork and find it! Who lives there? Where do you turn off at? Hey Pop, can't we turn off there?"

"We never have seen a house with a secret panel!" June Star shrieked. "Let's go to the house with the secret panel! Hey Pop, can't we go see the house with the secret panel!"

"It's not far from here, I know," the grandmother said. "It won't take over twenty minutes."

Bailey was looking straight ahead. His jaw was as rigid as a horseshoe. "No," he said.

The children began to yell and scream that they wanted to see the house with 50
the secret panel. John Wesley kicked the back of the front seat and June Star hung over her mother's shoulder and whined desperately into her ear that they never had any fun even on their vacation, that they could never do what THEY wanted to do. The baby began to scream and John Wesley kicked the back of the seat so hard that his father could feel the blows in his kidney.

"All right!" he shouted and drew the car to a stop at the side of the road. "Will you all shut up? Will you all just shut up for one second? If you don't shut up, we won't go anywhere."

"It would be very educational for them," the grandmother murmured.

"All right," Bailey said, "but get this: this is the only time we're going to stop for anything like this. This is the one and only time."

"The dirt road that you have to turn down is about a mile back," the grandmother directed. "I marked it when we passed."

"A dirt road," Bailey groaned. 55

After they had turned around and were headed toward the dirt road, the grandmother recalled other points about the house, the beautiful glass over the front doorway and the candle-lamp in the hall. John Wesley said that the secret panel was probably in the fireplace.

"You can't go inside this house," Bailey said. "You don't know who lives there."

"While you all talk to the people in front, I'll run around behind and get in a window," John Wesley suggested.

"We'll all stay in the car," his mother said.

They turned onto the dirt road and the car raced roughly along in a swirl of 60
pink dust. The grandmother recalled the times when there were no paved roads and thirty miles was a day's journey. The dirt road was hilly and there were sudden washes in it and sharp curves on dangerous embankments. All at once they would be on a hill, looking down over the blue tops of trees for miles around, then the next minute, they would be in a red depression with the dust-coated trees looking down on them.

"This place had better turn up in a minute," Bailey said, "or I'm going to turn around."

The road looked as if no one had traveled on it for months.

"It's not much farther," the grandmother said and just as she said it, a horrible thought came to her. The thought was so embarrassing that she turned red in the face and her eyes dilated and her feet jumped up, upsetting her valise in the corner. The instant the valise moved, the newspaper top she had over the basket under it rose with a snarl and Pitty Sing, the cat, sprang onto Bailey's shoulder.

The children were thrown to the floor and their mother, clutching the baby, was thrown out the door onto the ground; the old lady was thrown into the front seat. The car turned over once and landed right-side-up in a gulch off the side of the road. Bailey remained in the driver's seat with the cat—gray-striped with a broad white face and an orange nose—clinging to his neck like a caterpillar.

As soon as the children saw they could move their arms and legs, they scram- 65
bled out of the car, shouting, "We've had an ACCIDENT!" The grandmother was curled up under the dashboard, hoping she was injured so that Bailey's wrath would not come down on her all at once. The horrible thought she had before the accident was that the house she had remembered so vividly was not in Georgia but in Tennessee.

Bailey removed the cat from his neck with both hands and flung it out the window against the side of a pine tree. Then he got out of the car and started looking for the children's mother. She was sitting against the side of the red gutted ditch, holding the screaming baby, but she only had a cut down her face and a broken shoulder. "We've had an ACCIDENT!" the children screamed in a frenzy of delight.

"But nobody's killed," June Star said with disappointment as the grandmother limped out of the car, her hat still pinned to her head but the broken front brim standing up at a jaunty angle and the violet spray hanging off the side. They all sat down in the ditch, except the children, to recover from the shock. They were all shaking.

"Maybe a car will come along," said the children's mother hoarsely.

"I believe I have injured an organ," said the grandmother, pressing her side, but no one answered her. Bailey's teeth were clattering. He had on a yellow sport shirt with bright blue parrots designed in it and his face was as yellow as the shirt. The grandmother decided that she would not mention that the house was in Tennessee.

The road was about ten feet above and they could see only the tops of the 70
trees on the other side of it. Behind the ditch they were sitting in there were more woods, tall and dark and deep. In a few minutes they saw a car some distance away on top of a hill, coming slowly as if the occupants were watching them. The grandmother stood up and waved both arms dramatically to attract their attention. The car continued to come on slowly, disappeared around a bend and appeared again, moving even slower, on top of the hill they had gone over. It was a big black battered hearse-like automobile. There were three men in it.

It came to a stop just over them and for some minutes, the driver looked down with a steady expressionless gaze to where they were sitting, and didn't speak. Then he turned his head and muttered something to the other two and they got out. One was a fat boy in black trousers and a red sweat shirt with a silver stallion embossed on the front of it. He moved around on the right side of them and stood staring, his mouth partly open in a kind of loose grin. The other had on khaki pants and a blue striped coat and a gray hat pulled down very low, hiding most of his face. He came around slowly on the left side. Neither spoke.

The driver got out of the car and stood by the side of it, looking down at them. He was an older man than the other two. His hair was just beginning to gray and he wore silver-rimmed spectacles that gave him a scholarly look. He had a long creased face and didn't have on any shirt or undershirt. He had on blue jeans that were too tight for him and was holding a black hat and a gun. The two boys also had guns.

"We've had an ACCIDENT!" the children screamed.

The grandmother had the peculiar feeling that the bespectacled man was someone she knew. His face was as familiar to her as if she had known him all her life but she could not recall who he was. He moved away from the car and began to come down the embankment, placing his feet carefully so that he wouldn't slip. He had on tan and white shoes and no socks, and his ankles were red and thin. "Good afternoon," he said. "I see you all had you a little spill."

"We turned over twice!" said the grandmother. 75

"Oncet," he corrected. "We seen it happen. Try their car and see will it run, Hiram," he said quietly to the boy with the gray hat.

"What you got that gun for?" John Wesley asked. "Whatcha gonna do with that gun?"

"Lady," the man said to the children's mother, "would you mind calling them children to sit down by you? Children make me nervous. I want all you all to sit down right together there where you're at."

"What are you telling US what to do for?" June Star asked.

Behind them the line of woods gaped like a dark open mouth. "Come here," 80
said their mother.

"Look here now," Bailey said suddenly, "we're in a predicament! We're in..."

The grandmother shrieked. She scrambled to her feet and stood staring. "You're The Misfit!" she said. "I recognized you at once!"

"Yes'm," the man said, smiling slightly as if he were pleased in spite of himself to be known, "but it would have been better for all of you, lady, if you hadn't of reckernized me."

Bailey turned his head sharply and said something to his mother that shocked even the children. The old lady began to cry and The Misfit reddened.

"Lady," he said, "don't you get upset. Sometimes a man says things he don't 85
mean. I don't reckon he meant to talk to you thataway."

"You wouldn't shoot a lady, would you?" the grandmother said and removed a clean handkerchief from her cuff and began to slap at her eyes with it.

The Misfit pointed the toe of his shoe into the ground and made a little hole and then covered it up again. "I would hate to have to," he said.

"Listen," the grandmother almost screamed, "I know you're a good man. You don't look a bit like you have common blood. I know you must come from nice people!"

"Yes mam," he said, "finest people in the world." When he smiled he showed a row of strong white teeth. "God never made a finer woman than my mother and my daddy's heart was pure gold," he said. The boy with the red sweat shirt had come around behind them and was standing with his gun at his hip. The Misfit squatted down on the ground. "Watch them children, Bobby Lee," he said. "You know they make me nervous." He looked at the six of them huddled together in front of him and he seemed to be embarrassed as if he couldn't think of anything to say. "Ain't a cloud in the sky," he remarked, looking up at it. "Don't see no sun but don't see no cloud neither."

"Yes, it's a beautiful day," said the grandmother. "Listen," she said, "you shouldn't 90
call yourself The Misfit because I know you're a good man at heart. I can just look at you and tell."

"Hush!" Bailey yelled. "Hush! Everybody shut up and let me handle this!" He was squatting in the position of a runner about to sprint forward but he didn't move.

"I pre-chate that, lady," The Misfit said and drew a little circle in the ground with the butt of his gun.

"It'll take a half a hour to fix this here car," Hiram called, looking over the raised hood of it.

"Well, first you and Bobby Lee get him and that little boy to step over yonder with you," The Misfit said, pointing to Bailey and John Wesley. "The boys want to ast you something," he said to Bailey. "Would you mind stepping back in them woods there with them?"

"Listen," Bailey began, "we're in a terrible predicament! Nobody realizes what 95
this is," and his voice cracked. His eyes were as blue and intense as the parrots in his shirt and he remained perfectly still.

The grandmother reached up to adjust her hat brim as if she were going to the woods with him but it came off in her hand. She stood staring at it and after a second she let it fall to the ground. Hiram pulled Bailey up by the arm as if he were assisting an old man. John Wesley caught hold of his father's hand and Bobby Lee followed. They went off toward the woods and just as they reached the dark edge, Bailey turned and supporting himself against a gray naked pine trunk, he shouted, "I'll be back in a minute, Mamma, wait on me!"

"Come back this instant!" his mother shrilled but they all disappeared into the woods.

"Bailey Boy!" the grandmother called in a tragic voice but she found she was looking at The Misfit squatting on the ground in front of her. "I just know you're a good man," she said desperately. "You're not a bit common!"

"Nome, I ain't a good man," The Misfit said after a second as if he had considered her statement carefully, "but I ain't the worst in the world neither. My daddy said I was a different breed of dog from my brothers and sisters. 'You know,' Daddy said, 'it's some that can live their whole life out without asking about it and it's others has to know why it is, and this boy is one of the latters. He's going to be into everything!'" He put on his black hat and looked up suddenly and then away deep into the woods as if he were embarrassed again. "I'm sorry I don't have on a shirt before you ladies," he said, hunching his shoulders slightly. "We buried our clothes that we had on when we escaped and we're just making do until we can get better. We borrowed these from some folks we met," he explained.

"That's perfectly all right," the grandmother said. "Maybe Bailey has an extra 100
shirt in his suitcase."

"I'll look and see terrectly," The Misfit said.

"Where are they taking him?" the children's mother screamed.

"Daddy was a card himself," The Misfit said. "You couldn't put anything over on him. He never got in trouble with the Authorities though. Just had the knack of handling them."

"You could be honest too if you'd only try," said the grandmother. "Think how wonderful it would be to settle down and live a comfortable life and not have to think about somebody chasing you all the time."

The Misfit kept scratching in the ground with the butt of his gun as if he 105
were thinking about it. "Yes'm, somebody is always after you," he murmured.

The grandmother noticed how thin his shoulder blades were just behind his hat because she was standing up looking down on him. "Do you ever pray?" she asked.

He shook his head. All she saw was the black hat wiggle between his shoulder blades. "Nome," he said.

There was a pistol shot from the woods, followed closely by another. Then silence. The old lady's head jerked around. She could hear the wind move through the tree tops like a long satisfied insuck of breath. "Bailey Boy!" she called.

"I was a gospel singer for a while," The Misfit said. "I been most everything. Been in the arm service, both land and sea, at home and abroad, been twict married, been an undertaker, been with the railroads, plowed Mother Earth, been in a tornado, seen a man burnt alive oncet," and he looked up at the children's mother and the little girl who were sitting close together, their faces white and their eyes glassy; "I even seen a woman flogged," he said.

"Pray, pray," the grandmother began, "pray, pray. . . ." 110

"I never was a bad boy that I remember of," The Misfit said in an almost dreamy voice, "but somewheres along the line I done something wrong and got sent to the penitentiary. I was buried alive," and he looked up and held her attention to him by a steady stare.

"That's when you should have started to pray," she said. "What did you do to get sent to the penitentiary that first time?"

"Turn to the right, it was a wall," The Misfit said, looking up again at the cloudless sky. "Turn to the left, it was a wall. Look up it was a ceiling, look down it was a floor. I forget what I done, lady. I set there and set there, trying to remember what it was I done and I ain't recalled it to this day. Oncet in a while, I would think it was coming to me, but it never come."

"Maybe they put you in by mistake," the old lady said vaguely.

"Nome," he said. "It wasn't no mistake. They had the papers on me." 115

"You must have stolen something," she said.

The Misfit sneered slightly. "Nobody had nothing I wanted," he said. "It was a head-doctor at the penitentiary said what I had done was kill my daddy but I known that for a lie. My daddy died in nineteen ought nineteen of the epidemic flu and I never had a thing to do with it. He was buried in the Mount Hopewell Baptist churchyard and you can see for yourself."

"If you would pray," the old lady said, "Jesus would help you."

"That's right," The Misfit said.

"Well then, why don't you pray?" she asked trembling with delight suddenly. 120

"I don't want no hep," he said. "I'm doing all right by myself."

Bobby Lee and Hiram came ambling back from the woods. Bobby Lee was dragging a yellow shirt with bright blue parrots in it.

"Thow me that shirt, Bobby Lee," The Misfit said. The shirt came flying at him and landed on his shoulder and he put it on. The grandmother couldn't name what the shirt reminded her of. "No, lady," The Misfit said while he was buttoning it up, "I found out the crime don't matter. You can do one thing or you can do another, kill a man or take a tire off his car, because sooner or later you're going to forget what it was you done and just be punished for it."

The children's mother had begun to make heaving noises as if she couldn't get her breath. "Lady," he asked, "would you and that little girl like to step off yonder with Bobby Lee and Hiram and join your husband?"

"Yes, thank you," the mother said faintly. Her left arm dangled helplessly and 125
she was holding the baby, who had gone to sleep, in the other. "Hep that lady up, Hiram," The Misfit said as she struggled to climb out of the ditch, "and Bobby Lee, you hold onto that little girl's hand."

"I don't want to hold hands with him," June Star said. "He reminds me of a pig."

The fat boy blushed and laughed and caught her by the arm and pulled her off into the woods after Hiram and her mother.

Alone with The Misfit, the grandmother found that she had lost her voice. There was not a cloud in the sky nor any sun. There was nothing around her but woods. She wanted to tell him that he must pray. She opened and closed her mouth several times before anything came out. Finally she found herself saying, "Jesus, Jesus," meaning Jesus will help you, but the way she was saying it, it sounded as if she might be cursing.

"Yes'm," The Misfit said as if he agreed. "Jesus thrown everything off balance. It was the same case with Him as with me except He hadn't committed any crime and they could prove I had committed one because they had the papers on me. Of course," he said, "they never shown me my papers. That's why I sign myself now. I said long ago, you get your signature and sign everything you do and keep a copy of it. Then you'll know what you done and you can hold up the crime to the punishment and see do they match and in the end you'll have something to prove you ain't been treated right. I call myself The Misfit," he said, "because I can't make what all I done wrong fit what all I gone through in punishment."

There was a piercing scream from the woods, followed closely by a pistol re- 130
port. "Does it seem right to you, lady, that one is punished a heap and another ain't punished at all?"

"Jesus!" the old lady cried. "You've got good blood! I know you wouldn't shoot a lady! I know you come from nice people! Pray! Jesus, you ought not to shoot a lady. I'll give you all the money I've got!"

"Lady," The Misfit said, looking beyond her far into the woods, "there never was a body that give the undertaker a tip."

There were two more pistol reports and the grandmother raised her head like a parched old turkey hen crying for water and called, "Bailey Boy, Bailey Boy!" as if her heart would break.

"Jesus was the only One that ever raised the dead," The Misfit continued, "and He shouldn't have done it. He thrown everything off balance. If He did what He said, then it's nothing for you to do but throw away everything and follow Him, and if He didn't, then it's nothing for you to do but enjoy the few minutes you got left the best way you can—by killing somebody or burning down his house or doing some other meanness to him. No pleasure but meanness," he said and his voice had become almost a snarl.

"Maybe He didn't raise the dead," the old lady mumbled, not knowing what 135
she was saying and feeling so dizzy that she sank down in the ditch with her legs twisted under her.

"I wasn't there so I can't say He didn't," The Misfit said. "I wisht I had of been there," he said, hitting the ground with his fist. "It ain't right I wasn't there because if I had of been there I would of known. Listen lady," he said in a high voice, "if I had of been there I would of known and I wouldn't be like I am now." His voice seemed about to crack and the grandmother's head cleared for an instant. She saw the man's face twisted close to her own as if he were going to cry and she murmured, "Why you're one of my babies. You're one of my own children!" She reached out and touched him on the shoulder. The Misfit sprang back as if a snake had bitten him and shot her three times through the chest. Then he put his gun down on the ground and took off his glasses and began to clean them.

Hiram and Bobby Lee returned from the woods and stood over the ditch, looking down at the grandmother who half sat and half lay in a puddle of blood with her legs crossed under her like a child's and her face smiling up at the cloudless sky.

Without his glasses, The Misfit's eyes were red-rimmed and pale and defenseless-looking. "Take her off and thow her where you thown the others," he said, picking up the cat that was rubbing itself against his leg.

"She was a talker, wasn't she?" Bobby Lee said, sliding down the ditch with a yodel.

"She would of been a good woman," The Misfit said, "if it had been somebody 140
there to shoot her every minute of her life."

"Some fun!" Bobby Lee said.

"Shut up, Bobby Lee," The Misfit said. "It's no real pleasure in life."

(1953)

Questions for Discussion and Writing

1. What is disturbing about "A Good Man Is Hard to Find"? What is funny? How is it different from other stories you have read?
2. Consider the grandmother, the mother, and June Star as three different types of women. How is each type truly awful in her own way? Why is the grandmother the main character of the story?
3. What would a person ordinarily mean when using the phrases "a lady," "nice people," "a good man," and "a gentleman"? What do these phrases mean in the story? How do the portrayals of June Star and John Wesley relate to conventional ideas of childhood?
4. What line of reasoning does The Misfit follow to justify his behavior?
5. List details that foreshadow the violent ending. Nonetheless, were you surprised by the closing? Write an interpretation of the story, arguing that the ending is appropriate and inevitable.

Rosario Morales 1930–

Although raised in New York City, Rosario Morales spent her adult life in Puerto Rico, where she loved the beauty of the lush island but missed the freedom enjoyed by women in the mainland. She became a "Puerto Rican, Jewish, radical feminist" and complained that on the island there were "too many people nagging, harping, pushing you into line, into feminine behavior, into caution and fear, provocativeness and manipulativeness, full of predatory males who punish you for being female." Her credo is, "I am what I am. Take it or leave me alone."

The Day It Happened

The day it happened I was washing my hair. I had long hair then that went halfway down my back and I washed it once a week and rinsed it with lemon juice "to bring out the blond highlights" Mami said. Then I'd set it into pin-curls that took an age to do because there was so much to wind around and around my finger. But if Mami was in a good mood, and she looked like she might be that day, she curled the back for me. I usually did all this on Saturday so I would look great for church on Sunday, and for a date Saturday night if I ever had one. ¡ojala!

Naturally the moment when it all began I was rinsing the big soapy mess. Nosy Maria was leaning out the window drying her dark red fingernails in the breeze when Josie stepped out of our apartment house doorway with a suitcase in her hand. Maria sucked in her breath so hard the sound brought my mother, who took one look, crossed herself, or so Maria says, and started praying. Someone needed to pray for Josie. It was five o'clock and Ramón was due home any minute.

I wouldn't have known anything about any of this if Olga next door hadn't rung our doorbell and banged on the door just when Mami was too deep in prayer to hear and Maria was leaning out over the sill with her eyes bugging out. I cursed, very quietly of course, because if Mami or Papi heard me curse I'd get a slap across my face. I wrapped my sopping head in a towel and opened the door to Olga's "Oh my goodness, oh my dear. Oh honey, did you see? Look out the window this minute. I wouldn't have believed it if I hadn't seen it with my own two eyes. That poor little kid. I hate to think..." and on and on as we crossed the apartment to look out on the street.

Little Mikey from across the way was telling the rest of the kids how he'd found a taxi for Josie the minute he'd hit Southern Boulevard and how he'd hailed it and how the driver had let him ride back to Brook Street in the front seat—even though all of them had seen him arrive and step out with his back stiff with pride. Meantime Josie was back down in the street with Doña Toña from across the hall and Betty Murphy upstairs right behind her, all of them loaded down with two lamps, a typewriter and a big box of books. Doña Toña was muttering something we couldn't hear up here on the second story but it was probably either the prayer I was hearing on my right or the "...hurry oh hurry oh God he'll be here any minute are you mad girl, are you mad" that came at me from the left.

5 It was hard not to be scared as well as glad that Josie was packing up and leaving Ramón. They'd been married only six months but already they were in a pattern, like the Garcias down the block who did everything the same way on the same day, all year. Ramón worked late till seven every week day and five on Saturday. When he arrived he expected a good dinner to be on the table at the

right temperature exactly five minutes after he walked in the door. He yelled if she didn't get it right and sometimes even if she did.

Saturday evening they went out to a party or the bar down the avenue, both of them dressed up and Ramón looking proud and cheerful for a change. Josie always looked great. She's so cute. Small and plump with long lashes on her dark eyes and, get this, naturally curly hair. She smiled a lot when she was happy but she hadn't been happy much lately and not at all since she got pregnant. I wasn't supposed to know this. God, I was almost thirteen! But Maria, who was fourteen and a half and thought she was twenty, listened in on conversations in the living room by opening the door a sliver and she told me all about it.

Saturday nights there was sure to be a fight. Either it was that Josie was "no fun, a man can't be a man with such a wet rag around." Or it was that Josie was "a tramp. Why else was that guy staring at you, eating you up with his eyes?" The first time it happened, soon after they moved in, it woke me up from a deep sleep and I was so scared I crept into Maria's bed. I'd never heard such yelling in my life. When my parents fight it's during the day and in angry whispers. It sounds like a snake convention in my parents' bedroom. That's bad enough. Maria and I get real nervous and nothing's right until they make up and talk in normal voices again. But Ramón could be heard right through the floor at two in the morning. And then he took to throwing things and then he started hitting her. The first time that happened Josie didn't go to morning mass at St. Francis and Mami went down to her apartment to see if she was sick or something. Josie came to the door with a big bruise on her face. After that Mami went to fetch her every Sunday and stayed with her if she was too ashamed to go to church.

After she found out she was pregnant Josie had talked it over with Doña Toña and Doña Toña had talked it over with Mami and by and by we all knew she was scared he would hurt the little baby growing inside of her and worried about the child growing up with Ramón for a father. He expected too much of everyone and little kids hurt so when a parent thinks whatever they do is all wrong. Ha! Tell that to Mami and Papi, will you.

I don't think there was anyone in the neighborhood on Ramón's side, not even Joe who liked to bully his wife and daughters but didn't realize he did or Tito who talked all the time about "wearing the pants in this family." Ramón was too much, even for them. Josie was so clearly a fine person, a quiet homebody, a sweetypie. Ramón was out of his mind, that's what most of us thought. I mean you had to be to be so regularly mean to a person who adored you. And she did, at least at first. You could see it in the way she looked at him, boasted about his strength, his good job, his brains. The way she excused his temper. "He can't help himself. He doesn't mean it."

And now she was packed up and sitting in the taxi. Waiting for him to come 10
home, I guess. That was too much for Mami and she scooted out the door with Olga, Maria, Papi, no less, and me right behind her with that soaked blue towel wrapped sloppily around my head. "Ai Mamita! Jesus, Maria y José. Jesus Maria y José," came faintly up the stairs in the front of the hurrying line. I knew Mami and I knew she meant to stand in front of Josie to protect her from that bully and, sure as shooting, Papi was going to protect Mami who was going so fast in her house slippers she almost fell down except that Olga gripped her hard and kept her upright.

When we streamed out the door into the small crowd that had gathered by now it was to see Ramón coming down the street with a sour look on his face.

He looked up once or twice but mostly just stared at his feet as he strode up the block. He swept past us and almost into the house the way he did when he came home weary from the shipyard and the long ride home. He would have missed seeing Josie for sure, as I was praying he would, except that she called to him.

"Ramón," she said in her soft voice, stepping out of the taxi. "Ramón." He looked up and around then, took in the crowd, the taxi with a tall lamp lying on the back seat and Josie in her good suit. He stood looking at all this and especially at Josie for a long time. When he spoke it was only to Josie, as if we weren't there at all. He had to clear his throat to say "Josie?"

I was totally surprised and confused. He sounded so small, you know. So uncertain. It was Josie looked tall now and hard. If I hadn't known what I knew I would've said Josie was the bully in the family. She looked him straight in the eye and said stiffly, as if they were lines someone had given her to memorize, "I warned you. I said I would leave if you ever hit me again. I am not safe with you. Our child is not safe with you. I'm going now. I left arroz con pollo on the stove and the electric bill on the table." He didn't answer so she turned to hug Doña Toña and Mami before sitting herself back down. It was then that Ramón acted. Before I could blink he'd hurled himself at her, thrown himself on his knees and gripped her around her stockinged legs. "No! No te vayas. Tu no comprendes. Eres muy joven para comprender. Tu no puedes dejarme asi. Estamos casados para la vida. Te amo para siempre, para siempre. Josita, mi amor, no te vayas. Si te vas me mato. Te lo juro. No te puedes ir. No te puedes ir…" and on and on in a hoarse voice while Josie stood there frozen, fear on her face. There was no sound but Maria whispering occasional translations into Olga's impatient ear "Don't go." "You're too young to understand." "We're married for life." "I'll love you always." "I'll kill myself, I swear it."

It went on forever, Josie standing there, Ramón kneeling, all of us listening, tears running down my face, Josie's face, Mami's face. It was Olga who ended it, who walked up to Ramón, knelt down beside him, put an arm around him, and started talking, telling him Josie was a mother now and had to think about what was best for her baby, that it was his baby too, that he had to let her go now so she could bear a baby healthy in body and soul, that she knew he loved Josie, that his love would let him do what was best for them all. He was crying now, arguing with her while he slowly let go while he said he never could let her go, that she was his whole life, that he would die without her, while Josie kissed Toña quickly on the cheek and climbed in next to the taxi driver who sat there looking the way I probably looked, dazed, like he'd stumbled into a movie screen and couldn't get out. She had to tell him to drive off.

(1992)

Questions for Discussion and Writing

1. Why do Josie's neighbors and even her family treat her beatings as a drama to be observed rather than as an outrage that must be stopped?
2. Why is even Josie herself embarrassed by the beatings? Do you think she should be? What is her mother's attitude toward the abuse?
3. Can you make the argument that Josie would never have found the stamina to leave Ramón if she had not discovered she was pregnant? Support your claim with evidence from the story.

4. How would you describe the remarkable change that Ramón undergoes? Can you reconcile his machismo swaggering in the first part of the story with his contrite weeping at the end?
5. What do you think Morales's point is in telling this story? In other words, can you state her theme?

Chinua Achebe 1930–

Chinua Achebe was born in Ogidi, Nigeria, the son of an African teacher in a missionary school. Although he was christened Albert, after Queen Victoria's husband, he later took his Nigerian name, Chinua. His fiction depicts the effects of European culture on African traditions. His best-known novel, *Things Fall Apart*, has sold more than 8 million copies and been translated into fifty languages. Achebe defines himself as a cultural nationalist with a revolutionary mission "to help my society regain belief in itself and put away the complexes of the years of denigration and self-abasement." In 1990 Achebe was paralyzed from the waist down in a serious automobile accident. A short time later, he moved to the United States to teach at Bard College in New York.

Dead Men's Path

Michael Obi's hopes were fulfilled much earlier than he expected. He was appointed headmaster of Ndume Central School in January 1949. It had always been an unprogressive school, so the Mission authorities decided to send a young and energetic man to run it. Obi accepted this responsibility with enthusiasm. He had many wonderful ideas and this was an opportunity to put them into practice. He had had sound secondary school education which designated him a "pivotal teacher" in the official records and set him apart from the other headmasters in the mission field. He was outspoken in his condemnation of the narrow views of these older and often less-educated ones.

"We shall make a good job of it, shan't we?" he asked his young wife when they first heard the joyful news of his promotion.

"We shall do our best," she replied. "We shall have such beautiful gardens and everything will be just *modern* and delightful...." In their two years of married life she had become completely infected by his passion for "modern methods" and his denigration of "these old and superannuated people in the teaching field who would be better employed as traders in the Onitsha market." She began to see herself already as the admired wife of the young headmaster, the queen of the school.

The wives of the other teachers would envy her position. She would set the fashion in everything.... Then, suddenly, it occurred to her that there might not be other wives. Wavering between hope and fear, she asked her husband, looking anxiously at him.

"All our colleagues are young and unmarried," he said with enthusiasm 5
which for once she did not share. "Which is a good thing," he continued.

"Why?"

"Why? They will give all their time and energy to the school."

Nancy was downcast. For a few minutes she became skeptical about the new school; but it was only for a few minutes. Her little personal misfortune could not blind her to her husband's happy prospects. She looked at him as he sat folded up in a chair. He was stoop-shouldered and looked frail. But he sometimes surprised people with sudden bursts of physical energy. In his present posture, however, all his bodily strength seemed to have retired behind his deep-set eyes, giving them an extraordinary power of penetration. He was only twenty-six, but looked thirty or more. On the whole, he was not unhandsome.

"A penny for your thoughts, Mike," said Nancy after a while, imitating the woman's magazine she read.

"I was thinking what a grand opportunity we've got at last to show these people 10
how a school should be run."

Ndume school was backward in every sense of the word. Mr. Obi put his whole life into the work, and his wife hers too. He had two aims. A high standard of teaching was insisted upon, and the school compound was to be turned into a place of beauty. Nancy's dream-gardens came to life with the coming of the rains, and blossomed. Beautiful hibiscus and allamanda hedges in brilliant red and yellow marked out the carefully tended school compound from the rank neighbourhood bushes.

One evening as Obi was admiring his work he was scandalized to see an old woman from the village hobble right across the compound, through a marigold flower-bed and the hedges. On going up there he found faint signs of an almost disused path from the village across the school compound to the bush on the other side.

"It amazes me," said Obi to one of his teachers who had been three years in the school, "that you people allowed the villagers to make use of this footpath. It is simply incredible." He shook his head.

"The path," said the teacher apologetically, "appears to be very important to them. Although it is hardly used, it connects the village shrine with their place of burial."

"And what has that got to do with the school?" asked the headmaster. 15

"Well, I don't know," replied the other with a shrug of the shoulders. "But I remember there was a big row some time ago when we attempted to close it."

"That was some time ago. But it will not be used now," said Obi as he walked away. "What will the Government Education Officer think of this when he comes to inspect the school next week? The villagers might, for all I know, decide to use the schoolroom for a pagan ritual during the inspection."

Heavy sticks were planted closely across the path at the two places where it entered and left the school premises. These were further strengthened with barbed wire.

Three days later the village priest of *Ani* called on the headmaster. He was an old man and walked with a slight stoop. He carried a stout walking-stick which he usually tapped on the floor, by way of emphasis, each time he made a new point in his argument.

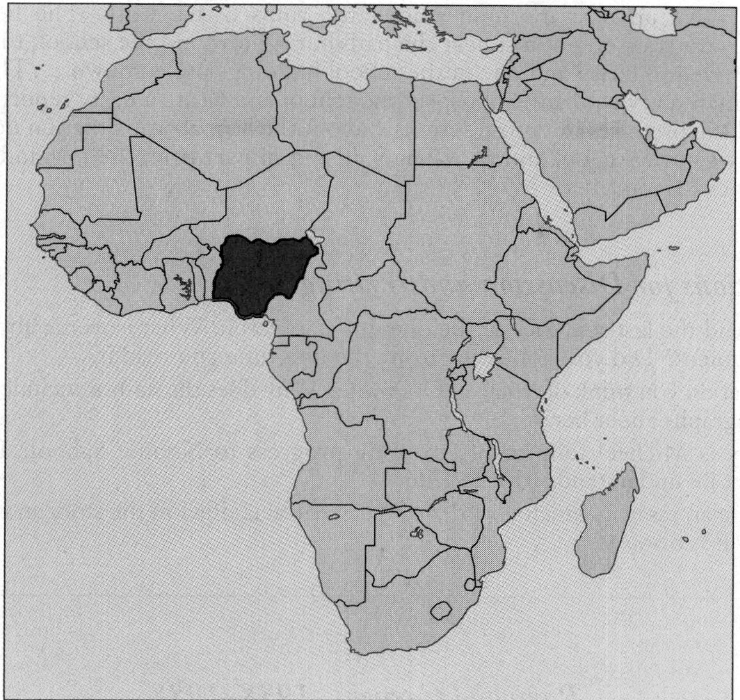

The most populous country in Africa, Nigeria gained independence from Great Britain in 1960. It is the setting for China Achebe's stories and novels.

"I have heard," he said after the usual exchange of cordialities, "that our ancestral footpath has recently been closed. . . ."

"Yes," replied Mr. Obi. "We cannot allow people to make a highway of our school compound."

"Look here, my son," said the priest bringing down his walking-stick, "this path was here before you were born and before your father was born. The whole life of this village depends on it. Our dead relatives depart by it and our ancestors visit us by it. But most important, it is the path of children coming in to be born. . . ."

Mr. Obi listened with a satisfied smile on his face.

"The whole purpose of our school," he said finally, "is to eradicate just such beliefs as that. Dead men do not require footpaths. The whole idea is just fantastic. Our duty is to teach your children to laugh at such ideas."

"What you say may be true," replied the priest, "but we follow the practices of our fathers. If you re-open the path we shall have nothing to quarrel about. What I always say is: let the hawk perch and let the eagle perch." He rose to go.

"I am sorry," said the young headmaster. "But the school compound cannot be a thoroughfare. It is against our regulations. I would suggest your constructing another path, skirting our premises. We can even get our boys to help in building it. I don't suppose the ancestors will find the little detour too burdensome."

"I have no more words to say," said the old priest, already outside.

Two days later, a young woman in the village died in childbed. A diviner was immediately consulted and he prescribed heavy sacrifices to propitiate ancestors insulted by the fence.

Obi woke up next morning among the ruins of his work. The beautiful hedges were torn up not just near the path but right round the school, the flowers trampled to death and one of the school buildings pulled down.... That day, the white Supervisor came to inspect the school and wrote a nasty report on the state of the premises but more seriously about the "tribal-war situation developing between the school and the village, arising in part from the misguided zeal of the new headmaster."

(1972)

Questions for Discussion and Writing

1. Reread the last sentence of the opening paragraph. What is ironic about that statement? Did you notice the irony the first time you read it?
2. What do you think of Michael Obi's wife? Why does the author include several paragraphs about her?
3. Why is Michael Obi unable to bring progress to Ndume School? Do you think he understands why he failed?
4. Write an essay in which you identify the central conflict in the story and explain how it is resolved.

Raymond Carver 1938–1988

Raymond Carver grew up poor in Yakima, Washington. Married at nineteen and a father of two by twenty, he moved to California, worked nights, attended college, divorced, and, as he put it, "took up drinking as a serious pursuit." At age thirty-nine, though, he gave up alcohol and observed, "In this second life, this post-drinking life, I still retain a certain sense of pessimism." But he did not give up smoking, declaring himself "a cigarette with a body attached to it." Two years before dying of lung cancer at age fifty, he and his partner, the poet Tess Gallagher, were married in a Reno chapel in a ceremony he described as a "high tacky affair."

What We Talk About When We Talk About Love

My friend Mel McGinnis was talking. Mel McGinnis is a cardiologist, and sometimes that gives him the right.

The four of us were sitting around his kitchen table drinking gin. Sunlight filled the kitchen from the big window behind the sink. There were Mel and me and his second wife, Teresa—Terri, we called her—and my wife, Laura. We lived in Albuquerque then. But we were all from somewhere else.

There was an ice bucket on the table. The gin and the tonic water kept going around, and we somehow got on the subject of love. Mel thought real love was nothing less than spiritual love. He said he'd spent five years in a seminary before quitting to go to medical school. He said he still looked back on those years in the seminary as the most important years in his life.

Terri said the man she lived with before she lived with Mel loved her so much he tried to kill her. Then Terri said, "He beat me up one night. He dragged me around the living room by my ankles. He kept saying, 'I love you, I love you, you bitch.' He went on dragging me around the living room. My head kept knocking on things." Terri looked around the table. "What do you do with love like that?"

She was a bone-thin woman with a pretty face, dark eyes, and brown hair that hung down her back. She liked necklaces made of turquoise, and long pendant earrings.

"My God, don't be silly. That's not love, and you know it," Mel said. "I don't know what you'd call it, but I sure know you wouldn't call it love."

"Say what you want to, but I know it was," Terri said. "It may sound crazy to you, but it's true just the same. People are different, Mel. Sure, sometimes he may have acted crazy. Okay. But he loved me. In his own way maybe, but he loved me. There was love there, Mel. Don't say there wasn't."

Mel let out his breath. He held his glass and turned to Laura and me. "The man threatened to kill me," Mel said. He finished his drink and reached for the gin bottle. "Terri's a romantic. Terri's of the kick-me-so-I'll-know-you-love-me school. Terri, hon, don't look that way." Mel reached across the table and touched Terri's cheek with his fingers. He grinned at her.

"Now he wants to make up," Terri said.

"Make up what?" Mel said. "What is there to make up? I know what I know. That's all."

"How'd we get started on this subject, anyway?" Terri said. She raised her glass and drank from it. "Mel always has love on his mind," she said. "Don't you, honey?" She smiled, and I thought that was the last of it.

"I just wouldn't call Ed's behavior love. That's all I'm saying, honey," Mel said. "What about you guys?" Mel said to Laura and me. "Does that sound like love to you?"

"I'm the wrong person to ask," I said. "I didn't even know the man. I've only heard his name mentioned in passing. I wouldn't know. You'd have to know the particulars. But I think what you're saying is that love is an absolute."

Mel said, "The kind of love I'm talking about is. The kind of love I'm talking about, you don't try to kill people."

Laura said, "I don't know anything about Ed, or anything about the situation. But who can judge anyone else's situation?"

I touched the back of Laura's hand. She gave me a quick smile. I picked up Laura's hand. It was warm, the nails polished, perfectly manicured. I encircled the broad wrist with my fingers, and I held her.

"When I left, he drank rat poison," Terri said. She clasped her arms with her hands. "They took him to the hospital in Santa Fe. That's where we lived then, about ten miles out. They saved his life. But his gums went crazy from it. I mean they pulled away from his teeth. After that, his teeth stood out like fangs. My God," Terri said. She waited a minute, then let go of her arms and picked up her glass.

"What people won't do!" Laura said.

"He's out of the action now," Mel said. "He's dead."

Mel handed me the saucer of limes. I took a section, squeezed it over my drink, and stirred the ice cubes with my finger.

"It gets worse," Terri said. "He shot himself in the mouth. But he bungled that too. Poor Ed," she said. Terri shook her head.

"Poor Ed nothing," Mel said. "He was dangerous."

Mel was forty-five years old. He was tall and rangy with curly soft hair. His face and arms were brown from the tennis he played. When he was sober, his gestures, all his movements, were precise, very careful.

"He did love me though, Mel. Grant me that," Terri said. "That's all I'm asking. He didn't love me the way you love me. I'm not saying that. But he loved me. You can grant me that, can't you?"

"What do you mean, he bungled it?" I said. 25

Laura leaned forward with her glass. She put her elbows on the table and held her glass in both hands. She glanced from Mel to Terri and waited with a look of bewilderment on her open face, as if amazed that such things happened to people you were friendly with.

"How'd he bungle it when he killed himself?" I said.

"I'll tell you what happened," Mel said. "He took this twenty-two pistol he'd bought to threaten Terri and me with. Oh, I'm serious, the man was always threatening. You should have seen the way we lived in those days. Like fugitives. I even bought a gun myself. Can you belive it? A guy like me? But I did. I bought one for self-defense and carried it in the glove compartment. Sometimes I'd have to leave the apartment in the middle of the night. To go to the hospital, you know? Terri and I weren't married then, and my first wife had the house and kids, the dog, everything, and Terri and I were living in this apartment here. Sometimes, as I say, I'd get a call in the middle of the night and have to go in to the hospital at two or three in the morning. It'd be dark out there in the parking lot, and I'd break into a sweat before I could even get to my car. I never knew if he was going to come up out of the shrubbery or from behind a car and start shooting. I mean, the man was crazy. He was capable of wiring a bomb, anything. He used to call my service at all hours and say he needed to talk to the doctor, and when I'd return the call, he'd say, 'Son of a bitch, your days are numbered.' Little things like that. It was scary, I'm telling you."

"I still feel sorry for him," Terri said.

"It sounds like a nightmare," Laura said. "But what exactly happened after he shot himself?" 30

Laura is a legal secretary. We'd met in a professional capacity. Before we knew it, it was a courtship. She's thirty-five, three years younger than I am. In addition to being in love, we like each other and enjoy one another's company. She's easy to be with.

"What happened?" Laura said.

Mel said, "He shot himself in the mouth in his room. Someone heard the shot and told the manager. They came in with a passkey, saw what had happened, and called an ambulance. I happened to be there when they brought him in, alive but past recall. The man lived for three days. His head swelled up to twice the size of a normal head. I'd never seen anything like it, and I hope I never do again. Terri wanted to go in and sit with him when she found out about it. We had a fight over it. I didn't think she should see him like that. I didn't think she should see him, and I still don't."

"Who won the fight?" Laura said.

"I was in the room with him when he died," Terri said. "He never came up out of it. But I sat with him. He didn't have anyone else." 35

"He was dangerous," Mel said. "If you call that love, you can have it."

"It was love," Terri said. "Sure, it's abnormal in most people's eyes. But he was willing to die for it. He did die for it."

"I sure as hell wouldn't call it love," Mel said. "I mean, no one knows what he did it for. I've seen a lot of suicides, and I couldn't say anyone ever knew what they did it for."

Mel put his hands behind his neck and tilted his chair back. "I'm not interested in that kind of love," he said. "If that's love, you can have it."

Terri said, "We were afraid. Mel even made a will out and wrote to his brother in California who used to be a Green Beret. Mel told him who to look for if something happened to him." 40

Terri drank from her glass. She said, "But Mel's right—we lived like fugitives. We were afraid. Mel was, weren't you, honey? I even called the police at one point, but they were no help. They said they couldn't do anything until Ed actually did something. Isn't that a laugh?" Terri said.

She poured the last of the gin into her glass and waggled the bottle. Mel got up from the table and went to the cupboard. He took down another bottle.

"Well, Nick and I know what love is," Laura said. "For us, I mean," Laura said. She bumped my knee with her knee. "You're supposed to say something now," Laura said, and turned her smile on me.

For an answer, I took Laura's hand and raised it to my lips. I made a big production out of kissing her hand. Everyone was amused.

"We're lucky," I said. 45

"You guys," Terri said. "Stop that now. You're making me sick. You're still on the honeymoon, for God's sake. You're still gaga, for crying out loud. Just wait. How long have you been together now? How long has it been? A year? Longer than a year?"

"Going on a year and a half," Laura said, flushed and smiling.

"Oh, now," Terri said. "Wait awhile."

She held her drink and gazed at Laura.

"I'm only kidding," Terri said. 50

Mel opened the gin and went around the table with the bottle.

"Here, you guys," he said. "Let's have a toast. I want to propose a toast. A toast to love. To true love," Mel said.

We touched glasses.

"To love," we said.

Outside in the backyard, one of the dogs began to bark. The leaves of the aspen that leaned past the window ticked against the glass. The afternoon sun was like a presence in this room, the spacious light of ease and generosity. We could have been anywhere, somewhere enchanted. We raised our glasses again and grinned at each other like children who had agreed on something forbidden. 55

"I'll tell you what real love is," Mel said. "I mean, I'll give you a good example. And then you can draw your own conclusions." He poured more gin into his glass. He added an ice cube and a sliver of lime. We waited and sipped our drinks. Laura and I touched knees again. I put a hand on her warm thigh and left it there.

"What do any of us really know about love?" Mel said. "It seems to me we're just beginners at love. We say we love each other and we do, I don't doubt it. I love Terri and Terri loves me, and you guys love each other too. You know the kind of love I'm talking about now. Physical love, that impulse that drives you to someone special, as well as love of the other person's being, his or her essence, as it were. Carnal love and, well, call it sentimental love, the day-to-day caring about the other person. But sometimes I have a hard time accounting for the fact that I must have loved my first wife too. But I did, I know I did. So I suppose I am like Terri in that regard. Terri and Ed." He thought about it and then he went on. "There was a time when I thought I loved my first wife more than life itself. But now I hate her guts. I do. How do you explain that? What happened to that love? What happened to it, is what I'd like to know. I wish someone could tell me. Then there's Ed. Okay, we're back to Ed. He loves Terri so much he tries to kill her and he winds up killing himself." Mel stopped talking and swallowed from his glass. "You guys have been together eighteen months and you love each other. It shows all over you. You glow with it. But you both loved other people before you met each other. You've both been married before, just like us. And you probably loved other people before that too, even. Terri and I have been together five years, been married for four. And the terrible thing, the terrible thing is, but the good thing too, the saving grace, you might say, is that if something happened to one of us—excuse me for saying this—but if something happened to one of us tomorrow, I think the other one, the other person, would grieve for a while, you know, but then the surviving party would go out and love again, have someone else soon enough. All this, all of this love we're talking about, it would just be a memory. Maybe not even a memory. Am I wrong? Am I way off base? Because I want you to set me straight if you think I'm wrong. I want to know. I mean, I don't know anything, and I'm the first one to admit it."

"Mel, for God's sake," Terri said. She reached out and took hold of his wrist. "Are you getting drunk? Honey? Are you drunk?"

"Honey, I'm just talking," Mel said. "All right? I don't have to be drunk to say what I think. I mean, we're all just talking, right?" Mel said. He fixed his eyes on her.

"Sweetie, I'm not criticizing," Terri said. 60

She picked up her glass.

"I'm not on call today," Mel said. "Let me remind you of that. I am not on call," he said.

"Mel, we love you," Laura said.

Mel looked at Laura. He looked at her as if he could not place her, as if she was not the woman she was.

"Love you too, Laura," Mel said. "And you, Nick, love you too. You know 65 something?" Mel said. "You guys are our pals," Mel said.

He picked up his glass.

Mel said, "I was going to tell you about something. I mean, I was going to prove a point. You see, this happened a few months ago, but it's still going on right now, and it ought to make us feel ashamed when we talk like we know what we're talking about when we talk about love."

"Come on now," Terri said. "Don't talk like you're drunk if you're not drunk."

"Just shut up for once in your life," Mel said very quietly. "Will you do me a favor and do that for a minute? So as I was saying, there's this old couple who had this car wreck out on the interstate. A kid hit them and they were all torn to shit and nobody was giving them much chance to pull through."

Terri looked at us and then back at Mel. She seemed anxious, or maybe that's too strong a word.

Mel was handing the bottle around the table.

"I was on call that night," Mel said. "It was May or maybe it was June. Terri and I had just sat down to dinner when the hospital called. There'd been this thing out on the interstate. Drunk kid, teenager, plowed his dad's pickup into this camper with this old couple in it. They were up in their mid-seventies, that couple. The kid—eighteen, nineteen, something—he was DOA. Taken the steering wheel through his sternum. The old couple, they were alive, you understand. I mean, just barely. But they had everything. Multiple fractures, internal injuries, hemorrhaging, contusions, lacerations, the works, and they each of them had themselves concussions. They were in a bad way, believe me. And, of course, their age was two strikes against them. I'd say she was worse off than he was. Ruptured spleen along with everything else. Both kneecaps broken. But they'd been wearing their seatbelts and, God knows, that's what saved them for the time being."

"Folks, this is an advertisement for the National Safety Council," Terri said. "This is your spokesman, Dr. Melvin R. McGinnis, talking." Terri laughed. "Mel," she said, "sometimes you're just too much. But I love you, hon," she said.

"Honey, I love you," Mel said.

He leaned across the table. Terri met him halfway. They kissed.

"Terri's right," Mel said as he settled himself again. "Get those seatbelts on. But seriously, they were in some shape, those oldsters. By the time I got down there, the kid was dead, as I said. He was off in a corner, laid out on a gurney. I took one look at the old couple and told the ER nurse to get me a neurologist and an orthopedic man and a couple of surgeons down there right away."

He drank from his glass. "I'll try to keep this short," he said. "So we took the two of them up to the OR and worked like fuck on them most of the night. They had these incredible reserves, those two. You see that once in a while. So we did everything that could be done, and toward morning we're giving them a fifty-fifty chance, maybe less than that for her. So here they are, still alive the next morning. So, okay, we move them into the ICU, which is where they both kept plugging away at it for two weeks, hitting it better and better on all the scopes. So we transfer them out to their own room."

Mel stopped talking. "Here," he said, "let's drink this cheapo gin the hell up. Then we're going to dinner, right? Terri and I know a new place. That's where we'll go, to this new place we know about. But we're not going until we finish up this cut-rate, lousy gin."

Terri said, "We haven't actually eaten there yet. But it looks good. From the outside, you know."

"I like food," Mel said. "If I had it to do all over again, I'd be a chef, you know? Right, Terri?" Mel said.

He laughed. He fingered the ice in his glass.

"Terri knows," he said. "Terri can tell you. But let me say this. If I could come back again in a different life, a different time and all, you know what? I'd like to come back as a knight. You were pretty safe wearing all that armor. It was all right being a knight until gunpowder and muskets and pistols came along."

"Mel would like to ride a horse and carry a lance," Terri said.

"Carry a woman's scarf with you everywhere," Laura said.

"Or just a woman," Mel said. 85

"Shame on you," Laura said.

Terri said, "Suppose you came back as a serf. The serfs didn't have it so good in those days," Terri said.

"The serfs never had it good," Mel said. "But I guess even the knights were vessels to someone. Isn't that the way it worked? But then everyone is always a vessel to someone. Isn't that right? Terri? But what I liked about knights, besides their ladies, was that they had that suit of armor, you know, and they couldn't get hurt very easy. No cars in those days, you know? No drunk teenagers to tear into your ass."

"Vassals," Terri said.

"What?" Mel said. 90

"Vassals," Terri said. "They were called vassals, not vessels."

"Vassals, vessels," Mel said, "what the fuck's the difference? You knew what I meant anyway. All right," Mel said. "So I'm not educated. I learned my stuff. I'm a heart surgeon, sure, but I'm just a mechanic. I go in and fuck around and I fix things. Shit," Mel said.

"Modesty doesn't become you," Terri said.

"He's just a humble sawbones," I said. "But sometimes they suffocated in all that armor, Mel. They'd even have heart attacks if it got too hot and they were too tired and worn out. I read somewhere that they'd fall off their horses and not be able to get up because they were too tired to stand with all that armor on them. They got trampled by their own horses sometimes."

"That's terrible," Mel said. "That's a terrible thing, Nicky. I guess they'd just lay 95
there and wait until somebody came along and made a shish kebab out of them."

"Some other vessel," Terri said.

"That's right," Mel said. "Some vassal would come along and spear the bastard in the name of love. Or whatever the fuck it was they fought over in those days."

"Same things we fight over these days," Terri said.

Laura said, "Nothing's changed."

The color was still high in Laura's cheeks. Her eyes were bright. She brought 100
her glass to her lips.

Mel poured himself another drink. He looked at the label closely as if studying a long row of numbers. Then he slowly put the bottle down on the table and slowly reached for the tonic water.

"What about the old couple?" Laura said. "You didn't finish that story you started."

Laura was having a hard time lighting her cigarette. Her matches kept going out.

The sunshine inside the room was different now, changing, getting thinner. But the leaves outside the window were still shimmering, and I stared at the pattern they made on the panes and on the Formica counter. They weren't the same patterns, of course.

"What about the old couple?" I said. 105

"Older but wiser," Terri said.

Mel stared at her.

Terri said, "Go on with your story, hon. I was only kidding. Then what happened?"

"Terri, sometimes," Mel said.

"Please, Mel," Terri said. "Don't always be so serious, sweetie. Can't you take 110
a joke?"

"Where's the joke?" Mel said.

He held his glass and gazed steadily at his wife.

"What happened?" Laura said.

Mel fastened his eyes on Laura. He said, "Laura, if I didn't have Terri and if I didn't love her so much, and if Nick wasn't my best friend, I'd fall in love with you. I'd carry you off, honey," he said.

"Tell your story," Terri said. "Then we'll go to that new place, okay?" 115

"Okay," Mel said. "Where was I?" he said. He started at the table and then he began again.

"I dropped in to see each of them every day, sometimes twice a day if I was up doing other calls anyway. Casts and bandages, head to foot, the both of them. You know, you've seen it in the movies. That's just the way they looked, just like in the movies. Little eye-holes and nose-holes and mouth-holes. And she had to have her legs slung up on top of it. Well, the husband was very depressed for the longest while. Even after he found out that his wife was going to pull through, he was still very depressed. Not about the accident, though. I mean, the accident was one thing, but it wasn't everything. I'd get up to his mouth-hole, you know, and he'd say no, it wasn't the accident exactly but it was because he couldn't see her through his eye-holes. He said that was what was making him feel so bad. Can you imagine? I'm telling you, the man's heart was breaking because he couldn't turn his goddamn head and *see* his goddamn wife."

Mel looked around the table and shook his head at what he was going to say.

"I mean, it was killing the old fart just because he couldn't *look* at the fucking woman."

We all looked at Mel. 120

"Do you see what I'm saying?" he said.

Maybe we were a little drunk by then. I know it was hard keeping things in focus. The light was draining out of the room, going back through the window where it had come from. Yet nobody made a move to get up from the table to turn on the overhead light.

"Listen," Mel said. "Let's finish this fucking gin. There's about enough here for one shooter all around. Then let's go eat. Let's go to the new place."

"He's depressed," Terri said. "Mel, why don't you take a pill?"

Mel shook his head. "I've taken everything there is." 125

"We all need a pill now and then," I said.

"Some people are born needing them," Terri said.

She was using her finger to rub at something on the table. Then she stopped rubbing.

"I think I want to call my kids," Mel said. "Is that all right with everybody? I'll call my kids," he said.

Terri said, "What if Marjorie answers the phone? You guys, you've heard us 130
on the subject of Marjorie? Honey, you know you don't want to talk to Marjorie. It'll make you feel even worse."

"I don't want to talk to Marjorie," Mel said. "But I want to talk to my kids."

"There isn't a day goes by that Mel doesn't say he wishes she'd get married again. Or else die," Terri said. "For one thing," Terri said, "she's bankrupting us. Mel says it's just to spite him that she won't get married again. She has a boyfriend who lives with her and the kids, so Mel is supporting the boyfriend too."

"She's allergic to bees," Mel said. "If I'm not praying she'll get married again, I'm praying she'll get herself stung to death by a swarm of fucking bees."

"Shame on you," Laura said.

"Bzzzzzzz," Mel said, turning his fingers into bees and buzzing them at 135
Terri's throat. Then he let his hands drop all the way to his sides.

"She's vicious," Mel said. "Sometimes I think I'll go up there dressed like a beekeeper. You know, that hat that's like a helmet with the plate that comes down over your face, the big gloves, and the padded coat? I'll knock on the door and let loose a hive of bees in the house. But first I'd make sure the kids were out, of course."

He crossed one leg over the other. It seemed to take him a lot of time to do it. Then he put both feet on the floor and leaned forward, elbows on the table, his chin cupped in his hands.

"Maybe I won't call the kids, after all. Maybe it isn't such a hot idea. Maybe we'll just go eat. How does that sound?"

"Sounds fine to me," I said. "Eat or not eat. Or keep drinking. I could head right on out into the sunset."

"What does that mean, honey?" Laura said. 140

"It just means what I said," I said. "It means I could just keep going. That's all it means."

"I could eat something myself," Laura said. "I don't think I've ever been so hungry in my life. Is there something to nibble on?"

"I'll put out some cheese and crackers," Terri said.

But Terri just sat there. She did not get up to get anything.

Mel turned his glass over. He spilled it out on the table. 145

"Gin's gone," Mel said.

Terri said, "Now what?"

I could hear my heart beating. I could hear everyone's heart. I could hear the human noise we sat there making, not one of us moving, not even when the room went dark.

(1981)

Questions for Discussion and Writing

1. What different definitions and descriptions of love come up during the conversation? Do the characters ever get anywhere with the subject? Why or why not?
2. What distinguishes this story from other stories you have read in this course? Do you think you could recognize another Raymond Carver story? How?
3. When the narrator says of himself and Laura, "In addition to being in love, we like each other and enjoy one another's company," what is he saying about his definition of love?
4. Reread the first two paragraphs of the story. What expository information do you get in these few sentences?
5. Is this story optimistic or pessimistic about love? Write an essay arguing your answer to this question.

Toni Cade Bambara 1939–1995

Toni Cade Bambara wrote under the name Toni Cade until 1970, when she adopted the African name Bambara. Early on, she championed the civil rights struggle and the women's liberation movement and, in the 1970s, visited both Cuba and Vietnam to meet with women's groups there. In her fiction, her colorful characters speak in black dialect, which she spoke of as "riffs" or "be-bop." For a while, she said, writing seemed to her "rather frivolous, like something you did because you didn't feel like doing any work. But…I've come to appreciate that it is a perfectly legitimate way to participate in a struggle." She fought colon cancer but died in 1995 at age fifty-six.

The Lesson

Back in the days when everyone was old and stupid or young and foolish and me and Sugar were the only ones just right, this lady moved on our block with nappy hair and proper speech and no makeup. And quite naturally we laughed at her, laughed the way we did at the junk man who went about his business like he was some big-time president and his sorry-ass horse his secretary. And we kinda hated her too, hated the way we did the winos who cluttered up our parks and pissed on our handball walls and stank up our hallways and stairs so you couldn't halfway play hide-and-seek without a goddamn gas mask. Miss Moore was her name. The only woman on the block with no first name. And she was black as hell, cept for her feet, which were fish white and spooky. And she was always planning these boring-ass things for us to do, us being my cousin, mostly, who lived on the block cause we all moved North the same time and to the same apartment then spread out gradual to breathe. And our parents would yank our heads into some kinda shape and crisp up our clothes so we'd be presentable for travel with Miss Moore, who always looked like she was going to church, though she never did. Which is just one of the things the grownups talked about when they talked behind her back like a dog. But when she came calling with some sachet she'd sewed up or some gingerbread she'd made or some book, why then they'd all be too embarrassed to turn her down and we'd get handed over all spruced up. She'd been to college and said it was only right that she should take responsibility for the young ones' education, and she not even related by marriage or blood. So they'd go for it. Specially Aunt Gretchen. She was the main gofer in the family. You got some ole dumb shit foolishness you want somebody to go for, you send for Aunt Gretchen. She been screwed into the go-along for so long, it's a blood-deep natural thing with her. Which is how she got saddled with me and Sugar and Junior in the first place while our mothers were in a la-de-da apartment up the block having a good ole time.

So this one day Miss Moore rounds us all up at the mailbox and it's puredee hot and she's knockin herself out about arithmetic. And school suppose to let up in summer I heard, but she don't never let up. And the starch in my pinafore scratching the shit outta me and I'm really hating this nappy-head bitch and her goddamn college degree. I'd much rather go to the pool or to the show where it's cool. So me and Sugar leaning on the mailbox being surly, which is a Miss Moore word. And Flyboy checking out what everybody brought for lunch. And Fat Butt already wasting his peanut-butter-and-jelly sandwich like the pig he is. And Junebug punchin on Q.T.'s arm for potato chips. And Rosie Giraffe shifting from one hip to the other waiting for somebody to step on her foot or ask her if she from Georgia so she can kick ass, preferably Mercedes'. And Miss Moore asking us do we know what money is, like we a bunch of retards. I mean real money, she say, like it's only poker chips or monopoly papers we lay on the grocer. So right away I'm tired of this and say so. And would much rather snatch Sugar and go to the Sunset and terrorize the West Indian kids and take their hair ribbons and their money too. And Miss Moore files that remark away for next week's lesson on brotherhood, I can tell. And finally I say we oughta get to the subway cause it's cooler and besides we might meet some cute boys. Sugar done swiped her mama's lipstick, so we ready.

So we heading down the street and she's boring us silly about what things cost and what our parents make and how much goes for rent and how money ain't divided up right in this country. And then she gets to the part about we all poor and live in the slums, which I don't feature. And I'm ready to speak on that, but she steps out in the street and hails two cabs just like that. Then she hustles half the crew in with her and hands me a five-dollar bill and tells me to calculate 10 percent tip for the driver. And we're off. Me and Sugar and Junebug and Flyboy hanging out the window and hollering to everybody, putting lipstick on each other cause Flyboy a faggot anyway, and making farts with our sweaty armpits. But I'm mostly trying to figure how to spend this money. But they all fascinated with the meter ticking and Junebug starts laying bets as to how much it'll read when Flyboy can't hold his breath no more. Then Sugar lays bets as to how much it'll be when we get there. So I'm stuck. Don't nobody want to go for my plan, which is to jump out at the next light and run off to the first bar-b-que we can find. Then the driver tells us to get the hell out cause we there already. And the meter reads eighty-five cents. And I'm stalling to figure out the tip and Sugar say give him a dime. And I decide he don't need it as bad as I do, so later for him. But then he tries to take off with Junebug still in the door so we talk about his mama something ferocious. Then we check out that we on Fifth Avenue and everybody dressed up in stockings. One lady in a fur coat, hot as it is. White folks crazy.

"This is the place," Miss Moore say, presenting it to us in the voice she uses at the museum. "Let's look in the windows before we go in."

5 "Can we steal?" Sugar asks very serious like she's getting the ground rules squared away before she plays. "I beg your pardon," say Miss Moore, and we fall out. So she leads us around the windows of the toy store and me and Sugar screamin, "This is mine, that's mine. I gotta have that, that was made for me, I was born for that," till Big Butt drowns us out.

"Hey, I'm going to buy that there."

"That there? You don't even know what it is, stupid."

"I do so," he say punchin on Rosie Giraffe. "It's a microscope."

"Whatcha gonna do with a microscope, fool?"

10 "Look at things."

"Like what, Ronald?" asks Miss Moore. And Big Butt ain't got the first notion. So here go Miss Moore gabbing about the thousands of bacteria in a drop of water and the somethinorother in a speck of blood and the million and one living things in the air around us is invisible to the naked eye. And what she say that for? Junebug go to town on that "naked" and we rolling. Then Miss Moore ask what it cost. So we all jam into the window smudgin it up and the price tag say $300. So then she ask how long'd take for Big Butt and Junebug to save up their allowances. "Too long," I say. "Yeh," adds Sugar, "outgrown it by that time." And Miss Moore say no, you never outgrow learning instruments. "Why, even medical students and interns and," blah, blah, blah. And we ready to choke Big Butt for bringing it up in the first damn place.

"This here costs four hundred eighty dollars," say Rosie Giraffe. So we pile up all over her to see what she pointin out. My eyes tell me it's a chunk of glass cracked with something heavy, and different-color inks dripped into the splits, then the whole thing put into a oven or something. But for $480 it don't make sense.

"That's a paperweight made of semi-precious stones fused together under tremendous pressure," she explains slowly, with her hands doing the mining and all the factory work.

"So what's a paperweight?" asks Rosie Giraffe.

"To weigh paper with, dumbbell," say Flyboy, the wise man from the East.

"Not exactly," say Miss Moore, which is what she say when you warm or way off too. "It's to weigh paper down so it won't scatter and make your desk untidy." So right away me and Sugar curtsey to each other and then to Mercedes who is more the tidy type.

"We don't keep paper on top of the desk in my class," say Junebug, figuring Miss Moore crazy or lyin one.

"At home, then," she say. "Don't you have a calendar and a pencil case and a blotter and a letter-opener on your desk at home where you do your homework?" And she know damn well what our homes look like cause she nosys around in them every chance she gets.

"I don't even have a desk," say Junebug. "Do we?"

"No. And I don't get no homework neither," say Big Butt.

"And I don't even have a home," say Flyboy like he do at school to keep the white folks off his back and sorry for him. Send this poor kid to camp posters, is his specialty.

"I do," says Mercedes. "I have a box of stationery on my desk and a picture of my cat. My godmother bought the stationery and the desk. There's a big rose on each sheet and the envelopes smell like roses."

"Who wants to know about your smelly-ass stationery," say Rosie Giraffe fore I can get my two cents in.

"It's important to have a work area all your own so that...."

"Will you look at this sailboat, please," say Flyboy, cuttin her off and pointin to the thing like it was his. So once again we tumble all over each other to gaze at this magnificent thing in the toy store which is just big enough to maybe sail two kittens across the pond if you strap them to the posts tight. We all start reciting the price tag like we in assembly. "Handcrafted sailboat of fiberglass at one thousand one hundred ninety-five dollars."

"Unbelievable," I hear myself say and am really stunned. I read it again for myself just in case the group recitation put me in a trance. Same thing. For some reason this pisses me off. We look at Miss Moore and she looking at us, waiting for I dunno what.

The interior of F.A.O. Schwartz, a glittering festival of toys that overwhelms Sylvia and the other underprivileged children in "The Lesson."

Who'd pay all that when you can buy a sailboat set for a quarter at Pop's, a tube of glue for a dime, and a ball of string for eight cents? "It must have a motor and a whole lot else besides," I say. "My sailboat cost me about fifty cents."

"But will it take water?" says Mercedes with her smart ass.

"Took mine to Alley Pond Park once," say Flyboy. "String broke. Lost it. Pity."

"Sailed mine in Central Park and it keeled over and sank. Had to ask my 30
father for another dollar."

"And you got the strap," laughs Big Butt. "The jerk didn't even have a string on it. My old man wailed on his behind."

Little Q.T. was staring hard at the sailboat and you could see he wanted it bad. But he too little and somebody'd just take it from him. So what the hell. "This boat for kids, Miss Moore?"

"Parents silly to buy something like that just to get all broke up," say Rosie Giraffe.

"That much money it should last forever," I figure.

"My father'd buy it for me if I wanted it." 35

"Your father, my ass," say Rosie Giraffe getting a chance to finally push Mercedes.

"Must be rich people shop here," say Q.T.

"You are a very bright boy," say Flyboy. "What was your first clue?" And he rap him on the head with the back of his knuckles, since Q.T. the only one he could get away with. Though Q.T. liable to come up behind you years later and get his licks in when you half expect it.

"What I want to know is," I says to Miss Moore though I never talk to her, I wouldn't give the bitch that satisfaction, "is how much a real boat costs? I figure a thousand'd get you a yacht any day."

"Why don't you check that out," she says, "and report back to the group?" Which really pains my ass. If you gonna mess up a perfectly good swim day least you could do is have some answers. "Let's go in," she say like she got something up her sleeve. Only she don't lead the way. So me and Sugar turn the corner to where the entrance is, but when we get there I kinda hang back. Not that I'm scared, what's there to be afraid of, just a toy store. But I feel funny, shame. But what I got to be shamed about? Got as much right to go in as anybody. But somehow I can't seem to get hold of the door, so I step away for Sugar to lead. But she hangs back too. And I look at her and she looks at me and this is ridiculous. I mean, damn, I have never ever been shy about doing nothing or going nowhere. But then Mercedes steps up and then Rosie Giraffe and Big Butt crowd in behind and shove, and next thing we all stuffed into the doorway with only Mercedes squeezing past us, smoothing out her jumper and walking right down the aisle. Then the rest of us tumble in like a glued-together jigsaw done all wrong. And people lookin at us. And it's like the time me and Sugar crashed into the Catholic church on a dare. But once we got in there and everything so hushed and holy and the candles and the bowin and the handkerchiefs on all the drooping heads, I just couldn't go through with the plan. Which was for me to run up to the altar and do a tap dance while Sugar played the nose flute and messed around in the holy water. And Sugar kept giving me the elbow. Then later teased me so bad I tied her up in the shower and turned it on and locked her in. And she'd be there till this day if Aunt Gretchen hadn't finally figured I was lyin about the boarder takin a shower.

Same thing in the store. We all walkin on tiptoe and hardly touchin the games and puzzles and things. And I watched Miss Moore who is steady watchin us like she waitin for a sign. Like Mama Drewery watches the sky and sniffs the air and takes note of just how much slant is in the bird formation. Then me and Sugar bump smack into each other, so busy gazing at the toys, 'specially the sailboat. But we don't laugh and go into our fat-lady bump-stomach routine. We just stare at that price tag. Then Sugar run a finger over the whole boat. And I'm jealous and want to hit her. Maybe not her, but I sure want to punch somebody in the mouth.

"Watcha bring us here for, Miss Moore?"

"You sound angry, Sylvia. Are you mad about something?" Givin me one of them grins like she tellin a grown-up joke that never turns out to be funny. And she's lookin very closely at me like maybe she plannin to do my portrait from memory. I'm mad, but I won't give her that satisfaction. So I slouch around the store bein very bored and say, "Let's go."

Me and Sugar at the back of the train watchin the tracks whizzin by large then small then gettin gobbled up in the dark. I'm thinkin about this tricky toy I saw in the store. A clown that somersaults on a bar then does chin-ups just cause you yank lightly at his leg. Cost $35. I could see me askin my mother for a $35 birthday clown. "You wanna who that costs what?" she'd say, cocking her head to the side to get a better view of the hole in my head. Thirty-five dollars could buy new bunk beds for Junior and Gretchen's boy. Thirty-five dollars and the whole household could go visit Granddaddy Nelson in the country. Thirty-five dollars would pay for the rent and the piano bill too. Who are these people that spend that much for performing clowns and $1,000 for toy sailboats? What kinda work they do and how they live and how come we ain't in on it? Where we are is who we are, Miss Moore always pointin out. But it don't necessarily have to be that way, she always adds then waits for somebody to say that poor people have to wake up and demand their share of the pie and don't one of us know what kind of pie she talkin about in the first damn place. But she ain't so smart cause I still got her four dollars from the taxi and she sure ain't gettin it. Messin up my day with this shit. Sugar nudges me in my pocket and winks.

Miss Moore lines us up in front of the mailbox where we started from, seem like 45
years ago, and I got a headache for thinkin so hard. And we lean all over each other so we can hold up under the draggy-ass lecture she always finishes us off with at the end before we thank her for borin us to tears. But she just looks at us like she readin tea leaves. Finally she say, "Well, what did you think of F.A.O. Schwartz?"

Rosie Giraffe mumbles, "White folks crazy."

"I'd like to go there again when I get my birthday money," says Mercedes, and we shove her out the pack so she has to lean on the mailbox by herself.

"I'd like a shower. Tiring day," say Flyboy.

Then Sugar surprises me by sayin, "You know, Miss Moore, I don't think all of us here put together eat in a year what that sailboat costs." And Miss Moore lights up like somebody goosed her. "And?" she say, urging Sugar on. Only I'm standin on her foot so she don't continue.

"Imagine for a minute what kind of society it is in which some people can spend 50
on a toy what it would cost to feed a family of six or seven. What do you think?"

"I think," say Sugar pushing me off her feet like she never done before, cause I whip her ass in a minute, "that this is not much of a democracy if you ask me. Equal chance to pursue happiness means an equal crack at the dough, don't it?" Miss Moore is besides herself and I am disgusted with Sugar's treachery. So I stand on her foot one more time to see if she'll shove me. She shuts up, and Miss Moore looks at me, sorrowfully I'm thinkin. And somethin weird is goin on, I can feel it in my chest.

"Anybody else learn anything today?" lookin dead at me. I walk away and Sugar has to run to catch up and don't even seem to notice when I shrug her arm off my shoulder.

"Well, we got four dollars anyway," she says.

"Uh hunh."

"We could go to Hascombs and get half a chocolate layer and then go to the 55
Sunset and still have plenty money for potato chips and ice-cream sodas."

"Uh hunh."

"Race you to Hascombs," she say.

We start down the block and she gets ahead which is O.K. by me cause I'm goin to the West End and then over to the Drive to think this day through. She can run if she want to and even run faster. But ain't nobody gonna beat me at nuthin.

(1972)

Questions for Discussion and Writing

1. How would you characterize Sylvia? What makes her first-person point of view effective? Is she a reliable narrator?
2. How would you characterize Miss Moore? Why doesn't Sylvia admire her, as the adults do? Why does Sugar not feel hostile toward Miss Moore, as Sylvia does?
3. Why doesn't Sylvia get the point of the lesson being taught by the visit to the expensive toy store? Why is she so angry that she wants "to punch somebody in the mouth"?
4. What is the significance of the last line of the story? How does it relate to the lesson Sylvia was supposed to learn?
5. Write an essay explaining how Bambara manages to convey her revolutionary "lesson" without seeming didactic or preachy.

Bharati Mukherjee 1940–

Bharati Mukherjee, born in India in 1940 to wealthy parents, taught herself to read and write when only three years old. She was educated in Calcutta, but desiring to become a writer, she attended the Writer's Workshop at the University of Iowa in 1961, where she met her future husband. They were married after a whirlwind courtship of only two weeks. Now a naturalized U.S. citizen, she is a Distinguished Professor of English at the University of California–Berkeley, and her husband teaches at the University of Iowa. Her fiction frequently explores the tensions in multicultural relationships.

A Father

One Wednesday morning in mid-May Mr. Bhowmick woke up as he usually did at 5:43 A.M., checked his Rolex against the alarm clock's digital readout, punched down the alarm (set for 5:45), then nudged his wife awake. She worked as a claims investigator for an insurance company that had an office in a nearby shopping mall. She didn't really have to leave the house until 8:30, but she liked to get up early and cook him a big breakfast. Mr. Bhowmick had to drive a long way to work. He was a naturally dutiful, cautious man, and he set the alarm clock early enough to accommodate a margin for accidents.

While his wife, in a pink nylon negligee she had paid for with her own MasterCard card, made him a new version of French toast from a clipping ("Eggs-cellent Recipes!") Scotchtaped to the inside of a kitchen cupboard, Mr. Bhowmick brushed his teeth. He brushed, he gurgled with the loud, hawking noises that he and his brother had been taught as children to make in order to flush clean not merely teeth but also tongue and palate.

After that he showered, then, back in the bedroom again, he recited prayers in Sanskrit to Kali, the patron goddess of his family, the goddess of wrath and vengeance. In the pokey flat of his childhood in Ranchi, Bihar, his mother had given over a whole bedroom to her collection of gods and goddesses. Mr. Bhowmick couldn't be that extravagant in Detroit. His daughter, twenty-six and an electrical engineer, slept in the other of the two bedrooms in his apartment. But he had done his best. He had taken Woodworking I and II at a nearby recreation center and built a grotto for the goddess. Kali-Mata was eight inches tall, made of metal and painted a glistening black so that the metal glowed like the oiled, black skin of a peasant woman. And though Kali-Mata was totally nude except for a tiny gilt crown and a garland strung together from sinners' chopped off heads, she looked warm, cozy, *pleased*, in her makeshift wooden shrine in Detroit. Mr. Bhowmick had gathered quite a crowd of admiring, fellow wood-workers in those final weeks of decoration.

"Hurry it up with the prayers," his wife shouted from the kitchen. She was an agnostic, a believer in ambition, not grace. She frequently complained that his prayers had gotten so long that soon he wouldn't have time to go to work, play duplicate bridge with the Ghosals, or play the tabla in the Bengali Association's one Sunday per month musical soirees. Lately she'd begun to drain him in a wholly new way. He wasn't praying, she nagged; he was shutting her out of his life. There'd be no peace in the house until she hid Kali-Mata in a suitcase.

5 She nagged, and he threatened to beat her with his shoe as his father had threatened his mother: it was the thrust and volley of marriage. There was no question of actually taking off a shoe and applying it to his wife's body. She was bigger than he was. And, secretly, he admired her for having the nerve, the agnosticism, which as a college boy in backward Bihar he too had claimed.

"I have time," he shot at her. He was still wrapped in a damp terry towel.

"You have time for everything but domestic life."

It was the fault of the shopping mall that his wife had started to buy pop psychology paperbacks. These paperbacks preached that for couples who could sit down and talk about their "relationship," life would be sweet again. His engineer daughter was on his wife's side. She accused him of holding things in.

"Face it, Dad," she said. "You have an affect deficit."

10 But surely everyone had feelings they didn't want to talk about or talk over. He definitely did not want to blurt out anything about the sick-in-the-guts sensations that came over him most mornings and that he couldn't bubble down with Alka-Seltzer or smother with Gas-X. The women in his family were smarter than him. They were cheerful, outgoing, more American somehow.

How could he tell these bright, mocking women that in the 5:43 A.M. darkness, he sensed invisible presences: gods and snakes frolicked in the master bedroom, little white sparks of cosmic static crackled up the legs of his pajamas. Something was out there in the dark, something that could invent accidents and coincidences to remind mortals that even in Detroit they were no more than mortal. His wife would label this paranoia and dismiss it. Paranoia, premonition: whatever it was, it had begun to undermine his composure.

Take this morning. Mr. Bhowmick had woken up from a pleasant dream about a man taking a Club Med vacation, and the postdream satisfaction had lasted through the shower, but when he'd come back to the shrine in the bedroom, he'd noticed all at once how scarlet and saucy was the tongue that

Kali-Mata stuck out at the world. Surely he had not lavished such alarming detail, such admonitory colors on that flap of flesh.

Watch out, ambulatory sinners. Be careful out there, the goddess warned him, and not with the affection of Sergeant Esterhaus,[1] either.

"French toast must be eaten hot-hot," his wife nagged. "Otherwise they'll taste like rubber."

Mr. Bhowmick laid the trousers of a two-trouser suit he had bought on sale 15
that winter against his favorite tweed jacket. The navy stripes in the trousers and the small, navy tweed flecks in the jacket looked quite good together. So what if the Chief Engineer had already started wearing summer cottons?

"I am coming, I am coming," he shouted back. "You want me to eat hot-hot, you start the frying only when I am sitting down. You didn't learn anything from Mother in Ranchi?"

"Mother cooked French toast from fancy recipes? I mean French Sandwich Toast with complicated filling?"

He came into the room to give her his testiest look. "You don't know the meaning of complicated cookery. And mother had to get the coal fire of the *chula* going first."

His daughter was already at the table. "Why don't you break down and buy her a microwave oven? That's what I mean about sitting down and talking things out." She had finished her orange juice. She took a plastic measure of Slim-Fast out of its can and poured the powder into a glass of skim milk. "It's ridiculous."

Babli was not the child he would have chosen as his only heir. She was brighter cer- 20
tainly than the sons and daughters of the other Bengalis he knew in Detroit, and she had been the only female student in most of her classes at Georgia Tech, but as she sat there in her beige linen business suit, her thick chin dropping into a polkadotted cravat, he regretted again that she was not the child of his dreams. Babli would be able to help him out moneywise if something happened to him, something so bad that even his pension plans and his insurance policies and his money market schemes wouldn't be enough. But Babli could never comfort him. She wasn't womanly or tender the way that unmarried girls had been in the wistful days of his adolescence. She could sing Hindi film songs, mimicking exactly the high, artificial voice of Lata Mungeshkar, and she had taken two years of dance lessons at Sona Devi's Dance Academy in Southfield, but these accomplishments didn't add up to real femininity. Not the kind that had given him palpitations in Ranchi.

Mr. Bhowmick did his best with his wife's French toast. In spite of its filling of marshmallows, apricot jam and maple syrup, it tasted rubbery. He drank two cups of Darjeeling tea, said, "Well, I'm off," and took off.

All might have gone well if Mr. Bhowmick hadn't fussed longer than usual about putting his briefcase and his trenchcoat in the backseat. He got in behind the wheel of his Oldsmobile, fixed his seatbelt and was just about to turn the key in the ignition when his neighbor, Al Stazniak, who was starting up his Buick Skylark, sneezed. A sneeze at the start of a journey brings bad luck. Al Stazniak's sneeze was fierce, made up of five short bursts, too loud to be ignored.

---

[1]A character from *Hill Street Blues*, a popular television program in the 1980s, who began each episode telling his officers, "Be careful out there."

Be careful out there! Mr. Bhowmick could see the goddess's scarlet little tongue tip wagging at him.

He was a modern man, an intelligent man. Otherwise he couldn't have had the options in life that he did have. He couldn't have given up a good job with perks in Bombay and found a better job with General Motors in Detroit. But Mr. Bhowmick was also a prudent enough man to know that some abiding truth lies bunkered within each wanton Hindu superstition. A sneeze was more than a sneeze. The heedless are carried off in ambulances. He had choices to make. He could ignore the sneeze, and so challenge the world unseen by men. Perhaps Al Stazniak had hay fever. For a sneeze to be a potent omen, surely it had to be unprovoked and terrifying, a thunderclap cleaving the summer skies. Or he could admit the smallness of mortals, undo the fate of the universe by starting over, and go back inside the apartment, sit for a second on the sofa, then re-start his trip.

Al Stazniak rolled down his window. "Everything okay?" 25

Mr. Bhowmick nodded shyly. They weren't really friends in the way neighbors can sometimes be. They talked as they parked or pulled out of their adjacent parking stalls. For all Mr. Bhowmick knew, Al Stazniak had no legs. He had never seen the man out of his Skylark.

He let the Buick back out first. Everything was okay, yes, please. All the same he undid his seatbelt. Compromise, adaptability, call it what you will. A dozen times a day he made these small trade-offs between new-world reasonableness and old-world beliefs.

While he was sitting in his parked car, his wife's ride came by. For fifty dollars a month, she was picked up and dropped off by a hard up, newly divorced woman who worked at a florist's shop in the same mall. His wife came out the front door in brown K-Mart pants and a burgundy windbreaker. She waved to him, then slipped into the passenger seat of the florist's rusty Japanese car.

He was a metallurgist. He knew about rust and ways of preventing it, secret ways, thus far unknown to the Japanese.

Babli's fiery red Mitsubishi was still in the lot. She wouldn't leave for work for 30
another eight minutes. He didn't want her to know he'd been undone by a sneeze. Babli wasn't tolerant of superstitions. She played New Wave music in her tapedeck. If asked about Hinduism, all she'd ever said to her American friends was that "it's neat." Mr. Bhowmick had heard her on the phone years before. The cosmos balanced on the head of a snake was like a beachball balanced on the snout of a circus seal. "This Hindu myth stuff," he'd heard her say, "is like a series of super graphics."

He'd forgiven her. He could probably forgive her anything. It was her way of surviving high school in a city that was both native to her, and alien.

There was no question of going back where he'd come from. He hated Ranchi. Ranchi was no place for dreamers. All through his teenage years, Mr. Bhowmick had dreamed of success abroad. What form that success would take he had left vague. Success had meant to him escape from the constant plotting and bitterness that wore out India's middle class.

Babli should have come out of the apartment and driven off to work by now. Mr. Bhowmick decided to take a risk, to dash inside and pretend he'd left his briefcase on the coffee table.

When he entered the living room, he noticed Babli's spring coat and large vinyl pocketbook on the sofa. She was probably sorting through the junk jewelry on her dresser to give her business suit a lift. She read hints about dressing in women's magazines and applied them to her person with seriousness. If his luck held, he could sit on the sofa, say a quick prayer and get back to the car without her catching on.

It surprised him that she didn't shout out from her bedroom, "Who's there?" 35
What if he had been a rapist?

Then he heard Babli in the bathroom. He heard unladylike squawking noises. She was throwing up. A squawk, a spitting, then the horrible gurgle of a waterfall.

A revelation came to Mr. Bhowmick. A woman vomiting in the privacy of the bathroom could mean many things. She was coming down with the flu. She was nervous about a meeting. But Mr. Bhowmick knew at once that his daughter, his untender, unloving daughter whom he couldn't love and hadn't tried to love, was not, in the larger world of Detroit, unloved. Sinners are everywhere, even in the bosom of an upright, unambitious family like the Bhowmicks. It was the goddess sticking out her tongue at him.

The father sat heavily on the sofa, shrinking from contact with her coat and pocketbook. His brisk, bright engineer daughter was pregnant. Someone had taken time to make love to her. Someone had thought her tender, feminine. Someone even now was perhaps mooning over her. The idea excited him. It was so grotesque and wondrous. At twenty-six Babli had found the man of her dreams; whereas at twenty-six Mr. Bhowmick had given up on truth, beauty and poetry and exchanged them for two years at Carnegie Tech.

Mr. Bhowmick's tweed-jacketed body sagged against the sofa cushions. Babli would abort, of course. He knew his Babli. It was the only possible option if she didn't want to bring shame to the Bhowmick family. All the same, he could see a chubby baby boy on the rug, crawling to his granddaddy. Shame like that was easier to hide in Ranchi. There was always a barren womb sanctified by marriage that could claim sudden fructifying by the goddess Parvati. Babli would do what she wanted. She was headstrong and independent and he was afraid of her.

Babli staggered out of the bathroom. Damp stains ruined her linen suit. It 40
was the first time he had seen his daughter look ridiculous, quite unprofessional. She didn't come into the living room to investigate the noises he'd made. He glimpsed her shoeless stockinged feet flip-flop on collapsed arches down the hall to her bedroom.

"Are you all right?" Mr. Bhowmick asked, standing in the hall. "Do you need Sinutab?"

She wheeled around. "What're you doing here?"

He was the one who should be angry. "I'm feeling poorly too," he said. "I'm taking the day off."

"I feel fine," Babli said.

Within fifteen minutes Babli had changed her clothes and left. Mr. Bhowmick 45
had the apartment to himself all day. All day for praising or cursing the life that had brought him along with its other surprises an illegitimate grandchild.

It was his wife that he blamed. Coming to America to live had been his wife's idea. After the wedding, the young Bhowmicks had spent two years in Pittsburgh on his student visa, then gone back home to Ranchi for nine years. Nine crushing years. Then the job in Bombay had come through. All during those nine years his wife had screamed and wept. She was a woman of wild, progressive ideas—she'd called them her "American" ideas—and she'd been martyred by her neighbors for them. American *memsahib. Markin mem, Markin mem.* In bazaars the beggar boys had trailed her and hooted. She'd done provocative things. She'd hired a *chamar* woman who by caste rules was forbidden to cook for higher caste families, especially for widowed mothers of decent men. This had caused a blowup in the neighborhood. She'd made other, lesser errors. While other wives shopped and cooked every day, his wife had cooked the whole week's menu on weekends.

"What's the point of having a refrigerator, then?" She'd been scornful of the Ranchi women.

His mother, an old-fashioned widow, had accused her of trying to kill her by poisoning. "You are in such a hurry? You want to get rid of me quick-quick so you can go back to the States?"

Family life had been turbulent.

50 He had kept aloof, inwardly siding with his mother. He did not love his wife now, and he had not loved her then. In any case, he had not defended her. He felt some affection, and he felt guilty for having shunned her during those unhappy years. But he had thought of it then as revenge. He had wanted to marry a beautiful woman. Not being a young man of means, only a young man with prospects, he had had no right to yearn for pure beauty. He cursed his fate and after a while, settled for a barrister's daughter, a plain girl with a wide, flat plank of a body and myopic eyes. The barrister had sweetened the deal by throwing in an all-expenses-paid two years' study at Carnegie Tech to which Mr. Bhowmick had been admitted. Those two years had changed his wife from pliant girl to ambitious woman. She wanted America, nothing less.

It was his wife who had forced him to apply for permanent resident status in the U.S. even though he had a good job in Ranchi as a government engineer. The putting together of documents for the immigrant visa had been a long and humbling process. He had had to explain to a chilly clerk in the Embassy that, like most Indians of his generation, he had no birth certificate. He had to swear out affidavits, suffer through police checks, bribe orderlies whose job it was to move his dossier from desk to desk. The decision, the clerk had advised him, would take months, maybe years. He hadn't dared hope that merit might be rewarded. Merit could collapse under bad luck. It was for grace that he prayed.

While the immigration papers were being processed, he had found the job in Bombay. So he'd moved his mother in with his younger brother's family, and left his hometown for good. Life in Bombay had been lighthearted, almost fulfilling. His wife had thrown herself into charity work with the same energy that had offended the Ranchi women. He was happy to be in a big city at last. Bombay was the Rio de Janeiro of the East; he'd read that in a travel brochure. He drove out to Nariman Point at least once a week to admire the necklace of municipal lights, toss coconut shells into the dark ocean, drink beer at the Oberoi-Sheraton where overseas Indian girls in designer jeans beckoned him in sly ways. His nights were full. He played duplicate bridge, went to the movies, took his wife to Bingo nights at his club. In Detroit he was a lonelier man.

Then the green card had come through. For him, for his wife, and for the daughter who had been born to them in Bombay. He sold what he could sell, and put in his brother's informal trust what he couldn't to save on taxes. Then he had left for America, and one more start.

All through the week, Mr. Bhowmick watched his daughter. He kept furtive notes on how many times she rushed to the bathroom and made hawking, wrenching noises, how many times she stayed late at the office, calling her mother to say she'd be taking in a movie and pizza afterwards with friends.

He had to tell her that he knew. And he probably didn't have much time. She 55
shouldn't be on Slim-Fast in her condition. He had to talk things over with her. But what would he say to her? What position could he take? He had to choose between public shame for the family, and murder.

For three more weeks he watched her and kept his silence. Babli wore shifts to the office instead of business suits, and he liked her better in those garments. Perhaps she was dressing for her young man, not from necessity. Her skin was pale and blotchy by turn. At breakfast her fingers looked stiff, and she had trouble with silverware.

Two Saturdays running, he lost badly at duplicate bridge. His wife scolded him. He had made silly mistakes. When was Babli meeting this man? Where? He must be American; Mr. Bhowmick prayed only that he was white. He pictured his grandson crawling to him, and the grandson was always fat and brown and buttery-skinned, like the infant Krishna. An American son-in-law was a terrifying notion. Why was she not mentioning men, at least, preparing the way for the major announcement? He listened sharply for men's names, rehearsed little lines like, "Hello, Bob, I'm Babli's old man," with a cracked little laugh. Bob, Jack, Jimmy, Tom. But no names surfaced. When she went out for pizza and a movie it was with the familiar set of Indian girls and their strange, unpopular, American friends, all without men. Mr. Bhowmick tried to be reasonable. Maybe she had already gotten married and was keeping it secret. "Well, Bob, you and Babli sure had Mrs. Bhowmick and me going there, heh-heh," he mumbled one night with the Sahas and Ghosals, over cards. "Pardon?" asked Pronob Saha. Mr. Bhowmick dropped two tricks, and his wife glared. "Such stupid blunders," she fumed on the drive back. A new truth was dawning; there would be no marriage for Babli. Her young man probably was not so young and not so available. He must be already married. She must have yielded to passion or been raped in the office. His wife seemed to have noticed nothing. Was he a murderer, or a conspirator? He kept his secret from his wife; his daughter kept her decision to herself.

Nights, Mr. Bhowmick pretended to sleep, but as soon as his wife began her snoring—not real snores so much as loud, gaspy gulpings for breath—he turned on his side and prayed to Kali-Mata.

In July, when Babli's belly had begun to push up against the waistless dresses she'd bought herself, Mr. Bhowmick came out of the shower one weekday morning and found the two women screaming at each other. His wife had a rolling pin in one hand. His daughter held up a *National Geographic* as a shield for her head. The crazy look that had been in his wife's eyes when she'd shooed away beggar kids was in her eyes again.

"Stop it!" His own boldness overwhelmed him. "Shut up! Babli's pregnant, so 60
what? It's your fault, you made us come to the States."

Girls like Babli were caught between rules, that's the point he wished to make. They were too smart, too impulsive for a backward place like Ranchi, but not tough nor smart enough for sex-crazy places like Detroit.

"My fault?" his wife cried. "I told her to do hanky-panky with boys? I told her to shame us like this?"

She got in one blow with the rolling pin. The second glanced off Babli's shoulder and fell on his arm which he had stuck out for his grandson's sake.

"I'm calling the police," Babli shouted. She was out of the rolling pin's range. "This is brutality. You can't do this to me." "This is brutality. You can't do this to me."

"Shut up! Shut your mouth, foolish woman." He wrenched the weapon from his wife's fist. He made a show of taking off his shoe to beat his wife on the face.

"What do you know? You don't know anything." She let herself down slowly on a dining chair. Her hair, curled overnight, stood in wild whorls around her head. "Nothing."

"And you do!" He laughed. He remembered her tormentors, and laughed again. He had begun to enjoy himself. Now *he* was the one with the crazy, progressive ideas.

"Your daughter is pregnant, yes," she said, "any fool knows that. But ask her the name of the father. Go, ask."

He stared at his daughter who gazed straight ahead, eyes burning with hate, jaw clenched with fury.

"Babli?"

"Who needs a man?" she hissed. "The father of my baby is a bottle and a syringe. Men louse up your lives. I just want a baby. Oh, don't worry—he's a certified fit donor. No diseases, college graduate, above average, and he made the easiest twenty-five dollars of his life—"

"Like animals," his wife said. For the first time he heard horror in her voice. His daughter grinned at him. He saw her tongue, thick and red, squirming behind her row of perfect teeth.

"Yes, yes, yes," she screamed, "like livestock. Just like animals. You should be happy—that's what marriage is all about, isn't it? Matching bloodlines, matching horoscopes, matching castes, matching, matching, matching..." and it was difficult to know if she was laughing or singing, or mocking and like a madwoman.

Mr. Bhowmick lifted the rolling pin high above his head and brought it down hard on the dome of Babli's stomach. In the end, it was his wife who called the police.

(1985)

Questions for Discussion and Writing

1. What kind of person is the father in this story? What details in the story reveal his character? How does his religion cause trouble in the family?
2. What kind of person is the mother? How is her character revealed?
3. What do we know about the grown daughter, Babli? How do you respond to her character?
4. How does the father regard his wife? How does he feel about his daughter? Do you think he has good reason to react this way?
5. Why does it seem unlikely that the events in this story would have happened if the family had remained in India?

Octavia E. Butler 1947–2006

Reared by her hardworking mother after her father died, Olivia Butler began writing while still a child. "I began with horse stories," she says, "because I was crazy over horses, even though I never got near one." She worked at a number of blue-collar jobs to earn her way through college. In 1969 she joined the Screen Writers' Guild Open Door Program, where she studied with Harlan Ellison. After five years, her stories began to be published. She won a MacArthur Foundation "genius" grant in 1995, the first one given to a writer of science fiction. "Writers use everything," she declares. "If it doesn't kill you, you probably wind up using it in your writing."

Speech Sounds

There was trouble aboard the Washington Boulevard bus. Rye had expected trouble sooner or later in her journey. She had put off going until loneliness and hopelessness drove her out. She believed she might have one group of relatives left alive—a brother and his two children twenty miles away in Pasadena. That was a day's journey one-way, if she were lucky. The unexpected arrival of the bus as she left her Virginia Road home had seemed to be a piece of luck—until the trouble began.

Two young men were involved in a disagreement of some kind, or, more likely, a misunderstanding. They stood in the aisle, grunting and gesturing at each other, each in his own uncertain T stance as the bus lurched over the potholes. The driver seemed to be putting some effort into keeping them off balance. Still, their gestures stopped just short of contact—mock punches, hand games of intimidation to replace lost curses.

People watched the pair, then looked at one another and made small anxious sounds. Two children whimpered.

Rye sat a few feet behind the disputants and across from the back door. She watched the two carefully, knowing the fight would begin when someone's nerve broke or someone's hand slipped or someone came to the end of his limited ability to communicate. These things could happen anytime.

One of them happened as the bus hit an especially large pothole and one 5
man, tall, thin, and sneering, was thrown into his shorter opponent.

Instantly, the shorter man drove his left fist into the disintegrating sneer. He hammered his larger opponent as though he neither had nor needed any weapon other than his left fist. He hit quickly enough, hard enough to batter his opponent down before the taller man could regain his balance or hit back even once.

People screamed or squawked in fear. Those nearby scrambled to get out of the way. Three more young men roared in excitement and gestured wildly. Then, somehow, a second dispute broke out between two of these three—probably because one inadvertently touched or hit the other.

As the second fight scattered frightened passengers, a woman shook the driver's shoulder and grunted as she gestured toward the fighting.

The driver grunted back through bared teeth. Frightened, the woman drew away.

Rye, knowing the methods of bus drivers, braced herself and held on to 10
the crossbar of the seat in front of her. When the driver hit the brakes, she was ready and the combatants were not. They fell over seats and onto screaming passengers, creating even more confusion. At least one more fight started.

The instant the bus came to a full stop, Rye was on her feet, pushing the back door. At the second push, it opened and she jumped out, holding her pack in one arm. Several other passengers followed, but some stayed on the bus. Buses were so rare and irregular now, people rode when they could, no matter what. There might not be another bus today—or tomorrow. People started walking, and if they saw a bus they flagged it down. People making intercity trips like Rye's from Los Angeles to Pasadena made plans to camp out, or risked seeking shelter with locals who might rob or murder them.

The bus did not move, but Rye moved away from it. She intended to wait until the trouble was over and get on again, but if there was shooting, she wanted the protection of a tree. Thus, she was near the curb when a battered blue Ford on the other side of the street made a U-turn and pulled up in front of the bus. Cars were rare these days—as rare as a severe shortage of fuel and of relatively unimpaired mechanics could make them. Cars that still ran were as likely to be used as weapons as they were to serve as transportation. Thus, when the driver of the Ford beckoned to Rye, she moved away warily. The driver got out—a big man, young, neatly bearded with dark, thick hair. He wore a long overcoat and a look of wariness that matched Rye's. She stood several feet from him, waiting to see what he would do. He looked at the bus, now rocking with the combat inside, then at the small cluster of passengers who had gotten off. Finally he looked at Rye again.

She returned his gaze, very much aware of the old forty-five automatic her jacket concealed. She watched his hands.

He pointed with his left hand toward the bus. The dark-tinted windows prevented him from seeing what was happening inside.

His use of the left hand interested Rye more than his obvious question. Left- 15
handed people tended to be less impaired, more reasonable and comprehending, less driven by frustration, confusion, and anger.

She imitated his gesture, pointing toward the bus with her own left hand, then punching the air with both fists.

The man took off his coat, revealing a Los Angeles Police Department uniform complete with baton and service revolver.

Rye took another step back from him. There was no more LAPD, no more *any* large organization, governmental or private. There were neighborhood patrols and armed individuals. That was all.

The man took something from his coat pocket, then threw the coat into the car. Then he gestured Rye back, back toward the rear of the bus. He had something made of plastic in his hand. Rye did not understand what he wanted until he went to the rear door of the bus and beckoned her to stand there. She obeyed mainly out of curiosity. Cop or not, maybe he could do something to stop the stupid fighting.

He walked around the front of the bus, to the street side where the driver's 20
window was open. There, she thought she saw him throw something into the bus. She was still trying to peer through the tinted glass when people began stumbling out the rear door, choking and weeping. Gas.

Rye caught an old woman who would have fallen, lifted two little children down when they were in danger of being knocked down and trampled. She could see the bearded man helping people at the front door. She caught a thin old man shoved out by one of the combatants. Staggered by the old man's weight, she was barely able to get out of the way as the last of the young men pushed his way out. This one, bleeding from nose and mouth, stumbled into another, and they grappled blindly, still sobbing from the gas.

The bearded man helped the bus driver out through the front door, though the driver did not seem to appreciate his help. For a moment, Rye thought there would be another fight. The bearded man stepped back and watched the driver gesture threateningly, watched him shout in wordless anger.

The bearded man stood still, made no sound, refused to respond to clearly obscene gestures. The least impaired people tended to do this—stand back unless they were physically threatened and let those with less control scream and jump around. It was as though they felt it beneath them to be as touchy as the less comprehending. This was an attitude of superiority, and that was the way people like the bus driver perceived it. Such "superiority" was frequently punished by beatings, even by death. Rye had had close calls of her own. As a result, she never went unarmed. And in this world where the only likely common language was body language, being armed was often enough. She had rarely had to draw her gun or even display it.

The bearded man's revolver was on constant display. Apparently that was enough for the bus driver. The driver spat in disgust, glared at the bearded man for a moment longer, then strode back to his gas-filled bus. He stared at it for a moment, clearly wanting to get in, but the gas was still too strong. Of the windows, only his tiny driver's window actually opened. The front door was open, but the rear door would not stay open unless someone held it. Of course, the air conditioning had failed long ago. The bus would take some time to clear. It was the driver's property, his livelihood. He had pasted old magazine pictures of items he would accept as fare on its sides. Then he would use what he collected to feed his family or to trade. If his bus did not run, he did not eat. On the other hand, if the inside of his bus was torn apart by senseless fighting, he would not eat very well either. He was apparently unable to perceive this. All he could see was that it would be some time before he could use his bus again. He shook his fist at the bearded man and shouted. There seemed to be words in his shout, but Rye could not understand them. She did not know whether this was his fault or hers. She had heard so little coherent human speech for the past three years, she was no longer certain how well she recognized it, no longer certain of the degree of her own impairment.

The bearded man sighed. He glanced toward his car, then beckoned to Rye. 25
He was ready to leave, but he wanted something from her first. No. No, he wanted her to leave with him. Risk getting into his car when, in spite of his uniform, law and order were nothing—not even words any longer.

She shook her head in a universally understood negative, but the man continued to beckon.

She waved him away. He was doing what the less impaired rarely did—drawing potentially negative attention to another of his kind. People from the bus had begun to look at her.

One of the men who had been fighting tapped another on the arm, then pointed from the bearded man to Rye, and finally held up the first two fingers of his right hand as though giving two-thirds of a Boy Scout salute. The gesture was very quick, its meaning obvious even at a distance. She had been grouped with the bearded man. Now what?

The man who had made the gesture started toward her.

30 She had no idea what he intended, but she stood her ground. The man was half a foot taller than she was and perhaps ten years younger. She did not imagine she could outrun him. Nor did she expect anyone to help her if she needed help. The people around her were all strangers.

She gestured once—a clear indication to the man to stop. She did not intend to repeat the gesture. Fortunately, the man obeyed. He gestured obscenely and several other men laughed. Loss of verbal language had spawned a whole new set of obscene gestures. The man, with stark simplicity, had accused her of sex with the bearded man and had suggested she accommodate the other men present—beginning with him.

Rye watched him wearily. People might very well stand by and watch if he tried to rape her. They would also stand and watch her shoot him. Would he push things that far?

He did not. After a series of obscene gestures that brought him no closer to her, he turned contemptuously and walked away.

And the bearded man still waited. He had removed his service revolver, holster and all. He beckoned again, both hands empty. No doubt his gun was in the car and within easy reach, but his taking it off impressed her. Maybe he was all right. Maybe he was just alone. She had been alone herself for three years. The illness had stripped her, killing her children one by one, killing her husband, her sister, her parents.

35 The illness, if it was an illness, had cut even the living off from one another. As it swept over the country, people hardly had time to lay blame on the Soviets (though they were falling silent along with the rest of the world), on a new virus, a new pollutant, radiation, divine retribution. . . . The illness was stroke-swift in the way it cut people down and strokelike in some of its effects. But it was highly specific. Language was always lost or severely impaired. It was never regained. Often there was also paralysis, intellectual impairment, death.

Rye walked toward the bearded man, ignoring the whistling and applauding of two of the young men and their thumbs-up signs to the bearded man. If he had smiled at them or acknowledged them in any way, she would almost certainly have changed her mind. If she had let herself think of the possible deadly consequences of getting into a stranger's car, she would have changed her mind. Instead, she thought of the man who lived across the street from her. He rarely washed since his bout with the illness. And he had gotten into the habit of urinating wherever he happened to be. He had two women already—one tending each of his large gardens. They put up with him in exchange for his protection. He had made it clear that he wanted Rye to become his third woman.

She got into the car and the bearded man shut the door. She watched as he walked around to the driver's door—watched for his sake because his gun was on the seat beside her. And the bus driver and a pair of young men had come a few steps closer. They did nothing, though, until the bearded man was in the car. Then one of them threw a rock. Others followed his example, and as the car drove away, several rocks bounced off harmlessly.

When the bus was some distance behind them, Rye wiped sweat from her forehead and longed to relax. The bus would have taken her more than halfway to Pasadena. She would have had only ten miles to walk. She wondered how far she would have to walk now—and wondered if walking a long distance would be her only problem.

At Figuroa and Washington, where the bus normally made a left turn, the bearded man stopped, looked at her, and indicated that she should choose a direction. When she directed him left and he actually turned left, she began to relax. If he was willing to go where she directed, perhaps he was safe.

As they passed blocks of burned, abandoned buildings, empty lots, and wrecked 40
or stripped cars, he slipped a gold chain over his head and handed it to her. The pendant attached to it was a smooth, glassy, black rock. Obsidian. His name might be Rock or Peter or Black, but she decided to think of him as Obsidian. Even her sometimes useless memory would retain a name like Obsidian.

She handed him her own name symbol—a pin in the shape of a large golden stalk of wheat. She had bought it long before the illness and the silence began. Now she wore it, thinking it was as close as she was likely to come to Rye. People like Obsidian who had not known her before probably thought of her as Wheat. Not that it mattered. She would never hear her name spoken again.

Obsidian handed her pin back to her. He caught her hand as she reached for it and rubbed his thumb over her calluses.

He stopped at First Street and asked which way again. Then, after turning right as she had indicated, he parked near the Music Center. There, he took a folded paper from the dashboard and unfolded it. Rye recognized it as a street map, though the writing on it meant nothing to her. He flattened the map, took her hand again, and put her index finger on one spot. He touched her, touched himself, pointed toward the floor. In effect, "We are here." She knew he wanted to know where she was going. She wanted to tell him, but she shook her head sadly. She had lost reading and writing. That was her most serious impairment and her most painful. She had taught history at UCLA. She had done freelance writing. Now she could not even read her own manuscripts. She had a houseful of books that she could neither read nor bring herself to use as fuel. And she had a memory that would not bring back to her much of what she had read before.

She stared at the map, trying to calculate. She had been born in Pasadena, had lived for fifteen years in Los Angeles. Now she was near L.A. Civic Center. She knew the relative positions of the two cities, knew streets, directions, even knew to stay away from freeways, which might be blocked by wrecked cars and destroyed overpasses. She ought to know how to point out Pasadena even though she could not recognize the word.

Hesitantly, she placed her hand over a pale orange patch in the upper right 45
corner of the map. That should be right. Pasadena.

Obsidian lifted her hand and looked under it, then folded the map and put it back on the dashboard. He could read, she realized belatedly. He could probably write, too. Abruptly, she hated him—deep, bitter hatred. What did literacy mean to him—a grown man who played cops and robbers? But he was literate and she was not. She never would be. She felt sick to her stomach with hatred, frustration, and jealousy. And only a few inches from her hand was a loaded gun.

She held herself still, staring at him, almost seeing his blood. But her rage crested and ebbed and she did nothing.

Obsidian reached for her hand with hesitant familiarity. She looked at him. Her face had already revealed too much. No person still living in what was left of human society could fail to recognize that expression, that jealousy.

She closed her eyes wearily, drew a deep breath. She had experienced longing for the past, hatred of the present, growing hopelessness, purposelessness, but she had never experienced such a powerful urge to kill another person. She had left her home, finally, because she had come near to killing herself. She had found no reason to stay alive. Perhaps that was why she had gotten into Obsidian's car. She had never before done such a thing.

50 He touched her mouth and made chatter motions with thumb and fingers. Could she speak?

She nodded and watched his milder envy come and go. Now both had admited what it was not safe to admit, and there had been no violence. He tapped his mouth and forehead and shook his head. He did not speak or comprehend spoken language. The illness had played with them, taking away, she suspected, what each valued most.

She plucked at his sleeve, wondering why he had decided on his own to keep the LAPD alive with what he had left. He was sane enough otherwise. Why wasn't he at home raising corn, rabbits, and children? But she did not know how to ask. Then he put his hand on her thigh and she had another question to deal with.

She shook her head. Disease, pregnancy, helpless, solitary agony…no.

He massaged her thigh gently and smiled in obvious disbelief.

55 No one had touched her for three years. She had not wanted anyone to touch her. What kind of world was this to chance bringing a child into even if the father were willing to stay and help raise it? It was too bad, though. Obsidian could not know how attractive he was to her—young, probably younger than she was, clean, asking for what he wanted rather than demanding it. But none of that mattered. What were a few moments of pleasure measured against a lifetime of consequences?

He pulled her closer to him and for a moment she let herself enjoy the closeness. He smelled good—male and good. She pulled away reluctantly.

He sighed, reached toward the glove compartment. She stiffened, not knowing what to expect, but all he took out was a small box. The writing on it meant nothing to her. She did not understand until he broke the seal, opened the box, and took out a condom. He looked at her, and she first looked away in surprise. Then she giggled. She could not remember when she had last giggled.

He grinned, gestured toward the backseat, and she laughed aloud. Even in her teens, she had disliked backseats of cars. But she looked around at the empty streets and ruined buildings, then she got out and into the backseat. He let her put the condom on him, then seemed surprised at her eagerness.

Sometime later, they sat together, covered by his coat, unwilling to become clothed near strangers again just yet. He made rock-the-baby gestures and looked questioningly at her.

60 She swallowd, shook her head. She did not know how to tell him her children were dead.

He took her hand and drew a cross in it with his index finger, then made his baby-rocking gesture again.

She nodded, held up three fingers, then turned away, trying to shut out a sudden flood of memories. She had told herself that the children growing up now were to be pitied. They would run through the downtown canyons with no real memory of what the buildings had been or even how they had come to be. Today's children gathered books as well as wood to be burned as fuel. They ran through the streets chasing one another and hooting like chimpanzees. They had no future. They were now all they would ever be.

He put his hand on her shoulder, and she turned suddenly, fumbling for his small box, then urging him to make love to her again. He could give her forgetfulness and pleasure. Until now, nothing had been able to do that. Until now, every day had brought her closer to the time when she would do what she had left home to avoid doing: putting her gun in her mouth and pulling the trigger.

She asked Obsidian if he would come home with her, stay with her.

65 He looked surprised and pleased once he understood. But he did not answer at once. Finally, he shook his head as she had feared he might. He was probably having too much fun playing cops and robbers and picking up women.

She dressed in silent disappointment, unable to feel any anger toward him. Perhaps he already had a wife and a home. That was likely. The illness had been harder on men than on women—had killed more men, had left male survivors more severely impaired. Men like Obsidian were rare. Women either settled for less or stayed alone. If they found an Obsidian, they did what they could to keep him. Rye suspected he had someone younger, prettier, keeping him.

He touched her while she was strapping her gun on and asked with a complicated series of gestures whether it was loaded.

She nodded grimly.

He patted her arm.

70 She asked once more if he would come home with her, this time using a different series of gestures. He had seemed hesitant. Perhaps he could be courted.

He got out and into the front seat without responding.

She took her place in front again, watching him. Now he plucked at his uniform and looked at her. She thought she was being asked something but did not know what it was.

He took off his badge, tapped it with one finger, then tapped his chest. Of course.

She took the badge from his hand and pinned her wheat stalk to it. If playing cops and robbers was his only insanity let him play. She would take him, uniform and all. It occurred to her that she might eventually lose him to someone he would meet as he had met her. But she would have him for a while.

75 He took the street map down again, tapped it, pointed vaguely northeast toward Pasadena, then looked at her.

She shrugged, tapped his shoulder, then her own, and held up her index and second fingers tight together, just to be sure.

He grasped the two fingers and nodded. He was with her.

She took the map from him and threw it onto the dashboard. She pointed back southwest—back toward home. Now she did not have to go to Pasadena. Now she could go on having a brother there and two nephews—three right-handed males. Now she did not have to find out for certain whether she was as alone as she feared. Now she was not alone.

Obsidian took Hill Street south, then Washington west, and she leaned back, wondering what it would be like to have someone again. With what she had scavenged, what she had preserved, and what she grew, there was easily enough food for them. There was certainly room enough in a four-bedroom house. He could move his possessions in. Best of all, the animal across the street would pull back and possibly not force her to kill him.

Obsidian had drawn her closer to him, and she had put her head on his shoulder when suddenly he braked hard, almost throwing her off the seat. Out of the corner of her eye, she saw that someone had run across the street in front of the car. One car on the street and someone had to run in front of it.

Straightening up, Rye saw that the runner was a woman, fleeing from an old frame house to a boarded-up storefront. She ran silently, but the man who followed her a moment later shouted what sounded like garbled words as he ran. He had something in his hand. Not a gun. A knife, perhaps.

The woman tried a door, found it locked, looked around desperately, finally snatched up a fragment of glass broken from the storefront window. With this she turned to face her pursuer. Rye thought she would be more likely to cut her own hand than to hurt anyone else with the glass.

Obsidian jumped from the car, shouting. It was the first time Rye had heard his voice—deep and hoarse from disuse. He made the same sound over and over the way some speechless people did, "Da, da, da!"

Rye got out of the car as Obsidian ran toward the couple. He had drawn his gun. Fearful, she drew her own and released the safety. She looked around to see who else might be attracted to the scene. She saw the man glance at Obsidian, then suddenly lunge at the woman. The woman jabbed his face with her glass, but he caught her arm and managed to stab her twice before Obsidian shot him.

The man doubled, then toppled, clutching his abdomen. Obsidian shouted, then gestured Rye over to help the woman.

Rye moved to the woman's side, remembering that she had little more than bandages and antiseptic in her pack. But the woman was beyond help. She had been stabbed with a long, slender boning knife.

She touched Obsidian to let him know the woman was dead. He had bent to check the wounded man who lay still and also seemed dead. But as Obsidian looked around to see what Rye wanted, the man opened his eyes. Face contorted, he seized Obsidian's just-holstered revolver and fired. The bullet caught Obsidian in the temple and he collapsed.

It happened just that simply, just that fast. An instant later, Rye shot the wounded man as he was turning the gun on her.

And Rye was alone—with three corpses.

She knelt beside Obsidian, dry-eyed, frowning, trying to understand why everything had suddenly changed. Obsidian was gone. He had died and left her—like everyone else.

Two very small children came out of the house from which the man and woman had run—a boy and girl perhaps three years old. Holding hands, they crossed the street toward Rye. They started at her, then edged past her and went to the dead woman. The girl shook the woman's arm as though trying to wake her.

This was too much. Rye got up, feeling sick to her stomach with grief and anger. If the children began to cry, she thought she would vomit.

They were on their own, those two kids. They were old enough to scavenge. She did not need any more grief. She did not need a stranger's children who would grow up to be hairless chimps.

She went back to the car. She could drive home, at least. She remembered how to drive.

95 The thought that Obsidian should be buried occurred to her before she reached the car, and she did vomit.

She had found and lost the man so quickly. It was as though she had been snatched from comfort and security and given a sudden, inexplicable beating. Her head would not clear. She could not think.

Somehow, she made herself go back to him, look at him. She found herself on her knees beside him with no memory of having knelt. She stroked his face, his beard. One of the children made a noise and she looked at them, at the woman who was probably their mother. The children looked back at her, obviously frightened. Perhaps it was their fear that reached her finally.

She had been about to drive away and leave them. She had almost done it, almost left two toddlers to die. Surely there had been enough dying. She would have to take the children home with her. She would not be able to live with any other decision. She looked around for a place to bury three bodies. Or two. She wondered if the murderer were the children's father. Before the silence, the police had always said some of the most dangerous calls they went out on were domestic disturbance calls. Obsidian should have known that—not that the knowledge would have kept him in the car. It would not have held her back either. She could not have watched the woman murdered and done nothing.

She dragged Obsidian toward the car. She had nothing to dig with her, and no one to guard for her while she dug. Better to take the bodies with her and bury them next to her husband and her children. Obsidian would come home with her after all.

100 When she had gotten him onto the floor in the back, she returned for the woman. The little girl, thin, dirty, solemn, stood up and unknowingly gave Rye a gift. As Rye began to drag the woman by her arms, the little girl screamed, "No!"

Rye dropped the woman and stared at the girl.

"No!" the girl repeated. She came to stand beside the woman. "Go away!" she told Rye.

"Don't talk," the little boy said to her. There was no blurring or confusing of sounds. Both children had spoken and Rye had understood. The boy looked at the dead murderer and moved further from him. He took the girl's hand. "Be quiet," he whispered.

Fluent speech! Had the woman died because she could talk and had taught her children to talk? Had she been killed by a husband's festering anger or by a stranger's jealous rage? And the children . . . they must have been born after the silence. Had the disease run its course, then? Or were these children simply immune? Certainly they had had time to fall sick and silent. Rye's mind leaped ahead. What if children of three or fewer years were safe and able to learn language? What if all they needed were teachers? Teachers and protectors.

105 Rye glanced at the dead murderer. To her shame, she thought she could understand some of the passions that must have driven him, whomever he was. Anger, frustration, hopelessness, insane jealousy . . . how many more of him were there—people willing to destroy what they could not have?

Obsidian had been the protector, had chosen that role for who knew what reason. Perhaps putting on an obsolete uniform and patrolling the empty streets had been what he did instead of putting a gun into his mouth. And now that there was something worth protecting, he was gone.

She had been a teacher. A good one. She had been a protector, too, though only of herself. She had kept herself alive when she had no reason to live. If the illness let these children alone, she could keep them alive.

Somehow she lifted the dead woman into her arms and placed her on the backseat of the car. The children began to cry, but she knelt on the broken pavement and whispered to them, fearful of frightening them with the harshness of her long unused voice.

"It's all right," she told them. "You're going with us, too. Come on." She lifted them both, one in each arm. They were so light. Had they been getting enough to eat?

110 The boy covered her mouth with his hand, but she moved her face away. "It's all right for me to talk," she told him. "As long as no one's around, it's all right." She put the boy down on the front seat of the car and he moved over without being told to, to make room for the girl. When they were both in the car, Rye leaned against the window, looking at them, seeing that they were less afraid now, that they watched her with at least as much curiosity as fear.

"I'm Valerie Rye," she said, savoring the words. "It's all right for you to talk to me."

(1983)

Questions for Discussion and Writing

1. What details in the first two paragraphs let readers know that the story takes place in the future following some breakdown in society?
2. Write an essay explaining how the names *Rye* and *Obsidian* suit their characters' roles and personalities?
3. How does the children's ability to speak affect the ending?
4. What is the major claim of this cautionary tale?
5. Write an essay explaining how Butler conveys the importance of language and human speech in maintaining a civil society.

T. Coraghessan Boyle 1948–

T. Coraghessan Boyle, born Thomas John Boyle, changed his middle name at age seventeen and explains how to pronounce it: "It's Cor-AG-hessan, accent on second syllable. As you may know, this is an old Gaelic term meaning 'Take two and call me in the morning.' " He was a radically alienated teenager but made it to college, where he "wandered into a creative writing class" and discovered that "writing was what I could do." He says now that hearing others reading or performing his stories "gives me—the disaffected, misanthropic non-player—a rush of pure joy and connection: somebody else is singing my song. I'm happy."

The Love of My Life

They wore each other like a pair of socks. He was at her house, she was at his. Everywhere they went—to the mall, to the game, to movies and shops and the classes that structured their days like a new kind of chronology—their fingers were entwined, their shoulders touching, their hips joined in the slow triumphant sashay of love. He drove her car, slept on the couch in the family room at her parents' house, played tennis and watched football with her father on the big, thirty-six-inch TV in the kitchen. She went shopping with his mother and hers, a triumvirate of tastes, and she would have played tennis with his father, if it came to it, but his father was dead. "I love you," he told her, because he did, because there was no feeling like this, no triumph, no high—it was like being immortal and unconquerable, like floating. And a hundred times a day she said it, too: " I love you. I love you."

They were together at his house one night when the rain froze on the streets and sheathed the trees in glass. It was her idea to take a walk and feel it in their hair and on the glistening shoulders of their parkas, an other-worldly drumming of pellets flung down out of the troposphere, alien and familiar at the same time, and they glided the length of the front walk and watched the way the power lines bellied and swayed. He built a fire when they got back, while she towelled her hair and made hot chocolate laced with Jack Daniel's. They'd rented a pair of slasher movies for the ritualized comfort of them—"Teens have sex," he said, "and then they pay for it in body parts"—and the maniac had just climbed out of the heating vent, with a meat hook dangling from the recesses of his empty sleeve, when the phone rang.

It was his mother, calling from the hotel room in Boston where she was curled up—shacked up?—for the weekend with the man she'd been dating. He tried to picture her, but he couldn't. He even closed his eyes a minute, to concentrate, but there was nothing there. Was everything all right? she wanted to know. With the storm and all? No, it hadn't hit Boston yet, but she saw on the Weather Channel that it was on its way. Two seconds after he hung up—before she could even hit the Start button on the VCR—the phone rang again, and this time it was her mother. Her mother had been drinking. She was calling from the restaurant, and China could hear a clamor of voices in the background. "Just stay put," her mother shouted into the phone. "The streets are like a skating rink. Don't you even think of getting in that car."

Well, she wasn't thinking of it. She was thinking of having Jeremy to herself, all night, in the big bed in his mother's room. They'd been having sex ever since they started going together at the end of their junior year, but it was always sex in the car or sex on a blanket or the lawn, hurried sex, nothing like she wanted it to be. She kept thinking of the way it was in the movies, where the stars ambushed each other on beds the size of small planets and then did it again and again until they lay nestled in a heap of pillows and blankets, her head on his chest, his arm flung over her shoulder, the music fading away to individual notes plucked softly on a guitar and everything in the frame glowing as if it had been sprayed with liquid gold. That was how it was supposed to be. That was how it was going to be. At least for tonight.

She'd been wandering around the kitchen as she talked, dancing with the 5
phone in an idle slow saraband, watching the frost sketch a design on the window over the sink, no sound but the soft hiss of the ice pellets on the roof, and now she

pulled open the freezer door and extracted a pint box of ice cream. She was in her socks, socks so thick they were like slippers, and a pair of black leggings under an oversize sweater. Beneath her feet, the polished floorboards were as slick as the sidewalk outside, and she liked the feel of that, skating indoors in her big socks. "Uh-huh," she said into the phone. "Uh-huh. Yeah, we're watching a movie." She dug a finger into the ice cream and stuck it in her mouth.

"Come on," Jeremy called from the living room, where the maniac rippled menacingly over the Pause button. "You're going to miss the best part."

"O.K., Mom, O.K.," she said into the phone, parting words, and then she hung up. "You want ice cream?" she called, licking her finger.

Jeremy's voice came back at her, a voice in the middle range, with a congenital scratch in it, the voice of a nice guy, a very nice guy who could be the star of a TV show about nice guys: "What kind?" He had a pair of shoulders and pumped-up biceps, too, a smile that jumped from his lips to his eyes, and close-cropped hair that stood up straight off the crown of his head. And he was always singing—she loved that—his voice so true he could do any song, and there was no lyric he didn't know, even on the oldies station. She scooped ice cream and saw him in a scene from last summer, one hand draped casually over the wheel of his car, the radio throbbing, his voice raised in perfect synch with Billy Corgan's, and the night standing still at the end of a long dark street overhung with maples.

"Chocolate. Swiss-chocolate almond."

"O.K.," he said, and then he was wondering if there was any whipped cream, 10
or maybe hot fudge—he was sure his mother had a jar stashed away somewhere, *Look behind the mayonnaise on the top row*—and when she turned around he was standing in the doorway.

She kissed him—they kissed whenever they met, no matter where or when, even if one of them had just stepped out of the room, because that was love, that was the way love was—and then they took two bowls of ice cream into the living room and, with a flick of the remote, set the maniac back in motion.

It was an early spring that year, the world gone green overnight, the thermometer twice hitting the low eighties in the first week of March. Teachers were holding sessions outside. The whole school, even the halls and the cafeteria, smelled of fresh-mowed grass and the unfolding blossoms of the fruit trees in the development across the street, and students—especially seniors—were cutting class to go out to the quarry or the reservoir or to just drive the backstreets with the sunroof and the windows open wide. But not China. She was hitting the books, studying late, putting everything in its place like pegs in a board, even love, even that. Jeremy didn't get it. "Look, you've already been accepted at your first-choice school, you're going to wind up in the top ten G.P.A.-wise, and you've got four years of tests and term papers ahead of you, and grad school after that. You'll only be a high-school senior once in your life. Relax. Enjoy it. Or at least *experience* it."

He'd been accepted at Brown, his father's alma mater, and his own G.P.A. would put him in the top ten percent of their graduating class, and he was content with that, skating through his final semester, no math, no science, taking art and music, the things he'd always wanted to take but never had time for—and Lit., of course, A.P. History, and Spanish 5. "*Tú eres el amor de mi vida*," he would tell her when they met at her locker or at lunch or when he picked her up for a movie on Saturday nights.

"*Y tú también*," she would say, "or is it '*yo también*'?"—French was her language. "But I keep telling you it really matters to me, because I know I'll never catch Margery Yu or Christian Davenport, I mean they're a lock for val and salut, but it'll kill me if people like Kerry Sharp or Jalapy Seegrand finish ahead of me—you should know that, you of all people—"

15 It amazed him that she actually brought her books along when they went backpacking over spring break. They'd planned the trip all winter and through the long wind tunnel that was February, packing away freeze-dried entrées, PowerBars, Gore-Tex windbreakers, and matching sweatshirts, weighing each item on a handheld scale with a dangling hook at the bottom of it. They were going up into the Catskills, to a lake he'd found on a map, and they were going to be together, without interruption, without telephones, automobiles, parents, teachers, friends, relatives, and pets, for five full days. They were going to cook over an open fire, they were going to read to each other and burrow into the double sleeping bag with the connubial zipper up the seam he'd found in his mother's closet, a relic of her own time in the lap of nature. It smelled of her, of his mother, a vague scent of her perfume that had lingered there dormant all these years, and maybe there was the faintest whiff of his father, too, though his father had been gone so long he didn't even remember what he looked like, let alone what he might have smelled like. Five days. And it wasn't going to rain, not a drop. He didn't even bring his fishing rod, and that was love.

When the last bell rang down the curtain on Honors Math, Jeremy was waiting at the curb in his mother's Volvo station wagon, grinning up at China through the windshield while the rest of the school swept past with no thought for anything but release. There were shouts and curses, T-shirts in motion, slashing legs, horns bleating from the seniors' lot, the school buses lined up like armored vehicles awaiting the invasion—chaos, sweet chaos—and she stood there a moment to savor it. "Your mother's car?" she said, slipping in beside him and laying both arms over his shoulders to pull him to her for a kiss. He'd brought her jeans and hiking boots along, and she was going to change as they drove, no need to go home, no more circumvention and delay, a stop at McDonald's, maybe, or Burger King, and then it was the sun and the wind and the moon and the stars. Five days. Five whole days.

"Yeah," he said, in answer to her question, "my mother said she didn't want to have to worry about us breaking down in the middle of nowhere—"

"So she's got your car? She's going to sell real estate in your car?"

He just shrugged and smiled. "Free at last," he said, pitching his voice down low till it was exactly like Martin Luther King's. "Thank God Almighty, we are free at last."

20 It was dark by the time they got to the trailhead, and they wound up camping just off the road in a rocky tumble of brush, no place on earth less likely or less comfortable, but they were together, and they held each other through the damp whispering hours of the night and hardly slept at all. They made the lake by noon the next day, the trees just coming into leaf, the air sweet with the smell of the sun in the pines. She insisted on setting up the tent, just in case—it could rain, you never knew—but all he wanted to do was stretch out on a gray neoprene pad and feel the sun on his face. Eventually, they both fell asleep in the sun, and when they woke they made love right there, beneath the trees, and with the wide blue expanse of the lake giving back the blue of the sky. For dinner, it was étouffée and rice, out of the foil pouch, washed down with hot chocolate and a few squirts of red wine from Jeremy's bota bag.

The next day, the whole day through, they didn't bother with clothes at all. They couldn't swim, of course—the lake was too cold for that—but they could bask and explore and feel the breeze out of the south on their bare legs and the places where no breeze had touched before. She would remember that always, the feel of that, the intensity of her motions, the simple unrefined pleasure of living in the moment. Wood smoke. Duelling flashlights in the night. The look on Jeremy's face when he presented her with the bag of finger-size crayfish he'd spent all morning collecting.

What else? The rain, of course. It came midway through the third day, clouds the color of iron filings, the lake hammered to iron, too, and the storm that crashed through the trees and beat at their tent with a thousand angry fists. They huddled in the sleeping bag, sharing the wine and a bag of trail mix, reading to each other from a book of Donne's love poems (she was writing a paper for Mrs. Masterson called "Ocular Imagery in the Poetry of John Donne") and the last third of a vampire novel that weighed eighteen-point-one ounces.

And the sex. They were careful, always careful—*I will never, never be like those breeders that bring their puffed-up squalling little red-faced babies to class*, she told him, and he agreed, got adamant about it, even, until it became a running theme in their relationship, the breeders overpopulating an overpopulated world and ruining their own lives in the process—but she had forgotten to pack her pills and he had only two condoms with him, and it wasn't as if there were a drug-store around the corner.

In the fall—or the end of August, actually—they packed their cars separately and left for college, he to Providence and she to Binghamton. They were separated by three hundred miles, but there was the telephone, there was e-mail, and for the first month or so there were Saturday nights in a motel in Danbury, but that was a haul, it really was, and they both agreed that they should focus on their course work and cut back to every second or maybe third week. On the day they'd left—and no, she didn't want her parents driving her up there, she was an adult and she could take care of herself—Jeremy followed her as far as the Bear Mountain Bridge and they pulled off the road and held each other till the sun fell down into the trees. She had a poem for him, a Donne poem, the saddest thing he'd ever heard. It was something about the moon. *More than moon*, that was it, lovers parting and their tears swelling like an ocean till the girl—the woman, the female—had more power to raise the tides than the moon itself, or some such. More than moon. That's what he called her after that, because she was white and round and getting rounder, and it was no joke, and it was no term of endearment.

She was pregnant. Pregnant, they figured, since the camping trip, and it was 25
their secret, a new constant in their lives, a fact, an inescapable fact that never varied no matter how many home-pregnancy kits they went through. Baggy clothes, that was the key, all in black, cargo pants, flowing dresses, a jacket even in summer. They went to a store in the city where nobody knew them and she got a girdle, and then she went away to school in Binghamton and he went to Providence. "You've got to get rid of it," he told her in the motel room that had become a prison. "Go to a clinic," he told her for the hundredth time, and outside it was raining—or, no, it was clear and cold that night, a foretaste of winter. "I'll find the money—you know I will."

She wouldn't respond. Wouldn't even look at him. One of the *Star Wars* movies was on TV, great flat thundering planes of metal roaring across the screen, and she was just sitting there on the edge of the bed, her shoulders hunched and hair hanging limp. Someone slammed a car door—two doors in rapid succession—and a child's voice shouted, "Me! Me first!"

"China," he said. "Are you listening to me?"

"I can't," she murmured, and she was talking to her lap, to the bed, to the floor. "I'm scared. I'm so scared." There were footsteps in the room next door, ponderous and heavy, then the quick tattoo of the child's feet and a sudden thump against the wall. "I don't want anyone to know," she said.

He could have held her, could have squeezed in beside her and wrapped her in his arms, but something flared in him. He couldn't understand it. He just couldn't. "What are you thinking? Nobody'll know. He's a doctor, for Christ's sake, sworn to secrecy, the doctor-patient compact and all that. What are you going to do, keep it? Huh? Just show up for English 101 with a baby on your lap and say, 'Hi, I'm the Virgin Mary'?"

She was crying. He could see it in the way her shoulders suddenly crumpled 30
and now he could hear it, too, a soft nasal complaint that went right through him. She lifted her face to him and held out her arms and he was there beside her, rocking her back and forth in his arms. He could feel the heat of her face against the hard fibre of his chest, a wetness there, fluids, her fluids. "I don't want a doctor," she said.

And that colored everything, that simple negative: life in the dorms, roommates, bars, bullshit sessions, the smell of burning leaves and the way the light fell across campus in great wide smoking bands just before dinner, the unofficial skateboard club, films, lectures, pep rallies, football—none of it mattered. He couldn't have a life. Couldn't be a freshman. Couldn't wake up in the morning and tumble into the slow steady current of the world. All he could think of was her. Or not simply her—her and him, and what had come between them. Because they argued now, they wrangled and fought and debated, and it was no pleasure to see her in that motel room with the queen-size bed and the big color TV and the soaps and shampoos they made off with as if they were treasure. She was pig-headed, stubborn, irrational. She was spoiled, he could see that now, spoiled by her parents and their standard of living and the socioeconomic expectations of her class—of his class—and the promise of life as you like it, an unscrolling vista of pleasure and acquistion. He loved her. He didn't want to turn his back on her. He would be there for her no matter what, but why did she have to be so stupid?

Big sweats, huge sweats, sweats that drowned and engulfed her, that was her campus life, sweats and the dining hall. Her dorm mates didn't know her, and so what if she was putting on weight? Everybody did. How could you shovel down all those carbohydrates, all that sugar and grease and the puddings and nachos and all the rest, without putting on ten or fifteen pounds the first semester alone? Half the girls in the dorm were waddling around like the Doughboy, their faces bloated and blotched with acne, with crusting pimples and whiteheads fed on fat. So she was putting on weight. Big deal. "There's more of me to love," she told her roommate, "and Jeremy likes it that way. And, really, he's the only one that matters." She was careful to shower alone, in the early morning, long before the light had begun to bump up against the windows.

On the night her water broke—it was mid-December, almost nine months, as best as she could figure—it was raining. Raining hard. All week she'd been having tense rasping sotto-voce debates with Jeremy on the phone—arguments, fights—and she told him that she would die, creep out into the woods like some animal and bleed to death, before she'd go to a hospital. "And what am I supposed to do?" he demanded in a high childish whine, as if he were the one who'd been knocked up, and she didn't want to hear it, she didn't.

"Do you love me?" she whispered. There was a long hesitation, a pause you could have poured all the affirmation of the world into.

35 "Yes," he said finally, his voice so soft and reluctant it was like the last gasp of a dying old man.

"Then you're going to have to rent the motel."

"And then what?"

"Then—I don't know." The door was open, her roommate framed there in the hall, a burst of rock and roll coming at her like an assault. "I guess you'll have to get a book or something."

By eight, the rain had turned to ice and every branch of every tree was coated with it, the highway littered with glistening black sticks, no moon, no stars, the tires sliding out from under her, and she felt heavy, big as a sumo wrestler, heavy and loose at the same time. She'd taken a towel from the dorm and put it under her, on the seat, but it was a mess, everything was a mess. She was cramping. Fidgeting with her hair. She tried the radio, but it was no help, nothing but songs she hated, singers that were worse. Twenty-two miles to Danbury and the first of the contractions came like a seizure, like a knife blade thrust into her spine. Her world narrowed to what the headlights would show her.

40 Jeremy was waiting for her at the door to the room, the light behind him a pale rinse of nothing, no smile on his face, no human expression at all. They didn't kiss—they didn't even touch—and then she was on the bed, on her back, her face clenched like a fist. She heard the rattle of the sleet at the window, the murmur of TV: *I can't let you go like this*, a man protested, and she could picture him, angular and tall, a man in a hat and overcoat in a black-and-white world that might have been another planet, *I just can't*. "Are you—?" Jeremy's voice drifted into the mix, and then stalled. "Are you ready? I mean, is it time? Is it coming now?"

She said one thing then, one thing only, her voice as pinched and hollow as the sound of the wind in the gutters: "Get it out of me."

It took a moment, and then she could feel his hands fumbling with her sweats.

Later, hours later, when nothing had happened but pain, a parade of pain with drum majors and brass bands and penitents crawling on their hands and knees till the streets were stained with their blood, she cried out and cried out again. "It's like *Alien*," she gasped, "like that thing in *Alien* when it, it—"

"It's O.K.," he kept telling her, "it's O.K.," but his face betrayed him. He looked scared, looked as if he'd been drained of blood in some evil experiment in yet another movie, and a part of her wanted to be sorry for him, but another part, the part that was so commanding and fierce it overrode everything else, couldn't begin to be.

45 He was useless, and he knew it. He'd never been so purely sick at heart and terrified in all his life, but he tried to be there for her, tried to do his best, and when the baby came out, the baby girl all slick with blood and mucus and the lumped white stuff that was like something spilled at the bottom of a garbage can, he was thinking of the ninth grade and how close he'd come to fainting

while the teacher went around the room to prick their fingers one by one so they each could smear a drop of blood across a slide. He didn't faint now. But he was close to it, so close he could feel the room dodging away under his feet. And then her voice, the first intelligible thing she'd said in an hour: "Get rid of it. Just get rid of it."

Of the drive back to Binghamton he remembered nothing. Or practically nothing. They took towels from the motel and spread them across the seat of her car, he could remember that much ... and the blood, how could he forget the blood? It soaked through her sweats and the towels and even the thick cotton bathmat and into the worn fabric of the seat itself. And it all came from inside her, all of it, tissue and mucus and the shining bright fluid, no end to it, as if she'd been turned inside out. He wanted to ask her about that, if that was normal, but she was asleep the minute she slid out from under his arm and dropped into the seat. If he focused, if he really concentrated, he could remember the way her head lolled against the doorframe while the engine whined and the car rocked and the slush threw a dark blanket over the windshield every time a truck shot past in the opposite direction. That and the exhaustion. He'd never been so tired, his head on a string, shoulders slumped, his arms like two pillars of concrete. And what if he'd nodded off? What if he'd gone into a skid and hurtled over an embankment into the filthy gray accumulation of the worst day of his life? What then?

She made it into the dorm under her own power, nobody even looked at her, and, no, she didn't need his help. "Call me," she whispered, and they kissed, her lips so cold it was like kissing a steak through the plastic wrap, and then he parked her car in the student lot and walked to the bus station. He made Danbury late that night, caught a ride out to the motel, and walked right through the "Do Not Disturb" sign on the door. Fifteen minutes. That was all it took. He bundled up everything, every trace, left the key in the box at the desk, and stood scraping the ice off the windshield of his car while the night opened up above him to a black glitter of sky. He never gave a thought to what lay discarded in the Dumpster out back, itself wrapped in plastic, so much meat, so much cold meat.

He was at the very pinnacle of his dream, the river dressed in its currents, the deep hole under the cutbank, and the fish like silver bullets swarming to his bait, when they woke him—when Rob woke him, Rob Greiner, his roommate, Rob with a face of crumbling stone and two policemen there at the door behind him and the roar of the dorm falling away to a whisper. And that was strange, policemen, a real anomaly in that setting, and at first—for the first thirty seconds, at least—he had no idea what they were doing there. Parking tickets? Could that be it? But then they asked him his name, just to confirm it, joined his hands together behind his back, and fitted two loops of naked metal over his wrists, and he began to understand. He saw McCaffrey and Tuttle from across the hall starting at him as if he were Jeffrey Dahmer or something, and the rest of them, all the rest, every head poking out of every door up and down the corridor, as the police led him away.

"What's all this about?" he kept saying, the cruiser nosing through the dark streets to the station house, the man at the wheel and the man beside him as incapable of speech as the seats or the wire mesh or the gleaming black dashboard that dragged them forward into the night. And then it was up the steps and into an explosion of light, more men in uniform, stand here, give me your hand, now the other one, and then the cage and the questions. Only then did he think of that thing in the garbage sack and the sound it had made—its body had made—when he flung it into the Dumpster like a sack of flour and the lid slammed down on it. He stared at the walls, and this was a movie, too. He'd never been in trouble before, never been inside a police station, but he knew his role well enough, because he'd seen it played out a thousand times on the tube: deny everything. Even as the two detectives settled in across from him at the bare wooden table in the little box of the overlit room he was telling himself just that: *Deny it, deny it all.*

The first detective leaned forward and set his hands on the table as if he'd come for a manicure. He was in his thirties, or maybe his forties, a tired-looking man with the scars of the turmoil he'd witnessed gouged into the flesh under his eyes. He didn't offer a cigarette ("I don't smoke," Jeremy was prepared to say, giving them that much at least), and he didn't smile or soften his eyes. And when he spoke his voice carried no freight at all, not outrage or threat or cajolery—it was just a voice, flat and tired. "Do you know a China Berkowitz?" he said.

And she. She was in the community hospital, where the ambulance had deposited her after her roommate had called 911 in a voice that was like a bone stuck in the back of her throat, and it was raining again. Her parents were there, her mother red-eyed and sniffling, her father looking like an actor who has forgotten his lines, and there was another woman there, too, a policewoman. The policewoman sat in an orange plastic chair in the corner, dipping her head to the knitting in her lap. At first, China's mother had tried to be pleasant to the woman, but pleasant wasn't what the circumstances called for, and now she ignored her, because the very unpleasant fact was that China was being taken into custody as soon as she was released from the hospital.

For a long while no one said anything—everything had already been said, over and over, one long flood of hurt and recrimination—and the antiseptic silence of the hospital held them in its grip while the rain beat at the windows and the machines at the foot of the bed counted off numbers. From down the hall came a snatch of TV dialogue, and for a minute China opened her eyes and thought she was back in the dorm. "Honey," her mother said, raising a purgatorial face to her, "are you all right? Can I get you anything?"

"I need to—I think I need to pee."

"Why?" her father demanded, and it was the perfect non sequitur. He was up out of the chair, standing over her, his eyes liked cracked porcelain. "Why didn't you tell us, or at least tell your mother—or Dr. Fredman? Dr.Fredman, at least. He's been—he's like a family member, you know that, and he could have, or he would have . . . What were you *thinking*, for Christ's sake?"

Thinking? She wasn't thinking anything, not then and not now. All she wanted—and she didn't care what they did to her, beat her, torture her, drag her weeping through the streets in a dirty white dress with "Baby Killer" stitched over her breast in scarlet letters—was to see Jeremy. Just that. Because what really mattered was what he was thinking.

The food at the Sarah Barnes Cooper Women's Correctional Institute was exactly what they served at the dining hall in college, heavy on the sugars, starches, and bad cholesterol, and that would have struck her as ironic if she'd been there under other circumstances—doing community outreach, say, or researching a paper for sociology class. But given the fact that she'd been locked up for more than a month now, the object of the other girls' threats, scorn, and just plain *nastiness*, given the fact that her life was ruined beyond any hope of redemption, and every newspaper in the country had her shrunken white face plastered across its front page under a headline that screamed **"MOTEL MOM,"** she didn't have much use for irony. She was scared twenty-four hours a day. Scared of the present, scared of the future, scared of the reporters waiting for the judge to set bail so that they could swarm all over her the minute she stepped out the door. She couldn't concentrate on the books and magazines her mother brought her, or even on the TV in the rec room. She sat in her room—it was a room, just like a dorm room, except that they locked you in at night—and stared at the walls, eating peanuts, M&M's, sunflower seeds by the handful, chewing for the pure animal gratification of it. She was putting on more weight, and what did it matter?

Jeremy was different. He'd lost everything—his walk, his smile, the muscles of his upper arms and shoulders. Even his hair lay flat now, as if he couldn't bother with a tube of gel and a comb. When she saw him at the arraignment, saw him for the first time since she'd climbed out of the car and limped into the dorm with the blood wet on her legs, he looked like a refugee, like a ghost. The room they were in—the courtroom—seemed to have grown up around them, walls, windows, benches, lights, and radiators already in place, along with the judge, the American flag, and the ready-made spectators. It was hot. People coughed into their fists and shuffled their feet, every sound magnified. The judge presided, his arms like bones twirled in a bag, his eyes searching and opaque as he peered over the top of his reading glasses.

China's lawyer didn't like Jeremy's lawyer, that much was evident, and the state prosecutor didn't like anybody. She watched him—Jeremy, only him—as the reporters held their collective breath and the judge read off the charges and her mother bowed her head and sobbed into the bucket of her hands. And Jeremy was watching her, too, his eyes locked on hers as if he defied them all, as if nothing mattered in the world but her, and when the judge said *First-degree murder* and *Murder by abuse or neglect* he never flinched.

She sent him a note that day—"I love you, will always love you no matter what, More than Moon"—and in the hallway, afterward, while their lawyers fended off the reporters and the bailiffs tugged impatiently at them, they had a minute, just a minute, to themselves. "What did you tell them?" he whispered. His voice was a rasp, almost a growl; she looked at him, inches away, and hardly recognized him.

"I told them it was dead." 60

"My lawyer—Mrs. Teagues?—she says they're saying it was alive when we, when we put it in the bag." His face was composed, but his eyes were darting like insects trapped inside his head.

"It was dead."

"It looked dead," he said, and already he was pulling away from her and some callous shit with a camera kept annihilating them with flash after flash of light, "and we certainly didn't—I mean, we didn't slap it or anything to get it breathing. . . ."

And then the last thing he said to her, just as they were pulled apart, and it was nothing she wanted to hear, nothing that had any love in it, or even the hint of love: "You told me to get rid of it."

65 There was no elaborate name for the place where they were keeping him. It was known as Drum Hill Prison, period. No reform-minded notions here, no verbal gestures toward rehabilitation or behavior modification, no benefactors, mayors, or role models to lend the place their family names, but then who in his right mind would want a prison named after him anyway? At least they kept him separated from the other prisoners, the gangbangers and dope dealers and sexual predators and the like. He was no longer a freshman at Brown, not officially, but he had his books and his course notes and he tried to keep up as best he could. Still, when the screams echoed through the cell block at night and the walls dripped with the accumulated breath of eight and a half thousand terminally angry sociopaths, he had to admit it wasn't the sort of college experience he'd bargained for.

And what had he done to deserve it? He still couldn't understand. That thing in the Dumpster—and he refused to call it human, let alone a baby—was nobody's business but his and China's. That's what he'd told his attorney, Mrs. Teagues, and his mother and her boyfriend, Howard, and he'd told them over and over again: *I didn't do anything wrong*. Even if it was alive, and it was, he knew in his heart that it was, even before the state prosecutor presented evidence of blunt-force trauma and death by asphyxiation and exposure, it didn't matter, or shouldn't have mattered. There was no baby. There was nothing but a mistake, a mistake clothed in blood and mucus. When he really thought about it, thought it through on its merits and dissected all his mother's pathetic arguments about where he'd be today if she'd felt as he did when she was pregnant herself, he hardened like a rock, like sand turning to stone under all the pressure the planet can bring to bear. Another unwanted child in an overpopulated world? They should have given him a medal.

It was the end of January before bail was set—three hundred and fifty thousand dollars his mother didn't have—and he was released to house arrest. He wore a plastic anklet that set off an alarm if he went out the door, and so did she, so did China, imprisoned like some fairy-tale princess at her parents' house. At first, she called him every day, but mostly what she did was cry—"I want to see it," she sobbed. "I want to see our daughter's *grave*." That froze him inside. He tried to picture her—her now, China, the love of his life—and he couldn't. What did she look like? What was her face like, her nose, her hair, her eyes and breasts and the slit between her legs? He drew a blank. There was no way to summon her the way she used to be or even the way she was in court, because all he could remember was the thing that had come out of her, four limbs and the equipment of a female, shoulders rigid and eyes shut tight, as if she were a mummy in a tomb … and the breath, the shuddering long gasping rattle of a breath he could feel ringing inside her even as the black plastic bag closed over her face and the lid of the Dumpster opened like a mouth.

He was in the den, watching basketball, a drink in his hand (7UP mixed with Jack Daniel's in a ceramic mug, so no one would know he was getting shit-faced at two o'clock on a Sunday afternoon), when the phone rang. It was Sarah Teagues. "Listen, Jeremy," she said in her crisp, equitable tones, "I thought you ought to know—the Berkowitzes are filing a motion to have the case against China dropped."

His mother's voice on the portable, too loud, a blast of amplified breath and static: "On what grounds?"

70 "She never saw the baby, that's what they're saying. She thought she had a miscarriage."

"Yeah, right," his mother said.

Sarah Teagues was right there, her voice as clear and present as his mother's. "Jeremy's the one that threw it in the Dumpster, and they're saying he acted alone. She took a polygraph test day before yesterday."

He could feel his heart pounding like it used to when he plodded up that last agonizing ridge behind the school with the cross-country team, his legs sapped, no more breath left in his body. He didn't say a word. Didn't even breathe.

"She's going to testify against him."

Outside was the world, puddles of ice clinging to the lawn under a weak 75
afternoon sun, all the trees stripped bare, the grass dead, the azalea under the window reduced to an armload of dead brown twigs. She wouldn't have wanted to go out today anyway. This was the time of year she hated most, the long interval between the holidays and spring break, when nothing grew and nothing changed—it didn't even seem to snow much anymore. What was out there for her anyway? They wouldn't let her see Jeremy, wouldn't even let her talk to him on the phone or write him anymore, and she wouldn't be able to show her face at the mall or even the movie theater without somebody shouting out her name as if she were a freak, as if she were another Monica Lewinsky or Heidi Fleiss. She wasn't China Berkowitz, honor student, not anymore—she was the punch line to a joke, a footnote to history.

She wouldn't mind going for a drive, though—that was something she missed, just following the curves out to the reservoir to watch the way the ice cupped the shore, or up to the turnout on Route 9 to look out over the river where it oozed through the mountains in a shimmering coil of light. Or to take a walk in the woods, just that. She was in her room, on her bed, posters of bands she'd outgrown staring down from the walls, her high-school books on two shelves in the corner, the closet door flung open on all the clothes she'd once wanted so desperately she could have died for each individual pair of boots or the cashmere sweaters that felt so good against her skin. At the bottom of her left leg, down there at the foot of the bed, was the anklet she wore now, the plastic anklet with the transmitter inside, no different, she supposed, than the collars they put on wolves to track them across all those miles of barren tundra or the bears sleeping in their dens. Except that hers had an alarm on it.

For a long while she just lay there gazing out the window, watching the rinsed-out sun slip down into the sky that had no more color in it than a TV tuned to an unsubscribed channel, and then she found herself picturing things the way they were an eon ago, when everything was green. She saw the azalea bush in bloom, the leaves knifing out of the trees, butterflies—or were they cabbage moths?—hovering over the flowers. Deep green. That was the color of the world. And she was remembering a night, summer before last, just after she and Jeremy started going together, the crickets thrumming, the air thick with humidity, and him singing along with the car radio, his voice so sweet and pure it was as if he'd written the song himself, just for her. And when they got to where they were going, at the end of that dark lane overhung with trees, to a place where it was private and hushed and the night fell in on itself as if it couldn't support the weight of the stars, he was as nervous as she was. She moved into his arms and they kissed, his lips groping for hers in the dark, his fingers trembling over the thin yielding silk of her blouse. He was Jeremy. He was the love of her life. And she closed her eyes and clung to him as if that were all that mattered.

(2000)

Questions for Discussion and Writing

1. How would you describe China and Jeremy at the beginning of the story—and at the end? Do you consider them to blame for what has happened to them?
2. Why is China so adamant in her refusal to deal with her pregnancy beyond simply hiding it?
3. Can you in any way justify China's telling Jeremy to "Just get rid of it" and then later agreeing to testify against him in court for getting rid of it?
4. Why does Jeremy feel he has done nothing wrong? Write an essay arguing for (or against) his position.
5. Write a continuation of the story telling what happens to China and Jeremy at the trial and what their lives are like afterward.

Sandra Cisneros 1954–

Sandra Cisneros, the daughter of a Mexican father and a Mexican-American mother, grew up with her six brothers in a barrio of Chicago that seemed to her "like France after World War II—empty lots and burned out buildings." Although the males in her family pressured her to adopt a subservient woman's role, she was determined to be "nobody's mother and nobody's wife." She achieved a higher education but has said, "If I had lived up to my teachers' expectations, I'd still be working in a factory." She has focused on the Latina experience in her sketches, short stories, novels, and poetry. In 1995 she was awarded a MacArthur "genius" grant of $500,000.

Geraldo No Last Name

She met him at a dance. Pretty too, and young. Said he worked in a restanrant, but she can't remember which one. Geraldo. That's all. Green pants and Saturday shirt. Geraldo. That's what he told her.

And how was she to know she'd be the last one to see him alive. An accident, don't you know. Hit and run. Marin, she goes to all those dances. Uptown. Logan. Embassy. Palmer. Aragon. Fontana. The Manor. She likes to dance. She knows how to do cumbias and salsas and rancheras even. And he was just someone she danced with. Somebody she met that night. That's right.

That's the story. That's what she said again and again. Once to the hospital people and twice to the police. No address. No name. Nothing in his pockets. Ain't it a shame.

Only Marin can't explain why it mattered, the hours and hours, for somebody she didn't even know. The hospital emergency room. Nobody but an intern working all alone. And maybe if the surgeon would've come, maybe if he hadn't lost so much blood, if the surgeon had only come, they would know who to notify and where.

But what difference does it make? He wasn't anything to her. He wasn't her 5
boyfriend or anything like that. Just another *brazer* who didn't speak English. Just another wetback. You know the kind. The ones who always look ashamed. And what was she doing out at three A.M. anyway? Marin who was sent home with her coat and some aspirin. How does she explain?

She met him at a dance. Geraldo in his shiny shirt and green pants. Geraldo going to a dance.

What does it matter?

They never saw the kitchenettes. They never knew about the two-room flats and sleeping rooms he rented, the weekly money orders sent home, the currency exchange. How could they?

His name was Geraldo. And his home is in another country. The ones he left behind are far away, will wonder, shrug, remember. Geraldo—he went north… we never heard from him again.

(1983)

Questions for Discussion and Writing

1. Why was only one intern working in the emergency room? Why didn't the surgeon come? Why are these facts included?
2. In the next-to-last paragraph, who is the "they" who never saw the kitchenettes and never knew about Geraldo's life? What is the point of this paragraph?
3. How would you describe the tone of the final paragraph? In what way does this paragraph sum up the story's main themes?
4. Write a paper in which you contrast the reactions of Marin with those of the unnamed narrator. Can you separate the two?
5. Write an essay from Geraldo's point of view. Let him speak for himself. What does he have to say about his life and what happened to him?

Louise Erdrich 1954–

Louise Erdrich was raised as a member of the Turtle Mountain Chippewas in North Dakota with her grandfather as the tribal chief. Growing up, she worked as a farmhand, a waitress, a lifeguard, and a construction worker. After graduating from Dartmouth, she eventually married one of her professors, the writer Michael Dorris. She was having no luck getting her first novel accepted until he sent submission letters on stationery he made himself with "Michael Dorris Agency" as the letterhead. The book became a best-seller, but the couple later separated, and he committed suicide. Erdrich presently lives, writes, and owns a bookstore in Minneapolis.

The Red Convertible

Lyman Lamartine

I was the first one to drive a convertible on my reservation. And of course it was red, a red Olds. I owned that car along with my brother Henry Junior. We owned it together until his boots filled with water on a windy night and he bought out my share. Now Henry owns the whole car, and his youngest brother Lyman (that's myself), Lyman walks everywhere he goes.

How did I earn enough money to buy my share in the first place? My own talent was I could always make money. I had a touch for it, unusual in a Chippewa. From the first I was different that way, and everyone recognized it. I was the only kid they let in the American Legion Hall to shine shoes, for example, and one Christmas I sold spiritual bouquets for the mission door to door. The nuns let me keep a percentage. Once I started, it seemed the more money I made the easier the money came. Everyone encouraged it. When I was fifteen I got a job washing dishes at the Joliet Cafe, and that was where my first big break happened.

It wasn't long before I was promoted to busing tables, and then the short-order cook quit and I was hired to take her place. No sooner than you know it I was managing the Joliet. The rest is history. I went on managing. I soon became part owner, and of course there was no stopping me then. It wasn't long before the whole thing was mine.

After I'd owned the Joliet for one year, it blew over in the worst tornado ever seen around here. The whole operation was smashed to bits. A total loss. The fryalator was up in a tree, the grill torn in half like it was paper. I was only sixteen. I had it all in my mother's name, and I lost it quick, but before I lost it I had every one of my relatives, and their relatives, to dinner, and I also bought that red Olds I mentioned, along with Henry.

The first time we saw it! I'll tell you when we first saw it. We had gotten a 5
ride to Winnipeg, and both of us had money. Don't ask me why, because we never mentioned a car or anything, we just had all our money. Mine was cash, a big bankroll from the Joliet's insurance. Henry had two checks—a week's extra pay for being laid off, and his regular check from the Jewel Bearing Plant.

We were walking down Portage anyway, seeing the sights, when we saw it. There it was, parked, large as life. Really as *if* it was alive. I thought of the word *repose*, because the car wasn't simply stopped, parked, or whatever. That car reposed, calm and gleaming, a FOR SALE sign in its left front window. Then, before we had thought it over at all, the car belonged to us and our pockets were empty. We had just enough money for gas back home.

We went places in that car, me and Henry. We took off driving all one whole summer. We started off toward the Little Knife River and Mandaree in Fort Berthold and then we found ourselves down in Wakpala somehow, and then suddenly we were over in Montana on the Rocky Boy, and yet the summer was not even half over. Some people hang on to details when they travel, but we didn't let them bother us and just lived our everyday lives here to there.

I do remember this place with willows. I remember I laid under those trees and it was comfortable. So comfortable. The branches bent down all around me like a tent or a stable. And quiet, it was quiet, even though there was a pow-wow close enough so I could see it going on. The air was not too still, not too windy either. When the dust rises up and hangs in the air around dancers like that, I feel good. Henry was asleep with his arms thrown wide. Later on, he woke up and we started driving again. We were somewhere in Montana, or maybe on the Blood Reserve—it could have been anywhere. Anyway it was where we met the girl.

All her hair was in buns around her ears, that's the first thing I noticed about her. She was posed alongside the road with her arm out, so we stopped. That girl was short, so short her lumber shirt looked comical on her, like a nightgown. She had jeans on and fancy moccasins and she carried a little suitcase.

"Hop on in," says Henry. So she climbs in between us. 10

"We'll take you home," I says. "Where do you live?"

"Chicken," she says.

"Where the hell's that?" I ask her.

"Alaska."

"Okay," says Henry, and we drive. 15

We got up there and never wanted to leave. The sun doesn't truly set there in summer, and the night is more a soft dusk. You might doze off, sometimes, but before you know it you're up again, like an animal in nature. You never feel like you have to sleep hard or put away the world. And things would grow up there. One day just dirt or moss, the next day flowers and long grass. The girl's name was Susy. Her family really took to us. They fed us and put us up. We had our own tent to live in by their house, and the kids would be in and out of there all day and night. They couldn't get over me and Henry being brothers, we looked so different. We told them we knew we had the same mother, anyway.

One night Susy came in to visit us. We sat around in the tent talking of this and that. The season was changing. It was getting darker by that time, and the cold was even getting just a little mean. I told her it was time for us to go. She stood up on a chair.

"You never seen my hair," Susy said.

That was true. She was standing on a chair, but still, when she unclipped her buns the hair reached all the way to the ground. Our eyes opened. You couldn't tell how much hair she had when it was rolled up so neatly. Then my brother Henry did something funny. He went up to the chair and said, "Jump on my shoulders." So she did that, and her hair reached down past his waist, and he started twirling, this way and that, so her hair was flung out from side to side.

"I always wondered what it was like to have long pretty hair," Henry says. 20 Well, we laughed. It was a funny sight, the way he did it. The next morning we got up and took leave of those people.

On to greener pastures, as they say. It was down through Spokane and across Idaho then Montana and very soon we were racing the weather right along under the Canadian border through Columbus, Des Lacs, and then were in Bottineau County and soon home. We'd made most of the trip, that summer, without putting up the car hood at all. We got home just in time.

I don't wonder that the army was so glad to get my brother that they turned him into a Marine. He was built like a brick outhouse anyway. We liked to tease him that they really wanted him for his Indian nose. He had a nose big and sharp as a hatchet, like the nose on Red Tomahawk, the Indian who killed Sitting Bull, whose profile is on signs all along the North Dakota highways.

Henry went off to training camp, came home once during Christmas, then the next thing you know we got an overseas letter from him. It was 1970, and he said he was stationed up in the northern hill country. Whereabouts I did not know. He wasn't such a hot letter writer, and only got off two before the enemy caught him. I could never keep it straight, which direction those good Vietnam soldiers were from.

I wrote him back several times, even though I didn't know if those letters would get through. I kept him informed all about the car. Most of the time I had it up on blocks in the yard or half taken apart, because that long trip did a hard job on it under the hood.

I always had good luck with numbers, and never worried about the draft myself. I never even had to think about what my number was. But Henry was never lucky in the same way as me. It was at least three years before Henry came home. By then I guess the whole war was solved in the government's mind, but for him it would keep on going. In those years I'd put his car into almost perfect shape. I always thought of it as his car while he was gone, even though when he left he said, "Now it's yours," and threw me his key.

"Thanks for the extra key," I'd said. "I'll put it in your drawer just in case I need it." He laughed.

When he came home, though, Henry was very different, and I'll say this: the change was no good. You could hardly expect him to change for the better, I know. But he was quiet, so quiet, and never comfortable sitting still anywhere but always up and moving around. I thought back to times we'd sat still for whole afternoons, never moving a muscle, just shifting our weight along the ground, talking to whoever sat with us, watching things. He'd always had a joke, then, too, and now you couldn't get him to laugh, or when he did it was more the sound of a man choking, a sound that stopped up the throats of other people around him. They got to leaving him alone most of the time, and I didn't blame them. It was a fact: Henry was jumpy and mean.

I'd bought a color TV set for my mom and the rest of us while Henry was away. Money still came very easy. I was sorry I'd ever bought it though, because of Henry. I was also sorry I'd bought color, because with black-and-white the pictures seem older and farther away. But what are you going to do? He sat in front of it, watching it, and that was the only time he was completely still. But it was the kind of stillness that you see in a rabbit when it freezes and before it will bolt. He was not easy. He sat in his chair gripping the armrests with all his might, as if the chair itself was moving at a high speed and if he let go at all he would rocket forward and maybe crash right through the set.

Once I was in the room watching TV with Henry and I heard his teeth click at something. I looked over, and he'd bitten through his lip. Blood was going down his chin. I tell you right then I wanted to smash that tube to pieces. I went over to it but Henry must have known what I was up to. He rushed from his chair and shoved me out of the way, against the wall. I told myself he didn't know what he was doing.

My mom came in, turned the set off real quiet, and told us she had made something for supper. So we went and sat down. There was still blood going down Henry's chin, but he didn't notice it and no one said anything, even though every time he took a bite of his bread his blood fell onto it until he was eating his own blood mixed in with the food.

While Henry was not around we talked about what was going to happen to him. There were no Indian doctors on the reservation, and my mom couldn't come around to trusting the old man, Moses Pillager, because he courted her long ago and was jealous of her husbands. He might take revenge through her son. We were afraid that if we brought Henry to a regular hospital they would keep him.

"They don't fix them in those places," Mom said; "they just give them drugs."

"We wouldn't get him there in the first place," I agreed, "so let's just forget about it."

Then I thought about the car.

Henry had not even looked at the car since he'd gotten home, though like I said, it was in tip-top condition and ready to drive. I thought the car might bring the old Henry back somehow. So I bided my time and waited for my chance to interest him in the vehicle.

One night Henry was off somewhere. I took myself a hammer. I went out to that car and I did a number on its underside. Whacked it up. Bent the tail pipe double. Ripped the muffler loose. By the time I was done with the car it looked worse than any typical Indian car that has been driven all its life on reservation roads, which they always say are like government promises—full of holes. It just about hurt me, I'll tell you that! I threw dirt in the carburetor and I ripped all the electric tape off the seats. I made it look just as beat up as I could. Then I sat back and waited for Henry to find it.

Still, it took him over a month. That was all right, because it was just getting warm enough, not melting, but warm enough to work outside.

"Lyman," he says, walking in one day, "that red car looks like shit."

"Well, it's old," I says. "You got to expect that."

"No way!" says Henry. "That car's a classic! But you went and ran the piss right out of it, Lyman, and you know it don't deserve that. I kept that car in A-one shape. You don't remember. You're too young. But when I left, that car was running like a watch. Now I don't even know if I can get it to start again, let alone get it anywhere near its old condition."

"Well, you try," I said, like I was getting mad, "but I say it's a piece of junk."

Then I walked out before he could realize I knew he'd strung together more than six words at once.

After that I thought he'd freeze himself to death working on that car. He was out there all day, and at night he rigged up a little lamp, ran a cord out the window, and had himself some light to see by while he worked. He was better than he had been before, but that's still not saying much. It was easier for him to do the things the rest of us did. He ate more slowly and didn't jump up and down during the meal to get this or that or look out the window. I put my hand in the back of the TV set, I admit, and fiddled around with it good, so that it was almost impossible now to get a clear picture. He didn't look at it very often anyway. He was always out with that car or going off to get parts for it. By the time it was really melting outside, he had it fixed.

I had been feeling down in the dumps about Henry around this time. We had always been together before. Henry and Lyman. But he was such a loner now that I didn't know how to take it. So I jumped at the chance one day when Henry seemed friendly. It's not that he smiled or anything. He just said, "Let's take that old shit-box for a spin." Just the way he said it made me think he could be coming around.

We went out to the car. It was spring. The sun was shining very bright. My only sister, Bonita, who was just eleven years old, came out and made us stand together for a picture. Henry leaned his elbow on the red car's windshield, and he took his other arm and put it over my shoulder, very carefully, as though it was heavy for him to lift and he didn't want to bring the weight down all at once.

"Smile," Bonita said, and he did. 45

That picture. I never look at it anymore. A few months ago, I don't know why, I got his picture out and tacked it on the wall. I felt good about Henry at the time, close to him. I felt good having his picture on the wall, until one night when I was looking at television. I was a little drunk and stoned. I looked up at the wall and Henry was staring at me. I don't know what it was, but his smile had changed, or maybe it was gone. All I know is I couldn't stay in the same room with that picture. I was shaking. I got up, closed the door, and went into the kitchen. A little later my friend Ray came over and we both went back into that room. We put the picture in a brown bag, folded the bag over and over tightly, then put it way back in a closet.

I still see that picture now, as if it tugs at me, whenever I pass that closet door. The picture is very clear in my mind. It was so sunny that day Henry had to squint against the glare. Or maybe the camera Bonita held flashed like a mirror, blinding him, before she snapped the picture. My face is right out in the sun, big and round. But he might have drawn back, because the shadows on his face are deep as holes. There are two shadows curved like little hooks around the ends of his smile, as if to frame it and try to keep it there—that one, first smile that looked like it might have hurt his face. He has his field jacket on and the wornin clothes he'd come back in and kept wearing ever since. After Bonita took the picture, she went into the house and we got into the car. There was a full cooler in the trunk. We started off, east, toward Pembina and the Red River because Henry said he wanted to see the high water.

The trip over there was beautiful. When everything starts changing, drying up, clearing off, you feel like your whole life is starting. Henry felt it, too. The top was down and the car hummed like a top. He'd really put it back in shape, even the tape on the seats was very carefully put down and glued back in layers. It's not that he smiled again or even joked, but his face looked to me as if it was clear, more peaceful. It looked as though he wasn't thinking of anything in particular except the bare fields and windbreaks and houses we were passing.

The river was high and full of winter trash when we got there. The sun was still out, but it was colder by the river. There were still little clumps of dirty snow here and there on the banks. The water hadn't gone over the banks yet, but it would, you could tell. It was just at its limit, hard swollen, glossy like an old gray scar. We made ourselves a fire, and we sat down and watched the current go. As I watched it I felt something squeezing inside me and tightening and trying to let go all at the same time. I knew I was not just feeling it myself; I knew I was feeling what Henry was going through at that moment. Except that I couldn't stand it, the closing and opening. I jumped to my feet. I took Henry by the shoulders and I started shaking him. "Wake up," I says, "wake up, wake up, wake up!" I didn't know what had come over me. I sat down beside him again.

50 His face was totally white and hard. Then it broke, like stones break all of a sudden when water boils up inside them.

"I know it," he says. "I know it. I can't help it. It's no use."

We start talking. He said he knew what I'd done with the car. It was obvious it had been whacked out of shape and not just neglected. He said he wanted to give the car to me for good now, it was no use. He said he'd fixed it just to give it back and I should take it.

"No way," I says. "I don't want it."

"That's okay," he says, "you take it."

55 "I don't want it, though," I says back to him, and then to emphasize, just to emphasize, you understand, I touch his shoulder. He slaps my hand off.

"Take that car," he says.

"No," I say. "Make me," I say, and then he grabs my jacket and rips the arm loose. That jacket is a class act, suede with tags and zippers. I push Henry backwards, off the log. He jumps up and bowls me over. We go down in a clinch and come up swinging hard, for all we're worth, with our fists. He socks my jaw so hard I feel like it swings loose. Then I'm at his rib cage and land a good one under his chin so his head snaps back. He's dazzled. He looks at me and I look at him and then his eyes are full of tears and blood and at first I think he's crying. But no, he's laughing. "Ha, ha!" he says. "Ha! Ha! Take good care of it."

"Okay," I says. "Okay, no problem. Ha! Ha!"

I can't help it, and I start laughing, too. My face feels fat and strange, and after a while I get a beer from the cooler in the trunk, and when I hand it to Henry he takes his shirt and wipes my germs off. "Hoof-and-mouth disease," he says. For some reason this cracks me up, and so we're really laughing for a while, and then we drink all the rest of the beers one by one and throw them in the river and see how far, how fast, the current takes them before they fill up and sink.

60 "You want to go on back?" I ask after a while. "Maybe we could snag a couple nice Kashpaw girls."

He says nothing. But I can tell his mood is turning again.

"They're all crazy, the girls up here, every damn one of them."

"You're crazy too," I say, to jolly him up. "Crazy Lamartine boys!"

He looks as though he will take this wrong at first. His face twists, then clears, and he jumps up on his feet. "That's right!" he says. "Crazier 'n hell. Crazy Indians!"

65 I think it's the old Henry again. He throws off his jacket and starts springing his legs up from the knees like a fancy dancer. He's down doing something between a grass dance and a bunny hop, no kind of dance I ever saw before, but neither has anyone else on all this green growing earth. He's wild. He wants to pitch whoopee! He's up and at me and all over. All this time I'm laughing so hard, so hard my belly is getting tied up in a knot.

"Got to cool me off!" he shouts all of a sudden. Then he runs over to the river and jumps in.

There's boards and other things in the current. It's so high. No sound comes from the river after the splash he makes, so I run right over. I look around. It's getting dark. I see he's halfway across the water already, and I know he didn't swim there but the current took him. It's far. I hear his voice, though, very clearly across it.

"My boots are filling," he says.

He says this in a normal voice, like he just noticed and he doesn't know what to think of it. Then he's gone. A branch comes by. Another branch. And I go in.

By the time I get out of the river, off the snag I pulled myself onto, the sun is down. I walk back to the car, turn on the high beams, and drive it up the bank. I put it in first gear and then I take my foot off the clutch. I get out, close the door, and watch it plow softly into the water. The headlights reach in as they go down, searching, still lighted even after the water swirls over the back end. I wait. The wires short out. It is all finally dark. And then there is only the water, the sound of it going and running and going and running and running.

(1984)

Questions for Discussion and Writing

1. How does the red Oldsmobile function as the story's central symbol? What changes does the car go through? How do these changes stand for what Lyman and Henry are going through?
2. Why is Lyman upset by the picture of himself and his brother? When does the picture begin to bother Lyman—before or after Henry's death? Do we know for sure? Does it make any difference?
3. Why does Lyman send the car into the river? Why are the car's lights left on?
4. Write an essay that makes a major claim about the brothers' relationship.
5. Analyze a single episode in the story (such as the visit to Alaska or Henry's watching TV), and discuss its relation to the story as a whole.

Ha Jin 1956–

Born in Liaoning, China, the son of a military officer, Ha Jin joined the army at age fourteen and served along China's border with Russia. When he finally embarked on his education and traveled to America to earn his doctorate, he fully intended to return to China to teach. But in 1989 Chinese soldiers attacked and killed student demonstrators in Tiananmen Square. "I was glued to the TV for three days," says Ha Jin. "I was in shock. I had served in the army to protect the people. Suddenly the whole thing was reversed." He has not been back since. Today, Ha Jin teaches at Boston University and lives in the suburbs; he became a U.S. citizen in 1997.

The Bridegroom

Before Beina's father died, I promised him that I'd take care of his daughter. He and I had been close friends for twenty years. He left his only child with me because my wife and I had no children of our own. It was easy to keep my word when Beina was still a teenager. As she grew older, it became more difficult, not because she was willful or troublesome, but because no man was interested in her, a short, homely girl. When she turned twenty-three and still had no boyfriend, I began to worry. Where could I find her a husband? Timid and quiet, she didn't know how to get close to a man. I was afraid she'd end up an old maid.

Then out of the blue, Huang Baowen proposed to her. I found myself at a loss, because they'd hardly known each other. How could he be serious about his offer? I feared he might make a fool of Beina, so I insisted they get engaged if he meant business. He came to my home with two trussed-up capons, four cartons of Ginseng cigarettes, two bottles of Five Grains' Sap, and one tall tin of oolong tea. I was pleased, though not very impressed by his gifts.

Two months later they got married. My colleagues congratulated me, saying, "That was fast, Old Cheng."

What a relief to me. But to many young women in our sewing machine factory, Beina's marriage was a slap in the face. They'd say, "A hen cooped up a peacock." Or, "A fool always lands in the arms of fortune." True, Baowen had been one of the most handsome unmarried men in the factory, and nobody had expected that Beina, stocky and stout, would win him. What's more, Baowen was good-natured and well educated—a middle school graduate—and he didn't smoke or drink or gamble. He had fine manners and often smiled politely, showing his bright, straight teeth. In a way he resembled a woman, delicate, clear-skinned, and soft-spoken; he even could knit things out of wool. But no men dared bully him because he was skilled at martial arts. Three times in a row he had won the first prize for kung fu at our factory's annual sports meet. He was very good at the long sword and freestyle boxing. When he was in middle school, bigger boys had often picked on him, so his stepfather had sent him to the martial arts school in their hometown. A year later, nobody would bug him again.

Sometimes I couldn't help wondering why Baowen had fallen for Beina. 5
What in her had caught his heart? Did he really like her fleshy face, which often reminded me of a blowfish? Although we had our doubts, my wife and I couldn't say anything negative about the marriage. Our only concern was that Baowen might be too good for our adopted daughter. Whenever I heard that somebody had divorced, I'd feel a sudden flutter of panic.

As the head of the Security Section in the factory, I had some pull and did what I could to help the young couple. Soon after their wedding, I secured them a brand-new two-bedroom apartment, which angered some people waiting in line for housing. I wasn't daunted by their criticism. I'd do almost anything to make Beina's marriage a success, because I believed that if it survived the first two years, it might last decades—once Baowen became a father, it would be difficult for him to break loose.

But after they'd been married for eight months, Beina still wasn't pregnant. I was afraid that Baowen would soon grow tired of her and run after another woman, as many young women in the factory were still attracted to him. A brazen one even declared that she'd leave her door open for him all night long. Some of them frequently offered him movie tickets and meat coupons. It seemed that they were determined to wreck Beina's marriage. I hated them, and just the thought of them would give me an earache or a sour stomach. Fortunately, Baowen hadn't yet done anything outside the bounds of a decent husband.

One morning in early November, Beina stepped into my office. "Uncle," she said in a tearful voice, "Baowen didn't come home last night."

I tried to remain clam, though my head began to swim. “Do you know where he’s been?” I asked.

“I don’t know. I looked for him everywhere.” She licked her cracked lips and took off her green work cap, her hair in a huge bun.

“When did you see him last?”

“At dinner yesterday evening. He said he was going to see somebody. He has lots of buddies in town.”

“Is that so?” I didn’t know he had many friends. “Don’t worry. Go back to your workshop and don’t tell anybody about this. I’ll call around and find him.”

She dragged herself out of my office. She must have gained at least a dozen pounds since the wedding. Her blue dungarees had become so tight that they seemed about to burst. Viewed from behind, she looked like a giant turnip.

I called the Rainbow Movie Theater, Victory park, and a few resturants in town. They all said they had not seen anyone matching Baowen’s description. Before I could phone the City Library, where Baowen sometimes spent his weekends, a call came in. It was from the city’s Public Security Bureau. The man on the phone said they’d detained a worker of ours, named Huang Baowen. He wouldn’t tell me what had happened. He just said, “Indecent activity. Come as soon as you can.”

It was a cold day. As I cycled toward downtown, the shrill north wind kept flipping up the front ends of my overcoat. My knees were sore, and I couldn’t help shivering. Soon my asthma tightened my throat and I began moaning. I couldn’t stop cursing Baowen. “I knew it. I just knew it,” I said to myself. I had sensed that sooner or later he’d seek pleasure with another woman. Now he was in the hands of the police, and the whole factory would talk about him. How would Beina take this blow?

At the Public Security Bureau I was surprised to see that about a dozen officials from other factories, schools, and companies were already there. I knew most of them—they were in charge of security affairs at their workplaces. A policewoman conducted us into a conference room upstairs where green silk curtains hung in the windows. We sat down around a long mahogany table and waited to be briefed about the case. The glass tabletop was brand-new, its edge still sharp. I saw worry and confusion on the other men’s faces. I figured Baowen must have been involved in a major crime—either an orgy or a gang rape. On second thought, I felt he couldn’t have been a rapist; by nature he was kindhearted, very gentle. I hoped this was not a political case, which would be absolutely unpardonable. Six or seven years ago, a half-wit and a high school graduate had started an association in our city, named the China Liberation Party, which eventually recruited nine members. Although the sparrow is small, it has a complete set of organs—their party elected a chairman, a secretary, and even a prime minister. But before they could print their manifesto, which expressed their intention to overthrow the government, the police rounded them up. Two of the top leaders were executed, and the rest of the members were jailed.

As I was wondering about the nature of Baowen’s crime, a middle-aged man came in. He had a solemn face, and his eyes were half-closed. He took off his dark-blue tunic, hung it on the back of a chair, and sat down at the end of the table. I recognized him; he was Chief Miao of the Investigation Department. Wearing a sheepskin jerkin, he somehow reminded me of Genghis Khan, thick-boned and round-faced. His hooded eyes were shrewd, though they looked sleepy. Without any opening remarks he declared that we had a case of homosexuality on our hands. At that, the room turned noisy. We'd heard that term before but didn't know what it meant exactly. Seeing many of us puzzled, Chief Miao explained, "It's a social disease, like gambling, or prostitution, or syphilis." He kept on squirming as if itchy with hemorrhoids.

A young man from the city's Fifth Middle School raised his hand. He asked, "What do homosexuals do?"

20 Miao smiled and his eyes almost disappeared. He said, "People of the same sex have a sexual relationship."

"Sodomy!" cried someone.

The room turned quiet for at least ten seconds. Then somebody asked what kind of crime this was.

Chief Miao explained, "Homosexuality originated in Western capitalism and bourgeois lifestyle. According to our law it's dealt with as a kind of hooliganism. Therefore, every one of the men we arrested will serve a sentence, from six months to five years, depending on the severity of his crime and his attitude toward it."

A truck blew its horn on the street and made my heart twinge. If Baowen went to prison, Beina would live like a widow, unless she divorced him. Why had he married her to begin with? Why did he ruin her this way?

25 What had happened was that a group of men, mostly clerks, artists, and schoolteachers, had formed a club called Men's World, a salon of sorts. Every Thursday evening they'd meet in a large room on the third floor of the office building of the Forestry Institute. Since the club admitted only men, the police suspected that it might be a secret association with a leaning toward violence, so they assigned two detectives to mix with the group. True, some of the men appeared to be intimate with one another in the club, but most of the time they talked about movies, books, and current events. Occasionally music was played, and they danced together. According to the detectives' account, it was a bizarre, emotional scene. A few men appeared in pairs, unashamed of necking and cuddling in the presence of others, and some would say with tears, "At last we men have a place for ourselves." A middle-aged painter wearing earrings exclaimed, "Now I feel alive! Only in here can I stop living in hypocrisy." Every week, two or three new faces would show up. When the club grew close to thirty men, the police took action and arrested them all.

After Chief Miao's briefing, we were allowed to meet with the criminals for fifteen minutes. A policeman led me into a small room in the basement and let me read Baowen's confession while he went to fetch him. I glanced through the four pages of interrogation notes, which stated that Baowen had been new to the club and that he'd joined them only twice, mainly because he was interested in their talks. Yet he didn't deny that he was a homosexual.

As it was next to a bathroom, the room smelled of urine. The policeman brought Baowen in and ordered him to sit opposite me at the table. Baowen, in handcuffs, avoided looking at me. His face was bloated, covered with bruises. A broad welt left by a baton, about four inches long, slanted across his forehead. The collar of his jacket was torn open. Yet he didn't appear frightened. His calm manner angered me, though I felt sorry for him.

I kept a hard face and said, "Baowen, do you know you committed a crime?"

"I didn't do anything. I just went there to listen to them talk."

30 "You mean you didn't do that thing with any man?" I wanted to make sure, so that I could help him.

He looked at me, then lowered his eyes, saying, "I thought about doing something, but, to be honest, I didn't."

"What's that supposed to mean?"

"I—I liked a man in the club, a lot. If he'd asked me, I might've agreed." His lips curled upward as if he prided himself on what he had said.

"You're sick!" I struck the table with my knuckles.

To my surprise, he said, "So? I'm a sick man. You think I don't know that?"

I was bewildered. He went on, "Years ago I tried everything to cure myself. I took a lot of herbs and boluses, and even ate baked scorpions, lizards, and toads. Nothing helped me. Still I'm fond of men. I don't know why I'm not interested in women. Whenever I'm with a woman my heart is as calm as a stone."

Outraged by his confession, I asked, "Then why did you marry my Beina? To make fun of her, eh? To throw mud in my face?"

"How could I be that mean? Before we got married, I told her I didn't like women and might not give her a baby."

"She believed you?"

"Yes. She said she wouldn't mind. She just wanted a husband, a home."

"She's an idiot!" I unfolded my hanky and blew my clogged nose into it, then asked, "Why did you choose her if you had no feelings for her at all?"

"What was the difference? For me she was similar to other women."

"You're a scoundrel!"

"If I didn't marry her, who would? The marriage helped us both, covering me and saving face for her. Besides, we could have a good apartment—a home. You see, I tried living like a normal man. I've never been mean to Beina."

"But the marriage is a fake! You lied to your mother too, didn't you?"

"She wanted me to marry."

The policeman signaled that our meeting was over. In spite of my anger, I told Baowen that I'd see what I could do, and that he'd better cooperate with the police and show a sincere attitude.

What should I do? I was sick of him, but he belonged to my family, at least in name, and I was obligated to help him.

On the way home I pedaled slowly, my mind heavy with thoughts. Gradually I realized that I might be able to do something to prevent him from going to jail. There were two steps I could take: first, I would maintain that he had done nothing in the club, so as to isolate him from the real criminals; second, I would present him as a sick man, so that he might receive medical treatment instead of a prison term. Once he became a criminal, he'd be marked forever as an enemy of society, no longer redeemable. Even his children might suffer. I ought to save him.

Fortunately both the Party secretary and the director of our factory were willing to accept Baowen as a sick man, particularly Secretary Zhu, who liked Baowen's kung fu style and had once let him teach his youngest son how to use a three-section cudgel. Zhu suggested we make an effort to rescue Baowen from the police. In the men's room inside our office building, he said to me, "Old Cheng, we must not let Baowen end up in prison." I was grateful for his words.

All of a sudden homosexuality became a popular topic in the factory. A few old workers said that some actors of the Beijing opera had slept together as lovers in the old days, because no women were allowed to perform in any troupe and the actors could associate only with men. Secretary Zhu, who was well read, said that some emperors in the Han Dynasty had kept male lovers in addition to their large harems. Director Liu had heard that the last emperor, Puyi, had often ordered his eunuchs to suck his penis and caress his testicles. Someone even claimed that homosexuality was an upper-class thing, not something for ordinary people. All this talk sickened me. I felt ashamed of my so-called son-in-law. I wouldn't join them in talking, and just listened, pretending I wasn't bothered.

As I expected, rumors went wild in the factory, especially in the foundry shop. Some people said Baowen was impotent. Some believed he was a hermaphrodite, otherwise his wife would've been pregnant long ago.

To console Beina, I went to see her one evening. She had a pleasant home, in which everything was in order. Two bookcases, filled with industrial manuals, biographies, novels, and medical books, stood against the whitewashed wall, on each side of the window. In one corner of the living room was a coat tree on which hung the red down parka Baowen had bought her before their wedding, and in another corner sat a floor lamp. At the opposite end of the room two pots of blooming flowers, one of cyclamens and the other of Bengal roses, were placed on a pair of low stools kept at an equal distance from each other and from the walls on both sides. Near the inner wall was a large sofa upholstered in orange imitation leather, and next to it, a yellow enamel spittoon. A black-and-white TV perched on an oak chest against the outer wall.

I was impressed, especially by the floor, inlaid with bricks and coated with bright red paint. Even my wife couldn't keep a home so neat. No doubt it was Baowen's work, because Beina couldn't be so tidy. Already the room showed the trace of her sloppy habits—in a corner were scattered an empty flour sack and a pile of soiled laundry. Sipping the tea she had poured me, I said, "Beina, I'm sorry about Baowen. I didn't know he was so bad."

"No, he's a good man." Her round eyes looked at me with a steady light.

"Why do you say that?"

"He's been good to me."

"But he can't be a good husband, can he?"

"What do you mean?"

I said bluntly, "He didn't go to bed with you very often, did he?"

"Oh, he can't do that because he practices kung fu. He said if he slept with a woman, all his many years' work would be gone. From the very beginning his master told him to avoid women."

"So you don't mind?" I was puzzled, saying to myself, What a stupid girl.

"Not really."

"But you two must've shared the bed a couple of times, haven't you?"

"No, we haven't."

"Really? Not even once?"

"No." She blushed a little and looked away, twisting her earlobe with her fingertips.

My head was reeling. After eight months' marriage she was still a virgin! And she didn't mind! I lifted the cup and took a large gulp of the jasmine tea.

A lull settled in. We both turned to watch the evening news; my numb mind couldn't take in what the anchorwoman was saying about a border skirmish between Vietnamese and Chinese troops.

A moment later I told Beina, "I'm sorry he has such a problem. If only we had known."

"Don't feel so bad, Uncle. In fact he's better than a normal man."

"How so?"

"Most men can't stay away from pretty women, but Baowen just likes to have a few buddies. What's wrong with that? It's better this way, 'cause I don't have to worry about those shameless bitches in our factory. He doesn't bother to give them a look. He'll never have a lifestyle problem."

I almost laughed, wondering how I should explain to her that he could have a sexual relationship with a man and that he'd been detained precisely because of a lifestyle problem. On second thought, I realized it might be better for her to continue to think that way. She didn't need more stress at the moment.

75 Then we talked about how to help Baowen. I told her to write a report emphasizing what a good, considerate husband he'd been. Of course she must not mention his celibacy in their marriage. Also, from now on, however vicious her fellow workers' remarks were, she should merely ignore them and never talk back, as if she'd heard nothing.

That night when I told my wife about Beina's silly notion, she smiled, saying, "Compared to most men, Baowen isn't so bad. Beina's not a fool."

I begged Chief Miao and a high-ranking officer to treat Baowen leniently and even gave each of them two bottles of brandy and a coupon for a Butterfly sewing machine. They seemed willing to help, but wouldn't promise me anything. For days I was so anxious that my wife was afraid my ulcer might recur.

One morning the Public Security Bureau called, saying they had accepted our factory's proposal and would have Baowen transferred to the mental hospital in a western suburb, provided our factory agreed to pay for his hospitalization. I accepted the offer readily, feeling relieved. Later, I learned that there wasn't enough space in the city's prison for twenty-seven gay men, who couldn't be mixed with other inmates and had to be put in solitary cells. So only four of them were jailed; the rest were either hospitalized (if their work units agreed to pay for the medical expenses) or sent to some labor farms to be reformed. The two Party members among them didn't go to jail, though they were expelled from the Party, a very severe punishment that ended their political lives.

The moment I put down the phone, I hurried to the assembly shop and found Beina. She broke into tears at the good news. She ran back home and filled a duffel bag with Baowen's clothes. We met at my office, then together set out for the Public Security Bureau. I pedaled my bicycle while she sat behind me, embracing the duffel as if it were a baby. With a strong tailwind, the cycling was easy and fast, so we arrived before Baowen left for the hospital. He was waiting for a van in front of the police station, accompanied by two policemen.

80 The bruises on his face had healed, and he looked handsome again. He smiled at us and said rather secretively, "I want to ask you a favor." He rolled his eyes as the dark-green van rounded the street corner, coming toward us.

"What?" I said.

"Don't let my mother know the truth. She's too old to take it. Don't tell her, please!"

"What should we say to her then?" I asked.

"Just say I have a temporary mental disorder."

85 Beina couldn't hold back her tears anymore, saying loudly, "Don't worry. We won't let her know. Take care of yourself and come back soon." She handed him the duffel, which he accepted without a word.

I nodded to assure him that I wouldn't reveal the truth. He smiled at her, then at me. For some reason his face turned rather sweet—charming and enticing, as though it were a mysterious female face. I blinked my eyes and wondered if he was really a man. It flashed through my mind that if he were a woman, he would've been quite a beauty—tall, slim, muscular, and slightly languid.

My thoughts were cut short by a metallic screech as the van stopped in front of us. Baowen climbed into it; so did the policemen. I walked around the van and shook his hand, saying that I'd visit him the next week, and that meanwhile, if he needed anything, just to give me a ring.

We waved goodbye as the van drew away, its tire chains clattering and flinging up bits of snow. After a blasting toot, it turned left and disappeared from the icy street. I got on my bicycle as a gust of wind blew up and almost threw me down. Beina followed me for about twenty yards, then leaped on the carrier, and together we headed home. She was so heavy. Thank heaven, I was riding a Great Golden Deer, one of the sturdiest makes.

During the following week I heard from Baowen once. He said on the phone that he felt better now and less agitated. Indeed his voice sounded calm and smooth. He asked me to bring him a few books when I came, specifically his *Dictionary of Universal Knowledge*, which was a hefty, rare book translated from the Russian in the late fifties. I had no idea how he had come by it.

I went to see him on Thursday morning. The hospital was on a mountain, 90
six miles southwest of Muji City. As I was cycling on the asphalt road, a few tall smokestacks fumed lazily beyond the larch woods in the west. To my right, the power lines along the roadside curved, heavy with fluffy snow, which would drop in little chunks whenever the wind blew across them. Now and then I overtook a horse cart loaded with earless sheaves of wheat, followed by one or two foals. After I pedaled across a stone bridge and turned into the mouth of a valley, a group of brick buildings emerged on a gentle slope, connected to one another by straight cement paths. Farther up the hill, past the buildings, there was a cow pen, in which about two dozen milk cows were grazing on dry grass while a few others huddled together to keep warm.

It was so peaceful here that if you hadn't known this was a mental hospital, you might have imagined it was a sanatorium for ranking officials. Entering Building 9, I was stopped by a guard, who then took me to Baowen's room on the ground floor. It happened that the doctor on duty, a tall fortyish man with tapering fingers, was making the morning rounds and examining Baowen. He shook hands with me and said that my son-in-law was doing fine. His surname was Mai; his whiskered face looked very intelligent. When he turned to give a male nurse instructions about Baowen's treatment, I noticed an enormous wart in his ear, almost blocking the earhole like a hearing aid. In a way he looked like a foreigner. I wondered if he had some Mongolian or Tibetan blood.

"We give him the electric bath," Doctor Mai said to me a moment later.

"What?" I asked, wincing.

"We treat him with the electric bath."

I turned to Baowen. "How is it?" 95

"It's good, really soothing." He smiled, but there was a churlish look in his eyes, and his mouth tightened.

The nurse was ready to take him for the treatment. Never having heard of such a bath, I asked Doctor Mai, "Can I see how it works?"

"All right, you may go with them."

Together we climbed the stairs to the second floor. There was another reason for me to join them. I wanted to find out whether Baowen was a normal man. The rumors in our factory had gotten on my nerves, particularly the one that said he had no penis—that was why he had always avoided bathing in the workers' bathhouse.

100 After taking off our shoes and putting on plastic slippers, we entered a small room that had pea-green walls and a parquet floor. At its center lay a porcelain bathtub, a ghastly thing, like an instrument of torture. Affixed along the interior wall of the tub were rectangles of black, perforated metal. Three thick rubber cords connected them to a tall machine standing by the wall. A control board full of buttons, gauges, and switches was mounted atop the machine. The young nurse, burly and square-faced, turned on the faucet; steaming water began to tumble into the tub. Then he went over to operate the machine. He seemed good-natured; his name was Long Fuhai. He said he came from the countryside, apparently of peasant stock, and had graduated from Jilin Nursing School.

Baowen smiled at me while unbuttoning his zebra-striped hospital robe. He looked fine now—all the bruises had disappeared from his face, which had become pinkish and smooth. I was frightened by the tub, however. It seemed more suitable for electrocuting a criminal. No matter how sick I might be, I would never lie in it with my back resting against that metal groove. What if there were a problem with the wiring?

"Does it hurt?" I asked Baowen.

"No."

He went behind a khaki screen in a corner and began taking off his clothes. When the water half filled the tub, the nurse took a small bag of white powder out of a drawer, cut it open with scissors, and poured the stuff into the water. It must be salt. He tucked up his shirt sleeves and bent double to agitate the solution with both hands, which were large and sinewy.

105 To my dismay, Baowen came out in a clean pair of shorts. Without hesitation he got into the tub and lay down, just as one would enter a lukewarm bathing pool. I was amazed. "Have you given him electricity yet?" I asked Nurse Long.

"Yes, some. I'll increase it little by little." He turned to the machine and adjusted a few buttons.

"You know," he said to me, "your son-in-law is a very good patient, always cooperative."

"He should be."

"That's why we give him the bath. Other patients get electric cuffs around their limbs or electric rods on their bodies. Some of them scream like animals every time. We have to tie them up."

110 "When will he be cured?"

"I'm not sure."

Baowen was noiseless in the electrified water, with his eyes shut and his head resting on a black rubber pad at the end of the tub. He looked fine, rather relaxed.

I drew up a chair and sat down. Baowen seemed reluctant to talk, preferring to concentrate on the treatment, so I remained silent, observing him. His body was wiry, his legs hairless, and the front of his shorts bulged quite a bit. He looked all right physically. Once in a while he breathed a feeble sigh.

As the nurse increased the electric current, Baowen began to squirm in the tub as if smarting from something. "Are you all right?" I asked but dared not touch him.

"Yeah."

He kept his eyes shut. Glistening beads of sweat gathered on his forehead. He looked pale, his lips curling now and again as though he were thirsty.

Then the nurse gave him more electricity. Baowen began writhing and moaning a little. Obviously he was suffering. This bath couldn't be so soothing as he'd claimed. With a white towel Nurse Long wiped the sweat off Baowen's face and whispered, "I'll turn it down in a few minutes."

"No, give me more!" Baowen said resolutely without opening his eyes, his face twisted.

I felt as though he were ashamed of himself. Perhaps my presence made this section of the treatment more uncomfortable for him. His hands gripped the rim of the tub, the arched wrists trembling. For a good three minutes nobody said a word; the room was so quiet that its walls seemed to be ringing.

As the nurse gradually reduced the electricity, Baowen calmed down. His toes stopped wiggling.

Not wanting to bother him further with my presence, I went out to look for Doctor Mai, to thank him and find out when Baowen would be cured. The doctor was not in his office, so I walked out of the building for a breath of air. The sun was high and the snow blazingly white. Once outside, I had to close my eyes for a minute to adjust them. I then sat down on a bench and lit a cigarette. A young woman in an ermine hat and army mittens passed by, holding an empty milk pail and humming the song "Comrade, Please Have a Cup of Tea." She looked handsome, and her crisp voice pleased me. I gazed at the pair of thick braids behind her, which swayed a little in the wind.

My heart was full of pity for Baowen. He was such a fine young man that he ought to be able to love a woman, have a family, and enjoy a normal life.

Twenty minutes later I rejoined him in his room. He looked tired, still shivering a little. He told me that as the electric currents increased, his skin had begun prickling as though stung by hundreds of mosquitoes. That was why he couldn't stay in the tub for longer than half an hour.

I felt for him and said, "I'll tell our leaders how sincere your attitude is and how cooperative you are."

"Oh, fine." He tilted his damp head. "Thanks for bringing the books."

"Do you need something else?"

"No." He sounded sad.

"Baowen, I hope you can come home before the New Year. Beina needs you."

"I know. I don't want to be locked up here forever."

I told him that Beina had written to his mother, saying he'd been away on a business trip. Then the bell for lunch rang in the building, and outside the loudspeaker began broadcasting the fiery music of "March of the Volunteers." Nurse Long walked in with a pair of chopsticks and a plate containing two corn buns. He said cheerily to Baowen, "I'll bring you the dish in a minute. We have tofu stewed with sauerkraut today, also bean sprout soup."

I stood up and took my leave.

When I reported Baowen's condition to the factory leaders, they seemed impressed. The term "electric bath" must have given their imagination free rein. Secretary Zhu kept shaking his head and said, "I'm sorry Baowen has to go through such a thing."

I didn't explain that the electric bath was a treatment less severe than the other kinds, nor did I describe what the bath was like. I just said, "They steep him in electrified water every day." Let the terror seize their brains, I thought, so that they might be more sympathetic toward Baowen when he is discharged from the hospital.

It was mid-December, and Baowen had been in the hospital for a month already. For days Beina went on saying that she wanted to see how her husband was doing; she was eager to bring him home before the New Year. Among her fellow workers rumors persisted. One said the electric bath had blistered Baowen; another claimed that his genitals had been shriveled up by the treatment; another added that he had become a vegetarian, nauseated at the mere sight of meat. The young woman who had once declared she'd leave her door open for him had just married and proudly told everybody she was pregnant. People began to be kind and considerate to Beina, treating her like an abused wife. The leaders of the assembly shop assigned her only the daytime shift. I was pleased that Finance still paid Baowen his wages as though he were on sick leave. Perhaps they did this because they didn't want to upset me.

On Saturday, Beina and I went to the mental hospital. She couldn't pedal, and it was too far for me to carry her on my bicycle, so we took the bus. She had been there by herself two weeks ago to deliver some socks and a pair of woolen pajamas she'd knitted for Baowen.

We arrived at the hospital early in the afternoon. Baowen looked healthy and in good spirits. It seemed that the bath had helped him. He was happy to see Beina and even cuddled her in my presence. He gave her two toffees; knowing I disliked candies, he didn't offer any to me. He poured a large mug of malted milk for both of us, since there was only one mug in the room. I didn't touch the milk, unsure whether homosexuality was communicable. I was glad to see that he treated his wife well. He took a genuine interest in what she said about their comrades in our factory, and now and then laughed heartily. What a wonderful husband he could have been if he were not sick.

Having sat with the couple for a few minutes, I left so that they could be alone. I went to the nurses' office upstairs and found Long Fuhai writing at a desk. The door was open, and I knocked on its frame. Startled, he closed his brown notebook and stood up.

"I didn't mean to scare you," I said.

"No, Uncle, only because I didn't expect anyone to come up here."

I took a carton of Peony cigarettes out of my bag and put it on the desk, saying, "I won't take too much of your time, young man. Please keep this as a token of my regards." I didn't mean to bribe him; I was sincerely grateful to him for treating Baowen well.

"Oh, don't give me this, please."

"You don't smoke?"

"I do. Tell you what, give it to Doctor Mai. He'll help Baowen more."

I was puzzled. Why didn't he want the top-quality cigarettes if he smoked? Seeing that I was confused, he went on, "I'll be nice to Baowen without any gift from you. He's a good man. It's the doctor's wheels that you should grease."

"I have another carton for him."

"One carton's nothing here. You should give him at least two."

I was moved by his thoughtfulness, thanked him, and said goodbye.

Doctor Mai happened to be in his office. When I walked in, he was reading the current issue of *Women's Life*, whose back cover carried a large photo of Madame Mao on trial—she wore black and stood, handcuffed, between two young policewomen. Doctor Mai put the magazine aside and asked me to sit down. In the room, tall shelves loaded with books and files lined the walls. A smell of rotten fruit hung in there. He seemed pleased to see me.

After we exchanged a few words, I took out both cartons of cigarettes and handed them to him. "This is just a small token of my gratitude, for the New Year," I said.

He took the cigarettes and put them away under his desk. "Thanks a lot," he 150
whispered.

"Doctor Mai, do you think Baowen will be cured before the holiday?" I asked.

"What did you say? Cured?" He looked surprised.

"Yes."

He shook his head slowly, then turned to check that the door was shut. It was. He motioned me to move closer. I pulled the chair forward a little and rested my forearms on the edge of his Bakelite desktop.

"To be honest, there's no cure," he said. 155

"What?"

"Homosexuality isn't an illness, so how can it have a cure? Don't tell anyone I said this."

"Then why torture Baowen like that?"

"The police sent him here and we couldn't refuse. Besides, we ought to make him feel better and hopeful."

"So it isn't disease?" 160

"Unfortunately, no. Let me say this again: there's no cure for your son-in-law, Old Cheng. It's not a disease. It's just a sexual preference; it may be congenital, like being left-handed. Got it?"

"Then why give him the electric bath?" Still I wasn't convinced.

"Electrotherapy is prescribed by the book—a standard treatment required by the Department of Public Health. I have no choice but to follow the regulations. That's why I didn't give him any of those harsher treatments. The bath is very mild by comparison. You see, I've done everything in my power to help him. Let me tell you another fact: according to the statistics, so far electrotherapy has cured only one out of a thousand homosexuals. I bet cod liver oil, or chocolate, or fried pork, anything, could produce a better result. All right, enough of this. I've said too much."

At last his words sank in. For a good while I sat there motionless with a numb mind. A flock of sparrows were flitting about in the naked branches outside the window, chasing the one that held a tiny ear of millet in its bill. Another of them dragged a yellow string tied around its leg, unable to fly as nimbly as the others. I rose to my feet and thanked the doctor for his candid words. He stubbed out his cigarette in the ashtray on the windowsill and said, "I'll take special care of your son-in-law. Don't worry."

I rejoined Beina downstairs. Baowen looked quite cheerful, and it seemed 165
they'd had a good time. He said to me, "If I can't come home soon, don't try too hard to get me out. They won't keep me here forever."

"I'll see what I can do."

In my heart I was exasperated, because if Doctor Mai's words were true, there'd be little I could do for Baowen. If homosexuality wasn't a disease, why had he felt sick and tried to have himself cured? Had he been shamming? It was unlikely.

Beina had been busy cleaning their home since her last visit to the hospital. She bought two young drakes and planned to make drunk duck, the dish she said Baowen liked best. My heart was heavy. On the one hand, I'd have loved to have him back for the holiday; on the other hand, I was unsure what would happen if his condition hadn't improved. I dared not reveal my thoughts to anybody, not even to my wife, who had a big mouth. Because of her, the whole factory knew that Beina was still a virgin, and some people called her the Virgin Bride.

For days I pondered what to do. I was confused. Everybody said that homosexuality was a disease except for Doctor Mai, whose opinion I dared not mention to others. The factory leaders would be mad at me if they knew there was no cure for homosexuality. We had already spent over three thousand yuan on Baowen. I kept questioning in my mind, If homosexuality is a natural thing, then why are there men and women? Why can't two men get married and make a baby? Why didn't nature give men another hole? I was beset by doubts. If only I could have seen a trustworthy doctor for a second opinion. If only I had a knowledgeable, honest friend to talk with.

I hadn't yet made up my mind about what to do when, five days before the holiday, Chief Miao called from the Public Security Bureau. He informed me that Baowen had repeated his crime, so the police had taken him out of the hospital and sent him to the prison in Tangyuan County. "This time he did it," said the chief.

"Impossible!" I cried.

"We have evidence and witnesses. He doesn't deny it himself."

"Oh." I didn't know how to continue.

"He has to be incarcerated now."

"Are you sure he's not a hermaphrodite?" I mentioned that as a last resort.

Miao chuckled drily. "No, he's not. We had him checked. Physically he's a man, healthy and normal. Obviously it's a mental, moral disease, like an addiction to opium."

Putting down the phone, I felt dizzy, cursing Baowen for having totally ruined himself. What had happened was that he and Long Fuhai had developed a relationship secretly. The nurse often gave him a double amount of meat or fish at dinner. Baowen, in return, unraveled his woolen pajamas and knitted Long a pullover with the wool. One evening when they were lying in each other's arms in the nurses' office, an old cleaner passed by in the corridor and coughed. Long Fuhai was terrified, convinced that the man saw what they had been doing. For days, however hard Baowen tried to talk him out of his conviction, Long wouldn't change his mind, blaming Baowen for having misled him. He said that the old cleaner often smiled at him meaningfully and was sure to turn them in. Finally Long Fuhai went to the hospital leaders and confessed everything. So unlike Baowen, who got three and a half years in jail, Nurse Long was merely put on probation; if he worked harder and criticized himself well, he might keep his current job.

That evening I went to tell Beina about the new development. As I spoke, she sobbed continually. Although she'd been cleaning the apartment for several days, her home was a shambles, most of the flowers half dead, and dishes and pots piled in the sink. Mopping her face with a pink towel, she asked me, "What should I tell my mother-in-law?"

"Tell her the truth."

She made no response. I said again, "You should consider a divorce."

"No!" Her sobbing turned into wailing. "He—he's my husband and I'm his wife. If I die my soul belongs to him. We've sworn never to leave each other. Let others say whatever they want, I know he's a good man."

"Then why did he go to bed with Long Fuhai?"

"He just wanted to have a good time. That was all. It's nothing like adultery or bigamy, is it?"

"But it's a crime that got him put in jail," I said. Although in my heart I admitted that Baowen in every way was a good fellow except for his fondness for men, I had to be adamant about my position. I was in charge of security for our factory; if I had a criminal son-in-law, who would listen to me? Wouldn't I be removed from my office soon? If I lost my job, who could protect Beina? Sooner or later she would be laid off, since a criminal's wife was not supposed to have the same employment opportunities as others. Beina remained silent; I asked again, "What are you going to do?"

"Wait for him."

I took a few spiced pumpkin seeds from a bowl, stood up, and went over to the window. Under the sill the radiator was hissing softly with a tiny steam leak. Outside, in the distance, firecrackers, one after another, scattered clusters of sparks in the indigo dusk. I turned around and said, "He's not worth waiting for. You must divorce him."

"No, I won't," she moaned.

"Well, it's impossible for me to have a criminal as my son-in-law. I've been humiliated enough. If you want to wait for him, don't come to see me again." I put the pumpkin seeds back into the bowl, picked up my fur hat, and dragged myself out the door.

(1999)

Questions for Discussion and Writing

1. What do you think of the narrator's views about homosexuality? Do you think they're the same as the author's views? How does Jin cast doubt on Cheng's attitudes toward homosexuals?
2. How does Cheng feel about Baowen? How do these feelings change in the course of the story? How does Cheng's position at the factory affect his feelings and reactions to Baowen's predicament?
3. Why does Long Fuhai confess his sexual activity to the hospital authorities? He blames Baowen for "having misled him." What do you think of that accusation?
4. In the end, the narrator tells Beina not to come see him again if she's going to wait for Baowen. Why does he say this? Do you think he will stick to his position?
5. What specific cultural issues does Jin identify in this story? Write an essay in which you make a claim about the author's purpose for writing about these issues.

Sherman Alexie 1966–

Sherman Alexie was born hydrocephalic (with water on the brain) and was expected to die or be severely retarded. Instead, he grew up on the Spokane Indian Reservation in Washington and attended the tribal school until he decided to seek a better education at an off-reservation high school, where he and the school mascot were the only Indians. While attending Washington State University, he joined a poetry workshop and became a creative writer. He has published eleven books of poetry, three short-story collections, four novels, and several screenplays. Some Native Americans criticize Alexie for perpetuating unflattering stereotypes, to which he replies that he reflects reality as he knows it. He adapted the following story for the film *Smoke Signals* in 1997.

This Is What It Means to Say Phoenix, Arizona

Just after Victor lost his job at the BIA,[1] he also found out that his father had died of a heart attack in Phoenix, Arizona. Victor hadn't seen his father in a few years, only talked to him on the telephone once or twice, but there still was a genetic pain, which was soon to be pain as real and immediate as a broken bone.

Victor didn't have any money. Who does have money on a reservation, except the cigarette and fireworks salespeople? His father had a savings account waiting to be claimed, but Victor needed to find a way to get to Phoenix. Victor's mother was just as poor as he was, and the rest of his family didn't have any use at all for him. So Victor called the Tribal Council.

"Listen," Victor said. "My father just died. I need some money to get to Phoenix to make arrangements."

"Now, Victor," the council said. "You know we're having a difficult time financially."

"But I thought the council had special funds set aside for stuff like this." 5

"Now, Victor, we do have some money available for the proper return of tribal members' bodies. But I don't think we have enough to bring your father all the way back from Phoenix."

"Well," Victor said. "It ain't going to cost all that much. He had to be cremated. Things were kind of ugly. He died of a heart attack in his trailer and nobody found him for a week. It was really hot, too. You get the picture."

"Now, Victor, we're sorry for your loss and the circumstances. But we can really only afford to give you one hundred dollars."

"That's not even enough for a plane ticket."

"Well, you might consider driving down to Phoenix." 10

"I don't have a car. Besides, I was going to drive my father's pickup back up here."

"Now, Victor," the council said. "We're sure there is somebody who could drive you to Phoenix. Or is there somebody who could lend you the rest of the money?"

"You know there ain't nobody around with that kind of money."

[1]The Bureau of Indian Affairs, which administers programs for federally recognized tribes.

"Well, we're sorry, Victor, but that's the best we can do."

15 Victor accepted the Tribal Council's offer. What else could he do? So he signed the proper papers, picked up his check, and walked over to the Trading Post to cash it.

While Victor stood in line, he watched Thomas Builds-the-Fire standing near the magazine rack, talking to himself. Like he always did. Thomas was a storyteller that nobody wanted to listen to. That's like being a dentist in a town where everybody has false teeth.

Victor and Thomas Builds-the-Fire were the same age, had grown up and played in the dirt together. Ever since Victor could remember, it was Thomas who always had something to say.

Once, when they were seven years old, when Victor's father still lived with the family, Thomas closed his eyes and told Victor this story: "Your father's heart is weak. He is afraid of his own family. He is afraid of you. Late at night he sits in the dark. Watches the television until there's nothing but that white noise. Sometimes he feels like he wants to buy a motorcycle and ride away. He wants to run and hide. He doesn't want to be found."

Thomas Builds-the-Fire had known that Victor's father was going to leave, knew it before anyone. Now Victor stood in the Trading Post with a one-hundred-dollar check in his hand, wondering if Thomas knew that Victor's father was dead, if he knew what was going to happen next.

20 Just then Thomas looked at Victor, smiled, and walked over to him.

"Victor, I'm sorry about your father," Thomas said.

"How did you know about it?" Victor asked.

"I heard it on the wind. I heard it from the birds. I felt it in the sunlight. Also, your mother was just in here crying."

"Oh," Victor said and looked around the Trading Post. All the other Indians stared, surprised that Victor was even talking to Thomas. Nobody talked to Thomas anymore because he told the same damn stories over and over again. Victor was embarrassed, but he thought that Thomas might be able to help him. Victor felt a sudden need for tradition.

25 "I can lend you the money you need," Thomas said suddenly. "But you have to take me with you."

"I can't take your money," Victor said. "I mean, I haven't hardly talked to you in years. We're not really friends anymore."

"I didn't say we were friends. I said you had to take me with you."

"Let me think about it."

Victor went home with his one hundred dollars and sat at the kitchen table. He held his head in his hands and thought about Thomas Builds-the-Fire, remembered little details, tears and scars, the bicycle they shared for a summer, so many stories.

---

30 Thomas Builds-the-Fire sat on the bicycle, waited in Victor's yard. He was ten years old and skinny. His hair was dirty because it was the Fourth of July.

"Victor," Thomas yelled. "Hurry up. We're going to miss the fireworks."

After a few minutes, Victor ran out of his house, jumped the porch railing, and landed gracefully on the sidewalk.

"And the judges award him a 9.95, the highest score of the summer," Thomas said, clapped, laughed.

Evan Adams as Thomas Builds-the-Fire and Adam Beach as Victor Joseph in *Smoke Signals*, the 1997 film version of "This Is What It Means to Say Phoenix, Arizona."

"That was perfect, cousin," Victor said. "And it's my turn to ride the bike."

Thomas gave up the bike and they headed for the fairgrounds. It was nearly dark and the fireworks were about to start.

"You know," Thomas said. "It's strange how us Indians celebrate the Fourth of July. It ain't like it was *our* independence everybody was fighting for."

"You think about things too much," Victor said. "It's just supposed to be fun. Maybe Junior will be there."

"Which Junior? Everybody on this reservation is named Junior."

And they both laughed.

The fireworks were small, hardly more than a few bottle rockets and a fountain. But it was enough for two Indian boys. Years later, they would need much more.

Afterwards, sitting in the dark, fighting off mosquitoes, Victor turned to Thomas Builds-the-Fire.

"Hey," Victor said. "Tell me a story."

Thomas closed his eyes and told this story: "There were these two Indian boys who wanted to be warriors. But it was too late to be warriors in the old way. All the horses were gone. So the two Indian boys stole a car and drove to the city. They parked the stolen car in front of the police station and then hitchhiked back home to the reservation. When they got back, all their friends cheered and their parents' eyes shone with pride. *You were very brave*, everybody said to the two Indian boys. *Very brave*."

"Ya-hey," Victor said. "That's a good one. I wish I could be a warrior."

"Me, too," Thomas said.

They went home together in the dark, Thomas on the bike now, Victor on foot. They walked through shadows and light from streetlamps.

"We've come a long ways," Thomas said. "We have outdoor lighting."

"All I need is the stars," Victor said. "And besides, you still think about things too much."

They separated then, each headed for home both laughing all the way.

Victor sat at his kitchen table. He counted his one hundred dollars again and again. He knew he needed more to make it to Phoenix and back. He knew he needed Thomas Builds-the-Fire. So he put his money in his wallet and opened the front door to find Thomas on the porch.

"Ya-hey, Victor," Thomas said. "I knew you'd call me."

Thomas walked into the living room and sat down on Victor's favorite chair.

"I've got some money saved up," Thomas said. "It's enough to get us down there, but you have to get us back."

"I've got this hundred dollars," Victor said. "And my dad had a savings account I'm going to claim."

"How much in your dad's account?"

"Enough. A few hundred."

"Sounds good. When we leaving?"

When they were fifteen and had long since stopped being friends, Victor and Thomas got into a fistfight. That is, Victor was really drunk and beat Thomas up for no reason at all. All the other Indian boys stood around and watched it happen. Junior was there and so were Lester, Seymour, and a lot of others. The beating might have gone on until Thomas was dead if Norma Many Horses hadn't come along and stopped it.

"Hey, you boys," Norma yelled and jumped out of her car. "Leave him alone."

If it had been someone else, even another man, the Indian boys would've just ignored the warnings. But Norma was a warrior. She was powerful. She could have picked up any two of the boys and smashed their skulls together. But worse than that, she would have dragged them all over to some tipi and made them listen to some elder tell a dusty old story.

The Indian boys scattered, and Norma walked over to Thomas and picked him up.

"Hey, little man, are you okay?" she asked.

Thomas gave her a thumbs up.

"Why they always picking on you?"

Thomas shook his head, closed his eyes, but no stories came to him, no words or music. He just wanted to go home, to lie in his bed and let his dreams tell his stories for him.

Thomas Builds-the-Fire and Victor sat next to each other in the airplane, coach section. A tiny white woman had the window seat. She was busy twisting her body into pretzels. She was flexible.

"I have to ask," Thomas said, and Victor closed his eyes in embarrassment.

"Don't," Victor said.

"Excuse me, miss," Thomas asked. "Are you a gymnast or something?"

"There's no something about it," she said. "I was first alternate on the 1980 Olympic team."

"Really?" Thomas asked.

"Really."

"I mean, you used to be a world-class athlete?" Thomas asked.

"My husband still thinks I am."

Thomas Builds-the-Fire smiled. She was a mental gymnast, too. She pulled her leg straight up against her body so that she could've kissed her kneecap.

"I wish I could do that," Thomas said.

Victor was ready to jump out of the plane. Thomas, that crazy Indian storyteller with ratty old braids and broken teeth, was flirting with a beautiful Olympic gymnast. Nobody back home on the reservation would ever believe it.

"Well," the gymnast said. "It's easy. Try it."

Thomas grabbed at his leg and tried to pull it up into the same position as the gymnast. He couldn't even come close, which made Victor and the gymnast laugh.

"Hey," she asked. "You two are Indian, right?"

"Full-blood," Victor said.

"Not me," Thomas said. "I'm half magician on my mother's side and half clown on my father's."

They all laughed.

"What are your names?" she asked.

"Victor and Thomas."

"Mine is Cathy. Pleased to meet you all."

The three of them talked for the duration of the flight. Cathy the gymnast complained about the government, how they screwed the 1980 Olympic team by boycotting.

"Sounds like you all got a lot in common with Indians," Thomas said.

Nobody laughed.

After the plane landed in Phoenix and they had all found their way to the terminal, Cathy the gymnast smiled and waved good-bye.

"She was really nice," Thomas said.

"Yeah, but everybody talks to everybody on airplanes," Victor said. "It's too bad we can't always be that way."

"You always used to tell me I think too much," Thomas said. "Now it sounds like you do."

"Maybe I caught it from you."

"Yeah."

Thomas and Victor rode in a taxi to the trailer where Victor's father died.

"Listen," Victor said as they stopped in front of the trailer. "I never told you I was sorry for beating you up that time."

"Oh, it was nothing. We were just kids and you were drunk."

"Yeah, but I'm still sorry."

"That's all right."

Victor paid for the taxi and the two of them stood in the hot Phoenix summer. They could smell the trailer.

"This ain't going to be nice," Victor said. "You don't have to go in."

"You're going to need help."

Victor walked to the front door and opened it. The stink rolled out and made them both gag. Victor's father had lain in that trailer for a week in hundred-degree temperatures before anyone found him. And the only reason anyone found him was because of the smell. They needed dental records to identify him. That's exactly what the coroner said. They needed dental records.

"Oh, man," Victor said. "I don't know if I can do this." 105

"Well, then don't."

"But there might be something valuable in there."

"I thought his money was in the bank."

"It is. I was talking about pictures and letters and stuff like that."

"Oh," Thomas said as he held his breath and followed Victor into the trailer. 110

When Victor was twelve, he stepped into an underground wasp nest. His foot was caught in the hole, and no matter how hard he struggled, Victor couldn't pull free. He might have died there, stung a thousand times, if Thomas Builds-the-Fire had not come by.

"Run," Thomas yelled and pulled Victor's foot from the hole. They ran then, hard as they ever had, faster than Billy Mills, faster than Jim Thorpe, faster than the wasps could fly.

Victor and Thomas ran until they couldn't breathe, ran until it was cold and dark outside, ran until they were lost and it took hours to find their way home. All the way back, Victor counted his stings.

"Seven," Victor said. "My lucky number."

Victor didn't find much to keep in the trailer. Only a photo album and a stereo. 115
Everything else had that smell stuck in it or was useless anyway.

"I guess this is all," Victor said. "It ain't much."

"Better than nothing," Thomas said.

"Yeah, and I do have the pickup."

"Yeah," Thomas said. "It's in good shape."

"Dad was good about that stuff." 120

"Yeah, I remember your dad."

"Really?" Victor asked. "What do you remember?"

Thomas Builds-the-Fire closed his eyes and told this story: "I remember when I had this dream that told me to go to Spokane, to stand by the Falls in the middle of the city and wait for a sign. I knew I had to go there but I didn't have a car. Didn't have a license. I was only thirteen. So I walked all the way, took me all day, and I finally made it to the Falls. I stood there for an hour waiting. Then your dad came walking up. *What the hell are you doing here?* he asked me. I said, *Waiting for a vision.* Then your father said, *All you're going to get here is mugged.* So he drove me over to Denny's, bought me dinner, and then drove me home to the reservation. For a long time I was mad because I thought my dreams had lied to me. But they didn't. Your dad was my vision. *Take care of each other* is what my dreams were saying. *Take care of each other.*"

Victor was quiet for a long time. He searched his mind for memories of his father, found the good ones, found a few bad ones, added it all up, and smiled.

"My father never told me about finding you in Spokane," Victor said. 125

"He said he wouldn't tell anybody. Didn't want me to get in trouble. But he said I had to watch out for you as part of the deal."

"Really?"

"Really. Your father said you would need the help. He was right."

"That's why you came down here with me, isn't it?" Victor asked.

"I came because of your father." 130

Victor and Thomas climbed into the pickup, drove over to the bank, and claimed the three hundred dollars in the savings account.

Thomas Builds-the-Fire could fly.

Once, he jumped off the roof of the tribal school and flapped his arms like a crazy eagle. And he flew. For a second, he hovered, suspended above all the other Indian boys who were too smart or too scared to jump.

"He's flying," Junior yelled, and Seymour was busy looking for the trick wires or mirrors. But it was real. As real as the dirt when Thomas lost altitude and crashed to the ground.

He broke his arm in two places. 135

"He broke his wing," Victor chanted, and the other Indian boys joined in, made it a tribal song.

"He broke his wing, he broke his wing, he broke his wing," all the Indian boys chanted as they ran off, flapping their wings, wishing they could fly, too. They hated Thomas for his courage, his brief moment as a bird. Everybody has dreams about flying. Thomas flew.

One of his dreams came true for just a second, just enough to make it real.

Victor's father, his ashes, fit in one wooden box with enough left over to fill a cardboard box.

"He always was a big man," Thomas said. 140

Victor carried part of his father and Thomas carried the rest out to the pickup. They set him down carefully behind the seats, put a cowboy hat on the wooden box and a Dodgers cap on the cardboard box. That's the way it was supposed to be.

"Ready to head back home?" Victor asked.

"It's going to be a long drive."

"Yeah, take a couple days, maybe."

"We can take turns," Thomas said. 145

"Okay," Victor said, but they didn't take turns. Victor drove for sixteen hours straight north, made it halfway up Nevada toward home before he finally pulled over.

"Hey, Thomas," Victor said. "You got to drive for a while."

"Okay."

Thomas Builds-the-Fire slid behind the wheel and started off down the road. All through Nevada, Thomas and Victor had been amazed at the lack of animal life, at the absence of water, of movement.

"Where is everything?" Victor had asked more than once. 150

Now when Thomas was finally driving they saw the first animal, maybe the only animal in Nevada. It was a long-eared jackrabbit.

"Look," Victor yelled. "It's alive."

Thomas and Victor were busy congratulating themselves on their discovery when the jackrabbit darted out into the road and under the wheels of the pickup.

"Stop the goddamn car," Victor yelled, and Thomas did stop, backed the pickup to the dead jackrabbit.

"Oh, man, he's dead," Victor said as he looked at the squashed animal. 155

"Really dead."

"The only thing alive in this whole state and we just killed it."

"I don't know," Thomas said. "I think it was suicide."

Victor looked around the desert, sniffed the air, felt the emptiness and loneliness, and nodded his head.

"Yeah," Victor said. "It had to be suicide."

"I can't believe this," Thomas said. "You drive for a thousand miles and there ain't even any bugs smashed on the windshield. I drive for ten seconds and kill the only living thing in Neveda."

"Yeah," Victor said. "Maybe I should drive."

"Maybe you should."

Thomas Builds-the-Fire walked through the corridors of the tribal school by himself. Nobody wanted to be anywhere near him because of all those stories. Story after story.

Thomas closed his eyes and his story came to him: "We are all given one thing by which our lives are measured, one determination. Mine are the stories which can change or not change the world. It doesn't matter which as long as I continue to tell the stories. My father, he died on Okinawa in World War II, died fighting for this country, which had tried to kill him for years. My mother, she died giving birth to me, died while I was still inside her. She pushed me out into the world with her last breath. I have no brothers or sisters. I have only my stories which came to me before I even had the words to speak. I learned a thousand stories before I took my first thousand steps. They are all I have. It's all I can do."

Thomas Builds-the-Fire told his stories to all those who would stop and listen. He kept telling them long after people had stopped listening.

Victor and Thomas made it back to the reservation just as the sun was rising. It was the beginning of a new day on earth, but the same old shit on the reservation.

"Good morning," Thomas said.

"Good morning."

The tribe was waking up, ready for work, eating breakfast, reading the newspaper, just like everybody else does. Willene LeBret was out in her garden wearing a bathrobe. She waved when Thomas and Victor drove by.

"Crazy Indians made it," she said to herself and went back to her roses.

Victor stopped the pickup in front of Thomas Builds-the-Fire's HUD house.[2] They both yawned, stretched a little, shook dust from their bodies.

"I'm tired," Victor said.

"Of everything," Thomas added.

They both searched for words to end the journey. Victor needed to thank Thomas for his help, for the money, and make the promise to pay it all back.

"Don't worry about the money," Thomas said. "It don't make any difference anyhow."

"Probably not, enit?"

"Nope."

---

[2]The Department of Housing and Urban Development, the federal agency that provides subsidized housing for low-income persons.

Victor knew that Thomas would remain the crazy storyteller-who talked to dogs and cars, who listened to the wind and pine trees. Victor knew that he couldn't really be friends with Thomas, even after all that had happened. It was cruel but it was real. As real as the ashes, as Victor's father, sitting behind the seats.

180 "I know how it is," Thomas said. "I know you ain't going to treat me any better than you did before. I know your friends would give you too much shit about it."

Victor was ashamed of himself. Whatever happened to the tribal ties, the sense of community? The only real thing he shared with anybody was a bottle and broken dreams. He owed Thomas something, anything.

"Listen," Victor said and handed Thomas the cardboard box which contained half of his father. "I want you to have this."

Thomas took the ashes and smiled, closed his eyes, and told this story: "I'm going to travel to Spokane Falls one last time and toss these ashes into the water. And your father will rise like a salmon, leap over the bridge, over me, and find his way home. It will be beautiful. His teeth will shine like silver, like a rainbow. He will rise, Victor, he will rise."

Victor smiled.

185 "I was planning on doing the same thing with my half," Victor said. "But I didn't imagine my father looking anything like a salmon. I thought it'd be like cleaning the attic or something. Like letting things go after they've stopped having any use."

"Nothing stops, cousin," Thomas said. "Nothing stops."

Thomas Builds-the-Fire got out of the pickup and walked up his driveway. Victor started the pickup and began the drive home.

"Wait," Thomas yelled suddenly from his porch. "I just got to ask one favor."

Victor stopped the pickup, leaned out the window, and shouted back. "What do you want?"

190 "Just one time when I'm telling a story somewhere, why don't you stop and listen?" Thomas asked.

"Just once?"

"Just once."

Victor waved his arms to let Thomas know that the deal was good. It was a fair trade, and that was all Victor had ever wanted from his whole life. So Victor drove his father's pickup toward home while Thomas went into his house, closed the door behind him, and heard a new story come to him in the silence afterwards.

(1993)

Questions for Discussion and Writing

1. Victor accuses Thomas of thinking too much. What does Thomas think about? Why does it bother Victor?
2. Why has Thomas evoked such dislike and hostility from Victor and the others in the tribe?
3. Does Victor change in the course of the story? Write an essay that argues for the growth and development of Victor.
4. Write an essay that describes the basic contrast between Victor and Thomas. Use this contrast to interpret the story's primary themes.
5. Write an account of the trip to Phoenix as Thomas might tell it.

A Portfolio of Humorous and Satirical Stories

As the poet Billy Collins says, "If you're majoring in English, you're majoring in death." Students often agree with Collins that serious literature can be seriously depressing. This group of humorous pieces is included to offset that effect, to lighten the load, so to speak. You can approach a humorous story the same way you would any other work of literature (through plot, character, point of view, and so on), or you can analyze the comic effects employed by the author. Each selection in this portfolio is designed to be funny, using common strategies such as irony to achieve the comic intent. Another technique at work in some of the stories is a more cutting form of humor—satire. Through exaggeration and striking contrasts, the object of the satire (a character, a theme, a style of writing) is openly or indirectly made fun of and criticized, often with the intent to provoke some form of improvement in a custom or institution or to change the reader's thinking about that custom or institution.

Frank O'Connor 1903–1966

Born Michael Francis O'Conner O'Donovan in Cork, Ireland, Frank O'Connor endured a difficult childhood. About his drunken, deadbeat father, he said, "Whenever he brandished the razor at Mother I went into hysterics, and a couple of times I threw myself on him with my fists." As an adult he joined the Irish Republican Army but lost faith in the cause when he realized that his own side could be as repressive and inhumane as their enemies. His short story "Guests of the Nation," which focuses on the ambiguities of the conflict, served as one inspiration for the motion picture *The Crying Game* (1992).

My Oedipus Complex

Father was in the army all through the war—the first war, I mean—so, up to the age of five, I never saw much of him, and what I saw did not worry me. Sometimes I woke and there was a big figure in khaki peering down at me in the candlelight. Sometimes in the early morning I heard the slamming of the front door and the clatter of nailed boots down the cobbles of the lane. These were Father's entrances and exits. Like Santa Claus he came and went mysteriously.

In fact, I rather liked his visits, though it was an uncomfortable squeeze between Mother and him when I got into the big bed in the early morning. He smoked, which gave him a pleasant musty smell, and shaved, an operation of astounding interest. Each time he left a trail of souvenirs—model tanks and Gurkha knives with handles made of bullet cases, and German helmets and cap badges and button-sticks, and all sorts of military equipment—carefully stowed away in a long box on top of the wardrobe, in case they ever came in handy. There was a bit of the magpie about Father; he expected everything to come in handy. When his back was turned, Mother let me get a chair and rummage through his treasures. She didn't seem to think so highly of them as he did.

The war was the most peaceful period of my life. The window of my attic faced southeast. My mother had curtained it, but that had small effect. I always woke with the first light and, with all the responsibilities of the previous day melted, feeling myself rather like the sun, ready to illumine and rejoice. Life never seemed so simple and clear and full of possibilities as then. I put my feet out from under the clothes—I called them Mrs. Left and Mrs. Right—and invented dramatic situations for them in which they discussed the problems of the day. At least Mrs. Right did; she was very demonstrative, but I hadn't the same control of Mrs. Left, so she mostly contented herself with nodding agreement.

They discussed what Mother and I should do during the day, what Santa Claus should give a fellow for Christmas, and what steps should be taken to brighten the home. There was that little matter of the baby, for instance. Mother and I could never agree about that. Ours was the only house in the terrace without a new baby, and Mother said we couldn't afford one till Father came back from the war because they cost seventeen and six. That showed how simple she was. The Geneys up the road had a baby, and everyone knew they couldn't afford seventeen and six. It was probably a cheap baby, and Mother wanted something really good, but I felt she was too exclusive. The Geneys' baby would have done us fine.

Having settled my plans for the day, I got up, put a chair under the attic 5
window, and lifted the frame high enough to stick out my head. The window overlooked the front gardens of the terrace behind ours, and beyond these it looked over a deep valley to the tall, red-brick houses terraced up the opposite hillside, which were all still in shadow, while those at our side of the valley were all lit up, though with long strange shadows that made them seem unfamiliar, rigid and painted.

After that I went into Mother's room and climbed into the big bed. She woke and I began to tell her of my schemes. By this time, though I never seem to have noticed it, I was petrified in my nightshirt, and I thawed as I talked until, the last frost melted, I fell asleep beside her and woke again only when I heard her below in the kitchen, making the breakfast.

After breakfast we went into town, heard Mass at St. Augustine's and said a prayer for Father, and did the shopping. If the afternoon was fine we either went for a walk in the country or a visit to Mother's great friend in the convent, Mother St. Dominic. Mother had them all praying for Father, and every night, going to bed, I asked God to send him back safe from the war to us. Little, indeed, did I know what I was praying for!

One morning, I got into the big bed, and there, sure enough, was Father in his usual Santa Claus manner, but later, instead of uniform, he put on his best blue suit, and Mother was as pleased as anything. I saw nothing to be pleased about, because, out of uniform, Father was altogether less interesting, but she only beamed, and explained that our prayers had been answered, and off we went to Mass to thank God for having brought Father safely home.

The irony of it! That very day when he came in to dinner he took off his boots and put on his slippers, donned the dirty old cap he wore about the house to save him from colds, crossed his legs, and began to talk gravely to Mother, who looked anxious. Naturally, I disliked her looking anxious, because it destroyed her good looks, so I interrupted him.

"Just a moment, Larry!" she said gently.

This was only what she said when we had boring visitors, so I attached no importance to it and went on talking.

"Do be quiet, Larry!" she said impatiently. "Don't you hear me talking to Daddy?"

This was the first time I had heard those ominous words, "talking to Daddy," and I couldn't help feeling that if this was how God answered prayers, he couldn't listen to them very attentively.

"Why are you talking to Daddy?" I asked with as great a show of indifference as I could muster.

"Because Daddy and I have business to discuss. Now, don't interrupt again!"

In the afternoon, at Mother's request, Father took me for a walk. This time we went into town instead of out to the country, and I thought at first, in my usual optimistic way, that it might be an improvement. It was nothing of the sort. Father and I had quite different notions of a walk in town. He had no proper interest in trams, ships, and horses, and the only thing that seemed to divert him was talking to fellows as old as himself. When I wanted to stop he simply went on, dragging me behind him by the hand; when he wanted to stop I had no alternative but to do the same. I noticed that it seemed to be a sign that he wanted to stop for a long time whenever he leaned against a wall. The second time I saw him do it I got wild. He seemed to be settling himself forever. I pulled him by the coat and trousers, but, unlike Mother who, if you were too persistent, got into a wax and said: "Larry if you don't behave yourself, I'll give you a good slap," Father had an extraordinary capacity for amiable inattention. I sized him up and wondered would I cry, but he seemed to be too remote to be annoyed even by that. Really, it was like going for a walk with a mountain! He either ignored the wrenching and pummelling entirely, or else glanced down with a grin of amusement from his peak. I had never met anyone so absorbed in himself as he seemed.

At teatime, "talking to Daddy" began again, complicated this time by the fact that he had an evening paper, and every few minutes he put it down and told Mother something new out of it. I felt this was foul play. Man for man, I was prepared to compete with him any time for Mother's attention, but when he had it all made up for him by other people it left me no chance. Several times I tried to change the subject without success.

"You must be quiet while Daddy is reading, Larry," Mother said impatiently. It was clear that she either genuinely liked talking to Father better than talking to me, or else that he had some terrible hold on her which made her afraid to admit the truth.

"Mummy," I said that night when she was tucking me up, "do you think if I prayed hard God would send Daddy back to the war?"

She seemed to think about that for a moment.

"No, dear," she said with a smile. "I don't think he would."

"Why wouldn't he, Mummy?"

"Because there isn't a war any longer, dear."

"But, Mummy, couldn't God make another war, if he liked?"

"He wouldn't like to, dear. It's not God who makes wars, but bad people."

"Oh!" I said.

I was disappointed about that. I began to think that God wasn't quite what he was cracked up to be.

Next morning I woke at my usual hour, feeling like a bottle of champagne. I put out my feet and invented a long conversation in which Mrs. Right talked of the trouble she had with her own father till she put him in the Home. I didn't quite know what the Home was but it sounded the right place for Father. Then I got my chair and stuck my head out of the attic window. Dawn was just breaking, with a guilty air that made me feel I had caught it in the act. My head bursting with stories and schemes, I stumbled in next door, and in the half-darkness scrambled into the big bed. There was no room at Mother's side so I had to get between her and Father. For the time being I had forgotten about him, and for several minutes I sat bolt upright, racking my brains to know what I could do with him. He was taking up more than his fair share of the bed, and I couldn't get comfortable, so I gave him several kicks that made him grunt and stretch. He made room all right, though. Mother waked and felt for me. I settled back comfortably in the warmth of the bed with my thumb in my mouth.

"Mummy!" I hummed, loudly and contentedly.

"Sssh! dear," she whispered. "Don't wake Daddy!"

This was a new development, which threatened to be even more serious than "talking to Daddy." Life without my early-morning conferences was unthinkable.

"Why?" I asked severely.

"Because poor Daddy is tired."

This seemed to me a quite inadequate reason, and I was sickened by the sentimentality of her "poor Daddy." I never liked that sort of gush; it always struck me as insincere.

"Oh!" I said lightly. Then in my most winning tone: "Do you know where I want to go with you today, Mummy?"

"No, dear," she sighed.

"I want to go down the Glen and fish for thornybacks with my new net, and then I want to go out to the Fox and Hounds, and—"

"Don't-wake-Daddy!" she hissed angrily, clapping her hand across my mouth.

But it was too late. He was awake, or nearly so. He grunted and reached for the matches. Then he stared incredulously at his watch.

"Like a cup of tea, dear?" asked Mother in a meek, hushed voice I had never heard her use before. It sounded almost as though she were afraid.

"Tea?" he exclaimed indignantly. "Do you know what the time is?"

"And after that I want to go up the Rathcooney Road," I said loudly, afraid I'd forget something in all those interruptions.

"Go to sleep at once, Larry!" she said sharply.

I began to snivel. I couldn't concentrate, the way that pair went on, and smothering my early-morning schemes was like burying a family from the cradle.

Father said nothing, but lit his pipe and sucked it, looking out into the shadows without minding Mother or me. I knew he was mad. Every time I made a remark Mother hushed me irritably. I was mortified. I felt it wasn't fair; there was even something sinister in it. Every time I had pointed out to her the waste of making two beds when we could both sleep in one, she had told me it was healthier like that, and now here was this man, this stranger, sleeping with her without the least regard for her health!

He got up early and made tea, but though he brought Mother a cup he brought none for me.

"Mummy," I shouted, "I want a cup of tea, too."

"Yes, dear," she said patiently. "You can drink from Mummy's saucer."

That settled it. Either Father or I would have to leave the house. I didn't want to drink from Mother's saucer; I wanted to be treated as an equal in my own home, so, just to spite her, I drank it all and left none for her. She took that quietly, too.

But that night when she was putting me to bed she said gently: "Larry, I want you to promise me something."

"What is it?" I asked.

"Not to come in and disturb poor Daddy in the morning. Promise?"

"Poor Daddy" again! I was becoming suspicious of everything involving that quite impossible man.

"Why?" I asked.

"Because poor Daddy is worried and tired and he doesn't sleep well."

"Why doesn't he, Mummy?"

"Well, you know, don't you, that while he was at the war Mummy got the pennies from the Post Office?"

"From Miss MacCarthy?"

"That's right. But now, you see, Miss MacCarthy hasn't any more pennies, so Daddy must go out and find us some. You know what would happen if he couldn't?"

"No," I said, "tell us."

"Well, I think we might have to go out and beg for them like the poor old woman on Fridays. We wouldn't like that, would we?"

"No," I agreed. "We wouldn't."

"So you'll promise not to come in and wake him?"

"Promise."

Mind you, I meant that. I knew pennies were a serious matter, and I was all against having to go out and beg like the old woman on Fridays. Mother laid out all my toys in a complete ring round the bed so that, whatever way I got out, I was bound to fall over one of them.

When I woke I remembered my promise all right. I got up and sat on the floor and played—for hours, it seemed to me. Then I got my chair and looked out the attic window for more hours. I wished it was time for Father to wake; I wished someone would make me a cup of tea. I didn't feel in the least like the sun; instead, I was bored and so very, very cold! I simply longed for the warmth and depth of the big featherbed.

At last I could stand it no longer. I went into the next room. As there was still no room at Mother's side I climbed over her and she woke with a start.

"Larry," she whispered, gripping my arm very tightly, "what did you promise?"

"But I did, Mummy," I wailed, caught in the very act. "I was quiet for ever so long."

"Oh, dear, and you're perished!" she said sadly, feeling me all over. "Now, if I let you stay will you promise not to talk?"

"But I want to talk, Mummy," I wailed.

"That has nothing to do with it," she said with a firmness that was new to me. "Daddy wants to sleep. Now, do you understand that?"

I understood it only too well. I wanted to talk, he wanted to sleep—whose house was it, anyway?

"Mummy," I said with equal firmness, "I think it would be healthier for Daddy to sleep in his own bed."

That seemed to stagger her, because she said nothing for a while. 75

"Now, once for all," she went on, "you're to be perfectly quiet or go back to your own bed. Which is it to be?"

The injustice of it got me down. I had convicted her out of her own mouth of inconsistency and unreasonableness, and she hadn't even attempted to reply. Full of spite, I gave Father a kick, which she didn't notice but which made him grunt and open his eyes in alarm.

"What time is it?" he asked in a panic-stricken voice, not looking at Mother but at the door, as if he saw someone there.

"It's early yet," she replied soothingly. "It's only the child. Go to sleep again.... Now, Larry," she added, getting out of bed, "you've wakened Daddy and you must go back."

This time, for all her quiet air, I knew she meant it, and knew that my princi- 80
pal rights and privileges were as good as lost unless I asserted them at once. As she lifted me, I gave a screech, enough to wake the dead, not to mind Father. He groaned.

"That damn child! Doesn't he ever sleep?"

"It's only a habit, dear," she said quietly, though I could see she was vexed.

"Well, it's time he got out of it," shouted Father, beginning to heave in the bed. He suddenly gathered all the bedclothes about him, turned to the wall, and then looked back over his shoulder with nothing showing, only two small, spiteful, dark eyes. The man looked very wicked.

To open the bedroom door, Mother had to let me down, and I broke free and dashed for the farthest corner, screeching. Father sat bolt upright in bed.

"Shut up, you little puppy!" he said in a choking voice. 85

I was so astonished that I stopped screeching. Never, never had anyone spoken to me in that tone before. I looked at him incredulously and saw his face convulsed with rage. It was only then that I fully realized how God had codded me, listening to my prayers for the safe return of this monster.

"Shut up, you!" I bawled, beside myself.

"What's that you said?" shouted Father, making a wild leap out of the bed.

"Mick, Mick!" cried Mother. "Don't you see the child isn't used to you?"

"I see he's better fed than taught," snarled Father, waving his arms wildly. 90
"He wants his bottom smacked."

All his previous shouting was as nothing to these obscene words referring to my person. They really made my blood boil.

"Smack your own!" I screamed hysterically. "Smack your own! Shut up! Shut up!"

At this he lost his patience and let fly at me. He did it with the lack of conviction you'd expect of a man under Mother's horrified eyes, and it ended up as a mere tap, but the sheer indignity of being struck at all by a stranger, a total stranger who had cajoled his way back from the war into our big bed as a result of my innocent intercession, made me completely dotty. I shrieked and shrieked, and danced in my bare feet, and Father, looking awkward and hairy in nothing but a short gray army shirt, glared down at me like a mountain out for murder. I think it must have been then that I realized he was jealous too. And there stood Mother in her nightdress, looking as if her heart was broken between us. I hoped she felt as she looked. It seemed to me that she deserved it all.

From that morning out my life was a hell. Father and I were enemies, open and avowed. We conducted a series of skirmishes against one another, he trying to steal my time with Mother and I his. When she was sitting on my bed, telling me a story, he took to looking for some pair of old boots which he alleged he had left behind him at the beginning of the war. While he talked to Mother I played loudly with my toys to show my total lack of concern. He created a terrible scene one evening when he came in from work and found me at his box, playing with his regimental badges, Gurkha knives and button-sticks. Mother got up and took the box from me.

"You mustn't play with Daddy's toys unless he lets you, Larry," she said severely. 95
"Daddy doesn't play with yours."

For some reason Father looked at her as if she had struck him and then turned away with a scowl.

"Those are not toys," he growled, taking down the box again to see had I lifted anything. "Some of those curios are very rare and valuable."

But as time went on I saw more and more how he managed to alienate Mother and me. What made it worse was that I couldn't grasp his method or see what attraction he had for Mother. In every possible way he was less winning than I. He had a common accent and made noises at his tea. I thought for a while that it might be the newspapers she was interested in, so I made up bits of news of my own to read to her. Then I thought it might be the smoking, which I personally thought attractive, and took his pipes and went round the house dribbling into them till he caught me. I even made noises at my tea, but Mother only told me I was disgusting. It all seemed to hinge round that unhealthy habit of sleeping together, so I made a point of dropping into their bedroom and nosing round, talking to myself, so that they wouldn't know I was watching them, but they were never up to anything that I could see. In the end it beat me. It seemed to depend on being grown-up and giving people rings, and I realized I'd have to wait.

But at the same time I wanted him to see that I was only waiting, not giving up the fight. One evening when he was being particularly obnoxious, chattering away well above my head, I let him have it.

"Mummy," I said, "do you know what I'm going to do when I grow up?" 100

"No, dear," she replied. "What?"

"I'm going to marry you," I said quietly.

Father gave a great guffaw out of him, but he didn't take me in. I knew it must only be pretense. And Mother, in spite of everything, was pleased. I felt she was probably relieved to know that one day Father's hold on her would be broken.

"Won't that be nice?" she said with a smile.

"It'll be very nice," I said confidently. "Because we're going to have lots and 105
lots of babies."

"That's right, dear," she said placidly. "I think we'll have one soon, and then you'll have plenty of company."

I was no end pleased about that because it showed that in spite of the way she gave in to Father she still considered my wishes. Besides, it would put the Geneys in their place.

It didn't turn out like that, though. To begin with, she was very preoccupied—I supposed about where she would get the seventeen and six—and though Father took to staying out late in the evenings it did me no particular good. She stopped taking me for walks, became as touchy as blazes, and smacked me for nothing at all. Sometimes I wished I'd never mentioned the confounded baby— I seemed to have genius for bringing calamity on myself.

And calamity it was! Sonny arrived in the most appalling hullabaloo—even that much he couldn't do without a fuss—and from the first moment I disliked him. He was a difficult child—so far as I was concerned he was always difficult—and demanded far too much attention. Mother was simply silly about him, and couldn't see when he was only showing off. As company he was worse than useless. He slept all day, and I had to go round the house on tiptoe to avoid waking him. It wasn't any longer a question of not waking Father. The slogan now was "Don't-wake-Sonny!" I couldn't understand why the child wouldn't sleep at the proper time, so whenever Mother's back was turned I woke him. Sometimes to keep him awake I pinched him as well. Mother caught me at it one day and gave me a most unmerciful flaking.

110 One evening, when Father was coming in from work, I was playing trains in the front garden. I let on not to notice him; instead, I pretended to be talking to myself, and said in a loud voice: "If another bloody baby comes into this house, I'm going out."

Father stopped dead and looked at me over his shoulder.

"What's that you said?" he asked sternly.

"I was only talking to myself," I replied, trying to conceal my panic. "It's private."

He turned and went in without a word. Mind you, I intended it as a solemn warning, but its effect was quite different. Father started being quite nice to me. I could understand that, of course. Mother was quite sickening about Sonny. Even at mealtimes she'd get up and gawk at him in the cradle with an idiotic smile, and tell Father to do the same. He was always polite about it, but he looked so puzzled you could see he didn't know what she was talking about. He complained of the way Sonny cried at night, but she only got cross and said that Sonny never cried except when there was something up with him—which was a flaming lie, because Sonny never had anything up with him, and only cried for attention. It was really painful to see how simple-minded she was. Father wasn't attractive, but he had a fine intelligence. He saw through Sonny, and now he knew that I saw through him as well.

115 One night I woke with a start. There was someone beside me in the bed. For one wild moment I felt sure it must be Mother, having come to her senses and left Father for good, but then I heard Sonny in convulsions in the next room, and Mother saying: "There! There! There!" and I knew it wasn't she. It was Father. He was lying beside me, wide awake, breathing hard and apparently as mad as hell.

After a while it came to me what he was mad about. It was his turn now. After turning me out of the big bed, he had been turned out himself. Mother had no consideration now for anyone but that poisonous pup, Sonny. I couldn't help feeling sorry for Father. I had been through it all myself, and even at that age I was magnanimous. I began to stroke him down and say: "There! There!" He wasn't exactly responsive.

"Aren't you asleep either?" he snarled.

"Ah, come on and put your arm around us, can't you?" I said, and he did, in a sort of way. Gingerly, I suppose, is how you'd describe it. He was very bony but better than nothing.

At Christmas he went out of his way to buy me a really nice model railway.

(1950)

Questions for Discussion and Writing

1. In the opening paragraph, the child narrator says that he rarely saw his father, "and what I saw did not worry me." Why would it worry him? What would be the expected reaction of a child to his father's rare appearances?
2. "My Oedipus Complex" is told completely from the child's point of view. How reliable is Larry as the narrator of events? How does this point of view provide humor? How is sexuality involved in the story's humor?
3. Why does Larry call it an "irony" that his prayers were answered?
4. What is Larry's concept of God—for example, when he says, "I began to think that God wasn't quite what he was cracked up to be"?
5. What is Freud's theory of the Oedipus complex? How does the theory fit the story? In what ways does the theory *not* fit the story?

Eudora Welty 1909–2001

Eudora Welty was born in Jackson, Mississippi, to devoted and prosperous parents who encouraged her literary bent. She recalled, "Any room in our house, at any time of day, was there to read in, or to be read to." She left Jackson to attend the University of Wisconsin and Columbia University, but returned to Jackson in 1932 to work for a radio station, several newspapers, and the WPA before launching her literary career. Welty's humor and astute observations give her portraits of small-town life a universal reality. One critic has observed, "Welty's career would seem to prove that an artist can thrive without benefit of poverty, obscurity, and neglect." She never married and when asked why, replied, "It never came up." The e-mail software Eudora was named after Welty because of her story "Why I Live at the P.O."

Why I Live at the P.O.

I was getting along fine with Mama, Papa-Daddy and Uncle Rondo until my sister Stella-Rondo just separated from her husband and came back home again. Mr. Whitaker! Of course I went with Mr. Whitaker first, when he first appeared here in China Grove, taking "Pose Yourself" photos, and Stella-Rondo broke us up. Told him I was one-sided. Bigger on one side than the other, which is a deliberate, calculated falsehood: I'm the same. Stella-Rondo is exactly twelve months to the day younger than I am and for that reason she's spoiled.

She's always had anything in the world she wanted and then she'd throw it away. Papa-Daddy gave her this gorgeous Add-a-Pearl necklace when she was eight years old and she threw it away playing baseball when she was nine, with only two pearls.

So as soon as she got married and moved away from home the first thing she did was separate! From Mr. Whitaker! This photographer with the popeyes she said she trusted. Came home from one of those towns up in Illinois and to our complete surprise brought this child of two.

Mama said she like to made her drop dead for a second. "Here you had this marvelous blonde child and never so much as wrote your mother a word about it," says Mama. "I'm thoroughly ashamed of you." But of course she wasn't.

Stella-Rondo just calmly takes off this *hat*, I wish you could see it. She says, 5
"Why, Mama, Shirley-T.'s adopted, I can prove it."

"How?" says Mama, but all I says was, "H'm!" There I was over the hot stove, trying to stretch two chickens over five people and a completely unexpected child into the bargain, without one moment's notice.

"What do you mean—'H'm!'?" says Stella-Rondo, and Mama says, "I heard that, Sister."

I said that oh, I didn't mean a thing, only that whoever Shirley-T. was, she was the spit-image of Papa-Daddy if he'd cut off his beard, which of course he'd never do in the world. Papa-Daddy's Mama's papa and sulks.

Stella-Rondo got furious! She said, "Sister, I don't need to tell you you got a lot of nerve and always did have and I'll thank you to make no future reference to my adopted child whatsoever."

"Very well," I said. "Very well, very well. Of course I noticed at once she 10
looks like Mr. Whitaker's side too. That frown. She looks like a cross between Mr. Whitaker and Papa-Daddy."

"Well, all I can say is she isn't."

"She looks exactly like Shirley Temple to me," says Mama, but Shirley-T. just ran away from her.

So the first thing Stella-Rondo did at the table was turn Papa-Daddy against me.

"Papa-Daddy," she says. He was trying to cut up his meat. "Papa-Daddy!" I was taken completely by surprise. Papa-Daddy is about a million years old and's got this long-long beard. "Papa-Daddy, Sister says she fails to understand why you don't cut off your beard."

So Papa-Daddy l-a-y-s down his knife and fork! He's real rich. Mama says he 15
is, he says he isn't. So he says, "Have I heard correctly? You don't understand why I don't cut off my beard?"

"Why," I says, "Papa-Daddy, of course I understand, I did not say any such of a thing, the idea!"

He says, "Hussy!"

I says, "Papa-Daddy, you know I wouldn't any more want you to cut off your beard than the man in the moon. It was the farthest thing from my mind! Stella Rondo sat there and made that up while she was eating breast of chicken."

But he says, "So the postmistress fails to understand why I don't cut off my beard. Which job I got you through my influence with the government. 'Bird's nest'—is that what you call it?"

Not that it isn't the next to smallest P.O. in the entire state of Mississippi. 20

I says, "Oh, Papa-Daddy," I says, "I didn't say any such of a thing, I never dreamed it was a bird's nest, I have always been grateful though this is the next to smallest P.O. in the state of Mississippi, and I do not enjoy being referred to as a hussy by my own grandfather."

But Stella-Rondo says, "Yes, you did say it too. Anybody in the world could of heard you, that had ears."

"Stop right there," says Mama, looking at me.

So I pulled my napkin straight back through the napkin ring and left the table.

As soon as I was out of the room Mama says, "Call her back, or she'll starve to death," but Papa-Daddy says, "This is the beard I started growing on the Coast when I was fifteen years old." He would of gone on till nightfall if Shirley-T. hadn't lost the Milky Way she ate in Cairo.

So Papa-Daddy says, "I am going out and lie in the hammock, and you can all sit here and remember my words: I'll never cut off my beard as long as I live, even one inch, and I don't appreciate it in you at all." Passed right by me in the hall and went straight out and got in the hammock.

It would be a holiday. It wasn't five minutes before Uncle Rondo suddenly appeared in the hall in one of Stella-Rondo's flesh-colored kimonos, all cut on the bias, like something Mr. Whitaker probably thought was gorgeous.

"Uncle Rondo!" I says. "I didn't know who that was! Where are you going?"

"Sister," he says, "get out of my way, I'm poisoned."

"If you're poisoned stay away from Papa-Daddy," I says. "Keep out of the hammock. Papa-Daddy will certainly beat you on the head if you come within forty miles of him. He thinks I deliberately said he ought to cut off his beard after he got me the P.O., and I've told him and told him and told him, and he acts like he just don't hear me. Papa-Daddy must of gone stone deaf."

"He picked a fine day to do it then," says Uncle Rondo, and before you could say "Jack Robinson" flew out in the yard.

What he'd really done, he'd drunk another bottle of that prescription. He does it every single Fourth of July as sure as shooting, and it's horribly expensive. Then he falls over in the hammock and snores. So he insisted on zigzagging right on out to the hammock, looking like a half-wit.

Papa-Daddy woke up with this horrible yell and right there without moving an inch he tried to turn Uncle Rondo against me. I heard every word he said. Oh, he told Uncle Rondo I didn't learn to read till I was eight years old and he didn't see how in the world I ever got the mail put up at the P.O., much less read it all, and he said if Uncle Rondo could only fathom the lengths he had gone to get me that job! And he said on the other hand he thought Stella-Rondo had a brilliant mind and deserved credit for getting out of town. All the time he was just lying there swinging as pretty as you please and looping out his beard, and poor Uncle Rondo was pleading with him to slow down the hammock, it was making him as dizzy as a witch to watch it. But that's what Papa-Daddy likes about a hammock. So Uncle Rondo was too dizzy to get turned against me for the time being. He's Mama's only brother and is a good case of a one-track mind. Ask anybody. A certified pharmacist.

Just then I heard Stella-Rondo raising the upstairs window. While she was married she got this peculiar idea that it's cooler with the windows shut and locked. So she has to raise the window before she can make a soul hear her outdoors.

So she raises the window and says, "Oh!" You would have thought she was mortally wounded.

Uncle Rondo and Papa-Daddy didn't even look up, but kept right on with what they were doing. I had to laugh.

I flew up the stairs and threw the door open! I says, "What in the wide world's the matter, Stella-Rondo? You mortally wounded?"

"No," she says, "I am not mortally wounded but I wish you would do me the favor of looking out that window there and telling me what you see."

So I shade my eyes and look out the window. 40

"I see the front yard," I says.

"Don't you see any human beings?" she says.

"I see Uncle Rondo trying to run Papa-Daddy out of the hammock," I says. "Nothing more. Naturally, it's so suffocating-hot in the house, with all the windows shut and locked, everybody who cares to stay in their right mind will have to go out and get in the hammock before the Fourth of July is over."

"Don't you notice anything different about Uncle Rondo?" asks Stella-Rondo.

"Why, no, except he's got on some terrible-looking flesh-colored contraption I wouldn't be found dead in, is all I can see," I says.

"Never mind, you won't be found dead in it, because it happens to be part of 45
my trousseau, and Mr. Whitaker took several dozen photographs of me in it," say Stella-Rondo. "What on earth could Uncle Rondo *mean* by wearing part of my trousseau out in the broad open daylight without saying so much as 'Kiss my foot,' *knowing* I only got home this morning after my separation and hung my negligee up on the bathroom door, just as nervous as I could be?"

"I'm sure I don't know, and what do you expect me to do about it?" I says. "Jump out the window?"

"No, I expect nothing of the kind. I simply declare that Uncle Rondo looks like a fool in it, that's all," she says. "It makes me sick to my stomach."

"Well, he looks as good as he can," I says. "As good as anybody in reason could." I stood up for Uncle Rondo, please remember. And I said to Stella Rondo, "I think I would do well not to criticize so freely if I were you and came home with a two-year-old child I had never said a word about, and no explanation whatever about my separation."

"I asked you the instant I entered this house not to refer one more time to my adopted child, and you gave me your word of honor you would not," was all Stella-Rondo would say, and started pulling out every one of her eyebrows with some cheap Kress tweezers.

So I merely slammed the door behind me and went down and made some 50
green-tomato pickle. Somebody had to do it. Of course Mama had turned both the niggers loose; she always said no earthly power could hold one anyway on the Fourth of July, so she wouldn't even try. It turned out that Jaypan fell in the lake and came within a very narrow limit of drowning.

So Mama trots in. Lifts up the lid and says, "H'm! Not very good for your Uncle Rondo in his precarious condition, I must say. Or poor little adopted Shirley-T. Shame on you!"

That made me tired. I says, "Well, Stella-Rondo had better thank her lucky stars it was her instead of me came trotting in with that very peculiar-looking child. Now if it had been me that trotted in from Illinois and brought a peculiar-looking child of two, I shudder to think of the reception I'd of got, much less controlled the diet of an entire family."

"But you must remember, Sister, that you were never married to Mr. Whitaker in the first place and didn't go up to Illinois to live," says Mama, shaking a spoon in my face. "If you had I would of been just as overjoyed to see you and your little adopted girl as I was to see Stella-Rondo, when you wound up with your separation and came on back home."

"You would not," I says.

"Don't contradict me, I would," says Mama.

But I said she couldn't convince me though she talked till she was blue in the face. Then I said, "Besides, you know as well as I do that that child is not adopted."

"She most certainly is adopted," says Mama, stiff as a poker.

I says, "Why, Mama, Stella-Rondo had her just as sure as anything in this world, and just too stuck up to admit it."

"Why, Sister," said Mama. "Here I thought we were going to have a pleasant Fourth of July, and you start right out not believing a word your own baby sister tells you!"

"Just like Cousin Annie Flo. Went to her grave denying the facts of life," I remind Mama.

"I told you if you ever mentioned Annie Flo's name I'd slap your face," says Mama, and slaps my face.

"All right, you wait and see," I says.

"I," says Mama, "*I* prefer to take my children's word for anything when it's humanly possible." You ought to see Mama, she weighs two hundred pounds and has real tiny feet.

Just then something perfectly horrible occurred to me.

"Mama," I says, "can that child talk?" I simply had to whisper! "Mama, I wonder if that child can be—you know—in any way? Do you realize," I says, "that she hasn't spoken one single, solitary word to a human being up to this minute? This is the way she looks," I says, and I looked like this.

Well, Mama and I just stood there and stared at each other. It was horrible!

"I remember well that Joe Whitaker frequently drank like a fish," says Mama. "I believed to my soul he drank *chemicals*." And without another word she marches to the foot of the stairs and calls Stella-Rondo.

"Stella-Rondo? O-o-o-o-o! Stella-Rondo!"

"What?" says Stella-Rondo from upstairs. Not even the grace to get up off the bed.

"Can that child of yours talk?" asks Mama.

Stella-Rondo says, "Can she what?"

"Talk! Talk!" says Mama. "Burdyburdyburdyburdy!"

So Stella-Rondo yells back, "Who says she can't talk?"

"Sister says so," says Mama.

"You didn't have to tell me, I know whose word of honor don't mean a thing in this house," says Stella-Rondo.

And in a minute the loudest Yankee voice I ever heard in my life yells out, "OE'm Pop-OE the Sailor-r-r-r Ma-a-an!" and then somebody jumps up and down in the upstairs hall. In another second the house would of fallen down.

"Not only talks, she can tap-dance!" calls Stella-Rondo, "Which is more than some people I won't name can do."

"Why, the little precious darling thing!" Mama says, so surprised. "Just as smart as she can be!" Starts talking baby talk right there. Then she turns on me. "Sister, you ought to be thoroughly ashamed! Run upstairs this instant and apologize to Stella-Rondo and Shirley-T."

"Apologize for what?" I says. "I merely wondered if the child was normal, that's all. Now that she's proved she is, why, I have nothing further to say."

But Mama just turned on her heel and flew out, furious. She ran right upstairs and hugged the baby. She believed it was adopted. Stella-Rondo hadn't done a thing but turn her against me from upstairs while I stood there helpless over the hot stove. So that made Mama, Papa-Daddy, and the baby all on Stella-Rondo's side.

Next, Uncle Rondo.

I must say that Uncle Rondo has been marvelous to me at various times in the past and I was completely unprepared to be made to jump out of my skin, the way it turned out. Once Stella-Rondo did something perfectly horrible to him—broke a chain letter from Flanders Field—and he took the radio back he had given her and gave it to me. Stella-Rondo was furious! For six months we all had to call her Stella instead of Stella-Rondo, or she wouldn't answer. I always thought Uncle Rondo had all the brains of the entire family. Another time he sent me to Mammoth Cave, with all expenses paid.

But this would be the day he was drinking that prescription, the Fourth of July.

So at supper Stella-Rondo speaks up and says she thinks Uncle Rondo ought to try to eat a little something. So finally Uncle Rondo said he would try a little cold biscuits and ketchup, but that was all. So she brought it to him.

"Do you think it wise to disport with ketchup in Stella-Rondo's flesh-colored kimono?" I says. Trying to be considerate! If Stella-Rondo couldn't watch out for her trousseau, somebody had to.

"Any objections?" asks Uncle Rondo, just about to pour out all the ketchup.

"Don't mind what she says, Uncle Rondo," says Stella-Rondo. "Sister has been devoting this solid afternoon to sneering out my bedroom window at the way you look."

"What's that?" says Uncle Rondo. Uncle Rondo has got the most terrible temper in the world. Anything is liable to make him tear the house down if it comes at the wrong time.

So Stella-Rondo says, "Sister says, 'Uncle Rondo certainly does look like a fool in that pink kimono!'"

Do you remember who it was really said that?

Uncle Rondo spills out all the ketchup and jumps out of his chair and tears off the kimono and throws it down on the dirty floor and puts his foot on it. It had to be sent all the way to Jackson to the cleaners and re-pleated.

"So that's your opinion of your Uncle Rondo, is it?" he says. "I look like a fool, do I? Well, that's the last straw. A whole day in this house with nothing to do, and then to hear you come out with a remark like that behind my back!"

"I didn't say any such of a thing, Uncle Rondo," I says, "and I'm not saying who did, either. Why, I think you look all right. Just try to take care of yourself and not talk and eat at the same time," I says. "I think you better go lie down."

"Lie down my foot," says Uncle Rondo. I ought to of known by that he was fixing to do something perfectly horrible.

So he didn't do anything that night in the precarious state he was in—just played Casino with Mama and Stella-Rondo and Shirley-T and gave Shirley-T. a nickel with a head on both sides. It tickled her nearly to death, and she called him "Papa." But at 6:30 A.M. the next morning, he threw a whole five-cent package of some unsold one-inch firecrackers from the store as hard as he could into my bedroom and they every one went off. Not one bad one in the string. Anybody else, there'd be one that wouldn't go off.

Well, I'm just terribly susceptible to noise of any kind, the doctor has always told me I was the most sensitive person he had ever seen in his whole life, and I was simply prostrated. I couldn't eat! People tell me they heard it as far as the cemetery, and old Aunt Jep Patterson, that had been holding her own so good, thought it was Judgment Day and she was going to meet her whole family. It's usually so quiet here.

And I'll tell you it didn't take me any longer than a minute to make up my mind what to do. There I was with the whole entire house on Stella-Rondo's side and turned against me. If I have anything at all I have pride.

So I just decided I'd go straight down to the P.O. There's plenty of room there in the back, I says to myself.

Well! I made no bones about letting the family catch on to what I was up to. I didn't try to conceal it.

The first thing they knew, I marched in where they were all playing Old 100
Maid and pulled the electric oscillating fan out by the plug, and everything got real hot. Next I snatched the pillow I'd done the needlepoint on right off the davenport from behind Papa-Daddy. He went "Ugh!" I beat Stella-Rondo up the stairs and finally found my charm bracelet in her bureau drawer under a picture of Nelson Eddy.

"So that's the way the land lies," says Uncle Rondo. There he was, piecing on the ham. "Well, Sister, I'll be glad to donate my army cot if you got any place to set it up, providing you'll leave right this minute and let me get some peace." Uncle Rondo was in France.

"Thank you kindly for the cot and 'peace' is hardly the word I would select if I had to resort to firecrackers at 6:30 A.M. in a young girl's bedroom," I says back to him. "And as to where I intend to go, you seem to forget my position as postmistress of China Grove, Mississippi," I says. "I've always got the P.O."

Well, that made them all sit up and take notice.

I went out front and started digging up some four-o'clocks to plant around the P.O.

"Ah-ah-ah!" says Mama, raising the window. "Those happen to be my 105
four-o'clocks. Everything planted in that star is mine. I've never known you to make anything grow in your life."

"Very well," I says. "But I take the fern. Even you, Mama, can't stand there and deny that I'm the one watered that fern. And I happen to know where I can send in a box top and get a packet of one thousand mixed seeds, no two the same kind, free."

"Oh, where?" Mama wants to know.

But I says, "Too late. You 'tend to your house, and I'll 'tend to mine. You hear things like that all the time if you know how to listen to the radio. Perfectly marvelous offers. Get anything you want free."

So I hope to tell you I marched in and got that radio, and they could of all bit a nail in two, especially Stella-Rondo, that it used to belong to, and she well knew she couldn't get it back, I'd sue for it like a shot. And I very politely took the sewing-machine motor I helped pay the most on to give Mama for Christmas back in 1929, and a good big calendar, with the first-aid remedies on it. The thermometer and the Hawaiian ukulele certainly were rightfully mine, and I stood on the step-ladder and got all my watermelon-rind preserves and every fruit and vegetable I'd put up, every jar. Then I began to pull the tacks out of the bluebird wall vases on the archway to the dining room.

"Who told you you could have those, Miss Priss?" says Mama, fanning as hard as she could.

"I bought 'em and I'll keep track of 'em," I says. "I'll tack 'em up one on each side the post-office window, and you can see 'em when you come to ask me for your mail, if you're so dead to see 'em."

"Not I! I'll never darken the door to that post office again if I live to be a hundred," Mama says. "Ungrateful child! After all the money we spent on you at the Normal."

"Me either," says Stella-Rondo. "You can just let my mail lie there and *rot*, for all I care. I'll never come and relieve you of a single, solitary piece."

"I should worry," I says. "And who you think's going to sit down and write you all those big fat letters and postcards, by the way? Mr. Whitaker? Just because he was the only man ever dropped down in China Grove and you got him—unfairly—is he going to sit down and write you a lengthy correspondence after you come home giving no rhyme nor reason whatsoever for your separation and no explanation for the presence of that child? I may not have your brilliant mind, but I fail to see it."

So Mama says, "Sister, I've told you a thousand times that Stella-Rondo simply got homesick, and this child is far too big to be hers," and she says, "Now, why don't you all just sit down and play Casino?"

Then Shirley-T. sticks out her tongue at me in this perfectly horrible way. She has no more manners than the man in the moon. I told her she was going to cross her eyes like that some day and they'd stick.

"It's too late to stop me now," I says. "You should have tried that yesterday. I'm going to the P.O. and the only way you can possibly see me is to visit me there."

So Papa-Daddy says, "You'll never catch me setting foot in that post office, even if I should take a notion into my head to write a letter some place." He says, "I won't have you reachin' out of that little old window with a pair of shears and cuttin' off any beard of mine. I'm too smart for you!"

"We all are," says Stella-Rondo.

But I said, "If you're so smart, where's Mr. Whitaker?"

So then Uncle Rondo says, "I'll thank you from now on to stop reading all the orders I get on postcards and telling everybody in China Grove what you think is the matter with them," but I says, "I draw my own conclusions and will continue in the future to draw them." I says, "If people want to write their inmost secrets on penny postcards, there's nothing in the wide world you can do about it, Uncle Rondo."

"And if you think we'll ever *write* another postcard you're sadly mistaken," says Mama.

"Cutting off your nose to spite your face then," I says. "But if you're all determined to have no more to do with the U.S. mail, think of this: What will Stella-Rondo do now, if she wants to tell Mr. Whitaker to come after her?"

"Wah!" says Stella-Rondo. I knew she'd cry. She had a conniption fit right there in the kitchen.

"It will be interesting to see how long she holds out," I says. "And now— I am leaving."

"Good-by," says Uncle Rondo.

"Oh, I declare," says Mama, "to think that a family of mine should quarrel on the Fourth of July, or the day after, over Stella-Rondo leaving old Mr. Whitaker and having the sweetest little adopted child! It looks like we'd all be glad!"

"Wah!" says Stella-Rondo, and has a fresh conniption fit.

"He left *her*—you mark my words," I says. "That's Mr. Whitaker. I know Mr. Whitaker. After all, I knew him first. I said from the beginning he'd up and leave her. I foretold every single thing that's happened."

"Where did he go?" asks Mama.

"Probably to the North Pole, if he knows what's good for him," I says.

But Stella-Rondo just bawled and wouldn't say another word. She flew to her room and slammed the door.

"Now look what you've gone and done, Sister," says Mama. "You go apologize."

"I haven't got time, I'm leaving," I says.

"Well, what are you waiting around for?" asks Uncle Rondo.

So I just picked up the kitchen clock and marched off, without saying "Kiss my foot" or anything, and never did tell Stella-Rondo good-by.

There was a nigger girl going along on a little wagon right in front.

"Nigger girl," I says, "come help me haul these things down the hill, I'm going to live in the post office."

Took her nine trips in her express wagon. Uncle Rondo came out on the porch and threw her a nickel.

And that's the last I've laid eyes on any of my family or my family laid eyes on me for five solid days and nights. Stella-Rondo may be telling the most horrible tales in the world about Mr. Whitaker, but I haven't heard them. As I tell everybody, I draw my own conclusions.

But oh, I like it here. It's ideal, as I've been saying. You see, I've got everything cater-cornered, the way I like it. Hear the radio? All the war news. Radio, sewing machine, book ends, ironing board, and that great big piano lamp—peace, that's what I like. Butter-bean vines planted all along the front where the strings are.

Of course, there's not much mail. My family are naturally the main people in China Grove, and if they prefer to vanish from the face of the earth, for all the mail they get or the mail they write, why, I'm not going to open my mouth. Some of the folks here in town are taking up for me and some turned against me. I know which is which. There are always people who will quit buying stamps just to get on the right side of Papa-Daddy.

But here I am, and here I'll stay. I want the world to know I'm happy.

And if Stella-Rondo should come to me this minute, on bended knees, and *attempt* to explain the incidents of her life with Mr. Whitaker, I'd simply put my fingers in both my ears and refuse to listen.

(1941)

Questions for Discussion and Writing

1. What are some of the verbal tactics that Sister uses to get us on her side as she tells this story? Find several examples of hyperbole and colloquial expressions that contribute to the humor of the story.
2. What does Sister's use of the racial epithet "nigger" tell you about her character? What does the last sentence in the story tell you about her?

3. How does Stella-Rondo's behavior intensify the sibling rivalry? Why do you think Mama takes her side against Sister?
4. When the family swears they will boycott the post office, Sister says, "Cutting off your nose to spite your face then." In what way is her response ironic?
5. Write a paper using evidence from the story making the claim that Sister was unfairly treated by her family or showing that Sister brought most of the trouble on herself.

John Updike 1932–2009

John Updike grew up in Pennsylvania, an only child who loved reading but suffered from stammering and psoriasis. He went to Harvard on a scholarship, got married during his junior year, and graduated summa cum laude in 1954. He briefly studied art at Oxford, then worked on the staff of the *New Yorker*, but after two years moved to Massachusetts. His prodigious output caused one critic to complain, "Updike can write faster than I can read." He has twice won the Pulitzer Prize, twice appeared on the cover of *Time*, and twice received the National Medal of Honor. Updike died of lung cancer in 2009 at the age of seventy-six.

A & P

In walks these three girls in nothing but bathing suits. I'm in the third checkout slot, with my back to the door, so I don't see them until they're over by the bread. The one that caught my eye first was the one in the plaid green two-piece. She was a chunky kid, with a good tan and a sweet broad soft-looking can with those two crescents of white just under it, where the sun never seems to hit, at the top of the backs of her legs. I stood there with my hand on a box of HiHo crackers trying to remember if I rang it up or not. I ring it up again and the customer starts giving me hell. She's one of these cash-register-watchers, a witch about fifty with rouge on her cheekbones and no eyebrows, and I know it made her day to trip me up. She'd been watching cash registers for fifty years and probably never seen a mistake before.

By the time I got her feathers smoothed and her goodies into a bag—she gives me a little snort in passing, if she'd been born at the right time they would have burned her over in Salem—by the time I get her on her way the girls had circled around the bread and were coming back, without a pushcart, back my way along the counters, in the aisle between the checkouts and the Special bins. They didn't even have shoes on. There was this chunky one, with the two-piece—it was bright green and the seams on the bra were still sharp and her belly was still pretty pale so I guessed she just got it (the suit)—there was this one, with one of those chubby berry-faces, the lips all bunched together under her nose, this one, and a tall one, with black hair that hadn't quite frizzed right, and one of these sunburns right across under the eyes and a chin that was too long—you know, the kind of girl other girls think is very "striking" and "attractive" but never quite makes it, as they very well know, which is why they like her so much—and then the third one, that wasn't quite so tall. She was the queen. She kind of led them, the other two peeking around and making their shoulders round. She didn't look around, not this queen, she just walked straight on slowly, on these long white prima-donna legs. She came down a little hard on her heels, as if she didn't walk in bare feet that much, putting down her heels and then letting the weight move along to her toes as if she was testing the floor with every step, putting a little deliberate extra action into it. You never know for sure how girls' minds work (do you really think it's a mind in there or just a little buzz like a bee in a glass jar?) but you got the idea she had talked the other two into coming in here with her, and now she was showing them how to do it, walk slow and hold yourself straight.

She had on a kind of dirty-pink—beige maybe, I don't know—bathing suit with a little nubble all over it and, what got me, the straps were down. They were off her shoulders looped loose around the cool tops of her arms, and I guess as a result the suit had slipped a little on her, so all around the top of the cloth there was this shining rim. If it hadn't been there you wouldn't have known there could have been anything whiter than those shoulders. With the straps pushed off, there was nothing between the top of the suit and the top of her head except just *her*, this clean bare plane of the top of her chest down from the shoulder bones like a dented sheet of metal tilted in the light. I mean, it was more than pretty.

She had a sort of oaky hair that the sun and salt had bleached, done up in a bun that was unraveling, and a kind of prim face. Walking into the A & P with your straps down, I suppose it's the only kind of face you *can* have. She held her head so high her neck, coming up out of those white shoulders, looked kind of stretched, but I didn't mind. The longer her neck was, the more of her there was.

5 She must have felt in the corner of her eye me and over my shoulder Stokesie in the second slot watching, but she didn't tip. Not this queen. She kept her eyes moving across the racks, and stopped, and turned so slow it made my stomach rub the inside of my apron, and buzzed to the other two, who kind of huddled against her for relief, and then they all three of them went up the cat-and-dog-food-breakfast-cereal-macaroni-rice-raisins-seasonings-spreads-spaghetti-soft-drinks-crackers-and-cookies aisle. From the third slot I look straight up this aisle to the meat counter, and I watched them all the way. The fat one with the tan sort of fumbled with the cookies, but on second thought she put the package back. The sheep pushing their carts down the aisle—the girls were walking against the usual traffic (not that we have one-way signs or anything)—were pretty hilarious. You could see them, when Queenie's white shoulders dawned on them, kind of jerk, or hop, or hiccup, but their eyes snapped back to their own baskets and on they pushed. I bet you could set off dynamite in an A & P and the people would by and large keep reaching and checking oatmeal off their lists and muttering "Let me see, there was a third thing, began with A, asparagus, no, ah, yes, applesauce!" or whatever it is they do mutter. But there was no doubt, this jiggled them. A few houseslaves in pin curlers even looked around after pushing their carts past to make sure what they had seen was correct.

You know, it's one thing to have a girl in a bathing suit down on the beach, where what with the glare nobody can look at each other much anyway, and another thing in the cool of the A & P, under the fluorescent lights, against all those stacked packages, with her feet paddling along naked over our checker-board green-and-cream rubber-tile floor.

"Oh Daddy," Stokesie said beside me. "I feel so faint."

"Darling," I said. "Hold me tight." Stokesie's married, with two babies chalked up on his fuselage already, but as far as I can tell that's the only difference. He's twenty-two, and I was nineteen this April.

"Is it done?" he asks, the responsible married man finding his voice. I forgot to say he thinks he's going to be manager some sunny day, maybe in 1990 when it's called the Great Alexandrov and Petrooshki Tea Company or something.

10 What he meant was, our town is five miles from a beach, with a big summer colony out on the Point, but we're right in the middle of town, and the women generally put on a shirt or shorts or something before they get out of the car into the street. And anyway these are usually women with six children and varicose veins mapping their legs and nobody, including them, could care less. As I say, we're right in the middle of town, and if you stand at our front doors you can see two banks and the Congregational church and the newspaper store and three real-estate offices and about twenty-seven old freeloaders tearing up Central Street because the sewer broke again. It's not as if we're on the Cape; we're north of Boston and there's people in this town haven't seen the ocean for twenty years.

The girls had reached the meat counter and were asking McMahon something. He pointed, they pointed, and they shuffled out of sight behind a pyramid of Diet Delight peaches. All that was left for us to see was old McMahon patting his mouth and looking after them sizing up their joints. Poor kids, I began to feel sorry for them, they couldn't help it.

Now here comes the sad part of the story, at least my family says it's sad, but I don't think it's so sad myself. The store's pretty empty, it being Thursday afternoon, so there was nothing much to do except lean on the register and wait for the girls to show up again. The whole store was like a pinball machine and I didn't know which tunnel they'd come out of. After a while they come around out of the far aisle, around the light bulbs, records at discount of the Caribbean Six or Tony Martin Sings or some such gunk you wonder they waste the wax on, six-packs of candy bars, and plastic toys done up in cellophane that fall apart when a kid looks at them anyway. Around they come, Queenie still leading the way, and holding a little gray jar in her hand. Slots Three through Seven are unmanned and I could see her wondering between Stokes and me, but Stokesie with his usual luck draws an old party in baggy gray pants who stumbles up with four giant cans of pineapple juice (what do these bums *do* with all that pineapple juice? I've often asked myself) so the girls come to me. Queenie puts down the jar and I take it into my fingers icy cold. Kingfish Fancy Herring Snacks in Pure Sour Cream: 49¢. Now her hands are empty, not a ring or a bracelet, bare as God made them, and I wonder where the money's coming from. Still with that prim look she lifts a folded dollar bill out of the hollow at the center of her nubbled pink top. The jar went heavy in my hand. Really, I thought that was so cute.

Then everybody's luck begins to run out. Lengel comes in from haggling with a truck full of cabbages on the lot and is about to scuttle into that door marked MANAGER behind which he hides all day when the girls touch his eye. Lengel's pretty dreary, teaches Sunday school and the rest, but he doesn't miss that much. He comes over and says, "Girls, this isn't the beach."

Queenie blushes, though maybe it's just a brush of sunburn I was noticing for the first time, now that she was so close. "My mother asked me to pick up a jar of herring snacks." Her voice kind of startled me, the way voices do when you see the people first, coming out so flat and dumb yet kind of tony, too, the way it ticked over "pick up" and "snacks." All of a sudden I slid right down her voice into her living room. Her father and the other men were standing around in ice-cream coats and bow ties and the women were in sandals picking up herring snacks on toothpicks off a big glass plate and they were all holding drinks the color of water with olives and sprigs of mint in them. When my parents have somebody over they get lemonade and if it's a real racy affair Schlitz in tall glasses with "They'll Do It Every Time" cartoons stencilled on.

"That's all right," Lengel said. "But this isn't the beach." His repeating this 15
struck me as funny, as if it had just occurred to him, and he had been thinking all these years the A & P was a great big dune and he was the head lifeguard. He didn't like my smiling—as I say he doesn't miss much—but he concentrates on giving the girls that sad Sunday-school-superintendent stare.

Queenie's blush is no sunburn now, and the plump one in plaid, that I liked better from the back—a really sweet can—pipes up, "We weren't doing any shopping. We just came in for the one thing."

"That makes no difference," Lengel tells her, and I could see from the way his eyes went that he hadn't noticed she was wearing a two-piece before. "We want you decently dressed when you come in here."

"We *are* decent," Queenie says suddenly, her lower lip pushing, getting sore now that she remembers her place, a place from which the crowd that runs the A & P must look pretty crummy. Fancy Herring Snacks flashed in her very blue eyes.

"Girls, I don't want to argue with you. After this come in here with your shoulders covered. It's our policy." He turns his back. That's policy for you. Policy is what the kingpins want. What the others want is juvenile delinquency.

All this while, the customers had been showing up with their carts but, you 20
know, sheep, seeing a scene, they had all bunched up on Stokesie, who shook open a paper bag as gently as peeling a peach, not wanting to miss a word. I could feel in the silence everybody getting nervous, most of all Lengel, who asks me, "Sammy, have you rung up their purchase?"

I thought and said "No" but it wasn't about that I was thinking. I go through the punches, 4, 9, GROC, TOT—it's more complicated than you think, and after you do it often enough, it begins to make a little song, that you hear words to, in my case "Hello (*bing*) there, you (*gung*) hap-py *pee*-pul (*splat*)!"—the *splat* being the drawer flying out. I uncrease the bill, tenderly as you may imagine, it just having come from between the two smoothest scoops of vanilla I had ever known there were, and pass a half and a penny into her narrow pink palm, and nestle the herrings in a bag and twist its neck and hand it over, all the time thinking.

The girls, and who'd blame them, are in a hurry to get out, so I say "I quit" to Lengel quick enough for them to hear, hoping they'll stop and watch me, their unsuspected hero. They keep right on going, into the electric eye; the door flies open and they flicker across the lot to their car, Queenie and Plaid and Big Tall

Goony-Goony (not that as raw material she was so bad), leaving me with Lengel and a kink in his eyebrow.

"Did you say something, Sammy?"

"I said I quit."

"I thought you did." 25

"You didn't have to embarrass them."

"It was they who were embarrassing us."

I started to say something that came out "Fiddle-de-do." It's a saying of my grandmother's, and I know she would have been pleased.

"I don't think you know what you're saying," Lengel said.

"I know you don't," I said. "But I do." 30

I pull the bow at the back of my apron and start shrugging it off my shoulders. A couple of customers that had been heading for my slot begin to knock against each other, like scared pigs in a chute.

Lengel sighs and begins to look very patient and old and gray. He's been a friend of my parents for years. "Sammy, you don't want to do this to your Mom and Dad," he tells me. It's true, I don't. But it seems to me that once you begin a gesture it's fatal not to go through with it. I fold the apron, "Sammy" stitched in red on the pocket, and put it on the counter, and drop the bow tie on top of it. The bow tie is theirs, if you've ever wondered. "You'll feel this for the rest of your life," Lengel says, and I know that's true, too, but remembering how he made that pretty girl blush makes me so scrunchy inside I punch the No Sale tab and the machine whirs "pee-pul" and the drawer splats out. One advantage to this scene taking place in summer, I can follow this up with a clean exit, there's no fumbling around getting your coat and galoshes, I just saunter into the electric eye in my white shirt that my mother ironed the night before, and the door heaves itself open, and outside the sunshine is skating around on the asphalt.

I look around for my girls, but they're gone, of course. There wasn't anybody but some young married screaming with her children about some candy they didn't get by the door of a powder-blue Falcon station wagon. Looking back in the big windows, over the bags of peat moss and aluminum lawn furniture stacked on the pavement, I could see Lengel in my place in the slot, checking the sheep through. His face was dark gray and his back stiff, as if he's just had an injection of iron, and my stomach kind of fell as I felt how hard the world was going to be to me hereafter.

(1962)

Questions for Discussion and Writing

1. What is Sammy's attitude toward his job, the people he works with, and his customers? List some of his descriptions, especially the metaphors (like "I got her feathers smoothed"), that reveal these attitudes.
2. Why does Sammy quit his job? Does he have more than one reason? Why does he see it as an act of heroism? Is it?
3. As the story closes, Sammy thinks "how hard the world was going to be to me hereafter." Will it? Why or why not?
4. Why do some readers find the story offensively sexist? Write an essay arguing your position on this question.

5. Rewrite a section of the story from a different point of view: Queenie's, Lengel's, the other shoppers', or an objective position. Show how point of view makes a difference in the story's interpretation.

Margaret Atwood 1939–

Perhaps best known for her feminist dystopian novel *The Handmaid's Tale* (1985), prize-winning novelist, poet, essayist, and activist Margaret Atwood is often described as Medusa-like, partly because of her unruly hair and the glint in her eye, but more for the intensity of her prolific literary output and political work. Although she is adamant that her first loyalty is always to her art, Atwood has served as president of PEN, an organization committed to the welfare of politically oppressed writers around the world, and has engaged in Green Party environmental politics in her native Canada. Her publisher described "Happy Endings" as intended to "reveal the logic of irrational behavior and the many textures lying beneath ordinary life."

Happy Endings

John and Mary meet.
What happens next?
If you want a happy ending, try A.

A.

John and Mary fall in love and get married. They both have worthwhile and remunerative jobs which they find stimulating and challenging. They buy a charming house. Real estate values go up. Eventually, when they can afford live-in help, they have two children, to whom they are devoted. The children turn out well. John and Mary have a stimulating and challenging sex life and worthwhile friends. They go on fun vacations together. They retire. They both have hobbies which they find stimulating and challenging. Eventually they die. This is the end of the story.

B.

Mary falls in love with John but John doesn't fall in love with Mary. He merely uses her body for selfish pleasure and ego gratification of a tepid kind. He comes to her apartment twice a week and she cooks him dinner, you'll notice that he doesn't even consider her worth the price of a dinner out, and after he's eaten dinner he fucks her and after that he falls asleep, while she does the dishes so he won't think she's untidy, having all those dirty dishes lying around, and puts on fresh lipstick so she'll look good when he wakes up, but when he wakes up he doesn't even notice, he puts on his socks and his shorts and his pants and his shirt and his tie and his shoes, the reverse order from the one in which he took them off. He doesn't take off Mary's clothes, she takes them off herself, she acts as if she's dying for it every time, not because she likes sex exactly, she doesn't, but she wants John to think she does because if they do it often enough surely he'll get used to her, he'll come to depend on her and they will get married, but John goes out the door with hardly so much as a good-night and three days later he turns up at six o'clock and they do the whole thing over again.

Mary gets run-down. Crying is bad for your face, everyone knows that and so does Mary but she can't stop. People at work notice. Her friends tell her John is a rat, a pig, a dog, he isn't good enough for her, but she can't believe it. Inside John, she thinks, is another John, who is much nicer. This other John will emerge like a butterfly from a cocoon, a Jack from a box, a pit from a prune, if the first John is only squeezed enough.

One evening John complains about the food. He has never complained about her food before. Mary is hurt.

Her friends tell her they've seen him in a restaurant with another woman, 5
whose name is Madge. It's not even Madge that finally gets to Mary: it's the restaurant. John has never taken Mary to a restaurant. Mary collects all the sleeping pills and aspirins she can find, and takes them and a half a bottle of sherry. You can see what kind of a woman she is by the fact that it's not even whiskey. She leaves a note for John. She hopes he'll discover her and get her to the hospital in time and repent and then they can get married, but this fails to happen and she dies.

John marries Madge and everything continues as in A.

C.

John, who is an older man, falls in love with Mary, and Mary, who is only twenty-two, feels sorry for him because he's worried about his hair falling out. She sleeps with him even though she's not in love with him. She met him at work. She's in love with someone called James, who is twenty-two also and not yet ready to settle down. John on the contrary settled down long ago: this is what is bothering him. John has a steady, respectable job and is getting ahead in his field, but Mary isn't impressed by him, she's impressed by James, who has a motorcycle and a fabulous record collection. But James is often away on his motorcycle, being free. Freedom isn't the same for girls, so in the meantime Mary spends Thursday evenings with John.

Thursdays are the only days John can get away.

John is married to a woman called Madge and they have two children, a charming house which they bought just before the real estate values went up, and hobbies which they find stimulating and challenging, when they have the time. John tells Mary how important she is to him, but of course he can't leave his wife because a commitment is a commitment. He goes on about this more than is necessary and Mary finds it boring, but older men can keep it up longer so on the whole she has a fairly good time.

One day James breezes in on his motorcycle with some top-grade California 10
hybrid and James and Mary get higher than you'd believe possible and they climb into bed. Everything becomes very underwater, but along comes John, who has a key to Mary's apartment. He finds them stoned and entwined. He's hardly in any position to be jealous, considering Madge, but nevertheless he's

overcome with despair. Finally he's middle-aged, in two years he'll be as bald as an egg and he can't stand it. He purchases a handgun, saying he needs it for target practice—this is the thin part of the plot, but it can be dealt with later—and shoots the two of them and himself. Madge, after a suitable period of mourning, marries an understanding man called Fred and everything continues as in A, but under different names.

D.

Fred and Madge have no problems. They get along exceptionally well and are good at working out any little difficulties that may arise. But their charming house is by the seashore and one day a giant tidal wave approaches. Real estate values go down. The rest of the story is about what caused the tidal wave and how they escape from it. They do, though thousands drown, but Fred and Madge are virtuous and grateful, and continue as in A.

E.

Yes, but Fred has a bad heart. The rest of the story is about how kind and understanding they both are until Fred dies. Then Madge devotes herself to charity work until the end of A. If you like, it can be "Madge," "cancer," "guilty and confused," and "bird watching."

F.

If you think this is all too bourgeois, make John a revolutionary and Mary a counterespionage agent and see how far that gets you. Remember, this is Canada. You'll still end up with A, though in between you may get a lustful brawling saga of passionate involvement, a chronicle of our times, sort of.

You'll have to face it, the endings are the same however you slice it. Don't be deluded by any other endings, they're all fake, either deliberately fake, with malicious intent to deceive, or just motivated by excessive optimism if not by downright sentimentality.

The only authentic ending is the one provided here: 15

John and Mary die. John and Mary die. John and Mary die.

So much for endings. Beginnings are always more fun. True connoisseurs, however, are known to favor the stretch in between, since it's the hardest to do anything with.

That's about all that can be said for plots, which anyway are just one thing after another, a what and a what and a what.

Now try How and Why.

(1983)

Questions for Discussion and Writing

1. What definitions of love and the good life emerge from each version of the story? What themes can be identified when all versions are read together?
2. Why does Atwood end story B with "and everything continues as in A"? Why does she repeat the phrase, with some variation, throughout the many

versions? In the end, how does this refrain contribute to your understanding of Atwood's view of the classic "happily-ever-after" story ending?

3. Why does Atwood repeat "John and Mary die. John and Mary die. John and Mary die" in section F?
4. How would you describe the tone of these phrases from story B: "you'll notice he doesn't even consider her worth the price of a dinner out" and "Crying is bad for your face, everyone knows that"? Is there a similar kind of commentary in version A? In the other versions? What accounts for any differences in tone between A and B?
5. Atwood has offered this advice on writing fiction: "Unless something has gone disastrously wrong, other people aren't that interesting to write about.... This is lesson No. 1 in narrative: Something has to happen. It can be good people to whom bad things happen, a nice person getting bitten in two by a shark or crushed by an earthquake, or their husbands run off on them. Or then it can be people of devious or shallow character getting into trouble or making trouble." Write an essay employing Atwood's claim to explain the relationship between plot and theme in "Happy Endings."

David Sedaris 1956–

In the tradition of satirists dating back to Jonathan Swift and Dorothy Parker, David Sedaris looks no further than his own life for the events and characters in his creative nonfiction, a hybrid form of autobiographical storytelling about real events that are passed through his humorous, fictionalizing lens. His work first appeared as broadcast stories on National Public Radio, including the annual rebroadcast of his 1992 "Santaland Diaries," an irreverent account of playing Crumpet the elf at New York's Macy's department store. Sedaris writes for radio and print, as well as for the stage with sister Amy, as the ironically named duo, the "Talent Family." Sedaris and his partner Hugh often live abroad, including rural France, the setting for "Nuit of the Living Dead."

Nuit of the Living Dead

I was on the front porch, drowning a mouse in a bucket when this van pulled up, which was strange. On an average day a total of fifteen cars might pass the house, but no one ever stops, not unless they live here. And this was late, three o'clock in the morning. The couple across the street are asleep by nine, and from what I can tell, the people next door turn in an hour or so later. There are no streetlamps in our village in Normandy, so when it's dark, it's really dark. And when it's quiet, you can hear everything.

"Did I tell you about the burglar who got stuck in the chimney?" That was the big story last summer. One time it happened in the village at the bottom of the hill, the pretty one bisected by a river, and another time it took place fifteen miles in the opposite direction. I heard the story from four people, and each time it happened in a different place.

"So this burglar," people said. "He tried the doors and windows and when those wouldn't open, he climbed up onto the roof."

It was always a summer house, a cottage owned by English people whose names no one seemed to remember. The couple left in early September and returned ten months later to find a shoe in their fireplace. "Is this yours?" the wife asked her husband.

The two of them had just arrived. There were beds to be made and closets to 5
air out, so between one thing and another the shoe was forgotten. It was early June, chilly, and as night fell, the husband decided to light a fire.

At this point in the story the tellers were beside themselves, their eyes aglow, as if reflecting the light of a campfire. "Do you honestly expect me to believe this?" I'd say. "I mean, *really*."

At the beginning of the summer the local paper devoted three columns to a Camembert-eating contest. Competitors were pictured, hands behind their backs, their faces buried in soft, sticky cheese. This on the front page. In an area so hard up for news, I think a death by starvation might command the headlines for, oh, about six years.

"But wait," I'm told. "There's more!"

As the room filled with smoke, the husband stuck a broom up the chimney. Something was blocking the flue, and he poked at it again and again, dislodging the now skeletal burglar, who fell feetfirst into the flames.

There was always a pause here, a break between the story and the practical 10
questions that would ultimately destroy it. "So who was this burglar?" I'd ask. "Did they identify his body?"

He was a Gypsy, a drifter, and, on two occasions, an Arab. No one remembered exactly where he was from. "But it's true," they said. "You can ask anyone," by which they meant the neighbor who had told them, or the person they themselves had told five minutes earlier.

I never believed that a burglar starved to death in a chimney. I don't believe that his skeleton dropped onto the hearth. But I do believe in spooks, especially when Hugh is away and I'm left alone in the country. During the war our house was occupied by Nazis. The former owner died in the bedroom, as did the owner before her, but it's not their ghosts that I worry about. It's silly, I know, but what frightens me is the possibility of zombies, former townspeople wandering about in pus-covered nightgowns. There's a church graveyard a quarter of a mile away, and were its residents to lurch out the gate and take a left, ours would be the third house they would stumble upon. Lying in bed with all the lights on, I draw up contingency plans on the off chance they might come a-callin'. The attic seems a wise hideout, but I'd have to secure the door, which would take time, time you do not have when zombies are steadily working their way through your windows.

I used to lie awake for hours, but now, if Hugh's gone for the night, I'll just stay up and keep myself busy: writing letters, cleaning the oven, replacing missing buttons. I won't put in a load of laundry, because the machine is too loud and would drown out other, more significant noises—namely, the shuffling footsteps of the living dead.

On this particular night, the night the van pulled up, I was in what serves as the combination kitchen/living room, trying to piece together a complex model of the Visible Man. The body was clear plastic, a shell for the organs, which ranged in color from bright red to a dull, liverish purple. We'd bought it as a birthday gift for a thirteen-year-old boy, the son of a friend, who pronounced it *null*, meaning "worthless, unacceptable." The summer before, he'd wanted to be a doctor, but over the next few months he seemed to have changed his mind, deciding instead that he might like to design shoes. I suggested that he at least keep the feet, but when he turned up his nose we gave him twenty euros and decided to keep the model for ourselves. I had just separated the digestive system when I heard a familiar noise coming from overhead, and dropped half the colon onto the floor.

There's a walnut tree in the side yard, and every year Hugh collects the fruit and lays it on the attic floor to dry. Shortly thereafter, the mice come in. I don't know how they climb the stairs, but they do, and the first thing on their list is to take Hugh's walnuts. They're much too big to be carried by mouth, so instead they roll them across the floor, pushing them toward the nests they build in the tight spaces between the walls and the eaves. Once there, they discover that the walnuts won't fit, and while I find this to be comic, Hugh thinks differently and sets the attic with traps I normally spring before the mice can get to them. Were they rats, it would be different, but a couple of mice? "Come on," I say. "What could be cuter?"

Sometimes, when the rolling gets on my nerves, I'll turn on the attic light and make like I'm coming up the stairs. This quiets them for a while, but on this night the trick didn't work. The noise kept up but sounded like something being dragged rather than rolled. A shingle? A heavy piece of toast? Again I turned on the attic light, and when the noise continued I went upstairs and found a mouse caught in one of the traps Hugh had set. The steel bar had come down on his back, and he was pushing himself in a tight circle, not in a death throe, but with a spirit of determination, an effort to work within this new set of boundaries. "I can live with this," he seemed to be saying. "Really. Just give me a chance."

I couldn't leave him that way, so I scooted the trapped mouse into a cardboard box and carried him down onto the front porch. The fresh air, I figured, would do him some good, and once released, he could run down the stairs and into the yard, free from the house that now held such bitter memories. I should have lifted the bar with my fingers, but instead, worried that he might try to bite me, I held the trap down with my foot and attempted to pry it open with the end of a metal ruler. Which was stupid. No sooner had the bar been raised than it snapped back, this time on the mouse's neck. My next three attempts were equally punishing, and when finally freed, he staggered onto the doormat, every imaginable bone broken in at least four different places. Anyone could see that he was not going to get any better. Not even a vet could have fixed this mouse, and so, to put him out of his misery, I decided to drown him.

The first step, and for me the most difficult, was going into the cellar to get the bucket. This involved leaving the well-lit porch, walking around to the side of the house, and entering what is surely the bleakest and most terrifying hole in all of Europe. Low ceiling, stone walls, a dirt floor stamped with paw prints. I never go in without announcing myself. "Hyaa!" I yell. "Hyaa. Hyaa!" It's the sound my father makes when entering his toolshed, the cry of cowboys as they round up dogies, and it suggests a certain degree of authority. Snakes, bats, weasels—it's time to head up and move on out. When retrieving the bucket, I carried a flashlight in each hand, holding them low, like pistols. Then I kicked in the door—"Hyaa! Hyaa!"—grabbed what I was looking for, and ran. I was back on the porch in less than a minute, but it took much longer for my hands to stop shaking.

The problem with drowning an animal—even a crippled one—is that it does not want to cooperate. This mouse had nothing going for him, and yet he struggled, using what, I don't really know. I tried to hold him down with a broom handle but it wasn't the right tool for the job and he kept breaking free and heading back to the surface. A creature that determined, you want to let it have its way, but this was for the best, whether he realized it or not. I'd just managed to pin his tail to the bottom of the bucket when this van drove up and stopped in front of the house. I say "van," but it was more like a miniature bus, with windows and three rows of seats. The headlights were on high, and the road before them appeared black and perfect.

After a moment or two the driver's window rolled down, and a man stuck his head into the pool of light spilling from the porch. "Bonsoir," he called. He said it the way a man in a lifeboat might yell, "Ahoy!" to a passing ship, giving the impression that he was very happy to see me. As he opened the door, a light came on and I could see five people seated behind him, two men and three women, each looking at me with the same expression of relief. All were adults, perhaps in their sixties or early seventies, and all of them had white hair.

The driver referred to a small book he held in his hand. Then he looked back at me and attempted to recite what he had just read. It was French, but just barely, pronounced phonetically, with no understanding of where the accents lay.

"Do you speak English?" I asked.

The man clapped his hands and turned around in his seat. "He speaks English!" The news was greeted with a great deal of excitement and then translated for one of the women, who apparently did not understand the significance. Meanwhile, my mouse had popped back to the surface and was using his good hand to claw at the sides of the bucket.

"We are looking for a particular place," the driver said. "A house we are renting with friends." He spoke loudly and with a slight accent. Dutch, I thought, or maybe Scandinavian.

I asked what town the house was in, and he said that it was not in a town, just a willage.

"A what?"

"A willage," he repeated.

Either he had a speech impediment or the letter *v* did not exist in his native language. Whatever the case, I wanted him to say it again.

"I'm sorry," I said. "But I couldn't quite hear you."

" A *willage*," he said. "Some friends have rented a house in a little willage and we can't seem to find it. We were supposed to be there hours ago, but now we are quite lost. Do you know the area?"

I said that I did, but drew a blank when he called out the name. There are countless small villages in our part of Normandy, clusters of stone buildings hidden by forests or knotted at the end of unpaved roads. Hugh might have known the place the man was looking for, but because I don't drive, I tend not to pay too much attention. "I have a map," the man said. "Do you think you could perhaps look at it?"

He stepped from the van and I saw that he was wearing a white nylon tracksuit, the pants puffy and gathered tight at the ankles. You'd expect to find sneakers attached to such an outfit, but instead he wore a pair of black loafers. The front gate was open, and as he made his way up the stairs, I remembered what it was that I'd been doing, and I thought of how strange it might look. It occurred to me to meet the man halfway, but by this time he had already reached the landing and was offering his hand in a gesture of friendship. We shook, and on hearing the faint, lapping noise, he squinted down into the bucket. "Oh," he said. "I see that you have a little swimming mouse." His tone did not invite explanation, and so I offered none. "My wife and I have a dog," he continued. "But we did not bring it with us. Too much trouble."

I nodded and he held out his map, a Xerox of a Xerox marked with arrows and annotated in a language I did not recognize. "I think I've got something better in the house," I said, and at my invitation, he followed me inside.

An unexpected and unknown visitor allows you to see a familiar place as if for the very first time. I'm thinking of the meter reader rooting through the kitchen at eight a.m., the Jehovah's Witness suddenly standing in your living room. "Here," they seem to say. "Use *my* eyes. The focus is much keener." I had always thought of our main room as cheerful, but walking through the door, I saw that I was mistaken. It wasn't dirty or messy, but like being awake when all decent people are fast asleep, there was something slightly suspicious about it. I looked at the Visible Man spread out on the table. The pieces lay in the shadow of a large taxidermied chicken that seemed to be regarding them, determining which organ might be the most appetizing. The table itself was pleasant to look at—oak and hand-hewn—but the chairs surrounding it were mismatched and in various states of disrepair. On the back of one hung a towel marked with the emblem of the Los Angeles County Coroner's Office. It had been a gift, not bought personally, but still it was there, leading the eye to an adjacent daybed, upon which lay two copies of a sordid true-crime magazine I purportedly buy to help me with my French. The cover of the latest issue pictured a young Belgian woman, a camper beaten to death with a cinder block. IS THERE A SERIAL KILLER IN *YOUR* REGION? The headline asked. The second copy was opened to the crossword puzzle I'd attempted earlier in the evening. One of the clues translated to "female sex organ," and in the space provided I had written the word for *vagina*. It was the first time I had ever answered a French crossword puzzle question, and in celebration I had marked the margins with bright exclamation points.

There seemed to be a theme developing, and everything I saw appeared to 35
substantiate it: the almanac of guns and firearms suddenly prominent on the bookshelf, the meat cleaver lying for no apparent reason upon a photograph of our neighbor's grandchild.

"It's more of a summer home," I said, and the man nodded. He was looking now at the fireplace, which was slightly taller than he was. I tend to see only the solid stone hearth and high oak mantel, but he was examining the meat hooks hanging from the clotted black interior.

"Every other house we passed was dark," he said. "We've been driving I think for hours, just looking for someone who was awake. We saw your lights, the open door..." His words were familiar from innumerable horror movies, the wayward soul announcing himself to the count, the mad scientist, the werewolf, moments before he changes.

"I hate to bother you, really."

"Oh, it's no bother, I was just drowning a mouse. Come in, please."

"So," the man said, "you say you have a map?" 40

I had several, and pulled the most detailed from a drawer containing, among other things, a short length of rope and a novelty pen resembling a dismembered finger. *Where does all this stuff come from?* I asked myself. There's a low cabinet beside the table, and pushing aside the delicate skull of a baby monkey, I spread the map upon the surface, identifying the road outside our house and then the village the man was looking for. It wasn't more than ten miles away. The route was fairly simple, but still I offered him the map, knowing he would feel better if he could refer to it on the road.

"Oh no," he said, "I couldn't," but I insisted, and watched from the porch as he carried it down the stairs and into the idling van. "If you have any problems, you know where I live," I said. "You and your friends can spend the night here if you like. Really, I mean it. I have plenty of beds." The man in the tracksuit waved good-bye, and then he drove down the hill, disappearing behind the neighbor's pitched roof.

The mouse that had fought so hard against my broom handle had lost his second wind and was floating, lifeless now, on the surface of the water. I thought of emptying the bucket into the field behind the house, but without the van, its headlights, and the comforting sound of the engine, the area beyond the porch seemed too menacing. The inside of the house suddenly seemed just as bad, and so I stood there, looking out at what I'd now think of as my willage. When the sun came up I would bury my dead and fill the empty bucket with hydrangeas, a bit of life and color, so perfect for the table. So pleasing to the eye.

(2004)

Questions for Discussion and Writing

1. How does Sedaris feel about the trapped mouse? Does this side of his character affect your response to Sedaris as the narrator of the other events in the story?
2. How many different stories does Sedaris tell in the course of recounting this one night's events? Describe the way he fits all of these stories together. Do you know people who tell stories in a similar way?
3. Once asked about critics' concerns over the line between truth and fiction in his stories, Sedaris quipped, "I had written that my spiders got so obese that their legs started chafing. I talked to the spider expert at the natural history museum, and he said that spiders' legs never rub together. I said, 'No, I know they wouldn't. I'm just saying it as a joke.'...To say that a humorist exaggerates to get big laughs, I don't see how that's big news." Find examples of his use of exaggeration in "Nuit of the Living Dead."
4. Closely examine paragraphs 12 and 13 for Sedaris's other methods of creating the right tone in his stories. Consider variation in word choice, such as "lurch out" and "come a-callin'."
5. When the "unknown visitor" enters the house, Sedaris re-sees all of the familiar objects around him with a more sinister view. Why? Write an essay about your

room or a similar familiar place. Argue for the many objects surrounding you as evidence of who you are—or are not.

6. What is the significance of the title? What movie is Sedaris alluding to? Why?

Daniel Orozco 1957–

Daniel Orozco is Professor of Creative Writing at the University of Idaho. His prize-winning fiction and essays earned him a prestigious National Endowment for the Arts (NEA) Literature Fellowship in 2006 and a spot in the *Pushcart Prize Anthology*. "Orientation," his best-known story, appeared on National Public Radio's *Selected Shorts* and was included in the 1995 edition of *The Best American Short Stories*. Speaking of his approach to writing, Orozco explained, "The impulse to write, for me, derives from figuring out a narrative problem: Can I tell this story in *this* way? Can I pull it off?" See how you would answer these questions when you have finished reading "Orientation."

Orientation

Those are the offices and these are the cubicles. That's my cubicle there, and this is your cubicle. This is your phone. Never answer your phone. Let the Voicemail System answer it. This is your Voicemail System Manual. There are no personal phone calls allowed. We do, however, allow for emergencies. If you must make an emergency phone call, ask your supervisor first. If you can't find your supervisor, ask Phillip Spiers, who sits over there. He'll check with Clarissa Nicks, who sits over there. If you make an emergency phone call without asking, you may be let go.

These are your IN and OUT boxes. All the forms in your IN box must be logged in by the date shown in the upper left-hand corner, initialed by you in the upper right-hand corner, and distributed to the Processing Analyst whose name is numerically coded in the lower left-hand corner. The lower right-hand corner is left blank. Here's your Processing Analyst Numerical Code Index. And here's your Forms Processing Procedures Manual.

You must pace your work. What do I mean? I'm glad you asked that. We pace our work according to the eight-hour workday. If you have twelve hours of work in your IN box, for example, you must compress that work into the eight-hour day. If you have one hour of work in your IN box, you must expand that work to fill the eight-hour day. That was a good question. Feel free to ask questions. Ask too many questions, however, and you may be let go.

That is our receptionist. She is a temp. We go through receptionists here. They quit with alarming frequency. Be polite and civil to the temps. Learn their names, and invite them to lunch occasionally. But don't get close to them, as it only makes it more difficult when they leave. And they always leave. You can be sure of that.

5 The men's room is over there. The women's room is over there. John LaFountaine, who sits over there, uses the women's room occasionally. He says it is accidental. We know better, but we let it pass. John LaFountaine is harmless, his forays into the forbidden territory of the women's room simply a benign thrill, a faint blip on the dull flat line of his life.

Russell Nash, who sits in the cubicle to your left, is in love with Amanda Pierce, who sits in the cubicle to your right. They ride the same bus together after work. For Amanda Pierce, it is just a tedious bus ride made less tedious by the idle nattering of Russell Nash. But for Russell Nash, it is the highlight of his day. It is the highlight of his life. Russell Nash has put on forty pounds, and grows fatter with each passing month, nibbling on chips and cookies while peeking glumly over the partitions at Amanda Pierce, and gorging himself at home on cold pizza and ice cream while watching adult videos on TV.

Amanda Pierce, in the cubicle to your right, has a six-year-old son named Jamie, who is autistic. Her cubicle is plastered from top to bottom with the boy's crayon artwork—sheet after sheet of precisely drawn concentric circles and ellipses, in black and yellow. She rotates them every other Friday. Be sure to comment on them. Amanda Pierce also has a husband, who is a lawyer. He subjects her to an escalating array of painful and humiliating sex games, to which Amanda Pierce reluctantly submits. She comes to work exhausted and freshly wounded each morning, wincing from the abrasions on her breasts, or the bruises on her abdomen, or the second-degree burns of the backs of her thighs.

But we're not supposed to know any of this. Do not let on. If you let on, you may be let go.

Amanda Pierce, who tolerates Russell Nash, is in love with Albert Bosch, whose office is over there. Albert Bosch, who only dimly registers Amanda Pierce's existence, has eyes only for Ellie Tapper, who sits over there. Ellie Tapper, who hates Albert Bosch, would walk through fire for Curtis Lance. But Curtis Lance hates Ellie Tapper. Isn't the world a funny place? Not in the ha-ha sense, of course.

10 Anika Bloom sits in that cubicle. Last year, while reviewing quarterly reports in a meeting with Barry Hacker, Anika Bloom's left palm began to bleed. She fell into a trance, stared into her hand, and told Barry Hacker when and how his wife would die. We laughed it off. She was, after all, a new employee. But Barry Hacker's wife is dead. So unless you want to know exactly when and how you'll die, never talk to Anika Bloom.

Colin Heavey sits in that cubicle over there. He was new once, just like you. We warned him about Anika Bloom. But at last year's Christmas Potluck, he felt sorry for her when he saw that no one was talking to her. Colin Heavey bought her a drink. He hasn't been himself since. Colin Heavey is doomed. There's nothing he can do about it, and we are powerless to help him. Stay away from Colin Heavey. Never give any of your work to him. If he asks to do something, tell him you have to check with me. If he asks again, tell him I haven't gotten back to you.

This is the Fire Exit. There are several on this floor, and they are marked accordingly. We have a Floor Evacuation Review every three months, and an Escape Route Quiz once a month. We have our Biannual Fire Drill twice a year, and our Annual Earthquake Drill once a year. These are precautions only. These things never happen.

For your information, we have a comprehensive health plan. Any catastrophic illness, any unforeseen tragedy is completely covered. All dependents are completely covered. Larry Bagdikian, who sits over there, has six daughters. If anything were to happen to any of his girls, or to all of them, if all six were to simultaneously fall victim to illness or injury—stricken with a hideous degenerative muscle disease or some rare toxic blood disorder, sprayed with semiautomatic gunfire while on a class field trip, or attacked in their bunk beds by some prowling nocturnal lunatic—if any of this were to pass, Larry's girls would all be taken care of. Larry Bagdikian would not have to pay one dime. He would have nothing to worry about.

We also have a generous vacation and sick leave policy. We have an excellent disability insurance plan. We have a stable and profitable pension fund. We get group discounts for the symphony, and block seating at the ballpark. We get commuter ticket books for the bridge. We have Direct Deposit. We are all members of Costco.

This is our kitchenette. And this, this is our Mr. Coffee. We have a coffee 15
pool, into which we each pay two dollars a week for coffee, filters, sugar, and CoffeeMate. If you prefer Cremora or half-and-half to CoffeeMate, there is a special pool for three dollars a week. If you prefer Sweet'n Low to sugar, there is a special pool for two-fifty a week. We do not do decaf. You are allowed to join the coffee pool of your choice, but you are not allowed to touch the Mr. Coffee.

This is the microwave oven. You are allowed to heat food in the microwave oven. You are not, however, allowed to cook food in the microwave oven.

We get one hour for lunch. We also get one fifteen-minute break in the morning, and one fifteen-minute break in the afternoon. Always take your breaks. If you skip a break, it is gone forever. For your information, your break is a privilege, not a right. If you abuse the break policy, we are authorized to rescind your breaks. Lunch, however, is a right, not a privilege. If you abuse the lunch policy, our hands will be tied, and we will be forced to look the other way. We will not enjoy that.

This is the refrigerator. You may put your lunch in it. Barry Hacker, who sits over there, steals food from this refrigerator. His petty theft is an outlet for his grief. Last New Year's Eve, while kissing his wife, a blood vessel burst in her brain. Barry Hacker's wife was two months pregnant at the time, and lingered in a coma for half a year before dying. It was a tragic loss for Barry Hacker. He hasn't been himself since. Barry Hacker's wife was a beautiful woman. She was also completely covered. Barry Hacker did not have to pay one dime. But his dead wife haunts him. She haunts all of us. We have seen her, reflected in the monitors of our computers, moving past our cubicles. We have seen the dim shadow of her face in our photocopies. She pencils herself in in the receptionist's appointment book, with the notation: To see Barry Hacker. She has left messages in the receptionist's Voicemail box, messages garbled by the electronic chirrups and buzzes in the phone line, her voice echoing from an immense distance within the ambient hum. But the voice is hers. And beneath the voice, beneath the tidal whoosh of static and hiss, the gurgling and crying of a baby can be heard.

In any case, if you bring a lunch, put a little something extra in the bag for Barry Hacker. We have four Barrys in this office. Isn't that a coincidence?

This is Matthew Payne's office. He is our Unit Manager, and his door is always 20
closed. We have never seen him, and you will never see him. But he is there. You can be sure of that. He is all around us.

This is the Custodian's Closet. You have no business in the Custodian's Closet.

And this, this is our Supplies Cabinet. If you need supplies, see Curtis Lance. He will log you in on the Supplies Cabinet Authorization Log, then give you a Supplies Authorization Slip. Present your pink copy of the Supplies Authorization Slip to Ellie Tapper. She will log you in on the Supplies Cabinet Key Log, then give you the key. Because the Supplies Cabinet is located outside the Unit Manager's office, you must be very quiet. Gather your supplies quietly. The Supplies Cabinet is divided into four sections. Section One contains letterhead stationery, blank paper and envelopes, memo and note pads, and so on. Section Two contains pens and pencils and typewriter and printer ribbons, and the like. In Section Three we have erasers, correction fluids, transparent tapes, glue sticks, et cetera. And in Section Four we have paper clips and push pins and scissors and razor blades. And here are the spare blades for the shredder. Do not touch the shredder, which is located over there. The shredder is of no concern to you.

Gwendolyn Stich sits in that office there. She is crazy about penguins, and collects penguin knickknacks: penguin posters and coffee mugs and stationery, penguin stuffed animals, penguin jewelry, penguin sweaters and T-shirts and socks. She has a pair of penguin fuzzy slippers she wears when working late at the office. She has a tape cassette of penguin sounds which she listens to for relaxation. Her favorite colors are black and white. She has personalized license plates that read PEN GWEN. Every morning, she passes through all the cubicles to wish each of us a good morning. She brings Danish on Wednesdays for Hump Day morning break, and doughnuts on Fridays for TGIF afternoon break. She organizes the Annual Christmas Potluck, and is in charge of the Birthday List. Gwendolyn Stich's door is always open to all of us. She will always lend an ear, and put in a good word for you; she will always give you a hand, or the shirt off her back, or a shoulder to cry on. Because her door is always open, she hides and cries in a stall in the women's room. And John LaFountaine—who, enthralled when a woman enters, sits quietly in his stall with his knees to his chest—John LaFountaine has heard her vomiting in there. We have come upon Gwendolyn Stich huddled in the stairwell, shivering in the updraft, sipping a Diet Mr. Pibb and hugging her knees. She does not let any of this interfere with her work. If it interfered with her work, she might have to be let go.

Kevin Howard sits in that cubicle over there. He is a serial killer, the one they call the Carpet Cutter, responsible for the mutilations across town. We're not supposed to know that, so do not let on. Don't worry. His compulsion inflicts itself on strangers only, and the routine established is elaborate and unwavering. The victim must be a white male, a young adult no older than thirty, heavyset, with dark hair and eyes, and the like. The victim must be chosen at random before sunset, from a public place; the victim is followed home, and must put up a struggle; et cetera. The carnage inflicted is precise: the angle and direction of the incisions; the layering of skin and muscle tissue; the rearrangement of visceral organs; and so on. Kevin Howard does not let any of this interfere with his work. He is, in fact, our fastest typist. He types as if he were on fire. He has a secret crush on Gwendolyn Stich, and leaves a red-foil-wrapped Hershey's Kiss on her desk every afternoon. But he hates Anika Bloom, and keeps well away from her. In his presence, she has uncontrollable fits of shaking and trembling. Her left palm does not stop bleeding.

In any case, when Kevin Howard gets caught, act surprised. Say that he seemed like a nice person, a bit of a loner, perhaps, but always quiet and polite.

This is the photocopier room. And this, this is our view. It faces southwest. West is down there, toward the water. North is back there. Because we are on the seventeenth floor, we are afforded a magnificent view. Isn't it beautiful? It overlooks the park, where the tops of those trees are. You can see a segment of the bay between those two buildings over there. You can see the sun set in the gap between those two buildings over there. You can see this building reflected in the glass panels of that building across the way. There. See? That's you, waving. And look there. There's Anika Bloom in the kitchenette, waving back.

Enjoy this view while photocopying. If you have problems with the photocopier, see Russell Nash. If you have any questions, ask your supervisor. If you can't find your supervisor, ask Phillip Spiers. He sits over there. He'll check with Clarissa Nicks. She sits over there. If you can't find them, feel free to ask me. That's my cubicle. I sit in there.

(1994)

Questions for Discussion and Writing

1. How familiar are the job benefits offered by the unnamed narrator of this story? If you were this new employee, is there a point at which you would begin to be uncomfortable or suspicious? Would you come back the next day?
2. Make a list of the formal and informal relationships that exist in the office and give examples of each. Do they remind you of any of the relationships in Atwood's "Happy Endings"? In what ways?
3. How would the narrator define the "good worker"? What is the narrator's attitude toward authority? Give examples to support each claim you make.
4. Study paragraphs 18 through 22. Trace the effects of the sequence of points made by the narrator, and analyze the use of various paragraph lengths by the author.
5. Why did Orozco add the outside "view" at the end of the story (para. 26)? What metaphor for the office space might Orozco be hoping to create with the scene?
6. Choose a commonly experienced event, and write a comic or satiric version similar to Orozco's description of the first day on the job. For example, you might present the dark yet funny underside of going on a first date, bringing home a new pet, remodeling a room, starting a research project, or trying out for a team.

Making Connections

1. Compare and/or contrast the main characters of the stories in this portfolio: Larry, Sister, Sammy, John and Mary, David, and the speaker in "Orientation." Discuss their similarities and differences, or adopt a central quality (like reliability, personality, motivation) as the basis for comparing them.
2. Analyze the effectiveness of point of view in each of the stories. All but "Happy Endings" use first-person narration, but are there variations in the authors' approaches to this method of storytelling? Consider, for example, the difference between a first-person account in the present tense and a first-person account recalled from the past. Explain a possible reason for Atwood's avoidance of the first person.
3. Choose a selection and consider its tone, diction, purpose, and plot. How do these elements function to make the story humorous? Do they also serve to convey a theme?
4. Which of these stories are satires? What institutions, beliefs, or human frailties are being mocked or ridiculed? What improvements or changes in attitude do the authors want to see made?
5. Prepare a script for dramatizing a key scene from one of the stories: describe the set and the characters; write the dialogue and the stage directions.

Part III

Writing About Poetry

The language of poetry is even more compressed than the language of the short story. You need to give yourself willingly to the understanding of poetry. The pleasure of reading it derives from the beauty of the language—the delight of the sounds and the images—as well as the power of the emotion and the depth of the insights conveyed. Poetry may seem difficult, but it can also be intensely rewarding.

12

How Do I Read Poetry?

In order to enjoy discovering the meaning of poetry, you must approach it with a positive attitude—a willingness to understand. Poetry invites your creative participation. More than any other form of literature, poetry allows you as reader to inform its meaning as you bring your own knowledge and experience to bear in interpreting images, motifs, and symbols.

Begin by reading the poem aloud—or at least by sounding the words aloud in your mind. Rhyme and rhythm work in subtle ways to emphasize key words and clarify meaning. As you reread, go slowly, paying careful attention to every word, looking up in a good dictionary any words that are unclear, and examining again and again any difficult lines.

Get the Literal Meaning First: Paraphrase

Before you begin interpreting a poem, you must be sure that you understand the literal meaning. Because one of the delights of poetry stems from the unusual ways in which poets put words together, you may sometimes need to straighten out the syntax. For instance, Thomas Hardy writes

> And why unblooms the best hope ever sown?

The usual way of expressing that question would be something like this:

> And why does the best hope ever sown not bloom?

Occasionally you may need to fill in words that the poet has deliberately omitted through ellipsis. When Walt Whitman writes

> But I with mournful tread,
> Walk the deck my Captain lies,
> Fallen cold and dead,

we can tell that he means "the deck on which my Captain lies, / Fallen cold and dead."

Pay close attention to punctuation; it can provide clues to meaning. But do not be distressed if you discover that poets (like Emily Dickinson and Stevie Smith) sometimes use punctuation in strange ways or (like E. E. Cummings) not at all. Along with the deliberate fracturing of syntax, this unusual use of punctuation comes under the heading of poetic license.

Always you must look up any words that you do not know—as well as any familiar words that fail to make complete sense in the context. When you read this line from Whitman:

> Passing the apple-tree blows of white and pink in the orchards,

the word "blows" seems a strange choice. If you consult your dictionary, you will discover an unusual definition of blows: "masses of blossoms," a meaning which fits exactly.

Make Associations for Meaning

Once you understand the literal meaning of a poem, you can begin to expand that meaning into an interpretation. As you do so, keep asking yourself questions: Who is the speaker? Who is being addressed? What is the message? What do the images contribute? What do the symbols suggest? How does it all fit together?

When, for instance, Emily Dickinson in the following lines envisions "Rowing in Eden," how do you respond to this image?

> Rowing in Eden—
> Ah, the Sea!
> Might I but moor—Tonight—
> In Thee!

Can she mean *literally* rowing in Eden? Not unless you picture a lake in the Garden, which is, of course, a possibility. What do you associate with Eden? Complete bliss? Surely. Innocence, perhaps—the innocence of Adam and Eve before the Fall? Or their lustful sensuality after the Fall? Given the opening lines of the poem,

> Wild Nights—Wild Nights!
> Were I with thee
> Wild Nights should be
> Our luxury!

one fitting response might be that "Rowing in Eden" suggests paddling through sexual innocence in a far from chaste anticipation of reaching the port of ecstasy: to "moor—Tonight— / In Thee!"

Sometimes poems, like stories and plays, contain *allusions* (indirect references to famous persons, events, places, or to other works of literature) that add to the meaning. Some allusions are fairly easy to perceive. When Eliot's Prufrock, in his famous love song, observes

> No! I am not Prince Hamlet, nor was meant to be,

we know that he declines to compare himself with Shakespeare's Hamlet, a character who also had difficulty taking decisive action. Some allusions, though, are more subtle. You need to know these lines from Ernest Dowson:

> Last night, ah, yesternight, betwixt her lips and mine,
> There fell thy shadow, Cynara!

in order to catch the allusion to them in Eliot's "The Hollow Men":

> Between the motion
> And the act
> Falls the shadow.

Many allusions you can simply look up. If you are puzzled by Swinburne's line

> Thou has conquered, O pale Galilean,

your dictionary will identify the Galilean as Jesus Christ. For less well-known figures or events, you may need to consult a dictionary of biblical characters, a dictionary of classical mythology, or a good encyclopedia.

Other valuable reference tools are Sir James Frazer's *The Golden Bough*, which discusses preclassical myth, magic, and religion, and Cirlot's *A Dictionary of Symbols*, which traces through mythology and world literature the significance of various ***archetypal*** (i.e., universal) symbols—the sea, the seasons, colors, numbers, islands, serpents, and a host of others.

Thus, learning to understand poetry—like learning to understand any imaginative literature—involves asking yourself questions and then speculating and researching until you come up with satisfying answers. Chart 12-1 on the next page will give you a starting list of questions.

Chart 12-1 Critical Questions for Reading Poetry

Before planning an analysis of any selection in the anthology of poetry, write out your answers to the following questions to confirm your understanding of the poem and to generate material for the paper.

1. Can you paraphrase the poem if necessary?
2. Who is the speaker in the poem? How would you describe this persona?
3. What is the speaker's tone? Which words reveal this tone? Is the poem perhaps ironic?
4. What heavily connotative words are used? What words have unusual or special meanings? Are any words or phrases repeated? If so, why? Which words do you need to look up?
5. What images does the poet use? How do the images relate to one another? Do these images form a unified pattern (a motif) throughout the poem? Is there a central, controlling image?
6. What figures of speech are used? How do they contribute to the tone and meaning of the poem?
7. Are there any symbols? What do they mean? Are they universal symbols, or do they arise from the particular context of this poem?
8. Is the occasion for or the setting of the poem important in understanding its meaning? If so, why?
9. What is the theme (the central idea) of this poem? Can you state it in a single sentence?
10. How important is the role of metrics (sound effects), such as rhyme and rhythm? How do they affect tone and meaning?
11. How important is the contribution of form, such as rhyme scheme and line arrangement? How does the form influence the overall effect of the poem?

13

Writing About Persona and Tone

Tone, which can be important in analyzing a short story, is crucial to the interpretation of poetry. Persona is closely related to tone. In order to identify persona and determine tone, you need (as usual) to ask yourself questions about the poem.

Who Is Speaking?

A good question to begin with is this: Who is the speaker in the poem? Often the most obvious answer seems to be "The poet," especially if the poem is written in the first person. When Emily Dickinson begins

> This is my letter to the world
> That never wrote to me—

we can be fairly sure that she is writing in her own voice—that the poem itself is her "letter to the world." But poets often adopt a ***persona***; that is, they speak through the voice of a character they have created. Stevie Smith, herself a middle-aged woman, adopts a persona of a different age and of the opposite sex in these lines:

> An old man of seventy-three
> I lay with my young bride in my arms. . . .

Thomas Hardy in "The Ruined Maid" (on page 468) composes a dramatic monologue with a dual persona (or two personae), two young women who converse throughout the poem. The speaker in Auden's "The Unknown Citizen" (on page 469) is apparently a spokesperson for the bureaucracy—but most certainly is not Auden himself. Thus, in order to be strictly accurate, you should avoid "The poet says . . ." and use instead "The speaker in the poem says . . ." or "The persona in the poem says. . . ."

What Is Tone?

After deciding who the speaker is, your next question might be "What is the tone of this poetic voice?" ***Tone*** in poetry is essentially the same as in fiction, drama, or expository prose: the attitude of the writer toward the subject matter of the work—the poem, story, play, or essay. And tone in a piece of writing is always similar to tone of voice in speaking. If a friend finds you on the verge of tears and comments, "You certainly look cheerful today," her tone of voice—as well as the absurdity of the statement—lets you know that your friend is using ***verbal irony***; that is, she means the opposite of what she says.

Recognizing Verbal Irony

Because verbal irony involves a reversal of meaning, it is the most important tone to recognize. To miss the irony is to miss the meaning in many cases. When Stephen Crane begins a poem

> Do not weep, maiden, for war is kind,

an alert reader will catch the ironic tone at once from the word *kind*, which war definitely is not. But irony can at times be much more subtle. Sometimes you need to put together a number of verbal clues in order to perceive the irony. W. H. Auden's poem "The Unknown Citizen," which appears in this chapter, is such a poem. Gradually as you read, you realize that the tribute being paid to this model worker (identified by number rather than name) is not the eulogy you are led to expect but an ironic commentary on the regimented society that molded the man. By the time you reach the last two lines, the irony has become apparent. (For a discussion of other types of irony that appear in drama and fiction but not often in poetry, look up ***irony*** in the Glossary.)

Describing Tone

One of the chief problems in identifying tone involves finding exactly the right word or words to describe it. Even after you have detected that a work's tone is ironic, you may need to decide whether the irony is gentle or bitter, or whether it is light or scathing in tone. Remember that you are trying to identify the tone of the poetic voice, just as you would identify the tone of anyone speaking to you.

You need a number of adjectives at your command to pinpoint tone. As you analyze poetic tone, keep the following terms in mind to see whether any may prove useful: *humorous, joyous, playful, light, hopeful, brisk, lyrical, admiring, celebratory, laudatory, expectant, wistful, sad, mournful, dreary, tragic, elegiac, solemn, somber, poignant, earnest, blasé, disillusioned, straightforward, curt, hostile, sarcastic, cynical, ambivalent, ambiguous.*

Looking at Persona and Tone

Read the following five poems for pleasure. Then, as you read through them again slowly and carefully, pay attention to the persona and try to identify the tone of this speaker's voice. Is the speaker angry, frightened, astonished, admiring? Or perhaps sincere, sarcastic, humorous, deceptive?

Theodore Roethke 1908–1963

Born in Saginaw, Michigan, Theodore Roethke was strongly influenced by his father, Otto, and his father's brother, stern German immigrants who co-owned a twenty-five-acre greenhouse complex. Much of the poet's childhood and adolescence was spent working there, as reflected by the images of nature and growth that pervade his poetry. In 1923, when Theodore was only fifteen, his uncle committed suicide and his father died from cancer. While an undergraduate at the University of Michigan, Roethke decided to pursue both poetry and teaching. He was awarded the Pulitzer Prize for poetry in 1953.

My Papa's Waltz

The whiskey on your breath
Could make a small boy dizzy;
But I hung on like death:
Such waltzing was not easy.

We romped until the pans
Slid from the kitchen shelf;
My mother's countenance
Could not unfrown itself.

The hand that held my wrist
Was battered on one knuckle;
At every step you missed
My right ear scraped a buckle.

You beat time on my head
With a palm caked hard by dirt,
Then waltzed me off to bed
Still clinging to your shirt.

(1948)

Thomas Hardy 1840–1928

An architect in London, Thomas Hardy first became interested in literature at age thirty, when he began to write novels. Among the sixteen he produced, the best-known are *The Return of the Native* (1878) and *Tess of the D'Urbervilles* (1891). When his novel *Jude the Obscure* (1895) was called immoral for criticizing marriage, Hardy became so angry that he wrote nothing but poetry for the rest of his life. Many modern poets, including W. H. Auden, Philip Larkin, and Dylan Thomas, were influenced by Hardy's use of irony and spoken language.

The Ruined Maid

"O 'Melia, my dear, this does everything crown!
Who could have supposed I should meet you in Town?
And whence such fair garments, such prosperi-ty?"—
"O didn't you know I'd been ruined?" said she.

—"You left us in tatters, without shoes or socks,
Tired of digging potatoes, and spudding up docks;
And now you've gay bracelets and bright feathers three!"—
"Yes: that's how we dress when we're ruined," said she.

—"At home in the barton° you said 'thee' and 'thou,'
And 'thik oon,' and 'theas oon,' and 't'other'; but now
Your talking quite fits 'ee for high compa-ny!"—
"Some polish is gained with one's ruin," said she.

—"Your hands were like paws then, your face blue and bleak,
But now I'm bewitched by your delicate cheek,
And your little gloves fit as on any la-dy!"—
"We never do work when we're ruined," said she.

—"You used to call home-life a hag-ridden dream,
And you'd sigh, and you'd sock,° but at present you seem
To know not of megrims° or melancho-ly!"—
"True. One's pretty lively when ruined," said she.

—"I wish I had feathers, a fine sweeping gown,
And a delicate face, and could strut about Town!"—
"My dear—a raw country girl, such as you be,
Cannot quite expect that. You ain't ruined," said she.

(1866)

---

9 barton Farmyard. 18 sock Moan. 19 megrims Sadness.

W. H. Auden 1907–1973

Although born and raised in England, W(ystan) H(ugh) Auden became a U.S. citizen in 1946. An extremely talented poet, he was the major literary voice of the 1930s, an "age of anxiety" that faced world war and global depression. Influenced by Freud, Auden often wrote about human guilt and fear, but he also celebrated the power of love to overcome anxiety. His volume of poetry *The Age of Anxiety* (1947) won the Pulitzer Prize. Auden also collaborated on verse plays and wrote librettos for operas.

The Unknown Citizen

(To JS/07/M/378
This Marble Monument
Is Erected by the State)

He was found by the Bureau of Statistics to be
One against whom there was no official complaint,
And all the reports on his conduct agree
That, in the modern sense of an old-fashioned word, he was a saint,
For in everything he did he served the Greater Community.
Except for the War till the day he retired
He worked in a factory and never got fired,
But satisfied his employers, Fudge Motors Inc.
Yet he wasn't a scab or odd in his views,
For his Union reports that he paid his dues,
(Our report on his Union shows it was sound)
And our Social Psychology workers found
That he was popular with his mates and liked a drink.
The Press are convinced that he bought a paper every day
And that his reactions to advertisements were normal in every way.
Policies taken out in his name prove that he was fully insured,
And his Health-card shows he was once in hospital but left it cured.
Both Producers Research and High-Grade Living declare
He was fully sensible to the advantages of the Installment Plan
And had everything necessary to the Modern Man,
A phonograph, a radio, a car and a frigidaire.
Our researchers into Public Opinion are content
That he held the proper opinions for the time of year;
When there was peace, he was for peace; when there was war, he went.
He was married and added five children to the population,
Which our Eugenist says was the right number for a parent of
his generation,
And our teachers report that he never interfered with their education.
Was he free? Was he happy? The question is absurd:
Had anything been wrong, we should certainly have heard.

(1940)

Edmund Waller 1606–1687

Edmund Waller was an English poet and a wealthy member of parliament. In 1643 he was arrested for his part in a plot to turn London over to the exiled king, Charles I. By betraying his co-conspirations and by making lavish bribes, Waller avoided death. His smooth, graceful verses were extremely popular and included both love poems and tributes to important public figures of the day.

Go, Lovely Rose

Go, lovely Rose,
Tell her that wastes her time and me,
that now she knows,
When I resemble her to thee,
How sweet and fair she seems to be.

Tell her that's young,
And shuns to have her graces spied,
that had'st thou sprung
In deserts where no men abide,
Thou must have uncommended died.

Small is the worth
Of beauty from the light retir'd:
Bid her come forth,
Suffer herself to be desir'd,
And not blush so to be admir'd.

Then die, that she
The common fate of all things rare
May read in thee,
How small a part of time they share,
That are so wondrous sweet and fair.

(1645)

Dorothy Parker 1893–1967

Known best for her acerbic wit, Dorothy Parker was actually a serious editor and writer. Fired from *Vanity Fair* for writing harsh theater reviews, she reviewed books for the *New Yorker*, which also published her stories, poems, and articles for over thirty years. Her lasting literary contributions include short stories such as "Big Blonde" and "The Waltz" and several collections of sardonic verse.

One Perfect Rose

A single flow'r he sent me, since we met.
All tenderly his messenger he chose;
Deep-hearted, pure, with scented dew still wet—
One perfect rose.

I knew the language of the floweret;
"My fragile leaves," it said, "his heart enclose."

Love long has taken for his amulet
    One perfect rose.

Why is it no one ever sent me yet
    One perfect limousine, do you suppose?
Ah no, it's always just my luck to get
    One perfect rose.

(1926)

PREWRITING

As you search for a fuller understanding of a poem and for a possible writing thesis, remember to keep rereading the poem (or at least pertinent parts of it). The questions you pose for yourself will become easier to answer and your responses more enlightened.

Asking Questions About the Speaker in "My Papa's Waltz"

If a poem lends itself to an approach through persona or tone, you will, of course, find something unusual or perhaps puzzling about the speaker or the poetic voice. Consider Theodore Roethke's "My Papa's Waltz," which you just read. Ask yourself first "Who is the speaker?" You know from line 2: "a small boy." But the past tense verbs suggest that the boy may be grown now, remembering a childhood experience. Sometimes this adult perspective requires additional consideration.

Next, ask yourself "What is the speaker's attitude toward his father?" The boy's feelings about his father become the crucial issue in determining the tone of the poem. You need to look carefully at details and word choice to discover your answer. Consider, for instance, these questions:

1. Try to recapture your own childhood perspective on some interaction with adults: being kissed and hugged by relatives, encountering an adult who acted oddly, relating to your first schoolteacher, meeting a babysitter. Was it fun? Were you uncomfortable? Write a description of the experience that includes only your point of view as a child.
2. Is it pleasant or unpleasant to be made dizzy from the smell of whiskey on someone's breath?
3. Does it sound like fun to hang on "like death"?
4. How does it change the usually pleasant experience of waltzing to call it "not easy"?
5. What sort of "romping" would be necessary to cause pans to slide from a shelf?
6. Is it unusual to hold your dancing partner by the wrist? How is this different from being held by the hand?

7. Would it be enjoyable or painful to have your ear scraped repeatedly by a buckle?
8. Would you like or resent having someone "beat time" on your head with a hard, dirty hand?
9. If the father is gripping the boy's wrist with one hand and thumping his head with the other, does this explain why the boy must hang on for dear life?
10. What other line in the poem does the last line echo?

If your answers to these questions lead you to conclude that this waltzing was not fun for the boy, then you could describe the tone as ironic (because of the discrepancy between the pleasant idea of the waltz and the boy's unpleasant experience). You could, possibly, describe the tone as detached, because the boy gives no clear indication of his feelings. We have to deduce them from details in the poem. You could even describe the tone as reminiscent, but this term is too general to indicate the meaning carried by the tone.

We all bring our own experience to bear in interpreting a poem. What you should be careful about is allowing your personal experience to carry too much weight in your response. If, for instance, you had an abusive father, you might so strongly identify with the boy's discomfort that you would call the tone resentful. On the other hand, if you enjoyed a loving relationship with your father, you might well find, as does X. J. Kennedy, "the speaker's attitude toward his father warmly affectionate" and take this recollection of childhood to be a happy one. Kennedy cites as evidence "the rollicking rhythms of the poem; the playfulness of a rhyme like *dizzy* and *easy*; the joyful suggestions of the words *waltz*, *waltzing*, and *romped*." He suggests that a reader who sees the tone as resentful fails "to visualize this scene in all its comedy, with kitchen pans falling and the father happily using his son's head for a drum." Kennedy also feels in the last line the suggestion of "the boy *still clinging* with persistent love."[1]

Devising a Thesis

Since your prewriting questioning has been directed toward discovering the attitude of the speaker in the poem, you could formulate a thesis that allows you to argue for the need to understand the persona in order to perceive the tone of the poem. Of course, the way you interpret the poem will determine the way you state your thesis. You could write a convincing paper on any one of the following claims:

The tone of Roethke's "My Papa's Waltz" reveals the speaker's ambivalent feelings toward his father.

The tone of Roethke's "My Papa's Waltz" subtly conveys the speaker's resentment toward his father.

The speaker's affection for his father is effectively captured in the tone of Roethke's "My Papa's Waltz."

---

[1] *An Introduction to Poetry*, 4th ed. (Boston: Little, Brown, 1971), 10.

If you wrote on the first claim, you would focus on the conflicting evidence suggesting that the boy is delighted by his father's attention but frightened by the coercion of the dance. If you wrote on the second claim, you would cite evidence of the boy's discomfort and argue that the "waltz" in the title and the rollicking meter are thus clearly ironic. If you wrote on the last claim, you would emphasize the sprightly meter and playful rhymes, which present the dance as a frisky romp and show that the boy is having a splendid time.

Describing the Tone in "The Ruined Maid"

You can see by now that speaker and tone are all but impossible to separate. In order to get at the tone of Hardy's poem, write out responses to the following questions and be prepared to discuss the tone in class.

1. Who are the two speakers in this poem?
2. What does the term *maid* mean in the title? Look it up in your dictionary if you are not sure.
3. What different meanings does your dictionary give for *ruined?* Which one applies in the poem?
4. How does the ruined maid probably make her living? What details suggest this?
5. Describe how the tone of the country maid's speeches changes during the course of the poem.
6. What tone does the ruined maid use in addressing her former friend?
7. How does the final line undercut the ruined maiden's boast that she gained "polish" with her ruin?
8. What is Hardy's tone—that is, the tone of the poem itself?

Discovering a Thesis

If you are going to write on tone in "The Ruined Maid," you might devise a major claim focusing on the way we, as readers, discover the irony in the poem. Your claim could read something like this:

> In Hardy's poem the discrepancy between the supposedly "ruined" woman's present condition and her previous wretched state reveals the ironic tone.

If you wanted, instead, to write about the dual personae in the poem, you might think about how they function—to figure out why Hardy chose to present the poem through two speakers instead of the usual one. Perhaps he chose this technique because the two voices enable him to convey his theme convincingly. You might invent a claim along these lines:

> Hardy employs dual personae in "The Ruined Maid" to convince us that prostitution, long considered "a fate worse than death," is actually much preferable to grinding poverty.

In each paper, although your focus would be different, the evidence you use in presenting the contrast would be essentially the same.

Describing the Tone in "The Unknown Citizen"

1. "The Unknown Citizen" begins with the citizen's epitaph. In a five- to ten-line poem, write your own epitaph as it might appear if you died in the next year. Think about what you would like to emphasize and what you prefer to downplay. Would you try to get a message across to people who read your gravestone?
2. How is the "he" being referred to in the poem identified in the italicized epigraph?
3. Who is the speaker in the poem? Why does the speaker use *our* and *we* instead of *my* and *I?*
4. Is *Fudge Motors Inc.* a serious name for a corporation? What is the effect of rhyming *Inc.* (line 8) with *drink* (line 13)?
5. Why does Auden capitalize so many words and phrases that normally would not be capitalized (like *Greater Community, Installment Plan, Modern Man,* and *Public Opinion*)?
6. What is the attitude of the poetic voice toward the Unknown Citizen? What is Auden's attitude toward the Unknown Citizen? What is Auden's attitude toward the speaker in the poem?
7. What, then, is the tone of the poem?

Discovering a Thesis

If you were going to write on tone in Auden's "The Unknown Citizen," you would focus on the features of the poem that reveal that tone— beginning or ending perhaps with the epigraph in which he is referred to as a number, not a name. You might frame a claim something like this:

> Auden's sharply ironic tone reveals to us that the Unknown Citizen is being honored not for his accomplishments but for being a model of conformity to the policies of the state.

As you develop this claim, you can focus on the discrepancies you recognize between the solemn praise offered by the speaker and your recognition of these qualities as far from admirable.

Discovering Tone in "Go, Lovely Rose"

1. What has happened between the speaker and the woman before the poem was written?
2. Why does he choose a rose to carry his message?
3. What does *uncommended* mean in line 10?
4. Can you detect a tone slightly different in lines 2 and 7 from the speaker's admiring tone in the poem as a whole?
5. How do you respond to his telling the rose to die so that the woman may be reminded of how quickly her beauty will also die?

6. Does the title "Song," as the poem is sometimes called, convey any hint about the tone?
7. How would you describe the tone of this poem?

Discovering Tone in "One Perfect Rose"

1. Think of a time when you received a gift that was not what you'd hoped for, or a gift that showed severe misjudgment of your preferences. Write a paragraph about your public and your private reactions to the gift.
2. What are the similarities between Parker's poem and Waller's?
3. What are the major differences?
4. Why does Parker put an apostrophe in *flow'r?*
5. What is an amulet?
6. How does the tone of the poem change in the last stanza? Can you explain why this happens?
7. What is the tone of the entire poem?

WRITING

Because you may find poetry more difficult to write about than short stories, first be sure that you understand the poem. If the poem is difficult, write a complete ***paraphrase*** in which you straighten out the word order and replace any unfamiliar words or phrases with everyday language. Yes, you damage the poem when you paraphrase it, but the poem will survive.

After you are sure you have a firm grasp on the literal level, you can then begin to examine the images, make associations, and flesh out the meanings that will eventually lead you to an interpretation of the poem. By this time, you should have generated sufficient material to write about the work. The writing process is essentially the same as it is for analyzing a short story.

Explicating and Analyzing

In explicating a poem, you proceed carefully through the text, interpreting it, usually, line by line. Because of the attention to detail, ***explication*** is best suited to writing about a short poem or a key section of a longer work. As an explicator you may look at any or all elements of the poem—tone, persona, images, symbolism, metrics—as you discuss the way these elements function together to form the poem. Although you may paraphrase an occasional line, your explication will be concerned mainly with revealing hidden meanings in the poem. Probably most of your class discussions involve a kind of informal explication of poems, stories, or plays.

A written explication is easy to organize: you start with the first line and work straight through the poem. But explicating well requires a discerning eye. You have to make numerous decisions about what to comment on and how far to pursue a point, and you also have to pull various strands together in the end to arrive at a conclusion involving a statement of the theme or purpose of the poem. This approach, if poorly handled, can be a mechanical task, but if well done, explication can prove a rewarding way to examine a rich and complex work.

A written ***analysis*** involves explication but differs by focusing on some element of the poem and examining how that element (tone, persona, imagery, symbolism, metrics) contributes to an understanding of the meaning or purpose of the whole. You can see that an analysis is more challenging to write because you must exercise more options in selecting and organizing your material. Your instructor will let you know if it matters which type of paper you compose.

IDEAS FOR WRITING

Ideas for Responsive Writing

1. Were you ever frightened or hurt as a child, like the boy in Roethke's poem, by being handled too roughly by an adult? Describe the experience, explaining not only how you felt but also what you now think the adult's motives might have been.
2. Using Dorothy Parker's "One Perfect Rose" as a guide, write an ironic or humorous response to Christopher Marlowe's "The Passionate Shepherd to His Love" (pages 667–68) or compose the woman's reply to Andrew Marvell's "To His Coy Mistress" (pages 570–71).
3. Do you know anyone well who is a conformist, a person very much like Auden's Unknown Citizen? If so, write an updated ironic tribute to the type of person who always goes along with the crowd. Write your satirical praise as a speech, an essay, or a poem.

Ideas for Critical Writing

1. Choose one of the sample claims included in the "Prewriting" section of this chapter and write an essay defending that claim.
2. Both "My Papa's Waltz" (page 467) by Theodore Roethke and "Piano" by D. H. Lawrence (page 602) concern the childhood experience of a young boy. Study both poems until you are sure you understand them; then compare or contrast their tones.
3. Compare Waller's "Go, Lovely Rose" with Parker's parody "One Perfect Rose" by focusing on the differences in tone.
4. Stevie Smith's "Not Waving but Drowning" (page 611) seems difficult until you realize that two voices are speaking—the "I" of the first and third stanzas and the "they" of the second. Once you understand the implications of this dual perspective, write an explication of the poem.

5. Explain the satirical effectiveness of Auden's deadpan narrator in "The Unknown Citizen."
6. CRITICAL APPROACHES: Review the formalist approach to literary interpretation (pages 689–90). Using evidence only from within "Go, Lovely Rose," explain the reasoning the narrator is presenting. What is his goal? What comparisons does he encourage the reader ("her") to make between herself and the rose? What point of argument is developed in each stanza?

Ideas for Researched Writing

1. To discover more about tone, consult reference works such as *A Handbook to Literature*, the *New Princeton Encyclopedia of Poetry and Poetics*, or the online *Glossary of Poetic Terms* at www.poeticbyway.com/glossary.html. Apply what you learn in an essay analyzing the tone of E. E. Cummings's "next to of course god america i" (pages 689–90).
2. Investigate the difference of opinion about the tone of "My Papa's Waltz." Locate at least three different interpretations, and write an essay in which you respond to and evaluate these views.

EDITING

In this section we will explain a few conventions that you should observe in writing about poetry. If you have often written papers analyzing poetry, you probably incorporate these small but useful bits of mechanical usage automatically. If not, take time during the revising or editing stage to get them right.

Quoting Poetry in Essays

The following are the main conventions to observe when quoting poetry in writing:

Inserting Slash Marks When quoting only a couple of lines, use a slash mark to indicate the end of each line (except the last).

> Whitman similarly describes the soul's position in the universe in these lines: "And you O my soul where you stand, / Surrounded, detached, in measureless oceans of space" (6–7).

Citing Line Numbers Cite line numbers in parentheses after the quotation marks and before the period when quoting complete lines, as in the previous example. When quoting only a phrase, cite the line number immediately after closing the quotation marks, even if your sentence continues.

In the italicized portion of the poem, the bird sings a carol in praise of "lovely and soothing death" (135) to help the persona overcome his grief.

Adjusting End Punctuation Because you are using the lines you quote in a different context from that in the poem, you may adjust the punctuation of the last line you quote to make it fit your sentence. Here is a line from Whitman's "When Lilacs Last in the Dooryard Bloom'd":

To adorn the burial-house of him I love?

Notice how the end punctuation is dropped in order to suit the writer's sentence:

The persona brings visions of the varying beauty of the entire country, as he says, "To adorn the burial-house of him I love" (80).

Using Ellipsis Dots To show omissions when quoting poetry, use three dots, just as you would if quoting prose.

The poet's sympathies are not for the living but for the dead: "They themselves were fully at rest. . . . / The living remain'd and suffer'd . . ." (181–82).

Using Square Brackets If you need to change a word, a capital letter, or some punctuation *within* the line or lines you quote, enclose the changed letter or mark of punctuation in square brackets (not parentheses).

The persona brings visions of the varying beauty of the entire country "[t]o adorn the burial-house of him [he] love[s]" (80).

Remember that you do not have to quote complete lines. Rather than clutter your sentence with three sets of brackets, you could quote only the telling phrase in that line.

The persona brings visions of the varying beauty of the entire country to "adorn the burial-house" (80) of the one he loves.

Quoting Multiple Lines If you are quoting more than two or three lines, indent ten spaces and omit the quotation marks (since the indention tells your readers that the material is quoted).

After describing the carnage of war dead, the persona realizes that his sympathies have been misplaced:

They themselves were fully at rest, they suffer'd not,
The living remain'd and suffer'd, the mother suffer'd,
And the wife and the child and the musing comrade suffer'd
And the armies that remain'd suffer'd. (181–84)

The indented material should still be double-spaced (unless your instructor asks you to single-space the lines).

Sample Student Response: Persona and Tone

The following student paper was written in response to A. E. Housman's poem "To an Athlete Dying Young" and is included here not as a model but to generate class discussion. Read the poem, which appears on page 589 and then decide whether you agree with the student's claims about the tone and persona of Housman's poem.

Sample Student Response: Persona and Tone

Bond 1

Kenric L. Bond

Professor Funk

English 1002

2 October 2005

Death at an Early Age

Wouldn't it be great to die in your prime, not to be remembered as old and feeble but as still strong and vibrant? A. E. Housman's poem "To an Athlete Dying Young" tells of an athlete who died a hero not too long after winning a record-setting race.

The first stanza tells of an athlete coming home after winning a race: "The time you won your town the race / We chaired you through the market-place" (1–2). But the next stanza begins, "To-day, the road all runners come, / Shoulder-high we bring you home" (5–6). The similarity between these two scenes is startling. We would not ordinarily link the picture of pallbearers carrying the deceased home in a casket with a hero being carried on the shoulders of his cheering fans. These first two stanzas set up the contrast between triumph and death that continues through the rest of the poem.

The third stanza deals with this issue of dying in one's prime by mentioning "the laurel," which grows "early" but "withers quicker than the rose" (11–12). The laurel represents fame for winning the race, but it is forgotten sooner than the brief life of a rose. This point about the brevity of fame is repeated in the last stanza:

> And round that early-laurelled head
> Will flock to gaze the strengthless dead,
> And find unwithered on its curls
> The garland briefer than a girl's. (25–28)

Bond 2

The victory garland, awarded after the race, is still green with life on the dead athlete's head; the fame of winning the race is shorter than a girl's innocence and purity. So, Housman implies, the time to die is while the recent victory is still being discussed among the living in the area coffee shops and beauty salons.

During the poem, A. E. Housman tries to convince us that it is best to die young: "Smart lad, to slip betimes away / From fields where glory does not stay" (9–10). Housman calls the athlete smart for dying while the memory of victory is still fresh in the minds of a society where positive accomplishments are easily forgotten. The poet also applauds the athlete's death because then the runner won't have to face the disheartening sight of a new runner breaking his records and stealing the glory he once enjoyed: "Eyes the shady night has shut / Cannot see the record cut" (13–14).

As a runner myself, I know that I will someday see all the records that I set in high school broken. I have already witnessed a few of my marks reset by other runners. If I had died right after my high school years, I could have missed these superficial disappointments. But an athlete shouldn't be so shallow that he or she can't bear to live and see such trivial things as records broken. They are just names on a wall or trophies in a case. I hope that somebody does break my records because that's why I made them—to be broken.

Housman seems to think that setting records and living in the limelight are all that athletes are looking for in their lives. The poet suggests that it would be too difficult for an athlete to live and see the record books rewritten and that a victorious athlete would be vain enough to worry about what other people think of his physical state after he's dead. Well, I think the poet is wrong. I'm one athlete who has more than records and glory to live for.

Analyzing the Student Response

After rereading Housman's poem, write an analysis of the preceding student response. (Or, if you prefer, write your own interpretation of "To an Athlete Dying Young.") The following questions may help you:

1. Does the student have a clear understanding of the poem's main theme? Where does he state the theme? Do you agree with his statement of the theme?
2. Does the student identify the speaker in the poem? Are the speaker and the poet the same person? How do you know?
3. Does the student identify the poem's tone? Could the speaker's attitude toward death be ironic? Does the student see any irony in the poem? Does the student ever use any irony himself?
4. Do you agree with the student's claim about Housman's purpose (first sentence of paragraph 5)? How does this claim relate to the student's interpretation of the poem's tone?
5. How do the student's own experiences influence his responses to the poem? How does the student feel about the poet's attitude toward athletes? Do you agree with the reactions expressed in the last two paragraphs?

Writing About Poetic Language

In no other form of literature are words so important as in poetry. As you study the language of poetry—its freshness, precision, and beauty— you can learn ways in which to use words effectively in your own prose writing.

What Do the Words Suggest?

Your sensitivity to poetic language will be enhanced if you learn the meaning of a few terms in literary criticism. (The important term *allusion* is defined in Chapter 12, page 463.)

Connotation and Denotation

Many single words carry a rich load of meaning, both denotative and connotative. The ***denotation*** of a word is the definition you will find in the dictionary. The ***connotation*** of a word is the emotional overtone you may feel when encountering the term. Consider the word *mother.* Most people would respond positively with feelings of warmth, security, and love associated with bedtime stories, a warm lap, and fresh apple pies. So, when Stephen Crane includes the word in these moving lines:

> Mother whose heart hung humble as a button
> On the bright splendid shroud of your son,
> Do not weep.
> War is kind,

the connotations of the word *mother* probably account for part of our emotional response.

Figures of Speech

The most common figures of speech—metaphor, simile, and personification—appear in our everyday language. You might say, if you keep forgetting things, "My mind is a sieve," creating a metaphor. Or you might note, "That dog looks like a dust mop without a handle," making a simile. Or you might complain, "My computer can't spell worth a darn," using personification. Of course, poets use figures of speech that are much fresher and more imaginative than the kind most of us employ—one of the cardinal reasons for considering them poets.

Metaphor and Simile

A ***metaphor*** is an imaginative comparison that makes use of the connotative values of words. When Shakespeare writes to a young lover, "Thy eternal summer shall not fade," he is comparing youth to the joys of summertime. In "Dulce et Decorum Est" (pages 688–89), a compelling antiwar poem, Wilfred Owen uses the metaphors "drunk with fatigue," "blood-shod," "like old beggars under sacks," "coughing like hags," "flound'ring like a man in fire or lime," and "his hanging face, like a devil's sick of sin." The last four of these singularly grim comparisons would usually be called ***similes*** because they include the connective *like*, but you can also find similes that use *as* and other explicitly comparative words. In fact, many people use the broader term *metaphor* to refer to any figure of speech that involves a comparison.

A metaphor goes beyond descriptive detail by making an association that can *only* be imaginary, one that is impossible in reality. A person's life does not have seasons except in a metaphorical way; nor do people really become intoxicated with fatigue. However, the mental stretch these comparisons demand is part of their power. "Drunk with fatigue" makes many imaginative associations: the tired soldiers have lost their ability to think straight; they are staggering along about to fall over; they are not physiologically alert. In the poem, it is this state that makes one of them unable to don his mask quickly when a chlorine gas bomb strikes. His reaction time is fatally impaired, just like a drunk's. You can see how the metaphor packs in meaning and guides our response to the poem's narrative.

These metaphorical ideas—life having seasons or people feeling drunk with fatigue—are not difficult to grasp, because they resonate with our own experiences. Some critics would say that the best metaphors demand a more intellectual leap, having a shocking or puzzling aspect. An example from "Dulce et Decorum Est" might be the description of the soldiers' hurry to grab their gas masks as "an ecstasy of fumbling." We usually associate "ecstasy" with happiness, yet this cannot be the meaning here. We are forced to think beyond the obvious, to the features of ecstasy that do apply—intensity, overpowering emotion, lack of thought, lack of conscious control. The student paper beginning on page 497 explicates several such unusual metaphors in John Donne's "A Valediction: Forbidding Mourning."

In this chapter, the poem "In the Long Hall" provides an example of an *extended metaphor.* An extended metaphor is exactly what it sounds like: an imaginative comparison worked out through several lines or perhaps even an entire poem, accruing meaning as it goes along. In this case, your understanding of the poem hinges on your understanding of the metaphor it develops.

Personification

"Daylight is nobody's friend," writes Anne Sexton in a metaphor that compares daylight to a friend. More exactly it is a ***personification***, because it makes a nonhuman thing sound like a human being. T. S. Eliot uses personification when he writes "the afternoon, the evening, sleeps so peacefully," as does Andrew Marvell in "Fate with jealous eyes does see."

Imagery

Perhaps personification is so widely used in poetry because it gives us a clear image of something otherwise vague or abstract, like daylight or fate. ***Imagery*** is the term we use to speak of these sensory impressions literature gives us. Robert Frost, in a famous poem, describes a sleigh driver "stopping here / To watch his woods fill up with snow," providing a visual image that most readers find easy to picture. In the same poem, Frost gives us an apt auditory image: "The only other sound's the sweep / Of easy wind and downy flake." And anyone who has spent time in a big airport surely agrees with Yvor Winters's image of one: "the light gives perfect vision, false and hard; / The metal glitters, deep and bright."

Symbol

A ***symbol*** is an image that becomes so suggestive that it takes on much more meaning than its descriptive value. The connotations of the words, the repetition, the placement, and the meaning it may gather from the rest of the poem help identify an image as a symbol. Blue skies and fresh spring breezes can certainly be just that, but they can also symbolize freedom. Look at the first stanza of a W. H. Auden poem:

As I walked out one evening
    Walking down Bristol Street
The people on the pavement
    Were fields of harvest wheat.

The image in lines 3 and 4 is descriptive: you can envision a crowd of moving people seeming to ripple like wheat. The observation is also symbolic, because harvest wheat is just about to be cut down; the rest of the poem endorses a rather dim view of human hopes and dreams.

Paradox

The same poem says, "You shall love your crooked neighbor / With your crooked heart." An inexperienced reader might say, "Now, that doesn't make any sense! *Crooked heart* and *love* seem contradictory." Others, though, would be sensitive to the paradox in those lines. A ***paradox*** is a phrase or statement that on the surface seems contradictory but makes some kind of emotional sense. Looking back at Yvor Winters's description of the San Francisco airport at night, you will find the phrase "perfect vision, false and hard." How can perfect vision be false instead of true? Only as a paradox. Paradoxical also are the "sounds of silence," which is the title of a Paul Simon song. And popular singer Carly Simon tells her lover paradoxically that "Nobody does it better / Makes me feel bad so good." The standard Christian paradox is stated in the motto of Mary, Queen of Scots: "In my end is my beginning." In order to make sense of that statement, all we need to know is the customary Christian belief that after death begins a better life in heaven.

Oxymoron

Another figure of speech that appears occasionally in both poetry and prose is an ***oxymoron***, an extreme paradox in which two words having opposite meanings are juxtaposed, as in "deafening silence" or "elaborately simple."

Looking at Poetic Language

The five poems you are about to study exemplify elements of poetic language. As you read them over several times, identify figures of speech, imagery, symbol, and paradox.

Walt Whitman 1819–1892

Born on an impoverished farm in Long Island, Whitman moved with his family to Brooklyn, where he worked for many years as a printer, teacher, journalist, and carpenter. In 1855, he published his own book of poetry, *Leaves of Grass*, a collection of twelve long poems, which he expanded and revised throughout his life. His work as a volunteer nurse in the Civil War inspired his next collection of poems, *Drum Taps* (1865). Whitman's bold experiments with free verse and his celebration of human sexuality shocked his contemporaries—but liberated American poetry and influenced generations of modern poets.

A Noiseless Patient Spider

A noiseless patient spider,
I mark'd where on a little promontory it stood isolated,

Mark'd how to explore the vacant vast surrounding,
It launched forth filament, filament, filament, out of itself,
Ever unreeling them, ever tirelessly speeding them.

And you O my soul where you stand,
Surrounded, detached, in measureless oceans of space,
Ceaselessly musing, venturing, throwing, seeking the
  spheres to connect them,
Till the bridge you will need be form'd, till the ductile anchor hold,
Till the gossamer thread you fling catch somewhere,
  O my soul.

(1881)

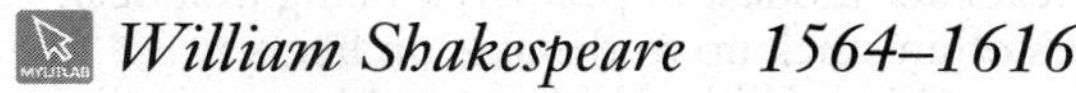

William Shakespeare 1564–1616

See page 889 for a biographical note about this author.

Shall I Compare Thee to a Summer's Day?

Shall I compare thee to a summer's day?
Thou art more lovely and more temperate:
Rough winds do shake the darling buds of May,
And summer's lease hath all too short a date:
Sometimes too hot the eye of heaven shines,
And often is his gold complexion dimmed;
And every fair from fair sometimes declines,
By chance or nature's changing course untrimmed;
But thy eternal summer shall not fade,
Nor lose possession of that fair thou ow'st;
Nor shall death brag thou wander'st in his shade,
When in eternal lines to time thou grow'st:
So long as men can breathe, or eyes can see,
So long lives this, and this gives life to thee.

(1609)

Kay Ryan 1945–

While a student at UCLA, Kay Ryan was denied membership in the university poetry club. In 2004 she was awarded the $100,000 Ruth Lilly Poetry Prize and in 2008 was named Poet Laureate of the United States. "All of us want instant success," she says. "I'm glad I was on a sort of slow drip." A lifetime Californian, she lives in Marin

County with her partner, Carol Adair, and has taught remedial English at the College of Marin for thirty years.

Turtle

Who would be a turtle who could help it?
A barely mobile hard roll, a four-oared helmet,
She can ill afford the chances she must take
In rowing toward the grasses that she eats.
Her track is graceless, like dragging
A packing-case places, and almost any slope
Defeats her modest hopes. Even being practical,
She's often stuck up to the axle on her way
To something edible. With everything optimal,
She skirts the ditch which would convert
Her shell into a serving dish. She lives
Below luck-level, never imagining some lottery
Will change her load of pottery to wings.
Her only levity is patience,
The sport of truly chastened things.

(1994)

Hayden Carruth 1921–2008

Hayden Carruth, who held a master's degree from the University of Chicago, spent eighteen months in his thirties in what he called "the loony bin," recovering from agoraphobia so severe that for five years he huddled in the attic of his parents' house, barely able to write—"like squeezing old glue out of the tube." Eventually he moved to Vermont, where he scraped out a hard living—chopping wood, smoking pigs, and typing manuscripts for a dollar a page. Married four times, he declared, "The women in my life got me through." He won the National Book Award in 1996 for his collection *Scrambled Eggs & Whiskey.*

In the Long Hall

On his knees he was weaving a tapestry
which was unraveling behind him. At first
he didn't mind it; the work was flawed,
loose ends, broken threads, a pattern
he could not control; but as his skill
improved he began to resent the way
his tapestry was undoing itself.
He resolved not to look back

but to keep going ahead, as he did
successfully for a long time. Still
later, however, he began to notice
that the part of the tapestry in front
of him was unraveling too; threads
he had just knotted became loose.
He tied them again. But before long
he could not keep up, his hands
were too slow, his fingers too weak.
The unraveling in front pushed
him toward the unraveling in back
until he found himself isolated
on a small part of the tapestry whose
pattern he could not see because
it was beneath his own body. He spun
this way and that. He worked as fast as
he could with trembling fingers
in futility, in frenzy, in despair.

(1978)

Donald Hall 1928–

Donald Hall was born in Connecticut and educated at Exeter Academy and at Harvard and Oxford universites. He met and married the poet Jane Kenyon in 1972, and the couple moved to Eagle Pond Farm in rural New Hampshire, where Hall remains affiliated with Bennington College. In 1989, he was diagnosed with colon cancer and given a slim chance of surviving five years. But in 1994 Kenyon developed leukemia and died within fifteen months. Hall's collection *Without: Poems* (1998) focuses on her illness and death. In 2006, he was named Poet Laureate of the United States.

My Son My Executioner

My son, my executioner,
  I take you in my arms,
Quiet and small and just astir,
  And whom my body warms.

Sweet death, small son, our instrument
  Of immortality,
Your cries and hungers document
  Our bodily decay.

We twenty-five and twenty-two,
  Who seemed to live forever,
Observe enduring life in you
  And start to die together.

(1955)

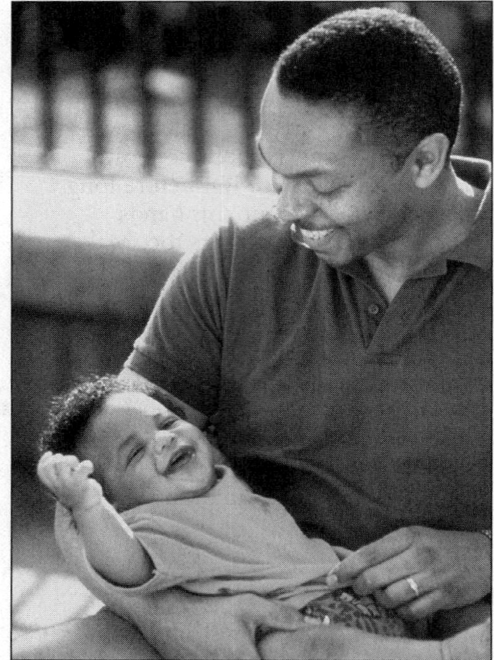

Father holding his son, who looks nothing like an executioner.

PREWRITING

The following exercises will help you analyze the use of language in the poems that you just read in preparation for writing a paper focusing on that approach.

Examining Poetic Language

1. Why could one say that "Shall I Compare Thee to a Summer's Day?" presents contrast rather than comparison?
2. In a group of classmates, attempt to write a companion poem to "Shall I Compare Thee to a Summer's Day?" using instead the extended metaphor "Shall I compare thee to a winter's day?" Try to use connotative language.
3. What is the main comparison made in "A Noiseless Patient Spider"? What is personified? Using a thesaurus, paraphrase the poem, substituting near synonyms for some of the original words. Comment on the differences in meaning and tone you create. (Imagine, for example, if the spider "launched forth string, string, string, out of itself.")
4. "Turtle" contains a number of figures of speech. Identify as many as you can. Which ones do you find fresh and effective? Which ones are less successful in your opinion?

5. What metaphor is developed through "In the Long Hall"? It may help you to fill in the blank: "________ is like weaving a tapestry." Within this metaphor, what do changes in the process of weaving mean?
6. Explain the paradox that is central to "My Son My Executioner."

WRITING

Poetic language is one of the richest veins of material for writing. You could, for example, analyze the role of nature imagery in "Turtle," in "Shall I Compare Thee to a Summer's Day?" or in "A Noiseless Patient Spider." Or you could examine the cumulative effect of the extended metaphor in "In the Long Hall."

Comparing and Contrasting

Noticing similarities and differences between poems will sharpen your sensitivity to each of them. If you listed all the words in the short poem "My Son My Executioner" and scrambled them and then listed all the words in "Turtle" and scrambled them, putting the two lists side by side, you might see for the first time that "Turtle" has few words longer than two syllables, that it has few abstract terms, and that in contrast with "My Son My Executioner" it has few words that convey emotion. Taking the comparison further, you might say that "Turtle" focuses on creating a strong, sensual image while "My Son My Executioner" focuses on expression of ideas and feelings.

The following writing assignments suggest some meaningful comparisons to explore.

IDEAS FOR WRITING

Ideas for Responsive Writing

1. Whitman's poem comparing the explorations of the spider to the searchings of his soul makes the totally abstract idea of the soul's search for meaning clear and concrete. Think of some abstraction that you might want to explain to a five-year-old child—something like gentleness, aggression, wisdom, slyness, or perseverance. Then think of an appropriate animal or insect to illustrate the quality, and write a poem or a fable to show the child why the quality is good or bad. Remember to keep your vocabulary simple and your lines or sentences short.
2. Who is the "he," the weaver, in "In the Long Hall"? Write an essay explaining whether "he" is everyone, a certain type of person, or a specific character created by Carruth. Be specific about how you came to your conclusion.
3. Write a detailed description of an animal, using personification and metaphors the way Kay Ryan does in her poem "Turtle."

Ideas for Critical Writing

1. In your study of literature and in your everyday life, you have come across many metaphors and similes for the life span (for example, the idea that life is a journey). Explain the extended metaphor in "In the Long Hall" in terms of similarities to and differences from other figures of speech that describe the life span.
2. Compare the two kinds of love described in "A Valediction: Forbidding Mourning" (pages 568–69), using the images associated with each kind, to discover what John Donne considers the nature of true love.
3. Interpret the symbol of the spider in "Design" (page 598) and in "A Noiseless Patient Spider" (pages 486–87).
4. Compare and contrast the nature imagery in Shakespeare's Sonnet 18 ("Shall I Compare Thee to a Summer's Day?" on page 487) and Sonnet 73 ("That Time of Year Thou Mayst in Me Behold" on page 565).
5. CRITICAL APPROACHES: Review the psychological approach to interpreting literature (pages 1159–60). Read D. H. Lawrence's "Piano" (page 602), looking for clues to the narrator's conscious and unconscious motivations, defenses, inner conflicts, and symbolic representations. Write an explication of the poem from a psychological point of view.

Ideas for Researched Writing

1. In the early twentieth century, a prominent group of poets developed an identity as *imagists,* dedicated to concrete, concentrated poetic language. The movement was called *imagism.* Several of these poets are represented in the poetry anthology in this text. Consult reference works and article databases for information about this movement and its followers. Write a paper explaining the principles of the movement, using examples from imagist poets.
2. Critic I. A. Richards coined two terms—*vehicle* and *tenor*—to describe the relationship between a writer's ideas and the metaphors used to objectify the ideas. Find out more about Richards's explanation of these terms. Then write a report explaining to your classmates how the terms can be used to analyze and understand metaphors. Use several poems from this book to illustrate your points.

REWRITING: STYLE

After looking so closely at poetic language, you should have a grasp of how important every word is to the total effect of a piece of writing.

Choosing Vivid, Descriptive Terms

Dudley Randall's "To the Mercy Killers" (page 623) draws its strength almost exclusively from the vividness of its language. He describes himself as "a clot, an aching clench, / a stub, a stump, a butt, a scab, a knob, / a screaming pain, a putrefying stench." While your expository prose should not be quite so packed with arresting terminology, it can probably be improved by some attention to descriptive wording. Look at several of your back papers from this class. See whether you can identify your favorite vacant words. Do you always express positive evaluations with *nice* or *beautiful*? Do you usually intensify an adjective with the word *very*? Do you refer to everything from ideas to irises as *things*? And do you describe anything that causes a faint stir in your being as *interesting*, causing you to come up with vapid sentences like "This beautiful poem is full of very interesting things"? If so, you need to find livelier, more exact terms.

Sample Student Paper: Poetic Language

Here are the second and final drafts of an Eastern Illinois University student's essay analyzing the love imagery in Donne's "A Valediction: Forbidding Mourning" (pages 568–69).

Comparison Exercise

After you have read both drafts, go over them again, making point-by-point comparisons. Notice that the writer went beyond the instructor's specific suggestions in her final revision. Write your response to the following topics, and be prepared to discuss your findings in class.

1. Identify five cases in which the writer made changes in word choice (diction). Using a dictionary, explain the rationale for the changes.
2. Identify two sentences that have been significantly changed. Explain the reasons for the changes.
3. Closely analyze all the alterations in the third paragraph of the essay.

Sample Student Paper: Second Draft

Sonya Weaver
Professor Funk
English 1002
April 3 2005

Images of a Love

The speaker in John Donne's poem "A Valediction: Forbidding Mourning" is an unromantic man who is sternly forbidding his wife to be sorrowful at his parting. This description is not true of course, but it is the way the speaker might be perceived if all comparisons, contrasts, and images were taken out of the poem. In order to appreciate the beauty of this poem and interpret it correctly, it is necessary to take a close look at each image or comparison.

punct.

wordy sentence.

The first comparison we come to likens the speaker's parting to the quiet and easy death of virtuous men. The speaker paints a picture of a virtuous or upright man who, because he does not fear it, is passing peacefully into death. His deathbed is surrounded by his friends who are having trouble deciding if he has actually passed away or if he is still quietly breathing. The speaker says that his departure from his wife should be just as calm. He says, "let us melt" (5) which implies slowly and easily parting without any noise or tears. He explains that showing great emotion would expose their love to the common people and he does not want this because he believes their love is special, and that exposure would lower their love.

vague reference

best word choice?

Weaver 2

The speaker next contrasts their love to the love of common people. He states that common people notice earthquakes, but not trepidations or tremblings that take place among the stars. He is illustrating that common people's love is earthly, but that their love is heavenly. He goes on to say that "sublunary" (13) or earthly lovers cannot be apart from each other because when they are, they lose their love because it is only physical. He claims that he and his wife are not like this. He feels that their love (his and his wife's) is spiritual and refined and that it is so great that it is above their understanding ("ourselves know not what it is" [18]). They do not have to worry about their spouse being unfaithful, as earthly lovers do, because their love is not just physical.

misleading reference?

needs rephrasing

weak reference

rephrase

Next the speaker compares the malleability of gold to the distance that their souls can stretch (21–24). The speaker says that temporary separation should not be viewed as a break. He believes that even though they may be many miles apart, they are still one. He claims their souls can expand over distances equal to the malleability of gold or 250 square feet. This is a truly beautiful image.

maybe expand with other associations of gold

clarify

The last image is another very beautiful one. It compares their two souls to twin compasses (25–36). The speaker believes that if their souls are two (instead of one), they are still linked to each other, as are the parts of a compass. He likens his wife to the foot in the center. She makes no attempt on her own to move. She does so only if he does. She is also like the center foot in that if he leaves, she leans after him

Weaver 3

and then becomes upright when he returns home as does the center foot of a compass when the outer foot is at a distance drawing a circle. He says that there will be times when he must leave but that he will always return to her even as a compass returns to its starting point upon completion of a circle.

Without its images, this poem would be nothing more than a husband prohibiting his wife from being sad at his departure. However, Donne's images transform this rough message into a beautiful and romantic love poem. Images are important! *Weak closing line*

Be sure to add Work Cited (on a separate page).

This is a good second draft showing sensitivity to the images. I have marked a few places where your style needs more clarity and grace as well as one paragraph that could be expanded.

Sample Student Paper: Final Draft

Weaver 1

Sonya Weaver
Professor Funk
English 1002
10 April 2005

Images of a Love

The speaker in John Donne's poem "A Valediction: Forbidding Mourning" is an unromantic man who is sternly forbidding his love to be sorrowful at his parting. This description is not true, of course, but it is the way the speaker might be perceived if all comparisons, contrasts, and images were taken out of the poem. In order to appreciate the beauty of this poem and interpret it accurately, each image or comparison must be closely analyzed.

The first comparison we come to likens the speaker's parting to the quiet and easy death of virtuous men. The speaker paints a picture of a virtuous or upright man who, because he does not fear it, is passing peacefully into death. His deathbed is surrounded by his friends, who are having trouble deciding if he has actually passed away or if he is still quietly breathing. The speaker suggests that his departure from his wife should be just as calm. He says, "let us melt" (5), which implies slow and easy movement, without any clamor or sobbing. He explains that showing great emotion would display their love to the common people, and he does not want this display because he believes it would make their special love seem common.

Weaver 2

The speaker next contrasts their special love to common love. He states that common people notice earthquakes, but not trepidations or tremblings that take place among the stars. He is illustrating that common people's love is earthly, but that the love between him and his wife is heavenly. He goes on to say that "sublunary" (13) or earthly lovers mourn physical separation because their love is limited to the physical realm. He claims that he and his wife are not thus limited. Their love is so spiritual and refined that it is even beyond their own understanding ("ourselves know not what it is" [18]). They do not have to worry about unfaithfulness, as earthly lovers do, because their love is not merely defined by the physical.

Next the speaker compares their love to the rare, precious, and beautiful metal gold (21–24). The comparison suggests not only that their love shares these three qualities, but also that it shares gold's malleability. An ounce of gold can be spread thin enough to cover 250 square feet. The speaker compares this span to the distance that their souls can stretch. The speaker says that temporary separation should not be viewed as a break. He believes that even though they may be many miles apart, they are still one, like a continuous sheet of spread gold—an unusual and expressive image.

The last image is another quite eloquent one. It compares their two souls to twin compasses (25–36). The speaker believes that if their souls are two (instead of one), they are still linked to each other, as are the parts of a drafting compass. He likens his wife to the foot in the center. She makes no attempt on her own to move but does so only if he does. She is also

Weaver 3

like the center foot in that if he leaves, she leans after him and then becomes upright when he returns home, behaving like the center foot of a compass when the outer foot draws a circle and then folds into the center. He says that there will be times when he must leave but that he will always return to her even as a compass returns to its starting point upon completion of a circle.

Without its images, this poem would be nothing more than a husband's prohibiting his wife from being sad at his departure. However, Donne's often extraordinary images transform this austere message into a beautiful and romantic love poem.

Weaver 4

Work Cited

Donne, John. "A Valediction: Forbidding Mourning." *Literature and the Writing Process*. Ed. Elizabeth McMahan, Susan X Day, and Robert Funk. 7th ed. Upper Saddle River: Prentice, 2005. 427. Print.

15

Writing About Poetic Form

When we say that poetry has *form*, we mean it has design or structure. All poems have some kind of form. Many elements go into making the forms of poetry, but they all involve arranging the words in patterns. Sometimes sound controls the pattern; sometimes the number of words or the length of the lines determines the form.

What Are the Forms of Poetry?

Poetic forms can be divided into those that use sound effects (rhythm, rhyme), those that involve the length and organization of lines (stanza), and those that artistically manipulate word order (syntax).

Rhythm and Rhyme

Sound effects are produced by organized repetition. Stressing or accenting words and syllables produces *rhythm*; repeating similar sounds in an effective scheme produces *rhyme*. Both effects intensify the meaning of a poem, arouse interest, and give pleasure. Once we notice a pattern of sound we expect it to continue, and this expectation makes us more attentive to subtleties in the entire poem.

Rhythm can affect us powerfully. We respond almost automatically to the beat of a drum, the thumping of our heart, the pulsing of an engine. Poetic rhythm, usually more subtle, is created by repeating stresses and pauses. Rhythm conveys no verbal meaning itself, but when used skillfully it reinforces the meaning and tone of a poem. Consider how Theodore Roethke captures the raucous spirit of "My Papa's Waltz" in the recurring three-stress rhythm of these lines.

> We rómped untíl the páns
> Slíd from the kítchen shélf;
>
> Then wáltzed me óff to béd
> Still clínging tó your shírt.

Chart 15-1 Rhythm and Meter in Poetry

When the rhythm has a regular pattern—that is, when the stress recurs at regular intervals—the result is *meter*. Not all poems are metered, but many are written in one dominant pattern.

Number of Feet Poetic meter is measured in feet, units of stressed and unstressed syllables. A line of poetry may be written in monometer (having one foot), dimeter (two feet), trimeter (three feet), tetrameter (four feet), pentameter (five feet), hexameter (six feet), and so on.

Kinds of Feet The syllables in a line can occur in regular patterns. The most common pattern for poetry written in English is *iambic*, an unstressed syllable (˘) followed by a stressed one (´). This line is written in iambic pentameter; it has five iambic feet:

My̆ mís | trĕss' eýes | ăre nó | thĭng líke | thĕ sún

Three other meters are of some importance in English poetry.

Trochaic (a stressed syllable followed by an unstressed one):

Téll mĕ | nót ĭn | móurn fŭl | núm bĕrs

Anapestic (two unstressed syllables followed by a stressed one):

'Twăs thĕ níght | bĕ fŏre Chríst | măs ănd áll | thrŏugh thĕ hóuse

Dactylic (a stressed syllable followed by two unstressed ones):

Híg glĕ dy̆ | píg glĕ dy̆ | Prés ĭ dĕnt | Jéff ĕr sŏn

For more details about the rhythms of poetry, see the above chart on meter.

Rhyme, a recurring pattern of similar sounds, also enhances tone and meaning. Because rhymed language is special language, it helps to set poetry apart from ordinary expression and calls attention to the sense, feeling, and tone of the words. Rhyme also gives a certain pleasure to the reader by fulfilling the expectation of the sound patterns. Rhyme, which usually depends on sound, not spelling, occurs when accented syllables contain the same or a similar vowel sound with identical consonant sounds following the vowel: *right* and *bite*, *knuckle* and *buckle*. Rhymes are commonly used at regular intervals within a poem, often at the ends of lines:

> Yet he wasn't a scab or odd in his views,
> For his Union reports that he paid his dues.

Alliteration, Assonance, and Consonance

Closely allied to rhyme are other verbal devices that depend on the correspondence of sounds. ***Alliteration*** is the repetition of consonant sounds either at the beginning of words or in stressed syllables: "The Soul selects her own Society—" or "Nature's first green is gold, /Her hardest hue to hold." ***Assonance*** is the repetition of similar vowel sounds that are not followed by identical consonant sounds: *grave* and *gain*, *shine* and *bright*. ***Consonance*** is a kind of half-rhyme in which the consonants are parallel but the vowels change: *blade* and *blood*, *flash* and *flesh*. Alliteration, assonance, and consonance are likely to be used occasionally and not in regular, recurring patterns; but these devices of sound do focus our attention and affect the tone, melody, and tempo of poetic expression.

Exercise on Poetic Form

Listen to a favorite popular song and copy down the lyrics (you may have to listen several times). Now arrange the lines on the page as you think they would be printed. What patterns of rhythm and sound do you see? Did you notice them before you wrote the words down and arranged the lines? Does the lineation (the arrangement into lines of poetry) help make the meaning any clearer? If possible, compare your written version with a printed one (on the CD cover or album liner or online lyrics site).

Stanzas: Closed and Open Forms

In the past, almost all poems were written in *closed form*: poetry with lines of equal length arranged in fixed patterns of stress and rhyme. Although these elements of form are still much in evidence today, modern poets prefer the greater freedom of *open-form poetry*, which uses lines of varying length and avoids prescribed patterns of rhyme or rhythm.

Closed forms give definition and shape to poetic expression. *Rhyme schemes* and *stanza patterns* demand the careful arrangement of words and lines into units of meaning that guide both writer and reader in understanding poetry.

Couplets and Quatrains Stanzas can be created on the basis of the number of lines, the length of the lines, the pattern of stressed syllables (the meter), and the rhyme scheme (the order in which rhymed words recur). The simplest stanza form is the ***couplet***: two rhymed lines, usually of equal length and similar meter. W. H. Auden's "The Unknown Citizen" (page 469) is written in rhyming couplets, although the lines vary in length and sometimes in rhythm. The most common stanza in English poetry is the ***quatrain***, a group of four lines with any number of rhyme schemes. "The Ruined Maid" (page 468) is composed of six quatrains in which the lines rhyme as couplets (critics indicate this pattern of rhyme with letters: *a a b b*). The same rhyme scheme and stanza form are used in "Aunt Jennifer's Tigers" (page 634), while the quatrains of "My Papa's Waltz" (page 467) employ an alternating rhyme pattern (*a b a b*). Longer stanza patterns are used, of course, but the quatrain and the couplet remain the basic components of closed-form poetry.

Sonnets The fixed form that has been used most frequently by the greatest variety of notable poets in England and America is the ***sonnet.*** Originated in Italy in the fourteenth century, the sonnet became a staple of English poetry in the sixteenth century and has continued to attract practitioners ever since.

The form of the sonnet is firmly fixed: fourteen lines, with ten syllables per line, arranged in a set rhyme scheme. The *Shakespearean sonnet* uses the rhyme scheme most common for sonnets in English: *a b a b, c d c d, e f e f, g g*. You will notice the rhyme scheme falls into three quatrains and an ending couplet, with a total of seven rhymes. "Shall I Compare Thee to a Summer's Day?" (page 487) and "That Time of Year Thou Mayst in Me Behold" (page 565) are splendid examples of Shakespeare's mastery of the sonnet (he wrote 154 of them) and illustrate why this traditional verse form continues to entice and stir both poets and readers. Dudley Randall's "To the Mercy Killers" (page 623) is an intriguing example of a modern Shakespearean sonnet.

The Italian sonnet, not very common in English poetry, uses fewer rhymes (five) and has only two groupings of lines, the first eight called the *octave* and the last six the *sestet*. Robert Frost created a chilling Italian sonnet in "Design" (page 598).

Free Verse A poem written in ***free verse*** or *open form* generally has no rhyme scheme and no basic meter for the entire selection. Rhyme and rhythm do occur, of course, but not in the fixed patterns that are required of stanzas and sonnets. Many readers think that open-form poetry is easy to write, but that is not the case. Only careless poetry is easy to write, and even closed forms can be sloppily written. Open forms demand their own special arrangements; without the fixed patterns of traditional forms to guide them, modern poets must discover these structures on their own. Walt Whitman's "A Noiseless Patient Spider" (pages 486–87) demonstrates how open form still uses sound and rhythm to create tone, enhance meaning, and guide the responses of the reader.

Poetic Syntax

Rhyme, rhythm, and stanza are not the only resources of form available to poets. Writers can also manipulate the way the words are arranged into sentences. For instance, the short, staccato sentences of "We Real Cool" (page 506) impress us in a way entirely different from the effect of the intricate expression of "The Silken Tent" (page 510), which is a single sentence stretching over fourteen lines. Words in English sentences must be arranged in fairly standard patterns. If we reverse the order of "John struck the ball" to "The ball struck John," the words take on a new meaning altogether. As with stanza form and rhyme scheme, poets can either stick with the rigidity of English sentence structure (syntax) or try to achieve unusual effects through inversion. E. E. Cummings, for example, forces his readers to pay close attention to the line "anyone lived in a pretty how town" by rearranging the words in an unexpected way. (In the standard pattern of an exclamation, the line would read "How pretty a town anyone lived in!")

Visual Poetry

Someone once defined poetry as "lines of words that don't go all the way to the margin." ***Concrete poetry***, however, makes extensive use of line breaks and spatial arrangements. A mix of conventional poetry and graphic art, a concrete poem takes on the shape of its subject. Some famous examples include George Herbert's "Easter Wings," which looks like a pair of wings on the page, and John Hollander's "Swan and Shadow," which arranges the words and lines to create the outline of a swan and its reflection in the water. More recent concrete poetry pays greater attention to the visual effect than to the content, such as the construction that uses only the phrase "au pair girl" displayed in the shape of a pear.

Looking at the Forms of Poetry

The following poems illustrate many of the variations of sound and organization that we have just discussed. As you read these poems, be alert for the special effects that the poets create with rhythm, rhyme, stanza form, and syntax. You may have to read some selections several times to appreciate how thoroughly form and meaning work together.

Gwendolyn Brooks 1917–2000

Gwendolyn Brooks once confessed that as a child she "was very ill-adjusted. I couldn't skate, I was never a good rope-jumper, and I can remember thinking I must be a very inferior kind of child since I couldn't play jacks." Although she grew up as a middle-class African American, in her poetry Brooks identified with the poor blacks of Chicago (where she spent most of her life) and the simplicity of her poetic voice successfully conveys the meager circumstance of her subjects. In 1950 she became the first black woman to win the Pulitzer Prize.

Looking cool shooting pool at the local hangout.

We Real Cool

The Pool Players
Seven at the Golden Shovel

We real cool. We
Left school. We

Lurk late. We
Strike straight. We

Sing sin. We
Thin gin. We

Jazz June. We
Die soon.

(1960)

A. E. Housman 1859–1936

After failing his finals at Oxford, A(lfred) E(dward) Housman became a clerk in the London Patent Office. An extremely capable scholar, he published several studies of classical authors and was eventually appointed a professor of Latin at London University and then at Cambridge University. Housman's own poetry, admired for its exquisite simplicity en deals with the tragedy of doomed youth. His poetic works 96) and *Last Poems* (1922).

Eight O'Clock

, and heard the steeple
e the quarters on the morning town.
, three, four, to market-place and people
d them down.

, noosed, nighing his hour,
od and counted them and cursed his luck;
the clock collected in the tower
ength, and struck.

(1922)

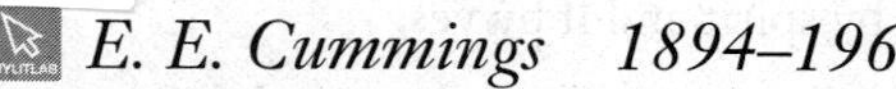

E. E. Cummings 1894–1962

Born in Cambridge, Massachusetts, E(dward) E(stlin) Cummings is perhaps best known for his eccentric antipathy toward capital letters—a style copied by many poetry students. His volumes of poetry include *Tulips and Chimneys* (1923) and *95 Poems* (1958). During World War I, Cummings served as an ambulance driver in France and was mistakenly committed to a French prison camp for three months, an experience he recounted in the prose journal *The Enormous Room* (1922).

anyone lived in a pretty how town

anyone lived in a pretty how town
(with up so floating many bells down)
spring summer autumn winter
he sang his didn't he danced his did.

Women and men (both little and small)
cared for anyone not at all
they sowed their isn't they reaped their same
sun moon stars rain

children guessed (but only a few
and down they forgot as up they grew
autumn winter spring summer)
that noone loved him more by more

when by now and tree by leaf
she laughed his joy she cried his grief
bird by snow and stir by still
anyone's any was all to her

someones married their everyones
laughed their cryings and did their dance
(sleep wake hope and then) they
said their nevers they slept their dream

stars rain sun moon
(and only the snow can begin to explain
how children are apt to forget to remember
with up so floating many bells down)

one day anyone died i guess
(and noone stooped to kiss his face)
busy folk buried them side by side
little by little and was by was

all by all and deep by deep
and more by more they dream their sleep
noone and anyone earth by april
wish by spirit and if by yes.

Women and men (both dong and ding)
summer autumn winter spring
reaped their sowing and went their came
sun moon stars rain

(1940)

Wole Soyinka 1934–

Wole Soyinka was born in Isara, Nigeria. An outspoken social critic, Soyinka had to flee Nigeria several times for criticizing the government and has been jailed twice. Educated at Leeds University in England, he has written twenty plays, two novels, five books of poetry, and numerous works of literary and social criticism. His works often concern the struggle between tradition and modernization in Africa. In 1986 he became the first black African to be awarded the Nobel Prize for Literature.

Telephone Conversation

The price seemed reasonable, location
Indifferent. The landlady swore she lived
Off premises. Nothing remained
But self-confession. 'Madam,' I warned,

'I hate a wasted journey—I am African.'
Silence. Silenced transmission of
Pressurized good-breeding. Voice, when it came,
Lipstick coated, long gold-rolled
Cigarette-holder pipped.° Caught I was, foully.
'HOW DARK?' ... I had not misheard ... 'ARE YOU LIGHT
OR VERY DARK?' Button B. Button A. Stench
Of rancid breath of public hide-and-speak.
Red booth. Red pillar-box. Red double-tiered
Omnibus squelching tar. It *was* real! Shamed
By ill-mannered silence, surrender
Pushed dumbfoundment to beg simplification.
Considerate she was, varying the emphasis—
'ARE YOU DARK? OR VERY LIGHT?' Revelation came.
'You mean—like plain or milk chocolate?'
Her assent was clinical, crushing in its light
Impersonality. Rapidly, wave-length adjusted,
I chose. 'West African sepia'—and as afterthought,
'Down in my passport.' Silence for spectroscopic
Flight of fancy, till truthfulness clanged her accent
Hard on the mouthpiece. 'WHAT'S THAT?' conceding
'DON'T KNOW WHAT THAT IS.' 'Like brunette.'
'THAT'S DARK, ISN'T IT?' 'Not altogether.
Facially, I am brunette, but madam, you should see
The rest of me. Palm of my hand, soles of my feet
Are a peroxide blond. Friction, caused—
Foolishly madam—by sitting down, has turned
My bottom raven black—One moment madam!'—sensing
Her receiver rearing on the thunderclap
About my ears—'Madam,' I pleaded, 'wouldn't you rather
See for yourself?'

(1960)

---

[9]**pipped** Made a short, high-pitched sound (British usage).

Robert Frost 1874–1963

One of the most popular and honored of American poets, Robert Frost was born in San Francisco, but as a young boy his family moved east, and much of his work reflects a love of the New England landscape. Before gaining success as a poet, Frost worked as a teacher, a chicken farmer, and a handyman. His poems are characterized by colloquial, restrained language that implies messages rather than openly stating them. Frost was awarded four Pultizer Prizes for his poetry.

The Silken Tent

She is as in a field a silken tent
At midday when the sunny summer breeze
Has dried the dew and all its ropes relent,
So that in guys it gently sways at ease,
And its supporting central cedar pole,
That is its pinnacle to heavenward
And signifies the sureness of the soul,
Seems to owe naught to any single cord,
But strictly held by none, is loosely bound
By countless silken ties of love and thought
To everything on earth the compass round,
And only by one's going slightly taut
In the capriciousness of summer air
Is of the slightest bondage made aware.

(1943)

Biily Collins 1941–

Born in New York City, William James (Billy) Collins has lived there ever since. His father is an electrician, his mother a nurse. Selected as Poet Laureate of the United States in 2000, he served two terms. He has managed to combine critical approval with unprecedented popular success: his last three collections of poems have broken sales records for poetry. "Usually," he says, "I try to create a hospitable tone at the beginning of the poem. Stepping from the title to the first lines is like stepping into a canoe. A lot of things can go wrong."

Sonnet

All we need is fourteen lines, well thirteen now,
and after this one just a dozen
to launch a little ship on love's storm-tossed seas,
then only ten more left like rows of beans.
How easily it goes unless you get Elizabethan
and insist the iambic bongos must be played
and rhymes positioned at the ends of lines,
one for every station of the cross.
But hang on here while we make the turn
into the final six where all will be resolved,
where longing and heartache will find an end,
where Laura will tell Petrarch to put down his pen,
take off those crazy medieval tights,
blow out the lights, and come at last to bed.

(1999)

Roger McGough 1937–

Award-winning poet, playwright, broadcaster, and children's author, Roger McGough has been one of the most successful poets in England for more than thirty years. His 1960s poems captured the verve and irreverence of that era. McGough has always used his wit to undermine the sad disappointments of life.

40 ------------------ Love

middle	aged
couple	playing
ten	nis
when	the
game	ends
and	they
go	home
the	net
will	still
be	be-
tween	them
	(1971)

PREWRITING

Writing about poetic form is challenging. Because it is impossible to separate form from meaning, you must be sure that you understand what a poem says before you try to analyze how its formal characteristics contribute to your understanding and appreciation. In completing the following exercises, you should read the poems aloud, if possible, and reread the difficult passages a number of times before you decide on your answers.

Experimenting with Poetic Forms

1. Examine "We Real Cool" by Gwendolyn Brooks (page 506). How would you describe the rhythm of this poem? How does the rhythm affect your perception of the speakers (the "We" of the poem)? Why are all the sentences in the last four stanzas only three words long? What is the effect of placing the subject of those sentences ("We") at the ends of the lines?
2. Look at the alliteration in "Eight O'Clock" by A. E. Housman (page 507). What events or feelings are emphasized by alliteration? How do other elements of form—rhyme, stress, stanza pattern—influence the tone and

point of the brief drama described in the poem? Write an objective account of the events in "Eight O'Clock." What did you have to leave out of your account?

3. Study the rhyme schemes and line variations of the following poems, all of which are written in quatrains:
   —"Eight O'Clock" (page 507)
   —"My Son My Executioner" (page 489)
   —"anyone lived in a pretty how town" (pages 507–08)
   —"One Perfect Rose" (pages 470–71)
   —"Piano" (page 602)
   —"A Valediction: Forbidding Mourning" (pages 568–69)

   In which of the poems do the stanza divisions indicate a change of time or a shift in thought? Do any of the poets disregard the stanza patterns? Try to decide why all of these poets used quatrains.
4. Rewrite the following lines—from "The Unknown Citizen" and "anyone lived in a pretty how town"—putting them in the word order you would expect them to follow in ordinary speech:

   For in everything he did he served the Greater Community.

   Except for the War till the day he retired
   He worked in a factory. . . .

   anyone lived in a pretty how town
   (with up so floating many bells down)

   Women and men (both little and small)
   cared for anyone not at all

WRITING

Because rhythm, rhyme, syntax, and stanza convey no meaning in themselves, you probably will not write an entire essay on form alone. Instead you can use what you have learned about poetic form to help you analyze and interpret a poem (or poems) with greater understanding and confidence.

Relating Form to Meaning

You can use observations about form to confirm and develop your ideas about the meaning or theme of a poem. Looking at a poem's formal characteristics will help you to answer such important questions as these: What is the tone? Is the speaker being ironic? What are the key words and images? And how does the main idea advance through the poem?

Specifically, elements of form offer clues like these:

1. Close, obvious rhyme often indicates a comic or ironic tone. Subtle rhymes support more serious tones.
2. Heavy stress can be humorous, but it can also suggest anger, defiance, strength, or fear.
3. Alliteration can be humorous, but it can also be chillingly serious; it serves to provide emphasis by slowing the reading of the line.
4. Assonance can provide a rich, solemn effect, a certain grandeur perhaps, or even a sensuous effect.
5. Rhythm and repetition emphasize key words.
6. Stanzas and rhyme schemes mark out patterns of thought and can serve as guides to development of theme.
7. Important images are often underscored with rhyme and stress.
8. Inverted or unusual syntax calls attention to complex ideas.
9. Various elements of form can be used to indicate a change in speaker or a shift in thought or tone.
10. Typographical effects can call attention to significant feelings or ideas.

This list does not exhaust the possibilities, but it should alert you to the various ways that form relates to thought and meaning in poetry.

IDEAS FOR WRITING

Ideas for Expressive Writing

1. Write an original haiku. A *haiku* is a rhymeless Japanese poem. Its form is based on syllables: seventeen syllables usually arranged in three lines, often following a pattern of five, seven, and five. Haiku written in English, however, do not always follow the original Japanese syllable pattern and may even be rhymed. Because of their brevity, haiku compress their expression by focusing on images and letting the closely observed details suggest the feelings and meanings. The following haiku, translated from Japanese originals and some written in English, provide a variety of models for you to follow.

   The piercing chill I feel:
   my dead wife's comb, in our bedroom,
   under my heel...
   —Taniguchi Buson (trans. Harold G. Henderson)

   Sprayed with strong poison
   my roses are crisp this year
   in the crystal vase.
   —Paul Goodman

the old woman holds
lilac buds
to her good ear—

—Raymond Roseliep

Heat-lightning streak—
    through darkness pierces
the heron's shriek.

—Matsuo Basho

Notice that the images in these haiku convey strong sensory experiences implying a great deal more than a mere description would suggest.

2. Write a concrete poem. Decide on a topic (an object, an activity, or an emotion), and then imagine how to make the appearance of the words on the page reflect what they mean. For example, if you were to write about running or driving, you might runthewordstogetherlikethis to suggest speed, or you could arrange the letters in the word *staircase* so they actually climb up the page. You can vary the typeface to represent different ways to emphasize the words, such as boldface to suggest anger or all capitals to indicated loudness. You might write the poem out first and then use your computer to format the type and the spaces to represent the meaning.

Ideas for Critical Writing

1. Explain how rhythm, repetition, and rhyme affect the tone and meaning in "We Real Cool" and "Eight O'Clock." Are the effects the same in both poems?
2. Write an interpretation of "anyone lived in a pretty how town" or "Telephone Conversation." Give particular attention to the way that meter, rhyme, alliteration, syntax, and stanza form contribute to your understanding of the poem.
3. CRITICAL APPROACHES: Review the discussion of the deconstructionists' approach to interpreting literature (pages 1161–62). Then analyze the poem "Sonnet" explaining how Billy Collins deconstructs the form and purposes of a traditional sonnet at the same time he uses them. Is the poem a parody or a clever treatment of the conventional form—or both?
4. Compare one of Shakespeare's sonnets (page 487 or pages 564–66) with a modern sonnet, such as Frost's "Design" (page 598) or Randall's "To the Mercy Killers" (page 623). Why do the modern poems *not* seem like sonnets? Pay close attention to the syntax and the way the rhyme scheme subdivides each poem.
5. Explain how the spacing and the arrangement of words contribute to the tone and meaning of "40 - - - Love" (page 511). You probably need to find out what "40-love" means in tennis.

Ideas for Researched Writing

1. What is a *villanelle* or a *sestina* or a *cinquain*? Examine the rules for writing one of these closed forms of poetry and read a number of examples.

Consult a reference work such as *The New Princeton Encyclopedia of Poetry* or *The Teachers & Writers Handbook of Poetic Forms.* Using illustrative examples, write a paper in which you describe the form to an audience of classmates and general readers.

2. Research the phenomenon of *slam poetry*. What happens at these events? What kinds of poetry do they produce? You might include the *spoken word movement*, which is a spinoff of slam poetry, in your investigation.

REWRITING: STYLE

As a writer, you must choose your words carefully. Many English words are to some extent synonymous, even interchangeable, but often the distinctions between synonyms are as important as their similarities. "The difference between the right word and the almost right word," said Mark Twain, "is the difference between lightning and the lightning bug." When you revise your essay, focus on the accuracy and precision of the words you use.

Finding the Exact Word

You must take care that both the denotations and the connotations of the words you use are the ones you intend. You do not want to write *heroics* when you really mean *heroism*. You do not want to "*expose* three main topics" when you really intend to *explore* them. The following are some problem areas to consider as you look at the words you have used in your essay.

1. **Distinguish among synonyms.**
   Exact writing demands that you choose among different shades of meaning. Although *feeling* and *sensation* are synonyms, they are certainly not interchangeable. Neither are *funny* and *laughable* or *famous* and *notorious*. Consult your dictionary for help in choosing the word that says exactly what you mean.

   Explain the differences in meaning among the following groups of words and phrases:

   a. a *renowned* politician, a *famous* politician, a *notorious* politician
   b. an *indifferent* parent, a *detached* parent, an *unconcerned* parent
   c. to *condone* an action, to *excuse* an action, to *forgive* an action
   d. *pilfer, steal, rob, burglarize, loot, ransack*
   e. an *apparent* error, a *visible* error, an *egregious* error

2. **Watch out for words with similar sound or spelling.**
   Homophones (words that have the same pronunciation but different meanings and different spellings) are sometimes a source of confusion.

The student who wrote that a song conveyed the composer's "piece of mind" let the sound of the word override her knowledge of spelling and meaning. Words that are similar in sound and spelling can also be confusing. If you are not careful, you can easily confuse *eminent* with *imminent* or write *quiet* when you mean *quite*.

Explain the difference in meaning in the following pairs of words:

a. *apprise, appraise*
b. *anecdote, antidote*
c. *elicit, illicit*
d. *martial, marital*
e. *statue, statute*
f. *human, humane*
g. *lose, loose*
h. *idol, idle*
i. *accept, except*
j. *simple, simplistic*
k. *beside, besides*
l. *weather, whether*
m. *incidence, incident*
n. *angle, angel*

3. **Choose the precise adjective form.**

Many words have two or more adjective forms: a *questioning* remark is not the same as a *questionable* remark. As with homophones and other words that sound alike, do not let the similarity in spelling and pronunciation mislead you.

Point out the connotative differences in meaning in the following pairs of adjectives.

a. an *intelligible* essay, an *intelligent* essay
b. a *hateful* sibling, a *hated* sibling
c. a *likely* roommate, a *likable* roommate
d. an *informed* speaker, an *informative* speaker
e. a *workable* thesis, a *working* thesis

4. **Watch out for malapropisms.**

Misused words are often unintentionally funny. These humorous confusions and near misses are called *malapropisms*. You may get a laugh from your readers if you write "My car insurance collapsed last week," but you will not be impressing them with your command of the language.

In the following sentences, what do you think the writer probably meant to say?

a. He has only a *supercilious* knowledge of the subject.
b. She was the *pineapple* of perfection.
c. They burned the *refuge*.
d. He passed his civil service *eliminations*.
e. They are in for a *shrewd* awakening.

5. **Be sure the words fit the context.**

Sentences can be disconcerting if all the words do not have the same emotional associations. For instance, "The thief brandished his gun and angrily requested the money" is confusing because *brandished* and *angrily* suggest a different emotion from *requested*. A better word choice would be "*demanded* the money."

Explain why the italicized words are inappropriate in the following sentences. What words would you use as replacements?

a. Her *stubbornness* in the face of danger saved our lives.
b. The use of violence to obtain a goal is too *poignantly* barbaric for most people to *sympathize* with.
c. The mob shouted in *displeasure*.

Sample Student Paper on Poetic Form

The following paper, written by a student at Eastern Illinois University, advances several claims about Robert Frost's use of the sonnet form in "The Silken Tent" (page 510).

Elizabeth Curvey
Professor Coleman
English 1003
12 December 2008

Consistency of Character and Form in "The Silken Tent"

The speaker in Robert Frost's poem "The Silken Tent" compares a woman he admires to a flexible shelter. In an extended metaphor, he conveys two distinct impressions: the soft femininity of a delicate fabric (silk) and the protective toughness of a tent. The speaker admires his subject, the woman, for being feminine and strong at the same time; but it is her seamless, genuine character that inspires his praise most. This inspiration is expressed in both the content and the form of the poem.

Frost's speaker uses detailed descriptions of the tent to illustrate the personality traits that he most admires. The woman's poise and self-confidence are first conveyed in the description of the tent's movements: "it gently sways at ease" (4), without rigidity. And the depiction of the tent's "supporting central cedar pole" (5) seems to stress the woman's pride and integrity. By comparing the woman's soul to a "pinnacle"—a sharp, straight, upright object—that points "heavenward" (6-7), the speaker reinforces his admiration of her firmness of character.

The admiration is intensified by the speaker's realization that everything the woman has and stands for is her own creation from materials in the world around her. This notion is expressed in the line "Seems to owe naught to any single cord" (8), a remark that implies that the woman is self-sustaining, not relying on someone else for her esteem. Yet the woman's self-confidence has not made her insensitive to others. She is connected "By countless silken ties of love and thought / To everything on earth the compass round" (10-11). The speaker suggests that the woman is capable of loving generously because she is self-assured.

Perhaps the most significant compliment comes in the last three lines of the poem, where the speaker comments on the woman's temperament:

And only by one's going slightly taut
In the capriciousness of summer air
Is of the slightest bondage made aware. (12-14)

Using the image of a summer breeze to suggest the tugs of change, the speaker indicates that the woman handles her obligations with ease and composure.

The form of "The Silken Tent" is a traditional Shakespearean sonnet: three quatrains with *abab, cdcd, efef* rhyme schemes, followed by a *gg* couplet. In the conventional sonnet, each quatrain expresses its own statement, topic, or question. The couplet sums up all the quatrains with a concluding comment. However, in "The Silken Tent" the thoughts and observations are not divided up into the conventional units set out by the patterns of rhyme.

The quatrains do not end with terminal punctuation: periods, semicolons, question marks, or colons. Instead, the whole poem comprises one long sentence. So the logic flows smoothly from one section into the next—for example, the last three lines (quoted above) are a logical unit, not the last two lines. The continuity and inner logic of the sonnet reflect the

Curvey 3

speaker's appraisal of the woman, as being both conventional and unique, a person with a wholeness and unity all her own. Though influenced by the demands of custom, she remains splendidly herself.

SAMPLE PUBLISHED ESSAY ON POETIC FORM

David Huddle's essay—"The 'Banked Fire' of Robert Hayden's 'Those Winter Sundays'"—on the following pages is an example of a published essay on poetic form. (The poem appears on pages 681–82.)

David Huddle

The "Banked Fire" of Robert Hayden's "Those Winter Sundays"

For twenty years I've been teaching Robert Hayden's most frequently anthologized poem to undergraduate poetry-writing students. By "teach," I mean that from our textbook I read the poem aloud in the classroom, I ask one of the students to read it aloud, I make some observations about it, I invite the students to make some observations about it, then we talk about it a while longer. Usually to wrap up the discussion, I'll read the poem through once more. Occasions for such teaching come up about half a dozen times a year, and so let's say that during my life I've been privileged to read this poem aloud approximately 240 times. "Those Winter Sundays" has withstood my assault upon it. It remains a poem I look forward to reading and discussing in my classroom. The poem remains alive to me, so that for hours and sometimes days after it visits my classroom, I'm hearing its lines in my mind's ear.

Though a fourteen-liner, "Those Winter Sundays" is only loosely a sonnet. Its stanzas are five, four, and five lines long. There are rhymes and near-rhymes, but no rhyme scheme. The poem's lines probably average about eight syllables. There are only three strictly iambic lines: the fourth, the eighth, and (significantly) the fourteenth. It's a poem that's powerfully informed by the sonnet form; it's a poem that "feels like" a sonnet—it has the density and gravity of a sonnet—which is to say that in its appearance on the page, in its diction and syntax, in its tone, cadence, and argumentative strategy, "Those Winter Sundays" presents the credentials of a work of literary art in the tradition of English letters. But it's also a poem that has gone its own way, a definite departure from that most conventional of all the poetic forms of English and American verse.

The abstract issue of this poem's sonnethood is of less value to my beginning poets than the tangible matter of the sounds the poem makes, especially those *k*-sounding words of the first eleven lines that one comes to associate with discomfort: "clothes . . . blueback cold . . . cracked . . . ached . . . weekday . . . banked . . . thanked . . . wake . . . cold . . . breaking . . . call . . . chronic . . . cold." What's missing from the final three lines? The *k* sounds have been driven from the poem, as the father has "driven out the cold" from the house. The sounds that have replaced those *k* sounds are the *o* sounds of "good . . . shoes . . . know . . . know . . . love . . . lonely offices." The poem lets us associate the *o* sounds with love and loneliness. Sonically the poem tells the same story the poem narrates for us. The noise of this poem moves us through its emotional journey from discomfort to lonely love. If ever there was a poem that could teach a beginning poet the viability of the element of sound-crafting, it is "Those Winter Sundays."

Quote its first two words, and a great many poets and English teachers will be able to finish the first line (if not the whole poem) from memory. Somewhat remarkably, the poem's thesis—that the office of love can be relentless, thankless, and more than a little mysterious—resides in that initially odd-sounding two-word beginning, "Sundays too." The rest of the line—the rest of the independent clause—is ordinary. Nowhere else in Anglo-American literature does the word *too* carry the weight it carries in "Those Winter Sundays."

Not as immediately apparent as its opening words but very nearly as important to the poem's overall strategy is the two-sentence engineering of the first stanza. Because they will appreciate it more if they discover it for themselves, I often maneuver Socratically to have my students describe the poem's first two sentences: long and complex, followed by short and simple. It almost always seems to me worthwhile to ask, "Why didn't Hayden begin his poem this way: 'No one ever thanked my father for getting up early on Sundays, too'? Wouldn't that be a more direct and hospitable way to bring the reader into the poem?" After I've taken my students that far, they are quick to see how that ordinary five-word unit, "No one ever thanked him," gains meaning and emotion, weight, and force, from the elaborate preparation given it by the thirty-two-word "Sundays too" first sentence.

So much depends on "No one ever thanked him" that it requires the narrative enhancement of the first four and a half lines. It is the crux of the poem. What is this poem about? It is about a son's remorse over never thanking his father not only for what he did for him but also for how (he now realizes) he felt about him. And what is the poem if not an elegantly fashioned, permanent expression of gratitude?

"Those Winter Sundays" tells a story, or it describes a circumstance, of father-son conflict, and it even makes some excuses for the son's "Speaking indifferently" to the father: there was a good deal of anger between them; "chronic angers of that house" suggests that the circumstances were complicated somewhat beyond the usual and ordinary conflict between fathers and sons. Of the father, we know that he labored outdoors with his hands. Of the son, we know that he was, in the classic manner of youth, heedless of the ways in which his father served him.

Though the evidence of his "labor" is visible in every stanza of this poem, the father himself is somewhere else. We don't see him. He is in some other room of the house than the one where our speaker is. That absence suggests the emotional distance between the father and the son as well as the current absence, through death, of the father on the occasion of this utterance. It's easy enough to imagine this poem as a graveside meditation, an elegy, and a rather impassioned one at that, "What did I know, what did I know?"

The grinding of past against present gives the poem its urgency. The story is being told with such clarity, thoughtfulness, and apparent calm that we are surprised by the outburst of the repeated question of the thirteenth line. The fourteenth line returns to a tone of tranquillity. Its diction is formal, even arch, and its phrasing suggests an extremely considered conclusion; the fourteenth line is the answer to a drastic rephrasing of the original question: *What is the precise name of what as a youth I was incapable of perceiving but that as a life-examining adult, I now suddenly understand?*

I tell my students that they may someday need this poem, they may someday be walking along downtown and find themselves asking aloud, "What did I know, what did I know?" But what I mean to suggest to them is that Hayden has made them the gift of this final phrase like a package that in ten years' time they may open and find immensely valuable: "love's austere and lonely offices." Like "the banked fires" his father made, Hayden has made a poem that will be of value to readers often years after they've first read it.

(1996)

Casebook
The Poetry and Prose of Langston Hughes

Contents

Langston Hughes: A Brief Biography

Langston Hughes was born in Joplin, Missouri, in 1902 and spent his youth in the Midwest. He went to grade school in Lawrence, Kansas, where he lived with his grandmother after his parents divorced. At the time, Lawrence's population of 12,000 was 20 percent African American. His father, a businessman, had moved to Mexico, where his mixed race (both grandfathers being white) was not a social barrier. After his mother remarried, Langston joined her to go to high school in Cleveland, Ohio. At a progressive, racially mixed school, he was class poet and published stories in the school magazine. He graduated in 1920 and went to Mexico in an attempt to reunite with his father. The emotional bond did not flourish. However, the Mexican experience was formative, particularly the culture's straightforward acceptance of his brown skin, and Hughes had links to the Hispanic literary world throughout his life. His most famous poem, "The Negro Speaks of Rivers," was written on the train to Mexico in 1921.

Such a background ensured that matters of skin color and class were ingrained in Hughes's consciousness. After one unhappy year at Columbia University, he embarked on a series of world travels as a seaman and menial worker in Africa and Europe. The various attitudes toward race and class became obvious to Hughes, and he endorsed a gut socialism and the primitivism popular in the 1920s and 1930s, which viewed dark-skinned people as more directly in touch with nature and emotional wisdom than others were. Hughes returned to finish school in the United States at the nation's first black college, Lincoln University in Pennsylvania, graduating in 1929. Meanwhile, he had become a noted poet through publishing in small literary and left-wing magazines.

Hughes's life was enriched by artistic innovations in New York's Harlem during this same period. He visited the city frequently to enjoy the theater, dance, music, and sociability of blacks from the South and the Caribbean who had moved to the district and created the Harlem Renaissance. Hughes was entranced by the jazz and blues of the era, as well as the diversity among people of color he found in Harlem and in the wider world. At Harlem clubs, he listened to music performed by Duke Ellington, Charlie Mingus, Count Basie, Bessie Smith, and Louis Armstrong, and echoes of their musical style can be heard in recordings of Hughes reading his own poetry.

Besides poetry, Hughes wrote short stories, novels, two autobiographies, newspaper columns, children's books, anthologies of African-American literature, plays, musicals, operettas, and translations of Spanish and French poetry. He maintained political activism through efforts such as composing poems and a play to protest the racist treatment of the Scottsboro Boys in Alabama, nine young black males wrongfully convicted of raping two white women in 1931. Because of his socialist opinions, the McCarthy committee investigating U.S. communists called him to testify in 1953, and under pressure Hughes essentially disowned his early writings. From then on, he avoided blatantly socialist messages in his publications until his final book of poetry, *The Panther and the Lash*, which came out after his death in 1967. During the second half of his life, Hughes nurtured the talents of many other African American writers and

Langston Hughes, a leading figure of the Harlem Renaissance in the 1920s and 1930s, who celebrated the vitality of African American culture in many genres. (The New York Public Library/Art Resource. Schomburg Collection of the New York Public Library.)

gained international admiration. Although a very public figure, Hughes was circumspect about private matters, and almost nothing is known about his intimate relationships with others.

Langston Hughes died alone in New York City after surgery for prostate cancer, in 1967.

Poetry

The Negro Speaks of Rivers

(To W. E. B. Du Bois)

I've known rivers:
I've known rivers ancient as the world and older than the
flow of human blood in human veins.

My soul has grown deep like the rivers.

I bathed in the Euphrates when dawns were young.
I built my hut near the Congo and it lulled me to sleep.

I looked upon the Nile and raised the pyramids above it.
I heard the singing of the Mississippi when Abe Lincoln
went down to New Orleans, and I've seen its muddy
bosom turn all golden in the sunset.

I've known rivers:
Ancient, dusky rivers.

My soul has grown deep like the rivers.

(1921)

Mother to Son

Well, son, I'll tell you:
Life for me ain't been no crystal stair.
It's had tacks in it,
And splinters,
And boards torn up,
And places with no carpet on the floor—
Bare.
But all the time
I'se been a-climbin' on,
And reachin' landin's,
And turnin' corners,
And sometimes goin' in the dark
Where there ain't been no light.
So boy, don't you turn back.
Don't you set down on the steps
'Cause you finds it's kinder hard.
Don't you fall now—
For I'se still goin', honey,
I'se still climbin',
And life for me ain't been no crystal stair.

(1922)

The Weary Blues

Droning a drowsy syncopated tune,
Rocking back and forth to a mellow croon,
I heard a Negro play.
Down on Lenox Avenue the other night
By the pale dull pallor of an old gas light
He did a lazy sway…
He did a lazy sway…
To the tune o' those Weary Blues.
With his ebony hands on each ivory key
He made that poor piano moan with melody.
O Blues!
Swaying to and fro on his rickety stool
He played the sad raggy tune like a musical fool.
Sweet Blues!

Coming from a black man's soul!
  O Blues!
In a deep song voice with a melancholy tone
I heard that Negro sing, that old piano moan—
  "Ain't got nobody in all this world,
    Aint' got nobody but ma self.
    I's gwine to quit ma frownin'
    And put ma troubles on the shelf."

Thump, thump, thump went his foot on the floor
He played a few chords then he sang some more—
  "I got the Weary Blues
    And I can't be satisfied.
    Got the Weary Blues
    And can't be satisfied—
    I ain't happy no mo'
    And I wish that I had died."
And far into the night he crooned that tune.
The stars went out and so did the moon.
The singer stopped playing and went to bed
While the Weary Blues echoed through his head.
He slept like a rock or a man that's dead.

(1925)

Saturday Night

Play it once.
O, play some more.
Charlie is a gambler
An' Sadie is a whore.
  A glass o' whiskey
  An' a glass o' gin:
  Strut, Mr. Charlie,
  Till de dawn comes in.
Pawn yo' gold watch
An' diamond ring.
Git a quart o' licker,
Let's shake dat thing!
  Skee-de-dad! De-dad!
  Doo-doo-doo!
  Won't be nothin' left
  When de worms git through
  An' you's a long time
  Dead
  When you is
  Dead, too.
  So beat dat drum, boy!
  Shout dat song:
  Shake 'em up an' shake 'em up
  All night long.

Hey! Hey!
Ho . . . Hum!
Do it, Mr. Charlie,
Till de red dawn come.

(1927)

Trumpet Player

The Negro
With the trumpet at his lips
Has dark moons of weariness
Beneath his eyes
Where the smoldering memory
Of slave ships
Blazed to the crack of whips
About his thighs.

The Negro
With the trumpet at his lips
Has a head of vibrant hair
Tamed down,
Patent-leathered now
Until it gleams
Like jet—
Were jet a crown.

The music
From the trumpet at his lips
Is honey
Mixed with liquid fire.
The rhythm
From the trumpet at his lips
Is ecstasy
Distilled from old desire—
Desire
That is longing for the moon
Where the moonlight's but a spotlight
In his eyes,
Desire
That is longing for the sea
Where the sea's a bar-glass
Sucker size.

The Negro
With the trumpet at his lips
Whose jacket
Has a *fine* one-button roll,
Does not know

Upon what riff the music slips
Its hypodermic needle
To his soul—
  But softly
  As the tune comes from his throat
  Trouble
  Mellows to a golden note.

(1947)

Harlem (A Dream Deferred)

What happens to a dream deferred?

Does it dry up
like a raisin in the sun?
Or fester like a sore—
And then run?
Does it stink like rotten meat?
Or crust and sugar over—
like a syrupy sweet?

Maybe it just sags
like a heavy load.

Or does it explode?

(1951)

A Great Day in Harlem: fifty-seven jazz musicians photographed on 126th Street in Harlem in 1958.

Theme for English B

The instructor said,

Go home and write
a page tonight.
And let that page come out of you—
Then, it will be true.

I wonder if it's that simple?
I am twenty-two, colored, born in Winston-Salem.
I went to school there, then Durham, then here
to this college on the hill above Harlem.
I am the only colored student in my class.
The steps from the hill lead down into Harlem,
through a park, then I cross St. Nicholas,
Eighth Avenue, Seventh, and I come to the Y,
the Harlem Branch Y, where I take the elevator
up to my room, sit down, and write this page:
It's not easy to know what is true for you or me
at twenty-two, my age. But I guess I'm what
I feel and see and hear, Harlem, I hear you:
hear you, hear me—we two—you, me, talk on this page.
(I hear New York, too.) Me—who?
Well, I like to eat, sleep, drink, and be in love.
I like to work, read, learn, and understand life.
I like a pipe for a Christmas present,
or records—Bessie,° bop,° or Bach.
I guess being colored doesn't make me *not* like
the same things other folks like who are other races.
So will my page be colored that I write?
Being me, it will not be white.
But it will be
a part of you, instructor.
You are white—
yet a part of me, as I am a part of you.
That's American.
Sometimes perhaps you don't want to be a part of me.
Nor do I often want to be a part of you.
But we are, that's true!
I guess you learn from me—
although you're older—and white—
and somewhat more free.

This is my page for English B.

(1951)

---

24 Bessie (Smith, 1894–1937), African American blues singer. **bop** A kind of jazz; also called be-bop.

Considering the Poems

1. Think about why a river is an apt metaphor for a human soul. Then consider Hughes's choice of specific rivers to mention in the poem "The Negro Speaks of Rivers." What makes each river appropriate to the poem's theme?
2. What is the extended metaphor in "Mother to Son"? Who is the speaker, and what has her life been like? What would a "crystal stair" life be like?
3. How would you describe the mood of "The Weary Blues"? Harold Bloom wrote that "the piano player brims with pathos and joy." Can you see these emotions in the poem, or was Bloom reading too much into it?
4. Recall your first response to reading "Saturday Night." Countee Cullen, another leading poet of the Harlem Renaissance, criticized Hughes's zeal for poems like this one, saying, "I wonder if jazz poems really belong to that dignified company, that select and austere circle of high literary expression which we call poetry." Do you agree with Cullen?
5. "Trumpet Player" describes a series of transformations, such as the transformation of slave memories to "dark moons of weariness" under the trumpet player's eyes. List and explain the other transformations suggested in the poem. Are the changes positive, negative, or both? How are they related to black heritage?
6. Examine the similes Hughes employs to evoke the effects of the "dream deferred." How is each simile different from the others, in terms of how it would be manifested in the real world? For example, what would be the difference between a *sagging* society and an *exploding* one?
7. In "Theme for English B," the belief that what comes out of a person is, by its very nature, "true" sounds strange to the student. The contrast between the English teacher's assumptions and the student writer's is clear. What different ways of describing himself truly does the student writer attempt? Are they satisfactory, in your opinion?

Prose

Salvation

I was saved from sin when I was going on thirteen. But not really saved. It happened like this. There was a big revival at my Auntie Reed's church. Every night for weeks there had been much preaching, singing, praying, and shouting, and some very hardened sinners had been brought to Christ, and the membership of the church had grown by leaps and bounds. Then just before the revival ended, they held a special meeting for children, "to bring the young lambs to the fold." My aunt spoke of it for days ahead. That night I was escorted to the front row and placed on the mourners' bench with all the other young sinners, who had not yet been brought to Jesus.

My aunt told me that when you were saved you saw a light, and something happened to you inside! And Jesus came into your life! And God was with you from then on! She said you could see and hear and feel Jesus in your soul. I believed her. I had heard a great many old people say the same thing and it seemed to me they ought to know. So I sat there calmly in the hot crowded church, waiting for Jesus to come to me.

The preacher preached a wonderful rhythmical sermon, all moans and shouts and lonely cries and dire pictures of hell, and then he sang a song about the ninety and nine safe in the fold, but one little lamb was left in the cold. Then he said, "Won't you come? Won't you come to Jesus? Young lambs, won't you come?" And he held out his arms to all us young sinners there on the mourners' bench. And the little girls cried. And some of them jumped up and went to Jesus right away. But most of us just sat there.

A great many old people came and knelt around us and prayed, old women with jet-black faces and braided hair, old men with work-gnarled hands. And the church sang a song about the lower lights are burning, some poor sinners to be saved. And the whole building rocked with prayer and song.

Still I kept waiting to see Jesus. 5

Finally all the young people had gone to the altar and were saved, but one boy and me. He was a rounder's son named Westley. Westley and I were surrounded by sisters and deacons praying. It was very hot in the church, and getting late now. Finally Westley said to me in a whisper: "Goddamn! I'm tired o' sitting here. Let's get up and be saved." So he got up and was saved.

Then I was left all alone on the mourners' bench. My aunt came and knelt at my knees and cried, while prayers and songs swirled all around me in the little church. The whole congregation prayed for me alone, in a mighty wail of moans and voices. And I kept waiting serenely for Jesus, waiting, waiting—but he didn't come. I wanted to see him, but nothing happened to me. Nothing! I wanted something to happen to me, but nothing happened.

I heard the songs and the minister saying: "Why don't you come? My dear child, why don't you come to Jesus? Jesus is waiting for you. He wants you. Why don't you come? Sister Reed, what is this child's name?"

"Langston," my aunt sobbed.

"Langston, why don't you come? Why don't you come and be saved? Oh, 10 Lamb of God! Why don't you come?"

Now it was really getting late. I began to be ashamed of myself, holding everything up so long. I began to wonder what God thought about Westley, who certainly hadn't seen Jesus either, but who was now sitting proudly on the platform, swinging his knickerbockered legs and grinning down at me, surrounded by deacons and old women on their knees praying. God had not struck Westley dead for taking his name in vain or for lying in the temple. So I decided that maybe to save further trouble, I'd better lie, too, and say that Jesus had come, and get up and be saved.

So I got up.

Suddenly the whole room broke into a sea of shouting, as they saw me rise. Waves of rejoicing swept the place. Women leaped into the air. My aunt threw her arms around me. The minister took me by the hand and led me to the platform.

When things quieted down, in a hushed silence, punctuated by a few ecstatic "Amens," all the new young lambs were blessed in the name of God. Then joyous singing filled the room.

That night, for the last time in my life but one—for I was a big boy twelve years old—I cried. I cried, in bed alone, and couldn't stop. I buried my head under the quilts, but my aunt heard me. She woke up and told my uncle I was crying because the Holy Ghost had come into my life, and because I had seen Jesus. But I was really crying because I couldn't bear to tell her that I had lied, that I had deceived everybody in the church, and I hadn't seen Jesus, and that now I didn't believe there was a Jesus any more, since he didn't come to help me.

(1940)

On the Road

He was not interested in the snow. When he got off the freight, one early evening during the depression, Sargeant never even noticed the snow. But he must have felt it seeping down his neck, cold, wet, sopping in his shoes. But if you had asked him, he wouldn't have known it was snowing. Sargeant didn't see the snow, not even under the bright lights of the main street, falling white and flaky against the night. He was too hungry, too sleepy, too tired.

The Reverend Mr. Dorset, however, saw the snow when he switched on his porch light, opened the front door of his parsonage, and found standing there before him a big black man with snow on his face, a human piece of night with snow on his face—obviously unemployed.

Said the Reverend Mr. Dorset before Sargeant even realized he'd opened his mouth: "I'm sorry. No! Go right on down this street four blocks and turn to your left, walk up seven and you'll see the Relief Shelter. I'm sorry. No!" He shut the door.

Sargeant wanted to tell the holy man that he had already been to the Relief Shelter, been to hundreds of relief shelters during the depression years, the beds were always gone and supper was over, the place was full, and they drew the color line anyhow. But the minister said, "No," and shut the door. Evidently he didn't want to hear about it. And he *had* a door to shut.

The big black man turned away. And even yet he didn't see the snow, walking right into it. Maybe he sensed it, cold, wet, sticking to his jaws, wet on his black hands, sopping in his shoes. He stopped and stood on the sidewalk hunched over—hungry, sleepy, cold—looking up and down. Then he looked right where he was—in front of a church. Of course! A church! Sure, right next to a parsonage, certainly a church.

It had *two* doors.

Broad white steps in the night all snowy white. Two high arched doors with slender stone pillars on either side. And way up, a round lacy window with a stone crucifix in the middle and Christ on the crucifix in stone. All this was pale in the street lights, solid and stony pale in the snow.

Sargeant blinked. When he looked up, the snow fell into his eyes. For the first time that night he *saw* the snow. He shook his head. He shook the snow from his coat sleeves, felt hungry, felt lost, felt not lost, felt cold. He walked up the steps of the church. He knocked at the door. No answer. He tried the handle. Locked. He put his shoulder against the door and his long black body slanted like a ramrod. He pushed. With loud rhythmic grunts, like the grunts in a chain-gang song, he pushed against the door.

"I'm tired . . . Huh! . . . Hongry . . . Uh! . . . I'm sleepy . . . Huh! I'm cold . . . I got to sleep somewheres," Sargeant said. "This here is a church, ain't it? Well, uh!"

He pushed against the door.

Suddenly, with an undue cracking and screaking, the door began to give way to the tall black Negro who pushed ferociously against it.

By now two or three white people had stopped in the street, and Sargeant was vaguely aware of some of them yelling at him concerning the door. Three or four more came running, yelling at him.

"Hey!" they said. "Hey!"

"Uh-huh," answered the big tall Negro, "I know it's a white folks' church, but I got to sleep somewhere." He gave another lunge at the door. "Huh!"

And the door broke open.

But just when the door gave way, two white cops arrived in a car, ran up the steps with their clubs, and grabbed Sargeant. But Sargeant for once had no intention of being pulled or pushed away from the door.

Sargeant grabbed, but not for anything so weak as a broken door. He grabbed for one of the tall stone pillars beside the door, grabbed at it and caught it. And held it. The cops pulled and Sargeant pulled. Most of the people in the street got behind the cops and helped them pull.

"A big black unemployed Negro holding onto our church!" thought the people. "The idea!"

The cops began to beat Sargeant over the head, and nobody protested. But he held on.

And then the church fell down.

Gradually, the big stone front of the church fell down, the walls and the rafters, the crucifix and the Christ. Then the whole thing fell down, covering the cops and the people with bricks and stones and debris. The whole church fell down in the snow.

Sargeant got out from under the church and went walking on up the street with the stone pillar on his shoulder. He was under the impression that he had buried the parsonage and the Reverend Mr. Dorset who said, "No!" So he laughed, and threw the pillar six blocks up the street and went on.

Sargeant thought he was alone, but listening to the *crunch, crunch, crunch* on the snow of his own footsteps, he heard other footsteps, too, doubling his own. He looked around, and there was Christ walking along beside him, the same Christ that had been on the cross on the church—still stone with a rough stone surface, walking along beside him just like he was broken off the cross when the church fell down.

"Well, I'll be dogged," said Sargeant. "This here's the first time I ever seed you off the cross."

" Yes," said Christ, crunching his feet in the snow. "You had to pull the church down to get me off the cross."

"You glad?" said Sargeant.

"I sure am," said Christ.

They both laughed.

"I'm a hell of a fellow, ain't I?" said Sargeant. "Done pulled the church down!"

"You did a good job," said Christ. "They have kept me nailed on a cross for nearly two thousand years."

"Whee-ee-e!" said Sargeant. "I know you are glad to get off."

"I sure am," said Christ.

They walked on in the snow. Sargeant looked at the man of stone.

"And you have been up there two thousand years?"

"I sure have," said Christ.

"Well, if I had a little cash," said Sargeant, "I'd show you around a bit."

"I been around," said Christ.

"Yeah, but that was a long time ago."

"All the same," said Christ, "I've been around."

They walked on in the snow until they came to the railroad yards. Sargeant was tired, sweating and tired.

"Where you goin'?" Sargeant said, stopping by the tracks. He looked at Christ. Sargeant said, "I'm just a bum on the road. How about you? Where you goin'?"

"God knows," Christ said, "but I'm leavin' here."

They saw the red and green lights of the railroad yard half veiled by the snow that fell out of the night. Away down the track they saw a fire in a hobo jungle.

"I can go there and sleep," Sargeant said.

"You can?"

"Sure," said Sargeant. "That place ain't got no doors."

Outside the town, along the tracks, there were barren trees and bushes below the embankment, snow-gray in the dark. And down among the trees and bushes there were makeshift houses made out of boxes and tin and old pieces of wood and canvas. You couldn't see them in the dark, but you knew they were there if you'd ever been on the road, if you had ever lived with the homeless and hungry in a depression.

"I'm side-tracking," Sargeant said. "I'm tired."

"I'm gonna make it on to Kansas City," said Christ.

"O.K.," Sargeant said. "So long!"

He went down into the hobo jungle and found himself a place to sleep. He never did see Christ no more. About 6:00 A.M. a freight came by. Sargeant scrambled out of the jungle with a dozen or so more hobos and ran along the track, grabbing at the freight. It was dawn, early dawn, cold and gray.

"Wonder where Christ is by now?" Sargeant thought. "He musta gone on way on down the road. He didn't sleep in this jungle."

Sargeant grabbed the train and started to pull himself up into a moving coal car, over the edge of a wheeling coal car. But strangely enough, the car was full of cops. The nearest cop rapped Sargeant soundly across the knuckles with his night stick. Wham! Rapped his big black hands for clinging to the top of the car. Wham! But Sargeant did not turn loose. He clung on and tried to pull himself into the car. He hollered at the top of his voice, "Damn it, lemme in this car!"

"Shut up," barked the cop. "You crazy coon!" He rapped Sargeant across the knuckles and punched him in the stomach. "You ain't out in no jungle now. This ain't no train. You in jail."

55 Wham! across his bare black fingers clinging to the bars of his cell. Wham! between the steel bars low down against his shins.

Suddenly Sargeant realized that he really was in jail. He wasn't on no train. The blood of the night before had dried on his face, his head hurt terribly, and a cop outside in the corridor was hitting him across the knuckles for holding onto the door, yelling and shaking the cell door.

"They musta took me to jail for breaking down the door last night," Sargeant thought, "that church door."

Sargeant went over and sat on a wooden bench against the cold stone wall. He was emptier than ever. His clothes were wet, clammy cold wet, and shoes sloppy with snow water. It was just about dawn. There he was, locked up behind a cell door, nursing his bruised fingers.

The bruised fingers were his, but not the *door*.

60 Not the *club*, but the fingers.

"You wait," mumbled Sargeant, black against the jail wall. "I'm gonna break down this door, too."

"Shut up—or I'll paste you one," said the cop.

"I'm gonna break down this door," yelled Sargeant as he stood up in his cell.

Then he must have been talking to himself because he said, "I wonder where Christ's gone? I wonder if he's gone to Kansas City?"

(1952)

Thank You, M'am

She was a large woman with a large purse that had everything in it but a hammer and nails. It had a long strap, and she carried it slung across her shoulder. It was about eleven o'clock at night, dark, and she was walking alone, when a boy ran up behind her and tried to snatch her purse. The strap broke with the sudden single tug the boy gave it from behind. But the boy's weight and the weight of the purse combined caused him to lose his balance. Instead of taking off full blast as he had hoped, the boy fell on his back on the sidewalk and his legs flew up. The large woman simply turned around and kicked him right square in his blue-jeaned sitter. Then she reached down, picked the boy up by his shirt front, and shook him until his teeth rattled.

After that the woman said, "Pick up my pocketbook, boy, and give it here."

She still held him tightly. But she bent down enough to permit him to stoop and pick up her purse. Then she said, "Now ain't you ashamed of yourself?"

Firmly gripped by his shirt front, the boy said, "Yes'm."

The woman said, "What did you want to do it for?"

The boy said, "I didn't aim to."

She said, "You a lie!"

By that time two or three people passed, stopped, turned to look, and some stood watching.

"If I turn you loose, will you run?" asked the woman.

"Yes'm," said the boy.

"Then I won't turn you loose," said the woman. She did not release him.

"Lady, I'm sorry," whispered the boy.

"Um-hum! Your face is dirty. I got a great mind to wash your face for you. Ain't you got nobody home to tell you to wash your face?"

"No'm," said the boy.

"Then it will get washed this evening," said the large woman, starting up the street, dragging the frightened boy behind her.

He looked as if he were fourteen or fifteen, frail and willow-wild, in tennis shoes and blue jeans.

The woman said, "You ought to be my son. I would teach you right from wrong. Least I can do right now is to wash your face. Are you hungry?"

"No'm," said the being-dragged boy. "I just want you to turn me loose."

"Was I bothering *you* when I turned that corner?" asked the woman.

"No'm."

"But you put yourself in contact with *me*," said the woman. "If you think that that contact is not going to last a while, you got another thought coming. When I get through with you, sir, you are going to remember Mrs. Luella Bates Washington Jones."

Sweat popped out on the boy's face and he began to struggle. Mrs. Jones stopped, jerked him around in front of her, put a half nelson about his neck, and continued to drag him up the street. When she got to her door, she dragged the boy inside, down a hall, and into a large kitchenette-furnished room at the rear of the house. She switched on the light and left the door open. The boy could hear other roomers laughing and talking in the large house. Some of their doors were open, too, so he knew he and the woman were not alone. The woman still had him by the neck in the middle of her room.

She said, "What is your name?"

"Roger," answered the boy.

"Then, Roger, you go to that sink and wash your face," said the woman, whereupon she turned him loose—at last. Roger looked at the door—looked at the woman—looked at the door—*and went to the sink*.

"Let the water run until it gets warm," she said. "Here's a clean towel."

"You gonna take me to jail?" asked the boy, bending over the sink.

"Not with that face, I would not take you nowhere," said the woman. "Here I am trying to get home to cook me a bite to eat, and you snatch my pocketbook! Maybe you ain't been to your supper either, late as it be. Have you?"

"There's nobody home at my house," said the boy.

"Then we'll eat," said the woman. "I believe you're hungry—or been hungry—to try to snatch my pocketbook!"

"I want a pair of blue suede shoes," said the boy.

"Well, you didn't have to snatch *my* pocketbook to get some suede shoes," said Mrs. Luella Bates Washington Jones. "You could of asked me."

"M'am?"

The water dripping from his face, the boy looked at her. There was a long pause. A very long pause. After he had dried his face, and not knowing what else to do, dried it again, the boy turned around, wondering what next. The door was open. He could make a dash for it down the hall. He could run, run, run, *run*!

The woman was sitting on the daybed. After a while she said, "I were young 35
once and I wanted things I could not get."

There was another long pause. The boy's mouth opened. Then he frowned, not knowing he frowned.

The woman said, "Um-hum! You thought I was going to say *but*, didn't you? You thought I was going to say, *but I didn't snatch people's pocketbooks*. Well, I wasn't going to say that." Pause. Silence. "I have done things, too, which I would not tell you, son—neither tell God, if He didn't already know. Everybody's got something in common. So you set down while I fix us something to eat. You might run that comb through your hair so you will look presentable."

In another corner of the room behind a screen was a gas plate and an ice-box. Mrs. Jones got up and went behind the screen. The woman did not watch the boy to see if he was going to run now, nor did she watch her purse, which she left behind her on the daybed. But the boy took care to sit on the far side of the room, away from the purse, where he thought she could easily see him out of the corner of her eye if she wanted to. He did not trust the woman *not* to trust him. And he did not want to be mistrusted now.

"Do you need somebody to go to the store," asked the boy, "maybe to get some milk or something?"

"Don't believe I do," said the woman, "unless you just want sweet milk yourself. 40
I was going to make cocoa out of this canned milk I got here."

"That will be fine," said the boy.

She heated some lima beans and ham she had in the icebox, made the cocoa, and set the table. The woman did not ask the boy anything about where he lived, or his folks, or anything else that would embarrass him. Instead, as they ate, she told him about her job in a hotel beauty shop that stayed open late, what the work was like, and how all kinds of women came in and out, blondes, redheads, and Spanish. Then she cut him a half of her ten-cent cake.

"Eat some more, son," she said.

When they were finished eating, she got up and said, "Now here, take this ten dollars and buy yourself some blue suede shoes. And next time, do not make the mistake of latching onto *my* pocketbook *nor nobody else's*—because shoes got by devilish ways will burn your feet. I got to get my rest now. But from here on in, son, I hope you will behave yourself."

She led him down the hall to the front door and opened it. "Good night! 45
Behave yourself, boy!" she said, looking out into the street as he went down the steps.

The boy wanted to say something other than, "Thank you, m'am," to Mrs. Luella Bates Washington Jones, but although his lips moved, he couldn't even say that as he turned at the foot of the barren stoop and looked up at the large woman in the door. Then she shut the door.

(1958)

Considering the Prose

1. "Salvation" is a narrative from Hughes's autobiography. Why does the young Langston finally stand up to be saved? Why does he later cry about it? Was he really "saved" in any sense?
2. Besides the sad and disturbing content of "On the Road," the story also contains humorous elements. What is funny in the tale, and how does the humor affect the meaning? Are there humorous elements in "Salvation" and "Thank You, M'am"? Why do you think a writer with a serious intent would include lighthearted moments?
3. Mrs. Luella Bates Washington Jones has an unusual response to being assaulted by Roger. Do you think her response is purposeful? If so, what is she trying to do? Is she successful? What would she think about the way your community deals with street crime?

Critical Commentaries

Onwuchekwa Jemie, "Hughes and the Black Controversy"

Perhaps the most remarkable fact about Langston Hughes's career is his singlemindedness. It would appear that relatively early in life he discovered what he wanted to do and how he wanted to do it, and he spent most of his life doing it. What he wanted was to record and interpret the lives of the common black folk, their thoughts and habits and dreams, their struggle for political freedom and economic well-being. He wanted to do this using their own forms of expression: their language, humor, music, and folk verse. And consistently, through a career of four decades and in the face of opposition not only from much of the white world which constituted the majority of his audience, but from an important portion of his black audience who objected to his matter and manner, Hughes did what he set out to do, and did it well. Unlike Countee Cullen, for instance, who wore his color like a shroud, Hughes wore his "Like a banner for the proud / . . . Like a song soaring high."

In his first book he demonstrated mastery of his craft and spoke in his own authentic voice, but still his technique improved over the years, and his angle of attack shifted with the times. What is unique, however, is that for a career that lasted so long, Hughes's subject matter and his commitment to black folk expression remained stubbornly undiluted. And literary history has vindicated him, for the "temples for tomorrow" which he and his fellow believers in a distinctive black art insisted on building, regardless of the pleasure or displeasure of their contemporaries, are the temples in which pan-African artists of the *negritude* school worshipped in the 1930s and 40s, and in which Afro-American artists of the 1960s and 70s still worship.

Langston Hughes: An Introduction to the Poetry, 1976: 1–2

Margaret Larkin, "A Poet for the People"

Ever since I first heard Langston Hughes read his verse, I am continually wanting to liken his poems to those of Bobby Burns. Burns caught three things in his poems: dialect, speech cadence, and character of the people, so that he seems more Scotch than all of bonnie Scotland. It is a poet's true business to distill this pure essence of life, more potent by far than life ever turns out to be, even for poets. I think that Hughes is doing for the Negro race what Burns did for the Scotch—squeezing out the beauty and rich warmth of a noble people into enduring poetry.

In hearing a group of young poets reading their new poems to each other recently, I was struck with their common tendency to intricacy, mysticism, and preoccupation with brilliant technique. Their poems are competent and beautiful, and the antithesis of simple. To any but other poets, skilled in the craft, they are probably as completely mysterious as though in a foreign tongue. The machine age and the consequent decline of the arts has driven many poets and artists into the philosophy that art is the precious possession of the few initiate. Poets now write for the appreciation of other poets, painters are scornful of all but painters, even music, most popular of all the arts, is losing the common touch. Perhaps this is an inevitable development. Yet the people perish. Beauty is not an outworn ideal, for they still search for it on Fourteenth Street. While the poets and artists hoard up beauty for themselves and each other, philosophizing upon the "aristocracy of art," some few prophets are calling for art to come out of rich men's closets and become the "proletarian art" of all the people.

Perhaps Langston Hughes does not relish the title of Proletarian Poet, but he deserves it just the same. "Railroad Avenue," "Brass Spitoons," "Prize Fighter," "Elevator Boy," "Porter," "Saturday Night," and the songs from the Georgia Roads, all have their roots deep in the lives of workers. They give voice to the philosophy of men of the people, more rugged, more beautiful, better food for poetry, than the philosophy of the "middle classes."

This is a valuable example for all poets of what can be done with simple technique and "every day" subjects, but it is particularly valuable, I believe, for other Negro poets. Booker T. Washington's adjuration to "educate yourself" has sunk too deep in the Race philosophy. As in all American life, there is a strong urge to escape life's problems by reaching another station. "The life of a professional man must surely be happier than that of a factory worker," America reasons. "A teacher must surely find greater satisfaction than a farmer." Poets, influenced by this group sentiment, want to write about "nicer" emotions than those of the prize fighter who reasons

Only dumb guys fight.
If I wasn't dumb
I wouldn't be fightin'

I could make six dollars a day
On the docks,
And I'd save more than I do now.
Only dumb guys fight.

Opportunity: Journal of Negro Life, 5 (March 1927): 84–85

Richard Wright, "Forerunner and Ambassador"

The double role that Langston Hughes has played in the rise of a realistic literature among the Negro people resembles in one phase the role that Theodore Dreiser played in freeing American literary expression from the restrictions of Puritanism. Not that Negro literature was ever Puritanical, but it was timid and vaguely lyrical and folkish. Hughes's early poems, "The Weary Blues" and "Fine Clothes to the Jew," full of irony and urban imagery, were greeted by a large section of the Negro reading public with suspicion and shock when they first appeared in the middle twenties. Since then the realistic position assumed by Hughes has become the dominant outlook of all those Negro writers who have something to say.

The other phase of Hughes's role has been, for the lack of a better term, that of a cultural ambassador. Performing his task quietly and almost casually, he has represented the Negroes' case, in his poems, plays, short stories and novels, at the court of world opinion. On the other hand he has brought the experiences of other nations within the orbit of the Negro writer by his translations from the French, Russian, and Spanish.

How Hughes became this forerunner and ambassador can best be understood in the cameo sequences of his own life that he gives us in his sixth and latest book, *The Big Sea*. Out of his experiences as a seaman, cook, laundry worker, farm helper, busboy, doorman, unemployed worker, have come his writings dealing with black gals who wore red stockings and black men who sang the blues all night and slept like rocks all day.

Unlike the sons and daughters of Negro "society," Hughes was not ashamed of those of his race who had to scuffle for their bread. The jerky transitions of his own life did not admit of his remaining in one place long enough to become a slave of prevailing Negro middle-class prejudices. So beneficial does this ceaseless movement seem to Hughes that he has made it one of his life principles: six months in one place, he says, is long enough to make one's life complicated. The result has been a range of artistic interest and expression possessed by no other Negro writer of his time.

The New Republic 103 (October 1940)

Karen Jackson Ford, "Do Right to Write Right: Langston Hughes's Aesthetics of Simplicity"

The one thing most readers of twentieth-century American poetry can say about Langston Hughes is that he has known rivers. "The Negro Speaks of Rivers" has become memorable for its lofty, oratorical tone, mythic scope, and powerful rhythmic repetitions.

> I've known rivers:
> I've known rivers ancient as the world and older than
> the flow of human blood in human veins.

But however beautiful its cadences, the poem is remembered primarily because it is Hughes's most frequently anthologized work. The fact is, "The Negro Speaks of Rivers" is one of Hughes's most uncharacteristic poems, and yet it has defined his reputation, along with a small but constant selection of other poems included in anthologies....

The repression of the great bulk of Hughes's poems is the result of chronic critical scorn for their simplicity. Throughout his long career, but especially after his first two volumes of poetry (readers were at first willing to assume that a youthful poet might grow to be more complex), his books received their harshest reviews for a variety of "flaws" that all originate in an aesthetics of simplicity. From his first book, *The Weary Blues* (1926), to his last one, *The Panther and the Lash* (1967), the reviews invoke a litany of faults: the poems are superficial, infantile, silly, small, unpoetic, common, jejune, iterative, and, of course, simple. Even his admirers reluctantly conclude that Hughes's poetics failed. Saunders Redding flatly opposes simplicity and artfulness. "While Hughes's rejection of his own growth shows an admirable loyalty to his self-commitment as the poet of the 'simple, Negro common-folk'...it does a disservice to his art." James Baldwin, who recognizes the potential of simplicity as an artistic principle, faults the poems for "tak[ing] refuge...in a fake simplicity in order to avoid the very difficult simplicity of the experience."

Despite a lifetime of critical disappointments, then, Hughes remained loyal to the aesthetic program he had outlined in 1926 in his decisive poetic treatise, "The Negro Artist and the Racial Mountain." There he had predicted that the common people would "give to this world its truly great Negro artist, the one who is not afraid to be himself," a poet who would explore the "great field of unused [folk] material ready for his art" and recognize that this source would provide "sufficient matter to furnish a black artist with a lifetime of creative work." This is clearly a portrait of the poet Hughes would become, and he maintained his fidelity to this ideal at great cost to his literary reputation.

Twentieth Century Literature 38.4 (1992): 436–37

Peter Townsend, "Jazz and Langston Hughes's Poetry"

Hughes's engagement with jazz was close and long-lived, from his "Weary Blues" of 1926 up to the time of his death in 1967. Jazz crops naturally out of the landscape of Hughes's poetry, which is largely that of the black communities of Harlem and Chicago, and it remains fluid in its significance....

Hughes responded with particular sympathy to jazz of the bebop period, which he saw as having great political significance. *Montage of a*

Dream Deferred, published in 1951, is one of Hughes's most substantial sequences of poems, and it is shot through with references to jazz. His editorial note to the sequence explains the stylistic influence of bebop on its composition:

> This poem on contemporary Harlem, like bebop, is marked by conflicting changes, sudden nuances, sharp and impudent interjections, and passages sometimes in the manner of the jam session, sometimes the popular song, punctuated by the riffs, runs, breaks and distortions of the music of a community in transition....

Bebop affected the forms of Hughes's poetry at the higher architectural levels, dictating the structural rhythm of longer works like "Dream Deferred," but otherwise he employed a small range of simple verse forms that originate in earlier styles of black music. A particular favourite was a two-stress line rhymed in quatrains, derived from spirituals, and he also frequently used a looser form drawn from the 12-bar blues. The first of these Hughes was able to use with remarkable flexibility, considering its brevity. The form is often used for aphoristic effect, as in "Motto":

I play it cool
And dig all jive.
That's the reason
I stay alive.

or in "Sliver," a comment on the form itself:

A cheap little tune
To cheap little rhymes
Can cut a man's
Throat sometimes.

Jazz in American Culture, 2001: 126–28

Langston Hughes, "Harlem Rent Parties"

Then [in the early thirties] it was that house-rent parties began to flourish—and not always to raise the rent either. But, as often as not, to have a get-together of one's own, where you could do the black-bottom with no stranger behind you trying to do it, too. Non-theatrical, non-intellectual Harlem was an unwilling victim of its own vogue. It didn't like to be stared at by white folks. But perhaps the downtowners never knew this—for the cabaret owners, the entertainers, and the speakeasy proprietors treated them fine—as long as they paid.

The Saturday night rent parties that I attended were often more amusing than any night club, in small apartments where God knows who lived—because the guests seldom did—but where the piano would often be augmented by a guitar, or an odd cornet, or somebody with a pair of drums walking in off the street. And where awful bootleg whiskey and good fried fish or steaming chitterling were sold at very low prices. And the dancing and singing and impromptu entertaining went on until dawn came in at the windows.

These parties, often termed whist parties or dances, were usually announced by brightly colored cards stuck in the grille of apartment house elevators. Some of the cards were highly entertaining in themselves:

We got yellow girls, we've got black and tan
Will you have a good time? - YEAH MAN!

A Social Whist Party

—GIVEN BY—

MARY WINSTON

147 West 145th Street Apt. 5

SATURDAY EVE., MARCH 19th, 1932

GOOD MUSIC REFRESHMENTS

Almost every Saturday night when I was in Harlem I went to a house-rent party. I wrote lots of poems about house-rent parties, and ate thereat many a fried fish and pig's foot—with liquid refreshments on the side. I met ladies' maids and truck drivers, laundry workers and shoe shine boys, seamstresses and porters. I can still hear their laughter in my ears, hear the soft slow music, and feel the floor shaking as the dancers danced.

The Big Sea, 1940: 228–30

Ideas for Writing About Langston Hughes

1. From reading about Hughes's life, and from the commentaries excerpted here, write an essay making claims about where he got his material and why he chose this subject matter. Use examples from the works you have read. Include a discussion of how it differed from the conventional subject matter of poetry in the early twentieth century.
2. Write an essay responding to various negative criticisms of Hughes's writing. When you first read the selections by Hughes reprinted here, did you see the same flaws as those reported in the commentaries? Do you think that Hughes's critics had valid literary points, or were they driven by political concerns, or a combination of both?
3. Music is a prominent element in Hughes's poetry. Write an essay in which you develop an argument about the musical features in the poem. Be sure to discuss how music and poetry are interconnected in general.

Ideas for Researched Writing

1. Some of the writers that Langston Hughes acknowledged as influences were Paul Dunbar, W. E. B. DuBois, Richard Wright, James Baldwin, Walt Whitman, and Carl Sandburg. Look up information on these writers. Biographies of Hughes often remark on their influence. Write an essay explaining what it was about each of these writers that affected Langston Hughes.
2. For a weekly newspaper column in the Chicago *Defender*, Hughes wrote a series of fictional editorials from the point of view of Jesse B. Semple, a black workingman who lived in a Harlem rooming house. This folksy character related humorous moral tales about the social, political, and economic disparities between the haves and have-nots in the United States. Investigate the history of the Jesse B. Semple stories and write about popular and critical responses to them. Start by reading Susan L. Blake, "Old John in Harlem: The Urban Folktales of Langston Hughes," *Black American Literature Forum* 14 (Fall 1980): 100–104, and Phyllis R. Klotman, "Jesse B. Semple and the Narrative Art of Langston Hughes," *Journal of Narrative Technique* 3 (January 1973): 66–75.

The Art of Poetry

Writers frequently find inspiration in what they see—the beauty of nature, the energy of a city street, the image of an odd stranger, or the message of a work of art. Each writer's interpretation of a work of art is highly individual because each of us sees through the lens of our own experience. In her poem "American Literature," Lisel Mueller describes this process of poetic interpretation as writers ponder the paintings of Edward Hopper.

LISEL MUELLER (1924–)

American Literature

Poets and storytellers
move into the vacancies
Edward Hopper left them.
They settle down in blank spaces,
where the light has been scoured and bleached
skull-white, and nothing grows
except absence. Where something is missing,
the man a woman waits for,
or furniture in a room
stripped like a hospital bed
after the patient has died.
Such bereft interiors
are just what they've been looking for,
the writers, who come with their baggage
of dowsing rods and dog-eared books,
their uneasy family photographs,
their lumpy beds, their predilection
for starting fires in empty rooms.

(1996)

Before you read each poem in this section, look closely at the reproduction of the work of art that goes with it, and write down words and phrases that describe your response to the art. Then you can see how your response compares to the poems we have selected.

Edward Hopper (American, 1882–1967), *Nighthawks*, 1942.
Oil on canvas, 84.1×152.4 cm. Friends of American Art Collection, 1942.51. (The Art Institute of Chicago. Photography ©The Art Institute of Chicago.)

Samuel Yellen (1906–1983)

Nighthawks

The place is the corner of Empty and Bleak,
The time is night's most desolate hour,
The scene is Al's Coffee Cup or the Hamburger Tower,
The persons in this drama do not speak.

We who peer through that curve of plate glass
Count three nighthawks seated there—patrons of life:
The counterman will be with you in a jiff,
The thick white mugs were never meant for demitasse.

The single man whose hunched back we see
Once put a gun to his head in Russian roulette,
Whirled the chamber, pulled the trigger, won the bet,
And now lives out his *x* years' guarantee.

And facing us, the two central characters
Have finished their coffee, and have lit
A contemplative cigarette;
His hand lies close, but not touching hers.

Not long ago together in a darkened room,
Mouth burned mouth, flesh beat and ground
On ravaged flesh, and yet they found
No local habitation and no name.

Oh, are we not lucky to be none of these!
We can look on with complacent eye:
Our satisfactions satisfy,
Our pleasures, our pleasures please.

(1951)

Susan Ludvigson (1942–)

Inventing My Parents

After Edward Hopper's *Nighthawks* (1942)

They sit in the bright cafe
discussing Hemingway, and how
this war will change them.
Sinclair Lewis' name comes up,
and Kay Boyle's, and then Fitzgerald's.
They disagree about the American Dream.
My mother, her bare arms
silver under fluorescent lights,
says she imagines it a hawk
flying over, its shadow sweeping
every town. Their coffee's getting cold
but they hardly notice. My mother's face
is lit by ideas. My father's gestures
are a Frenchman's. When he concedes
a point, he shrugs, an elaborate lift
of the shoulders, his hands and smile
declaring an open mind.

I am five months old, at home with a sitter
this August night, when the air outside
is warm as a bath. They decide,
though the car is parked nearby,
to walk the few blocks home, savoring
the fragrant night, their being alone together.
As they go out the door, he's reciting
Donne's "Canonization": "For God's sake
hold your tongue, and let me love,"
and she's laughing, light
as summer rain when it begins.

(1992)

Pieter Brueghel the Elder (c. 1525–1569), *Landscape with the Fall of Icarus*, c. 1554–1555. Oil on panel. (The Bridgeman Art Library International Ltd.)

W. H. AUDEN (1907–1973)

Musée des Beaux Arts

About suffering they were never wrong,
The Old Masters: how well they understood
Its human position; how it takes place
While someone else is eating or opening a window or just
walking dully along;
How, when the aged are reverently, passionately waiting
For the miraculous birth, there always must be
Children who did not specially want it to happen, skating
On a pond at the edge of the wood:
They never forgot
That even the dreadful martyrdom must run its course
Anyhow in a corner, some untidy spot
Where the dogs go on with their doggy life and the torturer's horse
Scratches its innocent behind on a tree.

In Brueghel's *Icarus*, for instance: how everything turns away
Quite leisurely from the disaster; the ploughman may
Have heard the splash, the forsaken cry,
But for him it was not an important failure; the sun shone
As it had to on the white legs disappearing into the green
Water; and the expensive delicate ship that must have seen
Something amazing, a boy falling out of the sky,
Had somewhere to get to and sailed calmly on.

(1940)

Paolo Uccello (1397–1475)
St. George and the Dragon, 1470.
Oil on canvas. (National Gallery, London, United Kingdom)

U. A. Fanthorpe (1929–2009)

Not My Best Side

I

Not my best side, I'm afraid.
The artist didn't give me a chance to
Pose properly, and as you can see,
Poor chap, he had this obsession with
Triangles, so he left off two of my
Feet. I didn't comment at the time
(What, after all, are two feet
To a monster?) but afterwards
I was sorry for the bad publicity.
Why, I said to myself, should my conqueror
Be so ostentatiously beardless, and ride
A horse with a deformed neck and square hoofs?
Why should my victim be so
Unattractive as to be inedible,
And why should she have me literally
On a string? I don't mind dying
Ritually, since I always rise again,
But I should have liked a little more blood
To show they were taking me seriously.

II

It's hard for a girl to be sure if
She wants to be rescued. I mean, I quite
Took to the dragon. It's nice to be
Liked, if you know what I mean. He was
So nicely physical, with his claws
And lovely green skin, and that sexy tail,
And the way he looked at me,
He made me feel he was all ready to
Eat me. And any girl enjoys that.
So when this boy turned up, wearing machinery,
On a really dangerous horse, to be honest
I didn't much fancy him. I mean,
What was he like underneath the hardware?
He might have acne, blackheads or even
Bad breath for all I could tell, but the dragon—
Well, you could see all his equipment
At a glance. Still, what could I do?
The dragon got himself beaten by the boy,
And a girl's got to think of her future.

III

I have diplomas in Dragon
Management and Virgin Reclamation.
My horse is the latest model, with
Automatic transmission and built-in
Obsolescence. My spear is custom-built,
And my prototype armour
Still on the secret list. You can't
Do better than me at the moment.
I'm qualified and equipped to the
Eyebrow. So why be difficult?
Don't you want to be killed and/or rescued
In the most contemporary way? Don't
You want to carry out the roles
That sociology and myth have designed for you?
Don't you realize that, by being choosy,
You are endangering job prospects
In the spear- and horse-building industries?
What, in any case, does it matter what
You want? You're in my way.

(1989)

Vincent van Gogh (1853–1890), *The Starry Night*, 1889
Oil on canvas, 29 × 36 1/4. Acquired through the Lillie P. Bliss Bequest (472.1941). The Museum of Modern Art. (Digital image ©The Museum of Modern Art / Licensed by SCALA/Art Resource, NY.)

ANNE SEXTON (1928–1974)

The Starry Night

"That does not keep me from having a terrible need of—shall I say the word—religion. Then I go out at night to paint the stars."
—Vincent van Gogh in a letter to his brother

The town does not exist
except where one black-haired tree slips
up like a drowned woman into the hot sky.
The town is silent. The night boils with eleven stars
Oh starry starry night! This is how
I want to die.

It moves. They are all alive.
Even the moon bulges in its orange irons
to push children, like a god, from its eye.
The old unseen serpent swallows up the stars.
Oh starry starry night! This is how
I want to die:

into that rushing beast of the night,
sucked up by that great dragon, to split
from my life with no flag,
no belly,
no cry.

(1961)

Henri Matisse (1869–1954) *The Red Studio*, 1911.
Oil on canvas, approximately 71 × 86. (The Museum of Modern Art, New York)

W. D. SNODGRASS (1926–2009)

Matisse: "The Red Studio"

There is no one here.
But the objects: they are real. It is not
As if he had stepped out or moved away;
There is no other room and no
Returning. Your foot or finger would pass
Through, as into unreflecting water
Red with clay, or into fire.
Still, the objects: they are real. It is
As if he had stood
Still in the bare center of this floor,

His mind turned in in concentrated fury,
Till he sank
Like a great beast sinking into sands
Slowly, and did not look up.
His own room drank him.
What else could generate this
Terra cotta raging through the floor and walls,
Through chests, chairs, the table and the clock,
Till all environments of living are
Transformed to energy—
Crude, definitive and gay.
And so gave birth to objects that are real.
How slowly they took shape, his children, here,
Grew solid and remain:
The crayons; these statues; the clear brandybowl;
The ashtray where a girl sleeps, curling among
    flowers;
This flask of tall glass, green, where a vine begins
Whose bines circle the other girl brown as a
    cypress knee.
Then, pictures, emerging on the walls:
Bathers; a landscape; a still life with a vase;
To the left, a golden blonde, lain in magentas with flowers
    scattering like stars;
Opposite, top right, these terra cotta women, living, in
    their world of living's colors;
Between, but yearning toward them, the sailor on his red
    cafe chair, dark blue, self-absorbed.
These stay, exact,
Within the belly of these walls that burn,
That must hum like the domed electric web
Within which, at the carnival, small cars bump
    and turn,
Toward which, for strength, they reach their
    iron hands:
Like the heavens' walls of flame that the old magi
    could see;
Or those ethereal clouds of energy
From which all constellations form,
Within whose love they turn.
They stand here real and ultimate.
But there is no one here.

(1967)

Kitagawa Utamaro (1754–1806), *Two Women Fixing Their Hair,* from the series *Daily Life of Women,* 1794–1795.
Nishiki-e print, oban format.
(Photo: Harry Brejat. Musée des Arts Asiatiques—Guimet, Paris. Photo Credit: Reunion des Musées Nationaux/ Art Resource, NY.)

Cathy Song (1952–)

Beauty and Sadness

for Kitagawa Utamaro

He drew hundreds of women
in studies unfolding
like flowers from a fan.
Teahouse waitresses, actresses,
geishas, courtesans and maids.
They arranged themselves
before this quick, nimble man
whose invisible presence
one feels in these prints
is as delicate
as the skinlike paper
he used to transfer
and retain their fleeting loveliness.

Crouching like cats,
they purred amid the layers of kimono
swirling around them
as though they were bathing
in a mountain pool with irises
growing in the silken sunlit water.
Or poised like porcelain vases,
slender, erect and tall; their heavy
brocaded hair was piled high
with sandalwood combs and blossom sprigs
poking out like antennae.
They resembled beautiful iridescent insects,
creatures from a floating world.

Utamaro absorbed these women of Edo
in their moments of melancholy.
He captured the wisp of shadows,
the half-draped body
emerging from a bath; whatever
skin was exposed
was powdered white as snow.
A private space disclosed.
Portraying another girl
catching a glimpse of her own vulnerable
face in the mirror, he transposed
the trembling plum lips
like a drop of blood
soaking up the white expanse of paper.

At times, indifferent to his inconsolable
eye, the women drifted
through the soft gray feathered light,
maintaining stillness, the moments in between.
Like the dusty ash-winged moths
that cling to the screens in summer
and that the Japanese venerate
as ancestors reincarnated;
Utamaro graced these women with immortality
in the thousand sheaves of prints
fluttering into the reverent hands of keepers:
the dwarfed and bespectacled painter
holding up to a square of sunlight
what he had carried home beneath his coat
one afternoon in winter.

(1983)

The Art of Poetry: Questions for Discussion and Writing

American Literature by Lisel Mueller [p. 548]

The daughter of two teachers, Lisel Mueller grew up in Hamburg, Germany, during the rise of Adolf Hitler. Fearing that their anti-Fascist beliefs would result in persecution (her father had been arrested once), the family fled the country when Mueller was fifteen, settling in Evansville, Indiana, where her father became a professor at the University of Evansville. Influenced early by the poetry of Carl Sandburg, Muller writes in a familiar, easy-to-understand style, but her poems are deceptively intricate and often layered with meaning. Her collection *Alive Together* won the 1997 Pulitzer Prize for poetry.

1. List the set of images related to Hopper's paintings. Look on the Internet or at an art collection for Hopper paintings besides *Nighthawks.* Do you see the types of images Mueller describes?
2. What images are related to the poets and storytellers in the poem? Explain what each image denotes. For example, what do dog-eared books and lumpy beds suggest to you? Why might you carry those into a new apartment? What is the function of a dowsing-rod? How do the poets' and storytellers' images contrast with the Hopper images?
3. Why are the Hopper paintings just what the poets and storytellers have been looking for? What relationship between real-life settings and poetic interpretations of them is suggested by Mueller's poems? Use details from the poem as evidence of this relationship.
4. Explain how the last image in particular brings together Hopper's rooms and the work of the writer. Think of the various nonliteral meanings of "starting fires." How do those relate to writing poetry? Use logical reasoning to support your ideas.

Nighthawks by Samuel Yellen [p. 549]

Born in Lithuania, Yellen attended college in the United States and settled permanently in Bloomington, Indiana, where he was an English professor at Indiana University. Besides many books of poems, Yellen wrote *American Labor Struggles* (1936), the story of ten significant union movements. Several of his poems have been set to music.

1. Which details in the poem best capture the tone of the painting?
2. What does having once played Russian roulette suggest about the man with the hunched shoulders?

3. Is the last stanza ironic? Argue your response.
4. Compose your own backstory for the three nighthawks in the painting.
5. Compare Yellen's handling of the three characters sketched in this poem with John Updike's presentation of the down-and-out Flick Webb in "Ex-Basketball Player" (pages 638–39).

Inventing My Parents by Susan Ludvigson [p. 550]

Writing poetry in both open and closed forms, Susan Ludvigson is renowned for giving voice to an astonishing range of characters in her works: rural women in Wisconsin with dark secrets, little girls playing house, the mistress of sculptor Auguste Rodin, a young man attempting suicide in the Paris Metro, a Japanese film crew building a sand castle. When Ludvigson was a child, her father owned two restaurants in a small town in Wisconsin, and images from that period may influence the poem here.

1. Explain how Ludvigson's envisioning of the painting creates a different tone from the stark one presented in Yellen's poem.
2. What do the details of the couple's conversation reveal about the kind of people the parents are?
3. What adjectives would you choose to describe the mother? Which might you choose to describe the father? Explain the reasoning behind your choices.
4. How does the depiction of the sexual relationship of the couple in Yellen's poem differ from that suggested in Ludvigson's version? Use details from the poems to argue your point.
5. Does Ludvigson's poem change the way you view Edward Hopper's *Nighthawks?* Or does the painting still seem to present the bleak café and alienated patrons seen by Yellen? Consider the title that Hopper chose.
6. Why do the two poets interpret the painting differently? What personal meanings do they seem to discover in the art? Which response is closer to yours?

Musée des Beaux Arts by W. H. Auden [p. 551]

See page 468 for a biographical note about this poet.

1. What are the two kinds of events contrasted in this poem?
2. What examples does Auden give of suffering that goes unnoticed in life?
3. Look up the myth of Icarus in an encyclopedia or other reference work. What comments about the human condition or human nature does the story deal with? Does the poem make the same point, or a different one? Use details from both the story and poem as evidence of similarity or difference.
4. Compare this poem with Frost's "'Out, Out—'" (pages 596–97). What does each poem say about the attitudes of people toward the

suffering of others? Are these poems cynical, ironic, disillusioned, truthful? Provide details from the poems to support your points.

5. What point does Auden make about the visual arrangement of Brueghel's painting? Does he make an accurate interpretation of the artwork? Devise a claim for your own reaction to the painting.
6. Choose a picture, either in a museum or a book, and write a reflection on it. If the picture is not well-known, include a photocopy or other reproduction of it when you give your writing to a reader or instructor.

Not My Best Side by U. A. Fanthorpe [p. 552]

A British poet who published her first book of verse at the age of fifty, Fanthorpe earlier made her living as an English teacher and then as a hospital ward clerk. These occupations no doubt lent the dark humor and appreciation of quirky individualism that characterize her unsentimental poetry. Fanthorpe rarely writes about herself, saying, "The people I want to write about are, on the whole, the ones whom nobody notices, whose voices aren't heard. I'm interested in neglected places, and in the boundaries of language, the language of small children, the inarticulate and the mentally confused."

1. When you first read this poem, at what point did you realize it was humorous? What made you realize this? What makes the poem funny?
2. The poem has three stanzas, each with a different speaker. Which character in the painting is speaking in each stanza? What kind of person is each one? What are the main goals of each speaker? If you were going to make the poem into a movie, what actor would you cast in each role? Explain the reasoning behind your choices.
3. Look up the story of St. George and the Dragon, the topic of Uccello's painting. Relate details of the story to details in the poem. How are they similar and different? What different main points do they make?
4. Review the forms of poetry (Chapter 15) and identify the form of "Not My Best Side." Argue that this is the most suitable form for the poem.
5. Find out trends and styles in Italian painting in the 15th century, when Uccello created *St. George and the Dragon.* Point out how the painting reflects these trends and styles. Does the poem allude to any of these? Give examples.
6. Choose Hopper's *Nighthawks* or Utamaro's *Two Women Fixing Their Hair*, paintings reproduced in this section. Write a humorous poem using the points of view of people in the paintings, as Fanthorpe did in "Not My Best Side."

The Starry Night by Anne Sexton [p. 553]

Instead of attending college, Anne Sexton eloped at nineteen, became a housewife and mother, and worked briefly as a fashion model. She suffered her first nervous breakdown when she was twenty-eight, and for

the rest of her life, she was "in and out of mental institutions, on and off psychiatric drugs." Her psychiatrist suggested writing poetry as therapy. She did, and her highly introspective poetry won her a wide and loyal audience. Sexton once wrote that poetry "should be a shock to the senses. It should hurt." Her collection of poems *Live or Die* (1966) won a Pulitzer Prize. She committed suicide at age forty-six.

1. Both van Gogh and Sexton, suffering from depression, sought death, and both spent periods when they lived only for their creative arts. How are these states of mind reflected in Sexton's "The Starry Night"? Use details from the poem to argue your point.
2. Review the types of poetic language in Chapter 14. Discuss the imagery, metaphor and simile, and connotations in "The Starry Night." Tie the poetic language to a main point about the poem's meaning.
3. The epigraph is from a letter of van Gogh's to his brother. Such letters are main sources for van Gogh's biographers. Describe the connection between the quotation and the poem.
4. If possible, find a bigger and clearer image of van Gogh's *The Starry Night* (see www.vangoghgallery.com, for instance). When you look at the painting, is your point of view similar to Sexton's? Why or why not?
5. In what ways does Sexton's poem *not* describe or evoke van Gogh's painting?
6. Write your own paragraph or poem responding to *The Starry Night* or to another van Gogh painting. Then reflect upon your experience looking at the painting as subject matter for writing. Did the effort to write about it change your thoughts or perceptions of the visual art?

The Red Studio by W. D. Snodgrass [pp. 554–55]

Some of W. D. Snodgrass's best-known poetry is filled with references to the wives and children from his three marriages. Although Snodgrass is usually named as a founder of the highly personal, self-examining confessional movement in poetry, he does not like the label himself. One of his decidedly nonconfessional books, *The Fuehrer Bunker*, consists of poems spoken by men and women in Hitler's bunker in 1945. One critic wrote of Snodgrass that he "has identified himself with exquisite suffering and guilt and with all those who barely manage to exist on the edge of life."

1. Throughout this poem, the artist (Henri Matisse) is "not here," but the objects in his studio are real. Look at the poem in terms of the artist's relationship to his work. What is this relationship like? Can you guess what has happened to the artist, at least in the poet's opinion? Use words and phrases from the poem as evidence for your claim.

2. Look at www.artchive.com for images of Matisse's paintings. Can you recognize any of them in the painting and the poem? Can you connect Matisse's other paintings to "The Red Studio" in style or content? Give some examples that demonstrate the connection you see.
3. In *The Shock of the New*, a book about modern art, Robert Hughes wrote about Matisse: "His studio was a world within the world: a place of equilibrium that, for sixty continuous years, produced images of comfort, refuge, and balanced satisfaction." Does your impression of the painting agree with Hughes's description? Do you think that the poet Snodgrass would agree with Hughes's description? Point out specific details from the painting and poem to support your claims.
4. Snodgrass closes the poem with three metaphors for the walls of Matisse's studio: the "domed electric web" of a carnival ride, the magi's "wall of flame," and "ethereal clouds of energy" that are the source of all things. Follow up on these comparisons and what they mean by doing some research. Then explain how they illuminate Snodgrass's interpretation of *The Red Studio.*
5. Can you think of a specific room or setting that you strongly associate with your identity, your activities, or your creations? Consider how you would present this place in a painting or in words. See whether this activity helps you understand the painting and poem "The Red Studio."
6. Where is the closest place you could go to see an actual Matisse painting? You might enjoy viewing an original painting and writing your impressions of it into a poem.

Beauty and Sadness by Cathy Song [page 556]

Cathy Song grew up in Hawaii, the daughter of Chinese and Korean Americans. As a young girl, she wished to become a songwriter like Joan Baez or Joni Mitchell, but she turned her attention to writing poetry while in high school. She won a prestigious award in 1982 for her book *Picture Bride*, where the subject matter clearly reflected her Asian American heritage. "Two Women Fixing Their Hair" appeared in that volume. However, Song's themes and content have broadened since that time, and her poetry today is known for its treatment of universal topics: love, death, motherhood, family, and aging.

1. In the first stanza, the speaker remarks on the "fleeting loveliness" of the women. What images and comparisons reinforce this idea in the rest of the poem?
2. What do the women look like in each stanza? How well does the poet's description match the visual art? Find other reproductions of drawings by Kitagawa Utamaro. Does Song's description fit these drawings too? Use details from the poem and drawings to support your ideas about the accuracy of Song's description.
3. What does the title mean? Why are the women sad? What is the connection between their sadness and their beauty?

4. Line 34 speaks of "A private space disclosed." What does this line mean?
5. Paraphrase the last stanza. What claim is the poet making about the artist and his mission? Relate details from the stanza to this claim.
6. Why does Song tell us that Utamaro was a "dwarfed and bespectacled painter"? Why does she wait until late in the poem to give these details? Use logical reasoning to explain your idea.
7. Write an essay on Song's use of imagery in this poem. What motifs does she develop? What themes do they support?
8. Look up information about Kitagawa Utamaro. Does what you learned help you to understand the poem? Explain by relating biographical material to the poem and the drawing or drawings.
9. Write your own response to Utamaro's drawing. If possible, try to make a claim or create an interpretation of the drawing that is different from Song's.

ANTHOLOGY of Poetry

Thomas Wyatt 1503–1542

Like many of his peers, Thomas Wyatt wrote poems of great charm and wit while pursuing a career as a politician and diplomat. He was rumored to have been Anne Boleyn's lover before she married King Henry VIII. On a diplomatic mission to Italy, he became acquainted with the poetry of Petrarch and, as a result, was one of the first poets to compose sonnets in English.

They Flee from Me

They flee from me, that sometime did me seek,
With naked foot, stalking in my chamber:
I have seen them gentle, tame, and meek,
That now are wild, and do not remember
That sometime they put themselves in danger
To take bread at my hand; and now they range,
Busily seeking with a continual change.

Thankèd be fortune, it hath been otherwise
Twenty times better; but once, in special,
In thin array, after a pleasant guise,
When her loose gown from her shoulders did fall,
And she me caught in her arms long and small,
Therewithal sweetly did me kiss,
And softly said, "Dear heart, how like you this?"

It was no dream; I lay broad waking.
But all is turned, thorough my gentleness,
Into a strange fashion of forsaking;
And I have leave to go of her goodness,
And she also to use new-fangleness.
But since that I so kindely am served,
I would fain know what she hath deserved.

(ca. 1535)

Questions for Discussion and Writing

1. What is the speaker's attitude toward the special woman of stanzas 2 and 3? Why does she stand out from the others?
2. Describe in your own words what happens in the second stanza. Why does the woman do what she does? How would you describe her?
3. What does the speaker suggest is the cause of his abandonment?
4. Write a character sketch of the speaker, paying particular attention to his views about love and women.

William Shakespeare 1564–1616

See page 889 for a biographical note about this author.

When in Disgrace with Fortune and Men's Eyes

When, in disgrace with fortune and men's eyes,
I all alone beweep my outcast state,
And trouble deaf heaven with my bootless° cries,
And look upon myself, and curse my fate,
Wishing me like to one more rich in hope,
Featured like him, like him with friends possessed,
Desiring this man's art and that man's scope,
With what I most enjoy contented least;
Yet in these thoughts myself almost despising,
Haply I think on thee—and then my state,°
Like to the lark at break of day arising
From sullen earth, sings hymns at heaven's gate;
For thy sweet love remembered such wealth brings
That then I scorn to change my state with kings.

(1609)

3 bootless Helpless. **10 state** Condition.

Questions for Discussion and Writing

1. Is it believable that the mere thought of his beloved could change the speaker's whole outlook on life?
2. Summarize the speaker's state of mind before the shift that occurs in line 10.
3. How does the meaning of the poem change if the reader interprets "thee" (line 10) and "thy" (line 13) to refer to God instead of a romantic lover?

Let Me Not to the Marriage of True Minds

Let me not to the marriage of true minds
Admit impediments. Love is not love
Which alters when it alteration finds,
Or bends with the remover to remove:
O, no! it is an ever-fixèd mark
That looks on tempests and is never shaken;
It is the star to every wandering bark,
Whose worth's unknown, although his height be taken.
Love's not Time's fool, though rosy lips and cheeks
Within his bending sickle's compass come;
Love alters not with his brief hours and weeks,
But bears it out even to the edge of doom.
If this be error and upon me proved,
I never writ, nor no man ever loved.

(1609)

Questions for Discussion and Writing

1. What familiar part of the traditional Christian marriage service is echoed in the first line?
2. Notice that the poem celebrates "the marriage of true minds," not of bodies. In a brief paragraph, summarize in your own words the nature of this kind of love.
3. What two comparisons does Shakespeare make in lines 5–8? What is the connection between "an ever-fixèd mark" and "the star"?

That Time of Year Thou Mayst in Me Behold

That time of year thou mayst in me behold
When yellow leaves, or none, or few, do hang
Upon those boughs which shake against the cold,
Bare ruined choirs, where late the sweet birds sang.
In me thou see'st the twilight of such day
As after sunset fadeth in the west,
Which by and by black night doth take away,
Death's second self that seals up all in rest.
In me thou see'st the glowing of such fire,
That on the ashes of his youth doth lie,
As the death-bed, whereon it must expire
Consumed with that which it was nourished by.
This thou perceiv'st, which makes thy love more strong
To love that well, which thou must leave ere long.

(1609)

Questions for Discussion and Writing

1. How does the speaker portray himself in this sonnet?
2. What are the controlling metaphors in each of the quatrains? How are they related?
3. How do you explain the idea expressed in the last two lines? Why would the loved one's love grow stronger when he/she sees that the speaker is getting older?

My Mistress' Eyes Are Nothing Like the Sun

My mistress' eyes are nothing like the sun;
Coral is far more red than her lips' red;
If snow be white, why then her breasts are dun;
If hairs be wires, black wires grow on her head.
I have seen roses damask'd, red and white,
But no such roses see I in her cheeks,
And in some perfumes there is more delight
Than in the breath that from my mistress reeks.
I love to hear her speak, yet well I know
That music hath a far more pleasing sound.
I grant I never saw a goddess go;
My mistress, when she walks, treads on the ground:
And yet, by heaven, I think my love as rare
As any she belied with false compare.

(1609)

Questions for Discussion and Writing

1. The comparisons that Shakespeare uses negatively in this sonnet were familiar enough in his time to be considered clichés even then. What is the poet's point in cataloging these overused images?
2. What is the speaker's attitude toward his mistress? Is he making fun of her? Do the "if...then" constructions help you to figure out the distinction the speaker is making between the artificial comparisons and his real-life girlfriend?
3. Paraphrase the last two lines of the poem.
4. Write your own parody of some form of writing that you think is sometimes overdone (such as advice columns, sports articles, celebrity profiles, articles in sensational tabloids like the *National Enquirer*, horoscopes).

John Donne 1572–1631

The first and perhaps greatest of the metaphysical poets, John Donne wrote erotic lyrics and cynical love poems in his youth. A politically disastrous marriage ruined his civil career, but in 1615 he converted to Anglicanism and later became dean of St. Paul's

Cathedral, the most influential preacher in England. In later years, he wrote religious sonnets, elegies, epigrams, and verse letters. Donne's use of complex conceits and compressed phrasing influenced many twentieth-century poets, especially T. S. Eliot.

Death, Be Not Proud

Death, be not proud, though some have callèd thee
Mighty and dreadful, for thou art not so,
For those whom thou think'st thou dost overthrow
Die not, poor Death, nor yet canst thou kill me.
From rest and sleep, which but thy pictures be,
Much pleasure, then from thee much more must flow;
And soonest our best men with thee do go—
Rest of their bones and souls' delivery!
Thou'rt slave to fate, chance, kings, and desperate men,
And dost with poison, war, and sickness dwell,
And poppy or charms can make us sleep as well,
And better than thy stroke; why swell'st thou then?
One short sleep past, we wake eternally,
And death shall be no more: Death, thou shalt die!

(1633)

Questions for Discussion and Writing

1. What is the speaker's attitude toward Death in this poem?
2. How are paradox and personification used in this sonnet to signify a victory over Death?
3. Summarize each step in the argument that "proves" Death not to be very powerful.
4. Upon what beliefs does the success of the argument depend? In what senses are the speaker's final claims about Death not justified?

The Flea

Mark but this flea, and mark in this
How little that which thou deny'st me is;
Me it sucked first, and now sucks thee,
And in this flea our two bloods mingled be;
Thou know'st that this cannot be said
A sin, or shame, or loss of maidenhead,
    Yet this enjoys before it woo,
    And pampered swells with one blood made of two,
    And this, alas, is more than we would do.

Oh stay, three lives in one flea spare,
Where we almost, nay more than married, are.
This flea is you and I, and this
Our marriage bed and marriage temple is;
Though parents grudge, and you, we're met
And cloistered in these living walls of jet.
Though use make you apt to kill me,
Let not to that, self-murder added be,
And sacrilege, three sins in killing three.

Cruel and sudden, has thou since
Purpled thy nail in blood of innocence?
Wherein could this flea guilty be,
Except in that drop which it sucked from thee?
Yet thou triumph'st, and say'st that thou
Find'st not thyself, nor me, the weaker now;
'Tis true; then learn how false fears be;
Just so much honor, when thou yield'st to me,
Will waste, as this flea's death took life from thee.

(1633)

Questions for Discussion and Writing

1. What is the "little" thing the lover says the lady is denying him (line 2)? Is it really a small matter? Be sure to put the poem in the context of Elizabethan times when you answer.
2. What action is the woman about to take at the beginning of stanza two? Whose are the three lives the speaker wants to spare?
3. What is the argument that her parents might not believe but he hopes the lady will (lines 12–15)? What are the "living walls of jet"?
4. In what sense will the lady be guilty of killing both the lover and herself if she kills the flea (lines 16–18)?
5. What has happened at the beginning of stanza three? Why is the lady's nail purple?
6. What do you think the lady's response might be to the speaker's argument?

A Valediction: Forbidding Mourning

As virtuous men pass mildly away,
And whisper to their souls, to go,
Whilst some of their sad friends do say,
"The breath goes now," and some say, "No,"

So let us melt, and make no noise,
No tear-floods, nor sigh-tempests move,

'Twere profanation of our joys
    To tell the laity our love.

Moving of th' earth brings harms and fears,
    Men reckon what it did and meant;
But trepidation of the spheres,
    Though greater far, is innocent.°

Dull sublunary lovers' love
    (Whose soul is sense) cannot admit
Absence, because it doth remove
    Those things which elemented° it.

But we, by a love so much refined
    That our selves know not what it is,
Inter-assurèd of the mind,
    Care less, eyes, lips, and hands to miss.

Our two souls therefore, which are one,
    Though I must go, endure not yet
A breach, but an expansion,
    Like gold to airy thinness beat.

If they be two, they are two so
    As stiff twin compasses are two:
Thy soul, the fixed foot, makes no show
    To move, but doth, if th' other do.

And though it in the center sit,
    Yet when the other far doth roam,
It leans, and hearkens after it,
    And grows erect, as that comes home.

Such wilt thou be to me, who must
    Like th' other foot, obliquely run;
Thy firmness makes my circle just,
    And makes me end, where I begun.

(1633)

12 innocent Innocuous, harmless. **16 elemented** Composed.

Questions for Discussion and Writing

1. What is a "valediction"? And why does the speaker forbid mourning?
2. Explain how the simile about the passing away of virtuous men (lines 1–4) relates to the couple (in lines 5–8).
3. What distinction does the speaker make between "dull sublunary lovers" and the love that he and his beloved share?
4. According to the speaker, why will he end where he began? Can you explain his reasons?

Andrew Marvell 1621–1678

Though not a Puritan himself, Andrew Marvell supported the Puritan cause in the English Civil War. He held a number of posts during the Commonwealth and was instrumental in saving John Milton from punishment after the Restoration. One of the metaphysical poets, Marvell is best known for his witty lyrics that often present a tacit debate about opposing values. He has been called "the most major minor poet" in English.

To His Coy Mistress

Had we but world enough, and time,
This coyness,° lady, were no crime.
We would sit down, and think which way
To walk, and pass our long love's day.
Thou by the Indian Ganges' side
Shouldst rubies find; I by the tide
Of Humber° would complain. I would
Love you ten years before the Flood:
And you should if you please refuse
Till the conversion of the Jews.
My vegetable love should grow
Vaster than empires, and more slow.
An hundred years should go to praise
Thine eyes, and on thy forehead gaze.
Two hundred to adore each breast:
But thirty thousand to the rest.
An age at least to every part,
And the last age should show your heart.
For, lady, you deserve this state;
Nor would I love at lower rate.
    But at my back I always hear
Time's wingèd chariot hurrying near:
And yonder all before us lie
Deserts of vast eternity.
Thy beauty shall no more be found,
Nor, in thy marble vault, shall sound
My echoing song; then worms shall try
That long preserved virginity:
And your quaint honour turn to dust;
And into ashes all my lust.
The grave's a fine and private place,
But none, I think, do there embrace.
    Now therefore, while the youthful hue
Sits on thy skin like morning dew,
And while thy willing soul transpires

---

2 coyness Modesty, reluctance. **7 Humber** A river in northern England.

At every pore with instant fires,
Now let us sport us while we may;
And now, like amorous birds of prey,
Rather at once our time devour,
Than languish in his slow-chapped° pow'r.
Let us roll all our strength, and all
Our sweetness, up into one ball:
And tear our pleasures with rough strife,
Through the iron gates of life.
Thus, though we cannot make our sun
Stand still, yet we can make him run.

(1681)

---

40 slow-chapped Slow chewing

Questions for Discussion and Writing

1. What is the tone of the assertion in the first 20 lines? How does the speaker's tone change after line 20?
2. In the second stanza (lines 21–23), why is time behind the speaker and eternity in front of him?
3. What words contribute to a second change in tone (after line 32)?
4. In the 17th century, a cannonball was simply called a "ball." What is the point, then, of the description of a cannonball ripping through the gates of a fortified city?
5. What universal human concern does this poem reflect? What basic human needs might be said to motivate the speaker?

William Blake 1757–1827

William Blake was both artist and poet, though he achieved little success as either during his lifetime. Of the more than half-dozen books he wrote and illustrated, only one of them was published conventionally; his wife helped him print the rest. A mystic and visionary, Blake created his own mythology, complete with illustrations. His best-known volumes of poetry are *Songs of Innocence* (1789) and *Songs of Experience* (1794).

The Lamb

From *Songs of Innocence*

Little Lamb, who made thee?
Dost thou know who made thee?
Gave thee life, and bid thee feed
By the stream and o'er the mead;

Gave thee clothing of delight,
Softest clothing, wooly, bright;
Gave thee such a tender voice,
Making all the vales rejoice?
Little Lamb, who made thee?
Dost thou know who made thee?

Little Lamb, I'll tell thee,
Little Lamb, I'll tell thee:
He is callèd by thy name,
For he calls himself a Lamb.
He is meek, and he is mild;
He became a little child.
I a child, and thou a lamb,
We are callèd by his name.
Little Lamb, God bless thee!
Little Lamb, God bless thee!

(1789)

Questions for Discussion and Writing

1. What symbolic meanings are conveyed by the image of the lamb?
2. What view of God and creation does this poem present?
3. How does Blake establish the Lamb as a symbol of creation?

The Tyger

From *Songs of Experience*

Tyger, Tyger, burning bright
In the forests of the night,
What immortal hand or eye
Could frame thy fearful symmetry?

In what distant deeps or skies
Burnt the fire of thine eyes?
On what wings dare he aspire?
What the hand dare seize the fire?

And what shoulder and what art
Could twist the sinews of thy heart?
And, when thy heart began to beat,
What dread hand? and what dread feet?

What the hammer? What the chain?
In what furnace was thy brain?

What the anvil? What dread grasp
Dare its deadly terrors clasp?

When the stars threw down their spears,
And watered heaven with their tears,
Did He smile his work to see?
Did He who made the lamb make thee?

Tyger, Tyger, burning bright
In the forests of the night,
What immortal hand or eye
Dare frame thy fearful symmetry?

(1794)

Questions for Discussion and Writing

1. What side of creation is presented in this poem? Is the creator of the tiger the same as the creator of the lamb?
2. What Christian metaphors do you find in this poem? What mythological allusions are contained in lines 7 and 8?
3. Explain why "The Tyger" and "The Lamb" should be considered as a pair, one the reverse of the other.
4. Why does an allegedly all-powerful and beneficent creator permit evil at all?

The Sick Rose

O Rose, thou art sick!
The invisible worm
That flies in the night,
In the howling storm,

Has found out thy bed
Of crimson joy,
And his dark secret love
Does thy life destroy.

(1794)

Questions for Discussion and Writing

1. Are there sexual implications in the poem?
2. What do you think the rose and the worm might represent?

Illustrated manuscript of "The Sick Rose" from *Songs of Experience* (1794), designed and printed by Blake himself. (The Bridgeman Art Library International Ltd.)

3. What causes the rose to be sick?
4. Write an allegorical interpretation of the poem, explaining its hidden meaning.

London

I wander through each chartered street,
Near where the chartered Thames does flow,

And mark in every face I meet
Marks of weakness, marks of woe.

In every cry of every man,
In every infant's cry of fear,
In every voice, in every ban,
The mind-forged manacles I hear.

How the chimney-sweeper's cry
Every black'ning church appalls;
And the hapless soldier's sigh
Runs in blood down palace walls.

But most through midnight streets I hear
How the youthful harlot's curse
Blasts the new-born infant's tear,
And blights with plagues the marriage hearse.

(1794)

Questions for Discussion and Writing

1. How does Blake convey the impression of pain and suffering?
2. "The youthful harlot's curse" is usually interpreted to mean venereal disease, which blinds the infant after birth. How does this information help you to understand Blake's metaphor in the final stanza? Why is this curse so important to the speaker?
3. What is the significance of the mention of a church, a soldier, and a palace?

William Wordsworth 1770–1850

An English poet recognized for his use of common language and his love of nature, William Wordsworth was educated at Cambridge University. He lived for a time in France, where he fathered an illegitimate daughter and experienced the French Revolution firsthand. When he returned to England, he began writing in earnest. His works include *Lyrical Ballads* (1798), *Poems in Two Volumes* (1807), and *The Excursion* (1814). A leader of English Romanticism, Wordsworth was named Poet Laureate in 1843.

The World Is Too Much with Us

The world is too much with us; late and soon,
Getting and spending, we lay waste our powers;

Little we see in Nature that is ours;
We have given our hearts away, a sordid boon!°
This Sea that bares her bosom to the moon,
The winds that will be howling at all hours,
And are up-gathered now like sleeping flowers,
For this, for everything, we are out of tune;
It moves us not.—Great God! I'd rather be
A Pagan suckled in a creed outworn;
So might I, standing on this pleasant lea,°
Have glimpses that would make me less forlorn;
Have sight of Proteus°rising from the sea;
Or hear old Triton°blow his wreathèd horn.

(1807)

---

4 boon Blessing. **11 lea** Meadow. **13 Proteus** A sea god who could change shape. **14 Triton** A sea god whose top half was man and bottom half was fish.

Questions for Discussion and Writing

1. In what way, according to the speaker in the poem, have we "given our hearts away" (line 4)?
2. The poem is a sonnet divided into an octave and a sestet. Where does the sestet begin?
3. How is the poem unified? What is the poem's theme?

George Gordon, Lord Byron 1788–1824

Born in London and educated at Cambridge, George Gordon, Lord Byron, became a public figure as much for his scandalous personal life as for his irreverent, satiric poetry. Rumors about an affair with his half-sister forced him to leave England in 1816. His masterpiece is the comic epic poem *Don Juan*, begun in 1819 and still unfinished when he died in Greece from a fever he contracted while fighting for Greek independence.

She Walks in Beauty

She walks in beauty, like the night
    Of cloudless climes and starry skies;
And all that's best of dark and bright
    Meet in her aspect and her eyes:

Thus mellowed to that tender light
Which Heaven to gaudy day denies.
One shade the more, one ray the less,
Had half impaired the nameless grace
Which waves in every raven tress,
Or softly lightens o'er her face;
Where thoughts serenely sweet express,
How pure, how dear their dwelling-place.

And on that cheek, and o'er that brow,
So soft, so calm, yet eloquent,
The smiles that win, the tints that glow,
But tell of days in goodness spent,
A mind at peace with all below,
A heart whose love is innocent!

(1814)

Questions for Discussion and Writing

1. The light image introduced in the first stanza is the foundation of the poem, but just which image of light is dominant?
2. What does the word "eloquent" refer to? In those same lines, are the smiles on the cheek and the glow on the brow? How does that description work?
3. What are the speaker's attitudes toward women and beauty?

Percy Bysshe Shelley 1792–1822

Percy Shelley married sixteen-year-old Harriet Westbrook in 1811, the same year he was expelled from Oxford for writing a pamphlet on atheism. In 1814 he went to France with Mary Wollstonecraft, later famous for writing *Frankenstein*. The two were wed in 1816 after Harriet committed suicide. The couple then settled in Italy, where Shelley wrote some of his best lyrics, including "Ozymandias," "Ode to the West Wind," and *Adonais*.

Ozymandias

I met a traveller from an antique land
Who said: Two vast and trunkless legs of stone
Stand in the desert.... Near them, on the sand,
Half sunk, a shattered visage lies, whose frown,
And wrinkled lip, and sneer of cold command,

Tell that its sculptor well those passions read
Which yet survive, stamped on these lifeless things,
The hand that mocked them, and the heart that fed:
And on the pedestal these words appear:
"My name is Ozymandias, king of kings:
Look on my works, ye Mighty, and despair!"
Nothing beside remains. Round the decay
Of that colossal wreck, boundless and bare
The lone and level sands stretch far away.

(1817)

Questions for Discussion and Writing

1. The statue that this poem is written about has been described as one of the largest in Egypt. It has this inscription: "I am Ozymandias, king of kings; if anyone wishes to know what I am and where I lie, let him surpass me in some of my exploits." Does having this information help your understanding of the poem?
2. What contrast is there between what the king said and how the statue now looks?
3. How does the final image (the "lone and level sands" stretching far away) work to reinforce the tone and theme of the poem?

John Keats 1795–1821

A major figure in the romantic period of English poetry, John Keats began writing at age eighteen and died of tuberculosis in Italy at age twenty-five, after having seen both his mother and brother die of the disease. His poems, which are rich in imagery and dignified in expression, include "Ode on a Grecian Urn," "To Autumn," and "The Eve of St. Agnes."

Ode on a Grecian Urn

Thou still unravished bride of quietness,
    Thou foster-child of silence and slow time,
Sylvan historian, who canst thus express
    A flowery tale more sweetly than our rhyme:
What leaf-fringed legend haunts about thy shape
Of deities or mortals, or of both,
    In Tempe° or the dales of Arcady?°

---

7 Tempe Valley in Thessaly, noted for its natural beauty. **Arcady** Region in Greece, a traditional setting for pastoral poetry.

What men or gods are these? What maidens loth?
What mad pursuit? What struggle to escape?
What pipes and timbrels? What wild ecstasy?

Heard melodies are sweet, but those unheard
Are sweeter; therefore, ye soft pipes, play on;
Not to the sensual ear, but, more endeared,
Pipe to the spirit ditties of no tone:
Fair youth, beneath the trees, thou canst not leave
Thy song, nor ever can those trees be bare;
Bold Lover, never, never canst thou kiss,
Though winning near the goal—yet, do not grieve;
She cannot fade, though thou hast not thy bliss,
For ever wilt thou love, and she be fair!

Ah, happy, happy boughs! that cannot shed
Your leaves, nor ever bid the spring adieu;
And, happy melodist, unwearièd,
For ever piping songs for ever new;
More happy love! more happy, happy love!
For ever warm and still to be enjoyed,
For ever panting, and for ever young;
All breathing human passion far above,
That leaves a heart high-sorrowful and cloyed,
A burning forehead, and a parching tongue.

Who are these coming to the sacrifice?
To what green altar, O mysterious priest,
Lead'st thou that heifer lowing at the skies,
And all her silken flanks with garlands dressed?
What little town by river or sea shore,
Or mountain-built with peaceful citadel,
Is emptied of this folk, this pious morn?
And, little town, thy streets for evermore
Will silent be; and not a soul to tell
Why thou art desolate, can e'er return.

O Attic° shape! Fair attitude! with brede°
Of marble men and maidens overwrought,
With forest branches and the trodden weed;
Thou, silent form, dost tease us out of thought
As doth eternity: Cold Pastoral!
When old age shall this generation waste,
Thou shalt remain, in midst of other woe
Than ours, a friend to man, to whom thou say'st,
"Beauty is truth, truth beauty,"—that is all
Ye know on earth, and all ye need to know.

(1819)

---

41 Attic Of Attica, thus, classic in grace and simplicity. **brede** Design, decoration.

Questions for Discussion and Writing

1. How can unheard melodies be sweeter than heard ones?
2. Why are the figures so lucky to exist on the urn (lines 15–27)? What disadvantages do living lovers experience (lines 28–30)?
3. How is the urn a "Cold Pastoral"? How is it a "friend to man"?
4. Explain the closing line and give your reactions to this assertion about beauty and truth.

Walt Whitman 1819–1892

See page 486 for a biographical note about this author.

When I Heard the Learn'd Astronomer

When I heard the learn'd astronomer,
When the proofs, the figures, were ranged in columns before me,
When I was shown the charts and diagrams, to add, divide, and
    measure them,
When I sitting heard the astronomer where he lectured with much
    applause in the lecture-room,
How soon unaccountable I became tired and sick,
Till rising and gliding out I wander'd off by myself,
In the mystical moist night-air, and from time to time,
Look'd up in perfect silence at the stars.

(1865)

Questions for Discussion and Writing

1. Why is the speaker in the poem unable to appreciate the astronomy lecture?
2. Whitman's lines neither rhyme nor scan, so what makes this a poem?
3. Do you think poetry and science are antithetical? Write an essay about the similarities and differences between the methods and purposes of science and poetry. Use specific poems to support your claims.

Song of Myself

SECTION 11

Twenty-eight young men bathe by the shore,
Twenty-eight young men and all so friendly;

Twenty-eight years of womanly life and all so lonesome.

She owns the fine house by the rise of the bank,
She hides handsome and richly drest aft the blinds of the window.

Which of the young men does she like the best?
Ah the homeliest of them is beautiful to her.

Where are you off to, lady? for I see you,
You splash in the water there, yet stay stock still in your room.

Dancing and laughing along the beach came the twenty-ninth bather,
The rest did not see her, but she saw them and loved them.

The beards of the young men glisten'd with wet, it ran from their
    long hair,
Little streams pass'd all over their bodies.

An unseen hand also pass'd over their bodies,
It descended tremblingly from their temples and ribs.

The young men float on their backs, their white bellies bulge to the
    sun, they do not ask who seizes fast to them,
They do not know who puffs and declines with pendant and
    bending arch,
They do not think whom they souse with spray.

(1881)

Questions for Discussion and Writing

1. Why does the woman hide "handsome and richly drest" behind the window blinds? What sort of life do you think she leads?
2. How can the woman splash in the water and also "stay stock still" in her room?
3. What is the sexual implication of the phrase "souse with spray"? What other sexually charged language is there in these lines?
4. What does this episode imply about the sexual differences between men and women? Do you think these implications are valid?
5. What is the effect of the repetition and the unusually long lines of verse?

Matthew Arnold 1822–1888

Matthew Arnold was born in Middlesex, England, studied classics at Oxford, and later taught there. He was appointed inspector of schools for England and remained at that post for thirty-five years. As a poet, Arnold took his inspiration from Greek tragedies, Keats, and Wordsworth. An eminent social and literary critic in later years, he lectured in America in 1883 and 1886.

Dover Beach

The sea is calm to-night,
The tide is full, the moon lies fair
Upon the Straits;—on the French coast, the light
Gleams, and is gone; the cliffs of England stand,
Glimmering and vast, out in the tranquil bay.
Come to the window, sweet is the night air!
Only, from the long line of spray
Where the sea meets the moon-blanched sand,
Listen! you hear the grating roar
Of pebbles which the waves draw back, and fling,
At their return, up the high strand,
Begin, and cease, and then again begin,

With tremulous cadence slow, and bring
The eternal note of sadness in.
Sophocles° long ago
Heard it on the Aegean, and it brought
Into his mind the turbid ebb and flow
Of human misery; we
Find also in the sound a thought,
Hearing it by this distant northern sea.

The Sea of Faith
Was once, too, at the full, and round earth's shore
Lay like the folds of a bright girdle furled;
But now I only hear
Its melancholy, long, withdrawing roar,
Retreating to the breath
Of the night-wind down the vast edges drear
And naked shingles° of the world.

Ah, love, let us be true
To one another! for the world, which seems
To lie before us like a land of dreams,
So various, so beautiful, so new,
Hath really neither joy, nor love, nor light,
Nor certitude, nor peace, nor help for pain;
And we are here as on a darkling° plain
Swept with confused alarms of struggle and flight,
Where ignorant armies clash by night.

(1867)

---

15 Sophocles In *Antigone* the Greek dramatist likens the curse of heaven to the ebb and flow of the sea. **28 shingles** Gravel beaches. **35 darkling** Darkened.

Questions for Discussion and Writing

1. Describe the setting of the poem. To whom is the persona speaking?
2. What could have caused the "Sea of Faith" to be retreating like the tide? Note the date of the poem.

3. What does the persona pose as a solution to the loss of religious faith?
4. Write an essay in which you argue that the images of sound and sight—or lack of sight—contribute to the effectiveness of the poem.

Emily Dickinson 1830–1886

Emily Dickinson is among the greatest of American poets. During most of her adult life, she was a recluse, confining herself to her father's home in Amherst, Massachusetts, wearing only white and shunning company. She produced more than 1,700 lyrics, which are characterized by startling imagery, ellipses, and unexpected juxtapositions. Only seven of her poems were published in her lifetime—and those without her permission. Her influence is still felt in modern poetry.

Faith Is a Fine Invention

Faith is a fine invention
For Gentlemen who *see*.
But *Microscopes* are prudent—
In an Emergency!

(1860)

Questions for Discussion and Writing

1. Consider "invention" as a key word choice. What kinds of things are usually called inventions? What does the word imply about faith?
2. According to the poem, when are microscopes better tools than faith? Why might this be so? How do microscopes improve on vision?
3. Write a paragraph interpreting this poem as a satire.

I'm Nobody! Who Are You?

I'm Nobody! Who are you?
Are you—Nobody—Too?
Then there's a pair of us!
Don't tell! they'd banish us—you know!

How dreary—to be—Somebody!
How public—like a Frog—
To tell your name—the livelong June—
To an admiring Bog!

(1861)

Questions for Discussion and Writing

1. Who are "they" in the first stanza? In what way would they "banish us"?
2. Explain the simile about the frog in the final stanza. What makes it effective?
3. What kind of person is the speaker in the poem? Do you know anyone like that? Are you perhaps a private person yourself, or are you an extrovert? Write a statement explaining why you want—or don't want—to be in the public eye.

He Put the Belt Around My Life

He put the Belt around my life—
I heard the Buckle snap—
And turned away, imperial,
My Lifetime folding up—
Deliberate, as a Duke would do
A Kingdom's Title Deed—
Henceforth, a Dedicated sort—
A Member of the Cloud.

Yet not too far to come at call—
And do the little Toils
That make the Circuit of the Rest—
And deal occasional smiles
To lives that stoop to notice mine—
And kindly ask it in—
Whose invitation, know you not
For Whom I must decline?

(ca. 1861)

Questions for Discussion and Writing

1. Who is the "He" in the poem? How does the persona feel toward him?
2. What could it mean to be a "Member of the Cloud"?
3. How would you describe the attitude of the persona? Polite? Modest? Submissive?
4. Write about an occasion when someone in authority (parent, teacher, law officer) put restrictions on your freedom. What was your response? Do you wish now that you had reacted differently?

Much Madness Is Divinest Sense

Much Madness is divinest Sense—
To a discerning Eye—
Much Sense—the starkest Madness—

'Tis the Majority
In this, as All, prevail—
Assent—and you are sane—
Demur—you're straightway dangerous—
And handled with a Chain—

(ca. 1862)

Questions for Discussion and Writing

1. Can you think of an example, perhaps historical, of something that was considered madness that turned out to be the truth?
2. Can you think of something that is accepted by most people in society that you consider "madness"?
3. What does Dickinson mean by "handled with a Chain"?

Because I Could Not Stop for Death

Because I could not stop for Death—
He kindly stopped for me—
The Carriage held but just Ourselves—
And Immortality—

We slowly drove—He knew no haste
And I had put away
My labor and my leisure too,
For His Civility—

We passed the School, where Children strove
At Recess—in the Ring—
We passed the Fields of Gazing Grain—
We passed the Setting Sun—

Or rather—He passed Us—
The Dews drew quivering and chill—
For only Gossamer,° my Gown
My Tippet°—only Tulle°—

We paused before a House that seemed
A Swelling of the Ground—
The Roof was scarcely visible—
The Cornice—in the Ground—

Since then—'tis Centuries—and yet
Feels shorter than the Day
I first surmised the Horses' Heads
Were toward Eternity—

(ca. 1863)

---

15 Gossamer Thin, sheer. **16 Tippet** Short cape covering just the shoulders. **Tulle** Soft net fabric.

Questions for Discussion and Writing

1. What is the action described in the poem? What do the images in stanza 3 suggest? What is the "House" in lines 17–20?
2. Death is personified in the poem. What sort of person is he?
3. What is the persona's attitude toward death?
4. Can you state a theme for the poem?

Some Keep the Sabbath Going to Church

Some keep the Sabbath going to Church—
I keep it, staying at Home—
With a Bobolink for a Chorister—
And an Orchard, for a Dome—

Some keep the Sabbath in Surplice—
I just wear my Wings—
And instead of tolling the Bell, for Church,
Our little Sexton—sings.

God preaches, a noted Clergyman—
And the sermon is never long
So instead of getting to Heaven, at last—
I'm going, all along.

(1864)

Questions for Discussion and Writing

1. Describe the persona in the poem.
2. How does the speaker celebrate the sabbath? Point out the contrasts with conventional religious observance.
3. What is the tone of the poem? Does it have a theme?

Wild Nights—Wild Nights!

Wild Nights—Wild Nights!
Were I with thee
Wild Nights should be
Our luxury!

Futile—the Winds—
To a Heart in port—
Done with the Compass—
Done with the Chart!

Rowing in Eden—
Ah, the Sea!
Might I but moor—Tonight—
In Thee!

(1861)

Questions for Discussion and Writing

1. What is the speaker looking forward to in this poem?
2. What does the word *luxury* mean in line 4?
3. Paraphrase the second stanza, adding any words that may have been omitted.
4. Explain the image of "a Heart in port" in stanza 2.
5. What does the speaker long for in the last two lines?

Gerard Manley Hopkins 1844–1889

Gerard Manley Hopkins was a major poet who was not recognized during his lifetime. Born in Essex, England, he attended Oxford, converted to Catholicism, and became a Jesuit priest. He died of typhoid fever at age forty-four, having never published his poetry. Nearly thirty years later, a friend brought out Hopkins's *Poems* (1918), and he has since been acknowledged as a major poet.

Pied Beauty

Glory be to God for dappled things—
For skies of couple-color as a brinded° cow;
For rose-moles all in stipple° upon trout that swim;
Fresh-firecoal chestnut-falls;° finches' wings;
Landscape plotted and pieced—fold, fallow, and plow;
And áll trádes, their gear and tackle and trim.°

All things counter, original, spare, strange;
Whatever is fickle, freckled (who knows how?)
With swift, slow; sweet, sour; adazzle, dim;
He fathers-forth whose beauty is past change:
Praise him.

(1877)

2 brinded Striped. **3 stipple** Small dots. **4 chestnut-falls** Chestnuts fresh from the fire with their hulls off. **6 trim** Tools.

Questions for Discussion and Writing

1. What words in the poem did Hopkins coin?
2. Can you describe what he means by "Landscape plotted and pieced"?
3. Why does the poet praise things made by human hands as well as things in nature?

Spring and Fall

To a Young Child

Márgarét áre you gríeving
Over Goldengrove unleaving?
Leáves, líke the things of man, you
With your fresh thoughts care for, can you?
Áh! ás the heart grows older
It will come to such sights colder
By and by, nor spare a sigh
Though worlds of wanwood°leafmeal° lie;
And yet you *will* weep and know why.
Now no matter, child, the name:
Sórrow's springs áre the same.
Nor mouth had, no nor mind, expressed
What heart heard of, ghost° guessed:
It ís the blight man was born for,
It is Margaret you mourn for.

(1880)

8 wanwood Pale woods, as though bloodless. **leafmeal** Fallen leaf by leaf. **13 ghost** Spirit, soul.

Questions for Discussion and Writing

1. What does Hopkins mean in his unusual phrase "Goldengrove unleaving"? In other words, why is Margaret grieving?
2. Does the fall of the leaves suggest any other kind of fall, perhaps a metaphorical one?
3. Explain why Margaret is, in effect, mourning for herself.

A. E. Housman 1859–1936

See pages 506–07 for a biographical note about this author.

To an Athlete Dying Young

The time you won your town the race
We chaired you through the market-place;
Man and boy stood cheering by,
And home we brought you shoulder-high.

To-day, the road all runners come,
Shoulder-high we bring you home,
And set you at your threshold down,
Townsman of a stiller town.

Smart lad, to slip betimes away
From fields where glory does not stay,
And early though the laurel grows
It withers quicker than the rose.

Eyes the shady night has shut
Cannot see the record cut,
And silence sounds no worse than cheers
After earth has stopped the ears.

Now you will not swell the rout
Of lads that wore their honors out,
Runners whom renown outran
And the name died before the man.

So set, before its echoes fade,
The fleet foot on the sill of shade,
And hold to the low lintel° up
The still-defended challenge-cup.

And round that early-laurelled° head
Will flock to gaze the strengthless dead,
And find unwithered on its curls
The garland briefer than a girl's.

(1896)

---

23 lintel Horizontal support above a door. **25 laurelled** In ancient times victors were crowned with laurel wreaths.

Questions for Discussion and Writing

1. What is "the road all runners come" in line 5? What is that "stiller town" the road leads to? What is the significance of the laurel in line 11?
2. How valuable is the approbation the lad receives in the final stanza? Would it have been worth dying for?
3. What point do you think Housman is making here?

Loveliest of Trees

Loveliest of trees, the cherry now
Is hung with bloom along the bough,
And stands about the woodland ride,°
Wearing white for Eastertide.

Now, of my threescore years and ten,
Twenty will not come again,
And take from seventy springs a score,
It only leaves me fifty more.

And since to look at things in bloom
Fifty springs are little room,
About the woodlands I will go
To see the cherry hung with snow.

(1896)

3 ride Path.

Questions for Discussion and Writing

1. How old is the speaker in the poem?
2. What associations can you make with the white blossoms in the first stanza and with "snow," the last word in the poem?
3. Does the poem have a theme? If so, can you state it?

William Butler Yeats 1865–1939

One of the most important poets of the twentieth century, William Butler Yeats was born near Dublin, attended art school for a time, but quit to devote himself to poetry, plays, and politics. He served as a senator in the Irish Free State (1922–1928), helped found the Irish National Theatre Society at the now famous Abbey Theatre, and was awarded the Nobel Prize for Literature in 1923.

The Second Coming

Turning and turning in the widening gyre°
The falcon cannot hear the falconer;
Things fall apart; the centre cannot hold;
Mere anarchy is loosed upon the world,
The blood-dimmed tide is loosed, and everywhere
The ceremony of innocence is drowned;
The best lack all conviction, while the worst

1 gyre A spiral motion, used by Yeats to suggest the cycles of history.

Are full of passionate intensity.

Surely some revelation is at hand;
Surely the Second Coming is at hand.
The Second Coming! Hardly are those words out
When a vast image out of *Spiritus Mundi*°
Troubles my sight: somewhere in sands of the desert
A shape with lion body and the head of a man,
A gaze blank and pitiless as the sun,
Is moving its slow thighs, while all about it
Reel shadows of the indignant desert birds.
The darkness drops again; but now I know
That twenty centuries of stony sleep
Were vexed to nightmare by a rocking cradle,
And what rough beast, its hour come round at last,
Slouches towards Bethlehem to be born?

(1921)

12 Spiritus Mundi The Soul of the World, a collective unconscious from which humans draw memories, symbols, dreams.

Questions for Discussion and Writing

1. What is the state of the world being described by the speaker in the first stanza?
2. What does the "ceremony of innocence" suggest?
3. Why does Yeats envision the "rough beast" as coming from the desert? What associations can you make with a desert?
4. Can you explain lines 19 and 20? Whose rocking cradle is it?
5. Write a brief essay explaining what the beast represents.

Sailing to Byzantium°*

That is no country for old men. The young
In one another's arms, birds in the trees
—Those dying generations—at their song,
The salmon-falls, the mackerel-crowded seas,
Fish, flesh, or fowl, commend all summer long
Whatever is begotten, born, and dies.
Caught in that sensual music all neglect
Monuments of unaging intellect.

An agéd man is but a paltry thing,
A tattered coat upon a stick, unless
Soul clap its hands and sing, and louder sing

Title: The capital of the Byzantine Empire, the city now called Istanbul; for Yeats, a symbol of life perfected by art.

For every tatter in its mortal dress,
Nor is there singing school but studying
Monuments of its own magnificence;
And therefore I have sailed the seas and come
To the holy city of Byzantium.

O sages standing in God's holy fire
As in the gold mosaic of a wall,
Come from the holy fire, perne in a gyre,°
And be the singing-masters of my soul.
Consume my heart away; sick with desire
And fastened to a dying animal
It knows not what it is; and gather me
Into the artifice of eternity.

Once out of nature I shall never take
My bodily form from any natural thing,
But such a form as Grecian goldsmiths make
Of hammered gold and gold enamelling
To keep a drowsy Emperor awake;
Or set upon a golden bough to sing
To lords and ladies of Byzantium
Of what is past, or passing, or to come.

(1928)

---

19 gyre The spiraling motion that Yeats associates with the whirling of fate; see "The Second Coming."

Questions for Discussion and Writing

1. What does the imagery in the first stanza suggest? Why does Yeats describe the young as "those dying generations"? Do you know the Renaissance meaning for the word "die"?
2. What is that "country" referred to in the first line?
3. Why does the speaker want to sail to Byzantium? Can you explain what Byzantium symbolizes? Why is it a perfect choice?
4. What is the "dying animal" in line 22 that the speaker wants to be freed from?
5. Write a paper explaining how the images interrelate to give the poem an almost perfect unity.

Paul Laurence Dunbar 1872–1906

Paul Laurence Dunbar was born in Dayton, Ohio, the son of former slaves. He graduated from high school but could not afford college and worked instead as an elevator operator. He published his first two books of poetry with his own money. Following the appearance of *Lyrics of Lowly Life* (1896), he became the first African American poet to win national recognition.

We Wear the Mask

We wear the mask that grins and lies,
It hides our cheeks and shades our eyes,—
This debt we pay to human guile;
With torn and bleeding hearts we smile,
And mouth with myriad subtleties.

Why should the world be overwise,
In counting all our tears and sighs?
Nay, let them only see us, while
    We wear the mask.

We smile, but, O great Christ, our cries
To thee from tortured souls arise.
We sing, but oh the clay is vile
Beneath our feet, and long the mile;
But let the world dream otherwise,
    We wear the mask!

(1895)

Questions for Discussion and Writing

1. Who is speaking in the poem? Who are the "we"?
2. The poet doesn't say why the mask is necessary. Can you tell why?
3. How would you state the theme of this poem?
4. People often appear happy although they are secretly seething over some real or imagined wrong—especially people who have little power, like children, women, or the members of minority groups. If you have ever had such an experience, describe it in writing and try to explain just how the incident made you feel. How do your feelings match those expressed in Dunbar's poem?

Robert Frost 1874–1963

See page 509 for a biographical note about this poet.

Mending Wall

Something there is that doesn't love a wall,
That sends the frozen-ground-swell under it
And spills the upper boulders in the sun,
And makes gaps even two can pass abreast.

The work of hunters is another thing:
I have come after them and made repair
Where they have left not one stone on a stone,
But they would have the rabbit out of hiding,
To please the yelping dogs. The gaps I mean,
No one has seen them made or heard them made,
But at spring mending-time we find them there.
I let my neighbor know beyond the hill;
And on a day we meet to walk the line
And set the wall between us once again.
We keep the wall between us as we go.
To each the boulders that have fallen to each.
And some are loaves and some so nearly balls
We have to use a spell to make them balance:
"Stay where you are until our backs are turned!"
We wear our fingers rough with handling them.
Oh, just another kind of outdoor game,
One on a side. It comes to little more:
There where it is we do not need the wall:
He is all pine and I am apple orchard.
My apple trees will never get across
And eat the cones under his pines, I tell him.
He only says, "Good fences make good neighbors."
Spring is the mischief in me, and I wonder
If I could put a notion in his head:
"*Why* do they make good neighbors? Isn't it
Where there are cows? But here there are no cows.
Before I built a wall I'd ask to know
What I was walling in or walling out,
And to whom I was like to give offense.
Something there is that doesn't love a wall,
That wants it down." I could say "Elves" to him,
But it's not elves exactly, and I'd rather
He said it for himself. I see him there,
Bringing a stone grasped firmly by the top
In each hand, like an old-stone savage armed.
He moves in darkness as it seems to me,
Not of woods only and the shade of trees.
He will not go behind his father's saying,
And he likes having thought of it so well
He says again, "Good fences make good neighbors."
(1914)

Questions for Discussion and Writing

1. Who is the speaker in the poem? What sort of person is he or she? What sort of person is the neighbor?
2. The line "Something there is that doesn't love a wall" appears twice. Why? What does the line mean? Does it state the poem's theme?

3. How does the speaker feel about walls? About hunters?
4. Do "Good fences make good neighbors," or are they "like to give offense"? Write an essay arguing your views on this issue.

Birches

When I see birches bend to left and right
Across the lines of straighter darker trees,
I like to think some boy's been swinging them.
But swinging doesn't bend them down to stay
As ice-storms do. Often you must have seen them
Loaded with ice a sunny winter morning
After a rain. They click upon themselves
As the breeze rises, and turn many-colored
As the stir cracks and crazes their enamel.
Soon the sun's warmth makes them shed crystal shells
Shattering and avalanching on the snow-crust—
Such heaps of broken glass to sweep away
You'd think the inner dome of heaven had fallen.
They are dragged to the withered bracken by the load,
And they seem not to break; though once they are bowed
So low for long, they never right themselves:
You may see their trunks arching in the woods
Years afterwards, trailing their leaves on the ground
Like girls on hands and knees that throw their hair
Before them over their heads to dry in the sun.
But I was going to say when Truth broke in
With all her matter-of-fact about the ice-storm,
I should prefer to have some boy bend them
As he went out and in to fetch the cows—
Some boy too far from town to learn baseball,
Whose only play was what he found himself,
Summer or winter, and could play alone.
One by one he subdued his father's trees
By riding them down over and over again
Until he took the stiffness out of them,
And not one but hung limp, not one was left
For him to conquer. He learned all there was
To learn about not launching out too soon
And so not carrying the tree away
Clear to the ground. He always kept his poise
To the top branches, climbing carefully
With the same pains you use to fill a cup
Up to the brim, and even above the brim.
Then he flung outward, feet first, with a swish,
Kicking his way down through the air to the ground.
So was I once myself a swinger of birches.

And so I dream of going back to be.
It's when I'm weary of considerations,
And life is too much like a pathless wood
Where your face burns and tickles with the cobwebs
Broken across it, and one eye is weeping
From a twig's having lashed across it open.
I'd like to get away from earth awhile
And then come back to it and begin over.
May no fate willfully misunderstand me
And half grant what I wish and snatch me away
Not to return. Earth's the right place for love:
I don't know where it's likely to go better.
I'd like to go by climbing a birch tree,
And climb black branches up a snow-white trunk,
Toward heaven, till the tree could bear no more,
But dipped its top and set me down again.
That would be good both going and coming back.
One could do worse than be a swinger of birches.

(1916)

Questions for Discussion and Writing

1. Why does the speaker prefer to think that the birches have been bent by boys instead of by ice storms? Refer to lines 23 to 27 for his image of the boy.
2. Explain the extended comparison in lines 41 through 49.
3. Why does the speaker insist that he would want to return to earth? He says, "Earth's the right place for love." Do you agree? What does this statement imply about the speaker's philosophy of life? How do you interpret the last line in terms of how one should live?
4. Write a short essay or long poem about some childhood pleasure you wish you could sometimes recapture.

"Out, Out—"

The buzz saw snarled and rattled in the yard
And made dust and dropped stove-length sticks of wood,
Sweet-scented stuff when the breeze drew across it.
And from there those that lifted eyes could count
Five mountain ranges one behind the other
Under the sunset far into Vermont.
And the saw snarled and rattled, snarled and rattled,
As it ran light, or had to bear a load.
And nothing happened: day was all but done.
Call it a day, I wish they might have said
To please the boy by giving him the half hour

That a boy counts so much when saved from work.
His sister stood beside them in her apron
To tell them 'Supper.' At the word, the saw,
As if to prove saws knew what supper meant,
Leaped out at the boy's hand, or seemed to leap—
He must have given the hand. However it was,
Neither refused the meeting. But the hand!
The boy's first outcry was a rueful laugh,
As he swung toward them holding up the hand
Half in appeal, but half as if to keep
The life from spilling. Then the boy saw all—
Since he was old enough to know, big boy
Doing a man's work, though a child at heart—
He saw all spoiled. 'Don't let him cut my hand off—
The doctor, when he comes. Don't let him, sister!'
So. But the hand was gone already.
The doctor put him in the dark of ether.
He lay and puffed his lips out with his breath.
And then—the watcher at his pulse took fright.
No one believed. They listened at his heart.
Little—less—nothing!—and that ended it.
No more to build on there. And they, since they
Were not the one dead, turned to their affairs.

(1916)

Questions for Discussion and Writing

1. Who is speaking this narrative poem? Why are the characters not named?
2. What does Frost achieve by personifying the saw?
3. What is the theme of the poem?
4. The title is an allusion to Shakespeare's *Macbeth*, Act 5, Scene 5, lines 23–28. Look up the passage and explain in writing how the title refers to the meaning of the poem.

Fire and Ice

Some say the world will end in fire,
Some say in ice.
From what I've tasted of desire
I hold with those who favor fire.
But if it had to perish twice,
I think I know enough of hate
To say that for destruction ice
Is also great
And would suffice.

(1923)

Questions for Discussion and Writing

1. Why does the persona associate "fire" with desire and "ice" with hate?
2. Why does he choose "fire" and "ice" as the two possible ways that the world might end?
3. How does the word "suffice" as a rhyme for "ice" affect the meaning of the poem?

Design

I found a dimpled spider, fat and white,
On a white heal-all,° holding up a moth
Like a white piece of rigid satin cloth—
Assorted characters of death and blight
Mixed ready to begin the morning right,
Like the ingredients of a witches' broth—
A snow-drop spider, a flower like a froth,
And dead wings carried like a paper kite.

What had that flower to do with being white,
The wayside blue and innocent heal-all?
What brought the kindred spider to that height,
Then steered the white moth thither in the night?
What but design of darkness to appall?—
If design govern in a thing so small.

(1936)

2 heal-all A low-growing plant, usually having violet-blue flowers.

Questions for Discussion and Writing

1. How does the title relate to the poem?
2. What associations do you get from the words used to describe the spider? How do you usually think of spiders?
3. What do the speaker's questions lead you to consider? What answers does the poem suggest?
4. Write an essay interpreting Frost's ironic use of white in the poem.

Carl Sandburg 1878–1967

Carl Sandburg was born in Galesburg, Illinois, and worked as a day laborer, soldier, political activist, and journalist. These experiences provided a rich palette of poetic colors to select from, and Sandburg painted boldly in vigorous free verse. He also wrote an acclaimed six-volume biography of Abraham Lincoln.

Fog

The fog comes
on little cat feet.

It sits looking
over harbor and city
on silent haunches
and then moves on.
(1916)

Questions for Discussion and Writing

1. Does this poem have a theme? What do you think its purpose is?
2. Compare this poem with the fog-as-cat image in lines 15 through 23 of Eliot's "The Love Song of J. Alfred Prufrock" (page 603). Which do you think puts a better picture in your mind?

Chicago

Hog Butcher for the World,
Tool Maker, Stacker of Wheat,
Player with Railroads and the Nation's Freight Handler;
Stormy, husky, brawling,
City of the Big Shoulders:
They tell me you are wicked and I believe them, for I have seen
your painted women under the gas lamps luring the farm boys.
And they tell me you are crooked and I answer: Yes, it is true I
have seen the gunman kill and go free to kill again.
And they tell me you are brutal and my reply is: On the faces of
women and children I have seen the marks of wanton hunger.
And having answered so I turn once more to those who sneer at this
my city, and I give them back the sneer and say to them:
Come and show me another city with lifted head singing so proud
to be alive and coarse and strong and cunning.
Flinging magnetic curses amid the toil of piling job on job, here is a tall
bold slugger set vivid against the little soft cities;
Fierce as a dog with tongue lapping for action, cunning as a savage
pitted against the wilderness,
Bareheaded,
Shoveling,
Wrecking,
Planning,
Building, breaking, rebuilding,
Under the smoke, dust all over his mouth, laughing with white teeth,
Under the terrible burden of destiny laughing as a young man laughs,

Laughing even as an ignorant fighter laughs who has never lost a battle,
Bragging and laughing that under his wrist is the pulse, and under his
ribs the heart of the people,
Laughing!
Laughing the stormy, husky, brawling laughter of Youth, half-naked,
sweating, proud to be Hog Butcher, Tool Maker, Stacker of
Wheat, Player with Railroads and Freight Handler to the Nation.

(1914)

Questions for Discussion and Writing

1. What are the defining characteristics of Sandburg's Chicago?
2. How does he handle the city's obvious drawbacks—its violence and brutality?
3. What makes this piece a poem? That is, what elements of poetry are functioning in this unpoetic-sounding poem?
4. Write an essay arguing for or against the effectiveness of Sandburg's personification of the city in the poem. Does it work throughout, or do you find it strained at times?

William Carlos Williams 1883–1963

William Carlos Williams spent almost his entire life as a physician in Rutherford, New Jersey. The "inarticulate poems" that he heard in the words of his patients inspired him to write, jotting down lines and phrases whenever he could find a moment. Williams wrote about common objects and experiences and imbued them with spiritual qualities. His works include *Pictures from Brueghel* (1962), which won a Pulitzer Prize, and his masterpiece, *Paterson* (1946–1958), a poem in five volumes.

Danse Russe

If when my wife is sleeping
and the baby and Kathleen
are sleeping
and the sun is a flame-white disc
in silken mists
above shining trees,—
if I in my north room
dance naked, grotesquely
before my mirror
waving my shirt round my head
and singing softly to myself:
"I am lonely, lonely.

I was born to be lonely,
I am best so!"
If I admire my arms, my face,
my shoulders, flanks, buttocks
against the yellow drawn shades,—
Who shall say I am not
the happy genius of my household?
(1916)

Questions for Discussion and Writing

1. What does the French phrase *Danse Russe* mean? Why do you think Williams chose that title for this poem?
2. Where is the speaker and what time is it?
3. Why is he dancing naked?

The Red Wheelbarrow

so much depends
upon

a red wheel
barrow

glazed with rain
water

beside the white
chickens.
(1923)

Questions for Discussion and Writing

1. Does the poem need to be interpreted, or should readers just enjoy the sharply revealed images?
2. What makes this a poem? Do you consider it a successful one?
3. Write your own "so much depends" passage or poem.

D. H. Lawrence 1885–1930

See page 267 for a biographical note about this author.

Piano

Softly, in the dusk, a woman is singing to me;
Taking me back down the vista of years, till I see
A child sitting under the piano, in the boom of the tingling strings
And pressing the small, poised feet of a mother who smiles as she sings.

In spite of myself, the insidious mastery of song
Betrays me back, till the heart of me weeps to belong
To the old Sunday evenings at home, with winter outside
And hymns in the cozy parlour, the tinkling piano our guide.

So now it is vain for the singer to burst into clamour
With the great black piano appassionato. The glamour
Of childish days is upon me, my manhood is cast
Down in the flood of remembrance, I weep like a child for the past.

(1918)

Questions for Discussion and Writing

1. Where is the speaker in the first line of the poem? In line 3?
2. Who is the woman in the first line? In line 4?
3. The speaker resists crying because in 1918 it was considered unmanly to weep. Does he try for any other reason to stem "the flood of remembrance"?

T. S. Eliot 1888–1965

Born in St. Louis, T(homas) S(tearns) Eliot studied at Harvard and emigrated to London, where he worked as a bank clerk and as an editor. In 1927 he became a British citizen and joined the Church of England. His landmark poem *The Waste Land* (1922) influenced a generation of young poets. As a critic, he revived interest in John Donne and other metaphysical poets. In later years, he wrote verse plays, such as *Murder in the Cathedral* (1935) and *The Cocktail Party* (1950), and won the Nobel Prize for Literature in 1948.

The Love Song of J. Alfred Prufrock

S'io credesse che mia risposta fosse
A persona che mai tornasse al mondo,
Questa fiamma staria senza piu scosse.
Ma perciocche giammai di questo fondo

Non torno vivo alcun, s'i'odo il vero,
Senze tema d'infamia ti rispondo.°

Let us go then, you and I,
When the evening is spread out against the sky
Like a patient etherised upon a table;
Let us go, through certain half-deserted streets,
The muttering retreats
Of restless nights in one-night cheap hotels
And sawdust restaurants with oyster-shells:
Streets that follow like a tedious argument
Of insidious intent
To lead you to an overwhelming question…
Oh, do not ask, "What is it?"
Let us go and make our visit.

In the room the women come and go
Talking of Michelangelo.

The yellow fog that rubs its back upon the window-panes,
The yellow smoke that rubs its muzzle on the window-panes
Licked its tongue into the corners of the evening,
Lingered upon the pools that stand in drains,
Let fall upon its back the soot that falls from chimneys,
Slipped by the terrace, made a sudden leap,
And seeing that it was a soft October night,
Curled once about the house, and fell asleep.

And indeed there will be time
For the yellow smoke that slides along the street
Rubbing its back upon the window-panes;
There will be time, there will be time
To prepare a face to meet the faces that you meet;
There will be time to murder and create,
And time for all the works and days of hands
That lift and drop a question on your plate;
Time for you and time for me,
And time yet for a hundred indecisions,
And for a hundred visions and revisions,
Before the taking of a toast and tea.

In the room the women come and go
Talking of Michelangelo.

And indeed there will be time
To wonder, "Do I dare? " and, "Do I dare?"
Time to turn back and descend the stair,
With a bald spot in the middle of my hair—
(They will say: "How his hair is growing thin!")
My morning coat, my collar mounting firmly to the chin,

Epigraph: From Dante's *Inferno*—the speech of one dead and damned, Count Guido da Montefe, who thinks his hearer is also going to remain in hell; he offers to tell Dante his story: "If I thought my reply were to someone who could ever return to the world, this flame would waver no more. But since, I'm told, nobody ever escapes from this pit, I'll tell you without fear of ill fame."

My necktie rich and modest, but asserted by a simple pin—
(They will say: "But how his arms and legs are thin!")
Do I dare
Disturb the universe?
In a minute there is time
For decisions and revisions which a minute will reverse.

For I have known them all already, known them all—
Have known the evenings, mornings, afternoons,
I have measured out my life with coffee spoons;
I know the voices dying with a dying fall
Beneath the music from a farther room.
    So how should I presume?

And I have known the eyes already, known them all—
The eyes that fix you in a formulated phrase,
And when I am formulated, sprawling on a pin,
When I am pinned and wriggling on the wall,
Then how should I begin
To spit out all the butt-ends of my days and ways?
    And how should I presume?

And I have known the arms already, known them all—
Arms that are braceleted and white and bare
(But in the lamplight, downed with light brown hair!)
Is it perfume from a dress
That makes me so digress?
Arms that lie along a table, or wrap about a shawl.
    And should I then presume?
    And how should I begin?

. . . .

Shall I say, I have gone at dusk through narrow streets
And watched the smoke that rises from the pipes
Of lonely men in shirt-sleeves, leaning out of windows? . . .
I should have been a pair of ragged claws
Scuttling across the floors of silent seas.

. . . .

And the afternoon, the evening, sleeps so peacefully!
Smoothed by long fingers,
Asleep . . . tired . . . or it malingers,
Stretched on the floor, here beside you and me.
Should I, after tea and cakes and ices,
Have the strength to force the moment to its crisis?
But though I have wept and fasted, wept and prayed,
Though I have seen my head (grown slightly bald) brought in upon a
    platter,°
I am no prophet—and here's no great matter;
I have seen the moment of my greatness flicker,

---

82 upon a platter The head of John the Baptist was presented to Salome on a platter. See Matthew 14:1–11.

And I have seen the eternal Footman hold my coat, and snicker,
And in short, I was afraid.

And would it have been worth it, after all,
After the cups, the marmalade, the tea,
Among the porcelain, among some talk of you and me,
Would it have been worth while,
To have bitten off the matter with a smile,
To have squeezed the universe into a ball
To roll it toward some overwhelming question,
To say: "I am Lazarus,° come from the dead,
Come back to tell you all, I shall tell you all"—
If one, settling a pillow by her head,
    Should say: "That is not what I meant at all;
    That is not it, at all."
And would it have been worth it, after all,
Would it have been worth while,
After the sunsets and the dooryards and the sprinkled streets,
After the novels, after the teacups, after the skirts that trail along the
    floor—
And this, and so much more?—
It is impossible to say just what I mean!
But as if a magic lantern threw the nerves in patterns on a screen:
Would it have been worth while
If one, settling a pillow or throwing off a shawl,
And turning toward the window, should say:
"That is not it at all,
That is not what I meant, at all."

. . . .

No! I am not Prince Hamlet, nor was meant to be;
Am an attendant lord, one that will do
To swell a progress, start a scene or two,
Advise the prince; no doubt, an easy tool,
Deferential, glad to be of use,
Politic, cautious, and meticulous;
Full of high sentence, but a bit obtuse;
At times, indeed, almost ridiculous—
Almost, at times, the Fool.

I grow old . . . I grow old . . .
I shall wear the bottoms of my trousers rolled.

Shall I part my hair behind? Do I dare to eat a peach?
I shall wear white flannel trousers, and walk upon the beach.
I have heard the mermaids singing, each to each.

I do not think that they will sing to me.

I have seen them riding seaward on the waves
Combing the white hair of the waves blown back
When the wind blows the water white and black.

---

94 Lazarus Jesus raised Lazarus from the dead. See John 11:1–41.

We have lingered in the chambers of the sea
By sea-girls wreathed with seaweed red and brown
Till human voices wake us, and we drown.

(1917)

Questions for Discussion and Writing

1. Who is speaking in the poem and to whom?
2. What is the situation depicted?
3. What sort of person is J. Alfred Prufrock? Why is he so wary about going to this party? Why does he consider parting his hair behind? What does it mean to measure out one's life with coffee spoons? Why do women make him so nervous? Why does he think he should have been a crab, "Scuttling across the floors of silent seas"? Why does he exaggerate so? Is he right in deciding that he's more like Polonius than Hamlet? Why does he wonder if he dares to eat a peach? Why does he decide the mermaids will not sing to him?

Claude McKay 1890–1948

Claude McKay was born in Sunny Ville, Jamaica. At the age of twenty-three, he moved to the United States, where he encountered the strong racial prejudice prevalent during this period. A prominent figure in the Harlem Renaissance, McKay was a catalyst among African American writers, preaching black vitality and social reform. He wrote four volumes of poetry, including *If We Must Die* (1919); a novel, *Home to Harlem* (1928); and an autobiography, *A Long Way from Home* (1937).

America

Although she feeds me bread of bitterness,
And sinks into my throat her tiger's tooth,
Stealing my breath of life, I will confess
I love this cultured hell that tests my youth!
Her vigor flows like tides into my blood,
Giving me strength erect against her hate.
Her bigness sweeps my being like a flood,
Yet as a rebel fronts a king in state,
I stand within her walls with not a shred
Of terror, malice, not a word of jeer.
Darkly I gaze into the days ahead,
And see her might and granite wonders there,
Beneath the touch of Time's unerring hand,
Like priceless treasures sinking in the sand.

(1920)

Questions for Discussion and Writing

1. Who is speaking in this poem?
2. Explain the metaphors in the first three lines.
3. What does the speaker love about America? What does he regard as a threat to her strength?

Edna St. Vincent Millay 1892–1950

Born in Maine and educated at Vassar, Edna St. Vincent Millay moved in 1917 to Greenwich Village and published her first book of poetry, *Renascence and Other Poems*. She won the Pulitzer Prize for *The Harp-Weaver* (1922), a collection of sonnets that deal wittily and flippantly with love. Although Millay became politically involved and used her poetry to speak out for social causes, she is known best for her poems about the bittersweet emotions of love and the brevity of life.

Oh, Oh, You Will Be Sorry for That Word!

Oh, oh, you will be sorry for that word!
Give back my book and take my kiss instead.
Was it my enemy or my friend I heard,
"What a big book for such a little head!"
Come, I will show you now my newest hat,
And you may watch me purse my mouth and prink!
Oh, I shall love you still, and all of that.
I never again shall tell you what I think.
I shall be sweet and crafty, soft and sly;
You will not catch me reading any more:
I shall be called a wife to pattern by;
And some day when you knock and push the door,
Some sane day, not too bright and not too stormy,
I shall be gone, and you may whistle for me.

(1923)

Questions for Discussion and Writing

1. Why is the speaker in the poem angry?
2. What does she plan to do in response to the insult?
3. In 1923 when the poem was written, what qualities would have been expected of "a wife to pattern by" (line 11)?

First Fig

My candle burns at both ends;
  It will not last the night;
But ah, my foes, and oh, my friends—
  It gives a lovely light!

(1920)

Questions for Discussion and Writing

1. Explain the metaphor in this little poem.
2. What is the attitude of the speaker? How do you know?
3. Why is the poem called "First Fig"?

E. E. Cummings 1894–1962

See page 507 for a biographical note about this author.

in Just-

in Just-
spring when the world is mud-
luscious the little
lame balloonman

whistles far and wee

and eddieandbill come
running from marbles and
piracies and it's
spring.

when the world is puddle-wonderful

the queer
old balloonman whistles

far and wee
and bettyandisbel come dancing

from hop-scotch and jump-rope and
it's
spring
and

  the

goat-footed°

balloonMan whistles
far
and
wee

(1923)

20 goat-footed The Greek god Pan, portrayed with the body of a man and the legs of a goat.

Questions for Discussion and Writing

1. Which children's names are run together? Which are separated? What activities is each pair engaged in before heeding the balloonman's whistle? Considering your answers to these questions, what does the poem emphasize about the children?
2. What do you know about the goat-footed god Pan? If you can't place him, look him up. Why is the balloonman described as Pan-like?
3. What is the powerful whistle that makes kids come running from their play? In other words, what is calling "far and wee" to the children? The change in the typography of balloonMan in line 21 may give you a clue.

pity this busy monster,manunkind

pity this busy monster,manunkind,

not. Progress is a comfortable disease:
your victim (death and life safely beyond)

plays with the bigness of his littleness
—electrons deify one razorblade
into a mountainrange; lenses extend

unwish through curving wherewhen till unwish
return on its unself.

A world of made
is not a world of born—pity poor flesh

and trees,poor stars and stones, but never this
fine specimen of hypermagical

ultraomnipotence. We doctors know

a hopeless case if—listen:there's a hell
of a good universe next door; let's go

(1944)

Questions for Discussion and Writing

1. How does the speaker define "Progress"? What extended metaphor is used?
2. Paraphrase the lines "A world of made / is not a world of born." What distinction do these lines stress? Why is that distinction so important?

3. What does the poem suggest about technological advancement? Write a short essay agreeing or disagreeing with the claim.

Jean Toomer 1894–1967

Jean Toomer grew up in Washington, D.C., attended several colleges, and worked briefly as the headmaster of a black school in Georgia. His best-known work, *Cane* (1923), combines poetry, fiction, and drama into an artistic vision of the black American experience. Widely acclaimed for its innovative style and penetrating insights, *Cane* is one of the most important works of the Harlem Renaissance, although Toomer later disavowed any connection with that movement.

Reapers

Black reapers with the sound of steel on stones
Are sharpening scythes. I see them place the hones°
In their hip-pockets as a thing that's done,
And start their silent swinging, one by one.

Black horses drive a mower through the weeds,
And there, a field rat, startled, squealing bleeds,
His belly close to ground. I see the blade,
Blood-stained, continue cutting weeds and shade.

(1923)

2 hones Whetstones for sharpening blades.

Questions for Discussion and Writing

1. Read the poem aloud. Notice several patterns of sound. How do they relate to the picture described in the poem?
2. Does the speaker of the poem, the viewer of the scene, see life as a joyful romp, a dashing adventure, or a predetermined grind? How do you know?
3. Death is sometimes called "The Grim Reaper." Do you think Toomer had this in mind when he wrote "Reapers"? Why?

Stevie Smith 1902–1971

Born Florence Margaret Smith in Hull, England, Stevie Smith worked as a secretary and occasionally as a writer and broadcaster for the BBC. She began publishing verse, which she often illustrated herself, in the 1930s but did not gain much recognition until 1962, when her *Selected Poems* appeared. Noted for her eccentricity and humor, Smith often aimed her satirical barbs at religion and made unexpected use of traditional hymns, songs, and nursery rhymes in her poems.

Not Waving but Drowning

Nobody heard him, the dead man,
But still he lay moaning:
I was much further out than you thought
And not waving but drowning.

Poor chap, he always loved larking
And now he's dead
It must have been too cold for him his heart gave way,
They said.

Oh, no no no, it was too cold always
(Still the dead one lay moaning)
I was much too far out all my life
And not waving but drowning.

(1957)

Questions for Discussion and Writing

1. Who are the two speakers in the poem? How does one misunderstand the other?
2. The lines "I was much too far out all my life /And not waving but drowning" are obviously meant to carry more than a literal meaning. What does the dead man mean?
3. In what ways might your outward demeanor be contrary to the "inner you"? Write an essay about how you or someone you know might give a false impression to others.

Countee Cullen 1903–1946

Countee Cullen was adopted by a Methodist minister and raised in Harlem. His first volume of poems, *Color* (1925), was published when he was a student at New York University. His early work established him as a leader of the Harlem Renaissance, but his collection *Copper Sun* (1927), which featured love poems, disappointed black nationalists. Cullen stopped writing poetry after he published *The Black Christ* in 1929. He taught school in New York City for the rest of his life.

Incident

(For Eric Walrond)

Once riding in old Baltimore,
Heart-filled, head-filled with glee,
I saw a Baltimorean
Keep looking straight at me.

Now I was eight and very small,
And he was no whit bigger,
And so I smiled, but he poked out
His tongue, and called me, "Nigger."

I saw the whole of Baltimore
From May until December;
Of all the things that happened there
That's all that I remember.

(1925)

Questions for Discussion and Writing

1. Though the main point of "Incident" is unstated, its theme is clear. How would you state it in a sentence?
2. "Incident" is very simple in form and language. Why do you think the author chose this simplicity?
3. Write an essay about your own introduction into a part of the adult world that you weren't aware of as a child or youth.

Pablo Neruda 1904–1973

Pablo Neruda was born in Parral, Chile. Despite his reputation as one of the greatest Spanish American poets in history, few of his works have been translated into English. Neruda was a radical poet who mixed meditations on political oppression with intensely personal lyrics about romantic love. He was awarded the Nobel Prize for Literature in 1971.

Sweetness, Always

Translated by Alastair Reid

Why such harsh machinery?
Why, to write down the stuff
and people of every day,
must poems be dressed up in gold,

in old and fearful stone?
I want verses of felt or feather
which scarcely weigh, mild verses
with the intimacy of beds
where people have loved and dreamed.
I want poems stained
by hands and everydayness.

Verses of pastry which melt
into milk and sugar in the mouth,
air and water to drink,
the bites and kisses of love.
I long for eatable sonnets,
poems of honey and flour.

Vanity keeps prodding us
to lift ourselves skyward
or to make deep and useless
tunnels underground.
So we forget the joyous
love-needs of our bodies.
We forget about pastries.
We are not feeding the world.

In Madras a long time since,
I saw a sugary pyramid,
a tower of confectionery—
one level after another,
and in the construction, rubies,
and other blushing delights,
medieval and yellow.

Someone dirtied his hands
to cook up so much sweetness.
Brother poets from here
and there, from earth and sky,
from Medellín, from Veracruz,
Abyssinia, Antofagasta,
do you know the recipe for honeycombs?

Let's forget all about that stone.

Let your poetry fill up
the equinoctial pastry shop
our mouths long to devour—
all the children's mouths
and the poor adults' also.
Don't go on without seeing,
relishing, understanding
all these hearts of sugar.

Don't be afraid of sweetness.

With us or without us,
sweetness will go on living

and is infinitely alive,
forever being revived,
for it's in a man's mouth,
whether he's eating or singing,
that sweetness has its place.

(1958)

Questions for Discussion and Writing

1. What types of poems are "harsh machinery," "dressed up in gold, in old and fearful stone"? Find examples of such poems, as Neruda would see them, in this anthology. In contrast, what images does the writer use to describe the kind of poetry he feels is needed?
2. What is the extended metaphor? Explain the comparison that is developed.
3. What are the connotations of the adjective "sweet," as in calling someone a sweet person? Why might poets object to having their poems called "sweet"?
4. Look carefully at the stanza division in the poem. Can you explain why stanzas are separated the way they are?

W. H. Auden 1907–1973

See page 468 for a biographical note about this author.

Funeral Blues

Stop all the clocks, cut off the telephone,
Prevent the dog from barking with a juicy bone,
Silence the pianos and with muffled drum
Bring out the coffin, let the mourners come.

Let aeroplanes circle moaning overhead
Scribbling on the sky the message He Is Dead,
Put crepe bows round the white necks of the public doves,
Let the traffic policemen wear black cotton gloves.

He was my North, my South, my East and West,
My working week and my Sunday rest,
My noon, my midnight, my talk, my song;
I thought that love would last for ever: I was wrong.

The stars are not wanted now: put out every one;
Pack up the moon and dismantle the sun;
Pour away the ocean and sweep up the wood;
For nothing now can ever come to any good.

(1936)

Questions for Discussion and Writing

1. What is the name for a poem that mourns and honors someone who has died? Is this one typical of the genre?
2. Do you think the lost lover in this poem is dead or merely departed?
3. What is the tone of the poem? What are your clues?
4. Do you think that the poem is just a parody, or do you think that Auden truly cared for his lost love? What makes you think so?
5. Write an elegy—serious or playful—about a person (or a pet) you loved and lost.

Lullaby

Lay your sleeping head, my love,
Human on my faithless arm;
Time and fevers burn away
Individual beauty from
Thoughtful children, and the grave
Proves the child ephemeral:
But in my arms till break of day
Let the living creature lie,
Mortal, guilty, but to me
The entirely beautiful.

Soul and body have no bounds:
To lovers as they lie upon
Her tolerant enchanted slope
In their ordinary swoon,
Grave the vision Venus sends
Of supernatural sympathy,
Universal love and hope;
While an abstract insight wakes
Among the galciers and the rocks
The hermit's carnal ecstasy.

Certainty, fidelity
On the stroke of midnight pass
Like vibrations of a bell
And fashionable madmen raise
Their pedantic boring cry:
Every farthing of the cost,
All the dreaded cards foretell,
Shall be paid, but from this night
Not a whisper, not a thought,
Not a kiss nor look be lost.

Beauty, midnight, vision dies:
Let the winds of dawn that blow

Softly round your dreaming head
Such a day of welcome show
Eye and knocking heart may bless,
Find our mortal world enough;
Noons of dryness find you fed
By the involuntary powers,
Night of insult let you pass
Watched by every human love.

(1937)

Questions for Discussion and Writing

1. What are lullabies usually like? For whom are they usually written? What is their tone and rhythm? What idea of human nature is usually expressed in a lullaby? Scrutinize the words of an actual lullaby to answer these questions.
2. Now read the first stanza of Auden's lullaby. Which of the conventions are maintained? Which words break the conventions? How does knowing that this lullaby was written for an adult lover explain some of the breaks with convention?
3. Summarize the first stanza in your own words. What ideas do the subsequent stanzas add to your impression of the first one?
4. The word *grave* is used in both the first and second stanzas. What does it mean in each case? What is the point of the repetition?
5. Compare Auden's depiction of the duality of love, both spiritual and earthly, with Donne's conception of this duality as expressed in "A Valediction: Forbidding Mourning" (pages 568–69).

Theodore Roethke 1908–1963

See page 467 for a biographical note about this author.

I Knew a Woman

I knew a woman, lovely in her bones,
When small birds sighed, she would sigh back at them;
Ah, when she moved, she moved more ways than one:
The shapes a bright container can contain!
Of her choice virtues only gods should speak,
Or English poets who grew up on Greek
(I'd have them sing in chorus, cheek to cheek).

How well her wishes went! She stroked my chin,
She taught me Turn, and Counter-turn, and Stand;
She taught me Touch, that undulant white skin;

I nibbled meekly from her proffered hand;
She was the sickle; I, poor I, the rake,
Coming behind her for her pretty sake
(But what prodigious mowing we did make).

Love likes a gander, and adores a goose:
Her full lips pursed, the errant note to seize;
She played it quick, she played it light and loose;
My eyes, they dazzled at her flowing knees;
Her several parts could keep a pure repose,
Or one hip quiver with a mobile nose
(She moved in circles, and those circles moved).

Let seed be grass, and grass turn into hay:
I'm martyr to a motion not my own;
What's freedom for? To know eternity.
I swear she cast a shadow white as stone.
But who would count eternity in days?
These old bones live to learn her wanton ways:
(I measure time by how a body sways).

(1958)

Questions for Discussion and Writing

1. List some of the things that the woman is compared to. What do they have in common? What comparisons strike you as unusual in a love poem?
2. Explain the image of the sickle and rake in stanza two.
3. Write an essay explaining how the speaker of the poem gently makes fun of himself for his obsession with the woman.

Elizabeth Bishop 1911–1979

Elizabeth Bishop was born in Massachusetts. Her father died when she was a baby and her mother was committed as insane when Elizabeth was five; she was raised by relatives in New England and Nova Scotia. Educated at Vassar, she lived mainly in Key West and in Brazil. Bishop's poetry, known for its understanding of the natural world, often provides meticulously detailed descriptions that focus on external reality. Her first book, *North & South*, was published in 1946; collected with her second book, *Cold Spring*, it won the 1955 Pulitzer Prize.

One Art

The art of losing isn't hard to master;
so many things seem filled with the intent
to be lost that their loss is no disaster.

Lose something every day. Accept the fluster
of lost door keys, the hour badly spent.
The art of losing isn't hard to master.

Then practice losing farther, losing faster:
places, and names, and where it was you meant
to travel. None of these will bring disaster.

I lost my mother's watch. And look! my last, or
next-to-last, of three loved houses went.
The art of losing isn't hard to master.

I lost two cities, lovely ones. And, vaster,
some realms I owned, two rivers, a continent.
I miss them, but it wasn't a disaster.

—Even losing you (the joking voice, a gesture
I love) I shan't have lied. It's evident
the art of losing's not too hard to master
though it may look like (*Write it!*) like disaster.
(1976)

Questions for Discussion and Writing

1. What is the form of this poem? What effect does the repetition have on the tone and point of the poem?
2. What experiences does the poem relate?
3. What kinds of loss does the speaker mention?
4. Is losing an art? Is it really "easy"? How does one "master" it? Has the speaker mastered it?

May Sarton 1912–1995

A prolific writer of poetry, novels, autobiography, screenplays, and journals, May Sarton was born in Belgium but emigrated to the United States in 1916. Sarton supported herself mainly through visiting professorships, poetry readings, and lectures. Her work deals with private human concerns such as love, loneliness, and creativity. Sarton's clear, simple style only appears effortless: she said some of her poems went through sixty drafts. Her poetry is compiled in *Collected Poems, 1930–1973* (1974) and *Selected Poems* (1978).

AIDS

We are stretched to meet a new dimension
Of love, a more demanding range

Where despair and hope must intertwine.
How grow to meet it? Intention
Here can neither move nor change
The raw truth. Death is on the line.
It comes to separate and estrange
Lover from lover in some reckless design.
Where do we go from here?

Fear. Fear. Fear. Fear.

Our world has never been more stark
Or more in peril.
It is very lonely now in the dark.
Lonely and sterile.
And yet in the simple turn of a head
Mercy lives. I heard it when someone said
"I must go now to a dying friend.
Every night at nine I tuck him into bed,
And give him a shot of morphine,"
And added, "I go where I have never been."
I saw he meant into a new discipline
He had not imagined before, and a new grace.

Every day now we meet face to face.
Every day now devotion is the test.
Through the long hours, the hard, caring nights
We are forging a new union. We are blest.

As closed hands open to each other
Closed lives open to strange tenderness.
We are learning the hard way how to mother.
Who says it is easy? But we have the power.
I watch the faces deepen all around me.
It is the time of change, the saving hour.
The word is not fear, the word we live,
But an old word suddenly made new,
As we learn it again, as we bring it alive:

Love. Love. Love. Love.

(1988)

Questions for Discussion and Writing

1. Who is the "we" in the poem?
2. When the friend in stanza four says, "I go where I have never been," what does he mean? How does his experience relate to the rest of the poem?
3. What does the line "We are blest" mean? How does the speaker manage to pull a positive meaning out of the AIDS experience? Do you know of other, similar experiences that bring about "a new grace"?

Karl Shapiro 1913–2000

Karl Shapiro believed that poems should convey not just ideas but "what ideas feel like—ideas on Sunday, thoughts on vacation." His poetry captures the authenticity of everyday experience rather than abstract philosophy. Without ever finishing a college degree, he won the Pulitzer Prize in 1944 for a collection of poems he wrote during his army service in World War II. Shapiro taught at several universities but remarked, "I have a sort of special status around English departments—I'm not really a professor, but sort of a mad guest."

Auto Wreck

Its quick soft silver bell beating, beating,
And down the dark one ruby flare
Pulsing out red light like an artery,
The ambulance at top speed floating down
Past beacons and illuminated clocks
Wings in a heavy curve, dips down,
And brakes speed, entering the crowd.
The doors leap open, emptying light;
Stretchers are laid out, the mangled lifted
And stowed into the little hospital.
Then the bell, breaking the hush, tolls once,
And the ambulance with its terrible cargo
Rocking, slightly rocking, moves away,
As the doors, an afterthought, are closed.

We are deranged, walking among the cops
Who sweep glass and are large and composed.
One is still making notes under the light.
One with a bucket douches ponds of blood
Into the street and gutter.
One hangs lanterns on the wrecks that cling,
Empty husks of locusts, to iron poles.

Our throats were tight as tourniquets,
Our feet were bound with splints, but now,
Like convalescents intimate and gauche,
We speak through sickly smiles and warn
With the stubborn saw of common sense,
The grim joke and the banal resolution.
The traffic moves around with care,
But we remain, touching a wound
That opens to our richest horror.

Already old, the question Who shall die?
Becomes unspoken Who is innocent?
For death in war is done by hands;
Suicide has cause and stillbirth, logic;

And cancer, simple as a flower, blooms.
But this invites the occult mind,
Cancels our physics with sneer,
And spatters all we knew of denouement
Across the expedient and wicked stones.

(1942)

Questions for Discussion and Writing

1. In what ways is an auto wreck an unusual subject for a poem? In what ways is the poem a conventional one?
2. Who is the "we" in the poem? How does witnessing the auto wreck affect them?
3. Point out images that appeal to senses other than sight.

Octavio Paz 1914–1998

The first Mexican to be awarded the Nobel Prize for Literature (1990), Octavio Paz was born in Mexico City, the son and grandson of prominent political activists. For twenty years, Paz served as a diplomat for the Mexican government with posts in New York, Paris, India, and Japan. In 1968, however, he resigned from the diplomatic service in protest against the government's violent suppression of the student demonstrations during the Olympic Games in Mexico. After that, Paz worked as an editor and publisher, founding two important magazines dedicated to the arts and politics. In 1980, he was named honorary doctor at Harvard University.

The Street

Translated by Muriel Rukeyser

A long silent street.
I walk in blackness and I stumble and fall
and rise, and I walk blind, my feet
stepping on silent stones and dry leaves.
Someone behind me also stepping on stones, leaves:
if I slow down, he slows;
if I run, he runs. I turn: nobody.
Everything dark and doorless.
Turning and turning among these corners
which lead forever to the street
where nobody waits for, nobody follows me,
where I pursue a man who stumbles
and rises and says when he sees me: nobody.

(1963)

Questions for Discussion and Writing

1. Reread the first four lines of the poem. What is familiar about this scene? How does it make you feel?
2. What are the main sensory appeals of the poem? List the words that carry this appeal.
3. Why do you think the leaves are dry rather than wet? What about the choice of the word "doorless" in line 8?

Dudley Randall 1914–2000

Dudley Randall was born in Washington, D.C., and graduated from Wayne State and the University of Michigan, where he earned degrees in English and library science. In 1969 he became librarian and poet-in-residence at the University of Detroit. A pioneer in the movement to publish the work of African-American writers, Randall founded Broadside Press, one of the most influential small publishing houses in America. Collections of his work include *Cities Burning* (1968), *More to Remember* (1971), *After the Killing* (1973), and *A Litany of Friends* (1981).

Ballad of Birmingham

"Mother dear, may I go downtown
instead of out to play,
and march the streets of Birmingham
in a Freedom March today?"

"No, baby, no, you may not go,
for the dogs are fierce and wild,
and clubs and hoses, guns and jails
aren't good for a little child."

"But, mother, I won't be alone.
Other children will go with me,
and march the streets of Birmingham
to make our country free."

"No, baby, no, you may not go,
for I fear those guns will fire.
But you may go to church instead
and sing in the children's choir."

She has combed and brushed her night-dark hair,
and bathed rose petal sweet,
and drawn white gloves on her small brown hands,
and white shoes on her feet.

The mother smiled to know her child
was in the sacred place,
but that smile was the last smile
to come upon her face.

For when she heard the explosion,
her eyes grew wet and wild.
She raced through the street of Birmingham
calling for her child.

She clawed through bits of glass and brick,
then lifted out a shoe.
"O, here is the shoe my baby wore,
but, baby, where are you?"

(1964)

Questions for Discussion and Writing

1. Explain the situational irony that is present in this poem.
2. Look up the conventions of a traditional ballad. Which ones does this poem employ? And how does it differ from the traditional form?
3. Find out about the actual incident that inspired this poem. How well does Randall's treatment of the events capture the emotions of the situation?
4. Try your hand at writing a ballad about a memorable event during your lifetime.

To the Mercy Killers

If ever mercy move you murder me,
I pray you, kindly killers, let me live.
Never conspire with death to set me free,
but let me know such life as pain can give.
Even though I be a clot, an aching clench,
a stub, a stump, a butt, a scab, a knob,
a screaming pain, a putrefying stench,
still let me live, so long as life shall throb.
Even though I turn such traitor to myself
as beg to die, do not accomplice me.
Even though I seem not human, a mute shelf
of glucose, bottled blood, machinery
to swell the lung and pump the heart—even so,
do not put out my life. Let me still glow.

(1973)

Questions for Discussion and Writing

1. Point out the ironic word choice in the first two lines of the poem.
2. Why does the speaker want to be allowed to live even when enduring the horrors he describes? Do you agree with his position?

3. What is the implied comparison in the last line?
4. Write a short response in which you agree or disagree with the poem's main argument.

Dylan Thomas 1914–1953

Dylan Thomas was born in Wales. Shunning school to pursue a writing career, he published his first book of poetry at age twenty. Limited by his lack of a degree, he had trouble making a living as a writer, and his early life was marked by poverty and heavy drinking. Calling his poetry a "record of my struggle from darkness towards some measure of light," Thomas delighted in sound, sometimes at the expense of sense.

The Force That Through the Green Fuse Drives the Flower

The force that through the green fuse drives the flower
Drives my green age; that blasts the roots of trees
Is my destroyer.
And I am dumb to tell the crooked rose
My youth is bent by the same wintry fever.

The force that drives the water through the rocks
Drives my red blood; that dries the mouthing streams
Turns mine to wax.
And I am dumb to mouth unto my veins
How at the mountain spring the same mouth sucks.

The hand that whirls the water in the pool
Stirs the quicksand; that ropes the blowing wind
Hauls my shroud sail.
And I am dumb to tell the hanging man
How of my clay is made the hangman's lime.

The lips of time leech to the fountain head;
Love drips and gathers, but the fallen blood
Shall calm her sores.
And I am dumb to tell a weather's wind
How time has ticked a heaven round the stars.

And I am dumb to tell the lover's tomb
How at my sheet° goes the same crooked worm.

(1934)

---

22 sheet Winding-sheet in which a corpse is wrapped.

Questions for Discussion and Writing

1. How would you define the force that the speaker insists runs throughout nature?
2. Divide the images in the poem into two groups, images of growth and life and images of death and decay. Which receive more emphasis? Can you explain this in the context of the poem's meaning?
3. What is the meaning of the repeated words "I am dumb"? Why is it a key phrase in interpreting the poem?

Do Not Go Gentle into That Good Night

Do not go gentle into that good night,
Old age should burn and rave at close of day;
Rage, rage against the dying of the light.

Though wise men at their end know dark is right,
Because their words had forked no lightning they
Do not go gentle into that good night.

Good men, the last wave by, crying how bright
Their frail deeds might have danced in a green bay,
Rage, rage against the dying of the light.

Wild men who caught and sang the sun in flight,
And learn, too late, they grieved it on its way,
Do not go gentle into that good night.

Grave men, near death, who see with blinding sight
Blind eyes could blaze like meteors and be gay,
Rage, rage against the dying of the light.

And you, my father, there on the sad height,
Curse, bless, me now with your fierce tears, I pray.
Do not go gentle into that good night.
Rage, rage against the dying of the light.

(1952)

Questions for Discussion and Writing

1. What do the repeated images "that good night" and "dying of the light" stand for?
2. What repeated pattern can you see in stanzas two through five? What kinds of people are described in these stanzas?
3. Explain the seeming contradiction in line 17.

Gwendolyn Brooks 1917–2000

See page 505 for a biographical note about this author.

Sadie and Maud

Maud went to college.
Sadie stayed at home.
Sadie scraped life
With a fine-tooth comb.

She didn't leave a tangle in.
Her comb found every strand.
Sadie was one of the livingest chits°
In all the land.

Sadie bore two babies
Under her maiden name.
Maud and Ma and Papa
Nearly died of shame.

When Sadie said her last so-long
Her girls struck out from home.
(Sadie had left as heritage
Her fine-tooth comb.)

Maud, who went to college,
Is a thin brown mouse.
She is living all alone
In this old house.

(1945)

---

7 **chits** A pert, lively young woman.

Questions for Discussion and Writing

1. What is the attitude of the speaker toward each young woman, Sadie and Maud?
2. What was Sadie's legacy, symbolized by her "fine-tooth comb"?
3. What is the meaning of the poem? Write an explication.
4. Do you agree with Brooks's theme? Why or why not?

The Bean Eaters

They eat beans mostly, this old yellow pair.
Dinner is a casual affair.

Plain chipware on a plain and creaking wood,
Tin flatware.

Two who are Mostly Good.
Two who have lived their day,
But keep on putting on their clothes
And putting things away.

And remembering…
Remembering, with twinklings and twinges,
As they lean over the beans in their rented back room that
is full of beads and receipts and dolls and cloths,
tobacco crumbs, vases and fringes.

(1945)

Questions for Discussion and Writing

1. Why is the couple eating beans? How do you know?
2. What overall impression does the list at the end of the poem give you?
3. Why does the writer include the phrase "Mostly Good"? Why aren't the people described as "Good"?
4. What is the significance of "putting on their clothes /And putting things away"?

Richard Wilbur 1921–

The son of a portrait artist, Richard Wilbur was born in New York City and educated at Amherst College. After serving as a staff sergeant in World War II, he earned an M.A. from Harvard, taught English at Wellesley College and Wesleyan University, and was writer in residence at Smith College. He won Pulitzer Prizes in poetry twice: in 1957 for *Things of This World* and in 1988 for *New and Collected Poems.* In 1987 he was named the second Poet Laureate of the United States. One commentator has said that "the smooth surface of [a] Wilbur poem can successfully distract us from recognizing how unusual and unexpected are the twists and leaps that structure the poem's narrative."

Love Calls Us to the Things of This World

The eyes open to a cry of pulleys,
And spirited from sleep, the astounded soul
Hangs for a moment bodiless and simple
As false dawn.
Outside the open window
The morning air is all awash with angels.

Some are in bed-sheets, some are in blouses,
Some are in smocks: but truly there they are.
Now they are rising together in calm swells
Of halcyon feeling, filling whatever they wear
With the deep joy of their impersonal breathing;

Now they are flying in place, conveying
The terrible speed of their omnipresence, moving
And staying like white water; and now of a sudden
They swoon down into so rapt a quiet
That nobody seems to be there.
The soul shrinks

From all that it is about to remember,
From the punctual rape of every blessèd day,
And cries,
"Oh, let there be nothing on earth but laundry,
Nothing but rosy hands in the rising steam
And clear dances done in the sight of heaven."

Yet, as the sun acknowledges
With a warm look the world's hunks and colors,
The soul descends once more in bitter love
To accept the waking body, saying now
In a changed voice as the man yawns and rises,

"Bring them down from their ruddy gallows;
Let there be clean linen for the backs of thieves;
Let lovers go fresh and sweet to be undone,
And the heaviest nuns walk in a pure floating
Of dark habits,
keeping their difficult balance."

(1956)

Laundry hung out to dry on a pulley-operated line above street level.

Questions for Discussion and Writing

1. In what state of consciousness is the speaker when his eyes open at the beginning of the poem? How might this account for what he sees out the window? What meaning does he assign to what he sees?
2. How do you respond to the word *rape* in line 17? Can you speculate on why the writer chose such a strong word there?
3. Describe the shift between stanzas four and five. What is happening to the speaker? What is the difference between "the soul" before and after this shift? Which relates to the title, the first or second state of consciousness?
4. What additional meanings can you ascribe to the "difficult balance" in the last line?

Philip Larkin 1922–1985

Philip Larkin came from a working-class background in the north of England. His father, the treasurer of the city of Coventry, was an admirer of Hitler. Larkin claimed that "Form holds little interest for me," and became the leader of the British anti-Romantic movement. His poetry often treats conventional themes, such as love and death, with searing wit and sophisticated roughness. Although he had a number of affairs, Larkin feared marriage and family, and never married. "Two can live as stupidly as one," he once said.

Home Is So Sad

Home is so sad. It stays as it was left,
Shaped to the comfort of the last to go
As if to win them back. Instead, bereft
Of anyone to please, it withers so,
Having no heart to put aside the theft
And turn again to what it started as,
A joyous shot at how things ought to be,
Long fallen wide. You can see how it was:
Look at the pictures and the cutlery.
The music in the piano stool. That vase.

(1964)

Questions for Discussion and Writing

1. Whose home is being described in the poem?
2. What effect is gained by the personification of the house?

3. Do you think the family was happy or otherwise?
4. Write a poem about your home, personifying the house to show how it might respond to activities of your family.

James Dickey 1923–1997

James Dickey was born in Atlanta, played football in college, served in the Army Air Force in World War II, worked in advertising, taught at several universities, and was poet-in-residence at the University of South Carolina. Dickey's poems are usually wedded to personal incidents and project an almost demonic view of life. His several volumes of poetry include *Buckdancer's Choice* (1965), winner of the National Book Award. He also wrote the best-selling novel *Deliverance* (1970).

The Leap

The only thing I have of Jane MacNaughton
Is one instant of a dancing-class dance.
She was the fastest runner in the seventh grade,
My scrapbook says, even when boys were beginning
To be as big as the girls,
But I do not have her running in my mind,
Though Frances Lane is there, Agnes Fraser,
Fat Betty Lou Black in the boys-against-girls
Relays we ran at recess: she must have run

Like the other girls, with her skirts tucked up
So they would be like bloomers,
But I cannot tell; that part of her is gone.
What I do have is when she came,
With the hem of her skirt where it should be
For a young lady, into the annual dance
Of the dancing class we all hated, and with a light
Grave leap, jumped up and touched the end
Of one of the paper-ring decorations

To see if she could touch it. She could.
And reached me now as well, hanging in my mind
From a brown chain of brittle paper, thin
And muscular, wide-mouthed, eager to prove
Whatever it proves when you leap
In a new dress, a new womanhood, among the boys
Whom you easily left in the dust
Of the passionless playground. If I said I saw
In the paper where Jane MacNaughton Hill,

Mother of four, leapt to her death from a window
Of a downtown hotel, and that her body crushed-in
The top of a parked taxi, and that I held
Without trembling a picture of her cradled
In that papery steel as though lying in the grass,
One shoe idly off, arms folded across her breast,
I would not believe myself. I would say
The convenient thing, that it was a bad dream
Of maturity, to see that eternal process

Most obsessively wrong with the world
Come out of her light, earth-spurning feet
Grown heavy: would say that in the dusty heels
Of the playground some boy who did not depend
On speed of foot, caught and betrayed her.
Jane, stay where you are in my first mind:
It was odd in that school, at that dance.
I and the other slow-footed yokels sat in corners
Cutting rings out of drawing paper

Before you leapt in your new dress
And touched the end of something I began,
Above the couples struggling on the floor,
New men and women clutching at each other
And prancing foolishly as bears: hold on
To that ring I made for you, Jane—
My feet are nailed to the ground
By dust I swallowed thirty years ago—
While I examine my hands.

(1967)

Questions for Discussion and Writing

1. What does the title of the poem mean?
2. What happens to boys and girls around seventh grade? What images show that the narrator here is aware of the significance of the time his memory reconstructs?
3. What is the "eternal process / Most obsessively wrong with the world"? What does the narrator think happened to Jane? What personal meaning does her suicide hold for him?

Maxine Kumin 1925–

When Maxine Kumin was in college, an instructor wrote this comment about her poetry: "Say it with flowers, but for God's sake don't try to write poems." So she didn't for a long time. But in her thirties, during her third pregnancy, she took up writing poetry again. "The grit of discontent, the acute misery of early and uninformed motherhood," she said, "worked under my skin to force out the writer." Kumin likes to write about what she calls "small overlooked things" and bring them "back to the world's attention." She won a Pulitzer Prize for *Up Country* (1972), poems inspired by her New Hampshire farm.

Woodchucks

Gassing the woodchucks didn't turn out right.
The knockout bomb from the Feed and Grain Exchange
was featured as merciful, quick at the bone
and the case we had against them was airtight,
both exits shoehorned shut with puddingstone,
but they had a sub-sub-basement out of range.

Next morning they turned up again, no worse
for the cyanide than we for our cigarettes
and state-store Scotch, all of us up to scratch.
They brought down the marigolds as a matter of course
and then took over the vegetable patch
nipping the broccoli shoots, beheading the carrots.

The food from our mouths, I said, righteously thrilling
to the feel of the .22, the bullets' neat noses.
I, a lapsed pacifist fallen from grace
puffed with Darwinian pieties for killing,
now drew a bead on the littlest woodchuck's face.
He died down in the everbearing roses.

Ten minutes later I dropped the mother. She
flipflopped in the air and fell, her needle teeth
still hooked in a leaf of early Swiss chard.
Another baby next. O one-two-three
the murderer inside me rose up hard,
the hawkeye killer came on stage forthwith.

There's one chuck left. Old wily fellow, he keeps
me cocked and ready day after day after day.
All night I hunt his humped-up form. I dream
I sight along the barrel in my sleep.
If only they'd all consented to die unseen
gassed underground the quiet Nazi way.

(1972)

Questions for Discussion and Writing

1. What kind of person is the speaker of the poem before she starts shooting woodchucks? What details let you know?
2. What side of her does the killing bring out? How is the order of the killings significant?

3. Why does the speaker assert that it would be better if the woodchucks had "consented to die unseen"?

Anne Sexton 1928–1974

See page 559 for a biographical note about this poet.

You All Know the Story of the Other Woman

It's a little Walden.
She is private in her breathbed
as his body takes off and flies,
flies straight as an arrow.
But it's a bad translation.
Daylight is nobody's friend.
God comes in like a landlord
and flashes on his brassy lamp.
Now she is just so-so.
He puts his bones back on,
turning the clock back an hour.
She knows flesh, that skin balloon,
the unbound limbs, the boards,
the roof, the removable roof.
She is his selection, part time.
You know the story too! Look,
when it is over he places her,
like a phone, back on the hook.

(1967)

Questions for Discussion and Writing

1. Concentrate on the title. Do you all know the story of the other woman? What is "the conventional wisdom" about what happens to the other woman?
2. This poem depends on metaphors and similes for its meaning. Identify and explain five of them. Why does the last simile make the point unmistakable?
3. How does the man behave after he has had sex with the woman? Write a paraphrase of lines 6 through 14.

Adrienne Rich 1929–

Born in Baltimore, Adrienne Rich graduated from Radcliffe College in 1951, the same year that her first book of poetry, *A Change in the World*, appeared in the Yale Series of Younger Poets. The Vietnam War and her teaching experience with minority youth in New York City heightened Rich's political awareness, and she became increasingly involved in the women's movement. Her poetry collection *Diving into the Wreck* (1973) won the National Book Award.

Aunt Jennifer's Tigers

Aunt Jennifer's tigers prance across a screen,
Bright topaz denizens of a world of green.
They do not fear the men beneath the tree;
They pace in sleek chivalric certainty.

Aunt Jennifer's fingers fluttering through her wool
Find even the ivory needle hard to pull.
The massive weight of Uncle's wedding band
Sits heavily upon Aunt Jennifer's hand.

When Aunt is dead, her terrified hands will lie
Still ringed with ordeals she was mastered by.
The tigers in the panel that she made
Will go on prancing, proud and unafraid.

(1951)

Questions for Discussion and Writing

1. What human traits do the tigers possess? What kind of life do they lead? What does "prancing" suggest?
2. What kind of life does Aunt Jennifer lead? How do the tigers help you to understand her plight? Why might she have chosen them for her tapestry?
3. What does Aunt Jennifer's wedding band symbolize? What is a wedding ring supposed to symbolize?
4. One critic says that the speaker in the poem is "almost callous in her disregard for Aunt's death," that the speaker cares more for the gorgeous tigers than for Aunt Jennifer. Argue your response to this interpretation.

Living in Sin

She had thought the studio would keep itself;
no dust upon the furniture of love.

Half heresy, to wish the taps less vocal,
the panes relieved of grime. A plate of pears,
a piano with a Persian shawl, a cat
stalking the picturesque amusing mouse
had risen at his urging.
Not that at five each separate stair would writhe
under the milkman's tramp; that morning light
so coldly would delineate the scraps
of last night's cheese and three sepulchral bottles;
that on the kitchen shelf among the saucers
a pair of beetle-eyes would fix her own—
envoy from some village in the moldings . . .
Meanwhile, he, with a yawn,
sounded a dozen notes upon the keyboard,
declared it out of tune, shrugged at the mirror,
rubbed at his beard, went out for cigarettes;
while she, jeered by the minor demons,
pulled back the sheets and made the bed and found
a towel to dust the table-top,
and let the coffee-pot boil over on the stove.
By evening she was back in love again,
though not so wholly but throughout the night
she woke sometimes to feel the daylight coming
like a relentless milkman up the stairs.

(1955)

Questions for Discussion and Writing

1. What two things are being contrasted in this poem? Which part is emphasized? Why?
2. How does the final image unify the poem and reinforce its meaning?
3. Write about an experience in which you expected one thing and got quite a different one.

Ruth Fainlight 1931–

Born in New York City, Ruth Fainlight moved to England at age fifteen and is considered a British poet. She has published thirteen collections of poems, some translated into Portuguese, French, and Spanish. In an unusual application of poetic skill, she has also written the libretti (the words) for several operas. In an interview Fainlight said, "When students or young poets proudly tell me that they do not work on their poems because they do not want to lose the first inspiration, . . . I try to explain that to make a poem sound simple and inevitable requires a great deal of time, thought, knowledge, and effort."

Flower Feet

Silk Shoes in the Whitworth Museum, Manchester, England

Real women's feet wore these objects
that look like toys or spectacle cases stitched
from bands of coral, jade, and apricot silk
embroidered with twined sprays of flowers.
Those hearts, tongues, crescents, and disks, leather
shapes an inch across, are the soles of shoes
no wider or longer than the span of my ankle.
If the feet had been cut off and the raw stumps
thrust inside the opening, surely
it could not hurt more than broken toes, twisted
back and bandaged tight. An old woman,
leaning on a cane outside her door
in a Chinese village, smiled to tell how
she fought and cried, how when she stood on points
of pain that gnawed like fire, nurse and mother
praised her tottering walk on flower feet.
Her friends nodded, glad the times had changed.
Otherwise, they would have crippled their daughters.

(1989)

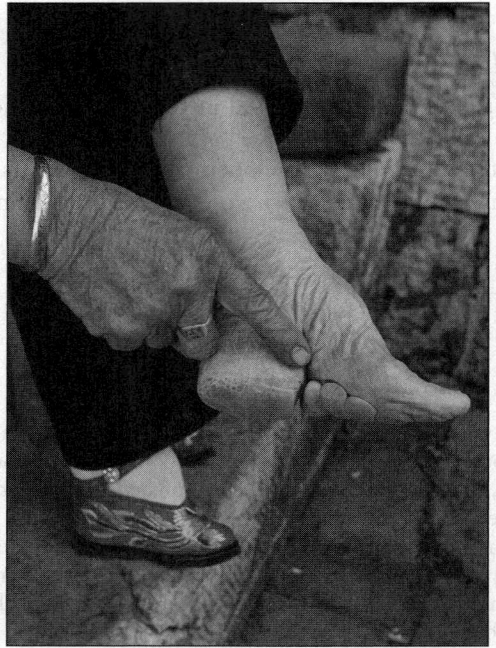

Feet were bound by breaking bones in four small toes and forcing them to grow underneath.

Questions for Discussion and Writing

1. Where is the narrator standing as she describes the shoes? Why is this setting important to understanding the poem?
2. Compare the imagery of the first stanza with the imagery of the second stanza. What contrast is emphasized by the difference in imagery?
3. What comment on the power of culture is made in the last two lines?
4. Look up historical information on Chinese foot-binding and write an informative short essay that would help other readers understand the poem.

Sylvia Plath 1932–1963

Sylvia Plath was born in Boston, where her father taught at Boston University. Her early years were filled with honors and awards. She won a Fulbright Scholarship to Cambridge, where she met and married English poet Ted Hughes. But beneath the conventional success was a woman whose acute perceptions and intolerable pain led her to commit suicide at age thirty. Plath produced three volumes of powerful poetry and an autobiographical novel, *The Bell Jar*(1963).

Mirror

I am silver and exact. I have no preconceptions.
Whatever I see I swallow immediately
Just as it is, unmisted by love or dislike.
I am not cruel, only truthful—
The eye of a little god, four-cornered.
Most of the time I meditate on the opposite wall.
It is pink, with speckles. I have looked at it so long
I think it is a part of my heart. But it flickers.
Faces and darkness separate us over and over.

Now I am a lake. A woman bends over me,
Searching my reaches for what she really is.
Then she turns to those liars, the candles or the moon.
I see her back, and reflect it faithfully.
She rewards me with tears and an agitation of hands.
I am important to her. She comes and goes.
Each morning it is her face that replaces the darkness.
In me she has drowned a young girl, and in me an old woman
Rises toward her day after day, like a terrible fish.

(1963)

Questions for Discussion and Writing

1. Consider the use of personification in this poem. What difference would it make if the mirror had no voice—for example, if the poem began "The mirror is silver and exact. It has no preconceptions"?
2. What reason can you see for the stanza division? What two characters does the mirror choose to describe itself?
3. Why does the mirror call candles and the moon "those liars"?

John Updike 1932–2009

See page 440 for a biographical note about this author.

Ex-Basketball Player

Pearl Avenue runs past the high-school lot,
Bends with the trolley tracks, and stops, cut off
Before it has a chance to go two blocks,
At Colonel McComsky Plaza. Berth's Garage
Is on the corner facing west, and there,
Most days, you'll find Flick Webb, who helps Berth out.

Flick stands tall among the idiot pumps—
Five on a side, the old bubble-head style,°
Their rubber elbows hanging loose and low.
One's nostrils are two S's, and his eyes
An E and O.°And one is squat, without
A head at all—more of a football type.

Once Flick played for the high-school team, the Wizards.
He was good: in fact, the best. In '46
He bucketed three hundred ninety points,
A county record still. The ball loved Flick.
I saw him rack up thirty-eight or forty
In one home game. His hands were like wild birds.

He never learned a trade, he just sells gas,
Checks oil, and changes flats. Once in a while,
As a gag, he dribbles an inner tube,
But most of us remember anyway.

---

8 bubble-head style Gasoline pumps with round glass globes on top.
11 E and O ESSO—a major oil company in the 1940s, the time frame of the poem.

An "old bubble-head" ESSO gasoline pump.

His hands are fine and nervous on the lug wrench.
It makes no difference to the lug wrench, though.

Off work, he hangs around Mae's luncheonette.
Grease-gray and kind of coiled, he plays pinball,
Smokes those thin cigars, nurses lemon phosphates.
Flick seldom says a word to Mae, just nods
Beyond her face toward bright applauding tiers
Of Necco Wafers, Nibs, and Juju Beads.

(1958)

Questions for Discussion and Writing

1. What is the story of Flick Webb's life? How do both his first and last names fit his life story?
2. Who is the narrator (the "I") of the poem? How old is he? Where does he live?
3. Though the poem has no regular rhyme, it follows patterns. Explain the logic of the stanza breaks and line breaks.
4. Do you think Flick would agree with this assessment of his life?

Imamu Amiri Baraka 1934–

Imamu Amiri Baraka was born LeRoi Jones in Newark, New Jersey. He attended Rutgers, graduated from Howard University, and spent three years in the Air Force. In the 1960s he became involved with black nationalist politics, changed his name to Imamu Amiri Baraka, and founded the Black Arts Theater in Harlem. His anger at the privileged status of whites is expressed in such plays as *Dutchman* and *The Slave* (both 1964) and in his collection of poetry *Black Magic* (1967).

Biography

Hangs.
whipped
blood
striped
meat pulled
clothes ripped
slobber
feet dangled
pointing
noised
noise
churns
face
black sky
and moon
leather night
red
bleeds
drips
ground
sucks
blood
hangs
life wetting
sticky
mud

laughs
bonnets
wolfmoon
crazyteeth

hangs

hangs

granddaddy
granddaddy, they tore
his

neck

(1969)

Questions for Discussion and Writing

1. How did the grandfather die? Who killed him? How do you know?
2. Point out places where the images do not fit together logically. How can you account for the author's use of confused images? Rewrite part of the poem in usual prose form (you will probably have to do some filling in).
3. What is the dictionary meaning of *biography?* What does the word suggest as a title for this poem?
4. In what way is this a concrete or "picture" poem?

Audre Lorde 1934–1992

Audre Lorde was born of West Indian parents in New York City. She was educated at the National University of Mexico, Hunter College, and Columbia University. Her poetry is passionate about love, angry about race, and feminist. Her first major work of prose, *The Cancer Journals* (1980), depicts her struggle with breast cancer and mastectomy and carries her message of the strength of women. *The Black Unicorn* (1978) is a volume of her poems about Africa.

Hanging Fire

I am fourteen
and my skin has betrayed me
the boy I cannot live without
still sucks his thumb
in secret
how come my knees are
always so ashy
what if I die
before morning
and momma's in the bedroom
with the door closed.

I have to learn how to dance
in time for the next party

my room is too small for me
suppose I die before graduation
they will sing sad melodies
but finally
tell the truth about me
There is nothing I want to do
and too much
that has to be done
and momma's in the bedroom
with the door closed.

Nobody even stops to think
about my side of it
I should have been on Math Team
my marks were better than his
why do I have to be
the one
wearing braces
I have nothing to wear tomorrow
will I live long enough
to grow up
and momma's in the bedroom
with the door closed.

(1978)

Questions for Discussion and Writing

1. Do you think that the teenager's thoughts in this poem are true to life? Can you remember similar thoughts when you were around fourteen? What kinds of concerns does the speaker have?
2. Find out what the title means. How is it appropriate for the poem and the speaker?
3. What do you think of the refrain, "and momma's in the bedroom /with the door closed"? Is the speaker a victim of neglect?

Marge Piercy 1936–

Marge Piercy was born in Detroit, Michigan. Concerned with depicting and dignifying women's experiences, Piercy has been accused of politicizing her work. In the introduction to her book of poetry *Circles on the Water* (1982), she explains how her writing can be "of use" to women: "To find ourselves spoken for in art gives dignity to our pain, our anger, our lust, our losses." Among her popular novels are *Small Changes* (1973), *Woman on the Edge of Time* (1976), and *Gone to Soldiers* (1987).

Barbie Doll

This girlchild was born as usual
and presented dolls that did pee-pee
and miniature GE stoves and irons
and wee lipsticks the color of cherry candy.
Then in the magic of puberty, a classmate said:
You have a great big nose and fat legs.

She was healthy, tested intelligent,
possessed strong arms and back,
abundant sexual drive and manual dexterity.
She went to and fro apologizing.
Everyone saw a fat nose on thick legs.

She was advised to play coy,
exhorted to come on hearty,
exercise, diet, smile and wheedle.
Her good nature wore out
like a fan belt.
So she cut off her nose and her legs
and offered them up.

In the casket displayed on satin she lay
with the undertaker's cosmetics painted on,
a turned-up putty nose,
dressed in a pink and white nightie.
Doesn's she look pretty? everyone said.
Consummation at last.
To every woman a happy ending.

(1973)

Questions for Discussion and Writing

1. What led to the suicide in the poem? In what way is it a happy ending?
2. Why is the poem titled "Barbie Doll"? What qualities do you associate with Barbie?
3. This poem was written in 1973. Do you think its view of female socialization is still relevant today? Write a paper arguing your answer to this question.

Seamus Heaney 1939–

Cited as Ireland's best poet since Yeats, Seamus Heaney was born on a farm in Northern Ireland, and his early poetry communicates a strong sense of the physical environment of his youth. His later work, often dense and poignant, concerns the cultural implications of words and their historical contexts. Heaney now divides his time between Dublin and the United

States, where he teaches at Harvard. His most recent books of poetry are *The Haw Lantern* (1987) and *Electric Light* (2001). He received the Nobel Prize for Literature in 1995.

Digging

Between my finger and my thumb
The squat pen rests; snug as a gun.

Under my window, a clean rasping sound
When the spade sinks into gravelly ground:
My father, digging. I look down

Till his straining rump among the flowerbeds
Bends low, comes up twenty years away
Stooping in rhythm through potato drills
Where he was digging.

The coarse boot nestled on the lug, the shaft
Against the inside knee was levered firmly.
He rooted out tall tops, buried the bright edge deep
To scatter new potatoes that we picked
Loving their cool hardness in our hands.

By God, the old man could handle a spade.
Just like his old man.

My grandfather cut more turf° in a day
Than any other man on Toner's bog.
Once I carried him milk in a bottle
Corked sloppily with paper. He straightened up
To drink it, then fell to right away
Nicking and slicing neatly, heaving sods
Over his shoulder, going down and down
For the good turf. Digging.

The cold smell of potato mould, the squelch and slap
Of soggy peat, the curt cuts of an edge
Through living roots awaken in my head.
But I've no spade to follow men like them.

Between my finger and my thumb
The squat pen rests.
I'll dig with it.

(1966)

---

17 turf Peat, used for fuel in Ireland.

Questions for Discussion and Writing

1. What does the speaker of the poem admire about his forefathers? Make a list of the qualities he seems to revere.

2. Do you have any feelings about carrying on the work of your parents or grandparents? Do you think most people do?
3. The speaker has chosen a profession very different from potato farming. He implies, though, in the last line, that it is similar. How is it the same?

Sharon Olds 1942–

Sharon Olds, born in San Francisco and educated at Stanford University, is the author of several books of poetry. Because of her intense focus on family and sexual relationships, she is often compared to confessional poets Sylvia Plath and Anne Sexton. Olds teaches creative writing at New York University and at the Goldwater Hospital, a facility for the physically disabled. A review of her book *The Unswept Room* (2002) calls her poetry "fiery, penetrating, and unnerving."

Sex Without Love

How do they do it, the ones who make love
without love? Beautiful as dancers,
gliding over each other like ice-skaters
over the ice, fingers hooked
inside each other's bodies, faces
red as steak, wine, wet as the
children at birth whose mothers are going to
give them away. How do they come to the
come to the   come to the   God   come to the
still waters, and not love
the one who came there with them, light
rising slowly as steam off their joined
skin? These are the true religious,
the purists, the pros, the ones who will not
accept a false Messiah, love the
priest instead of the God. They do not
mistake the lover for their own pleasure,
they are like great runners: they know they are alone
with the road surface, the cold, the wind,
the fit of their shoes, their over-all cardio-
vascular health—just factors, like the partner
in the bed, and not the truth, which is the
single body alone in the universe
against its own best time.

(1984)

Questions for Discussion and Writing

1. What other kinds of people are those who have sex without love compared with? Would you call these comparisons positive, negative, or mixed?
2. What do you think is the speaker's attitude toward people who have sex without love? What in the poem contributes to your opinion?
3. What ideas about love and sex are challenged in this poem?

The Death of Marilyn Monroe

The ambulance men touched her cold
body, lifted it, heavy as iron,
onto the stretcher, tried to close the
mouth, closed the eyes, tied the
arms to the sides, moved a caught
strand of hair, as if it mattered,
saw the shape of her breasts, flattened by
gravity, under the sheet,
carried her, as if it were she,
down the steps.

These men were never the same. They went out
afterwards, as they always did,
for a drink or two, but they could not meet
each other's eyes.
Their lives took
a turn—one had nightmares, strange
pains, impotence, depression, One did not
like his work, his wife looked
different, his kids. Even death
seemed different to him—a place where she
would be waiting,

and one found himself standing at night
in the doorway to a room of sleep, listening to a
woman breathing, just an ordinary
woman
breathing.

(1983)

Questions for Discussion and Writing

1. In the first stanza, why does the poet choose the specific physical details of Marilyn's body?
2. How would the ambulance carry her "as if it were she" (line 9)? Is it not "she"? Why would they carry her this way, knowing she is dead?
3. Why do you think the men always went out for a drink or two after their duties? What purpose did this routine serve?

4. How did the men respond to their experience? Write a paper explaining what the various responses to this unusual experience represent. In particular, consider the last man described. Why is the woman he listens to called "ordinary"?

Nikki Giovanni 1943–

Nikki Giovanni is noted for her often joyous poetry, which she shares, enthusiastically, with large audiences. She contributed to the outpouring of militant black poetry in the 1960s and 1970s, but she has since focused on writing about love and relationships. She has recorded several albums of her poetry, one of which uses gospel music in the background because she wanted her grandmother to like it. Giovanni's works include *Black Feeling, Black Talk* (1968), *A Poetic Equation* (1974), and several collections of poems for children.

Dreams

in my younger years
before i learned
black people aren't
suppose to dream
i wanted to be
a raelet
and say "dr o wn d in my youn tears"
or "tal kin bout tal kin bout"
or marjorie hendricks and grind
all up against the mic
and scream
"baaaaaby nightandday
baaaaaby nightandday"
then as i grew and matured
i became more sensible
and decided i would
settle down
and just become
a sweet inspiration

(1968)

Questions for Discussion and Writing

1. What youthful hope did the speaker hold? What image do you think she had of herself when she daydreamed?
2. Why does the speaker believe that black people aren't supposed to dream?

3. What youthful hope or aspiration did you have to give up? Why did you give it up? Write an essay about this experience.

Gina Valdés 1943–

Gina Valdés was born in Los Angeles, spent her childhood in Mexico, and returned to Los Angeles during adolescence. She attended the University of California, San Diego, and still lives in San Diego today. Her stories and poetry often focus on the plight of undocumented workers, Chicano alienation in the United States and the status of Chicanas. Her collection *Puentes y fronteras* [*Bridges and Frontiers*] (1982) takes the form of *coplas*, four-line stanzas from traditional Mexican folk poetry, with Valdés substituting a female for the conventional male narrator. In *Comiendo lumbre: Eating Fire* (1986), she experiments with alternating between Spanish and English in each poem.

My Mother Sews Blouses

My mother sews blouses
for a dollar a piece.
They must be working on
black cloth again, I see
her fingers sliding on
her eyelids.

Six months ago she went
to the old oculist, the
one who "knows all about

Women working in an apparel-industry sweatshop.

eyes," who turned her
eyelids inside out and
scraped them with a tiny
knife to get the black
lint out.

Her eyes were bright and
clear for a few months.
She's blinking now,
talking about night
school.

(1986)

Questions for Discussion and Writing

1. Why do you think the mother is so poorly paid for her sewing?
2. Consider possible symbolism in the poem. What do we usually associate with the inability to see? What could the black lint symbolize?
3. Why is the woman "thinking about night school"? What effect will her current job have on this goal? Does the poem suggest that she will succeed or fail? Explain.

Edward Hirsch 1950–

Edward Hirsch was born in Chicago. When he was eight years old, he "wandered down to the basement of our house to pick through some of my grandfather's forgotten books" and read a verse (by Emily Bronte) that captivated him. It was the beginning of a lifelong love affair with poetry, which he explored at Grinnell College and the University of Pennsylvania, where he received a Ph.D. in folklore. His book *How to Read a Poem and Fall in Love with Poetry* was a surprise bestseller in 1999 and remains in print today.

Execution

The last time I saw my high school football coach
He had cancer stenciled into his face
Like pencil marks from the sun, like intricate
Drawings on the chalkboard, small x's and o's
That he copied down in a neat numerical hand
Before practice in the morning. By day's end
The board was a spiderweb of options and counters,
Blasts and sweeps, a constellation of players
Shining under his favorite word, Execution,
Underlined in the upper right-hand corner of things.
He believed in football like a new religion

And had perfect unquestioning faith in the fundamentals
Of blocking and tackling, the idea of warfare
Without suffering or death, the concept of teammates
Moving in harmony like the planets—and yet
Our awkward adolescent bodies were always canceling
The flawless beauty of Saturday afternoons in September,
Falling away from the particular grace of autumn,
The clear weather, the ideal game he imagined.
And so he drove us through punishing drills
On weekday afternoons, and doubled our practice time,
And challenged us to hammer him with forearms,
And devised elaborate, last-second plays—a flea-
Flicker, a triple reverse—to save us from defeat.
Almost always they worked. He despised losing
And loved winning more than his own body, maybe even
More than himself. But the last time I saw him
He looked wobbly and stunned by illness,
And I remembered the game in my senior year
When we met a downstate team who loved hitting
More than we did, who battered us all afternoon
With a vengeance, who destroyed us with timing
And power, with deadly, impersonal authority,
Machine-like fury, perfect execution.

(1989)

Questions for Discussion and Writing

1. How does the coach feel about football? What comparisons does the speaker use to describe the coach's feelings?
2. What is the significance of the game with the downstate team (lines 29–34)? Why did the speaker remember that game the last time he saw the coach?
3. What do you think of the lines "He despised losing / And loved winning more than his own body"? What is the speaker implying?
4. What is the speaker's attitude toward his coach? Do you think he likes or admires him? Write a paper arguing your position on this issue.
5. Explain the ironies that you find in this poem. Start with the title.

Rita Dove 1952–

Rita Dove was born in Akron, Ohio, and educated at Miami University, the University of Tübingen, and the University of Iowa. She has earned praise for plainspoken poems that reflect her life and the experiences of African-Americans in general. In 1987 she won the Pulitzer Prize for *Thomas and Beulah*, a series of poems about the lives of the title characters, from their southern origins through their lives in Akron in the 1960s. In 1992 Dove was named Poet Laureate of the United States, the youngest person ever to be appointed to this post.

Daystar

She wanted a little room for thinking:
but she saw diapers steaming on the line,
a doll slumped behind the door.
So she lugged a chair behind the garage
to sit out the children's naps.

Sometimes there were things to watch—
the pinched armor of a vanished cricket,
a floating maple leaf. Other days
she stared until she was assured
when she closed her eyes
she'd see only her own vivid blood.

She had an hour, at best, before Liza appeared
pouting from the top of the stairs.
And just *what* was mother doing
out back with the field mice? Why,

building a palace. Later
that night when Thomas rolled over and
lurched into her, she would open her eyes
and think of the place that was hers
for an hour—where
she was nothing,
pure nothing, in the middle of the day.

(1986)

Questions for Discussion and Writing

1. What is a "daystar" and how does it apply to this poem?
2. Did you identify with the woman in the poem? When, if ever, do you want solitude? Why? Why does the persona want it?
3. Who are Liza and Thomas? Are they important characters? Why does the writer refrain from identifying them? Why is the woman not identified by name, as they are?
4. What is happening in the last stanza? Why would the woman want to be "pure nothing" while having sex?

Alberto Ríos 1952–

The son of a Guatemalan father and an English mother, Alberto Ríos grew up on the American side of the city of Nogales, Arizona, on the Mexican border. Having earned an M.F.A. in creative writing at the University of Arizona, he is the author of nine books of poems, three short-story collections, and a memoir. He won the Walt Whitman Award for his poetry, which has been adapted to dance and both classical and popular music. Ríos was also featured in the documentary *Birthwrite: Growing Up Hispanic* (1989). Since 1994, he has been Regents' Professor of English at Arizona State University.

In Second Grade Miss Lee I Promised Never to Forget You and I Never Did

In a letting-go moment
Miss Lee the Teacher
Who was not married
And who the next year was not at school,
Said to us, her second grade,
French lovers in the morning
Keep an apple next to the bed,
Each taking a bite
On first waking, to take away
The blackish breath of the night,
You know the kind.
A bite and then kissing,
And kissing like that was better.

I saw her once more
When she came to sell encyclopedias.
I was always her favorite—
The erasers, and the way she looked at me.
I promised, but not to her face,
Never to forget
The story of the apples.
Miss Lee all blond hair and thin,
Like *a real movie star*
If she would have just combed herself more.
Miss Lee, I promised,
I would keep apples
For you.

(2002)

Questions for Discussion and Writing

1. Put together a profile of Miss Lee from the details you know about her. Why do you think she was not at school the year after the time in the poem?
2. How old are second grade students? Why did the narrator remember forever the apple story Miss Lee told? Do you remember any single classroom incident from your grade school years? Why? Generally, what kinds of incidents stand out in a child's mind?

3. How does Ríos sustain the child's point of view in the poem? What would be different from an adult's point of view? For example, what would the point of view of the child's parents include?

Jimmy Santiago Baca 1952–

Jimmy Santiago Baca endured a family life shattered by matricide, a childhood in a state orphanage, and years in a state prison for supposed drug crimes. Baca managed to teach himself to read and write between state-ordered electroshock sessions to curb his combative nature. His poetry, especially that about prison life, has won him critical acclaim.

There Are Black

There are black guards slamming cell gates
on black men,
And brown guards saying hello to brown men
with numbers on their backs,
And white guards laughing with white cons,
and red guards, few, say nothing
to red inmates as they walk by to chow and cells.

There you have it, the little antpile…
convicts marching in straight lines, guards flying
on badged wings, permits to sting, to glut themselves
at the cost of secluding themselves from their people…
Turning off their minds like watertaps
wrapped in gunnysacks that insulate the pipes
carrying the pale weak water to their hearts.

It gets bad when you see these same guards
carrying buckets of blood out of cells,
see them puking at the smell, the people,
their own people slashing their wrists,
hanging themselves with belts from light outlets;
it gets bad to see them clean up the mess,
carry the blue cold body out under sheets,
and then retake their places in guard cages,
watching their people maul and mangle themselves,

And over this blood-rutted land,
the sun shines, the guards talk of horses and guns,
go to the store and buy new boots,
and the longer they work here the more powerful they become,
taking on the presence of some ancient mummy,
down in the dungeons of prison, a mummy

that will not listen, but has a strange power
in this dark world, to be so utterly disgusting in ignorance,
and yet so proudly command so many men....

And the convicts themselves, at the mummy's
feet, blood-splattered leather, at this one's feet,
they become cobras sucking life out of their brothers,
they fight for rings and money and drugs,
in this pit of pain their teeth bare fangs,
to fight for what morsels they can....

And the other convicts, guilty
of nothing but their born color, guilty of being innocent,
they slowly turn to dust in the nightly winds here,
flying in the wind back to their farms and cities.
From the gash in their hearts, sand flies up spraying
over houses and through trees,

look at the sand blow over this deserted place,
you are looking at them.

(1979)

Questions for Discussion and Writing

1. What is it about the prison guards that horrifies the speaker in "There Are Black"?
2. The speaker understands what motivates the guards to keep their jobs. What are their motivations?
3. What are the two types of convicts described in stanzas five and six?
4. Do you think that this subject matter is appropriate for poetry? Why or why not?

Judith Ortiz Cofer 1952–

Judith Ortiz Cofer was born in Puerto Rico; her family emigrated to the United States when she was six. This mixed heritage animates her writing, which often describes the experience of balancing two cultures in one life. Cofer wrote poetry as a graduate student and began focusing on prose in the late 1980s, publishing the novel *The Line of the Sun*, which was nominated for a 1989 Pulitzer Prize. She has also written widely published essays and a volume of stories for young adults.

Latin Women Pray

Latin women pray
In incense sweet churches
They pray in Spanish to an Anglo God

With a Jewish heritage.
And this Great White Father
Imperturbable in his marble pedestal
Looks down upon his brown daughters
Votive candles shining like lust
In his all seeing eyes
Unmoved by their persistent prayers.

Yet year after year
Before his image they kneel
Margarita Josefina Maria and Isabel
All fervently hoping
That if not omnipotent
At least he be bilingual

(1987)

Questions for Discussion and Writing

1. To what religion do the women belong? How can you tell?
2. List words that describe the God worshipped in the poem and words that describe the women. How are the two lists opposites? Do they contain any similarities? What other views of God may be compared with this one?
3. What are the women probably praying for "year after year"? Why do they never get it? Why do they persist?
4. Of all the ways possible to describe the reflection of votive candles in a statue's eyes, the writer chose the image "shining like lust." What does this image contribute to our understanding of the God in the poem?

Dorianne Laux 1952–

Dorianne Laux worked at lowly service jobs from the age of eighteen until thirty, raising a daughter as a single mother and taking writing classes and workshops at the local college when she could. Obtaining scholarships and grants, she was able to return to school full-time and graduated with honors from Mills College in 1988. In a 2006 interview with *Southern Hum*, Laux asserted, "It seems to me that all poems are odes in one way or another. Even poems of desperation or loss are odes to human emotion and endurance, to the spirit that rages quietly on."

What I Wouldn't Do

The only job I didn't like, quit
after the first shift, was selling
subscriptions to *TV Guide* over the phone.

Before that it was fast food, all
the onion rings I could eat, handing
sacks of deep fried burritos through
the sliding window, the hungry hands
grabbing back. And at the laundromat,
plucking bright coins from a palm
or pressing them into one, kids
screaming from the bathroom and twenty
dryers on high. Cleaning houses was fine,
polishing the knick-knacks of the rich.
I liked holding the hand-blown glass bell
from Czechoslovakia up to the light,
the jewelled clapper swinging lazily
from side to side, its foreign,
A-minor ping. I drifted, an itinerant,
from job to job, the sanatorium
where I pureed peas and carrots
and stringy beets, scooped them,
like pudding, onto flesh-colored
plastic plates, or the gas station
where I dipped the ten-foot measuring stick
into the hole in the blacktop,
pulled it up hand over hand
into the twilight, dripping
its liquid gold, pink-tinged.
I liked the donut shop best, 3 AM,
alone in the kitchen, surrounded
by sugar and squat mounds of dough,
the flashing neon sign strung from wire
behind the window, gilding my white uniform
yellow, then blue, then drop-dead red.
It wasn't that I hated calling them, hour
after hour, stuck in a booth with a list
of strangers' names, dialing their numbers
with the eraser end of a pencil and them
saying hello. It was that moment
of expectation, before I answered back,
the sound of their held breath,
their disappointment when they realized
I wasn't who they thought I was,
the familiar voice, or the voice they loved
and had been waiting all day to hear.

(1994)

Questions for Discussion and Writing

1. List the jobs the narrator describes before her telemarketing job. What do they have in common? What is similar in the way she describes each one?
2. What can you infer about the narrator by the way she describes the jobs? Why do you think she liked them all right?

3. How does the *TV Guide* job contrast with the others in the poem? Can you explain why she quit after the first shift? Does the nature of *TV Guide* play a role in the poem's meaning?
4. Write a descriptive paragraph or poem about a job you enjoyed or hated.

Tony Hoagland 1953–

Tony Hoagland was born in North Carolina. Unlike most widely published poets, Hoagland is known for his humorous, down-to-earth touch. In 2005, Hoagland was awarded the O. B. Hardison Jr. Prize by the Folger Shakespeare Library in recognition of his teaching as well as his writing. He also won the 2005 Mark Twain Award for his contributions to humor in American poetry. In making this award for The Poetry Foundation, Stephen Young said, "Wit and morality rarely consort these days; it's good to see them happily, often hilariously reunited in the winner's poetry."

The Change

The season turned like the page of a glossy fashion magazine.
In the park the daffodils came up
and in the parking lot, the new car models were on parade.

Sometimes I think that nothing really changes—

The young girls show the latest crop of tummies,
    and the new president proves that he's a dummy.

But remember the tennis match we watched that year?
Right before our eyes

some tough little European blonde
pitted against that big black girl from Alabama,
cornrowed hair and Zulu bangles on her arms,
some outrageous name like Vondella Aphrodite—
We were just walking past the lounge
    and got sucked in by the screen above the bar,
and pretty soon
we started to care about who won,

putting ourselves into each whacked return
as the volleys went back and forth and back
like some contest between
the old world and the new,

and you loved her complicated hair
and her to-hell-with-everybody stare,
and I,

Serena Williams, one of the most powerful players in women's tennis, smashes a return.

I couldn't help wanting
the white girl to come out on top,
because she was one of my kind, my tribe,
with her pale eyes and thin lips

and because the black girl was so big
and so black,
so unintimidated,

hitting the ball like she was driving the Emancipation Proclamation
down Abraham Lincoln's throat,
like she wasn't asking anyone's permission.

There are moments when history
passes you so close
you can smell its breath,
you can reach your hand out
and touch it on its flank,

and I don't watch all that much Masterpiece Theatre,
but I could feel the end of an era there

in front of those bleachers full of people
in their Sunday tennis-watching clothes

as that black girl wore down her opponent
then kicked her ass good
then thumped her once more for good measure

and stood up on the red clay court
holding her racket over her head like a guitar.

And the little pink judge
                had to climb up on a box
to put the ribbon on her neck,
still managing to smile into the camera flash,
even though everything was changing

and in fact, everything had already changed—

Poof, remember? It was the twentieth century almost gone,
we were there,

and when we went to put it back where it belonged,
it was past us
and we were changed.

(2003)

Questions for Discussion and Writing

1. The first three stanzas describe spring. What imagery is traditional in describing spring? What spiritual associations are usually connected with the coming of spring? What is expected and unexpected in Hoagland's imagery?
2. What symbolic meaning did the narrator attach to the tennis match? Why did he and his companion root for different players in the match?
3. Find two or three metaphors in the poem (see pages 484–85). In what way do these metaphors add meaning to the literal descriptive details?
4. Do some research to find out what year and what tennis match the narrator describes in "The Change." Write a short essay explaining how tennis history can help readers understand the poem.

Cornelius Eady 1954–

Cornelius Eady, an African-American poet. was born in Rochester, New York, currently resides in New York City, and directs the Poetry Center at the State University of New York at Stony Brook. Author of five books of poetry and winner of the Lamont Poetry Selection of the American Academy of Poets, he has been nominated for a Pulitzer Prize and has received fellowships from the Lila Wallace-Reader's Digest Foundation, the Guggenheim Foundation, and the National Endowment for the Arts.

The Supremes

We were born to be gray. We went to school,
Sat in rows, ate white bread,
Looked at the floor a lot. In the back
Of our small heads

A long scream. We did what we could,
And all we could do was
Turn on each other. How the fat kids suffered!
Not even being jolly could save them.

And then there were the anal retentives,
The terrified brown-noses, the desperately
Athletic or popular. This, of course,
Was training. At home

Our parents shook their heads and waited.
We learned of the industrial revolution,
The sectioning of the clock into pie slices.
We drank cokes and twiddled our thumbs. In the
Back of our minds

The Supremes—Mary Wilson, Diana Ross, and Cindy Birdsong—performing in vibrant, sequined gowns.

A long scream. We snapped butts in the showers,
Froze out shy girls on the dance floor,
Pin-pointed flaws like radar.
Slowly we understood: this was to be the world.

We were born insurance salesmen and secretaries,
Housewives and short order cooks,
Stock room boys and repairmen,
And it wouldn't be a bad life, they promised,
In a tone of voice that would force some of us
To reach in self-defense for wigs,
Lipstick,

Sequins.

(1991)

Questions for Discussion and Writing

1. What does the speaker mean when he says, "We were born to be gray"? Who is he talking about?
2. The speaker says that "all we could do was / Turn on each other" (lines 6–7). In what ways do they turn on each other? Is the speaker trying to justify this behavior?
3. Explain line 21: "Slowly we understood: this was to be the world."
4. What happens in the last two stanzas? Why do "some of us" reach for "wigs, / Lipstick, / Sequins"? What does that mean? And what is the "tone of voice" that would force them to do so? In what ways is it self-defense?

Louise Erdrich 1954–

See page 393 for a biographical note about this author.

Indian Boarding School: The Runaways

Home's the place we head for in our sleep.
Boxcars stumbling north in dreams
don't wait for us. We catch them on the run.
The rails, old lacerations that we love,
shoot parallel across the face and break
just under Turtle Mountains. Riding scars
you can't get lost. Home is the place they cross.

The lame guard strikes a match and makes the dark
less tolerant. We watch through cracks in boards

as the land starts rolling, rolling till it hurts
to be here, cold in regulation clothes.
We know the sheriff's waiting at midrun
to take us back. His car is dumb and warm.
The highway doesn't rock, it only hums
like a wing of long insults. The worn-down welts
of ancient punishments lead back and forth.

All runaways wear dresses, long green ones,
the color you would think shame was. We scrub
the sidewalks down because it's shameful work.
Our brushes cut the stone in watered arcs
and in the soak frail outlines shiver clear
a moment, things us kids pressed on the dark
face before it hardened, pale, remembering
delicate old injuries, the spines of names and leaves.

(1984)

Questions for Discussion and Writing

1. Tell the story recounted in the poem. Why do the children run away? What means do they use? How do they get caught? What is their punishment?
2. Underline the images of injury and pain throughout the poem. Why are they appropriate when no real violence befalls the runaways?
3. What do the children see when they scrub the sidewalk? Why do these impressions undercut the shame of the punishment? Will the children rebel again?

Martín Espada 1957–

Martin Espada came from a family of Puerto Rican immigrants, and his many volumes of poetry reflect these origins. His writing is openly political, expressing anger at injustice and racism. The poems often tell stories from the points of view of gutsy, vivid Latino characters, such as janitors, junkies, prisoners, or mental patients. Humor and empathy infuse his depictions of these characters' struggles. Espada's third book of poetry, *Rebellion Is the Circle of a Lover's Hands*, won the 1990 PEN/Revson Award and the Paterson Poetry Prize.

Bully

Boston, Massachusetts, 1987

In the school auditorium
the Theodore Roosevelt statue

is nostalgic
for the Spanish American War,
each fist lonely for a saber
or the reins of anguished horses,
or a podium to clatter with speeches
glorying in the malaria of conquest.

But now the Roosevelt school
is pronounced *Hernandez.*
Puerto Rico has invaded Roosevelt
with its army of Spanish-singing children
in the hallways,
brown children devouring
the stockpiles of the cafeteria,
children painting *Taíno* ancestors
that leap naked across murals.

Roosevelt is surrounded
by all the faces
he ever shoved in eugenic spite
and cursed as mongrels, skin of one race,
hair and cheekbones of another.

Once Marines tramped
from the newsreel of his imagination;
now children plot to spray graffiti
in parrot-brilliant colors
across the Victorian mustache
and monocle.

(1990)

Questions for Discussion and Writing

1. The poet depends on our knowing at least a few things about Teddy Roosevelt, the Spanish-American War, eugenics, and Taíno Puerto Rican ancestors. If you aren't familiar with any of this history, use an encyclopedia to fill in the gaps, and then explain how this information helps you to read the poem. Can you understand his main theme without these insights?
2. There are several surprising images in the poem, created by unexpected word combinations—for example, the linking of "lonely" and "fist," as well as "statue" and "nostalgic." Find other examples and discuss the tone created by these images.
3. There are four stanzas in the poem. Summarize the main point of each, and explain the reasons for the order in which Espada places his ideas.
4. Who is the "bully" in the poem? Why did Espada select this title? Why did he include "Boston, Massachusetts, 1987"? Write an essay in which you argue your position on these questions.

Essex Hemphill 1957–1995

The oldest of five children born into a working-class family in Chicago, Essex Hemphill took up writing as a teenager. "I was a skinny little 14-year-old black boy," he said, "growing up in a ghetto that had not yet suffered the fatal wounds and injuries caused by drugs and black-on-black crime." As an adult, he was an activist in the black gay rights movement, but he explained, "I love my race enough to know that I'm a Black man first and foremost and that my sexuality falls in line after that." He died at age thirty-eight from complications of AIDS.

Commitments

I will always be there.
When the silence is exhumed.
When the photographs are examined
I will be pictured smiling
among siblings, parents,
nieces and nephews.

In the background of the photographs
the hazy smoke of barbecue,
a checkered red-and-white tablecloth
laden with blackened chicken,
glistening ribs, paper plates,
bottles of beer, and pop.

In the photos
the smallest of children
are held by their parents.
My arms are empty, or around
the shoulders of unsuspecting aunts
expecting to throw rice at me someday.

Or picture tinsel, candles,
ornamented, imitation trees,
or another table, this one
set for Thanksgiving,
a turkey steaming the lens.

My arms are empty
in those photos, too,
so empty they would break around a lover.

I am always there
for critical emergencies,
graduations,
the middle of the night.

I am the invisible son.
In the family photos
nothing appears out of character.
I smile as I serve my duty.
(1992)

Questions for Discussion and Writing

1. Why are the speaker's arms "empty or around the shoulders of unsuspecting aunts"? Why are the aunts "unsuspecting"? Unsuspecting of what?
2. Why does the speaker think of himself as "the invisible son"?
3. Explain the title. What commitments does the speaker fulfill? Does his family have any commitments to him? How does he feel about his place in the family?
4. Did you ever feel invisible even though you were plainly in sight? What was the social situation? Did you welcome the invisibility, or did you wish someone would take notice of you? In an essay, poem, or story, express how this invisibility affected you.

Nancy A. Henry 1961–

Born in Chipley, Florida, Nancy A. Henry grew up in Gainesville, Florida. After graduating from college, she moved to Maine and took a law degree. Still a practicing attorney, she also teaches English at Southern Maine Community College and works as a child advocate. She lives in the western foothills of the White Mountains with her husband, who is a physicist. About her poetry, Gary Lawless writes, "These are poems from the hard world, poems from the heart, the soul, the deep interior, passing through a poet of wise intelligence, empathy and love."

People Who Take Care

People who take care of people
get paid less than anybody
people who take care of people
are not worth much
except to people who are
sick, old, helpless, and poor
people who take care of people
are not important to most other people
are not respected by many other people
come and go without much fuss
unless they don't show up

when needed
people who make more money
tell them what to do
never get shit on their hands
never mop vomit or wipe tears
don't stand in danger
of having plates thrown at them
sharing every cold
observing agonies
they cannot tell at home
people who take care of people
have a secret
that sees them through the double shift
that moves with them from room to room
that keeps them on the floor
sometimes they fill a hollow
no one else can fill
sometimes through the shit
and blood and tears
they go to a beautiful place, somewhere
those clean important people
have never been.

(2003)

Questions for Discussion and Writing

1. What is the irony conveyed by the first twelve lines of the poem?
2. Does caring for people sound like a job that should pay more? Why do you suppose it doesn't?
3. What secret do people who take care of people have?
4. Write a brief explanation of what the speaker means by that "beautiful place, somewhere / those clean important people / have never been."
5. Did you ever have a job that was hard, dirty, and ill paid? How did you feel about it? Write an argument for why you liked it or hated it.

PAIRED POEMS FOR COMPARISON

Poets are often inspired by the work of earlier poets. This section contains seven pairs of poems that respond to each other in some way. In the first pair, for example, the speaker in the second poem replies directly to the enticement made by the speaker in the first poem. In some cases the two poets present differing perspectives on the same topic. Other responses are light-hearted *parodies*—imitations that copy some features such as diction, style, or form, but change or exaggerate other features for humorous effect. As you read these pairs of poems, think about what each poet has to say and how the second poem modifies or complements the intent and meaning of the first one.

Christopher Marlowe 1564–1593

The son of a Canterbury shoemaker, Christopher Marlowe was one of the leading poets and dramatists of his day. His major plays, which include *Tamburlaine the Great* (1587), *Dr. Faustus* (1588), and *Edward II* (1592), concern heroic figures who are brought down by their own extravagant passions. He was one of the first to use blank verse in his plays, a practice that Shakespeare perfected. Marlowe's lyric poetry is graceful and warmly sensuous. He was killed in a quarrel over a tavern bill.

The Passionate Shepherd to His Love

Come live with me and be my love,
And we will all the pleasures prove,
That valleys, groves, hills and fields,
Woods, or steepy mountain yields.

And we will sit upon the rocks,
And see the shepherds feed their flocks,
By shallow rivers to whose falls
Melodious birds sing madrigals.

And I will make thee beds of roses
With a thousand fragrant posies,
A cap of flowers, and a kirtle
Embroidered all with leaves of myrtle;

A gown made of the finest wool
Which from our pretty lambs we pull;

Fair lined slippers for the cold,
With buckles of the purest gold;

A belt of straw and ivy buds,
With coral clasps and amber studs:
And if these pleasures may thee move,
Come live with me and be my love.

The shepherds' swains shall dance and sing
For thy delight each May morning:
If these delights thy mind may move,
Then live with me and be my love.

(1600)

Questions for Discussion and Writing

1. How does the young lover vary his appeals? Is there an implication that the object of his invitation is rejecting him?
2. Does the speaker go too far ("buckles of the purest gold") and lose credibility? Or is credibility even an issue in this kind of poem?
3. By the end of the poem, how convincing do you find the Shepherd's appeal? Just how "passionate" is he?

Sir Walter Raleigh ca. 1552–1618

Sir Walter Raleigh was an English soldier, explorer, courtier, and man of letters. A favorite of Queen Elizabeth I, he organized the colonizing expeditions to North America that ended tragically with the lost colony of Roanoke Island. Imprisoned for thirteen years in the Tower of London by James I, Raleigh was released to search for gold in South America. When he returned empty-handed, he was executed. A true court poet, he circulated his poems in manuscript; as a result, only a few have survived.

The Nymph's Reply to the Shepherd

If all the world and love were young,
And truth in every shepherd's tongue,
These pretty pleasures might me move,
To live with thee, and be thy love.

Time drives the flocks from field to fold,
When rivers rage, and rocks grow cold,
And Philomel becometh dumb,
The rest complains of cares to come.

The flowers do fade, and wanton fields,
To wayward winter reckoning yields:
A honey tongue, a heart of gall,
Is fancy's spring, but sorrow's fall.

Thy gowns, thy shoes, thy beds of roses,
Thy cap, thy kirtle, and thy posies,
Soon break, soon wither, soon forgotten:
In folly ripe, in reason rotten.

Thy belt of straw and ivy buds,
Thy coral clasps and amber studs,
All these in me no means can move,
To come to thee, and be thy love.

But could youth last, and love still breed,
Had joys no date, nor age no need,
Then these delights my mind might move
To live with thee and be thy love.

(1600)

Questions for Discussion and Writing

1. How does the nymph counter the shepherd's pleasant pastoral images?
2. Note how the nymph mentions all of the images drawn from nature that were used in the Marlowe poem. But what does she do with them?
3. Which of the two lovers, the shepherd or the nymph, do you like better? Which approach to love do you find more attractive? Write a comparison essay in which you defend your choice.

Robert Browning 1812–1889

Robert Browning was an English poet who experimented with diction and rhythm as well as with psychological portraits in verse. He secretly married Elizabeth Barrett, and they moved to Italy in 1846, partly to avoid her domineering father. Browning was a master of dramatic monologues, exemplified in "My Last Duchess" and "Porphyria's Lover." After the death of his wife, Browning returned to England where he wrote what some consider his masterwork, *The Ring and the Book* (1868–1869).

My Last Duchess

Ferrara

That's my last Duchess painted on the wall,
Looking as if she were alive; I call
That piece a wonder, now: Frà Pandolf's° hands
Worked busily a day, and there she stands.
Will't please you sit and look at her? I said
"Frà Pandolf" by design, for never read
Strangers like you that pictured countenance,
The depth and passion of its earnest glance,
But to myself they turned (since none puts by
The curtain I have drawn for you, but I)
And seemed as they would ask me, if they durst,
How such a glance came there; so, not the first
Are you to turn and ask thus. Sir, 'twas not
Her husband's presence only, called that spot
Of joy into the Duchess' cheek: perhaps
Frà Pandolf chanced to say "Her mantle laps
Over my Lady's wrist too much," or "Paint
Must never hope to reproduce the faint
Half-flush that dies along her throat": such stuff
Was courtesy, she thought, and cause enough
For calling up that spot of joy. She had
A heart—how shall I say?—too soon made glad,
Too easily impressed; she liked whate'er
She looked on, and her looks went everywhere.
Sir, 'twas all one! My favor at her breast,
The dropping of the daylight in the West,
The bough of cherries some officious fool
Broke in the orchard for her, the white mule
She rode with round the terrace—all and each
Would draw from her alike the approving speech,
Or blush, at least. She thanked men,—good; but thanked
Somehow—I know not how—as if she ranked
My gift of a nine-hundred-years-old name
With anybody's gift. Who'd stoop to blame
This sort of trifling? Even had you skill
In speech—(which I have not)—to make your will
Quite clear to such an one, and say, "Just this

3 Frà Pandolf's A fictitious artist.

Or that in you disgusts me; here you miss,
Or there exceed the mark"—and if she let
Herself be lessoned so, nor plainly set
Her wits to yours, forsooth, and made excuse,
—E'en then would be some stooping, and I choose
Never to stoop. Oh, Sir, she smiled, no doubt,
Whene'er I passed her; but who passed without
Much the same smile? This grew; I gave commands;
Then all smiles stopped together. There she stands
As if alive. Will't please you rise? We'll meet
The company below, then. I repeat,
The Count your Master's known munificence
Is ample warrant that no just pretence
Of mine for dowry will be disallowed;
Though his fair daughter's self, as I avowed
At starting, is my object. Nay, we'll go
Together down, Sir! Notice Neptune, though,
Taming a sea-horse, thought a rarity,
Which Claus of Innsbruck° cast in bronze for me.

(1842)

---

56 Claus of Innsbruck Another fictitious artist.

Questions for Discussion and Writing

1. Who is speaking to whom? What is the situation?
2. According to the Duke, what were the Duchess's faults? Do you trust the speaker's account of the Duchess and her "failings"?
3. Does the Duke's carefully controlled composure slip as he relates his story about the last duchess? Or is he intentionally letting the emissary know his (the Duke's) feelings about women and wives?
4. If you were the emissary for the Count whose daughter the Duke hopes to marry, what would you report to your master?

Gabriel Spera 1966–

Gabriel Spera is a technical writer and the director of the Aerospace Press in El Segundo, California. He was born in New York, grew up in New Jersey, and holds a B.A. from Cornell University and an M.F.A. from the University of North Carolina. His first collection of poems, *The Standing Wave,* received the 2004 PEN Center USA Literary Award. According to one critic, Spera's poetry "distinguishes itself with intelligence, wit, impeccable technique, and openness, and it has real substance to impart."

My Ex-Husband

That's my ex-husband pictured on the shelf,
Smiling as if in love. I took it myself
With his Leica, and stuck it in that frame
We got for our wedding. Kind of a shame
To waste it on him, but what could I do?
(Since I haven't got a photograph of you.)
I know what's on your mind—you want to know
Whatever could have made me let him go—
He seems like any woman's perfect catch,
What with his ruddy cheeks, the thin mustache,
Those close-set, baggy eyes, that tilted grin.
But snapshots don't show what's beneath the skin!
He had a certain charm, charisma, style,
That passionate, earnest glance he struck, meanwhile
Whispering the sweetest things, like "Your lips
Are like plump rubies, eyes like diamond chips,"
Could flush the throat of any woman, not
Just mine. He knew the most romantic spots
In town, where waiters, who all knew his face,
Reserved an intimately dim-lit place
Half-hidden in a corner nook. Such stuff
Was all too well rehearsed, I soon enough
Found out. He had an attitude—how should
I put it—smooth, self-satisfied, too good
For the rest of the world, too easily
Impressed with his officious self. And he
flirted—fine! but flirted somehow a bit
Too ardently, too blatantly, as if,
If someone ever noticed, no one cared
How slobbishly he carried on affairs.
Who'd lower herself to put up with shit
Like that? Even if you'd the patience—which
I have not—to go and see some counsellor
And say, "My life's a living hell," or
"Everything he does disgusts, the lout!"—
And even if you'd somehow worked things out,
Took a long trip together, made amends,
Let things get back to normal, even then
You'd still be on the short end of the stick;
And I choose never ever to get stuck.
Oh, no doubt, it always made my limbs go
Woozy when he kissed me, but what bimbo
In the steno pool went without the same
Such kisses? So, I made some calls, filed some claims,
All kisses stopped together. There he grins,
Almost lovable. Shall we go? I'm in
The mood for Chez Pierre's, perhaps, tonight,
Though anything you'd like would be all right

As well, of course, though I'd prefer not to go
To any place with checkered tables. No,
We'll take my car. By the way, have I shown
You yet these lovely champagne flutes, hand blown,
Imported from Murano, Italy,
Which Claus got in the settlement for me!

(1992)

Questions for Discussion and Writing

1. Look at this poem alongside the original, Browning's "My Last Duchess," and note the similarities. Make a list of parallels in the form and tone of the two poems. Then discuss parallels in content: what changes are made in the details of the situation?
2. What do the speakers of the poems have in common? What does the persona of "My Ex-Husband" do rather than have the spouse murdered?
3. Is there a difference in the ways you respond to the speakers? If so, how do you account for the difference?

Thomas Hardy 1840–1928

See pages 467–68 for a biographical note about this author.

The Convergence of the Twain

Lines on the Loss of the "Titanic"

I

In a solitude of the sea
Deep from human vanity,
And the Pride of Life that planned her, stilly couches she.

II

Steel chambers, late the pyres
Of her salamandrine fires,
Cold currents thrid,° and turn to rhythmic tidal lyres.

---

6 thrid Thread.

III

Over the mirrors meant
To glass the opulent
The sea-worm crawls—grotesque, slimed, dumb, indifferent.

IV

Jewels in joy designed
To ravish the sensuous mind
Lie lightless, all their sparkles bleared and black and blind.

V

Dim moon-eyed fishes near
Gaze at the gilded gear
And query: "What does this vaingloriousness down here?"

VI

Well: while was fashioning
This creature of cleaving wing,
The Immanent Will that stirs and urges everything

VII

Prepared a sinister mate
For her—so gaily great—
A Shape of Ice, for the time far and dissociate.

VIII

And as the smart ship grew
In stature, grace, and hue,
In shadowy silent distance grew the Iceberg too.

IX

Alien they seemed to be:
No mortal eye could see
The intimate welding of their later history,

X

Or sign that they were bent
By paths coincident
On being anon twin halves of one august event.

XI

Till the Spinner of the Years
Said "Now!" And each one hears,
And consummation comes, and jars two hemispheres.

(1912)

Questions for Discussion and Writing

1. Look up any words that are unfamiliar to you and decide what they mean in the context of the poem.
2. Paraphrase the first stanza, putting Hardy's statement into a familiar word order. Paraphrase any other stanzas that you have trouble understanding.
3. How would you describe Hardy's concept of the godhead (the "Immanent Will" of stanza VI)? What or who is the "Spinner of the Years" in stanza XI?
4. What themes do you find in the poem?

David R. Slavitt 1935–

David R. Slavitt was born in White Plains, New York, and educated at Andover, Yale, and Columbia. A scholar, poet, and serious novelist, he has also written best-sellers under the pseudonym Henry Sutton. Slavitt declares himself a poet at heart who writes novels only in order to support his penchant for writing poetry.

Titanic

Who does not love the *Titanic*?
If they sold passage tomorrow for that same crossing,
who would not buy?

To go down . . . We all go down, mostly
alone. But with crowds of people, friends, servants,
well fed, with music, with lights! Ah!

And the world, shocked, mourns, as it ought to do
and almost never does. There will be the books and movies
to remind our grandchildren who we were
and how we died, and give them a good cry.

Not so bad, after all. The cold
water is anesthetic and very quick.
The cries on all sides must be a comfort.

We all go: only a few, first-class.

(1983)

Photo of the *HMS Titanic*, the British luxury passenger liner that sank on April 14–15, 1912, during its maiden voyage to New York City from Southampton, England, killing about 1,500 passengers and ship personnel. (Hulton Getty/Getty Images, Inc.-Liaison.)

Questions for Discussion and Writing

1. Given the chance and knowing the ship's fate, would you book passage on the maiden voyage of the *Titanic*?
2. What reasons does the speaker give for thinking that we would all sign up? Are any of these valid reasons?
3. What is the tone of this poem? What makes you think so?
4. Write an essay responding to the opening line ("Who does not love the *Titanic*?"), explaining the legendary appeal of the famous ship and its fate.

Edwin Arlington Robinson 1869–1935

Edwin Arlington Robinson was born in Tide Head, Maine. Though now considered an important poet, Robinson spent many years depending on friends for a livelihood. The publication of his narrative poem *Tristram* (1927) brought him wide recognition and some measure of financial independence. Although his verse is traditional in form, he anticipated many twentieth-century poets with his emphasis on themes of alienation and failure. His poetry won three Pulitzer Prizes—in 1921, 1924, and 1927.

Richard Cory

Whenever Richard Cory went downtown,
We people on the pavement looked at him;
He was a gentleman from sole to crown,
Clean favored, and imperially slim.

And he was always quietly arrayed,
And he was always human when he talked;
But still he fluttered pulses when he said,
"Good-morning," and he glittered when he walked.

And he was rich—yes, richer than a king—
And admirably schooled in every grace:
In fine,° we thought that he was everything
To make us wish that we were in his place.

So on we worked, and waited for the light,
And went without the meat, and cursed the bread;
And Richard Cory, one calm summer night,
Went home and put a bullet through his head.

(1896)

---

11 In fine In short.

Questions for Discussion and Writing

1. Who is the speaker in this poem?
2. What sort of person is Richard Cory? What does it mean to be "a gentleman from sole to crown"?
3. Trace the motif of images of royalty in the poem. What do they suggest about Richard Cory and those who admired him?

Paul Simon 1942–

Paul Simon was born in Newark, New Jersey, and attended Queens College, where he majored in English. In 1964 he teamed with Art Garfunkel to form one of the most successful singing duos in rock history, recording such hits as "Mrs. Robinson," "Bridge over Troubled Waters," and "The Sounds of Silence." The team split in 1971. Simon's solo albums include *Still Crazy After All These Years* (1975) and *Graceland* (1986). He was inducted into the Rock and Roll Hall of Fame in 1990.

Richard Cory

They say that Richard Cory owns one half of this whole town
With political connections to spread his wealth around.
Born into society, a banker's only child,
He had everything a man could want: power, grace, and style.

But I work in his factory
And I curse the life I'm livin'
And I curse my poverty
And I wish that I could be
Oh I wish that I could be
Oh I wish that I could be
Richard Cory.

The papers print his picture almost everywhere he goes;
Richard Cory at the opera, Richard Cory at a show,
And the rumor of his parties and the orgies on his yacht,
Oh he surely must be happy with everything he's got.

But I work in his factory
And I curse the life I'm livin'
And I curse my poverty
And I wish that I could be
Oh I wish that I could be
Oh I wish that I could be
Richard Cory.

He freely gave to charity, he had the common touch,
And they were thankful for his patronage and they thanked him very much,
So my mind was filled with wonder when the evening headlines read:
"Richard Cory went home last night and put a bullet through his head."

But I work in his factory
And I curse the life I'm livin'
And I curse my poverty
And I wish that I could be
Oh I wish that I could be
Oh I wish that I could be
Richard Cory.

(1966)

Questions for Discussion and Writing

1. What difference in tone do you see between the Robinson and Simon versions of "Richard Cory"? Does the difference in time of composition (1896 and 1966) account for the change?

2. Choose a different poem from the nineteenth century or early twentieth century and write a modernized version, perhaps for a rock group to perform.

William Stafford 1914–1993

As a boy growing up in Kansas during the great depression, William Stafford helped support his family working in sugar beet fields, growing vegetables, and delivering papers. He was of a gentle nature, so during World War II he became a conscientious objector, refusing to be drafted, and spent the war years in work camps doing soil conservation, fighting fires, and building roads. After the war, he taught for many years at Lewis and Clark College in Portland, Oregon. Stafford said of his own writing, "I have woven a parachute out of everything broken."

Traveling Through the Dark

Traveling through the dark I found a deer
dead on the edge of the Wilson River road.
It is usually best to roll them into the canyon:
that road is narrow; to swerve might make more dead.
By glow of the tail-light I stumbled back of the car
and stood by the heap, a doe, a recent killing;
she had stiffened already, almost cold.
I dragged her off; she was large in the belly.

My fingers touching her side brought me the reason—
her side was warm; her fawn lay there waiting,
alive, still, never to be born.
Beside that mountain road I hesitated.

The car aimed ahead its lowered parking lights;
under the hood purred the steady engine.
I stood in the glare of the warm exhaust turning red;
around our group I could hear the wilderness listen.

I thought hard for us all—my only swerving—,
then pushed her over the edge into the river.

(1957)

Questions for Discussion and Writing

1. Brainstorm about possible interpretations of the poem's title.
2. Why does the speaker roll the dead deer into the canyon? Does the doe's pregnancy make any difference?
3. The poem includes vivid details about the speaker's car. How do they add to your understanding of the poem as a whole?
4. Look carefully at the last stanza. What do you think the speaker "thought hard" about? Who are "us all"? Why does he call his thought "my only swerving"?

Mary Oliver 1935–

Born in Maple Heights, Ohio, Mary Oliver attended Ohio State University and Vassar College but did not earn a degree. She worked for a time as secretary for the sister of Edna St. Vincent Millay, a poet whose influence is apparent in Oliver's early lyrics. She is the author of ten volumes of poetry, including the Pulitzer Prize-winning *American Primitive* (1983), which celebrates the natural world and the rewards of solitude in nature. One critic says that "her vision of nature is celebratory and religious in the deepest sense."

The Black Snake

When the black snake
flashed onto the morning road,
and the truck could not swerve—
death, that is how it happens.

Now he lies looped and useless
as an old bicycle tire.
I stop the car
and carry him into the bushes.

He is as cool and gleaming
as a braided whip, he is as beautiful and quiet
as a dead brother.
I leave him under the leaves

and drive on, thinking
about *death*: its suddenness,
its terrible weight,
its certain coming. Yet under

reason burns a brighter fire, which the bones
have always preferred.

It is the story of endless good fortune.
It says to oblivion: not me!

It is the light at the center of every cell.
It is what sent the snake coiling and flowing forward
happily all spring through the green leaves before
he came to the road.

(1979)

Questions for Discussion and Writing

1. What is the speaker's attitude toward the snake? How does she dispose of it? How does that contrast with the way the speaker in Stafford's poem disposed of the deer?
2. Why do you think Oliver chose to write about a black snake rather than another animal, like a squirrel or a raccoon?
3. What is the "brighter fire, which the bones / have always preferred"? Why do you think she chose the word "bones" instead of, say, "heart"?
4. What is the "light at the center of every cell," and how does it relate to the theme of the poem?

Robert Hayden 1913–1980

Born Asa Bundy Sheffey in Detroit, Robert Hayden was renamed by his foster parents. In the poetry of his first collection, *Heart-Shape in the Dust* (1940), he used facts about African American history that he unearthed as a researcher for the Federal Writers' Project (1936–40). Educated at Wayne State and the University of Michigan, Hayden taught at Fisk University and returned to teach at Michigan. He considered his writing "a form of prayer—a prayer for illumination, perfection."

Those Winter Sundays

Sundays too my father got up early
and put his clothes on in the blueblack cold,
then with cracked hands that ached
from labor in the weekday weather made
banked fires blaze. No one ever thanked him.

I'd wake and hear the cold splintering, breaking.
When the rooms were warm, he'd call,
and slowly I would rise and dress,
fearing the chronic angers of that house,

Speaking indifferently to him,
who had driven out the cold
and polished my good shoes as well.
What did I know, what did I know
of love's austere and lonely offices°?

(1966)

14 offices Duties.

Questions for Discussion and Writing

1. The speaker is clearly looking back at a pattern of life experienced as a child. What does the speaker know now that he or she didn't know then?
2. What kind of home was the speaker's? How do you know?
3. What are the various expressions of love? Which ones are "austere and lonely"?
4. What is the religious meaning of the word "office"? How does that connotation fit the use of the word in this poem?

George Bilgere 1951–

George Bligere survived an unhappy childhood in Riverside, California. His father was a drunk, his parents divorced, then his mother died. Yet he came out of it as a basically contented individual. Dealing with the pain of his own divorce, he has said, enabled him to use more "open" language in his poetry. Billy Collins observes that the poems are "balanced between humor and seriousness, between the sadness of loss and the joy of being alive to experience it. Whenever a parade of Bilgere poems goes by, I'll be there waving my little flag."

Like Riding a Bicycle

I would like to write a poem
About how my father taught me
To ride a bicycle one soft twilight,
A poem in which he was tired
And I was scared, unable to disbelieve

In gravity and believe in him,
As the fireflies were coming out
And only enough light remained
For one more run, his big hand at the small
Of my back, pulling away like the gantry
At a missile launch, and this time, this time
I wobbled into flight, caught a balance
I would never lose, and pulled away
From him as he eased, laughing, to a stop,
A poem in which I said that even today
As I make some perilous adult launch,
Like pulling away from my wife
Into the fragile new balance of our life
Apart, I can still feel that steadying hand,
Still hear that strong voice telling me
To embrace the sweet fall forward
Into the future's blue
Equilibrium. But,

Of course, he was drunk that night,
Still wearing his white shirt
And tie from the office, the air around us
Sick with scotch, and the challenge
Was keeping his own balance
As he coaxed his bulk into a trot
Beside me in the hot night, sweat
Soaking his armpits, the eternal flame
Of his cigarette flaring as he gasped
And I fell, again and again, entangled
In my gleaming Schwinn, until
He swore and stomped off
Into the house to continue
Working with my mother
On their own divorce, their balance
Long gone and the hard ground already
Rising up to smite them
While I stayed outside in the dark,
Still falling, until at last I wobbled
Into the frail, upright delight
Of feeling sorry for myself, riding
Alone down the neighborhood's
Black street like the lonely western hero
I still catch myself in the act
Of performing.

And yet, having said all this,
I must also say that this summer evening
Is very beautiful, and I am older
Than my father ever was
As I coast the Pacific shoreline
On my old bike, the gears clicking

Like years, the wind
Touching me for the first time, it seems,
In a very long time,
With soft urgency all over.

(2002)

Questions for Discussion and Writing

1. What is a "gantry" (line 10)? Explain why "gantry" is a perfect word choice in the poem.
2. How would you describe the boy's relationship with his father? On what specific words and phrases in the poem do you base your interpretation?
3. Why does the poet place the stanza breaks where they are? Summarize the meaning of each of the three stanzas.
4. Write an essay comparing this poem with Hayden's "Those Winter Sundays." Focus on the speaker's attitude toward his father in each poem.

A Portfolio of War Poetry

War stirs powerful feelings and has inspired an abundance of powerful poetry. Admirable emotions—courage, honor, bravery—are aroused by the excitement and passion of war. But at the same time, negative emotions—grief, anger, misery—are stoked by the senseless slaughter of war. Perhaps this emotional duality helps somewhat to explain why the eloquence and power of antiwar poems have done so little to halt humans' willingness to engage in war, despite its destruction and its staggering toll.

Richard Lovelace 1618–1657

A wealthy, handsome Cavalier poet and a loyal supporter of King Charles I, Richard Lovelace was twice imprisoned by the Puritan Parliament during the English Civil War. He died in poverty in a London slum. Much of Lovelace's poetry is labored and lifeless, but he did write several charming, graceful lyrics, such as "To Althea from Prison," "To Amarantha, That She Would Dishevel Her Hair," and "To Lucasta, on Going to the Wars."

To Lucasta, on Going to the Wars

Tell me not, sweet, I am unkind,
  That from the nunnery
Of thy chaste breast and quiet mind
  To war and arms I fly.

True, a new mistress now I chase,
  The first foe in the field;
And with stronger faith embrace
  A sword, a horse, a shield.

Yet this inconstancy is such
  As thou shalt adore;
I could not love thee, dear, so much,
  Loved I not honor more.

(1649)

Questions for Discussion and Writing

1. What seems to be the speaker's attitude toward war? How old do you imagine the speaker to be?
2. Who is the speaker's "new mistress"?
3. What values or virtues are contrasted in the poem?

Stephen Crane 1871–1900

Stephen Crane was born in Newark, New Jersey, the fourteenth child of a Methodist minister who died when Crane was nine. Leaving college early, he moved to New York City, where he observed firsthand the boozers and prostitutes who inhabited the slums. Crane's first novel, *Maggie: A Girl of the Streets* (1893), drew on these observations. At age twenty-four, and with no military experience, he wrote *The Red Badge of Courage* (1895), a Civil War novel that became an American classic and made Crane famous.

War Is Kind

Do not weep, maiden, for war is kind.
Because your lover threw wild hands toward the sky
And the affrighted steed ran on alone,
Do not weep.
War is kind.

> Hoarse, booming drums of the regiment,
> Little souls who thirst for fight,
> These men were born to drill and die.
> The unexplained glory flies above them,
> Great is the Battle-God, great, and his Kingdom—
> A field where a thousand corpses lie.

Do not weep, babe, for war is kind.
Because your father tumbled in the yellow trenches,
Raged at his breast, gulped and died,
Do not weep.
War is kind.

> Swift blazing flag of the regiment,
> Eagle with crest of red and gold,
> These men were born to drill and die.
> Point for them the virtue of slaughter,
> Make plain to them the excellence of killing
> And a field where a thousand corpses lie.

Mother whose heart hung humble as a button
On the bright splendid shroud of your son,
Do not weep.
War is kind.

(1899)

Questions for Discussion and Writing

1. Why do you think stanzas 2 and 4 are indented?

2. Why is the flag referred to as "the unexplained glory" (line 9)?
3. What is the tone of the poem? And the theme?

Carl Sandburg 1878–1967

See page 598 for a biographical note about this author.

Grass

Pile the bodies high at Austerlitz and Waterloo.°
Shovel them under and let me work—
I am the grass; I cover all.

And pile them high at Gettysburg°
And pile them high at Ypres and Verdun.°
Shovel them under and let me work.
Two years, ten years, and passengers ask the conductor:
What place is this?
Where are we now?

I am the grass.
Let me work.

(1918)

1 Austerlitz and Waterloo Battlefields of the Napoleonic Wars. **4 Gettysburg** Civil War battlefield. **5 Ypres and Verdun** Battlefields of World War I.

Questions for Discussion and Writing

1. Who are the "passengers" who "ask the conductor: / What place is this? / Where are we now?"
2. Does the work of the grass ("I cover all") serve a useful purpose or a sinister one?
3. Describe the tone of the poem. State its theme.

Wilfred Owen 1893–1918

Wilfred Owen began writing poetry at the University of London. After teaching English in France for a few years, he returned to England and joined the army. Owen was wounded in 1917 and killed in action a few days before the armistice was declared in

1918. Owen's poems, published only after his death, are some of the most powerful and vivid accounts of the horrors of war to emerge from World War I.

Dulce et Decorum Est

Bent double, like old beggars under sacks,
Knock-kneed, coughing like hags, we cursed through sludge,
Till on the haunting flares we turned our backs
And towards our distant rest began to trudge.
Men marched asleep. Many had lost their boots
But limped on, blood-shod. All went lame; all blind;
Drunk with fatigue; deaf even to the hoots
Of tired, outstripped Five-Nines° that dropped behind.

Gas! Gas! Quick, boys!—An ecstasy of fumbling,
Fitting the clumsy helmets just in time;
But someone still was yelling out and stumbling
And flound'ring like a man in fire or lime...
Dim, through the misty panes and thick green light,
As under a green sea, I saw him drowning.
In all my dreams before my helpless sight,
He plunges at me, guttering, choking, drowning.

If in some smothering dreams you too could pace
Behind the wagon that we flung him in,
And watch the white eyes writhing in his face,
His hanging face, like a devil's sick of sin;
If you could hear, at every jolt, the blood

John Singer Sargent's painting *Gassed* (1918) depicts World War I soldiers blinded by mustard gas being led back to hospital tents and dressing stations. *Source:* Imperial War Museum Negative Number Q1460.

8 Five-Nines Poison gas shells.

Come gargling from the froth-corrupted lungs,
Obscene as cancer, bitter as the cud
Of vile, incurable sores on innocent tongues,—
My friend, you would not tell with such high zest
To children ardent for some desperate glory,
The old Lie: Dulce et decorum est
Pro patria mori.°

(1920)

27–28 The old Lie The quotation is from the Latin poet Horace, meaning "It is sweet and fitting to die for one's country."

Questions for Discussion and Writing

1. What are "Five-Nines"? Why does the speaker describe them as "tired"?
2. To whom is this poem addressed (the "you" in the third stanza)? What is the tone of the phrase "My friend" (line 25)?
3. What is the "desperate glory" mentioned in line 26? Can you think of any examples of it from books or movies?
4. What is "the old Lie," and do people still tell it?

E. E. Cummings 1894–1962

See page 507 for a biographical note about this author.

next to of course god america i

"next to of course god america i
love you land of the pilgrims' and so forth oh
say can you see by the dawn's early my
country 'tis of centuries come and go
and are no more what of it we should worry
in every language even deafanddumb
thy sons acclaim your glorious name by gorry
by jingo by gee by gosh by gum
why talk of beauty what could be more beautiful
than these heroic happy dead
who rushed like lions to the roaring slaughter
they did not stop to think they died instead
then shall the voice of liberty be mute?"

He spoke. And drank rapidly a glass of water

(1926)

Questions for Discussion and Writing

1. Why does the poem begin with quotation marks?
2. At what point in the poem did you figure out that it is a parody? What is being parodied?
3. Point out several patriotic clichés in the quoted lines. Why are they jumbled together? Which ones contradict each other?
4. What does the last line of the poem reveal to you?

Wislawa Szymborska 1923–

Born near Pozan, Poland, Wislawa Szymborska has lived in Krakow since 1931, where she studied literature at Jagiellonian University and worked as a poetry editor of a well-known literary journal. Her work was virtually unknown outside Poland until she received the Nobel Prize for Literature in 1996 "for poetry that with ironic precision allows the historical and biological context to come to light in fragments of human reality." Her best-known volumes include *Selected Poems* (1967), *Sounds, Feelings, Thought: Seventy Poems* (1981), and *View with a Grain of Sand* (1995).

End and Beginning

Translated by Joseph Brodsky

After each war
somebody has to clear up
put things in order
by itself it won't happen.

Somebody's got to push
rubble to the highway shoulder
making way
for the carts filled up with corpses.

Someone might trudge
through muck and ashes,
sofa springs,
splintered glass
and blood-soaked rugs.

Somebody has to haul
beams for propping a wall,
another put glass in a window
and hang the door on hinges.

This is not photogenic
and takes years.

All the cameras have left already
for another war.

Bridges are needed
also new railroad stations.
Tatters turn into sleeves
for rolling up.

Somebody, broom in hand,
still recalls how it was,
Someone whose head was not
torn away listens nodding.
But nearby already
begin to bustle those
who'll need persuasion.

Somebody still at times
digs up from under the bushes
some rusty quibble
to add it to burning refuse.

Those who knew
what this was all about
must yield to those
who know little
or less than little
essentially nothing.

In the grass that has covered
effects in causes
somebody must recline,
a stalk of rye in the teeth,
ogling the clouds.

(1993)

Questions for Discussion and Writing

1. Who is the "somebody" or "someone" described in the first six stanzas of the poem? What are they doing?
2. How does the "somebody" or "someone" change after stanza six? What is the "somebody" doing in stanza 10?
3. Using points made in this poem, write a brief essay explaining why people do not learn from wars.

Peg Lauber 1938–

Born and reared in Detroit, Michigan, Peg Lauber now spends summers in Wisconsin and winters in New Orleans raising sandhill cranes. One critic says that in her collection, *New Orleans Suite*, she "captures the river, the birds, the fish, the snakes, the barge traffic, the strippers and prostitutes—all the sweetness and squalor, the festivity and fever, the miracle and mayhem of the human spectacle."

Six National Guardsmen Blown Up Together

Today the six come home for good,
those who grew up together on the bayous,
like those boys in the Civil War
who enlisted together, died together,
sometimes leaving small towns
with no young men—
a whole generation gone. These six hunted,
fished, trapped together, but someone
tracked them, hunted them
a world away from their usual prey—
alligators, nutrias, crawfish, bass.

Right across the canal out front
is the Naval base's runway approach
where we'll hear or even see
the big cargo plane carrying
what is left of the men coming in,
rumbling and lumbering along, scaring
the brown pelican and his mate
flying low up the channel
and scattering seventeen members
of the Cajun Air Force,
those bigger white pelicans,
cruising, then banking away.

Only the gulls will remain
gliding around with mournful
screeches, appropriate requiem.
Then silence, all planes grounded
in respect for the relatives, the wives
who huddle on folding chairs, bent
weeping into their small children's hair,
the children frightened, weeping with them,
now understanding that their father
in that flag-draped box will not,
like a Jack, pop out
if they touch a button—
that nothing, nothing
will ever be the same.

(2006)

Questions for Discussion and Writing

1. Why did the poet select the title "Six National Guardsmen Blown Up Together"? How does it shape your expectations for the poem?
2. What is the setting for this poem? How many different kinds of local animals are mentioned? How does their presence affect your feelings about the people and events in the poem?
3. What do you think of the Jack-in-the-Box simile in the final lines? How effectively does it capture the events and feelings of the moment being described?

Yusef Komunyakaa 1947–

Born James Willie Brown Jr., Yusef Komunyakaa was born and grew up in Bogalusa, Louisiana, just as the civil rights movement was gathering momentum. He later reclaimed the name *Komunyakaa* from his great-grandparents, who had been stowaways in a ship from Trinidad. He served in the U.S. Army in Vietnam from 1965 to 1967, and his war poems rank with the best on the subject. Komunyakaa has said, "Poetry is a kind of distilled insinuation. It's a way of expanding and talking around an idea or question. Sometimes more actually gets said through such a technique than a full-frontal assault." His collection *Neon Vernacular* won the Pulitzer Prize for poetry in 1994.

Facing It

My black face fades,
hiding inside the black granite.
I said I wouldn't,
Dammit: No tears.
I'm stone. I'm flesh.
My clouded reflection eyes me
like a bird of prey, the profile of night
slanted against morning. I turn
this way—the stone lets me go.
I turn that way—I'm inside
the Vietnam Veterans Memorial
again, depending on the light
to make a difference.
I go down the 58,002 names,
half-expecting to find
my own in letters like smoke.
I touch the name Andrew Johnson;
I see the booby trap's white flash.
Names shimmer on a woman's blouse
but when she walks away

The Vietnam Veterans Memorial in Washington, D. C., contains 58,325 names of the killed and missing from the Vietnam war. The wall's mirror-like surface (polished black granite) reflects the images of surrounding trees, lawns, monuments, and visitors. (Alan Schein/Corbis/Stock Market.)

the names stay on the wall.
Brushstrokes flash, a red bird's
wings cutting across my stare.
The sky. A plane in the sky.
A white vet's image floats
closer to me, then his pale eyes
look through mine. I'm a window.
He's lost his right arm
inside the stone. In the black mirror
a woman's trying to erase names:
No, she's brushing a boy's hair.

(1988)

Questions for Discussion and Writing

1. Explain the title of the poem. What is "It"?
2. Why is the speaker "half-expecting to find my own [name] in letters like smoke" (lines 15–16)?

3. From line 19 on, the speaker describes images he sees reflected in the Wall. Can you explain the choice of these particular images?
4. What is the significance of the error in perception that the speaker makes at the end of the poem? Why are the woman and boy present? How is their activity symbolic?

Dwight Okita 1958–

Dwight Okita, born in Chicago and still a resident there, describes himself as a gay Japanese American Buddhist. His parents were sent as teenagers to a relocation camp at the onset of World War II, and his mother served as the model for the young girl in the following poem. Okita explains that at the time of the experience she thought "the term 'camp' always sounded like fun, like summer camp. So I wrote the poem in the form of a kind of thank-you letter, which I imagined she might've written to the American government."

In Response to Executive Order 9066 All Americans of Japanese Descent Must Report to Relocation Centers

Dear Sirs:
Of course I'll come. I've packed my galoshes
and three packets of tomato seeds. Denise calls them
love apples. My father says where we're going
they won't grow.

I am a fourteen-year-old girl with bad spelling
and a messy room. If it helps any, I will tell you
I have always felt funny using chopsticks
and my favorite food is hot dogs.
My best friend is a white girl named Denise—
we look at boys together. She sat in front of me
all through grade school because of our names:
O'Connor, Ozawa. I know the back of Denise's head very well.
I tell her she's going bald. She tells me I copy on tests.
We're best friends.

I saw Denise today in Geography class.
She was sitting on the other side of the room.
"You're trying to start a war," she said, "giving secrets away
to the Enemy. Why can't you keep your big mouth shut?"
I didn't know what to say.

May 1942, Hayward, California—A Japanese American family, tagged and waiting for the bus that will take them to an internment camp.

I gave her a packet of tomato seeds
and asked her to plant them for me, told her
when the first tomato ripened
she'd miss me.

(1983)

Questions for Discussion and Writing

1. Log on to "YouTube Executive Order 9066," and watch a movie about the Japanese internment in 1942. Why is it ironic that the speaker in the poem is packing her galoshes?
2. Why does the first-person persona of a fourteen-year-old girl provide an effective voice for the poem?
3. Why does she mention that she has "always felt funny using chopsticks" (line 8) and that her favorite food is hot dogs?
5. What has happened to cause her "best friend" Denise to shun her? Why does the speaker not "know what to say" (line 20)? Do you think the tomato seeds she gives Denise are in any way symbolic?

Making Connections

1. Compare the speaker's attitude toward war in "To Lucasta, on Going to the Wars" with the attitudes of the speakers in at least three other poems in this portfolio.

2. Write a paper discussing the ways in which the memorial in Washington to the Vietnam War dead differs from the usual monuments honoring dead soldiers. Consider why some patriotic groups at first were offended by the monument.
3. Discuss the meaning of the phrases "desperate glory" (from "Dulce et Decorum Est"), "unexplained glory" (from "War Is Kind"), and "your glorious name" (from "next to of course god america i") to show how these phrases reinforce the themes of their poems.
4. Choose two poems that depict war's destruction of cities and landscapes, and contrast their imagery with the images in two poems depicting the destruction of human life.
5. Several poems directly or indirectly attack the causes of war. Make a list of as many of these causes as you can. Which ones seem valid to you? Which do you question?

A Portfolio of Humorous and Satirical Poetry

Oddly enough, many adults who claim not to enjoy poetry once loved it, in the form of nursery rhymes like this one:

Hey, diddle, diddle,
The cat and the fiddle,
The cow jumped over the moon.
The little dog laughed
To see such sport,
And the dish ran away with the spoon.

In this portfolio, we print ten poems which, though written for adults, use many of the same tactics to amuse the readers as "Hey Diddle Diddle" does. A little bit of nonsense, some unexpected combinations of familiar things, a funny shift in point of view, characters and objects performing unfeasible actions, a surprising set of incongruities, a lighthearted warmth in the tone—these are all qualities that made you giggle as a child, and you will see them in the poems to follow. But as you remember, some funny nursery rhymes lack that lighthearted tone, such as "Jack and Jill Went Up the Hill" and "Humpty Dumpty," whose characters come to no good end. And in our collection, poems appear that are also humorous in a dark, satiric way, showing a sharper intolerance for foolishness and inconsistency. We hope that through studying these ten poems, you regain your childhood pleasure in the genre.

Don Marquis 1878–1937

A popular columnist in New York City newspapers in the 1920s, Don Marquis created Archy and Mehitabel, a cockroach and an alley cat, who supposedly produced Marquis's copy. Archy typed the columns in free verse by diving onto the typewriter keys on his head, thus filling each column with fewer words than prose and without punctuation, taking some of the writing pressure off Marquis. Collections of Archy and Mehitabel's work have never gone out of print for the eighty-five years since their creation, with an annotated edition published as recently as 2006.

the lesson of the moth

i was talking to a moth
the other evening
he was trying to break into
an electric light bulb
and fry himself on the wires

why do you fellows
pull this stunt i asked him

because it is the conventional
thing for moths or why
if that had been an uncovered
candle instead of an electric
light bulb you would
now be a small unsightly cinder
have you no sense

plenty of it he answered
but at times we get tired
of using it
we get bored with the routine
and crave beauty
and excitement
fire is beautiful
and we know that if we get
too close it will kill us
but what does that matter
it is better to be happy
for a moment
and be burned up with beauty
than to live a long time
and be bored all the while
so we wad all our life up
into one little roll
and then we shoot the roll
that is what life is for
it is better to be a part of beauty
for one instant and then cease to
exist than to exist forever
and never be a part of beauty
our attitude toward life
is come easy go easy
we are like human beings
used to be before they became
too civilized to enjoy themselves

and before i could argue him
out of his philosophy
he went and immolated himself
on a patent cigar lighter
i do not agree with him
myself i would rather have
half the happiness and twice
the longevity

but at the same time i wish
there was something i wanted
as badly as he wanted to fry himself

archy

(1927)

Questions for Discussion and Writing

1. What is the moth's justification for throwing himself onto a flame? How does his point of view contrast with Archy the cockroach's attitude toward life and death?
2. Explain Archy's ambivalence, expressed in the last stanza of the poem.
3. Write a short essay speculating on how Marquis meant the poem to apply to the human beings reading his column.

Linda Pastan 1932–

Born in the Bronx, Linda Pastan was raised in a Jewish family. After graduating from college, she put her career on hold to get married and raise children. Ten years later she returned to poetry, publishing her first book at age thirty-nine. The poet May Sarton writes that Pastan offers "a wry unsentimental acceptance of hard truth." In a typical line, Pastan observes, "I made a list of things I have to remember and a list of things I want to forget, but I see they are the same list." Her works investigate the depths of seemingly mundane experience, using clear language and everyday metaphors.

Marks

My husband gives me an A
for last night's supper,
an incomplete for my ironing,
a B plus in bed.
My son says I am average,
an average mother, but if
I put my mind to it
I could improve.
My daughter believes
in Pass/Fail and tells me
I pass. Wait 'til they learn
I'm dropping out.

(1978)

Questions for Discussion and Writing

1. How would you describe the speaker in the poem? What is her status in the family? How do the other family members perceive her?
2. Explain the significance of the title. Make up another title that would also fit the poem.

3. What do the speaker's marks in different activities suggest about her? About the graders?
4. Did you ever feel that you were being evaluated on something that you really shouldn't be given marks for? Remember your feelings about this and relate them to the meaning of "Marks."

Lucille Clifton 1936–

Lucille Clifton grew up in Buffalo, New York, the child of parents without much formal schooling who instilled in their children the value of education and the love of reading. She began writing as a child but later remarked that "the only writers I ever saw in the New York public schools were portraits on the wall of old dead white men with beards from New England." But she developed the "respect and wonder and love for language" that enabled her to become a poet. "The only reason to write poetry," she declares, "is to assert the importance of being human."

homage to my hips

these hips are big hips.
they need space to
move around in.
they don't fit into little
petty places. these hips
are free hips.
they don't like to be held back.
these hips have never been enslaved.
they go where they want to go.
they do what they want to do.
these hips are mighty hips.
these hips are magic hips.
i have known them
to put a spell on a man and
spin him like a top!

(1987)

Questions for Discussion and Writing

1. What is the unexpected element in "homage to my hips"? Point out examples.
2. Any big-hipped woman could appreciate the speaker's sentiments on some level. Do you think that knowing that Lucille Clifton is African American adds anything to your appreciation of the poem? What details stand out

when you think of the author's race? Do you think this attention is fair or unfair? Argue for your answer.

3. Why are the last three lines especially impressive concerning the power of the speaker's hips?
4. Identify one of your physical or emotional qualities that others might see as a negative but that you believe makes you a stronger or better person. Write an essay arguing your point.

Ron Koertge 1940–

Ron Koertge, an only child, grew up "fairly happy" in a comfortable home in Olney, Illinois. As a teenager, he was taken ill with rheumatic fever, which weakened his heart and left him with "a sense of the insubstantiality of my body and made me alternately tentative and foolishly bold." He had a dramatic flair and loved attention, loved to shock people, "to leave them lurching, not laughing." He did not begin writing poetry until he was in graduate school. In fact, he claims, "I didn't so much plan to be a writer. Mostly I wrote a lot. Then people started to call me a writer."

Cinderella's Diary

I miss my stepmother. What a thing to say
but it's true. The prince is so boring: four
hours to dress and then the cheering throngs.
Again. The page who holds the door is cute
enough to eat. Where is he once Mr. Charming
kisses my forehead goodnight?

Every morning I gaze out a casement window
at the hunters, dark men with blood on their
boots who joke and mount, their black trousers
straining, rough beards, callused hands, selfish,
abrupt...

Oh, dear diary—I am lost in ever after:
Those insufferable birds, someone in every
room with a lute, the queen calling me to look
at another painting of her son, this time
holding the transparent slipper I wish
I'd never seen.

(2007)

Questions for Discussion and Writing

1. What do people usually write in diaries? How does your answer help you understand the poem?
2. What does Koertge's Cinderella really want? Support your answer with details. What is unexpected about her desires?
3. What is the writer's attitude toward Cinderella? Explain your answer using evidence from the poem. What is *your* attitude toward this Cinderella, and why?
4. Write a poem or prose narrative about what happens *after* the end of a well-known story. Imagine what happens after the close of a Disney fairy tale, a romantic movie, a war adventure, for example. If you like, choose one character from the story as the speaker, as Koertge does.

Billy Collins 1941–

Born in New York City, William James (Billy) Collins has lived there ever since. His father is an electrician, his mother a nurse. Selected as Poet Laureate of the United States in 2000, he served two terms. He has managed to combine critical approval with unprecedented popular success. His last three collections of poems have broken sales records for poetry. "Usually," he says, "I try to create a hospitable tone at the beginning of a poem. Stepping from the title to the first lines is like stepping into a canoe. A lot of things can go wrong."

Introduction to Poetry

I ask them to take a poem
and hold it up to the light
like a color slide

or press an ear against its hive.

I say drop a mouse into a poem
and watch him probe his way out,

or walk inside the poem's room
and feel the walls for a light switch.

I want them to water-ski
across the surface of a poem
waving at the author's name on the shore.

But all they want to do
is tie the poem to a chair with a rope
and torture a confession out of it.

They begin beating it with a hose
to find out what it really means.

(1988)

Questions for Discussion and Writing

1. Who is "I" in the poem? Who are "they"? Does the title help you identify who these people represent? In what two different ways could you take the title?
2. The "I" presents five metaphors as possible approaches to understanding a poem. Can you explain what type of approach each metaphor suggests? Even if not, can you identify which approach *you* usually take when studying a poem? How would you describe your usual process if you don't understand a poem right away?
3. While the "I" uses five metaphors, the "they" present only one metaphor. What is it? Why is the last metaphor humorous? Can you explain more than one reason why this metaphor for understanding a poem represents a bad approach?

Craig Raine 1944–

Born into a working-class family in Durham, England, Craig Raine says he "wasn't a religious boy," that he "never liked God." One of his early teachers described his attempts at poetry as "pimply Dylan Thomas," but he was not deterred. "I really have a free-floating acceptance of possibilities," he later declared; "I don't think anything is unthinkable. What the poet does is as ordinary and mysterious as digesting. I question. I break life down. I impose chaos on order."

A Martian Sends a Postcard Home

Caxtons are mechanical birds with many wings
and some are treasured for their markings—

they cause the eyes to melt
or the body to shriek without pain.

I have never seen one fly, but
sometimes they perch on the hand.

Mist is when the sky is tired of flight
and rests its soft machine on the ground:

then the world is dim and bookish
like engravings under tissue paper.

Rain is when the earth is television.
It has the properites of making colours darker.

Model T is a room with the lock inside—
a key is turned to free the world

for movement, so quick there is a film
to watch for anything missed.

But time is tied to the wrist
or kept in a box, ticking with impatience.

In homes, a haunted apparatus sleeps,
that snores when you pick it up.

If the ghost cries, they carry it
to their lips and soothe it to sleep

with sounds. And yet, they wake it up
deliberately, by tickling with a finger.

Only the young are allowed to suffer
openly. Adults go to a punishment room

with water but nothing to eat.
They lock the door and suffer the noises

alone. No one is exempt
and everyone's pain has a different smell.

At night, when all the colours die,
they hide in pairs

and read about themselves—
in colour, with their eyelids shut.

(1979)

Questions for Discussion and Writing

1. Craig Raine and his fellow poet Christopher Reid were main writers in the Martian Poetry movement in the 1970s and early 1980s in England. This poetry used odd and unusual metaphors to describe things through the eyes of a Martian, as the poem printed here does. Why would things look different to a Martian than they do to an Earthling? Have you ever felt like an alien trying to understand your surroundings? Describe the situation.
2. The postcard describes a series of common objects and phenomenon. In a small group of classmates, work to explain as many of these as you can identify and why the Martian sees them the way it does. As a whole class, see whether you can identify all of the images in the postcard.
3. Martian Poetry is conceptually related to other poetic traditions such as medieval riddles, which gave a description of something as well as apt metaphors and then asked the reader for the answer, "What am I?" Here's an example:

   My house is not quiet, I am not loud; But for us God fashioned our fate together.
   I am the swifter, at times the stronger, My house more enduring, longer to last.

At times I rest; my dwelling still runs; Within it I lodge as long as I live.
Should we two be severed, my death is sure.

The answer is, "A fish in water." Try to write a poem or prose poem in the form of a riddle.

Jan Beatty 1952–

Born in Pittsburgh, Jan Beatty, who directs the creative writing program at Carlow, a Catholic university in Pennsylvania, is in charge of their Madwomen in the Attic Writing Workshop—so named to challenge old traditions of women's writing (when these crazy ladies were kept shut away from view). One critic observes that her poems "question icons, invoke taboos, and walk the tightrope between sex and love." In April 2008 Beatty encountered difficulty at a poetry reading because her poems were considered "too sexually explicit."

A Waitress's Instructions on Tipping or Get the Cash Up and Don't Waste My Time

20% minimum as long as the waitress doesn't inflict bodily harm.
If you're two people at a four top, tip extra.
If you sit a long time, pay rent.
Double tips for special orders.
Always tip extra when using coupons.
Better yet, don't use coupons.
Never leave change instead of bills.
Never leave pennies at all.
Never hide a tip for fun.
Overtip, overtip, overtip.
Remember, I am somebody's mother or daughter.
Large parties *must* overtip, no separate piles of change.
If people in your party don't show up, tip *for* them.
Don't wait around for gratitude if you overtip.
Take a risk. Don't adjust your tip so your credit card total is even.
Don't ever, ever pull out a tipping guide in public.
If you leave 10% or less, eat at home.
If I call a taxi for you, tip me.
If I hang your coat for you, tip me.

If I get cigarettes for you, tip me.
Better yet, do it yourself.
If you buy a $50 bottle of wine, pull out a $10.
If I serve you one cocktail, don't hand me $.35
If you're just having coffee, leave a $5.
Don't fold a bill and hand it to me like you're a big shot.
Don't say, *there's a big tip in it for you if…*
Don't say, *I want to make sure you get this,* like a busboy would steal it.
Don't say, *Here, honey, this is for you.*—ever.
Don't say, *I'll make it worth your while.*
If you're miserable, there's not enough money in the world.

(1995)

Questions for Discussion and Writing

1. Who is the speaker? What is her attitude toward restaurant customers? Quote words and phrases that show this attitude. How would you describe the language used in the poem?
2. Did you learn anything about being a waitress or a customer from reading this poem? What was it? Do you think that Jan Beatty ever held a job as a waitress? Why?
3. Much of the poem tells us about the customers, but the last two lines tell us something more about the speaker. What may we conclude about her from these lines?
4. Write a poem in the same form as this one, giving a list of advice for customers, clients, or bosses you have worked with. Close with a line or two that tells something about you as a worker in the site you wrote about.

Peter Pereira 1959–

Born in Spokane, Washington, Peter Pereira is a family physician in Seattle and co-founder of Floating Bridge Press. His parents, who were pen pals after World War II, eventually met, fell in love, married, and raised ten kids together. As a Catholic during the restive 1960s, Pereira learned to question authority, social conventions, and Biblical constructs. "Reconsidering the Seven," he says, "is an example of such questioning." He has been happily united with his partner Dean for twenty-two years.

Reconsidering the Seven

Deadly Sins? Please—let's replace Pride
with Modesty, especially when it's false.

And thank goodness for Lust, without it
I wouldn't be here. Would you?

Envy, Greed—why not? If they lead us
to better ourselves, to Ambition.

And Gluttony, like a healthy belch, is a guest's
best response to being served a good meal.

I'll take Sloth over those busybodies
who can't sit still, watch a sunset

without yammering, or snapping a picture.
Now *that* makes me Wrathful.

(2007)

Questions for Discussion and Writing

1. What are the seven deadly sins? Where does the list come from originally?
2. Why does the speaker reconsider the seven deadly sins? What makes the reconsideration funny? Do you find the argument persuasive? Why or why not?
3. Write a poem or prose poem in which you suggest the positive side of something usually considered negative. Try to make your work humorous by using unexpected but not completely unreasonable points, as Pereira does.

Jeanne Marie Beaumont 1954–

Jeanne Marie Beaumont, born in Springfield, Pennsylvania, spent her childhood there in the suburbs, which she says she detested, "feeling stifled and rebellious." Her parents, who neither encouraged nor discouraged her writing, did instill in her "a sense of discipline." Her poetry is informed by her interest in folklore, fairy tales, history, modernism, surrealism, theatre of the absurd, and play. A three-minute film using the text of "Afraid So" read by Garrison Keillor has been shown in schools and at many film festivals since appearing in January 2000.

Afraid So

Is it starting to rain?
Did the check bounce?
Are we out of coffee?
Is this going to hurt?
Could you lose your job?

Did the glass break?
Was the baggage misrouted?
Will this go on my record?
Are you missing much money?
Was anyone injured?
Is the traffic heavy?
Do I have to remove my clothes?
Will it leave a scar?
Must you go?
Will this be in the papers?
Is my time up already?
Are we seeing the understudy?
Will it affect my eyesight?
Did all the books burn?
Are you still smoking?
Is the bone broken?
Will I have to put him to sleep?
Was the car totaled?
Am I responsible for these charges?
Are you contagious?
Will we have to wait long?
Is the runway icy?
Was the gun loaded?
Could this cause side effects?
Do you know who betrayed you?
Is the wound infected?
Are we lost?
Will it get any worse?

(2004)

Questions for Discussion and Writing

1. What is the answer to all of the questions that compose the poem? When you were reading the poem, when did you realize this was true? Did this realization add to the humor? Why or why not?
2. Reread the poem looking for some logical reason for the order of the questions. Can you make sense of the organization? What is it? Give some examples to support your idea.
3. Write a poem using the same form as Beaumont's with the title "Probably Not," "You Bet," or some other phrase that can answer all the questions you write.

Jay Leeming 1969–

Jay Leeming, born and raised in Ithaca, New York, now teaches, writes, and plays guitar, still in Ithaca, New York. His fellow poet Martin Prechtel writes about Leeming's collection *Dynamite on a China Plate* (2006), "Every poem in [it] drenches us like the wake of a blue whale suddenly breaching from someone's suburban lawn pool." And Robert Bly declares, "His poems are winged beings that dive straight to the playful, lunatic heart of human companionship." His friends simply testify that "he's a funny man."

Man Writes Poem

This just in a man has begun writing a poem
in a small room in Brooklyn. His curtains
are apparently blowing in the breeze. We go now
to our man Harry on the scene, what's

the story down there Harry? "Well Chuck
he has begun the second stanza and seems
to be doing fine, he's using a blue pen, most
poets these days use blue or black ink so blue

is a fine choice. His curtains are indeed blowing
in a breeze of some kind and what's more his radiator
is 'whistling' somewhat. No metaphors have been written yet,
but I'm sure he's rummaging around down there

in the tin cans of his soul and will turn up something
for us soon. Hang on—just breaking news here Chuck,
there are 'birds singing' outside his window, and a car
with a bad muffler has just gone by. Yes... definitely

a confirmation on the singing birds." Excuse me Harry
but the poem seems to be taking on a very auditory quality
at this point wouldn't you say? "Yes Chuck, you're right,
but after years of experience I would hesitate to predict

exactly where this poem is going to go. Why I remember
being on the scene with Frost in '47, and with Stevens in '53,
and if there's one thing about poems these days it's that
hang on, something's happening here, he's just compared the curtains

to his mother, and he's described the radiator as 'Roaring deep
with the red walrus of History.' Now that's a key line,
especially appearing here, somewhat late in the poem,
when all of the similes are about to go home. In fact he seems

a bit knocked out with the effort of writing that line,
and who wouldn't be? Looks like... yes, he's put down his pen
and has gone to brush his teeth. Back to you Chuck." Well
thanks Harry. Wow, the life of the artist. That's it for now,

but we'll keep you informed of more details as they arise.

(2006)

Questions for Discussion and Writing

1. Who is the speaker of the poem? Who is being spoken about? Who is being spoken to? Considering your answers, what type of discourse or talk is being imitated in the poem? Give some examples of wording that helped you see the situation being portrayed.
2. Why is the writing of poetry *not* a newsworthy event? Does the poem suggest that it should be, or that it should not? Give examples from the poem that support your idea.
3. Look up "Frost in '47" and "Stevens in '53." Why does Chuck bring up these two names to Harry and the audience? Does he make a point about them?
4. Think of another activity that isn't usually material for a broadcast, and describe it in a newsy style as Leeming does in "Man Writes Poem": "Child Throws Tantrum," "Teenager Sulks," "Student Procrastinates," "Cat Watches Bird," for instance.

Making Connections

1. Much of the humorous quality of poetry comes from its *tone*: that is, the attitude it conveys, such as in "tone of voice." Following is a list of words that can describe tone in literature. Look up any unfamiliar or vague terms in a dictionary so that you are clear on their meaning. Assign at least two of the terms to each of the ten poems in this portfolio. Get together with a group of classmates and discuss your choices, and report to the whole class the choices where you found most agreement.

whimsical	naive	intolerant
satiric	sympathetic	surprising
bitter	forgiving	intellectual
comical	sharp	ludicrous
warm		

2. Some of our pleased reaction to poems comes from the joy of figuring out some puzzle that they present. This principle is obvious in "A Martian Sends a Postcard Home." What other poems in this portfolio involve your unraveling a puzzle of some kind? Apply this principle to at least four other poems in the portfolio, and explain what the puzzle is that had to be solved by the reader. Then do the same to two poems in the Anthology of Poetry.

PART IV

Writing About Drama

This section, focusing on drama and including brief discussions of its beginnings and more recent developments in contemporary theater, completes our literary and rhetorical instruction.

16

How Do I Read a Play?

A play is written to be performed. Although most drama begins with a written script, the author of a play counts on the collaboration of others—actors, directors, set designers, costumers, makeup artists, lighting and sound engineers—to translate the written words into a performance on stage or film or videotape. Unlike novelists and poets, playwrights do not necessarily expect their words to be read by the audience.

The performance goal of drama does not mean, however, that you cannot read and study a play as you would a story or a poem. Plays share many literary qualities with other types of creative writing: character, plot, structure, atmosphere, theme, symbolism, and point of view. But it is important to recognize the differences between reading a play and seeing one performed.

Listen to the Lines

The major difference between reading and watching a play is that, as a reader, you do not have the actors' voices and gestures to interpret the lines and establish the characters for you. Because playwrights rely almost entirely on speeches or conversations (called *dialogue*) to define character, develop plot, and convey theme, it will be your task as a reader to listen to the lines in your mind. Read the dialogue as you would expect to hear it spoken. For example, when you read Antigone's response to Creon,

> So for me, at least, to meet this doom of yours
> is precious little pain. But if I had allowed
> my own mother's son to rot, an unburied corpse—
> that would have been an agony!

do you hear the assurance and passion in her voice? Or when you read the speech that Troy Maxson directs to "Mr. Death," do you detect the mixture of defiance and anger and fear in his words?

> I'm gonna tell you what I'm gonna do. I'm gonna take and build me a fence around this yard. See? I'm gonna build me a fence around what belongs to me. And then I want you to stay on the other side. See? You stay over there until you're ready for me. Then you come on. Bring your army. Bring your sickle. Bring your wrestling clothes. I ain't gonna fall down on my vigilance this time. You ain't gonna sneak up on me no more.

Of course, the tone of these lines is not as clear when they are taken out of context, but even these brief quotations illustrate the charged nature of language you should expect when you read a play.

You can actually read the lines out loud to yourself or enlist some fellow students to act out some scenes with you. These oral readings will force you to decide how to interpret the words. Most of the time, however, you will have to use your imagination to re-create the sound of the spoken medium. If you do get to see a performance of a play you are reading or to hear a recording of it, you will appreciate the extraordinary liveliness of dramatic literature when it is lifted from the page and provided with sound and action.

Reading a play does have some advantage over viewing a live performance. Unlike a theatergoer, a reader can stop and return to lines or speeches that seem especially complicated or meaningful. Close reading gives you the opportunity to examine and consider the playwright's exact words, which often fly by quickly, sometimes in altered form, in an actual performance.

Visualize the Scene

In addition to imagining the sound of the dialogue, you will want to picture in your mind what the stage looks like. In a traditional theater the audience sits out front while the actors perform on a raised stage separated from the viewers by a curtain and perhaps an orchestra. The arch from which the curtain hangs is called the *proscenium*; the space extending from the bottom of the curtain to the footlights is the *apron*. The stage directions (printed in italics) indicate where the playwright wants the actors to move. *Upstage* means toward the back; *downstage* means toward the apron. A traditional set, made of canvas-covered frames called *flats*, will look like a room—with one wall removed for the audience to see through. Sometimes the set will be constructed to resemble the battlements of a castle, an opening in a forest, or a lifeboat on the ocean. Occasionally the setting is only suggested: a character climbs a ladder to deliver lines supposedly from a balcony or from an upstairs room. In one modern play, the two protagonists are presented on a bare stage speaking throughout the production (with only their heads visible) from inside garbage cans.

Another kind of stage, called *theater in the round* or an *arena stage*, puts the audience in raised seats on all sides with the players performing in the round space in the middle. After the audience is seated, the lights are extinguished, and the actors enter through the same aisles used earlier by the audience. When the actors are in position, the lights come up, illuminating only the stage, and the play begins. At the end of a scene or an act, the lights go down again, signifying the fall of the curtain and allowing the actors to leave. Stagehands come on between acts or scenes, if needed, to rearrange the setting. Not all plays are suited to this intimate staging, of course, but the audience at an arena production gains an immediacy, a feeling almost of being involved in the action, that cannot be achieved in a traditional theater.

Envision the Action

Poet and playwright Ezra Pound pointed out that the "medium of drama is not words, but persons moving about on a stage using words." This observation underlines the importance of movement, gesture, and setting in the performance of a play. These nonverbal elements of the language of drama are sometimes described in the author's stage directions. Often, though, you will find the cues for gestures, movements, and facial expressions in the words themselves, just as the director and the actors do when they are preparing a script for production. For example, these lines of Othello, spoken when he has been roused from his bed by a fight among his men, suggest the physical performance that would accompany the words:

> Why, how now, ho! from whence ariseth this?
> Are we turn'd Turks, and to ourselves do that
> Which heaven hath forbid the Ottomites?
> For Christian shame, put by this barbarous brawl
> He that stirs next to carve for his own rage
> Holds his soul light; he dies upon his motion.
> Silence that dreadful bell.

Reading this speech with an actor's or director's imagination, you can see in your mind the character stride angrily into the fight scene, gesture threateningly at the men who are poised to continue the fight, and then point suddenly offstage in the direction of the clamoring alarm bell. Such a detailed reading will take time, but you will be rewarded by the fun and satisfaction of catching the full dramatic quality of the play.

In more recent years, playwrights like David Hwang and August Wilson have tried to keep artistic control over the interpretations of their works by including detailed stage directions in their scripts. The extensive production notes for Wilson's *Fences* sometimes read like descriptions from a novel or an essay.

> Troy is fifty-three years old, a large man with thick, heavy hands; it is his largeness that he strives to fill out and make an accommodation with. Together with his blackness, his largeness informs his sensibilities and the choices he has made in his life.

With or without notes like this, your imagination will be working full time when you read a play. You will not be at the mercy of some designer's taste or the personal interpretation of a director or actor. You will be free to produce the play in the theater of your mind.

Drama on Film

Many plays are available on videotape or digital videodiscs. These include filmed versions of stage performances, such as the Laurence Olivier production of Shakespeare's *Othello*, and movies adapted from plays, such as the screen version of David Hwang's *M. Butterfly* starring Jeremy Irons. You will find that many plays in this book are on video.

You can often gain insight and special pleasure from seeing a dramatic work on film. A video production provides you with an opportunity to compare your responses to the play as you read it with your responses as you watch the video. You will also be able to think about the decisions that the film director has made. Here are some points to consider when comparing a film to the written text of a play:

- What scenes or characters, if any, have been cut? What, if anything, has been added? Why do you think these changes were made? What is their effect?
- Are the characters portrayed as you imagined they would be? Has the film changed your perception of the characters or your understanding of the plot?
- Would you have cast the same actors in these roles? If not, whom would you have chosen? What difference do you think your choices would make?
- Does the film focus your attention on certain characters or actions through such techniques as close-ups or reaction shots? What are the results of these uses of the camera?
- How is the setting different from what you imagined as you read the play? Did the filmmaker take liberties with the setting suggested by the playwright? (For example, were indoor play scenes transferred outdoors in the film?)
- Does the play transfer effectively from the page to the screen? Do you think the play is better suited to the stage?
- Does the film version clarify the play for you? Does it enhance your appreciation of the play? Can you explain why or why not?
- Do you think the playwright would be pleased with the film version? Why or why not?

- Imagine that you are directing a film version of a play that you have read. What important decisions about character, setting, and pacing of the action would you have to make? Would you cut any scenes? Would you add any new scenes? What advice would you give to the performers about their roles?

Before writing about a play or a film, be sure to respond to the critical questions in Chart 16-1.

Chart 16-1 Critical Questions for Reading Plays

Before planning an analysis of any of the plays in this text, write out your answers to the following questions to be sure you understand the play and to help you generate material for your paper.

1. What is the central conflict in the play? How is it resolved?
2. Does the play contain any secondary conflicts (subplots)? How do they relate to the main conflict?
3. Does the play follow a traditional dramatic structure (see Chapter 17)? What is the climax? Is there a denouement?
4. Who is the main character or protagonist (see Chapter 17)? What sort of person is he or she? Does this protagonist have a fatal flaw? Is the protagonist a hero (see Chapter 18)?
5. Is the antagonist (the one who opposes the protagonist) a person, an environment, or a social force (see Chapter 17)? If a person, does the antagonist cause conflict intentionally?
6. Do the other characters provide exposition (background information)? Are they used as *foils* to oppose, contrast, criticize, and thus help develop the main characters?
7. What are the time and setting of the play? How important are these elements? Could the play be set just as effectively in another time or place?
8. Does the title provide any clues to an understanding of the play? If you had to give the play another title, what would it be?
9. What is the theme of the play? Can you state it in a single sentence?
10. Is the play a tragedy, a comedy, or a mixture (see Chapter 18)? Is this classification important?
11. Is the presentation realistic? Does the playwright use any special theatrical devices (such as lighting, music, costumes, distinctive or surreal settings)? If so, what effect do they have on your impression of the play?

17

Writing About Dramatic Structure

Drama is not as flexible as other forms of literature. A writer of fiction can take as much time as needed to inform the reader about character, setting, motivation, or theme. The dramatist must do everything quickly and clearly. Audiences will not sit through a tedious first act; neither can they stop the play, pick it up tomorrow, or go back to Act I to refresh their memories. Even with the technology of video recording, most plays, including film and television drama, are seen in a single, relatively brief sitting.

What Is Dramatic Structure?

More than two thousand years ago the Greek philosopher Aristotle pointed out that the most important element of drama is the ***fable***, what we call the *story*, or ***plot***. The fable, said Aristotle, has to have a beginning, a middle, and an end. As obvious as this observation seems, it emphasizes the dramatist's special need to engage an audience early and keep it engaged until the conclusion of the play.

Recognizing the drama's strict time limits, Aristotle set down a number of conditions for developing the fable, or plot, in a clear and interesting way. According to Aristotle, the heart of the dramatic story is the *agon*, or ***argument***, and the conflict surrounding this argument creates tension and incites interest. The two sides of the conflict, the pros and cons of the argument, are represented on stage by the ***protagonist*** and the ***antagonist***. The protagonist may be one person or many, and the antagonist may be a person, a group, a thing, or a force (supernatural or natural). We often call the protagonist of a play its ***hero*** or ***heroine***, and sometimes the antagonist is also the *villain*.

The fundamental struggle between the protagonist and the antagonist is developed according to a set pattern that theater audiences have come to recognize and expect. This conventional structure can be varied, of course, but most dramatic literature contains the following components:

1. ***Point of attack:*** the starting point from which the dramatist leads the audience into the plot. A playwright can begin at the story's beginning and allow the audience to discover what is going on at the same time the characters do; or the writer can begin in the middle of things (*in medias res*), or even near the end, and gradually reveal the events that have already taken place.
2. ***Exposition:*** the revelation of facts, circumstances, and past events. The essential facts about the characters and the conflict can be established in a number of ways, from having minor characters reveal information through conversation to plunging the audience right into the action.
3. ***Rising action:*** the building of interest through complication of the conflict. In this stage, the protagonist and antagonist move steadily toward a confrontation.
4. ***Climax:*** the play's high point, the decisive showdown between protagonist and antagonist. The climax—the play's turning point—can be a single moment or a series of events, but once reached, it becomes a point of no return.
5. ***Falling action:*** the unraveling of the plot, where events fall into place and the conflict moves toward final resolution.
6. ***Denouement:*** the play's conclusion, the explanation or outcome of the action. The term *denouement* (literally an "untying") may be applied to both comedy and tragedy, but the Greeks used the word *catastrophe* for a tragic denouement, probably because it involved the death of the hero or heroine. Comedies, of course, end happily, often with a wedding.

Whatever it is called, the denouement marks the end of the play: the lovers kiss, the bodies are carried off the stage, and the audience goes home. Most dramatists employ this traditional pattern. Even when they mix in other devices, rearrange elements, and invent new ways to exhibit their materials, dramatists still establish a conflict, develop both sides of the argument, and reach a credible conclusion. After centuries of theater history, the basic structure of drama has changed very little.

Looking at Dramatic Structure

As you read *Antigone*, written in 442 B.C., notice that the play's central conflict is introduced, developed, and resolved according to the pattern we have just described.

Although written first, *Antigone* is the third and last play in the chronology of events composing Sophocles's Oedipus cycle; the first two plays are *Oedipus the King* and *Oedipus at Colonus.*

According to Greek legend, King Laius of Thebes and his descendants were doomed by the god Apollo. Warned by the Oracle of Delphi that his own son would kill him, Laius leaves the son, Oedipus, to die in the mountains. But Oedipus survives and unknowingly kills his father, whom he encounters on the road to Thebes. Oedipus solves the riddle of the Sphinx for the Thebans and becomes their king, unwittingly marrying his mother, Jocasta, the widow of Laius. Several years later, when he learns what he has done, Oedipus blinds himself and leaves Thebes. Creon, brother of Jocasta, becomes the ruler of Thebes and is entrusted with caring for Oedipus's two daughters, Antigone and Ismene. Oedipus's two sons, Polynices and Eteocles, reject their father and struggle for power in Thebes. Polynices is driven from the city but returns with an army; in the ensuing battle he and Eteocles kill each other, while Creon succeeds to the throne. As the play opens, Antigone and Ismene are discussing Creon's first official decree.

Sophocles *ca. 496–ca. 405* B.C.

Sophocles wrote more than 120 plays, but only 7 have survived. Born in Colonus, near Athens, he studied under Aeschylus, the master of Greek tragedy. Sophocles did not question the justice of the gods; his plays assume a divine order that humans must follow. His strong-willed protagonists end tragically because of pride and lack of self-knowledge. His works include *Oedipus the King*, *Antigone*, *Electra*, and *Ajax*.

Antigone

Translated by Robert Fagles

CHARACTERS

ANTIGONE, *daughter of Oedipus and Jocasta*
ISMENE, *sister of Antigone*
A CHORUS *of old Theban citizens and their* LEADER
CREON, *king of Thebes, uncle of Antigone and Ismene*
A SENTRY
HAEMON, *son of Creon and Eurydice*
TIRESIAS, *a blind prophet*
A MESSENGER
EURYDICE, *wife of Creon*
GUARDS, ATTENDANTS, *and* A BOY

TIME AND SCENE

The royal house of Thebes. It is still night, and invading armies have just been driven from the city. Fighting on opposite sides, the sons of Oedipus, Eteocles and Polynices, have killed each other in combat. Their uncle, CREON, *is now king of Thebes.*

Enter ANTIGONE, *slipping through the central doors of the palace. She motions to her sister,* ISMENE, *who follows her cautiously toward an altar at the center of the stage.*

The opening scene from a modern-dress production (1946) of *Anitgone*, with Katharine Cornell in the title role. Antigone is seated alone to the left, with the Narrator, a substitute for the Greek chorus, gesturing in the center and Haemon and Ismene standing at the right. (AP/Wide World Photos)

ANTIGONE. My own flesh and blood—dear sister, dear Ismene,
how many griefs our father Oedipus handed down!
Do you know one, I ask you, one grief
that Zeus[1] will not perfect for the two of us
while we still live and breathe? There's nothing,
no pain—our lives are pain—no private shame,
no public disgrace, nothing I haven't seen
in your griefs and mine. And now this:
an emergency decree, they say, the Commander
has just declared for all of Thebes.
What, haven't you heard? Don't you see?
The doom reserved for enemies
marches on the ones we love the most.
ISMENE. Not I, I haven't heard a word, Antigone.
Nothing of loved ones,
no joy or pain has come my way, not since
the two of us were robbed of our two brothers,
both gone in a day, a double blow—
not since the armies of Argos vanished,
just this very night. I know nothing more,
whether our luck's improved or ruin's still to come.
ANTIGONE. I thought so. That's why I brought you out here,
past the gates, so you could hear in private.
ISMENE. What's the matter? Trouble, clearly…
you sound so dark, so grim.

[1]**Zeus** The highest Olympian deity.

Antigone. Why not? Our own brothers' burial!
Hasn't Creon graced one with all the rites,
disgraced the other? Eteocles, they say,
has been given full military honors,
rightly so—Creon's laid him in the earth
and he goes with glory down among the dead.
But the body of Polynices, who died miserably—
why, a city-wide proclamation, rumor has it,
forbids anyone to bury him, even mourn him.
He's to be left unwept, unburied, a lovely treasure
for birds that scan the field and feast to their heart's content.

Such, I hear, is the martial law our good Creon
lays down for you and me—yes, me, I tell you—
and he's coming here to alert the uninformed
in no uncertain terms,
and he won't treat the matter lightly. Whoever
disobeys in the least will die, his doom is sealed:
stoning to death inside the city walls!

There you have it. You'll soon show what you are,
worth your breeding, Ismene, or a coward—
for all your royal blood.
Ismene. My poor sister, if things have come to this,
who am I to make or mend them, tell me,
what good am I to you?
Antigone. Decide.
Will you share the labor, share the work?
Ismene. What work, what's the risk? What do you mean?
Antigone.
Raising her hands.
Will you lift up his body with these bare hands
and lower it with me?
Ismene. What? You'd bury him—
when a law forbids the city?
Antigone. Yes!
He is my brother and—deny it as you will—
your brother too.
No one will ever convict me for a traitor.
Ismene. So desperate, and Creon has expressly—
Antigone. No,
he has no right to keep me from my own.
Ismene. Oh my sister, think—
think how our own father died, hated,
his reputation in ruins, driven on
by the crimes he brought to light himself
to gouge out his eyes with his own hands—
then mother . . . his mother and wife, both in one,
mutilating her life in the twisted noose—
and last, our two brothers dead in a single day,

both shedding their own blood, poor suffering boys,
battling out their common destiny hand-to-hand.

Now look at the two of us, left so alone…
think what a death we'll die, the worst of all
if we violate the laws and override
the fixed decree of the throne, its power—
we must be sensible. Remember we are women,
we're not born to contend with men. Then too,
we're underlings, ruled by much stronger hands,
so we must submit in this, and things still worse.

I, for one, I'll beg the dead to forgive me—
I'm forced, I have no choice—I must obey
the ones who stand in power. Why rush to extremes?
It's madness, madness.

ANTIGONE. I won't insist,
no, even if you should have a change of heart,
I'd never welcome you in the labor, not with me.
So, do as you like, whatever suits you best—
I'll bury him myself.
And even if I die in the act, that death will be a glory.
I'll lie with the one I love and loved by him—
an outrage sacred to the gods! I have longer
to please the dead than please the living here:
in the kingdom down below I'll lie forever.
Do as you like, dishonor the laws
the gods hold in honor.

ISMENE. I'd do them no dishonor…
but defy the city? I have no strength for that.

ANTIGONE. You have your excuses. I am on my way,
I'll raise a mound for him, for my dear brother.

ISMENE. Oh Antigone, you're so rash—I'm so afraid for you!

ANTIGONE. Don't fear for me. Set your own life in order.

ISMENE. Then don't, at least, blurt this out to anyone.
Keep it a secret. I'll join you in that, I promise.

ANTIGONE . Dear god, shout it from the rooftops. I'll hate you
all the more for silence—tell the world!

ISMENE. So fiery—and it ought to chill your heart.

ANTIGONE. I know I please where I must please the most.

ISMENE. Yes, if you can, but you're in love with impossibility.

ANTIGONE. Very well then, once my strength gives out
I will be done at last.

ISMENE. You're wrong from the start.
You're off on a hopeless quest.

ANTIGONE. If you say so, you will make me hate you,
and the hatred of the dead, by all rights,
will haunt you night and day.
But leave me to my own absurdity, leave me
to suffer this—dreadful thing. I'll suffer

nothing as great as death without glory.
Exit to the side.
Ismene. Then go if you must, but rest assured,
wild, irrational as you are, my sister,
you are truly dear to the ones who love you.
Withdrawing to the palace. Enter a Chorus, *the old citizens of Thebes, chanting as the sun begins to rise.*
Chorus. Glory!—great beam of sun, brightest of all
that ever rose on the seven gates of Thebes,
you burn through night at last!
Great eye of the golden day,
mounting the Dirce's[2] banks you throw him back—
the enemy out of Argos, the white shield, the man of bronze—
he's flying headlong now
the bridle of fate stampeding him with pain!

And he had driven against our borders,
launched by the warring claims of Polynices—
like an eagle screaming, winging havoc
over the land, wings of armor
shielded white as snow,
a huge army massing,
crested helmets bristling for assault.

He hovered above our roofs, his vast maw gaping
closing down around our seven gates,
his spears thirsting for the kill
but now he's gone, look,
before he could glut his jaws with Theban blood
or the god of fire put our crown of towers to the torch.
He grappled the Dragon none can master—Thebes—
the clang of our arms like thunder at his back!

Zeus hates with a vengeance all bravado,
the mighty boasts of men. He watched them
coming on in a rising flood, the pride
of their golden armor ringing shrill—
and brandishing his lightning
blasted the fighter just at the goal,
rushing to shout his triumph from our walls.

Down from the heights he crashed, pounding down on the earth!
And a moment ago, blazing torch in hand—
mad for attack, ecstatic
he breathed his rage, the storm
of his fury hurling at our heads!

---

[2]**Dirce** A river near Thebes.

But now his high hopes have laid him low
and down the enemy ranks the iron god of war
deals his rewards, his stunning blows—Ares[3]
rapture of battle, our right arm in the crisis.

Seven captains marshaled at seven gates
seven against their equals, gave
their brazen trophies up to Zeus,
god of the breaking rout of battle,
all but two: those blood brothers,
one father, one mother—matched in rage,
spears matched for the twin conquest—
clashed and won the common prize of death.

But now for Victory! Glorious in the morning,
joy in her eyes to meet our joy
she is winging down to Thebes,
our fleets of chariots wheeling in her wake—
Now let us win oblivion from the wars,
thronging the temples of the gods
in singing, dancing choirs through the night!
Lord Dionysus,[4] god of the dance
that shakes the land of Thebes, now lead the way!

Enter CREON *from the palace, attended by his guard.*

But look, the king of the realm is coming,
Creon, the new man for the new day,
whatever the gods are sending now…
what new plan will he launch?
Why this, this special session?
Why this sudden call to the old men
summoned at one command?

CREON. My countrymen,
the ship of state is safe. The gods who rocked her,
after a long, merciless pounding in the storm,
have righted her once more.
Out of the whole city
I have called you here alone. Well I know,
first, your undeviating respect
for the throne and royal power of King Laius.
Next, while Oedipus steered the land of Thebes,
and even after he died, your loyalty was unshakable,
you still stood by their children. Now then,
since the two sons are dead—two blows of fate
in the same day, cut down by each other's hands,
both killers, both brothers stained with blood—
as I am next in kin to the dead,
I now possess the throne and all its powers.
Of course you cannot know a man completely,

---

[3]Ares God of war.
[4]Dionysus God of fertility and wine.

his character, his principles, sense of judgment,
not till he's shown his colors, ruling the people,
making laws. Experience, there's the test.
As I see it, whoever assumes the task,
the awesome task of setting the city's course,
and refuses to adopt the soundest policies
but fearing someone, keeps his lips locked tight,
he's utterly worthless. So I rate him now,
I always have. And whoever places a friend
above the good of his own country, he is nothing:
I have no use for him. Zeus my witness,
Zeus who sees all things, always—
I could never stand by silent, watching destruction
march against our city, putting safety to rout,
nor could I ever make that man a friend of mine
who menaces our country. Remember this:
our country *is* our safety.
Only while she voyages true on course
can we establish friendships, truer than blood itself.
Such are my standards. They make our city great.

Closely akin to them I have proclaimed,
just now, the following decree to our people
concerning the two sons of Oedipus.
Eteocles, who died fighting for Thebes,
excelling all in arms: he shall be buried,
crowned with a hero's honors, the cups we pour
to soak the earth and reach the famous dead.

But as for his blood brother, Polynices,
who returned from exile, home to his father-city
and the gods of his race, consumed with one desire—
to burn them roof to roots—who thirsted to drink
his kinsmen's blood and sell the rest to slavery:
that man—a proclamation has forbidden the city
to dignify him with burial, mourn him at all.
No, he must be left unburied, his corpse
carrion for the birds and dogs to tear,
an obscenity for the citizens to behold!

These are my principles. Never at my hands
will the traitor be honored above the patriot.
But whoever proves his loyalty to the state:
I'll prize that man in death as well as life.

Leader. If this is your pleasure, Creon, treating
our city's enemy and our friend this way...
The power is yours, I suppose, to enforce it
with the laws, both for the dead and all of us,
the living.

CREON. Follow my orders closely then,
be on your guard.
LEADER. We're too old.
Lay that burden on younger shoulders.
CREON. No, no,
I don't mean the body—I've posted guards already.
LEADER. What commands for us then? What other service?
CREON. See that you never side with those who break my orders.
LEADER. Never. Only a fool could be in love with death.
CREON. Death is the price—you're right. But all too often
the mere hope of money has ruined many men.

A SENTRY *enters from the side.*

SENTRY. My lord,
I can't say I'm winded from running, or set out
with any spring in my legs either—no sir,
I was lost in thought, and it made me stop, often,
dead in my tracks, wheeling, turning back,
and all the time a voice inside me muttering,
"Idiot, why? You're going straight to your death."
Then muttering, "Stopped again, poor fool?
If somebody gets the news to Creon first,
what's to save your neck?"

And so,
mulling it over, on I trudged, dragging my feet,
you can make a short road take forever...
but at last, common sense won out,
I'm here, and I'm all yours,
and even though I come empty-handed
I'll tell my story just the same, because
I've come with a good grip on one hope,
what will come will come, whatever fate—
CREON. Come to the point!
What's wrong—why so afraid?
SENTRY. First, myself, I've got to tell you,
I didn't do it, didn't see who did—
Be fair, don't take it out on me.
CREON. You're playing it safe, soldier,
barricading yourself from any trouble.
It's obvious, you've something strange to tell.
SENTRY. Dangerous too, and danger makes you delay
for all you're worth.
CREON. Out with it—then dismiss!
SENTRY. All right, here it comes. The body—
someone's just buried it, then run off...
sprinkled some dry dust on the flesh,
given it proper rites.
CREON. What?
What man alive would dare—

SENTRY. I've no idea, I swear it.
There was no mark of a spade, no pickaxe there,
no earth turned up, the ground packed hard and dry,
unbroken, no tracks, no wheelruts, nothing,
the workman left no trace. Just at sunup
the first watch of the day points it out—
it was a wonder! We were stunned…
a terrific burden too, for all of us, listen:
you can't see the corpse, not that it's buried,
really, just a light cover of road-dust on it,
as if someone meant to lay the dead to rest
and keep from getting cursed.
Not a sign in sight that dogs or wild beasts
had worried the body, even torn the skin.

But what came next! Rough talk flew thick and fast,
guard grilling guard—we'd have come to blows
at last, nothing to stop it; each man for himself
and each the culprit, no one caught red-handed,
all of us pleading ignorance, dodging the charges,
ready to take up red-hot iron in our fists,
go through fire, swear oaths to the gods—
"I didn't do it, I had no hand in it either,
not in the plotting, not in the work itself!"

Finally, after all this wrangling came to nothing,
one man spoke out and made us stare at the ground,
hanging our heads in fear. No way to counter him,
no way to take his advice and come through
safe and sound. Here's what he said:
"Look, we've got to report the facts to Creon,
we can't keep this hidden." Well, that won out,
and the lot fell on me, condemned me,
unlucky as ever, I got the prize. So here I am,
against my will and yours too, well I know—
no one wants the man who brings bad news.

LEADER. My king,
ever since he began I've been debating in my mind,
could this possibly be the work of the gods?

CREON. Stop—
before you make me choke with anger—the gods!
You, you're senile, must you be insane?
You say—why it's intolerable—say the gods
could have the slightest concern for that corpse?
Tell me, was it for meritorious service
they proceeded to bury him, prized him so? The hero
who came to burn their temples ringed with pillars,
their golden treasures—scorch their hallowed earth
and fling their laws to the winds.
Exactly when did you last see the gods
celebrating traitors? Inconceivable!

No, from the first there were certain citizens
who could hardly stand the spirit of my regime,
grumbling against me in the dark, heads together,
tossing wildly, never keeping their necks beneath
the yoke, loyally submitting to their king.
These are the instigators, I'm convinced—
they've perverted my own guard, bribed them
to do their work.
Money! Nothing worse
in our lives, so current, rampant, so corrupting.
Money—you demolish cities, root men from their homes,
you train and twist good minds and set them on
to the most atrocious schemes. No limit,
you make them adept at every kind of outrage,
every godless crime—money!
Everyone—
the whole crew bribed to commit this crime,
they've made one thing sure at least:
sooner or later they will pay the price.
Wheeling on the Sentry.
You—
I swear to Zeus as I still believe in Zeus,
if you don't find the man who buried that corpse,
the very man, and produce him before my eyes,
simple death won't be enough for you,
not till we string you up alive
and wring the immorality out of you.
Then you can steal the rest of your days,
better informed about where to make a killing.
You'll have learned, at last, it doesn't pay
to itch for rewards from every hand that beckons.
Filthy profits wreck most men, you'll see—
they'll never save your life.

Sentry. Please,
may I say a word or two, or just turn and go?
Creon. Can't you tell? Everything you say offends me.
Sentry. Where does it hurt you, in the ears or in the heart?
Creon. And who are you to pinpoint my displeasure?
Sentry. The culprit grates on your feelings,
I just annoy your ears.
Creon. Still talking?
You talk too much! A born nuisance—
Sentry. Maybe so,
but I never did this thing, so help me!
Creon. Yes, you did—
what's more, you squandered your life for silver!
Sentry. Oh it's terrible when the one who does the judging
judges things all wrong.
Creon. Well now,
you just be clever about your judgments—

if you fail to produce the criminals for me,
you'll swear your dirty money brought you pain.
Turning sharply, reentering the palace.

SENTRY. I hope he's found. Best thing by far.
But caught or not, that's in the lap of fortune;
I'll never come back, you've seen the last of me.
I'm saved, even now, and I never thought,
I never hoped—
dear gods, I owe you all my thanks!
Rushing out.

CHORUS. Numberless wonders
terrible wonders walk the world but none the match for man—
that great wonder crossing the heaving gray sea,
driven on by the blasts of winter
on through breakers crashing left and right,
holds his steady course
and the oldest of the gods he wears away—
the Earth, the immortal, the inexhaustible—
as his plows go back and forth, year in, year out
with the breed of stallions turning up the furrows.

And the blithe, lightheaded race of birds he snares,
the tribes of savage beasts, the life that swarms the depths—
with one fling of his nets
woven and coiled tight, he takes them all,
man the skilled, the brilliant!
He conquers all, taming with his techniques
the prey that roams the cliffs and wild lairs,
training the stallion, clamping the yoke across
his shaggy neck, and the tireless mountain bull.

And speech and thought, quick as the wind
and the mood and mind for law that rules the city—
all these he has taught himself
and shelter from the arrows of the frost
when there's rough lodging under the cold clear sky
and the shafts of lashing rain—
ready, resourceful man!
Never without resources
never an impasse as he marches on the future—
only Death, from Death alone he will find no rescue
but from desperate plagues he has plotted his escapes.

Man the master, ingenious past all measure
past all dreams, the skills within his grasp—
he forges on, now to destruction
now again to greatness. When he weaves in
the laws of the land, and the justice of the gods
that binds his oaths together
he and his city rise high—
but the city casts out

that man who weds himself to inhumanity
thanks to reckless daring. Never share my hearth
never think my thoughts, whoever does such things.

Enter ANTIGONE *from the side, accompanied by the* SENTRY.

Here is a dark sign from the gods—
what to make of this? I know her,
how can I deny it? That young girl's Antigone!
Wretched child of a wretched father,
Oedipus. Look, is it possible?
They bring you in like a prisoner—
why? did you break the king's laws?
Did they take you in some act of mad defiance?

SENTRY. She's the one, she did it single-handed—
we caught her burying the body. Where's Creon?

Enter CREON *from the palace.*

LEADER. Back again, just in time when you need him.

CREON. In time for what? What is it?

SENTRY. My king,
there's nothing you can swear you'll never do—
second thoughts make liars of us all.
I could have sworn I wouldn't hurry back
(what with your threats, the buffeting I just took),
but a stroke of luck beyond our wildest hopes,
what a joy, there's nothing like it. So,
back I've come, breaking my oath, who cares?
I'm bringing in our prisoner—this young girl—
we took her giving the dead the last rites.
But no casting lots this time; this is *my* luck,
my prize, no one else's.
Now, my lord,
here she is. Take her, question her,
cross-examine her to your heart's content.
But set me free, it's only right—
I'm rid of this dreadful business once for all.

CREON. Prisoner! Her? You took her—where, doing what?

SENTRY. Burying the man. That's the whole story.

CREON. What?
You mean what you say, you're telling me the truth?

SENTRY. She's the one. With my own eyes I saw her
bury the body, just what you've forbidden.
There. Is that plain and clear?

CREON. What did you see? Did you catch her in the act?

SENTRY. Here's what happened. We went back to our post,
those threats of yours breathing down our necks—
we brushed the corpse clean of the dust that covered it,
stripped it bare... it was slimy, going soft,
and we took to high ground, backs to the wind
so the stink of him couldn't hit us;
jostling, baiting each other to keep awake,
shouting back and forth—no napping on the job,

not this time. And so the hours dragged by
until the sun stood dead above our heads,
a huge white ball in the noon sky, beating,
blazing down, and then it happened—
suddenly, a whirlwind!
Twisting a great dust-storm up from the earth,
a black plague of the heavens, filling the plain,
ripping the leaves off every tree in sight,
choking the air and sky. We squinted hard
and took our whipping from the gods.

And after the storm passed—it seemed endless—
there, we saw the girl!
And she cried out a sharp, piercing cry,
like a bird come back to an empty nest,
peering into its bed, and all the babies gone…
Just so, when she sees the corpse bare
she bursts into a long, shattering wail
and calls down withering curses on the heads
of all who did the work. And she scoops up dry dust,
handfuls, quickly, and lifting a fine bronze urn,
lifting it high and pouring, she crowns the dead
with three full libations.
Soon as we saw
we rushed her, closed on the kill like hunters,
and she, she didn't flinch. We interrogated her,
charging her with offenses past and present—
she stood up to it all, denied nothing. I tell you,
it made me ache and laugh in the same breath.
It's pure joy to escape the worst yourself,
it hurts a man to bring down his friends.
But all that, I'm afraid, means less to me
than my own skin. That's the way I'm made.

CREON.
Wheeling on ANTIGONE
You,
with your eyes fixed on the ground—speak up.
Do you deny you did this, yes or no?

ANTIGONE. I did it. I don't deny a thing.

CREON.
To the SENTRY.
You, get out, wherever you please—
you're clear of a very heavy charge.
He leaves; CREON *turns back to* ANTIGONE.
You, tell me briefly, no long speeches—
were you aware a decree had forbidden this?

ANTIGONE. Well aware. How could I avoid it? It was public.

CREON. And still you had the gall to break this law?

ANTIGONE. Of course I did. It wasn't Zeus, not in the least,
who made this proclamation—not to me.
Nor did that Justice, dwelling with the gods

beneath the earth, ordain such laws for men.
Nor did I think your edict had such force
that you, a mere mortal, could override the gods,
the great unwritten, unshakable traditions.
They are alive, not just today or yesterday:
they live forever, from the first of time,
and no one knows when they first saw the light.

These laws—I was not about to break them,
not out of fear of some man's wounded pride,
and face the retribution of the gods.
Die I must, I've known it all my life—
how could I keep from knowing?—even without
your death-sentence ringing in my ears.
And if I am to die before my time
I consider that a gain. Who on earth,
alive in the midst of so much grief as I,
could fail to find his death a rich reward?
So for me, at least, to meet this doom of yours
is precious little pain. But if I had allowed
my own mother's son to rot, an unburied corpse—
that would have been an agony! This is nothing.
And if my present actions strike you as foolish,
let's just say I've been accused of folly
by a fool.

LEADER. Like father like daughter,
passionate, wild...
she hasn't learned to bend before adversity.

CREON. No? Believe me, the stiffest stubborn wills
fall the hardest; the toughest iron,
tempered strong in the white-hot fire,
you'll see it crack and shatter first of all.
And I've known spirited horses you can break
with a light bit—proud, rebellious horses.
There's no room for pride, not in a slave,
not with the lord and master standing by.

This girl was an old hand at insolence
when she overrode the edicts we made public.
But once she'd done it—the insolence,
twice over—to glory in it, laughing,
mocking us to our face with what she'd done.
I'm not the man, not now: she is the man
if this victory goes to her and she goes free.

Never! Sister's child or closer in blood
than all my family clustered at my altar
worshiping Guardian Zeus—she'll never escape,
she and her blood sister, the most barbaric death.
Yes, I accuse her sister of an equal part
in scheming this, this burial.

To his ATTENDANTS.
Bring her here!
I just saw her inside, hysterical, gone to pieces.
It never fails: the mind convicts itself
in advance, when scoundrels are up to no good,
plotting in the dark. Oh but I hate it more
when a traitor, caught red-handed,
tries to glorify his crimes.
ANTIGONE. Creon, what more do you want
than my arrest and execution?
CREON. Nothing. Then I have it all.
ANTIGONE. Then why delay? Your moralizing repels me,
every word you say—pray god it always will.
So naturally all I say repels you too.
Enough.
Give me glory! What greater glory could I win
than to give my own brother decent burial?
These citizens here would all agree,
To the CHORUS.
they'd praise me too
if their lips weren't locked in fear.
Pointing to CREON.
Lucky tyrants—the perquisites of power!
Ruthless power to do and say whatever pleases *them*.
CREON. You alone, of all the people in Thebes,
see things that way.
ANTIGONE. They see it just that way
but defer to you and keep their tongues in leash.
CREON. And you, aren't you ashamed to differ so from them?
So disloyal!
ANTIGONE. Not ashamed for a moment,
not to honor my brother, my own flesh and blood.
CREON. Wasn't Eteocles a brother too—cut down, facing him?
ANTIGONE. Brother, yes, by the same mother, the same father.
CREON. Then how can you render his enemy such honors,
such impieties in his eyes?
ANTIGONE. He'll never testify to that,
Eteocles dead and buried.
CREON. He will—
if you honor the traitor just as much as him.
ANTIGONE. But it was his brother, not some slave that died—
CREON. Ravaging our country!—
but Eteocles died fighting in our behalf.
ANTIGONE. No matter—Death longs for the same rites for all.
CREON. Never the same for the patriot and the traitor.
ANTIGONE. Who, Creon, who on earth can say the ones below
don't find this pure and uncorrupt?
CREON. Never. Once an enemy, never a friend,
not even after death.

ANTIGONE. I was born to join in love, not hate—
that is my nature.
CREON. Go down below and love,
if love you must—love the dead! While I'm alive,
no woman is going to lord it over me.
Enter ISMENE *from the palace, under guard.*
CHORUS. Look,
Ismene's coming, weeping a sister's tears,
loving sister, under a cloud...
her face is flushed, her cheeks streaming.
Sorrow puts her lovely radiance in the dark.
CREON. You—
in my house, you viper, slinking undetected,
sucking my life-blood! I never knew
I was breeding twin disasters, the two of you
rising up against my throne. Come, tell me,
will you confess your part in the crime or not?
Answer me. Swear to me.
ISMENE. I did it, yes—
if only she consents—I share the guilt,
the consequences too.
ANTIGONE. No,
Justice will never suffer that—not you,
you were unwilling. I never brought you in.
ISMENE. But now you face such dangers... I'm not ashamed
to sail through trouble with you,
make your troubles mine.
ANTIGONE. Who did the work?
Let the dead and the god of death bear witness!
I've no love for a friend who loves in words alone.
ISMENE. Oh no, my sister, don't reject me, please,
let me die beside you, consecrating
the dead together.
ANTIGONE. Never share my dying,
don't lay claim to what you never touched.
My death will be enough.
ISMENE. What do I care for life, cut off from you?
ANTIGONE. Ask Creon. Your concern is all for him.
ISMENE. Why abuse me so? It doesn't help you now.
ANTIGONE. You're right—
if I mock you, I get no pleasure from it,
only pain.
ISMENE. Tell me, dear one,
what can I do to help you, even now?
ANTIGONE. Save yourself. I don't grudge you your survival.
ISMENE. Oh no, no, denied my portion in your death?
ANTIGONE. You chose to live, I chose to die.
ISMENE. Not, at least,
without every kind of caution I could voice.

ANTIGONE. Your wisdom appealed to one world—mine, another.
ISMENE. But look, we're both guilty, both condemned to death.
ANTIGONE. Courage! Live your life. I gave myself to death,
long ago, so I might serve the dead.
CREON. They're both mad, I tell you, the two of them.
One's just shown it, the other's been that way
since she was born.
ISMENE. True, my king,
the sense we were born with cannot last forever...
commit cruelty on a person long enough
and the mind begins to go.
CREON. Yours did,
when you chose to commit your crimes with her.
ISMENE. How can I live alone, without her?
CREON. Her?
Don't even mention her—she no longer exists.
ISMENE. What? You'd kill your own son's bride?
CREON. Absolutely:
there are other fields for him to plow.
ISMENE. Perhaps,
but never as true, as close a bond as theirs.
CREON. A worthless woman for my son? It repels me.
ISMENE. Dearest Haemon, your father wrongs you so!
CREON. Enough, enough—you and your talk of marriage!
ISMENE. Creon—you're really going to rob your son of Antigone?
CREON. Death will do it for me—break their marriage off.
LEADER. So, it's settled then? Antigone must die?
CREON. Settled, yes—we both know that.
To the GUARDS.
Stop wasting time. Take them in.
From now on they'll act like women.
Tie them up, no more running loose;
even the bravest will cut and run,
once they see Death coming for their lives.
The GUARDS *escort* ANTIGONE *and* ISMENE *into the palace.* CREON *remains while the old citizens form their chorus.*
CHORUS. Blest, they are the truly blest who all their lives
have never tasted devastation. For others, once
the gods have rocked a house to its foundations
the ruin will never cease, cresting on and on
from one generation on throughout the race—
like a great mounting tide
driven on by savage northern gales,
surging over the dead black depths
roiling up from the bottom dark heaves of sand
and the headlands, taking the storm's onslaught full-force,
roar, and the low moaning
echoes on and on
and now
as in ancient times I see the sorrows of the house,

the living heirs of the old ancestral kings,
piling on the sorrows of the dead
and one generation cannot free the next—
some god will bring them crashing down,
the race finds no release.
And now the light, the hope
springing up from the late last root
in the house of Oedipus, that hope's cut down in turn
by the long, bloody knife swung by the gods of death
by a senseless word
by fury at the heart.
Zeus,
yours is the power, Zeus, what man on earth
can override it, who can hold it back?
Power that neither Sleep, the all-ensnaring
no, nor the tireless months of heaven
can ever overmaster—young through all time,
mighty lord of power, you hold fast
the dazzling crystal mansions of Olympus.
And throughout the future, late and soon
as through the past, your law prevails:
no towering form of greatness
enters into the lives of mortals
free and clear of ruin.
True,
our dreams, our high hopes voyaging far and wide
bring sheer delight to many, to many others
delusion, blithe, mindless lusts
and the fraud steals on one slowly . . . unaware
till he trips and puts his foot into the fire.
He was a wise old man who coined
the famous saying: "Sooner or later
foul is fair, fair is foul
to the man the gods will ruin"—
He goes his way for a moment only
free of blinding ruin.

Enter HAEMON *from the palace.*

Here's Haemon now, the last of all your sons.
Does he come in tears for his bride,
his doomed bride, Antigone—
bitter at being cheated of their marriage?

CREON. We'll soon know, better than seers could tell us.

Turning to HAEMON.

Son, you've heard the final verdict on your bride?
Are you coming now, raving against your father?
Or do you love me, no matter what I do?

HAEMON. Father, I'm your *son* . . . you in your wisdom
set my bearings for me—I obey you.
No marriage could ever mean more to me than you,
whatever good direction you may offer.

Creon. Fine, Haemon.
That's how you ought to feel within your heart,
subordinate to your father's will in every way.
That's what a man prays for: to produce good sons—
households full of them, dutiful and attentive,
so they can pay his enemy back with interest
and match the respect their father shows his friend.
But the man who rears a brood of useless children,
what has he brought into the world, I ask you?
Nothing but trouble for himself, and mockery
from his enemies laughing in his face.
Oh Haemon,
never lose your sense of judgment over a woman.
The warmth, the rush of pleasure, it all goes cold
in your arms, I warn you... a worthless woman
in your house, a misery in your bed.
What wound cuts deeper than a loved one
turned against you? Spit her out,
like a mortal enemy—let the girl go.
Let her find a husband down among the dead.

Imagine it: I caught her in naked rebellion,
the traitor, the only one in the whole city.
I'm not about to prove myself a liar,
not to my people, no, I'm going to kill her!
That's right—so let her cry for mercy, sing her hymns
to Zeus who defends all bonds of kindred blood.
Why, if I bring up my own kin to be rebels,
think what I'd suffer from the world at large.
Show me the man who rules his household well:
I'll show you someone fit to rule the state.
That good man, my son,
I have every confidence he and he alone
can give commands and take them too. Staunch
in the storm of spears he'll stand his ground,
a loyal, unflinching comrade at your side.

But whoever steps out of line, violates the laws
or presumes to hand out orders to his superiors,
he'll win no praise from me. But that man
the city places in authority, his orders
must be obeyed, large and small
right and wrong.
Anarchy—
show me a greater crime in all the earth!
She, she destroys cities, rips up houses,
breaks the ranks of spearmen into headlong rout.
But the ones who last it out, the great mass of them
owe their lives to discipline. Therefore
we must defend the men who live by law,

never let some woman triumph over us.
Better to fall from power, if fall we must,
at the hands of a man—never be rated
inferior to a woman, never.

LEADER. To us,
unless old age has robbed us of our wits,
you seem to say what you have to say with sense.

HAEMON. Father, only the gods endow a man with reason,
the finest of all their gifts, a treasure.
Far be it from me—I haven't the skill,
and certainly no desire, to tell you when,
if ever, you make a slip in speech . . . though
someone else might have a good suggestion.

Of course it's not for you,
in the normal run of things, to watch
whatever men say or do, or find to criticize.
The man in the street, you know, dreads your glance,
he'd never say anything displeasing to your face.
But it's for me to catch the murmurs in the dark,
the way the city mourns for this young girl.
"No woman," they say, "ever deserved death less,
and such a brutal death for such a glorious action.
She, with her own dear brother lying in his blood—
she couldn't bear to leave him dead, unburied,
food for the wild dogs or wheeling vultures.
Death? She deserves a glowing crown of gold!"
So they say, and the rumor spreads in secret,
darkly . . .

I rejoice in your success, father—
nothing more precious to me in the world.
What medal of honor brighter to his children
than a father's growing glory? Or a child's
to his proud father? Now don't, please,
be quite so single-minded, self-involved
or assume the world is wrong and you are right.
Whoever thinks that he alone possesses intelligence,
the gift of eloquence, he and no one else,
and character too . . . such men, I tell you,
spread them open—and you will find them empty.

No,
it's no disgrace for a man, even a wise man,
to learn many things and not to be too rigid.
You've seen trees by a raging winter torrent,
how many sway with the flood and salvage every twig,
but not the stubborn—they're ripped out, roots and all.
Bend or break. The same when a man is sailing:
haul your sheets too taut, never give an inch,
you'll capsize, go the rest of the voyage
keel up and the rowing-benches under.

Oh give way. Relax your anger—change!
I'm young, I know, but let me offer this:
it would be best by far, I admit,
if a man were born infallible, right by nature.
If not—and things don't often go that way,
it's best to learn from those with good advice.

LEADER. You'd do well, my lord, if he's speaking to the point,
to learn from him,

Turning to HAEMON.

and you, my boy, from him.
You both are talking sense.

CREON. So,
men our age, we're to be lectured, are we?—
schooled by a boy his age?

HAEMON. Only in what is right. But if I seem young,
look less to my years and more to what I do.

CREON. Do? Is admiring rebels an achievement?

HAEMON. I'd never suggest that you admire treason.

CREON. Oh?—
isn't that just the sickness that's attacked her?

HAEMON. The whole city of Thebes denies it, to a man.

CREON. And is Thebes about to tell me how to rule?

HAEMON. Now, you see? Who's talking like a child?

CREON. Am I to rule this land for others—or myself?

HAEMON. It's no city at all, owned by one man alone.

CREON. What? The city *is* the king's—that's the law!

HAEMON. What a splendid king you'd make of a desert island—
you and you alone.

CREON.

To the CHORUS.

This boy, I do believe,
is fighting on her side, the woman's side.

HAEMON. If you are a woman, yes;
my concern is all for you.

CREON. Why, you degenerate—bandying accusations,
threatening me with justice, your own father!

HAEMON. I see my father offending justice—wrong.

CREON. Wrong?
To protect my royal rights?

HAEMON. Protect your rights?
When you trample down the honors of the gods?

CREON. You, you soul of corruption, rotten through—
woman's accomplice!

HAEMON. That may be,
but you'll never find me accomplice to a criminal.

CREON. That's what *she* is,
and every word you say is a blatant appeal for her—

HAEMON. And you, and me, and the gods beneath the earth.

CREON. You'll never marry her, not while she's alive.

HAEMON. Then she'll die… but her death will kill another.

CREON. What, brazen threats? You go too far!

HAEMON. What threat?
Combating your empty, mindless judgments with a word?
CREON. You'll suffer for your sermons, you and your empty wisdom!
HAEMON. If you weren't my father, I'd say you were insane.
CREON. Don't flatter me with Father—you woman's slave!
HAEMON. You really expect to fling abuse at me
and not receive the same?
CREON. Is that so!
Now, by heaven, I promise you, you'll pay—
taunting, insulting me! Bring her out,
that hateful—she'll die now, here,
in front of his eyes, beside her groom!
HAEMON. No, no, she will never die beside me—
don't delude yourself. And you will never
see me, never set eyes on my face again.
Rage your heart out, rage with friends
who can stand the sight of you.
Rushing out.
LEADER. Gone, my king, in a burst of anger.
A temper young as his . . . hurt him once,
he may do something violent.
CREON. Let him do—
dream up something desperate, past all human limit!
Good riddance. Rest assured,
he'll never save those two young girls from death.
LEADER. Both of them, you really intend to kill them both?
CREON. No, not her, the one whose hands are clean;
you're quite right.
LEADER. But Antigone—
what sort of death do you have in mind for her?
CREON. I'll take her down some wild, desolate path
never trod by men, and wall her up alive
in a rocky vault, and set out short rations,
just a gesture of piety
to keep the entire city free of defilement.
There let her pray to the one god she worships:
Death—who knows?—may just reprieve her from death.
Or she may learn at last, better late than never,
what a waste of breath it is to worship Death.
Exit to the palace.
CHORUS. Love, never conquered in battle
Love the plunderer laying waste the rich!
Love standing the night-watch
guarding a girl's soft cheek,
you range the seas, the shepherds' steadings off in the wilds—
not even the deathless gods can flee your onset,
nothing human born for a day—
whoever feels your grip is driven mad.
Love
you wrench the minds of the righteous into outrage,
swerve them to their ruin—you have ignited this,

this kindred strife, father and son at war
and Love alone the victor—
warm glance of the bride triumphant, burning with desire!
Throned in power, side-by-side with the mighty laws!
Irresistible Aphrodite,[5] never conquered—
Love, you mock us for your sport.

ANTIGONE *is brought from the palace under guard.*

But now, even I'd rebel against the king,
I'd break all bounds when I see this—
I fill with tears, can't hold them back,
not any more... I see Antigone make her way
to the bridal vault where all are laid to rest.

ANTIGONE. Look at me, men of my fatherland,
setting out on the last road
looking into the last light of day
the last I'll ever see...
the god of death who puts us all to bed
takes me down to the banks of Acheron[6] alive—
denied my part in the wedding-songs,
no wedding-song in the dusk has crowned my marriage—
I go to wed the lord of the dark waters.

CHORUS. Not crowned with glory, crowned with a dirge,
you leave for the deep pit of the dead.
No withering illness laid you low,
no strokes of the sword—no law to yourself,
alone, no mortal like you, ever, you go down
to the halls of Death alive and breathing.

ANTIGONE. But think of Niobe[7]—well I know her story—
think what a living death she died,
Tantalus' daughter, stranger queen from the east:
there on the mountain heights, growing stone
binding as ivy, slowly walled her round
and the rains will never cease, the legends say
the snows will never leave her...
wasting away, under her brows the tears
showering down her breasting ridge and slopes—
a rocky death like hers puts me to sleep.

CHORUS. But she was a god, born of gods,
and we are only mortals born to die.
And yet, of course, it's a great thing
for a dying girl to hear, just hear
she shares a destiny equal to the gods,
during life and later, once she's dead.

ANTIGONE. O you mock me!
Why, in the name of all my fathers' gods
why can't you wait till I am gone—
must you abuse me to my face?

---

[5]**Aphrodite** Goddess of love.
[6]**Acheron** A river in the underworld, to which the dead go.
[7]**Niobe** A queen of Thebes who was punished by the gods for her pride and was turned into stone.

O my city, all your fine rich sons!
And you, you springs of the Dirce,
holy grove of Thebes where the chariots gather,
you at least, you'll bear me witness, look,
unmourned by friends and forced by such crude laws
I go to my rockbound prison, strange new tomb—
always a stranger, O dear god,
I have no home on earth and none below,
not with the living, not with the breathless dead.

CHORUS. You went too far, the last limits of daring—
smashing against the high throne of Justice!
Your life's in ruins, child—I wonder...
do you pay for your father's terrible ordeal?

ANTIGONE. There—at last you've touched it, the worst pain
the worst anguish! Raking up the grief for father
three times over, for all the doom
that's struck us down, the brilliant house of Laius.
O mother, your marriage-bed
the coiling horrors, the coupling there—
you with your own son, my father—doomstruck mother!
Such, such were my parents, and I their wretched child.
I go to them now, cursed, unwed, to share their home—
I am a stranger! O dear brother, doomed
in your marriage—your marriage murders mine,
your dying drags me down to death alive!

Enter CREON.

CHORUS. Reverence asks some reverence in return—
but attacks on power never go unchecked,
not by the man who holds the reins of power.
Your own blind will, your passion has destroyed you.

ANTIGONE. No one to weep for me, my friends,
no wedding-song—they take me away
in all my pain... the road lies open, waiting.
Never again, the law forbids me to see
the sacred eye of day. I am agony!
No tears for the destiny that's mine,
no loved one mourns my death.

CREON. Can't you see?
If a man could wail his own dirge *before* he dies,
he'd never finish.

To the GUARDS.

Take her away, quickly!
Wall her up in the tomb, you have your orders.
Abandon her there, alone, and let her choose—
death or a buried life with a good roof for shelter.
As for myself, my hands are clean. This young girl—
dead or alive, she will be stripped of her rights,
her stranger's rights, here in the world above.

ANTIGONE. O tomb, my bridal-bed—my house, my prison
cut in the solid rock, my everlasting watch!
I'll soon be there, soon embrace my own,

the great growing family of our dead
Persephone[8] has received among her ghosts.
I,
the last of them all, the most reviled by far,
go down before my destined time's run out.
But still I go, cherishing one good hope:
my arrival may be dear to father,
dear to you, my mother,
dear to you, my loving brother, Eteocles—
When you died I washed you with my hands,
I dressed you all, I poured the cups
across your tombs. But now, Polynices,
because I laid your body out as well,
this, this is my reward. Nevertheless
I honored you—the decent will admit it—
well and wisely too.
Never, I tell you,
if I had been the mother of children
or if my husband died, exposed and rotting—
I'd never have taken this ordeal upon myself,
never defied our people's will. What law,
you ask, do I satisfy with what I say?
A husband dead, there might have been another.
A child by another too, if I had lost the first.
But mother and father both lost in the halls of Death,
no brother could ever spring to light again.

For this law alone I held you first in honor.
For this, Creon, the king, judges me a criminal
guilty of dreadful outrage, my dear brother!
And now he leads me off, a captive in his hands,
with no part in the bridal-song, the bridal-bed,
denied all joy of marriage, raising children—
deserted so by loved ones, struck by fate,
I descend alive to the caverns of the dead.

What law of the mighty gods have I transgressed?
Why look to the heavens any more, tormented as I am?
Whom to call, what comrades now? Just think,
my reverence only brands me for irreverence!
Very well: if this is the pleasure of the gods,
once I suffer I will know that I was wrong.
But if these men are wrong, let them suffer
nothing worse than they mete out to me—
these masters of injustice!

LEADER. Still the same rough winds, the wild passion
raging through the girl.

---

[8]**Persephone** Queen of the underworld.

CREON.
To the GUARDS.
Take her away.
You're wasting time—you'll pay for it too.
ANTIGONE. Oh god, the voice of death. It's come, it's here.
CREON. True. Not a word of hope—your doom is sealed.
ANTIGONE. Land of Thebes, city of all my fathers—
O you gods, the first gods of the race!
They drag me away, now, no more delay.
Look on me, you noble sons of Thebes—
the last of a great line of kings,
I alone, see what I suffer now
at the hands of what breed of men—
all for reverence, my reverence for the gods!
She leaves under guard; the CHORUS *gathers.*
CHORUS. Danaë, Danaë[9]—
even she endured a fate like yours,
in all her lovely strength she traded
the light of day for the bolted brazen vault—
buried within her tomb, her bridal-chamber,
wed to the yoke and broken.
But she was of glorious birth
my child, my child
and treasured the seed of Zeus within her womb,
the cloudburst streaming gold!
The power of fate is a wonder,
dark, terrible wonder—
neither wealth nor armies
towered walls nor ships
black hulls lashed by the salt
can save us from that force.

The yoke tamed him too
young Lycurgus[10] flaming in anger
king of Edonia, all for his mad taunts
Dionysus clamped him down, encased
in the chain-mail of rock
and there his rage
his terrible flowering rage burst—
sobbing, dying away...at last that madman
came to know his god—
the power he mocked, the power
he taunted in all his frenzy
trying to stamp out
the women strong with the god—
the torch, the raving sacred cries—

---

[9]**Danaë** Locked in a cell by her father because it was prophesied that her son would kill him, but visited by Zeus in the form of a shower of gold. Their son was Perseus.

[10]**Lycurgus** Punished by Dionysus because he would not worship him.

enraging the Muses[11] who adore the flute.
And far north where the Black Rocks
cut the sea in half
and murderous straits
split the coast of Thrace
a forbidding city stands
where once, hard by the walls
the savage Ares thrilled to watch
a king's new queen, a Fury rearing in rage
against his two royal sons—
her bloody hands, her dagger-shuttle
stabbing out their eyes—cursed, blinding wounds—
their eyes blind sockets screaming for revenge!

They wailed in agony, cries echoing cries
the princes doomed at birth...
and their mother doomed to chains,
walled off in a tomb of stone—
but she traced her own birth back
to a proud Athenian line and the high gods
and off in caverns half the world away,
born of the wild North Wind
she sprang on her father's gales,
racing stallions up the leaping cliffs—
child of the heavens. But even on her the Fates
the gray everlasting Fates rode hard
my child, my child.

Enter TIRESIAS, *the blind prophet, led by a* BOY.

TIRESIAS. Lords of Thebes,
I and the boy have come together,
hand in hand. Two see with the eyes of one...
so the blind must go, with a guide to lead the way.

CREON. What is it, old Tiresias? What news now?

TIRESIAS. I will teach you. And you obey the seer.

CREON. I will,
I've never wavered from your advice before.

TIRESIAS. And so you kept the city straight on course.

CREON. I owe you a great deal, I swear to that.

TIRESIAS. Then reflect, my son: you are poised,
once more, on the razor-edge of fate.

CREON. What is it? I shudder to hear you.

TIRESIAS. You will learn
when you listen to the warnings of my craft.
As I sat on the ancient seat of augury,[12]
in the sanctuary where every bird I know
will hover at my hands—suddenly I heard it,
a strange voice in the wingbeats, unintelligible,

[11]**Muses** Goddesses of the arts.
[12]**Seat of augury** Where Tiresias looked for omens among birds.

barbaric, a mad scream! Talons flashing, ripping,
they were killing each other—that much I knew—
the murderous fury whirring in those wings
made that much clear!
I was afraid,
I turned quickly, tested the burnt-sacrifice,
ignited the altar at all points—but no fire,
the god in the fire never blazed.
Not from those offerings . . . over the embers
slid a heavy ooze from the long thighbones,
smoking, sputtering out, and the bladder
puffed and burst—spraying gall into the air—
and the fat wrapping the bones slithered off
and left them glistening white. No fire!
The rites failed that might have blazed the future
with a sign. So I learned from the boy here;
he is my guide, as I am guide to others.
And it's you—
your high resolve that sets this plague on Thebes.
The public altars and sacred hearths are fouled,
one and all, by the birds and dogs with carrion
torn from the corpse, the doomstruck son of Oedipus!
And so the gods are deaf to our prayers, they spurn
the offerings in our hands, the flame of holy flesh.
No birds cry out an omen clear and true—
they're gorged with the murdered victim's blood and fat.
Take these things to heart, my son, I warn you.
All men make mistakes, it is only human.
But once the wrong is done, a man
can turn his back on folly, misfortune too,
if he tries to make amends, however low he's fallen,
and stops his bullnecked ways. Stubbornness
brands you for stupidity—pride is a crime.
No, yield to the dead!
Never stab the fighter when he's down.
Where's the glory, killing the dead twice over?

I mean you well. I give you sound advice.
It's best to learn from a good adviser
when he speaks for your own good:
it's pure gain.

CREON. Old man—all of you! So,
you shoot your arrows at my head like archers at the target—
I even have *him* loosed on me, this fortune-teller.
Oh his ilk has tried to sell me short
and ship me off for years. Well,
drive your bargains, traffic—much as you like—
in the gold of India, silver-gold of Sardis.
You'll never bury that body in the grave,
not even if Zeus's eagles rip the corpse

and wing their rotten pickings off to the throne of god!
Never, not even in fear of such defilement
will I tolerate his burial, that traitor.
Well I know, we can't defile the gods—
no mortal has the power.
No,
reverend old Tiresias, all men fall,
it's only human, but the wisest fall obscenely
when they glorify obscene advice with rhetoric—
all for their own gain.

Tiresias. Oh god, is there a man alive
who knows, who actually believes...

Creon. What now?
What earth-shattering truth are you about to utter?
Tiresias.... just how much a sense of judgment, wisdom
is the greatest gift we have?

Creon. Just as much, I'd say,
as a twisted mind is the worst affliction going.

Tiresias. You are the one who's sick, Creon, sick to death.

Creon. I am in no mood to trade insults with a seer.

Tiresias. You have already, calling my prophecies a lie.

Creon. Why not?
You and the whole breed of seers are mad for money!

Tiresias. And the whole race of tyrants lusts to rake it in.

Creon. This slander of yours—
are you aware you're speaking to the king?

Tiresias. Well aware. Who helped you save the city?

Creon. You—
you have your skills, old seer, but you lust for injustice!

Tiresias. You will drive me to utter the dreadful secret in my heart.

Creon. Spit it out! Just don't speak it for profit.

Tiresias. Profit? No, not a bit of profit, not for you.

Creon. Know full well, you'll never buy off my resolve.

Tiresias. Then know this too, learn this by heart!
The chariot of the sun will not race through
so many circuits more, before you have surrendered
one born of your own loins, your own flesh and blood,
a corpse for corpses given in return, since you have thrust
to the world below a child sprung for the world above,
ruthlessly lodged a living soul within the grave—
then you've robbed the gods below the earth,
keeping a dead body here in the bright air,
unburied, unsung, unhallowed by the rites.

You, you have no business with the dead,
nor do the gods above—this is violence
you have forced upon the heavens.
And so the avengers, the dark destroyers late
but true to the mark, now lie in wait for you,
the Furies sent by the gods and the god of death

to strike you down with the pains that you perfected!
There. Reflect on that, tell me I've been bribed.
The day comes soon, no long test of time, not now,
that wakes the wails for men and women in your halls.
Great hatred rises against you—
cities in tumult, all whose mutilated sons
the dogs have graced with burial, or the wild beasts,
some wheeling crow that wings the ungodly stench of carrion
back to each city, each warrior's hearth and home.

These arrows for your heart! Since you've raked me
I loose them like an archer in my anger,
arrows deadly true. You'll never escape
their burning, searing force.
Motioning to his escort.
Come, boy, take me home.
So he can vent his rage on younger men,
and learn to keep a gentler tongue in his head
and better sense than what he carries now.
Exit to the side.

LEADER. The old man's gone, my king—
terrible prophecies. Well I know,
since the hair on this old head went gray,
he's never lied to Thebes.

CREON. I know it myself—I'm shaken, torn.
It's a dreadful thing to yield...but resist now?
Lay my pride bare to the blows of ruin?
That's dreadful too.

LEADER. But good advice,
Creon, take it now, you must.

CREON. What should I do? Tell me...I'll obey.

LEADER. Go! Free the girl from the rocky vault
and raise a mound for the body you exposed.

CREON. That's your advice? You think I should give in?

LEADER. Yes, my king, quickly. Disasters sent by the gods
cut short our follies in a flash.

CREON. Oh it's hard,
giving up the heart's desire...but I will do it—
no more fighting a losing battle with necessity.

LEADER. Do it now, go, don't leave it to others.

CREON. Now—I'm on my way! Come, each of you,
take up axes, make for the high ground,
over there, quickly! I and my better judgment
have come round to this—I shackled her,
I'll set her free myself. I am afraid...
it's best to keep the established laws
to the very day we die.
Rushing out, followed by his entourage. The CHORUS *clusters around the altar.*

CHORUS. God of a hundred names!

Great Dionysus—
Son and glory of Semele! Pride of Thebes—
Child of Zeus whose thunder rocks the clouds—
Lord of the famous lands of evening—
King of the Mysteries!
King of Eleusis, Demeter's plain[13]
her breasting hills that welcome in the world—
Great Dionysus!
Bacchus,[14] living in Thebes
the mother-city of all your frenzied women—
Bacchus
living along the Ismenus'[15] rippling waters
standing over the field sown with the Dragon's teeth!

You—we have seen you through the flaring smoky fires,
your torches blazing over the twin peaks
where nymphs of the hallowed cave climb onward
fired with you, your sacred rage—
we have seen you at Castalia's running spring[16]
and down from the heights of Nysa[17] crowned with ivy
the greening shore rioting vines and grapes
down you come in your storm of wild women
ecstatic, mystic cries—
Dionysus—
down to watch and ward the roads of Thebes!

First of all cities, Thebes you honor first
you and your mother, bride of the lightning—
come, Dionysus! now your people lie
in the iron grip of plague,
come in your racing, healing stride
down Parnassus' slopes[18]
or across the moaning straits.
Lord of the dancing—
dance, dance the constellations breathing fire!
Great master of the voices of the night!
Child of Zeus, God's offspring, come, come forth!
Lord, king, dance with your nymphs, swirling, raving
arm-in-arm in frenzy through the night
they dance you, Iacchus[19]—

---

[13]**Demeter's plain** The goddess of grain was worshiped at Eleusis, near Athens.
[14]**Bacchus** Another name for Dionysus.
[15]**Ismenus** A river near Thebes where the founders of the city were said to have sprung from a dragon's teeth.
[16]**Castalia's running spring** The sacred spring of Apollo's oracle at Delphi.
[17]**Nysa** A mountain where Dionysus was worshiped.
[18]**Parnassus** A mountain in Greece that was sacred to Dionysus as well as other gods and goddesses.
[19]**Iacchus** Dionysus.

Dance, Dionysus
giver of all good things!
Enter a MESSENGER *from the side.*

MESSENGER. Neighbors,
friends of the house of Cadmus[20] and the kings,
there's not a thing in this life of ours
I'd praise or blame as settled once for all.
Fortune lifts and Fortune fells the lucky
and unlucky every day. No prophet on earth
can tell a man his fate. Take Creon:
there was a man to rouse your envy once,
as I see it. He saved the realm from enemies;
taking power, he alone, the lord of the fatherland,
he set us true on course—flourished like a tree
with the noble line of sons he bred and reared...
and now it's lost, all gone.
Believe me,
when a man has squandered his true joys,
he's good as dead, I tell you, a living corpse.
Pile up riches in your house, as much as you like—
live like a king with a huge show of pomp,
but if real delight is missing from the lot,
I wouldn't give you a wisp of smoke for it,
not compared with joy.

LEADER. What now?
What new grief do you bring the house of kings?

MESSENGER. Dead, dead—and the living are guilty of their death!

LEADER. Who's the murderer? Who is dead? Tell us.

MESSENGER. Haemon's gone, his blood spilled by the very hand—

LEADER. His father's or his own?

MESSENGER. His own...
raging mad with his father for the death—

LEADER. Oh great seer,
you saw it all, you brought your word to birth!

MESSENGER. Those are the facts. Deal with them as you will.
As he turns to go, EURYDICE *enters from the palace.*

LEADER. Look, Eurydice. Poor woman, Creon's wife,
so close at hand. By chance perhaps,
unless she's heard the news about her son.

EURYDICE. My countrymen,
all of you—I caught the sound of your words
as I was leaving to do my part,
to appeal to queen Athena[21] with my prayers.
I was just loosing the bolts, opening the doors,
when a voice filled with sorrow, family sorrow,
struck my ears, and I fell back, terrified,

---

[20]**Cadmus** The legendary founder of Thebes.
[21]**Athena** Goddess of wisdom and protector of Greek cities.

into the women's arms—everything went black.
Tell me the news, again, whatever it is…
sorrow and I are hardly strangers;
I can bear the worst.

MESSENGER. I—dear lady,
I'll speak as an eye-witness. I was there.
And I won't pass over one word of the truth.
Why should I try to soothe you with a story,
only to prove a liar in a moment?
Truth is always best.
So,
I escorted your lord, I guided him
to the edge of the plain where the body lay,
Polynices, torn by the dogs and still unmourned.
And saying a prayer to Hecate of the Crossroads,
Pluto[22] too, to hold their anger and be kind,
we washed the dead in a bath of holy water
and plucking some fresh branches, gathering…
what was left of him, we burned them all together
and raised a high mound of native earth, and then
we turned and made for that rocky vault of hers,
the hollow, empty bed of the bride of Death.
And far off, one of us heard a voice,
a long wail rising, echoing
out of that unhallowed wedding-chamber;
he ran to alert the master and Creon pressed on,
closer—the strange, inscrutable cry came sharper,
throbbing around him now, and he let loose
a cry of his own, enough to wrench the heart,
"Oh god, am I the prophet now? going down
the darkest road I've ever gone? My son—
it's *his* dear voice, he greets me! Go, men,
closer, quickly! Go through the gap,
the rocks are dragged back—
right to the tomb's very mouth—and look,
see if it's Haemon's voice I think I hear,
or the gods have robbed me of my senses."

The king was shattered. We took his orders,
went and searched, and there in the deepest,
dark recesses of the tomb we found her…
hanged by the neck in a fine linen noose,
strangled in her veils—and the boy,
his arms flung around her waist,
clinging to her, wailing for his bride,
dead and down below, for his father's crimes

[22]**Hecate, Pluto** Gods of the underworld.

and the bed of his marriage blighted by misfortune.
When Creon saw him, he gave a deep sob,
he ran in, shouting, crying out to him,
"Oh my child—what have you done? what seized you,
what insanity? what disaster drove you mad?
Come out, my son! I beg you on my knees!"
But the boy gave him a wild burning glance,
spat in his face, not a word in reply,
he drew his sword—his father rushed out,
running as Haemon lunged and missed!—
and then, doomed, desperate with himself,
suddenly leaning his full weight on the blade,
he buried it in his body, halfway to the hilt.
And still in his senses, pouring his arms around her,
he embraced the girl and breathing hard,
released a quick rush of blood,
bright red on her cheek glistening white.
And there he lies, body enfolding body...
he has won his bride at last, poor boy,
not here but in the houses of the dead.

Creon shows the world that of all the ills
afflicting men the worst is lack of judgment.

EURYDICE *turns and reenters the palace.*

LEADER. What do you make of that? The lady's gone,
without a word, good or bad.

MESSENGER. I'm alarmed too
but here's my hope—faced with her son's death,
she finds it unbecoming to mourn in public.
Inside, under her roof, she'll set her women
to the task and wail the sorrow of the house.
She's too discreet. She won't do something rash.

LEADER. I'm not so sure. To me, at least,
a long heavy silence promises danger,
just as much as a lot of empty outcries.

MESSENGER. We'll see if she's holding something back,
hiding some passion in her heart.
I'm going in. You may be right—who knows?
Even too much silence has its dangers.

Exit to the palace. Enter CREON *from the side, escorted by* ATTENDANTS *carrying* HAEMON*'s body on a bier.*

LEADER. The king himself! Coming toward us,
look, holding the boy's head in his hands.
Clear, damning proof, if it's right to say so—
proof of his own madness, no one else's,
no, his own blind wrongs.

CREON. Ohhh,
so senseless, so insane... my crimes,
my stubborn, deadly—

Look at us, the killer, the killed,
father and son, the same blood—the misery!
My plans, my mad fanatic heart,
my son, cut off so young!
Ai, dead, lost to the world,
not through your stupidity, no, my own.

LEADER. Too late,
too late, you see what justice means.

CREON. Oh I've learned
through blood and tears! Then, it was then,
when the god came down and struck me—a great weight
shattering, driving me down that wild savage path,
ruining, trampling down my joy. Oh the agony!
the heartbreaking agonies of our lives.

Enter the MESSENGER *from the palace.*

MESSENGER. Master,
what a hoard of grief you have, and you'll have more.
The grief that lies to hand you've brought yourself—

Pointing to HAEMON*'s body.*

the rest, in the house, you'll see it all too soon.

CREON. What now? What's worse than this?

MESSENGER. The queen is dead.
The mother of this dead boy . . . mother to the end—
poor thing, her wounds are fresh.

CREON. No, no,
harbor of Death, so choked, so hard to cleanse!—
why me? why are you killing me?
Herald of pain, more words, more grief?
I died once, you kill me again and again!
What's the report, boy . . . some news for me?
My wife dead? O dear god!
Slaughter heaped on slaughter?

The doors open; the body of EURYDICE *is brought out on her bier.*

MESSENGER. See for yourself:
now they bring her body from the palace.

CREON. Oh no,
another, a second loss to break the heart.
What next, what fate still waits for me?
I just held my son in my arms and now,
look, a new corpse rising before my eyes—
wretched, helpless mother—O my son!

MESSENGER. She stabbed herself at the altar,
then her eyes went dark, after she'd raised
a cry for the noble fate of Megareus,[23] the hero
killed in the first assault, then for Haemon,
then with her dying breath she called down
torments on your head—you killed her sons.

---

[23]**Megareus** A son of Creon and Eurydice; he died when Thebes was attacked.

CREON. Oh the dread,
I shudder with dread! Why not kill me too?—
run me through with a good sharp sword?
Oh god, the misery, anguish—
I, I'm churning with it, going under.
MESSENGER. Yes, and the dead, the woman lying there,
piles the guilt of all their deaths on you.
CREON. How did she end her life, what bloody stroke?
MESSENGER. She drove home to the heart with her own hand,
once she learned her son was dead . . . that agony.
CREON. And the guilt is all mine—
can never be fixed on another man,
no escape for me. I killed you,
I, god help me, I admit it all!
To his ATTENDANTS.
Take me away, quickly, out of sight.
I don't even exist—I'm no one. Nothing.
LEADER. Good advice, if there's any good in suffering.
Quickest is best when troubles block the way.
CREON.
Kneeling in prayer.
Come, let it come!—that best of fates for me
that brings the final day, best fate of all.
Oh quickly, now—
so I never have to see another sunrise.
LEADER. That will come when it comes;
we must deal with all that lies before us.
The future rests with the ones who tend the future.
CREON. That prayer—I poured my heart into that prayer!
LEADER. No more prayers now. For mortal men
there is no escape from the doom we must endure.
CREON. Take me away, I beg you, out of sight.
A rash, indiscriminate fool!
I murdered you, my son, against my will—
you too, my wife . . .
Wailing wreck of a man,
whom to look to? where to lean for support?
Desperately turning from HAEMON *to* EURYDICE *on their biers.*
Whatever I touch goes wrong—once more
a crushing fate's come down upon my head.
The MESSENGER *and* ATTENDANTS *lead* CREON *into the palace.*
CHORUS. Wisdom is by far the greatest part of joy,
and reverence toward the gods must be safeguarded.
The mighty words of the proud are paid in full
with mighty blows of fate, and at long last
those blows will teach us wisdom.
The old citizens exit to the side.

(ca. 442 B.C.)

PREWRITING

Now that you have read *Antigone* and have some sense of its basic structure, read the play again carefully and write out the answers to the questions below. Your responses will not only help you to sharpen your understanding of dramatic structure; they will also lead you to clarify your reactions to *Antigone*'s characters and themes.

Analyzing Dramatic Structure

1. Think about a clash with authority that you have experienced in your own life. What caused the clash? How firmly did you stand your ground in the conflict? What were the consequences of your behavior?
2. What background are we given in the opening scene (lines 1–116)? List the main points of information that this exchange between Antigone and Ismene reveals.
3. What exposition does the Chorus give in lines 117–72?
4. How does Sophocles use the Sentry (lines 249 and following)? Does this character provide more than factual exposition?
5. What do you think the main conflict is? State it as specifically as you can in a single sentence.
6. Identify the protagonist and the antagonist. Is it fair to apply the labels *heroine* and *villain* to them?
7. Where does the climax occur? Identify the scene and describe what happens. Why do you think this is the play's turning point?
8. Does the climax seem to come early in the play? How does Sophocles maintain interest after the turning point? Did you expect such dramatic developments after the climax? Do you think Creon expected them?
9. When does the catastrophe occur? Was this outcome inevitable? Were your feelings about the outcome different the second time you read the play?
10. State what you consider the play's theme to be.
11. A *foil* is a contrasting character who sets off or helps to define another character. How is Ismene a foil to Antigone? Are there any foils to Creon?
12. Why is Eurydice included in the plot? How do you feel about her fate?

Having answered these questions about the structure of *Antigone*, devise a graph or chart that illustrates the pattern of events in the play. Make sure your graph shows the six structural components discussed on page 721.

WRITING

Your understanding of the structure of *Antigone* will enable you to write more easily about the play's arguments. As you watched the conflict develop between Antigone and Creon, you undoubtedly became aware of the opposing values that these two characters represent. As one critic has observed about *Antigone*, "The characters *are* the issues, and the issues the characters."[1] It is now your turn to examine these issues and decide where you stand.

Discovering a Workable Argumentative Thesis

Argument means dispute; it implies that there are opposing sides. Any matter worth arguing will involve at least one "issue"—that is, an essential point in question or disagreement. You need not always take sides, but once you have decided what issues are involved in an argument, you can write an effective paper by taking a stand and explaining why you have chosen one side over the other.

Your approach to *Antigone* will have to take into account the controversial nature of the play's conflict. Review your responses to the prewriting questions about the disagreement and about the antagonist and protagonist. Can you identify an issue that you think is central to the play's meaning? Are there other issues involved in the conflict? Try to get the main issues stated as clearly and specifically as you can before you begin to write. The ideas for writing that follow should help you to work out the important issues of the play.

You can argue an issue in two ways. You can devise a major claim about one side of the question and present reasons and evidence to support your stand. Or you can anticipate the claims of the opposing side and show how the evidence does not support this side, indicating where the fallacies or errors lie in the opposition's reasoning. You will probably want to combine both techniques in writing about *Antigone*.

Whatever your approach, you need to study the evidence and examine the ideas on both sides for flaws in logical thinking. One way to make this examination involves listing the main arguments, pro and con, in two columns on a sheet of paper.

Creon	**Antigone**
Public interest outweighs private loyalties.	Eternal unwritten laws take precedence.
Polynices made war on his own country.	All the dead deserve honor.

[1]Charles Paul Segal, "Sophocles' Praise of Man and the Conflicts of *Antigone*," in *Sophocles: A Collection of Critical Essays*, ed. T. Woodward (Englewood Cliffs, NJ: Prentice-Hall, 1966), 63.

You can make a similar listing of speeches or lines from the play that serve as evidence for the two sides of the argument. For instance, you may want to note such revealing statements by Creon as these:

> [W]hoever places a friend
> above the good of his own country, he is nothing. (203–04)
>
> [T]hat man
> the city places in authority, his orders
> must be obeyed, large and small,
> right and wrong. (748–51)

Compare these lists and see which side has the stronger arguments and the greater amount of evidence. You can then decide which side you are going to support; you also have a convenient listing of specific ideas and quotations to use in developing your essay.

Quoting from a Play

When writing a paper on a single play, instead of citing page numbers, you need to give act and scene numbers in parentheses at the end of the quoted material; for verse plays give act, scene, and line numbers. Because *Antigone* is not divided into acts and scenes, give the line numbers for the quotations you use. Long quotations (more than three lines) should be indented with *no* quotation marks. Also, indicate the speaker when quoting a passage in which more than one character speaks. Here are some samples:

> It is up to Ismene, then, to point out the obvious: "Remember we are women, / we're not born to contend with men" (74–75).

Only two lines are quoted, separated with a slash and enclosed in quotation marks.

> During her defense, Antigone declares her defiance:
>
> This is nothing.
> And if my present actions strike you as foolish,
> let's just say I've been accused of folly
> by a fool. (522–25)

A long quotation is indented with no quotation marks.

For plays *not* written in verse, give act and scene or page numbers in parentheses at the end of the quoted material.

IDEAS FOR WRITING

Ideas for Responsive Writing

1. Do you see yourself as approving of or opposing the rules and norms of the society you live in? How do you support, change, or disobey these rules and norms? Write about one rule or group of related rules (for example, sex roles or parent–child relationships) that you accept or reject.
2. In modern society, what might Creon and Antigone disagree about? Write an essay explaining where the two characters would probably stand on one of today's issues.

Ideas for Critical Writing

1. Is Creon a politician concerned with imposing and maintaining order? Is Antigone an anarchist whose action will destroy that order? Or is she a private citizen determined to follow the dictates of her personal beliefs? Write an essay that interprets *Antigone* as a struggle between public policy and individual conscience, supporting the side that you think is right.
2. CRITICAL APPROACHES: Read about gender-focused approaches to interpreting literature (pages 1160–61). Can you explain the conflict between Antigone and Creon as a psychological clash between a woman and a man? Write an essay that develops a claim about the male–female opposition in the play. You may want to work Ismene, Haemon, and Eurydice into your scheme of opposing values.

Ideas for Researched Writing

1. A. R. Gurney wrote *Another Antigone* (1988), an updated version of *Antigone* in which a classics professor and a headstrong college student clash over a term paper on Sophocles. Read this modern *Antigone*, and write an essay comparing and contrasting it to the original. Some topics to consider: What problems did the modern writer encounter in changing the setting? Are the same themes developed in both versions? Are the conflicts resolved in similar ways? Compare and contrast specific scenes. You may want to read reviews of productions of *Another Antigone* to see how critics and audiences respond to it.
2. Other transformations of *Antigone* include two plays with World War II settings: Jean Anouilh's 1942 version, also called *Antigone*, which was first produced in Paris in 1944 during the Nazi occupation of France; and Chiori Miyagawa's *Antigone's Red*, which is set in a Japanese-American internment camp in the 1940s. Find out more about these versions, and write an essay in which you evaluate how effectively the original themes and conflicts are used to comment on modern-day issues. Or write a comparison to the original using the approach previously described.

REWRITING

You will want to be certain that your arguments about *Antigone* are perfectly clear. Take some time to ensure that what you have written cannot be misunderstood. If you can, coax a friend or classmate into reading your first draft; ask your reader to point out sentences that do not make sense or that are unclear.

Avoiding Unclear Language

Multisyllabic words and long, involved sentences may dazzle your readers, but they can also hinder clear communication. Your first goal in writing should be to convey ideas and information. Trying to impress your readers with big words and fancy phrases may lead to one or more forms of unclear expression.

1. *Engfish:* Writing specialist Ken Macrorie uses this term to call attention to artificial language that does not represent a writer's own experience and education. Engfish is phony, pretentious, stuffy, and often impossible to decode. Writers use Engfish, it seems, when they are unsure of which attitude to take toward their subject and their audience. The student who wrote

   > Antigone's unacceptable posture toward the designated governmental powers inevitably entailed the termination of her existence,

   no doubt thought that this inflated diction was appropriate for a serious paper on a classical play. But most readers probably would prefer to see that sentence revised to read more clearly, like this one:

   > Antigone's defiance led to her death.

   In the long run, clarity will impress your readers more than Engfish ever can.
2. *Jargon:* This term applies to the specialized language used by a particular group of people. Computer operators, sociologists, teenagers, architects, hockey players, mobsters—all sorts of interest groups and professions—employ words and terms that relate only to their particular activities. The problem with jargon is that outsiders do not understand it. Writing about a "love game" or the "ad court" will be all right for an audience of tennis buffs, but you will have to change your language for more general readers. Jargon may not come up in your essay about *Antigone*, but it can creep in from other sources. For instance, the student who wrote

> Antigone's behavior is marked by regressive reaction formation toward authoritarian figures

was apparently influenced by the jargon of her psychology class. Unless you are writing for an audience of fellow psychoanalysts, you would do better to say the following:

> Antigone sometimes acted like a disobedient daughter.

3. *Abstract words:* Abstract terms and general expressions do not automatically make your writing intellectual and impressive. Although it is true that writing an argumentative essay requires using abstract ideas, your paper will be more persuasive if it is factual, concrete, and clear. Abstractions tend to be hazy and difficult to define. Words like *duty*, *anarchy*, *patriotism*, and *truth* have different meanings to different people. When writing about an abstract concept, make certain that you have a definite meaning in your own mind. If, for instance, you write that

> Antigone is a woman of honor

it is a good idea to check the dictionary to see if your understanding of the word *honor* coincides with a standard definition. *The American Heritage Dictionary* gives thirteen entries for *honor.* Which one does the above sentence convey? Would "a woman's chastity" be accurate in this context? It might be more meaningful to say

> Antigone is a woman of principle and integrity

although those words are also abstract. Try, if possible, to specify the meaning you want when using an abstract term.

> Above all, Creon is a master politician—a man of ambition intent on holding his power.

Sample Student Paper

In the following paper, Laurie Dahlberg, a student at Illinois State University, argues that the chief conflict in *Antigone* involves a power struggle between male and female. Notice how she uses and documents quoted material from the play to support her claims.

Sample Student Paper

Dahlberg 1

Laurie Dahlberg

Professor Day

English 102

April 2, 2005

"Never Be Rated Inferior to a Woman":
Gender Conflict in *Antigone*

Antigone is a drama built around two basic conflicts. Beneath the more obvious conflict of the individual versus the state lies a struggle of male against female. The protagonist, Antigone, becomes a criminal by choice but a feminist by chance. The antagonist, Creon, is fighting to retain control over Antigone, not only as king over subject but also as man over woman.

Antigone knows that she has violated the king's order not to bury her brother Polynices, but she seems not to notice that she has also violated the social code by stepping outside the boundaries of acceptable feminine behavior. Her act of defiance is courageous, self-reliant, and completely contrary to the obedience expected of women in her society. She fearlessly assures her sister, Ismene, that Creon "has no right to keep me from my own" (59). It is up to Ismene, then, to point out the obvious: "Remember we are women, / we're not born to contend with men" (74–75). A perfect foil for Antigone, Ismene epitomizes the good Theban woman—she is deferential, passive, and timid. Though she loves Antigone dearly, Ismene is still bound to her male masters and cannot follow her sister: "we're underlings, ruled by much stronger hands," she says. "I must obey / the ones who

Dahlberg 2

stand in power" (76, 79–80). Eventually, Ismene is rewarded for her passivity when Creon spares her life.

When Antigone is arrested, King Creon expresses shock that a woman in his court has committed the crime. But his disbelief soon turns to perverse pleasure at the opportunity to punish this woman for her audacity. Creon's threatening speeches to Antigone also bring out his contempt for women:

> Go down below and love,
> if love you must—love the dead!
> While I'm alive,
> no woman is going to lord it over
> me. (591–93)

Antigone, however, rises above the pettiness of sexual rivalry by responding only to the conflict between king and subject. Unlike Creon, Antigone acts out of a heartfelt moral obligation, proclaiming that she is "Not ashamed for a moment, / not to honor my brother, my own flesh and blood" (572–73). As Antigone calmly and eloquently argues the righteousness of her action instead of quivering with fear under Creon's threats, the king's feeling of triumph slowly turns to rage. During her defense, Antigone declares her defiance:

> This is nothing.
> And if my present actions strike you
> as foolish,
> let's just say I've been accused of
> folly
> by a fool. (522–25)

To which Creon angrily replies:

> This girl was an old hand at
> insolence

when she overrode the edicts we made
public.
But once she'd done it—the
insolence,
twice over—to glory in it,
laughing,
mocking us to our face with what
she'd done.
I'm not the man, not now: she is the
man
if this victory goes to her and she
goes free. (536–42)

Though Antigone's illegal act is punishable by death, it is the fact that a mere woman has defied him that enrages Creon. Her death alone will not satisfy him. He needs to master her willfulness and make her regret her arrogance. Instead of killing her, he entombs her, where she will die slowly. This method of execution, Creon says, will teach the woman a lesson:

There let her pray to the one god she
worships:
Death—who knows?—may just reprieve
her from death.
Or she may learn at last, better
late than never,
what a waste of breath it is to
worship Death. (875–78)

The key to Creon's personality is found in his comment to Haemon when he is explaining why he (the king) has sentenced his son's bride-to-be to death:

we must defend the men who live by
law,

never let some woman triumph over us.
Better to fall from power, if we
must,
at the hands of a man—never be
rated
inferior to a woman, never. (757–61)

Creon refuses to listen to Haemon's reasoning, and the young man, disgusted by his father's cruelty, rejects him. This rejection makes the king even more bitter. Creon's pride has made him blind to his mistake.

Throughout the course of the play, Creon changes from a strict but competent leader to a wildly insecure man, plagued by imaginary enemies. He has come to suspect that anyone who disagrees with him is involved in a plot against him, as these words to Ismene reveal:

You—
in my house, you viper, slinking
undetected,
sucking my life-blood! I never knew
I was breeding twin disasters, the
two of you
rising up against my throne. (597–601)

Creon has mistaken Antigone's act of piety for a wild attempt by a power-hungry woman to undermine his rule. Out of his own fear of being beaten by a woman, Creon begins a chain of events which finally destroys him, fulfilling Antigone's prediction:

But if these men are wrong, let them
suffer
nothing worse than they mete out to
me—
these masters of injustice! (1019–21)

Dahlberg 5

Work Cited

Sophocles. *Antigone.* Trans. Robert Fagles. *Literature and the Writing Process.* Ed. Elizabeth McMahan, Susan X Day, and Robert Funk. 7th ed. Upper Saddle River: Prentice, 2005. 592–627. Print.

Questions for Discussion

1. Do you think this essay overemphasizes the gender issue in analyzing the conflict between Creon and Antigone? Has the author slighted or ignored more important issues?
2. Can you find any additional evidence that the author of the essay overlooked or chose not to use? Would the case be strengthened by including Eurydice in the analysis?
3. The author says that Antigone rises above sexual rivalry in her defiant behavior. Is this view entirely true? Can you find any evidence to suggest that Antigone is also caught up in the power struggle between male and female?
4. In carrying out her approach, the author of the essay analyzes Creon more than Antigone. Why is that? Is this strategy productive? Do you agree with the conclusion about Creon's character development?

18

Writing About Character

Pondering people's characters comes quite naturally and easily. You will remember that we began our approach to literature with the study of character in the short story. Drama also provides us with carefully drawn examples of human speech and behavior. Whether the presentation is realistic or not, the characters are at the heart of the play.

What Is the Modern Hero?

In everyday life, we use the word *heroic* to describe people who save others' lives while risking their own, acts of great self-sacrifice or self-control, feats that we hold in awe. Before you read on, think of the last time you remember calling something heroic or referring to someone as a hero. Note the situation, and think about what you meant by the word. We often use it lightly—the person who supplies a much needed extension cord or an emergency ten-dollar loan may temporarily be a hero. But drama practically forces us into deeper consideration of what a hero is.

The Classical Tragic Hero

In the fourth century B.C., Aristotle described the classic concept of the tragic hero. He wrote that the hero must be someone "who is highly renowned and prosperous." Classical tragedy involves the inevitable destruction of a noble person by means of a character flaw, usually a disproportionate measure of a specific human attribute such as pride or jealousy or indecision. The Aristotelian definition implies this basic premise: there is a natural, right ordering and proportion of traits within the human being that, if violated, produces calamity. Many critics cite Antigone's "difficult willfulness" as the explanation of her fate. Charles Segal claims that "she can assert what she is only by staking her entire being, her life. It is by this extreme defense of her beliefs that she rises to heroic and deeply tragic stature."[1]

[1]Charles Paul Segal, "Sophocles' Praise of Man and the Conflicts of *Antigone*," in *Sophocles: A Collection of Critical Essays*, ed. T. Woodward (Englewood Cliffs, NJ: Prentice-Hall, 1966), 65.

The Modern Tragic Hero

In 1949, the famous playwright Arthur Miller described what he considered a new kind of hero. In an article titled "Tragedy and the Common Man" (*New York Times*, 27 Feb. 1949, 3.1.3.), he challenged Aristotle's idea that the hero must be a "highly renowned and prosperous" figure who has a tragic flaw. In contrast to a disorder exclusively within the personal traits of the hero, Miller's idea of the modern hero emphasizes a clash between the character and the environment, especially the social environment. He says that each person has a chosen image of self and position and that tragedy results when the character's environment denies the fulfillment of this self-concept. The hero no longer must be born into the nobility but gains stature in the action of pitting self against cosmos. The tragedy is "the disaster inherent in being torn away from our chosen image of what and who we are in this world." Feelings of displacement and indignity, then, are the driving forces for Miller's modern tragic hero. In his own play *Death of a Salesman*, the character Willy Loman imagines himself as a well-liked, successful, worldly businessman. Tragically, he is really an object of ridicule and contempt, always on the edge of poverty. Such conflicts between ideal self-image and reality occur over and over in the modern play you are about to read.

Looking at the Modern Hero

As you read for pleasure *Fences* by August Wilson, take special note of the characters. Who is the hero? the heroine?—or are there none? To which characters do you respond positively? Are there any to whom you respond negatively?

August Wilson 1945–2005

August Wilson earned fame writing a cycle of ten plays, each set during a decade from 1900 to 1990 in his boyhood home, the economically depressed neighborhood of The Hill in Pittsburgh. He said that his plays offer White Americans a different view of Blacks: "For instance, in *Fences* they see a garbageman, a person they don't really look at, although they see a garbageman every day. By looking at Troy's life, white people find out that the content of this black garbageman's life is affected by the same things—love, honor, beauty, betrayal, duty. Recognizing that these things are as much part of his life as theirs can affect how they think about and deal with black people in their lives." Wilson's plays were so successful and admired on the New York stage that when he died in 2005, Broadway's Virginia Theater was renamed the August Wilson Theater.

Fences

for Lloyd Richards,
who adds to whatever he touches

When the sins of our fathers visit us
We do not have to play host.
We can banish them with forgiveness
As God, in His Largeness and Laws.

—August Wilson

LIST OF CHARACTERS

Troy Maxson
Jim Bono, *Troy's friend*
Rose, *Troy's wife*
Lyons, *Troy's oldest son by previous marriage*
Gabriel, *Troy's brother*
Cory, *Troy and Rose's son*
Raynell, *Troy's daughter*

SETTING

The setting is the yard which fronts the only entrance to the Maxson household, an ancient two-story brick house set back off a small alley in a big-city neighborhood. The entrance to the house is gained by two or three steps leading to a wooden porch badly in need of paint.

A relatively recent addition to the house and running its full width, the porch lacks congruence. It is a sturdy porch with a flat roof. One or two chairs of dubious value sit at one end where the kitchen window opens onto the porch. An old-fashioned icebox stands silent guard at the opposite end.

The yard is a small dirt yard, partially fenced, except for the last scene, with a wooden saw horse, a pile of lumber, and other fence-building equipment set off to the side. Opposite is a tree from which hangs a ball made of rags. A baseball bat leans against the tree. Two oil drums serve as garbage receptacles and sit near the house at right to complete the setting.

THE PLAY

Near the turn of the century, the destitute of Europe sprang on the city with tenacious claws and an honest and solid dream. The city devoured them. They swelled its belly until it burst into a thousand furnaces and sewing machines, a thousand butcher shops and bakers' ovens, a thousand churches and hospitals and funeral parlors and money-lenders. The city grew. It nourished itself and offered each man a partnership limited only by his talent, his guile and his willingness and capacity for hard work. For the immigrants of Europe, a dream dared and won true.

The descendants of African slaves were offered no such welcome or participation. They came from places called the Carolinas and the Virginias, Georgia, Alabama, Mississippi, and Tennessee. They came strong, eager, searching. The city rejected them and they fled and settled along the riverbanks and under bridges in shallow, ramshackle houses made of sticks and tarpaper. They collected rags and wood. They sold the use of their muscles and their bodies. They cleaned houses and washed clothes, they shined shoes, and in quiet desperation and vengeful pride, they stole, and lived in pursuit of their own dream. That they could breathe free, finally, and stand to meet life with the force of dignity and whatever eloquence the heart could call upon.

By 1957, the hard-won victories of the European immigrants had solidified the industrial might of America. War had been confronted and won with new energies that used loyalty and patriotism as its fuel. Life was rich, full, and flourishing. The Milwaukee Braves won the World Series, and the hot winds of change that would make the sixties a turbulent, racing, dangerous, and provocative decade had not yet begun to blow full.

ACT 1

SCENE 1

It is 1957. TROY *and* BONO *enter the yard, engaged in conversation.* TROY *is fifty- three years old, a large man with thick, heavy hands; it is this largeness that he strives to fill out and make an accommodation with. Together with his blackness, his largeness informs his sensibilities and the choices he has made in his life.*

Of the two men, BONO *is obviously the follower. His commitment to their friendship of thirty-odd years is rooted in his admiration of* TROY'S *honesty, capacity for hard work, and his strength, which* BONO *seeks to emulate.*

It is Friday night, payday, and the one night of the week the two men engage in a ritual of talk and drink. TROY *is usually the most talkative and at times he can be crude and almost vulgar, though he is capable of rising to profound heights of expression. The men carry lunch buckets and wear or carry burlap aprons and are dressed in clothes suitable to their jobs as garbage collectors.*

BONO. Troy, you ought to stop that lying!

TROY. I ain't lying! The nigger had a watermelon this big. [*He indicates with his hands.*] Talking about… "What watermelon, Mr. Rand?" I liked to fell out! "What watermelon, Mr. Rand?"… And it sitting there big as life.

BONO. What did Mr. Rand say?

TROY. Ain't said nothing. Figure if the nigger too dumb to know he carrying a watermelon, he wasn't gonna get much sense out of him. Trying to hide that great big old watermelon under his coat. Afraid to let the white man see him carry it home.

BONO. I'm like you… I ain't got no time for them kind of people.

TROY. Now what he look like getting mad cause he see the man from the union talking to Mr. Rand?

BONO. He come to me talking about… "Maxson gonna get us fired." I told him to get away from me with that. He walked away from me calling you a troublemaker. What Mr. Rand say?

TROY. Ain't said nothing. He told me to go down the Commissioner's office next Friday. They called me down there to see them.

BONO. Well, as long as you got your complaint filed, they can't fire you. That's what one of them white fellows tell me.

TROY. I ain't worried about them firing me. They gonna fire me cause I asked a question? That's all I did. I went to Mr. Rand and asked him, "Why? Why you got the white mens driving and the colored lifting?" Told him, "What's the matter, don't I count? You think only white fellows got sense enough to drive a truck. That ain't no paper job! Hell, anybody can drive a truck. How come you got all whites driving and the colored lifting?" He told me "take it to the union." Well, hell, that's what I done! Now they wanna come up with this pack of lies.

BONO. I told Brownie if the man come and ask him any questions... just tell the truth! It ain't nothing but something they done trumped up on you cause you filed a complaint on them.

TROY. Brownie don't understand nothing. All I want them to do is change the job description. Give everybody a chance to drive the truck. Brownie can't see that. He ain't got that much sense.

BONO. How you figure he be making out with that gal be up at Taylor's all the time... that Alberta gal?

TROY. Same as you and me. Getting just as much as we is. Which is to say nothing.

BONO. It is, huh? I figure you doing a little better than me... and I ain't saying what I'm doing.

TROY. Aw, nigger, look here... I know you. If you had got anywhere near that gal, twenty minutes later you be looking to tell somebody. And the first one you gonna tell... that you gonna want to brag to... is me.

BONO. I ain't saying that, I see where you be eyeing her.

TROY. I eye all the women. I don't miss nothing. Don't never let nobody tell you Troy Maxson don't eye the women.

BONO. You been doing more than eyeing her. You done bought her a drink or two.

TROY. Hell yeah, I bought her a drink! What that mean? I bought you one, too. What that mean cause I buy her a drink? I'm just being polite.

BONO. It's all right to buy her one drink. That's what you call being polite. But when you wanna be buying two or three... that's what you call eyeing her.

TROY. Look here, as long as you known me... you ever known me to chase after women?

BONO. Hell yeah! Long as I done known you. You forgetting I knew you when.

TROY. Naw, I'm talking about since I been married to Rose?

BONO. Oh, not since you been married to Rose. Now, that's the truth, there, I can say that.

TROY. All right then! Case closed.

BONO. I see you be walking up around Alberta's house. You supposed to be at Taylors' and you be walking up around there.

TROY. What you watching where I'm walking for? I ain't watching after you.

BONO. I seen you walking around there more than once.

TROY. Hell, you liable to see me walking anywhere! That don't mean nothing cause you see me walking around there.

BONO. Where she come from anyway? She just kinda showed up one day.

TROY. Tallahassee. You can look at her and tell she one of them Florida gals. They got some big healthy women down there. Grow them right up out the ground. Got a little bit of Indian in her. Most of them niggers down in Florida got some Indian in them.

BONO. I don't know about that Indian part. But she damn sure big and healthy. Women wear some big stockings. Got them great big old legs and hips as wide as the Mississippi River.

TROY. Legs don't mean nothing. You don't do nothing but push them out of the way. But them hips cushion the ride!

BONO. Troy, you ain't got no sense.

TROY. It's the truth! Like you riding on Goodyears!

ROSE *enters from the house. She is ten years younger than* TROY, *her devotion to him stems from her recognition of the possibilities of her life without him: a succession of abusive men and their babies, a life of partying and running the streets, the Church, or aloneness with its attendant pain and frustration. She recognizes* TROY'S *spirit as a fine and illuminating one and she either ignores or forgives his faults, only some of which she recognizes. Though she doesn't drink, her presence is an integral part of the Friday night rituals. She alternates between the porch and the kitchen, where supper preparations are under way.*

ROSE. What you all out here getting into?

TROY. What you worried about what we getting into for? This is men talk, woman.

ROSE. What I care what you all talking about? Bono, you gonna stay for supper?

BONO. No, I thank you, Rose. But Lucille say she cooking up a pot of pigfeet.

TROY. Pigfeet! Hell, I'm going home with you! Might even stay the night if you got some pigfeet. You got something in there to top them pigfeet, Rose?

ROSE. I'm cooking up some chicken. I got some chicken and collard greens.

TROY. Well, go on back in the house and let me and Bono finish what we was talking about. This is men talk. I got some talk for you later. You know what kind of talk I mean. You go on and powder it up.

ROSE. Troy Maxson, don't you start that now!

TROY [*puts his arm around her*]. Aw, woman . . . come here. Look here. Bono . . . when I met this woman . . . I got out that place, say, "Hitch up my pony, saddle up my mare . . . there's a woman out there for me somewhere. I looked here. Looked there. Saw Rose and latched on to her." I latched on to her and told her—I'm gonna tell you the truth—I told her, "Baby, I don't wanna marry, I just wanna be your man." Rose told me . . . tell him what you told me, Rose.

ROSE. I told him if he wasn't the marrying kind, then move out the way so the marrying kind could find me.

TROY. That's what she told me. "Nigger, you in my way. You blocking the view! Move out the way so I can find me a husband." I thought it over two or three days. Come back—

ROSE. Ain't no two or three days nothing. You was back the same night.

TROY. Come back, told her . . . "Okay, baby . . . but I'm gonna buy me a banty rooster and put him out there in the backyard . . . and when he see a stranger come, he'll flap his wings and crow . . . ." Look here, Bono, I could watch the front door by myself . . . it was that back door I was worried about.

ROSE. Troy, you ought not talk like that. Troy ain't doing nothing but telling a lie.

TROY. Only thing is . . . when we first got married . . . forget the rooster . . . we ain't had no yard!

BONO. I hear you tell it. Me and Lucille was staying down there on Logan Street. Had two rooms with the outhouse in the back. I ain't mind the outhouse none. But when that goddamn wind blow through there in the winter . . . that's what I'm talking about! To this day I wonder why in the hell I ever stayed down there for six long years. But see, I didn't know I could do no better. I thought only white folks had inside toilets and things.

ROSE. There's a lot of people don't know they can do no better than they doing now. That's just something you got to learn. A lot of folks still shop at Bella's.

TROY. Ain't nothing wrong with shopping at Bella's. She got fresh food.

ROSE. I ain't said nothing about if she got fresh food. I'm talking about what she charge. She charge ten cents more than the A&P.

TROY. The A&P ain't never done nothing for me. I spends my money where I'm treated right. I go down to Bella, say, "I need a loaf of bread, I'll pay you Friday." She give it to me. What sense that make when I got money to go and spend it somewhere else and ignore the person who done right by me? That ain't in the Bible.

ROSE. We ain't talking about what's in the Bible. What sense it make to shop there when she overcharge?

TROY. You shop where you want to. I'll do my shopping where the people been good to me.

ROSE. Well, I don't think it's right for her to overcharge. That's all I was saying.

BONO. Look here…I got to get on. Lucille going be raising all kind of hell.

TROY. Where you going, nigger? We ain't finished this pint. Come here, finish this pint.

BONO. Well, hell, I am…if you ever turn the bottle loose.

TROY [*hands him the bottle*]. The only thing I say about the A&P is I'm glad Cory got that job down there. Help him take care of his school clothes and things. Gabe done moved out and things getting tight around here. He got that job.…He can start to look out for himself.

ROSE. Cory done went and got recruited by a college football team.

TROY. I told that boy about that football stuff. The white man ain't gonna let him get nowhere with that football. I told him when he first come to me with it. Now you come telling me he done went and got more tied up in it. He ought to go and get recruited in how to fix cars or something where he can make a living.

ROSE. He ain't talking about making no living playing football. It's just something the boys in school do. They gonna send a recruiter by to talk to you. He'll tell you he ain't talking about making no living playing football. It's a honor to be recruited.

TROY. It ain't gonna get him nowhere. Bono'll tell you that.

BONO. If he be like you in the sports…he's gonna be all right. Ain't but two men ever played baseball as good as you. That's Babe Ruth and Josh Gibson. Them's the only two men ever hit more home runs than you.

TROY. What it ever get me? Ain't got a pot to piss in or a window to throw it out of.

ROSE. Times have changed since you was playing baseball, Troy. That was before the war. Times have changed a lot since then.

TROY. How in hell they done changed?

ROSE. They got lots of colored boys playing ball now. Baseball and football.

BONO. You right about that, Rose. Times have changed, Troy. You just come along too early.

TROY. There ought not never have been no time called too early! Now you take that fellow…What's that fellow they had playing right field for the Yankees back then? You know who I'm talking about, Bono. Used to play right field for the Yankees.

ROSE. Selkirk?

TROY. Selkirk! That's it! Man batting .269, understand? .269. What kind of sense that make? I was hitting .432 with thirty-seven home runs! Man batting .269 and playing right field for the Yankees! I saw Josh Gibson's daughter yesterday. She walking around with raggedy shoes on her feet. Now I bet you Selkirk's daughter ain't walking around with raggedy shoes on the feet! I bet you that!

Rose. They got a lot of colored baseball players now. Jackie Robinson was the first. Folks had to wait for Jackie Robinson.

Troy. I done seen a hundred niggers play baseball better than Jackie Robinson. Hell, I know some teams Jackie Robinson couldn't even make! What you talking about Jackie Robinson. Jackie Robinson wasn't nobody. I'm talking about if you could play ball then they ought to have let you play. Don't care what color you were. Come telling me I come along too early. If you could play...then they ought to have let you play.

Troy *takes a long drink from the bottle.*

Rose. You gonna drink yourself to death. You don't need to be drinking like that.

Troy. Death ain't nothing. I done seen him. Done wrassled with him. You can't tell me nothing about death. Death ain't nothing but a fastball on the outside corner. And you know what I'll do to that! Lookee here, Bono...am I lying? You get one of them fastballs, about waist high, over the outside corner of the plate where you can get the meat of the bat on it...and good god! You can kiss it goodbye. Now, am I lying?

Bono. Naw, you telling the truth there. I seen you do it.

Troy. If I'm lying...that 450 feet worth of lying! [*Pause.*] That's all death is to me. A fastball on the outside corner.

Rose. I don't know why you want to get on talking about death.

Troy. Ain't nothing wrong with talking about death. That's part of life. Everybody gonna die. You gonna die, I'm gonna die. Bono's gonna die. Hell, we all gonna die.

Rose. But you ain't got to talk about it. I don't like to talk about it.

Troy. You the one brought it up. Me and Bono was talking about baseball...you tell me I'm gonna drink myself to death. Ain't that right, Bono? You know I don't drink this but one night out of the week. That's Friday night. I'm gonna drink just enough to where I can handle it. Then I cuts it loose. I leave it alone. So don't you worry about me drinking myself to death. 'Cause I ain't worried about Death. I done seen him. I done wrestled with him.

Look here, Bono...I looked up one day and Death was marching straight at me. Like Soldiers on Parade! The Army of Death was marching straight at me. The middle of July, 1941. It got real cold just like it be winter. It seem like Death himself reached out and touched me on the shoulder. He touched me just like I touch you. I got cold as ice and Death standing there grinning at me.

Rose. Troy, why don't you hush that talk.

Troy. I say...what you want, Mr. Death? You be wanting me? You done brought your army to be getting me? I looked him dead in the eye. I wasn't fearing nothing. I was ready to tangle. Just like I'm ready to tangle now. The Bible say be ever vigilant. That's why I don't get but so drunk. I got to keep watch.

Rose. Troy was right down there in Mercy Hospital. You remember he had pneumonia? Laying there with a fever talking plumb out of his head.

Troy (James Earl Jones) stands ready to take a swing at Death while Rose (Mary Alice) and Bono (Ray Aranha) look on. Photo from the original Broadway production of *Fences*.

TROY. Death standing there staring at me... carrying that sickle in his hand. Finally he say, "You want bound over for another year?" See, just like that... "You want bound over for another year?" I told him, "Bound over hell! Let's settle this now!"

It seem like he kinda fell back when I said that, and all the cold went out of me. I reached down and grabbed that sickle and threw it just as far as I could throw it... and me and him commenced to wrestling.

We wrestled for three days and three nights. I can't say where I found the strength from. Everytime it seemed like he was gonna get the best of me, I'd reach way down deep inside myself and find the strength to do him one better.

ROSE. Everytime Troy tell that story he find different ways to tell it. Different things to make up about it.

TROY. I ain't making up nothing. I'm telling you the facts of what happened. I wrestled with Death for three days and three nights and I'm standing here to tell you about it. [*Pause.*] All right. At the end of the third night we done weakened each other to where we can't hardly move. Death stood up, throwed on his robe... had him a white robe with a hood on it. He throwed on that robe and went off to look for his sickle. Say, "I'll be back." Just like that. "I'll be back." I told him, say, "Yeah, but... you gonna have to find me!" I wasn't no fool. I wasn't going looking for him. Death ain't nothing to play with. And I know he's gonna get me. I know I got to join his army... his camp followers. But as long as I keep my strength and see him coming... as long as I keep up my vigilance... he's gonna have to fight to get me. I ain't going easy.

BONO. Well, look here, since you got to keep up your vigilance... let me have the bottle.

TROY. Aw hell, I shouldn't have told you that part. I should have left out that part.

ROSE. Troy be talking that stuff and half the time don't even know what he be talking about.

TROY. Bono know me better than that.

BONO. That's right. I know you. I know you got some Uncle Remus in your blood. You got more stories than the devil got sinners.

TROY. Aw hell, I done seen him too! Done talked with the devil.

ROSE. Troy, don't nobody wanna be hearing all that stuff.

> LYONS *enters the yard from the street. Thirty-four years old,* TROY'S *son by a previous marriage, he sports a neatly trimmed goatee, sport coat, white shirt, tieless and buttoned at the collar. Though he fancies himself a musician, he is more caught up in the rituals and "idea" of being a musician than in the actual practice of the music. He has come to borrow money from* TROY, *and while he knows he will be successful, he is uncertain as to what extent his lifestyle will be held up to scrutiny and ridicule.*

LYONS. Hey, Pop.

TROY. What you come "Hey, Popping" me for?

LYONS. How you doing, Rose? [*He kisses her.*] Mr. Bono. How you doing?

BONO. Hey, Lyons... how you been?

TROY. He must have been doing all right. I ain't seen him around here last week.

ROSE. Troy, leave your boy alone. He come by to see you and you wanna start all that nonsense.

TROY. I ain't bothering Lyons. [*Offers him the bottle.*] Here... get you a drink. We got an understanding. I know why he come by to see me and he know I know.

LYONS. Come on, Pop... I just stopped by to say hi... see how you was doing.

TROY. You ain't stopped by yesterday.

ROSE. You gonna stay for supper, Lyons? I got some chicken cooking in the oven.

LYONS. No, Rose... thanks. I was just in the neighborhood and thought I'd stop by for a minute.

TROY. You was in the neighborhood all right, nigger. You telling the truth there. You was in the neighborhood 'cause it's my payday.

LYONS. Well, hell, since you mentioned it... let me have ten dollars.

TROY. I'll be damned! I'll die and go to hell and play blackjack with the devil before I give you ten dollars.

BONO. That's what I wanna know about... that devil you done seen.

LYONS. What... Pop done seen the devil? You too much, Pops.

TROY. Yeah, I done seen him. Talked to him too!

ROSE. You ain't seen no devil. I done told you that man ain't had nothing to do with the devil. Anything you can't understand, you want to call it the devil.

TROY. Look here, Bono... I went down to see Hertzberger about some furniture. Got three rooms for two-ninety-eight. That what it say on the radio. "Three rooms... two-ninety-eight." Even made up a little song about it. Go down there... man tell me I can't get no credit. I'm working every day and can't get no credit. What to do? I got an empty house with some raggedy furniture in it. Cory ain't got no bed. He's sleeping on a pile of rags on the floor. Working every day and can't get no credit. Come back here—Rose'll tell you—madder than hell. Sit down... try to figure what I'm gonna do. Come a knock on the door. Ain't been living here but three days. Who know I'm here? Open the door... devil standing there bigger than life. White fellow... got on good clothes and everything. Standing there with a clipboard in his hand. I ain't had to say nothing. First words come out of his mouth was... "I understand you need some furniture and can't get no credit." I liked to fell over. He say, "I'll give you all the credit you want, but you got to pay the interest on it." I told him, "Give me three rooms worth and charge whatever you want." Next day a truck pulled up here and two men unloaded them three rooms. Man what drove the truck give me a book. Say send ten dollars, first of every month to the address in the book and every thing will be all right. Say if I miss a payment the devil was coming back and it'll be hell to pay. That was fifteen years ago. To this day... the first of the month I send my ten dollars, Rose'll tell you.

ROSE. Troy lying.

TROY. I ain't never seen that man since. Now you tell me who else that could have been but the devil? I ain't sold my soul or nothing like that, you understand. Naw, I wouldn't have truck with the devil about nothing like that. I got my furniture and pays my ten dollars the first of the month just like clockwork.

BONO. How long you say you been paying this ten dollars a month?

TROY. Fifteen years!

BONO. Hell, ain't you finished paying for it yet? How much the man done charged you?

TROY. Ah hell, I done paid for it. I done paid for it ten times over! The fact is I'm scared to stop paying it.

ROSE. Troy lying. We got that furniture from Mr. Glickman. He ain't paying no ten dollars a month to nobody.

TROY. Aw hell, woman. Bono know I ain't that big a fool.

LYONS. I was just getting ready to say... I know where there's a bridge for sale.

TROY. Look here, I'll tell you this... it don't matter to me if he was the devil. It don't matter if the devil give credit. Somebody has got to give it.

ROSE. It ought to matter. You going around talking about having truck with the devil... God's the one you gonna have to answer to. He's the one gonna be at the Judgment.

LYONS. Yeah, well, look here, Pop... Let me have that ten dollars. I'll give it back to you. Bonnie got a job working at the hospital.

TROY. What I tell you, Bono? The only time I see this nigger is when he wants something. That's the only time I see him.

LYONS. Come on, Pop, Mr. Bono don't want to hear all that. Let me have the ten dollars. I told you Bonnie working.

TROY. What that mean to me? "Bonnie working." I don't care if she working. Go ask her for the ten dollars if she working. Talking about "Bonnie working." Why ain't you working?

LYONS. Aw, Pop, you know I can't find no decent job. Where am I gonna get a job at? You know I can't get no job.

TROY. I told you I know some people down there. I can get you on the rubbish if you want to work. I told you that the last time you came by here asking me for something.

LYONS. Naw, Pop... thanks. That ain't for me. I don't wanna be carrying nobody's rubbish. I don't wanna be punching nobody's time clock.

TROY. What's the matter, you too good to carry people's rubbish? Where you think that ten dollars you talking about come from? I'm just supposed to haul people's rubbish and give my money to you cause you too lazy to work. You too lazy to work and wanna know why you ain't got what I got.

ROSE. What hospital Bonnie working at? Mercy?

LYONS. She's down at Passavant working in the laundry.

TROY. I ain't got nothing as it is. I give you that ten dollars and I got to eat beans the rest of the week. Naw...you ain't getting no ten dollars here.

LYONS. You ain't got to be eating no beans. I don't know why you wanna say that.

TROY. I ain't got no extra money. Gabe done moved over to Miss Pearl's paying her the rent and things done got tight around here. I can't afford to be giving you every payday.

LYONS. I ain't asked you to give me nothing. I asked you to loan me ten dollars. I know you got ten dollars.

TROY. Yeah, I got it. You know why I got it? 'Cause I don't throw my money away out there in the streets. You living the fast life...wanna be a musician...running around in them clubs and things...then, you learn to take care of yourself. You ain't gonna find me going and asking nobody for nothing. I done spent too many years without.

LYONS. You and me is two different people, Pop.

TROY. I done learned my mistake and learned to do what's right by it. You still trying to get something for nothing. Life don't owe you nothing. You owe it to yourself. Ask Bono. He'll tell you I'm right.

LYONS. You got your way of dealing with the world...I got mine. The only thing that matters to me is the music.

TROY. Yeah, I can see that! It don't matter how you gonna eat...where your next dollar is coming from. You telling the truth there.

LYONS. I know I got to eat. But I got to live too. I need something that gonna help me to get out of the bed in the morning. Make me feel like I belong in the world. I don't bother nobody. I just stay with the music cause that's the only way I can find to live in the world. Otherwise there ain't no telling what I might do. Now I don't come criticizing you and how you live. I just come by to ask you for ten dollars. I don't wanna hear all that about how I live.

TROY. Boy, your mamma did a hell of a job raising you.

LYONS. You can't change me, Pop. I'm thirty-four years old. If you wanted to change me, you should have been there when I was growing up. I come by to see you...ask for ten dollars and you want to talk about how I was raised. You don't know nothing about how I was raised.

ROSE. Let the boy have ten dollars, Troy.

TROY [*to* LYONS]. What the hell you looking at me for? I ain't got no ten dollars. You know what I do with my money. [*To* ROSE.] Give him ten dollars if you want him to have it.

ROSE. I will. Just as soon as you turn it loose.

TROY [*handing* ROSE *the money*]. There it is. Seventy-six dollars and forty-two cents. You see this, Bono? Now, I ain't gonna get but six of that back.

ROSE. You ought to stop telling that lie. Here, Lyons. [*She hands him the money.*]

LYONS. Thanks, Rose. Look...I got to run...I'll see you later.

TROY. Wait a minute. You gonna say, "Thanks, Rose" and ain't gonna look to see where she got that ten dollars from? See how they do me, Bono?

LYONS. I know she got it from you, Pop. Thanks. I'll give it back to you.

TROY. There he go telling another lie. Time I see that ten dollars...he'll be owing me thirty more.

LYONS. See you, Mr. Bono.

BONO. Take care, Lyons!

LYONS. Thanks, Pop. I'll see you again.

LYONS *exits the yard.*

TROY. I don't know why he don't go and get him a decent job and take care of that woman he got.

BONO. He'll be all right, Troy. The boy is still young.

TROY. The *boy* is thirty-four years old.

ROSE. Let's not get off into all that.

BONO. Look here…I got to be going. I got to be getting on. Lucille gonna be waiting.

TROY [*puts his arm around* ROSE]. See this woman, Bono? I love this woman. I love this woman so much it hurts. I love her so much…I done run out of ways of loving her. So I got to go back to basics. Don't you come by my house Monday morning talking about time to go to work…'cause I'm still gonna be stroking!

ROSE. Troy! Stop it now!

BONO. I ain't paying him no mind, Rose. That ain't nothing but gin-talk. Go on, Troy. I'll see you Monday.

TROY. Don't you come by my house, nigger! I done told you what I'm gonna be doing.

The lights go down to black.

SCENE 2

The lights come up on ROSE *hanging up clothes. She hums and sings softly to herself. It is the following morning.*

ROSE [*sings*].

Jesus, be a fence all around me every day
Jesus, I want you to protect me as I travel on my way.
Jesus, be a fence all around me every day.

TROY *enters from the house.*

Jesus, I want you to protect me
As I travel on my way.

[*To* TROY.] Morning. You ready for breakfast? I can fix it soon as I finish hanging up these clothes.

TROY. I got the coffee on. That'll be all right. I'll just drink some of that this morning.

ROSE. That 651 hit yesterday. That's the second time this month. Miss Pearl hit for a dollar…seem like those that need the least always get lucky. Poor folks can't get nothing.

TROY. Them numbers don't know nobody. I don't know why you fool with them. You and Lyons both.

ROSE. It's something to do.

TROY. You ain't doing nothing but throwing your money away.

ROSE. Troy, you know I don't play foolishly. I just play a nickel here and a nickel there.

TROY. That's two nickels you done thrown away.

ROSE. Now I hit sometimes…that makes up for it. It always comes in handy when I do hit. I don't hear you complaining then.

TROY. I ain't complaining now. I just say it's foolish. Trying to guess out of six hundred ways which way the number gonna come. If I had all the money niggers, these Negroes, throw away on numbers for one week—just one week—I'd be a rich man.

ROSE. Well, you wishing and calling it foolish ain't gonna stop folks from playing numbers. That's one thing for sure. Besides... some good things come from playing numbers. Look where Pope done bought him that restaurant off of numbers.

TROY. I can't stand niggers like that. Man ain't had two dimes to rub together. He walking around with his shoes all run over bumming money for cigarettes. All right. Got lucky there and hit the numbers...

ROSE. Troy, I know all about it.

TROY. Had good sense, I'll say that for him. He ain't throwed his money away. I seen niggers hit the numbers and go through two thousand dollars in four days. Man bought him that restaurant down there... fixed it up real nice... and then didn't want nobody to come in it! A Negro go in there and can't get no kind of service. I seen a white fellow come in there and order a bowl of stew. Pope picked all the meat out of the pot for him. Man ain't had nothing but a bowl of meat! Negro come behind him and ain't got nothing but the potatoes and carrots. Talking about what numbers do for people, you picked a wrong example. Ain't done nothing but make a worser fool out of him than he was before.

ROSE. Troy, you ought to stop worrying about what happened at work yesterday.

TROY. I ain't worried. Just told me to be down there at the Commissioner's office on Friday. Everybody think they gonna fire me. I ain't worried about them firing me. You ain't got to worry about that. [*Pause.*] Where's Cory? Cory in the house? [*Calls.*] Cory?

ROSE. He gone out.

TROY. Out, huh? He gone out 'cause he know I want him to help me with this fence. I know how he is. That boy scared of work.

> GABRIEL *enters. He comes halfway down the alley and, hearing* TROY*'s voice, stops.*

TROY [*continues*]. He ain't done a lick of work in his life.

ROSE. He had to go to football practice. Coach wanted them to get in a little extra practice before the season start.

TROY. I got his practice... running out of here before he get his chores done.

ROSE. Troy, what is wrong with you this morning? Don't nothing set right with you. Go on back in there and go to bed... get up on the other side.

TROY. Why something got to be wrong with me? I ain't said nothing wrong with me.

ROSE. You got something to say about everything. First it's the numbers... then it's the way the man runs his restaurant... then you done got on Cory. What's it gonna be next? Take a look up there and see if the weather suits you... or is it gonna be how you gonna put up the fence with the clothes hanging in the yard.

TROY. You hit the nail on the head then.

ROSE. I know you like I know the back of my hand. Go on in there and get you some coffee... see if that straighten you up. 'Cause you ain't right this morning.

> TROY *starts into the house and sees* GABRIEL. GABRIEL *starts singing.* TROY's *brother, he is seven years younger than* TROY. *Injured in World War II, he has a metal plate in his head. He carries an old trumpet tied around his waist and*

believes with every fiber of his being that he is the Archangel Gabriel. He carries a chipped basket with an assortment of discarded fruits and vegetables he has picked up in the strip district and which he attempts to sell.

GABRIEL [*singing*].

Yes, ma'am I got plums
You ask me how I sell them
Oh ten cents apiece
Three for a quarter
Come and buy now
'Cause I'm here today
And tomorrow I'll be gone

GABRIEL *enters.*

Hey, Rose!

ROSE. How you doing Gabe?

GABRIEL. There's Troy... Hey, Troy!

TROY. Hey, Gabe.

Exit into kitchen.

ROSE [*to* GABRIEL]. What you got there?

GABRIEL. You know what I got, Rose. I got fruits and vegetables.

ROSE [*looking in basket*]. Where's all these plums you talking about?

GABRIEL. I ain't got no plums today, Rose. I was just singing that. Have some tomorrow. Put me in a big order for plums. Have enough plums tomorrow for St. Peter and everybody.

TROY *reenters from kitchen, crosses to steps.*

[*To* ROSE.] Troy's mad at me.

TROY. I ain't mad at you. What I got to be mad at you about? You ain't done nothing to me.

GABRIEL. I just moved over to Miss Pearl's to keep out from in your way. I ain't mean no harm by it.

TROY. Who said anything about that? I ain't said anything about that.

GABRIEL. You ain't mad at me, is you?

TROY. Naw... I ain't mad at you, Gabe. If I was mad at you I'd tell you about it.

GABRIEL. Got me two rooms. In the basement. Got my own door too. Wanna see my key? [*He holds up a key.*] That's my own key! My two rooms!

TROY. Well, that's good, Gabe. You got your own key... that's good.

ROSE. You hungry, Gabe? I was just fixing to cook Troy his breakfast.

GABRIEL. I'll take some biscuits. You got some biscuits? Did you know when I was in heaven... every morning me and St. Peter would sit down by the gate and eat some big fat biscuits? Oh, yeah! We had us a good time. We'd sit there and eat us them biscuits and then St. Peter would go off to sleep and tell me to wake him up when it's time to open the gates for the judgment.

ROSE. Well, come on... I'll make up a batch of biscuits.

ROSE *exits into the house.*

GABRIEL. Troy... St. Peter got your name in the book. I seen it. It say... Troy Maxson. I say... I know him! He got the same name like what I got. That's my brother!

TROY. How many times you gonna tell me that, Gabe?

GABRIEL. Ain't got my name in the book. Don't have to have my name. I done died and went to heaven. He got your name though. One morning St. Peter was looking at his book... marking it up for the judgment... and he let me see your name. Got it in there under M. Got Rose's name... I ain't seen it like I seen yours... but I know it's in there. He got a great big book. Got everybody's name what was ever been born. That's what he told me. But I seen your name. Seen it with my own eyes.

TROY. Go on in the house there. Rose going to fix you something to eat.

GABRIEL. Oh, I ain't hungry. I done had breakfast with Aunt Jemimah. She come by and cooked me up a whole mess of flapjacks. Remember how we used to eat them flapjacks?

TROY. Go on in the house and get you something to eat now.

GABRIEL. I got to sell my plums. I done sold some tomatoes. Got me two quarters. Wanna see? [*He shows* TROY *his quarters.*] I'm gonna save them and buy me a new horn so St. Peter can hear me when it's time to open the gates. [GABRIEL *stops suddenly. Listens.*] Hear that? That's the hellhounds. I got to chase them out of here. Go on get out of here! Get out!

GABRIEL *exits singing.*

Better get ready for the judgment
Better get ready for the judgment
My Lord is coming down

ROSE *enters from the house.*

TROY. He's gone off somewhere.

GABRIEL [*offstage*].

Better get ready for the judgment
Better get ready for the judgment morning
Better get ready for the judgment
My God is coming down

ROSE. He ain't eating right. Miss Pearl say she can't get him to eat nothing.

TROY. What you want me to do about it, Rose? I done did everything I can for the man. I can't make him get well. Man got half his head blown away... what you expect?

ROSE. Seem like something ought to be done to help him.

TROY. Man don't bother nobody. He just mixed up from that metal plate he got in his head. Ain't no sense for him to go back into the hospital.

ROSE. Least he be eating right. They can help him take care of himself.

TROY. Don't nobody wanna be locked up, Rose. What you wanna lock him up for? Man go over there and fight the war... messin' around with them Japs, get half his head blow off... and they give him a lousy three thousand dollars. And I had to swoop down on that.

ROSE. Is you fixing to go into that again?

TROY. That's the only way I got a roof over my head... cause of that metal plate.

ROSE. Ain't no sense you blaming yourself for nothing. Gabe wasn't in no condition to manage that money. You done what was right by him. Can't nobody say you ain't done what was right by him. Look how long you took care of him... till he wanted to have his own place and moved over there with Miss Pearl.

TROY. That ain't what I'm saying woman! I'm just stating the facts. If my brother didn't have that metal plate in his head... I wouldn't have a pot to piss in or a window to throw it out of. And I'm fifty-three years old. Now see if you can understand that!

TROY *gets up from the porch and starts to exit the yard.*

ROSE. Where you going off to? You been running out of here every Saturday for weeks. I thought you was gonna work on this fence?

TROY. I'm gonna walk down to Taylors'. Listen to the ball game. I'll be back in a bit. I'll work on it when I get back.

He exits the yard. The lights go to black.

SCENE 3

The lights come up on the yard. It is four hours later. ROSE *is taking down the clothes from the line.* CORY *enters carrying his football equipment.*

ROSE. Your daddy like to had a fit with you running out of here this morning without doing your chores.

CORY. I told you I had to go to practice.

ROSE. He say you were supposed to help him with this fence.

CORY. He been saying that the last four or five Saturdays, and then he don't never do nothing, but go down to Taylors'. Did you tell him about the recruiter?

ROSE. Yeah, I told him.

CORY. What he say?

ROSE. He ain't said nothing too much. You get in there and get started on your chores before he gets back. Go on and scrub down them steps before he gets back here hollering and carrying on.

CORY. I'm hungry. What you got to eat, Mama?

ROSE. Go on and get started on your chores. I got some meat loaf in there. Go on and make you a sandwich...and don't leave no mess in there.

CORY *exits into the house.* ROSE *continues to take down the clothes.* TROY *enters the yard and sneaks up and grabs her from behind.*

Troy! Go on, now. You liked to scared me to death. What was the score of the game? Lucille had me on the phone and I couldn't keep up with it.

TROY. What I care about the game? Come here, woman.

[*He tries to kiss her.*]

ROSE. I thought you went down Taylors' to listen to the game. Go on, Troy! You supposed to be putting up this fence.

TROY [*attempting to kiss her again*]. I'll put it up when I finish with what is at hand.

ROSE. Go on, Troy. I ain't studying you.

TROY [*chasing after her*]. I'm studying you...fixing to do my homework!

ROSE. Troy, you better leave me alone.

TROY. Where's Cory? That boy brought his butt home yet?

ROSE. He's in the house doing his chores.

TROY [*calling*]. Cory! Get your butt out here, boy!

ROSE *exits into the house with the laundry.* TROY *goes over to the pile of wood, picks up a board, and starts sawing.* CORY *enters from the house.*

TROY. You just now coming in here from leaving this morning?

CORY. Yeah, I had to go to football practice.

TROY. Yeah, what?

CORY. Yessir.

TROY. I ain't but two seconds off you noway. The garbage sitting in there overflowing . . . you ain't done none of your chores . . . and you come in here talking about "Yeah."

CORY. I was just getting ready to do my chores now, Pop . . .

TROY. Your first chore is to help me with this fence on Saturday. Everything else come after that. Now get that saw and cut them boards.

CORY takes the saw and begins cutting the boards. TROY continues working. There is a long pause.

CORY. Hey, Pop . . . why don't you buy a TV?

TROY. What I want with a TV? What I want one of them for?

CORY. Everybody got one. Earl, Ba Bra . . . Jesse!

TROY. I ain't asked you who had one. I say what I want with one?

CORY. So you can watch it. They got lots of things on TV. Baseball games and everything. We could watch the World Series.

TROY. Yeah . . . and how much this TV cost?

CORY. I don't know. They got them on sale for around two hundred dollars.

TROY. Two hundred dollars, huh?

CORY. That ain't that much, Pop.

TROY. Naw, it's just two hundred dollars. See that roof you got over your head at night? Let me tell you something about that roof. It's been over ten years since that roof was last tarred. See now . . . the snow come this winter and sit up there on that roof like it is . . . and it's gonna seep inside. It's just gonna be a little bit . . . ain't gonna hardly notice it. Then the next thing you know, it's gonna be leaking all over the house. Then the wood rot from all that water and you gonna need a whole new roof. Now, how much you think it cost to get that roof tarred?

CORY. I don't know.

TROY. Two hundred and sixty-four dollars . . . cash money. While you thinking about a TV, I got to be thinking about the roof . . . and whatever else go wrong here. Now if you had two hundred dollars, what would you do . . . fix the roof or buy a TV?

CORY. I'd buy a TV. Then when the roof started to leak . . . when it needed fixing . . . I'd fix it.

TROY. Where you gonna get the money from? You done spent it for a TV. You gonna sit up and watch the water run all over your brand new TV.

CORY. Aw, Pop. You got money. I know you do.

TROY. Where I got it at, huh?

CORY. You got it in the bank.

TROY. You wanna see my bankbook? You wanna see that seventy-three dollars and twenty-two cents I got sitting up in there?

CORY. You ain't got to pay for it all at one time. You can put a down payment on it and carry it on home with you.

TROY. Not me. I ain't gonna owe nobody nothing if I can help it. Miss a payment and they come and snatch it right out of your house. Then what you got? Now, soon as I get two hundred dollars clear, then I'll buy a TV. Right now, as soon as I get two hundred and sixty-four dollars, I'm gonna have this roof tarred.

CORY. Aw . . . Pop!

TROY. You go on and get you two hundred dollars and buy one if ya want it. I got better things to do with my money.

CORY. I can't get no two hundred dollars. I ain't never seen two hundred dollars.

TROY. I'll tell you what...you get you a hundred dollars and I'll put the other hundred with it.

CORY. All right, I'm gonna show you.

TROY. You gonna show me how you can cut them boards right now.

CORY *begins to cut the boards. There is a long pause.*

CORY. The Pirates won today. That makes five in a row.

TROY. I ain't thinking about the Pirates. Got an all-white team. Got that boy...that Puerto Rican boy...Clemente. Don't even half-play him. That boy could be something if they give him a chance. Play him one day and sit him on the bench the next.

CORY. He gets a lot of chances to play.

TROY. I'm talking about playing regular. Playing every day so you can get your timing. That's what I'm talking about.

CORY. They got some white guys on the team that don't play every day. You can't play everybody at the same time.

TROY. If they got a white fellow sitting on the bench...you can bet your last dollar he can't play! That colored guy got to be twice as good before he get on the team. That's why I don't want you to get all tied up in them sports. Man on the team and what it get him? They got colored on the team and don't use them. Same as not having them. All them teams the same.

CORY. The Braves got Hank Aaron and Wes Covington. Hank Aaron hit two home runs today. That makes forty-three.

TROY. Hank Aaron ain't nobody. That what you supposed to do. That's how you supposed to play the game. Ain't nothing to it. It's just a matter of timing...getting the right follow-through. Hell, I can hit forty-three home runs right now!

CORY. Not off no major-league pitching, you couldn't.

TROY. We had better pitching in the Negro leagues. I hit seven home runs off of Satchel Paige. You can't get no better than that!

CORY. Sandy Koufax. He's leading the league in strikeouts.

TROY. I ain't thinking of no Sandy Koufax.

CORY. You got Warren Spahn and Lew Burdette. I bet you couldn't hit no home runs off of Warren Spahn.

TROY. I'm through with it now. You go on and cut them boards. [*Pause.*] Your mama tell me you done got recruited by a college football team? Is that right?

CORY. Yeah. Coach Zellman say the recruiter gonna be coming by to talk to you. Get you to sign the permission papers.

TROY. I thought you supposed to be working down there at the A&P. Ain't you suppose to be working down there after school?

CORY. Mr. Stawicki say he gonna hold my job for me until after the football season. Say starting next week I can work weekends.

TROY. I thought we had an understanding about this football stuff? You suppose to keep up with your chores and hold that job down at the A&P. Ain't been around here all day on a Saturday. Ain't none of your chores done...and now you telling me you done quit your job.

CORY. I'm going to be working weekends.

TROY. You damn right you are! And ain't no need for nobody coming around here to talk to me about signing nothing.

CORY. Hey, Pop...you can't do that. He's coming all the way from North Carolina.

TROY. I don't care where he coming from. The white man ain't gonna let you get nowhere with that football noway. You go on and get your book-learning so you can work yourself up in that A&P or learn how to fix cars or build houses or something, get you a trade. That way you have something can't nobody take away from you. You go on and learn how to put your hands to some good use. Besides hauling people's garbage.

CORY. I get good grades, Pop. That's why the recruiter wants to talk with you. You got to keep up your grades to get recruited. This way I'll be going to college. I'll get a chance...

TROY. First you gonna get your butt down there to the A&P and get your job back.

CORY. Mr. Stawicki done already hired somebody else 'cause I told him I was playing football.

TROY. You a bigger fool than I thought...to let somebody take away your job so you can play some football. Where you gonna get your money to take out your girlfriend and whatnot? What kind of foolishness is that to let somebody take away your job?

CORY. I'm still gonna be working weekends.

TROY. Naw...naw. You getting your butt out of here and finding you another job.

CORY. Come on, Pop! I got to practice. I can't work after school and play football too. The team needs me. That's what Coach Zellman say...

TROY. I don't care what nobody else say. I'm the boss...you understand? I'm the boss around here. I do the only saying what counts.

CORY. Come on, Pop!

TROY. I asked you...did you understand?

CORY. Yeah...

TROY. What?!

CORY. Yessir.

TROY. You go on down there to that A&P and see if you can get your job back. If you can't do both...then you quit the football team. You've got to take the crookeds with the straights.

CORY. Yessir. [*Pause.*] Can I ask you a question?

TROY. What the hell you wanna ask me? Mr. Stawicki the one you got the questions for.

CORY. How come you ain't never liked me?

TROY. Liked you? Who the hell say I got to like you? What law is there say I got to like you? Wanna stand up in my face and ask a damn fool-ass question like that. Talking about liking somebody. Come here, boy, when I talk to you.

CORY *comes over to where* TROY *is working. He stands slouched over and* TROY *shoves him on his shoulder.*

Straighten up, goddammit! I asked you a question...what law is there say I got to like you?

CORY. None.

TROY. Well, all right then! Don't you eat every day? [*Pause.*] Answer me when I talk to you! Don't you eat every day?

CORY. Yeah.

TROY. Nigger, as long as you in my house, you put that sir on the end of it when you talk to me.

CORY. Yes . . . sir.

TROY. You eat every day.

CORY. Yessir!

TROY. Got a roof over your head.

CORY. Yessir!

TROY. Got clothes on your back.

CORY. Yessir.

TROY. Why you think that is?

CORY. 'Cause of you.

TROY. Ah, hell I know it's 'cause of me . . . but why do you think that is?

CORY [*hesitant*]. 'Cause you like me.

TROY. Like you? I go out of here every morning . . . bust my butt . . . putting up with them crackers every day . . . 'cause I like you? You are the biggest fool I ever saw. [*Pause.*] It's my job. It's my responsibility! You understand that? A man got to take care of his family. You live in my house . . . sleep you behind on my bedclothes . . . fill you belly up with my food . . . cause you my son. You my flesh and blood. Not 'cause I like you! 'Cause it's my duty to take care of you. I owe a responsibility to you! Let's get this straight right here . . . before it go along any further . . . I ain't got to like you. Mr. Rand don't give me my money come payday 'cause he likes me. He gives me 'cause he owe me. I done give you everything I had to give you. I gave you your life! Me and your mama worked that out between us. And liking your black ass wasn't part of the bargain. Don't you try and go through life worrying about if somebody like you or not. You best be making sure they doing right by you. You understand what I'm saying boy?

CORY. Yessir.

TROY. Then get the hell out of my face, and get on down to that A&P.

ROSE *has been standing behind the screen door for much of the scene. She enters as* CORY *exits.*

ROSE. Why don't you let the boy go ahead and play football, Troy? Ain't no harm in that. He's just trying to be like you with the sports.

TROY. I don't want him to be like me! I want him to move as far away from my life as he can get. You the only decent thing that ever happened to me. I wish him that. But I don't wish him a thing else from my life. I decided seventeen years ago that boy wasn't getting involved in no sports. Not after what they did to me in the sports.

ROSE. Troy, why don't you admit you was too old to play in the major leagues? For once . . . why don't you admit that?

TROY. What do you mean too old? Don't come telling me I was too old. I just wasn't the right color. Hell, I'm fifty-three years old and can do better than Selkirk's .269 right now!

ROSE. How's was you gonna play ball when you were over forty? Sometimes I can't get no sense out of you.

TROY. I got good sense, woman. I got sense enough not to let my boy get hurt over playing no sports. You been mothering that boy too much. Worried about if people like him.

ROSE. Everything that boy do . . . he do for you. He wants you to say "Good job, son." That's all.

TROY. Rose, I ain't got time for that. He's alive. He's healthy. He's got to make his own way. I made mine. Ain't nobody gonna hold his hand when he get out there in that world.

ROSE. Times have changed from when you was young, Troy. People change. The world's changing around you and you can't even see it.

TROY [*slow, methodical*]. Woman...I do the best I can do. I come in here every Friday. I carry a sack of potatoes and a bucket of lard. You all line up at the door with your hands out. I give you the lint from my pockets. I give you my sweat and my blood. I ain't got no tears. I done spent them. We go upstairs in that room at night...and I fall down on you and try to blast a hole into forever. I get up Monday morning...find my lunch on the table. I go out. Make my way. Find my strength to carry me through to the next Friday. [*Pause.*] That's all I got, Rose. That's all I got to give. I can't give nothing else.

TROY *exits into the house. The lights go down to black.*

SCENE 4

It is Friday. Two weeks later. CORY *starts out of the house with his football equipment. The phone rings.*

CORY [*calling*]. I got it! [*He answers the phone and stands in the screen door talking.*] Hello? Hey, Jesse. Naw...I was just getting ready to leave now.

ROSE [*calling*]. Cory!

CORY. I told you, man, them spikes is all tore up. You can use them if you want, but they ain't no good. Earl got some spikes.

ROSE [*calling*]. Cory!

CORY [*calling to* ROSE]. Mam? I'm talking to Jesse. [*Into phone.*] When she say that? [*Pause.*] Aw, you lying, man. I'm gonna tell her you said that.

ROSE [*calling*]. Cory, don't you go nowhere!

CORY. I got to go to the game, Ma! [*Into the phone.*] Yeah, hey, look, I'll talk to you later. Yeah, I'll meet you over Earl's house. Later. Bye, Ma.

CORY *exits the house and starts out the yard.*

ROSE. Cory, where you going off to? You got that stuff all pulled out and thrown all over your room.

CORY [*in the yard*]. I was looking for my spikes. Jesse wanted to borrow my spikes.

ROSE. Get up there and get that cleaned up before your daddy get back in here.

CORY. I got to go to the game! I'll clean it up *when I get back.*

CORY *exits.*

ROSE. That's all he need to do is see that room all messed up.

ROSE *exits into the house.* TROY *and* BONO *enter the yard.* TROY *is dressed in clothes other than his work clothes.*

BONO. He told him the same thing he told you. Take it to the union.

TROY. Brownie ain't got that much sense. Man wasn't thinking about nothing. He wait until I confront them on it...then he wanna come crying seniority. [*Calls.*] Hey, Rose!

BONO. I wish I could have seen Mr. Rand's face when he told you.

TROY. He couldn't get it out of his mouth! Liked to bit his tongue! When they called me down there to the Commissioner's office...he thought they was gonna fire me. Like everybody else.

BONO. I didn't think they was gonna fire you. I thought they was gonna put you on the warning paper.

TROY. Hey, Rose! [*To* BONO.] Yeah, Mr. Rand like to bit his tongue.

TROY *breaks the seal on the bottle, takes a drink, and hands it to* BONO.

BONO. I see you run right down to Taylors' and told that Alberta gal.

TROY [*calling*]. Hey Rose! [*To* BONO.] I told everybody. Hey, Rose! I went down there to cash my check.

ROSE [*entering from the house*]. Hush all that hollering, man! I know you out here. What they say down there at the Commissioner's office?

TROY. You supposed to come when I call you, woman. Bono'll tell you that. [*To* BONO.] Don't Lucille come when you call her?

ROSE. Man, hush your mouth. I ain't no dog…talk about "come when you call me."

TROY [*puts his arm around* ROSE]. You hear this, Bono? I had me an old dog used to get uppity like that. You say, "C'mere, Blue!"…and he just lay there and look at you. End up getting a stick and chasing him away trying to make him come.

ROSE. I ain't studying you and your dog. I remember you used to sing that old song.

TROY [*he sings*].

> Hear it ring! Hear it ring!
> I had a dog his name was Blue.

ROSE. Don't nobody wanna hear you sing that old song.

TROY [*sings*]. You know Blue was mighty true.

ROSE. Used to have Cory running around here singing that song.

BONO. Hell, I remember that song myself.

TROY [*sings*].

> You know Blue was a good old dog.
> Blue treed a possum in a hollow log.

That was my daddy's song. My daddy made up that song.

ROSE. I don't care who made it up. Don't nobody wanna hear you sing it.

TROY [*makes a song like calling a dog*]. Come here, woman.

ROSE. You come in here carrying on, I reckon they ain't fired you. What they say down there at the Commissioner's office?

TROY. Look here, Rose…Mr. Rand called me into his office today when I got back from talking to them people down there…it come from up top…he called me in and told me they was making me a driver.

ROSE. Troy, you kidding!

TROY. No I ain't. Ask Bono.

ROSE. Well, that's great, Troy. Now you don't have to hassle them people no more.

LYONS *enters from the street.*

TROY. Aw hell, I wasn't looking to see you today. I thought you was in jail. Got it all over the front page of the *Courier* about them raiding Sefus's place…where you be hanging out with all them thugs.

LYONS. Hey, Pop…that ain't got nothing to do with me. I don't go down there gambling. I go down there to sit in with the band. I ain't got nothing to do with the gambling part. They got some good music down there.

TROY. They got some rogues... is what they got.

LYONS. How you been, Mr. Bono? Hi, Rose.

BONO. I see where you playing down at the Crawford Grill tonight.

ROSE. How come you ain't brought Bonnie like I told you? You should have brought Bonnie with you, she ain't been over in a month of Sundays.

LYONS. I was just in the neighborhood... thought I'd stop by.

TROY. Here he come...

BONO. Your daddy got a promotion on the rubbish. He's gonna be the first colored driver. Ain't got to do nothing but sit up there and read the paper like them white fellows.

LYONS. Hey, Pop... if you knew how to read you'd be all right.

BONO. Naw... naw... you mean if the nigger knew how to drive he'd be all right. Been fighting with them people about driving and ain't even got a license. Mr. Rand know you ain't got no driver's license?

TROY. Driving ain't nothing. All you do is point the truck where you want it to go. Driving ain't nothing.

BONO. Do Mr. Rand know you ain't got no driver's license? That's what I'm talking about. I ain't asked if driving was easy. I asked if Mr. Rand know you ain't got no driver's license.

TROY. He ain't got to know. The man ain't got to know my business. Time he find out, I have two or three driver's licenses.

LYONS [*going into his pocket*]. Say, look here, Pop...

TROY. I knew it was coming. Didn't I tell you, Bono? I know what kind of "Look here, Pop" that was. The nigger fixing to ask me for some money. It's Friday night. It's my payday. All them rogues down there on the avenue... the ones that ain't in jail... and Lyons is hopping in his shoes to get down there with them.

LYONS. See, Pop... if you give somebody else a chance to talk sometimes, you'd see that I was fixing to pay you back your ten dollars like I told you. Here... I told you I'd pay you when Bonnie got paid.

TROY. Naw... you go ahead and keep that ten dollars. Put it in the bank. The next time you feel like you wanna come by here and ask me for something... you go on down there and get that.

LYONS. Here's your ten dollars, Pop. I told you I don't want you to give me nothing. I just wanted to borrow ten dollars.

TROY. Naw... you go on and keep that for the next time you want to ask me.

LYONS. Come on, Pop... here go your ten dollars.

ROSE. Why don't you go on and let the boy pay you back, Troy?

LYONS. Here you go, Rose. If you don't take it I'm gonna have to hear about it for the next six months. [*He hands her the money.*]

ROSE. You can hand yours over here too, Troy.

TROY. You see this, Bono. You see how they do me.

BONO. Yeah, Lucille do me the same way.

GABRIEL *is heard singing off stage. He enters.*

GABRIEL. Better get ready for the Judgment! Better get ready for... Hey!... Hey!... There's Troy's boy!

LYONS. How are you doing, Uncle Gabe?

GABRIEL. Lyons... The King of the Jungle! Rose... hey, Rose. Got a flower for you. [*He takes a rose from his pocket.*] Picked it myself. That's the same rose like you is!

ROSE. That's right nice of you, Gabe.
LYONS. What you been doing, Uncle Gabe?
GABRIEL. Oh, I been chasing hellhounds and waiting on the time to tell St. Peter to open the gates.
LYONS. You been chasing hellhounds, huh? Well... you doing the right thing, Uncle Gabe. Somebody got to chase them.
GABRIEL. Oh, yeah... I know it. The devil's strong. The devil ain't no pushover. Hellhounds snipping at everybody's heels. But I got my trumpet waiting on the Judgment time.
LYONS. Waiting on the Battle of Armageddon, huh?
GABRIEL. Ain't gonna be too much of a battle when God get to waving that Judgment sword. But the people's gonna have a hell of a time trying to get into heaven if them gates ain't open.
LYONS [*putting his arm around* GABRIEL]. You hear this, Pop. Uncle Gabe, you all right!
GABRIEL [*laughing with* LYONS]. Lyons! King of the Jungle.
ROSE. You gonna stay for suppper, Gabe? Want me to fix you a plate?
GABRIEL. I'll take a sandwich, Rose. Don't want no plate. Just wanna eat with my hands. I'll take a sandwich.
ROSE. How about you, Lyons? You staying? Got some short ribs cooking.
LYONS. Naw, I won't eat nothing till after we finished playing. [*Pause.*] You ought to come down and listen to me play, Pop.
TROY. I don't like that Chinese music. All that noise.
ROSE. Go on in the house and wash up, Gabe... I'll fix you a sandwich.
GABRIEL [*to* LYONS, *as he exits*]. Troy's mad at me.
LYONS. What you mad at Uncle Gabe for, Pop?
ROSE. He thinks Troy's mad at him 'cause he moved over to Miss Pearl's.
TROY. I ain't mad at the man. He can live where he want to live at.
LYONS. What he move over there for? Miss Pearl don't like nobody.
ROSE. She don't mind him none. She treats him real nice. She just don't allow all that singing.
TROY. She don't mind that rent he be paying... That's what she don't mind.
ROSE. Troy, I ain't going through that with you no more. He's over there cause he want to have his own place. He can come and go as he please.
TROY. Hell, he could come and go as he please here. I wasn't stopping him. I ain't put no rules on him.
ROSE. It ain't the same thing, Troy. And you know it.

GABRIEL *comes to the door.*

Now, that's the last I wanna hear about that. I don't wanna hear nothing else about Gabe and Miss Pearl. And next week...
GABRIEL. I'm ready for my sandwich, Rose.
ROSE. And next week... when that recruiter come from that school... I want you to sign that paper and go on and let Cory play football. Then that'll be the last I have to hear about that.
TROY [*to* ROSE *as she exits into the house*]. I ain't thinking about Cory nothing.
LYONS. What... Cory got recruited? What school he going to?
TROY. That boy walking around here smelling his piss... thinking he's grown. Thinking he's gonna do what he want, irrespective of what I say. Look here, Bono... I left the Commissioner's office and went down to the A&P... that

boy ain't working down there. He lying to me. Telling me he got his job back . . . telling me he working weekends . . . telling me he working after school . . . Mr. Stawicki tell me he ain't working down there at all!

LYONS. Cory just growing up. He's just busting at the seams trying to fill out your shoes.

TROY. I don't care what he's doing. When he get to the point where he wanna disobey me . . . then it's time for him to move on. Bono'll tell you that. I bet he ain't never disobeyed his daddy without paying the consequences.

BONO. I ain't never had a chance. My daddy came on through . . . but I ain't never knew him to see him . . . or what he had on his mind or where he went. Just moving on through. Searching out the New Land. That's what the old folks used to call it. See a fellow moving around from place to place . . . woman to woman . . . called it searching out the New Land. I can't say if he ever found it. I come along, didn't want no kids. Didn't know if I was gonna be in one place long enough to fix on them right as their daddy. I figured I was going searching too. As it turned out I been hooked up with Lucille near about as long as your daddy been with Rose. Going on sixteen years.

TROY. Sometimes I wish I hadn't known my daddy. He ain't cared nothing about no kids. A kid to him wasn't nothing. All he wanted was for you to learn how to walk so he could start you to working. When it come time for eating . . . he ate first. If there was anything left over, that's what you got. Man would sit down and eat two chickens and give you the wing.

LYONS. You ought to stop that, Pop. Everybody feed their kids. No matter how hard times is . . . everybody care about their kids. Make sure they have something to eat.

TROY. The only thing my daddy cared about was getting them bales of cotton in to Mr. Lubin. That's the only thing that mattered to him. Sometimes I used to wonder why he was living. Wonder why the devil hadn't come and got him. "Get them bales of cotton in to Mr. Lubin" and find out he owe him money . . .

LYONS. He should have just went on and left when he saw he couldn't get nowhere. That's what I would have done.

TROY. How he gonna leave with eleven kids? And where he gonna go? He ain't knew how to do nothing but farm. No, he was trapped and I think he knew it. But I'll say this for him . . . he felt a responsibility toward us. Maybe he ain't treated us the way I felt he should have . . . but without that responsibility he could have walked off and left us . . . made his own way.

BONO. A lot of them did. Back in those days what you talking about . . . they walk out their front door and just take on down one road or another and keep on walking.

LYONS. There you go! That's what I'm talking about.

BONO. Just keep on walking till you come to something else. Ain't you never heard of nobody having the walking blues? Well, that's what you call it when you just take off like that.

TROY. My daddy ain't had them walking blues! What you talking about? He stayed right there with his family. But he was just as evil as he could be. My mama couldn't stand him. Couldn't stand that evilness. She run off when I was about eight. She sneaked off one night after he had gone to sleep. Told me she was coming back for me. I ain't never seen her no more. All his women run off and left him. He wasn't good for nobody.

When my turn come to head out, I was fourteen and got to sniffing around Joe Canewell's daughter. Had us an old mule we called Greyboy. My daddy sent me out to do some plowing and I tied up Greyboy and went to fooling around with Joe Canewell's daughter. We done found us a nice little spot, got real cozy with each other. She about thirteen and we done figured we was grown anyway... so we down there enjoying ourselves... ain't thinking about nothing. We didn't know Greyboy had got loose and wandered back to the house and my daddy was looking for me. We down there by the creek enjoying ourselves when my daddy come up on us. Surprised us. He had them leather straps off the mule and commenced to whupping me like there was no tomorrow. I jumped up, mad and embarrassed. I was scared of my daddy. When he commenced to whupping on me... quite naturally I run to get out of the way. [*Pause.*] Now I thought he was mad 'cause I ain't done my work. But I see where he was chasing me off so he could have the gal for himself. When I see what the matter of it was, I lost all fear of my daddy. Right there is where I become a man... at fourteen years of age. [*Pause.*] Now it was my turn to run him off. I picked up them same reins that he had used on me. I picked up them reins and commenced to whupping on him. The gal jumped up and run him off... and when my daddy turned to face me, I could see why the devil had never come to get him... 'cause he was the devil himself. I don't know what happened. When I woke up, I was laying right there by the creek, and Blue... this old dog we had... was licking my face. I thought I was blind. I couldn't see nothing. Both my eyes were swollen shut. I laid there and cried. I didn't know what I was gonna do. The only thing I knew was the time had come for me to leave my daddy's house. And right there the world suddenly got big. And it was a long time before I could cut it down to where I could handle it.

Part of that cutting down was when I got to the place where I could feel him kicking in my blood and knew that the only thing that separated us was the matter of a few years.

Gabriel *enters from the house with a sandwich.*

Lyons. What you got there, Uncle Gabe?

Gabriel. Got me a ham sandwich. Rose gave me a ham sandwich.

Troy. I don't know what happened to him. I done lost touch with everybody except Gabriel. But I hope he's dead. I hope he found some peace.

Lyons. That's a heavy story, Pop. I didn't know you left home when you was fourteen.

Troy. And didn't know nothing. The only part of the world I knew was the forty-two acres of Mr. Lubin's land. That's all I knew about life.

Lyons. Fourteen's kinda young to be out on your own. [*Phone rings.*] I don't even think I was ready to be out on my own at fourteen. I don't know what I would have done.

Troy. I got up from the creek and walked on down to Mobile. I was through with farming. Figured I could do better in the city. So I walked the two hundred miles to Mobile.

Lyons. Wait a minute... you ain't walked no two hundred miles, Pop. Ain't nobody gonna walk no two hundred miles. You talking about some walking there.

Bono. That's the only way you got anywhere back in them days.

LYONS. Shhh. Damn if I wouldn't have hitched a ride with someday!

TROY. Who you gonna hitch it with? They ain't had no cars and things like they got now. We talking about 1918.

ROSE [*entering*]. What you all out here getting into?

TROY [*to* ROSE]. I'm telling Lyons how good he got it. He don't know nothing about this I'm talking.

ROSE. Lyons, that was Bonnie on the phone. She say you supposed to pick her up.

LYONS. Yeah, okay Rose.

TROY. I walked on down to Mobile and hitched up with some of them fellows that was heading this way. Got up here and found out... not only couldn't you get a job... you couldn't find no place to live. I thought I was in freedom. Shhh. Colored folks living down there on the river banks in whatever kind of shelter they could find for themselves. Right down there under the Brady Street Bridge. Living in shacks made of sticks and tarpaper. Messed around there and went from bad to worse. Started stealing. First it was food. Then I figured, hell, if I steal money I can buy me some food. Buy me some shoes too! One thing led to another. Met your mama. I was young and anxious to be a man. Met your mama and had you. What I do that for? Now I got to worry about feeding you and her. Got to steal three times as much. Went out one day looking for somebody to rob... that's what I was, a robber. I'll tell you the truth. I'm ashamed of it today. But it's the truth. Went to rob this fellow... pulled out my knife... and he pulled out a gun. Shot me in the chest. I felt just like somebody had taken a hot branding iron and laid it on me. When he shot me I jumped at him with my knife. They told me I killed him and they put me in the penitentiary and locked me up for fifteen years. That's where I met Bono. That's where I learned how to play baseball. Got out that place and your mama had taken you and went on to make life without me. Fifteen years was a long time for her to wait. But that fifteen years cured me of that robbing stuff. Rose'll tell you. She asked me when I met her if I had gotten all that foolishness out of my system. And I told her, "Baby, it's you and baseball all what count with me." You hear me, Bono? I meant it too. She say, "Which one comes first?" I told her, "Baby, ain't no doubt it's baseball... but you stick and get old with me and we'll both outlive this baseball." Am I right, Rose? And it's true.

ROSE. Man, hush your mouth. You ain't said no such thing. Talking about, "Baby you know you'll always be number one with me." That's what you was talking.

TROY. You hear that, Bono. That's why I love her.

BONO. Rose'll keep you straight. You get off the track, she'll straighten you up.

ROSE. Lyons, you better get on up and get Bonnie. She waiting on you.

LYONS [*gets up to go*]. Hey, Pop, why don't you come on down to the Grill and hear me play?

TROY. I ain't going down there. I'm too old to be sitting around in them clubs.

BONO. You got to be good to play down at the Grill.

LYONS. Come on, Pop...

TROY. I got to get up in the morning.

LYONS. You ain't got to stay long.

TROY. Naw, I'm gonna get my supper and go on to bed.

LYONS. Well, I got to go. I'll see you again.

TROY. Don't you come around my house on my payday.

ROSE. Pick up the phone and let somebody know you coming. And bring Bonnie with you. You know I'm always glad to see her.

LYONS. Yeah, I'll do that, Rose. You take care now. See you, Pop. See you, Mr. Bono. See you, Uncle Gabe.

GABRIEL. Lyons! King of the Jungle!

LYONS *exits*

TROY. Is supper ready, woman? Me and you got some business to take care of. I'm gonna tear it up too.

ROSE. Troy, I done told you now!

TROY [*puts his arm around* BONO]. Aw hell, woman... this is Bono. Bono like family. I done known this nigger since... how long I done know you?

BONO. It's been a long time.

TROY. I done know this nigger since Skippy was a pup. Me and him done been through some times.

BONO. You sure right about that.

TROY. Hell, I done know him longer than I known you. And we still standing shoulder to shoulder. Hey look here, Bono... a man can't ask for no more than that. [*Drinks to him.*] I love you, nigger.

BONO. Hell, I love you too... I got to get home see my woman. You got yours in hand. I got to get mine.

BONO *starts to exit as* CORY *enters the yard, dressed in his football uniform. He gives* TROY *a hard, uncompromising look.*

CORY. What you do that for, Pop?

He throws his helmet down in the direction of TROY.

ROSE. What's the matter? Cory... What's the matter?

CORY. Papa done went up to the school and told Coach Zellman I can't play football no more. Wouldn't even let me play the game. Told him to tell the recruiter not to come.

ROSE. Troy...

TROY. What you Troying me for. Yeah, I did it. And the boy know why I did it.

CORY. Why you wanna do that to me? That was the one chance I had.

ROSE. Ain't nothing wrong with Cory playing football, Troy.

TROY. The boy lied to me. I told the nigger if he wanna play football... to keep up his chores and hold down that job at the A&P. That was the conditions. Stopped down there to see Mr. Stawicki...

CORY. I can't work after school during the football season, Pop! I tried to tell you that Mr. Stawicki's holding my job for me. You don't never want to listen to nobody. And then you wanna go and do this to me!

TROY. I ain't done nothing to you. You done it to yourself.

CORY. Just cause you didn't have a chance! You just scared I'm gonna be better than you, that's all.

TROY. Come here.

ROSE. Troy...

CORY *reluctantly crosses over to* TROY.

TROY. All right! See. You done made a mistake.

CORY. I didn't even do nothing!

TROY. I'm gonna tell you what your mistake was. See... you swung at the ball and didn't hit it. That's strike one. See, you in the batter's box now. You swung and you missed. That's strike one. Don't you strike out!

Lights fade to black.

ACT 2

SCENE 1

The following morning. CORY *is at the tree hitting the ball with the bat. He tries to mimic* TROY, *but his swing is awkward, less sure.* ROSE *enters from the house.*

ROSE. Cory, I want you to help me with this cupboard.

CORY. I ain't quitting the team. I don't care what Poppa say.

ROSE. I'll talk to him when he gets back. He had to go see about your Uncle Gabe. The police done arrested him. Say he was disturbing the peace. He 'll be back directly. Come on in here and help me clean out the top of this cupboard.

CORY *exits into the house.* ROSE *sees* TROY *and* BONO *coming down the alley.*

Troy... what they say down there?

TROY. Ain't said nothing. I give them fifty dollars and they let him go. I'll talk to you about it. Where's Cory?

ROSE. He's in there helping me clean out these cupboards.

TROY. Tell him to get his butt out here.

TROY *and* BONO *go over to the pile of wood.* BONO *picks up the saw and begins sawing.*

TROY [*to* BONO]. All they want is the money. That makes six or seven times I done went down there and got him. See me coming they stick out their hands.

BONO. Yeah. I know what you mean. That's all they care about... that money. They don't care about what's right. [*Pause.*] Nigger, why you got to go and get some hard wood? You ain't doing nothing but building a little old fence. Get you some soft pine wood. That's all you need.

TROY. I know what I'm doing. This is outside wood. You put pine wood inside the house. Pine wood is inside wood. This here is outside wood. Now you tell me where the fence is gonna be?

BONO. You don't need this wood. You can put it up with pine wood and it'll stand as long as you gonna be here looking at it.

TROY. How you know how long I'm gonna be here, nigger? Hell, I might just live forever. Live longer than old man Horsely.

BONO. That's what Magee used to say.

TROY. Magee's damn fool. Now you tell me who you ever heard of gonna pull their own teeth with a pair of rusty pliers.

BONO. The old folks... my granddaddy used to pull his teeth with pliers. They ain't had no dentists for the colored folks back then.

TROY. Get clean pliers! You understand? Clean pliers! Sterilize them! Besides we ain't living back then. All Magee had to do was walk over to Doc Goldblum's.

BONO. I see where you and that Tallahassee gal... that Alberta... I see where you all done got tight.

TROY. What you mean "got tight"?
BONO. I see where you be laughing and joking with her all the time.
TROY. I laughs and jokes with all of them, Bono. You know me.
BONO. That ain't the kind of laughing and joking I'm talking about.

CORY *enters from the house.*

CORY. How you doing, Mr. Bono?
TROY. Cory? Get that saw from Bono and cut some wood. He talking about the wood's too hard to cut. Stand back there, Jim, and let that young boy show you how it's done.
BONO. He's sure welcome to it.

CORY *takes the saw and begins to cut the wood.*

Whew-e-e! Look at that. Big old strong boy. Look like Joe Louis. Hell, must be getting old the way I'm watching that boy whip through that wood.
CORY. I don't see why Mama want a fence around the yard noways.
TROY. Damn if I know either. What the hell she keeping out with it? She ain't got nothing nobody want.
BONO. Some people build fences to keep people out...and other people build fences to keep people in. Rose wants to hold on to you all. She loves you.
TROY. Hell, nigger, I don't need nobody to tell me my wife loves me. Cory...go on in the house and see if you can find that other saw.
CORY. Where's it at?
TROY. I said find it! Look for it till you find it!

CORY *exits into the house.*

What's that supposed to mean? Wanna keep us in?
BONO. Troy...I done known you seem like damn near my whole life. You and Rose both. I done know both of you all for a long time. I remember when you met Rose. When you was hitting them baseball out the park. A lot of them old gals was after you then. You had the pick of the litter. When you picked Rose, I was happy for you. That was the first time I knew you had any sense. I said...My man Troy knows what he's doing...I'm gonna follow this nigger...he might take me somewhere. I been following you too. I done learned a whole heap of things about life watching you. I done learned how to tell where the shit lies. How to tell it from the alfalfa. You done learned me a lot of things. You showed me how to not make the same mistakes...to take life as it comes along and keep putting one foot in front of the other. [*Pause.*] Rose a good woman, Troy.
TROY. Hell, nigger, I know she a good woman. I been married to her for eighteen years. What you got on your mind, Bono?
BONO. I just say she a good woman. Just like I say anything. I ain't got to have nothing on my mind.
TROY. You just gonna say she a good woman and leave it hanging out there like that? Why you telling me she a good woman?
BONO. She loves you, Troy. Rose loves you.
TROY. You saying I don't measure up. That's what you trying to say. I don't measure up cause I'm seeing this other gal. I know what you trying to say.
BONO. I know what Rose means to you, Troy. I'm just trying to say I don't want to see you mess up.

TROY. Yeah, I appreciate that, Bono. If you was messing around on Lucille I'd be telling you the same thing.

BONO. Well, that's all I got to say. I just say that because I love you both.

TROY. Hell, you know me ... I wasn't out there looking for nothing. You can't find a better woman than Rose. I know that. But seems like this woman just stuck onto me where I can't shake her loose. I done wrestled with it, tried to throw her off me ... but she just stuck on tighter. Now she's stuck on for good.

BONO. You's in control ... that's what you tell me all the time. You responsible for what you do.

TROY. I ain't ducking the responsibility of it. As long as it sets right in my heart ... then I'm okay. 'Cause that's all I listen to. It'll tell me right from wrong every time. And I ain't talking about doing Rose no bad turn. I love Rose. She done carried me a long ways and I love and respect her for that.

BONO. I know you do. That's why I don't want to see you hurt her. But what you gonna do when she find out? What you got then? If you try and juggle both of them ... sooner or later you gonna drop one of them. That's common sense.

TROY. Yeah, I hear what you saying, Bono. I been trying to figure a way to work it out.

BONO. Work it out right, Troy. I don't want to be getting all up between you and Rose's business ... but work it so it come out right.

TROY. Ah hell, I get all up between you and Lucille's business. When you gonna get that woman that refrigerator she been wanting? Don't tell me you ain't got no money now. I know who your banker is. Mellon don't need that money bad as Lucille want that refrigerator. I'll tell you that.

BONO. Tell you what I'll do ... when you finish building this fence for Rose ... I'll buy Lucille that refrigerator.

TROY. You done stuck your foot in your mouth now!

TROY *grabs up a board and begins to saw.* BONO *starts to walk out the yard.*

Hey, nigger ... where you going?

BONO. I'm going home. I know you don't expect me to help you now. I'm protecting my money. I wanna see you put that fence up by yourself. That's what I want to see. You'll be here another six months without me.

TROY. Nigger, you ain't right.

BONO. When it comes to my money ... I'm right as fireworks on the Fourth of July.

TROY. All right, we gonna see now. You better get out your bankbook.

BONO *exits, and* TROY *continues to work.* ROSE *enters from the house.*

ROSE. What they say down there? What's happening with Gabe?

TROY. I went down there and got him out. Cost me fifty dollars. Say he was disturbing the peace. Judge set up a hearing for him in three weeks. Say to show cause why he shouldn't be recommitted.

ROSE. What was he doing that cause them to arrest him?

TROY. Some kids was teasing him and he run them off home. Say he was howling and carrying on. Some folks seen him and called the police. That's all it was.

ROSE. Well, what's you say? What'd you tell the judge?

TROY. Told him I'd look after him. It didn't make no sense to recommit the man. He stuck out his big greasy palm and told me to give him fifty dollars and take him on home.

ROSE. Where's he at now? Where'd he go off to?

TROY. He's gone about his business. He don't need nobody to hold his hand.

ROSE. Well, I don't know. Seem like that would be the best place for him if they did put him into the hospital. I know what you're gonna say. But that's what I think would be best.

TROY. The man done had his life ruined fighting for what? And they wanna take and lock him up. Let him be free. He don't bother nobody.

ROSE. Well, everybody got their own way of looking at it I guess. Come on and get your lunch. I got a bowl of lima beans and some cornbread in the oven. Come and get something to eat. Ain't no sense you fretting over Gabe.

ROSE *turns to go into the house.*

TROY. Rose...got something to tell you.

ROSE. Well, come on...wait till I get this food on the table.

TROY. Rose!

She stops and turns around.

I don't know how to say this. [*Pause.*] I can't explain it none. It just sort of grows on you till it gets out of hand. It starts out like a little bush...and the next thing you know it's a whole forest.

ROSE. Troy...what is you talking about?

TROY. I'm talking, woman, let me talk. I'm trying to find a way to tell you...I'm gonna be a daddy. I'm gonna be somebody's daddy.

ROSE. Troy...you're not telling me this? You're gonna be...what?

TROY. Rose...now...see...

ROSE. You telling me you gonna be somebody's daddy? You telling your *wife* this?

GABRIEL *enters from the street. He carries a rose in his hand.*

GABRIEL. Hey, Troy! Hey, Rose!

ROSE. I have to wait eighteen years to hear something like this.

GABRIEL. Hey, Rose...I got a flower for you. [*He hands it to her.*] That's a rose. Same rose like you is.

ROSE. Thanks, Gabe.

GABRIEL. Troy, you ain't mad at me is you? Them bad mens come and put me away. You ain't mad at me is you?

TROY. Naw, Gabe, I ain't mad at you.

ROSE. Eighteen years and you wanna come with this.

GABRIEL [*takes a quarter out of his pocket*]. See what I got? Got a brand new quarter.

TROY. Rose...it's just...

ROSE. Ain't nothing you can say, Troy. Ain't no way of explaining that.

GABRIEL. Fellow that give me this quarter had a whole mess of them. I'm gonna keep this quarter till it stop shining.

ROSE. Gabe, go on in the house there. I got some watermelon in the Frigidaire. Go on and get you a piece.

GABRIEL. Say, Rose...you know I was chasing hellhounds and them bad mens come and get me and take me away. Troy helped me. He come down there and told them they better let me go before he beat them up. Yeah, he did!

ROSE. You go on and get you a piece of watermelon, Gabe. Them bad mens is gone now.

GABRIEL. Okay, Rose... gonna get me some watermelon. The kind with the stripes on it.

GABRIEL *exits into the house.*

ROSE. Why, Troy? Why? After all these years to come dragging this in to me now. It don't make no sense at your age. I could have expected this ten or fifteen years ago, but not now.

TROY. Age ain't got nothing to do with it, Rose.

ROSE. I done tried to be everything a wife should be. Everything a wife could be. Been married eighteen years and I got to live to see the day you tell me you been seeing another woman and done fathered a child by her. And you know I ain't never wanted no half nothing in my family. My whole family is half. Everybody got different fathers and mothers... my two sisters and my brother. Can't hardly tell who's who. Can't never sit down and talk about Papa and Mama. It's your papa and your mama and my papa and my mama...

TROY. Rose... stop it now.

ROSE. I ain't never wanted that for none of my children. And now you wanna drag your behind in here and tell me something like this.

TROY. You ought to know. It's time for you to know.

ROSE. Well, I don't want to know, goddamn it!

TROY. I can't just make it go away. It's done now. I can't wish the circumstance of the thing away.

ROSE. And you don't want to either. Maybe you want to wish me and my boy away. Maybe that's what you want? Well, you can't wish us away. I've got eighteen years of my life invested in you. You ought to have stayed upstairs in my bed where you belong.

TROY. Rose... now listen to me... we can get a handle on this thing. We can talk this out... come to an understanding.

ROSE. All of a sudden it's "we." Where was "we" at when you was down there rolling around with some godforsaken woman? "We" should have come to an understanding before you started making a damn fool of yourself. You're a day late and a dollar short when it comes to an understanding with me.

TROY. It's just... She gives me a different idea... a different understanding about myself. I can step out of this house and get away from the pressures and problems... be a different man. I ain't got to wonder how I'm gonna pay the bills or get the roof fixed. I can just be a part of myself that I ain't never been.

ROSE. What I want to know... is do you plan to continue seeing her? That's all you can say to me.

TROY. I can sit up in her house and laugh. Do you understand what I'm saying? I can laugh out loud... and it feels goods. It reaches all the way down to the bottom of my shoes. [*Pause.*] Rose, I can't give that up.

ROSE. Maybe you ought to go on and stay down there with her... if she's a better woman than me.

TROY. It ain't about nobody being a better woman or nothing. Rose, you ain't the blame. A man couldn't ask for no woman to be a better wife than you've been. I'm responsible for it. I done locked myself into a pattern trying to take care of you all that I forgot about myself.

ROSE. What the hell was I there for? That was my job, not somebody else's.

TROY. Rose, I done tried all my life to live decent... to live a clean... hard... useful life. I tried to be a good husband to you. In every way I knew how. Maybe I come into the world backwards, I don't know. But...you born with two strikes on you before you come to the plate. You got to guard it closely...always looking for the curve ball on the inside corner. You can't afford to let none get past you. You can't afford a call strike. If you going down...you going down swinging. Everything lined up against you. What you gonna do. I fooled them, Rose. I bunted. When I found you and Cory and a halfway decent job...I was safe. Couldn't nothing touch me. I wasn't gonna strike out no more. I wasn't going back to the penitentiary. I wasn't gonna lay in the streets with a bottle of wine. I was safe. I had me a family. A job. I wasn't gonna get that last strike. I was on first looking for one of them boys to knock me in. To get me home.

ROSE. You should have stayed in my bed, Troy.

TROY. Then when I saw that gal...she firmed up my backbone. And I got to thinking that if I tried...I just might be able to steal second. Do you understand after eighteen years I wanted to steal second.

ROSE. You should have held me tight. You should have grabbed me and held on.

TROY. I stood on first base for eighteen years and I thought...well, goddamn it...go on for it!

ROSE. We're not talking about baseball! We're talking about you going off to lay in bed with another woman...and then bring it home to me. That's what we're talking about. We ain't talking about no baseball.

TROY. Rose, you're not listening to me. I'm trying the best I can to explain it to you. It's not easy for me to admit that I been standing in the same place for eighteen years.

ROSE. I been standing with you! I been right here with you, Troy. I got a life too. I gave eighteen years of my life to stand in the same spot with you. Don't you think I ever wanted other things? Don't you think I had dreams and hopes? What about my life? What about me? Don't you think it ever crossed my mind to want to know other men? That I wanted to lay up somewhere and forget about my responsibilities? That I wanted someone to make me laugh so I could feel good? You not the only one who's got wants and needs. But I held on to you, Troy. I took all my feelings, my wants and needs, my dreams...and I buried them inside you. I planted a seed and watched and prayed over it. I planted myself inside you and waited to bloom. And it didn't take me no eighteen years to find out the soil was hard and rocky and it wasn't never gonna bloom.

But I held on to you, Troy. I held you tighter. You was my husband. I owed you everything I had. Every part of me I could find to give you. And upstairs in that room...with the darkness falling in on me...I gave everything I had to try and erase the doubt that you wasn't the finest man in the world. And wherever you was going...I wanted to be there with you. 'Cause you was my husband. 'Cause that's the only way I was gonna survive as your wife. You always talking about what you give...and what you don't have to give. But you take too. You take...and don't even know nobody's giving!

ROSE *turns to exit into the house;* TROY *grabs her arm.*

TROY. You say I take and don't give!

ROSE. Troy! You're hurting me!

TROY. You say I take and don't give!

ROSE. Troy...you're hurting my arm! Let go!

TROY. I done give you everything I got. Don't you tell that lie on me.

ROSE. Troy!
TROY. Don't you tell that lie on me!

CORY *enters from the house.*

CORY. Mama!
ROSE. Troy. You're hurting me.
TROY. Don't you tell me about no taking and giving.

CORY *comes up behind* TROY *and grabs him.* TROY, *surprised, is thrown off balance just as* CORY *throws a glancing blow that catches him on the chest and knocks him down.* TROY *is stunned, as is* CORY.

ROSE. Troy. Troy. No!

TROY *gets to his feet and starts at* CORY.

Troy…no. Please! Troy!

ROSE *pulls on* TROY *to hold him back.* TROY *stops himself.*

TROY [*to* CORY]. All right. That's strike two. You stay away from around me, boy. Don't you strike out. You living with a full count. Don't you strike out.

TROY *exits out the yard as the lights go down.*

SCENE 2

It is six months later, early afternoon. TROY *enters from the house and starts to exit the yard.* ROSE *enters from the house.*

ROSE. Troy, I want to talk to you.
TROY. All of a sudden, after all this time, you want to talk to me, huh? You ain't wanted to talk to me for months. You ain't wanted to talk to me last night. You ain't wanted no part of me then. What you wanna talk to me about now?
ROSE. Tomorrow's Friday.
TROY. I know what day tomorrow is. You think I don't know tomorrow's Friday? My whole life I ain't done nothing but look to see Friday coming and you got to tell me it's Friday.
ROSE. I want to know if you're coming home.
TROY. I always come home, Rose. You know that. There ain't never been a night I ain't come home.
ROSE. That ain't what I mean…and you know it. I want to know if you're coming straight home after work.
TROY. I figure I'd cash my check…hang out at Taylors' with the boys…maybe play a game of checkers…
ROSE. Troy, I can't live like this. I won't live like this. You livin' on borrowed time with me. It's been going on six months now you ain't been coming home.
TROY. I be here every night. Every night of the year. That's 365 days.
ROSE. I want you to come home tomorrow after work.
TROY. Rose…I don't mess up my pay. You know that now. I take my pay and I give it to you. I don't have no money but what you give me back. I just want to have little time to myself…a little time to enjoy life.
ROSE. What about me? When's my time to enjoy life?
TROY. I don't know what to tell you, Rose. I'm doing the best I can.

ROSE. You ain't been home from work but time enough to change your clothes and run out...and you wanna call that the best you can do?

TROY. I'm going over to the hospital to see Alberta. She went into the hospital this afternoon. Look like she might have the baby early. I won't be gone long.

ROSE. Well, you ought to know. They went over to Miss Pearl's and got Gabe today. She said you told them to go ahead and lock him up.

TROY. I ain't said no such thing. Whoever told you that is telling a lie. Pearl ain't doing nothing but telling a big fat lie.

ROSE. She ain't had to tell me. I read it on the papers.

TROY. I ain't told them nothing of the kind.

ROSE. I saw it right there on the papers.

TROY. What it say, huh?

ROSE. It said you told them to take him.

TROY. Then they screwed that up, just the way they screw up everything. I ain't worried about what they got on the paper.

ROSE. Say the government sent part of his check to the hospital and the other part to you.

TROY. I ain't got nothing to do with that if that's the way it works. I ain't made up the rules about how it work.

ROSE. You did Gabe just like you did Cory. You wouldn't sign the paper for Cory...but you signed for Gabe. You signed that paper.

The telephone is heard ringing inside the house.

TROY. I told you I ain't signed nothing, woman! The only thing I signed was the release form. Hell, I can't read, I don't know what they had on that paper! I ain't signed nothing about sending Gabe away.

ROSE. I said send him to the hospital...you said let him be free...now you done went down there and signed him to the hospital for half his money. You went back on yourself, Troy. You gonna have to answer for that.

TROY. See now...you been over there talking to Miss Pearl. She done got mad 'cause she ain't getting Gabe's rent money. That's all it is. She's liable to say anything.

ROSE. Troy, I seen where you signed the paper.

TROY. You ain't seen nothing I signed. What she doing got papers on my brother anyway? Miss Pearl telling a big fat lie. And I'm gonna tell her about it too! You ain't seen nothing I signed. Say...you ain't seen nothing I signed.

ROSE *exits into the house to answer the telephone. Presently she returns.*

ROSE. Troy...that was the hospital. Alberta had the baby.

TROY. What she have? What is it?

ROSE. It's a girl.

TROY. I better get on down to the hospital to see her.

ROSE. Troy...

TROY. Rose...I got to go see her now. That's only right...what's the matter...the baby's all right, ain't it?

ROSE. Alberta died having the baby.

TROY. Died...you say she's dead? Alberta's dead?

ROSE. They said they done all they could. They couldn't do nothing for her.

TROY. The baby? How's the baby?

Rose. They say it's healthy. I wonder who's gonna bury her.

Troy. She had family, Rose. She wasn't living in the world by herself.

Rose. I know she wasn't living in the world by herself.

Troy. Next thing you gonna want to know if she had any insurance.

Rose. Troy, you ain't got to talk like that.

Troy. That's the first thing that jumped out your mouth. "Who's gonna bury her?" Like I'm fixing to take on that task for myself.

Rose. I am your wife. Don't push me away.

Troy. I ain't pushing nobody away. Just give me some space. That's all. Just give me some room to breathe.

Rose *exits into the house.* Troy *walks about the yard.*

Troy [*with a quiet rage that threatens to consume him*]. All right...Mr. Death. See now...I'm gonna tell you what I'm gonna do. I'm gonna take and build me a fence around this yard. See? I'm gonna build me a fence around what belongs to me. And then I want you to stay on the other side. See? You stay over there until you're ready for me. Then you come on. Bring your army. Bring your sickle. Bring your wrestling clothes. I ain't gonna fall down on my vigilance this time. You ain't gonna sneak up on me no more. When you ready for me...when the top of your list say Troy Maxson...that's when you come around here. You come up and knock on the front door. Ain't nobody else got nothing to do with this. This is between you and me. Man to man. You stay on the other side of that fence until you ready for me. Then you come up and knock on the front door. Anytime you want. I'll be ready for you.

The lights go down to black.

SCENE 3

The lights come up on the porch. It is late evening three days later. Rose *sits listening to the ball game waiting for* Troy. *The final out of the game is made and* Rose *switches off the radio.* Troy *enters the yard carrying an infant wrapped in blankets. He stands back from the house and calls.*

Rose *enters and stands on the porch. There is a long, awkward silence, the weight of which grows heavier with each passing second.*

Troy. Rose...I'm standing here with my daughter in my arms. She ain't but a wee bittie little old thing. She don't know nothing about grownups' business. She innocent...and she ain't got no mama.

Rose. What you telling me for, Troy?

She turns and exits into the house.

Troy. Well...I guess we'll just sit out here on the porch.

He sits down on the porch. There is an awkward indelicateness about the way he handles the baby. His largeness engulfs and seems to swallow it. He speaks loud enough for Rose *to hear.*

A man's got to do what's right for him. I ain't sorry for nothing I done. It felt right in my heart. [*To the baby.*] What you smiling at? Your daddy's a big man. Got these great big old hands. But sometimes he's scared. And right now your daddy's scared cause we sitting out here and ain't got no home. Oh, I been homeless before. I ain't had no little baby with me. But I been homeless. You just be out on the road by your lonesome and you see one of them trains coming and you just kinda go like this...

He sings as a lullaby.

Please, Mr. Engineer let a man ride the line
Please, Mr. Engineer let a man ride the line
I ain't got no ticket please let me ride the blinds.

ROSE *enters from the house.* TROY, *hearing her steps behind him, stands and faces her.*

She's my daughter, Rose. My own flesh and blood. I can't deny her no more than I can deny them boys. [*Pause.*] You and them boys is my family. You and them and this child is all I got in the world. So I guess what I'm saying is...I'd appreciate it if you'd help me take care of her.

ROSE. Okay, Troy...you're right. I'll take care of your baby for you...'cause...like you say...she's innocent...and you can't visit the sins of the father upon the child. A motherless child has got a hard time. [*She takes the baby from him.*] From right now...this child got a mother. But you a womanless man.

ROSE *turns and exits into the house with the baby. Lights go down to black.*

SCENE 4

It is two months later. LYONS *enters the street. He knocks on the door and calls.*

LYONS. Hey, Rose! [*Pause.*] Rose!

ROSE [*from inside the house*]. Stop that yelling. You gonna wake up Raynell. I just got her to sleep.

LYONS. I just stopped by to pay Papa this twenty dollars I owe him. Where's Papa at?

ROSE. He should be here in a minute. I'm getting ready to go down to the church. Sit down and wait on him.

LYONS. I got to go pick up Bonnie over her mother's house.

ROSE. Well, sit it down there on the table. He'll get it.

LYONS [*enters the house and sets the money on the table*]. Tell Papa I said thanks. I'll see you again.

ROSE. All right, Lyons. We'll see you.

LYONS *starts to exit as* CORY *enters.*

CORY. Hey, Lyons.

LYONS. What's happening, Cory? Say man, I'm sorry I missed your graduation. You know I had a gig and couldn't get away. Otherwise, I would have been there, man. So what you doing?

CORY. I'm trying to find a job.

LYONS. Yeah I know how that go, man. It's rough out here. Jobs are scarce.

CORY. Yeah, I know.

LYONS. Look here, I got to run. Talk to Papa...he know some people. He'll be able to help get you a job. Talk to him...see what he say.

CORY. Yeah...all right, Lyons.

LYONS. You take care. I'll talk to you soon. We'll find some time to talk.

LYONS *exits the yard.*

CORY *wanders over to the tree, picks up the bat, and assumes a batting stance. He studies an imaginary pitcher and swings. Dissatisfied with the result, he tries again.* TROY *enters. They eye each other for a beat.* CORY *puts the bat down and exits the yard.* TROY *starts into the house as* ROSE *exits with* RAYNELL. *She is carrying a cake.*

TROY. I'm coming in and everybody's going out.

ROSE. I'm taking this cake down to the church for the bake sale. Lyons was by to see you. He stopped by to pay you your twenty dollars. It's laying in there on the table.

TROY [*going into his pocket*]. Well... here go this money.

ROSE. Put it in there on the table, Troy. I'll get it.

TROY. What time you coming back?

ROSE. Ain't no use in you studying me. It don't matter what time I come back.

TROY. I just asked you a question, woman. What's the matter... can't I ask you a question?

ROSE. Troy, I don't want to go into it. Your dinner's in there on the stove. All you got to do is heat it up. And don't you be eating the rest of them cakes in there. I'm coming back for them. We having a bake sale at the church tomorrow.

ROSE *exits the yard.* TROY *sits down on the steps, takes a pint bottle from his pocket, opens it, and drinks. He begins to sing.*

TROY.

Hear it ring! Hear it ring!
Had an old dog his name was Blue
You know Blue was mighty true
You know Blue as a good old dog
Blue trees a possum in a hollow log
You know from that he was a good old dog.

BONO *enters the yard.*

BONO. Hey, Troy.

TROY. Hey, what's happening, Bono?

BONO. I just thought I'd stop by to see you.

TROY. What you stop by and see me for? You ain't stopped by in a month of Sundays. Hell, I must owe you money or something.

BONO. Since you got your promotion I can't keep up with you. Used to see you every day. Now I don't even know what route you working.

TROY. They keep switching me around. Got me out in Greentree now... hauling white folks' garbage.

BONO. Greentree, huh? You lucky, at least you ain't got to be lifting them barrels. Damn if they ain't getting heavier. I'm gonna put in my two years and call it quits.

TROY. I'm thinking about retiring myself.

BONO. You got it easy. You can drive for another five years.

TROY. It ain't the same, Bono. It ain't like working the back of the truck. Ain't got nobody to talk to... feel like you working by yourself. Naw, I'm thinking about retiring. How's Lucille?

BONO. She all right. Her arthritis get to acting up on her sometime. Saw Rose on my way in. She going down to the church, huh?

TROY. Yeah, she took up going down there. All them preachers looking for somebody to fatten their pockets. [*Pause.*] Got some gin here.

BONO. Naw, thanks. I just stopped by to say hello.

TROY. Hell, nigger…you can take a drink. I ain't never known you to say no to a drink. You ain't got to work tomorrow.

BONO. I just stopped by. I'm fixing to go over to Skinner's. We got us a domino game going over his house every Friday.

TROY. Nigger, you can't play no dominoes. I used to whup you four games out of five.

BONO. Well, that learned me. I'm getting better.

TROY. Yeah? Well, that's all right.

BONO. Look here…I got to be getting on. Stop by sometime, huh?

TROY. Yeah, I'll do that, Bono. Lucille told Rose you bought her a new refrigerator.

BONO. Yeah, Rose told Lucille you had finally built your fence…so I figured we'd call it even.

TROY. I knew you would.

BONO. Yeah…okay. I'll be talking to you.

TROY. Yeah, take care, Bono. Good to see you. I'm gonna stop over.

BONO. Yeah. Okay, Troy.

BONO *exits.* TROY *drinks from the bottle.*

TROY.

Old Blue died and I dig his grave
Let him down with a golden chain
Every night when I hear old Blue bark
I know Blue treed a possum in Noah's Ark
Hear it ring! Hear it ring!

CORY *enters the yard. They eye each other for a beat.* TROY *is sitting in the middle of the steps.* CORY *walks over.*

CORY. I got to get by.

TROY. Say what? What's you say?

CORY. You in my way. I got to get by.

TROY. You got to get by where? This is my house. Bought and paid for. In full. Took me fifteen years. And if you wanna go in my house and I'm sitting on the steps…you say excuse me. Like your mama taught you.

CORY. Come on, Pop…I got to get by.

CORY *starts to maneuver his way past* TROY. TROY *grabs his leg and shoves him back.*

TROY. You just gonna walk over top of me?

CORY. I live here too!

TROY [*advancing toward him*]. You just gonna walk over top of me in my own house?

CORY. I ain't scared of you.

TROY. I ain't asked if you was scared of me. I asked you if you was fixing to walk over top of me in my own house? That's the question. You ain't gonna say excuse me? You just gonna walk over top of me?

CORY. If you wanna put it like that.

TROY. How else am I gonna put it?

CORY. I was walking by you to go into the house cause you sitting on the steps drunk, singing to yourself. You can put it like that.

TROY. Without saying excuse me???

CORY *doesn't respond.*

I asked you a question. Without saying excuse me???

CORY. I ain't got to say excuse me to you. You don't count around here no more.

TROY. Oh, I see . . . I don't count around here no more. You ain't got to say excuse me to your daddy. All of a sudden you done got so grown that your daddy don't count around here no more . . . Around here in his own house and yard that he done paid for with the sweat of his brow. You done got so grown to where you gonna take over. You gonna take over my house. Is that right? You gonna wear my pants. You gonna go in there and stretch out on my bed. You ain't got to say excuse me cause I don't count around here no more. Is that right?

CORY. That's right. You always talking this dumb stuff. Now, why don't you just get out my way?

TROY. I guess you got someplace to sleep and something to put in your belly. You got that, huh? You got that? That's what you need. You got that, huh?

CORY. You don't know what I got. You ain't got to worry about what I got.

TROY. You right! You one hundred percent right! I done spent the last seventeen years worrying about what you got. Now it's your turn, see? I'll tell you what to do. You grown . . . we done established that. You a man. Now, let's see you act like one. Turn your behind around and walk out this yard. And when you get out there in the alley . . . you can forget about this house. See? 'Cause this is my house. You go on and be a man and get your own house. You can forget about this. 'Cause this is mine. You go on and get yours cause I'm through with doing for you.

CORY. You talking about what you did for me . . . what'd you ever give me?

TROY. Them feet and bones! That pumping heart, nigger! I give you more than anybody else is ever gonna give you.

CORY. You ain't never gave me nothing! You ain't never done nothing but hold me back. Afraid I was gonna be better than you. All you ever did was try and make me scared of you. I used to tremble every time you called my name. Every time I heard your footsteps in the house. Wondering all the time . . . what's Papa gonna say if I do this? . . . What's he gonna say if I do that? . . . What's Papa gonna say if I turn on the radio? And mama, too . . . she tries . . . but she's scared of you.

TROY. You leave your mama out of this. She ain't got nothing to do with this.

CORY. I don't know how she stand you . . . after what you did to her.

TROY. I told you to leave your mama out of this!

He advances toward CORY.

CORY. What you gonna do . . . give me a whupping? You can't whup me no more. You're too old. You just an old man.

TROY [*shoves him on his shoulder*]. Nigger! That's what you are. You just another nigger on the street to me!

CORY. You crazy! You know that?

TROY. Go on now! You got the devil in you. Get on away from me!

CORY. You just a crazy old man . . . talking about I got the devil in me.

TROY. Yeah, I'm crazy! If you don't get on the other side of that yard . . . I'm gonna show you how crazy I am! Go on . . . get the hell out of my yard.

CORY. It ain't your yard. You took Uncle Gabe's money he got from the army to buy this house and then you put him out.

TROY [*advances on* CORY]. Get your black ass out of my yard!

TROY'*s advance backs* CORY *up against the tree.* CORY *grabs up the bat.*

CORY. I ain't going nowhere! Come on . . . put me out! I ain't scared of you.

TROY. That's my bat!

Cory. Come on!
Troy. Put my bat down!
Cory. Come on, put me out.

Cory *swings at* Troy, *who backs across the yard.*

What's the matter? You so bad . . . put me out!

Troy *advances toward* Cory.

Cory [*backing up*]. Come on! Come on!
Troy. You're gonna have to use it! You wanna draw that bat back on me . . . you're gonna have to use it.
Cory. Come on! . . . Come on!

Cory *swings the bat at* Troy *a second time. He misses.* Troy *continues to advance toward him.*

Troy. You're gonna have to kill me! You wanna draw that bat back on me. You're gonna have to kill me.

Cory, *backed up against the tree, can go no farther.* Troy *taunts him. He sticks out his head and offers him a target.*

Come on! Come on!

Cory *is unable to swing the bat.* Troy *grabs it.*

Troy. Then I'll show you.

Cory *and* Troy *struggle over the bat. The struggle is fierce and fully engaged.* Troy *ultimately is the stronger and takes the bat from* Cory *and stands over him ready to swing. He stops himself.*

Go on and get away from around my house.

Cory, *stung by his defeat, picks himself up, walks slowly out of the yard and up the alley.*

Cory. Tell Mama I'll be back for my things.
Troy. They'll be on the other side of that fence.

Cory *exits.*

I can't taste nothing. Helluljah! I can't taste nothing no more. [Troy *assumes a batting posture and begins to taunt Death, the fastball on the outside corner.*] Come on! It's between you and me now! Come on! Anytime you want! Come on! I be ready for you . . . but I ain't gonna be easy.

The lights go down on the scene.

SCENE 5

The time is 1965. The lights come up in the yard. It is the morning of Troy's *funeral. A funeral plaque with a light hangs beside the door. There is a small garden plot off to the side. There is noise and activity in the house as* Rose, Lyons, *and* Bono *have gathered. The door opens and* Raynell, *seven years old, enters dressed in a flannel nightgown. She crosses to the garden and pokes around with a stick.* Rose *calls from the house.*

Rose. Raynell!
Raynell. Mam?

ROSE. What you doing out there?
RAYNELL. Nothing.

ROSE *comes to the door.*

ROSE. Girl, get in here and get dressed. What you doing?
RAYNELL. Seeing if my garden growed.
ROSE. I told you it ain't gonna grow overnight. You got to wait.
RAYNELL. It don't look like it never gonna grow. Dag!
ROSE. I told you a watched pot never boils. Get in here and get dressed.
RAYNELL. This ain't even no pot, Mama.
ROSE. You just have to give it a chance. It'll grow. Now you come on and do what I told you. We got to be getting ready. This ain't no morning to be playing around. You hear me?
RAYNELL. Yes, mam.

ROSE *exits into the house.* RAYNELL *continues to poke at her garden with a stick.* CORY *enters. He is dressed in a Marine corporal's uniform, and carries a duffelbag. His posture is that of a military man, and his speech has a clipped sternness.*

CORY [*to* RAYNELL]. Hi. [*Pause.*] I bet your name is Raynell.
RAYNELL. Uh huh.
CORY. Is your mama home?

RAYNELL *runs up on the porch and calls through the screen door.*

RAYNELL. Mama... there's some man out here. Mama?

ROSE *comes to the door.*

ROSE. Cory? Lord have mercy! Look here, you all!

ROSE *and* CORY *embrace in a tearful reunion as* BONO *and* LYONS *enter from the house dressed in funeral clothes.*

BONO. Aw, looka here...
ROSE. Done got all grown up!
CORY. Don't cry, Mama. What you crying about?
ROSE. I'm just so glad you made it.
CORY. Hey Lyons. How you doing, Mr. Bono.

LYONS *goes to embrace* CORY.

LYONS. Look at you, man. Look at you. Don't he look good, Rose. Got them Corporal stripes.
ROSE. What took you so long?
CORY. You know how the Marines are, Mama. They got to get all their paperwork straight before they let you do anything.
ROSE. Well, I'm sure glad you made it. They let Lyons come. Your Uncle Gabe's still in the hospital. They don't know if they gonna let him out or not. I just talked to them a little while ago.
LYONS. A Corporal in the United States Marines.
BONO. Your daddy knew you had it in you. He used to tell me all the time.
LYONS. Don't he look good, Mr. Bono?
BONO. Yeah, he remind me of Troy when I first met him. [*Pause.*] Say, Rose, Lucille's down at the church with the choir. I'm gonna go down and get the pallbearers lined up. I'll be back to get you all.

ROSE. Thanks, Jim.
CORY. See you, Mr. Bono.
LYONS [*with his arm around* RAYNELL]. Cory... look at Raynell. Ain't she precious? She gonna break a whole lot of hearts.
ROSE. Raynell, come and say hello to your brother. This is your brother, Cory. You remember Cory.
RAYNELL. No, Mam.
CORY. She don't remember me, Mama.
ROSE. Well, we talk about you. She heard us talk about you. [*To* RAYNELL.] This is your brother, Cory. Come on and say hello.
RAYNELL. Hi.
CORY. Hi. So you're Raynell. Mama told me a lot about you.
ROSE. You all come on into the house and let me fix you some breakfast. Keep up your strength.
CORY. I ain't hungry, Mama.
LYONS. You can fix me something, Rose. I'll be in there in a minute.
ROSE. Cory, you sure you don't want nothing? I know they ain't feeding you right.
CORY. No, Mama... thanks. I don't feel like eating. I'll get something later.
ROSE. Raynell... get on upstairs and get that dress on like I told you.

ROSE *and* RAYNELL *exit into the house.*

LYONS. So... I hear you thinking about getting married.
CORY. Yeah, I done found the right one, Lyons. It's about time.
LYONS. Me and Bonnie been split up about four years now. About the time Papa retired. I guess she just got tired of all them changes I was putting her through. [*Pause.*] I always knew you was gonna make something out yourself. Your head was always in the right direction. So... you gonna stay in... make it a career... put in your twenty years?
CORY. I don't know. I got six already, I think that's enough.
LYONS. Stick with Uncle Sam and retire early. Ain't nothing out here. I guess Rose told you what happened with me. They got me down the workhouse. I thought I was being slick cashing other people's checks.
CORY. How much time you doing?
LYONS. They give me three years. I got that beat now. I ain't got but nine more months. It ain't so bad. You learn to deal with it like anything else. You got to take the crookeds with the straights. That's what Papa used to say. He used to say that when he struck out. I seen him strike out three times in a row... and the next time up he hit the ball over the grandstand. Right out there in Homestead Field. He wasn't satisfied hitting in the seats... he want to hit it over everything! After the game he had two hundred people standing around waiting to shake his hand. You got to take the crookeds with the straights. Yeah, Papa was something else.
CORY. You still playing?
LYONS. Cory... you know I'm gonna do that. There's some fellows down there we got us a band... we gonna try and stay together when we get out... but yeah, I'm still playing. It still helps me to get out of bed in the morning. As long as it do that I'm gonna be right there playing and trying to make some sense out of it.
ROSE [*calling*]. Lyons, I got these eggs in the pan.
LYONS. Let me go on and get these eggs, man. Get ready to go bury Papa. [*Pause.*] How you doing? You doing all right?

CORY *nods.* LYONS *touches him on the shoulder and they share a moment of silent grief.* LYONS *exits into the house.* CORY *wanders about the yard.* RAYNELL *enters.*

RAYNELL. Hi.
CORY. Hi.
RAYNELL. Did you used to sleep in my room?
CORY. Yeah... that used to be my room.
RAYNELL. That's what Papa call it. "Cory's room." It got your football in the closet.

ROSE *comes to the door.*

ROSE. Raynell, get in there and get them good shoes on.
RAYNELL. Mama, can't I wear these? Them other one hurt my feet.
ROSE. Well, they just gonna have to hurt your feet for a while. You ain't said they hurt your feet when you went down to the store and got them.
RAYNELL. They didn't hurt then. My feet done got bigger.
ROSE. Don't you give me no backtalk now. You get in there and get them shoes on.

RAYNELL *exits into the house.*

Ain't too much changed. He still got that piece of rag tied to that tree. He was out here swinging that bat. I was just ready to go back in the house. He swung that bat and then he just fell over. Seem like he swung it and stood there with this grin on his face... and then he just fell over. They carried him on down to the hospital, but I knew there wasn't no need... why don't you come on in the house?
CORY. Mama... I got something to tell you. I don't know how to tell you this... but I've got to tell you... I'm not going to Papa's funeral.
ROSE. Boy, hush your month. That's your daddy you talking about. I don't want hear that kind of talk this morning. I done raised you to come to this? You standing there all healthy and grown talking about you ain't going to your daddy's funeral?
CORY. Mama... listen...
ROSE. I don't want to hear it, Cory. You just get that thought out of your head.
CORY. I can't drag Papa with me everywhere I go. I've got to say no to him. One time in my life I've got to say no.
ROSE. Don't nobody have to listen to nothing like that. I know you and your daddy ain't seen eye to eye, but I ain't got to listen to that kind of talk this morning. Whatever was between you and your daddy... the time has come to put it aside. Just take it and set it over there on the shelf and forget about it. Disrespecting your daddy ain't gonna make you a man, Cory. You got to find a way to come to that on your own. Not going to your daddy's funeral ain't gonna make you a man.
CORY. The whole time I was growing up... living in his house... Papa was like a shadow that followed you everywhere. It weighed on you and sunk into your flesh. It would wrap around you and lay there until you couldn't tell which one was you anymore. That shadow digging in your flesh. Trying to crawl in. Trying to live through you. Everywhere I looked, Troy Maxson was staring back at me... hiding under the bed... in the closet. I'm just saying I've got to find a way to get rid of that shadow, Mama.
ROSE. You just like him. You got him in you good.

CORY. Don't tell me that, Mama.
ROSE. You Troy Maxson all over again.
CORY. I don't want to be Troy Maxson. I want to be me.
ROSE. You can't be nobody but who you are, Cory. That shadow wasn't nothing but you growing into yourself. You either got to grow into it or cut it down to fit you. But that's all you got to make life with. That's all you got to measure yourself against that world out there. Your daddy wanted you to be everything he wasn't...and at the same time he tried to make you into everything he was. I don't know if he was right or wrong...but I do know he meant to do more good than he meant to do harm. He wasn't always right. Sometimes when he touched he bruised. And sometimes when he took me in his arms he cut.

When I first met your daddy I thought...Here is a man I can lay down with and make a baby. That's the first thing I thought when I seen him. I was thirty years old and had done seen my share of men. But when he walked up to me and said, "I can dance a waltz that'll make you dizzy," I thought, Rose Lee, here is a man that you can open yourself up to and be filled to bursting. Here is a man that can fill all them empty spaces you been tipping around the edges of. One of them empty spaces was being somebody's mother.

I married your daddy and settled down to cooking his supper and keeping clean sheets on the bed. When your daddy walked through the house he was so big he filled it up. That was my first mistake. Not to make him leave some room for me. For my part in the matter. But at that time I wanted that. I wanted a house that I could sing in. And that's what your daddy gave me. I didn't know to keep up his strength I had to give up little pieces of mine. I did that. I took on his life as mine and mixed up the pieces so that you couldn't hardly tell which was which anymore. It was my choice. It was my life and I didn't have to live it like that. But that's what life offered me in the way of being a woman and I took it. I grabbed hold of it with both hands.

By the time Raynell came into the house, me and your daddy had done lost touch with one another. I didn't want to make my blessing off of nobody's misfortune...but I took on to Raynell like she was all them babies I had wanted and never had.

The phone rings.

Like I'd been blessed to relive a part of my life. And if the Lord see fit to keep up my strength...I'm gonna do her just like your daddy did you...I'm gonna give her the best of what's in me.

RAYNELL [*entering, still with her old shoes*]. Mama...Reverend Tollivier on the phone.

ROSE *exits into the house.*

RAYNELL. Hi.
CORY. Hi.
RAYNELL. You in the Army or the Marines?
CORY. Marines.
RAYNELL. Papa said it was the Army. Did you know Blue?
CORY. Blue? Who's Blue?
RAYNELL. Papa's dog what he sing about all the time.
CORY [*singing*].

Hear it ring! Hear it ring!
I had a dog his name was Blue
You know Blue was mighty true
You know Blue was a good old dog
Blue treed a possum in a hollow log
You know from that he was a good old dog.
Hear it ring! Hear it ring!

RAYNELL *joins in singing.*

CORY AND RAYNELL.

Blue treed a possum out on a limb
Blue looked at me and I looked at him
Grabbed that possum and put him in a sack
Blue stayed there till I came back
Old Blue's feets was big and round
Never allowed a possum to touch the ground.

Old Blue died and I dug his grave
I dug his grave with a silver spade
Let him down with a golden chain
Any every night I call his name
Go on Blue, you good dog you
Go on Blue, you good dog you.

RAYNELL.

Blue laid down and died like a man
Blue laid down and died…

BOTH.

Blue laid down and died like a man
Now he's treeing possums in the Promised Land
I'm gonna tell you this to let you know
Blue's gone where the good dogs go
When I hear old Blue bark
When I hear old Blue bark
Blue treed a possum in Noah's Ark
Blue treed a possum in Noah's Ark.

ROSE *comes to the screen door.*

ROSE. Cory, we gonna be ready to go in a minute.

CORY [*to* RAYNELL]. You go on in the house and change them shoes like Mama told you so we can go to Papa's funeral.

RAYNELL. Okay, I'll be back.

RAYNELL *exits into the house.* CORY *gets up and crosses over to the tree.* ROSE *stands in the screen door watching him.* GABRIEL *enters from the alley.*

GABRIEL [*calling*]. Hey, Rose!

ROSE. Gabe?

GABRIEL. I'm here, Rose. Hey Rose, I'm here!

ROSE *enters from the house.*

ROSE. Lord... Look here, Lyons!
LYONS. See, I told you, Rose... I told you they'd let him come.
CORY. How you doing, Uncle Gabe?
LYONS. How you doing, Uncle Gabe?
GABRIEL. Hey, Rose. It's time. It's time to tell St. Peter to open the gates. Troy, you ready? You ready, Troy. I'm gonna tell St. Peter to open the gates. You get ready now.

GABRIEL, *with great fanfare, braces himself to blow. The trumpet is without a mouthpiece. He puts the end of it into his mouth and blows with great force, like a man who has been waiting some twenty-odd years for this single moment. No sound comes out of the trumpet. He braces himself and blows again with the same results. A third time he blows. There is a weight of impossible description that falls away and leaves him bare and exposed to a frightful realization. It is a trauma that a sane and normal mind would be unable to withstand. He begins to dance. A slow, strange dance, eerie and life-giving. A dance of atavistic signature and ritual.* LYONS *attempts to embrace him.* GABRIEL *pushes* LYONS *away. He begins to howl in what is an attempt at song, or perhaps a song turning back into itself in an attempt at speech. He finishes his dance and the gates of heaven stand open as wide as God's closet.*

That's the way that go!

(Blackout)

[1987]

PREWRITING

Begin your study of *Fences* by writing about and discussing the following ideas.

Analyzing the Characters

1. One way to look at this play is as a story of deceptions. List five or six deceptions that occur in the play. Compare your list with those of others in your class. Discuss how you would rank the seriousness or harmlessness of the deceptions you have identified. Be sure to consider possible self-deceptions for each character.
2. Reread the opening scene involving Troy, Rose, and Bono (pp. 774–78). With two other people, prepare an oral reading of the scene, choosing one quality to emphasize in each of the characters. Present the scene to your class, asking them to identify the qualities you chose. Listen to the other students' interpretations of the scene.
3. In Act 1, scene 4, Rose tells Troy, "Times have changed from when you was young, Troy. People change. The world's changing around you and you can't even see it." How does this statement fit in with

Arthur Miller's concept of tragic heroism? Find statements by other characters that imply being out of step with the times. How is the idea important to understanding the characters?

4. Follow the prominent money motif through the play: losing it, winning it, saving it, spending it, gambling it, lending it, paying it back, and so forth. What does money mean to the characters? Does it mean different things to different characters?
5. Reread Rose's closing speech, Act 2, scene 5 (p. 815). Does this monolog encourage a hopeful or a pessimistic reading of the play as a whole?
6. Choose a character from *Fences* and argue that he or she is the hero. Can you argue for more than one character as a hero?

WRITING

In your prewriting, you gathered a list of deceptions that you found in *Fences*. Looking at that list, you may come up with a thesis for an essay on the play. "Deception is an important element in *Fences*" is not enough, even though that may be your first reaction to such a long list. You must say *why* deception is important. Here are some possible thesis ideas:

Troy's ideal roles for himself will never be enacted in the real world, and he maintains a staggering level of illusion to avoid this fact.

The line between outright lies and self-deceptions is not always clear in *Fences* (and even the audience is left without knowing which is which in some cases), suggesting that truth is less clear-cut than it sometimes seems.

Though Troy is presented as a person with both good and bad traits, his betrayal of Rose precludes his being acceptable as a tragic hero.

Choosing a Structure

Your choice of thesis should determine how you organize your raw material—in this case, your list of examples from the prewriting activity. Perhaps your list looks something like this:

Deception and Lies

- Cory not working at the A&P
- Signing papers to put Gabe away in an institution
- Watching the game at Taylors'
- How Troy courted Rose
- Lyons's talent as a musician
- Troy's talent as a baseball player
- Walking 200 miles to Mobile
- The wholesale animosity of whites
- Troy's fantasy self-image when he's with Alberta

- Troy's betrayal of Rose with Alberta
- Gabe's identity
- Playing the numbers
- Troy's encounter with Death
- Rose tries to erase her doubts about Troy
- Other people's beliefs that Gabe either needs or doesn't need to be put away
- Why Gabe moved out
- Troy pretends no anger toward Gabe

This unorganized jumble can be structured in several ways. For the first thesis we mentioned, you would probably pull from the list all of Troy's illusions and lies, concentrating on their relation to his real situation and history. For the second thesis, you would separate items that are outright, conscious lies from those that are self-deceptions, and then make a category of matters whose truth the characters and audience never can be sure about. For the last thesis, you would focus on the illusions embraced by Troy and Rose about their relationship, intending to show that Troy's secret affair with Alberta casts him as a scoundrel, not a hero.

IDEAS FOR WRITING

Ideas for Responsive Writing

1. Cory asserts that he will not attend his father's funeral, but then does go in the end. Consider what he is thinking and feeling about Troy at the end of the play. Write a speech for him to deliver explaining his change of mind.
2. One character, Alberta, never appears on the stage. What do you think is her side of the story about her affair and the conception of Raynell? Write a plausible account of the play's events from her point of view.
3. Take the stance of the director of this play. Explain how you would direct the actor playing Gabriel. In addition, how should the other actors on stage react to Gabriel when they're in a scene with him? Write an explanation of your handling of Gabriel's role, aimed at your entire cast of actors.

Ideas for Critical Writing

1. Devise and support a major claim about the role of imagination and fantasy in each character's life.
2. Expand on Rose's statement about Troy in Act 2, scene 5: "I don't know if he was right or wrong... but I do know he meant to do more good than he meant to do harm." Is the statement true, a lie to appease Cory, or a self-protective illusion?
3. Trace the idea of father-son legacies through the play. Are these legacies positive? negative? unavoidable? superstitious?

4. CRITICAL APPROACHES: Review the discussion of mythological and archetypal approaches to interpreting literature (page 1160). Then argue that the character of Rose is a mythic or archetypal figure, using other sources about such figures to support your claims.
5. CRITICAL APPROACHES: Read about cultural criticism in Chapter 19 and in the Critical Approaches to Literature. In your paper, explain how the dynamics of *Fences* are understandable in terms of its time: the late 1950s.
6. Write an essay explaining why Troy's one real triumph, desegregating the job assignments at work, means little to him.

Ideas for Researched Writing

1. Consider the influence of the African traditions and myth in *Fences.* Two sources on the topic are *The Past as Present in the Drama of August Wilson* (2004) by Harry J. Elam, Jr., and *August Wilson and the African-American Odyssey* (1995) by Kim Pereira. These books will lead you to other reference materials on the topic.
2. CRITICAL APPROACHES: Read about cultural criticism in Chapter 19 and in the Critical Approaches to Literature. Write a paper explaining how the history of baseball is significant in understanding the play.

REWRITING

The more specifically you support your claims about the work, the more credible you will be to your readers. Another crucial advantage of forcing yourself to be specific is that you will prevent yourself from straying from the printed page into the fields of your own mind, which may be rich and green but not relevant.

Developing Paragraphs Specifically

The following paragraph makes several good observations but lacks specifics:

> Each family member pursues a life's work that is alien to his or her chosen self-image. They each make choices that preclude the fulfillment of their dreams, and they live in an environment that frustrates their attempts to pursue their ideals.

Although these statements are true, the writer has given the reader no particular cause to believe them. The paragraph should have additional details from the play. Compare the following:

> In several ways, the Maxson family fits Arthur Miller's characterization of modern tragedy. Each family member pursues a life's work that is alien to his or her chosen self-image. Troy envisions his potential as a major league

> baseball player, while laboring as a garbage man. The poignant contrast between his dreams and his real possibilities makes him an object of pity. Cory, instead of gaining a college education through a football scholarship, becomes a Marine Corporal with a marked lack of enthusiasm, thinking he'll get out in six years. Lyons, who idealized an exciting musical career for himself, turned to robbery and ends up with a sentence in the workhouse. Gabe, the war hero, is delusional from his injuries and lives on government disability funds. Even Rose, who seems to embody feminine domestic virtues so naturally, reveals her derailment as she berates the unfaithful Troy: "Don't you think I ever wanted other things? Don't you think I had dreams and hopes? What about my life?... You not the only one who's got wants and needs. But I held on to you, Troy. I took all my feelings, my wants and needs, my dreams... and I buried them inside you" (803).

The references to the text of the play specifically support the writer's contentions. The exercise that follows will give you practice in finding such support.

Exercise on Providing Quotations

For each general statement, provide appropriate quotations from the play. Some of these generalizations may give you further ideas for papers.

1. Throughout the play, Rose confronts Troy only on minor flaws, while supporting his self-image as a good, strong, capable man.
2. Though they are affected by an inhospitable environment, the characters also worsen their situations through their own questionable choices.
3. Troy's strategies to make Rose agree to mother his illegitimate child consist of crass manipulation and self-serving sentimentality.
4. The fence has several symbolic meanings in the play.
5. Evidence from the play suggests that Raynell is destined for a life of misery and self-deception.

CASEBOOK
Fences: Interpreting Troy Maxson

Troy Maxson is one of the great male characters of modern American drama, a marvelously complex and contradictory protagonist who elicits a broad range of responses from audiences and readers alike. Is he, as one critic says, "the ultimate warrior" who is also "pensive, sensitive, and lovable"? Or is he, as another claims, "stubborn, pessimistic, and deliberately self-limiting"? Lloyd Richards, who directed *Fences* on Broadway, sums up Troy's paradoxical nature in this way:

> How is this reformed criminal perceived? What should be learned from him? What accepted? What passed on? Is his life to be discarded or honored? That is the story of *Fences*, which we build to keep things and people out or in.

This brief casebook presents excerpts from published critical writings that argue for different interpretations of Troy's character. They should help you to enjoy and understand the play more fully by providing insights, raising questions, and challenging your own responses.

Six Critical Interpretations

Frank Rich, "Family Ties in Wilson's **Fences***"*

In his review of the first New York production of *Fences*, critic Frank Rich expresses admiration for the contradictory nature of the play's protagonist.

> To hear his wife tell it, Troy Maxson, the middle-aged Pittsburgh sanitation worker at the center of *Fences*, is "so big" that he fills up his tenement house just by walking through it. Needless to say, that description could also apply to James Earl Jones, the actor who has found what may be the best role of his career in August Wilson's new play.... But the remarkable stature of the character and of the performance is not a matter of sheer size. If Mr. Jones's Troy is a mountainous man prone to tyrannical eruptions of rage, he is also a dignified, delicate figure capable of cradling a tiny baby, of pleading gravely to his wife for understanding, of standing still to stare death unflinchingly in the eye. A black man, a free man, a descendant of slaves, a menial laborer, a father, a husband, a lover—Mr. Jones's Troy embraces all the contradictions of being black and male and American in his time.
>
> *New York Times*, 27 March 1987, C3

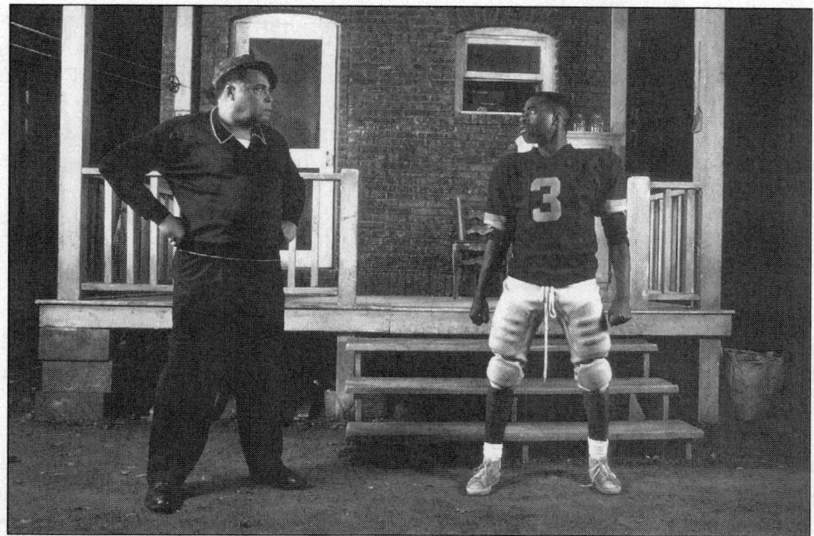

Troy (James Earl Jones) and Cory (Courtney Vance) in one of many standoffs. Photo from the original Broadway production of *Fences*.

Brent Staples, "Fences: *No Barrier to Emotion*"

Also responding to the contradictions in Troy's character, Brent Staples offers a more personal and less compassionate point of view.

Many of us who were born black and male in the late 1940s or early '50s were born into the poor families that would in time issue forth the nation's first substantial group of black intellectuals and professionals. We were born, too, into houses like the one in the set of *Fences*, a sagging-porched, red brick affair vacated by the first round of European immigrants who had come to what are now called rust-belt cities to labor in mills, shipyards and factories.

Our fathers had by circumstances become nearly impossible to love. They were hard men, tall in green work clothes—just like the ones James Earl Jones wears in the first act of this play. Theirs was the steely love of men who view the world from the angle of one who toils with his muscles. In their childhoods, they had never been guaranteed food or shelter; they clothed and fed us, and that, they left us to think, was love. They rarely kissed us. They watched us grow, were determined to mold us, to keep us out of jail, to see us out of their houses with jobs, at the very least....

When James Earl Jones enters into the set of *Fences*, tall, powerful, clad in my father's green, he carries a sack of potatoes brought from some farmer (my father brought bushels of tomatoes and corn). He is so familiar that I can faintly make out the odor of the man who has sweated all day. He, my father, seems to have come back over 20 years, and in this yard, among these familiar people, we go once again over this battle that seems never to be finished....

A once-stellar baseball player in the old Negro Leagues, [Troy] is embittered by the forces—time, racism—that have kept him from his sport. He is, too, a philandering, absentee father with children by three women (that we know of), and he is a powerful, often terrifying patriarch who, by turns, seems capable of breaking every bone in every character in the play, or of drawing them to his breast, to kiss them—male or female—lovingly.

New York Times, 5 April, 1987, 2.1

August Wilson, "Talking About Fences"

In a 1987 interview, the playwright himself offers a context for judging Troy's actions with sympathy and understanding.

Interviewer: In reading *Fences*, I came to view Troy more and more critically as the play progressed, sharing Rose's point of view. We see that Troy has been crippled by his father. That's being replayed in Troy's relationship with Cory. Do you think there's a way out of that cycle?

Wilson: Surely. First of all, we're all like our parents. The things we are taught early in life, how to respond to the world, our sense of morality—everything, we get from them. Now you can take that legacy and do with it anything you want to do. It's in your hands. Cory is Troy's son. How can he be Troy's son without sharing Troy's values? I was trying to get at why Troy made the choices he made, how they have influenced his values and how he attempts to pass those along to his son. Each generation gives the succeeding generation what they think they need. One question in the play is, "Are the tools we are given sufficient to compete in a world that is different from the one our parents knew?" I think they are—it's just that we have to do different things with the tools. That's all Troy has to give. Troy's flaw is that he does not recognize that the world was changing. That's because he spent fifteen years in a penitentiary.

In Their Own Words: Contemporary American Playwrights, 1988: 289

Christine Birdwell, "Death as a Fastball on the Outside Corner"

Dr. Christine Birdwell of Michigan State University explains Troy's character by focusing on his disappointing experience with the sport of baseball.

An abusive father, poverty, and the inevitable pain of aging stacked the odds against Troy, odds increased by Troy's sports experience. For Troy, who did not grow up playing baseball but came to it later in life, the sport was a salvation and a hope. It was (as music is for Lyons) a "way…to live in the world." But when the 1950s' "hot winds of change"…began to blow, they did not blow for Troy Maxson in Pittsburgh.…The long-delayed integration [of professional baseball] also brought about the demise of the Negro Leagues and of sandlot baseball, where men like Troy could have played past their prime years. Troy was not only too old for the majors, he had no other place to play. Part of the sacred American Trinity—Mom's apple pie, hot dogs, and baseball—had let them down.

Nevertheless, August Wilson shows us that as destructive as racial rejection has been to Troy, the man has made some bad plays on his own.... He was ultimately a man both made and broken by the conflicting elements of his life. Though outside forces fenced him out of professional status and economic security, his own choices fenced him out of the rest of the American Dream: family, and the comfort and security it provides.

Aethlon: The Journal of Sports Literature 8.1 (1990): 87–96.

Carla J. McDonough, "August Wilson: Performing Black Masculinity"

Looking at Troy through the lens of gender criticism, Professor Carla McDonough explicates his character in terms of his need to establish and bolster his masculine identity.

Troy's personality has been shaped by the harshness of his life: first in his contention with his father, a sharecropper in the South who drove Troy out on his own at age 14, and then in his contention with the white world. Although his responsibility to his current family drives Troy to work long hours at an undesirable job, the harshness he has cultivated in order to survive does not leave much room for him to express his love for his family. Troy has developed a pose of emotional detachment to buffer the disappointments in his life and to help him endure the brutal routine that keeps his family fed and clothed. His job means money for food and shelter, which he believes he owes his son and wife and which is a duty he fulfills while denying that it comes out of any sense of love. Troy prefers, instead, to define his actions as his responsibility. As he tells his son Cory, "It's my job. It's my responsibility! You understand that? A *man* got to take care of his family..."

Aside from his job, Troy's relationship with his wife Rose helps him to structure his identity along traditional gender lines.... [I]t becomes clear that Troy's sexuality is central to his manhood—so much so that he is willing to betray the wife he loves in order to prove to himself that he is still desirable and virile. Yet Troy still manages to evoke sympathy, for Wilson's portrait of him suggests that the hardness in his character results from the harshness of his life.

Staging Masculinity, 1997: 147–48.

Mary Ellen Snodgrass, "Fences"

In contrast to McDonough's judgment, Mary Ellen Snodgrass finds little about Troy Maxson to praise and admire.

Wilson establishes the price of perpetual malcontent and marital disloyalty by depicting Troy as a loner cut off from friends and family. After Troy's advancement to driver, Jim Bono shares less off-duty time with Troy, who must continue his payday drinking alone without the sustaining camaraderie of his work buddy. Troy's son knocks him to the ground for manhandling Rose and disclaims his fatherhood with a telling accusation, "You don't count around here no more." Rose withdraws from the toxic home environment into church work, taking with her Raynell, who cares more for her surrogate mother than for her biological father. To his shame, Troy relinquishes care of Gabe to a state institution as a way to reclaim half of his government check. The arrangement portrays Troy as heartless and mercenary.

Demeaned by difficult choices and self-aggrandizement, Troy seems unworthy of the reunited family that gathers for his funeral and burial or of the blessing that Gabe confers with his howl of farewell and primitive dance. Wilson exalts Rose to head of household and faithful nurturer as she shepherds the Maxson men to the church. To Cory, who battles internally much as his father did, she redeems the father figure posthumously: "I do know he meant to do more good than he meant to do harm."

August Wilson: A Literary Companion, 2004: 85

Responding to the Critics

1. What do you think of Troy? Which of the critics' views do you most agree with? Which do you disagree with? Write your own interpretation of Troy's character. You might begin by reacting to one or more of the critical viewpoints you just read.
2. Wilson says that "Troy's flaw is that he does not recognize that the world was changing. That's because he spent fifteen years in a penitentiary." How does this flaw affect Troy and his family?
3. Robert Brustein, theater critic and artistic director of Harvard's American Repertory Theater, has argued that "Wilson's larger purpose [in *Fences*] depends on his conviction that Troy's potential was stunted not [by] 'his own behavior' but by centuries of racist oppression." Do you agree? Do you think Wilson wants us to see Troy as a victim of racism? Or has Brustein missed or ignored other themes?

Ideas for Researched Writing

1. Actor James Earl Jones's interpretation of Troy Maxson in the 1987 Broadway production of *Fences* is often cited as one of the chief reasons for the play's success. Find out as much as you can about Jones's performance. How did he interpret the role? Write a paper in which you describe Jones's characterization of Troy and explain its contribution to the play's positive reception.
2. In the winter of 1997, Dr. Margaret Booker of Stanford University directed an all-Chinese production of *Fences* at the People's Art Theatre in Beijing, China. Research this production: Was it successful? How was it received? Share the results of your research with your class.

19

Writing About Culture

Works of literature that have been around for generations, yet still appeal to modern readers, are sometimes called *timeless.* However, each work did begin in a certain time, and the set of beliefs, attitudes, material conditions, and worldviews of that time influenced its creator. Meanwhile, the time setting in which you read literature affects how you read it. For example, Mark Twain's *Adventures of Huckleberry Finn* (1884) was a remarkably antiracist novel for its time; yet, readers today cringe at the use of the word *nigger* in the novel. While this outdated language doesn't change the egalitarian theme of the book, the setting we read it in today influences our reaction.

What Is Cultural Analysis?

Culture is a broad word including habits of thought, feeling, and behavior that were invented by humans, taught to other humans, and passed down to descendants, but not practiced among all human groups. It is often entwined with racial identity, ethnic category, and geographical background. Because culture changes from time to time, place to place, and social category to social category, we can speak about American culture of the 1990s, lesbian culture, deaf culture, Apostolic Christian culture, traditional Japanese culture, Victorian upper-class culture, 1950s middle-class U.S. culture, and so forth. A cultural approach to literature assumes that a work is part of its social context—both a product of its culture and a contribution to that culture. For example, we may read *Antigone* as a way of understanding ancient Greek culture, or we may study the culture of ancient Greece as a way of understanding *Antigone.* Because drama and fiction tend to present critiques of social and cultural problems, they are likely subjects for cultural analysis. Works that are specifically designed to attack or support some cultural value or practice (such as racism or apathy) are especially appropriate to such an approach. Many works, too, unwittingly embody elements of the culture that engendered them. The worlds of Henrik Ibsen, Ernest

Hemingway, Kate Chopin, and Walt Whitman were not like ours, and cultural analysis can throw light on the values and beliefs underlying their writings. The conditions of the world at the time of a literary creation affect how it presents themes, even when the themes are timeless.

Looking at Cultural Issues

In his play *M. Butterfly*, David Henry Hwang takes the cultural stereotype of the submissive Oriental female and turns it inside out. By combining elements of the opera *Madame Butterfly* with the true story of a French diplomat who carried on a lengthy affair with a Chinese actress without realizing that "she" was a man, the playwright has fashioned a complex drama about politics, race, gender, and sexuality.

David Henry Hwang 1957–

David Henry Hwang, the son of immigrant Chinese-American parents, was born in Los Angeles and educated at Stanford University. His first play, *F.O.B.*, which dramatizes the tensions between a "fresh off the boat" Chinese immigrant and his assimilated friends, won the 1981 Obie Award for best new off-Broadway play of the season. Hwang addressed similar issues in *The Dance and the Railroad* (1981) and *Rich Relations* (1986). *M. Butterfly* (1988), a brilliant critique of Western attitudes toward Asia, established Hwang as an important voice in American theater. It was a Broadway hit and claimed

John Lithgow as Rene Gallimard and B. D. Wong as Song Liling in the opening tableau of the Broadway production (1988) of *M. Butterfly*. (Martha Swope/Getty Images/Time Life Pictures.)

several major prizes, including the Tony Award for best play of the year. In 1993 it was made into a popular film starring Jeremy Irons.

M. Butterfly

CHARACTERS

RENE GALLIMARD	COMRADE CHIN / SUZUKI / SHU-FANG
SONG LILING	HELGA
MARC / MAN NO. 2 / CONSUL SHARPLESS	TOULON / MAN NO. 1 / JUDGE
RENEE / WOMAN AT PARTY / PINUP GIRL	DANCERS

PLAYWRIGHT'S NOTE:

This play was suggested by international newspaper accounts of a recent espionage trial. For purposes of dramatization, names have been changed, characters created, and incidents devised or altered, and this play does not purport to be a factual record of real events or real people.

A former French diplomat and a Chinese opera singer have been sentenced to six years in jail for spying for China after a two-day trial that traced a story of clandestine love and mistaken sexual identity....

Mr. Bouriscot was accused of passing information to China after he fell in love with Mr. Shi, whom he believed for twenty years to be a woman.

—*New York Times*, May 11, 1986

I could escape this feeling
With my China girl...

—David Bowie & Iggy Pop

TIME AND PLACE

The action of the play takes place in a Paris prison in the present, and, in recall, during the decade 1960–1970 in Beijing, and from 1966 to the present in Paris.

ACT I

SCENE I

M. GALLIMARD'S prison cell. Paris. 1988.

Lights fade up to reveal RENE GALLIMARD, *sixty-five, in a prison cell. He wears a comfortable bathrobe, and looks old and tired. The sparsely furnished cell contains a wooden crate, upon which sits a hot plate with a kettle, and a portable tape recorder.* GALLIMARD *sits on the crate staring at the recorder, a sad smile on his face.*

Upstage SONG, *who appears as a beautiful woman in traditional Chinese garb, dances a traditional piece from the Peking Opera, surrounded by the percussive clatter of Chinese music.*

Then, slowly, lights and sound cross-fade; the Chinese opera music dissolves into a Western opera, the "Love Duet" from Puccini's Madame Butterfly. *Song continues dancing, now to the Western accompaniment. Though her movements are the same, the difference in music now gives them a balletic quality.*

Gallimard *rises, and turns upstage towards the figure of* Song, *who dances without acknowledging him.*

Gallimard. Butterfly, Butterfly…

[He forces himself to turn away, as the image of Song *fades out, and talks to us.]*

Gallimard. The limits of my cell are as such: four-and-a-half meters by five. There's one window against the far wall; a door, very strong, to protect me from autograph hounds. I'm responsible for the tape recorder, the hot plate, and this charming coffee table.

When I want to eat, I'm marched off to the dining room—hot, steaming slop appears on my plate. When I want to sleep, the light bulb turns itself off—the work of fairies. It's an enchanted space I occupy. The French—we know how to run a prison.

But, to be honest, I'm not treated like an ordinary prisoner. Why? Because I'm a celebrity. You see, I make people laugh.

I never dreamed this day would arrive. I've never been considered witty or clever. In fact, as a young boy, in an informal poll among my grammar school classmates, I was voted "least likely to be invited to a party." It's a title I managed to hold on to for many years. Despite some stiff competition.

But now, how the tables turn! Look at me: the life of every social function in Paris. Paris? Why be modest: My fame has spread to Amsterdam, London, New York. Listen to them! In the world's smartest parlors, I'm the one who lifts their spirits!

[*With a flourish,* Gallimard *directs our attention to another part of the stage.*]

SCENE II

A party. 1988.

Lights go up on a chic-looking parlor, where a well-dressed trio, two men and one woman, make conversation. Gallimard *also remains lit; he observes them from his cell.*

Woman. And what of Gallimard?

Man 1. Gallimard?

Man 2. Gallimard!

Gallimard [*to us*]. You see? They're all determined to say my name, as if it were some new dance.

Woman. He still claims not to believe the truth.

Man 1. What? Still? Even since the trial?

Woman. Yes. Isn't it mad?

Man 2 [*laughing*]. He says…it was dark…and she was very modest!

[*The trio break into laughter.*]

Man 1. So—what? He never touched her with his hands?

Man 2. Perhaps he did, and simply misidentified the equipment. A compelling case for sex education in the schools.

Woman. To protect the National Security—the Church can't argue with that.

MAN 1. That's impossible! How could he not know?
MAN 2. Simple ignorance.
MAN 1. For twenty years?
MAN 2. Time flies when you're being stupid.
WOMAN. Well, I thought the French were ladies' men.
MAN 2. It seems Monsieur Gallimard was overly anxious to live up to his national reputation.
WOMAN. Well, he's not very good-looking.
MAN 1. No, he's not.
MAN 2. Certainly not.
WOMAN. Actually, I feel sorry for him.
MAN 2. A toast! To Monsieur Gallimard!
WOMAN. Yes! To Gallimard!
MAN 1. To Gallimard!
MAN 2. *Vive la différence!*

[They toast, laughing. Lights down on them.]

SCENE III

M. GALLIMARD's cell.

GALLIMARD [*smiling*]. You see? They toast me. I've become a patron saint of the socially inept. Can they really be so foolish? Men like that—they should be scratching at my door, begging to learn my secrets! For I, Rene Gallimard, you see, I have known, and been loved by . . . the Perfect Woman.

Alone in this cell, I sit night after night, watching our story play through my head, always searching for a new ending, one which redeems my honor, where she returns at last to my arms. And I imagine you—my ideal audience—who come to understand and even, perhaps just a little, to envy me.

[*He turns on his tape recorder. Over the house speakers, we hear the opening phrases of* Madame Butterfly.]

GALLIMARD. In order for you to understand what I did and why, I must introduce you to my favorite opera: *Madame Butterfly*. By Giacomo Puccini. First produced at La Scala, Milan, in 1904, it is now beloved throughout the Western world.

[*As* GALLIMARD *describes the opera, the tape segues in and out to sections he may be describing.*]

GALLIMARD. And why not? Its heroine, Cio-Cio-San, also known as Butterfly, is a feminine ideal, beautiful and brave. And its hero, the man for whom she gives up everything, is—[*He pulls out a naval officer's cap from under his crate, pops it on his head, and struts about*]—not very good-looking, not too bright, and pretty much a wimp: Benjamin Franklin Pinkerton of the U.S. Navy. As the curtain rises, he's just closed on two great bargains: one on a house, the other on a woman—call it a package deal.

Pinkerton purchased the rights to Butterfly for one hundred yen—in modern currency, equivalent to about . . . sixty-six cents. So, he's feeling pretty pleased with himself as Sharpless, the American consul, arrives to witness the marriage.

[MARC, *wearing an official cap to designate* SHARPLESS, *enters and plays the character.*]

SHARPLESS/MARC. Pinkerton!

PINKERTON/GALLIMARD. Sharpless! How's it hangin'? It's a great day, just great. Between my house, my wife, and the rickshaw ride in from town, I've saved nineteen cents just this morning.

SHARPLESS. Wonderful. I can see the inscription on your tombstone already: "I saved a dollar, here I lie." [*He looks around.*] Nice house.

PINKERTON. It's artistic. Artistic, don't you think? Like the way the shoji screens slide open to reveal the wet bar and disco mirror ball? Classy, huh? Great for impressing the chicks.

SHARPLESS. "Chicks"? Pinkerton, you're going to be a married man!

PINKERTON. Well, sort of.

SHARPLESS. What do you mean?

PINKERTON. This country—Sharpless, it is okay. You got all these geisha girls running around—

SHARPLESS. I know! I live here!

PINKERTON. Then, you know the marriage laws, right? I split for one month, it's annulled!

SHARPLESS. Leave it to you to read the fine print. Who's the lucky girl?

PINKERTON. Cio-Cio-San. Her friends call her Butterfly. Sharpless, she eats out of my hand!

SHARPLESS. She's probably very hungry.

PINKERTON. Not like American girls. It's true what they say about Oriental girls. They want to be treated bad!

SHARPLESS. Oh, please!

PINKERTON. It's true!

SHARPLESS. Are you serious about this girl?

PINKERTON. I'm marrying her, aren't I?

SHARPLESS. Yes—with generous trade-in terms.

PINKERTON. When I leave, she'll know what it's like to have loved a real man. And I'll even buy her a few nylons.

SHARPLESS. You aren't planning to take her with you?

PINKERTON. Huh? Where?

SHARPLESS. Home!

PINKERTON. You mean, America? Are you crazy? Can you see her trying to buy rice in St. Louis?

SHARPLESS. So, you're not serious.

[*Pause.*]

PINKERTON/GALLIMARD [*as* PINKERTON]. Consul, I am a sailor in port. [*As* GALLIMARD.] They then proceed to sing the famous duet, "The Whole World Over."

[*The duet plays on the speakers.* GALLIMARD, *as* PINKERTON, *lip-syncs his lines from the opera.*]

GALLIMARD. To give a rough translation: "The whole world over, the Yankee travels, casting his anchor wherever he wants. Life's not worth living unless he can win the hearts of the fairest maidens, then hotfoot it off the premises

ASAP." [*He turns towards* MARC.] In the preceding scene, I played Pinkerton, the womanizing cad, and my friend Marc from school… [MARC *bows grandly for our benefit.*] played Sharpless, the sensitive soul of reason. In life, however, our positions were usually—no, always—reversed.

SCENE IV

École Nationale.[1] Aix-en-Provence. 1947.

GALLIMARD. No, Marc, I think I'd rather stay home.
MARC. Are you crazy?! We are going to Dad's condo in Marseilles! You know what happened last time?
GALLIMARD. Of course I do.
MARC. Of course you don't! You never know.… They stripped, Rene!
GALLIMARD. Who stripped?
MARC. The girls!
GALLIMARD. Girls? Who said anything about girls?
MARC. Rene, we're a buncha university guys goin' up to the woods. What are we gonna do—talk philosophy?
GALLIMARD. What girls? Where do you get them?
MARC. Who cares? The point is, they come. On trucks. Packed in like sardines. The back flips open, babes hop out, we're ready to roll.
GALLIMARD. You mean, they just—?
MARC. Before you know it, every last one of them—they're stripped and splashing around my pool. There's no moon out, they can't see what's going on, their boobs are flapping, right? You close your eyes, reach out—it's grab bag, get it? Doesn't matter whose ass is between whose legs, whose teeth are sinking into who. You're just in there, going at it, eyes closed, on and on for as long as you can stand. [*Pause.*] Some fun, huh?
GALLIMARD. What happens in the morning?
MARC. In the morning, you're ready to talk some philosophy. [*Beat.*] So how 'bout it?
GALLIMARD. Marc, I can't… I'm afraid they'll say no—the girls. So I never ask.
MARC. You don't have to ask! That's the beauty—don't you see? They don't have to say yes. It's perfect for a guy like you, really.
GALLIMARD. You go ahead… I may come later.
MARC. Hey, Rene—it doesn't matter that you're clumsy and got zits—they're not looking!
GALLIMARD. Thank you very much.
MARC. Wimp.

[MARC *walks over to the other side of the stage, and starts waving and smiling at women in the audience.*]

GALLIMARD [*to us*]. We now return to my version of *Madame Butterfly* and the events leading to my recent conviction for treason.

[GALLIMARD *notices* MARC *making lewd gestures.*]

GALLIMARD. Marc, what are you doing?

---

[1]National School.

MARC. Huh? [*Sotto voce.*] Rene, there're a lotta great babes out there. They're probably lookin' at me and thinking, "What a dangerous guy."

GALLIMARD. Yes—how could they help but be impressed by your cool sophistication?

[GALLIMARD *pops the* SHARPLESS *cap on* MARC*'s head, and points him offstage.* MARC *exits, leering.*]

SCENE V

M. GALLIMARD's cell.

GALLIMARD. Next, Butterfly makes her entrance. We learn her age—fifteen...but very mature for her years.

[*Lights come up on the area where we saw* SONG *dancing at the top of the play. She appears there again, now dressed as Madame Butterfly, moving to the "Love Duet."* GALLIMARD *turns upstage slightly to watch, transfixed.*]

GALLIMARD. But as she glides past him, beautiful, laughing softly behind her fan, don't we who are men sigh with hope? We, who are not handsome, nor brave, nor powerful, yet somehow believe, like Pinkerton, that we deserve a Butterfly. She arrives with all her possessions in the folds of her sleeves, lays them all out, for her man to do with as he pleases. Even her life itself—she bows her head as she whispers that she's not even worth the hundred yen he paid for her. He's already given too much, when we know he's really had to give nothing at all.

[*Music and lights on* SONG *out.* GALLIMARD *sits at his crate.*]

GALLIMARD. In real life, women who put their total worth at less than sixty-six cents are quite hard to find. The closest we come is in the pages of these magazines. [*He reaches into his crate, pulls out a stack of girlie magazines, and begins flipping through them.*] Quite a necessity in prison. For three or four dollars, you get seven or eight women.

I first discovered these magazines at my uncle's house. One day, as a boy of twelve. The first time I saw them in his closet...all lined up—my body shook. Not with lust—no, with power. Here were women—a shelfful—who would do exactly as I wanted.

[*The "Love Duet" creeps in over the speakers. Special comes up, revealing, not* SONG *this time, but a* PINUP GIRL *in a sexy negligee, her back to us.* GALLIMARD *turns upstage and looks at her.*]

GIRL. I know you're watching me.

GALLIMARD. My throat...it's dry.

GIRL. I leave my blinds open every night before I go to bed.

GALLIMARD. I can't move.

GIRL. I leave my blinds open and the lights on.

GALLIMARD. I'm shaking. My skin is hot, but my penis is soft. Why?

GIRL. I stand in front of the window.

GALLIMARD. What is she going to do?

GIRL. I toss my hair, and I let my lips part...barely.

GALLIMARD. I shouldn't be seeing this. It's so dirty. I'm so bad.

GIRL. Then, slowly, I lift off my nightdress.

GALLIMARD. Oh, god. I can't believe it. I can't—
GIRL. I toss it to the ground.
GALLIMARD. Now, she's going to walk away. She's going to—
GIRL. I stand there, in the light, displaying myself.
GALLIMARD. No. She's—why is she naked?
GIRL. To you.
GALLIMARD. In front of a window? This is wrong. No—
GIRL. Without shame.
GALLIMARD. No, she must...like it.
GIRL. I like it.
GALLIMARD. She...she wants me to see.
GIRL. I want you to see.
GALLIMARD. I can't believe it! She's getting excited!
GIRL. I can't see you. You can do whatever you want.
GALLIMARD. I can't do a thing. Why?
GIRL. What would you like me to do...next?

[*Lights go down on her. Music off. Silence, as* GALLIMARD *puts away his magazines. Then he resumes talking to us.*]

GALLIMARD. Act Two begins with Butterfly staring at the ocean. Pinkerton's been called back to the U.S., and he's given his wife a detailed schedule of his plans. In the column marked "return date," he's written "when the robins nest." This failed to ignite her suspicions. Now, three years have passed without a peep from him. Which brings a response from her faithful servant, Suzuki.

[*Comrade* CHIN *enters, playing* SUZUKI.]

SUZUKI. Girl, he's a loser. What'd he ever give you? Nineteen cents and those ugly Day-Glo stockings? Look, it's finished! Kaput! Done! And you should be glad! I mean, the guy was a woofer! He tried before, you know—before he met you, he went down to geisha central and plunked down his spare change in front of the usual candidates—everyone else gagged! These are hungry prostitutes, and they were not interested, get the picture? Now, stop slathering when an American ship sails in, and let's make some bucks—I mean, yen! We are broke!

Now, what about Yamadori? Hey, hey—don't look away—the man is a prince—figuratively, and, what's even better, literally. He's rich, he's handsome, he says he'll die if you don't marry him—and he's even willing to overlook the little fact that you've been deflowered all over the place by a foreign devil. What do you mean, "But he's Japanese"? What do you think you are? You think you've been touched by the whitey god? He was a sailor with dirty hands!

[SUZUKI *stalks offstage.*]

GALLIMARD. She's also visited by Consul Sharpless, sent by Pinkerton on a minor errand.

[MARC *enters, as* SHARPLESS.]

SHARPLESS. I hate this job.
GALLIMARD. This Pinkerton—he doesn't show up personally to tell his wife he's abandoning her. No, he sends a government diplomat...at taxpayers' expense.

SHARPLESS. Butterfly? Butterfly? I have some bad—I'm going to be ill. Butterfly, I came to tell you—

GALLIMARD. Butterfly says she knows he'll return and if he doesn't she'll kill herself rather than go back to her own people. [*Beat.*] This causes a lull in the conversation.

SHARPLESS. Let's put it this way...

GALLIMARD. Butterfly runs into the next room, and returns holding—

[*Sound cue: a baby crying.* SHARPLESS, *"seeing" this, backs away.*]

SHARPLESS. Well, good. Happy to see things going so well. I suppose I'll be going now. Ta ta. Ciao. [*He turns away. Sound cue out.*] I hate this job.

[*He exits.*]

GALLIMARD. At that moment, Butterfly spots in the harbor an American ship—the *Abramo Lincoln!*

[*Music cue: "The Flower Duet."* SONG, *still dressed as Butterfly, changes into a wedding kimono, moving to the music.*]

GALLIMARD. This is the moment that redeems her years of waiting. With Suzuki's help, they cover the room with flowers—

[CHIN, *as* SUZUKI, *trudges onstage and drops a lone flower without much enthusiasm.*]

GALLIMARD. —and she changes into her wedding dress to prepare for Pinkerton's arrival.

[SUZUKI *helps Butterfly change.* HELGA *enters, and helps* GALLIMARD *change into a tuxedo.*]

GALLIMARD. I married a woman older than myself—Helga.

HELGA. My father was ambassador to Australia. I grew up among criminals and kangaroos.

GALLIMARD. Hearing that brought me to the altar—

[HELGA *exits.*]

GALLIMARD. —where I took a vow renouncing love. No fantasy woman would ever want me, so, yes, I would settle for a quick leap up the career ladder. Passion, I banish, and in its place—practicality!

But my vows had long since lost their charm by the time we arrived in China. The sad truth is that all men want a beautiful woman, and the uglier the man, the greater the want.

[SUZUKI *makes final adjustments of Butterfly's costume, as does* GALLIMARD *of his tuxedo.*]

GALLIMARD. I married late, at age thirty-one. I was faithful to my marriage for eight years. Until the day when, as a junior-level diplomat in puritanical Peking, in a parlor at the German ambassador's house, during the "Reign of a Hundred Flowers,"[2] I first saw her...singing the death scene from *Madame Butterfly.*

[SUZUKI *runs offstage.*]

---

[2]Name given to a brief period of free expression in China.

SCENE VI

German ambassador's house. Beijing. 1960.

The upstage special area now becomes a stage. Several chairs face upstage, representing seating for some twenty guests in the parlor. A few "diplomats"—RENEE, MARC, TOULON—*in formal dress enter and take seats.*

GALLIMARD *also sits down, but turns towards us and continues to talk. Orchestral accompaniment on the tape is now replaced by a simple piano.* SONG *picks up the death scene from the point where Butterfly uncovers the hara-kiri knife.*

GALLIMARD. The ending is pitiful. Pinkerton, in an act of great courage, stays home and sends his American wife to pick up Butterfly's child. The truth, long deferred, has come up to her door.

[SONG, *playing Butterfly, sings the lines from the opera in her own voice—which, though not classical, should be decent.*]

SONG. *"Con onor muore / chi non puo serbar / vita con onore."*

GALLIMARD [*simultaneously*]. "Death with honor / Is better than life / Life with dishonor."

[*The stage is illuminated; we are now completely within an elegant diplomat's residence.* SONG *proceeds to play out an abbreviated death scene. Everyone in the room applauds.* SONG, *shyly, takes her bows. Others in the room rush to congratulate her.* GALLIMARD *remains with us.*]

GALLIMARD. They say in opera the voice is everything. That's probably why I'd never before enjoyed opera. Here...here was a Butterfly with little or no voice—but she had the grace, the delicacy...I believed this girl. I believed her suffering. I wanted to take her in my arms—so delicate, even I could protect her, take her home, pamper her until she smiled.

[*Over the course of the preceding speech,* SONG *has broken from the upstage crowd and moved directly upstage of* GALLIMARD.]

SONG. Excuse me. Monsieur...?

[GALLIMARD *turns upstage, shocked.*]

GALLIMARD. Oh! Gallimard. Mademoiselle...? A beautiful...

SONG. Song Liling.

GALLIMARD. A beautiful performance.

SONG. Oh, please.

GALLIMARD. I usually—

SONG. You make me blush. I'm no opera singer at all.

GALLIMARD. I usually don't like *Butterfly*.

SONG. I can't blame you in the least.

GALLIMARD. I mean, the story—

SONG. Ridiculous.

GALLIMARD. I like the story, but...what?

SONG. Oh, you like it?

GALLIMARD. I...what I mean is, I've always seen it played by huge women in so much bad makeup.

SONG. Bad makeup is not unique to the West.

GALLIMARD. But, who can believe them?
SONG. And you believe me?
GALLIMARD. Absolutely. You were utterly convincing. It's the first time—
SONG. Convincing? As a Japanese woman? The Japanese used hundreds of our people for medical experiments during the war, you know. But I gather such an irony is lost on you.
GALLIMARD. No! I was about to say, it's the first time I've seen the beauty of the story.
SONG. Really?
GALLIMARD. Of her death. It's a . . . a pure sacrifice. He's unworthy, but what can she do? She loves him . . . so much. It's a very beautiful story.
SONG. Well, yes, to a Westerner.
GALLIMARD. Excuse me?
SONG. It's one of your favorite fantasies, isn't it? The submissive Oriental woman and the cruel white man.
GALLIMARD. Well, I didn't quite mean . . .
SONG. Consider it this way: what would you say if a blonde homecoming queen fell in love with a short Japanese businessman? He treats her cruelly, then goes home for three years, during which time she prays to his picture and turns down marriage from a young Kennedy. Then, when she learns he has remarried, she kills herself. Now, I believe you would consider this girl to be a deranged idiot, correct? But because it's an Oriental who kills herself for a Westerner—ah!—you find it beautiful.

[*Silence.*]

GALLIMARD. Yes . . . well . . . I see your point . . .
SONG. I will never do Butterfly again, Monsieur Gallimard. If you wish to see some real theater, come to the Peking Opera sometime. Expand your mind.

[SONG *walks offstage. Other guests exit with her.*]

GALLIMARD [*to us*]. So much for protecting her in my big Western arms.

SCENE VII

M. GALLIMARD's apartment. Beijing. 1960.
GALLIMARD *changes from his tux into a casual suit.* HELGA *enters.*

GALLIMARD. The Chinese are an incredibly arrogant people.
HELGA. They warned us about that in Paris, remember?
GALLIMARD. Even Parisians consider them arrogant. That's a switch.
HELGA. What is it that Madame Su says? "We are a very old civilization." I never know if she's talking about her country or herself.
GALLIMARD. I walk around here, all I hear every day, everywhere is how *old* this culture is. The fact that "old" may be synonymous with "senile" doesn't occur to them.
HELGA. You're not going to change them. "East is east, west is west, and . . ." whatever that guy said.
GALLIMARD. It's just that—silly. I met . . . at Ambassador Koening's tonight—you should've been there.
HELGA. Koening? Oh god, no. Did he enchant you all again with the history of Bavaria?

GALLIMARD. No. I met, I suppose, the Chinese equivalent of a diva. She's a singer in the Chinese opera.

HELGA. They have an opera, too? Do they sing in Chinese? Or maybe—in Italian?

GALLIMARD. Tonight, she did sing in Italian.

HELGA. How'd she manage that?

GALLIMARD. She must've been educated in the West before the Revolution. Her French is very good also. Anyway, she sang the death scene from *Madame Butterfly*.

HELGA. *Madame Butterfly!* Then I should have come. [*She begins humming, floating around the room as if dragging long kimono sleeves.*] Did she have a nice costume? I think it's a classic piece of music.

GALLIMARD. That's what *I* thought, too. Don't let her hear you say that.

HELGA. What's wrong?

GALLIMARD. Evidently the Chinese hate it.

HELGA. She hated it, but she performed it anyway? Is she perverse?

GALLIMARD. They hate it because the white man gets the girl. Sour grapes if you ask me.

HELGA. Politics again? Why can't they just hear it as a piece of beautiful music? So, what's in their opera?

GALLIMARD. I don't know. But, whatever it is, I'm sure it must be *old*.

[HELGA *exits.*]

SCENE VIII

Chinese opera house and the streets of Beijing. 1960.
The sound of gongs clanging fills the stage.

GALLIMARD. My wife's innocent question kept ringing in my ears. I asked around, but no one knew anything about the Chinese opera. It took four weeks, but my curiosity overcame my cowardice. This Chinese diva—this unwilling Butterfly—what did she do to make her so proud?

The room was hot, and full of smoke. Wrinkled faces, old women, teeth missing—a man with a growth on his neck, like a human toad. All smiling, pipes falling from their mouths, cracking nuts between their teeth, a live chicken pecking at my foot—all looking, screaming, gawking... at her.

[*The upstage area is suddenly hit with a harsh white light. It has become the stage for the Chinese opera performance. Two dancers enter, along with* SONG. GALLIMARD *stands apart, watching.* SONG *glides gracefully amidst the two dancers. Drums suddenly slam to a halt.* SONG *strikes a pose, looking straight at* GALLIMARD. *Dancers exit. Light change. Pause, then* SONG *walks right off the stage and straight up to* GALLIMARD.]

SONG. Yes. You. White man. I'm looking straight at you.

GALLIMARD. Me?

SONG. You see any other white men? It was too easy to spot you. How often does a man in my audience come in a tie?

[SONG *starts to remove her costume. Underneath, she wears simple baggy clothes. They are now backstage. The show is over.*]

SONG. So, you are an adventurous imperialist?

GALLIMARD. I...thought it would further my education.
SONG. It took you four weeks. Why?
GALLIMARD. I've been busy.
SONG. Well, education has always been undervalued in the West, hasn't it?
GALLIMARD [*laughing*]. I don't think that's true.
SONG. No, you wouldn't. You're a Westerner. How can you objectively judge your own values?
GALLIMARD. I think it's possible to achieve some distance.
SONG. Do you? [*Pause.*] It stinks in here. Let's go.
GALLIMARD. These are the smells of your loyal fans.
SONG. I love them for being my fans, I hate the smell they leave behind. I too can distance myself from my people. [*She looks around, then whispers in his ear.*] "Art for the masses" is a shitty excuse to keep artists poor. [*She pops a cigarette in her mouth.*] Be a gentleman, will you? And light my cigarette.

[GALLIMARD *fumbles for a match.*]

GALLIMARD. I don't...smoke.
SONG [*lighting her own*]. Your loss. Had you lit my cigarette, I might have blown a puff of smoke right between your eyes. Come.

[*They start to walk about the stage. It is a summer night on the Beijing streets. Sounds of the city play on the house speakers.*]

SONG. How I wish there were even a tiny café to sit in. With cappuccinos, and men in tuxedos and bad expatriate jazz.
GALLIMARD. If my history serves me correctly, you weren't even allowed into the clubs in Shanghai before the Revolution.
SONG. Your history serves you poorly, Monsieur Gallimard. True, there were signs reading "No dogs and Chinamen." But a woman, especially a delicate Oriental woman—we always go where we please. Could you imagine it otherwise? Clubs in China filled with pasty, big-thighed white women, while thousands of slender lotus blossoms wait just outside the door? Never. The clubs would be empty. [*Beat.*] We have always held a certain fascination for you Caucasian men, have we not?
GALLIMARD. But...that fascination is imperialist, or so you tell me.
SONG. Do you believe everything I tell you? Yes. It is always imperialist. But sometimes...sometimes, it is also mutual. Oh—this is my flat.
GALLIMARD. I didn't even—
SONG. Thank you. Come another time and we will further expand your mind.

[SONG *exits.* GALLIMARD *continues roaming the streets as he speaks to us.*]

GALLIMARD. What was that? What did she mean, "Sometimes...it is mutual"? Women do not flirt with me. And I normally can't talk to them. But tonight, I held up my end of the conversation.

SCENE IX

GALLIMARD's bedroom. Beijing. 1960.

[HELGA *enters.*]

HELGA. You didn't tell me you'd be home late.
GALLIMARD. I didn't intend to. Something came up.

Helga. Oh? Like what?

Gallimard. I went to the... to the Dutch ambassador's home.

Helga. Again?

Gallimard. There was a reception for a visiting scholar. He's writing a six-volume treatise on the Chinese revolution. We all gathered that meant he'd have to live here long enough to actually write six volumes, and we all expressed our deepest sympathies.

Helga. Well, I had a good night too. I went with the ladies to a martial arts demonstration. Some of those men—when they break those thick boards—[*She mimes fanning herself.*] whoo-whoo!

[Helga *exits. Lights dim.*]

Gallimard. I lied to my wife. Why? I've never had any reason to lie before. But what reason did I have tonight? I didn't do anything wrong. That night, I had a dream. Other people, I've been told, have dreams when angels appear. Or dragons, or Sophia Loren in a towel. In my dream, Marc from school appeared.

[Marc *enters, in a nightshirt and cap.*]

Marc. Rene! You met a girl!

[Gallimard *and* Marc *stumble down the Beijing streets. Night sounds over the speakers.*]

Gallimard. It's not that amazing, thank you.

Marc. No! It's so monumental, I heard about it halfway around the world in my sleep!

Gallimard. I've met girls before, you know.

Marc. Name one. I've come across time and space to congratulate you. [*He hands* Gallimard *a bottle of wine.*]

Gallimard. Marc, this is expensive.

Marc. On those rare occasions when you become a formless spirit, why not steal the best?

[Marc *pops open the bottle, begins to share it with* Gallimard.]

Gallimard. You embarrass me. She... there's no reason to think she likes me.

Marc. "Sometimes, it is mutual"?

Gallimard. Oh.

Marc. "Mutual"? "Mutual"? What does that mean?

Gallimard. You heard?

Marc. It means the money is in the bank, you only have to write the check!

Gallimard. I am a married man!

Marc. And an excellent one too. I cheated after... six months. Then again and again, until now—three hundred girls in twelve years.

Gallimard. I don't think we should hold that up as a model.

Marc. Of course not! My life—it is disgusting! Phooey! Phooey! But, you—you are the model husband.

Gallimard. Anyway, it's impossible. I'm a foreigner.

Marc. Ah, yes. She cannot love you, it is taboo, but something deep inside her heart... she cannot help herself... she must surrender to you. It is her destiny.

GALLIMARD. How do you imagine all this?

MARC. The same way you do. It's an old story. It's in our blood. They fear us, Rene. Their women fear us. And their men—their men hate us. And, you know something? They are all correct.

[*They spot a light in a window.*]

MARC. There! There, Rene!

GALLIMARD. It's her window.

MARC. Late at night—it burns. The light—it burns for you.

GALLIMARD. I won't look. It's not respectful.

MARC. We don't have to be respectful. We're foreign devils.

[*Enter* SONG, *in a sheer robe, her face completely swathed in black cloth. The "One Fine Day" aria creeps in over the speakers. With her back to us,* SONG *mimes attending to her toilette. Her robe comes loose, revealing her white shoulders.*]

MARC. All your life you've waited for a beautiful girl who would lay down for you. All your life you've smiled like a saint when it's happened to every other man you know. And you see them in magazines and you see them in movies. And you wonder, what's wrong with me? Will anyone beautiful ever want me? As the years pass, your hair thins and you struggle to hold on to even your hopes. Stop struggling, Rene. The wait is over. [*He exits.*]

GALLIMARD. Marc? Marc?

[*At that moment,* SONG, *her back still towards us, drops her robe. A second of her naked back, then a sound cue: a phone ringing, very loud. Blackout, followed in the next beat by a special up on the bedroom area, where a phone now sits.* GALLIMARD *stumbles across the stage and picks up the phone. Sound cue out. Over the course of his conversation, area lights fill in the vicinity of his bed. It is the following morning.*]

GALLIMARD. Yes? Hello?

SONG [*offstage*]. Is it very early?

GALLIMARD. Why, yes.

SONG [*offstage*]. How early?

GALLIMARD. It's . . . it's 5: 30. Why are you—?

SONG [*offstage*]. But it's light outside. Already.

GALLIMARD. It is. The sun must be in confusion today.

[*Over the course of* SONG'*s next speech, her upstage special comes up again. She sits in a chair, legs crossed, in a robe, telephone to her ear.*]

SONG. I waited until I saw the sun. That was as much discipline as I could manage for one night. Do you forgive me?

GALLIMARD. Of course . . . for what?

SONG. Then I'll ask you quickly. Are you really interested in the opera?

GALLIMARD. Why, yes. Yes I am.

SONG. Then come again next Thursday. I am playing *The Drunken Beauty.* May I count on you?

GALLIMARD. Yes. You may.

SONG. Perfect. Well, I must be getting to bed. I'm exhausted. It's been a very long night for me.

[SONG *hangs up; special on her goes off.* GALLIMARD *begins to dress for work.*]

SCENE X

SONG LILING's apartment. Beijing. 1960.

GALLIMARD. I returned to the opera that next week, and the week after that...she keeps our meetings so short—perhaps fifteen, twenty minutes at most. So I am left each week with a thirst which is intensified. In this way, fifteen weeks have gone by. I am starting to doubt the words of my friend Marc. But no, not really. In my heart, I know she has...an interest in me. I suspect this is her way. She is outwardly bold and outspoken, yet her heart is shy and afraid. It is the Oriental in her at war with her Western education.

SONG [*offstage*]. I will be out in an instant. Ask the servant for anything you want.

GALLIMARD. Tonight, I have finally been invited to enter her apartment. Though the idea is almost beyond belief, I believe she is afraid of me.

[GALLIMARD *looks around the room. He picks up a picture in a frame, studies it. Without his noticing,* SONG *enters, dressed elegantly in a black gown from the twenties. She stands in the doorway looking like Anna May Wong.*[3]]

SONG. That is my father.

GALLIMARD [*surprised*]. Mademoiselle Song...

[*She glides up to him, snatches away the picture.*]

SONG. It is very good that he did not live to see the Revolution. They would, no doubt, have made him kneel on broken glass. Not that he didn't deserve such a punishment. But he is my father. I would've hated to see it happen.

GALLIMARD. I'm very honored that you've allowed me to visit your home.

[SONG *curtseys.*]

SONG. Thank you. Oh! Haven't you been poured any tea?

GALLIMARD. I'm really not—

SONG [*to her offstage servant*]. Shu-Fang! Cha! Kwai-lah! [*To* GALLIMARD.] I'm sorry. You want everything to be perfect—

GALLIMARD. Please.

SONG. —and before the evening even begins—

GALLIMARD. I'm really not thirsty.

SONG. —it's ruined.

GALLIMARD [*sharply*]. Mademoiselle Song!

[SONG *sits down.*]

SONG. I'm sorry.

GALLIMARD. What are you apologizing for now?

[*Pause;* SONG *starts to giggle.*]

SONG. I don't know!

[GALLIMARD *laughs.*]

GALLIMARD. Exactly my point.

SONG. Oh, I am silly. Light-headed. I promise not to apologize for anything else tonight, do you hear me?

---

[3]Chinese American actress (1905–1961).

Gallimard. That's a good girl.

[Shu-Fang, *a servant girl, comes out with a tea tray and starts to pour.*]

Song [*to Shu-Fang*]. No! I'll pour myself for the gentleman!

[Shu-Fang, *staring at* Gallimard, *exits.*]

Gallimard. You have a beautiful home.
Song. No, I...I don't even know why I invited you up.
Gallimard. Well, I'm glad you did.

[Song *looks around the room.*]

Song. There is an element of danger to your presence.
Gallimard. Oh?
Song. You must know.
Gallimard. It doesn't concern me. We both know why I'm here.
Song. It doesn't concern me either. No...well perhaps...
Gallimard. What?
Song. Perhaps I am slightly afraid of scandal.
Gallimard. What are we doing?
Song. I'm entertaining you. In my parlor.
Gallimard. In France, that would hardly—
Song. France. France is a country living in the modern era. Perhaps even ahead of it. China is a nation whose soul is firmly rooted two thousand years in the past. What I do, even pouring the tea for you now...it has...implications. The walls and windows say so. Even my own heart, strapped inside this Western dress...even it says things—things I don't care to hear.

[Song *hands* Gallimard *a cup of tea.* Gallimard *puts his hand over both the teacup and* Song*'s hand.*]

Gallimard. This is a beautiful dress.
Song. Don't.
Gallimard. What?
Song. I don't even know if it looks right on me.
Gallimard. Believe me—
Song. You are from France. You see so many beautiful women.
Gallimard. France? Since when are the European women—?
Song. Oh! What am I trying to do, anyway?!

[Song *runs to the door, composes herself, then turns towards* Gallimard.]

Song. Monsieur Gallimard, perhaps you should go.
Gallimard. But...why?
Song. There's something wrong about this.
Gallimard. I don't see what.
Song. I feel...I am not myself.
Gallimard. No. You're nervous.
Song. Please. Hard as I try to be modern, to speak like a man, to hold a Western woman's strong face up to my own...in the end, I fail. A small, frightened heart beats too quickly and gives me away. Monsieur Gallimard, I'm a Chinese girl. I've never...never invited a man up to my flat before. The forwardness of my actions makes my skin burn.

GALLIMARD. What are you afraid of? Certainly not me, I hope.
SONG. I'm a modest girl.
GALLIMARD. I know. And very beautiful. [*He touches her hair.*]
SONG. Please—go now. The next time you see me, I shall again be myself.
GALLIMARD. I like you the way you are right now.
SONG. You are a cad.
GALLIMARD. What do you expect? I'm a foreign devil.

[GALLIMARD *walks downstage.* SONG *exits.*]

GALLIMARD [*to us*]. Did you hear the way she talked about Western women? Much differently than the first night. She does—she feels inferior to them—and to me.

SCENE XI

The French embassy. Beijing. 1960.
GALLIMARD *moves towards a desk.*

GALLIMARD. I determined to try an experiment. In *Madame Butterfly*, Cio-Cio-San fears that the Western man who catches a butterfly will pierce its heart with a needle, then leave it to perish. I began to wonder: had I, too, caught a butterfly who would writhe on a needle?

[MARC *enters, dressed as a bureaucrat, holding a stack of papers. As* GALLIMARD *speaks,* MARC *hands papers to him. He peruses, then signs, stamps, or rejects them.*]

GALLIMARD. Over the next five weeks, I worked like a dynamo. I stopped going to the opera, I didn't phone or write her. I knew this little flower was waiting for me to call, and, as I wickedly refused to do so, I felt for the first time that rush of power—the absolute power of a man.

[MARC *continues acting as the bureaucrat, but he now speaks as himself.*]

MARC. Rene! It's me.
GALLIMARD. Marc—I hear your voice everywhere now. Even in the midst of work.
MARC. That's because I'm watching you—all the time.
GALLIMARD. You were always the most popular guy in school.
MARC. Well, there's no guarantee of failure in life like happiness in high school. Somehow I knew I'd end up in the suburbs working for Renault and you'd be in the Orient picking exotic women off the trees. And they say there's no justice.
GALLIMARD. That's why you were my friend?
MARC. I gave you a little of my life, so that now you can give me some of yours. [*Pause.*] Remember Isabelle?
GALLIMARD. Of course I remember! She was my first experience.
MARC. We all wanted to ball her. But she only wanted me.
GALLIMARD. I had her.
MARC. Right. You balled her.
GALLIMARD. You were the only one who ever believed me.
MARC. Well, there's a good reason for that. [*Beat.*] C'mon. You must've guessed.
GALLIMARD. You told me to wait in the bushes by the cafeteria that night. The next thing I knew, she was on me. Dress up in the air.

MARC. She never wore underwear.
GALLIMARD. My arms were pinned to the dirt.
MARC. She loved the superior position. A girl ahead of her time.
GALLIMARD. I looked up, and there was this woman... bouncing up and down on my loins.
MARC. Screaming, right?
GALLIMARD. Screaming, and breaking off the branches all around me, and pounding my butt up and down into the dirt.
MARC. Huffing and puffing like a locomotive.
GALLIMARD. And in the middle of all this, the leaves were getting into my mouth, my legs were losing circulation, I thought, "God. So this is *it*?"
MARC. You thought that?
GALLIMARD. Well, I was worried about my legs falling off.
MARC. You didn't have a good time?
GALLIMARD. No, that's not what I—I had a great time!
MARC. You're sure?
GALLIMARD. Yeah. Really.
MARC. 'Cuz I wanted you to have a good time.
GALLIMARD. I did.

[*Pause.*]

MARC. Shit. [*Pause.*] When all is said and done, she was kind of a lousy lay, wasn't she? I mean, there was a lot of energy there, but you never knew what she was doing with it. Like when she yelled "I'm coming!"—hell, it was so loud, you wanted to go, "Look, it's not that big a deal."
GALLIMARD. I got scared. I thought she meant someone was actually coming. [*Pause.*] But, Marc?
MARC. What?
GALLIMARD. Thanks.
MARC. Oh, don't mention it.
GALLIMARD. It was my first experience.
MARC. Yeah. You got her.
GALLIMARD. I got her.
MARC. Wait! Look at that letter again!

[GALLIMARD *picks up one of the papers he's been stamping, and rereads it.*]

GALLIMARD [*to us*]. After six weeks, they began to arrive. The letters.

[*Upstage special on* SONG, *as Madame Butterfly. The scene is underscored by the "Love Duet."*]

SONG. Did we fight? I do not know. Is the opera no longer of interest to you? Please come—my audiences miss the white devil in their midst.

[GALLIMARD *looks up from the letter, towards us.*]

GALLIMARD [*to us*]. A concession, but much too dignified. [*Beat; he discards the letter.*] I skipped the opera again that week to complete a position paper on trade.

[*The bureaucrat hands him another letter.*]

SONG. Six weeks have passed since last we met. Is this your practice—to leave friends in the lurch? Sometimes I hate you, sometimes I hate myself, but always I miss you.

GALLIMARD [*to us*]. Better, but I don't like the way she calls me "friend." When a woman calls a man her "friend," she's calling him a eunuch or a homosexual. [*Beat; he discards the letter.*] I was absent from the opera for the seventh week, feeling a sudden urge to clean out my files.

[*Bureaucrat hands him another letter.*]

SONG. Your rudeness is beyond belief. I don't deserve this cruelty. Don't bother to call. I'll have you turned away at the door.

GALLIMARD [*to us*]. I didn't. [*He discards the letter; bureaucrat hands him another.*] And then finally, the letter that concluded my experiment.

SONG. I am out of words. I can hide behind dignity no longer. What do you want? I have already given you my shame.

[GALLIMARD *gives the letter back to* MARC, *slowly. Special on* SONG *fades out.*]

GALLIMARD [*to us*]. Reading it, I became suddenly ashamed. Yes, my experiment had been a success. She was turning on my needle. But the victory seemed hollow.

MARC. Hollow?! Are you crazy?

GALLIMARD. Nothing, Marc. Please go away.

MARC [*exiting, with papers*]. Haven't I taught you anything?

GALLIMARD. "I have already given you my shame." I had to attend a reception that evening. On the way, I felt sick. If there is a God, surely he would punish me now. I had finally gained power over a beautiful woman, only to abuse it cruelly. There must be justice in the world. I had the strange feeling that the axe would fall this very evening.

SCENE XII

Ambassador Toulon's residence. Beijing. 1960.

Sound cue: party noises. Light change. We are now in a spacious residence. TOULON, *the French ambassador, enters and taps* GALLIMARD *on the shoulder.*

TOULON. Gallimard? Can I have a word? Over here.

GALLIMARD [*to us*]. Manuel Toulon. French ambassador to China. He likes to think of us all as his children. Rather like God.

TOULON. Look, Gallimard, there's not much to say. I've liked you. From the day you walked in. You were no leader, but you were tidy and efficient.

GALLIMARD. Thank you, sir.

TOULON. Don't jump the gun. Okay, our needs in China are changing. It's embarrassing that we lost Indochina. Someone just wasn't on the ball there. I don't mean you personally, of course.

GALLIMARD. Thank you, sir.

TOULON. We're going to be doing a lot more information-gathering in the future. The nature of our work here is changing. Some people are just going to have to go. It's nothing personal.

GALLIMARD. Oh.

TOULON. Want to know a secret? Vice-Consul LeBon is being transferred.

GALLIMARD [*to us*]. My immediate superior!

TOULON. And most of his department.
GALLIMARD [*to us*]. Just as I feared! God has seen my evil heart—
TOULON. But not you.
GALLIMARD [*to us*].—and he's taking her away just as... [*To* TOULON.] Excuse me, sir?
TOULON. Scare you? I think I did. Cheer up, Gallimard. I want you to replace LeBon as vice-consul.
GALLIMARD. You—? Yes, well, thank you, sir.
TOULON. Anytime.
GALLIMARD. I... accept with great humility.
TOULON. Humility won't be part of the job. You're going to coordinate the revamped intelligence division. Want to know a secret? A year ago, you would've been out. But the past few months, I don't know how it happened, you've become this new aggressive, confident... thing. And they also tell me you get along with the Chinese. So I think you're a lucky man, Gallimard. Congratulations.

[*They shake hands.* TOULON *exits. Party noises out.* GALLIMARD *stumbles across a darkened stage.*]

GALLIMARD. Vice-consul? Impossible! As I stumbled out of the party, I saw it written across the sky: There is no God. Or, no—say that there is a God. But that God... understands. Of course! God who creates Eve to serve Adam, who blesses Solomon with his harem but ties Jezebel to a burning bed[4]—that God is a man. And he understands! At age thirty-nine, I was suddenly initiated into the way of the world.

SCENE XIII

SONG LILING's apartment. Beijing. 1960.

SONG *enters, in a sheer dressing gown.*

SONG. Are you crazy?
GALLIMARD. Mademoiselle Song—
SONG. To come here—at this hour? After... after eight weeks?
GALLIMARD. It's the most amazing—
SONG. You bang on my door? Scare my servants, scandalize the neighbors?
GALLIMARD. I've been promoted. To vice-consul.

[*Pause.*]

SONG. And what is that supposed to mean to me?
GALLIMARD. Are you my Butterfly?
SONG. What are you saying?
GALLIMARD. I've come tonight for an answer: are you my Butterfly?
SONG. Don't you know already?
GALLIMARD. I want you to say it.
SONG. I don't want to say it.
GALLIMARD. So, that is your answer?
SONG. You know how I feel about—
GALLIMARD. I do remember one thing.

---

[4]Biblical allusions; see Genesis 2:18–25, I Kings 11:1–8, and II Kings 9:30–37.

SONG. What?
GALLIMARD. In the letter I received today.
SONG. Don't.
GALLIMARD. "I have already given you my shame."
SONG. It's enough that I even wrote it.
GALLIMARD. Well, then—
SONG. I shouldn't have it splashed across my face.
GALLIMARD. —if that's all true—
SONG. Stop!
GALLIMARD. Then what is one more short answer?
SONG. I don't want to!
GALLIMARD. Are you my Butterfly? [*Silence; he crosses the room and begins to touch her hair.*] I want from you honesty. There should be nothing false between us. No false pride.

[*Pause.*]

SONG. Yes, I am. I am your Butterfly.
GALLIMARD. Then let me be honest with you. It is because of you that I was promoted tonight. You have changed my life forever. My little Butterfly, there should be no more secrets: I love you.

[*He starts to kiss her roughly. She resists slightly.*]

SONG. No…no…gently…please, I've never…
GALLIMARD. No?
SONG. I've tried to appear experienced, but…the truth is…no.
GALLIMARD. Are you cold?
SONG. Yes. Cold.
GALLIMARD. Then we will go very, very slowly.

[*He starts to caress her; her gown begins to open.*]

SONG. No…let me…keep my clothes…
GALLIMARD. But…
SONG. Please…it all frightens me. I'm a modest Chinese girl.
GALLIMARD. My poor little treasure.
SONG. I am your treasure. Though inexperienced, I am not…ignorant. They teach us things, our mothers, about pleasing a man.
GALLIMARD. Yes?
SONG. I'll do my best to make you happy. Turn off the lights.

[GALLIMARD *gets up and heads for a lamp.* SONG, *propped up on one elbow, tosses her hair back and smiles.*]

SONG. Monsieur Gallimard?
GALLIMARD. Yes, Butterfly?
SONG. "*Vieni, vieni!*"
GALLIMARD. "Come, darling."
SONG. "*Ah! Dolce notte!*"
GALLIMARD. "Beautiful night."
SONG. "*Tutto estatico d'amor ride il ciel!*"
GALLIMARD. "All ecstatic with love, the heavens are filled with laughter."

[*He turns off the lamp. Blackout.*]

ACT II

SCENE I

M. GALLIMARD's cell. Paris. 1988.

Lights up on GALLIMARD. *He sits in his cell, reading from a leaflet.*

GALLIMARD. This, from a contemporary critic's commentary on Madame Butterfly: "Pinkerton suffers from... being an obnoxious bounder whom every man in the audience itches to kick." Bully for us men in the audience! Then, in the same note: "Butterfly is the most irresistibly appealing of Puccini's 'Little Women.' Watching the succession of her humiliations is like watching a child under torture." [*He tosses the pamphlet over his shoulder.*] I suggest that, while we men may all want to kick Pinkerton, very few of us would pass up the opportunity to *be* Pinkerton.

[GALLIMARD *moves out of his cell.*]

SCENE II

GALLIMARD and Butterfly's flat. Beijing. 1960.

We are in a simple but well-decorated parlor. GALLIMARD *moves to sit on a sofa, while* SONG, *dressed in a chong sam,*[5] *enters and curls up at his feet.*

GALLIMARD [*to us*]. We secured a flat on the outskirts of Peking. Butterfly, as I was calling her now, decorated our "home" with Western furniture and Chinese antiques. And there, on a few stolen afternoons or evenings each week, Butterfly commenced her education.

SONG. The Chinese men—they keep us down.

GALLIMARD. Even in the "New Society"?

SONG. In the "New Society," we are all kept ignorant equally. That's one of the exciting things about loving a Western man. I know you are not threatened by a woman's education.

GALLIMARD. I'm no saint, Butterfly.

SONG. But you come from a progressive society.

GALLIMARD. We're not always reminding each other how "old" we are, if that's what you mean.

SONG. Exactly. We Chinese—once, I suppose, it is true, we ruled the world. But so what? How much more exciting to be part of the society ruling the world today. Tell me—what's happening in Vietnam?

GALLIMARD. Oh, Butterfly—you want me to bring my work home?

SONG. I want to know what you know. To be impressed by my man. It's not the particulars so much as the fact that you're making decisions which change the shape of the world.

GALLIMARD. Not the world. At best, a small corner.

[TOULON *enters, and sits at a desk downstage.*]

[5]Tight-fitting dress with slits in the sides of the skirt.

SCENE III

French embassy. Beijing. 1961.

GALLIMARD *moves downstage, to* TOULON*'s desk.* SONG *remains upstage, watching.*

TOULON. And a more troublesome corner is hard to imagine.

GALLIMARD. So, the Americans plan to begin bombing?

TOULON. This is very secret, Gallimard: yes. The Americans don't have an embassy here. They're asking us to be their eyes and ears. Say Jack Kennedy signed an order to bomb North Vietnam, Laos. How would the Chinese react?

GALLIMARD. I think the Chinese will squawk—

TOULON. Uh-huh.

GALLIMARD. —but, in their hearts, they don't even like Ho Chi Minh.[6]

[*Pause.*]

TOULON. What a bunch of jerks. Vietnam was *our* colony. Not only didn't the Americans help us fight to keep them, but now, seven years later, they've come back to grab the territory for themselves. It's very irritating.

GALLIMARD. With all due respect, sir, why should the Americans have won our war for us back in 'fifty-four if we didn't have the will to win it ourselves?

TOULON. You're kidding, aren't you?

[*Pause.*]

GALLIMARD. The Orientals simply want to be associated with whoever shows the most strength and power. You live with the Chinese, sir. Do you think they like Communism?

TOULON. I live in China. Not with the Chinese.

GALLIMARD. Well, I—

TOULON. *You* live with the Chinese.

GALLIMARD. Excuse me?

TOULON. I can't keep a secret.

GALLIMARD. What are you saying?

TOULON. Only that I'm not immune to gossip. So, you're keeping a native mistress? Don't answer. It's none of my business. [*Pause.*] I'm sure she must be gorgeous.

GALLIMARD. Well…

TOULON. I'm impressed. You had the stamina to go out into the streets and hunt one down. Some of us have to be content with the wives of the expatriate community.

GALLIMARD. I do feel…fortunate.

TOULON. So, Gallimard, you've got the inside knowledge—what *do* the Chinese think?

GALLIMARD. Deep down, they miss the old days. You know, cappuccinos, men in tuxedos—

TOULON. So what do we tell the Americans about Vietnam?

GALLIMARD. Tell them there's a natural affinity between the West and the Orient.

[6]President of North Vietnam, 1945–1969.

Toulon. And that you speak from experience?

Gallimard. The Orientals are people too. They want the good things we can give them. If the Americans demonstrate the will to win, the Vietnamese will welcome them into a mutually beneficial union.

Toulon. I don't see how the Vietnamese can stand up to American firepower.

Gallimard. Orientals will always submit to a greater force.

Toulon. I'll note your opinions in my report. The Americans always love to hear how "welcome" they'll be. [*He starts to exit.*]

Gallimard. Sir?

Toulon. Mmmm?

Gallimard. This . . . rumor you've heard.

Toulon. Uh-huh?

Gallimard. How . . . widespread do you think it is?

Toulon. It's only widespread within this embassy. Where nobody talks because everybody is guilty. We were worried about you, Gallimard. We thought you were the only one here without a secret. Now you go and find a lotus blossom . . . and top us all. [*He exits.*]

Gallimard [*to us*]. Toulon knows! And he approves! I was learning the benefits of being a man. We form our own clubs, sit behind thick doors, smoke—and celebrate the fact that we're still boys. [*He starts to move upstage, towards* Song.] So, over the—

[*Suddenly* Comrade Chin *enters.* Gallimard *backs away.*]

Gallimard [*to* Song]. No! Why does she have to come in?

Song. Rene, be sensible. How can they understand the story without her? Now, don't embarrass yourself.

[Gallimard *moves down center.*]

Gallimard [*to us*]. Now, you will see why my story is so amusing to so many people. Why they snicker at parties in disbelief. Please—try to understand it from my point of view. We are all prisoners of our time and place. [*He exits.*]

SCENE IV

Gallimard and Butterfly's flat. Beijing. 1961.

Song [*to us*]. 1961. The flat Monsieur Gallimard rented for us. An evening after he has gone.

Chin. Okay, see if you can find out when the Americans plan to start bombing Vietnam. If you can find out what cities, even better.

Song. I'll do my best, but I don't want to arouse his suspicions.

Chin. Yeah, sure, of course. So, what else?

Song. The Americans will increase troops in Vietnam to 170,000 soldiers with 120,000 militia and 11,000 American advisors.

Chin [*writing*]. Wait, wait, 120,000 militia and—

Song. —11,000 American—

Chin. —American advisors. [*Beat.*] How do you remember so much?

Song. I'm an actor.

Chin. Yeah. [*Beat.*] Is that how come you dress like that?

Song. Like what, Miss Chin?

CHIN. Like that dress! You're wearing a dress. And every time I come here, you're wearing a dress. Is that because you're an actor? Or what?
SONG. It's a . . . disguise, Miss Chin.
CHIN. Actors, I think they're all weirdos. My mother tells me actors are like gamblers or prostitutes or—
SONG. It helps me in my assignment.

[*Pause.*]

CHIN. You're not gathering information in any way that violates Communist Party principles, are you?
SONG. Why would I do that?
CHIN. Just checking. Remember: when working for the Great Proletarian State, you represent our Chairman Mao in every position you take.
SONG. I'll try to imagine the Chairman taking my positions.
CHIN. We all think of him this way. Good-bye, comrade. [*She starts to exit.*] Comrade?
SONG. Yes?
CHIN. Don't forget: there is no homosexuality in China!
SONG. Yes, I've heard.
CHIN. Just checking. [*She exits.*]
SONG [*to us*]. What passes for a woman in modern China.

[GALLIMARD *sticks his head out from the wings.*]

GALLIMARD. Is she gone?
SONG. Yes, Rene. Please continue in your own fashion.

SCENE V

Beijing. 1961–1963.

GALLIMARD *moves to the couch where* SONG *still sits. He lies down in her lap, and she strokes his forehead.*

GALLIMARD [*to us*]. And so, over the years 1961, '62, '63, we settled into our routine, Butterfly and I. She would always have prepared a light snack and then, ever so delicately, and only if I agreed, she would start to pleasure me. With her hands, her mouth . . . too many ways to explain, and too sad, given my present situation. But mostly we would talk. About my life. Perhaps there is nothing more rare than to find a woman who passionately listens.

[SONG *remains upstage, listening, as* HELGA *enters and plays a scene downstage with* GALLIMARD.]

HELGA. Rene, I visited Dr. Bolleart this morning.
GALLIMARD. Why? Are you ill?
HELGA. No, no. You see, I wanted to ask him . . . that question we've been discussing.
GALLIMARD. And I told you, it's only a matter of time. Why did you bring a doctor into this? We just have to keep trying—like a crapshoot, actually.
HELGA. I went, I'm sorry. But listen: he says there's nothing wrong with me.
GALLIMARD. You see? Now, will you stop—?
HELGA. Rene, he says he'd like you to go in and take some tests.
GALLIMARD. Why? So he can find there's nothing wrong with both of us?

HELGA. Rene, I don't ask for much. One trip! One visit! And then, whatever you want to do about it—you decide.

GALLIMARD. You're assuming he'll find something defective!

HELGA. No! Of course not! Whatever he finds—if he finds nothing, we decide what to do about nothing! But go!

GALLIMARD. If he finds nothing, we keep trying. Just like we do now.

HELGA. But at least we'll know! [*Pause.*] I'm sorry. [*She starts to exit.*]

GALLIMARD. Do you really want me to see Dr. Bolleart?

HELGA. Only if you want a child, Rene. We have to face the fact that time is running out. Only if you want a child.

[*She exits.*]

GALLIMARD [*to* SONG]. I'm a modern man, Butterfly. And yet, I don't want to go. It's the same old voodoo. I feel like God himself is laughing at me if I can't produce a child.

SONG. You men of the West—you're obsessed by your odd desire for equality. Your wife can't give you a child, and *you're* going to the doctor?

GALLIMARD. Well, you see, she's already gone.

SONG. And because this incompetent can't find the defect, you now have to subject yourself to him? It's unnatural.

GALLIMARD. Well, what is the "natural" solution?

SONG. In Imperial China, when a man found that one wife was inadequate, he turned to another—to give him his son.

GALLIMARD. What do you—? I can't . . . marry you, yet.

SONG. Please. I'm not asking you to be my husband. But I am already your wife.

GALLIMARD. Do you want to . . . have my child?

SONG. I thought you'd never ask.

GALLIMARD. But, your career . . . your—

SONG. Phooey on my career! That's your Western mind, twisting itself into strange shapes again. Of course I love my career. But what would I love most of all? To feel something inside me—day and night—something I know is yours. [*Pause.*] Promise me . . . you won't go to this doctor. Who is this Western quack to set himself as judge over the man I love? I know who is a man, and who is not.

[*She exits.*]

GALLIMARD [*to us*]. Dr. Bolleart? Of course I didn't go. What man would?

SCENE VI

Beijing. 1963.

Party noises over the house speakers. RENEE *enters, wearing a revealing gown.*

GALLIMARD. 1963. A party at the Austrian embassy. None of us could remember the Austrian ambassador's name, which seemed somehow appropriate. [*To Renee.*] So, I tell the Americans, Diem[7] must go. The U.S. wants to be respected by the Vietnamese, and yet they're propping up this nobody seminarian as her president. A man whose claim to fame is his sister-in-law imposing fanatic "moral

---

[7]Ngo Dinh Diem (1901–1963), president of South Vietnam, 1955–1963; assassinated in a U.S.-supported coup.

order" campaigns? Oriental women—when they're good, they're very good, but when they're bad, they're Christians.

RENEE. Yeah.

GALLIMARD. And what do you do?

RENEE. I'm a student. My father exports a lot of useless stuff to the Third World.

GALLIMARD. How useless?

RENEE. You know. Squirt guns, confectioner's sugar, Hula Hoops...

GALLIMARD. I'm sure they appreciate the sugar.

RENEE. I'm here for two years to study Chinese.

GALLIMARD. Two years!

RENEE. That's what everybody says.

GALLIMARD. When did you arrive?

RENEE. Three weeks ago.

GALLIMARD. And?

RENEE. I like it. It's primitive, but...well, this is the place to learn Chinese, so here I am.

GALLIMARD. Why Chinese?

RENEE. I think it'll be important someday.

GALLIMARD. You do?

RENEE. Don't ask me when, but...that's what I think.

GALLIMARD. Well, I agree with you. One hundred percent. That's very farsighted.

RENEE. Yeah. Well of course, my father thinks I'm a complete weirdo.

GALLIMARD. He'll thank you someday.

RENEE. Like when the Chinese start buying Hula Hoops?

GALLIMARD. There're a billion bellies out there.

RENEE. And if they end up taking over the world—well, then I'll be lucky to know Chinese too, right?

[*Pause.*]

GALLIMARD. At this point, I don't see how the Chinese can possibly take—

RENEE. You know what I *don't* like about China?

GALLIMARD. Excuse me? No—what?

RENEE. Nothing to do at night.

GALLIMARD. You come to parties at embassies like everyone else.

RENEE. Yeah, but they get out at ten. And then what?

GALLIMARD. I'm afraid the Chinese idea of a dance hall is a dirt floor and a man with a flute.

RENEE. Are you married?

GALLIMARD. Yes. Why?

RENEE. You wanna...fool around?

[*Pause.*]

GALLIMARD. Sure.

RENEE. I'll wait for you outside. What's your name?

GALLIMARD. Gallimard. Rene.

RENEE. Weird. I'm Renee too. [*She exits.*]

GALLIMARD [*to us*]. And so, I embarked on my first extra-extramarital affair. Renee was picture perfect. With a body like those girls in the magazines. If I put a tissue paper over my eyes, I wouldn't have been able to tell the difference. And it was exciting to be with someone who wasn't afraid to be seen completely naked. But is it possible for a woman to be *too* uninhibited, *too* willing, so as to seem almost too... masculine?

[*Chuck Berry blares from the house speakers, then comes down in volume as* RENEE *enters, toweling her hair.*]

RENEE. You have a nice weenie.

GALLIMARD. What?

RENEE. Penis. You have a nice penis.

GALLIMARD. Oh. Well, thank you. That's very...

RENEE. What—can't take a compliment?

GALLIMARD. No, it's very... reassuring.

RENEE. But most girls don't come out and say it, huh?

GALLIMARD. And also... what did you call it?

RENEE. Oh. Most girls don't call it a "weenie," huh?

GALLIMARD. It sounds very—

RENEE. Small, I know.

GALLIMARD. I was going to say, "young."

RENEE. Yeah. Young, small, same thing. Most guys are pretty, uh, sensitive about that. Like, you know, I had a boyfriend back home in Denmark. I got mad at him once and called him a little weeniehead. He got so mad! He said at least I should call him a great big weeniehead.

GALLIMARD. I suppose I just say "penis."

RENEE. Yeah. That's pretty clinical. There's "cock," but that sounds like a chicken. And "prick" is painful, and "dick" is like you're talking about someone who's not in the room.

GALLIMARD. Yes. It's a... bigger problem than I imagined.

RENEE. I—I think maybe it's because I really don't know what to do with them—that's why I call them "weenies."

GALLIMARD. Well, you did quite well with... mine.

RENEE. Thanks, but I mean, really *do* with them. Like, okay, have you ever looked at one? I mean, really?

GALLIMARD. No, I suppose when it's part of you, you sort of take it for granted.

RENEE. I guess. But, like, it just hangs there. This little... flap of flesh. And there's so much fuss that we make about it. Like, I think the reason we fight wars is because we wear clothes. Because no one knows—between the men, I mean—who has the biggest... weenie. So, if I'm a guy with a small one, I'm going to build a really big building or take over a really big piece of land or write a really long book so the other men don't know, right? But, see, it never really works, that's the problem. I mean, you conquer the country, or whatever, but you're still wearing clothes, so there's no way to prove absolutely whose is bigger or smaller. And that's what we call a civilized society. The whole world run by a bunch of men with pricks the size of pins.

[*She exits.*]

GALLIMARD [*to us*]. This was simply not acceptable.

[*A high-pitched chime rings through the air.* SONG, *dressed as Butterfly, appears in the upstage special. She is obviously distressed. Her body swoons as she attempts to clip the stems of flowers she's arranging in a vase.*]

GALLIMARD. But I kept up our affair, wildly, for several months. Why? I believe because of Butterfly. She knew the secret I was trying to hide. But, unlike a Western woman, she didn't confront me, threaten, even pout. I remembered the words of Puccini's *Butterfly*:

SONG. "*Noi siamo gente avvezza / alle piccole cose / umili e silenziose.*"

GALLIMARD. "I come from a people / Who are accustomed to little / Humble and silent." I saw Pinkerton and Butterfly, and what she would say if he were unfaithful . . . nothing. She would cry, alone, into those wildly soft sleeves, once full of possessions, now empty to collect her tears. It was her tears and her silence that excited me, every time I visited Renee.

TOULON [*offstage*]. Gallimard!

[TOULON *enters.* GALLIMARD *turns towards him. During the next section,* SONG, *up center, begins to dance with the flowers. It is a drunken, reckless dance, where she breaks small pieces off the stems.*]

TOULON. They're killing him.

GALLIMARD. Who? I'm sorry? What?

TOULON. Bother you to come over at this late hour?

GALLIMARD. No . . . of course not.

TOULON. Not after you hear my secret. Champagne?

GALLIMARD. Um . . . thank you.

TOULON. You're surprised. There's something that you've wanted, Gallimard. No, not a promotion. Next time. Something in the world. You're not aware of this, but there's an informal gossip circle among intelligence agents. And some of ours heard from some of the Americans—

GALLIMARD. Yes?

TOULON. That the U.S. will allow the Vietnamese generals to stage a coup . . . and assassinate President Diem.

[*The chime rings again.* TOULON *freezes.* GALLIMARD *turns upstage and looks at Butterfly, who slowly and deliberately clips a flower off its stem.* GALLIMARD *turns back towards* TOULON.]

GALLIMARD. I think . . . that's a very wise move!

[TOULON *unfreezes.*]

TOULON. It's what you've been advocating. A toast?

GALLIMARD. Sure. I consider this a vindication.

TOULON. Not exactly. "To the test. Let's hope you pass."

[*They drink. The chime rings again.* TOULON *freezes.* GALLIMARD *turns upstage, and* SONG *clips another flower.*]

GALLIMARD [*to* TOULON]. The test?

TOULON [*unfreezing*]. It's a test of everything you've been saying. I personally think the generals probably will stop the Communists. And you'll be a hero. But if anything goes wrong, then your opinions won't be worth a pig's ear. I'm sure that won't happen. But sometimes it's easier when they don't listen to you.

GALLIMARD. They're your opinions too, aren't they?

TOULON. Personally, yes.

GALLIMARD. So we agree.

TOULON. But my opinions aren't on that report. Yours are. Cheers.

[TOULON *turns away from* GALLIMARD *and raises his glass. At that instant* SONG *picks up the vase and hurls it to the ground. It shatters.* SONG *sinks down amidst the shards of the vase, in a calm, childlike trance. She sings softly, as if reciting a child's nursery rhyme.*]

SONG [*repeat as necessary*]. "The whole world over, the white man travels, setting anchor, wherever he likes. Life's not worth living, unless he finds, the finest maidens, of every land. . . ."

[GALLIMARD *turns downstage towards us.* SONG *continues singing.*]

GALLIMARD. I shook as I left his house. That coward! That worm! To put the burden for his decisions on my shoulders!

I started for Renee's. But no, that was all I needed. A schoolgirl who would question the role of the penis in modern society. What I wanted was revenge. A vessel to contain my humiliation. Though I hadn't seen her in several weeks, I headed for Butterfly's.

[GALLIMARD *enters* SONG*'s apartment.*]

SONG. Oh! Rene . . . I was dreaming!

GALLIMARD. You've been drinking?

SONG. If I can't sleep, then yes, I drink. But then, it gives me these dreams which—Rene, it's been almost three weeks since you visited me last.

GALLIMARD. I know. There's been a lot going on in the world.

SONG. Fortunately I am drunk. So I can speak freely. It's not the world, it's you and me. And an old problem. Even the softest skin becomes like leather to a man who's touched it too often. I confess I don't know how to stop it. I don't know how to become another woman.

GALLIMARD. I have a request.

SONG. Is this a solution? Or are you ready to give up the flat?

GALLIMARD. It may be a solution. But I'm sure you won't like it.

SONG. Oh well, that's very important. "Like it?" Do you think I "like" lying here alone, waiting, always waiting for your return? Please—don't worry about what I may not "like."

GALLIMARD. I want to see you . . . naked.

[*Silence.*]

SONG. I thought you understood my modesty. So you want me to—what—strip? Like a big cowboy girl? Shiny pasties on my breasts? Shall I fling my kimono over my head and yell "ya-hoo" in the process? I thought you respected my shame!

GALLIMARD. I believe you gave me your shame many years ago.

SONG. Yes—and it is just like a white devil to use it against me. I can't believe it. I thought myself so repulsed by the passive Oriental and the cruel white man. Now I see—we are always most revolted by the things hidden within us.

GALLIMARD. I just mean—

SONG. Yes?

GALLIMARD. —that it will remove the only barrier left between us.

SONG. No, Rene. Don't couch your request in sweet words. Be yourself—a cad—and know that my love is enough, that I submit—submit to the worst you can give me. [*Pause.*] Well, come. Strip me. Whatever happens, know that you have willed it. Our love, in your hands. I'm helpless before my man.

[GALLIMARD *starts to cross the room.*]

GALLIMARD. Did I not undress her because I knew, somewhere deep down, what I would find? Perhaps. Happiness is so rare that our mind can turn somersaults to protect it.

At the time, I only knew that I was seeing Pinkerton stalking towards his Butterfly, ready to reward her love with his lecherous hands. The image sickened me, pulled me to my knees, so I was crawling towards her like a worm. By the time I reached her, Pinkerton . . . had vanished from my heart. To be replaced by something new, something unnatural, that flew in the face of all I'd learned in the world—something very close to love.

[*He grabs her around the waist; she strokes his hair.*]

GALLIMARD. Butterfly, forgive me.
SONG. Rene . . .
GALLIMARD. For everything. From the start.
SONG. I'm . . .
GALLIMARD. I want to—
SONG. I'm pregnant. [*Beat.*] I'm pregnant. [*Beat.*] I'm pregnant.

[*Beat.*]

GALLIMARD. I want to marry you!

SCENE VII

GALLIMARD and Butterfly's flat. Beijing. 1963.

Downstage, SONG *paces as* COMRADE CHIN *reads from her notepad. Upstage, GALLIMARD is still kneeling. He remains on his knees throughout the scene, watching it.*

SONG. I need a baby.
CHIN [*from pad*]. He's been spotted going to a dorm.
SONG. I need a baby.
CHIN. At the Foreign Language Institute.
SONG. I need a baby.
CHIN. The room of a Danish girl. . . . What do you mean, you need a baby?!
SONG. Tell Comrade Kang—last night, the entire mission, it could've ended.
CHIN. What do you mean?
SONG. Tell Kang—he told me to strip.
CHIN. Strip?!
SONG. Write!
CHIN. I tell you, I don't understand nothing about this case anymore. Nothing.
SONG. He told me to strip, and I took a chance. Oh, we Chinese, we know how to gamble.
CHIN [*writing*]. ". . . told him to strip."
SONG. My palms were wet, I had to make a split-second decision.
CHIN. Hey! Can you slow down?!

[*Pause.*]

SONG. You write faster, I'm the artist here. Suddenly, it hit me—"All he wants is for her to submit. Once a woman submits, a man is always ready to become 'generous.'"
CHIN. You're just gonna end up with rough notes.
SONG. And it worked! He gave in! Now, if I can just present him with a baby. A Chinese baby with blond hair—he'll be mine for life!

CHIN. Kang will never agree! The trading of babies has to be a counterrevolutionary act!

SONG. Sometimes, a counterrevolutionary act is necessary to counter a counterrevolutionary act.

[*Pause.*]

CHIN. Wait.

SONG. I need one...in seven months. Make sure it's a boy.

CHIN. This doesn't sound like something the Chairman would do. Maybe you'd better talk to Comrade Kang yourself.

SONG. Good. I will.

[CHIN *gets up to leave.*]

SONG. Miss Chin? Why, in the Peking Opera, are women's roles played by men?

CHIN. I don't know. Maybe, a reactionary remnant of male—

SONG. No. [*Beat.*] Because only a man knows how a woman is supposed to act.

[CHIN *exits.* SONG *turns upstage, towards* GALLIMARD.]

GALLIMARD [*calling after* CHIN]. Good riddance! [*To* SONG.] I could forget all that betrayal in an instant, you know. If you'd just come back and become Butterfly again.

SONG. Fat chance. You're here in prison, rotting in a cell. And I'm on a plane, winging my way back to China. Your President pardoned me of our treason, you know.

GALLIMARD. Yes, I read about that.

SONG. Must make you feel...lower than shit.

GALLIMARD. But don't you, even a little bit, wish you were here with me?

SONG. I'm an artist, Rene. You were my greatest...acting challenge. [*She laughs.*] It doesn't matter how rotten I answer, does it? You still adore me. That's why I love you, Rene. [*She points to us.*] So—you were telling your audience about the night I announced I was pregnant.

[GALLIMARD *puts his arms around* SONG*'s waist. He and* SONG *are in the positions they were in at the end of SCENE VI.*]

SCENE VIII

Same.

GALLIMARD. I'll divorce my wife. We'll live together here, and then later in France.

SONG. I feel so...ashamed.

GALLIMARD. Why?

SONG. I had begun to lose faith. And now, you shame me with your generosity.

GALLIMARD. Generosity? No, I'm proposing for very selfish reasons.

SONG. Your apologies only make me feel more ashamed. My outburst a moment ago!

GALLIMARD. Your outburst? What about my request?!

SONG. You've been very patient dealing with my...eccentricities. A Western man, used to women freer with their bodies—

GALLIMARD. It was sick! Don't make excuses for me.

SONG. I have to. You don't seem willing to make them for yourself.

[*Pause.*]

GALLIMARD. You're crazy.
SONG. I'm happy. Which often looks like crazy.
GALLIMARD. Then make me crazy. Marry me.

[*Pause.*]

SONG. No.
GALLIMARD. What?
SONG. Do I sound silly, a slave, if I say I'm not worthy?
GALLIMARD. Yes. In fact you do. No one has loved me like you.
SONG. Thank you. And no one ever will. I'll see to that.
GALLIMARD. So what is the problem?
SONG. Rene, we Chinese are realists. We understand rice, gold, and guns. You are a diplomat. Your career is skyrocketing. Now, what would happen if you divorced your wife to marry a Communist Chinese actress?
GALLIMARD. That's not being realistic. That's defeating yourself before you begin.
SONG. We conserve our strength for the battles we can win.
GALLIMARD. That sounds like a fortune cookie!
SONG. Where do you think fortune cookies come from!
GALLIMARD. I don't care.
SONG. You do. So do I. And we should. That is why I say I'm not worthy. I'm worthy to love and even to be loved by you. But I am not worthy to end the career of one of the West's most promising diplomats.
GALLIMARD. It's not that great a career! I made it sound like more than it is!
SONG. Modesty will get you nowhere. Flatter yourself, and you flatter me. I'm flattered to decline your offer.

[*She exits.*]

GALLIMARD [*to us*]. Butterfly and I argued all night. And, in the end, I left, knowing I would never be her husband. She went away for several months—to the countryside, like a small animal. Until the night I received her call.

[*A baby's cry from offstage.* SONG *enters, carrying a child.*]

SONG. He looks like you.
GALLIMARD. Oh! [*Beat; he approaches the baby.*] Well, babies are never very attractive at birth.
SONG. Stop!
GALLIMARD. I'm sure he'll grow more beautiful with age. More like his mother.
SONG. "*Chi vide mai/a bimbo del Giappon...*"
GALLIMARD. "What baby, I wonder, was ever born in Japan"—or China, for that matter—
SONG. "*...occhi azzurrini?*"
GALLIMARD. "With azure eyes"—they're actually sort of brown, wouldn't you say?
SONG. "*E il labbro.*"
GALLIMARD. "And such lips!" [*He kisses* SONG.] And such lips.
SONG. "*E i ricciolini d'oro schietto?*"
GALLIMARD. "And such a head of golden"—if slightly patchy—"curls?"
SONG. I'm going to call him "Peepee."
GALLIMARD. Darling, could you repeat that because I'm sure a rickshaw just flew by overhead.
SONG. You heard me.

Gallimard. "Song Peepee"? May I suggest Michael, or Stephan, or Adolph?
Song. You may, but I won't listen.
Gallimard. You can't be serious. Can you imagine the time this child will have in school?
Song. In the West, yes.
Gallimard. It's worse than naming him Ping Pong or Long Dong or—
Song. But he's never going to live in the West, is he?

[*Pause.*]

Gallimard. That wasn't my choice.
Song. It is mine. And this is my promise to you: I will raise him, he will be our child, but he will never burden you outside of China.
Gallimard. Why do you make these promises? I want to be burdened! I want a scandal to cover the papers!
Song [*to us*]. Prophetic.
Gallimard. I'm serious.
Song. So am I. His name is as I registered it. And he will never live in the West.

[Song *exits with the child.*]

Gallimard [*to us*]. It is possible that her stubbornness only made me want her more. That drawing back at the moment of my capitulation was the most brilliant strategy she could have chosen. It is possible. But it is also possible that by this point she could have said, could have done . . . anything, and I would have adored her still.

SCENE IX

Beijing. 1966.
A driving rhythm of Chinese percussion fills the stage.

Gallimard. And then, China began to change. Mao became very old, and his cult became very strong. And, like many old men, he entered his second childhood. So he handed over the reins of state to those with minds like his own. And children ruled the Middle Kingdom[8] with complete caprice. The doctrine of the Cultural Revolution[9] implied continuous anarchy. Contact between Chinese and foreigners became impossible. Our flat was confiscated. Her fame and my money now counted against us.

[*Two dancers in Mao suits and red-starred caps enter, and begin crudely mimicking revolutionary violence, in an agitprop fashion.*]

Gallimard. And somehow the American war went wrong too. Four hundred thousand dollars were being spent for every Viet Cong[10] killed; so General Westmoreland's[11] remark that the Oriental does not value life the way Americans do was oddly accurate. Why weren't the Vietnamese people giving in? Why were they content instead to die and die and die again?

[Toulon *enters. Percussion and dancers continue upstage.*]

---

[8]From earliest history, the Chinese have called their country the Middle Kingdom.
[9]Name given to the era of fierce suppression of ideologies contrary to the ideas of Chinese leader Mao Tse-tung, 1965–1967.
[10]Vietnamese communists who sought to overthrow the South Vietnam government.
[11]William Westmoreland, commander of U.S. military forces in Vietnam, 1964–1968.

TOULON. Congratulations, Gallimard.
GALLIMARD. Excuse me, sir?
TOULON. Not a promotion. That was last time. You're going home.
GALLIMARD. What?
TOULON. Don't say I didn't warn you.
GALLIMARD. I'm being transferred . . . because I was wrong about the American war?
TOULON. Of course not. We don't care about the Americans. We care about your mind. The quality of your analysis. In general, everything you've predicted here in the Orient . . . just hasn't happened.
GALLIMARD. I think that's premature.
TOULON. Don't force me to be blunt. Okay, you said China was ready to open to Western trade. The only thing they're trading out there are Western heads. And, yes, you said the Americans would succeed in Indochina. You were kidding, right?
GALLIMARD. I think the end is in sight.
TOULON. Don't be pathetic. And don't take this personally. You were wrong. It's not your fault.
GALLIMARD. But I'm going home.
TOULON. Right. Could I have the number of your mistress? [*Beat.*] Joke! Joke! Eat a croissant for me.

[TOULON *exits.* SONG, *wearing a Mao suit, is dragged in from the wings as part of the upstage dance. They "beat" her, then lampoon the acrobatics of the Chinese opera, as she is made to kneel onstage.*]

GALLIMARD [*simultaneously*]. I don't care to recall how Butterfly and I said our hurried farewell. Perhaps it was better to end our affair before it killed her.

[GALLIMARD *exits. Percussion rises in volume. The lampooning becomes faster, more frenetic. At its height, Comrade* CHIN *walks across the stage with a banner reading: "The Actor Renounces His Decadent Profession!" She reaches the kneeling* SONG. *At the moment* CHIN *touches* SONG'*s chin, percussion stops with a thud. Dancers strike poses.*]

CHIN. Actor-oppressor, for years you have lived above the common people and looked down on their labor. While the farmer ate millet—
SONG. I ate pastries from France and sweetmeats from silver trays.
CHIN. And how did you come to live in such an exalted position?
SONG. I was a plaything for the imperialists!
CHIN. What did you do?
SONG. I shamed China by allowing myself to be corrupted by a foreigner. . . .
CHIN. What does this mean? The People demand a full confession!
SONG. I engaged in the lowest perversions with China's enemies!
CHIN. What perversions? Be more clear!
SONG. I let him put it up my ass!

[*Dancers look over, disgusted.*]

CHIN. Aaaa-ya! How can you use such sickening language?!

SONG. *My* language…is only as foul as the crimes I committed….
CHIN. Yeah. That's better. So—what do you want to do…now?
SONG. I want to serve the people

[*Percussion starts up, with Chinese strings.*]

CHIN. What?
SONG. I want to serve the people!

[*Dancers regain their revolutionary smiles, and begin a dance of victory.*]

CHIN. What?!
SONG. I want to serve the people!!

[*Dancers unveil a banner: "The Actor Is Re-Habilitated!"* SONG *remains kneeling before* CHIN, *as the dancers bounce around them, then exit. Music out.*]

SCENE X

A commune. Hunan Province. 1970.

CHIN. How you planning to do that?
SONG. I've already worked four years in the fields of Hunan, Comrade Chin.
CHIN. So? Farmers work all their lives. Let me see your hands.

[SONG *holds them out for her inspection.*]

CHIN. Goddamn! Still so smooth! How long does it take to turn you actors into good anythings? Hunh. You've just spent too many years in luxury to be any good to the Revolution.
SONG. I served the Revolution.
CHIN. Served the Revolution? Bullshit! You wore dresses! Don't tell me—I was there. I saw you! You and your white vice-consul! Stuck up there in your flat, living off the People's Treasury! Yeah, I knew what was going on! You two…homos! Homos! Homos! [*Pause; she composes herself.*] Ah! Well…you will serve the people, all right. But not with the Revolution's money. This time, you use your own money.
SONG. I have no money.
CHIN. Shut up! And you won't stink up China anymore with your pervert stuff. You'll pollute the place where pollution begins—the West.
SONG. What do you mean?
CHIN. Shut up! You're going to France. Without a cent in your pocket. You find your consul's house, you make him pay your expenses—
SONG. No.
CHIN. And you give us weekly reports! Useful information!
SONG. That's crazy. It's been four years.
CHIN. Either that, or back to the rehabilitation center!
SONG. Comrade Chin, he's not going to support me! Not in France! He's a white man! I was just his plaything—
CHIN. Oh yuck! Again with the sickening language? Where's my stick?
SONG. You don't understand the mind of a man.

[*Pause.*]

CHIN. Oh no? No I don't? Then how come I'm married, huh? How come I got a man? Five, six years ago, you always tell me those kind of things, I felt very bad. But not now! Because what does the Chairman say? He tells us *I'm* now the smart one, you're now the nincompoop! *You're* the blockhead, the hare-brain, the nitwit! You think you're so smart? You understand "The Mind of a Man"? Good! Then *you* go to France and be a pervert for Chairman Mao!

[CHIN *and* SONG *exit in opposite directions.*]

SCENE XI

Paris. 1968–1970.

[GALLIMARD *enters.*]

GALLIMARD. And what was waiting for me back in Paris? Well, better Chinese food than I'd eaten in China. Friends and relatives. A little accounting, regular schedule, keeping track of traffic violations in the suburbs. . . . And the indignity of students shouting the slogans of Chairman Mao at me—in French.

HELGA. Rene? Rene? [*She enters, soaking wet.*] I've had a . . . problem. [*She sneezes.*]

GALLIMARD. You're wet.

HELGA. Yes, I . . . coming back from the grocer's. A group of students, waving red flags, they—

[GALLIMARD *fetches a towel.*]

HELGA. —they ran by, I was caught up along with them. Before I knew what was happening—

[GALLIMARD *gives her the towel.*]

HELGA. Thank you. The police started firing water cannons at us. I tried to shout, to tell them I was the wife of a diplomat, but—you know how it is . . . [*Pause.*] Needless to say, I lost the groceries. Rene, what's happening to France?

GALLIMARD. What's—? Well, nothing, really.

HELGA. Nothing?! The storefronts are in flames, there's glass in the streets, buildings are toppling—and I'm wet!

GALLIMARD. Nothing! . . . . that I care to think about.

HELGA. And is that why you stay in this room?

GALLIMARD. Yes, in fact.

HELGA. With the incense burning? You know something? I hate incense. It smells so sickly sweet.

GALLIMARD. Well, I hate the French. Who just smell—period!

HELGA. And the Chinese were better?

GALLIMARD. Please—don't start.

HELGA. When we left, this exact same thing, the riots—

GALLIMARD. No, no . . .

HELGA. Students screaming slogans, smashing down doors—

GALLIMARD. Helga—

HELGA. It was all going on in China, too. Don't you remember?!

GALLIMARD. Helga! Please! [*Pause.*] You have never understood China, have you? You walk in here with these ridiculous ideas, that the West is falling apart, that China was spitting in our faces. You come in, dripping of the streets, and you leave water all over my floor. [He *grabs* HELGA*'s towel, begins mopping up the floor.*]

HELGA. But it's the truth!

GALLIMARD. Helga, I want a divorce.

[*Pause;* GALLIMARD *continues mopping the floor.*]

HELGA. I take it back. China is... beautiful. Incense, I like incense.

GALLIMARD. I've had a mistress.

HELGA. So?

GALLIMARD. For eight years.

HELGA. I knew you would. I knew you would the day I married you. And now what? You want to marry her?

GALLIMARD. I can't. She's in China.

HELGA. I see. You know that no one else is ever going to marry me, right?

GALLIMARD. I'm sorry.

HELGA. And you want to leave. For someone who's not here, is that right?

GALLIMARD. That's right.

HELGA. You can't live with her, but still you don't want to live with me.

GALLIMARD. That's right.

[*Pause.*]

HELGA. Shit. How terrible that I can figure that out. [*Pause.*] I never thought I'd say it. But, in China, I was happy. I knew, in my own way, I knew that you were not everything you pretended to be. But the pretense—going on your arm to the embassy ball, visiting your office and the guards saying, "Good morning, good morning, Madame Gallimard"—the pretense.... was very good indeed. [*Pause.*] I hope everyone is mean to you for the rest of your life.

[*She exits.*]

GALLIMARD [*to us*]. Prophetic.

[MARC *enters with two drinks.*]

GALLIMARD [*to* MARC]. In China, I was different from all other men.

MARC. Sure. You were white. Here's your drink.

GALLIMARD. I felt... touched.

MARC. In the head? Rene, I don't want to hear about the Oriental love goddess. Okay? One night—can we just drink and throw up without a lot of conversation?

GALLIMARD. You still don't believe me, do you?

MARC. Sure I do. She was the most beautiful, et cetera, et cetera, blasé, blasé.

[*Pause.*]

GALLIMARD. My life in the West has been such a disappointment.

MARC. Life in the West is like that. You'll get used to it. Look, you're driving me away. I'm leaving. Happy, now? [*He exits, then returns.*] Look, I have a date tomorrow night. You wanna come? I can fix you up with—

GALLIMARD. Of course. I would love to come.

[*Pause.*]

MARC. Uh—on second thought, no. You'd better get a hold of yourself first.

[*He exits*; GALLIMARD *nurses his drink*.]

GALLIMARD [*to us*]. This is the ultimate cruelty, isn't it? That I can talk and talk and to anyone listening, it's only air—too rich a diet to be swallowed by a mundane world. Why can't anyone understand? That in China, I once loved, and was loved by, very simply, the Perfect Woman.

[SONG *enters, dressed as Butterfly in wedding dress.*]

GALLIMARD [*to* SONG]. Not again. My imagination is hell. Am I asleep this time? Or did I drink too much?
SONG. Rene!
GALLIMARD. God, it's too painful! That you speak?
SONG. What are you talking about? Rene—touch me.
GALLIMARD. Why?
SONG. I'm real. Take my hand.
GALLIMARD. Why? So you can disappear again and leave me clutching at the air? For the entertainment of my neighbors who—?

[SONG *touches* GALLIMARD.]

SONG. Rene?

[GALLIMARD *takes* SONG*'s hand. Silence.*]

GALLIMARD. Butterfly? I never doubted you'd return.
SONG. You hadn't... forgotten—?
GALLIMARD. Yes, actually, I've forgotten everything. My mind, you see—there wasn't enough room in this hard head—not for the world *and* for you. No, there was only room for one. [*Beat.*] Come, look. See? Your bed has been waiting, with the Klimt[12] poster you like, and—see? The *xiang lu*[13] you gave me?
SONG. I... I don't know what to say.
GALLIMARD. There's nothing to say. Not at the end of a long trip. Can I make you some tea?
SONG. But where's your wife?
GALLIMARD. She's by my side. She's by my side at last.

[GALLIMARD *reaches to embrace* SONG. SONG *sidesteps, dodging him.*]

GALLIMARD. Why?!
SONG [*to us*]. So I did return to Rene in Paris. Where I found—
GALLIMARD. Why do you run away? Can't we show them how we embraced that evening?
SONG. Please. I'm talking.
GALLIMARD. You have to do what I say! I'm conjuring you up in *my* mind!
SONG. Rene, I've never done what you've said. Why should it be any different in your mind? Now split—the story moves on, and I must change.
GALLIMARD. I welcomed you into my home! I didn't have to, you know! I could've left you penniless on the streets of Paris! But I took you in!

---

[12]Gustav Klimt (1862–1918), an Austrian painter.
[13]Incense burner.

SONG. Thank you.
GALLIMARD. So... please... don't change.
SONG. You know I have to. You know I will. And anyway, what difference does it make? No matter what your eyes tell you, you can't ignore the truth. You already know too much.

[GALLIMARD *exits.* SONG *turns to us.*]

SONG. The change I'm going to make requires about five minutes. So I thought you might want to take this opportunity to stretch your legs, enjoy a drink, or listen to the musicians. I'll be here, when you return, right where you left me.

[SONG *goes to a mirror in front of which is a washbasin of water. She starts to remove her makeup as stagelights go to half and houselights come up.*]

ACT III

SCENE I

A courthouse in Paris. 1986.

As he promised, SONG *has completed the bulk of his transformation onstage by the time the houselights go down and the stagelights come up full. As he speaks to us, he removes his wig and kimono, leaving them on the floor. Underneath, he wears a well-cut suit.*

SONG. So I'd done my job better than I had a right to expect. Well, give him some credit, too. He's right—I was in a fix when I arrived in Paris. I walked from the airport into town, then I located, by blind groping, the Chinatown district. Let me make one thing clear: whatever else may be said about the Chinese, they are stingy! I slept in doorways three days until I could find a tailor who would make me this kimono on credit. As it turns out, maybe I didn't even need it. Maybe he would've been happy to see me in a simple shift and mascara. But... better safe than sorry.

That was 1970, when I arrived in Paris. For the next fifteen years, yes, I lived a very comfy life. Some relief, believe me, after four years on a fucking commune in Nowheresville, China. Rene supported the boy and me, and I did some demonstrations around the country as part of my "cultural exchange" cover. And then there was the spying.

[SONG *moves upstage, to a chair.* TOULON *enters as a judge, wearing the appropriate wig and robes. He sits near* SONG. *It's 1986, and* SONG *is testifying in a courtroom.*]

SONG. Not much at first. Rene had lost all his high-level contacts. Comrade Chin wasn't very interested in parking-ticket statistics. But finally, at my urging, Rene got a job as a courier, handling sensitive documents. He'd photograph them for me, and I'd pass them on to the Chinese embassy.
JUDGE. Did he understand the extent of his activity?
SONG. He didn't ask. He knew that I needed those documents, and that was enough.
JUDGE. But he must've known he was passing classified information.
SONG. I can't say.
JUDGE. He never asked what you were going to do with them?

SONG. Nope.

[*Pause.*]

JUDGE. There is one thing that the court—indeed, that all of France—would like to know.

SONG. Fire away.

JUDGE. Did Monsieur Gallimard know you were a man?

SONG. Well, he never saw me completely naked. Ever.

JUDGE. But surely, he must've...how can I put this?

SONG. Put it however you like. I'm not shy. He must've felt around?

JUDGE. Mmmmm.

SONG. Not really. I did all the work. He just laid back. Of course we did enjoy more...complete union, and I suppose he *might* have wondered why I was always on my stomach, but...But what you're thinking is, "Of course a wrist must've brushed...a hand hit...over twenty years!" Yeah. Well, Your Honor, it was my job to make him think I was a woman. And chew on this: it wasn't all that hard. See, my mother was a prostitute along the Bundt before the Revolution. And, uh, I think it's fair to say she learned a few things about Western men. So I borrowed her knowledge. In service to my country.

JUDGE. Would you care to enlighten the court with this secret knowledge? I'm sure we're all very curious.

SONG. I'm sure you are. [*Pause.*] Okay, Rule One is: Men always believe what they want to hear. So a girl can tell the most obnoxious lies and the guys will believe them every time—"This is my first time"—"That's the biggest I've ever seen"—or *both*, which, if you really think about it, is not possible in a single lifetime. You've maybe heard those phrases a few times in your own life, yes, Your Honor?

JUDGE. It's not my life, Monsieur Song, which is on trial today.

SONG. Okay, okay, just trying to lighten up the proceedings. Tough room.

JUDGE. Go on.

SONG. Rule Two: As soon as a Western man comes into contact with the East—he's already confused. The West has sort of an international rape mentality towards the East. Do you know rape mentality?

JUDGE. Give us your definition, please.

SONG. Basically, "Her mouth says no, but her eyes say yes."

The West thinks of itself as masculine—big guns, big industry, big money—so the East is feminine—weak, delicate, poor...but good at art, and full of inscrutable wisdom—the feminine mystique.

Her mouth says no, but her eyes say yes. The West believes the East, deep down, *wants* to be dominated—because a woman can't think for herself.

JUDGE. What does this have to do with my question?

SONG. You expect Oriental countries to submit to your guns, and you expect Oriental women to be submissive to your men. That's why you say they make the best wives.

JUDGE. But why would that make it possible for you to fool Monsieur Gallimard? Please—get to the point.

SONG. One, because when he finally met his fantasy woman, he wanted more than anything to believe that she was, in fact, a woman. And second, I am an Oriental. And being an Oriental, I could never be completely a man.

[*Pause.*]

JUDGE. Your armchair political theory is tenuous, Monsieur Song.
SONG. You think so? That's why you'll lose in all your dealings with the East.
JUDGE. Just answer my question: did he know you were a man?

[*Pause.*]

SONG. You know, Your Honor, I never asked.

SCENE II

Same.

Music from the "Death Scene" from Butterfly blares over the house speakers. It is the loudest thing we've heard in this play.

[GALLIMARD *enters, crawling towards* SONG*'s wig and kimono.*]

GALLIMARD. Butterfly? Butterfly?

[SONG *remains a man, in the witness box, delivering a testimony we do not hear.*]

GALLIMARD [*to us*]. In my moment of greatest shame, here, in this courtroom—with that...person up there, telling the world.... What strikes me especially is how shallow he is, how glib and obsequious...completely...without substance! The type that prowls around discos with a gold medallion stinking of garlic. So little like my Butterfly.

Yet even in this moment my mind remains agile, flip-flopping like a man on a trampoline. Even now, my picture dissolves, and I see that...witness...talking to me.

[SONG *suddenly stands straight up in his witness box, and looks at* GALLIMARD.]

SONG. Yes. You. White man.

[SONG *steps out of the witness box, and moves downstage towards* GALLIMARD. *Light change.*]

GALLIMARD [*to Song*]. Who? Me?
SONG. Do you see any other white men?
GALLIMARD. Yes. There're white men all around. This is a French courtroom.
SONG. So you are an adventurous imperialist. Tell me, why did it take you so long? To come back to this place?
GALLIMARD. What place?
SONG. This theater in China. Where we met many years ago.
GALLIMARD [*to us*]. And once again, against my will, I am transported.

[*Chinese opera music comes up on the speakers.* SONG *begins to do opera moves, as he did the night they met.*]

SONG. Do you remember? The night you gave your heart?
GALLIMARD. It was a long time ago.
SONG. Not long enough. A night that turned your world upside down.
GALLIMARD. Perhaps.
SONG. Oh, be honest with me. What's another bit of flattery when you've already given me twenty years' worth? It's a wonder my head hasn't swollen to the size of China.
GALLIMARD. Who's to say it hasn't?

SONG. Who's to say? And what's the shame? In pride? You think I could've pulled this off if I wasn't already full of pride when we met? No, not just pride. Arrogance. It takes arrogance, really—to believe you can will, with your eyes and your lips, the destiny of another. [*He dances.*] C'mon. Admit it. You still want me. Even in slacks and a button-down collar.

GALLIMARD. I don't see what the point of—

SONG. You don't? Well maybe, Rene, just maybe—I want you.

GALLIMARD. You do?

SONG. Then again, maybe I'm just playing with you. How can you tell? [*Reprising his feminine character, he sidles up to* GALLIMARD.] "How I wish there were even a small café to sit in. With men in tuxedos, and cappuccinos, and bad expatriate jazz." Now you want to kiss me, don't you?

GALLIMARD [*pulling away*]. What makes you—?

SONG. —so sure? See? I take the words from your mouth. Then I wait for you to come and retrieve them. [*He reclines on the floor.*]

GALLIMARD. Why?! Why do you treat me so cruelly?

SONG. Perhaps I *was* treating you cruelly. But now—I'm being nice. Come here, my little one.

GALLIMARD. I'm not your little one!

SONG. My mistake. It's I who am *your* little one, right?

GALLIMARD. Yes, I—

SONG. So come get your little one. If you like, I may even let you strip me.

GALLIMARD. I mean, you were! Before... but not like this!

SONG. I was? Then perhaps I still am. If you look hard enough. [*He starts to remove his clothes.*]

GALLIMARD. What—what are you doing?

SONG. Helping you to see through my act.

GALLIMARD. Stop that! I don't want to! I don't—

SONG. Oh, but you asked me to strip, remember?

GALLIMARD. What? That was years ago! And I took it back!

SONG. No. You postponed it. Postponed the inevitable. Today, the inevitable has come calling.

[*From the speakers, cacophony*: Butterfly *mixed in with Chinese gongs.*]

GALLIMARD. No! Stop! I don't want to see!

SONG. Then look away.

GALLIMARD. You're only in my mind! All this is in my mind! I order you! To stop!

SONG. To what? To strip? That's just what I'm—

GALLIMARD. No! Stop! I want you—!

SONG. You want me?

GALLIMARD. To stop!

SONG. You know something, Rene? Your mouth says no, but your eyes say yes. Turn them away. I dare you.

GALLIMARD. I don't have to! Every night, you say you're going to strip, but then I beg you and you stop!

SONG. I guess tonight is different.

GALLIMARD. Why? Why should that be?

SONG. Maybe I've become frustrated. Maybe I'm saying "Look at me, you fool!" Or maybe I'm just feeling... sexy. [*He is down to his briefs.*]

GALLIMARD. Please. This is unnecessary. I know what you are.

SONG. You do? What am I?

GALLIMARD. A—a man.

SONG. You don't really believe that.

GALLIMARD. Yes I do! I knew all the time somewhere that my happiness was temporary, my love a deception. But my mind kept the knowledge at bay. To make the wait bearable.

SONG. Monsieur Gallimard—the wait is over.

[SONG *drops his briefs. He is naked. Sound cue out. Slowly, we and* SONG *come to the realization that what we had thought to be* GALLIMARD*'s sobbing is actually his laughter.*]

GALLIMARD. Oh god! What an idiot! Of course!

SONG. Rene—what?

GALLIMARD. Look at you! You're a man! [*He bursts into laughter again.*]

SONG. I fail to see what's so funny!

GALLIMARD. "You fail to see—!" I mean, you never did have much of a sense of humor, did you? I just think it's ridiculously funny that I've wasted so much time on just a man!

SONG. Wait. I'm not "just a man."

GALLIMARD. No? Isn't that what you've been trying to convince me of?

SONG. Yes, but what I mean—

GALLIMARD. And now, I finally believe you, and you tell me it's not true? I think you must have some kind of identity problem.

SONG. Will you listen to me?

GALLIMARD. Why?! I've been listening to you for twenty years. Don't I deserve a vacation?

SONG. I'm not just any man!

GALLIMARD. Then, what exactly are you?

SONG. Rene, how can you ask—? Okay, what about this?

[*He picks up Butterfly's robes, starts to dance around. No music.*]

GALLIMARD. Yes, that's very nice. I have to admit.

[SONG *holds out his arm to* GALLIMARD.]

SONG. It's the same skin you've worshipped for years. Touch it.

GALLIMARD. Yes, it does feel the same.

SONG. Now—close your eyes.

[SONG *covers* GALLIMARD*'s eyes with one hand. With the other,* SONG *draws* GALLIMARD*'s hand up to his face.* GALLIMARD, *like a blind man, lets his hands run over* SONG*'s face.*]

GALLIMARD. This skin, I remember. The curve of her face, the softness of her cheek, her hair against the back of my hand…

SONG. I'm your Butterfly. Under the robes, beneath everything, it was always me. Now, open your eyes and admit it—you adore me. [*He removes his hand from* GALLIMARD*'s eyes.*]

GALLIMARD. You, who knew every inch of my desires—how could you, of all people, have made such a mistake?

SONG. What?

GALLIMARD. You showed me your true self. When all I loved was the lie. A perfect lie, which you let fall to the ground—and now, it's old and soiled.

SONG. So—you never really loved me? Only when I was playing a part?

GALLIMARD. I'm a man who loved a woman created by a man. Everything else—simply falls short.

[*Pause.*]

SONG. What am I supposed to do now?

GALLIMARD. You were a fine spy, Monsieur Song, with an even finer accomplice. But now I believe you should go. Get out of my life!

SONG. Go where? Rene, you can't live without me. Not after twenty years.

GALLIMARD. I certainly can't live with you—not after twenty years of betrayal.

SONG. Don't be stubborn! Where will you go?

GALLIMARD. I have a date... with my Butterfly.

SONG. So, throw away your pride. And come....

GALLIMARD. Get away from me! Tonight, I've finally learned to tell fantasy from reality. And, knowing the difference, I choose fantasy.

SONG. *I'm* your fantasy!

GALLIMARD. You? You're as real as hamburger. Now get out! I have a date with my Butterfly and I don't want your body polluting the room! [*He tosses* SONG*'s suit at him.*] Look at these—you dress like a pimp.

SONG. Hey! These are Armani slacks and—! [*He puts on his briefs and slacks.*] Let's just say... I'm disappointed in you, Rene. In the crush of your adoration, I thought you'd become something more. More like... a woman.

But no. Men. You're like the rest of them. It's all in the way we dress, and make up our faces, and bat our eyelashes. You really have so little imagination!

GALLIMARD. You, Monsieur Song? Accuse me of too little imagination? You, if anyone, should know—I am pure imagination. And in imagination I will remain. Now get out!

[GALLIMARD *bodily removes* SONG *from the stage, taking his kimono.*]

SONG. Rene! I'll never put on those robes again! You'll be sorry!

GALLIMARD [*to* SONG]. I'm already sorry! [*Looking at the kimono in his hands.*] Exactly as sorry... as a Butterfly.

SCENE III

M. GALLIMARD's prison cell. Paris. 1988.

GALLIMARD. I've played out the events of my life night after night, always searching for a new ending to my story, one where I leave this cell and return forever to my Butterfly's arms.

Tonight I realize my search is over. That I've looked all along in the wrong place. And now, to you, I will prove that my love was not in vain—by returning to the world of fantasy where I first met her.

[*He picks up the kimono; dancers enter.*]

GALLIMARD. There is a vision of the Orient that I have. Of slender women in chong sams and kimonos who die for the love of unworthy foreign devils. Who are born and raised to be the perfect women. Who take whatever punishment we give them, and bounce back, strengthened by love, unconditionally. It is a vision that has become my life.

[*Dancers bring the washbasin to him and help him make up his face.*]

GALLIMARD. In public, I have continued to deny that Song Liling is a man. This brings me headlines, and is a source of great embarrassment to my French colleagues, who can now be sent into a coughing fit by the mere mention of Chinese food. But alone, in my cell, I have long since faced the truth.

And the truth demands a sacrifice. For mistakes made over the course of a lifetime. My mistakes were simple and absolute—the man I loved was a cad, a bounder. He deserved nothing but a kick in the behind, and instead I gave him . . . all my love.

Yes—love. Why not admit it all? That was my undoing, wasn't it? Love warped my judgment, blinded my eyes, rearranged the very lines on my face . . . until I could look in the mirror and see nothing but . . . a woman.

[*Dancers help him put on the Butterfly wig.*]

GALLIMARD. I have a vision. Of the Orient. That, deep within its almond eyes, there are still women. Women willing to sacrifice themselves for the love of a man. Even a man whose love is completely without worth.

[*Dancers assist* GALLIMARD *in donning the kimono. They hand him a knife.*]

GALLIMARD. Death with honor is better than life . . . life with dishonor. [*He sets himself center stage, in a seppuku position.*[14]] The love of a Butterfly can withstand many things—unfaithfulness, loss, even abandonment. But how can it face the one sin that implies all others? The devastating knowledge that, underneath it all, the object of her love was nothing more, nothing less than . . . a man. [*He sets the tip of the knife against his body.*] It is 1988. And I have found her at last. In a prison on the outskirts of Paris. My name is Rene Gallimard—also known as Madame Butterfly.

[GALLIMARD *turns upstage and plunges the knife into his body, as music from the "Love Duet" blares over the speakers. He collapses into the arms of the dancers, who lay him reverently on the floor. The image holds for several beats. Then a tight special up on* SONG, *who stands as a man, staring at the dead* GALLIMARD. *He smokes a cigarette; the smoke filters up through the lights. Two words leave his lips.*]

SONG. Butterfly? Butterfly?

[*Smoke rises as lights fade slowly to black.*]

(1988)

[14]The position assumed in committing *hara kiri* (ritual suicide).

PREWRITING

Because cultural analysis usually involves sources outside the literary work, the prewriting stage is necessarily more complex than simply gathering ideas for writing from only your own thoughts. You still need to understand the work well, but your task is complicated by the need to find, read, and assimilate other documents, being careful to credit these ideas when you incorporate them into your own writing.

You can begin a cultural analysis by taking notes on your own responses to the play, and then considering them in terms of the customs, habits, beliefs, practices, and values of your own time, place, and social position. For example, Figure 19-1 shows a page of notes on *M. Butterfly* taken by Linda Samuel, the writer of the student paper in this chapter.

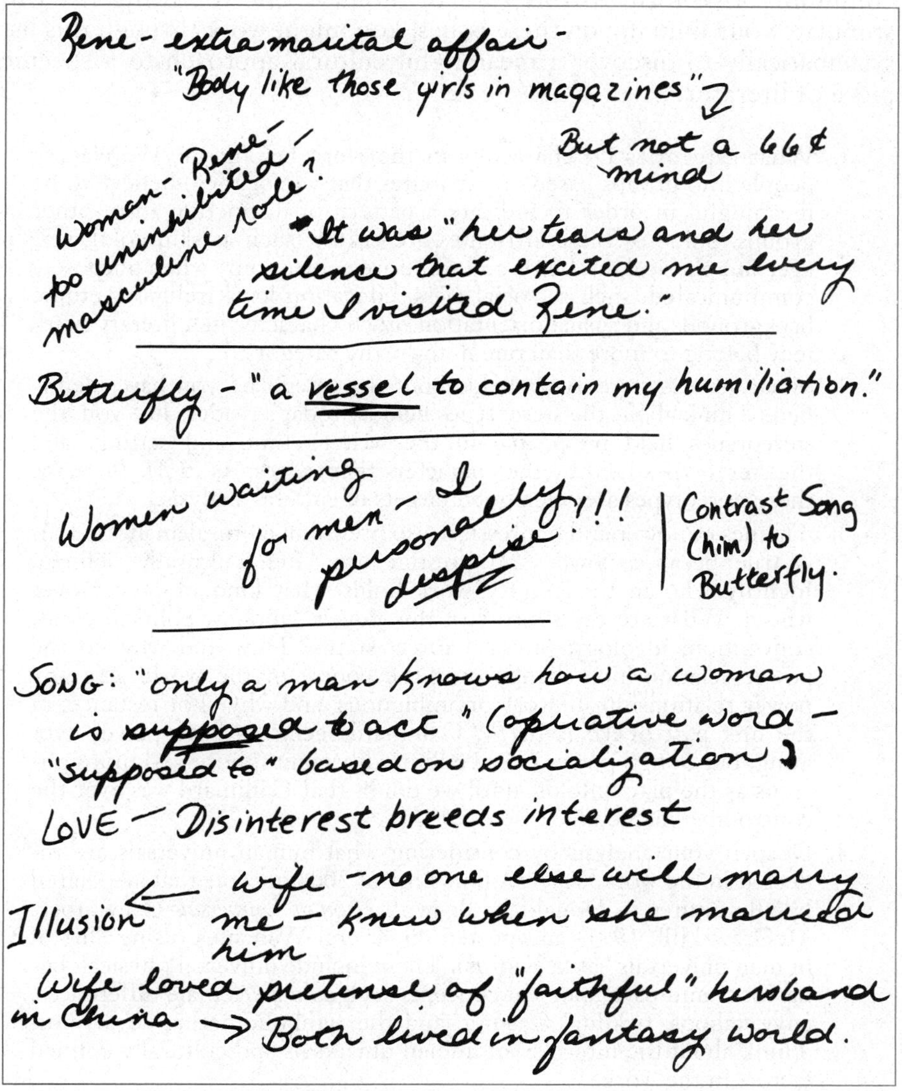

Rene - extramarital affair -
"Body like those girls in magazines"
But not a 66¢ mind

Woman - Rene - too uninhibited - masculine role?

* It was "her tears and her silence that excited me every time I visited Rene."

Butterfly - "a vessel to contain my humiliation."

Women waiting for men - I personally despise!!!

Contrast Song (him) to Butterfly.

SONG: "only a man knows how a woman is supposed to act" (operative word - "supposed to" based on socialization)

LOVE - Disinterest breeds interest

Illusion ← wife - no one else will marry me - knew when she married him

Wife loved pretense of "faithful" husband in China → Both lived in fantasy world.

Figure 19-1 Reading Notes

Pondering these notes, Linda saw that she had focused on the relations between the sexes. She generated some further questions about this topic, finally deciding that her specific interest was in the fantasies embraced by both sexes. She decided that fantasy versus reality was a good subject to start with, involving sexual and cultural stereotypes.

Exploring Cultural Themes

When you wish to do a cultural analysis of literary work, you can develop your ideas by considering some themes and questions that commonly give form to this type of inquiry. The following list will stimulate your thinking on these issues. You might work through this list systematically to discover a meaningful cultural approach to a specific piece of literature.

1. What categories do characters in the work belong to? We classify people into groups based on attributes that we (or they) believe to be meaningful in order to indicate a pattern of distinction from other groups. Some of these attributes are visible, such as skin color, sex, age, and physical disability, and some are evident only when purposely communicated, such as social class, education level, religion, ethnic background, and sexual orientation. Each character in a literary work may belong to more than one noteworthy category.
2. What are the stereotypes held about the categories you have identified? Think about the stereotypes held by today's readers like you, the stereotypes held by people in the writer's time and setting, and the stereotypes held by the characters themselves. As in *M. Butterfly*, these stereotypes are often good targets of cultural analysis.
3. Themes of power and oppression also prevail in cultural analysis. This is true because power and prestige are often culturally defined. Identify who in the literary work holds what kind of power over whom. What are the sources of this power—money, political clout, convention, ideology, physical force, status? How and why do the power relationships change over the course of the work? Are any power relationships illusory or ambiguous, and why? For instance, in the first part of *M. Butterfly*, Gallimard seems to have power over Song, but Song's power over Gallimard becomes more and more obvious as the play unfolds, until we doubt that Gallimard was ever the controlling character.
4. Deepen your analysis by considering what human universals are reflected in the work. You can find a list of 200 concepts that are shared by all cultures in Donald E. Brown's *Human Universals* (New York: McGraw-Hill, 1991) and posted on several Web sites (using "list of human universals" as keywords). These include universal physical, behavioral, and psychological concepts such as male/female differences, envy, taboos, tickling, feasting, and the symbolic nature of dreams. Think about the interplay of human universals and culturally defined factors in the work.

5. Cultural analysis makes use of documents beyond literary criticism and essays. Brainstorm about where you might find materials that reflect the attitudes, beliefs, customs, and conditions that prevailed in the period when the work was written or the era in which it is set. For example, Linda Samuel looked up the 1986 *New York Times* article that reported the real-life espionage case of the French diplomat and Chinese opera singer. In her paper, she used the "Afterword" that author David Hwang wrote for the print version of *M. Butterfly*, as well as *Time* magazine's review of the 1993 movie that was based on the play. You might also think about documents from other fields that may be relevant, like psychological theory, sociology, popular culture of the time, the arts of the time, and political science.

Posing Yourself a Problem

You will write with greater engagement if you can develop a question concerning one of the topics in the above list as it applies to your chosen literary work. Do you wonder, as most readers do, whether Gallimard was *really* ignorant of his lover's biological sex for twenty years? The question you might express and try to answer in your paper would be this:

> Is Gallimard thoroughly deceived about Song's biological sex, and if so, how and why?

The question comes from thinking about cultural stereotypes of masculinity and femininity and thinking about the universal concept of illusion versus reality. Another cultural analysis might come from this question:

> How are sexual and racial stereotypes active in Gallimard's life story?

After coming up with one or two questions like this, work on collecting and reading sources that will help you develop an answer, as suggested by item 5 in the preceding list of themes and topics.

WRITING

Before you begin writing your first draft, turn the questions you are investigating into a thesis statement—a sentence that sets out the major claim you want to make after studying your primary source and reading your other sources. At this point, you will be able to indicate how you intend to explain and support your interpretation.

Refining Your Thesis

For instance, you might begin by investigating this question:

> Why did *M. Butterfly*, a play that ridicules much mainstream American thought, win the 1993 Tony Award for best play of the year, as well as many other awards?

You might, after doing your research, end up with a thesis statement something like this:

> By 1993, the social criticisms brought up by *M. Butterfly* were already common in American artistic and intellectual culture, so New York audiences were ready to respond favorably to their portrayal on the stage.

By the time you devise that claim, you have probably come up with a reasonable answer to your question. Your sources, in this case, would provide evidence to show what social criticisms were alive and well in artistic and intellectual circles around 1993. You would also need to show that New York audiences came from these circles.

Your thesis may change as you work with your material, but you need a fairly clear idea of what you want to say and how you will go about saying it before you begin.

IDEAS FOR WRITING

Ideas for Responsive Writing

1. Write an essay about fantasy in relationships. Have you ever had a romance or friendship built on fantasy more than on reality? If so, explain how this relationship came about and how it ended (if it did). Does the experience help you understand Gallimard's illusions?
2. What do you think of Gallimard's experiment in which he neglected Song for seven weeks? Why did he do it? Why does Song respond as she does? Is Gallimard's strategy still used in your culture? Explain how and why, as well as giving your evaluation of the strategy.

Ideas for Critical Writing

1. Review the scenes between Gallimard and Marc. Write an essay explaining their friendship. What roles do they play in the relationship? What does each one get from the relationship? Does the friendship change over the course of time—if so, how and why?
2. Find all the instances of generalizations about groups of people—Chinese, French, Westerners, Americans, actors, men, and so forth. Write about how stereotypes function, using examples from the play and from your own experience.

3. Find and read the 1986 *New York Times* article that inspired David Hwang to write *M. Butterfly* (Richard Bernstein, "France Jails 2 in Odd Case of Espionage," May 11, 1986, section 1, column 1, page 7). What elements of *M. Butterfly* came from the real story? What features of Hwang's culture informed his embellishments on the news story? Investigate the differences between the fictional and the journalistic stories.

Ideas for Researched Writing

1. Read documents related to Puccini's *Madame Butterfly.* These might be liner notes from recordings, reviews of stage productions, historical accounts, and so forth. Discuss how Hwang's version deals with the original themes and characters to make the story relevant to late-twentieth-century culture.
2. A document retrieved from the Internet using "stereotypes of Asian women" as keywords includes these remarks by a Chinese-American woman:

   > I believe that stereotypes of Asian women in general stem largely (and wrongly) from stereotypes of Japanese women. The fantasy Asian is intelligent yet pliable, mysterious yet ornamental. She's also perpetually prepubescent—ageless and petite, hairless, high-pitched, girly—while simultaneously being exotic and wise beyond her years...I've definitely seen one too many dorky white-guy musicians who play "oriental fusion" music, wear their hair in a samurai bun, and have Chinese characters tattooed on their pecs—all in the interest of aligning themselves with "ethnicity" in some way. I've seen China-doll blindness that affects men to the point where no matter how many burritos you eat, no matter how many Young Ones videos you watch, no matter how many combinations of combat boots, 501s, and tatty Goodwill coats you wear, they still see a little Oriental flower. ("How come you never wear a kimono? You'd look really nice in one. Will you wear one so I can at least take a picture?")

   Find other documents about this subject. Are the stereotypes held by Gallimard and other characters in M. Butterfly still endorsed in your culture? Why do you think these stereotypes have stayed alive or have faded over time? Focus your essay on why these stereotypes live and die in modern cultures.
3. Analyze the wardrobe of *M. Butterfly.* You might use photos and reviews of stage productions of the play, descriptions of costumes within the play, and sources on the styles described (e.g., chong sam, Mao suit, Armani). Explain how the costuming of the play supports its messages.
4. Examine the staging of *M. Butterfly.* Look at stage directions and scene design notes within the play, photographs of productions, and sources on technical aspects of the theater in the late twentieth century. You might also interview a scene designer or theatrical lighting specialist for material. Was *M. Butterfly* typical of or unusual for its era in theater history? Explain the intended effects and meaning of the stagecraft.

REWRITING

Writing is often an act of discovery—that is why we encourage you to use freewriting and clustering to develop your ideas. Your ideas also develop as you write a preplanned essay, and you may find yourself saying something much more interesting than you originally conceived. You also get warmed up as you go along, and your style becomes more natural and straightforward than it was in the beginning.

Coordinating Your Introduction and Conclusion

The changes that come from your growing comfort in writing the essay are great outcomes—but they demand that you go back to your opening and revise it to match the rest. We often find that deleting the original first paragraph entirely is a good idea. Then choose the best sentence from your conclusion—written after your warm-up and your discoveries midstream—and move it up front as the central sentence of a new introduction. Finally, see whether the closing needs smoothing out after you remove the sentence. It may need only a loose paraphrase of what you removed. Try this tactic on one of your old essays to see whether the introduction acquires new life. Consider it after you draft your essay for this chapter as well.

Sample Student Paper on Cultural Issues

The following paper was written by a student at Illinois State University.

Sample Student Paper

Linda Samuel

Professor Day

English 102

28 September 2008

The Choice for Illusion in *M. Butterfly*

David Henry Hwang's *M. Butterfly* captivates the audience through a tense, cynical interplay of racial, sexual, and cultural stereotypes in a barely believable plot. The most compelling challenge to belief that transfixes Hwang's audience is Gallimard's admitted ignorance of his lover's sex after twenty years of intimacy.

James S. Moy, associate professor of theater and drama at the University of Wisconsin, reflects upon the audience's reservation regarding Gallimard's lack of intimate knowledge about his lover: "As audiences leave the theater, then, racial/sexual identity is not an issue; rather, most are simply incredulous at how for twenty years Gallimard could have confused Song's rectum for a woman's vagina" (54). Moy further remarks that "the audience is left to ponder how a sophisticated western diplomat could fall victim to so amusing a case of gender confusion" (49).

Even the judge, at the play's culmination, dares to ask Song what every reader begs to know: "There is one thing that the court—indeed, that all of France—would like to know. . . . Did Monsieur Gallimard know you were a man?" (745). Readers of *M. Butterfly* silently repeat the judge's question. Did Gallimard know that Song was a man, or did ignorance somehow supplant intelligence, illusion supplant reality? These questions play havoc with rationality. How could Gallimard not know? How dare he not know? Readers scoff at the implausible concept that Gallimard could not know his lover's true sex.

Might Gallimard be guilty of a greater flaw than ignorance? Might his greater offense be that of knowingly placing fantasy over reality? John Simon, theater critic for *New York* magazine, questions Gallimard's supposed ignorance when he asks, "Can love be *that* blind? Can wish-fulfillment fantasy be *that* strong?" (117). Gallimard's actions from the play's genesis to its conclusion not only suggest his choice of fantasy over reality but confirm that it is a choice most of the characters make. Gallimard is more whole-heartedly involved in his illusion and is ennobled by his total immersion.

Henry David Hwang, writer of *M. Butterfly*, gives credibility to this conclusion in an Afterword, asserting that racial as well as sexual fantasy held Gallimard in its grip: Gallimard's "assumption was consistent with a certain stereotyped view of Asians as bowing, blushing flowers. I therefore concluded that the diplomat must have fallen in love, not with a person, but with a fantasy stereotype" (Afterword 95). Theater critic Richard Corliss provides further insight into Gallimard's world of illusion, insisting that "the heart sees what it sees" (85). What does Gallimard's heart see? In Song Liling, Gallimard sees a beautiful butterfly, despite initial evidence to the contrary. Her westernized words and tone combined with equal amounts of brass and sass stand in stark contrast to the Oriental butterfly that Gallimard seeks. Notice how Song questions Gallimard: "It's one of your favorite fantasies, isn't it? The submissive Oriental woman and the cruel white man" (715). Any evidence of a gentle butterfly here?

Although Song's harsh statements clearly do not reflect the submissive Oriental butterfly that consumes Gallimard's fantasies, his heart nevertheless "sees what it sees." Gallimard chooses fantasy over reality by rationalizing her attitude. "She is outwardly bold and outspoken, yet her heart is shy and afraid" (720). Fact or fantasy? He convinces himself, despite evidence to the contrary, that Song is a butterfly.

Why is Gallimard driven toward illusion over reality? For Gallimard, up to the time of meeting Song, reality was disappointing in both his professional and personal worlds. By his own admission, he was not a "true man." Recall Gallimard's statement, "The sad truth is that all men want a beautiful woman, and the uglier the man, the greater the want" (714). He acknowledges his status by concluding, "We, who are not handsome, nor brave, nor powerful, yet somehow believe, like Pinkerton, that we deserve a Butterfly" (712).

In Gallimard's world of fantasy, here finally is beautiful Song, who not only is attracted to Gallimard but has also conceded, "I have already given you my shame" (724). Song is not only beautiful but under Gallimard's power as well. His response to Song's concession is "I had finally gained power over a beautiful woman" (724). It is a dual fantasy come true. First, he gains power over a woman, apparently for the first time in his life. Second, he gains power over a *beautiful* woman. This fantasy come true is worth clinging to and defending even in the face of clues about gender deception. The illusion of heterosexual romance with Song makes room for dreams of political power and paternity to come true. *New York Times* critic Frank Rich emphasizes this point: "Gallimard believes he can become a real man only if he can exercise power over a beautiful and submissive woman, which is why he's so ripe to be duped by Song Liling's impersonation of a shrinking butterfly" (C13).

However, is Song solely responsible for duping Gallimard? Song does her part in making the fantasy real; as playwright Hwang comments, "The Chinese spy encouraged these misperceptions" (95). However, the principal weight of the fantasy rests with Gallimard's willingness to be duped and refusal to betray his own illusion. Although he states quite emphatically in the concluding act, "Tonight, I've finally learned to tell fantasy from reality. And, knowing the difference, I choose fantasy" (749), the truth is that Gallimard fully chooses fantasy over reality throughout the play, in the only authentic choice of his life.

Gallimard's wife, Helga, cannot conceive a child by Gallimard through intercourse. That Song can conceive a child by Gallimard is the illusion. Which "truth" would Gallimard believe? Leo Sauvage, theater critic, mentions the absurdity of the situation: "As for the baby Song convinces him s/he has had (surely the most preposterous unexplained item in the actual news story)[1] the play shows Chinese intelligence officers supplying it to their agent" (22). Gallimard once again chooses fantasy by accepting the Eurasian child as his own, never having witnessed its development within Song's body.

Gallimard is not the only character in the play who endorses illusion. Other characters likewise choose illusion in the face of reality. Recall what Comrade Chin says to Song, "Don't forget: there is no homosexuality in China" (730). In reality, however, does Chin really believe that Song could procure political secrets from Gallimard over a twenty-year period without engaging in homosexual acts? Chin is well aware that Song is a man; however, like Gallimard, she promotes the illusion.

Even Gallimard's wife, upon hearing Gallimard's request for a divorce, responds:

> I knew in my own way, I knew that you were not everything you pretended to be. But the pretense—going on your arm to the embassy ball, visiting your office and the guards saying, "Good morning, good morning, Madame Gallimard"—the pretense...was very good indeed. (743)

The greatest distinction between Helga's and Chin's fantasy and Gallimard's is that Helga and Chin recognize the illusion for what it is—and isn't—more clearly.

Ambassador Toulon, Gallimard's superior, also chooses fantasy over reality by promoting Gallimard to vice-consul and accepting his ideas on international policy, knowing at the same time that Gallimard is inexperienced in international affairs (outside his affair with the Butterfly). Toulon accepts Gallimard's political fantasizing based on his personal stereotype that "Orientals will always submit to a greater force" (729). Moy notes, "This, of course, was the mistake of the Vietnam War" (50). In the end, Toulon's illusion proves to be as costly and tragic as Gallimard's.

The question raised by the judge still begs for an answer. At what level does Gallimard know that Song is a man? Gallimard incriminates himself at the play's conclusion in his efforts to prevent Song from displaying evidence beyond all shadow of a doubt that he indeed is a man. At this point, Gallimard announces, "I know what you are . . . a man" (748).

Gallimard comes face-to-face with fact and fantasy. For the first time throughout the entire play, he acknowledges fact. However, he wastes no time in moving from this uncomfortable reality to a position closer to home. Gallimard exchanges his old fantasy of making his Butterfly "writhe on a needle" (722) for a new fantasy in which he is the butterfly, as he places the wig on his head and wraps himself in the kimono. Now, clothed within this new fantasy, Gallimard proudly announces, "My name is Rene Gallimard—also known as Madame Butterfly" (750). Like Chin and Helga, he now is able to sustain two contradictory beliefs at once.

As with his previous illusions, Gallimard pushes this fatal fantasy of being Madame Butterfly to the limit. He mimics the dying words and actions of Madame Butterfly, "Death with honor is better than life . . . life with dishonor" (750), as he pierces his heart with the knife. We must conclude that the dishonor equals an existence where fantasy and reality know each other's face.

Note

[1]Hwang based this play on a brief story that appeared in the *New York Times* ("France Jails 2 in Odd Case of Espionage": 11 May 1986), but he did not do any further research into the incident.

Samuel 8

Works Cited

Corliss, Richard. "Cinema: Betrayal in Beijing." *Time* 4 Oct. 1993: 85. *Expanded Academic ASAP.* Web. 10 Sept. 2008.

Hwang, David H. Afterword. *M. Butterfly.* New York: New American, 1988. 94–100. Print.

---. *M. Butterfly. Literature and the Writing Process.* 8th ed. Ed. Elizabeth McMahan, Susan X Day, and Robert Funk. Upper Saddle River: Prentice, 2005. 706–50. Print.

Moy, James S. "David Henry Hwang's *M. Butterfly* and Philip Kan Gotanda's *Yankee Dawg You Die*: Repositioning Chinese American Marginality on the American Stage." *Theatre Journal* 42 (1990): 48–56. *JSTOR.* Web. 11 Sept. 2008.

Rich, Frank. "*M. Butterfly*: A Story of a Strange Love, Conflict and Betrayal." *New York Times* 21 Mar. 1988: C13. *LexisNexis.* Web. 10 Sept. 2008.

Sauvage, Leo. "On Stage: Spring Salad." *New Leader* 11 April 1988: 22–23. Print.

Simon, John. "Finding Your Song." *New York* 11 Apr. 1988: 117. Print.

ANTHOLOGY of Drama

William Shakespeare 1564–1616

William Shakespeare is the most widely known author in all English literature. He was born in Stratford-on-Avon, probably attended grammar school there, and at eighteen married Anne Hathaway, who bore him three children. In 1585 or shortly thereafter, he went to London and began his apprenticeship as an actor. By 1594 he had won recognition as a poet, but it was in the theater that he made his strongest reputation. Shakespeare produced perhaps thirty-five plays in twenty-five years, including historical dramas, comedies, romances, and the great tragedies: *Hamlet* (1602), *Othello* (1604), *King Lear* (1605), and *Macbeth* (1606). His 154 sonnets are supreme examples of the form.

Othello, the Moor of Venice

THE NAMES OF THE ACTORS

OTHELLO, *the Moor.*
BRABANTIO, *a senator, father to Desdemona.*
CASSIO, *an honourable lieutenant to Othello.*
IAGO, *Othello's ancient, a villain.*
RODERIGO, *a gulled gentleman.*
DUKE OF VENICE.
SENATORS *of Venice.*
MONTANO, *governor of Cyprus.*
LODOVICO *and* GRATIANO, *kinsmen to Brabantio, two noble Venetians.*
SAILORS.
CLOWN.
DESDEMONA, *daughter to Brabantio and wife to Othello.*
EMILIA, *wife to Iago.*
BIANCA, *a courtezan and mistress to Cassio.*
MESSENGER, HERALD, OFFICERS, GENTLEMEN, MUSICIANS, *and* ATTENDANTS.

[SCENE: VENICE; A SEA-PORT IN CYPRUS]

ACT I

SCENE I

Venice. A street.

[*Enter* RODERIGO *and* IAGO.]

RODERIGO. Tush! never tell me; I take it much unkindly
That thou, Iago, who hast had my purse
As if the strings were thine, shouldst know of this.
IAGO. 'Sblood,[1] but you'll not hear me:
If ever I did dream of such a matter,
Abhor me.
RODERIGO. Thou told'st me thou didst hold him in thy hate.
IAGO. Despise me, if I do not. Three great ones of the city,[2]
In personal suit to make me his lieutenant,
Off-capp'd to him:[3] and, by the faith of man,
I know my price, I am worth no worse a place:
But he, as loving his own pride and purposes,
Evades them, with a bombast circumstance
Horribly stuff'd with epithets of war;
And, in conclusion,
Nonsuits[4] my mediators; for, "Certes," says he,
"I have already chose my officer."
And what was he?
Forsooth, a great arithmetician,[5]
One Michael Cassio, a Florentine,
A fellow almost damn'd in a fair wife;[6]
That never set a squadron in the field,
Nor the division[7] of a battle knows
More than a spinster; unless the bookish theoric,[8]
Wherein the toged[9] consuls can propose[10]
As masterly as he: mere prattle, without practice,
Is all his soldiership. But he, sir, had th' election:
And I, of whom his eyes had seen the proof

[1]**'Sblood** an oath, "by God's blood."
[2]**great ones of the city** Iago means to indicate his importance in the community; this is suggested also by his use of the word *worth* in line 11.
[3]**him** Othello.
[4]**Nonsuits** rejects.
[5]**arithmetician** a man whose military knowledge was merely theoretical, based on books of tactics.
[6]**A...wife** Cassio does not seem to be married, but his counterpart in Shakespeare's source did have a wife.
[7]**division** disposition of a battle line.
[8]**theoric** theory.
[9]**toged** wearing the toga.
[10]**propose** discuss.

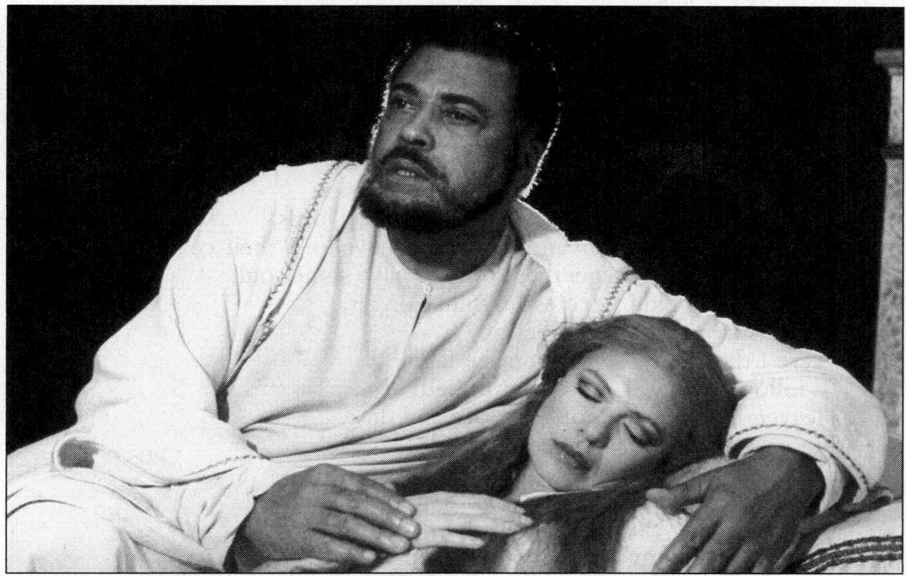

James Earl Jones as Othello and Irene Jacob as Desdemona in the 1995 film of *Othello*, directed by Oliver Parker. (Martha Swope/Getty Images/Time Life Pictures.)

At Rhodes, at Cyprus[11] and on other grounds
Christian and heathen, must be be-lee'd and calm'd
By debitor and creditor: this counter-caster,[12]
He, in good time,[13] must his lieutenant be,
And I—God bless the mark![14] —Moorship's ancient.[15]

RODERIGO. By heaven, I rather would have been his hangman.

IAGO. Why, there's no remedy; 'tis the curse of service,
Preferment goes by letter and affection,
And not by old gradation,[16] where each second
Stood heir to th' first. Now, sir, be judge yourself,
Whether I in any just term am affin'd[17]
To love the Moor.

RODERIGO. I would not follow then.

IAGO. O, sir, content you;
I follow him to serve my turn upon him:
We cannot all be masters, nor all masters
Cannot be truly follow'd. You shall mark

[11]**Rhodes, Cyprus** islands in the Mediterranean south of Asia Minor, long subject to contention between the Venetians and the Turks.

[12]**counter-caster** a sort of bookkeeper; contemptuous term.

[13]**in good time** opportunely.

[14]**God bless the mark** anciently, a pious interjection to avert evil omens.

[15]**ancient** standardbearer, ensign.

[16]**old gradation** seniority; Iago here expresses a characteristic prejudice of professional soldiers.

[17]**affin'd** bound.

Many a duteous and knee-crooking knave,
That, doting on his own obsequious bondage,
Wears out his time, much like his master's ass,
For nought but provender, and when he's old, cashier'd:
Whip me such honest knaves. Others there are
Who, trimm'd in forms and visages of duty,
Keep yet their hearts attending on themselves,
And, throwing but shows of service on their lords,
Do well thrive by them and when they have lin'd their coats
Do themselves homage: these fellows have some soul;
And such a one do I profess myself. For, sir,
It is as sure as you are Roderigo,
Were I the Moor, I would not be Iago:[18]
In following him, I follow but myself;
Heaven is my judge, not I for love and duty,
But seeming so, for my peculiar end:
For when my outward action doth demonstrate
The native act and figure of my heart
In compliment extern,[19] 'tis not long after
But I will wear my heart upon my sleeve
For daws to peck at: I am not what I am.

RODERIGO. What a full fortune does the thick-lips[20] owe,
If he can carry 't thus!

IAGO. Call up her father,
Rouse him: make after him, poison his delight,
Proclaim him in the streets, incense her kinsmen,
And, though he in a fertile climate dwell,
Plague him with flies: though that his joy be joy,
Yet throw such changes of vexation on 't,
As it may lose some colour.

RODERIGO. Here is her father's house; I'll call aloud.

IAGO. Do, with like timorous[21] accent and dire yell
As when, by night and negligence, the fire
Is spied in populous cities.

RODERIGO. What, ho, Brabantio! Signior Brabantio, ho!

IAGO. Awake! what, ho, Brabantio! thieves! thieves! thieves!
Look to your house, your daughter and your bags!
Thieves! thieves!

[BRABANTIO *appears above at a window*.]

BRABANTIO. What is the reason of this terrible summons?
What is the matter there?

RODERIGO. Signior, is all your family within?

IAGO. Are your doors lock'd?

BRABANTIO. Why, wherefore ask you this?

---

[18]**Were . . . Iago** Were I in the position of the Moor, I should not feel as Iago feels.
[19]**compliment extern** outward civility.
[20]**thick-lips** Elizabethans often applied the term Moor to Negroes.
[21]**timorous** frightening.

IAGO. 'Zounds, sir, y' are robb'd; for shame, put on your gown;
Your heart is burst, you have lost half your soul;
Even now, now, very now, an old black ram
Is tupping your white ewe. Arise, arise:
Awake the snorting[22] citizens with the bell,
Or else the devil will make a grandsire of you:
Arise, I say.

BRABANTIO. What, have you lost your wits?

RODERIGO. Most reverend signior, do you know my voice?

BRABANTIO. Not I: what are you?

RODERIGO. My name is Roderigo.

BRABANTIO. The worser welcome:
I have charg'd thee not to haunt about my doors:
In honest plainness thou has heard me say
My daughter is not for thee; and now, in madness,
Being full of supper and distemp'ring draughts,
Upon malicious bravery,[23] doest thou come
To start[24] my quiet.

RODERIGO. Sir, sir, sir,—

BRABANTIO. But thou must needs be sure
My spirit and my place have in them power
To make this bitter to thee.

RODERIGO. Patience, good sir.

BRABANTIO. What tell'st thou me of robbing? this is Venice;
My house is not a grange.[25]

RODERIGO. Most grave Brabantio,
In simple and pure soul I come to you.

IAGO. 'Zounds, sir, you are one of those that will not serve God, if the devil bid you. Because we come to do you service and you think we are ruffians, you'll have your daughter covered with a Barbary horse; you'll have your nephews[26] neigh to you; you'll have coursers for cousins and gennets[27] for germans.[28]

BRABANTIO. What profane wretch are thou?

IAGO. I am one, sir, that comes to tell you your daughter and the
Moor are now making the beast with two backs.

BRABANTIO. Thou art a villain.

IAGO. You are—a senator.

BRABANTIO. This thou shalt answer; I know thee, Roderigo.

RODERIGO. Sir, I will answer any thing. But, I beseech you,
If 't be your pleasure and most wise consent,
As partly I find it is, that your fair daughter,
At this odd-even[29] and dull watch o' th' night,

---

[22]**snorting** snoring.
[23]**bravery** defiance, bravado.
[24]**start** disrupt.
[25]**grange** isolated farmhouse.
[26]**nephews** grandsons.
[27]**gennets** small Spanish horses.
[28]**germans** near relatives.
[29]**odd-even** between night and morning.

Transported, with no worse nor better guard
But with a knave of common hire, a gondolier,
To the gross clasps of a lascivious Moor,—
If this be known to you and your allowance,[30]
We then have done you bold and saucy wrongs;
But if you know not this, my manners tell me
We have your wrong rebuke. Do not believe
That, from[31] the sense of all civility,
I thus would play and trifle with your reverence:
Your daughter, if you have not given her leave,
I say again, hath made a gross revolt;
Tying her duty, beauty, wit and fortunes
In an extravagant[32] and wheeling[33] stranger
Of here and every where. Straight satisfy yourself:
If she be in her chamber or your house,
Let loose on me the justice of the state
For thus deluding you.

BRABANTIO. Strike on the tinder,[34] ho!
Give me a taper! call up all my people!
This accident[35] is not unlike my dream:
Belief of it oppresses me already.
Light, I say! light!

[*Exit above.*]

IAGO. Farewell; for I must leave you:
It seems not meet, nor wholesome to my place,
To be produc'd—as, if I stay, I shall—
Against the Moor: for, I do know, the state,
However this may gall him with some check,[36]
Cannot with safety cast[37] him, for he's embark'd
With such loud reason to the Cyprus wars,
Which even now stand in act,[38] that, for their souls,
Another of his fathom[39] they have none,
To lead their business: in which regard,
Though I do hate him as I do hell-pains,
Yet, for necessity of present life,
I must show out a flag and sign of love,
Which is indeed but sign. That you shall surely find him,
Lead to the Sagittary[40] the raised search:
And there will I be with him. So, farewell.

[*Exit.*]

---

[30]**allowance** permission.
[31]**from** contrary to.
[32]**extravagant** wandering.
[33]**wheeling** vagabond.
[34]**tinder** charred linen kept in a metal box, and ignited by a spark from flint and steel.
[35]**accident** occurrence, event.
[36]**check** rebuke.
[37]**cast** dismiss.
[38]**stand in act** are going on.
[39]**fathom** ability.
[40]**Sagitarry** probably an inn.

[*Enter below* BRABANTIO, *with* SERVANTS *and torches.*]

BRABANTIO. It is too true an evil: gone she is;
And what's to come of my despised time
Is nought but bitterness. Now, Roderigo,
Where didst thou see her? O unhappy girl!
With the Moor, say'st thou? Who would be a father!
How didst thou know 'twas she? O, she deceives me
Past thought! What said she to you? Get moe[41] tapers:
Raise all my kindred. Are they married, think you?
RODERIGO. Truly, I think they are.
BRABANTIO. O heaven! How got she out? O treason of the blood!
Fathers, from hence trust not your daughters' minds
By what you see them act. Is[42] there not charms
By which the property[43] of youth and maidhood
May be abus'd? Have you not read, Roderigo,
Of some such thing?
RODERIGO. Yes, sir, I have indeed.
BRABANTIO. Call up my brother. O, would you[44] had had her!
Some one way, some another. Do you know
Where we may apprehend her and the Moor?
RODERIGO. I think I can discover him, if you please
To get good guard and go along with me.
BRABANTIO. Pray you, lead on. At every house I'll call;
I may command at most. Get weapons, ho!
And raise some special officers of night.[45]
On, good Roderigo: I will deserve your pains.

[*Exeunt.*]

SCENE II

Another street.

[*Enter* OTHELLO, IAGO, ATTENDANTS *with torches.*]

IAGO. Though in the trade of war I have slain men,
Yet do I hold it very stuff o' th' conscience
To do no contriv'd murder: I lack iniquity
Sometime to do me service: nine or ten times
I had thought t' have yerk'd[46] him here under the ribs.
OTHELLO. 'Tis better as it is.
IAGO. Nay, but he prated,
And spoke such scurvy and provoking terms
Against your honour

[41]**moe** more.
[42]**Is** are.
[43]**property** special quality.
[44]**you** Roderigo.
[45]**officers of night** police.
[46]**yerk'd** stabbed.

That, with the little godliness I have,
I did full hard forbear him. But, I pray you, sir,
Are you fast married? Be assur'd of this,
That the magnifico[47] is much belov'd,
And hath in his effect[48] a voice potential[49]
As double[50] as the duke's: he will divorce you;
Or put upon you what restraint and grievance
The law, with all his might to enforce it on,
Will give him cable.

OTHELLO. Let him do his spite;
My services, which I have done the signiory[51]
Shall out-tongue his complaints. 'Tis yet to know—
Which, when I know that boasting is an honour,
I shall promulgate—I fetch my life and being
From men of royal siege,[52] and my demerits[53]
May speak unbonneted[54] to as proud a fortune
As this that I have reach'd: for know, Iago,
But that I love the gentle Desdemona,
I would not my unhoused free condition
Put into circumscription and confine
For the sea's worth. But, look! what lights come yond?

IAGO. Those are the raised father and his friends:
You were best go in.

OTHELLO. Not I; I must be found:
My parts, my title and my perfect soul[55]
Shall manifest me rightly. Is it they?

IAGO. By Janus, I think no.

[*Enter* CASSIO *and certain* OFFICERS *with torches.*]

OTHELLO. The servants of the duke, and my lieutenant.
The goodness of the night upon you, friends!
What is the news?

CASSIO. The duke does greet you, general,
And he requires your haste-post-haste appearance,
Even on the instant.

OTHELLO. What is the matter, think you?

CASSIO. Something from Cyprus, as I may divine:
It is a business of some heat: the galleys
Have sent a dozen sequent[56] messengers
This very night at one another's heels,

---

[47]**magnifico** Venetian grandee (i.e., Brabantio).
[48]**effect** influence.
[49]**potential** powerful.
[50]**double** twice as influential as most men's.
[51]**signiory** Venetian government.
[52]**siege** rank.
[53]**demerits** deserts.
[54]**unbonneted** on equal terms.
[55]**perfect soul** unflawed conscience.
[56]**sequent** successive.

And many of the consuls,[57] rais'd and met,
Are at the duke's already: you have been hotly call'd for;
When, being not at your lodging to be found,
The senate hath sent about three several[58] quests
To search you out.

OTHELLO. 'Tis well I am found by you.
I will but spend a word here in the house,
And go with you.

[*Exit.*]

CASSIO. Ancient, what makes he here?

IAGO. 'Faith, he to-night hath boarded a land carack:[59]
If it prove lawful prize, he's made for ever.

CASSIO. I do not understand.

IAGO. He's married.

CASSIO. To who?

[*Enter* OTHELLO.]

IAGO. Marry, to—Come, captain will you?

OTHELLO. Have with you.

CASSIO. Here comes another troop to seek for you.

[*Enter* BRABANTIO, RODERIGO, *with* OFFICERS *and torches.*]

IAGO. It is Brabantio. General, be advis'd;
He comes to bad intent.

OTHELLO. Holla! stand there!

RODERIGO. Signoir, it is the Moor.

BRABANTIO. Down with him, thief!

[*They draw on both sides.*]

IAGO. You, Roderigo! come, sir, I am for you.

OTHELLO. Keep up your bright swords, for the dew will rust them.
Good Signior, you shall more command with years
Than with your weapons.

BRABANTIO. O thou foul thief, where hast thou stow'd my daughter?
Damn'd as thou art, thou has enchanted her;
For I'll refer me to all things of sense,[60]
If she in chains of magic were not bound,
Whether a maid so tender, fair and happy,
So opposite to marriage that she shunn'd
The wealthy curled darlings of our nation,
Would ever have, t' incur a general mock,
Run from her guardage[61] to the sooty bosom
Of such a thing as thou, to fear, not to delight.

---

[57]**consuls** senators.
[58]**several** separate.
[59]**carack** large merchant ship.
[60]**things of sense** commonsense understandings of the natural order.
[61]**guardage** guardianship.

Judge me the world, if 'tis not gross in sense[62]
That thou has practis'd on her with foul charms,
Abus'd her delicate youth with drugs or minerals[63]
That weaken motion:[64] I'll have't disputed on;[65]
'Tis probable and palpable to thinking.
I therefore apprehend and do attach thee
For an abuser of the world,[66] a practiser
Of arts inhibited[67] and out of warrant.
Lay hold upon him: if he do resist,
Subdue him at his peril.

OTHELLO. Hold your hands,
Both you of my inclining,[68] and the rest:
Were it my cue to fight, I should have known it
Without a prompter. Whither will you that I go
To answer this charge?

BRABANTIO. To prison, till fit time
Of law and course of direct session[69]
Call thee to answer.

OTHELLO. What if I do obey?
How may the duke be therewith satisfied,
Whose messengers are here about my side,
Upon some present business of the state
To bring me to him?

FIRST OFFICER. 'Tis true, most worthy signior;
The duke's in council, and your noble self,
I am sure, is sent for.

BRABANTIO. How! the duke in council!
In this time of night! Bring him away:
Mine's not an idle cause: the duke himself,
Or any of my brothers of the state,
Cannot but feel this wrong as 'twere their own;
For if such actions may have passage free,
Bond-slaves and pagans[70] shall our statesmen be.

[*Exeunt.*]

SCENE III

A council-chamber

[*Enter* DUKE, SENATORS *and* OFFICERS *set at a table, with lights and* ATTENDANTS.]

DUKE. There is no composition in these news
That gives them credit.

---

[62]**gross in sense** easily discernible in apprehension or perception.
[63]**minerals** medicine, poison.
[64]**motion** thought, reason.
[65]**disputed on** argued in court by professional counsel.
[66]**abuser of the world** corrupter of society.
[67]**inhibited** prohibited.
[68]**inclining** following, party.
[69]**course of direct session** regular legal proceedings.
[70]**Bond-slaves and pagans** contemptuous reference to Othello's past history.

FIRST SENATOR. Indeed, they are disproportion'd;[71]
My letters say a hundred and seven galleys.
DUKE. And mine, a hundred forty.
SECOND SENATOR. And mine, two hundred:
But though they jump[72] not on a just account,—
As in these cases, where the aim[73] reports,
'Tis oft with difference—yet do they all confirm
A Turkish fleet, and bearing up to Cyprus.
DUKE. Nay, it is possible enough to judgment:
I do not so secure me[74] in the error,
But the main article[75] I do approve
In fearful sense.
SAILOR. [*Within*] What, ho! what, ho! what, ho!
FIRST OFFICE. A messenger from the galleys.

[*Enter* SAILOR.]

DUKE. Now, what's the business?
SAIL. The Turkish preparation makes for Rhodes;
So was I bid report here to the state
By Signior Angelo.
DUKE. How say you by this change?
FIRST SENATOR. This cannot be,
By no assay[76] of reason: 'tis a pageant,
To keep us in false gaze. When we consider
Th' importancy of Cyprus to the Turk,
And let ourselves again but understand,
That as it more concerns the Turk than Rhodes,
So may he with more facile question[77] bear it,
For that it stands not in such warlike brace,[78]
But altogether lacks th' abilities
That Rhodes is dress'd in: if we make thought of this,
We must not think the Turk is so unskilful
To leave that latest which concerns him first,
Neglecting an attempt of ease and gain,
To wake and wage a danger profitless.
DUKE. Nay, in all confidence, he's not for Rhodes.
FIRST OFFICE. Here is more news.

[*Enter a* MESSENGER.]

MESSENGER. The Ottomites, reverend and gracious,
Steering with due course toward the isle of Rhodes,
Have there injointed them with an after fleet.

---

[71]**disproportion'd** inconsistent.
[72]**jump** agree.
[73]**aim** conjecture.
[74]**secure me** feel myself secure.
[75]**main article** i.e., that the Turkish fleet is threatening.
[76]**assay** test.
[77]**more facile question** greater facility of effort.
[78]**brace** state of defense.

FIRST SENATOR. Ay, so I thought. How many, as you guess?
MESSENGER. Of thirty sail: and now they do re-stem[79]
Their backward course, bearing with frank appearance
Their purposes toward Cyprus. Signior Montano,
Your trusty and most valiant servitor,
With his free duty recommends you thus,
And prays you to believe him.
DUKE. 'Tis certain, then, for Cyprus.
Marcus Luccicos, is not he in town?
FIRST SENATOR. He's now in Florence.
DUKE. Write from us to him; post-post-haste dispatch.
FIRST SENATOR. Here comes Brabantio and the valiant Moor.

[*Enter* BRABANTIO, OTHELLO, CASSIO, IAGO, RODERIGO, *and* OFFICERS.]

DUKE. Valiant Othello, we must straight employ you
Against the general enemy Ottoman.
[*To* BRABANTIO.] I did not see you; welcome, gentle signior;
We lack'd your counsel and your help to-night.
BRABANTIO. So did I yours. Good your grace, pardon me;
Neither my place nor aught I heard of business
Hath rais'd me from my bed, nor doth the general care
Take hold on me, for my particular grief
Is of so flood-gate and o'erbearing nature
That it engluts[80] and swallows other sorrows
And it is still itself.
DUKE. Why, what's the matter?
BRABANTIO. My daughter! O, my daughter!
DUKE *and* SENATOR. Dead?
BRABANTIO. Ay, to me;
She is abus'd, stol'n from me, and corrupted
By spells and medicines bought of mountebanks;
For nature so preposterously to err,
Being not deficient, blind, or lame of sense,
Sans witchcraft could not.
DUKE. Whoe'er he be that in this foul proceeding
Hath thus beguil'd your daughter of herself
And you of her, the bloody book of law
You shall yourself read in the bitter letter
After your own sense, yea, though our proper son
Stood in your action.[81]
BRABANTIO. Humbly I thank your grace.
Here is the man, this Moor, whom now, it seems,
Your special mandate for the state-affairs
Hath hither brought.

[79]**re-stem** steer again.
[80]**engluts** engulfs.
[81]**Stood…action** was under your accusation.

DUKE *and* SENATOR. We are very sorry for 't.
DUKE [*To Othello.*] What, in your own part, can you say to this?
BRABANTIO. Nothing, but this is so.
OTHELLO. Most potent, grave, and reverend signiors,
My very noble and approv'd good masters,
That I have ta'en away this old man's daughter,
It is most true; true, I have married her:
The very head and front of my offending
Hath this extent, no more. Rude am I in my speech,
And little bless'd with the soft phrase of peace;
For since these arms of mine had seven years' pith,[82]
Till now some nine moons wasted, they have us'd
Their dearest action in the tented field,
And little of this great world can I speak,
More than pertains to feats of broil and battle,
And therefore little shall I grace my cause
In speaking for myself. Yet, by your gracious patience,[83]
I will a round unvarnish'd tale deliver
Of my whole course of love; what drugs, what charms,
What conjuration and what mighty magic,
For such proceeding I am charg'd withal,
I won his daughter.
BRABANTIO. A maiden never bold;
Of spirit so still and quiet, that her motion
Blush'd at herself,[84] and she, in spite of nature,
Of years, of country, credit, every thing,
To fall in love with what she fear'd to look on!
It is a judgement maim'd and most imperfect
That will confess perfection so could err
Against all rules of nature, and must be driven
To find out practices of cunning hell,
Why this should be. I therefore vouch[85] again
That with some mixtures pow'rful o'er the blood,
Or with some dram conjur'd to this effect,
He wrought upon her.
DUKE. To vouch this is no proof,
Without more wider and more overt test
Than these thin habits and poor likelihoods
Of modern seeming do prefer against him.
FIRST SENATOR. But, Othello, speak:
Did you by indirect and forced courses
Subdue and poison this young maid's affections?
Or came it by request and such fair question
As soul to soul affordeth?

---

[82]**pith** strength, vigor.
[83]**patience** suffering, permission.
[84]**motion . . . herself** inward impulses blushed at themselves.
[85]**vouch** assert.

OTHELLO. I do beseech you,
Send for the lady to the Sagittary,
And let her speak of me before her father:
If you do find me foul in her report,
The trust, the office I do hold of you,
Not only take away, but let your sentence
Even fall upon my life.
DUKE. Fetch Desdemona hither.
OTHELLO. Ancient, conduct them; you best know the place.
[*Exeunt* IAGO *and* ATTENDANTS.]
And, till she come, as truly as to heaven
I do confess the vices of my blood,
So justly to your grave ear I'll present
How I did thrive in this fair lady's love,
And she in mine.
DUKE. Say it, Othello.
OTHELLO. Her father lov'd me; oft invited me;
Still question'd me the story of my life,
From year to year, the battles, sieges, fortunes,
That I have pass'd.
I ran it through, even from my boyish days,
To th' very moment that he bade me tell it;
Wherein I spake of most disastrous chances,
Of moving accidents by flood and field,
Of hair-breadth scapes i' th' imminent[86] deadly breach,
Of being taken by the insolent foe
And sold to slavery, of my redemption thence
And portance[87] in my travels' history:
Wherein of antres[88] vast and deserts idle,[89]
Rough quarries, rocks and hills whose heads touch heaven,
It was my hint[90] to speak,—such was the process;
And of the Cannibals that each other eat,[91]
The Anthropophagi[92] and men whose heads
Do grow beneath their shoulders. This to hear
Would Desdemona seriously incline:
But still the house-affairs would draw her thence:
Which ever as she could with haste dispatch,
She 'd come again, and with a greedy ear
Devour up my discourse: which I observing,
Took once a pliant hour, and found good means
To draw from her a prayer of earnest heart

[86]**imminent** i.e., impending parts when a gap has been made in a fortification.
[87]**portance** conduct.
[88]**antres** caverns.
[89]**idle** barren, unprofitable.
[90]**hint** occasion.
[91]**eat** ate.
[92]**Anthropophagi** man-eaters.

That I would all my pilgrimage dilate,[93]
Whereof by parcels she had something heard,
But not intentively:[94] I did consent,
And often did beguile her of her tears,
When I did speak of some distressful stroke
That my youth suffer'd. My story being done,
She gave me for my pains a world of sighs:
She swore, in faith, 'twas strange, 'twas passing strange,
'Twas pitiful, 'twas wondrous pitiful:
She wish'd she had not heard it, yet she wish'd
That heaven had made her such a man: she thank'd me,
And bade me, if I had a friend that lov'd her,
I should but teach him how to tell my story,
And that would woo her. Upon this hint I spake:
She lov'd me for the dangers I had pass'd,
And I lov'd her that she did pity them.
This only is the witchcraft I have us'd:
Here comes the lady; let her witness it.

[*Enter* DESDEMONA, IAGO, *and* ATTENDANTS.]

DUKE. I think this tale would win my daughter too.
Good Brabantio,
Take up this mangled matter at the best:
Men do their broken weapons rather use
Than their bare hands.

BRABANTIO. I pray you, hear her speak:
If she confess that she was half the wooer,
Destruction on my head, if my bad blame
Light on the man! Come hither, gentle mistress:
Do you perceive in all this noble company
Where most you owe obedience?

DESDEMONA. My noble father,
I do perceive here a divided duty:[95]
To you I am bound for life and education;
My life and education both do learn me
How to respect you; you are the lord of duty;
I am hitherto your daughter: but here's my husband,
And so much duty as my mother show'd
To you, preferring you before her father,
So much I challenge that I may profess
Due to the Moor my lord.

BRABANTIO. God be with you! I have done.
Please it your grace, on to[96] the state-affairs:
I had rather to adopt a child than get[97] it.
Come hither, Moor:

---

[93]**dilate** relate in detail.
[94]**intentively** with full attention.
[95]**divided duty** Desdemona recognizes that she still owes a duty to her father even after marriage.
[96]**on to** i.e., proceed with.
[97]**get** beget.

I here do give thee that with all my heart
Which, but thou hast already, with all my heart
I would keep from thee. For your sake,[98] jewel,
I am glad at soul I have no other child;
For thy escape would teach me tyranny,
To hang clogs on them. I have done, my lord.

DUKE. Let me speak like yourself,[99] and lay a sentence,[100]
Which, as a grise[101] or step, may help these lovers
Into your favour.
When remedies are past, the griefs are ended
By seeing the worst, which late on hopes depended.
To mourn a mischief that is past and gone
Is the next[102] way to draw new mischief on.
What cannot be preserv'd when fortune takes,
Patience her injury a mock'ry makes.
The robb'd that smiles steals something from the thief;
He robs himself that spends a bootless grief.

BRABANTIO. So let the Turk of Cyprus us beguile;
We lost it not, so long as we can smile.
He bears the sentence well that nothing bears
But the free comfort[103] which from thence he hears,
But he bears both the sentence and the sorrow
That, to pay grief, must of poor patience borrow.
These sentences, to sugar, or to gall,
Being strong on both sides, are equivocal:
But words are words; I never yet did hear
That the bruis'd heart was pierced through the ear.
I humbly beseech you, proceed to th' affairs of state.

DUKE. The Turk with a most mighty preparation makes for Cyprus. Othello, the fortitude[104] of the place is best known to you; and though we have there a substitute of most allowed[105] sufficiency, yet opinion, a sovereign mistress of effects, throws a more safer voice on you:[106] you must therefore be content to slubber[107] the gloss of your new fortunes with this more stubborn and boisterous expedition.

OTHELLO. The tyrant custom, most grave senators,
Hath made the flinty and steel couch of war
My thrice-driven[108] bed of down: I do agnize[109]

---

[98] **For your sake** on your account.
[99] **like yourself** i.e., as you would, in your proper temper.
[100] **sentence** maxim.
[101] **grise** step.
[102] **next** nearest.
[103] **comfort** i.e., the consolation that it may be borne with patience.
[104] **fortitude** strength.
[105] **allowed** acknowledged.
[106] **opinion . . . on you** public opinion, an important determiner of affairs, chooses you as the best man.
[107] **slubber** soil, sully.
[108] **thrice-driven** thrice sifted.
[109] **agnize** know in myself.

A natural and prompt alacrity
I find in hardness[110] and do undertake
These present wars against the Ottomites.
Most humbly therefore bending to your state,
I crave fit disposition for my wife,
Due reference of place and exhibition,[111]
With such accommodation and besort[112]
As levels with her breeding.

DUKE. If you please,
Be 't at her father's.

BRABANTIO. I'll not have it so.

OTHELLO. Nor I.

DESDEMONA. Nor I; I would not there reside,
To put my father in impatient thoughts
By being in his eye. Most gracious duke,
To my unfolding lend your prosperous[113] ear;
And let me find a charter[114] in your voice,
T' assist my simpleness.[115]

DUKE. What would you, Desdemona?

DESDEMONA. That I did love the Moor to live with him,
My downright violence and storm of fortunes,
May trumpet to the world: my heart's subdu'd
Even to the very quality of my lord:
I saw Othello's visage in his mind,
And to his honours and his valiant parts
Did I my soul and fortunes consecrate.
So that, dear lords, if I be left behind,
A moth of peace, and he go to the war,
The rites for why I love him are bereft me,
And I a heavy interim shall support
By his dear absence. Let me go with him.

OTHELLO. Let her have your voices.
Vouch with me, heaven, I therefore beg it not,
To please the palate of my appetite,
Nor to comply with heat—the young affects[116]
In me defunct—and proper satisfaction,
But to be free and bounteous to her mind:
And heaven defend your good souls, that you think
I will your serious and great business scant
When she is with me. No, when light-wing'd toys
Of feather'd Cupid seel[117] with wanton dullness

---

[110]**hardness** hardship.
[111]**exhibition** allowance.
[112]**besort** suitable company.
[113]**prosperous** propitious.
[114]**charter** privilege.
[115]**simpleness** simplicity.
[116]**affects** inclinations, desires.
[117]**seel** in falconry, to make blind by sewing up the eyes of the hawk in training.

My speculative and offic'd instruments,[118]
That[119] my disports[120] corrupt and taint[121] my business,
Let housewives make a skillet of my helm,
And all indign[122] and base adversities
Make head against my estimation![123]
DUKE. Be it as you shall privately determine,
Either for her stay or going: th' affair cries haste,
And speed must answer it.
FIRST SENATOR. You must away to-night.
OTHELLO. With all my heart.
DUKE. At nine i' th' morning here we'll meet again.
Othello, leave some officer behind,
And he shall our commission bring to you;
With such things else of quality and respect
As doth import[124] you.
OTHELLO. So please your grace, my ancient;
A man he is of honesty and trust:
To his conveyance I assign my wife,
With what else needful your good grace shall think
To be sent after me.
DUKE. Let it be so.
Good night to every one. [*To* BRABANTIO.] And, noble signior,
If virtue no delighted[125] beauty lack,
Your son-in-law is far more fair than black.
FIRST SENATOR. Adieu, brave Moor; use Desdemona well.
BRABANTIO. Look to her, Moor, if thou hast eyes to see;
She has deceiv'd her father, and may thee.
[*Exeunt* DUKE, SENATORS, OFFICERS, *etc.*]
OTHELLO. My life upon her faith! Honest Iago,[126]
My Desdemona must I leave to thee:
I prithee, let thy wife attend on her;
And bring them after in the best advantage.
Come, Desdemona; I have but an hour
Of love, of wordly matters and direction,
To spend with thee: we must obey the time.
[*Exit with* DESDEMONA.]
RODERIGO. Iago—
IAGO. What say'st thou, noble heart?
RODERIGO. What will I do, thinkest thou?
IAGO. Why, go to bed, and sleep.
RODERIGO. I will incontinently[127] drown myself.

---

[118]**speculative...instruments** ability to see and reason clearly.
[119]**That** so that.
[120]**disports** pastimes.
[121]**taint** impair.
[122]**indign** unworthy, shameful.
[123]**estimation** reputation.
[124]**import** concern.
[125]**delighted** delightful.
[126]**Honest Iago** an evidence of Iago's carefully built reputation.
[127]**incontinently** immediately.

IAGO. If thou dost, I shall never love thee after. Why, thou silly gentleman!

RODERIGO. It is silliness to live when to live is torment; and then have we a prescription to die when death is our physician.

IAGO. O villainous! I have looked upon the world for four times seven years; and since I could distinguish betwixt a benefit and an injury, I never found man that knew how to love himself. Ere I would say, I would drown myself for the love of a guinea-hen, I would change my humanity with a baboon.

RODERIGO. What should I do? I confess it is my shame to be so fond; but it is not in my virtue[128] to amend it.

IAGO. Virtue! a fig! 'tis in ourselves that we are thus or thus. Our bodies are our gardens, to the which our wills are gardeners; so that if we will plant nettles, or sow lettuce, set hyssop[129] and weed up thyme, supply it with one gender[130] of herbs, or distract it with many, either to have it sterile with idleness,[131] or manured with industry, why, the power and corrigible authority[132] of this lies in our wills. If the balance of our lives had not one scale of reason to poise another of sensuality, the blood and baseness of our natures would conduct us to most preposterous conclusions:[133] but we have reason to cool our raging motions,[134] our carnal stings, our unbitted[135] lusts, whereof I take this that you call love to be a sect[136] or scion.

RODERIGO. It cannot be.

IAGO. It is merely a lust of the blood and a permission of the will. Come, be a man. Drown thyself! Drown cats and blind puppies. I have professed me thy friend and I confess me knit to thy deserving with cables of perdurable[137] toughness; I could never better stead thee than now. Put money in thy purse; follow thou the wars; defeat thy favour[138] with an usurped beard; I say, put money in thy purse. It cannot be that Desdemona should long continue her love to the Moor,—put money in thy purse,—nor he his to her: it was a violent commencement in her, and thou shalt see an answerable sequestration:[139]—put but money in thy purse. These Moors are changeable in their wills:—fill thy purse with money:—the food that to him now is as luscious as locusts,[140] shall be to him shortly as bitter as coloquintida.[141] She must change for youth: when she is sated with his body, she will find the

---

[128]**virtue** strength.

[129]**hyssop** an herb of the mint family.

[130]**gender** kind.

[131]**idleness** want of cultivation.

[132]**corrigible authority** the power to correct.

[133]**reason...conclusions** Iago understands the warfare between reason and sensuality, but his ethics are totally inverted; reason works in him not good, as it should according to natural law, but evil, which he has chosen for his good.

[134]**motions** appetites.

[135]**unbitted** uncontrolled.

[136]**sect** cutting.

[137]**perdurable** very durable.

[138]**defeat thy favour** disguise and disfigure thy face.

[139]**answerable sequestration** a corresponding separation or estrangement.

[140]**locusts** of doubtful meaning; defined as fruit of the carob tree, as honeysuckle, and as lollipops or sugar sticks.

[141]**coloquintida** colocynth, or bitter apple, a purgative.

error of her choice: she must have change, she must: therefore put money in thy purse. If thou wilt needs damn thyself, do it a more delicate way than drowning. Make all the money thou canst: if sanctimony and a frail vow betwixt an erring[142] barbarian and a supersubtle Venetian be not too hard for my wits and all the tribe of hell, thou shalt enjoy her; therefore make money. A pox of drowning thyself! it is clean out of the way: seek thou rather to be hanged in compassing the joy than to be drowned and go without her.

RODERIGO. Wilt thou be fast to my hopes, if I depend on the issue?

IAGO. Thou art sure of me: —go, make money:—I have told thee often, and I re-tell thee again and again, I hate the Moor: my cause is hearted;[143] thine hath no less reason. Let us be conjunctive[144] in our revenge against him; if thou canst cuckold him, thou dost thyself a pleasure, me a sport. There are many events in the womb of time which will be delivered. Traverse![145] go, provide thy money. We will have more of this to-morrow. Adieu.

RODERIGO. Where shall we meet i' the morning?

IAGO. At my lodging.

RODERIGO. I'll be with thee betimes.

IAGO. Go to; farewell. Do you hear, Roderigo?

RODERIGO. What say you?

IAGO. No more of drowning, do you hear?

RODERIGO. I am changed. I'll go sell all my land. [*Exit.*]

IAGO. Thus do I ever make my fool my purse;
For I mine own gain'd knowledge should profane,
If I would time expend with such a snipe,[146]
But for my sport and profit. I hate the Moor;
And it is thought abroad, that 'twixt my sheets
H' as done my office: I know not if 't be true;
But I, for mere suspicion in that kind,
Will do as if for surety. He holds me well;
The better shall my purpose work on him.
Cassio's a proper man: let me see now:
To get his place and to plume up[147] my will
In double knavery—How, how?—Let's see:—
After some time, to abuse Othello's ears
That he[148] is too familiar with his wife.
He hath a person and a smooth dispose[149]
To be suspected, fram'd to make women false.
The Moor is of a free[150] and open nature,

---

[142]**erring** wandering.
[143]**hearted** fixed in the heart.
[144]**conjunctive** united.
[145]**Traverse** go (military term).
[146]**snipe** gull, fool.
[147]**plume up** glorify, gratify.
[148]**he** i.e., Cassio.
[149]**dispose** external manner.
[150]**free** frank.

That thinks men honest that but seem to be so,
And will as tenderly be led by th' nose
As asses are.
I have 't. It is engend'red. Hell and night
Must bring this monstrous birth to the world's light.

[*Exit.*]

ACT II

SCENE I

A Sea-port in Cyprus. An open place near the quay.

[*Enter* MONTANO *and two* GENTLEMEN.]

MONTANO. What from the cape can you discern at sea?
FIRST GENTLEMAN. Nothing at all: it is a high-wrought flood;
I cannot, 'twixt the heaven and the main,
Descry a sail.
MONTANO. Methinks the wind hath spoke aloud at land;
A fuller blast ne'er shook our battlements:
If it hath ruffian'd[1] so upon the sea,
What ribs of oak, when mountains melt on them,
Can hold the mortise?[2] What shall we hear of this?
SECOND GENTLEMAN. A segregation[3] of the Turkish fleet:
For do but stand upon the foaming shore,
The chidden billow seems to pelt the clouds:
The wind-shak'd surge, with high and monstrous mane,
Seems to cast water on the burning bear,[4]
And quench the guards[5] of th' ever-fixed pole:
I never did like molestation view
On the enchafed[6] flood.
MONTANO. If that the Turkish fleet
Be not enshelter'd and embay'd, they are drown'd;
It is impossible they bear it out.

[*Enter a third* GENTLEMAN.]

THIRD GENTLEMAN. News, lads! our wars are done.
The desperate tempest hath so bang'd the Turks,
That their designment[7] halts: a noble ship of Venice
Hath seen a grievous wrack and sufferance[8]
On most part of their fleet.
MONTANO. How! is this true?

---

[1]**ruffian'd** raged.
[2]**mortise** the socket hollowed out in fitting timbers.
[3]**segregation** dispersion.
[4]**bear** a constellation.
[5]**quench the guards** overwhelm the stars near the polestar.
[6]**enchafed** angry.
[7]**designment** enterprise.
[8]**sufferance** disaster.

THIRD GENTLEMAN. The ship is here put in,
A Veronesa; Michael Cassio,
Lieutenant to the warlike Moor Othello,
Is come on shore: the Moor himself at sea,
And is in full commission here for Cyprus.
MONTANO. I am glad on 't; 'tis a worthy governor.
THIRD GENTLEMAN. But this same Cassio, though he speak of comfort
Touching the Turkish loss, yet he looks sadly,
And prays the Moor be safe; for they were parted
With foul and violent tempest.
MONTANO. Pray heavens he be;
For I have serv'd him, and the man commands
Like a full[9] soldier. Let's to the seaside, ho!
As well to see the vessel that's come in
As to throw out our eyes for brave Othello,
Even till we make the main and th' aerial blue
An indistinct regard.[10]
THIRD GENTLEMAN. Come, let's do so;
For every minute is expectancy
Of more arrivance.[11]

[*Enter* CASSIO.]

CASSIO. Thanks, you the valiant of this warlike isle,
That so approve the Moor! O, let the heavens
Give him defence against the elements,
For I have lost him on a dangerous sea.
MONTANO. Is he well shipp'd?
CASSIO. His bark is stoutly timber'd, and his pilot
Of very expert and approv'd allowance;[12]
Therefore my hopes, not surfeited to death,
Stand in bold cure. [*A cry within.*] "A sail, a sail, a sail!"

[*Enter a fourth* GENTLEMAN.]

CASSIO. What noise?

FOURTH GENTLEMAN. The town is empty; on the brow o' th' sea
Stand ranks of people, and they cry "A sail!"
CASSIO. My hopes do shape him for the governor. [*Guns heard.*]
SECOND GENTLEMAN. They do discharge their shot of courtesy:
Our friends at least.
CASSIO. I pray you, sir, go forth,
And give us truth who 'tis that is arriv'd.
SECOND GENTLEMAN. I shall.

[*Exit.*]

MONTANO. But, good lieutenant, is your general wiv'd?
CASSIO. Most fortunately: he hath achiev'd a maid

---

[9]**full** perfect.
[10]**make . . . regard** cause the blue of the sea and the air to grow indistinguishable in our view.
[11]**arrivance** arrival.
[12]**allowance** reputation.

That paragons[13] description and wild fame;
One that excels the quirks[14] of blazoning[15] pens,
And in th' essential vesture of creation[16]
Does tire the ingener.[17]

[*Enter second* GENTLEMAN.]

How now! who has put in?
SECOND GENTLEMAN. 'Tis one Iago, ancient to the general.
CASSIO. Has had most favourable and happy speed:
Tempests themselves, high seas and howling winds,
The gutter'd[18] rocks and congregated sands,—
Traitors ensteep'd[19] to clog the guiltless keel,—
As having sense of beauty, do omit
Their mortal[20] natures, letting go safely by
The divine Desdemona.
MONTANO. What is she?
CASSIO. She that I spake of, our great captain's captain,
Left in the conduct of the bold Iago,
Whose footing here anticipates our thoughts
A se'nnight's[21] speed. Great Jove, Othello guard,
And swell his sail with thine own powr'ful breath,
That he may bless this bay with his tall ship,
Make love's quick pants in Desdemona's arms,
Give renew'd fire to our extincted spirits,
And bring all Cyprus comfort!

[*Enter* DESDEMONA, IAGO, RODERIGO, *and* EMILIA *with* ATTENDANTS.]

O, behold,
The riches of the ship is come on shore!
You men of Cyprus, let her have your knees.
Hail to thee, lady! and the grace of heaven,
Before, behind thee and on every hand,
Enwheel thee round!
DESDEMONA. I thank you, valiant Cassio.
What tidings can you tell me of my lord?
CASSIO. He is not yet arriv'd: nor know I aught
But that he's well and will be shortly here.
DESDEMONA. O, but I fear—How lost you company?
CASSIO. The great contention of the sea and skies

---

[13]**paragons** surpasses.
[14]**quirks** witty conceits.
[15]**blazoning** setting forth honorably in words.
[16]**vesture of creation** the real qualities with which creation has invested her.
[17]**ingener** inventor, praiser.
[18]**gutter'd** jagged, trenched.
[19]**ensteep'd** lying under water.
[20]**mortal** deadly.
[21]**se'nnight's** week's.

Parted our fellowship—But, hark! a sail.
[*Within*] "A sail, a sail!" [*Guns heard.*]

Second Gentleman. They give their greeting to the citadel:
This likewise is a friend.

Cassio. See for the news.

[*Exit* Gentleman.]

Good ancient, you are welcome. [*To* Emilia.] Welcome, mistress:
Let it not gall your patience, good Iago,
That I extend my manners; 'tis my breeding
That gives me this bold show of courtesy. [*Kissing her.*]

Iago. Sir, would she give you so much of her lips
As of her tongue she oft bestows on me,
You would have enough.

Desdemona. Alas, she has no speech.

Iago. In faith, too much;
I find it still, when I have list to sleep:
Marry, before your ladyship, I grant,
She puts her tongue a little in her heart,
And chides with thinking.

Emilia. You have little cause to say so.

Iago. Come on, come on; you are pictures out of doors,
Bells in your parlours, wild-cats in your kitchens,
Saints in your injuries, devils being offended,
Players in your housewifery, and housewives[22] in your beds.

Desdemona. O, fie upon thee, slanderer!

Iago. Nay, it is true, or else I am a Turk:
You rise to play and go to bed to work.

Emilia. You shall not write my praise.

Iago. No, let me not.

Desdemona. What wouldst thou write of me, if thou shouldst praise me?

Iago. O gentle lady, do not put me to 't;
For I am nothing, if not critical.[23]

Desdemona. Come on, assay. There's one gone to the harbour?

Iago. Ay, madam.

Desdemona. I am not merry; but I do beguile
The thing I am, by seeming otherwise.
Come, how wouldst thou praise me?

Iago. I am about it; but indeed my invention
Comes from my pate as birdlime[24] does from frieze;[25]
It plucks out brains and all: but my Muse labours,
And thus she is deliver'd.
If she be fair and wise, fairness and wit,
The one's for use, the other useth it.

Desdemona. Well praised! How if she be black and witty?

Iago. If she be black, and thereto have a wit,

[22]**housewives** hussies.
[23]**critical** censorious.
[24]**birdlime** sticky substance smeared on twigs to catch small birds.
[25]**frieze** coarse woolen cloth.

She'll find a white[26] that shall her blackness fit.
DESDEMONA. Worse and worse.
EMILIA. How if fair and foolish?
IAGO. She never yet was foolish that was fair;
For even her folly help'd her to an heir.

DESDEMONA. These are old fond[27] paradoxes to make fools laugh i' the alehouse. What miserable praise hast Thou for her that's foul and foolish?

IAGO. There's none so foul and foolish thereunto,
But does foul pranks which fair and wise ones do.

DESDEMONA. O heavy ignorance! thou praisest the worst best. But what praise couldst thou bestow on a deserving woman indeed, one that, in the authority of her merit, did justly put on the vouch[28] of her malice itself?

IAGO. She that was ever fair and never proud,
Had tongue at will and yet was never loud,
Never lack'd gold and yet went never gay,
Fled from her wish and yet said "Now I may,"
She that being ang'red, her revenge being nigh,
Bade her wrong stay and her displeasure fly,
She that in wisdom never was so frail
To change the cod's head for the salmon's tail,[29]
She that could think and ne'er disclose her mind,
See suitors following and not look behind,
She was a wight, if ever such wight were,—
DESDEMONA. To do what?
IAGO. To suckle fools and chronicle small beer.[30]

DESDEMONA. O most lame and impotent conclusion! Do not learn of him, Emilia, though he be thy husband. How say you, Cassio? Is he not a most profane and liberal[31] counsellor?

CASSIO. He speaks home,[32] madam: you may relish him more in the soldier than in the scholar.

IAGO [*Aside*]. He takes her by the palm: ay, well said, whisper: with as little a web as this will I ensnare as great a fly as Cassio. Ay, smile upon her, do; I will gyve[33] thee in thine own courtship.[34] You say true; 'tis so, indeed: if such tricks as these strip you out of your lieutenantry, it had been better you had not kissed your three fingers[35] so oft, which now again you are most apt to play the sir[36] in. Very good; well kissed! an excellent courtesy! 'tis so, indeed. Yet again your fingers to your lips? would they were clyster-pipes[37] for your sake. [*Trumpet within.*] The Moor! I know his trumpet.

---

[26]**white** a fair person, with a wordplay on *wight*.
[27]**fond** foolish.
[28]**put on the vouch** compel the approval.
[29]**To change . . . tail** to exchange a delicacy for mere refuse.
[30]**chronicle small beer** keep petty household accounts.
[31]**liberal** licentious.
[32]**speaks home** i.e., without reserve.
[33]**gyve** fetter, shackle.
[34]**courtship** courtesy.
[35]**kissed your three fingers** he kisses his own hand as a token of reverence.
[36]**the sir** i.e., the fine gentleman.
[37]**clyster-pipes** tubes used for enemas.

CASSIO. 'Tis truly so.
DESDEMONA. Let's meet him and receive him.
CASSIO. Lo, where he comes!

[*Enter* OTHELLO *and* ATTENDANTS.]

OTHELLO. O my fair warrior!
DESDEMONA. My dear Othello!
OTHELLO. It gives me wonder great as my content
To see you here before me. O my soul's joy!
If after every tempest comes such calms,
May the winds blow till they have waken'd death!
And let the labouring bark climb hills of seas
Olympus-high and duck again as low
As hell 's from heaven! If it were now to die,
'Twere now to be most happy; for, I fear,
My soul hath her content so absolute
That not another comfort like to this
Succeeds in unknown fate.
DESDEMONA. The heavens forbid
But that our loves and comforts should increase,
Even as our days do grow!
OTHELLO. Amen to that, sweet powers!
I cannot speak enough of this content;
It stops me here; it is too much of joy:
And this, and this, the greatest discords be [*Kissing her*.]
That e'er our hearts shall make!
IAGO. [*Aside*.] O, you are well tun'd now!
But I'll set down the pegs[38] that make this music,
As honest as I am.
OTHELLO. Come, let us to the castle.
News, friends; our wars are done, the Turks are drowned.
How does my old acquaintance of this isle?
Honey, you shall be well desir'd in Cyprus;
I have found great love amongst them. O my sweet,
I prattle out of fashion, and I dote
In mine own comforts. I prithee, good Iago,
Go to the bay and disembark my coffers:
Bring thou the master to the citadel;
He is a good one, and his worthiness
Does challenge much respect. Come, Desdemona,
Once more, well met at Cyprus.

[*Exeunt* OTHELLO *and* DESDEMONA *and all but* IAGO *and* RODERIGO.]

IAGO [*To an* ATTENDANT]. Do thou meet me presently at the harbour. [*To* RODERIGO]. Come hither. If thou be'st valiant,—as, they say, base men being in love have then a nobility in their natures more than is native to them,—list me. The lieutenant tonight watches on the court of guard.[39] I must tell thee this—Desdemona is directly in love with him.

---

[38]**set down the pegs** lower the pitch of the strings, i.e., disturb the harmony.
[39]**court of guard** guardhouse.

RODERIGO. With him! why 'tis not possible.

IAGO. Lay thy finger thus, and let thy soul be instructed. Mark me with what violence she first loved the Moor, but for bragging and telling her fantastical lies: and will she love him still for prating? Let not thy discreet heart think it. Her eye must be fed; and what delight shall she have to look on the devil? When the blood is made dull with the act of sport, there should be, again to inflame it and to give satiety a fresh appetite, loveliness in favour, sympathy in years, manners and beauties; all which the Moor is defective in: now, for want of these required conveniences, her delicate tenderness will find itself abused, begin to heave the gorge, disrelish and abhor the Moor; very nature will instruct her in it and compel her to some second choice. Now, sir, this granted,—as it is a most pregnant and unforced position—who stands so eminent in the degree of this fortune as Cassio does? a knave very voluble; no further conscionable[40] than in putting on the mere form of civil and humane seeming, for the better compassing of his salt[41] and most hidden loose affection? why, none; why, none: a slipper[42] and subtle knave, a finder of occasions, that has an eye can stamp and counterfeit advantages, though true advantage never present itself; a devilish knave. Besides, the knave is handsome, young, and hath all those requisites in him that folly and green minds look after: a pestilent complete knave; and the woman hath found him already.

RODERIGO. I cannot believe that in her; she's full of most blessed condition.

IAGO. Blessed fig's-end! the wine she drinks is made of grapes: if she had been blessed, she would never have loved the Moor. Blessed pudding! Didst thou not see her paddle with the palm of his hand? didst not mark that?

RODERIGO. Yes, that I did; but that was but courtesy.

IAGO. Lechery, by his hand; an index and obscure prologue to the history of lust and foul thoughts. They met so near with their lips that their breaths embraced together. Villainous thoughts, Roderigo! when these mutualities so marshall the way, hard at hand comes the master and main exercise, the incorporate conclusion. Pish! But, sir, be you ruled by me: I have brought you from Venice. Watch you to-night; for the command, I'll lay't upon you. Cassio knows you not. I'll not be far from you: do you find some occasion to anger Cassio, either by speaking too loud, or tainting[43] his discipline; or from what other course you please, which the time shall more favourably minister.

RODERIGO. Well.

IAGO. Sir, he is rash and very sudden in choler, and haply may strike at you: provoke him, that he may; for even out of that will I cause these of Cyprus to mutiny; whose qualification[44] shall come into no true taste again but by the displanting of Cassio. So shall you have a shorter journey to your desires by the means I shall then have to prefer them; and the impediment most profitably removed, without the which there were no expectation of our prosperity.

RODERIGO. I will do this, if I can bring it to any opportunity.

---

[40]**conscionable** conscientious.
[41]**salt** licentious.
[42]**slipper** slippery.
[43]**tainting** disparaging.
[44]**qualification** appeasement.

IAGO. I warrant thee. Meet me by and by[45] at the citadel: I must fetch his necessaries ashore. Farewell.

RODERIGO. Adieu.

[*Exit.*]

IAGO. That Cassio loves her, I do well believe 't;
That she loves him, 'tis apt[46] and of great credit:[47]
The Moor, howbeit that I endure him not,
Is of a constant, loving, noble nature,
And I dare think he'll prove to Desdemona
A most dear husband. Now, I do love her too;
Not out of absolute lust, though peradventure
I stand accountant for as great a sin,
But partly led to diet my revenge,
For that I do suspect the lusty Moor
Hath leap'd into my seat; the thought whereof
Doth, like a poisonous mineral, gnaw my inards;
And nothing can or shall content my soul
Till I am even'd with him, wife for wife,
Or failing so, yet that I put the Moor
At least into a jealousy so strong
That judgement cannot cure. Which thing to do,
If this poor trash[48] of Venice, whom I trash[49]
For his quick hunting, stand the putting on,[50]
I'll have our Michael Cassio on the hip,[51]
Abuse him to the Moor in the rank garb—
For I fear Cassio with my night-cap too—
Make the Moor thank me, love me and reward me,
For making him egregiously an ass
And practicing upon his peace and quiet
Even to madness. 'Tis here, but yet confus'd:
Knavery's plain face is never seen till us'd.

[*Exit.*]

SCENE II

A street.

[*Enter Othello's* HERALD *with a proclamation.*]

HERALD. It is Othello's pleasure, our noble and valiant general, that, upon certain tidings now arrived, importing the mere perdition[52] of the Turkish fleet, every man put himself into triumph; some to dance, some to make bonfires, each man to what sport and revels his addiction leads him: for,

---

[45]**by and by** immediately.
[46]**apt** probable.
[47]**credit** credibility.
[48]**trash** worthless thing (Roderigo).
[49]**trash** hold in check.
[50]**putting on** incitement to quarrel.
[51]**on the hip** at my mercy (wrestling term).
[52]**mere perdition** complete destruction.

besides these beneficial news, it is the celebration of his nuptial. So much was his pleasure should be proclaimed. All offices[53] are open, and there is full liberty of feasting from this present hour of five till the bell have told eleven. Heaven bless the isle of Cyprus and our general Othello!

[*Exit.*]

SCENE III

A hall in the castle.

[*Enter* OTHELLO, DESDEMONA, CASSIO, *and* ATTENDANTS.]

OTHELLO. Good Michael, look you to the guard to-night:
Let's teach ourselves that honourable stop,[54]
Not to outsport discretion.

CASSIO. Iago hath direction what to do;
But, notwithstanding, with my personal eye
Will I look to 't.

OTHELLO. Iago is most honest.
Michael, goodnight: to-morrow with your earliest
Let me have speech with you. [*To* DESDEMONA.] Come, my dear love,
The purchase made, the fruits are to ensue;
That profit's yet to come 'tween me and you.
Good night.

[*Exit* OTHELLO, *with* DESDEMONA *and* ATTENDANTS.]

[*Enter* IAGO.]

CASSIO. Welcome, Iago; we must to the watch.

IAGO. Not this hour, lieutenant; 'tis not yet ten o' the clock. Our general cast[55] us thus early for the love of his Desdemona; who let us not therefore blame: he hath not yet made wanton the night with her; and she is sport for Jove.

CASSIO. She's a most exquisite lady.

IAGO. And, I'll warrant her, full of game.

CASSIO. Indeed, she's a most fresh and delicate creature.

IAGO. What an eye she has! Methinks it sounds a parley of provocation.

CASSIO. An inviting eye; and yet methinks right modest.

IAGO. And when she speaks, is it not an alarum to love?

CASSIO. She is indeed perfection.

IAGO. Well, happiness to their sheets! Come, lieutenant, I have a stoup[56] of wine; and here without are a brace of Cyprus gallants that would fain have a measure to the health of black Othello.

CASSIO. Not to-night, good Iago: I have very poor and unhappy brains for drinking: I could well wish courtesy would invent some other custom of entertainment.

IAGO. O, they are our friends, but one cup: I'll drink for you.

---

[53]**offices** rooms where food and drink were kept.
[54]**stop** restraint.
[55]**cast** dismissed.
[56]**stoup** measure of liquor, two quarts.

CASSIO. I have drunk but one cup tonight, and that was craftily qualified[57] too, and, behold, what innovation[58] it makes here:[59] I am unfortunate in the infirmity, and dare not task my weakness with any more.

IAGO. What, man! 'tis a night of revels: the gallants desire it.

CASSIO. Where are they?

IAGO. Here at the door; I pray you, call them in.

CASSIO. I'll do 't; but it dislikes me. [*Exit.*]

IAGO. If I can fasten but one cup upon him,
With that which he hath drunk to-night already,
He'll be as full of quarrel and offence
As my young mistress' dog. Now, my sick fool Roderigo,
Whom love hath turn'd almost the wrong side out,
To Desdemona hath to-night carous'd
Potations pottle-deep;[60] and he's to watch:
Three lads of Cyprus, noble swelling spirits,
That hold their honours in a wary distance,[61]
The very elements[62] of this warlike isle,
Have I to-night fluster'd with flowing cups,
And they watch[63] too. Now, 'mongst this flock of drunkards,
Am I to put our Cassio in some action
That may offend the isle.—But here they come:

[*Enter* CASSIO, MONTANO, *and* GENTLEMEN; SERVANTS *following with wine.*]

If consequence do but approve[64] my dream,
My boat sails freely, both with wind and stream.

CASSIO. 'Fore God, they have given me a rouse[65] already.

MONTANO. Good faith, a little one; not past a pint, as I am a soldier.

IAGO. Some wine, ho!
[*Sings.*] And let me the canakin[66] clink, clink;
And let me the canakin clink
A soldier's a man;
A life's but a span;
Why, then, let a soldier drink.
Some wine, boys!

CASSIO. 'Fore God, an excellent song.

IAGO. I learned it in England, where, indeed, they are most potent in potting your Dane, your German, and your swag-bellied Hollander—Drink, ho!—are nothing to your English.

CASSIO. Is your Englishman so expert in his drinking?

---

[57]**qualified** diluted.
[58]**innovation** disturbance.
[59]**here** i.e., in Cassio's head.
[60]**pottle-deep** to the bottom of the tankard.
[61]**hold . . . distance** i.e., are extremely sensitive of their honor.
[62]**very elements** true representatives.
[63]**watch** are members of the guard.
[64]**approve** confirm.
[65]**rouse** full draft of liquor.
[66]**canakin** small drinking vessel.

IAGO. Why, he drinks you, with facility, your Dane dead drunk; he sweats not to overthrow your Almain;[67] he gives your Hollander a vomit, ere the next pottle can be filled.

CASSIO. To the health of our general!

MONTANO. I am for it, lieutenant; and I'll do you justice.[68]

IAGO. O sweet England! [*Sings.*]

King Stephen was a worthy peer,
His breeches cost him but a crown;
He held them sixpence all too dear,
With that he call'd the tailor lown.[69]

He was a wight of high renown,
And thou art but of low degree:
'Tis pride that pulls the country down;
Then take thine auld cloak about thee.
Some wine, ho!

CASSIO. Why, this is a more exquisite song than the other.

IAGO. Will you hear 't again?

CASSIO. No; for I hold him to be unworthy of his place that does those things. Well, God's above all; and there be souls must be saved, and there be souls must not be saved.

IAGO. It's true, good lieutenant.

CASSIO. For mine own part,—no offence to the general, nor any man of quality,—I hope to be saved.

IAGO. And so do I too, lieutenant.

CASSIO. Ay, but, by your leave, not before me; the lieutenant is to be saved before the ancient. Let 's have no more of this; let 's to our affairs.—God forgive us our sins!—Gentlemen, let 's look to our business. Do not think, gentlemen, I am drunk: this is my ancient; this is my right hand, and this is my left: I am not drunk now: I can stand well enough, and speak well enough.

ALL. Excellent well.

CASSIO. Why, very well then; you must not think then that I am drunk. [*Exit.*]

MONTANO. To th' platform, masters; come, let's set the watch.

IAGO. You see this fellow that is gone before;
He's soldier fit to stand by Caesar
And give direction and do but see his vice;
'Tis to his virtue a just equinox,[70]
The one as long as th' other 'tis pity of him.
I fear the trust Othello puts him in,
On some odd time of his infirmity,
Will shake this island.

MONTANO. But is he often thus?

IAGO. 'Tis evermore the prologue to his sleep:

---

[67]**Almain** German.
[68]**I'll . . . justice** i.e., drink as much as you.
[69]**lown** lout, loon.
[70]**equinox** equal length of days and nights; used figuratively to mean "counterpart."

He'll watch the horologe[71] a double set,[72]
If drink rock not his cradle.

Montano. It were well
The general were put in mind of it.
Perhaps he sees it not; or his good nature
Prizes the virtue that appears in Cassio,
And looks not on his evils: is not this true?

[*Enter* Roderigo.]

Iago [*Aside to him*]. How now, Roderigo!
I pray you, after the lieutenant; go.

[*Exit* Roderigo.]

Montano. And 'tis great pity that the noble Moor
Should hazard such a place as his own second
With one of an ingraft[73] infirmity:
It were an honest action to say
So to the Moor.

Iago. Not I, for this fair island:
I do love Cassio well; and would do much
To cure him of this evil—But, hark! what noise?
[*Cry within:* "Help! help!"]

[*Enter* Cassio, *pursing* Roderigo.]

Cassio. 'Zounds, you rogue! you rascal!

Montano. What's the matter, lieutenant?

Cassio. A knave teach me my duty!
I'll beat the knave into a twiggen[74] bottle.

Roderigo. Beat me!

Cassio. Dost thou prate, rogue? [*Striking* Roderigo.]

Montano. Nay, good lieutenant; [*Staying him.*]
I pray you, sir, hold your hand.

Cassio. Let me go, sir,
Or I'll knock you o'er the mazzard.[75]

Montano. Come, come, you're drunk.

Cassio. Drunk! [*They fight.*]

Iago [*aside to* Roderigo]. Away, I say; go out, and cry a mutiny.

[*Exit* Roderigo.]

Nay, good lieutenant,—God's will, gentlemen;—
Help, ho!—Lieutenant,—sir,—Montano,—sir,—
Help, masters!—Here's a goodly watch indeed! [*Bell rings.*]
Who's that which rings the bell?—Diablo,[76] ho!
The town will rise:[77] God's will, lieutenant, hold!
You'll be asham'd for ever.

[*Enter* Othello *and* Attendants.]

---

[71]**horologe** clock.
[72]**double set** twice around.
[73]**ingraft** ingrafted, inveterate.
[74]**twiggen** covered with woven twigs.
[75]**mazzard** head.
[76]**Diablo** the devil.
[77]**rise** grow riotous.

OTHELLO. What is the matter here?
MONTANO. 'Zounds, I bleed still; I am hurt to th' death.
He dies! [*Thrusts at* CASSIO.]
OTHELLO. Hold, for your lives!
IAGO. Hold, ho! Lieutenant,—sir,—Montano,—gentlemen,—
Have you forgot all sense of place and duty?
Hold! the general speaks to you; hold, for shame!
OTHELLO. Why, how now, ho! from whence ariseth this?
Are we turn'd Turks[78] and to ourselves do that
Which heaven hath forbid the Ottomites?
For Christian shame, put by this barbarous brawl:
He that stirs next to carve for[79] his own rage
Holds his soul light; he dies upon his motion.
Silence that dreadful bell: it frights the isle
From her propriety.[80] What is the matter, masters?
Honest Iago, that looks dead with grieving,
Speak, who began this? on thy love, I charge thee.
IAGO. I do not know: friends all but now, even now,
In quarter,[81] and in terms like bride and groom
Devesting them for bed; and then, but now—
As if some planet had unwitted men—
Swords out, and tilting one at other's breast,
In opposition bloody. I cannot speak
Any beginning to this peevish odds;[82]
And would in action glorious I had lost
Those legs that brought me to a part of it!
OTHELLO. How comes it, Michael, you are thus forgot?
CASSIO. I pray you, pardon me; I cannot speak.
OTHELLO. Worthy Montano, you were wont be civil;
The gravity and stillness of your youth
The world hath noted, and your name is great
In mouths of wisest censure.[83] What's the matter,
That you unlace[84] your reputation thus
And spend your rich opinion for the name
Of a night-brawler? Give me answer to it.
MONTANO. Worthy Othello, I am hurt to danger:
Your officer, Iago, can inform you,—
While I spare speech, which something now offends me,—
Of all that I do know: nor know I aught
By me that's said or done amiss this night;
Unless self-charity be sometimes a vice,
And to defend ourselves it be a sin
When violence assails us.
OTHELLO. Now, by heaven,

---

[78]**turn'd Turks** changed completely for the worse; proverbial.
[79]**carve for** indulge.
[80]**propriety** proper state or condition.
[81]**In quarter** on terms.
[82]**peevish odds** childish quarrel.
[83]**censure** judgment.
[84]**unlace** degrade.

My blood begins my safer guides to rule;
And passion, having my best judgment collied,[85]
Assays to lead the way: if I once stir,
Or do but lift this arm, the best of you
Shall sink in my rebuke. Give me to know
How this foul rout began, who set it on;
And he that is approv'd in[86] this offence,
Though he had twinn'd with me, both at a birth,
Shall lose me. What! in a town of war,
Yet wild, the people's hearts brimful of fear,
To manage private and domestic quarrel,
In night, and on the court and guard[87] of safety!
'Tis monstrous. Iago, who began 't?

MONTANO [*to* IAGO]. If partially affin'd,[88] or leagu'd in office,
Thou dost deliver more or less than truth,
Thou art no soldier.

IAGO. Touch me not so near:
I had rather have this tongue cut from my mouth
Than it should do offense to Michael Cassio;
Yet, I persuade myself, to speak the truth
Shall nothing wrong him. Thus it is, general.
Montano and myself being in speech,
There comes a fellow crying out for help;
And Cassio following him with determin'd sword,
To execute[89] upon him. Sir, this gentleman
Steps in to Cassio, and entreats his pause:
Myself the crying fellow did pursue,
Lest by his clamour—as it so fell out—
The town might fall in fright: he, swift of foot,
Outran my purpose; and I return'd the rather
For that I heard the clink and fall of swords,
And Cassio high in oath; which till to-night
I ne'er might say before. When I came back—
For this was brief—I found them close together,
At blow and thrust; even as again they were
When you yourself did part them.
More of this matter cannot I report:
But men are men; the best sometimes forget:
Though Cassio did some little wrong to him,
As men in rage strike those that wish them best,
Yet surely, Cassio, I believe, receiv'd
From him that fled some strange indignity,
Which patience could not pass.

OTHELLO. I know, Iago,

---

[85] **collied** darkened.
[86] **approv'd in** found guilty of.
[87] **court and guard** spot and guarding place, i.e., the main guardhouse.
[88] **affin'd** bound by a tie.
[89] **execute** give effect to (his anger).

Thy honesty and love doth mince this matter,
Making it light to Cassio. Cassio, I love thee;
But never more be officer of mine.

[*Enter* DESDEMONA, *attended.*]

Look, if my gentle love be not rais'd up!
I'll make thee an example.

DESDEMONA. What's the matter?

OTHELLO. All's well now, sweeting; come away to bed.
Sir, for your hurts, myself will be your surgeon:
Lead him off. [*To* MONTANO, *who is led off.*]
Iago, look with care about the town,
And silence those whom this vile brawl distracted.
Come, Desdemona: 'tis the soldiers' life
To have their balmy slumbers wak'd with strife.

[*Exit with all but* IAGO *and* CASSIO.]

IAGO. What, are you hurt, lieutenant?

CASSIO. Ay, past all surgery.

IAGO. Marry, God forbid!

CASSIO. Reputation, reputation, reputation! O, I have lost my reputation! I have lost the immortal part of myself, and what remains is bestial. My reputation, Iago, my reputation!

IAGO. As I am an honest man, I thought you had received some bodily wound; there is more sense in that than in reputation. Reputation is an idle and most false imposition; oft got without merit, and lost without deserving: you have lost no reputation at all, unless you repute yourself such a loser. What, man! there are ways to recover the general again: you are but now cast in his mood, a punishment more in policy than in malice; even so as one would beat his offenseless dog to affright an imperious lion: sue to him again, and he 's yours.

CASSIO. I will rather sue to be despised than to deceive so good a commander with so slight, so drunken, and so indiscreet an officer. Drunk? and speak parrot?[90] and squabble? swagger? swear? and discourse fustian[91] with one's own shadow? O thou invisible spirit of wine, if thou hast no name to be known by, let us call thee devil!

IAGO. What was he that you followed with your sword? What had he done to you?

CASSIO. I know not.

IAGO. Is 't possible?

CASSIO. I remember a mass of things, but nothing distinctly; a quarrel, but nothing wherefore. O God, that men should put an enemy in their mouths to steal away their brains! that we should, with joy, pleasance, revel and applause, transform ourselves into beasts!

IAGO. Why, but you are now well enough. How came you thus recovered?

CASSIO. It hath pleased the devil drunkenness to give place to the devil wrath: one unperfectness[92] shows me another, to make me frankly despise myself.

---

[90]**speak parrot** talk nonsense.
[91]**discourse fustian** talk nonsense.
[92]**unperfectness** imperfection.

IAGO. Come, you are too severe a moraler: as the time, the place, and the condition of this country stands, I could heartily wish this had not befallen; but, since it is as it is, mend it for your own good.

CASSIO. I will ask him for my place again; he shall tell me I am a drunkard! Had I as many mouths as Hydra,[93] such an answer would stop them all. To be now a sensible man, by and by a fool, and presently a beast! O strange! Every inordinate cup is unblessed and the ingredient is a devil.

IAGO. Come, come, good wine is a good familiar creature, if it be well used: exclaim no more against it. And, good lieutenant, I think you think I love you.

CASSIO. I have well approved[94] it, sir. I drunk!

IAGO. You or any man living may be a drunk at a time, man. I'll tell you what you shall do. Our general's wife is now the general: I may say so in this respect, for that he hath devoted and given up himself to the contemplation, mark, and denotement[95] of her parts and graces: confess yourself freely to her; importune her help to put you in your place again: she is of so free, so kind, so apt, so blessed a disposition, she holds it a vice in her goodness not to do more than she is requested: this broken joint between you and her husband entreat her to splinter;[96] and, my fortunes against any lay[97] worth naming, this crack of your love shall grow stronger than it was before.

CASSIO. You advise me well.

IAGO. I protest, in the sincerity of love and honest kindness.

CASSIO. I think it freely; and betimes in the morning I will beseech the virtuous Desdemona to undertake for me. I am desperate of my fortunes if they check[98] me here.

IAGO. You are in the right. Good night, lieutenant; I must to the watch.

CASSIO. Good night, honest Iago. [*Exit* CASSIO.]

IAGO. And what 's he then that says I play the villain?
When this advice is free I give and honest,
Probal[99] to thinking and indeed the course
To win the Moor again? For 'tis most easy
Th' inclining[100] Desdemona to subdue[101]
In any honest suit: she 's fram'd as fruitful
As the free elements. And then for her
To win the Moor—were 't to renounce his baptism,
All seals and symbols of redeemed sin,
His soul is so enfetter'd to her love,
That she may make, unmake, do what she list,
Even as her appetite shall play the god
With his weak function. How am I then a villain
To counsel Cassio to this parallel[102] course,

---

[93]**Hydra** a monster with many heads, slain by Hercules as the second of his twelve labors.
[94]**approved** proved.
[95]**denotement** observation.
[96]**splinter** bind with splints.
[97]**lay** stake, wager.
[98]**check** repulse.
[99]**Probal** probable.
[100]**inclining** favorably disposed.
[101]**subdue** persuade.
[102]**parallel** corresponding to his best interest.

Directly to his good? Divinity of hell!
When devils will the blackest sins put on,[103]
They do suggest[104] at first with heavenly shows,
As I do now: for whiles this honest fool
Plies Desdemona to repair his fortunes
And she for him pleads strongly to the Moor,
I'll pour this pestilence into his ear,
That she repeals him[105] for her body's lust;
And by how much she strives to do him good,
She shall undo her credit with the Moor.
So will I turn her virtue into pitch,
And out of her own goodness make the net
That shall enmesh them all.

[*Enter* RODERIGO.]

How now, Roderigo!

RODERIGO. I do not follow here in the chase, not like a hound that hunts, but one that fills up the cry.[106] My money is almost spent; I have been tonight exceedingly well cudgellèd; and I think the issue will be, I shall have so much experience for my pains, and so, with no money at all and a little more wit, return again to Venice.

IAGO. How poor are they that have not patience!
What wound did ever heal but by degrees?
Thou know'st we work by wit, and not by witchcraft;
And wit depends on dilatory time.
Does 't not go well? Cassio hath beaten thee,
And thou, by that small hurt, hast cashier'd[107] Cassio.
Though other things grow fair against the sun,
Yet fruits that blossom first will first be ripe.
Content thyself awhile. By th' mass, 'tis morning;
Pleasure and action make the hours seem short.
Retire thee; go where thou art billeted.
Away, I say; thou shalt know more hereafter:
Nay, get thee gone. [*Exit* RODERIGO.]
Two things are to be done:
My wife must move for Cassio to her mistress;
I'll set her on;
Myself the while to draw the Moor apart,
And bring him jump[108] when he may Cassio find
Soliciting his wife: ay, that's the way:
Dull not device by coldness and delay.

[*Exit.*]

---

[103]**put on** further.
[104]**suggest** tempt.
[105]**repeals him** i.e., attempts to get him restored.
[106]**cry** pack.
[107]**cashier'd** dismissed from service.
[108]**jump** precisely.

ACT III

SCENE I

Before the castle.

[*Enter* CASSIO *and* MUSICIANS.]

CASSIO. Masters, play here; I will content[1] your pains;
Something that 's brief; and bid "Good morrow, general." [*They play.*]

[*Enter* CLOWN.]

CLOWN. Why, masters, have your instruments been in Naples, that they speak i' the nose[2] thus?

FIRST MUSICIAN. How, sir, how!

CLOWN. Are these, I pray you, wind-instruments?

FIRST MUSICIAN. Ay, marry, are they, sir.

CLOWN. O, thereby hangs a tail.

FIRST MUSICIAN. Whereby hangs a tale,[3] sir?

CLOWN. Marry, sir, by many a wind-instrument that I know. But, masters, here's money for you: and the general so likes your music, that he desires you, for love's sake, to make no more noise with it.

FIRST MUSICIAN. Well, sir, we will not.

CLOWN. If you have any music that may not be heard, to 't again: but, as they say, to hear music the general does not greatly care.

FIRST MUSICIAN. We have none such, sir.

CLOWN. Then put up your pipes in your bag, for I'll away: go; vanish into air; away! [*Exeunt* MUSICIANS.]

CASSIO. Dost thou hear, my honest friend?

CLOWN. No, I hear not your honest friend; I hear you.

CASSIO. Prithee, keep up thy quillets. There 's a poor piece of gold for thee: if the gentlewoman that attends the general's wife be stirring, tell her there 's one Cassio entreats her a little favour of speech; wilt thou do this?

CLOWN. She is stirring, sir: if she will stir hither, I shall seem to notify unto her.

CASSIO. Do, good my friend. [*Exit* CLOWN.]

[*Enter* IAGO.]

In happy time, Iago.

IAGO. You have not been a-bed, then?

CASSIO. Why, no; the day had broke
Before we parted. I have made bold, Iago,
To send in to your wife: my suit to her
Is, that she will to virtuous Desdemona
Procure me some access.

IAGO. I'll send her to you presently;

---

[1]**content** reward.

[2]**speak i' the nose** i.e., like Neapolitans, who spoke a nasal dialect (with a joke on syphilis, which attacks the nose).

[3]**tale** pun on *tail*, a wind instrument of sorts.

And I'll devise a means to draw the Moor
Out of the way, that your converse and business
May be more free.

CASSIO. I humbly thank you for 't. [*Exit* IAGO.]
I never knew
A Florentine more kind and honest.

[*Enter* EMILIA.]

EMILIA. Good morrow, good lieutenant. I am sorry
For your displeasure; but all will sure be well.
The general and his wife are talking of it;
And she speaks for you stoutly: the Moor replies,
That he you hurt is of great fame in Cyprus
And great affinity[4] and that in wholesome wisdom
He might not but refuse you, but he protests he loves you
And needs no other suitor but his likings
To take the safest occasion by the front[5]
To bring you in again.

CASSIO. Yet, I beseech you,
If you think fit, or that it may be done,
Give me advantage of some brief discourse
With Desdemona alone.

EMILIA. Pray you, come in:
I will bestow you where you shall have time
To speak your bosom freely.

CASSIO. I am much bound to you. [*Exeunt*.]

SCENE II

A room in the castle.

[*Enter* OTHELLO, IAGO, *and* GENTLEMEN.]

OTHELLO. These letters give, Iago, to the pilot;
And by him do my duties to the senate.
That done, I will be walking on the works.[6]
Repair there to me.

IAGO. Well, my good lord, I'll do 't.

OTHELLO. This fortification, gentlemen, shall we see't?

GENTLEMEN. We'll wait upon your lordship. [*Exeunt*.]

SCENE III

The garden of the castle.

[*Enter* DESDEMONA, CASSIO, *and* EMILIA.]

DESDEMONA. Be thou assur'd, good Cassio, I will do
All my abilities in thy behalf.

---

[4]**affinity** kindred, family connection.
[5]**by the front** i.e., by the forelock.
[6]**works** earthworks, fortifications.

EMILIA. Good madam, do. I warrant it grieves my husband,
As if the case were his.
DESDEMONA. O, that 's an honest fellow. Do not doubt, Cassio,
But I will have my lord and you again
As friendly as you were.
CASSIO. Bounteous madam,
Whatever shall become of Michael Cassio,
He's never any thing but your true servant.
DESDEMONA. I know 't; I thank you. You do love my lord:
You have known him long; and be you well assur'd
He shall in strangeness[7] stand no farther off
Than in a politic distance.
CASSIO. Ay, but lady,
That policy may either last so long
Or feed upon such nice and waterish diet,
Or breed itself so out of circumstance,[8]
That, I being absent and my place supplied,
My general will forget my love and service.
DESDEMONA. Do not doubt[9] that; before Emilia here
I give thee warrant of thy place: assure thee,
If I do vow a friendship, I'll perform it
To the last article: my lord shall never rest;
I'll watch him tame[10] and talk him out of patience;
His bed shall seem a school, his board a shrift;[11]
I'll intermingle every thing he does
With Cassio's suit: therefore be merry, Cassio;
For thy solicitor shall rather die
Than give thy cause away.[12]

[*Enter* OTHELLO *and* IAGO *at a distance*.]

EMILIA. Madam, here comes my lord.
CASSIO. Madam, I'll take my leave.
DESDEMONA. Why, stay, and hear me speak.
CASSIO. Madam, not now. I am very ill at ease,
Unfit for mine own purposes.
DESDEMONA. Well, do your discretion. [*Exit* CASSIO.]
IAGO. Ha! I like not that.
OTHELLO. What dost thou say?
IAGO. Nothing, my lord or if—I know not what.
OTHELLO. Was not that Cassio parted from my wife?
IAGO. Cassio, my lord! No, sure, I cannot think it,
That he would steal away so guilty-like,
Seeing you coming.

---

[7]**strangeness** distant behavior.
[8]**breed . . . circumstance** increase itself so on account of accidents.
[9]**doubt** fear.
[10]**watch him tame** tame him by keeping him from sleeping (a term from falconry).
[11]**shrift** confessional.
[12]**away** up.

OTHELLO. I do believe 'twas he.
DESDEMONA. How now, my lord!
I have been talking with a suitor here,
A man that languishes in your displeasure.
OTHELLO. Who is 't you mean?
DESDEMONA. Why, your lieutenant, Cassio. Good my lord,
If I have any grace or power to move you,
His present reconciliation take;
For if he be not one that truly loves you,
That errs in ignorance and not in cunning,
I have no judgment in an honest face:
I prithee, call him back.
OTHELLO. Went he hence now?
DESDEMONA. Ay, sooth; so humbled
That he hath left part of his grief with me,
To suffer with him. Good love, call him back.
OTHELLO. Not now, sweet Desdemona; some other time.
DESDEMONA. But shall 't be shortly?
OTHELLO. The sooner, sweet, for you.
DESDEMONA. Shall 't be to-night at supper?
OTHELLO. No, not to-night.
DESDEMONA. To-morrow dinner, then?
OTHELLO. I shall not dine at home;
I meet the captain at the citadel.
DESDEMONA. Why, then, to-morrow night; or Tuesday morn;
On Tuesday noon, or night; on Wednesday morn:
I prithee, name the time, but let it not
Exceed three days: in faith, he's penitent;
And yet his trespass, in our common reason[13]—
Save that, they say, the wars must make examples
Out of their best—is not almost a fault
T' incur a private check. When shall he come?
Tell me, Othello. I wonder in my soul,
What you would ask me, that I should deny,
Or stand so mamm'ring on.[14] What! Michael Cassio,
That came a-wooing with you, and so many a time,
When I have spoke of you dispraisingly,
Hath ta'en your part; to have so much to do
To bring him in! Trust me, I could do much,—
OTHELLO. Prithee, no more: let him come when he will;
I will deny thee nothing.
DESDEMONA. Why, this is not a boon;
'Tis as I should entreat you wear your gloves,
Or feed on nourishing dishes, or keep you warm,
Or sue to you to do a peculiar profit
To your own person: nay, when I have a suit

[13]**common reason** everyday judgments.
[14]**mamm'ring on** wavering.

Wherein I mean to touch your love indeed,
It shall be full of poise[15] and difficult weight
And fearful to be granted.

OTHELLO. I will deny thee nothing:
Whereon, I do beseech thee, grant me this,
To leave me but a little to myself.

DESDEMONA. Shall I deny you? No: farewell, my lord.

OTHELLO. Farewell, my Desdemona. I'll come to thee straight.

DESDEMONA. Emilia, come. Be as your fancies teach you;
Whate'er you be, I am obedient. [*Exit with* EMILIA.]

OTHELLO. Excellent wretch![16] Perdition catch my soul,
But I do love thee! And when I love thee not,
Chaos is come again.

IAGO. My noble lord—

OTHELLO. What dost thou say, Iago?

IAGO. Did Michael Cassio, when you woo'd my lady,
Know of your love?

OTHELLO. He did, from first to last: why dost thou ask?

IAGO. But for a satisfaction of my thought;
No further harm.

OTHELLO. Why of thy thought, Iago?

IAGO. I did not think he had been acquainted with her.

OTHELLO. O, yes; and went between us very oft.

IAGO. Indeed!

OTHELLO. Indeed! Ay, indeed: discern'st thou aught in that?
Is he not honest?

IAGO. Honest, my lord!

OTHELLO. Honest! ay, honest.

IAGO. My lord, for aught I know.

OTHELLO. What dost thou think?

IAGO. Think, my lord!

OTHELLO. Think, my lord!
By heaven, he echoes me,
As if there were some monster in his thought
Too hideous to be shown. Thou dost mean something.
I heard thee say even now, thou lik'st not that,
When Cassio left my wife: what didst not like?
And when I told thee he was of my counsel
In my whole course of wooing, thou criedst "Indeed!"
And didst contract and purse thy brow together,
As if thou then hadst shut up in thy brain
Some horrible conceit: if thou dost love me,
Show me thy thought.

IAGO. My lord, you know I love you.

OTHELLO. I think thou dost;
And, for I know thou 'rt full of love and honesty,

---

[15]**poise** heaviness.
[16]**wretch** term of affectionate endearment with a connotation of pity.

And weigh'st thy words before thou giv'st them breath,
Therefore these stops of thine fright me the more:
For such things in a false disloyal knave
Are tricks of custom, but in a man that's just
They 're close delations,[17] working from the heart
That passion cannot rule.

IAGO. For Michael Cassio,
I dare be sworn I think that he is honest.

OTHELLO. I think so too.

IAGO. Men should be what they seem;
Or those that be not, would they might seem none!

OTHELLO. Certain, men should be what they seem.

IAGO. Why, then, I think Cassio 's an honest man.

OTHELLO. Nay, yet there 's more in this.
I prithee, speak to me as to thy thinkings,
As thou dost ruminate, and give thy worst of thoughts
The worst of words.

IAGO. Good my lord, pardon me:
Though I am bound to every act of duty,
I am not bound to that all slaves are free to.
Utter my thoughts? Why, say they are vile and false;
As where 's that palace whereinto foul things
Sometimes intrude not? Who has a breast so pure,
But some uncleanly apprehensions
Keep leets[18] and law-days[19] and in sessions sit
With meditations lawful?

OTHELLO. Thou dost conspire against thy friend, Iago,
If thou but think'st him wrong'd and mak'st his ear
A stranger to thy thoughts.

IAGO. I do beseech you—
Though I perchance am vicious[20] in my guess,
As, I confess, it is my nature's plague
To spy into abuses, and oft my jealousy[21]
Shapes faults that are not—that your wisdom yet,
From one that so imperfectly conceits,[22]
Would take no notice, nor build yourself a trouble
Out of his scattering and unsure observance.
It were not for your quiet nor your good,
Nor for my manhood, honesty, or wisdom,
To let you know my thoughts.

OTHELLO. What dost thou mean?

IAGO. Good name in man and woman, dear my lord,

---

[17]**close delations** secret or involuntary accusations.
[18]**Keep leets** hold courts.
[19]**law-days** court days.
[20]**vicious** wrong.
[21]**jealousy** suspicion of evil.
[22]**conceits** judges.

Is the immediate jewel of their souls.
Who steals my purse steals trash: 'tis something, nothing;
'Twas mine, 'tis his, and has been slave to thousands;
But he that filches from me my good name
Robs me of that which not enriches him
And makes me poor indeed.

OTHELLO. By heaven, I'll know thy thoughts.

IAGO. You cannot, if my heart were in your hand;
Nor shall not, whilst 'tis in my custody.

OTHELLO. Ha!

IAGO. Oh, beware, my lord, of jealousy;
It is the green-ey'd monster which doth mock
The meat it feeds on: that cuckold lives in bliss
Who, certain of his fate, loves not his wronger;
But, O, what damned minutes tells he o'er
Who dotes, yet doubts, suspects, yet strongly loves!

OTHELLO. O misery!

IAGO. Poor and content is rich and rich enough,
But riches fineless[23] is as poor as winter
To him that ever fears he shall be poor.
Good God, the souls of all my tribe defend
From jealousy!

OTHELLO. Why, why is this?
Think'st thou I'd make a life of jealousy,
To follow still the changes of the moon
With fresh suspicions? No; to be once in doubt
Is once to be resolv'd: exchange me for a goat,
When I shall turn the business of my soul
To such exsufflicate and blown[24] surmises,
Matching thy inference. 'Tis not to make me jealous
To say my wife is fair, feeds well, loves company,
Is free of speech, sings, plays and dances well;
Where virtue is, these are more virtuous;
Nor from mine own weak merits will I draw
The smallest fear or doubt of her revolt:
For she had eyes, and chose me. No, Iago;
I'll see before I doubt; when I doubt, prove;
And on the proof, there is no more but this,—
Away at once with love or jealousy!

IAGO. I am glad of this; for now I shall have reason
To show the love and duty that I bear you
With franker spirit: therefore, as I am bound,
Receive it from me. I speak not yet of proof.
Look to your wife; observe her well with Cassio;
Wear your eye thus, not jealous nor secure:[25]

---

[23]**fineless** boundless.
[24]**exsufflicate and blown** unsubstantial and inflated, flyblown.
[25]**secure** free from uneasiness.

I would not have your free and noble nature,
Out of self-bounty,[26] be abus'd; look to 't.
I know our country disposition well;
In Venice they do let heaven see the pranks
They dare not show their husbands; their best conscience
Is not to leave 't undone, but keep 't unknown.

OTHELLO. Dost thou say so?

IAGO. She did deceive her father, marrying you;
And when she seem'd to shake and fear your looks,
She lov'd them most.

OTHELLO. And so she did.

IAGO. Why, go to then;
She that, so young, could give out such a seeming,[27]
To seel[28] her father's eyes up close as oak—
He thought 'twas witchcraft—but I am much to blame;
I humbly do beseech you of your pardon
For too much loving you.

OTHELLO. I am bound to thee for ever.

IAGO. I see this hath a little dash'd your spirits.

OTHELLO. Not a jot, not a jot.

IAGO. I' faith, I fear it has.
I hope you will consider what is spoke
Comes from my love. But I do see y' are mov'd.
I am to pray you not to strain my speech
To grosser issues nor to larger reach[29]
Than to suspicion.

OTHELLO. I will not.

IAGO. Should you do so, my lord,
My speech should fall into such vile success
As my thoughts aim not at. Cassio 's my worthy friend—
My lord, I see y' are mov'd.

OTHELLO. No, not much mov'd.
I do not think but Desdemona's honest.

IAGO. Long live she so! and long live you to think so!

OTHELLO. And yet, how nature erring from itself,—

IAGO. Ay, there's the point: as—to be bold with you—
Not to affect many proposed matches
Of her own clime, complexion, and degree,
Whereto we see in all things nature tends—
Foh! one may smell in such a will[30] most rank,
Foul disproportion,[31] thoughts unnatural.
But pardon me; I do not in position[32]

---

[26]**self-bounty** inherent or natural goodness.
[27]**seeming** false appearance.
[28]**seel** blind (a term from falconry).
[29]**reach** meaning.
[30]**will** sensuality.
[31]**disproportion** abnormality.
[32]**position** general argument.

Distinctly speak of her; though I may fear
Her will, recoiling to[33] her better judgment,
May fall to match you with her country forms[34]
And happily repent.[35]
OTHELLO. Farewell, farewell:
If more thou dost perceive, let me know more;
Set on thy wife to observe. Leave me, Iago.
IAGO [*going*]. My lord, I take my leave.
OTHELLO. Why did I marry? This honest creature doubtless
Sees and knows more, much more, than he unfolds.
IAGO [*returning*]. My Lord, I would I might entreat your honour
To scan this thing no farther; leave it to time:
Although 'tis fit that Cassio have his place,
For, sure, he fills it up with great ability,
Yet, if you please to hold him off awhile,
You shall by that perceive him and his means:
Note, if your lady strain his entertainment[36]
With any strong or vehement importunity;
Much will be seen in that. In the mean time,
Let me be thought too busy in my fears—
As worthy cause I have to fear I am—
And hold her free,[37] I do beseech your honour.
OTHELLO. Fear not my government.[38]
IAGO. I once more take my leave. [*Exit.*]
OTHELLO. This fellow 's of exceeding honesty,
And knows all qualities; with a learned spirit,
Of human dealings. If I do prove her haggard,[39]
Though that her jesses[40] were my dear heartstrings,
I'd whistle her off and let her down the wind,
To prey at fortune.[41] Haply, for I am black
And have not those soft parts of conversation
That chamberers[42] have, or for I am declin'd
Into the vale of years,—yet that 's not much—
She 's gone. I am abus'd, and my relief
Must be to loathe her. O curse of marriage,
That we can call these delicate creatures ours,
And not their appetites! I had rather be a toad,
And live upon the vapour of a dungeon,
Than keep a corner in the thing I love

---

[33]**recoiling to** falling back upon, or recoiling against.
[34]**fall...forms** happen to compare you with Venetian norms of handsomeness.
[35]**repent** i.e., of her marriage.
[36]**strain his entertainment** urge his reinstatement.
[37]**hold her free** regard her as innocent.
[38]**government** self-control.
[39]**haggard** a wild female duck.
[40]**jesses** straps fastened around the legs of a trained hawk.
[41]**at fortune** at random.
[42]**chamberers** gallants.

For others' uses. Yet, 'tis the plague of great ones;
Prerogativ'd[43] are they less than the base;
'Tis destiny unshunnable, like death:
Even then this forked[44] plague is fated to us
When we do quicken.[45] Look where she comes:

[*Enter* DESDEMONA *and* EMILIA.]

If she be false, O, then heaven mocks itself!
I'll not believe 't.
DESDEMONA. How now, my dear Othello!
Your dinner, and the generous[46] islanders
By you invited, do attend your presence.
OTHELLO. I am to blame.
DESDEMONA. Why do you speak so faintly?
Are you not well?
OTHELLO. I have a pain upon my forehead here.
DESDEMONA. 'Faith, that 's with watching;[47]'twill away again.
Let me but bind it hard, within this hour
It will be well.
OTHELLO. Your napkin is too little

[*He puts the handkerchief from him; and it drops.*]

Let it alone. Come, I'll go in with you.
DESDEMONA. I am very sorry that you are not well. [*Exit with* OTHELLO.]
EMILIA. I am glad I have found this napkin.
This was her first remembrance from the Moor.
My wayward husband hath a hundred times
Woo'd me to steal it; but she so loves the token,
For he conjur'd her she should ever keep it,
That she reserves it evermore about her
To kiss and talk to. I'll have the work ta'en out,[48]
And give 't Iago: what he will do with it
Heaven knows, not I;
I nothing but to please his fantasy.

[*Enter* IAGO.]

IAGO. How now! what do you here alone?
EMILIA. Do not you chide; I have a thing for you.
IAGO. A thing for me? it is a common thing[49]—
EMILIA. Ha!
IAGO. To have a foolish wife.
EMILIA. O, is that all? What will you give me now

---

[43]**Prerogativ'd** privileged.
[44]**forked** an allusion to the horns of the cuckold.
[45]**quicken** receive life.
[46]**generous** noble.
[47]**watching** working late.
[48]**work ta'en out** design copied.
[49]**common thing** *common* suggests coarseness and availability to all, and *thing* is slang for female sexual organs.

For that same handkerchief?
IAGO. What handkerchief?
EMILIA. What handkerchief!
Why, that the Moor first gave to Desdemona;
That which so often you did bid me steal.
IAGO. Hast stol'n it from her?
EMILIA. No, 'faith; she let it drop by negligence,
And, to th' advantage, I, being here, took 't up.
Look, here it is.
IAGO. A good wench; give it me.
EMILIA. What will you do with 't, that you have been so earnest
To have me filch it?
IAGO. [*Snatching it.*] Why, what is that to you?
EMILIA. If it be not for some purpose of import,
Give 't me again: poor lady, she'll run mad
When she shall lack it.
IAGO. Be not acknown on 't;[50] I have use for it.
Go, leave me. [*Exit* EMILIA.]
I will in Cassio's lodging lose this napkin,
And let him find it. Trifles light as air
Are to the jealous confirmations strong
As proofs of holy writ: this may do something.
The Moor already changes with my poison:
Dangerous conceits are, in their natures, poisons,
Which at the first are scarce found to distaste,
But with a little act[51] upon the blood,
Burn like the mines of sulphur. I did say so.

[*Enter* OTHELLO.]

Look, where he comes! Not poppy, nor mandragora,
Nor all the drowsy syrups of the world,
Shall ever medicine thee to that sweet sleep
Which thou owedst yesterday.
OTHELLO. Ha! ha! false to me?
IAGO. Why, how now, general! no more of that.
OTHELLO. Avaunt! be gone! thou has set me on the rack;
I swear 'tis better to be much abus'd
Than but to know 't a little.
IAGO. How now, my lord!
OTHELLO. What sense had I of her stol'n hours of lust?
I saw 't not, thought it not, it harm'd not me:
I slept the next night well, fed well, was free and merry;
I found not Cassio's kisses on her lips.
He that is robb'd, not wanting what is stol'n,
Let him not know 't, and he 's not robb'd at all.
IAGO. I am sorry to hear this.
OTHELLO. I had been happy, if the general camp,

---

[50]**Be... on't** do not confess knowledge of it.
[51]**act** action, working.

Pioners[52] and all, had tasted her sweet body,
So I had nothing known. O, now, for ever
Farewell the tranquil mind! farewell content!
Farewell the plumed troop, and the big wars,
That make ambition virtue! O, farewell!
Farewell the neighing steed, and the shrill trump,
The spirit-stirring drum, th' ear-piercing fife,
The royal banner, and all quality,
Pride, pomp and circumstance[53] of glorious war!
And, O you mortal engines,[54] whose rude throats
Th' immortal Jove's dread clamours counterfeit,
Farewell! Othello's occupation 's gone!

IAGO. Is 't possible, my lord?

OTHELLO. Villain, be sure thou prove my love a whore,
Be sure of it; give me the ocular proof;
Or, by the worth of mine eternal soul,
Thou hadst been better have been born a dog
Than answer my wak'd wrath!

IAGO. Is 't come to this?

OTHELLO. Make me see 't; or, at the least, so prove it,
That the probation bear no hinge nor loop
To hang a doubt on; or woe upon thy life!

IAGO. My noble lord,—

OTHELLO. If thou dost slander her and torture me,
Never pray more; abandon all remorse;
On horror's head horrors[55] accumulate;
Do deeds to make heaven weep, all earth amaz'd;
For nothing canst thou to damnation add
Greater than that.

IAGO. O grace! O heaven forgive me!
Are you a man? Have you a soul or sense?
God be wi' you; take mine office. O wretched fool,
That liv'st to make thine honesty a vice!
O monstrous world! Take note, take note, O world,
To be direct and honest is not safe.
I thank you for this profit; and from hence
I'll love no friend, sith love breeds such offense.

OTHELLO. Nay, stay: thou shouldst be honest.

IAGO. I should be wise, for honesty 's a fool
And loses that it works for.

OTHELLO. By the world,
I think my wife be honest and think she is not;
I think that thou are just and think thou art not.
I'll have some proof. Her name, that was as fresh
As Dian's visage, is now begrim'd and black

---

[52]**Pioners** sappers, a low grade of soldiers.
[53]**circumstance** attendant fact; here, formal display.
[54]**mortal engines** i.e., cannon.
[55]**horrors** object of *accumulate*.

As mine own face. If there be cords, or knives,
Poison, or fire, or suffocating streams,
I'll not endure it. Would I were satisfied!
IAGO. I see, sir, you are eaten up with passion:
I do repent me that I put it to you.
You would be satisfied?
OTHELLO. Would! nay, I will.
IAGO. And may: but, how? how satisfied, my lord?
Would you, the supervisor, grossly gape on—
Behold her topp'd?
OTHELLO. Death and damnation! O!
IAGO. It were a tedious difficulty, I think,
To bring them to that prospect: damn them then,
If ever mortal eyes do see them bolster[56]
More than their own! What then? how then?
What shall I say? Where 's satisfaction?
It is impossible you should see this,
Were they as prime as goats, as hot as monkeys,
As salt[57] as wolves in pride, and fools as gross
As ignorance made drunk. But yet, I say,
If imputation[58] and strong circumstances,
Which lead directly to the door of truth,
Will give you satisfaction, you may have 't.
OTHELLO. Give me a living reason she 's disloyal.
IAGO. I do not like the office.
But, sith I am ent'red in this cause so far,
Prick'd to 't by foolish honesty and love,
I will go on. I lay with Cassio lately;
And, being troubled with a raging tooth,
I could not sleep.
There are a kind of men so loose of soul,
That in their sleeps will mutter their affairs.
One of this kind is Cassio.
In sleep I heard him say "Sweet Desdemona,
Let us be wary, let us hide our loves";
And then, sir, would he grip and wring my hand,
Cry "O sweet creature!" and then kiss me hard,
As if he pluck'd up kisses by the roots
That grew upon my lips: then laid his leg
Over my thigh, and sigh'd and kiss'd; and then
Cried "Cursed fate that gave thee to the Moor!"
OTHELLO. O monstrous! monstrous!
IAGO. Nay, this was but his dream.
OTHELLO. But this denoted a foregone conclusion.[59]

---

[56]**bolster** lie together.
[57]**salt** wanton, sensual.
[58]**imputation** i.e., opinion founded on strong circumstantial evidence.
[59]**foregone conclusion** previous trial or experience (not used in our sense).

'Tis a shrewd doubt, though it be but a dream.
IAGO. And this may help to thicken other proofs
That do demonstrate thinly.
OTHELLO. I'll tear her all to pieces.
IAGO. Nay, but be wise: yet we see nothing done;
She may be honest yet. Tell me but this,
Have you not sometimes seen a handkerchief
Spotted with strawberries in your wife's hand?
OTHELLO. I gave her such a one; 'twas my first gift.
IAGO. I know not that: but such a handkerchief—
I am sure it was your wife's—did I to-day
See Cassio wipe his beard with.
OTHELLO. If it be that,—
IAGO. If it be that, or any that was hers,
It speaks against her with the other proofs.
OTHELLO. O, that the slave had forty thousand lives!
One is too poor, too weak for my revenge.
Now do I see 'tis true. Look here, Iago;
All my fond love thus do I blow to heaven.
'Tis gone.
Arise, black vengeance, from the hollow hell!
Yield up, O love, thy crown and hearted[60] throne
To tyrannous hate! Swell, bosom, with thy fraught,[61]
For 'tis of aspics'[62] tongues!
IAGO. Yet be content.
OTHELLO. O, blood, blood, blood!
IAGO. Patience, I say; your mind perhaps may change.
OTHELLO. Never, Iago. Like to the Pontic sea,
Whose icy current and compulsive course
Ne'er feels retiring ebb, but keeps due on
To the Propontic and the Hellespont,
Even so my bloody thoughts, with violent pace,
Shall ne'er look back, ne'er ebb to humble love,
Till that a capable and wide revenge
Swallow them up. Now, by yond marble[63] heaven,
[*Kneels*] In the due reverence of a sacred vow
I here engage my words.
IAGO. Do not rise yet.
[*Kneels.*] Witness, you ever-burning lights above,
You elements that clip us round about,
Witness that here Iago doth give up
The execution[64] of his wit, hands, heart,
To wrong'd Othello's service! Let him command,

---

[60]**hearted** fixed in the heart.
[61]**fraught** freight, burden.
[62]**aspics'** venemous serpents'.
[63]**marble** i.e., gleaming like marble.
[64]**execution** exercise.

And to obey shall be in me remorse,[65]
What bloody business ever. [*They rise.*]
OTHELLO. I greet thy love,
Not with vain thanks, but with acceptance bounteous,
And will upon the instant put thee to 't.
Within these three days let me hear thee say
That Cassio 's not alive.
IAGO. My friend is dead; 'tis done at your request:
But let her live.
OTHELLO. Damn her, lewd minx! O, damn her! damn her!
Come, go with me apart; I will withdraw,
To furnish me with some swift means of death
For the fair devil. Now art thou my lieutenant.
IAGO. I am your own for ever. [*Exeunt.*]

SCENE IV

Before the castle.

[*Enter* DESDEMONA, EMILIA, *and* CLOWN.]

DESDEMONA. Do you know, sirrah, where Lieutenant Cassio lies?
CLOWN. I dare not say he lies any where.
DESDEMONA. Why, man?
CLOWN. He's a soldier, and for one to say a soldier lies, is stabbing.
DESDEMONA. Go to: where lodges he?
CLOWN. To tell you where he lodges, is to tell you where I lie.
DESDEMONA. Can any thing be made of this?
CLOWN. I know not where he lodges, and for me to devise a lodging and say he lies here or he lies there, were to lie in mine own throat.
DESDEMONA. Can you inquire him out, and be edified by report?
CLOWN. I will catechize the world for him; that is, make questions, and by them answer.
DESDEMONA. Seek him, bid him come hither: tell him I have moved my lord on his behalf, and hope all will be well.
CLOWN. To do this is within the compass of man's wit; and therefore I will attempt the doing it. [*Exit* CLOWN.]

DESDEMONA. Where should I lose that handkerchief, Emilia?
EMILIA. I know not, madam.
DESDEMONA. Believe me, I had rather have lost my purse
Full of crusadoes[66] and but my noble Moor
Is true of mind and made of no such baseness
As jealous creatures are, it were enough
To put him to ill thinking.
EMILIA. Is he not jealous?

---

[65]**remorse** pity for Othello's wrongs.
[66]**crusadoes** Portuguese gold coins.

DESDEMONA. Who, he? I think the sun where he was born
Drew all such humours from him.
EMILIA. Look, where he comes.
[*Enter* OTHELLO.]
DESDEMONA. I will not leave him now till Cassio
Be call'd to him.—How is 't with you, my lord?
OTHELLO. Well, my good lady. [*Aside*] O, hardness to dissemble!—
How do you, Desdemona?
DESDEMONA. Well, my good lord.
OTHELLO. Give me your hand. This hand is moist, my lady.
DESDEMONA. It yet hath felt no age nor known no sorrow.
OTHELLO. This argues fruitfulness and liberal heart.
Hot, hot, and moist this hand of yours requires
A sequester[67] from liberty, fasting and prayer,
Much castigation, exercise devout;
For here 's a young and sweating devil here,
That commonly rebels. 'Tis a good hand,
A frank one.
DESDEMONA. You may, indeed, say so,
For 'twas that hand that gave away my heart.
OTHELLO. A liberal hand: the hearts of old gave hands;
But our new heraldry is hands, not hearts.[68]
DESDEMONA. I cannot speak of this. Come now, your promise.
OTHELLO. What promise, chuck?
DESDEMONA. I have sent to bid Cassio come speak with you.
OTHELLO. I have a salt and sorry rheum[69] offends me;
Lend me thy handkerchief.
DESDEMONA. Here, my lord.
OTHELLO. That which I gave you.
DESDEMONA. I have it not about me.
OTHELLO. Not?
DESDEMONA. No, indeed, my lord.
OTHELLO. That 's a fault.
That handkerchief
Did an Egyptian[70] to my mother give;
She was a charmer, and could almost read
The thoughts of people. She told her, while she kept it,
'Twould make her amiable and subdue my father
Entirely to her love, but if she lost it
Or made a gift of it, my father's eye
Should hold her loathed and his spirits should hunt
After new fancies: she, dying, gave it me;
And bid me, when my fate would have me wive,
To give it her. I did so: and take heed on 't;

[67]**sequester** separation, sequestration.
[68]**new...hearts** a current expression referring to marriages in which there is a joining of hands without the giving of hearts.
[69]**sorry rheum** distressful head cold.
[70]**Egyptian** gypsy.

Make it a darling like your precious eye;
To lose 't or give 't away were such perdition
As nothing else could match.

Desdemona. Is 't possible?

Othello. 'Tis true. There 's magic in the web of it:
A sibyl, that had numb'red in the world
The sun to course two hundred compasses,
In her prophetic fury sew'd the work;
The worms were hallow'd that did breed the silk;
And it was dy'd in mummy[71] which the skilful
Conserv'd of[72] maidens' hearts.

Desdemona. Indeed! is 't true?

Othello. Most veritable; therefore look to 't well.

Desdemona. Then would to God that I had never seen 't!

Othello. Ha! wherefore?

Desdemona. Why do you speak so startingly and rash?

Othello. Is 't lost? is 't gone? speak, is it out o' th' way?

Desdemona. Heaven bless us!

Othello. Say you?

Desdemona. It is not lost; but what an if it were?

Othello. How!

Desdemona. I say, it is not lost.

Othello. Fetch 't, let me see 't.

Desdemona. Why, so I can, sir, but I will not now.
This is a trick to put me from my suit:
Pray you, let Cassio be receiv'd again.

Othello. Fetch me the handkerchief: my mind misgives.

Desdemona. Come, come;
You'll never meet a more sufficient man.

Othello. The handkerchief!

Desdemona. I pray, talk me of Cassio.

Othello. The handkerchief!

Desdemona. A man that all his time
Hath founded his good fortunes on your love,
Shar'd dangers with you,—

Othello. The handkerchief!

Desdemona. In sooth, you are to blame.

Othello. Away! [*Exit* Othello.]

Emilia. Is not this man jealous?

Desdemona. I ne'er saw this before.
Sure, there 's some wonder in this handkerchief:
I am most unhappy in the loss of it.

Emilia. 'Tis not a year or two shows us a man:
They are all but stomachs, and we all but food;
They eat us hungerly, and when they are full,
They belch us.

---

[71]**mummy** medicinal or magical preparation drained from the flesh of mummified bodies.
[72]**Conserv'd of** preserved out of.

[*Enter* IAGO *and* CASSIO.]

Look you, Cassio and my husband!
IAGO. There is no other way; 'tis she must do 't:
And, lo, the happiness! go, and importune her.
DESDEMONA. How now, good Cassio! what 's the news with you?
CASSIO. Madam, my former suit. I do beseech you
That by your virtuous means I may again
Exist, and be a member of his love
Whom I with all the office of my heart
Entirely honour. I would not be delay'd.
If my offense be of such mortal kind
That nor my service past, nor present sorrows,
Nor purpos'd merit in futurity,
Can ransom me into his love again,
But to know so much be my benefit;[73]
So shall I clothe me in a forc'd content,
And shut myself up in some other course,
To fortune's alms.
DESDEMONA. Alas, thrice-gentle Cassio!
My advocation[74] is not now in tune;
My lord is not my lord; nor should I know him,
Were he in favour as in humour alter'd.
So help me every spirit sanctified
As I have spoken for you all my best
And stood within the blank[75] of his displeasure
For my free speech! You must awhile be patient.
What I can do I will; and more I will
Than for myself I dare: let that suffice you.
IAGO. Is my lord angry?
EMILIA. He went hence but now,
And certainly in strange unquietness.
IAGO. Can he be angry? I have seen the cannon,
When it hath blown his ranks into the air,
And, like the devil, from his very arm
Puff'd his own brother:—and can he be angry?
Something of moment then. I will go meet him:
There 's matter in 't indeed, if he be angry.
DESDEMONA. I prithee, do so. [*Exit* IAGO.]

Something, sure, of state,
Either from Venice, or some unhatch'd practice
Made demonstrable here in Cyprus to him,
Hath puddled[76] his clear spirit; and in such cases
Men's natures wrangle with inferior things,
Though great ones are their object. 'Tis even so;

---

[73]**to know . . . benefit** to know that my case is hopeless will end my vain endeavor.
[74]**advocation** advocacy.
[75]**blank** white spot in the center of a target; here, range.
[76]**puddled** sullied the purity of.

For let our finger ache, and it indues[77]
Our other healthful members even to a sense
Of pain. Nay, we must think men are not gods,
Nor of them look for such observancy
As fits the bridal. Beshrew me much, Emilia,
I was, unhandsome[78] warrior as I am,
Arraigning his unkindness with my soul;
But now I find I had suborn'd the witness,
And he 's indicted falsely.

EMILIA. Pray heaven it be state-matters, as you think,
And no conception[79] nor no jealous toy
Concerning you.

DESDEMONA. Alas the day! I never gave him cause.

EMILIA. But jealous souls will not be answer'd so;
They are not ever jealous for the cause,
But jealous for they are jealous: 'tis a monster
Begot upon itself, born on itself.

DESDEMONA. Heaven keep that monster from Othello's mind!

EMILIA. Lady, amen.

DESDEMONA. I will go seek him. Cassio, walk here about:
If I do find him fit, I'll move your suit
And seek to effect it to my uttermost.

CASSIO. I humbly thank your ladyship. [*Exit* DESDEMONA *with* EMILIA.]

[*Enter* BIANCA.]

BIANCA. Save you, friend Cassio!

CASSIO. What make you from home?
How is 't with you, my most fair Bianca?
I' faith, sweet love, I was coming to your house.

BIANCA. And I was going to your lodging, Cassio.
What, keep a week away? seven days and nights?
Eight score eight hours? and lovers' absent hours,
More tedious than the dial eight score times?
O weary reck'ning!

CASSIO. Pardon me, Bianca.
I have this while with leaden thoughts been press'd;
But I shall, in a more continuate[80] time,
Strike off this score of absence. Sweet Bianca,

[*Giving her* DESDEMONA'S *handkerchief.*]

Take me this work out.[81]

BIANCA. O Cassio, whence came this?
This is some token from a newer friend:
To the felt absence now I feel a cause:

---

[77]**indues** brings to the same condition.
[78]**unhandsome** unfair.
[79]**conception** mere fancy.
[80]**continuate** uninterrupted.
[81]**Take . . . out** i.e., copy this embroidery for me.

Is 't come to this? Well, well.
CASSIO. Go to, woman!
Throw your vile guesses in the devil's teeth,
From whence you have them. You are jealous now
That this is from some mistress, some remembrance:
No, in good troth, Bianca.
BIANCA. Why, whose is it?
CASSIO. I know not, sweet. I found it in my chamber.
I like the work well. Ere it be demanded—
As like enough it will—I would have it copied:
Take it, and do 't; and leave me for this time.
BIANCA. Leave you! wherefore?
CASSIO. I do attend here on the general;
And think it no addition, nor my wish,
To have him see me woman'd.
BIANCA. Why, I pray you?
CASSIO. Not that I love you not.
BIANCA. But that you do not love me.
I pray you, bring me on the way a little,
And say if I shall see you soon at night.
CASSIO. 'Tis but a little way that I can bring you;
For I attend here, but I'll see you soon.
BIANCA. 'Tis very good; I must be circumstance'd.[82] [*Exeunt omnes.*]

ACT IV

SCENE I

Cyprus. Before the castle.

[*Enter* OTHELLO *and* IAGO.]

IAGO. Will you think so?
OTHELLO. Think so, Iago!
IAGO. What,
To kiss in private?
OTHELLO. An unauthoriz'd kiss.
IAGO. Or to be naked with her friend in bed
An hour or more, not meaning any harm?
OTHELLO. Naked in bed, Iago, and not mean harm!
It is hypocrisy against the devil:
They that mean virtuously, and yet do so,
The devil their virtue tempts, and they tempt heaven.
IAGO. So[1] they do nothing, 'tis a venial slip:
But if I give my wife a handkerchief,—
OTHELLO. What then?
IAGO. Why, then, 'tis hers, my lord: and, being hers,

---

[82]**circumstance'd** governed by circumstances.
[1]**So** so long as.

She may, I think, bestow 't on any man.
OTHELLO. She is protectress of her honour too:
May she give that?
IAGO. Her honour is an essence that 's not seen;
They have it very oft that have it not:
But, for the handkerchief,—
OTHELLO. By heaven, I would most gladly have forgot it.
Thou said'st—O, it comes o'er my memory,
As doth the raven o'er the infected house,[2]
Boding to all—he had my handkerchief.
IAGO. Ay, what of that?
OTHELLO. That 's not so good now.
IAGO. What,
If I had said I had seen him do you wrong?
Or heard him say,—as knaves be such abroad,
Who having, by their own importunate suit,
Or voluntary dotage of some mistress,
Convinced or supplied[3] them, cannot choose
But they must blab—
OTHELLO. Hath he said any thing?
IAGO. He hath, my lord; but be you well assur'd,
No more than he'll unswear.
OTHELLO. What hath he said?
IAGO. 'Faith, that he did—I know not what he did.
OTHELLO. What? what?
IAGO. Lie—
OTHELLO. With her?
IAGO. With her, on her; what you will.

OTHELLO. Lie with her! lie on her! We say lie on her, when they belie her. Lie with her! that's fulsome.—Handkerchief—confessions—handkerchief—To confess, and be hanged for his labour;—first, to be hanged, and then to confess.—I tremble at it. Nature would not invest herself in such shadowing passion without some instruction.[4] It is not words that shakes me thus. Pish! Noses, ears, and lips.—Is 't possible? Confess—handkerchief—O devil!

[*Falls in a trance.*]

IAGO. Work on,
My medicine, work! Thus credulous fools are caught;
And many worthy and chaste dames even thus,
All guiltless, meet reproach. What, ho! my lord!
My lord, I say! Othello!

[*Enter* CASSIO.]

How now, Cassio!
CASSIO. What 's the matter?
IAGO. My lord is fall'n into an epilepsy:

---

[2]**raven . . . house** allusion to the belief that the raven hovered over a house of sickness or infection.

[3]**Convinced or supplied** i.e., mistresses gained by importunity and those who doted voluntarily.

[4]**Nature . . . instruction** i.e., my jealousy cannot be merely the result of natural imagination, but must have some foundation in fact.

This is his second fit; he had one yesterday.
CASSIO. Rub him about the temples.
IAGO. No, forbear;
The lethargy[5] must have his quiet course:
If not, he foams at mouth and by and by
Breaks out to savage madness. Look, he stirs:
Do you withdraw yourself a little while,
He will recover straight. When he is gone,
I would on great occasion speak with you.
[*Exit* CASSIO.]
How is it, general? Have you not hurt your head?
OTHELLO. Dost thou mock me?
IAGO. I mock you! no, by heaven.
Would you would bear your fortune like a man!
OTHELLO. A horned man's a monster and a beast.
IAGO. There's many a beast then in a populous city,
And many a civil[6] monster.
OTHELLO. Did he confess it?
IAGO. Good sir, be a man;
Think every bearded fellow that's but yok'd
May draw with you.[7] There's millions now alive
That nightly lie in those unproper[8] beds
Which they dare swear peculiar:[9] your case is better.
O, 'tis the spite of hell, the fiend's arch-mock,
To lip a wanton in a secure couch,
And to suppose her chaste! No, let me know;
And knowing what I am, I know what she shall be.
OTHELLO. O, thou are wise; 'tis certain.
IAGO. Stand you awhile apart;
Confine yourself but in a patient list.[10]
Whilst you were here o'erwhelmed with your grief—
A passion most unsuiting such a man—
Cassio came hither. I shifted him away,
And laid good 'scuse upon your ecstasy,
Bade him anon return and here speak with me;
The which he promis'd. Do but encave[11] yourself,
And mark the fleers,[12] the gibes, and notable scorns,
That dwell in every region of his face;
For I will make him tell the tale anew,
Where, how, how oft, how long ago, and when
He hath, and is again to cope your wife:
I say, but mark his gesture. Marry, patience;

---

[5]**lethargy** unconscious condition.
[6]**civil** i.e., in civilized society.
[7]**draw with you** i.e, share your fate as cuckold.
[8]**unproper** not belonging exclusively to an individual.
[9]**peculiar** private, one's own.
[10]**patient list** within the bounds of patience.
[11]**encave** conceal.
[12]**fleers** sneers.

Or I shall say y' are all in all in spleen,
And nothing of a man.

OTHELLO. Dost thou hear, Iago?
I will be found most cunning in my patience;
But—dost thou hear?—most bloody.

IAGO. That 's not amiss;
But yet keep time[13] in all. Will you withdraw?

[OTHELLO *retires*.]

Now will I question Cassio of Bianca,
A housewife that by selling her desires
Buys herself bread and clothes: it is a creature
That dotes on Cassio; as 'tis the strumpet's plague
To beguile many and be beguil'd by one:
He, when he hears of her, cannot refrain
From the excess of laughter. Here he comes:

[*Enter* CASSIO.]

As he shall smile, Othello shall go mad;
And his unbookish[14] jealousy must conster[15]
Poor Cassio's smiles, gestures and light behaviour,
Quite in the wrong. How do you know, lieutenant?

CASSIO. The worser that you give me the addition[16]
Whose want even kills me.

IAGO. Ply Desdemona well, and you are sure on 't.
[*Speaking lower*] Now, if this suit lay in Bianca's power,
How quickly should you speed!

CASSIO. Alas, poor caitiff!

OTHELLO. Look, how he laughs already!

IAGO. I never knew woman love man so.

CASSIO. Alas, poor rogue! I think, i' faith, she loves me.

OTHELLO. Now he denies it faintly, and laughs it out.

IAGO. Do you hear, Cassio?

OTHELLO. Now he importunes him
To tell o'er: go to; well said, well said.

IAGO. She gives it out that you shall marry her:
Do you intend it?

CASSIO. Ha, ha, ha!

OTHELLO. Do you triumph, Roman?[17] do you triumph?

CASSIO. I marry her! what? a customer![18] Prithee, bear some charity to my wit; do not think it so unwholesome. Ha, ha, ha!

OTHELLO. So, so, so, so they laugh that win.

IAGO. 'Faith, the cry goes that you shall marry her.

CASSIO. Prithee, say true.

---

[13]**keep time** use judgment and order.
[14]**unbookish** uninstructed.
[15]**conster** construe.
[16]**addition** title.
[17]**Roman** epithet arising from the association of the Romans with the idea of triumph.
[18]**customer** prostitute.

IAGO. I am a very villain else.

OTHELLO. Have you scored me?[19] Well.

CASSIO. This is the monkey's own giving out: she is persuaded I will marry her, out of her own love and flattery, not out of my promise.

OTHELLO. Iago beckons me; now he begins the story.

CASSIO. She was here even now; she haunts me in every place. I was the other day talking on the seabank with certain Venetians; and thither comes the bauble,[20] and, by this hand, she falls me thus about my neck—

OTHELLO. Crying, 'O dear Cassio!' as it were: his gesture imports it.

CASSIO. So hangs, and lolls, and weeps upon me; so shakes, and pulls me ha, ha, ha!

OTHELLO. Now he tells how she plucked him to my chamber. O, I see that nose of yours, but not that dog I shall throw it to.

CASSIO. Well, I must leave her company.

IAGO. Before me![21] look, where she comes.

[*Enter* BIANCA.]

CASSIO. 'Tis such another fitchew![22] marry, a perfumed one.—What do you mean by this haunting of me?

BIANCA. Let the devil and his dam haunt you! What did you mean by that same handkerchief you gave me even now? I was a fine fool to take it. I must take out the work?—A likely piece of work, that you should find it in your chamber, and not know who left it there! This is some minx's token, and I must take out the work? There; give it your hobby-horse.[23] Wheresoever you had it, I'll take out no work on 't.

CASSIO. How now, my sweet Bianca! how now! how now!

OTHELLO. By heaven, that should be my handkerchief!

BIANCA. If you'll come to supper to-night, you may; if you will not, come when you are next prepared for. [*Exit*.]

IAGO. After her, after her.

CASSIO. 'Faith, I must; she'll rail in the street else.

IAGO. Will you sup there?

CASSIO. Yes, I intend so.

IAGO. Well, I may chance to see you; for I would very fain speak with you.

CASSIO. Prithee, come; will you?

IAGO. Go to; say no more. [*Exit* CASSIO.]

OTHELLO [*Advancing*]. How shall I murder him, Iago?

IAGO. Did you perceive how he laughed at his vice?

OTHELLO. O Iago!

IAGO. And did you see the handkerchief?

OTHELLO. Was that mine?

IAGO. Yours, by this hand: and to see how he prizes the foolish woman your wife! She gave it him, and he hath given it his whore.

---

[19]**scored me** made up my reckoning, or branded me.
[20]**bauble** plaything.
[21]**Before me!** On my soul!
[22]**fitchew** polecat (because of her strong perfume; also, slang word for a prostitute).
[23]**hobby-horse** harlot.

Othello. I would have him nine years a-killing. A fine woman! a fair woman! a sweet woman!

Iago. Nay, you must forget that.

Othello. Ay, let her rot, and perish, and be damned to-night; for she shall not live: no, my heart is turned to stone; I strike it, and it hurts my hand. O, the world hath not a sweeter creature: she might lie by an emperor's side and command him tasks.

Iago. Nay, that 's not your way.[24]

Othello. Hang her! I do but say what she is: so delicate with her needle: an admirable musician: O! she will sing the savageness out of a bear: of so high and plenteous wit and invention:—

Iago. She 's the worse for all this.

Othello. O, a thousand thousand times: and then, of so gentle a condition!

Iago. Ay, too gentle.

Othello. Nay, that 's certain: but yet the pity of it, Iago! O Iago, the pity of it, Iago!

Iago. If you are so fond over her iniquity, give her patent[25] to offend; for, if it touch not you, it comes near nobody.

Othello. I will chop her into messes;[26] cuckold me!

Iago. O, 'tis foul in her.

Othello. With mine officer!

Iago. That 's fouler.

Othello. Get me some poison, Iago; this night I'll not expostulate with her, lest her body and beauty unprovide[27] my mind again: this night, Iago.

Iago. Do it not with poison, strangle her in her bed, even the bed she hath contaminated.

Othello. Good, good: the justice of it pleases: very good.

Iago. And for Cassio, let me be his undertaker.[28] You shall hear more by midnight.

Othello. Excellent good. [*A trumpet within.*] What trumpet is that same?

Iago. I warrant something from Venice.

[*Enter* Lodovico, Desdemona, *and* Attendants.]

'Tis Lodovico.
This comes from the duke: and, see, your wife's with him.

Lodovico. God save you, worthy general!

Othello. With all my heart, sir.

Lodovico. The duke and the senators of Venice greet you. [*Gives him a letter.*]

Othello. I kiss the instrument of their pleasures. [*Opens the letter, and reads.*]

Desdemona. And what's the news, good cousin Lodovico?

Iago. I am very glad to see you, signior;
Welcome to Cyprus.

Lodovico. I thank you. How does Lieutenant Cassio?

Iago. Lives, sir.

Desdemona. Cousin, there's fall'n between him and my lord
An unkind breach, but you shall make all well.

---

[24]**your way** i.e., the way you should think of her.
[25]**patent** license.
[26]**messes** dishes of food.
[27]**unprovide** weaken, unfit.
[28]**let . . . undertaker** i.e., let me settle with him.

OTHELLO. Are you sure of that?
DESDEMONA. My lord?
OTHELLO [*Reads*]. "This fail you not to do, as you will—"
LODOVICO. He did not call; he's busy in the paper.
Is there division 'twixt my lord and Cassio?
DESDEMONA. A most unhappy one. I would do much
T' atone them, for the love I bear to Cassio.
OTHELLO. Fire and brimstone!
DESDEMONA. My lord?
OTHELLO. Are you wise?
DESDEMONA. What, is he angry?
LODOVICO. May be the letter mov'd him:
For, as I think, they do command him home,
Deputing Cassio in his government.[29]
DESDEMONA. Trust me, I am glad on 't.
OTHELLO. Indeed!
DESDEMONA. My lord?
OTHELLO. I am glad to see you mad.
DESDEMONA. Why, sweet Othello,—
OTHELLO [*Striking her*]. Devil!
DESDEMONA. I have not deserv'd this.
LODOVICO. My lord, this would not be believ'd in Venice,
Though I should swear I saw 't; 'tis very much.
Make her amends; she weeps.
OTHELLO. O devil, devil!
If that the earth could teem with woman's tears,
Each drop she falls would prove a crocodile.[30]
Out of my sight!
DESDEMONA. I will not stay to offend you. [*Going*.]
LODOVICO. Truly, an obedient lady.
I do beseech your lordship, call her back.
OTHELLO. Mistress!
DESDEMONA. My lord?
OTHELLO. What would you with her, sir?
LODOVICO. Who, I, my lord?
OTHELLO. Ay; you did wish that I would make her turn:
Sir, she can turn, and turn, and yet go on,
And turn again; and she can weep, sir, weep;
And she 's obedient, as you say, obedient,
Very obedient. Proceed you in your tears.
Concerning this, sir,—O well-painted passion!—[31]
I am commanded home. Get you away;
I'll send for you anon. Sir, I obey the mandate,
And will return to Venice. Hence, avaunt!
[*Exit* DESDEMONA.]

---

[29]**government** office.
[30]**prove a crocodile** i.e., by weeping crocodile tears; it was believed the crocodile shed tears over the body of the person it was eating.
[31]**well-painted passion** well-simulated emotion.

Cassio shall have my place. And, sir, to-night,
I do entreat that we may sup together.
You are welcome, sir, to Cyprus.—Goats and monkeys! [*Exit.*]

LODOVICO. Is this the noble Moor whom our full senate
Call all in all sufficient? Is this the nature
Whom passion could not shake? whose solid virtue
The shot of accident, nor dart of chance,
Could neither graze nor pierce?

IAGO. He is much chang'd.

LODOVICO. Are his wits safe? Is he not light of brain?

IAGO. He's that he is. I may not breathe my censure
What he might be: if what he might he is not,
I would to heaven he were!

LODOVICO. What, strike his wife!

IAGO. 'Faith, that was not so well; yet would I knew
That stroke would prove the worst!

LODOVICO. Is it his use?
Or did the letters work upon his blood,
And new-create this fault?

IAGO. Alas, alas!
It is not honesty in me to speak
What I have seen and known. You shall observe him,
And his own courses will denote him so
That I may save my speech: do but go after,
And mark how he continues.

LODOVICO. I am sorry that I am deceiv'd in him. [*Exeunt.*]

SCENE II

A room in the castle.

[*Enter* OTHELLO *and* EMILIA.]

OTHELLO. You have seen nothing then?

EMILIA. Nor ever heard, nor ever did suspect.

OTHELLO. Yes, you have seen Cassio and she together.

EMILIA. But then I saw no harm, and then I heard
Each syllable that breath made up between them.

OTHELLO. What, did they never whisper?

EMILIA. Never, my lord.

OTHELLO. Nor send you out 'o th' way?

EMILIA. Never.

OTHELLO. To fetch her fan, her gloves, her mask, nor nothing?

EMILIA. Never, my lord.

OTHELLO. That 's strange.

EMILIA. I durst, my lord, to wager she is honest,
Lay down my soul at stake: if you think other,
Remove your thought; it doth abuse your bosom.
If any wretch have put this in your head,
Let heaven requite it with the serpent's curse!

For, if she be not honest, chaste, and true,
There's no man happy; the purest of their wives
Is foul as slander.

OTHELLO. Bid her come hither: go. [*Exit* EMILIA.]

She says enough; yet she's a simple bawd
That cannot say as much. This is a subtle whore,
A closet lock and key[32] of villainous secrets:
And yet she'll kneel and pray; I have seen her do't.

[*Enter* DESDEMONA *and* EMILIA.]

DESDEMONA. My lord, what is your will?
OTHELLO. Pray, chuck, come hither.
DESDEMONA. What is your pleasure?
OTHELLO. Let me see your eyes;
Look in my face.
DESDEMONA. What horrible fancy 's this?
OTHELLO [*to* Emilia]. Some of your function,[33] mistress;
Leave procreants[34] alone and shut the door;
Cough, or cry "hem," if any body come.
Your mystery, your mystery:[35] nay, dispatch. [*Exit* Emilia.]
DESDEMONA. Upon my knees, what doth your speech import?
I understand a fury in your words,
But not the words.
OTHELLO. Why, what art thou?
DESDEMONA. Your wife, my lord; your true
And loyal wife.
OTHELLO. Come, swear it, damn thyself;
Lest, being like one of heaven, the devils themselves
Should fear to seize thee: therefore be double damn'd:
Swear thou are honest.
DESDEMONA. Heaven doth truly know it.
OTHELLO. Heaven truly knows that thou are false as hell.
DESDEMONA. To whom, my lord? with whom? how am I false?
OTHELLO. O Desdemon! away! away! away!
DESDEMONA. Alas the heavy day! Why do you weep?
Am I the motive of these tears, my lord?
If haply you my father do suspect
An instrument of this your calling back,
Lay not your blame on me: if you have lost him,
Why, I have lost him too.
OTHELLO. Had it pleas'd heaven
To try me with affliction; had they[36] rain'd
All kinds of sores and shames on my bare head,

[32]**closet lock and key** complete storeroom.
[33]**Some...function** i.e., set to work in your chosen profession, that of bawd.
[34]**procreants** mating couples.
[35]**mystery** trade, occupation.
[36]**they** heavenly powers.

Steep'd me in poverty to the very lips,
Given to captivity me and my utmost hopes,
I should have found in some place of my soul
A drop of patience: but, alas, to make me
A fixed figure for the time of scorn
To point his slow unmoving finger at![37]
Yet could I bear that too; well, very well.
But there, where I have garner'd up my heart,
Where either I must live, or bear no life;
The fountain from the which my current runs,
Or else dries up; to be discarded thence!
Or keep it as a cistern for foul toads
To knot and gender[38] in! Turn thy complexion[39] there,
Patience, thou young and rose-lipp'd cherubin,—
Ay, there, look grim as hell!

DESDEMONA. I hope my noble lord esteems me honest.

OTHELLO. O, ay; as summer flies are in the shambles,[40]
That quicken[41] even with blowing. O thou weed,
Who are so lovely fair and smell'st so sweet
That the sense aches at thee, would thou hads't ne'er been born!

DESDEMONA. Alas, what ignorant sin have I committed?

OTHELLO. Was this fair paper, this most goodly book,
Made to write "whore" upon? What committed!
Committed! O thou public commoner![42]
I should make very forges of my cheeks,
That would to cinders burn up modesty,
Did I but speak thy deeds. What committed!
Heaven stops the nose at it and the moon winks,
The bawdy wind that kisses all it meets
Is hush'd within the hollow mine of earth,
And will not hear it. What committed!
Impudent strumpet!

DESDEMONA. By heaven, you do me wrong.

OTHELLO. Are not you a strumpet?

DESDEMONA. No, as I am a Christian.
If to preserve this vessel[43] for my lord
From any other foul unlawful touch
Be not to be a strumpet, I am none.

OTHELLO. What, not a whore?

DESDEMONA. No, as I shall be sav'd.

OTHELLO. Is't possible?

---

[37]**A . . . at** Othello possibly thinks of himself as a man set in a pillory at whom the scornful world points in mockery. There seems to be a comparison with the sundial, whose gnomon, or indicator, becomes the finger of scornful time.

[38]**gender** engender.

[39]**Turn thy complexion** grow pale.

[40]**shambles** slaughterhouse.

[41]**quicken** come to life.

[42]**commoner** prostitute.

[43]**vessel** body.

DESDEMONA. O, heaven forgive us!
OTHELLO. I cry you mercy, then.
I took you for the cunning whore of Venice
That married with Othello. [*Raising his voice*] You, mistress,
That have the office opposite to Saint Peter,
And keep the gate of hell!

[*Enter* EMILIA.]

You, you, ay, you!
We have done our course; there's money for your pains.
I pray you, turn the key and keep our counsel. [*Exit.*]

EMILIA. Alas, what does this gentleman conceive?
How do you, madam? how do you, my good lady?
DESDEMONA. 'Faith, half asleep.
EMILIA. Good madam, what 's the matter with my lord?
DESDEMONA. With who?
EMILIA. Why, with my lord, madam.
DESDEMONA. Who is thy lord?
EMILIA. He that is yours, sweet lady.
DESDEMONA. I have none: do not talk to me, Emilia;
I cannot weep; nor answers have I none,
But what should go by water.[44] Prithee, tonight
Lay on my bed my wedding sheets, remember;
And call thy husband hither.
EMILIA. Here 's a change indeed! [*Exit.*]
DESDEMONA. 'Tis meet I should be us'd so, very meet.
How have I been behav'd, that he might stick
The small'st opinion on my least misuse?[45]

[*Enter* IAGO *and* EMILIA.]

IAGO. What is your pleasure, madam? How is 't with you?
DESDEMONA. I cannot tell. Those that do teach young babes
Do it with gentle means and easy tasks:
He might have chid me so; for, in good faith,
I am a child to chiding.
IAGO. What is the matter, lady?
EMILIA. Alas, Iago, my lord hath so bewhor'd her,
Thrown such despite[46] and heavy terms upon her,
As true hearts cannot bear.
DESDEMONA. Am I that name, Iago?
IAGO. What name, fair lady?
DESDEMONA. Such as she said my lord did say I was.
EMILIA. He call'd her whore: a beggar in his drink
Could not have laid such terms upon his callet.[47]
IAGO. Why did he so?
DESDEMONA. I do not know; I am sure I am none such.

[44]**go by water** be expressed by tears.
[45]**misuse** evil conduct.
[46]**despite** contempt, scorn.
[47]**callet** lewd woman.

IAGO. Do not weep, do not weep. Alas the day!
EMILIA. Hath she forsook so many noble matches,
Her father and her country and her friends,
To be call'd whore? Would it not make one weep?
DESDEMONA. It is my wretched fortune.
IAGO. Beshrew him for 't!
How comes this trick upon him?
DESDEMONA. Nay, heaven doth know.
EMILIA. I will be hang'd, if some eternal villain,
Some busy and insinuating rogue,
Some cogging,[48] cozening slave, to get some office,
Have not devis'd this slander; I will be hang'd else.
IAGO. Fie, there is no such man; it is impossible.
DESDEMONA. If any such there be, heaven pardon him!
EMILIA. A halter pardon him! and hell gnaw his bones!
Why should he call her whore? who keeps her company?
What place? what time? what form? what likelihood?
The Moor's abus'd by some most villainous knave,
Some base notorious knave, some scurvy fellow.
O heaven, that such companions thou 'dst unfold,
And put in every honest hand a whip
To lash the rascals naked through the world
Even from the east to th' west!
IAGO. Speak within door.[49]
EMILIA. O, fie upon them! Some such squire he was
That turn'd your wit the seamy side without,
And made you to suspect me with the Moor.
IAGO. You are a fool; go to.
DESDEMONA. Alas, Iago.
What shall I do to win my lord again?
Good friend, go to him; for, by this light of heaven,
I know not how I lost him. Here I kneel:
If e'er my will did trespass 'gainst his love,
Either in discourse of thought or actual deed,
Or that mine eyes, mine ears, or any sense,
Delighted them in any other form;
Or that I do not yet, and ever did,
And ever will—though he do shake me off
To beggarly divorcement—love him dearly,
Comfort forswear me! Unkindness may do much;
And his unkindness may defeat my life,
But never taint my love. I cannot say "whore":
It doth abhor me now I speak the word;
To do the act that might the addition[50] earn
Not the world's mass of vanity could make me.
IAGO. I pray you, be content; 'tis but his humour:

[48]**cogging** cheating.
[49]**Speak . . . door** i.e., not so loud.
[50]**addition** title.

The business of the state does him offense,
And he does chide with you.

DESDEMONA. If 'twere no other,—

IAGO. 'Tis but so, I warrant. [*Trumpets within.*]
Hark, how these instruments summon to supper!
The messengers of Venice stay the meat;[51]
Go in, and weep not; all things shall be well.

[*Exeunt* DESDEMONA *and* EMILIA.]

[*Enter* RODERIGO.]

How now, Roderigo!

RODERIGO. I do not find that thou dealest justly with me.

IAGO. What in the contrary?

RODERIGO. Every day thou daffest me[52] with some device, Iago; and rather, as it seems to me now, keepest from me all conveniency[53] than suppliest me with the least advantage of hope. I will indeed no longer endure it, nor am I yet persuaded to put up[54] in peace what already I have foolishly suffered.

IAGO. Will you hear me, Roderigo?

RODERIGO. 'Faith, I have heard too much, for your words and performances are no kin together.

IAGO. You charge me most unjustly.

RODERIGO. With nought but truth. I have wasted myself out of my means. The jewels you have had from me to deliver to Desdemona would half have corrupted a votarist.[55] You have told me she hath received them and returned me expectations and comforts of sudden respect and acquaintance, but I find none.

IAGO. Well; go to; very well.

RODERIGO. Very well! go to! I cannot go to, man; nor 'tis not very well: nay, I think it is scurvy, and begin to find myself fopped[56] in it.

IAGO. Very well.

RODERIGO. I tell you 'tis not very well. I will make myself known to Desdemona: if she will return me my jewels, I will give over my suit and repent my unlawful solicitation; if not, assure yourself I will seek satisfaction of you.

IAGO. You have said now.[57]

RODERIGO. Ay, and said nothing but what I protest intendment[58] of doing.

IAGO. Why, now I see there 's mettle in thee, and even from this instance do build on thee a better opinion than ever before. Give my thy hand, Roderigo. Thou hast taken against me a most just exception; but yet, I protest, I have dealt most directly in thy affair.

RODERIGO. It hath not appeared.

IAGO. I grant indeed it hath not appeared, and your suspicion is not without wit and judgment. But, Roderigo, if thou hast that in thee indeed, which I have

---

[51]**stay the meat** are waiting for supper.
[52]**daffest me** put me off with an excuse.
[53]**conveniency** advantage, opportunity.
[54]**put up** submit to.
[55]**votarist** nun.
[56]**fopped** fooled.
[57]**You...now** well said, quite right.
[58]**intendment** purpose, intention.

greater reason to believe now than ever, I mean purpose, courage and valour, this night show it; if thou the next night following enjoy not Desdemona, take me from this world with treachery and devise engines for[59] my life.

RODERIGO. Well, what is it? Is it within reason and compass?

IAGO. Sir, there is especial commission come from Venice to depute Cassio in Othello's place.

RODERIGO. Is that true? Why, then Othello and Desdemona return again to Venice.

IAGO. O, no; he goes into Mauritania[60] and takes away with him the fair Desdemona, unless his abode be lingered here by some accident: wherein none can be so determinate[61] as the removing of Cassio.

RODERIGO. How do you mean, removing of him?

IAGO. Why, by making him uncapable of Othello's place; knocking out his brains.

RODERIGO. And that you would have me to do?

IAGO. Ay, if you dare do yourself a profit and a right. He sups to-night with a harlotry,[62] and thither will I go to him: he knows not yet of his honourable fortune. If you will watch his going thence, which I will fashion to fall out between twelve and one, you may take him at your pleasure: I will be near to second your attempt, and he shall fall between us. Come, stand not amazed at it, but go along with me; I will show you such a necessity in his death that you shall think yourself bound to put it on him. It is now high[63] suppertime, and the night grows to waste: about it.

RODERIGO. I will hear further reason for this.

IAGO. And you shall be satisfied.

[*Exeunt.*]

SCENE III

Another room in the castle.

[*Enter* OTHELLO, LODOVICO, DESDEMONA, EMILIA, *and* ATTENDANTS.]

LODOVICO. I do beseech you, sir, trouble yourself no further.

OTHELLO. O, pardon me; 'twill do me good to walk.

LODOVICO. Madam, good night. I humbly thank your ladyship.

DESDEMONA. Your honour is most welcome.

OTHELLO. Will you walk, sir?
O,—Desdemona,—

DESDEMONA. My lord?

OTHELLO. Get you to bed on th' instant; I will be returned forthwith. Dismiss your attendant there: look 't be done.

DESDEMONA. I will, my lord.

[*Exit* OTHELLO, *with* LODOVICO *and* ATTENDANTS.]

EMILIA. How goes it now? He looks gentler than he did.

DESDEMONA. He says he will return incontinent.[64]

---

[59] **engines for** plots against.
[60] **Mauritania** Roman name of northwest Africa, supposed land of the Moors.
[61] **determinate** decisive.
[62] **harlotry** courtesan.
[63] **high** quite.
[64] **incontinent** immediately.

He hath commanded me to go to bed,
And bade me to dismiss you.

EMILIA. Dismiss me!

DESDEMONA. It was his bidding; therefore, good Emilia,
Give me my nightly wearing, and adieu.
We must not now displease him.

EMILIA. I would you had never seen him!

DESDEMONA. So would not I. My love doth so approve him,
That even his stubbornness,[65] his checks,[66] his frowns,—
Prithee, unpin me,—have grace and favour in them.

EMILIA. I have laid those sheets you bade me on the bed.

DESDEMONA. All's one. Good faith, how foolish are our minds!
If I do die before thee, prithee, shroud me
In one of those same sheets.

EMILIA. Come, come, you talk.

DESDEMONA. My mother had a maid call'd Barbary.
She was in love, and he she lov'd prov'd mad
And did forsake her. She had a song of 'willow';
An old thing 'twas, but it express'd her fortune,
And she died singing it. That song to-night
Will not go from my mind; I have much to do,
But to[67] go hang my head all at one side,
And sing it like poor Barbary. Prithee, dispatch.

EMILIA. Shall I go fetch your night-gown?[68]

DESDEMONA. No, unpin me here.
This Lodovico is a proper man.

EMILIA. A very handsome man.

DESDEMONA. He speaks well.

EMILIA. I know a lady in Venice would have walked barefoot to Palestine for a touch of his nether lip.

DESDEMONA [*Singing*]. "The poor soul sat sighing by a sycamore tree,
Sing all a green willow;
Her hand on her bosom, her head on her knee,
Sing willow, willow, willow.
The fresh streams ran by her, and murmur'd her moans;
Sing willow, willow, willow;
Her salt tears fell from her, and soft'ned the stones;—"
Lay by these —
[*Singing*]. "Sing willow, willow, willow"
Prithee, hie thee; he'll come anon —
[*Singing*]. "Sing all a green willow must be my garland.
Let nobody blame him; his scorn I approve,—"
Nay, that's not next.—Hark! who is 't that knocks?

EMILIA. It 's the wind.

---

[65]**stubbornness** harshness.
[66]**checks** rebukes.
[67]**But to** not to.
[68]**night-gown** dressing gown.

DESDEMONA [*Singing*]. "I call'd my love false love; but what said he then?
Sing willow, willow, willow:
If I court moe women, you'll couch with moe men.—"
So, get thee gone; good night. Mine eyes do itch;
Doth that bode weeping?
EMILIA. 'Tis neither here nor there.
DESDEMONA. I have heard it said so. O, these men, these men!
Dost thou in conscience think,—tell me, Emilia,—
That there be women do abuse their husbands
In such gross kind?
EMILIA. There be some such, no question.
DESDEMONA. Wouldst thou do such a deed for all the world?
EMILIA. Why, would not you?
DESDEMONA. No, by this heavenly light!
EMILIA. Nor I neither by this heavenly light; I might do 't as well i' the dark.
DESDEMONA. Wouldst thou do such a deed for all the world?
EMILIA. The world 's a huge thing: it is a great price
For a small vice.
DESDEMONA. In troth, I think thou wouldst not.
EMILIA. In troth, I think I should; and undo 't when I had done. Marry, I would not do such a thing for a joint-ring,[69] nor for measures of lawn, nor for gowns, petticoats, nor caps, nor any petty exhibition;[70] for all the whole world,—why, who would not make her husband a cuckold to make him a monarch? I should venture purgatory for 't.
DESDEMONA. Beshrew me, if I would do such a wrong
For the whole world.
EMILIA. Why, the wrong is but a wrong i' the world; and having the world for your labour, 'tis a wrong in your own world, and you might quickly make it right.
DESDEMONA. I do not think there is any such woman.
EMILIA. Yes, a dozen; and as many
To the vantage[71] as would store the world they played for.
But I do think it is their husband's faults
If wives do fall. Say that they slack their duties,
And pour our treasures into foreign laps,[72]
Or else break out in peevish jealousies,
Throwing restraint upon us; or say they strike us,
Or scant our former having in despite;[73]
Why, we have galls,[74] and though we have some grace,[75]
Yet have we some revenge. Let husbands know
Their wives have sense like them: they see and smell
And have their palates both for sweet and sour,

---

[69]**joint-ring** a ring made in separable halves as a lover's token.
[70]**exhibition** gift, present.
[71]**to the vantage** in addition.
[72]**pour . . . laps** i.e., are unfaithful.
[73]**scant . . . despite** reduce our allowance to spite us.
[74]**have galls** are capable of resenting injury and insult.
[75]**grace** i.e., to forgive.

As husbands have. What is it that they do
When they change us for others? Is it sport?
I think it is. And doth affection breed it?
I think it doth. Is 't frailty that thus errs?
It is so too. And have not we affections,
Desires for sport, and frailty, as men have?
Then let them use us well: else let them know,
The ills we do, their ills instruct us so.

DESDEMONA. Good night, good night: heaven me such uses send,
Not to pick bad from bad, but by bad mend! [*Exeunt.*]

ACT V

SCENE I

Cyprus. A street

[*Enter* IAGO *and* RODERIGO.]

IAGO. Here stand behind this bulk;[1] straight will he come:
Wear thy good rapier bare, and put it home:
Quick, quick; fear nothing; I'll be at thy elbow:
It makes us, or it mars us; think on that,
And fix most firm thy resolution.

RODERIGO. Be near at hand; I may miscarry in 't.

IAGO. Here, at thy hand: be bold, and take thy stand. [*Retires.*]

RODERIGO. I have no great devotion to the deed;
And yet he hath given me satisfying reasons:
'Tis but a man gone. Forth, my sword: he dies.

IAGO. I have rubb'd this young quat[2] almost to the sense,[3]
And he grows angry. Now, whether he kill Cassio,
Or Cassio him, or each do kill the other,
Every way makes my gain. Live Roderigo,
He calls me to a restitution large
Of gold and jewels that I bobb'd[4] from him,
As gifts to Desdemona;
It must not be. If Cassio do remain,
He hath a daily beauty in his life
That makes me ugly; and, besides, the Moor
May unfold me to him; there stand I in much peril:
No, he must die. But so: I hear him coming.

[*Enter* CASSIO.]

RODERIGO. I know his gait, 'tis he.—Villain, thou diest!
[*Makes a pass at* CASSIO.]

CASSIO. That thrust had been mine enemy indeed,

---

[1]**bulk** framework projecting from the front of a shop.
[2]**quat** pimple, pustule; used contemptuously.
[3]**to the sense** to the quick.
[4]**bobb'd** filched cunningly.

But that my coat[5] is better than thou know'st.
I will make proof of thine. [*Draws, and wounds* RODERIGO.]

RODERIGO. O, I am slain!

[IAGO *from behind wounds* CASSIO *in the leg, and exits.*]

CASSIO. I am maim'd for ever. Help, ho! murder! murder! [*Falls.*]

[*Enter* OTHELLO.]

OTHELLO. The voice of Cassio. Iago keeps his word.

RODERIGO. O, villain that I am!

OTHELLO. It is even so.

CASSIO. O, help, ho! light! a surgeon!

OTHELLO. 'Tis he: —O brave Iago, honest and just,
That hast such noble sense of thy friend's wrong!
Thou teachest me. Minion, your dear lies dead,
And your unblest fate hies: strumpet, I come.
Forth of my heart those charms, thine eyes, are blotted;
Thy bed, lust-stain'd, shall with lust's blood be spotted.

[*Exit* OTHELLO.]

[*Enter* LODOVICO *and* GRATIANO.]

CASSIO. What, ho! no watch? no passage?[6] murder! murder!

GRATIANO. 'Tis some mischance; the cry is very direful.

CASSIO. O, help!

LODOVICO. Hark!

RODERIGO. O wretched villain!

LODOVICO. Two or three groan. It is a heavy[7] night;
These may be counterfeits. Let 's think 't unsafe
To come in to the cry without more help.

RODERIGO. Nobody come? Then shall I bleed to death.

LODOVICO. Hark!

[*Enter* IAGO with a light.]

GRATIANO. Here's one comes in his shirt, with light and weapons.

IAGO. Who's there? Whose noise is this that cries on[8] murder?

LODOVICO. We do not know.

IAGO. Did not you hear a cry?

CASSIO. Here, here! for heaven's sake, help me!

IAGO. What's the matter?

GRATIANO. This is Othello's ancient, as I take it.

LODOVICO. The same indeed; a very valiant fellow.

IAGO. What are you here that cry so grievously?

CASSIO. Iago? O, I am spoil'd, undone by villains!
Give me some help.

IAGO. O me, lieutenant! what villains have done this?

CASSIO. I think that one of them is hereabout,
And cannot make away.

---

[5]**coat** coat of mail.
[6]**passage** people passing.
[7]**heavy** thick, cloudy.
[8]**cries on** cries out.

IAGO. O treacherous villains!
What are you there? Come in, and give some help.
[*To* LODOVICO *and* GRATIANO.]

RODERIGO. O, help me here!

CASSIO. That's one of them.

IAGO. O murd'rous slave! O villain!
[*Stabs* RODERIGO.]

RODERIGO. O damn'd Iago! O inhuman dog!

IAGO. Kill men i' th' dark!—Where be these bloody thieves?—
How silent in this town!—Ho! murder! murder!—
What[9] you be? Are you of good or evil?

LODOVICO. As you shall prove us, praise us.

IAGO. Signior Lodovico?

LODOVICO. He, sir.

IAGO. I cry you mercy. Here's Cassio hurt by villains.

GRATIANO. Cassio!

IAGO. How is 't, brother!

CASSIO. My leg is cut in two.

IAGO. Marry, heaven forbid!
Light, gentlemen. I'll bind it with my shirt.

[*Enter* BIANCA.]

BIANCA. What is the matter, ho? Who is 't that cried?

IAGO. Who is 't that cried?

BIANCA. O my dear Cassio! my sweet Cassio!
O Cassio, Cassio, Cassio!

IAGO. O notable strumpet! Cassio, may you suspect
Who they should be that have thus mangled you?

CASSIO. No.

GRATIANO. I am sorry to find you thus: I have been to seek you.

IAGO. Lend me a garter. So. O, for a chair,[10]
To bear him easily hence!

BIANCA. Alas, he faints! O Cassio, Cassio, Cassio!

IAGO. Gentlemen all, I do suspect this trash[11]
To be a party in this injury.
Patience awhile, good Cassio. Come, come;
Lend me a light. Know we this face or no?
Alas, my friend and my dear countryman
Roderigo! no:—yes, sure:—O heaven! Roderigo.

GRATIANO. What, of Venice?

IAGO. Even he, sir: did you know him?

GRATIANO. Know him! ay.

IAGO. Signior Gratiano? I cry your gentle pardon;
These bloody accidents must excuse my manners,
That so neglected you.

GRATIANO. I am so glad to see you.

IAGO. How do you, Cassio? O, a chair, a chair!

---

[9]**What** who.
[10]**chair** sedan chair.
[11]**trash** worthless thing—i.e., Bianca.

GRATIANO. Roderigo!
IAGO. He, he, 'tis he. [*A chair brought in.*] O, that's well said; the chair.
Some good man bear him carefully from hence;
I'll fetch the general's surgeon. [*To* BIANCA] For you, mistress,
Save you your labour. He that lies slain here, Cassio,
Was my dear friend: what malice was between you?
CASSIO. None in the world; nor do I know the man.
IAGO [*To* BIANCA]. What, look you pale? O, bear him out o' th' air.
[CASSIO *and* RODERIGO *are borne off.*]
Stay you, good gentlemen. Look you pale, mistress?
Do you perceive the gastness[12] of her eye?
Nay, if you stare, we shall hear more anon.
Behold her well; I pray you, look upon her:
Do you see, gentlemen? Nay, guiltiness will speak,
Though tongues were out of use.

[*Enter* EMILIA.]

EMILIA. 'Las, what's the matter? what's the matter, husband?
IAGO. Cassio hath here been set on in the dark
By Roderigo and fellows that are scap'd:
He's almost slain, and Roderigo dead.
EMILIA. Alas, good gentlemen! alas, good Cassio!
IAGO. This is the fruit of whoring. Prithee, Emilia,
Go know of Cassio where he supp'd to-night.
[*To* BIANCA] What, do you shake at that?
BIANCA. He supp'd at my house; but I therefore shake not.
IAGO. O, did he so? I charge you, go with me.
EMILIA. Fie, fie upon thee, strumpet!
BIANCA. I am no strumpet; but of life as honest
As you that thus abuse me.
EMILIA. As I! foh! fie upon thee!
IAGO. Kind gentlemen, let's go see poor Cassio dress'd.
Come, mistress, you must tell's another tale.
Emilia, run you to the citadel,
And tell my lord and lady what hath happ'd.
Will you go on afore? [*Aside*] This is the night
That either makes me or fordoes[13] me quite. [*Exeunt.*]

SCENE II

A bedchamber in the castle.

[*Enter* OTHELLO *with a light;* DESDEMONA *in her bed.*]

OTHELLO. It is the cause, it is the cause,[14] my soul,—
Let me not name it to you, you chaste stars!—

---

[12] **gastness** terror, ghastliness.
[13] **fordoes** undoes, ruins.
[14] **It is the cause** i.e., the cause of justice on which Othello must act, Desdemona's deed, which is too unmentionable to be named to the chaste stars.

It is the cause. Yet I'll not shed her blood;
Nor scar that whiter skin of hers than snow,
And smooth as monumental alabaster.
Yet she must die, else she'll betray more men.
Put out the light, and then put out the light:
If I quench thee, thou flaming minister,
I can again thy former light restore,
Should I repent me: but once put out thy light,
Thou cunning'st pattern of excelling nature,
I know not where is that Promethean heat[15]
That can thy light relume.[16] When I have pluck'd the rose,
I cannot give it vital growth again,
It needs must wither: I'll smell thee on the tree. [*Kissing her.*]
O balmy breath, that dost almost persuade
Justice to break her sword! One more, one more.
Be thus when thou art dead, and I will kill thee,
And love thee after. One more, and that's the last:
So sweet was ne'er so fatal. I must weep,
But they are cruel tears: this sorrow 's heavenly;[17]
It strikes where it doth love. She wakes.

DESDEMONA. Who's there? Othello?
OTHELLO. Ay, Desdemona.
DESDEMONA. Will you come to bed, my lord?
OTHELLO. Have you pray'd to-night, Desdemon?
DESDEMONA. Ay, my lord.
OTHELLO. If you bethink yourself of any crime
Unreconcil'd as yet to heaven and grace,
Solicit for it straight.
DESDEMONA. Alack, my lord, what may you mean by that?
OTHELLO. Well, do it, and be brief; I will walk by:
I would not kill thy unprepared spirit;
No; heaven forfend! I would not kill thy soul.
DESDEMONA. Talk you of killing?
OTHELLO. Ay, I do.
DESDEMONA. Then heaven
Have mercy on me!
OTHELLO. Amen, with all my heart!
DESDEMONA. If you say so, I hope you will not kill me.
OTHELLO. Hum!
DESDEMONA. And yet I fear you; for you're fatal then
When your eyes roll so: why I should fear I know not,
Since guiltiness I know not; but yet I feel I fear.
OTHELLO. Think on thy sins.
DESDEMONA. They are loves I bear to you.

[15]**Promethean heat** divine fire; allusion to the theft of fire from heaven by Prometheus.
[16]**relume** rekindle.
[17]**this...heavenly** this tenderness, with which I lament the punishment which justice compels me to inflict, is a holy passion.

OTHELLO. Ay, and for that thou diest.
DESDEMONA. That death 's unnatural that kills for loving.
Alas, why gnaw you so your nether lip?
Some bloody passion shakes your very frame:
These are portents; but yet I hope, I hope,
They do not point on me.
OTHELLO. Peace, and be still!
DESDEMONA. I will so. What 's the matter?
OTHELLO. That handkerchief which I so lov'd and gave thee
Thou gav'st to Cassio.
DESDEMONA. No, by my life and soul!
Send for the man, and ask him.
OTHELLO. Sweet soul, take heed,
Take heed of perjury; thou are on thy deathbed.
DESDEMONA. Ay, but not yet to die.
OTHELLO. Yes, presently:
Therefore confess thee freely of thy sin;
For to deny each article with oath
Cannot remove nor choke the strong conception[18]
That I do groan withal. Thou art to die.
DESDEMONA. Then Lord have mercy on me!
OTHELLO. I say, amen.
DESDEMONA. And have you mercy too! I never did
Offend you in my life; never lov'd Cassio
But with such general warranty of heaven
As I might love; I never gave him token.
OTHELLO. By heaven, I saw my handkerchief in 's hand.
O perjur'd woman! thou dost stone[19] my heart,
And makes me call what I intend to do
A murder, which I thought a sacrifice:
I saw the handkerchief.
DESDEMONA. He found it then;
I never gave it him: send for him hither;
Let him confess a truth.
OTHELLO. He hath confess'd.
DESDEMONA. What, my Lord?
OTHELLO. That he hath us'd thee.
DESDEMONA. How? unlawfully?
OTHELLO. Ay.
DESDEMONA. He will not say so.
OTHELLO. No, his mouth is stopp'd;
Honest Iago hath ta'en order[20] for 't.
DESDEMONA. O! my fear interprets: what, is he dead?
OTHELLO. Had all his hairs been lives, my great revenge
Had stomach for them all.

---

[18]**conception** plan, intention.

[19]**stone** turn to stone, harden; Othello means that he will be tempted to kill her in sheer anger because of her perjury.

[20]**ta'en order** taken measures.

DESDEMONA. Alas! he is betray'd and I undone.
OTHELLO. Out, strumpet! weep'st thou for him to my face?
DESDEMONA. O, banish me, my lord, but kill me not!
OTHELLO. Down, strumpet!
DESDEMONA. Kill me to-morrow: let me live to-night!
OTHELLO. Nay, if you strive,—
DESDEMONA. But half an hour!
OTHELLO. Being done, there is no pause.[21]
DESDEMONA. But while I say one prayer!
OTHELLO. It is too late. [*Smothers her.*]
EMILIA [*at the door*]. My lord, my lord! what, ho! my lord, my lord!
OTHELLO. What noise is this? Not dead? not yet quite dead?
I that am cruel am yet merciful;
I would not have thee linger in thy pain:
So, so.
EMILIA [*within*]. What, ho! my lord, my lord!
OTHELLO. Who's there?
EMILIA [*within*]. O, good my lord, I would speak a word with you!
OTHELLO. Yes: 'tis Emilia. By and by. She 's dead.
'Tis like she comes to speak of Cassio's death.—
The noise was here. Ha! no more moving?
Still as the grave. Shall she come in? were 't good?—
I think she stirs again:—no. What 's best to do?
If she come in, she'll sure speak to my wife.
My wife! my wife! what wife? I have no wife.
O, insupportable! O heavy hour!
Methinks it should be now a huge eclipse
Of sun and moon, and that th' affrighted globe
Should yawn[22] at alteration.[23]
EMILIA. [*Within*] I do beseech you
That I may speak with you, O, good my lord!
OTHELLO. I had forgot thee: O, come in, Emilia:
Soft; by and by. Let me the curtains draw.
Where art thou? [*Closes bed-curtains and opens door.*]

[*Enter* EMILIA.]

What's the matter with thee now?
EMILIA. O, my good lord, yonder's foul murders done!
OTHELLO. What, now?
EMILIA. But now, my lord.
OTHELLO. It is the very error[24] of the moon;
She comes more nearer earth than she was wont,
And makes men mad.

---

[21]**Being...pause** i.e., when the execution of the deed has once begun, there is no stopping.
[22]**yawn** gape in amazement.
[23]**at alteration** at the change.
[24]**error** irregularity.

EMILIA. Cassio, my lord, hath kill'd a young Venetian
Call'd Roderigo.
OTHELLO. Roderigo kill'd!
And Cassio kill'd!
EMILIA. No, Cassio is not kill'd.
OTHELLO. Not Cassio kill'd! Then murder 's out of tune,
And sweet revenge grows harsh.
DESDEMONA. O, falsely, falsely murder'd!
EMILIA. Alas, what cry is that?
OTHELLO. That! what?
EMILIA. Out, and alas! that was my lady's voice.
Help, help, ho! help. O lady, speak again!
Sweet Desdemona! O sweet mistress, speak!
DESDEMONA. A guiltless death I die.
EMILIA. O, who hath done this deed?
DESDEMONA. Nobody; I myself. Farewell:
Commend me to my kind lord: O, farewell! [*Dies.*]
OTHELLO. Why, how should she be murd'red?
EMILIA. Alas, who knows?
OTHELLO. You heard her say herself, it was not I.
EMILIA. She said so: I must needs report the truth.
OTHELLO. She's, like a liar, gone to burning hell:
'Twas I that kill'd her.
EMILIA. O, the more angel she,
And you the blacker devil!
OTHELLO. She turn'd to folly,[25] and she was a whore.
EMILIA. Thou dost belie her, and thou art a devil.
OTHELLO. She was false as water.
EMILIA. Thou art rash as fire, to say
That she was false: O, she was heavenly true!
OTHELLO. Cassio did top her; ask thy husband else.
O, I were damned beneath all depth in hell,
But that I did proceed upon just grounds
To this extremity. Thy husband knew it all.
EMILIA. My husband!
OTHELLO. Thy husband.
EMILIA. That she was false to wedlock?
OTHELLO. Ay, with Cassio. Nay, had she been true,
If heaven would make me such another world
Of one entire and perfect chrysolite,[26]
I'ld not have sold her for it.
EMILIA. My husband!
OTHELLO. Ay, 'twas he that told me first:
An honest man he is, and hates the slime
That sticks on filthy deeds.

[25]**folly** unchastity.
[26]**chrysolite** the golden stone; a name given to various precious stones of green color.

EMILIA. My husband!
OTHELLO. What needs this iterance,[27] woman? I say thy husband.
EMILIA. O mistress, villainy hath made mocks with[28] love!
My husband say that she was false!
OTHELLO. He, woman;
I say thy husband: dost understand the word?
My friend, thy husband, honest, honest Iago.
EMILIA. If he say so, may his pernicious soul
Rot half a grain a day! He lies to th' heart:
She was too fond of her most filthy bargain.
OTHELLO. Ha!
EMILIA. Do thy worst:
This deed of thine is no more worthy heaven
Than thou wast worthy her.
OTHELLO. Peace, you were best.
EMILIA. Thou hast not half that power to do me harm
As I have to be hurt.[29] O gull! O dolt!
As ignorant as dirt! thou has done a deed—
I care not for thy sword; I'll make thee known,
Though I lost twenty lives.—Help! help, ho! help!
The Moor hath kill'd my mistress! Murder! murder!

[*Enter* MONTANO, GRATIANO, *and* IAGO *with others.*]

MONTANO. What is the matter? How now, general!
EMILIA. O, are you come, Iago? You have done well,
That men must lay their murders on your neck.
GRATIANO. What is the matter?
EMILIA. Disprove this villain, if thou be'st a man:
He says thou told'st him that his wife was false:
I know thou didst not, thou'rt not such a villain:
Speak, for my heart is full.
IAGO. I told him what I thought, and told no more
Than what he found himself was apt[30] and true.
EMILIA. But did you ever tell him she was false?
IAGO. I did.
EMILIA. You told a lie; an odious, damned lie;
Upon my soul, a lie, a wicked lie.
She false with Cassio!—did you say with Cassio?
IAGO. With Cassio, mistress. Go to, charm[31] your tongue.
EMILIA. I will not charm my tongue; I am bound to speak:
My mistress here lies murdered in her bed,—
ALL. O heavens forfend!
EMILIA. And your reports have set the murder on.

---

[27]**iterance** iteration, repetition.
[28]**made mocks with** derided, made sport of.
[29]**to be hurt** i.e., to endure hurting.
[30]**apt** natural, likely.
[31]**charm** keep silent.

OTHELLO. Nay, stare not, masters: it is true, indeed.
GRATIANO. 'Tis a strange truth.
MONTANO. O monstrous act!
EMILIA. Villainy, villainy, villainy!
I think upon't, I think: I smell't: O villainy—
I thought so then:[32] I'll kill myself for grief:—
O villainy, villainy!
IAGO. What, are you mad? I charge you, get you home.
EMILIA. Good gentlemen, let me have leave to speak:
'Tis proper I obey him, but not now.
Perchance, Iago, I will ne'er go home.
OTHELLO. O! O! O! [*He falls on the bed.*]
EMILIA. Nay, lay thee down and roar;
For thou hast kill'd the sweetest innocent
That e'er did lift up eye.
OTHELLO. [*Rising*] O, she was foul!
I scarce did know you, uncle: there lies your niece,
Whose breath, indeed, these hands have newly stopp'd:
I know this act shows horrible and grim.
GRATIANO. Poor Desdemon! I am glad thy father 's dead:
Thy match was mortal to him, and pure grief
Shore[33] his old thread in twain: did he live now,
This sight would make him do a desperate turn,
Yea, curse his better angel from his side,
And fall to reprobation.[34]
OTHELLO. 'Tis pitiful; but yet Iago knows
That she with Cassio hath the act of shame
A thousand times committed; Cassio confess'd it:
And she did gratify his amorous works
With that recognizance[35] and pledge of love
Which I first gave her; I saw it in his hand:
It was a handkerchief, an antique token
My father gave my mother.
EMILIA. O heaven! O heavenly pow'rs!
IAGO. Come, hold your peace.
EMILIA. ' Twill out, 'twill out: I peace!
No, I will speak as liberal as the north:[36]
Let heaven and men and devils, let them all,
All, all, cry shame against me, yet I'll speak.
IAGO. Be wise, and get you home.
EMILIA. I will not! [IAGO *offers to stab* EMILIA.]
GRATIANO. Fie!
Your sword upon a woman?
EMILIA. O thou dull Moor! that handkerchief thou speak'st of

[32]**then** i.e., at some earlier time, probably IV, ii, when she suspected the machinations of *some eternal villain*; she did not, however, know that villain to be Iago until this moment.
[33]**Shore** cut.
[34]**reprobation** damnation, rejection by God.
[35]**recognizance** token.
[36]**liberal as the north** freely as the north wind.

I found by fortune[37] and did give my husband;
For often, with solemn earnestness,
More than indeed belong'd to such a trifle,
He begg'd me to steal it.

IAGO. Villainous whore!

EMILIA. She give it Cassio! no, alas! I found it,
And I did give't my husband.

IAGO. Filth, thou liest!

EMILIA. By heaven, I do not, I do not, gentlemen.
O murd'rous coxcomb![38] what should such a fool
Do with so good a wife!

OTHELLO. Are there no stones in heaven[39]
But what serves for the thunder?—Precious villain!

[*He runs at* IAGO; IAGO, *from behind, stabs* EMILIA, *and exits*.]

GRATIANO. The woman falls; sure, he hath kill'd his wife.

EMILIA. Ay, ay: O, lay me by my mistress' side.

GRATIANO. He 's gone, but his wife 's kill'd.

MONTANO. 'Tis a notorious villain. Take you this weapon,
Which I have here recover'd from the Moor:
Come, guard the door without; let him not pass,
But kill him rather. I'll after that same villain,
For 'tis a damned slave. [*Exit with all but* OTHELLO *and* EMILIA.]

OTHELLO. I am not valiant neither,
But every puny whipster[40] gets my sword:
But why should honour outlive honesty?[41]
Let it go all.

EMILIA. What did thy song bode, lady?
Hark, canst thou hear me? I will play the swan,
And die in music. [*Singing*] "Willow, willow, willow.—"
Moor, she was chaste; she lov'd thee, cruel Moor;
So come my soul to bliss, as I speak true;
So speaking as I think, I die, I die. [*Dies*.]

OTHELLO. I have another weapon in this chamber;
It is a sword of Spain, the ice-brook's temper[42]:—
O, here it is. Uncle, I must come forth.

GRATIANO [*within*]. If thou attempt it, it will cost thee dear:
Thou hast no weapon, and perforce must suffer.

OTHELLO. Look in upon me then and speak with me,
Or, naked[43] as I am, I will assault thee.

[*Enter* GRATIANO.]

---

[37]**fortune** chance.

[38]**coxcomb** fool; addressed to Othello.

[39]**stones in heaven** thunderbolts. It was supposed that real stones fell with the thunder and caused the damage.

[40]**whipster** contemptible fellow.

[41]**honour outlive honesty** Othello realizes that he has done a shameful deed; he asks why his reputation for valor should endure.

[42]**ice-brook's temper** usually defined as "tempered in ice-cold water."

[43]**naked** unarmed.

GRATIANO. What is the matter?
OTHELLO. Behold, I have a weapon;
A better never did itself sustain
Upon a soldier's thigh: I have seen the day,
That, with this little arm and this good sword,
I have made my way through more impediments
Than twenty times your stop:[44] but, O vain boast!
Who can control his fate? 'tis not so now.
Be not afraid, though you do see me weapon'd;
Here is my journey's end, here is my butt,[45]
And very sea-mark[46] of my utmost sail.
Do you go back dismay'd? 'tis a lost fear;
Man[47] but a rush[48] against Othello's breast,
And he retires. Where should Othello go?
Now, how dost thou look now? O ill-starr'd wench!
Pale as thy smock! when we shall meet at compt,[49]
This look of thine will hurl my soul from heaven,
And fiends will snatch at it. Cold, cold, my girl!
Even like thy chastity. O cursed, cursed slave!
Whip me, ye devils,
From the possession of this heavenly sight!
Blow me about in winds! roast me in sulphur!
Wash me in steep-down gulfs of liquid fire!
O Desdemona! Dead Desdemona! dead!
Oh! Oh!

[*Enter* LODOVICO, CASSIO *carried in a chair*, MONTANO, *and* IAGO, *prisoner, with* OFFICERS.]

LODOVICO. Where is this rash and most unfortunate man?
OTHELLO. That's he that was Othello: here I am.
LODOVICO. Where is that viper? Bring the villain forth.
OTHELLO. I look down towards his feet;[50] but that's a fable.
If that thou be'st a devil, I cannot kill thee. [*Wounds* IAGO.]
LODOVICO. Wrench his sword from him.
IAGO. I bleed sir; but not kill'd.
OTHELLO. I am not sorry neither: I 'd have thee live;
For, in my sense, 'tis happiness to die.
LODOVICO. O thou Othello, that wert once so good,
Fall'n in the practice of a damned slave,
What shall be said to thee?
OTHELLO. Why, any thing:
An honourable murderer, if you will;
For nought I did in hate, but all in honour.

[44]**stop** power.
[45]**butt** mark for archery, goal, limit.
[46]**sea-mark** beacon (marking his destination or limit).
[47]**Man** provide, as in manning a gun.
[48]**rush** reed.
[49]**compt** account, judgment day.
[50]**towards his feet** i.e., to see if they were cloven like a devil's.

LODOVICO. This wretch hath part confess'd his villainy:
Did you and he consent in Cassio's death?
OTHELLO. Ay.
CASSIO. Dear general, I never gave you cause.
OTHELLO. I do believe it, and I ask your pardon.
Will you, I pray, demand that demi-devil
Why he hath thus ensnar'd my soul and body?
IAGO. Demand me nothing: what you know, you know:
From this time forth I never will speak word.
LODOVICO. What, not to pray?
GRATIANO. Torments will ope your lips.
OTHELLO. Well, thou dost best.
LODOVICO. Sir, you shall understand what hath befall'n,
Which, as I think, you know not. Here is a letter
Found in the pocket of the slain Roderigo;
And here another: the one of them imports
The death of Cassio to be undertook
By Roderigo.
OTHELLO. O villain!
CASSIO. Most heathenish and most gross!
LODOVICO. Now here's another discontented[51] paper,
Found in his pocket too; and this, it seems,
Roderigo meant t' have sent this damned villain;
But that belike Iago in the interim
Came in and satisfied him.
OTHELLO. O thou pernicious caitiff[52]—
How came you, Cassio, by that handkerchief
That was my wife's?
CASSIO. I found it in my chamber:
And he himself confess'd but even now
That there he dropp'd it for a special purpose
Which wrought to his desire.
OTHELLO. O fool! O fool! fool!
CASSIO. There is besides in Roderigo's letter,
How he upbraids Iago, that he made him
Brave[53] me upon the watch; whereon it came
That I was cast:[54] and even but now he spake,
After long seeming dead, Iago hurt him,
Iago set him on.
LODOVICO. You must forsake this room, and go with us:
Your power and your command is taken off,[55]
And Cassio rules in Cyprus. For this slave,
If there be any cunning cruelty
That can torment him much and hold him long,

---

[51]**discontented** expressing dissatisfaction.
[52]**caitiff** wretch.
[53]**Brave** defy.
[54]**cast** dismissed.
[55]**taken off** taken away.

It shall be his. You shall close prisoner rest,
Till that the nature of your fault be known
To the Venetian state. Come, bring him away.

OTHELLO. Soft you; a word or two before you go.
I have done the state some service, and they know 't.
No more of that. I pray you, in your letters,
When you shall these unlucky deeds relate,
Speak of me as I am; nothing extenuate,[56]
Nor set down aught in malice: then must you speak
Of one that lov'd not wisely but too well;
Of one not easily jealous, but being wrought,
Perplex'd[57] in the extreme; of one whose hand,
Like the base Judean,[58] threw a pearl away
Richer than all his tribe; of one whose subdu'd eyes,
Albeit unused to the melting mood,
Drop tears as fast as the Arabian trees
Their medicinable gum. Set you down this;
And say besides, that in Aleppo[59] once,
Where a malignant and a turban'd Turk
Beat a Venetian and traduc'd the state,
I took by th' throat the circumcised dog,
And smote him, thus. [*Stabs himself.*]

LODOVICO. O bloody period![60]

GRATIANO. All that is spoke is marr'd.

OTHELLO. I kiss'd thee ere I kill'd thee: no way but this;
Killing myself, to die upon a kiss. [*Falls on the bed, and dies.*]

CASSIO. This did I fear, but thought he had no weapon;
For he was great of heart.

LODOVICO. [*To* IAGO] O Spartan dog,[61]
More fell than anguish, hunger, or the sea!
Look on the tragic loading of this bed;
This is thy work: the object poisons sight;
Let it be hid. Gratiano, keep the house,
And seize upon the fortunes of the Moor,
For they succeed on you. To you, lord governor,
Remains the censure of this hellish villain;
The time, the place, the torture: O, enforce it!
Myself will straight abroad; and to the state
This heavy act with heavy heart relate. [*Exeunt.*]

(1604)

---

[56]**extenuate** diminish, depreciate; the idea is contrasted with the thought of *malice* in the following line.

[57]**Perplex'd** confounded, distracted.

[58]**Judean** infidel or disbeliever.

[59]**Aleppo** a Turkish city where the Venetians had special trading privileges. It is stated that it was immediate death for a Christian to strike a Turk in Aleppo; Othello risked his life for the honor of Venice.

[60]**period** termination, conclusion.

[61]**Spartan dog** Spartan dogs were noted for their savagery.

Questions for Discussion and Writing

1. How does Shakespeare establish the dignity, nobility, and heroism of Othello early in the play? Does Othello regain any of his lost stature in the end? How?
2. Analyze the relationship between Othello and Desdemona, and explain how tragedy enters their lives.
3. Why is Iago committed, above all else, to destroying Desdemona?
4. Explain Desdemona's behavior in the scene in which Othello accuses her of being a whore (Act IV, Scene II). Why can't Othello perceive her goodness and innocence?
5. How do race and racism contribute to Othello's downfall?
6. Shakespearean scholar M. R. Ridley suggests that the theme of *Othello* centers on the conflict between "reason" and "instinct." Write an essay in which you explore this theme in the play.
7. Professor Carol Neely maintains that "the play's central theme is love—especially marital love; its central conflict is between the men and the women." Write an essay in which you argue for or against these claims.
8. Some people think Othello acts with unjustified haste and violence, that it is inexcusable for him to suspect his wife and unbelievable that he would not suspect Iago. Write an essay in which you answer these charges.

Henrik Ibsen 1828–1906

Henrik Ibsen, a Norwegian dramatist, was one of the most influential figures in modern theater. He worked as a stage manager, playwright, and director and is best known for breaking away from the romantic tradition in drama in order to portray life realistically. His social plays, such as *A Doll's House* (1879), *Ghosts* (1881), and *Hedda Gabler* (1890), shocked audiences with subject matter (venereal disease, suicide, women's independence) that was considered unmentionable in public. In these and other plays, Ibsen explored the conflict between social restrictions and the psychological, often unconscious demands of individual freedom.

A Doll's House

Translated by R. Farquharson Sharp

CHARACTERS

TORVALD HELMER, *a lawyer and bank manager*
NORA, *his wife*
IVAR, BOB, *and* EMMY, *the Helmers' three young children*
ANNE, *their nurse*

DOCTOR RANK
MRS. CHRISTINE LINDE
NILS KROGSTAD, *a lawyer and bank clerk*
HELEN, *a housemaid*
A PORTER

The action takes place in HELMERS' *apartment*

ACT 1

SCENE. *A room, furnished comfortably and tastefully, but not extravagantly. At the back, a door to the right leads to the entrance hall, another to the left leads to* HELMER'S *study. Between the doors stands a piano. In the middle of the left-hand wall is a door, and beyond it a window. Near the window are a round table, armchairs and a small sofa. In the right-hand wall, at the farther end, another door; and on the same side, nearer the footlights, a stove, two easy chairs and a rocking-chair; between the stove and the door, a small table. Engravings on the walls; a cabinet with china and other small objects, a small book case with well-bound books. The floors are carpeted, and a fire burns in the stove. It is winter.*

A bell rings in the hall; shortly afterwards the door is heard to open. Enter NORA, *humming a tune and in high spirits. She is in outdoor dress and carries a number of parcels; these she lays on the table to the right. She leaves the outer door open after her, and through it is seen a* PORTER *who is carrying a Christmas Tree and a basket, which he gives to the* MAID *who has opened the door.*

Anthony Hopkins as Torvald and Claire Bloom as Nora in the 1973 film adaptation of *A Doll's House*. (Picture Desk, Inc./Kobal Collection)

NORA. Hide the Christmas Tree away carefully, Helen. Be sure the children do not see it till this evening, when it is dressed. [*to the* PORTER, *taking out her purse*] How much?

PORTER. Sixpence.

NORA. There is a shilling. No, keep the change.

[*The* PORTER *thanks her, and goes out.* NORA *shuts the door. She is laughing to herself, as she takes off her hat and coat. She takes a packet of macaroons from her pocket and eats one or two; then goes cautiously to her husband's door and listens.*]

Yes, he is in.

[*Still humming, she goes to the table on the right.*]

HELMER. [*calls out from his room*] Is that my little lark twittering out there?

NORA. [*busy opening some of the parcels*] Yes, it is!

HELMER. Is my little squirrel bustling about?

NORA. Yes!

HELMER. When did my squirrel come home?

NORA. Just now. [*puts the bag of macaroons into her pocket and wipes her mouth*] Come in here, Torvald, and see what I have bought.

HELMER. Don't disturb me. [*A little later, he opens the door and looks into the room, pen in his hand.*] Bought, did you say? All these things? Has my little spendthrift been wasting money again?

NORA. Yes, but, Torvald, this year we really can let ourselves go a little. This is the first Christmas that we have not needed to economise.

HELMER. Still, you know, we can't spend money recklessly.

NORA. Yes, Torvald, we may be a wee bit more reckless now, mayn't we? Just a tiny wee bit! You are going to have a big salary and earn lots and lots of money.

HELMER. Yes, after the New Year; but then it will be a whole quarter before the salary is due.

NORA. Pooh! We can borrow till then.

HELMER. Nora! [*goes up to her and takes her playfully by the ear*] The same little featherhead! Suppose, now, that I borrowed fifty pounds to-day, and you spent it all in the Christmas week, and then on New Year's Eve a slate fell on my head and killed me, and—

NORA. [*putting her hands over his mouth*] Oh! don't say such horrid things.

HELMER. Still, suppose that happened—what then?

NORA. If that were to happen, I don't suppose I should care whether I owed money or not.

HELMER. Yes, but what about the people who had lent it?

NORA. They? Who would bother about them? I should not know who they were.

HELMER. That is like a woman! But seriously, Nora, you know what I think about that. No debt, no borrowing. There can be no freedom or beauty about a home life that depends on borrowing and debt. We two have kept bravely on the straight road so far, and we will go on the same way for the short time longer that there need be any struggle.

NORA. [*moving towards the stove*] As you please, Torvald.

HELMER. [*following her*] Come, come, my little skylark must not droop her wings. What is this! Is my little squirrel out of temper? [*taking out his purse*] Nora, what do you think I have got here?

NORA. [*turning around quickly*] Money!

Helmer. There you are. [*gives her some money*] Do you think I don't know what a lot is wanted for housekeeping at Christmas-time?

Nora. [*counting*] Ten shillings—a pound—two pounds! Thank you, thank you, Torvald; that will keep me going for a long time.

Helmer. Indeed it must.

Nora. Yes, yes, it will. But come here and let me show you what I have bought. And all so cheap! Look, here is a new suit for Ivar, and a sword; and a horse and a trumpet for Bob; and a doll and dolly's bedstead for Emmy—they are very plain, but anyway she will soon break them in pieces. And here are dress-lengths and handkerchiefs for the maids; old Anne ought really to have something better.

Helmer. And what is in this parcel?

Nora. [*crying out*] No, no! You mustn't see that till this evening.

Helmer. Very well. But now tell me, you extravagant little person, what would you like for yourself?

Nora. For myself? Oh, I am sure I don't want anything.

Helmer. Yes, but you must. Tell me something reasonable that you would particularly like to have.

Nora. No, I really can't think of anything—unless, Torvald—

Helmer. Well?

Nora. [*playing with his coat buttons, and without raising her eyes to his*] If you really want to give me something, you might—you might—

Helmer. Well, out with it!

Nora. [*speaking quickly*] You might give me money, Torvald. Only just as much as you can afford; and then one of these days I will buy something with it.

Helmer. But, Nora—

Nora. Oh, do! dear Torvald; please, please do! Then I will wrap it up in beautiful gilt paper and hang it on the Christmas Tree. Wouldn't that be fun?

Helmer. What are little people called that are always wasting money?

Nora. Spendthrifts—I know. Let us do as you suggest, Torvald, and then I shall have time to think what I am most in want of. That is a very sensible plan, isn't it?

Helmer. [*smiling*] Indeed it is—that is to say, if you were really to save out of the money I give you, and then really buy something for yourself. But if you spend it all on the housekeeping and any number of unnecessary things, then I merely have to pay up again.

Nora. Oh but, Torvald—

Helmer. You can't deny it, my dear little Nora. [*puts his arm round her waist*] It's a sweet little spendthrift, but she uses up a deal of money. One would hardly believe how expensive such little persons are!

Nora. It's a shame to say that. I do really save all I can.

Helmer. [*laughing*] That's very true—all you can. But you can't save anything!

Nora. [*smiling quietly and happily*] You haven't any idea how many expenses we skylarks and squirrels have, Torvald.

Helmer. You are an odd little soul. Very like your father. You always find some new way of wheedling money out of me, and, as soon as you have got it, it seems to melt in your hands. You never know where it has gone. Still, one must take you as you are. It is in the blood; for indeed it is true that you can inherit these things, Nora.

Nora. Ah, I wish I had inherited many of papa's qualities.

HELMER. And I would not wish you to be anything but just what you are, my sweet little skylark. But, do you know, it strikes me that you are looking rather—what shall I say—rather uneasy to-day?

NORA. Do I?

HELMER. You do, really. Look straight at me.

NORA. [*looks at him*] Well?

HELMER. [*wagging his finger at her*] Hasn't Miss Sweet-Tooth been breaking rules in town to-day?

NORA. No; what makes you think that?

HELMER. Hasn't she paid a visit to the confectioner's?

NORA. No, I assure you, Torvald—

HELMER. Not been nibbling sweets?

NORA. No, certainly not.

HELMER. Not even taken a bite at a macaroon or two?

NORA. No, Torvald, I assure you really—

HELMER. There, there, of course I was only joking.

NORA. [*going to the table on the right*] I should not think of going against your wishes.

HELMER. No, I am sure of that! besides, you gave me your word—[*going up to her*] Keep your little Christmas secrets to yourself, my darling. They will all be revealed tonight when the Christmas Tree is lit, no doubt.

NORA. Did you remember to invite Doctor Rank?

HELMER. No. But there is no need; as a matter of course he will come to dinner with us. However, I will ask him when he comes in this morning. I have ordered some good wine. Nora, you can't think how I am looking forward to this evening.

NORA. So am I! And how the children will enjoy themselves, Torvald!

HELMER. It is splendid to feel that one has a perfectly safe appointment, and a big enough income. It's delightful to think of, isn't it?

NORA. It's wonderful!

HELMER. Do you remember last Christmas? For a full three weeks beforehand you shut yourself up every evening till long after midnight, making ornaments for the Christmas Tree and all the other fine things that were to be a surprise to us. It was the dullest three weeks I ever spent!

NORA. I didn't find it dull.

HELMER. [*smiling*] But there was precious little result, Nora.

NORA. Oh, you shouldn't tease me about that again. How could I help the cat's going in and tearing everything to pieces?

HELMER. Of course you couldn't, poor little girl. You had the best of intentions to please us all, and that's the main thing. But it is a good thing that our hard times are over.

NORA. Yes, it is really wonderful.

HELMER. This time I needn't sit here and be dull all alone, and you needn't ruin your dear eyes and your pretty little hands—

NORA. [*clapping her hands*] No, Torvald, I needn't any longer, need I! It's wonderfully lovely to hear you say so! [*taking his arm*] Now I will tell you how I have been thinking we ought to arrange things, Torvald. As soon as Christmas is over— [*A bell rings in the hall.*] There's the bell. [*She tidies the room a little.*] There's someone at the door. What a nuisance!

HELMER. If it is a caller, remember I am not at home.

MAID. [*in the doorway*] A lady to see you, ma'am—a stranger.
NORA. Ask her to come in.
MAID. [*to* HELMER] The doctor came at the same time, sir.
HELMER. Did he go straight into my room?
MAID. Yes sir.

[HELMER *goes into his room. The* MAID *ushers in* MRS. LINDE, *who is in travelling dress, and shuts the door.*]

MRS. LINDE. [*in a dejected and timid voice*] How do you do, Nora?
NORA. [*doubtfully*] How do you do—
MRS. LINDE. You don't recognize me, I suppose.
NORA. No, I don't know—yes, to be sure, I seem to—[*suddenly*] Yes! Christine! Is it really you?
MRS. LINDE. Yes, it is I.
NORA. Christine! To think of my not recognising you! And yet how could I—[*in a gentle voice*] How you have altered, Christine!
MRS. LINDE. Yes, I have indeed. In nine, ten long years—
NORA. Is it so long since we met? I suppose it is. The last eight years have been a happy time for me, I can tell you. And so now you have come into the town, and have taken this long journey in winter—that was plucky of you.
MRS. LINDE. I arrived by steamer this morning.
NORA. To have some fun at Christmas-time, of course. How delightful! We will have such fun together! But take off your things. You are not cold, I hope. [*helps her*] Now we will sit down by the stove, and be cosy. No, take this arm-chair; I will sit here in the rocking-chair. [*takes her hands*] Now you look like your old self again; it was only the first moment—You are a little paler, Christine, and perhaps a little thinner.
MRS. LINDE. And much, much older, Nora.
NORA. Perhaps a little older; very, very little; certainly not much. [*stops suddenly and speaks seriously*] What a thoughtless creature I am, chattering away like this. My poor, dear Christine, do forgive me.
MRS. LINDE. What do you mean, Nora?
NORA. [*gently*] Poor Christine, you are a widow.
MRS. LINDE. Yes; it is three years ago now.
NORA. Yes, I knew; I saw it in the papers. I assure you, Christine, I meant ever so often to write to you at the time, but I always put it off and something always prevented me.
MRS. LINDE. I quite understand, dear.
NORA. It was very bad of me, Christine. Poor thing, how you must have suffered. And he left you nothing?
MRS. LINDE. No.
NORA. And no children?
MRS. LINDE. No.
NORA. Nothing at all, then?
MRS. LINDE. Not even any sorrow or grief to live upon.
NORA. [*looking incredulously at her*] But, Christine, is that possible?
MRS. LINDE. [*smiles sadly and strokes her hair*] It sometimes happens, Nora.
NORA. So you are quite alone. How dreadfully sad that must be. I have three lovely children. You can't see them just now, for they are out with their nurse. But now you must tell me all about it.

MRS. LINDE. No, no; I want to hear you.

NORA. No, you must begin. I mustn't be selfish to-day; to-day I must only think of your affairs. But there is one thing I must tell you. Do you know we have just had a great piece of good luck?

MRS. LINDE. No, what is it?

NORA. Just fancy, my husband has been made manager of the Bank!

MRS. LINDE. Your husband? What good luck!

NORA. Yes, tremendous! A barrister's profession is such an uncertain thing, especially if he won't undertake unsavoury cases; and naturally Torvald has never been willing to do that, and I quite agree with him. You may imagine how pleased we are! He is to take up his work in the Bank at the New Year, and then he will have a big salary and lots of commissions. For the future we can live quite differently—we can do just as we like. I feel so relieved and so happy, Christine! It will be splendid to have heaps of money and not need to have any anxiety, won't it?

MRS. LINDE. Yes, anyhow I think it would be delightful to have what one needs.

NORA. No, not only what one needs, but heaps and heaps of money.

MRS. LINDE. [*smiling*] Nora, Nora haven't you learnt sense yet? In our schooldays you were a great spendthrift.

NORA. [*laughing*] Yes, that is what Torvald says now. [*wags her finger at her*] But "Nora, Nora" is not so silly as you think. We have not been in a position for me to waste money. We have both had to work.

MRS. LINDE. You too?

NORA. Yes; odds and ends, needlework, crochet-work, embroidery, and that kind of thing. [*dropping her voice*] And other things as well. You know Torvald left his office when we were married? There was no prospect of promotion there, and he had to try and earn more than before. But during the first year he overworked himself dreadfully. You see, he had to make money every way he could, and he worked early and late; but he couldn't stand it, and fell dreadfully ill, and the doctors said it was necessary for him to go south.

MRS. LINDE. You spent a whole year in Italy didn't you?

NORA. Yes. It was no easy matter to get away, I can tell you. It was just as Ivar was born; but naturally we had to go. It was a wonderfully beautiful journey, and it saved Torvald's life. But it cost a tremendous lot of money, Christine.

MRS. LINDE. So I should think.

NORA. It cost about two hundred and fifty pounds. That's a lot, isn't it?

MRS. LINDE. Yes, and in emergencies like that it is lucky to have the money.

NORA. I ought to tell you that we had it from papa.

MRS. LINDE. Oh, I see. It was just about that time that he died, wasn't it?

NORA. Yes; and, just think of it, I couldn't go and nurse him. I was expecting little Ivar's birth every day and I had my poor sick Torvald to look after. My dear, kind father—I never saw him again, Christine. That was the saddest time I have known since our marriage.

MRS. LINDE. I know how fond you were of him. And then you went off to Italy?

NORA. Yes; you see we had money then, and the doctors insisted on our going, so we started a month later.

MRS. LINDE. And your husband came back quite well?

NORA. As sound as a bell!

MRS. LINDE. But—the doctor?

NORA. What doctor?

MRS. LINDE. I thought your maid said the gentleman who arrived here just as I did was the doctor?

NORA. Yes, that was Doctor Rank, but he doesn't come here professionally. He is our greatest friend, and comes in at least once every day. No, Torvald has not had an hour's illness since then, and our children are strong and healthy and so am I. [*jumps up and claps her hands*] Christine! Christine! it's good to be alive and happy!—But how horrid of me; I am talking of nothing but my own affairs. [*sits on a stool near her, and rests her arms on her knees*] You mustn't be angry with me. Tell me, is it really true that you did not love your husband? Why did you marry him?

MRS. LINDE. My mother was alive then, and was bedridden and helpless, and I had to provide for my two younger brothers; so I did not think I was justified in refusing his offer.

NORA. No, perhaps you were quite right. He was rich at that time, then?

MRS. LINDE. I believe he was quite well off. But his business was a precarious one; and, when he died, it all went to pieces and there was nothing left.

NORA. And then?—

MRS. LINDE. Well, I had to turn my hand to anything I could find—first a small shop, then a small school, and so on. The last three years have seemed like one long working-day, with no rest. Now it is at an end, Nora. My poor mother needs me no more, for she is gone; and the boys do not need me either; they have got situations and can shift for themselves.

NORA. What a relief you must feel it—

MRS. LINDE. No, indeed; I only feel my life unspeakably empty. No one to live for any more. [*gets up restlessly*] That was why I could not stand the life in my little backwater any longer. I hope it may be easier here to find something which will busy me and occupy my thoughts. If only I could have the good luck to get some regular work—office work of some kind—

NORA. But, Christine, that is so frightfully tiring, and you look tired out now. You had far better go away to some watering-place.

MRS. LINDE. [*walking to the window*] I have no father to give me money for a journey, Nora.

NORA. [*rising*] Oh, don't be angry with me.

MRS. LINDE. [*going up to her*] It is you that must not be angry with me, dear. The worst of a position like mine is that it makes one so bitter. No one to work for, and yet obliged to be always on the look-out for chances. One must live, and so one becomes selfish. When you told me of the happy turn your fortunes have taken—you will hardly believe it—I was delighted not so much on your account as on my own.

NORA. How do you mean?—Oh, I understand. You mean that perhaps Torvald could get you something to do.

MRS. LINDE. Yes, that was what I was thinking of.

NORA. He must, Christine. Just leave it to me; I will broach the subject very cleverly—I will think of something that will please him very much. It will make me so happy to be of some use to you.

MRS. LINDE. How kind you are, Nora, to be so anxious to help me! It is doubly kind in you, for you know so little of the burdens and troubles of life.

NORA. I—? I know so little of them?

MRS. LINDE. [*smiling*] My dear! Small household cares and that sort of thing!—You are a child, Nora.

NORA. [*tosses her head and crosses the stage*] You ought not to be so superior.
MRS. LINDE. No?
NORA. You are just like the others. They all think that I am incapable of anything really serious—
MRS. LINDE. Come, come—
NORA. —that I have gone through nothing in this world of cares.
MRS. LINDE. But, my dear Nora, you have just told me all your troubles.
NORA. Pooh!—those were trifles. [*lowering her voice*] I have not told you the important thing.
MRS. LINDE. The important thing? What do you mean?
NORA. You look down upon me altogether, Christine—but you ought not to. You are proud, aren't you, of having worked so hard and so long for your mother?
MRS. LINDE. Indeed, I don't look down on any one. But it is true that I am both proud and glad to think that I was privileged to make the end of my mother's life almost free from care.
NORA. And you are proud to think of what you have done for your brothers.
MRS. LINDE. I think I have the right to be.
NORA. I think so, too. But now, listen to this; I too have something to be proud of and glad of.
MRS. LINDE. I have no doubt you have. But what do you refer to?
NORA. Speak low. Suppose Torvald were to hear! He mustn't on any account—no one in the world must know, Christine, except you.
MRS. LINDE. But what is it?
NORA. Come here. [*pulls her down on the sofa beside her*] Now I will show you that I too have something to be proud and glad of. It was I who saved Torvald's life.
MRS. LINDE. "Saved"? How?
NORA. I told you about our trip to Italy. Torvald would never have recovered if he had not gone there—
MRS. LINDE. Yes, but your father gave you the necessary funds.
NORA. [*smiling*] Yes, that is what Torvald and all the others think, but—
MRS. LINDE. But—
NORA. Papa didn't give us a shilling. It was I who procured the money.
MRS. LINDE. You? All that large sum?
NORA. Two hundred and fifty pounds. What do you think of that?
MRS. LINDE. But, Nora, how could you possibly do it? Did you win a prize in the Lottery?
NORA. [*contemptuously*] In the Lottery? There would have been no credit in that.
MRS. LINDE. But where did you get it from, then?
NORA. [*humming and smiling with an air of mystery*] Hm, hm! Aha!
MRS. LINDE. Because you couldn't have borrowed it.
NORA. Couldn't I? Why not?
MRS. LINDE. No, a wife cannot borrow without her husband's consent.
NORA. [*tossing her head*] Oh, if it is a wife who has any head for business—a wife who has the wit to be a little bit clever—
MRS. LINDE. I don't understand it at all, Nora.
NORA. There is no need you should. I never said I had borrowed the money. I may have got it some other way. [*lies back on the sofa*] Perhaps I got it from some other admirer. When anyone is as attractive as I am—
MRS. LINDE. You are a mad creature.
NORA. Now, you know you're full of curiosity, Christine.

Mrs. Linde. Listen to me, Nora dear. Haven't you been a little bit imprudent?

Nora. [*sits up straight*] Is it imprudent to save your husband's life?

Mrs. Linde. It seems to me imprudent, without his knowledge, to—

Nora. But it was absolutely necessary that he should not know! My goodness, can't you understand that? It was necessary he should have no idea what a dangerous condition he was in. It was to me that the doctors came and said that his life was in danger, and that the only thing to save him was to live in the south. Do you suppose I didn't try, first of all, to get what I wanted as if it were for myself? I told him how much I should love to travel abroad like other young wives; I tried tears and entreaties with him; I told him that he ought to remember the condition I was in, and that he ought to be kind and indulgent to me; I even hinted that he might raise a loan. That nearly made him angry, Christine. He said I was thoughtless, and that it was his duty as my husband not to indulge me in my whims and caprices—as I believe he called them. Very well I thought, you must be saved—and that was how I came to devise a way out of the difficulty—

Mrs. Linde. And did your husband never get to know from your father that the money had not come from him?

Nora. No, never. Papa died just at that time. I had meant to let him into the secret and beg him never to reveal it. But he was so ill then—alas, there never was any need to tell him.

Mrs. Linde. And since then have you never told your secret to your husband?

Nora. Good Heavens, no! How could you think so? A man who has such strong opinions about these things! And besides, how painful and humiliating it would be for Torvald, with his manly independence, to know that he owed me anything! It would upset our mutual relations altogether; our beautiful happy home would no longer be what it is now.

Mrs. Linde. Do you mean never to tell him about it?

Nora. [*meditatively, and with a half smile*] Yes—some day, perhaps, after many years, when I am no longer as nice-looking as I am now. Don't laugh at me! I mean of course, when Torvald is no longer as devoted to me as he is now; when my dancing and dressing-up and reciting have palled on him; then it may be a good thing to have something in reserve—[*breaking off*] What nonsense! That time will never come. Now, what do you think of my great secret, Christine? Do you still think I am of no use? I can tell you, too, that this affair has caused me a lot of worry. It has been by no means easy for me to meet my engagements punctually. I may tell you that there is something that is called, in business, quarterly interest, and another thing called payment in instalments, and it is always so dreadfully difficult to manage them. I have had to save a little here and there, where I could, you understand. I have not been able to put aside much from my housekeeping money, for Torvald must have a good table. I couldn't let my children be shabbily dressed; I have felt obliged to use up all he gave me for them, the sweet little darlings!

Mrs. Linde. So it has all had to come out of your own necessaries of life, poor Nora?

Nora. Of course. Besides, I was the one responsible for it. Whenever Torvald has given me the money for new dresses and such things, I have never spent more than half of it; I have always bought the simplest and cheapest things. Thank Heaven, any clothes look well on me, and so Torvald has never noticed it. But it was often very hard on me, Christine—because it is delightful to be really well dressed, isn't it?

MRS. LINDE. Quite so.

NORA. Well, then I have found other ways of earning money. Last winter I was lucky enough to get a lot of copying to do; so I locked myself up and sat writing every evening until quite late at night. Many a time I was desperately tired; but all the same it was a tremendous pleasure to sit there working and earning money. It was like being a man.

MRS. LINDE. How much have you been able to pay off in that way?

NORA. I can't tell you exactly. You see, it is very difficult to keep an account of a business matter of that kind. I only know that I have paid every penny that I could scrape together. Many a time I was at my wit's end. [*smiles*] Then I used to sit here and imagine that a rich old gentleman had fallen in love with me—

MRS. LINDE. What! Who was it?

NORA. Be quiet!—that he had died; and that when his will was opened it contained, written in big letters, the instruction "The lovely Mrs. Nora Helmer is to have all I possess paid over to her at once in cash."

MRS. LINDE. But, my dear Nora—who could the man be?

NORA. Good gracious, can't you understand? There was no old gentleman at all; it was only something that I used to sit here and imagine, when I couldn't think of any way of procuring money. But it's all the same now; the tiresome old person can stay where he is, as far as I am concerned; I don't care about him or his will either, for I am free from care now. [*jumps up*] My goodness, it's delightful to think of, Christine! Free from care! To be able to be free from care, quite free from care; to be able to play and romp with the children; to be able to keep the house beautifully and have everything just as Torvald likes it! And, think of it, soon the spring will come and the big blue sky! Perhaps we shall be able to take a little trip—perhaps I shall see the sea again! Oh, it's a wonderful thing to be alive and be happy. [*A bell is heard in the hall.*]

MRS. LINDE. [*rising*] There is the bell; perhaps I had better go.

NORA. No, don't go; no one will come in here; it is sure to be for Torvald.

SERVANT. [*at the hall door*] Excuse me, ma'am—there is a gentleman to see the master, and as the doctor is with him—

NORA. Who is it?

KROGSTAD. [*at the door*] It is I, Mrs. Helmer. [MRS. LINDE *starts, trembles, and turns to the window.*]

NORA. [*takes a step towards him, and speaks in a strained, low voice*] You? What is it? What do you want to see my husband about?

KROGSTAD. Bank business—in a way. I have a small post in the Bank, and I hear your husband is to be our chief now—

NORA. Then it is—

KROGSTAD. Nothing but dry business matters, Mrs. Helmer; absolutely nothing else.

NORA. Be so good as to go into the study, then. [*She bows indifferently to him and shuts the door into the hall; then comes back and makes up the fire in the stove.*]

MRS. LINDE. Nora—who was that man?

NORA. A lawyer, of the name of Krogstad.

MRS. LINDE. Then it really was he.

NORA. Do you know the man?

MRS. LINDE. I used to—many years ago. At one time he was a solicitor's clerk in our town.

NORA. Yes, he was.

Mrs. Linde. He is greatly altered.

Nora. He made a very unhappy marriage.

Mrs. Linde. He is a widower now, isn't he?

Nora. With several children. There now, it is burning up.

[*Shuts the door of the stove and moves the rocking-chair aside.*]

Mrs. Linde. They say he carries on various kinds of business.

Nora. Really! Perhaps he does; I don't know anything about it. But don't let us think of business; it is so tiresome.

Doctor Rank. [*comes out of* Helmer*'s study. Before he shuts the door he calls to him.*] No, my dear fellow, I won't disturb you; I would rather go in to your wife for a little while. [*shuts the door and sees* Mrs. Linde] I beg your pardon; I am afraid I am disturbing you too.

Nora. No, not at all. [*introducing him*] Doctor Rank, Mrs. Linde.

Rank. I have often heard Mrs. Linde's name mentioned here. I think I passed you on the stairs when I arrived, Mrs. Linde?

Mrs. Linde. Yes, I go up very slowly; I can't manage stairs well.

Rank. Ah! some slight internal weakness?

Mrs. Linde. No, the fact is I have been overworking myself.

Rank. Nothing more than that? Then I suppose you have come to town to amuse yourself with our entertainments?

Mrs. Linde. I have come to look for work.

Rank. Is that a good cure for overwork?

Mrs. Linde. One must live, Doctor Rank.

Rank. Yes, the general opinion seems to be that it is necessary.

Nora. Look here, Doctor Rank—you know you want to live.

Rank. Certainly. However wretched I may feel, I want to prolong the agony as long as possible. All my patients are like that. And so are those who are morally diseased; one of them, and a bad case too, is at this very moment with Helmer—

Mrs. Linde. [*sadly*] Ah!

Nora. Whom do you mean?

Rank. A lawyer of the name of Krogstad, a fellow you don't know at all. He suffers from a diseased moral character, Mrs. Helmer; but even he began talking of its being highly important that he should live.

Nora. Did he? What did he want to speak to Torvald about?

Rank. I have no idea; I only heard that it was something about the Bank.

Nora. I didn't know this—what's his name—Krogstad had anything to do with the Bank.

Rank. Yes, he has some sort of appointment there. [*to* Mrs. Linde] I don't know whether you find also in your part of the world that there are certain people who go zealously snuffing about to smell out moral corruption, and, as soon as they have found some, put the person concerned into some lucrative position where they can keep their eye on him. Healthy natures are left out in the cold.

Mrs. Linde. Still I think the sick are those who most need taking care of.

Rank. [*shrugging his shoulders*] Yes, there you are. That is the sentiment that is turning Society into a sickhouse.

[Nora, *who has been absorbed in her thoughts, breaks out into smothered laughter and claps her hands.*]

RANK. Why do you laugh at that? Have you any notion what Society really is?

NORA. What do I care about tiresome Society? I am laughing at something quite different, something extremely amusing. Tell me, Doctor Rank, are all the people who are employed in the Bank dependent on Torvald now?

RANK. Is that what you find so extremely amusing?

NORA. [*smiling and humming*] That's my affair! [*walking about the room*] It's perfectly glorious to think that we have—that Torvald has so much power over so many people. [*takes the packet from her pocket*] Doctor Rank, what do you say to a macaroon?

RANK. What, macaroons? I thought they were forbidden here.

NORA. Yes, but these are some Christine gave me.

MRS. LINDE. What! I?—

NORA. Oh, well, don't be alarmed! You couldn't know that Torvald had forbidden them. I must tell you that he is afraid they will spoil my teeth. But, bah!—once in a while—That's so, isn't it, Doctor Rank? By your leave? [*puts a macaroon into his mouth*] You must have one too, Christine. And I shall have one, just a little one—or at most two. [*walking about*] I am tremendously happy. There is just one thing in the world now that I should dearly love to do.

RANK. Well, what is that?

NORA. It's something I should dearly love to say, if Torvald could hear me.

RANK. Well, why can't you say it?

NORA. No, I daren't; it's so shocking.

MRS. LINDE. Shocking?

RANK. Well, I should not advise you to say it. Still, with us you might. What is it you would so much like to say if Torvald could hear you?

NORA. I should just love to say—Well, I'm damned!

RANK. Are you mad?

MRS. LINDE. Nora, dear—

RANK. Say it, here he is!

NORA. [*hiding the packet*] Hush! Hush! Hush!

[HELMER *comes out of his room, with his coat over his arm and his hat in his hands.*]

NORA. Well, Torvald dear, have you got rid of him?

HELMER. Yes, he has just gone.

NORA. Let me introduce you—this is Christine, who has come to town.

HELMER. Christine—? Excuse me, but I don't know—

NORA. Mrs. Linde, dear; Christine Linde.

HELMER. Of course. A school friend of my wife's, I presume?

MRS. LINDE. Yes, we have known each other since then.

NORA. And just think, she has taken a long journey in order to see you.

HELMER. What do you mean?

MRS. LINDE. No, really, I—

NORA. Christine is tremendously clever at book-keeping, and she is frightfully anxious to work under some clever man, so as to perfect herself—

HELMER. Very sensible, Mrs. Linde.

NORA. And when she heard you had been appointed manager of the Bank—the news was telegraphed, you know—she travelled here as quick as she could. Torvald, I am sure you will be able to do something for Christine, for my sake, won't you?

HELMER. Well, it is not altogether impossible. I presume you are a widow, Mrs. Linde?

MRS. LINDE. Yes.

HELMER. And have had some experience of book-keeping?

MRS. LINDE. Yes, a fair amount.

HELMER. Ah! well, it's very likely I may be able to find something for you—

NORA. [*clapping her hands*] What did I tell you? What did I tell you?

HELMER. You have just come at a fortunate moment, Mrs. Linde.

MRS. LINDE. How am I to thank you?

HELMER. There is no need. [*puts on his coat*] But to-day you must excuse me—

RANK. Wait a minute; I will come with you.

[*Brings his fur coat from the hall and warms it at the fire.*]

NORA. Don't be long away, Torvald dear.

HELMER. About an hour, not more.

NORA. Are you going too, Christine?

MRS. LINDE. [*putting on her cloak*] Yes, I must go and look for a room.

HELMER. Oh, well then, we can walk down the street together.

NORA. [*helping her*] What a pity it is we are so short of space here: I am afraid it is impossible for us—

MRS. LINDE. Please don't think of it! Good-bye, Nora dear, and many thanks.

NORA. Good-bye for the present. Of course you will come back this evening. And you too, Dr. Rank. What do you say? If you are well enough? Oh, you must be! Wrap yourself up well.

[*They go to the door all talking together. Children's voices are heard on the staircase.*]

NORA. There they are. There they are! [*She runs to open the door: The Nurse comes in with the children.*] Come in! Come in! [*stoops and kisses them*] Oh, you sweet blessings! Look at them, Christine! Aren't they darlings?

RANK. Don't let us stand here in the draught.

HELMER. Come along, Mrs. Linde; the place will only be bearable for a mother now!

[RANK, HELMER *and* MRS. LINDE *go downstairs. The* NURSE *comes forward with the children;* NORA *shuts the hall door.*]

NORA. How fresh and well you look! Such red cheeks!—like apples and roses. [*The children all talk at once while she speaks to them.*] Have you had great fun? That's splendid! What, you pulled both Emmy and Bob along on the sledge?—both at once?—that *was* good. You are a clever boy, Ivar. Let me take her for a little, Anne. My sweet little baby doll! [*takes the baby from the* MAID *and dances it up and down*] Yes, yes, mother will dance with Bob too. What! Have you been snowballing? I wish I had been there too! No, no, I will take their things off, Anne; please let me do it, it is such fun. Go in now, you look half frozen. There is some coffee for you on the stove.

[*The* NURSE *goes into the room on the left.* NORA *takes off the children's things and throws them about, while they all talk to her at once.*]

NORA. Really! Did a big dog run after you? But it didn't bite you? No, dogs don't bite nice little dolly children. You mustn't look at the parcels, Ivar. What are they? Ah, I daresay you would like to know. No, no—it's something nasty! Come, let us have a game! What shall we play at? Hide and Seek? Yes, we'll play Hide and Seek. Bob shall hide first. Must I hide? Very well, I'll hide first.

[*She and the children laugh and shout, and romp in and out of the room; at last* NORA *hides under the table, the children rush in and look for her, but do not see her; they hear her smothered laughter, run to the table, lift up the cloth and find her. Shouts of laughter. She crawls forward and pretends to frighten them. Fresh laughter. Meanwhile there has been a knock at the hall door, but none of them has noticed it. The door is half opened, and Krogstad appears. He waits a little; the game goes on.*]

KROGSTAD. Excuse me, Mrs. Helmer.

NORA. [*with a stifled cry, turns round and gets up on to her knees*] Ah! what do you want?

KROGSTAD. Excuse me, the outer door was ajar; I suppose someone forgot to shut it.

NORA. [*rising*] My husband is out, Mr. Krogstad.

KROGSTAD. I know that.

NORA. What do you want here, then?

KROGSTAD. A word with you.

NORA. With me?—[*to the children, gently*] Go in to nurse. What? No, the strange man won't do mother any harm. When he has gone we will have another game. [*She takes the children into the room on the left, and shuts the door after them.*] You want to speak to me?

KROGSTAD. Yes, I do.

NORA. To-day? It is not the first of the month yet.

KROGSTAD. No, it is Christmas Eve, and it will depend on yourself what sort of a Christmas you will spend.

NORA. What do you want? To-day it is absolutely impossible for me—

KROGSTAD. We won't talk about that till later on. This is something different. I presume you can give me a moment?

NORA. Yes—yes, I can—although—

KROGSTAD. Good. I was in Olsen's Restaurant and saw your husband going down the street—

NORA. Yes?

KROGSTAD. With a lady.

NORA. What then?

KROGSTAD. May I make so bold as to ask if it was a Mrs. Linde?

NORA. It was.

KROGSTAD. Just arrived in town?

NORA. Yes, to-day.

KROGSTAD. She is a great friend of yours, isn't she?

NORA. She is. But I don't see—

KROGSTAD. I knew her too, once upon a time.

NORA. I am aware of that.

KROGSTAD. Are you? So you know all about it; I thought as much. Then I can ask you, without beating about the bush—is Mrs. Linde to have an appointment in the Bank?

NORA. What right have you to question me, Mr. Krogstad?—You, one of my husband's subordinates! But since you ask, you shall know. Yes, Mrs. Linde *is* to have an appointment. And it was I who pleaded her cause, Mr. Krogstad, let me tell you that.

Krogstad. I was right in what I thought, then.

Nora. [*walking up and down the stage*] Sometimes one has a tiny little bit of influence, I should hope. Because one is a woman, it does not necessarily follow that—. When anyone is in a subordinate position, Mr. Krogstad, they should really be careful to avoid offending anyone who—who—

Krogstad. Who has influence?

Nora. Exactly.

Krogstad. [*changing his tone*] Mrs. Helmer, you will be so good as to use your influence on my behalf.

Nora. What? What do you mean?

Krogstad. You will be so kind as to see that I am allowed to keep my subordinate position in the Bank.

Nora. What do you mean by that? Who proposes to take your post away from you?

Krogstad. Oh, there is no necessity to keep up the pretence of ignorance. I can quite understand that your friend is not very anxious to expose herself to the chance of rubbing shoulders with me; and I quite understand, too, whom I have to thank for being turned out.

Nora. But I assure you—

Krogstad. Very likely; but, to come to the point, the time has come when I should advise you to use your influence to prevent that.

Nora. But, Mr. Krogstad, I *have* no influence.

Krogstad. Haven't you? I thought you said yourself just now—

Nora. Naturally I did not mean you to put that construction on it. I! What should make you think I have any influence of that kind with my husband?

Krogstad. Oh, I have known your husband from our student days. I don't suppose he is any more unassailable than other husbands.

Nora. If you speak slightingly of my husband, I shall turn you out of the house.

Krogstad. You are bold, Mrs. Helmer.

Nora. I am not afraid of you any longer. As soon as the New Year comes, I shall in a very short time be free of the whole thing.

Krogstad. [*controlling himself*] Listen to me, Mrs. Helmer. If necessary, I am prepared to fight for my small post in the Bank as if I were fighting for my life.

Nora. So it seems.

Krogstad. It is not only for the sake of the money; indeed, that weighs least with me in the matter. There is another reason—well, I may as well tell you. My position is this. I daresay you know, like everybody else, that once, many years ago, I was guilty of an indiscretion.

Nora. I think I have heard something of the kind.

Krogstad. The matter never came into court; but every way seemed to be closed to me after that. So I took to the business that you know of. I had to do something; and, honestly, I don't think I've been one of the worst. But now I must cut myself free from all that. My sons are growing up; for their sake I must try and win back as much respect as I can in the town. This post in the Bank was like the first step up for me—and now your husband is going to kick me downstairs again into the mud.

Nora. But you must believe me, Mr. Krogstad; it is not in my power to help you at all.

KROGSTAD. Then it is because you haven't the will; but I have means to compel you.
NORA. You don't mean that you will tell my husband that I owe you money?
KROGSTAD. Hm!—suppose I were to tell him?
NORA. It would be perfectly infamous of you. [*sobbing*] To think of his learning my secret, which has been my joy and pride, in such an ugly, clumsy way—that he should learn it from you! And it would put me in a horribly disagreeable position—
KROGSTAD. Only disagreeable?
NORA. [*impetuously*] Well, do it, then!—and it will be the worse for you. My husband will see for himself what a blackguard you are, and you certainly won't keep your post then.
KROGSTAD. I asked you if it was only a disagreeable scene at home that you were afraid of?
NORA. If my husband does get to know of it, of course he will at once pay you what is still owing, and we shall have nothing more to do with you.
KROGSTAD. [*coming a step nearer*] Listen to me, Mrs. Helmer. Either you have a very bad memory or you know very little of business. I shall be obliged to remind you of a few details.
NORA. What do you mean?
KROGSTAD. When your husband was ill, you came to me to borrow two hundred and fifty pounds.
NORA. I didn't know any one else to go to.
KROGSTAD. I promised to get you that amount—
NORA. Yes, and you did so.
KROGSTAD. I promised to get you that amount, on certain conditions. Your mind was so taken up with your husband's illness, and you were so anxious to get the money for your journey, that you seem to have paid no attention to the conditions of our bargain. Therefore it will not be amiss if I remind you of them. Now, I promised to get the money on the security of a bond which I drew up.
NORA. Yes, and which I signed.
KROGSTAD. Good. But below your signature there were a few lines constituting your father a surety for the money; those lines your father should have signed.
NORA. Should? He did sign them.
KROGSTAD. I had left the date blank; that is to say your father should himself have inserted the date on which he signed the paper. Do you remember that?
NORA. Yes, I think I remember—
KROGSTAD. Then I gave you the bond to send by post to your father. Is that not so?
NORA. Yes.
KROGSTAD. And you naturally did so at once, because five or six days afterwards you brought me the bond with your father's signature. And then I gave you the money.
NORA. Well, haven't I been paying it off regularly?
KROGSTAD. Fairly so, yes. But—to come back to the matter in hand—that must have been a very trying time for you, Mrs. Helmer?
NORA. It was, indeed.
KROGSTAD. Your father was very ill, wasn't he?

Nora. He was very near his end.

Krogstad. And died soon afterwards?

Nora. Yes.

Krogstad. Tell me, Mrs. Helmer, can you by any chance remember what day your father died?—on what day of the month, I mean.

Nora. Papa died on the 29th of September.

Krogstad. That is correct; I have ascertained it for myself. And, as that is so, there is a discrepancy [*taking a paper from his pocket*] which I cannot account for.

Nora. What discrepancy? I don't know—

Krogstad. The discrepancy consists, Mrs. Helmer, in the fact that your father signed this bond three days after his death.

Nora. What do you mean? I don't understand—

Krogstad. Your father died on the 29th of September. But, look here; your father has dated his signature the 2nd of October. It is a discrepancy, isn't it? [Nora *is silent.*] Can you explain it to me? [Nora *is still silent.*] It is a remarkable thing, too, that the words "2nd of October," as well as the year, are not written in your father's handwriting but in one that I think I know. Well, of course it can be explained; your father may have forgotten to date his signature, and someone else may have dated it haphazard before they knew of his death. There is no harm in that. It all depends on the signature of the name; and that is genuine, I suppose, Mrs. Helmer? It was your father himself who signed his name here?

Nora. [*after a short pause, throws her head up and looks defiantly at him*] No, it was not. It was I that wrote papa's name.

Krogstad. Are you aware that is a dangerous confession?

Nora. In what way? You shall have your money soon.

Krogstad. Let me ask you a question; why did you not send the paper to your father?

Nora. It was impossible; papa was so ill. If I had asked him for his signature, I should have had to tell him what the money was to be used for; and when he was so ill himself I couldn't tell him that my husband's life was in danger—it was impossible.

Krogstad. It would have been better for you if you had given up your trip abroad.

Nora. No, that was impossible. That trip was to save my husband's life; I couldn't give that up.

Krogstad. But did it never occur to you that you were committing a fraud on me?

Nora. I couldn't take that into account; I didn't trouble myself about you at all. I couldn't bear you, because you put so many heartless difficulties in my way, although you knew what a dangerous condition my husband was in.

Krogstad. Mrs. Helmer, you evidently do not realise clearly what it is that you have been guilty of. But I can assure you that my one false step, which lost me all my reputation, was nothing more or nothing worse than what you have done.

Nora. You? Do you ask me to believe that you were brave enough to run a risk to save your wife's life?

Krogstad. The law cares nothing about motives.

Nora. Then it must be a very foolish law.

KROGSTAD. Foolish or not, it is the law by which you will be judged, if I produce this paper in court.

NORA. I don't believe it. Is a daughter not to be allowed to spare her dying father anxiety and care? Is a wife not to be allowed to save her husband's life? I don't know much about law; but I am certain that there must be laws permitting such things as that. Have you no knowledge of such laws—you who are a lawyer? You must be a very poor lawyer, Mr. Krogstad.

KROGSTAD. Maybe. But matters of business—such business as you and I have had together—do you think I don't understand that? Very well. Do as you please. But let me tell you this—if I lose my position a second time, you shall lose yours with me.

[*He bows, and goes out through the hall.*]

NORA. [*appears buried in thought for a short time, then tosses her head*] Nonsense! Trying to frighten me like that!—I am not so silly as he thinks. [*begins to busy herself putting the children's things in order*] And yet—? No, it's impossible! I did it for love's sake.

THE CHILDREN. [*in the doorway on the left*] Mother, the stranger man has gone out through the gate.

NORA. Yes, dears, I know. But, don't tell anyone about the stranger man. Do you hear? Not even papa.

CHILDREN. No, mother; but will you come and play again?

NORA. No, no—not now.

CHILDREN. But, mother, you promised us.

NORA. Yes, but I can't now. Run away in; I have such a lot to do. Run away in, my sweet little darlings. [*She gets them into the room by degrees and shuts the door on them; then sits down on the sofa, takes up a piece of needlework and sews a few stitches, but soon stops.*] No! [*throws down the work, gets up, goes to the hall door and calls out*] Helen! bring the Tree in. [*goes to the table on the left, opens a drawer, and stops again*] No, no! it is quite impossible!

MAID. [*coming in with the Tree*] Where shall I put it, ma'am?

NORA. Here, in the middle of the floor.

MAID. Shall I get you anything else?

NORA. No, thank you. I have all I want.

[*Exit Maid.*]

NORA. [*begins dressing the tree*] A candle here—and flowers here—. The horrible man! It's all nonsense—there's nothing wrong. The Tree shall be splendid! I will do everything I can think of to please you, Torvald!—I will sing for you, dance for you—[HELMER *comes in with some papers under his arm*] Oh! are you back already?

HELMER. Yes. Has anyone been here?

NORA. Here? No.

HELMER. That is strange. I saw Krogstad going out of the gate.

NORA. Did you? Oh yes, I forgot, Krogstad was here for a moment.

HELMER. Nora, I can see from your manner that he has been here begging you to say a good word for him.

NORA. Yes.

HELMER. And you were to appear to do it of your own accord; you were to conceal from me the fact of his having been here; didn't he beg that of you too?

NORA. Yes, Torvald, but—

Helmer. Nora, Nora, and you would be a party to that sort of thing? To have any talk with a man like that, and give him any sort of promise? And to tell me a lie into the bargain?

Nora. A lie—?

Helmer. Didn't you tell me no one had been here? [*shakes his finger at her*] My little song-bird must never do that again. A song-bird must have a clean beak to chirp with—no false notes! [*puts his arm round her waist*] That is so, isn't it? Yes, I am sure it is. [*lets her go*] We will say no more about it. [*sits down by the stove*] How warm and snug it is here!

[*Turns over his papers.*]

Nora. [*after a short pause, during which she busies herself with the Christmas Tree*] Torvald!

Helmer. Yes.

Nora. I am looking forward tremendously to the fancy dress ball at the Stenborgs' the day after to-morrow.

Helmer. And I am tremendously curious to see what you are going to surprise me with.

Nora. It was very silly of me to want to do that.

Helmer. What do you mean?

Nora. I can't hit upon anything that will do; everything I think of seems so silly and insignificant.

Helmer. Does my little Nora acknowledge that at last?

Nora. [*standing behind his chair with her arms on the back of it*] Are you very busy, Torvald?

Helmer. Well—

Nora. What are all those papers?

Helmer. Bank business.

Nora. Already?

Helmer. I have got authority from the retiring manager to undertake the necessary changes in the staff and in the rearrangement of the work; and I must make use of the Christmas week for that, so as to have everything in order for the new year.

Nora. Then that was why this poor Krogstad—

Helmer. Hm!

Nora. [*leans against the back of his chair and strokes his hair*] If you hadn't been so busy I should have asked you a tremendously big favour, Torvald.

Helmer. What is that? Tell me.

Nora. There is no one has such good taste as you. And I do so want to look nice at the fancy-dress ball. Torvald, couldn't you take me in hand and decide what I shall go as, and what sort of a dress I shall wear?

Helmer. Aha! so my obstinate little woman is obliged to get someone to come to her rescue?

Nora. Yes, Torvald, I can't get along a bit without your help.

Helmer. Very well, I will think it over, we shall manage to hit upon something.

Nora. That is nice of you. [*Goes to the Christmas Tree. A short pause.*] How pretty the red flowers look—. But, tell me, was it really something very bad that this Krogstad was guilty of?

Helmer. He forged someone's name. Have you any idea what that means?

Nora. Isn't it possible that he was driven to do it by necessity?

HELMER. Yes; or, as in so many cases, by imprudence. I am not so heartless as to condemn a man altogether because of a single false step of that kind.

NORA. No you wouldn't, would you, Torvald?

HELMER. Many a man has been able to retrieve his character, if he has openly confessed his fault and taken his punishment.

NORA. Punishment—?

HELMER. But Krogstad did nothing of that sort; he got himself out of it by a cunning trick, and that is why he has gone under altogether.

NORA. But do you think it would—?

HELMER. Just think how a guilty man like that has to lie and play the hypocrite with everyone, how he has to wear a mask in the presence of those near and dear to him, even before his own wife and children. And about the children—that is the most terrible part of it all, Nora.

NORA. How?

HELMER. Because such an atmosphere of lies infects and poisons the whole life of a home. Each breath the children take in such a house is full of the germs of evil.

NORA. [*coming nearer him*] Are you sure of that?

HELMER. My dear, I have often seen it in the course of my life as a lawyer. Almost everyone who has gone to the bad early in life has had a deceitful mother.

NORA. Why do you only say—mother?

HELMER. It seems most commonly to be the mother's influence, though naturally a bad father's would have the same result. Every lawyer is familiar with the fact. This Krogstad, now, has been persistently poisoning his own children with lies and dissimulation; that is why I say he has lost all moral character. [*holds out his hands to her*] That is why my sweet little Nora must promise me not to plead his cause. Give me your hand on it. Come, come, what is this? Give me your hand. There now, that's settled. I assure you it would be quite impossible for me to work with him; I literally feel physically ill when I am in the company of such people.

NORA. [*takes her hand out of his and goes to the opposite side of the Christmas Tree*] How hot it is in here; and I have such a lot to do.

HELMER. [*getting up and putting his papers in order*] Yes, and I must try and read through some of these before dinner; and I must think about your costume, too. And it is just possible I may have something ready in gold paper to hang up on the Tree. [*Puts his hand on her head.*] My precious little singing-bird!

[*He goes into his room and shuts the door after him.*]

NORA. [*after a pause, whispers*] No, no—it isn't true. It's impossible; it must be impossible.

[*The* NURSE *opens the door on the left.*]

NURSE. The little ones are begging so hard to be allowed to come in to mamma.

NORA. No, no, no! Don't let them come in to me! You stay with them, Anne.

NURSE. Very well, ma'am.

[*Shuts the door.*]

NORA. [*pale with terror*] Deprave my little children? Poison my home? [*a short pause. Then she tosses her head.*] It's not true. It can't possibly be true.

ACT 2

THE SAME SCENE. *The Christmas Tree is in the corner by the piano, stripped of its ornaments and with burnt-down candle-ends on its dishevelled branches.* NORA'S *cloak and hat are lying on the sofa. She is alone in the room, walking about uneasily. She stops by the sofa and takes up her cloak.*

NORA. [*drops the cloak*] Someone is coming now! [*goes to the door and listens*] No—it is no one. Of course, no one will come to-day, Christmas Day—nor tomorrow either. But, perhaps—[*opens the door and looks out*] No, nothing in the letter-box; it is quite empty. [*comes forward*] What rubbish! of course he can't be in earnest about it. Such a thing couldn't happen; it is impossible—I have three little children.

[*Enter the* NURSE *from the room on the left, carrying a big cardboard box.*]

NURSE. At last I have found the box with the fancy dress.

NORA. Thanks; put it on the table.

NURSE. [*doing so*] But it is very much in want of mending.

NORA. I should like to tear it into a hundred thousand pieces.

NURSE. What an idea! It can easily be put in order—just a little patience.

NORA. Yes, I will go and get Mrs. Linde to come and help me with it.

NURSE. What, out again? In this horrible weather? You will catch cold, ma'am, and make yourself ill.

NORA. Well, worse than that might happen. How are the children?

NURSE. The poor little souls are playing with their Christmas presents, but—

NORA. Do they ask much for me?

NURSE. You see, they are so accustomed to have their mamma with them.

NORA. Yes, but, nurse, I shall not be able to be so much with them now as I was before.

NURSE. Oh well, young children easily get accustomed to anything.

NORA. Do you think so? Do you think they would forget their mother if she went away altogether?

NURSE. Good heavens!—went away altogether?

NORA. Nurse, I want you to tell me something I have often wondered about—how could you have the heart to put your own child out among strangers?

NURSE. I was obliged to, if I wanted to be little Nora's nurse.

NORA. Yes, but how could you be willing to do it?

NURSE. What, when I was going to get such a good place by it? A poor girl who has got into trouble should be glad to. Besides, that wicked man didn't do a single thing for me.

NORA. But I suppose your daughter has quite forgotten you.

NURSE. No, indeed she hasn't. She wrote to me when she was confirmed, and when she was married.

NORA. [*putting her arms round her neck*] Dear old Anne, you were a good mother to me when I was little.

NURSE. Little Nora, poor dear, had no other mother but me.

NORA. And if my little ones had no other mother, I am sure you would—What nonsense I am talking! [*opens the box*] Go in to them. Now I must—. You will see tomorrow how charming I shall look.

NURSE. I am sure there will be no one at the ball so charming as you, ma'am.

[*Goes into the room on the left.*]

NORA. [*begins to unpack the box, but soon pushes it away from her*] If only I dared go out. If only no one would come. If only I could be sure nothing would happen here in the meantime. Stuff and nonsense! No one will come. Only I mustn't think about it. I will brush my muff. What lovely gloves! Out of my thoughts, out of my thoughts! One, two, three, four, five, six—[*Screams.*] Ah! there is someone coming—

[*Makes a movement towards the door, but stands irresolute.*]

[*Enter* MRS. LINDE *from the hall, where she has taken off her cloak and hat.*]

NORA. Oh, it's you, Christine. There is no one else out there, is there? How good of you to come!

MRS. LINDE. I heard you were up asking for me.

NORA. Yes, I was passing by. As a matter of fact, it is something you could help me with. Let us sit down here on the sofa. Look here. To-morrow evening there is to be a fancy-dress ball at the Stenborgs', who live above us; and Torvald wants me to go as a Neapolitan fisher-girl, and dance the Tarantella that I learnt at Capri.

MRS. LINDE. I see; you are going to keep up the character.

NORA. Yes, Torvald wants me to. Look, here is the dress; Torvald had it made for me there, but now it is all so torn, and I haven't any idea—

MRS. LINDE. We will easily put that right. It is only some of the trimming come unsewn here and there. Needle and thread? Now then, that's all we want.

NORA. It *is* nice of you.

MRS. LINDE. [*sewing*] So you are going to be dressed up to-morrow, Nora. I will tell you what—I shall come in for a moment and see you in your fine feathers. But I have completely forgotten to thank you for a delightful evening yesterday.

NORA. [*gets up, and crosses the stage*] Well I don't think yesterday was as pleasant as usual. You ought to have come to town a little earlier, Christine. Certainly Torvald does understand how to make a house dainty and attractive.

MRS. LINDE. And so do you, it seems to me; you are not your father's daughter for nothing. But tell me, is Doctor Rank always as depressed as he was yesterday?

NORA. No; yesterday it was very noticeable. I must tell you that he suffers from a very dangerous disease. He has consumption of the spine, poor creature. His father was a horrible man who committed all sorts of excesses; and that is why his son was sickly from childhood, do you understand?

MRS. LINDE. [*dropping her sewing*] But, my dearest Nora, how do you know anything about such things?

NORA. [*walking about*] Pooh! When you have three children, you get visits now and then from—from married women, who know something of medical matters, and they talk about one thing and another.

MRS. LINDE. [*goes on sewing. A short silence*] Does Doctor Rank come here every day?

NORA. Every day regularly. He is Torvald's most intimate friend, and a great friend of mine too. He is just like one of the family.

MRS. LINDE. But tell me this—is he perfectly sincere? I mean, isn't he the kind of man that is very anxious to make himself agreeable?

NORA. Not in the least. What makes you think that?

Mrs. Linde. When you introduced him to me yesterday, he declared he had often heard my name mentioned in this house; but afterwards I noticed that your husband hadn't the slightest idea who I was. So how could Doctor Rank—?

Nora. That is quite right, Christine. Torvald is so absurdly fond of me that he wants me absolutely to himself, as he says. At first he used to seem almost jealous if I mentioned any of the dear folk at home, so naturally I gave up doing so. But I often talk about such things with Doctor Rank, because he likes hearing about them.

Mrs. Linde. Listen to me, Nora. You are still very like a child in many things, and I am older than you in many ways and have a little more experience. Let me tell you this—you ought to make an end of it with Doctor Rank.

Nora. What ought I to make an end of?

Mrs. Linde. Of two things, I think. Yesterday you talked some nonsense about a rich admirer who was to leave you money—

Nora. An admirer who doesn't exist, unfortunately! But what then?

Mrs. Linde. Is Doctor Rank a man of means?

Nora. Yes, he is.

Mrs. Linde. And has no one to provide for?

Nora. No, no one; but—

Mrs. Linde. And comes here every day?

Nora. Yes, I told you so.

Mrs. Linde. But how can this well-bred man be so tactless?

Nora. I don't understand you at all.

Mrs. Linde. Don't prevaricate, Nora. Do you suppose I don't guess who lent you the two hundred and fifty pounds?

Nora. Are you out of your senses? How can you think of such a thing! A friend of ours, who comes here every day! Do you realise what a horribly painful position that would be?

Mrs. Linde. Then it really isn't he?

Nora. No, certainly not. It would never have entered into my head for a moment. Besides, he had no money to lend then; he came into his money afterwards.

Mrs. Linde. Well, I think that was lucky for you, my dear Nora.

Nora. No, it would never have come into my head to ask Doctor Rank. Although I am quite sure that if I had asked him—

Mrs. Linde. But of course you won't.

Nora. Of course not. I have no reason to think it could possibly be necessary. But I am quite sure that if I told Doctor Rank—

Mrs. Linde. Behind your husband's back?

Nora. I *must* make an end of it with the other one, and that will be behind his back too. I *must* make an end of it with him.

Mrs. Linde. Yes, that is what I told you yesterday, but—

Nora. [*walking up and down*] A man can put a thing like that straight much easier than a woman—

Mrs. Linde. One's husband, yes.

Nora. Nonsense! [*standing still*] When you pay off a debt you get your bond back, don't you?

Mrs. Linde. Yes, as a matter of course.

NORA. And can tear it into a hundred thousand pieces, and burn it up—the nasty dirty paper!

MRS. LINDE. [*looks hard at her, lays down her sewing and gets up slowly*] Nora, you are concealing something from me.

NORA. Do I look as if I were?

MRS. LINDE. Something has happened to you since yesterday morning. Nora, what is it?

NORA. [*going nearer to her*] Christine! [*listens*] Hush! there's Torvald come home. Do you mind going in to the children for the present? Torvald can't bear to see dressmaking going on. Let Anne help you.

MRS. LINDE. [*gathering some of the things together*] Certainly—but I am not going away from here till we have had it out with one another.

[*She goes into the room on the left, as* HELMER *comes in from the hall.*]

NORA. [*going up to* HELMER] I have wanted you so much, Torvald dear.

HELMER. Was that the dressmaker?

NORA. No, it was Christine; she is helping me to put my dress in order. You will see I shall look quite smart.

HELMER. Wasn't that a happy thought of mine, now?

NORA. Splendid! But don't you think it is nice of me, too, to do as you wish?

HELMER. Nice?—because you do as your husband wishes? Well, well, you little rogue, I am sure you did not mean it in that way. But I am not going to disturb you; you will want to be trying on your dress, I expect.

NORA. I suppose you are going to work.

HELMER. Yes. [*shows her a bundle of papers*] Look at that. I have just been into the bank. [*Turns to go into his room.*]

NORA. Torvald.

HELMER. Yes.

NORA. If your little squirrel were to ask you for something very, very prettily—?

HELMER. What then?

NORA. Would you do it?

HELMER. I should like to hear what it is, first.

NORA. Your squirrel would run about and do all her tricks if you would be nice, and do what she wants.

HELMER. Speak plainly.

NORA. Your skylark would chirp about in every room, with her song rising and falling—

HELMER. Well, my skylark does that anyhow.

NORA. I would play the fairy and dance for you in the moonlight, Torvald.

HELMER. Nora—you surely don't mean that request you made of me this morning?

NORA. [*going near him*] Yes, Torvald, I beg you so earnestly—

HELMER. Have you really the courage to open up that question again?

NORA. Yes, dear, you *must* do as I ask; you *must* let Krogstad keep his post in the Bank.

HELMER. My dear Nora, it is his post that I have arranged Mrs. Linde shall have.

NORA. Yes, you have been awfully kind about that; but you could just as well dismiss some other clerk instead of Krogstad.

Helmer. This is simply incredible obstinacy! Because you chose to give him a thoughtless promise that you would speak for him, I am expected to—

Nora. That isn't the reason, Torvald. It is for your own sake. This fellow writes in the most scurrilous newspapers; you have told me so yourself. He can do you an unspeakable amount of harm. I am frightened to death of him—

Helmer. Ah, I understand; it is recollections of the past that scare you.

Nora. What do you mean?

Helmer. Naturally you are thinking of your father.

Nora. Yes—yes, of course. Just recall to your mind what these malicious creatures wrote in the papers about papa, and how horribly they slandered him. I believe they would have procured his dismissal if the Department had not sent you over to inquire into it, and if you had not been so kindly disposed and helpful to him.

Helmer. My little Nora, there is an important difference between your father and me. Your father's reputation as a public official was not above suspicion. Mine is, and I hope it will continue to be so, as long as I hold my office.

Nora. You never can tell what mischief these men may contrive. We ought to be so well off, so snug and happy here in our peaceful home, and have no cares—you and I and the children. Torvald! That is why I beg you so earnestly—

Helmer. And it is just by interceding for him that you make it impossible for me to keep him. It is already known at the Bank that I mean to dismiss Krogstad. Is it to get about now that the new manager has changed his mind at his wife's bidding—

Nora. And what if it did?

Helmer. Of course!—if only this obstinate little person can get her way! Do you suppose I am going to make myself ridiculous before my whole staff, to let people think that I am a man to be swayed by all sorts of outside influence? I should very soon feel the consequences of it, I can tell you! And besides, there is one thing that makes it quite impossible for me to have Krogstad in the Bank as long as I am manager.

Nora. Whatever is that?

Helmer. His moral failings I might perhaps have overlooked, if necessary—

Nora. Yes, you could—couldn't you?

Helmer. And I hear he is a good worker, too. But I knew him when we were boys. It was one of those rash friendships that so often prove an incubus in after life. I may as well tell you plainly, we were once on very intimate terms with one another. But this tactless fellow lays no restraint on himself when other people are present. On the contrary, he thinks it gives him the right to adopt a familiar tone with me, and every minute it is "I say, Helmer, old fellow!" and that sort of thing. I assure you it is extremely painful for me. He would make my position in the Bank intolerable.

Nora. Torvald, I don't believe you mean that.

Helmer. Don't you? Why not?

Nora. Because it is such a narrow-minded way of looking at things.

Helmer. What are you saying? Narrow-minded? Do you think I am narrow-minded?

Nora. No, just the opposite, dear—and it is exactly for that reason.

HELMER. It's the same thing. You say my point of view is narrow-minded, so I must be so too. Narrow-minded! Very well—I must put an end to this. [*Goes to the hall-door and calls.*] Helen!

NORA. What are you going to do?

HELMER. [*looking among his papers*] Settle it. [*Enter* MAID.] Look here; take this letter and go downstairs with it at once. Find a messenger and tell him to deliver it, and be quick. The address is on it, and here is the money.

MAID. Very well, sir.

[*Exits with the letter.*]

HELMER. [*putting his papers together*] Now then, little Miss Obstinate.

NORA. [*breathlessly*] Torvald—what was that letter?

HELMER. Krogstad's dismissal.

NORA. Call her back, Torvald! There is still time. Oh Torvald, call her back! Do it for my sake—for your own sake—for the children's sake! Do you hear me, Torvald? Call her back!! You don't know what that letter can bring upon us.

HELMER. It's too late.

NORA. Yes, it's too late.

HELMER. My dear Nora, I can forgive the anxiety you are in, although really it is an insult to me. It is, indeed. Isn't it an insult to think that I should be afraid of a starving quill-driver's vengeance? But I forgive you nevertheless, because it is such eloquent witness to your great love for me. [*takes her in his arms*] And that is as it should be, my own darling Nora. Come what will, you may be sure I shall have both courage and strength if they be needed. You will see I am man enough to take everything upon myself.

NORA. [*in a horror-stricken voice*] What do you mean by that?

HELMER. Everything, I say—

NORA. [*recovering herself*] You will never have to do that.

HELMER. That's right. Well, we will share it, Nora, as man and wife should. That is how it shall be. [*caressing her*] Are you content now? There! there!—not these frightened dove's eyes! The whole thing is only the wildest fancy!—Now, you must go and play through the Tarantella and practise with your tambourine. I shall go into the inner office and shut the door, and I shall hear nothing; you can make as much noise as you please. [*turns back at the door*] And when Rank comes, tell him where he will find me.

[*Nods to her, takes his papers and goes into his room, and shuts the door after him.*]

NORA. [*bewildered with anxiety, stands as if rooted to the spot, and whispers*] He is capable of doing it. He will do it. He will do it in spite of everything.—No, not that! Never, never! Anything rather than that! Oh, for some help, some way out of it! [*The door-bell rings.*] Doctor Rank! Anything rather than that—anything, whatever it is!

[*She puts her hands over her face, pulls herself together, goes to the door and opens it.* RANK *is standing without, hanging up his coat. During the following dialogue it begins to grow dark.*]

NORA. Good-day, Doctor Rank. I knew your ring. But you mustn't go in to Torvald now; I think he is busy with something.

RANK. And you?
NORA. [*brings him in and shuts the door after him*] Oh, you know very well I always have time for you.
RANK. Thank you. I shall make use of as much of it as I can.
NORA. What do you mean by that? As much of it as you can?
RANK. Well, does that alarm you?
NORA. It was such a strange way of putting it. Is anything likely to happen?
RANK. Nothing but what I have long been prepared for. But I certainly didn't expect it to happen so soon.
NORA. [*gripping him by the arm*] What have you found out? Doctor Rank, you must tell me.
RANK. [*sitting down by the stove*] It is all up with me. And it can't be helped.
NORA. [*with a sigh of relief*] Is it about yourself?
RANK. Who else? It is no use lying to one's self. I am the most wretched of all my patients, Mrs. Helmer. Lately I have been taking stock of my internal economy. Bankrupt! Probably within a month I shall lie rotting in the churchyard.
NORA. What an ugly thing to say!
RANK. The thing itself is cursedly ugly, and the worst of it is that I shall have to face so much more that is ugly before that. I shall only make one more examination of myself; when I have done that, I shall know pretty certainly when it will be that the horrors of dissolution will begin. There is something I want to tell you. Helmer's refined nature gives him an unconquerable disgust at everything that is ugly; I won't have him in my sick-room.
NORA. Oh, but, Doctor Rank—
RANK. I won't have him there. Not on any account. I bar my door to him. As soon as I am quite certain that the worst has come, I shall send you my card with a black cross on it, and then you will know that the loathsome end has begun.
NORA. You are quite absurd to-day. And I wanted you so much to be in a really good humour.
RANK. With death stalking beside me?—To have to pay this penalty for another man's sin! Is there any justice in that? And in every single family, in one way or another, some such inexorable retribution is being exacted—
NORA. [*putting her hands over her ears*] Rubbish! Do talk of something cheerful.
RANK. Oh, it's a mere laughing matter, the whole thing. My poor innocent spine has to suffer for my father's youthful amusements.
NORA. [*sitting at the table on the left*] I suppose you mean that he was too partial to asparagus and pâté de foie gras, don't you.
RANK. Yes, and to truffles.
NORA. Truffles, yes. And oysters too, I suppose?
RANK. Oysters, of course, that goes without saying.
NORA. And heaps of port and champagne. It is sad that all these nice things should take their revenge on our bones.
RANK. Especially that they should revenge themselves on the unlucky bones of those who have not had the satisfaction of enjoying them.
NORA. Yes, that's the saddest part of it all.
RANK. [*with a searching look at her*] Hm!—
NORA. [*after a short pause*] Why did you smile?
RANK. No, it was you that laughed.

NORA. No, it was you that smiled, Doctor Rank!

RANK. [*rising*] You are a greater rascal than I thought.

NORA. I am in a silly mood to-day.

RANK. So it seems.

NORA. [*putting her hands on his shoulders*] Dear, dear Doctor Rank, death mustn't take you away from Torvald and me.

RANK. It is a loss you would easily recover from. Those who are gone are soon forgotten.

NORA. [*looking at him anxiously*] Do you believe that?

RANK. People form new ties, and then—

NORA. Who will form new ties?

RANK. Both you and Helmer, when I am gone. You yourself are already on the high road to it, I think. What did that Mrs. Linde want here last night?

NORA. Oho!—you don't mean to say you are jealous of poor Christine?

RANK. Yes, I am. She will be my successor in this house. When I am done for, this woman will—

NORA. Hush! don't speak so loud. She is in that room.

RANK. To-day again. There, you see.

NORA. She has only come to sew my dress for me. Bless my soul, how unreasonable you are! [*sits down on the sofa*] Be nice now, Doctor Rank, and tomorrow you will see how beautifully I shall dance, and you can imagine I am doing it all for you—and for Torvald too, of course. [*takes various things out of the box*] Doctor Rank, come and sit down here, and I will show you something.

RANK. [*sitting down*] What is it?

NORA. Just look at those!

RANK. Silk stockings.

NORA. Flesh-coloured. Aren't they lovely? It is so dark here now, but tomorrow—. No, no, no! you must only look at the feet. Oh well, you may have leave to look at the legs too.

RANK. Hm!—

NORA. Why are you looking so critical? Don't you think they will fit me?

RANK. I have no means of forming an opinion about that.

NORA. [*looks at him for a moment*] For shame! [*hits him lightly on the ear with the stockings*] That's to punish you. [*folds them up again*]

RANK. And what other nice things am I to be allowed to see?

NORA. Not a single thing more, for being so naughty. [*She looks among the things, humming to herself.*]

RANK. [*after a short silence*] When I am sitting here, talking to you as intimately as this, I cannot imagine for a moment what would have become of me if I had never come into this house.

NORA. [*smiling*] I believe you do feel thoroughly at home with us.

RANK. [*in a lower voice, looking straight in front of him*] And to be obliged to leave it all—

NORA. Nonsense, you are not going to leave it.

RANK. [*as before*] And not be able to leave behind one the slightest token of one's gratitude, scarcely even a fleeting regret—nothing but an empty place which the first comer can fill as well as any other.

NORA. And if I asked you now for a—? No!

RANK. For what?

Nora. For a big proof of your friendship—

Rank. Yes, yes!

Nora. I mean a tremendously big favour—

Rank. Would you really make me so happy for once?

Nora. Ah, but you don't know what it is yet.

Rank. No—but tell me.

Nora. I really can't, Doctor Rank. It is something out of all reason; it means advice, and help, and a favour—

Rank. The bigger a thing is, the better. I can't conceive what it is you mean. Do tell me. Haven't I your confidence?

Nora. More than anyone else. I know you are my truest and best friend, and so I will tell you what it is. Well, Doctor Rank, it is something you must help me to prevent. You know how devotedly, how inexpressibly deeply Torvald loves me; he would never for a moment hesitate to give his life for me.

Rank. [*leaning towards her*] Nora—do you think he is the only one—?

Nora. [*with a slight start*] The only one—?

Rank. The only one who would gladly give his life for your sake.

Nora. [*sadly*] Is that it?

Rank. I was determined you should know it before I went away, and there will never be a better opportunity than this. Now you know it, Nora. And now you know, too, that you can trust me as you would trust no one else.

Nora. [*rises, deliberately and quietly*] Let me pass.

Rank. [*makes room for her to pass him, but sits still*] Nora!

Nora. [*at the hall door*] Helen, bring in the lamp. [*goes over to the stove*] Dear Doctor Rank, that was really horrid of you.

Rank. To have loved you as much as anyone else does? Was that horrid?

Nora. No, but to go and tell me so. There was really no need—

Rank. What do you mean? Did you know—? [Maid *enters with lamp, puts it down on the table, and goes out.*] Nora—Mrs. Helmer—tell me, had you any idea of this?

Nora. Oh, how do I know whether I had or whether I hadn't? I really can't tell you—To think you could be so clumsy, Doctor Rank! We were getting on so nicely.

Rank. Well, at all events you know now that you can command me, body and soul. So won't you speak out?

Nora. [*looking at him*] After what happened?

Rank. I beg you to let me know what it is.

Nora. I can't tell you anything now.

Rank. Yes, yes. You mustn't punish me in that way. Let me have permission to do for you whatever a man may do.

Nora. You can do nothing for me now. Besides, I really don't need any help at all. You will find that the whole thing is merely fancy on my part. It really is so—of course it is! [*Sits down in the rocking-chair, and looks at him with a smile.*] You are a nice sort of man, Doctor Rank!—don't you feel ashamed of yourself, now the lamp has come?

Rank. Not a bit. But perhaps I had better go—for ever?

Nora. No, indeed, you shall not. Of course you must come here just as before. You know very well Torvald can't do without you.

Rank. Yes, but you?

NORA. Oh, I am always tremendously pleased when you come.

RANK. It is just that, that put me on the wrong track. You are a riddle to me. I have often thought that you would almost as soon be in my company as in Helmer's.

NORA. Yes—you see there are some people one loves best, and others whom one would almost rather have as companions.

RANK. Yes, there is something in that.

NORA. When I was at home, of course I loved papa best. But I always thought it tremendous fun if I could steal down into the maid's room, because they never moralised at all, and talked to each other about such entertaining things.

RANK. I see—it is *their* place I have taken.

NORA. [*jumping up and going to him*] Oh, dear, nice Doctor Rank, I never meant that at all. But surely you can understand that being with Torvald is a little like being with papa—

[*Enter* MAID *from the hall.*]

MAID. If you please, ma'am. [*whispers and hands her a card*]

NORA. [*glancing at the card*] Oh! [*puts it in her pocket*]

RANK. Is there anything wrong?

NORA. No, no, not in the least. It is only something—it is my new dress—

RANK. What? Your dress is lying there.

NORA. Oh, yes, that one; but this is another. I ordered it. Torvald mustn't know about it—

RANK. Oho! Then that was the great secret.

NORA. Of course. Just go in to him; he is sitting in the inner room. Keep him as long as—

RANK. Make your mind easy; I won't let him escape. [*goes into* HELMER*'s room.*]

NORA. [*to the* MAID] And he is standing waiting in the kitchen?

MAID. Yes; he came up the back stairs.

NORA. But didn't you tell him no one was in?

MAID. Yes, but it was no good.

NORA. He won't go away?

MAID. No; he says he won't until he has seen you, ma'am.

NORA. Well, let him come in—but quietly. Helen, you mustn't say anything about it to anyone. It is a surprise for my husband.

MAID. Yes, ma'am, I quite understand.

NORA. This dreadful thing is going to happen! It will happen in spite of me! No, no, no, it can't happen—it shan't happen!

[*She bolts the door of* HELMER*'s room. The* MAID *opens the hall door for* KROGSTAD *and shuts it after him. He is wearing a fur coat, high boots and a fur cap.*]

NORA. [*advancing towards him*] Speak low—my husband is at home.

KROGSTAD. No matter about that.

NORA. What do you want of me?

KROGSTAD. An explanation of something.

NORA. Make haste then. What is it?

KROGSTAD. You know, I suppose, that I have got my dismissal.

NORA. I couldn't prevent it, Mr. Krogstad. I fought as hard as I could on your side, but it was no good.

KROGSTAD. Does your husband love you so little, then? He knows that what I can expose you to, and yet he ventures—

NORA. How can you suppose that he has any knowledge of the sort?

KROGSTAD. I didn't suppose so at all. It would not be the least like our dear Torvald Helmer to show so much courage—

NORA. Mr. Krogstad, a little respect for my husband, please.

KROGSTAD. Certainly—all the respect he deserves. But since you have kept the matter so carefully to yourself, I make bold to suppose that you have a little clearer idea, than you had yesterday, of what it actually is that you have done?

NORA. More than you could ever teach me.

KROGSTAD. Yes, such a bad lawyer as I am.

NORA. What is it you want of me?

KROGSTAD. Only to see how you were, Mrs. Helmer. I have been thinking about you all day long. A mere cashier, a quill-driver, a—well, a man like me—even he has a little of what is called feeling, you know.

NORA. Show it, then; think of my little children.

KROGSTAD. Have you and your husband thought of mine? But never mind about that. I only wanted to tell you that you need not take this matter too seriously. In the first place there will be no accusation made on my part.

NORA. No, of course not; I was sure of that.

KROGSTAD. The whole thing can be arranged amicably; there is no reason why anyone should know anything about it. It will remain a secret between us three.

NORA. My husband must never get to know anything about it.

KROGSTAD. How will you be able to prevent it? Am I to understand that you can pay the balance that is owing?

NORA. No, not just at present.

KROGSTAD. Or perhaps that you have some expedient for raising the money soon?

NORA. No expedient that I mean to make use of.

KROGSTAD. Well, in any case, it would have been of no use to you now. If you stood there with ever so much money in your hand, I would never part with your bond.

NORA. Tell me what purpose you mean to put it to.

KROGSTAD. I shall only preserve it—keep it in my possession. No one who is not concerned in the matter shall have the slightest hint of it. So that if the thought of it has driven you to any desperate resolution—

NORA. It has.

KROGSTAD. If you had it in your mind to run away from your home—

NORA. I had.

KROGSTAD. Or even something worse—

NORA. How could you know that?

KROGSTAD. Give up the idea.

NORA. How did you know I had thought of *that*?

KROGSTAD. Most of us think of that at first. I did, too—but I hadn't the courage.

NORA. [*faintly*] No more had I.

KROGSTAD. [*in a tone of relief*] No, that's it, isn't it—you hadn't the courage either?

NORA. No, I haven't—I haven't.

KROGSTAD. Besides, it would have been a great piece of folly. Once the first storm at home is over—. I have a letter for your husband in my pocket.

NORA. Telling him everything?

KROGSTAD. In as lenient a manner as I possibly could.

NORA. [*quickly*] He mustn't get the letter. Tear it up. I will find some means of getting money.

KROGSTAD. Excuse me, Mrs. Helmer, but I think I told you just now—

NORA. I am not speaking of what I owe you. Tell me what sum you are asking my husband for, and I will get the money.

KROGSTAD. I am not asking your husband for a penny.

NORA. What do you want, then?

KROGSTAD. I will tell you. I want to rehabilitate myself, Mrs. Helmer; I want to get on; and in that your husband must help me. For the last year and a half I have not had a hand in anything dishonourable, and all that time I have been struggling in most restricted circumstances. I was content to work my way up step by step. Now I am turned out, and I am not going to be satisfied with merely being taken into favour again. I want to get on, I tell you. I want to get into the Bank again, in a higher position. Your husband must make a place for me—

NORA. That he will never do!

KROGSTAD. He will; I know him; he dare not protest. And as soon as I am in there again with him, then you will see! Within a year I shall be the manager's right hand. It will be Nils Krogstad and not Torvald Helmer who manages the Bank.

NORA. That's a thing you will never see!

KROGSTAD. Do you mean that you will—?

NORA. I have courage enough for it now.

KROGSTAD. Oh, you can't frighten me. A fine, spoilt lady like you—

NORA. You will see, you will see.

KROGSTAD. Under the ice, perhaps? Down into the cold, coal-black water? And then, in the spring, to float up to the surface, all horrible and unrecognisable, with your hair fallen out—

NORA. You can't frighten me.

KROGSTAD. Nor you me. People don't do such things, Mrs. Helmer. Besides, what use would it be? I should have him completely in my power all the same.

NORA. Afterwards? When I am no longer—

KROGSTAD. Have you forgotten that it is I who have the keeping of your reputation? [NORA *stands speechlessly looking at him.*] Well, now, I have warned you. Do not do anything foolish. When Helmer has had my letter, I shall expect a message from him. And be sure you remember that it is your husband himself who has forced me into such ways as this again. I will never forgive him for that. Good-bye, Mrs. Helmer.

[*Exit through the hall.*]

NORA. [*goes to the hall door, opens it slightly and listens*] He is going. He is not putting the letter in the box. Oh no, no! that's impossible! [*opens the door by degrees*] What is that? He is standing outside. He is not going downstairs. Is he hesitating? Can he—

[*A letter drops into the box; then* KROGSTAD*'s footsteps are heard, till they die away as he goes downstairs.* NORA *utters a stifled cry and runs across the room to the table by the sofa. A short pause.*]

NORA. In the letter-box. [*steals across to the hall door*] There it lies—Torvald, Torvald, there is no hope for us now!

[MRS. LINDE *comes in from the room on the left, carrying the dress.*]

MRS. LINDE. There, I can't see anything more to mend now. Would you like to try it on—?

NORA. [*in a hoarse whisper*] Christine, come here.

MRS. LINDE. [*throwing the dress down on the sofa*] What is the matter with you? You look so agitated!

NORA. Come here. Do you see that letter? There, look—you can see it through the glass in the letter-box.

MRS. LINDE. Yes, I see it.

NORA. That letter is from Krogstad.

MRS. LINDE. Nora—it was Krogstad who lent you the money!

NORA. Yes, and now Torvald will know all about it.

MRS. LINDE. Believe me, Nora, that's the best thing for both of you.

NORA. You don't know all. I forged a name.

MRS. LINDE. Good heavens—!

NORA. I only want to say this to you, Christine—you must be my witness.

MRS. LINDE. Your witness? What do you mean? What am I to—?

NORA. If I should go out of my mind—and it might easily happen—

MRS. LINDE. Nora!

NORA. Or if anything else should happen to me—anything, for instance, that might prevent my being here—

MRS. LINDE. Nora! Nora! you are quite out of your mind.

NORA. And if it should happen that there were someone who wanted to take all the responsibility, all the blame, you understand—

MRS. LINDE. Yes, yes—but how can you suppose—?

NORA. Then you must be my witness, that it is not true, Christine. I am not out of my mind at all; I am in my right senses now, and I tell you no one else has known anything about it; I, and I alone, did the whole thing. Remember that.

MRS. LINDE. I will, indeed. But I don't understand all this.

NORA. How should you understand it? A wonderful thing is going to happen.

MRS. LINDE. A wonderful thing?

NORA. Yes a wonderful thing!—But it is so terrible, Christine; it *mustn't* happen, not for all the world.

MRS. LINDE. I will go at once and see Krogstad.

NORA. Don't go to him; he will do you some harm.

MRS. LINDE. There was a time when he would gladly do anything for my sake.

NORA. He?

MRS. LINDE. Where does he live?

NORA. How should I know—? Yes [*feeling in her pocket*] here is his card. But the letter, the letter—!

HELMER. [*calls from his room, knocking at the door*] Nora!

NORA. [*cries out anxiously*] Oh, what's that? What do you want?

HELMER. Don't be so frightened. We are not coming in; you have locked the door. Are you trying on your dress?

NORA. Yes, that's it. I look so nice, Torvald.

MRS. LINDE. [*who has read the card*] I see he lives at the corner here.

NORA. Yes but it's no use. It is hopeless. The letter is lying there in the box.

MRS. LINDE. And your husband keeps the key?

NORA. Yes, always.

MRS. LINDE. Krogstad must ask for his letter back unread, he must find some pretence—

NORA. But it is just at this time that Torvald generally—

MRS. LINDE. You must delay him. Go in to him in the meantime. I will come back as soon as I can.

[*She goes out hurriedly through the hall door.*]

NORA. [*goes to* HELMER*'s door, opens it and peeps in*] Torvald!

HELMER. [*from the inner room*] Well? May I venture at last to come into my own room again? Come along, Rank, now you will see—[*halting in the doorway*] But what is this?

NORA. What is what, dear?

HELMER. Rank led me to expect a splendid transformation.

RANK. [*in the doorway*] I understood so, but evidently I was mistaken.

NORA. Yes, nobody is to have the chance of admiring me in my dress until tomorrow.

HELMER. But, my dear Nora, you look so worn out. Have you been practising too much?

NORA. No, I have not practised at all.

HELMER. But you will need to—

NORA. Yes, indeed I shall, Torvald. But I can't get on a bit without you to help me; I have absolutely forgotten the whole thing.

HELMER. Oh, we will soon work it up again.

NORA. Yes, help me, Torvald. Promise that you will! I am so nervous about it—all the people—. You must give yourself up to me entirely this evening. Not the tiniest bit of business—you mustn't even take a pen in your hand. Will you promise, Torvald dear?

HELMER. I promise. This evening I will be wholly and absolutely at your service, you helpless little mortal. Ah, by the way, first of all I will just—

[*Goes towards the hall door.*]

NORA. What are you going to do there?

HELMER. Only see if any letters have come.

NORA. No, no! don't do that, Torvald!

HELMER. Why not?

NORA. Torvald, please don't. There is nothing there.

HELMER. Well, let me look. [*Turns to go to the letter-box.* NORA, *at the piano, plays the first bars of the Tarantella.* HELMER *stops in the doorway.*] Aha!

NORA. I can't dance to-morrow if I don't practise with you.

HELMER. [*going up to her*] Are you really so afraid of it, dear.

NORA. Yes, so dreadfully afraid of it. Let me practise at once; there is time now, before we go to dinner. Sit down and play for me, Torvald dear; criticise me, and correct me as you play.

HELMER. With great pleasure, if you wish me to.

[*Sits down at the piano.*]

NORA. [*takes out of the box a tambourine and a long variegated shawl. She hastily drapes the shawl round her. Then she springs to the front of the stage and calls out.*] Now play for me! I am going to dance!

[HELMER *plays and* NORA *dances.* RANK *stands by the piano behind* HELMER *and looks on.*]

HELMER. [*as he plays*] Slower, slower!

NORA. I can't do it any other way.

HELMER. Not so violently, Nora!

NORA. This is the way.

HELMER. [*stops playing*] No, no—that is not a bit right.

NORA. [*laughing and swinging the tambourine*] Didn't I tell you so?

RANK. Let me play for her.

HELMER. [*getting up*] Yes, do. I can correct her better then.

[RANK *sits down at the piano and plays.* NORA *dances more and more wildly.* HELMER *has taken up a position beside the stove, and during her dance gives her frequent instructions. She does not seem to hear him; her hair comes down and falls over her shoulders; she pays no attention to it, but goes on dancing. Enter* MRS. LINDE.]

MRS. LINDE. [*standing as if spell-bound in the doorway*] Oh!—

NORA. [*as she dances*] Such fun, Christine!

HELMER. My dear darling Nora, you are dancing as if your life depended on it.

NORA. So it does.

HELMER. Stop, Rank; this is sheer madness. Stop, I tell you! [RANK *stops playing, and* NORA *suddenly stands still.* HELMER *goes up to her.*] I could never have believed it. You have forgotten everything I taught you.

NORA. [*throwing away the tambourine*] There, you see.

HELMER. You will want a lot of coaching.

NORA. Yes, you see how much I need it. You must coach me up to the last minute. Promise me that, Torvald!

HELMER. You can depend on me.

NORA. You must not think of anything but me, either to-day or to-morrow; you mustn't open a single letter—not even open the letter-box—

HELMER. Ah, you are still afraid of that fellow—

NORA. Yes, indeed I am.

HELMER. Nora, I can tell from your looks that there is a letter from him lying there.

NORA. I don't know; I think there is; but you must not read anything of that kind now. Nothing horrid must come between us till this is all over.

RANK. [*whispers to Helmer*] You mustn't contradict her.

HELMER. [*taking her in his arms*] The child shall have her way. But to-morrow night, after you have danced—

NORA. Then you will be free.

[*Maid appears in the doorway to the right.*]

MAID. Dinner is served, ma'am.

NORA. We will have champagne, Helen.

MAID. Very good, ma'am.

[*Exit.*]

HELMER. Hullo!—are we going to have a banquet?

NORA. Yes a champagne banquet till the small hours. [*calls out*] And a few macaroons, Helen—lots, just for once!

HELMER. Come, come, don't be so wild and nervous. Be my own little skylark, as you used.

NORA. Yes, dear, I will. But go in now and you too, Doctor Rank. Christine, you must help me to do up my hair.

RANK. [*whispers to* HELMER *as they go out*] I suppose there is nothing—she is not expecting anything?

HELMER. Far from it, my dear fellow; it is simply nothing more than this childish nervousness I was telling you of.

[*They go into the right-hand room.*]

NORA. Well!

MRS. LINDE. Gone out of town.

NORA. I could tell from your face.

MRS. LINDE. He is coming home to-morrow evening. I wrote a note for him.

NORA. You should have let it alone; you must prevent nothing. After all, it is splendid to be waiting for a wonderful thing to happen.

MRS. LINDE. What is it that you are waiting for?

NORA. Oh you wouldn't understand. Go in to them, I will come in a moment. [MRS. LINDE *goes into the dining-room.* NORA *stands still for a little while, as if to compose herself. Then she looks at her watch.*] Five o'clock. Seven hours till midnight; and then four-and-twenty hours till the next midnight. Then the Tarantella will be over. Twenty-four and seven? Thirty-one hours to live.

HELMER. [*from the doorway on the right*] Where's my little skylark?

NORA. [*going to him with her arms outstretched*] Here she is!

ACT 3

THE SAME SCENE. *The table has been placed in the middle of the stage, with chairs round it. A lamp is burning on the table. The door into the hall stands open. Dance music is heard in the room above.* MRS. LINDE *is sitting at the table idly turning over the leaves of a book; she tries to read, but does not seem able to collect her thoughts. Every now and then she listens intently for a sound at the outer door.*

MRS. LINDE. [*looking at her watch*] Not yet—and the time is nearly up. If only he does not—. [*listens again*] Ah, there he is. [*Goes into the hall and opens the outer door carefully. Light footsteps are heard on the stairs. She whispers.*] Come in. There is no one here.

KROGSTAD. [*in the doorway*] I found a note from you at home. What does this mean?

MRS. LINDE . It is absolutely necessary that I should have a talk with you.

KROGSTAD. Really? And is it absolutely necessary that it should be here?

MRS. LINDE . It is impossible where I live; there is no private entrance to my rooms. Come in; we are quite alone. The maid is asleep, and the Helmers are at the dance upstairs.

KROGSTAD. [*coming into the room*] Are the Helmers really at a dance to-night?

Mrs. Linde . Yes, why not?

Krogstad. Certainly—Why not?

Mrs. Linde . Now, Nils, let us have a talk.

Krogstad. Can we two have anything to talk about?

Mrs. Linde . We have a great deal to talk about.

Krogstad. I shouldn't have thought so.

Mrs. Linde. No, you have never properly understood me.

Krogstad. Was there anything else to understand except what was obvious to all the world—a heartless woman jilts a man when a more lucrative chance turns up?

Mrs. Linde. Do you believe I am as absolutely heartless as all that? And do you believe that I did it with a light heart?

Krogstad. Didn't you?

Mrs. Linde. Nils, did you really think that?

Krogstad. If it were as you say, why did you write to me as you did at the time?

Mrs. Linde. I could do nothing else. As I had to break with you, it was my duty also to put an end to all that you felt for me.

Krogstad. [*wringing his hands*] So that was it, and all this—only for the sake of money!

Mrs. Linde. You must not forget that I had a helpless mother and two little brothers. We couldn't wait for you, Nils; your prospects seemed hopeless then.

Krogstad. That may be so, but you had no right to throw me over for any one else's sake.

Mrs. Linde. Indeed I don't know. Many a time did I ask myself if I had the right to do it.

Krogstad. [*more gently*] When I lost you, it was as if all the solid ground went from under my feet. Look at me now—I am a shipwrecked man clinging to a bit of wreckage.

Mrs. Linde. But help may be near.

Krogstad. It *was* near; but then you came and stood in my way.

Mrs. Linde. Unintentionally, Nils. It was only to-day that I learnt it was your place I was going to take in the Bank.

Krogstad. I believe you, if you say so. But now that you know it, are you not going to give it up to me?

Mrs. Linde. No, because that would not benefit you in the least.

Krogstad. Oh, benefit, benefit—I would have done it whether or no.

Mrs. Linde. I have learnt to act prudently. Life, and hard, bitter necessity have taught me that.

Krogstad. And life has taught me not to believe in fine speeches.

Mrs. Linde. Then life has taught you something very reasonable. But deeds you must believe in.

Krogstad. What do you mean by that?

Mrs. Linde. You said you were like a shipwrecked man clinging to some wreckage.

Krogstad. I had good reason to say so.

Mrs. Linde. Well, I am like a shipwrecked woman clinging to some wreckage—no one to mourn for, no one to care for.

Krogstad. It was your own choice.

Mrs. Linde. There was no other choice—then.

KROGSTAD. Well, what now?

MRS. LINDE. Nils, how would it be if we two shipwrecked people could join forces?

KROGSTAD. What are you saying?

MRS. LINDE. Two on the same piece of wreckage would stand a better chance than each on their own.

KROGSTAD. Christine!

MRS. LINDE. What do you suppose brought me to town?

KROGSTAD. Do you mean that you gave me a thought?

MRS. LINDE. I could not endure life without work. All my life, as long as I can remember, I have worked, and it has been my greatest and only pleasure. But now I am quite alone in the world—my life is so dreadfully empty and I feel so forsaken. There is not the least pleasure in working for one's self. Nils, give me someone and something to work for.

KROGSTAD. I don't trust that. It is nothing but a woman's overstrained sense of generosity that prompts you to make such an offer of yourself.

MRS. LINDE. Have you ever noticed anything of the sort in me?

KROGSTAD. Could you really do it? Tell me—do you know all about my past life?

MRS. LINDE. Yes.

KROGSTAD. And do you know what they think of me here?

MRS. LINDE. You seemed to me to imply that with me you might have been quite another man.

KROGSTAD. I am certain of it.

MRS. LINDE. Is it too late now?

KROGSTAD. Christine, are you saying this deliberately? Yes, I am sure you are. I see it in your face. Have you really the courage, then—?

MRS. LINDE. I want to be a mother to someone, and your children need a mother. We two need each other. Nils, I have faith in your real character—I can dare anything together with you.

KROGSTAD. [*grasps her hands*] Thanks, thanks, Christine! Now I shall find a way to clear myself in the eyes of the world. Ah, but I forgot—

MRS. LINDE. [*listening*] Hush! The Tarantella! Go, go!

KROGSTAD. Why? What is it?

MRS. LINDE. Do you hear them up there? When that is over, we may expect them back.

KROGSTAD. Yes, yes—I will go. But it is all no use. Of course you are not aware what steps I have taken in the matter of the Helmers.

MRS. LINDE. Yes. I know all about that.

KROGSTAD. And in spite of that have you the courage to—?

MRS. LINDE. I understand very well to what lengths a man like you might be driven by despair.

KROGSTAD. If I could only undo what I have done!

MRS. LINDE. You can. Your letter is lying in the letter-box now.

KROGSTAD. Are you sure of that?

MRS. LINDE. Quite sure, but—

KROGSTAD. [*with a searching look at her*] Is that what it all means?—that you want to save your friend at any cost? Tell me frankly. Is that it?

MRS. LINDE. Nils, a woman who has once sold herself for another's sake, doesn't do it a second time.

KROGSTAD. I will ask for my letter back.

MRS. LINDE. No, no.

KROGSTAD. Yes, of course I will. I will wait here till Helmer comes; I will tell him he must give me my letter back—that it only concerns my dismissal—that he is not to read it—

MRS. LINDE. No, Nils, you must not recall your letter.

KROGSTAD. But, tell me, wasn't it for that very purpose that you asked me to meet you here?

MRS. LINDE. In my first moment of fright, it was. But twenty-four hours have elapsed since then, and in that time I have witnessed incredible things in this house. Helmer must know all about it. This unhappy secret must be disclosed; they must have a complete understanding between them, which is impossible with all this concealment and falsehood going on.

KROGSTAD. Very well, if you will take the responsibility. But there is one thing I can do in any case, and I shall do it at once.

MRS. LINDE. [*listening*] You must be quick and go! The dance is over; we are not safe a moment longer.

KROGSTAD. I will wait for you below.

MRS. LINDE. Yes, do. You must see me back to my door.

KROGSTAD. I have never had such an amazing piece of good fortune in my life.

[*Goes out through the outer door. The door between the room and the hall remains open.*]

MRS. LINDE. [*tidying up the room and laying her hat and cloak ready*] What a difference! what a difference! Someone to work for and live for—a home to bring comfort into. That I will do, indeed. I wish they would be quick and come—[*listens*] Ah, there they are now. I must put on my things.

[*Takes up her hat and cloak.* HELMER*'s and* NORA*'s voices are heard outside; a key is turned, and* HELMER *brings* NORA *almost by force into the hall. She is in an Italian costume with a large black shawl round her; he is in evening dress and a black domino which is flying open.*]

NORA. [*hanging back in the doorway, and struggling with him*] No, no, no!—don't take me in. I want to go upstairs again; I don't want to leave so early.

HELMER. But, my dearest Nora—

NORA. Please, Torvald dear—please, *please*—only an hour more.

HELMER. Not a single minute, my sweet Nora. You know that was our agreement. Come along into the room; you are catching cold standing there.

[*He brings her gently into the room, in spite of her resistance.*]

MRS. LINDE. Good evening.

NORA. Christine!

HELMER. You here, so late, Mrs. Linde?

MRS. LINDE. Yes, you must excuse me; I was so anxious to see Nora in her dress.

NORA. Have you been sitting here waiting for me?

MRS. LINDE. Yes, unfortunately I came too late, you had already gone upstairs; and I thought I couldn't go away without having seen you.

HELMER. [*taking off Nora's shawl*] Yes, take a good look at her. I think she is worth looking at. Isn't she charming, Mrs. Linde?

MRS. LINDE. Yes, indeed she is.

HELMER. Doesn't she look remarkably pretty? Everyone thought so at the dance. But she is terribly self-willed, this sweet little person. What are we to do with her? You will hardly believe that I had almost to bring her away by force.

NORA. Torvald, you will repent not having let me stay, even if it were only for half an hour.

HELMER. Listen to her, Mrs. Linde! She had danced her Tarantella, and it had been a tremendous success, as it deserved—although possibly the performance was a trifle too realistic—a little more so, I mean, than was strictly compatible with the limitations of art. But never mind about that! The chief thing is, she had made a success—she had made a tremendous success. Do you think I was going to let her remain there after that, and spoil the effect? No indeed! I took my charming little Capri maiden—my capricious little Capri maiden, I should say—on my arm; took one quick turn round the room; a curtsey on either side, and, as they say in novels, the beautiful apparition disappeared. An exit ought always to be effective, Mrs. Linde; but that is what I cannot make Nora understand. Pooh! this room is hot. [*throws his domino on a chair and opens the door of his room*] Hullo! it's all dark in here. Oh, of course—excuse me—.

[*He goes in and lights some candles.*]

NORA. [*in a hurried and breathless whisper*] Well?

MRS. LINDE. [*in a low voice*] I have had a talk with him.

NORA. Yes, and—

MRS. LINDE. Nora, you must tell your husband all about it.

NORA. [*in an expressionless voice*] I knew it.

MRS. LINDE. You have nothing to be afraid of as far as Krogstad is concerned; but you must tell him.

NORA. I won't tell him.

MRS. LINDE. Then the letter will.

NORA. Thank you, Christine. Now I know what I must do. Hush—!

HELMER. [*coming in again*] Well, Mrs. Linde, have you admired her?

MRS. LINDE. Yes, and now I will say good-night.

HELMER. What already? Is this yours, this knitting?

MRS. LINDE. [*taking it*] Yes, thank you, I had very nearly forgotten it.

HELMER. So you knit?

MRS. LINDE. Of course.

HELMER. Do you know, you ought to embroider.

MRS. LINDE. Really? Why?

HELMER. Yes, it's far more becoming. Let me show you. You hold the embroidery thus in your left hand, and use the needle with the right—like this—with a long, easy sweep. Do you see?

MRS. LINDE. Yes, perhaps—

HELMER. But in the case of knitting—that can never be anything but ungraceful; look here—the arms close together, the knitting-needles going up and down—it has a sort of Chinese effect—. That was really excellent champagne they gave us.

MRS. LINDE. Well,—good-night, Nora, and don't be self-willed any more.

HELMER. That's right, Mrs. Linde.

MRS. LINDE. Good-night, Mr. Helmer.

HELMER. [*accompanying her to the door*] Good-night, good-night. I hope you will get home all right. I should be very happy to—but you haven't any great distance to go. Good-night, good-night. [*She goes out; he shuts the door after her, and comes in again.*] Ah!—at last we have got rid of her. She is a frightful bore, that woman.

NORA. Aren't you very tired, Torvald?

HELMER. No, not in the least.

NORA. Nor sleepy?

HELMER. Not a bit. On the contrary, I feel extraordinarily lively. And you?—you really look both tired and sleepy.

NORA. Yes, I am very tired. I want to go to sleep at once.

HELMER. There, you see it was quite right of me not to let you stay there any longer.

NORA. Everything you do is quite right, Torvald.

HELMER. [*kissing her on the forehead*] Now my little skylark is speaking reasonably. Did you notice what good spirits Rank was in this evening?

NORA. Really? Was he? I didn't speak to him at all.

HELMER. And I very little, but I have not for a long time seen him in such good form. [*looks for a while at her and then goes nearer to her*] It is delightful to be at home by ourselves again, to be all alone with you—you fascinating, charming little darling!

NORA. Don't look at me like that, Torvald.

HELMER. Why shouldn't I look at my dearest treasure?—at all the beauty that is mine, all my very own?

NORA. [*going to the other side of the table*] You mustn't say things like that to me tonight.

HELMER. [*following her*] You have still got the Tarantella in your blood, I see. And it makes you more captivating than ever. Listen—the guests are beginning to go now. [*in a lower voice*] Nora—soon the whole house will be quiet.

NORA. Yes, I hope so.

HELMER. Yes, my own darling Nora. Do you know, when I am out at a party with you like this, why I speak so little to you, keep away from you, and only send a stolen glance in your direction now and then?—do you know why I do that? It is because I make believe to myself that we are secretly in love, and you are my secretly promised bride, and that no one suspects there is anything between us.

NORA. Yes, yes—I know very well your thoughts are with me all the time.

HELMER. And when we are leaving, and I am putting the shawl over your beautiful young shoulders—on your lovely neck—then I imagine that you are my young bride and that we have just come from the wedding, and I am bringing you for the first time into our home—to be alone with you for the first time—quite alone with my shy little darling! All this evening I have longed for nothing but you. When I watched the seductive figures of the Tarantella, my blood was on fire; I could endure it no longer, and that was why I brought you down so early—

NORA. Go away, Torvald! You must let me go. I won't—

HELMER. What's that? You're joking, my little, Nora! You won't? Am I not your husband—?

[*A knock is heard at the outer door.*]

NORA. [*starting*] Did you hear—?

HELMER. [*going into the hall*] Who is it?
RANK. [*outside*] It is I. May I come in for a moment?
HELMER. [*in a fretful whisper*] Oh, what does he want now? [*aloud*] Wait a minute! [*unlocks the door*] Come, that's kind of you not to pass by our door.
RANK. I thought I heard your voice, and felt as if I should like to look in. [*with a swift glance round*] Ah, yes!—these dear familiar rooms. You are very happy and cosy in here, you two.
HELMER. It seems to me that you looked after yourself pretty well upstairs too.
RANK. Excellently. Why shouldn't I? Why shouldn't one enjoy everything in this world?—at any rate as much as one can, and as long as one can. The wine was capital—
HELMER. Especially the champagne.
RANK. So you noticed that too? It is almost incredible how much I managed to put away!
NORA. Torvald drank a great deal of champagne tonight, too.
RANK. Did he?
NORA. Yes, and he is always in such good spirits afterwards.
RANK. Well, why should one not enjoy a merry evening after a well-spent day?
HELMER. Well spent? I am afraid I can't take credit for that.
RANK. [*clapping him on the back*] But I can, you know!
NORA. Doctor Rank, you must have been occupied with some scientific investigation to-day.
RANK. Exactly.
HELMER. Just listen!—little Nora talking about scientific investigations!
NORA. And may I congratulate you on the result?
RANK. Indeed you may.
NORA. Was it favourable, then?
RANK. The best possible, for both doctor and patient—certainty.
NORA. [*quickly and searchingly*] Certainty?
RANK. Absolute certainty. So wasn't I entitled to make a merry evening of it after that?
NORA. Yes, you certainly were, Doctor Rank.
HELMER. I think so too, so long as you don't have to pay for it in the morning.
RANK. Oh well, one can't have anything in this life without paying for it.
NORA. Doctor Rank—are you fond of fancy-dress balls?
RANK. Yes, if there is a fine lot of pretty costumes.
NORA. Tell me—what shall we two wear at the next?
HELMER. Little featherbrain!—are you thinking of the next already?
RANK. We two? Yes, I can tell you. You shall go as a good fairy—
HELMER. Yes, but what do you suggest as an appropriate costume for that?
RANK. Let your wife go dressed just as she is in everyday life.
HELMER. That was really very prettily turned. But can't you tell us what you will be?
RANK. Yes, my dear friend, I have quite made up my mind about that.
HELMER. Well?
RANK. At the next fancy dress ball I shall be invisible.
HELMER. That's a good joke!
RANK. There is a big black hat—have you never heard of hats that make you invisible? If you put one on, no one can see you.
HELMER. [*suppressing a smile*] Yes, you are quite right.

Rank. But I am clean forgetting what I came for. Helmer, give me a cigar—one of the dark Havanas.

Helmer. With the greatest pleasure. [*offers him his case*]

Rank. [*takes a cigar and cuts off the end*] Thanks.

Nora. [*striking a match*] Let me give you a light.

Rank. Thank you. [*she holds the match for him to light his cigar.*] And now good-bye!

Helmer. Good-bye, good-bye, dear old man!

Nora. Sleep well, Doctor Rank.

Rank. Thank you for that wish.

Nora. Wish me the same.

Rank. You? Well, if you want me to sleep well! And thanks for the light.

[*He nods to them both and goes out.*]

Helmer. [*in a subdued voice*] He has drunk more than he ought.

Nora. [*absently*] Maybe. [Helmer *takes a bunch of keys out of his pocket and goes into the hall.*] Torvald! what are you going to do there?

Helmer. Empty the letter-box; it is quite full; there will be no room to put the newspaper in to-morrow morning.

Nora. Are you going to work to-night?

Helmer. You know quite well I'm not. What is this? Some one has been at the lock.

Nora. At the lock—

Helmer. Yes, someone has. What can it mean? I should never have thought the maid—. Here is a broken hairpin. Nora, it is one of yours.

Nora. [*quickly*] Then it must have been the children—

Helmer. Then you must get them out of those ways. There, at last I have got it open. [*Takes out the contents of the letter-box, and calls to the kitchen.*] Helen!—Helen, put out the light over the front door. [*Goes back into the room and shuts the door into the hall. He holds out his hand full of letters.*] Look at that—look what a heap of them there are. [*turning them over*] What on earth is that?

Nora. [*at the window*] The letter—No! Torvald, no!

Helmer. Two cards—of Rank's.

Nora. Of Doctor Rank's?

Helmer. [*looking at them*] Doctor Rank. They were on the top. He must have put them in when he went out.

Nora. Is there anything written on them?

Helmer. There is a black cross over the name. Look there—what an uncomfortable idea! It looks as if he were announcing his own death.

Nora. It is just what he is doing.

Helmer. What? Do you know anything about it? Has he said anything to you?

Nora. Yes. He told me that when the cards came it would be his leave-taking from us. He means to shut himself up and die.

Helmer. My poor old friend. Certainly I knew we should not have him very long with us. But so soon! And so he hides himself away like a wounded animal.

Nora. If it has to happen, it is best it should be without a word—don't you think so, Torvald?

Helmer. [*walking up and down*] He had so grown into our lives. I can't think of him as having gone out of them. He, with his sufferings and his loneliness, was like a cloudy background to our sunlit happiness. Well, perhaps it is best so. For him, anyway. [*standing still*] And perhaps for us too, Nora. We two are thrown quite upon each other now. [*puts his arms round her*] My darling wife, I don't feel as if I could hold you tight enough. Do you know, Nora, I have often wished that you might be threatened by some great danger, so that I might risk my life's blood, and everything, for your sake.

NORA. [*disengages herself, and says firmly and decidedly*] Now you must read your letters Torvald.

HELMER. No, no; not to-night. I want to be with you, my darling wife.

NORA. With the thought of your friend's death—

HELMER. You are right, it has affected us both. Something ugly has come between us—the thought of the horrors of death. We must try and rid our minds of that. Until then—we will each go to our own room.

NORA. [*hanging on his neck*] Good-night, Torvald—Good-night!

HELMER. [*kissing her on the forehead.*] Good-night, my little singing-bird. Sleep sound, Nora. Now I will read my letters through.

[*He takes his letters and goes into his room, shutting the door after him.*]

NORA. [*gropes distractedly about, seizes* HELMER*'s domino, throws it round her, while she says in quick, hoarse, spasmodic whispers*] Never to see him again. Never! Never! [*puts her shawl over her head*] Never to see my children again either—never again. Never! Never!—Ah! the icy, black water—the unfathomable depths—If only it were over! He has got it now—now he is reading it. Good-bye, Torvald and my children!

[*She is about to rush out through the hall, when* HELMER *opens his door hurriedly and stands with an open letter in his hand.*]

HELMER. Nora!

NORA. Ah!—

HELMER. What is this? Do you know what is in this letter?

NORA. Yes, I know. Let me go! Let me get out!

HELMER. [*holding her back*] Where are you going?

NORA. [*trying to get free*] You shan't save me, Torvald!

HELMER. [*reeling*] True? Is this true, that I read here? Horrible! No, no—it is impossible that it can be true.

NORA. It is true. I have loved you above everything else in the world.

HELMER. Oh, don't let us have any silly excuses.

NORA. [*taking a step towards him*] Torvald—!

HELMER. Miserable creature—what have you done?

NORA. Let me go. You shall not suffer for my sake. You shall not take it upon yourself.

HELMER. No tragedy airs, please. [*locks the hall door*] Here you shall stay and give me an explanation. Do you understand what you have done? Answer me? Do you understand what you have done?

NORA. [*looks steadily at him and says with a growing look of coldness in her face*] Yes, now I am beginning to understand thoroughly.

HELMER. [*walking about the room*] What a horrible awakening! All these eight years—she who was my joy and pride—a hypocrite, a liar—worse, worse—a criminal! The unutterable ugliness of it all! For shame! For shame! [NORA *is silent and looks steadily at him. He stops in front of her.*] I ought to have suspected that something of the sort would happen. I ought to have foreseen it. All your father's want of principle—be silent!—all your father's want of principle has come out in you. No religion, no morality, no sense of duty—. How I am punished for having winked at what he did! I did it for your sake, and this is how you repay me.

NORA. Yes, that's just it.

HELMER. Now you have destroyed all my happiness. You have ruined all my future. It is horrible to think of! I am in the power of an unscrupulous man; he can do what he likes with me, ask anything he likes of me, give me any orders he pleases—I dare not refuse. And I must sink to such miserable depths because of a thoughtless woman!

NORA. When I am out of the way, you will be free.

HELMER. No fine speeches, please. Your father had always plenty of those ready, too. What good would it be to me if you were out of the way, as you say? Not the slightest. He can make the affair known everywhere; and if he does, I may be falsely suspected of having been a party to your criminal action. Very likely people will think I was behind it all—that it was I who prompted you! And I have to thank you for all this—you whom I have cherished during the whole of our married life. Do you understand now what it is you have done for me?

NORA. [*coldly and quietly*] Yes.

HELMER. It is so incredible that I can't take it in. But we must come to some understanding. Take off that shawl. Take it off, I tell you. I must try and appease him some way or another. The matter must be hushed up at any cost. And as for you and me, it must appear as if everything between us were just as before—but naturally only in the eyes of the world. You will still remain in my house, that is a matter of course. But I shall not allow you to bring up the children; I dare not trust them to you. To think that I should be obliged to say so to one whom I have loved so dearly, and whom I still—. No, that is all over. From this moment happiness is not the question; all that concerns us is to save the remains, the fragments, the appearance—

[*A ring is heard at the front-door bell.*]

HELMER. [*with a start*] What is that? So late! Can the worst—? Can he—? Hide yourself, Nora. Say you are ill.

[NORA *stands motionless.* HELMER *goes and unlocks the hall door.*]

MAID. [*half-dressed, comes to the door*] A letter for the mistress.

HELMER. Give it to me. [*takes the letter, and shuts the door*] Yes, it is from him. You shall not have it; I will read it myself.

NORA. Yes, read it.

HELMER. [*standing by the lamp*] I scarcely have the courage to do it. It may mean ruin for both of us. No, I must know. [*tears open the letter, runs his eye over a few lines, looks at a paper enclosed and gives a shout of joy*] Nora! [*she looks at him questioningly.*] Nora!—No, I must read it once again—. Yes, it is true! I am saved! Nora, I am saved!

NORA. And I?

HELMER. You too, of course; we are both saved, both you and I. Look, he sends you your bond back. He says he regrets and repents—that a happy change in his life—never mind what he says! We are saved, Nora! No one can do anything to you. Oh, Nora, Nora!—no, first I must destroy these hateful things. Let me see—[*takes a look at the bond*] No, no, I won't look at it. The whole thing shall be nothing but a bad dream to me. [*tears up the bond and both letters, throws them all into the stove, and watches them burn*] There—now it doesn't exist any longer. He says that since Christmas Eve you—. These must have been three dreadful days for you, Nora.

NORA. I have fought a hard fight these three days.

HELMER. And suffered agonies, and seen no way out but—. No, we won't call any of the horrors to mind. We will only shout with joy, and keep saying "It's all over! It's all over!" Listen to me, Nora. You don't seem to realise that it is all over. What is this?—such a cold, set face! My poor little Nora, I quite understand; you don't feel as if you could believe that I have forgiven you. But it is true, Nora, I swear it; I have forgiven you everything. I know that what you did, you did out of love for me.

NORA. That is true.

HELMER. You have loved me as a wife ought to love her husband. Only you had not sufficient knowledge to judge of the means you used. But do you suppose you are any the less dear to me, because you don't understand how to act on your own responsibility? No, no; only lean on me; I will advise you and direct you. I should not be a man if this womanly helplessness did not just give you a double attractiveness in my eyes. You must not think any more about the hard things I said in my first moment of consternation, when I thought everything was going to overwhelm me. I have forgiven you, Nora; I swear to you I have forgiven you.

NORA. Thank you for your forgiveness.

[*She goes out through the door to the right.*]

HELMER. No, don't go—. [*looks in*] What are you doing in there?

NORA. [*from within*] Taking off my fancy dress.

HELMER. [*standing at the open door*] Yes, do. Try and calm yourself, and make your mind easy again, my frightened little singing-bird. Be at rest, and feel secure; I have broad wings to shelter you under. [*walks up and down by the door*] How warm and cosy our home is, Nora. Here is shelter for you; here I will protect you like a hunted dove that I have saved from a hawk's claws. I will bring peace to your poor beating heart. It will come, little by little, Nora, believe me. Tomorrow morning you will look upon it all quite differently; soon everything will be just as it was before. Very soon you won't need me to assure you that I have forgiven you; you will yourself feel the certainty that I have done so. Can you suppose I should ever think of such a thing as repudiating you, or even reproaching you? You have no idea what a true man's heart is like, Nora. There is something so indescribably sweet and satisfying, to a man, in the knowledge that he has forgiven his wife—forgiven her freely, and with all his heart. It seems as if that had made her, as it were, doubly his own; he has given her a new life, so to speak; and she has in a way become both wife and child to him. So you shall be for me after this, my little scared, helpless darling. Have no anxiety about anything, Nora; only be frank and open with me, and I will serve as will and conscience both to you—. What is this? Not gone to bed? Have you changed your things?

NORA. [*in everyday dress*] Yes, Torvald, I have changed my things now.

HELMER. But what for?—so late as this.

NORA. I shall not sleep to-night.

HELMER. But, my dear Nora—

NORA. [*looking at her watch*] It is not so very late. Sit down here, Torvald. You and I have much to say to one another.

[*She sits down at one side of the table*.]

HELMER. Nora—what is this?—this cold, set face?

NORA. Sit down, it will take some time; I have a lot to talk over with you.

HELMER. [*sits down at the opposite side of the table*] You alarm me, Nora!—and I don't understand you.

NORA. No, that is just it. You don't understand me, and I have never understood you either—before to-night. No, you mustn't interrupt me. You must simply listen to what I say. Torvald, this is a settling of accounts.

HELMER. What do you mean by that?

NORA. [*after a short silence*] Isn't there one thing that strikes you as strange in our sitting here like this?

HELMER. What is that?

NORA. We have been married now eight years. Does it not occur to you that this is the first time we two, you and I, husband and wife, have had a serious conversation?

HELMER. What do you mean by serious?

NORA. In all these eight years—longer than that—from the very beginning of our acquaintance, we have never exchanged a word on any serious subject.

HELMER. Was it likely that I would be continually and forever telling you about worries that you could not help me to bear?

NORA. I am not speaking about business matters. I say that we have never sat down in earnest together to try and get at the bottom of anything.

HELMER. But, dearest Nora, would it have been any good to you?

NORA. That is just it; you have never understood me. I have been greatly wronged, Torvald—first by papa and then by you.

HELMER. What! By us two—by us two, who have loved you better than anyone else in the world?

NORA. [*shaking her head*] You have never loved me. You have only thought it pleasant to be in love with me.

HELMER. Nora, what do I hear you saying?

NORA. It is perfectly true, Torvald. When I was at home with papa, he told me his opinion about everything, and so I had the same opinions; and if I differed from him I concealed the fact, because he would not have liked it. He called me his doll-child, and he played with me just as I used to play with my dolls. And when I came to live with you—

HELMER. What sort of an expression is that to use about our marriage?

NORA. [*undisturbed*] I mean that I was simply transferred from papa's hands into yours. You arranged everything according to your own taste, and so I got the same tastes as you—or else I pretended to, I am really not quite sure which—I think sometimes the one and sometimes the other. When I look back on it, it seems to me as if I had been living here like a poor woman—just from hand to mouth. I have existed merely to perform tricks for you, Torvald. But you would have it so. You and papa have committed a great sin against me. It is your fault that I have made nothing of my life.

HELMER. How unreasonable and how ungrateful you are, Nora! Have you not been happy here?

NORA. No, I have never been happy. I thought I was, but it has never really been so.

HELMER. Not—not happy!

NORA. No, only merry. And you have always been so kind to me. But our home has been nothing but a playroom. I have been your doll-wife, just as at home I was papa's doll-child; and here the children have been my dolls. I thought it great fun when you played with me, just as they thought it great fun when I played with them. That is what our marriage has been, Torvald.

HELMER. There is some truth in what you say—exaggerated and strained as your view of it is. But for the future it shall be different. Playtime shall be over, and lesson-time shall begin.

NORA. Whose lessons? Mine, or the children's?

HELMER. Both yours and the children's, my darling Nora.

NORA. Alas, Torvald, you are not the man to educate me into being a proper wife for you.

HELMER. And you can say that!

NORA. And I—how am I fitted to bring up the children?

HELMER. Nora!

Torvald Helmer (Sam Waterston) begs Nora (Liv Ullmann) to reconsider her decision to leave home in the Joseph Papp New York Shakespeare Festival production (1995) of *A Doll's House* (director, Tormod Skagestad).

Nora. Didn't you say so yourself a little while ago—that you dare not trust me to bring them up?

Helmer. In a moment of anger! Why do you pay any heed to that?

Nora. Indeed, you were perfectly right. I am not fit for the task. There is another task I must undertake first. I must try and educate myself—you are not the man to help me in that. I must do that for myself. And that is why I am going to leave you now.

Helmer. [*springing up*] What do you say?

Nora. I must stand quite alone, if I am to understand myself and everything about me. It is for that reason that I cannot remain with you any longer.

Helmer. Nora! Nora!

Nora. I am going away from here now, at once. I am sure Christine will take me in for the night—

Helmer. You are out of your mind! I won't allow it! I forbid you!

Nora. It is no use forbidding me anything any longer. I will take with me what belongs to myself. I will take nothing from you, either now or later.

Helmer. What sort of madness is this!

Nora. To-morrow I shall go home—I mean, to my old home. It will be easiest for me to find something to do there.

Helmer. You blind, foolish woman!

Nora. I must try and get some sense, Torvald.

Helmer. To desert your home, your husband and your children! And you don't consider what people will say!

Nora. I cannot consider that at all. I only know that it is necessary for me.

Helmer. It's shocking. This is how you would neglect your most sacred duties.

Nora. What do you consider my most sacred duties?

Helmer. Do I need to tell you that? Are they not your duties to your husband and your children?

Nora. I have other duties just as sacred.

Helmer. That you have not. What duties could those be?

Nora. Duties to myself.

Helmer. Before all else, you are a wife and a mother.

Nora. I don't believe that any longer. I believe that before all else I am a reasonable human being, just as you are—or, at all events, that I must try and become one. I know quite well, Torvald, that most people would think you right, and that views of that kind are to be found in books; but I can no longer content myself with what most people say, or with what is found in books. I must think over things for myself and get to understand them.

Helmer. Can you not understand your place in your own home? Have you not a reliable guide in such matters as that?—have you no religion?

Nora. I am afraid, Torvald, I do not exactly know what religion is.

Helmer. What are you saying?

Nora. I know nothing but what the clergyman said when I went to be confirmed. He told us that religion was this, and that, and the other. When I am away from all this, and am alone, I will look into that matter too. I will see if what the clergyman said is true, or at all events if it is true for me.

Helmer. This is unheard of in a girl of your age! But if religion cannot lead you aright, let me try and awaken your conscience. I suppose you have some moral sense? Or—answer me—am I to think you have none?

NORA. I assure you, Torvald, that is not an easy question to answer. I really don't know. The thing perplexes me altogether. I only know that you and I look at it in quite a different light. I am learning, too, that the law is quite another thing from what I supposed; but I find it impossible to convince myself that the law is right. According to it a woman has no right to spare her old dying father, or to save her husband's life. I can't believe that.

HELMER. You talk like a child. You don't understand the conditions of the world in which you live.

NORA. No, I don't. But now I am going to try. I am going to see if I can make out who is right, the world or I.

HELMER. You are ill, Nora; you are delirious; I almost think you are out of your mind.

NORA. I have never felt my mind so clear and certain as to-night.

HELMER. And is it with a clear and certain mind that you forsake your husband and your children?

NORA. Yes, it is.

HELMER. Then there is only one possible explanation.

NORA. What is that?

HELMER. You do not love me any more.

NORA. No, that is just it.

HELMER. Nora!—and you can say that?

NORA. It gives me great pain, Torvald, for you have always been so kind to me, but I cannot help it. I do not love you any more.

HELMER. [*regaining his composure*] Is that a clear and certain conviction too?

NORA. Yes, absolutely clear and certain. That is the reason why I will not stay here any longer.

HELMER. And can you tell me what I have done to forfeit your love?

NORA. Yes, indeed I can. It was to-night, when the wonderful thing did not happen; then I saw you were not the man I had thought you.

HELMER. Explain yourself better—I don't understand you.

NORA. I have waited so patiently for eight years; for, goodness knows, I knew very well that wonderful things don't happen every day. Then this horrible misfortune came upon me; and then I felt quite certain that the wonderful thing was going to happen at last. When Krogstad's letter was lying out there, never for a moment did I imagine that you would consent to accept this man's conditions. I was so absolutely certain that you would say to him: Publish the thing to the whole world. And when that was done—

HELMER. Yes, what then?—when I had exposed my wife to shame and disgrace?

NORA. When that was done, I was so absolutely certain, you would come forward and take everything upon yourself, and say I am the guilty one.

HELMER. Nora—!

NORA. You mean that I would never have accepted such a sacrifice on your part? No, of course not. But what would my assurances have been worth against yours? That was the wonderful thing which I hoped for and feared; and it was to prevent that, that I wanted to kill myself.

HELMER. I would gladly work night and day for you, Nora—bear sorrow and want for your sake. But no man would sacrifice his honour for the one he loves.

NORA. It is a thing hundreds of thousands of women have done.

HELMER. Oh, you think and talk like a heedless child.

Nora. Maybe. But you neither think nor talk like the man I could bind myself to. As soon as your fear was over—and it was not fear for what threatened me, but for what might happen to you—when the whole thing was past, as far as you were concerned it was exactly as if nothing at all had happened. Exactly as before, I was your little skylark, your doll, which you would in future treat with doubly gentle care, because it was so brittle and fragile. [*getting up*] Torvald—it was then it dawned upon me that for eight years I had been living here with a strange man, and had borne him three children—. Oh, I can't bear to think of it! I could tear myself into little bits!

Helmer. [*sadly*] I see, I see. An abyss has opened between us—there is no denying it. But, Nora, would it not be possible to fill it up?

Nora. As I am now, I am no wife for you.

Helmer. I have it in me to become a different man.

Nora. Perhaps—if your doll is taken away from you.

Helmer. But to part!—to part from you! No, no, Nora, I can't understand that idea.

Nora. [*going out to the right*] That makes it all the more certain that it must be done.

[*She comes back with her cloak and hat and a small bag which she puts on a chair by the table.*]

Helmer. Nora, Nora, not now! Wait till to-morrow.

Nora. [*putting on her cloak*] I cannot spend the night in a strange man's room.

Helmer. But can't we live here like brother and sister—?

Nora. [*putting on her hat*] You know very well that would not last long. [*puts the shawl round her*] Good-bye, Torvald. I won't see the little ones. I know they are in better hands than mine. As I am now, I can be of no use to them.

Helmer. But some day, Nora—some day?

Nora. How can I tell? I have no idea what is going to become of me.

Helmer. But you are my wife, whatever becomes of you.

Nora. Listen, Torvald. I have heard that when a wife deserts her husband's house, as I am doing now, he is legally freed from all obligations towards her. In any case I set you free from all your obligations. You are not to feel yourself bound in the slightest way, any more than I shall. There must be perfect freedom on both sides. See here is your ring back. Give me mine.

Helmer. That too?

Nora. That too.

Helmer. Here it is.

Nora. That's right. Now it is all over. I have put the keys here. The maids know all about everything in the house—better than I do. To-morrow, after I have left her, Christine will come here and pack up my own things that I brought with me from home. I will have them sent after me.

Helmer. All over! All over!—Nora, shall you never think of me again?

Nora. I know I shall often think of you and the children and this house.

Helmer. May I write to you, Nora?

Nora. No—never. You must not do that.

Helmer. But at least let me send you—

Nora. Nothing—nothing—

Helmer. Let me help you if you are in want.

Nora. No. I can receive nothing from a stranger.

Helmer. Nora—can I never be anything more than a stranger to you?

NORA. [*taking her bag*] Ah, Torvald, the most wonderful thing of all would have to happen.

HELMER. Tell me what that would be!

NORA. Both you and I would have to be so changed that—. Oh, Torvald, I don't believe any longer in wonderful things happening.

HELMER. But I will believe in it. Tell me? So changed that—?

NORA. That our life together would be a real wedlock. Good-bye.

[*She goes out through the hall.*]

HELMER. [*sinks down on a chair at the door and buries his face in his hands*] Nora! Nora! [*looks round, and rises*] Empty. She is gone. [*A hope flashes across his mind.*] The most wonderful thing of all—?

[*The sound of a door slamming is heard from below.*]

(1879)

Questions for Discussion and Writing

1. What do the early conversations between Nora and Torvald tell us about their relationship?
2. At what point did you realize that Nora was going to leave her husband?
3. What or who is the main antagonist? Is it a person, an environment, or a social force? Is there more than one?
4. This play follows traditional dramatic structure rather closely. What point would you identify as the climax?
5. Why do Torvald's arguments against Nora's leaving fail?
6. Is Ibsen attacking marriage? What else may he be attacking?
7. What will become of Nora? Will she find happiness and fulfillment? Write an essay about Nora's future.
8. Write an essay in which you support this claim: "*A Doll's House* concerns the trouble caused by clinging to illusions."

Susan Glaspell 1882–1948

Born in Davenport, Iowa, Susan Glaspell took a degree in philosophy from Drake University before becoming a newspaper reporter in Des Moines. She turned her play *Trifles*, based on a murder case she covered on the job, into a widely anthologized short story, "A Jury of Her Peers." She married a freethinker who also believed in free love and unfettered drinking, making her life with him difficult. The couple moved to the East Coast, where they founded the Provincetown Players, an experimental theater group. Glaspell won the 1931 Pulitzer Prize for her play *Alison's House*, which depicted the life of Emily Dickinson. She said she promoted "all progressive movements, whether feminist, social, or economic."

Trifles

CHARACTERS

COUNTY ATTORNEY	HALE
MRS. PETERS	MRS. HALE
SHERIFF	

SCENE

The kitchen in the now abandoned farmhouse of JOHN WRIGHT, *a gloomy kitchen, and left without having been put in order—the walls covered with a faded wallpaper. Down right is a door leading to the parlor. On the right wall above this door is a built-in kitchen cupboard with shelves in the upper portion and drawers below. In the rear wall at right, up two steps is a door opening onto stairs leading to the second floor. In the rear wall at left is a door to the shed and from there to the outside. Between these two doors is an old-fashioned black iron stove. Running along the left wall from the shed door is an old iron sink and sink shelf, in which is set a hand pump. Downstage of the sink is an uncurtained window. Near the window is an old wooden rocker. Center stage is an unpainted wooden kitchen table with straight chairs on either side. There is a small chair down right. Unwashed pans under the sink, a loaf of bread outside the breadbox, a dish towel on the table—other signs of incompleted work. At the rear the shed door opens and the* SHERIFF *comes in followed by the* COUNTY ATTORNEY *and* HALE. *The* SHERIFF *and* HALE *are men in middle life, the* COUNTY ATTORNEY *is a young man; all are much bundled up and go at once to the stove. They are followed by the two women—the* SHERIFF*'s wife,* MRS. PETERS, *first; she is a slight wiry woman, a thin nervous face.* MRS. HALE *is larger and would ordinarily be called more comfortable looking, but she is disturbed now and looks fearfully about as she enters. The women have come in slowly, and stand close together near the door.*

COUNTY ATTORNEY [*at the stove rubbing his hands*]. This feels good. Come up to the fire, ladies.

MRS. PETERS [*after taking a step forward*]. I'm not—cold.

SHERIFF [*unbuttoning his overcoat and stepping away from the stove to right of the table as if to mark the beginning of official business*]. Now, Mr. Hale, before we move things about, you explain to Mr. Henderson just what you saw when you came here yesterday morning.

COUNTY ATTORNEY [*crossing down to left of the table*]. By the way, has anything been moved? Are things just as you left them yesterday?

SHERIFF [*looking about*]. It's just the same. When it dropped below zero last night I thought I'd better send Frank out this morning to make a fire for us—[*sits right of center table*] no use getting pneumonia with a big case on, but I told him not to touch anything except the stove—and you know Frank.

COUNTY ATTORNEY. Somebody should have been left here yesterday.

SHERIFF. Oh—yesterday. When I had to send Frank to Morris Center for that man who went crazy—I want you to know I had my hands full yesterday. I knew you could get back from Omaha by today and as long as I went over everything here myself—

COUNTY ATTORNEY. Well, Mr. Hale, tell just what happened when you came here yesterday morning.

A photo of the original 1916 production of *Trifles*. (The New York Public Library for the perfoming Arts/Art Resource, Billy Rose Theatre Collection, The New York Public Library for the Performing Arts. Astor, Lenox and Tilden Foundations)

HALE [*crossing down to above table*]. Harry and I had started to town with a load of potatoes. We came along the road from my place and as I got here I said, "I'm going to see if I can't get John Wright to go in with me on a party telephone." I spoke to Wright about it once before and he put me off, saying folks talked too much anyway, and all he asked was peace and quiet—I guess you know about how much he talked himself; but I thought maybe if I went to the house and talked about it before his wife, though I said to Harry that I didn't know as what his wife wanted made much difference to John—

COUNTY ATTORNEY. Let's talk about that later, Mr. Hale. I do want to talk about that, but tell now just what happened when you got to the house.

HALE. I didn't hear or see anything; I knocked at the door, and still it was all quiet inside. I knew they must be up, it was past eight o'clock. So I knocked again, and I thought I heard somebody say, "Come in." I wasn't sure, I'm not sure yet, but I opened the door—this door [*indicating the door by which the two women are still standing*] and there in that rocker—[*pointing to it*] sat Mrs. Wright. [*They all look at the rocker down left.*]

COUNTY ATTORNEY. What—what was she doing?

HALE. She was rockin' back and forth. She had her apron in her hand and was kind of—pleating it.

COUNTY ATTORNEY. And how did she—look?

HALE. Well, she looked queer.

COUNTY ATTORNEY. How do you mean—queer?

HALE. Well, as if she didn't know what she was going to do next. And kind of done up.

COUNTY ATTORNEY [*takes out notebook and pencil and sits left of center table*]. How did she seem to feel about your coming?

HALE. Why, I don't think she minded—one way or other. She didn't pay much attention. I said, "How do, Mrs. Wright, it's cold, ain't it?" And she said, "Is it?"—and went on kind of pleating at her apron. Well, I was surprised; she didn't ask me to come up to the stove, or to set down, but just sat there, not even looking at me, so I said, "I want to see John." And then she—laughed. I guess you would call it a laugh. I thought of Harry and the team outside, so I said a little sharp: "Can't I see John?" "No," she says, kind o' dull like. "Ain't he home?" says I. "Yes," says she, "he's home." "Then why can't I see him?" I asked her, out of patience. "'Cause he's dead," says she. "*Dead?*" says I. She just nodded her head, not getting a bit excited, but rockin' back and forth. "Why—where is he?" says I, not knowing what to say. She just pointed upstairs—like that. [*Himself pointing to the room above.*] I started for the stairs, with the idea of going up there. I walked from there to here—then I says, "Why, what did he die of?" "He died of a rope round his neck," says she, and just went on pleatin' at her apron. Well, I went out and called Harry. I thought I might—need help. We went upstairs and there he was lyin'—

COUNTY ATTORNEY. I think I'd rather have you go into that upstairs, where you can point it all out. Just go on now with the rest of the story.

HALE. Well, my first thought was to get that rope off. It looked... [*stops, his face twitches*] ... but Harry, he went up to him, and he said, "No, he's dead all right, and we'd better not touch anything." So we went back downstairs. She was still sitting that same way. "Has anybody been notified?" I asked. "No," says she, unconcerned. "Who did this, Mrs. Wright?" said Harry. He said it business-like—and she stopped pleatin' on her apron. "I don't know," she says. "You don't *know*?" says Harry. "No," says she. "Weren't you sleepin' in the bed with him?" says Harry. "Yes," says she, "but I was on the inside." "Somebody slipped a rope round his neck and strangled him and you didn't wake up?" says Harry. "I didn't wake up," she said after him. We musta looked as if we didn't see how that could be, for after a minute she said, "I sleep sound." Harry was going to ask her more questions but I said maybe we ought to let her tell her story first to the coroner, or the sheriff, so Harry went fast as he could to Rivers' place, where there's a telephone.

COUNTY ATTORNEY. And what did Mrs. Wright do when she knew that you had gone for the coroner?

HALE. She moved from the rocker to that chair over there [*pointing to a small chair in the down right corner*] and just sat there with her hands held together and looking down. I got a feeling that I ought to make some conversation, so I said I had come in to see if John wanted to put in a telephone, and at that she started to laugh, and then she stopped and looked at me—scared. [*The* COUNTY ATTORNEY, *who has had his notebook out, makes a note.*] I dunno, maybe it wasn't scared. I wouldn't like to say it was. Soon Harry got back, and then Dr. Lloyd came, and you, Mr. Peters, and so I guess that's all I know that you don't.

COUNTY ATTORNEY [*rising and looking around*]. I guess we'll go upstairs first—and then out to the barn and around there. [*To the* SHERIFF.] You're convinced that there was nothing important here—nothing that would point to any motive?

SHERIFF. Nothing here but kitchen things. [*The* COUNTY ATTORNEY, *after again looking around the kitchen, opens the door of a cupboard closet in right wall. He brings a small chair from right—gets up on it and looks on a shelf. Pulls his hand away, sticky.*]

COUNTY ATTORNEY. Here's a nice mess. [*The women draw nearer up center.*]

MRS. PETERS [*to the other woman*]. Oh, her fruit; it did freeze. [*To the* LAWYER.] She worried about that when it turned so cold. She said the fire'd go out and her jars would break.

SHERIFF [*rises*]. Well, can you beat the women! Held for murder and worryin' about her preserves.

COUNTY ATTORNEY [*getting down from chair*]. I guess before we're through she may have something more serious than preserves to worry about. [*Crosses down right center.*]

HALE. Well, women are used to worrying over trifles. [*The two women move a little closer together.*]

COUNTY ATTORNEY [*with the gallantry of a young politician*]. And yet, for all their worries, what would we do without the ladies? [*The women do not unbend. He goes below the center table to the sink, takes a dipperful of water from the pail and pouring it into a basin, washes his hands. While he is doing this the* SHERIFF *and* HALE *cross to cupboard, which they inspect. The* COUNTY ATTORNEY *starts to wipe his hands on the roller towel, turns it for a cleaner place.*] Dirty towels! [*Kicks his foot against the pans under the sink.*] Not much of a housekeeper, would you say, ladies?

MRS. HALE [*stiffly*]. There's a great deal of work to be done on a farm.

COUNTY ATTORNEY. To be sure. And yet [*with a little bow to her*] I know there are some Dickson County farmhouses which do not have such roller towels. [*He gives it a pull to expose its full length again.*]

MRS. HALE. Those towels get dirty awful quick. Men's hands aren't always as clean as they might be.

COUNTY ATTORNEY. Ah, loyal to your sex, I see. But you and Mrs. Wright were neighbors. I suppose you were friends, too.

MRS. HALE [*shaking her head*]. I've not seen much of her of late years. I've not been in this house—it's more than a year.

COUNTY ATTORNEY [*crossing to women up center*]. And why was that? You didn't like her?

MRS. HALE. I liked her all well enough. Farmers' wives have their hands full, Mr. Henderson. And then—

COUNTY ATTORNEY. Yes——?

MRS. HALE [*looking about*]. It never seemed a very cheerful place.

COUNTY ATTORNEY. No—it's not cheerful. I shouldn't say she had the homemaking instinct.

MRS. HALE. Well, I don't know as Wright had, either.

COUNTY ATTORNEY. You mean that they didn't get on very well?

MRS. HALE. No, I don't mean anything. But I don't think a place'd be any cheerfuller for John Wright's being in it.

COUNTY ATTORNEY. I'd like to talk more of that a little later. I want to get the lay of things upstairs now. [*He goes past the women to up right where steps lead to a stair door.*]

SHERIFF. I suppose anything Mrs. Peters does'll be all right. She was to take in some clothes for her, you know, and a few little things. We left in such a hurry yesterday.

County Attorney. Yes, but I would like to see what you take, Mrs. Peters, and keep an eye out for anything that might be of use to us.

Mrs. Peters. Yes, Mr. Henderson.

[*The men leave by up right door to stairs. The women listen to the men's steps on the stairs, then look about the kitchen.*]

Mrs. Hale [*crossing left to sink*]. I'd hate to have men coming into my kitchen, snooping around and criticizing. [*She arranges the pans under sink which the Lawyer had shoved out of place.*]

Mrs. Peters. Of course it's no more than their duty. [*Crosses to cupboard up right.*]

Mrs. Hale. Duty's all right, but I guess that deputy sheriff that came out to make the fire might have got a little of this on. [*Gives the roller towel a pull.*] Wish I'd thought of that sooner. Seems mean to talk about her for not having things slicked up when she had to come away in such a hurry. [*Crosses right to Mrs. Peters at cupboard.*]

Mrs. Peters [*who has been looking through the cupboard, lifts one end of a towel that covers a pan*]. She had bread set. [*Stands still.*]

Mrs. Hale [*eyes fixed on a loaf of bread beside the breadbox, which is on a low shelf of the cupboard*]. She was going to put this in there. [*Picks up loaf, then abruptly drops it. In a manner of returning to familiar things.*] It's a shame about her fruit. I wonder if it's all gone. [*Gets up on the chair and looks.*] I think there's some here that's all right, Mrs. Peters. Yes—here; [*holding it toward the window*] this is cherries, too. [*Looking again.*] I declare I believe that's the only one. [*Gets down, jar in her hand. Goes to the sink and wipes it off on the outside.*] She'll feel awful bad after all her hard work in the hot weather. I remember the afternoon I put up my cherries last summer. [*She puts the jar on the big kitchen table, center of the room. With a sigh, is about to sit down in the rocking chair. Before she is seated realizes what chair it is; with a slow look at it, steps back. The chair which she has touched rocks back and forth.* Mrs. Peters *moves to center table and they both watch the chair rock for a moment or two.*]

Mrs. Peters [*shaking off the mood which the empty rocking chair has evoked. Now in a businesslike manner she speaks*]. Well, I must get those things from the front room closet. [*She goes to the door at the right, but, after looking into the other room, steps back.*] You coming with me, Mrs. Hale? You could help me carry them. [*They go in the other room; reappear,* Mrs. Peters *carrying a dress, petticoat and skirt,* Mrs. Hale *following with a pair of shoes.*] My, it's cold in there. [*She puts the clothes on the big table, and hurries to the stove.*]

Mrs. Hale [*right of center table examining the skirt*]. Wright was close. I think maybe that's why she kept so much to herself. She didn't even belong to the Ladies' Aid. I suppose she felt she couldn't do her part, and then you don't enjoy things when you feel shabby. I heard she used to wear pretty clothes and be lively, when she was Minnie Foster, one of the town girls singing in the choir. But that—oh, that was thirty years ago. This all you was to take in?

Mrs. Peters. She said she wanted an apron. Funny thing to want, for there isn't much to get you dirty in jail, goodness knows. But I suppose just to make her feel more natural. [*Crosses to cupboard.*] She said they was in the top drawer of this cupboard. Yes, here. And then her little shawl that always hung behind the door. [*Opens stair door and looks.*] Yes, here it is. [*Quickly shuts door leading upstairs.*]

Mrs. Hale [*abruptly moving toward her*]. Mrs. Peters?

Mrs. Peters. Yes, Mrs. Hale? [*At up right door.*]

MRS. HALE. Do you think she did it?

MRS. PETERS [*in a frightened voice*]. Oh, I don't know.

MRS. HALE. Well, I don't think she did. Asking for an apron and her little shawl. Worrying about her fruit.

MRS. PETERS [*starts to speak, glances up, where footsteps are heard in the room above. In a low voice*]. Mr. Peters says it looks bad for her. Mr. Henderson is awful sarcastic in a speech and he'll make fun of her sayin' she didn't wake up.

MRS. HALE. Well, I guess John Wright didn't wake when they was slipping that rope under his neck.

MRS. PETERS [*crossing slowly to table and placing shawl and apron on table with other clothing*]. No, it's strange. It must have been done awful crafty and still. They say it was such a—funny way to kill a man, rigging it all up like that.

MRS. HALE [*crossing to left of* MRS. PETERS *at table*]. That's just what Mr. Hale said. There was a gun in the house. He says that's what he can't understand.

MRS. PETERS. Mr. Henderson said coming out that what was needed for the case was a motive; something to show anger, or—sudden feeling.

MRS. HALE [*who is standing by the table*]. Well, I don't see any signs of anger around here. [*She puts her hand on the dish towel which lies on the table, stands looking down at table, one-half of which is clean, the other half messy.*] It's wiped to here. [*Makes a move as if to finish work, then turns and looks at loaf of bread outside the breadbox. Drops towel. In that voice of coming back to familiar things.*] Wonder how they are finding things upstairs. [*Crossing below table to down right.*] I hope she had it a little more red-up[1] up there. You know, it seems kind of *sneaking*. Locking her up in town and then coming out here and trying to get her own house to turn against her!

MRS. PETERS. But, Mrs. Hale, the law is the law.

MRS. HALE. I s'pose 'tis. [*Unbuttoning her coat.*] Better loosen up your things, Mrs. Peters. You won't feel them when you go out. [MRS. PETERS *takes off her fur tippet,*[2] *goes to hang it on chair back left of table, stands looking at the work basket on floor near down left window.*]

MRS. PETERS. She was piecing a quilt. [*She brings the large sewing basket to the center table and they look at the bright pieces,* MRS. HALE *above the table and* MRS. PETERS *left of it.*]

MRS. HALE. It's a log cabin pattern. Pretty, isn't it? I wonder if she was goin' to quilt it or just knot it? [*Footsteps have been heard coming down the stairs. The* SHERIFF *enters followed by* HALE *and the* COUNTY ATTORNEY.]

SHERIFF. They wonder if she was going to quilt it or just knot it! [*The men laugh, the women look abashed.*]

COUNTY ATTORNEY [*rubbing his hands over the stove*]. Frank's fire didn't do much up there, did it? Well, let's go out to the barn and get that cleared up.

[*The men go outside by up left door.*]

MRS. HALE [*resentfully*]. I don't know as there's anything so strange, our takin' up our time with little things while we're waiting for them to get the evidence. [*She sits in chair right of table smoothing out a block with decision.*] I don't see as it's anything to laugh about.

MRS. PETERS [*apologetically*]. Of course they've got awful important things on their minds. [*Pulls up a chair and joins* MRS. HALE *at the left of the table.*]

---

[1]**red-up** cleaned up, neat.
[2]**tippet** a scarf-like wrap.

Mrs. Hale. [*examining another block*]. Mrs. Peters, look at this one. Here, this is the one she was working on, and look at the sewing! All the rest of it has been so nice and even. And look at this! It's all over the place! Why, it looks as if she didn't know what she was about! [*After she has said this they look at each other, then start to glance back at the door. After an instant* Mrs. Hale *has pulled at a knot and ripped the sewing.*]

Mrs. Peters. Oh, what are you doing, Mrs. Hale?

Mrs. Hale. [*mildly*]. Just pulling out a stitch or two that's not sewed very good. [*Threading a needle.*] Bad sewing always made me fidgety.

Mrs. Peters [*with a glance at door, nervously*]. I don't think we ought to touch things.

Mrs. Hale. I'll just finish up this end. [*Suddenly stopping and leaning forward.*] Mrs. Peters?

Mrs. Peters. Yes, Mrs. Hale?

Mrs. Hale. What do you suppose she was so nervous about?

Mrs. Peters. Oh—I don't know. I don't know as she was nervous. I sometimes sew awful queer when I'm just tired. [Mrs. Hale *starts to say something, looks at* Mrs. Peters, *then goes on sewing.*] Well, I must get these things wrapped up. They may be through sooner than we think. [*Putting apron and other things together.*] I wonder where I can find a piece of paper, and string. [*Rises.*]

Mrs. Hale. In that cupboard, maybe.

Mrs. Peters [*crosses right looking in cupboard*]. Why, here's a bird-cage. [*Holds it up.*] Did she have a bird, Mrs. Hale?

Mrs. Hale. Why, I don't know whether she did or not—I've not been here for so long. There was a man around last year selling canaries cheap, but I don't know as she took one; maybe she did. She used to sing real pretty herself.

Mrs. Peters [*glancing around*]. Seems funny to think of a bird here. But she must have had one, or why would she have a cage? I wonder what happened to it?

Mrs. Hale. I s'pose maybe the cat got it.

Mrs. Peters. No, she didn't have a cat. She's got that feeling some people have about cats—being afraid of them. My cat got in her room and she was real upset and asked me to take it out.

Mrs. Hale. My sister Bessie was like that. Queer, ain't it?

Mrs. Peters [*examining the cage*]. Why, look at this door. It's broke. One hinge is pulled apart. [*Takes a step down to* Mrs. Hale*'s right.*]

Mrs. Hale. [*looking too*]. Looks as if someone must have been rough with it.

Mrs. Peters. Why, yes. [*She brings the cage forward and puts it on the table.*]

Mrs. Hale. [*glancing toward up left door*]. I wish if they're going to find any evidence they'd be about it. I don't like this place.

Mrs. Peters. But I'm awful glad you came with me, Mrs. Hale. It would be lonesome for me setting here alone.

Mrs. Hale. It would, wouldn't it? [*Dropping her sewing.*] But I tell you what I do wish, Mrs. Peters. I wish I had come over sometimes when *she* was here. I—[*looking around the room*]—wish I had.

Mrs. Peters. But of course you were awful busy, Mrs. Hale—your house and your children.

Mrs. Hale [*rises and crosses left*]. I could've come. I stayed away because it weren't cheerful—and that's why I ought to have come. I—[*looking out left window*]—I've never liked this place. Maybe because it's down in a hollow and you don't see the road. I dunno what it is, but it's a lonesome place and always was. I wish I had come over to see Minnie Foster sometimes. I can see now—[*Shakes her head.*]

MRS. PETERS [*left of table and above it*]. Well, you mustn't reproach yourself, Mrs. Hale. Somehow we just don't see how it is with other folks until—something turns up.

MRS. HALE. Not having children makes less work—but it makes a quiet house, and Wright out to work all day, and no company when he did come in. [*Turning from window.*] Did you know John Wright, Mrs. Peters?

MRS. PETERS. Not to know him; I've seen him in town. They say he was a good man.

MRS. HALE. Yes—good; he didn't drink, and kept his word as well as most, I guess, and paid his debts. But he was a hard man, Mrs. Peters. Just to pass the time of day with him—[*Shivers.*] Like a raw wind that gets to the bone. [*Pauses, her eye falling on the cage.*] I should think she woulda wanted a bird. But what do you suppose went wrong with it?

MRS. PETERS. I don't know, unless it got sick and died. [*She reaches over and swings the broken door, swings it again; both women watch it.*]

MRS. HALE. You weren't raised round here, were you? [MRS. PETERS *shakes her head.*] You didn't know—her?

MRS. PETERS. Not till they brought her yesterday.

MRS. HALE. She—come to think of it, she was kind of like a bird herself—real sweet and pretty, but kind of timid and—fluttery. How—she—did—change. [*Silence; then as if struck by a happy thought and relieved to get back to everyday things. Crosses right above* MRS. PETERS *to cupboard, replaces small chair used to stand on to its original place down right.*] Tell you what, Mrs. Peters, why don't you take the quilt in with you? It might take up her mind.

MRS. PETERS. Why, I think that's a real nice idea, Mrs. Hale. There couldn't possibly be any objection to it, could there? Now, just what would I take? I wonder if her patches are in here—and her things. [*They look in the sewing basket.*]

MRS. HALE [*crosses to right of table*]. Here's some red. I expect this has got sewing things in it. [*Brings out a fancy box.*] What a pretty box. Looks like something somebody would give you. Maybe her scissors are in here. [*Opens box. Suddenly puts her hand to her nose.*] Why—[MRS. PETERS *bends nearer, then turns her face away.*] There's something wrapped up in this piece of silk.

MRS. PETERS. Why, this isn't her scissors.

MRS. HALE [*lifting the silk*]. Oh, Mrs. Peters—it's—[MRS. PETERS *bends closer.*]

MRS. PETERS. It's the bird.

MRS. HALE. But, Mrs. Peters—look at it! Its neck! Look at its neck! It's all—other side *to*.

MRS. PETERS. Somebody—wrung—its—neck. [*Their eyes meet. A look of growing comprehension, of horror. Steps are heard outside.* MRS. HALE *slips box under quilt pieces, and sinks into her chair. Enter* SHERIFF *and* COUNTY ATTORNEY. MRS. PETERS *steps down left and stands looking out of window.*]

COUNTY ATTORNEY [*as one turning from serious things to little pleasantries*]. Well, ladies, have you decided whether she was going to quilt it or knot it? [*Crosses to center above table.*]

MRS. PETERS. We think she was going to—knot it. [SHERIFF *crosses to right of stove, lifts stove lid and glances at fire, then stands warming hands at stove.*]

COUNTY ATTORNEY. Well, that's interesting, I'm sure. [*Seeing the bird-cage.*] Has the bird flown?

MRS. HALE [*putting more quilt pieces over the box*]. We think the—cat got it.

COUNTY ATTORNEY [*preoccupied*]. Is there a cat? [*Mrs. Hale glances in a quick covert way at Mrs. Peters.*]

MRS. PETERS [*turning from window takes a step in*]. Well, not now. They're superstitious, you know. They leave.

COUNTY ATTORNEY [*to* SHERIFF PETERS, *continuing an interrupted conversation*]. No sign at all of anyone having come from the outside. Their own rope. Now let's go up again and go over it piece by piece. [*They start upstairs.*] It would have to have been someone who knew just the—[MRS. PETERS *sits down left of table. The two women sit there not looking at one another, but as if peering into something and at the same time holding back. When they talk now it is in the manner of feeling their way over strange ground, as if afraid of what they are saying, but as if they cannot help saying it.*]

MRS. HALE [*hesitatively and in hushed voice*]. She liked the bird. She was going to bury it in that pretty box.

MRS. PETERS [*in a whisper*]. When I was a girl—my kitten—there was a boy took a hatchet, and before my eyes—and before I could get there—[*Covers her face an instant.*] If they hadn't held me back I would have—[*catches herself, looks upstairs where steps are heard, falters weakly*]—hurt him.

MRS. HALE [*with a slow look around her*]. I wonder how it would seem never to have had any children around. [*Pause.*] No, Wright wouldn't like the bird—a thing that sang. She used to sing. He killed that, too.

MRS. PETERS [*moving uneasily*]. We don't know who killed the bird.

MRS. HALE. I knew John Wright.

MRS. PETERS. It was an awful thing done in this house that night, Mrs. Hale. Killing a man while he slept, slipping a rope around his neck that choked the life out of him.

MRS. HALE. His neck. Choked the life out of him. [*Her hand goes out and rests on the bird-cage.*]

MRS. PETERS [*with rising voice*]. We don't know who killed him. We don't *know*.

MRS. HALE [*her own feeling not interrupted*]. If there'd been years and years of nothing, then a bird to sing to you, it would be awful—still, after the bird was still.

MRS. PETERS [*something within her speaking*]. I know what stillness is. When we homesteaded in Dakota, and my first baby died—after he was two years old, and me with no other then—

MRS. HALE [*moving*]. How soon do you suppose they'll be through looking for the evidence?

MRS. PETERS. I know what stillness is. [*Pulling herself back.*] The law has got to punish crime, Mrs. Hale.

MRS. HALE [*not as if answering that*]. I wish you'd seen Minnie Foster when she wore a white dress with blue ribbons and stood up there in the choir and sang. [*A look around the room.*] Oh, I *wish* I'd come over here once in a while! That was a crime! That was a crime! Who's going to punish that?

MRS. PETERS [*looking upstairs*]. We mustn't—take on.

MRS. HALE. I might have known she needed help! I know how things can be—for women. I tell you, it's queer, Mrs. Peters. We live close together and we live far apart. We all go through the same things—it's all just a different kind of the same thing. [*Brushes her eyes, noticing the jar of fruit, reaches out for it.*] If I was you I wouldn't tell her her fruit was gone. Tell her it ain't. Tell her it's all right. Take this in to prove it to her. She—she may never know whether it was broke or not.

MRS. PETERS [*takes the jar, looks about for something to wrap it in; takes petticoat from the clothes brought from the other room, very nervously begins winding this around the jar. In a false voice*]. My, it's a good thing the men couldn't hear us. Wouldn't they just laugh! Getting all stirred up over a little thing like a—dead canary. As if that could have anything to do with—with—wouldn't they *laugh*! [*The men are heard coming downstairs.*]

MRS. HALE [*under her breath*]. Maybe they would—maybe they wouldn't.

COUNTY ATTORNEY. No, Peters, it's all perfectly clear except a reason for doing it. But you know juries when it comes to women. If there was some definite thing. [*Crosses slowly to above table.* SHERIFF *crosses down right.* MRS. HALE *and* MRS. PETERS *remain seated at either side of table.*] Something to show—something to make a story about—a thing that would connect up with this strange way of doing it—[*The women's eyes meet for an instant. Enter* HALE *from outer door.*]

HALE [*remaining up left by door*]. Well, I've got the team around. Pretty cold out there.

COUNTY ATTORNEY. I'm going to stay awhile by myself. [*To the* SHERIFF.] You can send Frank out for me, can't you? I want to go over everything. I'm not satisfied that we can't do better.

SHERIFF. Do you want to see what Mrs. Peters is going to take in? [*The* LAWYER *picks up the apron, laughs.*]

COUNTY ATTORNEY. Oh, I guess they're not very dangerous things the ladies have picked out. [*Moves a few things about, disturbing the quilt pieces which cover the box. Steps back.*] No, Mrs. Peters doesn't need supervising. For that matter a sheriff's wife is married to the law. Ever think of it that way, Mrs. Peters?

MRS. PETERS. Not—just that way.

SHERIFF [*chuckling*]. Married to the law. [*Moves to down right door to the other room.*] I just want you to come in here a minute, George. We ought to take a look at these windows.

COUNTY ATTORNEY [*scoffingly*]. Oh, windows!

SHERIFF. We'll be right out, Mr. Hale. [HALE *goes outside. The* SHERIFF *follows the* COUNTY ATTORNEY *into the other room. Then* MRS. HALE *rises, hands tight together, looking intensely at* MRS. PETERS, *whose eyes make a slow turn, finally meeting* MRS. HALE'S. *A moment* MRS. HALE *holds her, then her own eyes point the way to where the box is concealed. Suddenly* MRS. PETERS *throws back quilt pieces and tries to put the box in the bag she is carrying. It is too big. She opens box, starts to take bird out, cannot touch it, goes to pieces, stands there helpless. Sound of a knob turning in the other room.* MRS. HALE *snatches the box and puts it in the pocket of her big coat. Enter* COUNTY ATTORNEY *and* SHERIFF, *who remains down right.*]

COUNTY ATTORNEY [*crosses to up left door; facetiously*]. Well, Henry, at least we found out that she was not going to quilt it. She was going to—what is it you call it, ladies?

MRS. HALE [*standing center below table facing front, her hand against her pocket*]. We call it—knot it, Mr. Henderson.

CURTAIN.

(1916)

Questions for Discussion and Writing

1. Describe the atmosphere evoked by the play's setting.
2. How would you characterize the men in the play?
3. What is the point of the women's concern about the quilt and whether Mrs. Wright "was going to quilt it or knot it"? What is the significance of the last line of the play and why is it ironic?
4. What sort of person was Minnie Foster before she married? What do you think happened to her?
5. Describe your reaction to the decision made by Mrs. Peters and Mrs. Hale to hide the dead bird from the men. Did they do the right thing? Write an essay in which you explain your answer to this question.

Lorraine Hansberry 1930–1965

Born into an extended family of black middle-class intellectuals and businesspeople on the south side of Chicago, Lorraine Hansberry learned at the age of eight the lessons that would shape the events in the prize-winning play you are about to read. Her parents moved the family to a white neighborhood only to be confronted one night by a hostile white mob. This led to an anti-segregation lawsuit that Carl Hansberry eventually won in the Illinois Supreme Court. Believing that "All art is ultimately social: that which agitates and that which prepares the mind for slumber," Hansberry saw her work as implicitly political and a way to increase understanding between blacks and whites. "The intimacy of knowledge which the Negro may culturally have of white Americans," she observed, "does not exist in reverse." *Raisin in the Sun* was the first drama by a black woman to reach the Broadway stage.

A Raisin in the Sun*

CHARACTERS IN ORDER OF APPEARANCE

RUTH YOUNGER, *Walter's wife, about thirty*
TRAVIS YOUNGER, *her son and Walter's*
WALTER LEE YOUNGER (BROTHER), *Ruth's husband, mid-thirties*
BENEATHA YOUNGER, *Walter's sister, about twenty*
LENA YOUNGER (MAMA), *mother of Walter and Beneatha*
JOSEPH ASAGAI, *Nigerian, Beneatha's suitor*
GEORGE MURCHISON, *Beneatha's date, wealthy*
KARL LINDNER, *white, chairman of the Clybourne Park New Neighbors Orientation Committee*
BOBO, *one of Walter's business partners*
MOVING MEN

*Hansberry's title is taken from Langston Hughes's poem "Harlem (A Dream Deferred)," which appears on page 531.

Walter (Sidney Poitier) electrifies his sister Beneatha (Diana Sans) while his wife Ruth (Ruby Dee) looks on, in Act II of the original Broadway production (1959) of *A Raisin in the Sun.* (The New York Public Library for the Performing Arts/Art Resource. The New York Public Library for the Performing Arts. Friedman-Abeles Collection)

The action of the play is set in Chicago's Southside, sometime between World War II and the present.

ACT I

SCENE I *Friday morning.*

SCENE II *The following morning.*

ACT II

SCENE I *Later, the same day.*

SCENE II *Friday night, a few weeks later.*

SCENE III *Moving day, one week later.*

ACT III

An hour later.

ACT I

SCENE I

The Younger living room would be a comfortable and well-ordered room if it were not for a number of indestructible contradictions to this state of being. Its furnishings are typical and undistinguished and their primary feature now is that they have clearly had to accommodate the living of too many people for too many years—and they are tired. Still, we can see that at some time, a time probably no longer remembered by the family (except perhaps for MAMA*), the furnishings of this room were actually selected with care and love and even hope—and brought to this apartment and arranged with taste and pride.*

That was a long time ago. Now the once loved pattern of the couch upholstery has to fight to show itself from under acres of crocheted doilies and couch covers which have themselves finally come to be more important than the upholstery. And here a table or a chair has been moved to disguise the worn places in the carpet; but the carpet has fought back by showing its weariness, with depressing uniformity, elsewhere on its surface.

Weariness has, in fact, won in this room. Everything has been polished, washed, sat on, used, scrubbed too often. All pretenses but living itself have long since vanished from the very atmosphere of this room.

Moreover, a section of this room, for it is not really a room unto itself, though the landlord's lease would make it seem so, slopes backward to provide a small kitchen area, where the family prepares the meals that are eaten in the living room proper, which must also serve as dining room. The single window that has been provided for these "two" rooms is located in this kitchen area. The sole natural light the family may enjoy in the course of a day is only that which fights its way through this little window.

At left, a door leads to a bedroom which is shared by MAMA *and her daughter,* BENEATHA. *At right, opposite, is a second room (which in the beginning of the life of this apartment was probably a breakfast room) which serves as a bedroom for* WALTER *and his wife,* RUTH.

Time: Sometime between World War II and the present.

Place: Chicago's Southside.

At Rise: It is morning dark in the living room. TRAVIS *is asleep on the make-down bed at center. An alarm clock sounds from within the bedroom at right, and presently* RUTH *enters from that room and closes the door behind her. She crosses sleepily toward the window. As she passes her sleeping son she reaches down and shakes him a little. At the window she raises the shade and a dusky Southside morning light comes in feebly. She fills a pot with water and puts it on to boil. She calls to the boy, between yawns, in a slightly muffled voice.*

RUTH *is about thirty. We can see that she was a pretty girl, even exceptionally so, but now it is apparent that life has been little that she expected, and disappointment has already begun to hang in her face. In a few years, before thirty-five even, she will be known among her people as a "settled woman."*

She crosses to her son and gives him a good, final, rousing shake.

RUTH. Come on now, boy, it's seven thirty! [*Her son sits up at last, in a stupor of sleepiness.*] I say hurry up, Travis! You ain't the only person in the world got to use a bathroom! [*The child, a sturdy, handsome little boy of ten or eleven, drags himself out of the bed and almost blindly takes his towels and "today's clothes" from drawers and a closet and goes out to the bathroom, which is in an outside hall and which is shared by another family or families on the same floor.* RUTH *crosses to the bedroom door at right and opens it and calls in to her husband*] Walter Lee!... It's after seven thirty! Lemme see you do some waking up in there now! [*She waits*] You better get up from there, man! It's after seven thirty I tell you. [*She waits again*] All right, you just go ahead and lay there and next thing you know Travis be finished and Mr. Johnson'll be in there and you'll be fussing and cussing round here like a mad man! And be late too! [*She waits, at the end of patience*] Walter Lee—it's time for you to get up! [*She waits another second and then starts to go into the bedroom, but is apparently satisfied that her husband has begun to get up. She stops, pulls the door to, and returns to the kitchen area. She wipes her face with a moist cloth and runs her fingers through her sleep-disheveled hair in a vain effort and ties an apron around her housecoat. The bedroom door at right opens and her husband stands in the doorway in his pajamas, which are rumpled and mismated. He is a lean, intense young man in his middle thirties, inclined to quick nervous movements and erratic speech habits—and always in his voice there is a quality of indictment*]

WALTER. Is he out yet?

RUTH. What you mean *out*? He ain't hardly got in there good yet.

WALTER [*Wandering in, still more oriented to sleep than to a new day*]. Well, what was you doing all that yelling for if I can't even get in there yet? [*Stopping and thinking*] Check coming today?

RUTH. They *said* Saturday and this is just Friday and I hopes to God you ain't going to get up here first thing this morning and start talking to me 'bout no money—'cause I 'bout don't want to hear it.

WALTER. Something the matter with you this morning?

RUTH. No—I'm just sleepy as the devil. What kind of eggs you want?

WALTER. Not scrambled. [RUTH *starts to scramble eggs*] Paper come? [RUTH *points impatiently to the rolled up* TRIBUNE *on the table, and he gets it and spreads it out and vaguely reads the front page*] Set off another bomb yesterday.

RUTH [*Maximum indifference*]. Did they?

WALTER [*Looking up*]. What's the matter with you?

RUTH. Ain't nothing the matter with me. And don't keep asking me that this morning.

WALTER. Ain't nobody bothering you. [*Reading the news of the day absently again*] Say Colonel McCormick is sick.

RUTH [*Affecting tea-party interest*]. Is he now? Poor thing.

WALTER [*Sighing and looking at his watch*]. Oh, me. [*He waits*] Now what is that boy doing in that bathroom all this time? He just going to have to start getting up earlier. I can't be being late to work on account of him fooling around in there.

RUTH [*Turning on him*]. Oh, no, he ain't going to be getting up earlier no such thing! It ain't his fault that he can't get to bed no earlier nights 'cause he got a bunch of crazy good-for-nothing clowns sitting up running their mouths in what is supposed to be his bedroom after ten o'clock at night...

WALTER. That's what you mad about, ain't it? The things I want to talk about with my friends just couldn't be important in your mind, could they? [*He rises and finds a cigarette in her handbag on the table and crosses to the little window and looks out, smoking and deeply enjoying this first one*]

RUTH [*Almost matter of factly, a complaint too automatic to deserve emphasis*]. Why you always got to smoke before you eat in the morning?

WALTER [*At the window*]. Just look at 'em down there...Running and racing to work...[*He turns and faces his wife and watches her a moment at the stove, and then, suddenly*] You look young this morning, baby.

RUTH [*Indifferently*]. Yeah?

WALTER. Just for a second—stirring them eggs. It's gone now—just for a second it was—you looked real young again. [*Then, drily*] It's gone now—you look like yourself again.

RUTH. Man, if you don't shut up and leave me alone.

WALTER [*Looking out to the street again*]. First thing a man ought to learn in life is not to make love to no colored woman first thing in the morning. You all some evil people at eight o'clock in the morning. [TRAVIS *appears in the hall doorway, almost fully dressed and quite wide awake now, his towels and pajamas across his shoulders. He opens the door and signals for his father to make the bathroom in a hurry*]

TRAVIS [*Watching the bathroom*]. Daddy, come on! [WALTER *gets his bathroom utensils and flies out to the bathroom*]

RUTH. Sit down and have your breakfast, Travis.

TRAVIS. Mama, this is Friday. [*Gleefully*] Check coming tomorrow, huh?

RUTH. You get your mind off money and eat your breakfast.

TRAVIS [*Eating*]. This is the morning we supposed to bring the fifty cents to school.

RUTH. Well, I ain't got no fifty cents this morning.

TRAVIS. Teacher say we have to.

RUTH. I don't care what teacher say. I ain't got it. Eat your breakfast, Travis.

TRAVIS. I *am* eating.

RUTH. Hush up now and just eat! [*The boy gives her an exasperated look for her lack of understanding, and eats grudgingly*]

TRAVIS. You think Grandmama would have it?

RUTH. No! And I want you to stop asking your grandmother for money, you hear me?

TRAVIS [*Outraged*]. Gaaaleee! I don't ask her, she just gimme it sometimes!

RUTH. Travis Willard Younger—I got too much on me this morning to be—

TRAVIS. Maybe Daddy—

RUTH. *Travis!* [*The boy hushes abruptly. They are both quiet and tense for several seconds*]

TRAVIS [*Presently*]. Could I maybe go carry some groceries in front of the supermarket for a little while after school then?

RUTH. Just hush, I said. [TRAVIS *jabs his spoon into his cereal bowl viciously, and rests his head in anger upon his fists*] If you through eating, you can get over there and make up your bed. [*The boy obeys stiffly and crosses the room, almost mechanically, to the bed and more or less carefully folds the covering. He carries the bedding into his mother's room and returns with his books and cap*]

TRAVIS [*Sulking and standing apart from her unnaturally*]. I'm gone.

RUTH [*Looking up from the stove to inspect him automatically*]. Come here. [*He crosses to her and she studies his head*] If you don't take this comb and fix this here head, you better! [TRAVIS *puts down his books with a great sigh of oppression, and crosses to the mirror. His mother mutters under her breath about his "stubbornness"*] 'Bout to march out of here with that head looking just like chickens slept in it! I just don't know where you get your stubborn ways…And get your jacket, too. Looks chilly out this morning.

TRAVIS [*With conspicuously brushed hair and jacket*]. I'm gone.

RUTH. Get carfare and milk money—[*Waving one finger*]—and not a single penny for no caps, you hear me?

TRAVIS [*With sullen politeness*]. Yes'm. [*He turns in outrage to leave. His mother watches after him as in his frustration he approaches the door almost comically. When she speaks to him, her voice has become a very gentle tease*]

RUTH [*Mocking; as she thinks he would say it*]. Oh, Mama makes me so mad sometimes, I don't know what to do! [*She waits and continues to his back as he stands stock-still in front of the door*] I wouldn't kiss that woman good-bye for nothing in this world this morning! [*The boy finally turns around and rolls his eyes at her, knowing the mood has changed and he is vindicated; he does not, however, move toward her yet*] Not for nothing in this world! [*She finally laughs aloud at him and holds out her arms to him and we see that it is a way between them, very old and practiced. He crosses to her and allows her to embrace him warmly but keeps his face fixed with masculine rigidity. She holds him back from her presently and looks at him and runs her fingers over the features of his face. With utter gentleness*—] Now—whose little old angry man are you?

TRAVIS [*The masculinity and gruffness start to fade at last*]. Aw gaalee—Mama …

RUTH [*Mimicking*]. Aw—gaaaaalleeeee, Mama! [*She pushes him, with rough playfulness and finality, toward the door*] Get on out of here or you going to be late.

TRAVIS [*In the face of love, new aggressiveness*]. Mama, could I *please* go carry groceries?

Ruth. Honey, it's starting to get so cold evenings.

WALTER [*Coming in from the bathroom and drawing a make-believe gun from a make-believe holster and shooting at his son*]. What is it he wants to do?

RUTH. Go carry groceries after school at the supermarket.

WALTER. Well, let him go…

TRAVIS [*Quickly, to the ally*]. I *have* to—she won't gimme the fifty cents…

WALTER [*To his wife only*]. Why not?

RUTH [*Simply, and with flavor*].'Cause we don't have it.

WALTER [*To* RUTH *only*]. What you tell the boy things like that for? [*Reaching down into his pants with a rather important gesture*] Here, son—[*He hands the boy the coin, but his eyes are directed to his wife's.* TRAVIS *takes the money happily*]

TRAVIS. Thanks, Daddy. [*He starts out.* RUTH *watches both of them with murder in her eyes. Walter stands and stares back at her with defiance, and suddenly reaches into his pocket again on an afterthought*]

WALTER [*Without even looking at his son, still staring hard at his wife*]. In fact, here's another fifty cents…Buy yourself some fruit today—or take a taxicab to school or something!

TRAVIS. Whoopee—[*He leaps up and clasps his father around the middle with his legs, and they face each other in mutual appreciation; slowly* WALTER LEE *peeks around the boy to catch the violent rays from his wife's eyes and draws his head back as if shot*]

WALTER. You better get down now—and get to school, man.

TRAVIS [*At the door*]. O.K. Good-bye. [*He exits*]

WALTER [*After him, pointing with pride*]. That's *my* boy. [*She looks at him in disgust and turns back to her work*] You know what I was thinking 'bout in the bathroom this morning?

RUTH. No.

WALTER. How come you always try to be so pleasant!

RUTH. What is there to be pleasant 'bout!

WALTER. You want to know what I was thinking 'bout in the bathroom or not!

RUTH. I know what you thinking 'bout.

WALTER [*Ignoring her*].'Bout what me and Willy Harris was talking about last night.

RUTH [*Immediately—a refrain*]. Willy Harris is a good-for-nothing loud mouth.

WALTER. Anybody who talks to me has got to be a good-for-nothing loud mouth, ain't he? And what you know about who is just a good-for-nothing loud mouth? Charlie Atkins was just a "good-for-nothing loud mouth" too, wasn't he! When he wanted me to go in the dry-cleaning business with him. And now—he's grossing a hundred thousand a year. A hundred thousand dollars a year! You still call him a loud mouth!

RUTH [*Bitterly*]. Oh, Walter Lee...[*She folds her head on her arms over the table*]

WALTER [*Rising and coming to her and standing over her*]. You tired, ain't you? Tired of everything. Me, the boy, the way we live—this beat-up hole—everything. Ain't you? [*She doesn't look up, doesn't answer*] So tired—moaning and groaning all the time, but you wouldn't do nothing to help, would you? You couldn't be on my side that long for nothing, could you?

RUTH. Walter, please leave me alone.

WALTER. A man needs for a woman to back him up ...

RUTH. Walter—

WALTER. Mama would listen to you. You know she listen to you more than she do me and Bennie. She think more of you. All you have to do is just sit down with her when you drinking your coffee one morning and talking 'bout things like you do and—[*He sits down beside her and demonstrates graphically what he thinks her methods and tone should be*]—you just sip your coffee, see, and say easy like that you been thinking 'bout that deal Walter Lee is so interested in, 'bout the store and all, and sip some more coffee, like what you saying ain't really that important to you—And the next thing you know, she be listening good and asking you questions and when I come home—I can tell her the details. This ain't no fly-by-night proposition, baby. I mean we figured it out, me and Willy and Bobo.

RUTH [*With a frown*]. Bobo?

WALTER. Yeah. You see, this little liquor store we got in mind cost seventy-five thousand and we figured the initial investment on the place be 'bout thirty thousand, see. That be ten thousand each. Course, there's a couple of hundred you got to pay so's you don't spend your life just waiting for them clowns to let your license get approved—

RUTH. You mean graft?

WALTER [*Frowning impatiently*]. Don't call it that. See there, that just goes to show you what women understand about the world. Baby, don't *nothing* happen for you in this world 'less you pay *somebody* off!

RUTH. Walter, leave me alone! [*She raises her head and stares at him vigorously—then says, more quietly*] Eat your eggs, they gonna be cold.

WALTER [*Straightening up from her and looking off*]. That's it. There you are. Man say to his woman: I got me a dream. His woman say: Eat your eggs. [*Sadly, but gaining in power*] Man say: I got to take hold of this here world, baby! And a woman will say: Eat your eggs and go to work. [*Passionately now*] Man say: I got to change my life, I'm choking to death, baby! And his woman say—[*In utter anguish as he brings his fists down on his thighs*]—Your eggs is getting cold!

RUTH [*Softly*]. Walter, that ain't none of our money.

WALTER [*Not listening at all or even looking at her*]. This morning, I was lookin' in the mirror and thinking about it…I'm thirty-five years old; I been married eleven years and I got a boy who sleeps in the living room—[*Very, very quietly*]—and all I got to give him is stories about how rich white people live …

RUTH. Eat your eggs, Walter.

WALTER. *Damn my eggs…damn all the eggs that ever was!*

RUTH. Then go to work.

WALTER [*Looking up at her*]. See—I'm trying to talk to you 'bout myself—[*Shaking his head with the repetition*]—and all you can say is eat them eggs and go to work.

RUTH [*Wearily*]. Honey, you never say nothing new. I listen to you every day, every night and every morning, and you never say nothing new. [*Shrugging*] So you would rather *be* Mr. Arnold than be his chauffeur. So—I would *rather* be living in Buckingham Palace.

WALTER. That is just what is wrong with the colored woman in this world … Don't understand about building their men up and making 'em feel like they somebody. Like they can do something.

RUTH [*Drily, but to hurt*]. There *are* colored men who do things.

WALTER. No thanks to the colored woman.

RUTH. Well, being a colored woman, I guess I can't help myself none. [*She rises and gets the ironing board and sets it up and attacks a huge pile of rough-dried clothes, sprinkling them in preparation for the ironing and then rolling them into tight fat balls.*]

WALTER [*Mumbling*]. We one group of men tied to a race of women with small minds. [*His sister* BENEATHA *enters. She is about twenty, as slim and intense as her brother. She is not as pretty as her sister-in-law, but her lean, almost intellectual face has a handsomeness of its own. She wears a bright-red flannel nightie, and her thick hair stands wildly about her head. Her speech is a mixture of many things; it is different from the rest of the family's insofar as education has permeated her sense of English—and perhaps the Midwest rather than the South has finally—at last—won out in her inflection; but not altogether, because over all of it is a soft slurring and transformed use of vowels which is the decided influence of the Southside. She passes through the room without looking at either* RUTH *or* WALTER *and goes to the outside door and looks, a little blindly, out to the bathroom. She sees that it has been lost to the Johnsons. She closes the door with a sleepy vengeance and crosses to the table and sits down a little defeated*]

BENEATHA. I am going to start timing those people.

Walter. You should get up earlier.

Beneatha [*Her face in her hands. She is still fighting the urge to go back to bed*]. Really—would you suggest dawn? Where's the paper?

Walter [*Pushing the paper across the table to her as he studies her almost clinically, as though he has never seen her before*]. You a horrible-looking chick at this hour.

Beneatha [*Drily*]. Good morning, everybody.

Walter [*Senselessly*]. How is school coming?

Beneatha [*In the same spirit*]. Lovely. Lovely. And you know, biology is the greatest. [*Looking up at him*] I dissected something that looked just like you yesterday.

Walter. I just wondered if you've made up your mind and everything.

Beneatha [*Gaining in sharpness and impatience*]. And what did I answer yesterday morning—and the day before that?

Ruth [*From the ironing board, like someone disinterested and old*]. Don't be so nasty, Bennie.

Beneatha [*Still to her brother*]. And the day before that and the day before that!

Walter [*Defensively*]. I'm interested in you. Something wrong with that? Ain't many girls who decide—

Walter *and* Beneatha [*In unison*].—"to be a doctor." [*Silence*]

Walter. Have we figured out yet just exactly how much medical school is going to cost?

Ruth. Walter Lee, why don't you leave that girl alone and get out of here to work?

Beneatha [*Exits to the bathroom and bangs on the door*]. Come on out of there, please! [*She comes back into the room*]

Walter [*Looking at his sister intently*]. You know the check is coming tomorrow.

Beneatha [*Turning on him with a sharpness all her own*]. That money belongs to Mama, Walter, and it's for her to decide how she wants to use it. I don't care if she wants to buy a house or a rocket ship or just nail it up somewhere and look at it. It's hers. Not ours—*hers*.

Walter [*Bitterly*]. Now ain't that fine! You just got your mother's interest at heart, ain't you, girl? You such a nice girl—but if Mama got that money she can always take a few thousand and help you through school too—can't she?

Beneatha. I have never asked anyone around here to do anything for me!

Walter. No! And the line between asking and just accepting when the time comes is big and wide—ain't it!

Beneatha [*With fury*]. What do you want from me, Brother—that I quit school or just drop dead, which!

Walter. I don't want nothing but for you to stop acting holy 'round here. Me and Ruth done made some sacrifices for you—why can't you do something for the family?

Ruth. Walter, don't be dragging me in it.

Walter. You are in it—Don't you get up and go work in somebody's kitchen for the last three years to help put clothes on her back?

Ruth. Oh, Walter—that's not fair...

Walter. It ain't that nobody expects you to get on your knees and say thank you, Brother; thank you, Ruth; thank you, Mama—and thank you, Travis, for wearing the same pair of shoes for two semesters—

Beneatha [*Dropping to her knees*]. Well—I *do*—all right?—thank everybody... and forgive me for ever wanting to be anything at all... forgive me, forgive me!

RUTH. Please stop it! Your mama'll hear you.

WALTER. Who the hell told you you had to be a doctor? If you so crazy 'bout messing 'round with sick people—then go be a nurse like other women—or just get married and be quiet …

BENEATHA. Well—you finally got it said…It took you three years but you finally got it said. Walter, give up; leave me alone—it's Mama's money.

WALTER. *He was my father, too!*

BENEATHA. So what? He was mine, too—and Travis' grandfather—but the insurance money belongs to Mama. Picking on me is not going to make her give it to you to invest in any liquor stores—[*Underbreath, dropping into a chair*]—and I for one say, God bless Mama for that!

WALTER [*To* RUTH]. See—did you hear? Did you hear!

RUTH. Honey, please go to work.

WALTER. Nobody in this house is ever going to understand me.

BENEATHA. Because you're a nut.

WALTER. Who's a nut?

BENEATHA. You—you are a nut. Thee is mad, boy.

WALTER [*Looking at his wife and his sister from the door, very sadly*]. The world's most backward race of people, and that's a fact.

BENEATHA [*Turning slowly in her chair*]. And then there are all those prophets who would lead us out of the wilderness—[WALTER *slams out of the house*]—into the swamps!

RUTH. Bennie, why you always gotta be pickin' on your brother? Can't you be a little sweeter sometimes? [*Door opens.* WALTER *walks in*]

WALTER [*to* RUTH]. I need some money for carfare.

RUTH [*Looks at him, then warms; teasing, but tenderly*]. Fifty cents? [*She goes to her bag and gets money*] Here, take a taxi. [WALTER *exits.* MAMA *enters. She is a woman in her early sixties, full-bodied and strong. She is one of those women of a certain grace and beauty who wear it so unobtrusively that it takes a while to notice. Her dark-brown face is surrounded by the total whiteness of her hair, and, being a woman who has adjusted to many things in life and overcome many more, her face is full of strength. She has, we can see, wit and faith of a kind that keep her eyes lit and full of interest and expectancy. She is, in a word, a beautiful woman. Her bearing is perhaps most like the noble bearing of the women of the Hereros of Southwest Africa—rather as if she imagines that as she walks she still bears a basket or a vessel upon her head. Her speech, on the other hand, is as careless as her carriage is precise—she is inclined to slur everything—but her voice is perhaps not so much quiet as simply soft*]

MAMA. Who that 'round here slamming doors at this hour? [*She crosses through the room, goes to the window, opens it, and brings in a feeble little plant growing doggedly in a small pot on the window sill. She feels the dirt and puts it back out*]

RUTH. That was Walter Lee. He and Bennie was at it again.

MAMA. My children and they tempers. Lord, if this little old plant don't get more sun than it's been getting it ain't never going to see spring again. [*She turns from the window*] What's the matter with you this morning, Ruth? You looks right peaked. You aiming to iron all them things? Leave some for me. I'll get to 'em this afternoon. Bennie honey, it's too drafty for you to be sitting 'round half dressed. Where's your robe?

BENEATHA. In the cleaners.

MAMA. Well, go get mine and put it on.

Beneatha. I'm not cold, Mama, honest.

Mama. I know—but you so thin …

Beneatha [*Irritably*]. Mama, I'm not cold.

Mama [*Seeing the make-down bed as* Travis *has left it*]. Lord have mercy, look at that poor bed. Bless his heart—he tries, don't he? [*She moves to the bed* Travis *has sloppily made up*]

Ruth. No—he don't half try at all 'cause he knows you going to come along behind him and fix everything. That's just how come he don't know how to do nothing right now—you done spoiled that boy so.

Mama. Well—he's a little boy. Ain't supposed to know 'bout housekeeping. My baby, that's what he is. What you fix for his breakfast this morning?

Ruth [*Angrily*]. I feed my son, Lena!

Mama. I ain't meddling—[*Underbreath; busy-bodyish*]. I just noticed all last week he had cold cereal, and when it starts getting this chilly in the fall a child ought to have some hot grits or something when he goes out in the cold—

Ruth [*Furious*]. I gave him hot oats—is that all right!

Mama. I ain't meddling. [*Pause*] Put a lot of nice butter on it? [Ruth *shoots her an angry look and does not reply*] He likes lots of butter.

Ruth [*Exasperated*]. Lena—

Mama [*To* Beneatha. Mama *is inclined to wander conversationally sometimes*]. What was you and your brother fussing 'bout this morning?

Beneatha. It's not important, Mama. [*She gets up and goes to look out at the bathroom, which is apparently free, and she picks up her towels and rushes out*]

Mama. What was they fighting about?

Ruth. Now you know as well as I do.

Mama [*Shaking her head*]. Brother still worrying hisself sick about that money?

Ruth. You know he is.

Mama. You had breakfast?

Ruth. Some coffee.

Mama. Girl, you better start eating and looking after yourself better. You almost thin as Travis.

Ruth. Lena—

Mama. Uh-hunh?

Ruth. What are you going to do with it?

Mama. Now don't you start, child. It's too early in the morning to be talking about money. It ain't Christian.

Ruth. It's just that he got his heart set on that store—

Mama. You mean that liquor store that Willy Harris want him to invest in?

Ruth. Yes—

Mama. We ain't no business people, Ruth. We just plain working folks.

Ruth. Ain't nobody business people till they go into business. Walter Lee say colored people ain't never going to start getting ahead till they start gambling on some different kinds of things in the world—investments and things.

Mama. What done got into you, girl? Walter Lee done finally sold you on investing.

Ruth. No. Mama, something is happening between Walter and me. I don't know what it is—but he needs something—something I can't give him any more. He needs this chance, Lena.

Mama [*Frowning deeply*]. But liquor, honey—

RUTH. Well—like Walter say—I spec people going to always be drinking themselves some liquor.

MAMA. Well—whether they drinks it or not ain't none of my business. But whether I go into business selling it to 'em *is*, and I don't want that on my ledger this late in life. [*Stopping suddenly and studying her daughter-in-law*] Ruth Younger, what's the matter with you today? You look like you could fall over right there.

RUTH. I'm tired.

MAMA. Then you better stay home from work today.

RUTH. I can't stay home. She'd be calling up the agency and screaming at them, "My girl didn't come in today—send me somebody! My girl didn't come in!" Oh, she just have a fit ...

MAMA. Well, let her have it. I'll just call her up and say you got the flu—

RUTH [*Laughing*]. Why the flu?

MAMA. 'Cause it sounds respectable to 'em. Something white people get, too. They know 'bout the flu. Otherwise they think you been cut up or something when you tell 'em you sick.

RUTH. I got to go in. We need the money.

MAMA. Somebody would of thought my children done all but starved to death the way they talk about money here late. Child, we got a great big old check coming tomorrow.

RUTH [*Sincerely, but also self-righteously*]. Now that's your money. It ain't got nothing to do with me. We all feel like that—Walter and Bennie and me—even Travis.

MAMA [*Thoughtfully, and suddenly very far away*]. Ten thousand dollars—

RUTH. Sure is wonderful.

MAMA. Ten thousand dollars.

RUTH. You know what you should do, Miss Lena? You should take yourself a trip somewhere. To Europe or South America or someplace—

MAMA [*Throwing up her hands at the thought*]. Oh, child!

RUTH. I'm serious. Just pack up and leave! Go on away and enjoy yourself some. Forget about the family and have yourself a ball for once in your life—

MAMA [*Drily*]. You sound like I'm just about ready to die. Who'd go with me? What I look like wandering 'round Europe by myself?

RUTH. Shoot—these here rich white women do it all the time. They don't think nothing of packing up they suitcases and piling on one of them big steamships and—swoosh!—they gone, child.

MAMA. Something always told me I wasn't no rich white woman.

RUTH. Well—what are you going to do with it then?

MAMA. I ain't rightly decided. [*Thinking. She speaks now with emphasis*] Some of it got to be put away for Beneatha and her schoolin'—and ain't nothing going to touch that part of it. Nothing. [*She waits several seconds, trying to make up her mind about something, and looks at* RUTH *a little tentatively before going on*] Been thinking that we maybe could meet the notes on a little old two-story somewhere, with a yard where Travis could play in the summertime, if we use part of the insurance for a down payment and everybody kind of pitch in. I could maybe take on a little day work again, few days a week—

RUTH [*Studying her mother-in-law furtively and concentrating on her ironing, anxious to encourage without seeming to*]. Well, Lord knows, we've put enough rent into this here rat trap to pay for four houses by now...

MAMA [*Looking up at the words "rat trap" and then looking around and leaning back and sighing—in a suddenly reflective mood—*]."Rat trap"—yes, that's all it is. [*Smiling*] I remember just as well the day me and Big Walter moved in here. Hadn't been married but two weeks and wasn't planning on living here no more than a year. [*She shakes her head at the dissolved dream*] We was going to set away, little by little, don't you know, and buy a little place out in Morgan Park. We had even picked out the house. [*Chuckling a little*] Looks right dumpy today. But Lord, child, you should know all the dreams I had 'bout buying that house and fixing it up and making me a little garden in the back—[*She waits and stops smiling*] And didn't none of it happen. [*Dropping her hands in a futile gesture*]

RUTH [*Keeps her head down, ironing*]. Yes, life can be a barrel of disappointments, sometimes.

MAMA. Honey, Big Walter would come in here some nights back then and slump down on that couch there and just look at the rug, and look at me and look at the rug and then back at me—and I'd know he was down then...really down. [*After a second very long and thoughtful pause; she is seeing back to times that only she can see*] And then, Lord, when I lost that baby—little Claude—I almost thought I was going to lose Big Walter too. Oh, that man grieved hisself! He was one man to love his children.

RUTH. Ain't nothin' can tear at you like losin' your baby.

MAMA. I guess that's how come that man finally worked hisself to death like he done. Likely he was fighting his own war with this here world that took his baby from him.

RUTH. He sure was a fine man, all right. I always liked Mr. Younger.

MAMA. Crazy 'bout his children! God knows there was plenty wrong with Walter Younger—hard-headed, mean, kind of wild with women—plenty wrong with him. But he sure loved his children. Always wanted them to have something—be something. That's where Brother gets all these notions, I reckon. Big Walter used to say, he'd get right wet in the eyes sometimes, lean his head back with the water standing in his eyes and say, "Seem like God didn't see fit to give the black man nothing but dreams—but He did give us children to make them dreams seem worth while." [*She smiles*] He could talk like that, don't you know.

RUTH. Yes, he sure could. He was a good man, Mr. Younger.

MAMA. Yes, a fine man—just couldn't never catch up with his dreams, that's all.
[BENEATHA *comes in, brushing her hair and looking up to the ceiling, where the sound of a vacuum cleaner has started up*]

BENEATHA. What could be so dirty on that woman's rugs that she has to vacuum them every single day?

RUTH. I wish certain young women 'round here who I could name would take inspiration about certain rugs in a certain apartment I could also mention.

BENEATHA [*Shrugging*]. How much cleaning can a house need, for Christ's sakes?

MAMA [*Not liking the Lord's name used thus*]. Bennie!

RUTH. Just listen to her—just listen!

BENEATHA. Oh, God!

MAMA. If you use the Lord's name just one more time—

BENEATHA [*A bit of a whine*]. Oh, Mama—

RUTH. Fresh—just fresh as salt, this girl!

BENEATHA [*Drily*]. Well—if the salt loses its savor—

MAMA. Now that will do. I just ain't going to have you 'round here reciting the scriptures in vain—you hear me?

BENEATHA. How did I manage to get on everybody's wrong side by just walking into a room?

RUTH. If you weren't so fresh—

BENEATHA. Ruth, I'm twenty years old.

MAMA. What time you be home from school today?

BENEATHA. Kind of late. [*With enthusiasm*] Madeline is going to start my guitar lessons today. [MAMA *and* RUTH *look up with the same expression*]

MAMA. Your *what* kind of lessons?

BENEATHA. Guitar.

RUTH. Oh, Father!

MAMA. How come you done taken it in your mind to learn to play the guitar?

BENEATHA. I just want to, that's all.

MAMA [*Smiling*]. Lord, child, don't you know what to do with yourself? How long it going to be before you get tired of this now—like you got tired of that little play-acting group you joined last year? [*Looking at* RUTH] And what was it the year before that?

RUTH. The horseback-riding club for which she bought that fifty-five-dollar riding habit that's been hanging in the closet ever since!

MAMA [*To* BENEATHA]. Why you got to flit so from one thing to another, baby?

BENEATHA [*Sharply*]. I just want to learn to play the guitar. Is there anything wrong with that?

MAMA. Ain't nobody trying to stop you. I just wonders sometimes why you has to flit so from one thing to another all the time. You ain't never done nothing with all that camera equipment you brought home—

BENEATHA. I don't flit! I—I experiment with different forms of expression—

RUTH. Like riding a horse?

BENEATHA. —People have to express themselves one way or another.

MAMA. What is it you want to express?

BENEATHA [*Angrily*]. Me! [MAMA *and* RUTH *look at each other and burst into raucous laughter*] Don't worry—I don't expect you to understand.

MAMA [*To change the subject*]. Who you going out with tomorrow night?

BENEATHA [*With displeasure*]. George Murchison again.

MAMA [*Pleased*]. Oh—you getting a little sweet on him?

RUTH. You ask me, this child ain't sweet on nobody but herself—[*Underbreath*] Express herself! [*They laugh*]

BENEATHA. Oh—I like George all right, Mama. I mean I like him enough to go out with him and stuff, but—

RUTH [*For devilment*]. What does *and stuff* mean?

BENEATHA. Mind your own business.

MAMA. Stop picking at her now, Ruth. [*A thoughtful pause, and then a suspicious sudden look at her daughter as she turns in her chair for emphasis*] What *does* it mean?

BENEATHA [*Wearily*]. Oh, I just mean I couldn't ever really be serious about George. He's—he's so shallow.

RUTH. Shallow—what do you mean he's shallow? He's *rich!*

MAMA. Hush, Ruth.

BENEATHA. I know he's rich. He knows he's rich, too.

RUTH. Well—what other qualities a man got to have to satisfy you, little girl?

Beneatha. You wouldn't even begin to understand. Anybody who married Walter could not possibly understand.

Mama [*Outraged*]. What kind of way is that to talk about your brother?

Beneatha. Brother is a flip—let's face it.

Mama [*To* Ruth, *helplessly*]. What's a flip?

Ruth [*Glad to add kindling*]. She's saying he's crazy.

Beneatha. Not crazy. Brother isn't really crazy yet—he—he's an elaborate neurotic.

Mama. Hush your mouth!

Beneatha. As for George. Well. George looks good—he's got a beautiful car and he takes me to nice places and, as my sister-in-law says, he is probably the richest boy I will ever get to know and I even like him sometimes—but if the Youngers are sitting around waiting to see if their little Bennie is going to tie up the family with the Murchisons, they are wasting their time.

Ruth. You mean you wouldn't marry George Murchison if he asked you someday? That pretty, rich thing? Honey, I knew you was odd—

Beneatha. No, I would not marry him if all I felt for him was what I feel now. Besides, George's family wouldn't really like it.

Mama. Why not?

Beneatha. Oh, Mama—The Murchisons are honest-to-God-real-live-rich colored people, and the only people in the world who are more snobbish than rich white people are rich colored people. I thought everybody knew that. I've met Mrs. Murchison. She's a scene!

Mama. You must not dislike people 'cause they well off, honey.

Beneatha. Why not? It makes just as much sense as disliking people 'cause they are poor, and lots of people do that.

Ruth [*A wisdom-of-the-ages manner. To* Mama]. Well, she'll get over some of this—

Beneatha. Get over it? What are you talking about, Ruth? Listen, I'm going to be a doctor. I'm not worried about who I'm going to marry yet—if I ever get married.

Mama *and* Ruth. *If!*

Mama. Now, Bennie—

Beneatha. Oh, I probably will . . . but first I'm going to be a doctor, and George, for one, still thinks that's pretty funny. I couldn't be bothered with that. I am going to be a doctor and everybody around here better understand that!

Mama [*Kindly*].'Course you going to be a doctor, honey, God willing.

Beneatha [*Drily*]. God hasn't got a thing to do with it.

Mama. Beneatha—that just wasn't necessary.

Beneatha. Well—neither is God. I get sick of hearing about God.

Mama. Beneatha!

Beneatha. I mean it! I'm just tired of hearing about God all the time. What has He got to do with anything? Does he pay tuition?

Mama. You 'bout to get your fresh little jaw slapped!

Ruth. That's just what she needs, all right!

Beneatha. Why? Why can't I say what I want to around here, like everybody else?

Mama. It don't sound nice for a young girl to say things like that—you wasn't brought up that way. Me and your father went to trouble to get you and Brother to church every Sunday.

Beneatha. Mama, you don't understand. It's all a matter of ideas, and God is just one idea I don't accept. It's not important. I am not going out and be immoral or commit crimes because I don't believe in God. I don't even think about it. It's just that I get tired of Him getting credit for all the things the human race achieves through its own stubborn effort. There simply is no blasted God—there is only man and it is he who makes miracles! [MAMA *absorbs this speech, studies her daughter and rises slowly and crosses to* BENEATHA *and slaps her powerfully across the face. After, there is only silence and the daughter drops her eyes from her mother's face, and* MAMA *is very tall before her*]

MAMA. Now—you say after me, in my mother's house there is still God. [*There is a long pause and* BENEATHA *stares at the floor wordlessly.* MAMA *repeats the phrase with precision and cool emotion*] In my mother's house there is still God.

BENEATHA. In my mother's house there is still God. [*A long pause*]

MAMA [*Walking away from* BENEATHA, *too disturbed for triumphant posture. Stopping and turning back to her daughter*]. There are some ideas we ain't going to have in this house. Not long as I am at the head of this family.

BENEATHA. Yes, ma'am. [MAMA *walks out of the room*]

RUTH [*Almost gently, with profound understanding*]. You think you a woman, Bennie—but you still a little girl. What you did was childish—so you got treated like a child.

BENEATHA. I see. [*Quietly*] I also see that everybody thinks it's all right for Mama to be a tyrant. But all the tyranny in the world will never put a God in the heavens! [*She picks up her books and goes out*]

RUTH [*Goes to* MAMA*'s door*]. She said she was sorry.

MAMA [*Coming out, going to her plant*]. They frightens me, Ruth. My children.

RUTH. You got good children, Lena. They just a little off sometimes—but they're good.

MAMA. No—There's something come down between me and them that don't let us understand each other and I don't know what it is. One done almost lost his mind thinking 'bout money all the time and the other done commence to talk about things I can't seem to understand in no form or fashion. What is it that's changing, Ruth?

RUTH [*Soothingly, older than her years*]. Now...you taking it all too seriously. You just got strong-willed children and it takes a strong woman like you to keep 'em in hand.

MAMA [*Looking at her plant and sprinkling a little water on it*]. They spirited all right, my children. Got to admit they got spirit—Bennie and Walter. Like this little old plant that ain't never had enough sunshine or nothing—and look at it...[*She has her back to* RUTH, *who has had to stop ironing and lean against something and put the back of her hand to her forehead*]

RUTH [*Trying to keep* MAMA *from noticing*]. You...sure...loves that little old thing, don't you? ...

MAMA. Well, I always wanted me a garden like I used to see sometimes at the back of the houses down home. This plant is close as I ever got to having one. [*She looks out of the window as she replaces the plant*] Lord, ain't nothing as dreary as the view from this window on a dreary day, is there? Why ain't you singing this morning, Ruth? Sing that "No Ways Tired." That song always lifts me up so—[*She turns at last to see that* RUTH *has slipped quietly into a chair, in a state of semiconsciousness*] Ruth! Ruth honey—what's the matter with you...Ruth!

CURTAIN.

SCENE II

It is the following morning; a Saturday morning, and house cleaning is in progress at the YOUNGERS. *Furniture has been shoved hither and yon and* MAMA *is giving the kitchen-area walls a washing down.* BENEATHA, *in dungarees, with a handkerchief tied around her face, is spraying insecticide into the cracks in the walls. As they work, the radio is on and a Southside disk-jockey program is inappropriately filling the house with a rather exotic saxophone blues.* TRAVIS, *the sole idle one, is leaning on his arms, looking out of the window.*

TRAVIS. Grandmama, that stuff Bennie is using smells awful. Can I go downstairs, please?

MAMA. Did you get all them chores done already? I ain't seen you doing much.

TRAVIS. Yes'm—finished early. Where did Mama go this morning?

MAMA [*Looking at* BENEATHA]. She had to go on a little errand.

TRAVIS. Where?

MAMA. To tend to her business.

TRAVIS. Can I go outside then?

MAMA. Oh, I guess so. You better stay right in front of the house, though... and keep a good lookout for the postman.

TRAVIS. Yes'm. [*He starts out and decides to give his* AUNT BENEATHA *a good swat on the legs as he passes her*] Leave them poor little old cockroaches alone, they ain't bothering you none. [*He runs as she swings the spray gun at him both viciously and playfully.* WALTER *enters from the bedroom and goes to the phone*]

MAMA. Look out there, girl, before you be spilling some of that stuff on that child!

TRAVIS [*Teasing*]. That's right—look out now! [*He exits*]

BENEATHA [*Drily*]. I can't imagine that it would hurt him—it has never hurt the roaches.

MAMA. Well, little boys' hides ain't as tough as Southside roaches.

WALTER [*Into phone*]. Hello—Let me talk to Willy Harris.

MAMA. You better get over there behind the bureau. I seen one marching out of there like Napoleon yesterday.

WALTER. Hello, Willy? It ain't come yet. It'll be here in a few minutes. Did the lawyer give you the papers?

BENEATHA. There's really only one way to get rid of them, Mama—

MAMA. How?

BENEATHA. Set fire to this building.

WALTER. Good. Good. I'll be right over.

BENEATHA. Where did Ruth go, Walter?

WALTER. I don't know. [*He exits abruptly*]

BENEATHA. Mama, where did Ruth go?

MAMA [*Looking at her with meaning*]. To the doctor, I think.

BENEATHA. The doctor? What's the matter? [*They exchange glances*] You don't think—

MAMA [*With her sense of drama*]. Now I ain't saying what I think. But I ain't never been wrong 'bout a woman neither. [*The phone rings*]

BENEATHA [*At the phone*]. Hay-lo... [*Pause, and a moment of recognition*] Well—when did you get back!... And how was it?... Of course I've missed you—in my way... This morning? No... house cleaning and all that and Mama hates it if I let people come over when the house is like this... You *have?* Well, that's different... What is it—Oh, what the hell, come on over... Right, see you then. [*She hangs up*]

MAMA [*Who has listened vigorously, as is her habit*]. Who is that you inviting over here with this house looking like this? You ain't got the pride you was born with!

BENEATHA. Asagai doesn't care how houses look, Mama—he's an intellectual.

MAMA. *Who*?

BENEATHA. Asagai—Joseph Asagai. He's an African boy I met on campus. He's been studying in Canada all summer.

MAMA. What's his name?

BENEATHA. Asagai, Joseph. Ah-sah-guy... He's from Nigeria.

MAMA. Oh, that's the little country that was founded by slaves way back...

BENEATHA. No, Mama—that's Liberia.

MAMA. I don't think I never met no African before.

BENEATHA. Well, do me a favor and don't ask him a whole lot of ignorant questions about Africans. I mean, do they wear clothes and all that—

MAMA. Well, now, I guess if you think we so ignorant 'round here maybe you shouldn't bring your friends here—

BENEATHA. It's just that people ask such crazy things. All anyone seems to know about when it comes to Africa is Tarzan—

MAMA [*Indignantly*]. Why should I know anything about Africa?

BENEATHA. Why do you give money at church for the missionary work?

MAMA. Well, that's to help save people.

BENEATHA. You mean save them from *heathenism*—

MAMA [*Innocently*]. Yes.

BENEATHA. I'm afraid they need more salvation from the British and the French. [RUTH *comes in forlornly and pulls off her coat with dejection. They both turn to look at her*]

RUTH [*Dispiritedly*]. Well, I guess from all the happy faces—everybody knows.

BENEATHA. You pregnant?

MAMA. Lord have mercy, I sure hope it's a little old girl. Travis ought to have a sister. [BENEATHA *and* RUTH *give her a hopeless look for this grandmotherly enthusiasm*]

BENEATHA. How far along are you?

RUTH. Two months.

BENEATHA. Did you mean to? I mean did you plan it or was it an accident?

MAMA. What do you know about planning or not planning?

BENEATHA. Oh, Mama.

RUTH [*Wearily*]. She's twenty years old, Lena.

BENEATHA. Did you plan it, Ruth?

RUTH. Mind your own business.

BENEATHA. It is my business—where is he going to live, on the roof? [*There is silence following the remark as the three women react to the sense of it*] Gee—I didn't mean that, Ruth, honest. Gee, I don't feel like that at all. I—I think it is wonderful.

RUTH [*Dully*]. Wonderful.

BENEATHA. Yes—really.

MAMA [*Looking at* RUTH, *worried*]. Doctor say everything going to be all right?

RUTH [*Far away*]. Yes—she says everything is going to be fine …

MAMA [*Immediately suspicious*]. "She"—What doctor you went to? [RUTH *folds over, near hysteria*]

MAMA [*Worriedly hovering over* RUTH]. Ruth, honey—what's the matter with you—you sick? [RUTH *has her fists clenched on her thighs and is fighting hard to suppress a scream that seems to be rising in her*]

BENEATHA. What's the matter with her, Mama?

MAMA [*Working her fingers in* RUTH'S *shoulder to relax her*]. She be all right. Women gets right depressed sometimes when they get her way. [*Speaking softly, expertly, rapidly*] Now you just relax. That's right…just lean back, don't think 'bout nothing at all…nothing at all—

RUTH. I'm all right…[*The glassy-eyed look melts and then she collapses into a fit of heavy sobbing. The bell rings*]

BENEATHA. Oh, my God—that must be Asagai.

MAMA [TO RUTH]. Come on now, honey. You need to lie down and rest awhile…then have some nice hot food. [*They exit,* RUTH'S *weight on her mother-in-law.* BENEATHA, *herself profoundly disturbed, opens the door to admit a rather dramatic-looking young man with a large package*]

ASAGAI. Hello, Alaiyo—

BENEATHA [*Holding the door open and regarding him with pleasure*]. Hello…[*Long pause*] Well—come in. And please excuse everything. My mother was very upset about my letting anyone come here with the place like this.

ASAGAI [*Coming into the room*]. You look disturbed too…Is something wrong?

BENEATHA [*Still at the door, absently*]. Yes…we've all got acute ghetto-itus. [*She smiles and comes toward him, finding a cigarette and sitting*] So—sit down! How was Canada?

ASAGAI [*A sophisticate*]. Canadian.

BENEATHA [*Looking at him*]. I'm very glad you are back.

ASAGAI [*Looking back at her in turn*]. Are you really?

BENEATHA. Yes—very.

ASAGAI. Why—you were quite glad when I went away. What happened?

BENEATHA. You went away.

ASAGAI. Ahhhhhhhh.

BENEATHA. Before—you wanted to be so serious before there was time.

ASAGAI. How much time must there be before one knows what one feels?

BENEATHA [*Stalling this particular conversation. Her hands pressed together, in a deliberately childish gesture*]. What did you bring me?

ASAGAI [*Handing her the package*]. Open it and see.

BENEATHA [*Eagerly opening the package and drawing out some records and the colorful robes of a Nigerian woman*]. Oh, Asagai!…You got them for me!…How beautiful…and the records too! [*She lifts out the robes and runs to the mirror with them and holds the drapery up in front of herself*]

ASAGAI [*Coming to her at the mirror*]. I shall have to teach you how to drape it properly. [*He flings the material about her for the moment and stands back to look at her*] Ah—Oh-pay-gay-day, oh-gbah-mu-shay. [*A Yoruba exclamation for admiration*] You wear it well…very well…mutilated hair and all.

BENEATHA [*Turning suddenly*]. My hair—what's wrong with my hair?

ASAGAI [*Shrugging*]. Were you born with it like that?

BENEATHA [*Reaching up to touch it*]. No…of course not. [*She looks back to the mirror, disturbed*]

ASAGAI [*Smiling*]. How then?

BENEATHA. You know perfectly well how... as crinkly as yours... that's how.

ASAGAI. And it is ugly to you that way?

BENEATHA [*Quickly*]. Oh, no—not ugly... [*More slowly, apologetically*] But it's so hard to manage when it's, well—raw.

ASAGAI. And so to accommodate that—you mutilate it every week?

BENEATHA. It's not mutilation!

ASAGAI [*Laughing aloud at her seriousness*]. Oh... please! I am only teasing you because you are so very serious about these things. [*He stands back from her and folds his arms across his chest as he watches her pulling at her hair and frowning in the mirror*] Do you remember the first time you met me at school?... [*He laughs*] You came up to me and said—and I thought you were the most serious little thing I had ever seen—you said: [*He imitates her*] "Mr. Asagai—I want very much to talk with you. About Africa. You see, Mr. Asagai, I am looking for my *identity*!" [*He laughs*]

BENEATHA [*Turning to him, not laughing*]. Yes—[*Her face is quizzical, profoundly disturbed*]

ASAGAI [*Still teasing and reaching out and taking her face in his hands and turning her profile to him*]. Well... it is true that this is not so much a profile of a Hollywood queen as perhaps a queen of the Nile—[*A mock dismissal of the importance of the question*] But what does it matter? Assimilationism is so popular in your country.

BENEATHA [*Wheeling, passionately, sharply*]. I am not an assimilationist!

ASAGAI [*The protest hangs in the room for a moment and* ASAGAI *studies her, his laughter fading*]. Such a serious one. [*There is a pause*] So—you like the robes? You must take excellent care of them—they are from my sister's personal wardrobe.

BENEATHA [*With incredulity*]. You—you sent all the way home—for me?

ASAGAI [*With charm*]. For you—I would do much more... Well, that is what I came for. I must go.

BENEATHA. Will you call me Monday?

ASAGAI. Yes... We have a great deal to talk about. I mean about identity and time and all that.

BENEATHA. Time?

ASAGAI. Yes. About how much time one needs to know what one feels.

BENEATHA. You never understood that there is more than one kind of feeling which can exist between a man and a woman—or, at least, there should be.

ASAGAI [*Shaking his head negatively but gently*]. No. Between a man and a woman there need be only one kind of feeling. I have that for you... Now even... right this moment ...

BENEATHA. I know—and by itself—it won't do. I can find that anywhere.

ASAGAI. For a woman it should be enough.

BENEATHA. I know—because that's what it says in all the novels that men write. But it isn't. Go ahead and laugh—but I'm not interested in being someone's little episode in America or—[*With feminine vengeance*]—one of them! [ASAGAI *has burst into laughter again*] That's funny as hell, huh!

ASAGAI. It's just that every American girl I have known has said that to me. White—black—in this you are all the same. And the same speech, too!

BENEATHA [*Angrily*]. Yuk, yuk, yuk!

ASAGAI. It's how you can be sure that the world's most liberated women are not liberated at all. You all talk about it too much! [MAMA *enters and is immediately all social charm because of the presence of a guest*]

Beneatha. Oh—Mama—this is Mr. Asagai.

Mama. How do you do?

Asagai [*Total politeness to an elder*]. How do you do, Mrs. Younger. Please forgive me for coming at such an outrageous hour on a Saturday.

Mama. Well, you are quite welcome. I just hope you understand that our house don't always look like this. [*Chatterish*] You must come again. I would love to hear all about—[*Not sure of the name*]—your country. I think it's so sad the way our American Negroes don't know nothing about Africa 'cept Tarzan and all that. And all that money they pour into these churches when they ought to be helping you people over there drive out them French and Englishmen done taken away your land. [*The mother flashes a slightly superior look at her daughter upon completion of the recitation*]

Asagai [*Taken aback by this sudden and acutely unrelated expression of sympathy*]. Yes... yes ...

Mama [*Smiling at him suddenly and relaxing and looking him over*]. How many miles is it from here to where you come from?

Asagai. Many thousands.

Mama [*Looking at him as she would* Walter]. I bet you don't half look after yourself, being away from your mama either. I spec you better come 'round here from time to time and get yourself some decent homecooked meals ...

Asagai [*Moved*]. Thank you. Thank you very much. [*They are all quiet, then*—] Well... I must go. I will call you Monday, Alaiyo.

Mama. What's that he call you?

Asagai. Oh—"Alaiyo." I hope you don't mind. It is what you would call a nickname, I think. It is a Yoruba word. I am a Yoruba.

Mama [*Looking at* Beneatha]. I—I thought he was from—

Asagai [*Understanding*]. Nigeria is my country. Yoruba is my tribal origin—

Beneatha. You didn't tell us what Alaiyo means... for all I know, you might be calling me Little Idiot or something...

Asagai. Well... let me see... I do not know how just to explain it... The sense of a thing can be so different when it changes languages.

Beneatha. You're evading.

Asagai. No—really it is difficult... [*Thinking*] It means... it means One for Whom Bread—Food—Is Not Enough. [*He looks at her*] Is that all right?

Beneatha [*Understanding, softly*]. Thank you.

Mama [*Looking from one to the other and not understanding any of it*]. Well... that's nice... You must come see us again—Mr.—

Asagai. Ah-sah-guy....

Mama. Yes... Do come again.

Asagai. Good-bye. [*He exits*]

Mama [*After him*]. Lord, that's a pretty thing just went out here! [*Insinuatingly, to her daughter*] Yes, I guess I see why we done commence to get so interested in Africa 'round here. Missionaries my aunt Jenny! [*She exits*]

Beneatha. Oh, Mama!... [*She picks up the Nigerian dress and holds it up to her in front of the mirror again. She sets the headdress on haphazardly and then notices her hair again and clutches at it and then replaces the headdress and frowns at herself. Then she starts to wriggle in front of the mirror as she thinks a Nigerian woman might.* Travis *enters and regards her*]

Travis. You cracking up?

BENEATHA. Shut up. [*She pulls the headdress off and looks at herself in the mirror and clutches at her hair again and squinches her eyes as if trying to imagine something. Then, suddenly, she gets her raincoat and kerchief and hurriedly prepares for going out*]

MAMA [*Coming back into the room*]. She's resting now. Travis, baby, run next door and ask Miss Johnson to please let me have a little kitchen cleanser. This here can is empty as Jacob's kettle.

TRAVIS. I just came in.

MAMA. Do as you told. [*He exits and she looks at her daughter*] Where you going?

BENEATHA [*Halting at the door*]. To become a queen of the Nile! [*She exits in a breathless blaze of glory.* RUTH *appears in the bedroom doorway*]

MAMA. Who told you to get up?

RUTH. Ain't nothing wrong with me to be lying in no bed for. Where did Bennie go?

MAMA [*Drumming her fingers*]. Far as I could make out—to Egypt. [RUTH *just looks at her*] What time is it getting to?

RUTH. Ten twenty. And the mailman going to ring that bell this morning just like he done every morning for the last umpteen years. [TRAVIS *comes in with the cleanser can*]

TRAVIS. She say to tell you that she don't have much.

MAMA [*Angrily*]. Lord, some people I could name sure is tight-fisted! [*Directing her grandson*] Mark two cans of cleanser down on the list there. If she that hard up for kitchen cleanser, I sure don't want to forget to get her none!

RUTH. Lena—maybe the woman is just short on cleanser—

MAMA [*Not listening*].—Much baking powder as she done borrowed from me all these years, she could of done gone into the baking business! [*The bell sounds suddenly and sharply and all three are stunned—serious and silent—mid-speech. In spite of all the other conversation and distractions of the morning, this is what they have been waiting for, even* TRAVIS, *who looks helplessly from his mother to his grandmother.* RUTH *is the first to come to life again*]

RUTH [*to* TRAVIS]. Get down them steps, boy! [TRAVIS *snaps to life and flies out to get the mail*]

MAMA [*Her eyes wide, her hand to her breast*]. You mean it done really come?

RUTH [*Excited*]. Oh, Miss Lena!

MAMA [*Collecting herself*]. Well... I don't know what we all so excited about 'round here for. We known it was coming for months.

RUTH. That's a whole lot different from having it come and being able to hold it in your hands... a piece of paper worth ten thousand dollars... [TRAVIS *bursts back into the room. He holds the envelope high above his head, like a little dancer, his face is radiant and he is breathless. He moves to his grandmother with sudden slow ceremony and puts the envelope into her hands. She accepts it, and then merely holds it and looks at it*] Come on! Open it... Lord have mercy, I wish Walter Lee was here!

TRAVIS. Open it, Grandmama!

MAMA [*Staring at it*]. Now you all be quiet. It's just a check.

RUTH. Open it ...

MAMA [*Still staring at it*]. Now don't act silly... We ain't never been no people to act silly 'bout no money—

RUTH [*Swiftly*]. We ain't never had none before—open it! [MAMA *finally makes a good strong tear and pulls out the thin blue slice of paper and inspects it closely. The boy and his mother study it raptly over* MAMA*'s shoulders*]

MAMA. Travis! [*She is counting off with doubt*] Is that the right number of zeros?

TRAVIS. Yes'm... ten thousand dollars. Gaalee, Grandmama, you rich.

MAMA [*She holds the check away from her, still looking at it. Slowly her face sobers into a mask of unhappiness*]. Ten thousand dollars. [*She hands it to* RUTH] Put it away somewhere, Ruth. [*She does not look at* RUTH; *her eyes seem to be seeing something somewhere very far off*] Ten thousand dollars they give you. Ten thousand dollars.

TRAVIS [*To his mother, sincerely*]. What's the matter with Grandmama—don't she want to be rich?

RUTH [*Distractedly*]. You go on out and play now, baby. [TRAVIS *exits.* MAMA *starts wiping dishes absently, humming intently to herself.* RUTH *turns to her, with kind exasperation*] You've gone and got yourself upset.

MAMA [*Not looking at her*]. I spec if it wasn't for you all... I would just put that money away or give it to the church or something.

RUTH. Now what kind of talk is that. Mr. Younger would just be plain mad if he could hear you talking foolish like that.

MAMA [*Stopping and staring off*]. Yes... he sure would. [*Sighing*] We got enough to do with that money, all right. [*She halts then, and turns and looks at her daughter-in-law hard;* RUTH *avoids her eyes and* MAMA *wipes her hands with finality and starts to speak firmly to* RUTH] Where did you go today, girl?

RUTH. To the doctor.

MAMA [*Impatiently*]. Now, Ruth... you know better than that. Old Doctor Jones is strange enough in his way but there ain't nothing 'bout him make somebody slip and call him "she"—like you done this morning.

RUTH. Well, that's what happened—my tongue slipped.

MAMA. You went to see that woman, didn't you?

RUTH [*Defensively, giving herself away*]. What woman you talking about?

MAMA [*Angrily*]. That woman who—[WALTER *enters in great excitement*]

WALTER. Did it come?

MAMA [*Quietly*]. Can't you give people a Christian greeting before you start asking about money?

WALTER [*To* RUTH]. Did it come? [RUTH *unfolds the check and lays it quietly before him, watching him intently with thoughts of her own.* WALTER *sits down and grasps it close and counts off the zeros*] Ten thousand dollars—[*He turns suddenly, frantically to his mother and draws some papers out of his breast pocket*] Mama—look. Old Willy Harris put everything on paper—

MAMA. Son—I think you ought to talk to your wife... I'll go on out and leave you alone if you want—

WALTER. I can talk to her later—Mama, look—

MAMA. Son—

WALTER. WILL SOMEBODY PLEASE LISTEN TO ME TODAY!

MAMA [*Quietly*]. I don't 'low no yellin' in this house, Walter Lee, and you know it—[WALTER *stares at them in frustration and starts to speak several times*] And there ain't going to be no investing in no liquor stores. I don't aim to have to speak on that again. [*A long pause*]

WALTER. Oh—so you don't aim to have to speak on that again? So *you* have decided... [*Crumpling his papers*]. Well, *you* tell that to my boy tonight when you put him to sleep on the living-room couch... [*Turning to* MAMA *and speaking directly to her*]. Yeah—and tell it to my wife, Mama, tomorrow when she has to go out of here to look after somebody else's kids. And tell it to *me*,

Mama, every time we need a new pair of curtains and I have to watch *you* go out and work in somebody's kitchen. Yeah, you tell me then! [*Walter starts out*]

RUTH. Where you going?

WALTER. I'm going out!

RUTH. Where?

WALTER. Just out of this house somewhere—

RUTH [*Getting her coat*]. I'll come too.

WALTER. I don't want you to come!

RUTH. I got something to talk to you about, Walter.

WALTER. That's too bad.

MAMA [*Still quietly*]. Walter Lee—[*She waits and he finally turns and looks at her*] Sit down.

WALTER. I'm a grown man, Mama.

MAMA. Ain't nobody said you wasn't grown. But you still in my house and my presence. And as long as you are—you'll talk to your wife civil. Now sit down.

RUTH [*Suddenly*]. Oh, let him go on out and drink himself to death! He makes me sick to my stomach! [*She flings her coat against him*]

WALTER [*Violently*]. And you turn mine, too, baby! [RUTH *goes into their bedroom and slams the door behind her.*] That was my greatest mistake—

MAMA [*Still quietly*]. Walter, what is the matter with you?

WALTER. Matter with me? Ain't nothing the matter with *me!*

MAMA. Yes there is. Something eating you up like a crazy man. Something more than me not giving you this money. The past few years I been watching it happen to you. You get all nervous acting and kind of wild in the eyes—[WALTER *jumps up impatiently at her words*] I said sit there now, I'm talking to you!

WALTER. Mama—I don't need no nagging at me today.

MAMA. Seem like you getting to a place where you always tied up in some kind of knot about something. But if anybody ask you 'bout it you just yell at 'em and bust out the house and go out and drink somewheres. Walter Lee, people can't live with that. Ruth's a good, patient girl in her way—but you getting to be too much. Boy, don't make the mistake of driving that girl away from you.

WALTER. Why—what she do for me?

MAMA. She loves you.

WALTER. Mama—I'm going out. I want to go off somewhere and be by myself for a while.

MAMA. I'm sorry 'bout your liquor store, son. It just wasn't the thing for us to do. That's what I want to tell you about—

WALTER. I got to go out, Mama—[*He rises*]

MAMA. It's dangerous, son.

WALTER. What's dangerous?

MAMA. When a man goes outside his home to look for peace.

WALTER [*Beseechingly*]. Then why can't there never be no peace in this house then?

MAMA. You done found it in some other house?

WALTER. No—there ain't no woman! Why do women always think there's a woman somewhere when a man gets restless. [*Coming to her*] Mama—Mama—I want so many things . . .

MAMA. Yes, son—

WALTER. I want so many things that they are driving me kind of crazy... Mama—look at me.

MAMA. I'm looking at you. You a good-looking boy. You got a job, a nice wife, a fine boy and—

WALTER. A job. [*Looks at her*] Mama, a job? I open and close car doors all day long. I drive a man around in his limousine and I say, "Yes, sir; no, sir; very good, sir; shall I take the Drive, sir?" Mama, that ain't no kind of job... that ain't nothing at all. [*Very quietly*] Mama, I don't know if I can make you understand.

MAMA. Understand what, baby?

WALTER [*Quietly*]. Sometimes it's like I can see the future stretched out in front of me—just plain as day. The future, Mama. Hanging over there at the edge of my days. Just waiting for me—a big, looming blank space—full of *nothing*. Just waiting for *me*. [*Pause*] Mama—sometimes when I'm downtown and I pass them cool, quiet-looking restaurants where them white boys are sitting back and talking 'bout things... sitting there turning deals worth millions of dollars... sometimes I see guys don't look much older than me—

MAMA. Son—how come you talk so much 'bout money?

WALTER [*With immense passion*]. Because it is life, Mama!

MAMA [*Quietly*]. Oh—[*Very quietly*] So now it's life. Money is life. Once upon a time freedom used to be life—now it's money. I guess the world really do change ...

WALTER. No—it was always money, Mama. We just didn't know about it.

MAMA. No... something has changed. [*She looks at him*] You something new, boy. In my time we was worried about not being lynched and getting to the North if we could and how to stay alive and still have a pinch of dignity too... Now here come you and Beneatha—talking 'bout things we ain't never even thought about hardly, me and your daddy. You ain't satisfied or proud of nothing we done. I mean that you had a home; that we kept you out of trouble till you was grown; that you don't have to ride to work on the back of nobody's streetcar. You my children—but how different we done become.

WALTER. You just don't understand, Mama, you just don't understand.

MAMA. Son—do you know your wife is expecting another baby? [WALTER *stands, stunned, and absorbs what his mother has said*] That's what she wanted to talk to you about. [WALTER sinks down into a chair] This ain't for me to be telling—but you ought to know. [*She waits*] I think Ruth is thinking 'bout getting rid of that child.

WALTER [*Slowly understanding*]. No—no—Ruth wouldn't do that.

MAMA. When the world gets ugly enough—a woman will do anything for her family. *The part that's already living.*

WALTER. You don't know Ruth, Mama, if you think she would do that. [RUTH *opens the bedroom door and stands there a little limp*]

RUTH [*Beaten*]. Yes I would too, Walter. [*Pause*] I gave her a five-dollar down payment. [*There is total silence as the man stares at his wife and the mother stares at her son*]

MAMA [*Presently*]. Well—[*Tightly*] Well—son, I'm waiting to hear you say something... I'm waiting to hear how you be your father's son. Be the man he was... [*Pause*] Your wife say she going to destroy your child. And I'm waiting to hear you talk like him and say we a people who give children life, not who destroys them—[*She rises*] I'm waiting to see you stand up and look like your daddy and say we done give up one baby to poverty and that we ain't going to give up nary another one…I'm waiting.

WALTER. Ruth—

MAMA. If you a son of mine, tell her! [WALTER *turns, looks at her and can say nothing. She continues, bitterly*] You…you are a disgrace to your father's memory. Somebody get me my hat.

CURTAIN.

ACT II

SCENE I

Time: Later the same day.

At rise: RUTH *is ironing again. She has the radio going. Presently* BENEATHA*'s bedroom door opens and* RUTH*'s mouth falls and she puts down the iron in fascination.*

RUTH. What have we got on tonight!

BENEATHA [*Emerging grandly from the doorway so that we can see her thoroughly robed in the costume* ASAGAI *brought*]. You are looking at what a well-dressed Nigerian woman wears—[*She parades for* RUTH, *her hair completely hidden by the headdress; she is coquettishly fanning herself with an ornate oriental fan, mistakenly more like Butterfly than any Nigerian that ever was*] Isn't it beautiful? [*She promenades to the radio and, with an arrogant flourish, turns off the good loud blues that is playing*] Enough of this assimilationist junk! [RUTH *follows her with her eyes as she goes to the phonograph and puts on a record and turns and waits ceremoniously for the music to come up. Then with a shout*] OCOMOGOSIAY! [RUTH *jumps. The music comes up, a lovely Nigerian melody.* BENEATHA *listens, enraptured, her eyes far away—"back to the past." She begins to dance.* RUTH *is dumbfounded*]

RUTH. What kind of dance is that?

BENEATHA. A folk dance.

RUTH [*Pearl Bailey*]. What kind of folks do that, honey?

BENEATHA. It's from Nigeria. It's a dance of welcome.

RUTH. Who you welcoming?

BENEATHA. The men back to the village.

RUTH. Where they been?

BENEATHA. How should I know—out hunting or something. Anyway, they are coming back now…

RUTH. Well, that's good.

BENEATHA [*With the record*]. *Alundi, alundi*
Alundi alunya
Jop pu a jeepua
Ang gu sooooooooo
Ai yai yae …

Ayehaye—alundi… [WALTER *comes in during this performance; he has obviously been drinking. He leans against the door heavily and watches his sister, at first with distaste. Then his eyes look off—"back to the past"—as he lifts both his fists to the roof, screaming*]

WALTER. YEAH... AND ETHIOPIA STRETCH FORTH HER HANDS AGAIN!...

RUTH [*Drily, looking at him*]. Yes—and Africa sure is claiming her own tonight. [*She gives them both up and starts ironing again*]

WALTER [*All in a drunken, dramatic shout*]. Shut up!... I'm digging them drums... them drums move me!... [*He makes his weaving way to his wife's face and leans in close to her*] In my *heart of hearts*—[*He thumps his chest*]—I am much warrior!

RUTH [*Without even looking up*]. In your heart of hearts you are much drunkard.

WALTER [*Coming away from her and starting to wander around the room, shouting*]. Me and Jomo... [*Intently, in his sister's face. She has stopped dancing to watch him in this unknown mood*] That's my man, Kenyatta. [*Shouting and thumping his chest*] FLAMING SPEAR! HOT DAMN! [*He is suddenly in possession of an imaginary spear and actively spearing enemies all over the room*] OCOMOGOSIAY... THE LION IS WAKING... OWIMOWEH! [*He pulls his shirt open and leaps up on a table and gestures with his spear. The bell rings.* RUTH *goes to answer*]

BENEATHA [*To encourage* WALTER, *thoroughly caught up with this side of him*]. OCOMOGOSIAY, FLAMING SPEAR!

WALTER [*On the table, very far gone, his eyes pure glass sheets. He sees what we cannot, that he is a leader of his people, a great chief, a descendant of Chaka, and that the hour to march has come*]. Listen, my black brothers—

BENEATHA. OCOMOGOSIAY!

WALTER. —Do you hear the waters rushing against the shores of the coastlands—

BENEATHA. OCOMOGOSIAY!

WALTER. —Do you hear the screeching of the cocks in yonder hills beyond where the chiefs meet in council for the coming of the mighty war—

BENEATHA. OCOMOGOSIAY!

WALTER. —Do you hear the beating of the wings of the birds flying low over the mountains and the low places of our land—[RUTH *opens the door*; GEORGE MURCHISON *enters*]

BENEATHA. OCOMOGOSIAY!

WALTER. —Do you hear the singing of the women, singing the war songs of our fathers to the babies in the great houses... singing the sweet war songs? oh, do you hear, my black brothers?

BENEATHA [*Completely gone*]. We hear you, Flaming Spear—

WALTER. Telling us to prepare for the greatness of the time—[*To* GEORGE] Black Brother! [*He extends his hand for the fraternal clasp*]

GEORGE. Black Brother, hell!

RUTH [*Having had enough, and embarrassed for the family*]. Beneatha, you got company—what's the matter with you? Walter Lee Younger, get down off that table and stop acting like a fool... [WALTER *comes down off the table suddenly and makes a quick exit to the bathroom*]

RUTH. He's had a little to drink... I don't know what her excuse is.

GEORGE [*To* BENEATHA]. Look honey, we're going *to* the theatre—we're not going to be *in* it... so go change, huh?

RUTH. You expect this boy to go out with you looking like that?

BENEATHA [*Looking at* GEORGE]. That's up to George. If he's ashamed of his heritage—

GEORGE. Oh, don't be so proud of yourself, Bennie—just because you look eccentric.

BENEATHA. How can something that's natural be eccentric?

GEORGE. That's what being eccentric means—being natural. Get dressed.

BENEATHA. I don't like that, George.

RUTH. Why must you and your brother make an argument out of everything people say?

BENEATHA. Because I hate assimilationist Negroes!

RUTH. Will somebody please tell me what assimila-who-ever means!

GEORGE. Oh, it's just a college girl's way of calling people Uncle Toms—but that isn't what it means at all.

RUTH. Well, what does it mean?

BENEATHA [*Cutting* GEORGE *off and staring at him as she replies to* RUTH]. It means someone who is willing to give up his own culture and submerge himself completely in the dominant, and in this case, *oppressive* culture!

GEORGE. Oh, dear, dear, dear! Here we go! A lecture on the African past! On our Great West African Heritage! In one second we will hear all about the great Ashanti empires; the great Songhay civilizations; and the great sculpture of Bénin—and then some poetry in the Bantu—and the whole monologue will end with the word *heritage!* [*Nastily*] Let's face it, baby, your heritage is nothing but a bunch of raggedy-assed spirituals and some grass huts!

BENEATHA. *Grass huts!* [RUTH *crosses to her and forcibly pushes her toward the bedroom*] See there... you are standing there in your splendid ignorance talking about people who were the first to smelt iron on the face of the earth! [RUTH *is pushing her through the door*] The Ashanti were performing surgical operations when the English—[RUTH *pulls the door to, with* BENEATHA *on the other side, and smiles graciously at* GEORGE. BENEATHA *opens the door and shouts the end of the sentence defiantly at* GEORGE]—were still tattooing themselves with blue dragons... [*She goes back inside*]

RUTH. Have a seat, George. [*They both sit.* RUTH *folds her hands rather primly on her lap, determined to demonstrate the civilization of the family*] Warm, ain't it? I mean for September. [*Pause*] Just like they always say about Chicago weather: If it's too hot or cold for you, just wait a minute and it'll change. [*She smiles happily at this cliché of clichés*] Everybody say it's got to do with them bombs and things they keep setting off. [*Pause*] Would you like a nice cold beer?

GEORGE. No, thank you. I don't care for beer. [*He looks at his watch*] I hope she hurries up.

RUTH. What time is the show?

GEORGE. It's an eight-thirty curtain. That's just Chicago, though. In New York standard curtain time is eight forty. [*He is rather proud of this knowledge*]

RUTH [*Properly appreciating it*]. You get to New York a lot?

GEORGE [*Offhand*]. Few times a year.

RUTH. Oh—that's nice. I've never been to New York. [WALTER *enters. We feel he has relieved himself, but the edge of unreality is still with him*]

WALTER. New York ain't got nothing Chicago ain't. Just a bunch of hustling people all squeezed up together—being "Eastern." [*He turns his face into a screw of displeasure*]

GEORGE. Oh—you've been?

WALTER. *Plenty* of times.

RUTH [*Shocked at the lie*]. Walter Lee Younger!

Walter [*Staring her down*]. Plenty! [*Pause*] What we got to drink in this house? Why don't you offer this man some refreshment. [*To* George] They don't know how to entertain people in this house, man.

George. Thank you—I don't really care for anything.

Walter [*Feeling his head; sobriety coming*]. Where's Mama?

Ruth. She ain't come back yet.

Walter [*Looking* Murchison *over from head to toe, scrutinizing his carefully casual tweed sports jacket over cashmere V-neck sweater over soft eyelet shirt and tie, and soft slacks, finished off with white buckskin shoes*]. Why all you college boys wear them fairyish-looking white shoes?

Ruth. Walter Lee! [George Murchison *ignores the remark*]

Walter [*To* Ruth]. Well, they look crazy as hell—white shoes, cold as it is.

Ruth [*Crushed*]. You have to excuse him—

Walter. No he don't! Excuse me for what? What you always excusing me for! I'll excuse myself when I needs to be excused! [*A pause*] They look as funny as them black knee socks Beneatha wears out of here all the time.

Ruth. It's the college *style*, Walter.

Walter. Style, hell. She looks like she got burnt legs or something!

Ruth. Oh, Walter—

Walter [*An irritable mimic*]. Oh, Walter! Oh, Walter! [*To* Murchison] How's your old man making out? I understand you all going to buy that big hotel on the Drive?[1] [*He finds a beer in the refrigerator, wanders over to Murchison, sipping and wiping his lips with the back of his hand, and straddling a chair backwards to talk to the other man*] Shrewd move. Your old man is all right, man. [*Tapping his head and half winking for emphasis*] I mean he knows how to operate. I mean he thinks *big*, you know what I mean, I mean for a *home*, you know?[2] But I think he's kind of running out of ideas now. I'd like to talk to him. Listen, man, I got some plans that could turn this city upside down. I mean I think like he does. *Big*. Invest big, gamble big, hell, lose *big* if you have to, you know what I mean. It's hard to find a man on this whole Southside who understands my kind of thinking—you dig? [*He scrutinizes* Murchison *again, drinks his beer, squints his eyes and leans in close, confidential, man to man*] Me and you ought to sit down and talk sometimes, man. Man, I got me some ideas...

Murchison [*With boredom*]. Yeah—sometime we'll have to do that, Walter.

Walter [*Understanding the indifference, and offended*]. Yeah—well, when you get the time, man. I know you a busy little boy.

Ruth. Walter, please—

Walter [*Bitterly, hurt*]. I know ain't nothing in this world as busy as you colored college boys with your fraternity pins and white shoes...

Ruth [*Covering her face with humiliation*]. Oh, Walter Lee—

Walter. I see you all all the time—with the books tucked under your arms—going to your [*British A—a mimic*] "clahsses." And for what! What the hell you learning over there? Filling up your heads—[*Counting off on his fingers*]—with the sociology and the psychology—but they teaching you how to be a man? How to take over and run the world? They teaching you how to run a rubber plantation or a steel mill? Naw—just to talk proper and read books and wear white shoes...

---

[1]**Drive** Chicago's Outer Drive running along Lake Michigan.

[2]**Home** Home-boy; one of us.

GEORGE [*Looking at him with distaste, a little above it all*]. You're all wacked up with bitterness, man.

WALTER [*Intently, almost quietly, between the teeth, glaring at the boy*]. And you—ain't you bitter, man? Ain't you just about had it yet? Don't you see no stars gleaming that you can't reach out and grab? You happy?—You contented son-of-a-bitch—you happy? You got it made? Bitter? Man, I'm a volcano. Bitter? Here I am a giant—surrounded by ants! Ants who can't even understand what it is the giant is talking about.

RUTH [*Passionately and suddenly*]. Oh, Walter—ain't you with nobody!

WALTER [*Violently*]. No! 'Cause ain't nobody with me! Not even my own mother!

RUTH. Walter, that's a terrible thing to say! [BENEATHA *enters, dressed for the evening in a cocktail dress and earrings*]

GEORGE. Well—hey, you look great.

BENEATHA. Let's go, George. See you all later.

RUTH. Have a nice time.

GEORGE. Thanks. Good night. [*To* WALTER, *sarcastically*] Good night, Prometheus. [BENEATHA *and* GEORGE *exit*]

WALTER [*To* RUTH]. Who is Prometheus?

RUTH. I don't know. Don't worry about it.

WALTER [*In fury, pointing after* GEORGE]. See there—they get to a point where they can't insult you man to man—they got to go talk about something ain't nobody never heard of!

RUTH. How do you know it was an insult? [*To humor him*] Maybe Prometheus is a nice fellow.

WALTER. Prometheus! I bet there ain't even no such thing! I bet that simple-minded clown—

RUTH. Walter—[*She stops what she is doing and looks at him*]

WALTER [*Yelling*]. Don't start!

RUTH. Start what?

WALTER. Your nagging! Where was I? Who was I with? How much money did I spend?

RUTH [*Plaintively*]. Walter Lee—why don't we just try to talk about it...

WALTER [*Not listening*]. I been out talking with people who understand me. People who care about the things I got on my mind.

RUTH [*Wearily*]. I guess that means people like Willy Harris.

WALTER. Yes, people like Willy Harris.

RUTH [*With a sudden flash of impatience*]. Why don't you all just hurry up and go into the banking business and stop talking about it!

WALTER. Why? You want to know why? 'Cause we all tied up in a race of people that don't know how to do nothing but moan, pray and have babies! [*The line is too bitter even for him and he looks at her and sits down*]

RUTH. Oh, Walter... [*Softly*] Honey, why can't you stop fighting me?

WALTER [*Without thinking*]. Who's fighting you? Who even cares about you? [*This line begins the retardation of his mood*]

RUTH. Well—[*She waits a long time, and then with resignation starts to put away her things*] I guess I might as well go on to bed... [*More or less to herself*] I don't know where we lost it... but we have... [*Then, to him*] I—I'm sorry about this new baby, Walter. I guess maybe I better go on and do what I started... I guess I just didn't realize how bad things was with us... I guess I just didn't really realize—[*She starts out to the bedroom and stops*] You want some hot milk?

WALTER. Hot milk?

RUTH. Yes—hot milk.

WALTER. Why hot milk?

RUTH. 'Cause after all that liquor you come home with you ought to have something hot in your stomach.

WALTER. I don't want no milk.

RUTH. You want some coffee then?

WALTER. No, I don't want no coffee. I don't want nothing hot to drink. [*Almost plaintively*] Why you always trying to give me something to eat?

RUTH [*Standing and looking at him helplessly*]. What else can I give you, Walter Lee Younger? [*She stands and looks at him and presently turns to go out again. He lifts his head and watches her going away from him in a new mood which began to emerge when he asked her "Who cares about you?"*]

WALTER. It's been rough, ain't it, baby? [*She hears and stops but does not turn around and he continues to her back*] I guess between two people there ain't never as much understood as folks generally thinks there is. I mean like between me and you—[*She turns to face him*] How we gets to the place where we scared to talk softness to each other. [*He waits, thinking hard himself*] Why you think it got to be like that? [*He is thoughtful, almost as a child would be*] Ruth, what is it gets into people ought to be close?

RUTH. I don't know, honey. I think about it a lot.

WALTER. On account of you and me, you mean? The way things are with us. The way something done come down between us.

RUTH. There ain't so much between us, Walter... Not when you come to me and try to talk to me. Try to be with me... a little even.

WALTER [*Total honesty*]. Sometimes... sometimes... I don't even know how to try.

RUTH. Walter—

WALTER. Yes?

RUTH [*Coming to him, gently and with misgiving, but coming to him*]. Honey... life don't have to be like this. I mean sometimes people can do things so that things are better... You remember how we used to talk when Travis was born... about the way we were going to live... the kind of house... [*She is stroking his head*] Well, it's all starting to slip away from us... [MAMA *enters, and* WALTER *jumps up and shouts at her*]

WALTER. Mama, where have you been?

MAMA. My—them steps is longer than they used to be. Whew! [*She sits down and ignores him*] How you feeling this evening, Ruth! [RUTH *shrugs, disturbed some at having been prematurely interrupted and watching her husband knowingly*]

WALTER. Mama, where have you been all day?

MAMA [*Still ignoring him and leaning on the table and changing to more comfortable shoes*]. Where's Travis?

RUTH. I let him go out earlier and he ain't come back yet. Boy, is he going to get it!

WALTER. Mama!

MAMA [*As if she has heard him for the first time*]. Yes, son?

WALTER. Where did you go this afternoon?

MAMA. I went downtown to tend to some business that I had to tend to.

WALTER. What kind of business?

MAMA. You know better than to question me like a child, Brother.

WALTER [*Rising and bending over the table*]. Where were you, Mama? [*Bringing his fists down and shouting*] Mama, you didn't go do something with that insurance money, something crazy? [*The front door opens slowly, interrupting him, and Travis peeks his head in, less than hopefully*]

TRAVIS [*To his mother*]. Mama, I—

RUTH. "Mama I" nothing! You're going to get it, boy! Get on in that bedroom and get yourself ready!

TRAVIS. But I—

MAMA. Why don't you all never let the child explain hisself.

RUTH. Keep out of it now, Lena. [MAMA *clamps her lips together, and* RUTH *advances toward her son menacingly*]

RUTH. A thousand times I have told you not to go off like that—

MAMA [*Holding out her arms to her grandson*]. Well—at least let me tell him something. I want him to be the first one to hear…Come here, Travis. [*The boy obeys, gladly*] Travis—[*She takes him by the shoulder and looks into his face*]—you know that money we got in the mail this morning?

TRAVIS. Yes'm—

MAMA. Well—what you think your grandmama gone and done with that money?

TRAVIS. I don't know, Grandmama.

MAMA [*Putting her finger on his nose for emphasis*]. She went out and she bought you a house! [*The explosion comes from* WALTER *at the end of the revelation and he jumps up and turns away from all of them in a fury.* MAMA *continues, to* TRAVIS] You glad about the house? It's going to be yours when you get to be a man.

TRAVIS. Yeah—I always wanted to live in a house.

MAMA. All right, gimme some sugar then—[TRAVIS *puts his arms around her neck as she watches her son over the boy's shoulder. Then, to* TRAVIS, *after the embrace*] Now when you say your prayers tonight, you thank God and your grandfather—'cause it was him who give you the house—in his way.

RUTH [*Taking the boy from* MAMA *and pushing him toward the bedroom*]. Now you get out of here and get ready for your beating.

TRAVIS. Aw, Mama—

RUTH. Get on in there—[*Closing the door behind him and turning radiantly to her mother-in-law*] So you went and did it!

MAMA [*Quietly, looking at her son with pain*]. Yes, I did.

RUTH [*Raising both arms classically*]. Praise God! [*Looks at* WALTER *a moment, who says nothing. She crosses rapidly to her husband*] Please, honey—let me be glad…you be glad too. [*She has laid her hands on his shoulders, but he shakes himself free of her roughly, without turning to face her*] Oh, Walter…a home…a home. [*She comes back to* MAMA] Well—where is it? How big is it? How much it going to cost?

MAMA. Well—

RUTH. When we moving?

MAMA [*Smiling at her*]. First of the month.

RUTH [*Throwing back her head with jubilance*]. *Praise God!*

MAMA [*Tentatively, still looking at her son's back turned against her and* RUTH]. It's—it's a nice house too…[*She cannot help speaking directly to him. An imploring quality in her voice, her manner, makes her almost like a girl now*] Three bedrooms—nice big one for you and Ruth…Me and Beneatha still have to share our room, but Travis have one of his own—and [*With difficulty*] I figure if the—new baby—is a boy, we could get one of them double-decker outfits…And there's a yard with a little patch of dirt where I could maybe get to grow me a few flowers…And a nice big basement…

RUTH. Walter honey, be glad—

MAMA [*Still to his back, fingering things on the table*].'Course I don't want to make it sound fancier than it is... It's just a plain little old house—but it's made good and solid—and it will be *ours*. Walter Lee—it makes a difference in a man when he can walk on floors that belong to *him*...

RUTH. Where is it?

MAMA [*Frightened at this telling*]. Well—well—it's out there in Clybourne Park— [RUTH*'s radiance fades abruptly, and* WALTER *finally turns slowly to face his mother with incredulity and hostility*]

RUTH. Where?

MAMA [*Matter-of-factly*]. Four o six Clybourne Street, Clybourne Park.

RUTH. Clybourne Park? Mama, there ain't no colored people living in Clybourne Park.

MAMA [*Almost idiotically*]. Well, I guess there's going to be some now.

WALTER [*Bitterly*]. So that's the peace and comfort you went out and bought for us today!

MAMA [*Raising her eyes to meet his finally*]. Son—I just tried to find the nicest place for the least amount of money for my family.

RUTH [*Trying to recover from the shock*]. Well—well—'course I ain't one never been 'fraid of no crackers, mind you—but—well, wasn't there no other houses nowhere?

MAMA. Them houses they put up for colored in them areas way out all seem to cost twice as much as other houses. I did the best I could.

RUTH [*Struck senseless with the news, in its various degrees of goodness and trouble, she sits a moment, her fists propping her chin in thought, and then she starts to rise, bringing her fists down with vigor, the radiance spreading from cheek to cheek again*]. Well—well!—All I can say is—if this is my time in life—*my time*—to say good-bye—[*And she builds with momentum as she starts to circle the room with an exuberant, almost tearfully happy release*]—to these Goddamned cracking walls!—[*She pounds the walls*]—and these marching roaches!—[*She wipes at an imaginary army of marching roaches*]—and this cramped little closet which ain't now or never was no kitchen!... then I say it loud and good, *Hallelujah! and good-bye misery... I don't never want to see your ugly face again!* [*She laughs joyously, having practically destroyed the apartment, and flings her arms up and lets them come down happily, slowly, reflectively, over her abdomen, aware for the first time perhaps that the life therein pulses with happiness and not despair*] Lena?

MAMA [*Moved, watching her happiness*]. Yes, honey?

RUTH [*Looking off*]. Is there—is there a whole lot of sunlight?

MAMA [*Understanding*]. Yes, child, there's a whole lot of sunlight. [*Long pause*]

RUTH [*Collecting herself and going to the door of the room* TRAVIS *is in*]. Well—I guess I better see 'bout Travis. [*To* MAMA] Lord, I sure don't feel like whipping nobody today! [*She exits*]

MAMA [*The mother and son are left alone now and the mother waits a long time, considering deeply, before she speaks*]. Son—you—you understand what I done, don't you? [WALTER *is silent and sullen*] I—I just seen my family falling apart today... just falling to pieces in front of my eyes... We couldn't of gone on like we was today. We was going backwards 'stead of forwards—talking 'bout killing babies and wishing each other was dead... When it gets like that in life—you just got to do something different, push on out and do something bigger... [*She waits*] I wish you'd say something, son... I wish you'd say how deep inside you you think I done the right thing—

WALTER [*Crossing slowly to his bedroom door and finally turning there and speaking measuredly*]. What you need me to say you done right for? *You* the head of this family. You run our lives like you want to. It was your money and you did what you wanted with it. So what you need for me to say it was all right for? [*Bitterly, to hurt her as deeply as he knows is possible*] So you butchered up a dream of mine—you—who always talking 'bout your children's dreams...

MAMA. Walter Lee—[*He just closes the door behind him. Mama sits alone, thinking heavily*]

CURTAIN.

SCENE II

Time: Friday night. A few weeks later.

At rise: Packing crates mark the intention of the family to move. BENEATHA *and* GEORGE *come in, presumably from an evening out again.*

GEORGE. O.K.... O.K., whatever you say... [*They both sit on the couch. He tries to kiss her. She moves away*] Look, we've had a nice evening; let's not spoil it, huh?... [*He again turns her head and tries to nuzzle in and she turns away from him, not with distaste but with momentary lack of interest; in a mood to pursue what they were talking about*]

BENEATHA. I'm *trying* to talk to you.

GEORGE. We always talk.

BENEATHA. Yes—and I love to talk.

GEORGE [*Exasperated; rising*]. I know it and I don't mind it sometimes... I want you to cut it out, see—The moody stuff, I mean. I don't like it. You're a nice-looking girl... all over. That's all you need, honey, forget the atmosphere. Guys aren't going to go for the atmosphere—they're going to go for what they see. Be glad for that. Drop the Garbo routine. It doesn't go with you. As for myself, I want a nice—[*Groping*]—simple [*Thoughtfully*]—sophisticated girl... not a poet—O.K.? [*She rebuffs him again and he starts to leave*]

BENEATHA. Why are you angry?

GEORGE. Because this is stupid! I don't go out with you to discuss the nature of "quiet desperation" or to hear all about your thoughts—because the world will go on thinking what it thinks regardless—

BENEATHA. Then why read books? Why go to school?

GEORGE [*With artificial patience, counting on his fingers*]. It's simple. You read books—to learn facts—to get grades—to pass the course—to get a degree. That's all—it has nothing to do with thoughts. [*A long pause*]

BENEATHA. I see. [*A longer pause as she looks at him*] Good night, George. [GEORGE *looks at her a little oddly, and starts to exit. He meets* MAMA *coming in*]

GEORGE. Oh—hello, Mrs. Younger.

MAMA. Hello, George, how you feeling?

GEORGE. Fine—fine, how are you?

MAMA. Oh, a little tired. You know them steps can get you after a day's work. You all have a nice time tonight?

GEORGE. Yes—a fine time. Well, good night.

MAMA. Good night. [*He exits.* MAMA *closes the door behind her*] Hello, honey. What you sitting like that for?

BENEATHA. I'm just sitting.

MAMA. Didn't you have a nice time?

BENEATHA. No.

MAMA. No? What's the matter?

BENEATHA. Mama, George is a fool—honest. [*She rises*]

MAMA [*Hustling around unloading the packages she has entered with. She stops*]. Is he, baby?

BENEATHA. Yes. [BENEATHA *makes up* TRAVIS' *bed as she talks*]

MAMA. You sure?

BENEATHA. Yes.

MAMA. Well—I guess you better not waste your time with no fools. [BENEATHA *looks up at her mother, watching her put groceries in the refrigerator. Finally she gathers up her things and starts into the bedroom. At the door she stops and looks back at her mother*]

BENEATHA. Mama—

MAMA. Yes, baby—

BENEATHA. Thank you.

MAMA. For what?

BENEATHA. For understanding me this time. [*She exits quickly and the mother stands, smiling a little, looking at the place where* BENEATHA *had stood.* RUTH *enters*]

RUTH. Now don't you fool with any of this stuff, Lena—

MAMA. Oh, I just thought I'd sort a few things out. [*The phone rings.* RUTH *answers*]

RUTH [*At the phone*]. Hello—Just a minute. [*Goes to door*] Walter, it's Mrs. Arnold. [*Waits. Goes back to the phone. Tense*] Hello. Yes, this is his wife speaking... He's lying down now. Yes... well, he'll be in tomorrow. He's been very sick. Yes—I know we should have called, but we were so sure he'd be able to come in today. Yes—yes, I'm very sorry. Yes... Thank you very much. [*She hangs up. Walter is standing in the doorway of the bedroom behind her*] That was Mrs. Arnold.

WALTER [*Indifferently*]. Was it?

RUTH. She said if you don't come in tomorrow that they are getting a new man...

WALTER. Ain't that sad—ain't that crying sad.

RUTH. She said Mr. Arnold has had to take a cab for three days... Walter, you ain't been to work for three days! [*This is a revelation to her*] Where you been, Walter Lee Younger? [WALTER *looks at her and starts to laugh*] You're going to lose your job.

WALTER. That's right ...

RUTH. Oh, Walter, and with your mother working like a dog every day—

WALTER. That's sad too—Everything is sad.

MAMA. What you been doing for these three days, son?

WALTER. Mama—you don't know all the things a man what got leisure can find to do in this city... What's this—Friday night? Well—Wednesday I borrowed Willy Harris' car and I went for a drive... just me and myself and I drove and drove... Way out... way past South Chicago, and I parked the car and I sat and looked at the steel mills all day long. I just sat in the car and looked at them big black chimneys for hours. Then I drove back and I went to the Green Hat. [*Pause*] And Thursday—Thursday I borrowed the car again and I got in it and I pointed it the other way and I drove the other way—for hours—way, way up to Wisconsin, and I looked at the farms. I just drove and looked at the farms. Then I drove back and I went to the Green Hat. [*Pause*] And today—today I didn't get the car. Today I just walked. All over the Southside. And I looked at the Negroes and they looked at me and finally I just sat down on the curb at Thirty-ninth and South Parkway and I just sat there and watched the Negroes go by. And then I went to the Green Hat. You all sad? You all depressed? And you know where I am going right now— [RUTH *goes out quietly*]

MAMA. Oh, Big Walter, is this the harvest of our days?

WALTER. You know what I like about the Green Hat? [*He turns the radio on and a steamy, deep blues pours into the room*] I like this little cat they got there who blows a sax... He blows. He talks to me. He ain't but 'bout five feet tall and he's got a conked head and his eyes is always closed and he's all music—

MAMA [*Rising and getting some papers out of her handbag*]. Walter—

WALTER. And there's this other guy who plays the piano... and they got a sound. I mean they can work on some music... They got the best little combo in the world in the Green Hat... You can just sit there and drink and listen to them three men play and you realize that don't nothing matter worth a damn, but just being there—

MAMA. I've helped do it to you, haven't I, son? Walter, I been wrong.

WALTER. Naw—you ain't never been wrong about nothing, Mama.

MAMA. Listen to me, now. I say I been wrong, son. That I been doing to you what the rest of the world been doing to you. [*She stops and he looks up slowly at her and she meets his eyes pleadingly*] Walter—what you ain't understood is that I ain't got nothing, don't own nothing, ain't never really wanted nothing that wasn't for you. There ain't nothing as precious to me... There ain't nothing worth holding on to, money, dreams, nothing else—if it means—if it means it's going to destroy my boy. [*She puts her papers in front of him and he watches her without speaking or moving*] I paid the man thirty-five hundred dollars down on the house. That leaves sixty-five hundred dollars. Monday morning I want you to take this money and take three thousand dollars and put it in a savings account for Beneatha's medical schooling. The rest you put in a checking account—with your name on it. And from now on any penny that come out of it or that go in it is for you to look after. For you to decide. [*She drops her hands a little helplessly*] It ain't much, but it's all I got in the world and I'm putting it in your hands. I'm telling you to be the head of this family from now on like you supposed to be.

WALTER [*Stares at the money*]. You trust me like that, Mama?

MAMA. I ain't never stop trusting you. Like I ain't never stop loving you. [*She goes out, and* WALTER *sits looking at the money on the table as the music continues in its idiom, pulsing in the room. Finally, in a decisive gesture, he gets up, and, in mingled joy and desperation, picks up the money. At the same moment,* TRAVIS *enters for bed*]

TRAVIS. What's the matter, Daddy? You drunk?

WALTER [*Sweetly, more sweetly than we have ever known him*]. No, Daddy ain't drunk. Daddy ain't going to never be drunk again...

TRAVIS. Well, good night, Daddy. [*The father has come from behind the couch and leans over, embracing his son*]

WALTER. Son, I feel like talking to you tonight.

TRAVIS. About what?

WALTER. Oh, about a lot of things. About you and what kind of man you going to be when you grow up.... Son—son, what do you want to be when you grow up?

TRAVIS. A bus driver.

WALTER [*Laughing a little*]. A what? Man, that ain't nothing to want to be!

TRAVIS. Why not?

WALTER. 'Cause, man—it ain't big enough—you know what I mean.

TRAVIS. I don't know then. I can't make up my mind. Sometimes Mama asks me that too. And sometimes when I tell her I just want to be like you—she says she don't want me to be like that and sometimes she says she does....

WALTER [*Gathering him up in his arms*]. You know what, Travis? In seven years you going to be seventeen years old. And things is going to be very different with us in seven years, Travis.... One day when you are seventeen I'll come home—home from my office downtown somewhere—

TRAVIS. You don't work in no office, Daddy.

WALTER. No—but after tonight. After what your daddy gonna do tonight, there's going to be offices—a whole lot of offices....

TRAVIS. What you gonna do tonight, Daddy?

WALTER. You wouldn't understand yet, son, but your daddy's gonna make a transaction...a business transaction that's going to change our lives...That's how come one day when you 'bout seventeen years old I'll come home and I'll be pretty tired, you know what I mean, after a day of conferences and secretaries getting things wrong the way they do...'cause an executive's life is hell, man—[*The more he talks the farther away he gets*] And I'll pull the car up on the driveway...just a plain black Chrysler, I think, with white walls—no—black tires. More elegant. Rich people don't have to be flashy...though I'll have to get something a little sportier for Ruth—maybe a Cadillac convertible to do her shopping in ... And I'll come up the steps to the house and the gardener will be clipping away at the hedges and he'll say, "Good evening, Mr. Younger." And I'll say, "Hello, Jefferson, how are you this evening?" And I'll go inside and Ruth will come downstairs and meet me at the door and we'll kiss each other and she'll take my arm and we'll go up to your room to see you sitting on the floor with the catalogues of all the great schools in America around you.... All the great schools in the world! And—and I'll say, all right son—it's your seventeenth birthday, what is it you've decided?...Just tell me where you want to go to school and you'll *go*. Just tell me, what it is you want to be—and you'll *be* it... Whatever you want to be—Yessir! [*He holds his arms open for* TRAVIS] You just name it, son...[TRAVIS *leaps into them*] and I hand you the world! [WALTER*'s voice has risen in pitch and hysterical promise and on the last line he lifts* TRAVIS *high*]

BLACKOUT.

SCENE III

Time: Saturday, moving day, one week later.

Before the curtain rises, RUTH*'s voice, a strident, dramatic church alto, cuts through the silence.*

It is, in the darkness, a triumphant surge, a penetrating statement of expectation: "Oh, Lord, I don't feel no ways tired! Children, oh, glory hallelujah!"

As the curtain rises we see that RUTH *is alone in the living room, finishing up the family's packing. It is moving day. She is nailing crates and tying cartons.* BENEATHA *enters, carrying a guitar case, and watches her exuberant sister-in-law.*

RUTH. Hey!

BENEATHA [*Putting away the case*]. Hi.

RUTH [*Pointing at a package*]. Honey—look in that package there and see what I found on sale this morning at the South Center. [RUTH *gets up and moves to the package and draws out some curtains*] Lookahere—hand-turned hems!

BENEATHA. How do you know the window size out there?

RUTH [*Who hadn't thought of that*]. Oh—Well, they bound to fit something in the whole house. Anyhow, they was too good a bargain to pass up. [RUTH *slaps her head, suddenly remembering something*] Oh, Bennie—I meant to put a special note on that carton over there. That's your mama's good china and she wants 'em to be very careful with it.

BENEATHA. I'll do it. [BENEATHA *finds a piece of paper and starts to draw large letters on it*]

RUTH. You know what I'm going to do soon as I get in that new house?

BENEATHA. What?

RUTH. Honey—I'm going to run me a tub of water up to here... [*With her fingers practically up to her nostrils*] And I'm going to get in it—and I am going to sit... and sit... and sit in that hot water and the first person who knocks to tell *me* to hurry up and come out—

BENEATHA. Gets shot at sunrise.

RUTH [*Laughing happily*]. You said it, sister! [*Noticing how large* BENEATHA *is absent-mindedly making the note*] Honey, they ain't going to read that from no airplane.

BENEATHA [*Laughing herself*]. I guess I always think things have more emphasis if they are big, somehow.

RUTH [*Looking up at her and smiling*]. You and your brother seem to have that as a philosophy of life. Lord, that man—done changed so 'round here. You know—you know what we did last night? Me and Walter Lee?

BENEATHA. What?

RUTH [*Smiling to herself*]. We went to the movies. [*Looking at* BENEATHA *to see if she understands*] We went to the movies. You know the last time me and Walter went to the movies together?

BENEATHA. No.

RUTH. Me neither. That's how long it been. [*Smiling again*] But we went last night. The picture wasn't much good, but that didn't seem to matter. We went—and we held hands.

BENEATHA. Oh, Lord!

RUTH. We held hands—and you know what?

BENEATHA. What?

RUTH. When we come out of the show it was late and dark and all the stores and things was closed up... and it was kind of chilly and there wasn't many people on the streets... and we was still holding hands, me and Walter.

BENEATHA. You're killing me. [WALTER *enters with a large package. His happiness is deep in him; he cannot keep still with his new-found exuberance. He is singing and wiggling and snapping his fingers. He puts his package in a corner and puts a phonograph record, which he has brought in with him, on the record player. As the music comes up he dances over to* RUTH *and tries to get her to dance with him. She gives in*

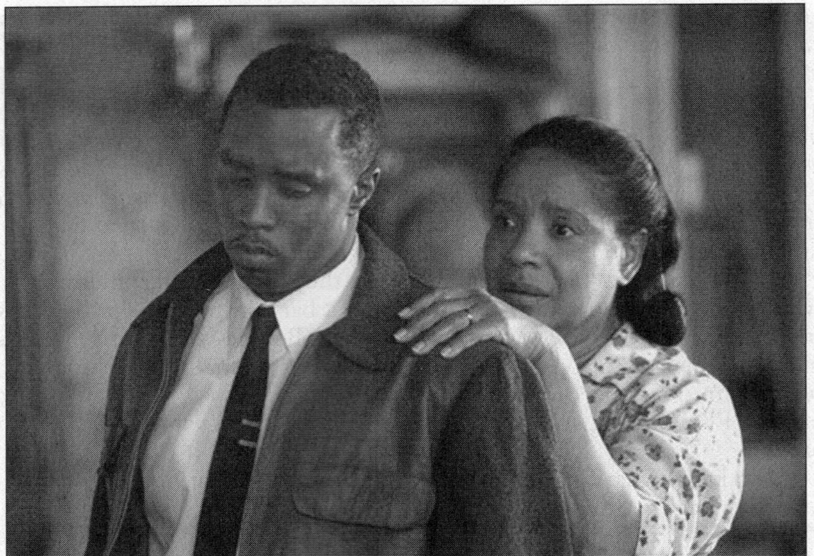

Mama (Phylicia Rashad) tries to comfort Walter (Sean Combs) in the 2008 ABC-TV production of *A Raisin in the Sun*.

at last to his raunchiness and in a fit of giggling allows herself to be drawn into his mood and together they deliberately burlesque an old social dance of their youth]

BENEATHA [*Regarding them a long time as they dance, then drawing in her breath for a deeply exaggerated comment which she does not particularly mean*]. Talk about—oldddddddddd—fashionedddddd—Negroes!

WALTER [*Stopping momentarily*]. What kind of Negroes? [*He says this in fun. He is not angry with her today, nor with anyone. He starts to dance with his wife again*]

BENEATHA. Old-fashioned.

WALTER [*As he dances with* RUTH]. You know, when these *New Negroes* have their convention—[*Pointing at his sister*]—that is going to be the chairman of the Committee on Unending Agitation. [*He goes on dancing, then stops*] Race, race, race!... Girl, I do believe you are the first person in the history of the entire human race to successfully brainwash yourself. [BENEATHA *breaks up and he goes on dancing. He stops again, enjoying his tease*] Damn, even the N double A C P takes a holiday sometimes! [BENEATHA *and* RUTH *laugh. He dances with Ruth some more and starts to laugh and stops and pantomimes someone over an operating table*] I can just see that chick someday looking down at some poor cat on an operating table before she starts to slice him, saying... [*Pulling his sleeves back maliciously*] "By the way, what are your views on civil rights down there?..." [*He laughs at her again and starts to dance happily. The bell sounds*]

BENEATHA. Sticks and stones may break my bones but... words will never hurt me! [BENEATHA *goes to the door and opens it as* WALTER *and* RUTH *go on with the clowning.* BENEATHA *is somewhat surprised to see a quiet-looking middle-aged white man in a business suit holding his hat and a briefcase in his hand and consulting a small piece of paper*]

MAN. Uh—how do you do, miss. I am looking for a Mrs.—[*He looks at the slip of paper*] Mrs. Lena Younger?

BENEATHA [*Smoothing her hair with slight embarrassment*]. Oh—yes, that's my mother. Excuse me. [*She closes the door and turns to quiet the other two*] Ruth! Brother! Somebody's here. [*Then she opens the door. The man casts a curious quick glance at all of them*] Uh—come in please.

MAN [*Coming in*]. Thank you.

BENEATHA. My mother isn't here just now. Is it business?

MAN. Yes... well, of a sort.

WALTER [*Freely, the Man of the House*]. Have a seat. I'm Mrs. Younger's son. I look after most of her business matters. [RUTH *and* BENEATHA *exchange amused glances*]

MAN [*Regarding* WALTER, *and sitting*]. Well—My name is Karl Lindner ...

WALTER [*Stretching out his hand*]. Walter Younger. This is my wife—[RUTH *nods politely*]—and my sister.

LINDNER. How do you do.

WALTER [*Amiably, as he sits himself easily on a chair, leaning with interest forward on his knees and looking expectantly into the newcomer's face*]. What can we do for you, Mr. Lindner!

LINDNER [*Some minor shuffling of the hat and briefcase on his knees*]. Well—I am a representative of the Clybourne Park Improvement Association—

WALTER [*Pointing*]. Why don't you sit your things on the floor?

LINDNER. Oh—yes. Thank you. [*He slides the briefcase and hat under the chair*] And as I was saying—I am from the Clybourne Park Improvement Association and we have had it brought to our attention at the last meeting that you people—or at least your mother—has bought a piece of residential property at—[*He digs for the slip of paper again*]—four o six Clybourne Street...

WALTER. That's right. Care for something to drink? Ruth, get Mr. Lindner a beer.

LINDNER [*Upset for some reason*]. Oh—no, really. I mean thank you very much, but no thank you.

RUTH [*Innocently*]. Some coffee?

LINDNER. Thank you, nothing at all. [BENEATHA *is watching the man carefully*]

LINDNER. Well, I don't know how much you folks know about our organization. [*He is a gentle man; thoughtful and somewhat labored in his manner*] It is one of these community organizations set up to look after—oh, you know, things like block upkeep and special projects and we also have what we call our New Neighbors Orientation Committee...

BENEATHA [*Drily*]. Yes—and what do they do?

LINDNER [*Turning a little to her and then returning the main force to* WALTER]. Well—it's what you might call a sort of welcoming committee, I guess. I mean they, we—I'm the chairman of the committee—go around and see the new people who move into the neighborhood and sort of give them the low-down on the way we do things out in Clybourne Park.

BENEATHA [*With appreciation of the two meanings, which escape* RUTH *and* WALTER]. Uh-huh.

LINDNER. And we also have the category of what the association calls—[*He looks elsewhere*]—uh—special community problems...

BENEATHA. Yes—and what are some of those?

WALTER. Girl, let the man talk.

LINDNER [*With understated relief*]. Thank you. I would sort of like to explain this thing in my own way. I mean I want to explain to you in a certain way.

WALTER. Go ahead.

LINDNER. Yes. Well. I'm going to try to get right to the point. I'm sure we'll all appreciate that in the long run.

BENEATHA. Yes.

WALTER. Be still now!

LINDNER. Well—

RUTH [*Still innocently*]. Would you like another chair—you don't look comfortable.

LINDNER [*More frustrated than annoyed*]. No, thank you very much. Please. Well—to get right to the point I—[*A great breath, and he is off at last*] I am sure you people must be aware of some of the incidents which have happened in various parts of the city when colored people have moved into certain areas—[BENEATHA *exhales heavily and starts tossing a piece of fruit up and down in the air*] Well—because we have what I think is going to be a unique type of organization in American community life—not only do we deplore that kind of thing—but we are trying to do something about it. [BENEATHA *stops tossing and turns with a new and quizzical interest to the man*] We feel—[*Gaining confidence in his mission because of the interest in the faces of the people he is talking to*]—we feel that most of the trouble in this world, when you come right down to it—[*He hits his knee for emphasis*]—most of the trouble exists because people just don't sit down and talk to each other.

RUTH [*Nodding as she might in church, pleased with the remark*]. You can say that again, mister.

LINDNER [*More encouraged by such affirmation*]. That we don't try hard enough in this world to understand the other fellow's problem. The other guy's point of view.

RUTH. Now that's right. [BENEATHA *and* WALTER *merely watch and listen with genuine interest*]

LINDNER. Yes—that's the way we feel out in Clybourne Park. And that's why I was elected to come here this afternoon and talk to you people. Friendly like, you know, the way people should talk to each other and see if we couldn't find some way to work this thing out. As I say, the whole business is a matter of *caring* about the other fellow. Anybody can see that you are a nice family of folks, hard working and honest I'm sure. [BENEATHA *frowns slightly, quizzically, her head tilted regarding him*] Today everybody knows what it means to be on the outside of *something*. And of course, there is always somebody who is out to take the advantage of people who don't always understand.

WALTER. What do you mean?

LINDNER. Well—you see our community is made of people who've worked hard as the dickens for years to build up that little community. They're not rich and fancy people; just hard-working, honest people who don't really have much but those little homes and a dream of the kind of community they want to raise their children in. Now, I don't say we are perfect and there is a lot wrong in some of the things they want. But you've got to admit that a man, right or wrong, has the right to want to have the neighborhood he lives in a certain kind of way. And at the moment the overwhelming majority of our people out there feel that people get along better, take more of a common interest in the life of the community, when they share a common background. I want you to believe me when I tell you that race prejudice simply doesn't enter into it. It is a matter of the people of Clybourne Park believing, rightly or wrongly, as I say, that for the happiness of all concerned that our Negro families are happier when they live in their *own* communities.

BENEATHA [*With a grand and bitter gesture*]. This, friends, is the Welcoming Committee!

WALTER [*Dumbfounded, looking at* LINDNER]. Is this what you came marching all the way over here to tell us?

LINDNER. Well, now we've been having a fine conversation. I hope you'll hear me all the way through.

WALTER [*Tightly*]. Go ahead, man.

LINDNER. You see—in the face of all things I have said, we are prepared to make your family a very generous offer...

BENEATHA. Thirty pieces and not a coin less!

WALTER. Yeah?

LINDNER [*Putting on his glasses and drawing a form out of the briefcase*]. Our association is prepared, through the collective effort of our people, to buy the house from you at a financial gain to your family.

RUTH. Lord have mercy, ain't this the living gall!

WALTER. All right, you through?

LINDNER. Well, I want to give you the exact terms of the financial arrangement—

WALTER. We don't want to hear no exact terms of no arrangements. I want to know if you got any more to tell us 'bout getting together?

LINDNER [*Taking off his glasses*]. Well—I don't suppose that you feel...

WALTER. Never mind how I feel—you got any more to say 'bout how people ought to sit down and talk to each other?...Get out of my house, man. [*He turns his back and walks to the door*]

LINDNER [*Looking around at the hostile faces and reaching and assembling his hat and briefcase*]. Well—I don't understand why you people are reacting this way. What do you think you are going to gain by moving into a neighborhood where you just aren't wanted and where some elements—well—people can get awful worked up when they feel that their whole way of life and everything they've ever worked for is threatened.

WALTER. Get out.

LINDNER [*At the door, holding a small card*]. Well—I'm sorry it went like this.

WALTER. Get out.

LINDNER [*Almost sadly regarding* WALTER]. You just can't force people to change their hearts, son. [*He turns and put his card on a table and exits.* WALTER *pushes the door to with stinging hatred, and stands looking at it.* RUTH *just sits and* BENEATHA *just stands. They say nothing.* MAMA *and* TRAVIS *enter*]

MAMA. Well—this all the packing got done since I left out of here this morning. I testify before God that my children got all the energy of the dead. What time the moving men due?

BENEATHA. Four o'clock. You had a caller, Mama. [*She is smiling, teasingly*]

MAMA. Sure enough—who?

BENEATHA [*Her arms folded saucily*]. The Welcoming Committee. [WALTER *and* RUTH *giggle*]

MAMA [*Innocently*]. Who?

BENEATHA. The Welcoming Committee. They said they're sure going to be glad to see you when you get there.

WALTER [*Devilishly*]. Yeah, they said they can't hardly wait to see your face. [*Laughter*]

MAMA [*Sensing their facetiousness*]. What's the matter with you all?

WALTER. Ain't nothing the matter with us. We just telling you 'bout the gentleman who came to see you this afternoon. From the Clybourne Park Improvement Association.

MAMA. What he want?

RUTH [*In the same mood as* BENEATHA *and* WALTER]. To welcome you, honey.

WALTER. He said they can't hardly wait. He said the one thing they don't have, that they just dying to have out there is a fine family of colored people! [*To* RUTH *and* BENEATHA] Ain't that right!

RUTH *and* Beneatha [*Mockingly*]. Yeah! He left his card in case—[*They indicate the card, and* MAMA *picks it up and throws it on the floor—understanding and looking off as she draws her chair up to the table on which she has put her plant and some sticks and some cord*]

MAMA. Father, give us strength. [*Knowingly—and without fun*] Did he threaten us?

BENEATHA. Oh—Mama—they don't do it like that any more. He talked Brotherhood. He said everybody ought to learn how to sit down and hate each other with good Christian fellowship. [*She and* WALTER *shake hands to ridicule the remark*]

MAMA [*Sadly*]. Lord, protect us…

RUTH. You should hear the money those folks raised to buy the house from us. All we paid and then some.

BENEATHA. What they think we going to do—eat 'em?

RUTH. No, honey, marry 'em.

MAMA [*Shaking her head*]. Lord, Lord, Lord…

RUTH. Well—that's the way the crackers crumble. Joke.

BENEATHA [*Laughingly noticing what her mother is doing*]. Mama, what are you doing?

MAMA. Fixing my plant so it won't get hurt none on the way…

BENEATHA. Mama, you going to take *that* to the new house?

MAMA. Un-huh—

BENEATHA. That raggedy-looking old thing?

MAMA [*Stopping and looking at her*]. It expresses *me*.

RUTH [*With delight, to* BENEATHA]. So there, Miss Thing! [WALTER *comes to* MAMA *suddenly and bends down behind her and squeezes her in his arms with all his strength. She is overwhelmed by the suddenness of it and, though delighted, her manner is like that of* RUTH *with* TRAVIS]

MAMA. Look out now, boy! You make me mess up my thing here!

WALTER [*His face lit, he slips down on his knees beside her, his arms still about her*]. Mama…you know what it means to climb up in the chariot?

MAMA [*Gruffly, very happy*]. Get on away from me now…

RUTH [*Near the gift-wrapped package, trying to catch* WALTER*'s eye*]. Psst—

WALTER. What the old song say, Mama…

RUTH. Walter—Now? [*She is pointing at the package*]

WALTER [*Speaking the lines, sweetly, playfully, in his mother's face*].

I got wings… you got wings…
All God's children got wings…

MAMA. Boy—get out of my face and do some work…

WALTER.

When I get to heaven gonna put on my wings,
Gonna fly all over God's heaven…

BENEATHA [*Teasingly, from across the room*]. Everybody talking 'bout heaven ain't going there!

WALTER [*To* RUTH, *who is carrying the box across to them*]. I don't know, you think we ought to give her that... Seems to me she ain't been very appreciative around here.

MAMA [*Eying the box, which is obviously a gift*]. What is that?

WALTER [*Taking it from* RUTH *and putting it on the table in front of* MAMA]. Well—what you all think? Should we give it to her?

RUTH. Oh—she was pretty good today.

MAMA. I'll good you—[*She turns her eyes to the box again*]

BENEATHA. Open it, Mama. [*She stands up, looks at it, turns and looks at all of them, and then presses her hands together and does not open the package*]

WALTER [*Sweetly*]. Open it, Mama. It's for you. [MAMA *looks in his eyes. It is the first present in her life without its being Christmas. Slowly she opens her package and lifts out, one by one, a brand-new sparkling set of gardening tools.* WALTER *continues, prodding*] Ruth made up the note—read it...

MAMA [*Picking up the card and adjusting her glasses*]."To our own Mrs. Miniver—Love from Brother, Ruth and Beneatha." Ain't that lovely...

TRAVIS [*Tugging at his father's sleeve*]. Daddy, can I give her mine now?

WALTER. All right, son. [TRAVIS *flies to get his gift*] Travis didn't want to go in with the rest of us, Mama. He got his own. [*Somewhat amused*] We don't know what it is...

TRAVIS [*Racing back in the room with a large hatbox and putting it in front of his grandmother*]. Here!

MAMA. Lord have mercy, baby. You done gone and bought your grandmother a hat?

TRAVIS [*Very proud*]. Open it! [*She does and lifts out an elaborate, but very elaborate, wide gardening hat, and all the adults break up at the sight of it*]

RUTH. Travis, honey, what is that?

TRAVIS [*Who thinks it is beautiful and appropriate*]. It's a gardening hat! Like the ladies always have on in the magazines when they work in their gardens.

BENEATHA [*Giggling fiercely*]. Travis—we were trying to make Mama Mrs. Miniver—not Scarlett O'Hara!

MAMA [*Indignantly*]. What's the matter with you all! This here is a beautiful hat! [*Absurdly*] I always wanted me one just like it! [*She pops it on her head to prove it to her grandson, and the hat is ludicrous and considerably oversized*]

RUTH. Hot dog! Go, Mama!

WALTER [*Doubled over with laughter*]. I'm sorry, Mama—but you look like you ready to go out and chop you some cotton sure enough! [*They all laugh except* MAMA, *out of deference to* TRAVIS*'s feelings*]

MAMA [*Gathering the boy up to her*]. Bless your heart—this is the prettiest hat I ever owned—[WALTER, RUTH *and* BENEATHA *chime in—noisily, festively and insincerely congratulating* TRAVIS *on his gift*] What are we all standing around here for? We ain't finished packin' yet. Bennie, you ain't packed one book. [*The bell rings*]

BENEATHA. That couldn't be the movers... it's not hardly two o'clock yet—[BENEATHA *goes into her room. Mama starts for door*]

WALTER [*Turning, stiffening*]. Wait—wait—I'll get it. [*He stands and looks at the door*]

MAMA. You expecting company, son?

WALTER [*Just looking at the door*]. Yeah—yeah... [MAMA *looks at* RUTH, *and they exchange innocent and unfrightened glances*]

MAMA [*Not understanding*]. Well, let them in, son.

BENEATHA [*From her room*]. We need some more string.

MAMA. Travis—you run to the hardware and get me some string cord. [MAMA *goes out and* WALTER *turns and looks at* RUTH. *Travis goes to a dish for money*]

RUTH. Why don't you answer the door, man?

WALTER [*Suddenly bounding across the floor to her*]. 'Cause sometimes it hard to let the future begin! [*Stooping down in her face*]

I got wings! You got wings!
All God's children got wings!

[*He crosses to the door and throws it open. Standing there is a very slight little man in a not too prosperous business suit and with haunted frightened eyes and a hat pulled down tightly, brim up, around his forehead.* TRAVIS *passes between the men and exits.* WALTER *leans deep in the man's face, still in his jubilance*]

When I get to heaven gonna put on my wings,
Gonna fly all over God's heaven...

[*The little man just stares at him*]

Heaven—

[*Suddenly he stops and looks past the little man into the empty hallway*] Where's Willy, man?

BOBO. He ain't with me.

WALTER [*Not disturbed*]. Oh—come on in. You know my wife.

BOBO [*Dumbly, taking off his hat*]. Yes—h'you, Miss Ruth.

RUTH [*Quietly, a mood apart from her husband already, seeing* BOBO]. Hello, Bobo.

WALTER. You right on time today...Right on time. That's the way! [*He slaps* BOBO *on his back*] Sit down...lemme hear. [RUTH *stands stiffly and quietly in back of them, as though somehow she senses death, her eyes fixed on her husband*]

BOBO [*His frightened eyes on the floor, his hat in his hands*]. Could I please get a drink of water, before I tell you about it, Walter Lee? [WALTER *does not take his eyes off the man.* RUTH *goes blindly to the tap and gets a glass of water and brings it to* BOBO]

WALTER. There ain't nothing wrong, is there?

BOBO. Lemme tell you—

WALTER. Man—didn't nothing go wrong?

BOBO. Lemme tell you—Walter Lee. [*Looking at* RUTH *and talking to her more than to* WALTER] You know how it was. I got to tell you how it was. I mean first I got to tell you how it was all the way...I mean about the money I put in, Walter Lee...

WALTER [*With taut agitation now*]. What about the money you put in?

BOBO. Well—it wasn't much as we told you—me and Willy—[*He stops*] I'm sorry, Walter. I got a bad feeling about it. I got a real bad feeling about it...

WALTER. Man, what you telling me about all this for?...Tell me what happened in Springfield...

BOBO. Springfield.

RUTH [*Like a dead woman*]. What was supposed to happen in Springfield?

BOBO [*To her*]. This deal that me and Walter went into with Willy—Me and Willy was going to go down to Springfield and spread some money 'round so's we wouldn't have to wait so long for the liquor license...That's what we were going to do. Everybody said that was the way you had to do, you understand, Miss Ruth?

WALTER. Man—what happened down there?

BOBO [*A pitiful man, near tears*]. I'm trying to tell you, Walter.

WALTER [*Screaming at him suddenly*]. THEN TELL ME, GODDAMMIT . . . WHAT'S THE MATTER WITH YOU?

BOBO. Man . . . I didn't go to no Springfield, yesterday.

WALTER [*Halted, life hanging in the moment*]. Why not?

BOBO [*The long way, the hard way to tell*].'Cause I didn't have no reasons to . . .

WALTER. Man, what are you talking about!

BOBO. I'm talking about the fact that when I got to the train station yesterday morning—eight o'clock like we planned . . . Man—*Willy didn't never show up*.

WALTER. Why . . . where was he . . . where is he?

BOBO. That's what I'm trying to tell you . . . I don't know . . . I waited six hours . . . I called his house . . . and I waited . . . six hours . . . I waited in that train station six hours . . . [*Breaking into tears*] That was all the extra money I had in the world . . . [*Looking up at* WALTER *with the tears running down his face*] Man, *Willy is gone*.

WALTER. Gone, what you mean Willy is gone? Gone where? You mean he went by himself. You mean he went off to Springfield by himself—to take care of getting the license—[*Turns and looks anxiously at* RUTH] You mean maybe he didn't want too many people in on the business down there? [*Looks to* RUTH *again, as before*] You know Willy got his own ways. [*Looks back to* BOBO] Maybe you was late yesterday and he just went on down there without you. Maybe—maybe—he's been callin' you at home tryin' to tell you what happened or something. Maybe—maybe—he just got sick. He's somewhere—he's got to be somewhere. We just got to find him—me and you got to find him. [*Grabs* BOBO *senselessly by the collar and starts to shake him*] We got to!

BOBO [*In sudden angry, frightened agony*]. What's the matter with you, Walter! *When a cat take off with your money he don't leave you no maps!*

WALTER [*Turning madly, as though he is looking for* WILLY *in the very room*]. Willy! . . . Willy . . . don't do it . . . Please don't do it . . . Man, not with that money . . . Man, please, not with that money . . . Oh, God . . . Don't let it be true . . . [*He is wandering around, crying out for* WILLY *and looking for him or perhaps for help from God*] Man . . . I trusted you . . . Man, I put my life in your hands . . . [*He starts to crumple down on the floor as* RUTH *just covers her face in horror.* MAMA *opens the door and comes into the room, with* BENEATHA *behind her*] Man . . . [*He starts to pound the floor with his fists, sobbing wildly*] That money is made out of my father's flesh . . .

BOBO [*Standing over him helplessly*]. I'm sorry, Walter . . . [*Only* WALTER'S *sobs reply.* BOBO *puts on his hat*] I had my life staked on this deal, too . . . [*He exits*]

MAMA [*To* WALTER]. Son—[*She goes to him, bends down to him, talks to his bent head*] Son . . . Is it gone? Son, I gave you sixty-five hundred dollars. Is it gone? All of it? Beneatha's money too?

WALTER [*Lifting his head slowly*]. Mama . . . I never . . . went to the bank at all . . .

MAMA [*Not wanting to believe him*]. You mean . . . your sister's school money . . . you used that too . . . Walter? . . .

WALTER. Yessss! . . . All of it . . . It's all gone . . .

[*There is total silence.* RUTH *stands with her face covered with her hands; Beneatha leans forlornly against a wall, fingering a piece of red ribbon from the mother's gift.* MAMA *stops and looks at her son without recognition and then, quite without thinking about it, starts to beat him senselessly in the face.* BENEATHA *goes to them and stops it*]

BENEATHA. Mama! [MAMA *stops and looks at both of her children and rises slowly and wanders vaguely, aimlessly away from them*]

MAMA. I seen...him...night after night...come in...and look at that rug...and then look at me...the red showing in his eyes...the veins moving in his head...I seen him grow thin and old before he was forty...working and working and working like somebody's old horse...killing himself...and you—you give it all away in a day...

BENEATHA. Mama—

MAMA. Oh, God...[*She looks up to Him*] Look down here—and show me the strength.

BENEATHA. Mama—

MAMA [*Folding over*]. Strength...

BENEATHA [*Plaintively*]. Mama...

MAMA. Strength!

CURTAIN.

ACT III

An hour later.

At curtain, there is a sullen light of gloom in the living room, gray light not unlike that which began the first scene of Act I. At left we can see WALTER *within his room, alone with himself. He is stretched out on the bed, his shirt out and open, his arms under his head. He does not smoke, he does not cry out, he merely lies there, looking up at the ceiling, much as if he were alone in the world.*

In the living room BENEATHA *sits at the table, still surrounded by the now almost ominous packing crates. She sits looking off. We feel that this is a mood struck perhaps an hour before, and it lingers now, full of the empty sound of profound disappointment. We see on a line from her brother's bedroom the sameness of their attitudes. Presently the bell rings and* BENEATHA *rises without ambition or interest in answering. It is* ASAGAI, *smiling broadly, striding into the room with energy and happy expectation and conversation.*

ASAGAI. I came over...I had some free time. I thought I might help with the packing. Ah, I like the look of packing crates! A household in preparation for a journey! It depresses some people...but for me...it is another feeling. Something full of the flow of life, do you understand? Movement, progress...It makes me think of Africa.

BENEATHA. Africa!

ASAGAI. What kind of a mood is this? Have I told you how deeply you move me?

BENEATHA. He gave away the money, Asagai...

ASAGAI. Who gave away what money?

BENEATHA. The insurance money. My brother gave it away.

ASAGAI. Gave it away?

BENEATHA. He made an investment! With a man even Travis wouldn't have trusted.

ASAGAI. And it's gone?

BENEATHA. Gone!

ASAGAI. I'm very sorry...And you, now?

BENEATHA. Me?...Me?...Me, I'm nothing...Me. When I was very small...we used to take our sleds out in the wintertime and the only hills we had were the ice-covered stone steps of some houses down the street. And we used to fill them in with snow and make them smooth and slide down them all day...and it was very dangerous, you know...far too steep...and sure enough one day a kid named Rufus came down too fast and hit the sidewalk...and we saw his face just split open right there in front of us...And I remember standing there looking at his bloody open face thinking that was the end of Rufus. But the ambulance came and they took him to the hospital and they fixed the broken bones and they sewed it all up...and the next time I saw Rufus he just had a little line down the middle of his face...I never got over that...[WALTER *sits up, listening on the bed. Throughout this scene it is important that we feel his reaction at all times, that he visibly respond to the words of his sister and* ASAGAI]

ASAGAI. What?

BENEATHA. That that was what one person could do for another, fix him up—sew up the problem, make him all right again. That was the most marvelous thing in the world...I wanted to do that. I always thought it was the one concrete thing in the world that a human being could do. Fix up the sick, you know—and make them whole again. This was truly being God...

ASAGAI. You wanted to be God?

BENEATHA. No—I wanted to cure. It used to be so important to me. I wanted to cure. It used to matter. I used to care. I mean about people and how their bodies hurt...

ASAGAI. And you've stopped caring?

BENEATHA. Yes—I think so.

ASAGAI. Why? [WALTER *rises, goes to the door of his room and is about to open it, then stops and stands listening, leaning on the door jamb*]

BENEATHA. Because it doesn't seem deep enough, close enough to what ails mankind—I mean this thing of sewing up bodies or administering drugs. Don't you understand? It was a child's reaction to the world. I thought that doctors had the secret to all the hurts...That's the way a child sees things—or an idealist.

ASAGAI. Children see things very well sometimes—and idealists even better.

BENEATHA. I know that's what you think. Because you are still where I left off—you still care. This is what you see for the world, for Africa. You with the dreams of the future will patch up all Africa—you are going to cure the Great Sore of colonialism with Independence—

ASAGAI. Yes!

BENEATHA. Yes—and you think that one word is the penicillin of the human spirit: "Independence!" But then what?

ASAGAI. That will be the problem for another time. First we must get there.

BENEATHA. And where does it end?

ASAGAI. End? Who even spoke of an end? To life? To living?

BENEATHA. An end to misery!

ASAGAI [*Smiling*]. You sound like a French intellectual.

BENEATHA. No! I sound like a human being who just had her future taken right out of her hands! While I was sleeping in my bed in there, things were happening in this world that directly concerned me—and nobody asked me, consulted me—they just went out and did things—and changed my life. Don't you see there isn't any real progress, Asagai, there is only one large circle that we march in, around and around, each of us with our own little picture—in front of us—our own little mirage that we think is the future.

ASAGAI. That is the mistake.

BENEATHA. What?

ASAGAI. What you just said—about the circle. It isn't a circle—it is simply a long line—as in geometry, you know, one that reaches into infinity. And because we cannot see the end—we also cannot see how it changes. And it is very odd but those who see the changes are called "idealist"—and those who cannot, or refuse to think, they are the "realists." It is very strange, and amusing too, I think.

BENEATHA. You—you are almost religious.

ASAGAI. Yes…I think I have the religion of doing what is necessary in the world—and of worshipping man—because he is so marvelous, you see.

BENEATHA. Man is foul! And the human race deserves its misery!

ASAGAI. You see: *you* have become the religious one in the old sense. Already, and after such a small defeat, you are worshipping despair.

BENEATHA. From now on, I worship the truth—and the truth is that people are puny, small and selfish…

ASAGAI. Truth? Why is it that you despairing ones always think that only you have the truth? I never thought to see *you* like that. You! Your brother made a stupid, childish mistake—and you are grateful to him. So that now you can give up the ailing human race on account of it. You talk about what good is struggle; what good is anything? Where are we all going? And why are we bothering?

BENEATHA. *And you cannot answer it!* All your talk and dreams about Africa and Independence. Independence and then what? What about all the crooks and petty thieves and just plain idiots who will come into power to steal and plunder the same as before—only now they will be black and do it in the name of the new Independence. You cannot answer that.

ASAGAI [*Shouting over her*]. *I live the answer!* [*Pause*] In my village at home it is the exceptional man who can even read a newspaper…or who ever *sees* a book at all. I will go home and much of what I will have to say will seem strange to the people of my village…But I will teach and work and things will happen, slowly and swiftly. At times it will seem that nothing changes at all…and then again…the sudden dramatic events which make history leap into the future. And then quiet again. Retrogression even. Guns, murder, revolution. And I even will have moments when I wonder if the quiet was not better than all that death and hatred. But I will look about my village at the illiteracy and disease and ignorance and I will not wonder long. And perhaps…perhaps I will be a great man…I mean perhaps I will hold on to the substance of truth and find my way always with the right course…and perhaps for it I will be butchered in my bed some night by the servants of empire…

BENEATHA. *The martyr!*

ASAGAI. …or perhaps I shall live to be a very old man, respected and esteemed in my new nation…And perhaps I shall hold office and this is what I'm trying to tell you, Alaiyo; perhaps the things I believe now for my country will be wrong and outmoded, and I will not understand and do terrible things to have things my way or merely to keep my power. Don't you see that there will be young men and women, not British soldiers then, but my own black countrymen…to step out of the shadows some evening and slit my then useless throat? Don't you see they have always been there…that they always will be.

And that such a thing as my own death will be an advance? They who might kill me even . . . actually replenish me!

BENEATHA. Oh, Asagai, I know all that.

ASAGAI. Good! Then stop moaning and groaning and tell me what you plan to do.

BENEATHA. Do?

ASAGAI. I have a bit of a suggestion.

BENEATHA. What?

ASAGAI [*Rather quietly for him*]. That when it is all over—that you come home with me—

BENEATHA [*Slapping herself on the forehead with exasperation born of misunderstanding*]. Oh—Asagai—at this moment you decide to be romantic!

ASAGAI [*Quickly understanding the misunderstanding*]. My dear, young creature of the New World—I do not mean across the city—I mean across the ocean; home—to Africa.

BENEATHA [*Slowly understanding and turning to him with murmured amazement*]. To—to Nigeria?

ASAGAI. Yes! . . . [*Smiling and lifting his arms playfully.*] Three hundred years later the African Prince rose up out of the seas and swept the maiden back across the middle passage over which her ancestors had come—

BENEATHA [*Unable to play*]. Nigeria?

ASAGAI. Nigeria. Home. [*Coming to her with genuine romantic flippancy*] I will show you our mountains and our stars; and give you cool drinks from gourds and teach you the old songs and the ways of our people—and, in time, we will pretend that—[*Very softly*]—you have only been away for a day—[*She turns her back to him, thinking. He swings her around and takes her full in his arms in a long embrace which proceeds to passion*]

BENEATHA [*Pulling away*]. You're getting me all mixed up—

ASAGAI. Why?

BENEATHA. Too many things—too many things have happened today. I must sit down and think. I don't know what I feel about anything right this minute. [*She promptly sits down and props her chin on her fist*]

ASAGAI [*Charmed*]. All right, I shall leave you. No—don't get up. [*Touching her, gently, sweetly*] Just sit awhile and think . . . Never be afraid to sit awhile and think. [*He goes to door and looks at her*] How often I have looked at you and said, "Ah—so this is what the New World hath finally wrought . . ." [*He exits.* BENEATHA *sits on alone. Presently* WALTER *enters from his room and starts to rummage through things, feverishly looking for something. She looks up and turns in her seat*]

BENEATHA [*Hissingly*]. Yes—just look at what the New World hath wrought! . . . Just look! [*She gestures with bitter disgust*] There he is! *Monsieur le petit bourgeous noir*—himself! There he is—Symbol of a Rising Class! Entrepreneur! Titan of the system! [WALTER *ignores her completely and continues frantically and destructively looking for something and hurling things to the floor and tearing things out of their place in his search.* BENEATHA *ignores the eccentricity of his actions and goes on with the monologue of insult*] Did you dream of yachts on Lake Michigan, Brother? Did you see yourself on that Great Day sitting down at the Conference Table, surrounded by all the mighty bald-headed men in America? All halted, waiting, breathless, waiting for your pronouncements on industry? Waiting for you—Chairman of the

Board? [WALTER *finds what he is looking for—a small piece of white paper—and pushes it in his pocket and puts on his coat and rushes out without ever having looked at her. She shouts after him*] I look at you and I see the final triumph of stupidity in the world! [*The door slams and she returns to just sitting again.* RUTH *comes quickly out of* MAMA*'s room*]

RUTH. Who was that?

BENEATHA. Your husband.

RUTH. Where did he go?

BENEATHA. Who knows—maybe he has an appointment at U.S. Steel.

RUTH [*Anxiously, with frightened eyes*]. You didn't say nothing bad to him, did you?

BENEATHA. Bad? Say anything bad to him? No—I told him he was a sweet boy and full of dreams and everything is strictly peachy keen, as the ofay[3] kids say! [MAMA *enters from her bedroom. She is lost, vague, trying to catch hold, to make some sense of her former command of the world, but it still eludes her. A sense of waste overwhelms her gait; a measure of apology rides on her shoulders. She goes to her plant, which has remained on the table, looks at it, picks it up and takes it to the window sill and sets it outside, and she stands and looks at it a long moment. Then she closes the window, straightens her body with effort and turns around to her children*]

MAMA. Well—ain't it a mess in here, though? [*A false cheerfulness, a beginning of something*] I guess we all better stop moping around and get some work done. All this unpacking and everything we got to do. [RUTH *raises her head slowly in response to the sense of the line; and* BENEATHA *in similar manner turns very slowly to look at her mother*] One of you all better call the moving people and tell 'em not to come.

RUTH. Tell 'em not to come?

MAMA. Of course, baby. Ain't no need in 'em coming all the way here and having to go back. They charges for that too. [*She sits down, fingers to her brow, thinking*] Lord, ever since I was a little girl, I always remembers people saying, "Lena—Lena Eggleston, you aims too high all the time. You needs to slow down and see life a little more like it is. Just slow down some." That's what they always used to say down home—"Lord, that Lena Eggleston is a high-minded thing. She'll get her due one day!"

RUTH. No, Lena...

MAMA. Me and Big Walter just didn't never learn right.

RUTH. Lena, no! We gotta go. Bennie—tell her... [*She rises and crosses to* BENEATHA *with her arms outstretched.* BENEATHA *doesn't respond*] Tell her we can still move... the notes ain't but a hundred and twenty-five a month. We got four grown people in this house—we can work...

MAMA [*To herself*]. Just aimed too high all the time—

RUTH [*Turning and going to* MAMA *fast—the words pouring out with urgency and desperation*]. Lena—I'll work... I'll work twenty hours a day in all the kitchens in Chicago... I'll strap my baby on my back if I have to and scrub all the floors in America and wash all the sheets in America if I have to—but we got to move... We got to get out of here... [MAMA *reaches out absently and pats* RUTH*'s hand*]

---

[3]**Ofay** white (pig Latin meaning *foe*).

MAMA. No—I sees things differently now. Been thinking 'bout some of the things we could do to fix this place up some. I seen a second-hand bureau over on Maxwell Street just the other day that could fit right there. [*She points to where the new furniture might go.* RUTH *wanders away from her*] Would need some new handles on it and then a little varnish and then it look like something brand-new. And—we can put up them new curtains in the kitchen… Why this place be looking fine. Cheer us all up so that we forget trouble ever came… [*To* RUTH] And you could get some nice screens to put up in your room round the baby's bassinet… [*She looks at both of them, pleadingly*] Sometimes you just got to know when to give up some things… and hold on to what you got. [WALTER *enters from the outside, looking spent and leaning against the door, his coat hanging from him*]

MAMA. Where you been, son?

WALTER [*Breathing hard*]. Made a call.

MAMA. To who, son?

WALTER. To The Man.

MAMA. What man, baby?

WALTER. The Man, Mama. Don't you know who The Man is?

RUTH. Walter Lee?

WALTER. *The Man.* Like the guys in the street say—*The Man.* Captain Boss—Mistuh Charley… Old Captain Please Mr. Bossman…

BENEATHA [*Suddenly*]. Lindner!

WALTER. That's right! That's good. I told him to come right over.

BENEATHA [*Fiercely, understanding*]. For what? What do you want to see him for?

WALTER [*Looking at his sister*]. We are going to do business with him.

MAMA. What you talking 'bout, son?

WALTER. Talking 'bout life, Mama. You all always telling me to see life like it is. Well—I laid in there on my back today… and I figured it out. Life just like it is. Who gets and who don't get. [*He sits down with his coat on and laughs*] Mama, you know it's all divided up. Life is. Sure enough. Between the takers and the "tooken." [*He laughs*] I've figured it out finally. [*He looks around at them*] Yeah. Some of us always getting "tooken." [*He laughs*] People like Willy Harris, they don't never get "tooken." And you know why the rest of us do? 'Cause we all mixed up. Mixed up bad. We get to looking 'round for the right and the wrong; and we worry about it and cry about it and stay up nights trying to figure out 'bout the wrong and the right of things all the time… And all the time, man, them takers is out there operating, just taking and taking. Willy Harris? Shoot—Willy Harris don't even count. He don't even count in the big scheme of things. But I'll say one thing for old Willy Harris… he's taught me something. He's taught me to keep my eye on what counts in this world. Yeah—[*Shouting out a little*] Thanks, Willy!

RUTH. What did you call that man for, Walter Lee!

WALTER. Called him to tell him to come on over to the show. Gonna put on a show for the man. Just what he wants to see. You see, Mama, the man came here today and he told us that them people out there where you want us to move—well they so upset they willing to pay us not to move out there. [*He laughs again*] And—and oh, Mama—you would of been proud of the way me and Ruth and Bennie acted. We told him to get out… Lord have mercy! We told the man to get out. Oh, we was some proud folks this afternoon, yeah. [*He lights a cigarette*] We were still full of that old-time stuff…

RUTH [*Coming toward him slowly*]. You talking 'bout taking them people's money to keep us from moving in that house?

WALTER. I ain't just talking 'bout it, baby—I'm telling you that's what's going to happen.

BENEATHA. Oh, God! Where is the bottom! Where is the real honest-to-God bottom so he can't go any farther!

WALTER. See—that's the old stuff. You and that boy that was here today. You all want everybody to carry a flag and a spear and sing some marching songs, huh? You wanna spend your life looking into things and trying to find the right and the wrong part, huh? Yeah. You know what's going to happen to that boy someday—he'll find himself sitting in a dungeon, locked in forever—and the takers will have the key! Forget it, baby! There ain't no causes—there ain't nothing but taking in this world, and he who takes most is smartest—and it don't make a damn bit of difference *how*.

MAMA. You making something inside me cry, son. Some awful pain inside me.

WALTER. Don't cry, Mama. Understand. That white man is going to walk in that door able to write checks for more money than we ever had. It's important to him and I'm going to help him... I'm going to put on the show, Mama.

MAMA. Son—I come from five generations of people who was slaves and sharecroppers—but ain't nobody in my family never let nobody pay 'em no money that was a way of telling us we wasn't fit to walk the earth. We ain't never been that poor. [*Raising her eyes and looking at him*] We ain't never been that dead inside.

BENEATHA. Well—we are dead now. All the talk about dreams and sunlight that goes on in this house. All dead.

WALTER. What's the matter with you all! I didn't make this world! It was give to me this way! Hell, yes, I want me some yachts someday! Yes, I want to hang some real pearls 'round my wife's neck. Ain't she supposed to wear no pearls? Somebody tell me—tell me, who decides which women is suppose to wear pearls in this world. I tell you I am a *man*—and I think my wife should wear some pearls in this world! [*This last line hangs a good while and* WALTER *begins to move about the room. The word "Man" has penetrated his consciousness; he mumbles it to himself repeatedly between strange agitated pauses as he moves about*]

MAMA. Baby, how you going to feel on the inside?

WALTER. Fine!... Going to feel fine... a man...

MAMA. You won't have nothing left then, Walter Lee.

WALTER [*Coming to her*]. I'm going to feel fine, Mama. I'm going to look that son-of-a-bitch in the eyes and say—[*He falters*]—and say, "All right, Mr. Lindner—[*He falters even more*]—that's your neighborhood out there. You got the right to keep it like you want. You got the right to have it like you want. Just write the check and—the house is yours." And, and I am going to say—[*His voice almost breaks*] "And you—you people just put the money in my hand and you won't have to live next to this bunch of stinking niggers!"... [*He straightens up and moves away from his mother, walking around the room*] Maybe—maybe I'll just get down on my black knees... [*He does so;* RUTH *and Bennie and Mama watch him in frozen horror*] Captain, Mistuh, Bossman. [*He starts crying*] A-hee-hee-hee! [*Wringing his hands in profoundly anguished imitation*] Yasssssuh! Great White Father, just gi' ussen de money, fo' God's sake, and we's ain't gwine come out deh and dirty up yo' white folks neighborhood... [*He breaks down completely, then gets up and goes into the bedroom*]

BENEATHA. That is not a man. That is nothing but a toothless rat.

MAMA. Yes—death done come in this here house. [*She is nodding, slowly, reflectively*] Done come walking in my house. On the lips of my children. You what supposed to be my beginning again. You—what supposed to be my harvest. [*To* BENEATHA] You—you mourning your brother?

BENEATHA. He's no brother of mine.

MAMA. What you say?

BENEATHA. I said that that individual in that room is no brother of mine.

MAMA. That's what I thought you said. You feeling like you better than he is today? [BENEATHA *does not answer*] Yes? What you tell him a minute ago? That he wasn't a man? Yes? You give him up for me? You done wrote his epitaph too—like the rest of the world? Well, who give you the privilege?

BENEATHA. Be on my side for once! You saw what he just did, Mama! You saw him—down on his knees. Wasn't it you who taught me—to despise any man who would do that? Do what he's going to do.

MAMA. Yes—I taught you that. Me and your daddy. But I thought I taught you something else too . . . I thought I taught you to love him.

BENEATHA. Love him? There is nothing left to love.

MAMA. There is always something left to love. And if you ain't learned that, you ain't learned nothing. [*Looking at her*] Have you cried for that boy today? I don't mean for yourself and for the family 'cause we lost the money. I mean for him; what he been through and what it done to him. Child, when do you think is the time to love somebody the most; when they done good and made things easy for everybody? Well then, you ain't through learning—because that ain't the time at all. It's when he's at his lowest and can't believe in hisself 'cause the world done whipped him so. When you starts measuring somebody, measure him right, child, measure him right. Make sure you done taken into account what hills and valleys he come through before he got to wherever he is. [TRAVIS *bursts into the room at the end of the speech, leaving the door open*]

TRAVIS. Grandmama—the moving men are downstairs! The truck just pulled up.

MAMA [*Turning and looking at him*]. Are they, baby? They downstairs? [*She sighs and sits. Lindner appears in the doorway. He peers in and knocks lightly, to gain attention, and comes in. All turn to look at him*]

LINDNER [*Hat and briefcase in hand*]. Uh—hello . . . [RUTH *crosses mechanically to the bedroom door and opens it and lets it swing open freely and slowly as the lights come up on Walter within, still in his coat, sitting at the far corner of the room. He looks up and out through the room to* LINDNER]

RUTH. He's here. [*A long minute passes and* WALTER *slowly gets up*]

LINDNER [*Coming to the table with efficiency, putting his briefcase on the table and starting to unfold papers and unscrew fountain pens*]. Well, I certainly was glad to hear from you people. [WALTER *has begun the trek out of the room, slowly and awkwardly, rather like a small boy, passing the back of his sleeve across his mouth from time to time*] Life can really be so much simpler than people let it be most of the time. Well—with whom do I negotiate? You, Mrs. Younger, or your son here? [MAMA *sits with her hands folded on her lap and her eyes closed as* WALTER *advances.* TRAVIS *goes close to* LINDNER *and looks at the papers curiously*] Just some official papers, sonny.

RUTH. Travis, you go downstairs.

MAMA [*Opening her eyes and looking into* WALTER'*s*]. No. Travis, you stay right here. And you make him understand what you doing, Walter Lee. You teach him good. Like Willy Harris taught you. You show where our five generations done come to. Go ahead, son—

WALTER [*Looks down into his boy's eyes. Travis grins at him merrily and* WALTER *draws him beside him with his arm lightly around his shoulders*]. Well, Mr. Lindner. [BENEATHA *turns away*] We called you—[*There is a profound, simple groping quality in his speech*]—because, well, me and my family [*He looks around and shifts from one foot to the other*] Well—we are very plain people...

LINDNER. Yes—

WALTER. I mean—I have worked as a chauffeur most of my life—and my wife here, she does domestic work in people's kitchens. So does my mother. I mean—we are plain people...

LINDNER. Yes, Mr. Younger—

WALTER [*Really like a small boy, looking down at his shoes and then up at the man*]. And—uh—well, my father, well, he was a laborer most of his life.

LINDNER [*Absolutely confused*]. Uh, yes—

WALTER [*Looking down at his toes once again*]. My father almost beat a man to death once because this man called him a bad name or something, you know what I mean?

LINDNER. No, I'm afraid I don't.

WALTER [*Finally straightening up*]. Well, what I mean is that we come from people who had a lot of pride. I mean—we are very proud people. And that's my sister over there and she's going to be a doctor—and we are very proud—

LINDNER. Well—I am sure that is very nice, but—

WALTER [*Starting to cry and facing the man eye to eye*]. What I am telling you is that we called you over here to tell you that we are very proud and that this is—this is my son, who makes the sixth generation of our family in this country, and that we have all thought about your offer and we have decided to move into our house because my father—my father—he earned it. [MAMA *has her eyes closed and is rocking back and forth as though she were in church, with her head nodding the amen yes*] We don't want to make no trouble for nobody or fight no causes—but we will try to be good neighbors. That's all we got to say. [*He looks the man absolutely in the eyes*] We don't want your money. [*He turns and walks away from the man*]

LINDNER [*Looking around at all of them*]. I take it then that you have decided to occupy.

BENEATHA. That's what the man said.

LINDNER [*To* MAMA *in her reverie*]. Then I would like to appeal to you, Mrs. Younger. You are older and wiser and understand things better I am sure ...

MAMA [*Rising*]. I am afraid you don't understand. My son said we was going to move and there ain't nothing left for me to say. [*Shaking her head with double meaning*] You know how these young folks is nowadays, mister. Can't do a thing with 'em. Good-bye.

LINDNER [*Folding up his materials*]. Well—if you are that final about it... There is nothing left for me to say. [*He finishes. He is almost ignored by the family, who are concentrating on* WALTER LEE. *At the door* LINDNER *halts and looks around*] I sure hope you people know what you're doing. [*He shakes his head and exits*]

RUTH [*Looking around and coming to life*]. Well, for God's sake—if the moving men are here—LET'S GET THE HELL OUT OF HERE!

MAMA [*Into action*]. Ain't it the truth! Look at all this here mess. Ruth, put Travis' good jacket on him... Walter Lee, fix your tie and tuck your shirt in, you look just like somebody's hoodlum. Lord have mercy, where is my plant? [*She flies to get it amid the general bustling of the family, who are deliberately trying to ignore the nobility of the past moment*] You all start on down... Travis child, don't go empty-handed... Ruth, where did I put that box with my skillets in it? I want to be in charge of it myself... I'm going to make us the biggest dinner we ever ate tonight... Beneatha, what's the matter with them stockings? Pull them things up, girl... [*The family starts to file out as two* MOVING MEN *appear and begin to carry out the heavier pieces of furniture, bumping into the family as they move about*]

BENEATHA. Mama, Asagai—asked me to marry him today and go to Africa—

MAMA [*In the middle of her getting-ready activity*]. He did? You ain't old enough to marry nobody—[*Seeing the* MOVING MEN *lifting one of her chairs precariously*] Darling, that ain't no bale of cotton, please handle it so we can sit in it again. I had that chair twenty-five years... [*The* MOVERS *sigh with exasperation and go on with their work*]

BENEATHA [*Girlishly and unreasonably trying to pursue the conversation*]. To go to Africa, Mama—be a doctor in Africa ...

MAMA [*Distracted*]. Yes, baby—

WALTER. Africa! What he want you to go to Africa for?

BENEATHA. To practice there ...

WALTER. Girl, if you don't get all them silly ideas out your head! You better marry yourself a man with some loot ...

BENEATHA [*Angrily, precisely as in the first scene of the play*]. What have you got to do with who I marry!

WALTER. Plenty. Now I think George Murchison—[*He and* BENEATHA *go out yelling at each other vigorously;* BENEATHA *is heard saying that she would not marry* GEORGE MURCHISON *if he were Adam and she were Eve, etc. The anger is loud and real till their voices diminish.* RUTH *stands at the door and turns to* MAMA *and smiles knowingly*]

MAMA [*Fixing her hat at last*]. Yeah—they something all right, my children ...

RUTH. Yeah—they're something. Let's go, Lena.

MAMA [*Stalling, starting to look around at the house*]. Yes—I'm coming. Ruth—

RUTH. Yes?

MAMA [*Quietly, woman to woman*]. He finally come into his manhood today, didn't he? Kind of like a rainbow after the rain ...

RUTH [*Biting her lip lest her own pride explode in front of* MAMA]. Yes, Lena. [WALTER*'s voice calls for them raucously*]

MAMA [*Waving* RUTH *out vaguely*]. All right, honey—go on down. I be down directly. [RUTH *hesitates, then exits.* MAMA *stands, at last alone in the living room, her plant on the table before her as the lights start to come down. She looks around at all the walls and ceilings and suddenly, despite herself, while the children call below, a great heaving thing rises in her and she puts her fist to her mouth, takes a final desperate look, pulls her coat about her, pats her hat and goes out. The lights dim down. The door opens and she comes back in, grabs her plant, and goes out for the last time.*]

CURTAIN.

(1958)

Questions for Discussion and Writing

1. The title comes from a poem by Langston Hughes. Look up the poem (page 531) and explain why you think Hansberry chose this phrase for her title.
2. Compare and contrast the dreams of Walter, Mama, Beneatha, and Ruth. Which one of these characters do you find most admirable?
3. How would you answer the charge that the play celebrates consumerism and material values?
4. Does the play promote the idea that blacks should want to be just like whites? Look up the words *assimilation* and *assimilationism*. Do these terms apply to the Youngers?
5. Is the play dated? Have the conflicts it presents been resolved?
6. What conflicts between men and women do you see in the play? How do they compare to similar conflicts in other stories and plays in this book? Write an essay making a major claim about the gender issues in this play.

A Portfolio of Humorous and Satirical Plays

You watch humorous plays—in various types and sizes—all the time: skits on *Saturday Night Live* and *MADtv*, episodes of *30 Rock* and reruns of *Frasier*, movies by Jim Carrey and Tyler Perry, musicals like *Hairspray* and *Grease*, school productions of *Arsenic and Old Lace* and community theater performances of *The Odd Couple*. Comedy is big business and always has been. Audiences like to laugh, and playwrights like to make money by making their audiences laugh. But the humor isn't always sunny and happy; it can also include anger, criticism, and ridicule. The four plays in this portfolio use comedy to mock human folly or denounce social wrongs. *Picnic on the Battlefield* contrives a ridiculous situation to expose the grim absurdity of war; *Beauty* combines irony with theatrical fantasy to comment on human vanity; *Los Vendidos* exploits exaggerated stereotypes to rail against racial bigotry; and *Sure Thing* pokes witty fun at the vicissitudes of dating. You will enjoy reading and responding to these plays for both their humor and their satirical perspectives.

Fernando Arrabal 1933–

Born in Morocco, Fernando Arrabal grew up in Spain. In the 1960s, after settling in France, he developed *Panic Theatre* (named after the god Pan). The *Panic* man was an anti-hero who dodged danger, lacked courage, and hid from heroics. Arrabal's theatre has been described as "a dramatic carnival in which the carcass of our advanced civilization is barbecued over the spits of a permanent revolution." Awarded the French Legion of Honor in 2005, he now travels worldwide lecturing about his work and defending human rights. "I have no politics," he declares, "except that I am against tyrants."

Picnic on the Battlefield

Translated by Barbara Wright

CHARACTERS

ZAPO, *a soldier.*
MONSIEUR TÉPAN, *the soldier's father.*
MADAME TÉPAN, *the soldier's mother.*
ZÉPO, *an enemy soldier.*
FIRST STRETCHER BEARER
SECOND STRETCHER BEARER

A battlefield. The stage is covered with barbed wire and sandbags. The battle is at its height. Rifle shots, exploding bombs and machine guns can be heard.
ZAPO *is alone on the stage, flat on his stomach, hidden among the sandbags. He is very frightened. The sound of the fighting stops. Silence.*

Zépo confronts Zapo in a 2001 production of Picnic on the Battlefield.

ZAPO *takes a ball of wool and some needles out of a canvas workbag and starts knitting a pullover, which is already quite far advanced. The field telephone, which is by his side, suddenly starts ringing.*

ZAPO. Hallo, hallo . . . yes, Captain . . . yes, I'm the sentry of sector 47 . . . Nothing new, Captain . . . Excuse me, Captain, but when's the fighting going to start again? And what am I supposed to do with the hand-grenades? Do I chuck them in front of me or behind me? . . . Don't get me wrong. I didn't mean to annoy you . . . Captain, I really feel terribly lonely, couldn't you send me someone to keep me company? . . . even if it's only a nanny-goat? [*The* CAPTAIN *is obviously severely reprimanding him*]. Whatever you say, Captain, whatever you say. [Zapo *hangs up. He mutters to himself. Silence. Enter* MONSIEUR *and* MADAME TÉPAN, *carrying baskets as if they were going on a picnic. They address their son, who has his back turned and doesn't see them come in.*]

MONS. T. [*ceremoniously*]. Stand up, my son, and kiss your mother on the brow. [Zapo, *surprised, gets up and kisses his mother very respectfully on the forehead. He is about to speak, but his father doesn't give him a chance.*] And now, kiss *me*.

ZAPO. But, dear Father and dear Mother, how did you dare to come all this way, to such a dangerous place? You must leave at once.

MONS. T. So you think you've got something to teach your father about war and danger, do you? All this is just a game to me. How many times—to take the first example that comes to mind—have I got off an underground train while it was still moving.

MME. T. We thought you must be bored, so we came to pay you a little visit. This war must be a bit tedious, after all.

ZAPO. It all depends.

MONS. T. I know exactly what happens. To start with you're attracted by the novelty of it all. It's fun to kill people, and throw hand-grenades about, and wear uniforms—you feel smart, but in the end you get bored stiff. You'd have found it much more interesting in my day. Wars were much more lively, much more highly colored. And then, the best thing was that there were horses, plenty of horses. It was a real pleasure; if the Captain ordered us to attack, there we all were immediately, on horseback, in our red uniforms. It was a sight to be seen. And then there were the charges at the gallop, sword in hand, and suddenly you found yourself face to face with the enemy, and he was equal to the occasion too—with his horses—there were always horses, lots of horses, with their well-rounded rumps—in his highly-polished boots, and his green uniform.

MME. T. No, no, the enemy uniform wasn't green. It was blue. I remember distinctly that it was blue.

MONS. T. I tell you it was green.

MME. T. When I was little, how many times did I go out on to the balcony to watch the battle and say to the neighbour's little boy: "I bet you a gum-drop the blues win." And the blues were our enemies.

MONS. T. Oh, well, you must be right, then.

MME. T. I've always liked battles. As a child I always said that when I grew up I wanted to be a Colonel of dragoons. But my mother wouldn't hear of it, you know how she will stick to her principles at all costs.

MONS. T. Your mother's just a half-wit.

ZAPO. I'm sorry, but you really must go. You can't come into a war unless you're a soldier.

MONS. T. I don't give a damn, we came here to have a picnic with you in the country and to enjoy our Sunday.

MME. T. And I've prepared an excellent meal, too. Sausage, hard-boiled eggs—you know how you like them!—ham sandwiches, red wine, salad, and cakes.

ZAPO. All right, let's have it your way. But if the Captain comes he'll be absolutely furious. Because he isn't at all keen on us having visits when we're at the front. He never stops telling us: "Discipline and hand-grenades are what's wanted in war, not visits."

MONS. T. Don't worry, I'll have a few words to say to your Captain.

ZAPO. And what if we have to start fighting again?

MONS. T. You needn't think that'll frighten me, it won't be the first fighting I've seen. Now if only it was battles on horseback! Times have changed, you can't understand. [*Pause.*] We came by motor bike. No one said a word to us.

ZAPO. They must have thought you were the referees.

MONS. T. We had enough trouble getting through, though. What with all the tanks and jeeps.

MME. T. And do you remember the bottle-neck that cannon caused, just when we got here?

MONS. T. You musn't be surprised at anything in wartime, everyone knows that.

MME. T. Good, let's start our meal.

MONS. T. You're quite right, I feel as hungry as a hunter. It's the smell of gunpowder.

MME. T. We'll sit on the rug while we're eating.

ZAPO. Can I bring my rifle with me?

MME. T. You leave your rifle alone. It's not good manners to bring your rifle to table with you. [*Pause.*] But you're absolutely filthy, my boy. How on earth did you get into such a state? Let's have a look at your hands.

ZAPO [*ashamed, holding out his hands*]. I had to crawl about on the ground during the manoeuvres.

MME. T. And what about your ears?

ZAPO. I washed them this morning.

MME. T. Well that's all right, then. And your teeth? [*He shows them.*] Very good. Who's going to give her little boy a great big kiss for cleaning his teeth so nicely? [*To her husband*] Well, go on, kiss your son for cleaning his teeth so nicely. [M. TÉPAN *kisses his son.*] Because, you know, there's one thing I *will* not have, and that's making fighting a war an excuse for not washing.

ZAPO. Yes, Mother. [*They eat.*]

MONS. T. Well, my boy, did you make a good score?

ZAPO. When?

MONS. T. In the last few days, of course.

ZAPO. Where?

MONS. T. At the moment, since you're fighting a war.

ZAPO. No, nothing much. I didn't make a good score. Hardly ever scored a bull.

MONS. T. Which are you best at shooting, enemy horses or soldiers?

ZAPO. No, not horses, there aren't any horses any more.

MONS. T. Well, soldiers then?

ZAPO. Could be.

MONS. T. Could be? Aren't you sure?

ZAPO. Well you see . . . I shoot without taking aim, [*pause*] and at the same time I say a Pater Noster for the chap I've shot.

MONS. T. You must be braver than that. Like your father.

MME. T. I'm going to put a record on. [*She puts a record on the gramophone—a pasodoble. All three are sitting on the ground, listening.*]

MONS.T. That really *is* music. Yes indeed, Ole! [*The music continues. Enter an enemy soldier:* ZÉPO. *He is dressed like* ZAPO. *The only difference is the colour of their uniforms.* ZÉPO *is in green and* ZAPO *is in grey.* ZÉPO *listens to the music openmouthed. He is behind the family so they can't see him. The record ends. As he gets up* ZAPO *discovers* ZÉPO. *Both put their hands up.* M. *and* MME. TÉPAN, *look at them in surprise.*] What's going on? [ZAPO *reacts—he hesitates. Finally, looking as if he's made up his mind, he points his rifle at* ZÉPO.]

ZAPO. Hands up! [ZÉPO *puts his hands up even higher, looking even more terrified.* ZAPO *doesn't know what to do. Suddenly he goes over quickly to* ZÉPO *and touches him gently on the shoulder, like a child playing a game of 'tag'.*] Got you! [*To his father, very pleased.*] There we are! A prisoner!

MONS. T. Fine. And now what're you going to do with him?

ZAPO. I don't know, but, well, could be—they might make me a corporal.

MONS. T. In the meantime, you'd better tie him up.

ZAPO. Tie him up? Why?

MONS. T. Prisoners always get tied up!

ZAPO. How?

MONS. T. Tie up his hands.

MME. T. Yes, there's no doubt about it, you must tie up his hands, I've always seen them do that.

ZAPO. Right. [*To his prisoner*] Put your hands together, if you please.

ZÉPO. Don't hurt me too much.

ZAPO. I won't.

ZÉPO. Ow! You're hurting me.

MONS. T. Now now, don't maltreat your prisoner.

MME. T. Is that the way I brought you up? How many times have I told you that we must be considerate of our fellow-men?

ZAPO. I didn't do it on purpose. [*To* ZÉPO.] And like that, does it hurt?
ZÉPO. No, it's all right like that.
MONS. T. Tell him straight out, say what you mean, don't mind us.
ZÉPO. It's all right like that.
MONS. T. Now his feet.
ZAPO. His feet as well, whatever next?
MONS. T. Didn't they teach you the rules?
ZAPO. Yes.
MONS. T. Well then!
ZAPO [*very politely, to* ZÉPO]. Would you be good enough to sit on the ground, please?
ZÉPO. Yes, but don't hurt me.
MME. T. You'll see, he'll take a dislike to you.
ZAPO. No he won't, no he won't. I'm not hurting you, am I?
ZÉPO. No, that's perfect.
ZAPO. Papa, why don't you take a photo of the prisoner on the ground and me with my foot on his stomach?
MONS. T. Oh, yes that'd look good.
ZÉPO. Oh no, not that!
MME. T. Say yes, don't be obstinate.
ZÉPO. No, I said no, and no it is.
MME. T. But just a little teeny weeny photo, what harm could that do you? And we could put it in the dining room, next to the life-saving certificate my husband won thirteen years ago.
ZÉPO. No—you won't shift me.
ZAPO. But why won't you let us?
ZÉPO. I'm engaged. And if she sees the photo one day, she'll say I don't know how to fight a war properly.
ZAPO. No she won't, all you'll need to say is that it isn't you, it's a panther.
MME. T. Come on, do say yes.
ZÉPO. All right then. But only to please you.
ZAPO. Lie down flat. [ZÉPO *lies down.* ZAPO *puts a foot on his stomach and grabs his rifle with a martial air.*]
MME. T. Stick your chest out a bit further.
ZAPO. Like this?
MME. T. Yes like that, and don't breathe.
MONS. T. Try to look like a hero.
ZAPO. What d'you mean, like a hero?
MONS. T. It's quite simple; try and look like the butcher does when he's boasting about his successes with the girls.
ZAPO. Like this?
MONS. T. Yes, like that.
MME. T. The most important thing is to puff your chest out and not breathe.
ZÉPO. Have you nearly finished?
MONS. T. Just be patient a moment. One . . . two . . . three.
ZAPO. I hope I'll come out well.
MME. T. Yes, you looked very martial.
MONS. T. You were fine.
MME. T. It makes me want to have my photo taken with you.
MONS. T. Now there's a good idea.

ZAPO. Right. I'll take it if you like.
MME. T. Give me your helmet to make me look like a soldier.
ZÉPO. I don't want any more photos. Even one's far too many.
ZAPO. Don't take it like that. After all, what harm can it do you?
ZÉPO. It's my last word.
MONS. T. [*to his wife*]. Don't press the point, prisoners are always very sensitive. If we go on he'll get cross and spoil our fun.
ZAPO. Right, what're we going to do with him, then?
MME. T. We could invite him to lunch. What do you say?
MONS. T. I don't see why not.
ZAPO. [*to* ZÉPO]. Well, will you have lunch with us, then?
ZÉPO. Er…
MONS. T. We brought a good bottle with us.
ZÉPO. Oh well, all right then.
MME. T. Make yourself at home, don't be afraid to ask for anything you want.
ZÉPO. All right.
MONS. T. And what about you, did you make a good score?
ZÉPO. When?
MONS. T. In the last few days, of course.
ZÉPO. Where?
MONS. T. At the moment, since you're fighting a war.
ZÉPO. No, nothing much. I didn't make a good score, hardly ever scored a bull.
MONS. T. Which are you best at shooting? Enemy horses or soldiers?
ZÉPO. No, not horses, they aren't any horses any more.
MONS. T. Well, soldiers, then?
ZÉPO. Could be.
MONS. T. Could be? Aren't you sure?
ZÉPO. Well you see…I shoot without taking aim [*pause*], and at the same time I say an Ave Maria for the chap I've shot.
ZAPO. An Ave Maria? I'd have thought you'd have said a Pater Noster.
ZÉPO. No, always an Ave Maria. [*Pause*] It's shorter.
MONS. T. Come come, my dear fellow, you must be brave.
MME. T. [*to* ZÉPO]. We can untie you if you like.
ZÉPO. No, don't bother, it doesn't matter.
MONS. T. Don't start getting stand-offish with us now. If you'd like us to untie you, say so.
MME. T. Make yourself comfortable.
ZÉPO. Well, if that's how you feel, you can untie my feet, but it's only to please you.
MONS. T. Zapo, untie him. [ZAPO *unties him.*]
MME. T. Well, do you feel better?
ZÉPO. Yes, of course. I really am putting you to a lot of inconvenience.
MONS. T. Not at all, just make yourself at home. And if you'd like us to untie your hands you only have to say so.
ZÉPO. No, not my hands, I don't want to impose upon you.
MONS. T. No no, my dear chap, no no. I tell you, it's no trouble at all.
ZÉPO. Right…Well then, untie my hands too. But only for lunch, eh? I don't want you think that you give me an inch and I take an ell.[1]

[1]A unit of measure equal to forty-five inches.

MONS. T. Untie his hands, son.

MME. T. Well, since our distinguished prisoner is so charming, we're going to have a marvellous day in the country.

ZÉPO. Don't call me your distinguished prisoner; just call me your prisoner.

MME. T. Won't that embarrass you?

ZÉPO. No, no, not at all.

MONS. T. Well, I must say you're modest. [*Noise of aeroplanes.*]

ZAPO. Aeroplanes. They're sure to be coming to bomb us. [ZAPO *and* ZÉPO *throw themselves on the sandbags and hide.*] [*To his parents*]. Take cover. The bombs will fall on you. [*The noise of the aeroplanes overpowers all the other noises. Bombs immediately start to fall. Shells explode very near the stage but not on it. A deafening noise.* ZAPO *and* ZÉPO *are cowering down between the sandbags.* M. TÉPAN *goes on talking calmly to his wife, and she answers in the same unruffled way. We can't hear what they are saying because of the bombing.* MME. TÉPAN *goes over to one of the baskets and takes an umbrella out of it. She opens it.* M. *and* MME. TÉPAN *shelter under it as if it were raining. They are standing up. They shift rhythmically from one foot to the other and talk about their personal affairs. The bombing continues. Finally the aeroplanes go away. Silence.* M. TÉPAN *stretches an arm outside the umbrella to make sure that nothing more is falling from the heavens.*]

MONS. T. [*to his wife*]. You can shut your umbrella. [MME. TÉPAN *does so. They both go over to their son and tap him lightly on the behind with the umbrella.*] Come on, out you come. The bombing's over. [ZAPO *and* ZÉPO *come out of their hiding place.*]

ZAPO. Didn't you get hit?

MONS. T. What d'you think could happen to your father? [*Proudly.*] Little bombs like that! Don't make me laugh! [*Enter, left, two* RED CROSS SOLDIERS. *They are carrying a stretcher.*]

1ST STRETCHER BEARER. Any dead here?

ZAPO. No, no one around these parts.

1ST STRETCHER BEARER. Are you sure you've looked properly?

ZAPO. Sure.

1ST STRETCHER BEARER. And there isn't a single person dead?

ZAPO. I've already told you there isn't.

1ST STRETCHER BEARER. No one wounded, even?

ZAPO. Not even that.

2ND STRETCHER BEARER [*to the* 1ST S. B.]. Well, now we're in a mess! [*To* ZAPO *persuasively.*] Just look again, search everywhere, and see if you can't find us a stiff.

1ST STRETCHER BEARER. Don't keep on about it, they've told you quite clearly there aren't any.

2ND STRETCHER BEARER. What a lousy trick!

ZAPO. I'm terribly sorry. I promise you I didn't do it on purpose.

2ND STRETCHER BEARER. That's what they all say. That no one's dead and that they didn't do it on purpose.

1ST STRETCHER BEARER. Oh, let the chap alone!

MONS. T. [*obligingly*]. We should be only too pleased to help you. At your service.

2ND STRETCHER BEARER. Well, really, if things go on like this I don't know what the Captain will say to us.

MONS. T. But what's it all about?

2ND STRETCHER BEARER. Quite simply that the others' wrists are aching with carting so many corpses and wounded men about, and that we haven't found any yet. And it's not because we haven't looked!

MONS. T. Well, yes, that really is annoying. [*To* ZAPO.] Are you quite sure no one's dead?

ZAPO. Obviously, Papa.

MONS. T. Have you looked under all the sandbags?

ZAPO. Yes, Papa.

MONS. T. [*angrily*]. Well then, you might as well say straight out that you don't want to lift a finger to help these gentlemen, when they're so nice, too!

1ST STRETCHER BEARER. Don't be angry with him. Let him be. We must just hope we'll have more luck in another trench and that all the lot'll be dead.

MONS. T. I should be delighted.

MME. T. Me too. There's nothing I like more than people who put their hearts into their work.

MONS. T. [*indignantly, addressing his remarks to the wings*]. Then is no one going to do anything for these gentlemen?

ZAPO. If it only rested with me, it'd already be done.

ZÉPO. I can say the same.

MONS. T. But look here, is neither of you even wounded?

ZAPO. [*ashamed*]. No, not me.

MONS. T. [*to* ZÉPO]. What about you?

ZÉPO [*ashamed*]. Me neither. I never have any luck.

MME. T. [*pleased*]. Now I remember! This morning, when I was peeling the onions, I cut my finger. Will that do you?

MONS. T. Of course it will! [*Enthusiastically.*] They'll take you off at once!

1ST STRETCHER BEARER. No, that won't work. With ladies it doesn't work.

MONS. T. We're no further advanced, then.

1ST STRETCHER BEARER. Never mind.

2ND STRETCHER BEARER. We may be able to make up for it in the other trenches. [*They start to go off.*]

MONS. T. Don't worry! If we find a dead man we'll keep him for you! No fear of us giving him to anyone else!

2ND STRETCHER BEARER. Thank you very much, sir.

MONS. T. Quite all right, old chap, think nothing of it. [*The two stretcher bearers say goodbye. All four answer them. The stretcher bearers go out.*]

MME. T. That's what's so pleasant about spending a Sunday in the country. You always meet such nice people.

MONS. T. [*pause*]. But why are you enemies?

ZÉPO. I don't know, I'm not very well educated.

MME. T. Was it by birth, or did you become enemies afterwards?

ZÉPO. I don't know, I don't know anything about it.

MONS. T. Well then, how did you come to be in the war?

ZÉPO. One day, at home, I was just mending my mother's iron, a man came and asked me: "Are you Zépo?" "Yes." "Right, you must come to the war." And so I asked him: "But what war?" and he said: "Don't you read the papers then? You're just a peasant!" I told him I did read the papers but not the war bits. . . .

ZAPO. Just how it was with me—exactly how it was with me.

MONS. T. Yes, they came to fetch you too.

MME. T. No, it wasn't quite the same; that day you weren't mending an iron, you were mending the car.

MONS. T. I was talking about the rest of it. [*To* ZÉPO.] Go on, what happened then?

ZÉPO. Then I told him I had a fiancée and that if I didn't take her to the pictures on Sundays she wouldn't like it. He said that that wasn't the least bit important.

ZAPO. Just how it was with me—exactly how it was with me.

ZÉPO. And then my father came down, and he said I couldn't go to the war because I didn't have a horse.

ZAPO. Just what my father said.

ZÉPO. The man said you didn't need a horse any more, and I asked him if I could take my fiancée with me. He said no. Then I asked whether I could take my aunt with me so that she could make me one of her custards on Thursdays; I'm very fond of them.

MME. T. [*realizing that she'd forgotten it*]. Oh! The custard!

ZÉPO. He said no again.

ZAPO. Same as with me.

ZÉPO. And ever since then I've been alone in the trench nearly all the time.

MME. T. I think you and your distinguished prisoner might play together this afternoon, as you're so close to each other and so bored.

ZAPO. Oh no, Mother, I'm too afraid, he's an enemy.

MONS. T. Now now, you mustn't be afraid.

ZAPO. If you only knew what the General was saying about the enemy!

MME. T. What did he say?

ZAPO. He said the enemy are very nasty people. When they take prisoners they put little stones in their shoes so that it hurts them to walk.

MME. T. How awful! What barbarians!

MONS. T. [*indignantly, to* ZÉPO]. And aren't you ashamed to belong to an army of criminals?

ZÉPO. I haven't done anything. I don't do anybody any harm.

MME. T. He was trying to take us in, pretending to be such a little saint!

MONS. T. We oughtn't to have untied him. You never know, we only need to turn our backs and he'll be putting a stone in our shoes.

ZÉPO. Don't be so nasty to me.

MONS. T. What'd you think we *should* be, then? I'm indignant. I know what I'll do. I'll go and find the Captain and ask him to let me fight in the war.

ZAPO. He won't let you, you're too old.

MONS. T. Then I'll buy myself a horse and a sword and come and fight on my own account.

MME. T. Bravo! If I were a man I'd do the same.

ZÉPO. Don't be like that with me, Madame. Anyway I'll tell you something—our General told us the same thing about you.

MME. T. How could he dare tell such a lie!

ZAPO. No—but the same thing really?

ZÉPO. Yes, the same thing.

MONS. T. Perhaps it was the same man who talked to you both?

MME. T. Well if it was the same man he might at least have said something different. That's a fine thing—saying the same thing to everyone!

MONS. T. [*to* ZÉPO *in a different tone of voice*]. Another little drink?

MME. T. I hope you liked our lunch?

MONS. T. In any case, it was better than last Sunday.

ZÉPO. What happened?

MONS. T. Well, we went to the country and we put the food on the rug. While we'd got our backs turned a cow ate up all our lunch, and the napkins as well.

ZÉPO. What a greedy cow!

MONS. T. Yes, but afterwards, to get our own back, we ate the cow. [*They laugh.*]

ZAPO [*to* ZÉPO]. They couldn't have been very hungry after that!

MONS. T. Cheers! [*They all drink.*]

MME. T. [*to* ZÉPO]. And what do you do to amuse yourself in the trench?

ZÉPO. I spend my time making flowers out of rags, to amuse myself. I get terribly bored.

MME. T. And what do you do with the flowers?

ZÉPO. At the beginning I used to send them to my fianceé, but one day she told me that the greenhouse and the cellar were already full of them and that she didn't know what to do with them any more, and she asked me, if I didn't mind, to send her something else.

MME. T. And what did you do?

ZÉPO. I tried to learn to make something else, but I couldn't so I go on making rag flowers to pass the time.

MME. T. Do you throw them away afterwards, then?

ZÉPO. No, I've found a way to use them now. I give one flower for each pal who dies. That way I know that even if I make an awful lot there'll never be enough.

MONS. T. That's a good solution you've hit on.

ZÉPO [*shyly*]. Yes.

ZAPO. Well, what I do is knit, so as not to get bored.

MME. T. But tell me, are all the soldiers as bored as you?

ZÉPO. It all depends on what they do to amuse themselves.

ZAPO. It's the same on our side.

MONS. T. Then let's stop the war.

ZÉPO. How?

MONS. T. It's very simple. [*To* ZAPO.] You just tell your pals that the enemy soldiers don't want to fight a war, and you [*to* ZÉPO] say the same to your comrades. And then everyone goes home.

ZAPO. Marvellous!

MME. T. And then you'll be able to finish mending the iron.

ZAPO. How is it that no one thought of such a good idea before?

MME. T. Your father is the only one who's capable of thinking of such ideas; don't forget he's a former student of the École Normale, *and* a philatelist.[2]

ZÉPO. But what will the sergeant-majors and corporals do?

MONS. T. We'll give them some guitars and castanets to keep them quiet!

ZÉPO. Very good idea.

MONS. T. You see how easy it is. Everything's fixed.

ZÉPO. We shall have a tremendous success.

ZAPO. My pals will be terribly pleased.

---

[2]Student of the Teacher's College and a stamp collector.

MME. T. What d'you say to putting on the pasodoble we were playing just now, to celebrate?

ZÉPO. Perfect.

ZAPO. Yes, put the record on, Mother. [MME. TÉPAN *puts a record on. She turns the handle. She waits. Nothing can be heard.*]

MONS. T. I can't hear a thing.

MME. T. Oh, how silly of me! Instead of putting a record on I put on a beret. *[She puts the record on. A gay pasodoble is heard. Zapo dances with Zépo and Mme. Tépan with her husband. They are all very gay. The field telephone rings. None of the four hears it. They go on dancing busily. The telephone rings again.*

The dance continues.

The battle starts up again with a terrific din of bombs, shots and bursts of machine-gun fire. None of the four has seen anything and they go on dancing merrily. A burst of machine-gun fire mows them all down. They fall to the ground, stone dead. A shot must have grazed the gramophone; the record keeps repeating the same thing, like a scratched record. The music of the scratched record can be heard till the end of the play. The two Stretcher Beares enter left. They are carrying the empty stretcher.]

SUDDEN CURTAIN

(1959)

Questions for Discussion and Writing

1. Did you find this play puzzling or confusing? Why? What dramatic expectations does it overturn?
2. How does each character in the play view the war? How do their views affect the relationships with one another?
3. Why are Zapo and Zépo's names so similar? What human values does Zapo exhibit in his actions toward Zépo? Does Zépo seem to share these values?
4. Write an essay in which you argue that Arrabal portrays humans as innocent yet cruel.
5. Find out about the movement called ***Theater of the Absurd.*** Write an essay explaining how this play illustrates the principles of this approach to drama.

Jane Martin 1938?–

Jane Martin is a woman of mystery. She has never been seen, has given no interviews, and there are no pictures. Theater critics speculate that her spokesperson, Jon Jory, retired artistic director of the Actors Theatre of Louisville, wrote the plays in collaboration with his wife. He firmly denies it, saying simply, "I'm not going to talk about that." But he has been the first to produce all of her plays and has accepted all of her awards for her. When asked whether her identity would be disclosed after her death, Jory responded, "That's a press conference that no one will come to. By the time I die, no one will care anyway." So Jane Martin remains, as one critic attests, "The best-known unknown playwright in America."

Beauty

CHARACTERS
CARLA
BETHANY

An apartment. Minimalist set. A young woman, Carla, on the phone.

CARLA. In love with me? You're in love with me? Could you describe yourself again? Uh-huh. Uh-huh. And you spoke to me? [*A knock at the door.*] Listen, I always hate to interrupt a marriage proposal, but…could you possibly hold that thought? [*Puts phone down and goes to door. Bethany, the same age as Carla and a friend, is there. She carries the sort of Mideastern lamp we know of from Aladdin.*]

BETHANY. Thank God you were home. I mean, you're not going to believe this!

CARLA. Somebody on the phone. [*Goes back to it.*]

BETHANY. I mean, I just had a beach urge, so I told them at work my uncle was dying…

CARLA [*motions to Bethany for quiet*]. And you were the one in the leather jacket with the tattoo? What was the tatoo? [*Carla again asks Bethany, who is gesturing wildly that she should hang up, to cool it.*] Look, a screaming eagle from shoulder to shoulder, maybe. There were a lot of people in the bar.

BETHANY [*gesturing and mouthing*]. I have to get back to work.

CARLA [*on phone*]. See, the thing is, I'm probably not going to marry someone I can't remember … particularly when I don't drink. Sorry. Sorry. Sorry. [*She hangs up.*] Madness.

BETHANY. So I ran out to the beach …

CARLA. This was some guy I never met who apparently offered me a beer …

BETHANY. … low tide and this … [*The lamp.*] … was just sitting there, lying there …

CARLA. … and he tracks me down …

BETHANY. … on the beach, and I lift this lid thing …

CARLA. … and seriously proposes marriage.

BETHANY. … and a genie comes out.

CARLA. I mean, that's twice in a … what?

BETHANY. A genie comes out of this thing.

CARLA. A genie?

BETHANY. I'm not kidding, the whole Disney kind of thing, swirling smoke, and then this twenty-foot-high, see-through guy in like an Arabian outfit.

CARLA. Very funny.

BETHANY. Yes, funny, but twenty feet high! I look up and down the beach, I'm alone. I don't have my pepper spray or my hand alarm. You know me, when I'm petrified I joke. I say his voice is too high for Robin Williams, and he says he's a castrati. Naturally. Who else would I meet?

CARLA. What's a castrati?

BETHANY. You know …

[*The appropriate gesture.*]

CARLA. Bethany, dear one, I have three modeling calls. I am meeting Ralph Lauren!

BETHANY. Okay, good. Ralph Lauren. Look, I am not kidding!

CARLA. You're not kidding what?!

BETHANY. There is a genie in this thingamajig.
CARLA. Uh-huh. I'll be back around eight.
BETHANY. And he offered me *wishes!*
CARLA. Is this some elaborate practical joke because it's my birthday?
BETHANY. No, happy birthday, but I'm like crazed because I'm on this deserted beach with a twenty-foot-high, see-through genie, so like sarcastically ... you know how I need a new car ... I said fine, gimme 25,000 dollars ...
CARLA. On the beach with the genie?
BETHANY. Yeah, right, exactly, and it rains down out of the sky.
CARLA. Oh sure.
BETHANY [*pulling a wad out of her purse*]. Count it, those are thousands. I lost one in the surf.

[*Carla sees the top bill. Looks at Bethany, who nods encouragement. Carla thumbs through them.*]

CARLA. These look real.
BETHANY. Yeah.
CARLA. And they rained down out of the sky?
BETHANY. Yeah.
CARLA. You've been really strange lately, are you dealing?
BETHANY. Dealing what, I've even given up chocolate.
CARLA. Let me see the genie.
BETHANY. Wait, wait.
CARLA. Bethany, I don't have time to screw around. Let me see the genie or let me go on my appointments.
BETHANY. Wait! So I pick up the money...see, there's sand on the money ... and I'm like nuts so I say, you know, "Okay, look, ummm, big guy, my uncle is in the hospital" ... because as you know when I said to the people at work my uncle was dying, I was on one level telling the truth although it had nothing to do with the beach, but he was in Intensive Care after the accident, and that's on my mind, so I say, okay, Genie, heal my uncle ... which is like impossible given he was hit by two trucks, and the genie says, "Yes, Master" ... like they're supposed to say, and he goes into this like kind of whirlwind, kicking up sand and stuff, and I'm like, "Oh my God!" and the air clears, and he bows, you know, and says, "It is done, Master," and I say, "Okay, whatever-you-are, I'm calling on my cell phone," and I get it out and I get this doctor who is like dumbstruck who says my uncle came to, walked out of Intensive Care and left the hospital! I'm not kidding, Carla.
CARLA. On your mother's grave?
BETHANY. On my mother's grave.

[*They look at each other.*]

CARLA. Let me see the genie.
BETHANY. No, no, look, that's the whole thing ... I was just, like, reacting, you know, responding, and that's already two wishes ... although I'm really pleased about my uncle, the $25,000 thing, I could have asked for $10 million, and there is only one wish left.
CARLA. So ask for $10 million.
BETHANY. I don't think so. I don't think so. I mean, I gotta focus in here. Do you have a sparkling water?
CARLA. No. Bethany, I'm missing Ralph Lauren now. Very possibly my one chance to go from catalogue model to the very, very big time, so, if you are joking, stop joking.

BETHANY. Not joking. See, see, the thing is, I know what I want. In my guts. Yes. Underneath my entire bitch of a life is this unspoken, ferocious, all-consuming urge…

CARLA [*trying to get her to move this along*]. Ferocious, all-consuming urge …

BETHANY. I want to be like you.

CARLA. Me?

BETHANY. Yes.

CARLA. Half the time you don't even like me.

BETHANY. Jealous. The ogre of jealousy.

CARLA. You're the one with the $40,000 job straight out of school. You're the one who has published short stories. I'm the one hanging on by her fingernails in modeling. The one who has creeps calling her on the phone. The one who had to have a nose job.

BETHANY. I want to be beautiful.

CARLA. You are beautiful.

BETHANY. Carla, I'm not beautiful.

CARLA. You have charm. You have personality. You know perfectly well you're pretty.

BETHANY. "Pretty," see, that's it. Pretty is the minor leagues of beautiful. Pretty is what people discover about you after they know you. Beautiful is what knocks them out across the room. Pretty, you get called a couple of times a year; *beautiful* is twenty-four hours a day.

CARLA. Yeah? So?

BETHANY. So?! We're talking *beauty* here. Don't say "So?" Beauty is the real deal. You are the center of any moment of your life. People stare. Men flock. I've seen you get offered discounts on makeup for no reason. Parents treat beautiful children better. Studies show your income goes up. You can have sex anytime you want it. Men have to know me. That takes up to a year. I'm continually horny.

CARLA. Bethany, I don't even like sex. I can't have a conversation without men coming on to me. I have no privacy. I get hassled on the street. They start pressuring me from the beginning. Half the time, it never occurs to them to start with a conversation. Smart guys like you. You've had three long-term relationships, and you're only twenty-three. I haven't had one. The good guys, the smart guys are scared to death of me. I'm surrounded by male bimbos who think a preposition is when you go to school away from home. I have no woman friends except you. I don't even want to talk about this!

BETHANY. I knew you'd say something like this. See, you're "in the club" so you can say this. It's the way beauty functions as an elite. You're trying to keep it all for yourself.

CARLA. I'm trying to tell you it's no picnic.

BETHANY. But it's what everybody wants. It's the nasty secret at large in the world. It's the unspoken tidal desire in every room and on every street. It's the unspoken, the soundless whisper…millions upon millions of people longing hopelessly and forever to stop being whatever they are and be beautiful, but the difference between those ardent multitudes and me is that I have a goddamn genie and one more wish!

CARLA. Well, it's not what I want. This is me, Carla. I have never read a whole book. Page six, I can't remember page four. The last thing I read was *The Complete Idiot's Guide to WordPerfect*. I leave dinner parties right after the dessert because I'm out of conversation. You know the dumb blond joke about the application where it says, "Sign here," she put Sagittarius? I've done that.

Only beautiful guys approach me, and that's because they want to borrow my eye shadow. I barely exist outside a mirror! You don't want to be me.

BETHANY. None of you tell the truth. That's why you have no friends. We can all see you're just trying to make us feel better because we aren't in your league. This only proves to me it should be my third wish. Money can only buy things. Beauty makes you the center of the universe.

[*Bethany picks up the lamp.*]

CARLA. Don't do it. Bethany, don't wish it! I am telling you you'll regret it.

[*Bethany lifts the lid. There is a tremendous crash, and the lights go out. Then they flicker and come back up, revealing Bethany and Carla on the floor where they have been thrown by the explosion. We don't realize it at first, but they have exchanged places.*]

CARLA/BETHANY. Oh God.

BETHANY/CARLA. Oh God.

CARLA/BETHANY. Am I bleeding? Am I dying?

BETHANY/CARLA. I'm so dizzy. You're not bleeding.

CARLA/BETHANY. Neither are you.

BETHANY/CARLA. I feel so weird.

CARLA/BETHANY. Me too. I feel ... [*Looking at her hands.*] Oh, my God, I'm wearing your jewelry. I'm wearing your nail polish.

BETHANY/CARLA. I know I'm over here, but I can see myself over there.

CARLA/BETHANY. I'm wearing your dress. I have your legs!!

BETHANY/CARLA. These aren't my shoes. I can't meet Ralph Lauren wearing these shoes!

CARLA/BETHANY. I wanted to be beautiful, but I didn't want to be you.

BETHANY/CARLA. Thanks a lot!!

CARLA/BETHANY. I've got to go. I want to pick someone out and get laid.

BETHANY/CARLA. You can't just walk out of here in my body!

CARLA/BETHANY. Wait a minute. Wait a minute. What's eleven eighteenths of 1,726?

BETHANY/CARLA. Why?

CARLA/BETHANY. I'm a public accountant. I want to know if you have my brain.

BETHANY/CARLA. One hundred thirty-two and a half.

CARLA/BETHANY. You have my brain.

BETHANY/CARLA. What shade of Rubenstein lipstick does Cindy Crawford wear with teal blue?

CARLA/BETHANY. Raging Storm.

BETHANY/CARLA. You have my brain. You poor bastard.

CARLA/BETHANY. I don't care. Don't you see?

BETHANY/CARLA. See what?

CARLA/BETHANY. We both have the one thing, the one and only thing everybody wants.

BETHANY/CARLA. What is that?

CARLA/BETHANY. It's better than beauty for me; it's better than brains for you.

BETHANY/CARLA. What? What?!

CARLA/BETHANY. Different problems.

Blackout.

END OF PLAY

(2001)

Questions for Discussion and Writing

1. What values and obsessions does this play satirize?
2. What stereotype does each character represent? Are they both objects of derision? Do you think one of them gets a better deal in the end?
3. Why does Bethany not believe Carla when she (Carla) tries to explain the downside of beauty?
4. Does this play have to be about females? Write an essay explaining how you would adapt the play to satirize two young men.

Luis Valdez 1940–

Born into a migrant farm-worker family in Delano, California, Luis Valdez often worked in the fields with his parents. After graduating from San Jose State in 1964 with a degree in drama, he formed a theater company of farm workers, E1 Teatro Campesino, to support the strikers at the Delano grape plantations by performing short, improvised, satirical skits in community centers and in the fields. By the 1980s, Valdez expanded his interests to film and television, in part to counter the broad ethnic stereotypes of Mexican Americans. His work included a film based on his widely successful play *Zoot Suit* (1978), and *La Bamba* (1987), a bio-pic of Chicano rock star Ritchie Valens. Critic John Leonard described Valdez's televised play *La Pastorela* (1991) as "the Nativity... tricked up to look like a road-show amalgam of *The Wizard of Oz* and *Cats.*"

Los Vendidos[1]

CHARACTERS

HONEST SANCHO	JOHNNY
SECRETARY	REVOLUCIONARIO
FARM WORKER	MEXICAN-AMERICAN

SCENE

HONEST SANCHO'S *Used Mexican Lot and Mexican Curio Shop. Three models are on display in* HONEST SANCHO'S *shop: to the right, there is a* REVOLUCIONARIO, *complete with sombrero, carrilleras*[2] *and carabina 30–30. At center, on the floor, there is the* FARM WORKER, *under a broad straw sombrero. At stage left is the* PACHUCO, *filero*[3] *in hand.*

---

[1]**Los Vendidos** The Sellouts.
[2]**carrilleras** cartridge belts.
[3]**Pachuco** Chicano slang for an urban tough guy; **filero** blade.

[HONEST SANCHO *is moving among his models, dusting them off and preparing for another day of business.*]

SANCHO. Bueno, bueno, mis monos, vamos a ver a quien vendemos ahora, ¿no?[4] [*To audience.*] ¡Quihubo! I'm Honest Sancho and this is my shop. Antes fui contratista pero ahora logré tener mi negocito.[5] All I need now is a customer. [*A bell rings offstage.*] Ay, a customer!

SECRETARY [*Entering*]. Good morning, I'm Miss Jiménez from—

SANCHO ¡Ah, una chicana! Welcome, welcome Señorita Jiménez.

SECRETARY [*Anglo pronunciation*]. JIM-enez.

SANCHO. ¿Qué?

SECRETARY. My name is Miss JIM-enez. Don't you speak English? What's wrong with you?

SANCHO. Oh, nothing, Señorita JIM-enez. I'm here to help you.

SECRETARY. That's better. As I was starting to say, I'm a secretary from Governor Reagan's office, and we're looking for a Mexican type for the administration.

SANCHO. Well, you come to the right place, lady. This is Honest Sancho's Used Mexican lot, and we got all types here. Any particular type you want?

SECRETARY. Yes, we were looking for somebody suave—

SANCHO. Suave.

SECRETARY. Debonair.

SANCHO. De buen aire.

SECRETARY. Dark.

SANCHO. Prieto.

SECRETARY. But of course not too dark.

SANCHO. No muy prieto.

SECRETARY. Perhaps, beige.

SANCHO. Beige, just the tone. Así como cafecito con leche,[6] ¿no?

SECRETARY. One more thing. He must be hard-working.

SANCHO. That could only be one model. Step right over here to the center of the shop, lady. [*They cross to the* FARM WORKER.] This is our standard farm worker model. As you can see, in the words of our beloved Senator George Murphy, he is "built close to the ground." Also take special notice of his four-ply Goodyear huaraches, made from the rain tire. This wide-brimmed sombrero is an extra added feature—keeps off the sun, rain, and dust.

SECRETARY. Yes, it does look durable.

SANCHO. And our farm worker model is friendly. Muy amable.[7] Watch. [*Snaps his fingers.*]

FARM WORKER [*Lifts up head*]. Buenos días, señorita. [*His head drops.*]

SECRETARY. My, he's friendly.

SANCHO. Didn't I tell you? Loves his patrones! But his most attractive feature is that he's hard-working. Let me show you. [*Snaps fingers.* FARM WORKER *stands.*]

---

[4]**Bueno ... no?** Well, well, my cute ones, let's see who we can sell now, O.K?
[5]**Antes ... negocito** I used to be a contractor, but now I'm successful with my own little business.
[6]**Asi ... leche** like coffee with milk.
[7]**Muy amable** very friendly.

FARM WORKER. ¡El jale![8] [*He begins to work.*]

SANCHO. As you can see, he is cutting grapes.

SECRETARY. Oh, I wouldn't know.

SANCHO. He also picks cotton. [*Snap.* FARM WORKER *begins to pick cotton.*]

SECRETARY. Versatile isn't he?

SANCHO. He also picks melons. [*Snap.* FARM WORKER *picks melons.*] That's his slow speed for late in the season. Here's his fast speed. [*Snap.* FARM WORKER *picks faster.*]

SECRETARY. ¡Chihuahua! . . . I mean, goodness, he sure is a hard worker.

SANCHO [*Pulls the* FARM WORKER *to his feet*]. And that isn't the half of it. Do you see these little holes on his arms that appear to be pores? During those hot sluggish days in the field, when the vines or the branches get so entangled, it's almost impossible to move; these holes emit a certain grease that allows our model to slip and slide right through the crop with no trouble at all.

SECRETARY. Wonderful. But is he economical?

SANCHO. Economical? Señorita, you are looking at the Volkswagen of Mexicans. Pennies a day is all it takes. One plate of beans and tortillas will keep him going all day. That, and chile. Plenty of chile. Chile jalapenos, chile verde, chile colorado. But, of course, if you do give him chile [*Snap.* FARM WORKER *turns left face. Snap.* FARM WORKER *bends over.*] then you have to change his oil filter once a week.

SECRETARY. What about storage?

SANCHO. No problem. You know these new farm labor camps our Honorable Governor Reagan has built out by Parlier or Raisin City? They were designed with our model in mind. Five, six, seven, even ten in one of those shacks will give you no trouble at all. You can also put him in old barns, old cars, river banks. You can even leave him out in the field overnight with no worry!

SECRETARY. Remarkable.

SANCHO. And here's an added feature: Every year at the end of the season, this model goes back to Mexico and doesn't return, automatically, until next Spring.

SECRETARY. How about that. But tell me: does he speak English?

SANCHO. Another outstanding feature: is that last year this model was programmed to go out on STRIKE! [*Snap.*]

FARM WORKER. ¡HUELGA! ¡HUELGA! Hermanos, sálganse de esos files.[9] [*Snap. He stops.*]

SECRETARY. No! Oh no, we can't strike in the State Capitol.

SANCHO. Well, he also scabs. [*Snap.*]

FARM WORKER. Me vendo barato, ¿y qué?[10] [*Snap.*]

SECRETARY. That's much better, but you didn't answer my question. Does he speak English?

SANCHO. Bueno . . . no, pero[11] he has other—

SECRETARY. No.

SANCHO. Other features.

---

[8]**El jale** the job.
[9]**Huelga! . . . files** Strike! Strike! Brothers, leave those rows.
[10]**Me . . . qué?** I come cheap, so what?
[11]**Bueno . . . no, pero** Well, no, but.

SECRETARY. No! He just won't do!
SANCHO. Okay, okay pues. We have other models.
SECRETARY. I hope so. What we need is something a little more sophisticated.
SANCHO. Sophisti—¿qué?
SECRETARY. An urban model.
SANCHO. Ah, from the city! Step right back. Over here in this corner of the shop is exactly what you're looking for. Introducing our new 1969 JOHNNY PACHUCO model! This is our fast-back model. Streamlined. Built for speed, low-riding, city life. Take a look at some of these features. Mag shoes, dual exhausts, green chartreuse paint-job, dark-tint windshield, a little poof on top. Let me just turn him on. [*Snap.* JOHNNY *walks to stage center with a pachuco bounce.*]
SECRETARY. What was that?
SANCHO. That, señorita, was the Chicano shuffle.
SECRETARY. Okay, what does he do?
SANCHO. Anything and everything necessary for city life. For instance, survival: He knife fights. [*Snap.* JOHNNY *pulls out switch blade and swings at* SECRETARY.]
[SECRETARY *screams.*]
SANCHO. He dances. [*Snap.*]
JOHNNY [*Singing*]. "Angel Baby, my Angel Baby…" [*Snap.*]
SANCHO. And here's a feature no city model can be without. He gets arrested, but not without resisting, of course. [*Snap.*]
JOHNNY. ¡En la madre, la placa![12] I didn't do it! I didn't do it! [JOHNNY *turns and stands up against an imaginary wall, legs spread out, arms behind his back.*]
SECRETARY. Oh no, we can't have arrests! We must maintain law and order.
SANCHO. But he's bilingual!
SECRETARY. Bilingual?
SANCHO. Simón que yes.[13] He speaks English! Johnny, give us some English. [*Snap.*]
JOHNNY [*Comes downstage*]. Fuck-you!
SECRETARY [*Gasps*]. Oh! I've never been so insulted in my whole life!
SANCHO. Well, he learned it in your school.
SECRETARY. I don't care where he learned it.
SANCHO. But he's economical!
SECRETARY. Economical?
SANCHO. Nickels and dimes. You can keep Johnny running on hamburgers, Taco Bell tacos, Lucky Lager beer, Thunderbird wine, yesca—
SECRETARY. Yesca?
SANCHO. Mota.
SECRETARY. Mota?
SANCHO. Leños[14]… Marijuana. [*Snap;* JOHNNY *inhales on an imaginary joint.*]
SECRETARY. That's against the law!
JOHNNY [*Big smile, holding his breath*]. Yeah.
SANCHO. He also sniffs glue. [*Snap.* JOHNNY *inhales glue, big smile.*]
JOHNNY. Tha's too much man, ése.
SECRETARY. No, Mr. Sancho, I don't think this—

[12]**En … la placa!** Wow, the cops!
[13]**Simón que yes** Yeah, sure.
[14]**Leños** joints (of marijuana).

SANCHO. Wait a minute, he has other qualities I know you'll love. For example, an inferiority complex. [*Snap.*]

JOHNNY [*To* SANCHO]. You think you're better than me, huh ése?[15] [*Swings switch blade.*]

SANCHO. He can also be beaten and he bruises, cut him and he bleeds; kick him and he—[*He beats, bruises and kicks* PACHUCO.] Would you like to try it?

SECRETARY. Oh, I couldn't.

SANCHO. Be my guest. He's a great scapegoat.

SECRETARY. No, really.

SANCHO. Please.

SECRETARY. Well, all right. Just once. [*She kicks* PACHUCO.] Oh, he's so soft.

SANCHO. Wasn't that good? Try again.

SECRETARY [*Kicks* PACHUCO]. Oh, he's so wonderful! [*She kicks him again.*]

SANCHO. Okay, that's enough, lady. You ruin the merchandise. Yes, our Johnny Pachuco model can give you many hours of pleasure. Why, the L.A.P.D. just bought twenty of these to train their rookie cops on. And talk about maintenance. Señorita, you are looking at an entirely self-supporting machine. You're never going to find our Johnny Pachuco model on the relief rolls. No, sir, this model knows how to liberate.

SECRETARY. Liberate?

SANCHO. He steals. [*Snap.* JOHNNY *rushes the* SECRETARY *and steals her purse.*]

JOHNNY. ¡Dame esa bolsa, vieja![16] [*He grabs the purse and runs. Snap by* SANCHO. *He stops.*]

[SECRETARY *runs after* JOHNNY *and grabs purse away from him, kicking him as she goes.*]

SECRETARY. No, no, no! We can't have any *more* thieves in the State Administration. Put him back.

SANCHO. Okay, we still got other models. Come on, Johnny, we'll sell you to some old lady. [SANCHO *takes* JOHNNY *back to his place.*]

SECRETARY. Mr. Sancho, I don't think you quite understand what we need. What we need is something that will attract the women voters. Something more traditional, more romantic.

SANCHO. Ah, a lover. [*He smiles meaningfully.*] Step right over here, señorita. Introducing our standard Revolucionario and/or Early California Bandit type. As you can see he is well-built, sturdy, durable. This is the International Harvester of Mexicans.

SECRETARY. What does he do?

SANCHO. You name it, he does it. He rides horses, stays in the mountains, crosses deserts, plains, rivers, leads revolutions, follows revolutions, kills, can be killed, serves as a martyr, hero, movie star—did I say movie star? Did you ever see *Viva Zapata? Viva Villa? Villa Rides? Pancho Villa Returns? Pancho Villa Goes Back? Pancho Villa Meets Abbott and Costello—*

SECRETARY. I've never seen any of those.

SANCHO. Well, he was in all of them. Listen to this. [*Snap.*]

REVOLUCIONARIO [*Scream*]. ¡VIVA VILLAAAAA!

SECRETARY. That's awfully loud.

---

[15] **ése** fellow, buddy.

[16] **Dame ... vieja!** Give me that bag, old lady.

SANCHO. He has a volume control. [*He adjusts volume. Snap.*]
REVOLUCIONARIO [*Mousey voice*]. ¡Viva Villa!
SECRETARY. That's better.
SANCHO. And even if you didn't see him in the movies, perhaps you saw him on TV. He makes commercials. [*Snap.*]
REVOLUCIONARIO. Is there a Frito Bandito in your house?
SECRETARY. Oh yes, I've seen that one!
SANCHO. Another feature about this one is that he is economical. He runs on raw horsemeat and tequila!
SECRETARY. Isn't that rather savage?
SANCHO. Al contrario,[17] it makes him a lover. [*Snap.*]
REVOLUCIONARIO [*To* SECRETARY]. ¡Ay, mamasota, cochota, ven pa'ca.[18] [*He grabs* SECRETARY *and folds her back—Latin-lover style.*]
SANCHO [*Snap.* REVOLUCIONARIO *goes back upright*]. Now wasn't that nice?
SECRETARY. Well, it was rather nice.
SANCHO. And finally, there is one outstanding feature about this model I know the ladies are going to love: He's a GENUINE antique! He was made in Mexico in 1910!
SECRETARY. Made in Mexico?
SANCHO. That's right. Once in Tijuana, twice in Guadalajara, three times in Cuernavaca.
SECRETARY. Mr. Sancho, I thought he was an American product.
SANCHO. No, but—
SECRETARY. No, I'm sorry. We can't buy anything but American-made products. He just won't do.
SANCHO. But he's an antique!
SECRETARY. I don't care. You still don't understand what we need. It's true we need Mexican models such as these, but it's more important that he be *American.*
SANCHO. American?
SECRETARY. That's right, and judging from what you've shown me, I don't think you have what we want. Well, my lunch hour's almost over; I better—
SANCHO. Wait a minute! Mexican but American?
SECRETARY. That's correct.
SANCHO. Mexican but... [*A sudden flash.*] AMERICAN! Yeah, I think we've got exactly what you want. He just came in today! Give me a minute. [*He exits. Talks from backstage.*] Here he is in the shop. Let me just get some papers off. There. Introducing our new 1970 Mexican-American! Ta-ra-ra-ra-ra-ra-RA-RAAA!

[SANCHO *brings out the* MEXICAN-AMERICAN *model, a clean-shaven middle-class type in business suit, with glasses.*]

SECRETARY [*Impressed*]. Where have you been hiding this one?
SANCHO. He just came in this morning. Ain't he a beauty? Feast your eyes on him! Sturdy US STEEL frame, streamlined, modern. As a matter of fact, he is built exactly like our Anglo models except that he comes in a variety of darker shades: naugahyde, leather, or leatherette.
SECRETARY. Naugahyde.

---

[17]**Al contrario** On the contrary.
[18]**Ay ... pa'ca!** Get over here!

SANCHO. Well, we'll just write that down. Yes, señorita, this model represents the apex of American engineering! He is bilingual, college educated, ambitious! Say the word "acculturate" and he accelerates. He is intelligent, well-mannered, clean—did I say clean? [*Snap.* MEXICAN-AMERICAN *raises his arm.*] Smell.

SECRETARY [*Smells*]. Old Sobaco, my favorite.

SANCHO [*Snap.* MEXICAN-AMERICAN *turns toward* SANCHO]. Eric! [*To* SECRETARY.] We call him Eric Garcia. [*To* ERIC.] I want you to meet Miss JIM-enez, Eric.

MEXICAN-AMERICAN. Miss JIM-enez, I am delighted to make your acquaintance. [*He kisses her hand.*]

SECRETARY. Oh, my, how charming!

SANCHO. Did you feel the suction? He has seven especially engineered suction cups right behind his lips. He's a charmer all right!

SECRETARY. How about boards? Does he function on boards?

SANCHO. You name them, he is on them. Parole boards, draft boards, school boards, taco quality control boards, surf boards, two-by-fours.

SECRETARY. Does he function in politics?

SANCHO. Señorita, you are looking at a political MACHINE. Have you ever heard of the OEO, EOC, COD, WAR ON POVERTY? That's our model! Not only that, he makes political speeches.

SECRETARY. May I hear one?

SANCHO. With pleasure. [*Snap.*] Eric, give us a speech.

MEXICAN-AMERICAN. Mr. Congressman, Mr. Chairman, members of the board, honored guests, ladies and gentlemen. [SANCHO *and* SECRETARY *applaud.*] Please, please, I come before you as a Mexican-American to tell you about the problems of the Mexican. The problems of the Mexican stem from one thing and one thing alone. He's stupid. He's uneducated. He needs to stay in school. He needs to be ambitious, forward-looking, harder-working. He needs to think American, American, American, AMERICAN, AMERICAN, AMERICAN. GOD BLESS AMERICA! GOD BLESS AMERICA! GOD BLESS AMERICA!! [*He goes out of control.*]

[SANCHO *snaps frantically and the* MEXICAN-AMERICAN *finally slumps forward, bending at the waist.*]

SECRETARY. Oh my, he's patriotic too!

SANCHO. Sí, señorita, he loves his country. Let me just make a little adjustment here. [*Stands* MEXICAN-AMERICAN *up.*]

SECRETARY. What about upkeep? Is he economical?

SANCHO. Well, no, I won't lie to you. The Mexican-American costs a little bit more, but you get what you pay for. He's worth every extra cent. You can keep him running on dry martinis, Langendorf bread.

SECRETARY. Apple pie?

SANCHO. Only Mom's. Of course, he's also programmed to eat Mexican food on ceremonial functions, but I must warn you an overdose of beans will plug up his exhaust.

SECRETARY. Fine! There's just one more question: HOW MUCH DO YOU WANT FOR HIM?

SANCHO. Well, I tell you what I'm gonna do. Today and today only, because you've been so sweet, I'm gonna let you steal this model from me! I'm gonna let you drive him off the lot for the simple price of—let's see taxes and license included—$15,000.

SECRETARY. Fifteen thousand DOLLARS? For a MEXICAN!

SANCHO. Mexican? What are you talking, lady? This is a Mexican-AMERICAN! We had to melt down two pachucos, a farm worker and three gabachos[19] to make this model! You want quality, but you gotta pay for it! This is no cheap run-about. He's got class!
SECRETARY. Okay, I'll take him.
SANCHO. You will?
SECRETARY. Here's your money.
SANCHO. You mind if I count it?
SECRETARY. Go right ahead.
SANCHO. Well, you'll get your pink slip in the mail. Oh, do you want me to wrap him up for you? We have a box in the back.
SECRETARY. No, thank you. The Governor is having a luncheon this afternoon, and we need a brown face in the crowd. How do I drive him?
SANCHO. Just snap your fingers. He'll do anything you want.

[SECRETARY *Snaps.* MEXICAN–AMERICAN *steps forward.*]

MEXICAN -AMERICAN. RAZA QUERIDA, ¡VAMOS LEVANTANDO ARMAS PARA LIBERARNOS DE ESTOS DESGRACIADOS GABACHOS QUE NOS EXPLOTAN! VAMOS.[20]
SECRETARY. What did he say?
SANCHO. Something about lifting arms, killing white people, etc.
SECRETARY. But he's not supposed to say that!
SANCHO. Look, lady, don't blame me for bugs from the factory. He's your Mexican-American; you bought him, now drive him off the lot!
SECRETARY. But he's broken!
SANCHO. Try snapping another finger.

[SECRETARY *snaps.* MEXICAN-AMERICAN *comes to life again.*]

MEXICAN-AMERICAN. ¡ESTA GRAN HUMANIDAD HA DICHO BASTA! Y SE HA PUESTO EN MARCHA! ¡BASTA! ¡BASTA! ¡VIVA LA RAZA! ¡VIVA LA CAUSA! ¡VIVA LA HUELGA! ¡VIVAN LOS BROWN BERETS! ¡VIVAN LOS ESTUDIANTES! ¡CHICANO POWER![21]

[*The* MEXICAN-AMERICAN *turns toward the* SECRETARY, *who gasps and backs up. He keeps turning toward the* PACHUCO, FARM WORKER, *and* REVOLUCIONARIO, *snapping his fingers and turning each of them on, one by one.*]

PACHUCO [*Snap. To* SECRETARY]. I'm going to get you, baby! ¡Viva La Raza!
FARM WORKER [*Snap. To* SECRETARY]. ¡Viva la huelga! ¡Viva la Huelga! ¡VIVA LA HUELGA!
REVOLUCIONARIO [*Snap. To* SECRETARY] ¡Viva la revolución! ¡VIVA LA REVOLUCIÓN!

[*The three models join together and advance toward the* SECRETARY *who backs up and runs out of the shop screaming.* SANCHO *is at the other end of the shop holding his money in his hand. All freeze. After a few seconds of silence, the* PACHUCO *moves and stretches, shaking his arms and loosening up. The* FARM WORKER *and* REVOLUCIONARIO *do the same.* SANCHO *stays where he is, frozen to his spot.*]

JOHNNY. Man, that was a long one, ése. [*Others agree with him.*]

---

[19]**gabachos** whites.
[20]**RAZA . . . VAMOS** Beloved Raza [people of Mexican descent], let's take up arms to liberate ourselves from those damned whites who exploit us! Let's go.
[21]**ESTA . . . CHICANO POWER**! This great mass of humanity has said enough! And it has begun to march! Enough! Enough! Long live La Raza! Long live the Cause! Long live the strike! Long live the Brown Berets! Long live the students! Chicano Power!

FARM WORKER. How did we do?

JOHNNY. Perty good, look at all that lana,[22] man! [*He goes over to* SANCHO *and removes the money from his hand.* SANCHO *stays where he is.*]

REVOLUCIONARIO. En la madre, look at all the money.

JOHNNY. We keep this up, we're going to be rich.

FARM WORKER. They think we're machines.

REVOLUCIONARIO. Burros.

JOHNNY. Puppets.

MEXICAN-AMERICAN. The only thing I don't like is—how come I always got to play the godamn Mexican-American?

JOHNNY. That's what you get for finishing high school.

FARM WORKER. How about our wages, ése?

JOHNNY. Here it comes right now. $3,000 for you, $3,000 for you, $3,000 for you, and $3,000 for me. The rest we put back into the business.

MEXICAN-AMERICAN. Too much, man–. Heh, where you vatos[23] going tonight?

FARM WORKER. I'm going over to Concha's. There's a party.

JOHNNY. Wait a minute, vatos. What about our salesman? I think he needs an oil job.

REVOLUCIONARIO. Leave him to me.

[*The* PACHUCO, FARM WORKER. *and* MEXICAN-AMERICAN *exit, talking loudly about their plans for the night. The* REVOLUCIONARIO *goes over to* SANCHO, *removes his derby hat and cigar, lifts him up and throws him over his shoulder.* SANCHO *hangs loose, lifeless.*]

REVOLUCIONARIO [*To audience*]. He's the best model we got! ¡Ajua! [*Exit.*]

(1967)

---

[22]**lana** money.
[23]**vatos** guys.

Questions for Discussion and Writing

1. What is the meaning of the play's title? Who are the "sellouts" that the title alludes to?
2. What stereotypes of Mexican-Americans does the play present? Are these stereotypes offensive? Why does Valdez use them?
3. What change occurs in the end of the play? Does this change clarify or explain the reason for using stereotypes?
4. What social or political messages does the play convey? Do the politics interfere with the play's dramatic effectiveness?

David Ives 1950–

Born and raised on Chicago's south side, David Ives began his career in Hollywood writing scripts for TV movies. After moving to New York, he did humorous pieces for the *New York Times Magazine* and the *New Yorker* before turning to playwriting. He describes one of his short plays featuring a cross-dressing corporate executive as being about "the ontological problem of lingerie" and says that he's grateful for the shortness of his plays because "when the lights go down, at least the audience isn't thinking, 'Oh, God, two more hours of this.'" Asked by a reporter, "If you weren't a writer, what would you be?" he responded, "I'd be a hawk. Or maybe a seal in the waters off Alaska. Preferably with my wife Martha as my fellow hawk or fellow seal."

Sure Thing

CHARACTERS

BILL, *in his late twenties* BETTY, *in her late twenties*

SETTING

A café table, with a couple of chairs.

SCENE

[BETTY, *reading at the table. An empty chair opposite her.* BILL *enters.*]

BILL. Excuse me. Is this chair taken?
BETTY. Excuse me?
BILL. Is this taken?
BETTY. Yes, it is.
BILL. Oh. Sorry.
BETTY. Sure thing.

[*A bell rings softly*]

BILL. Excuse me. Is this chair taken?
BETTY. Excuse me?
BILL. Is this taken?
BETTY. No, but I'm expecting somebody in a minute.
BILL. Oh. Thanks anyway.
BETTY. Sure thing.

[*A bell rings softly*]

BILL. Excuse me. Is this chair taken?
BETTY. No, but I'm expecting somebody very shortly.
BILL. Would you mind if I sit here till he or she or it comes?
BETTY [*Glances at her watch*]. They seem to be pretty late…
BILL. You never know who you might be turning down.
BETTY. Sorry. Nice try, though.
BILL. Sure thing.

[*Bell*]

BILL. Is this seat taken?
BETTY. No, it's not.
BILL. Would you mind if I sit here?

BETTY. Yes, I would.
BILL. Oh.

[*Bell*]

BILL. Is this chair taken?
BETTY. No, it's not.
BILL. Would you mind if I sit here?
BETTY. No. Go ahead.
BILL. Thanks. [*He sits. She continues reading*] Everyplace else seems to be taken.
BETTY. Mm-hm.
BILL. Great place.
BETTY. Mm-hm.
BILL. What's the book?
BETTY. I just wanted to read in quiet, if you don't mind.
BILL. No. Sure thing.

[*Bell*]

BILL. Everyplace else seems to be taken.
BETTY. Mm-hm.
BILL. Great place for reading.
BETTY. Yes, I like it.
BILL. What's the book?
BETTY. *The Sound and the Fury.*
BILL. Oh. Hemingway.

[*Bell*]

BILL. What's the book?
BETTY. *The Sound and the Fury.*
BILL. Oh. Faulkner.
BETTY. Have you read it?
BILL. Not … actually. I've read *about* it, though. It's supposed to be great.
BETTY. It is great.
BILL. I hear it's great. [*Small pause*] Waiter?

[*Bell*]

BILL. What's the book?
BETTY. *The Sound and the Fury.*
BILL. Oh. Faulkner.
BETTY. Have you read it?
BILL. I'm a Mets fan, myself.

[*Bell*]

BETTY. Have you read it?
BILL. Yeah, I read it in college.
BETTY. Where was college?
BILL. I went to Oral Roberts University.

[*Bell*]

BETTY. Where was college?
BILL. I was lying. I never really went to college. I just like to party.

[*Bell*]

BETTY. Where was college?

BILL. Harvard.
BETTY. Do you like Faulkner?
BILL. I love Faulkner. I spent a whole winter reading him once.
BETTY. I've just started.
BILL. I was so excited after ten pages that I went out and bought everything else he wrote. One of the greatest reading experiences of my life. I mean, all that incredible psychological understanding. Page after page of gorgeous prose. His profound grasp of the mystery of time and human existence. The smells of the earth... What do you think?
BETTY. I think it's pretty boring.

[*Bell*]

BILL. What's the book?
BETTY. *The Sound and the Fury*.
BILL. Oh! Faulkner!
BETTY. Do you like Faulkner?
BILL. I love Faulkner.
BETTY. He's incredible.
BILL. I spent a whole winter reading him once.
BETTY. I was so excited after ten pages that I went out and bought everything else he wrote.
BILL. All that incredible psychological understanding.
BETTY. And the prose is so gorgeous.
BILL. And the way he's grasped the mystery of time—
BETTY. —and human existence. I can't believe I've waited this long to read him.
BILL. You never know. You might not have liked him before.
BETTY. That's true.
BILL. You might not have been ready for him. You have to hit these things at the right moment or it's no good.
BETTY. That's happened to me.
BILL. It's all in the timing. [*Small pause*] My name's Bill, by the way.
BETTY. I'm Betty.
BILL. Hi.
BETTY. Hi.

[*Small pause*]

BILL. Yes, I thought reading Faulkner was ... a great experience.
BETTY. Yes.

[*Small pause*]

BILL. *The Sound and the Fury* ...

[*Another small pause*]

BETTY. Well. Onwards and upwards. [*She goes back to her book*]
BILL. Waiter—?

[*Bell*]

BILL. You have to hit these things at the right moment or it's no good.
BETTY. That's happened to me.
BILL. It's all in the timing. My name's Bill, by the way.
BETTY. I'm Betty.

BILL. Hi.
BETTY. Hi.
BILL. Do you come in here a lot?
BETTY. Actually I'm just in town for two days from Pakistan.
BILL. Oh. Pakistan.

[*Bell*]

BILL. My name's Bill, by the way.
BETTY. I'm Betty.
BILL. Hi.
BETTY. Hi.
BILL. Do you come in here a lot?
BETTY. Every once in a while. Do you?
BILL. Not much anymore. Not as much as I used to. Before my nervous breakdown.

[*Bell*]

BILL. Do you come in here a lot?
BETTY. Why are you asking?
BILL. Just interested.
BETTY. Are you really interested, or do you just want to pick me up?
BILL. No, I'm really interested.
BETTY. Why would you be interested in whether I come in here a lot?
BILL. Just . . . getting acquainted.
BETTY. Maybe you're only interested for the sake of making small talk long enough to ask me back to your place to listen to some music, or because you've just rented some great tape for your VCR, or because you've got some terrific unknown Django Reinhardt record, only all you'll really want to do is fuck—which you won't do very well—after which you'll go into the bathroom and pee very loudly, then pad into the kitchen and get yourself a beer from the refrigerator without asking me whether I'd like anything, and then you'll proceed to lie back down beside me and confess that you've got a girlfriend named Stephanie who's away at medical school in Belgium for a year, and that you've been involved with her—*off and on*—in what you'll call a very intricate relationship, for about *seven* YEARS. None of which *interests* me, mister!
BILL. Okay.

[*Bell*]

BILL. Do you come in here a lot?
BETTY. Every other day, I think.
BILL. I come in here quite a lot and I don't remember seeing you.
BETTY. I guess we must be on different schedules.
BILL. Missed connections.
BETTY. Yes. Different time zones.
BILL. Amazing how you can live right next door to somebody in this town and never even know it.
BETTY. I know.
BILL. City life.
BETTY. It's crazy.
BILL. We probably pass each other in the street every day. Right in front of this place, probably.

BETTY. Yep.

BILL [*Looks around*]. Well, the waiters here sure seem to be in some different time zone. I don't see one anywhere... Waiter! [*He looks back*] So what do you...

[*He sees that she's gone back to her book*]

BETTY. I beg pardon?

BILL. Nothing. Sorry.

[*Bell*]

BETTY. I guess we must be on different schedules.

BILL. Missed connections.

BETTY. Yes. Different time zones.

BILL. Amazing how you can live right next door to somebody in this town and never even know it.

BETTY. I know.

BILL. City life.

BETTY. It's crazy.

BILL. You weren't waiting for somebody when I came in, were you?

BETTY. Actually I was.

BILL. Oh. Boyfriend?

BETTY. Sort of.

BILL. What's a sort-of boyfriend?

BETTY. My husband.

BILL. Ah-ha.

[*Bell*]

BILL. You weren't waiting for somebody when I came in, were you?

BETTY. Actually I was.

BILL. Oh. Boyfriend?

BETTY. Sort of.

BILL. What's a sort-of boyfriend?

BETTY. We were meeting here to break up.

BILL. Mm-hm...

[*Bell*]

BILL. What's a sort-of boyfriend?

BETTY. My lover. Here she comes right now!

[*Bell*]

BILL. You weren't waiting for somebody when I came in, were you?

BETTY. No, just reading.

BILL. Sort of a sad occupation for a Friday night, isn't it? Reading here, all by yourself?

BETTY. Do you think so?

BILL. Well sure. I mean, what's a good-looking woman like you doing out alone on a Friday night?

BETTY. Trying to keep away from lines like that.

BILL. No, listen—

[*Bell*]

BILL. You weren't waiting for somebody when I came in, were you?

BETTY. No, just reading.

BILL. Sort of a sad occupation for a Friday night, isn't it? Reading here all by yourself?
BETTY. I guess it is, in a way.
BILL. What's a good-looking woman like you doing out alone on a Friday night anyway? No offense, but…
BETTY. I'm out alone on a Friday night for the first time in a very long time.
BILL. Oh.
BETTY. You see, I just recently ended a relationship.
BILL. Oh.
BETTY. Of rather long standing.
BILL. I'm sorry—Well listen, since reading by yourself *is* such a sad occupation for a Friday night, would you like to go elsewhere?
BETTY. No…
BILL. Do something else?
BETTY. No thanks.
BILL. I was headed out to the movies in a while anyway.
BETTY. I don't think so.
BILL. Big chance to let Faulkner catch his breath. All those long sentences get him pretty tired.
BETTY. Thanks anyway.
BILL. Okay.
BETTY. I appreciate the invitation.
BILL. Sure thing.

[*Bell*]

BILL. You weren't waiting for somebody when I came in, were you?
BETTY. No, just reading.
BILL. Sort of a sad occupation for a Friday night, isn't it? Reading here all by yourself?
BETTY. I guess I was trying to think of it as existentially romantic. You know—capuccino, great literature, rainy night….
BILL. That only works in Paris. We *could* hop the late plane to Paris. Get on a Concorde. Find a café…
BETTY. I'm a little short on plane fare tonight.
BILL. Darn it, so am I.
BETTY. To tell you the truth, I was headed to the movies after I finished this section. Would you like to come along? Since you can't locate a waiter?
BILL. That's a very nice offer, but—I can't.
BETTY. Uh-huh. Girlfriend?
BILL. Two of them, actually. One of them's pregnant, and Stephanie—

[*Bell*]

BETTY. Girlfriend?
BILL. No, I don't have a girlfriend. Not if you mean the castrating bitch I dumped last night.

[*Bell*]

BETTY. Girlfriend?
BILL. Sort of. Sort of…
BETTY. What's a sort-of girlfriend?
BILL. My mother.

[*Bell*]

BILL. I just ended a relationship, actually.
BETTY. Oh.
BILL. Of rather long standing.
BETTY. I'm sorry to hear it.
BILL. This is my first night out alone in a long time. I feel a little bit at sea, to tell you the truth.
BETTY. So you didn't stop to talk because you're a Moonie, or you have some weird political affiliation—?
BILL. Nope. Straight-down-the-ticket Republican.

[*Bell*]

Straight-down-the-ticket Democrat.

[*Bell*]

Can I tell you something about politics?

[*Bell*]

I consider myself a citizen of the universe.

[*Bell*]

I'm unaffiliated.

BETTY. That's a relief. So am I.
BILL. I vote my beliefs.
BETTY. Labels are not important.
BILL. Labels are not important, exactly. Like me, for example. I mean, what does it matter if I had a two-point—

[*Bell*]

—three-point—

[*Bell*]

—four-point at college, or if I did come from Pittsburgh—

[*Bell*]

—Cleveland—

[*Bell*]

—Westchester County?

BETTY. Sure.
BILL. I believe that a man is what he is.

[*Bell*]

A person is what he is.

[*Bell*]

A person is what they are.

BETTY. I think so, too.
BILL. So what if I admire Trotsky?

[*Bell*]

So what if I once had a total body liposuction?

[*Bell*]

So what if I don't have a penis?

[*Bell*]

So what if I spent a year in the Peace Corps? I was acting on my convictions.

BETTY. Convictions are important.
BILL. You just can't hang a sign on a person.
BETTY. Absolutely. I'll bet you're a Scorpio.

[*Many bells ring*]

BETTY. Listen, I was headed to the movies after I finished this section. Would you like to come along?
BILL. That sounds like fun. What's playing?
BETTY. A couple of the really early Woody Allen movies.
BILL. Oh.
BETTY. Don't you like Woody Allen?
BILL. Sure, I like Woody Allen.
BETTY. But you're not crazy about Woody Allen.
BILL. Those early ones kind of get on my nerves.
BETTY. Uh-huh.

[*Bell*]

BILL. [*Simultaneously*] BETTY.
Y'know, I was headed to the … I was thinking about …

BILL. I'm sorry.
BETTY. No, go ahead.
BILL. I was just going to say that I was headed to the movies in a little while, and…
BETTY. So was I.
BILL. The Woody Allen festival?
BETTY. Just up the street.
BILL. Do you like the early ones?
BETTY. I think anybody who doesn't ought to be run off the planet.
BILL. How many times have you seen *Bananas*?
BETTY. Eight times.
BILL. Twelve. So are you still interested?
BETTY. Do you like Entenmann's crumb cake?
BILL. I went out at two o'clock this morning to buy one. Did you have an Etch-a-Sketch as a child?
BETTY. Yes! Do you like brussel sprouts?
BILL. I think they're gross.
BETTY. They *are* gross!
BILL. Do you still believe in marriage in spite of current sentiments against it?
BETTY. Yes.
BILL. And children?
BETTY. Three of them.
BILL. Two girls and a boy.

BETTY. Harvard, Vassar, and Brown.
BILL. And will you love me?
BETTY. Yes.
BILL. And cherish me forever?
BETTY. Yes.
BILL. Do you still want to go to the movies?
BETTY. Sure thing.
BILL *and* BETTY [*Together*]. Waiter!

BLACKOUT

(1988)

Questions for Discussion and Writing

1. The play was originally set at a bus stop. What does its setting in a café say about the characters?
2. At one point Bill says, "You have to hit these things at the right moment or it's no good." Explain how this statement describes the play's basic dramatic premise.
3. What is the purpose of the ringing bell?
4. Describe the play's plot. What is its central conflict and how is it resolved? Where does the climax occur?
5. In 2001 a theater company in Denver put on *Sure Thing* by using three separate couples, each with the names Bill and Betty. The lines shifted from one couple to the next after each ring of the bell. Can you picture how this performance would work? Try reading the play this way out loud in class. You can make it easier to follow if you put numbers in the margin of the script to indicate which couple should read.

Making Connections

1. How would you describe the tone of each play? Which of the plays is harshest in its satire? Which is the friendliest? Did each play make your laugh? Why or why not?
2. Examine the theatrical devices used in the plays: the Aladdin's lamp, the ringing bell, the models that come to life. Write an essay explaining their purpose(s) and evaluating their effectiveness.
3. Comment on the title of each play. Which ones are most helpful? The original Spanish title for *Picnic on the Battlefield* is *Los Soldados*, which means "the soldiers." Do you think this is a better title for the play?
4. Write a two-character skit that satirizes some human foible, like greed, laziness, procrastination, gullibility.
5. Explain how you might adapt *Los Vendidos* to fit another minority.

6. Rewrite a key scene from another play using the bell device from *Sure Thing*. For example, you might write a sequence of possible drafts of Othello's dying words or Torvald's attempts to keep Nora from leaving (in *The Doll House*).
7. Write an essay explaining how you would stage one or more of the plays. You might draw a diagram to help you explain your ideas.

Handbook for Correcting Errors

Once you have become a good editor and proofreader, you will find editing the easiest part of the writing process. But just because locating and correcting errors is less taxing than composing the paper, do not consider it unimportant. Correcting errors is crucial. Errors will lower your grades in college and undermine the confidence of your readers in any writing that you do.

Proofreading

As we suggested in Chapter 3, you will need to proofread at least twice, concentrating on catching different types of errors each time. Here are some general rules to follow:

1. Read the essay aloud to catch words accidentally repeated or left out.
2. Read sentence by sentence from the bottom of the page to the top (to keep your attention focused on finding errors).
3. Read again, looking for any particular errors that you know you tend to make: fragments, comma splices, typical misspellings, and so on.
4. When in doubt about either spelling or meaning, use your dictionary.
5. If the piece of writing is important, find a literate friend to read it over for mistakes after you have completed all of the above.

Correcting Sentence Boundary Errors

Probably the most serious errors you need to check for are those that involve faulty sentence punctuation: fragments, comma splices, and run-on sentences. These errors reflect uncertainty or carelessness about the acceptable boundaries for written sentences.

Phrases and Clauses

To punctuate correctly, you need to know the difference between phrases and clauses. Charts A through C will help you remember.

Chart A Examples of Phrases and Clauses

Phrases

to the lighthouse
having been converted
a still, eerie, deserted beach

Phrases do not have subject and verb combinations.

Clauses

Independent	**Dependent (incomplete sentences)**
Clarissa finished.	after Clarissa finished
She completed her essay	which completed the essay
John gave her the pen.	because John gave her the pen.

All clauses have subject and verb combinations.

Fragments

As the term suggests, a sentence *fragment* is an incomplete group of words punctuated as a complete sentence. Fragments occur often in speech and are often used by professional writers for emphasis and convenience. But a fragmentary sentence may also represent a fragmentary idea that would be more effective if it were completed or connected to another idea. The following are typical sentence fragments that need to be revised.

1. Phrases that can be joined to the preceding sentence

Questionable fragment: Eveline gripped the iron railing and stared ahead. With no glimmer of "love or recognition" in her eyes.

[The fragment is a prepositional phrase without a subject or verb; see Charts A and B.]

Revision: Eveline gripped the iron railing and stared ahead with no glimmer of "love or recognition" in her eyes.

2. Explanatory phrases that begin with such expressions as *for example, that is,* and *such as* belong in the sentence with the material they are explaining

Questionable fragment: As Eveline looked around the room, she noticed familiar objects that she might

Chart B Kinds of Phrases

Phrase: a string of related words that does not contain a subject and verb combination

1. *Noun phrase:* a noun plus modifiers

   an old yellowed photograph

2. *Prepositional phrase:* a preposition plus its object and modifiers of the object

   against the dusty curtains

3. *Verbal phrase:* a verbal (word derived from a verb) plus modifiers and objects or completers

   a. *Infinitive:* verb with *to* before it

      to leave her father

   b. *Gerund: -ing* word used as a noun

      leaving her father

   c. *Participle: -ing* or *-ed* word used as an adjective

      leaning against the curtains
      frightened by her father

4. *Verb phrase:* an action or being verb plus its auxiliary verbs

   have been
   might be leaving
   will go

never see again. For instance, the yellowing photograph of the priest and the broken harmonium.

Revision: As Eveline looked around the room, she noticed familiar objects that she might never see again—for instance, the yellowing photograph of the priest and the broken harmonium.

3. Dependent (or subordinate) clauses that can be added to another sentence or rewritten as complete sentences

Questionable fragment: Eveline decided to stay with her family. Even though she felt she could forget her worries and be happy forever with Frank.

Chart C Kinds of Clauses

Clause: a group of related words containing a subject and verb combination

1. *Independent (main) clause:*

   subject + verb: Her hands trembled

   subject + verb + completer: Her hands gripped the railing.

2. *Dependent (subordinate) clause:* incomplete sentence that depends on an independent clause to complete its meaning

   a. *Noun clause:* used as a noun

   (direct object)

   She could not believe *what Frank told her*.

   (subject)

   Whoever called her did not identify himself.

   b. *Adjective clause*: modifies a noun or pronoun

   The promise *that Eveline made to her mother* weighed heavily on her conscience.

   She loved her younger brother, *who had died some years ago*.

An adjective clause is introduced by a relative pronoun: *who, which, that, whose, whom*.

   c. *Adverb clause*: modifies a verb, adjective, or adverb

   After Eveline wrote the letters, she held them in her lap.

   She could not leave with Frank *because she was afraid*.

An adverb clause is introduced by a subordinating conjunction: *after, although, as, as if, because, before, if, only, since, so as, as far as, so that, than, though, till, unless, until, when, whenever, while, whereas*.

[adverb clause, beginning with *even though;* see Chart C]

Revision: Even though she felt she could forget her worries and be happy forever with Frank, Eveline decided to stay with her family.

Questionable fragment: Frank had told Eveline numerous stories about his adventures on the high seas. Many of which seemed suspiciously vague and predictably romantic.

[adjective clause, indicated by *which;* see Chart C]

Revision: Frank had told Eveline numerous stories about his adventures on the high seas. Many of his tales seemed suspiciously vague and predictably romantic.

TIP! In English we typically begin sentences with adverbial clauses. But if you often write fragments, you may not be attaching those dependent clauses to independent clauses.

Remember that a group of words beginning with a subordinating word like *although, if, because, since, unless, when, which*, or *who* will be a fragment unless connected to an independent clause. If you typically have problems with fragments, put a sticky note at Charts B and C for quick consultation.

4. Verbal phrases that do not contain a complete verb

Questionable fragment: Eveline sat by the window and thought about her home and family. Leaning her head against the dusty curtains.

[The second group of words is a participle phrase; *leaning* is not a complete verb. See Chart B.]

Revision: Leaning her head against the dusty curtains, Eveline sat by the window and thought about her home and family.

TIP! Words ending in *-ing* or *-ed* sound like verbs, but often they are verbals (verb forms used as adjectives or nouns) and do not function as full verbs for a sentence.

5. Semicolon fragments

Questionable fragment: Eveline was fearful of her father and helplessly trapped; feeling immobile, like the dust on the curtains.

[The words that follow the semicolon do not constitute a full sentence. See Chart B.]

Revision: Eveline was fearful of her father and helplessly trapped; she felt immobile, like the dust on the curtains.

TIP! A semicolon is often used as a weak period to separate independent clauses that are closely related. Be sure you have written an independent clause before and after a semicolon (unless the semicolon separates items in a series that themselves contain commas).

Comma Splices

A comma splice (or comma fault or comma blunder) occurs when a writer places two independent clauses together with only a comma between them. Because the result appears to be a single sentence, it can momentarily confuse the reader.

Comma splice: Frank has become the Prince Charming in Eveline's fairy tale world, the other man in her life is much more real.

Because the two clauses joined here are independent (i.e., each could stand alone as a sentence), the two clauses should be linked by a stronger mark than a comma. Here are some options:

1. Punctuate both clauses as complete sentences.

   Frank has become the Prince Charming in Eveline's fairy tale world. The other man in her life is much more real.
2. Use a semicolon.

   Frank has become the Prince Charming in Eveline's fairy tale world; the other man in her life is much more real.
3. Keep the comma and add a coordinating conjunction (*and, but, or, nor, for, yet, so*).

   Frank has become the Prince Charming in Eveline's fairy tale world, but the other man in her life is much more real.
4. Subordinate one of the independent clauses.

   Although Frank has become the Prince Charming in Eveline's fairy tale world, the other man in her life is much more real.

To avoid comma splices, follow this general advice:

1. Be careful with commas.

   If you understand sentence structure, your writing probably won't contain many comma splices. But if you are not paying attention to sentence boundaries, you may, without realizing it, be joining independent clauses and separating them with commas.
2. Check your conjunctive adverbs.

   Transitional expressions like *indeed, however, thus, therefore, nevertheless, furthermore*, and *consequently* may lead you to use just a comma when connecting two independent clauses with these words. Do not do it. These words are called *conjunctive adverbs;* they do not serve to join clauses the way coordinating conjunctions do. Their main force is adverbial. Thus, you still need a semicolon (or a period and a capital letter) when you use these connectives.

Comma splice: Eveline's father is violent and overbearing, however, he is the man who really loves her.

Correct: Eveline's father is violent and overbearing; however, he is the man who really loves her.

3. Use commas with short clauses.

Although we advise you not to use commas to join independent clauses, many professional writers intentionally violate this advice if the clauses are short, if they are parallel in structure, if they are antithetical, or if there is no chance of misunderstanding.

He's not brave, he's crazy.

She felt one way, she acted another.

It was sunny, it was crisp, it was a perfect day.

Run-On Sentences

A run-on sentence (also called a fused sentence) is similar to a comma splice, except that there is no punctuation at all to separate the independent clauses.

Run-on: Eveline realizes that she leads a dull and unhappy home life she is also safely and securely encircled in her own little world.

Few writers ignore sentence boundaries so completely. Most people at least put a comma in (and thus produce a comma splice). When you edit, make sure that you have not run any sentences together. Run-ons will confuse and annoy your readers.

Clearing Up Confused Sentences

Carelessness can sometimes cause you to lose track of the way a sentence is developing. The result is called a *confused sentence* or *a mixed construction*. Repunctuating will not correct this kind of error. You will have to rewrite the garbled passage into readable prose.

Confused: One reason to conclude Eveline's hopeless situation would have to be related to her indecisive and timid lifestyle.

Revised: One reason for Eveline's hopeless situation is her indecisive and timid personality.

Sentences can go astray in many ways. The only sure defense against sentence confusion is to understand the basic principles of sentence structure. Checking your writing carefully and reading your sentences aloud will also help.

Solving Faulty Predication Problems

Another kind of sentence confusion occurs when you carelessly complete a linking verb (*is, am, are, was, were, will be, has been, becomes, appears,* etc.[1]) with a predicate noun or predicate adjective that does not match the subject of the sentence. This error is called *faulty predication*. In this kind of sentence the linking verb acts as an equals sign and sets up a verbal equation: the subject = the predicate noun (or predicate adjective).

Logical: Eveline is a passive, sheltered young woman.

Logical: At least at home Eveline would be secure.

In the first sentence, Eveline = young woman; and in the second, *secure* (predicate adjective) logically modifies *Eveline* (the subject). Here are some faulty predications followed by logical revisions:

Faulty: The importance of religion in the story is crucial to Eveline's decision.

Logical: Religion is important to Eveline's decision.

Faulty: The theme of the poem is thousands of dead soldiers.

Logical: The theme of the poem is the deplorable slaughter of thousands of soldiers.

Faulty: The setting for the advertisement is a man and a woman walking through a jungle in safari suits.

Logical: The setting for the advertisement is a jungle; a man and a woman in safari suits are walking through it.

The phrases *is where* and *is when* are likely culprits in producing faulty predication. Remember, *where* refers to a place, and *when* refers to a time. Use those words only in a place or time context, not in a context that equates them with an abstract quality. Here are examples:

Faulty: Dramatic irony is when Jim says Whitey is a card.

Logical: We recognize the dramatic irony when Jim says Whitey is a card.

Faulty: Visual imagery is where Owen describes the soldier's death.

Logical: Owen uses visual imagery to describe the soldier's death.

Fixing Subject–Verb Agreement Errors

1. Verbs agree with their subjects in number (that is, in being either singular or plural).

Victorian novels are usually long.

A Victorian novel is often moral.

A Victorian novel and a postmodernist novel are radically different.

---

[1]The most common linking verb is *be* in its various forms: *is, are, was, were, has been, will be, might be*. Other linking verbs include *seem* and *appear* and, in some instances, *feel, grow, act, look, smell, taste,* and *sound*.

2. Be sure to find the grammatical subject.

a. Sometimes a clause or phrase comes between the subject and verb to confuse you, like this.

Wrong: The good movies that come out in the fall makes up for the summer's trash.

The clause—*that come out in the fall*—intervenes between the subject *movies* and the verb, which should be *make* (plural to agree with *movies*).

Right: The good movies that come out in the fall make up for the summer's trash.

TIP! The plural form of the verb drops the *s*, unlike nouns, which add an *s* to form the plural (one villain *lies*, two villains *lie*).

b. Sometimes—especially in questions—the subject will come after the verb.

Right: Why are Romeo and Juliet so impetuous?

Right: From boredom, restlessness, and ignorance comes an otherwise senseless crime.

c. If you begin a sentence with *here*, *there*, *what*, *where*, *when*, or *why*, these words can rarely be subjects. Find the real subject (or subjects) and make the verb agree.

Wrong: Where is the climax and the denouement?

Wrong: There is suspense and tension in DuMaurier's novel.

The subjects in both of those examples are compound, requiring a plural verb.

Right: Where are the climax and the denouement?

Right: There are suspense and tension in DuMaurier's novel.

3. Compound singular subjects connected by correlative conjunctions (*either … or, not only … but also, neither … nor, not … but,* etc.) require a singular verb.

Right: Either Antigone or Creon is going to prevail.

Right: Not a beau but a husband is what Amanda wants for Laura.

If both subjects are plural, make the verb plural.

Right: Either poems or stories are fine with me.

If one subject is singular and the other one plural, make the verb agree with the subject closer to it.

Right: Either poems or a story is a good choice.

Right: Either a story or some poems are fine.

4. Some prepositions sound like conjunctions—*with, like, along with, as well as, no less than, including, besides*—and may appear to connect compound subjects, but they do not; the subject, if singular, remains singular.

Right: My career, as well as my reputation, is lost.
Right: Alcohol, together with my passion for filmy underthings, is responsible.
Right: My mother, like my aunt Chloe, my uncle Zeke, and my cousin Zelda, is not speaking to me.

5. Collective nouns (like *jury, family, company, staff, group, committee*) take either singular or plural verbs, depending on your meaning.

If the group is acting in unison, use the singular.

Right: The jury has agreed on a verdict.

If the group is behaving as separate individuals, use the plural.

Right: The jury still are not in agreement.

Or avoid the problem this way.

Right: The members of the jury still are not in agreement.

Fixing Pronoun Errors

1. Avoid ambiguous or unclear pronoun reference.

Ambiguous: Marvin gave Tom *his* pen back, but *he* swore it wasn't *his*.
Clear: Marvin gave Tom's pen back, but Tom swore it wasn't his.

Sometimes it is necessary to replace an inexact pronoun with a noun.

Unclear: She did not know how to make quiche until I wrote *it* out for her.
Clear: She did not know how to make quiche until I wrote out *the recipe* for her.

2. Use *this* and *which* with care.

These pronouns often refer to whole ideas or situations, and the reference is sometimes not clear.

Unclear: Renaldo runs three miles a day and works out with weights twice a week. He says *this* controls his high blood pressure and prevents heart attacks.
Clear: Renaldo runs three miles a day and works out with weights twice a week. He says *this exercise program* controls his high blood pressure and prevents heart attacks.

Avoid using *this* without a noun following it. Get in the habit of writing *this idea*, *this point*, or *this remark*, instead of having a pronoun that means nothing in particular.

The pronoun *which* can cause similar problems.

Unclear: Craig told me that he didn't like the movie, *which* upset me.

Clear: Craig told me that he didn't like the movie. His opinion upset me.

Clear: Craig told me that he didn't like the movie. This film upset me, too.

3. Be sure your pronouns agree with their antecedents in number (singular or plural).

Agreement errors occur when the pronoun is separated from its antecedent (the preceding noun which the pronoun replaces).

Incorrect: Although the average *American* believes in the ideal of justice for all, *they* do not always practice it.

Correct: Although most *Americans* believe in the ideal of justice for all, *they* do not always practice it.

4. Take care with indefinite pronouns.

Many indefinite pronouns sound plural but are considered grammatically singular: *anybody*, *anyone*, *everyone*, *everybody*, *someone*, *none*, *no one*, *neither*, *either*. If you follow this grammatical guideline in all cases, you may produce an illogical sentence.

Everybody applauded my speech, and I was glad *he* did.

It is now acceptable to use plural pronouns when referring to indefinite words.

Everyone should have *their* own pinking shears.

None of the students would admit *they* were cheating.

Some readers still question this practice and will insist that you refer to *everyone* and *none* with singular pronouns. You can sometimes avoid this dilemma by recasting your sentence or by writing in the plural.

Questionable: None of the students would admit he was cheating.

Recast: None of the students would admit to cheating.

Questionable: *Each* of the contestants must supply *their* own water skis.

No question: *All contestants* must supply *their* own water skis.

If you prefer to write in the singular, you may have to revise sentences with indefinite pronouns or stick to the old rule of referring to such words as *anyone*, *somebody*, *everyone*, *none*, and *neither* with singular pronouns.

Singular agreement: *Neither* of the drivers escaped the crash with *his* life.

That sentence is all right if both drivers were indeed males. But if one was a woman or if you are not sure of the gender of both drivers, you may want to use *his or her* to make your statement completely accurate. Or you can revise and avoid the problem altogether.

> *Revised:* Neither driver survived the crash.

5. Choose the proper case.

Except for possessives and plurals, nouns do not change form when used in different ways in a sentence. You can write "Ernie was watching the new kitten" or "The new kitten was watching Ernie" and neither noun (*Ernie*, *kitten*) changes. But pronouns do change with their function.

> *He* watched the kitten.
>
> The kitten watched *him.*

In the first sentence the subjective form *(he)* is used because the pronoun acts as the subject. In the second sentence the pronoun is the direct object of *watched*, so the objective form *(him)* is used. (The objective form is used for any objects—objects of prepositions, indirect objects, and direct objects.) The forms vary according to the *case* of the pronoun; in English there are three cases of pronouns.

Subjective	*Objective*	*Possessive*
I	me	mine
he	him	his
she	her	hers
you	your	yours
it	it	its
we	us	ours
they	them	theirs
who	whom	whose
whoever	whomever	whosever

You probably select the correct case for most of the pronouns you use, but you may need to keep the following warnings in mind:

a. **Do not confuse the possessive *its* with the contraction *it's*.**

If you look at the list of case forms in the preceding list, you will notice that possessive pronouns do *not* include an apostrophe. This information may confuse you because the possessives of nouns and indefinite words *do* contain an apostrophe.

> my mother's jewels
>
> the students' books
>
> everyone's appetite

TIP! *It's* is a contraction of *it is; its* is a possessive like *his*, *hers*, and *ours*.

b. **Be careful of pronouns in compound subjects and objects.**

Faulty: Nanouchka and *me* went to the movies.
Preferred: Nanouchka and *I* went to the movies.

Faulty: Shelly went with Nan and *I*.
Preferred: Shelly went with Nan and *me*.

If you are uncertain about which pronoun to use, drop the first part of the compound and see how the pronoun sounds alone.

I went? or *me* went?
with *I?* or with *me?*

You will recognize at once that *me went* and *with I* are not standard constructions.

c. **Watch out for pronouns used with appositives.**

The pronoun should be in the same case as the word it is in apposition with.

Faulty: Us video game addicts are slaves to our hobby.
Preferred: We video game addicts are slaves to our hobby.

Faulty: Video games are serious business to *we* addicts.
Preferred: Video games are serious business to *us* addicts.

Again, you can test this construction by dropping the noun and letting the sound guide you: *us are slaves* and *to we* should sound unacceptable to you.

d. **Take care with pronouns in comparisons.**

Faulty: Ernie is a lot stronger than *me*.
Preferred: Ernie is a lot stronger than *I*.

This comparison is not complete. There is an implied (or understood) verb after *than:* "stronger than I am." If you complete such comparative constructions in your mind, you will be able to choose the appropriate case for the pronoun.

e. **Choose carefully between *who* and *whom*.**

Preferred: My ex-roommate was a con artist *whom* we all trusted too much.

Although informal usage would allow you to use *who* in this sentence, the objective case form *(whom)* is preferred in most writing because the pronoun is the direct object in the clause it introduces: "we all trusted *him* too much." You can get around the choice between *who* and *whom* in this instance by using *that*.

Acceptable: My ex-roommate was a con artist *that* we all trusted too much.

Some people will still insist that you use *whom* in this sentence, even though the use of *that* is now considered standard. But you should not substitute *which* for *who* or *whom*, because standard usage does not permit *which* to refer to people.

Preferred: the taxidermist *whom* I often dated
Acceptable: the taxidermist *that* I often dated
Faulty: the taxidermist *which* I often dated

Correcting Shifts in Person

Decide before you begin writing whether to use first, second, or third person, and then be consistent.

1. Formal usage requires third person:

The reader senses foreboding in Poe's opening lines.

One senses foreboding in Poe's opening lines.

or first-person plural:

We sense foreboding in Poe's opening lines.

2. Informal usage allows first-person singular:

I find his characters too one-dimensional.

and many readers accept second person (as long as *you* means you, the reader):

If you examine his plots, you discover that the success of his tales lies elsewhere.

3. Do not switch person carelessly once you have begun:

Wrong: The *reader* feels the tension mount as *you* wait for the beast to spring.

Right: *We* feel the tension mount as *we* wait for the beast to spring.

Correcting Shifts in Tense

Stay in the same tense unless you have cause to change.

1. Sometimes you need to switch tenses because you are discussing events that happened (or will happen) at different times (past, present, or future).

Right: Although I *saw* Split Banana in concert last week, I *am going* to hear them again tonight when they *perform* in Chicago.

2. Do not change tense, though, without a reason.

Wrong: The group *appears* on stage, obviously drunk; the drummer *dropped* his sticks, the lead singer *trips* over the microphone cord, and the bass player *had* his back to the audience during the entire show.

3. When writing about literature, you may use the historical present tense even when discussing authors long dead.

Right: Hawthorne, in the opening scene of *The Scarlet Letter*, creates a somber setting relieved only by the flowers on a single rosebush.

Or you may write in the past tense.

Right: Hawthorne, in the opening scene of *The Scarlet Letter*, created a somber setting.

But do not switch carelessly back and forth.

Wrong: Hawthorne *creates* a somber setting into which Hester *stepped* with Pearl in her arms.

Finding Modifier Mistakes

A modifier is a word, phrase, or clause that describes, limits, or qualifies something else in the sentence. Be sure that every modifier has only one thing to refer to and that the relationship is clear.

1. Avoid dangling modifiers.

An introductory adjective phrase that does not modify the subject of the sentence is called a *dangling modifier*.

Dangling: Wheezing and shivering from the cold, the warm fire slowly revived Orville.

Improved: Wheezing and shivering from the cold, Orville slowly revived in front of the warm fire.

Sometimes you need to add a subject, making the phrase into a clause.

Dangling: While asleep in class, the instructor called on Jocasta to recite.

Improved: While Jocasta was asleep in class, the instructor called on her to recite.

2. Avoid misplaced modifiers.

Do not allow modifiers to stray too far from the thing they modify or you may produce confusing (and sometimes unintentionally amusing) sentences.

Misplaced: I can jog to the grocery store; then we can have lox and bagels for breakfast in just three minutes.

Improved: In just three minutes I can jog to the grocery store; then we can have lox and bagels for breakfast.

Dangling: Seymour was caught taking a nap in the restroom where he works.

Improved: While supposedly working, Seymour was caught taking a nap in the restroom.

3. Avoid squinting modifiers.

Be sure your modifiers have only one possible word to modify, or you may puzzle your readers.

Squinting: Arvilla suspects privately Agnes reads Harlequin romances.

Improved: Arvilla privately suspects that Agnes reads Harlequin romances.

Improved: Arvilla suspects that Agnes privately reads Harlequin romances.

Coping with Irregular Verbs

Some verbs are irregular; their principal parts must be memorized. Here is a list of the most common ones.

Present	*Past*	*Past Participle*
begin	began	begun
break	broke	broken
burst	burst	burst (*not* busted)
choose	chose	chosen
come	came	come
do	did	done
drag	dragged	dragged (*not* drug)
drink	drank	drunk
forget	forgot	forgotten (*not* forgot)

Present	*Past*	*Past Participle*
get	got	got (*or* gotten)
lay	laid	laid (*meaning* "placed")
lead	led	led
lie	lay	lain (*meaning* "reclined")
ride	rode	ridden
rise	rose	risen
run	ran	run
see	saw	seen
swim	swam	swum
take	took	taken
wake	waked (*or* woke)	waked (*or* woke)

If you find yourself wondering whether someone's heart was *broke* or *broken*, whether the sun has *rose* or *risen*, your dictionary can clear up your difficulty. Each dictionary has a guide to itself in the front, explaining how to use it and how the entries are arranged. Look up *inflected forms* and *principal parts of verbs* in this guide. Those sections will tell you how your dictionary lists irregular verb forms. Usually, the past and past participle are given in boldface type within the entry for the present-tense verb.

Getting Verbs Right

Even regular verbs sometimes cause trouble, for two reasons.

1. The third-person singular adds an *-s* (or *-es*), whereas with nouns, the plural adds an *-s* or *-es*.

   Plural nouns: two aardvarks, ten kisses
   Singular verbs: cream rises, a horse gallops, a goose hisses

2. The regular *-ed* ending that forms the past tense often is not heard in speech.

   talked deliberately — supposed to come
   used to go — locked the gate

Writing in Active Voice

Unless you have a clear reason for using passive voice, use *active voice*. Active voice usually leads to stronger, less wordy sentences. In passive voice, the grammatical subject of the sentence does *not* perform the action suggested by the verb; frequently, the performer is tacked onto the sentence in a separate phrase.

> In the story "Everyday Use," the quilts are coveted by both sisters.

Who covets the quilts? Both sisters, even though *quilts* is the subject of the sentence. In active voice, the sentence reads this way:

> In the story "Everyday Use," both sisters covet the quilts.

This version cuts two words and emphasizes the sisters' rivalry. (If you had some reason to emphasize the quilts instead, the first version would be better.)

All passive verbs use at least two words: some form of the verb *to be* as an auxiliary and the past participle of a verb. Even when the sentence is in the present tense, the past participle is there.

> The meaning of Stephen Crane's poem *is communicated* by the word "bitter."

The emphasis shifts when the sentence is written in active voice.

> The word "bitter" communicates the meaning of Stephen Crane's poem.

Solving Punctuation Problems

The most direct approach to punctuating your writing involves two questions.

1. What kinds of word groups are concerned?
2. What pieces of punctuation are standard and appropriate for this situation?

To answer the first question, remember the terms *phrase*, *dependent clause*, and *independent clause*. See Charts A, B, and C, at the beginning of this Handbook for Correcting Errors, for a refresher. Using these terms, you can probably identify any group of words you are trying to punctuate and classify it into one of the four writing situations we describe in this section. Under each situation, we list guidelines for deciding what punctuation to use.

1. Punctuation between two independent clauses

A *period*, usually:

> I enjoy a strong plot in a novel. Allen cares about style more than plot.

A *comma*, only if the two independent clauses are connected by *and*, *or*, *for*, *but*, *nor*, *yet*, or *so:*

> I enjoy a strong plot in a novel, so I liked *The Skull Beneath the Skin*.

A *semicolon*, to show a close relationship in meaning between the two:

> I enjoy a strong plot in a novel; however, Allen cares more about style.

A *colon*, if the second independent clause restates or exemplifies the first:

> I enjoy a strong plot in a novel: I read *The Skull Beneath the Skin* in just three days.

2. Punctuation between a phrase or dependent clause and an independent clause

A *comma*, if the phrase or dependent clause comes first and is long or transitional:

> When we were discussing epidemics this morning, Helen provided some new information. In fact, she had researched the subject recently. As a result, her knowledge was up to date.

No punctuation, usually, if the independent clause comes first:

> Helen described recent research when we were discussing epidemics this morning.

A *comma*, if the independent clause comes first and is followed by a transitional phrase or a tacked-on thought:

> She had researched the subject recently, in fact. She told us what she had found out, at least the main points.

3. Punctuation in an independent clause interrupted by a phrase or dependent clause

No punctuation if the interrupter (italicized in the example) limits the meaning of the word before it:

> Students *who are living alone for the first time* make several mistakes. Mistakes *that make them feel foolish* include accidentally dyeing all their underwear blue. Mistakes *that are more serious* include not budgeting their time and money.

Commas on both ends of the interrupter (italicized) if it simply adds information or detail about the word before it:

> Students, *who usually lead hectic lives*, must learn to budget their time and money. A night of cramming, *no matter how thorough*, cannot substitute for seven weeks of steady studying. And snacks at fast-food restaurants, *which seem cheap*, can be expensive if they are a nightly habit.

Parentheses to play down the interrupter:

> Sue went to the concert with Pam (her friend from Denver) to hear the all-female rock 'n' roll band.

Dashes to emphasize the interrupter:

> The music—although some might call it noise—made Sue and Pam get up and dance.

4. Punctuation in a list or series of words, phrases, or clauses

A *comma* between all parallel items:

> Pam planned to trim Sue's hair, do some paperwork, make dinner for seven, and take her granddaughter shopping all in the same day.

A *semicolon* to separate each of the items when one of them already has a comma in it:

> To me, the ideal novel has a strong plot; is intelligent, touching, and funny; and involves characters I would like to know personally.

A *colon* after an independent clause followed by a list:

> I usually read three kinds of fiction for pleasure: detective stories, feminist science fiction, and long nineteenth-century novels.

Using Necessary Commas Only

Commas *are* necessary to separate certain sentence elements. In brief, we need them in the following situations.

1. To set off transitional or dependent elements before the main clause

> As a matter of fact, Frank is an imaginary hero.
>
> After Eveline finally decides to run away with Frank, she finds herself unable to do so.

2. To set off elements that interrupt the main sentence

> I told you, Frank, not to set foot on that boat without me.
>
> My mother, a devout Catholic, made me promise to take care of my insufferable father.

3. To separate two independent clauses (sentences) when they are connected with *and, or, nor, yet, but, so,* or *for*

> No one will listen to you, so you will have to talk to your horse.
>
> Does this wallpaper look odd to you, or am I just seeing things?

4. To separate three or more items in a series

> I am writing about the relationship of setting, atmosphere, and structure in the story "A Hunger Artist."
>
> Those boys are famous for staying up all night, hooting like owls, and setting fire to barns.

5. To mark off an element tacked on at the end of the main clause

It sure looks like Emily, doesn't it?

The setting of the story is Japan, making it even harder to understand.

Sometimes commas are needed for clarity—to keep the reader from running words together inappropriately, for example. But many writers clutter their prose with unnecessary commas. These extra commas crop up frequently between the main parts of a subject–verb–object sentence.

1. Do not place a comma between the subject and the verb if no interrupter needing commas intervenes.

Faulty: The key to understanding difficult poetry, lies in finding a central image.

Revised: The key to understanding difficult poetry lies in finding a central image.

2. Do not place a comma between the verb and its object if no interrupter needing commas intervenes.

Faulty: Eveline's problem with leaving her dull home is, that she feels too guilty.

Revised: Eveline's problem with leaving her dull home is that she feels too guilty.

3. Do not place a comma before a coordinating conjunction (*and, but, or, nor, for, yet,* or *so*) unless it marks the conclusion of a series or the division between two complete sentences.

Faulty: Women from certain backgrounds can understand Aunt Jennifer, and know the reasons for her timidity.

Revised: Women from certain backgrounds can understand Aunt Jennifer and know the reasons for her timidity.

TIP! These three places where unnecessary commas creep in have something in common: they are places where someone might pause in speaking the sentences aloud. Perhaps the extra commas are a remnant of an old prescription to put commas wherever you would pause in speech. That old prescription expired many years ago.

Using Apostrophes

1. Use an apostrophe to indicate the possessive form of nouns.

a. Use an apostrophe followed by *s* to form the possessive of any singular noun or any plural noun not ending in *s*.

a child's toy

the boss's tie

the children's toys

James's parents

b. Use an apostrophe without *s* to form the possessive of a plural noun that ends in *s*.

the boys' locker room

my parents' house

c. Use an apostrophe with *s* to indicate the possessive of indefinite pronouns.

everybody's business

someone's book

d. Do *not* use an apostrophe for possessive pronouns.

his

hers

its

ours

yours

theirs

whose

2. Use an apostrophe to indicate that some letters or figures have been omitted in contractions.

isn't

the best film of '68

it's

o'clock

I'll

class of '82

3. An apostrophe is optional in forming the plural of letters, figures, and words referred to as words.

Your 2's look like 7's. *or* Your 2s look like 7s.

You use too many *and*'s in your sentences. *or*

You use too many *and*s.

Dot your *i*'s and cross your *t*'s.

Distinguishing Hyphens from Dashes

Do not confuse hyphens and dashes. Your keyboard has a hyphen key. Hit it once for a hyphen with no space between the words or syllables being hyphenated. To make a dash, hit the hyphen key twice—with no space between the two marks and no space between the words on either side of the dash.

Integrating Quotations Gracefully

In any literary essay you will need quotations from the text of the work you are examining. Be sure to enclose these borrowings in quotation marks as you gracefully introduce them or integrate them into your own sentences, like this.

> We feel the danger of Edna's relationship with Arobin when the excitement of an afternoon with him is described as "a remittent fever" (219).
>
> Underscoring the physical dimension of the relationship, Chopin writes that "the touch of his [Arobin's] lips upon her hand had acted like a narcotic upon her" (221).

That last example shows how to add your own words to explain a possibly confusing word in the quotation: use brackets. Most of the time, though, you can avoid this awkwardness by rewriting the sentence.

> The physical dimension of the relationship between Edna and Arobin is underscored by Chopin's imagery: "The touch of his lips upon her hand had acted like a narcotic upon her" (221).

Punctuating Quoted Material

1. Put quotation marks around words that you copy from any source.
   a. A quoted complete sentence introduced by *writes*, *says*, *notes*, and so on, needs a comma.

   > As Joan Didion points out, "Almost everything can trigger an attack of migraine: stress, allergy, fatigue, an abrupt change in barometric pressure, a contretemps over a parking ticket" (103).

   b. A quoted complete sentence introduced by *that* needs no comma.

   > Didion asserts that "Migraine is something more than the fancy of a neurotic imagination" (102).

   c. A quoted partial sentence that readers can clearly tell is a partial sentence needs no punctuation.

   > Didion explains that migraines stem from various causes, even so minor a trauma as "a contretemps over a parking ticket" (103).
   >
   > Didion is clearly irritated by people who attribute migraine to "the fancy of a neurotic imagination" (102).

   d. In a quoted partial sentence in which readers *cannot* tell something has been omitted, use ellipsis dots (three spaced periods) to show the omission. Show an omission at the beginning of a quoted sentence by using a lowercase letter.

> According to Didion, "Once the attack is under way. . . , no drug touches it" (104).

Original sentence: "Once the attack is under way, however, no drug touches it."

> Didion complains that "nothing so tends to prolong an attack as the accusing eye of someone who has never had a headache" (104).

Original sentence: "My husband also has migraine, which is unfortunate for him but fortunate for me: perhaps nothing so tends to prolong an attack as the accusing eye of someone who has never had a headache."

> Didion attests that "All of us who have migraine suffer not only from the attacks themselves but from this common conviction that we are perversely refusing to cure ourselves by taking a couple of aspirin. . . ." (104).

Original sentence: "All of us who have migraine suffer not only from the attacks themselves but from this common conviction that we are perversely refusing to cure ourselves by taking a couple of aspirin, that we are making ourselves sick, that we 'bring it on ourselves.'"

TIP! When the omission occurs at the end of the sentence, use *four dots*, not three. The extra dot is the period.

2. **When you quote material already containing quotation marks, use single quotation marks or indent the passage.**

   a. If quoted material within quotation marks is short, enclose within single quotation marks, using the apostrophe on your keyboard.

   > Didion observes, "There certainly is what doctors call a 'migraine personality,' and that personality tends to be ambitious, inward, intolerant of error, rather rigidly organized, perfectionist" (103).

   b. If quoting extensive conversation, set off the entire passage by indenting *one inch* or *ten spaces* and double-spacing the quotation.

   > Howell's attitude toward the sentimental novel is made clear when the dinner conversation turns to discussion of a current bestseller, *Tears, Idle Tears:*
   >
   > > "Ah, that"s the secret of its success," said Bromfield Corey. "It flatters the reader by painting the characters colossal,

> but with his limp and stoop, so that he feels himself of their supernatural proportions. You've read it, Nanny?"
>
> "Yes," said his daughter. "It ought to have been called *Slop, Silly Slop*." (237)

This same scorn for sentimentality is reflected in the subplot involving Lapham's daughters.

c. If quoted conversation is *brief*, use single quotation marks within double ones.

> We soon realize that the characters are hopelessly lost: "'It's a funny thing,' said Rabbit ten minutes later, 'how everything looks the same in a mist. Have you noticed it, Pooh?'" (142).

3. Put periods and commas inside quotation marks, except when citing a page or line number in parentheses at the end of a quotation.

> Kurt Vonnegut advises that "[s]implicity of language is not only reputable, but perhaps even sacred."
>
> "Simplicity of language," advises Kurt Vonnegut, "is not only reputable, but perhaps even sacred."
>
> As Kurt Vonnegut advises, "Simplicity of language is not only reputable, but perhaps even sacred" (113).
>
> Iago, in soliloquy, reveals his devious intentions toward Othello early in the play: "Though I do hate him as I do hell-pains, / Yet, for necessity of present life, / I must show out a flag and sign of love" (1.1.152–54).

4. Put question marks and exclamation marks inside the quotation marks if they belong with the quotation; put these marks outside if they punctuate the whole sentence.

> Is this an exact quotation from Twain, "Truth is more of a stranger than fiction"?
>
> E. M. Forster asks, "How do I know what I think until I see what I say?"

5. Put colons, semicolons, and dashes outside the quotation marks.

> Avoid clichés like these in stating the theme of a work: "Appearances can be deceiving"; "Do unto others . . . "; "The love of money is the root of all evil."

6. Put quotation marks around words used as words, or italicize them (or underline to indicate italics).

> The term "sentimentality" carries a negative meaning when applied to literature.

7. Put quotation marks around the titles of works that are short (essays and articles in magazines, short stories and poems, chapters in books).

> "A Hanging" (essay by George Orwell)
>
> "Rope" (short story by Katherine Anne Porter)

"Living in Sin" (poem by Adrienne Rich)

"Paper Pills" (chapter title in Sherwood Anderson's *Winesburg, Ohio*)

8. Italicize the titles of works that are long (books, movies, plays, long poems, names of magazines and newspapers).

   Adventures of Huckleberry Finn

   Casablanca

   Death of a Salesman

   Paradise Lost

   Sports Illustrated

   Detroit Free Press

TIP! Do not italicize or put in quotation marks the title of your own essay.

9. Put square brackets around words or letters that you add to clarify a quotation or change the verb tense.

   Iago early declares his ill feelings: "Though I do hate [Othello] as I do hell-pains, / Yet, for necessity of present life, / I must show out a flag and sign of love" (1.1.152–54).

   The crowd is hushed; then "Mr. Graves open[s] the slip of paper and there [is] a general sigh through the crowd . . . ," as his proves to be blank.

Writing Smooth Transitions

The transitions between paragraphs serve to set up expectations in your reader about what will follow—expectations that you will then fulfill. Look at these transitions and decide what you would expect from a paragraph opening with each:

On the other hand,

Furthermore,

In brief,

Probably, you would expect a paragraph opening with "On the other hand" to provide some contrast with the topic of the paragraph before it. But "Furthermore" suggests that the new paragraph will add development along the same lines as the paragraph just above it. "In brief" would lead you to expect a summary of earlier points. In fact, if the paragraphs did *not* fulfill the expectations elicited by the transitions, you would feel decidedly unsatisfied with the writing.

Transitions in good essays not only set up accurate expectations but also do so gracefully. Experienced writers use the *echo transition* to achieve this purpose. This technique echoes a word, phrase, or idea from the last sentence of one paragraph to provide the transition at the beginning of the next. Here is an example, beginning with the closing of a paragraph and showing the transition to the next:

> ... Throughout the story, the husband's word is considered law, and the wife barely dares to question it.
>
> *This unequal marriage* fits perfectly into the historical period of the setting....

The words *this unequal marriage* echo the inequality described in the previous sentence. Another echo transition might reuse exact words in this way:

> ...Throughout the story, the husband's word is considered law, and the wife barely dares to question it.
>
> *This husband-wife relationship* fits perfectly into the historical period of the setting....

Consider for a moment the information given by the sample transitional sentences above. The echo of *this unequal marriage* or *this husband-wife relationship* suggests that the subject matter is similar to the subject of the preceding paragraph, whereas the rest of the sentence leads you to expect material linking the marriage to its historical context. Rework at least a few of your own paragraph transitions so that they will provide such subtle but easily followed continuity.

Catching Careless Mistakes

These are errors that you make, even though you know better, because you are paying more attention to your thoughts than to the mechanical act of getting them down properly. In rough drafts, careless mistakes are no real problem, but in a finished paper, they are an extreme embarrassment. Some of the most common ones follow.

1. Skipping a word or letter

As you race along on an inspired part, your thoughts run ahead of your hand, and you may write sentences like

> Without knowing it, Emilia been an aid to an evil plot,

leaving the auxiliary verb *has* out before the *been*. Or you could end up with

> Five of the main characters die violently befor the end of the play.

2. Repeating a word

Most people have pens or keyboards that stutter sometimes, producing sentences like

> The characters who survive are are dramatically altered.

Short words like *the* and *of* seem to invite careless repetition more than long ones do.

3. Creative capitalization

Out of habit or because of the idiosyncrasies of your handwriting, you sometimes capitalize or fail to capitalize on impulse rather than by the rules. For example, one student wrote,

> Last thursday I took my Final Exam in History.

Though the capitalization surely reflects what the student considers important in the sentence, it should be altered to conform to standard capitalization. These rules are listed in the front of your collegiate dictionary.

4. Typographical errors

In a final draft, there is no such thing as "*just* a typing error." Most readers are irritated, some even offended, by negligent proofreading. Correct typographical errors neatly in ink, or print out a new page after correcting errors on your computer. Reading your manuscript aloud sometimes allows you to catch a number of careless surface errors, as well as more serious problems like sentence fragments.

Critical Approaches for Interpreting Literature

We are all critics. That is, we find ourselves in conversations about books, movies, and TV shows, conversations in which we express our likes and dislikes, approval and disapproval, often disagreeing with one another. You may devour romance novels in your spare time, while your best friend thinks those same novels are silly and a waste of time. Meanwhile, that friend seeks out the latest in experimental science fiction, which you find confusing and pointless. The two of you are coming from different tastes, for sure, but you are both taking different critical stances about what makes a book good. You value emotional involvement and absorption, as well as a satisfying beginning–middle–happy-ending structure, and that's what you get in romance novels. Your friend doesn't care at all about a predictable structure and an absorbing love story but values mental playfulness, challenge, and the element of surprise in her leisure reading. No one can say that one or the other is right. In using the word *criticism* in relation to the arts, we do not mean faultfinding as in everyday conversation; literary criticism has to do with interpretation of a work. Some literary criticism does evaluate or judge a work as good or bad, but appraisal is not the main point in most cases.

Just as friends can be separated into groups according to what they look for in leisure reading, literary critics can be loosely grouped according to what they look for in written works. They apply a systematic method to the interpretation of a piece and usually have a preferred method or combination of methods. For example, one critic may customarily think about a work in terms of how it reflects the historical period in which it was written, whereas another likes to focus on the images of femininity and masculinity depicted in the work. You can learn the various points of view that people use to interpret and judge literature. Probably some of them are the points of view you already use informally, and seeing them laid out in an orderly way will help you study and write about literature. You will want to be acquainted with all the standard approaches, because you need to match the critical point of view with the specific work you are studying. There is no one-size-fits-all option.

Formalism

A formalist critic looks at a piece of literature as complete within itself. The formalist approach appreciates the way in which all the features of a piece work together in a unified, meaningful whole. These features are, for the most part, what you study in this textbook: structure, imagery, character development, setting, language, and so on. The term *formalist,* instead of being directly related to the idea of formality, is related to the idea of *form.* In this book we encourage you to perceive the form and content of literature as deeply entwined. For example, on page 513, rhythm and rhyme are considered for the way they enhance tone and meaning. A prominent technique of the formalist critic is *close reading*, which we have promoted in this textbook as essential in making a first attempt at interpreting literature.

A strictly formalist reading does not bring in outside sources. The main tools are imagination and skill in analyzing the various features of literature. Support for an interpretation comes from evidence within the poem, story, or play.

Historical Approaches

In contrast with formalism, several approaches emphasize that the writer was leading a life in a certain time in history and that events in personal life and in the world affect the literature produced. Historical critics examine a work in the context of its time. They try to see the work as people in the original audience would. For example, Ibsen's *A Doll's House*, published in 1879, shocked its original nineteenth-century audience with its endorsement of Nora's self-liberation from a stifling marriage to a benevolent patriarch. Such separations are commonplace in our time, so it helps us understand the play to know that in its own day a sympathetic portrayal of Nora was considered outrageous.

Several types of historical approach are possible, focusing on specialized aspects of the past. These aspects may be biographical, cultural, or political.

Biographical

Diaries, letters, journals, biographies, and autobiographies are tools of the critic who investigates how an author's life is reflected in his or her imaginative writing. Emily Dickinson's hermitlike seclusion in real life often serves to help illuminate her difficult poems, because we can speculate on how her unusual solitude gave her an extraordinary point of view on things others take for granted or do not see at all. Similarly, we can appreciate Wilfred Owen's "Dulce et Decorum Est" more fully when we know that he served in World War I, was wounded in 1917 (shortly before the poem was written), and died in action in 1918. The powerful, detailed imagery of the poem is rooted in real-life experience.

Cultural

Cultural critics use materials beyond the standard biographical information and history books to examine literature. They are likely to look at cultural artifacts like the period's advertisements, architecture, journalism, campaign speeches, political tracts, fads, and popular literature such as comic books when they set a work in historical context. May Sarton's 1988 poem "AIDS" lends itself to such an approach, because it was written during the time of the nation's awakening to the horrors of the disease, and the poem draws much from the atmosphere of the era. A cultural critic might use various late-1980s journalistic writings about the epidemic, leaflets from demonstrations, and political speeches in analyzing the poem. A cultural critic would be more likely than a formalist to examine a work of literature in terms of its time. For example, such a critic might argue that Sarton's poem focuses on positive individual growth in the AIDS sphere, without mentioning the larger and uglier political struggle involved. Bharati Mukherjee's story "A Father" must be examined in terms of two cultures at two time periods: Bombay, India, at the time when the Bhowmick family lived there, and Detroit, Michigan, USA, during the time of the story, when the Bhowmicks have immigrated there. The clashes between the cultures illuminate the shocking family violence in the story if you learn about the battling conditions and beliefs in the two settings.

Marxist

Another historical point of view that may include judgment or evaluation of literature is the Marxist approach. Marxist critics take the stance that literature is an artifact of history, which is driven by economic forces and class struggle. They see the fine arts as frequently a reflection of the values of the privileged class, endorsing the status quo rather than challenging it. A Marxist critic would probably point out that Alice Walker's "Everyday Use" demonstrates the shift from a barter-based to a cash-based economy, in which a homemade quilt is detached from its natural purpose and instead elevated as a fetish, a work of folk art never to be used. Many works of literature do lend themselves to a more fruitful Marxist analysis; for example, one professional critic productively analyzes D. H. Lawrence's "The Rocking-Horse Winner" in terms of the parents' relentless, socially driven quest for more money and their exploitation of the child's labor.

Psychological Approaches

"The Rocking-Horse Winner" could also be approached from a psychological point of view. The family in the story shows signs of obsessive-compulsive disorder, in which people have uncontrollable, intrusive thoughts and behaviors that interfere with leading their everyday lives. Because a grasp of human motivation is key to understanding so much literature, psychology comes into play continually, and many critics make a practice of looking at literature through the lenses of psychological theories. It is difficult to discuss a poem like Robert Browning's "My Last Duchess" without psychoanalyzing the speaker, the Duke, who seems narcissistic as well as paranoid. Freud's early twentieth-century theories inform much psychological literary criticism, so explorations of characters' subconscious motivations, defenses, inner conflicts, and symbolic acts are commonplace. Frank O'Connor's "My Oedipus Complex" humorously hinges on the Freudian notion that little boys want to marry their mothers and be rid of their competitors (their dads) but eventually change their loyalty and identify with their fathers. Contemporary psychological research often comes into play as well, because literature so often entails emotional experience and its sequelae. Louis Erdrich's "The Red Convertible" involves a portrait of post-traumatic stress disorder (PTSD), a common syndrome among soldiers returning from the Vietnam War.

Sometimes psychological critics use their tools not to examine the characters but to analyze the author in their search for meaning in the literary work, and in such cases their pursuit combines the biographical and psychological approaches.

Mythological and Archetypal Approaches

Another approach is related to mass psychology rather than individual idiosyncrasies. Mythological or archetypal critics look at commonalities among dreams, myths, legends, religions, visual arts, and literature, and they see the same threads running through human imaginative work throughout the ages and across cultures. One such thread, for instance, is the quest or journey, during which the main character is challenged sorely (often three times), gaining wisdom and insight along the way to a heroic ending point (or not, having failed the challenge). Another thread is the hero who dies for the salvation of all humankind. Archetypal plots and characters are associated with the theories of the Swiss psychologist Carl Jung, who believed that every person is born equipped with a collective unconscious, a set of images including many universal fictional characters such as the wise old man, the fool, the trickster, the manly rescuer, the earth mother, and the mysterious stranger, as well as others. Our attraction to certain types of stories and characters comes from the way they appeal to our collective unconscious. Arnold Friend, the menacing yet magnetic visitor in Joyce Carol Oates's "Where Are You Going, Where Have You Been?" can be seen as a trickster archetype.

Gender Focus

Drawing from psychological, sociological, and political thought as well as from literary studies, many critics in the twentieth and twenty-first centuries look at art through the lenses of gender. They ponder how sex roles, sexual identity, and relationships between the sexes affect the way that a work is written and read. A gender-based reading of Tillie Olsen's "I Stand Here Ironing" would emphasize that all three main characters are female, with experiences different from those they would have if they were men. Within the fold of gender-focused critics are feminist critics, who would analyze the story in terms of women's strategies to cope with their powerlessness in the male-oriented world. Feminists explain the disparate experiences of the sexes by analyzing the effects of the differences in power, privilege, and expectations. Hisaye Yamamoto's "Seventeen Syllables" is ripe for a feminist approach, especially for understanding the mother's motivations. Feminist critics are interested in the images of women and men as presented in literature, often pointing out negative portrayals of women that might otherwise go unnoticed.

Another gender focus involves the lives and lifestyles of gay and lesbian authors, characters, and readers. As a minority culture, gays and lesbians have a distinctive experience that has often been ignored, despised, or treated as exotic. These attitudes frequently affect the way they write and are written about (or avoided). Sherwood Anderson's "Hands" would be baffling without the allusions to fear-ridden stereotypes of gay men, especially gay teachers.

Reader Response

The critical approaches discussed so far share the idea that a work of literature has a meaning, probably one that is stable and coherent. The last two we will take up do not share this idea but focus on the variety of interpretation that is possible. The reader response approach accepts that each person brings his or her own experiences and points of view to bear while reading. No one reads a work in exactly the same way as anyone else, as you have probably noticed in discussions with classmates and friends. In fact, you may have read the same work differently within your own life as you get older. One of our colleagues claims that no one can possibly understand *Macbeth* before the age of thirty! Although reader response critics will not allow totally far-fetched interpretations of a work, they are interested in individuals' different reactions to ambiguous clues. For example, when J. Alfred Prufrock asks, "Do I dare to eat a peach?" one reader may think that Prufrock is worried about the embarrassing messiness of consuming a ripe peach, another may think that he fears looking greedy, and another may decide that the peach is a feminine symbol and Prufrock fears the sex act. All of these thoughts are defensible using other evidence within the poem, and all are probably projections of the reader's own fears.

Deconstruction

Deconstructionists take a step beyond reader response critics by viewing a work of literature as unstable and therefore vulnerable to being taken apart (de-constructed). Whereas formalists look for the way that all the elements of a piece fit together, deconstructionists look for the way these elements contradict each other and undermine coherence. Their point of view is rooted in a philosophy of language which says that words are incapable of accurately expressing meaning, that every utterance contains a lie by omitting all other possible utterances at the moment. Other critical stances reject interpretations that cannot be supported by evidence within the work, but deconstructionists delight in bizarre and contradictory claims. For example, while most people view J. Alfred Prufrock as a timid, self-effacing, and fearful fellow, deconstructionists might ask why a timid person would present such a lengthy, detailed, self-absorbed introspection (the poem itself). They could argue that J. Alfred is a braggart and narcissist, enchanted with his own superhuman sensitivity.

Intertextual Approaches

The meaning of literature is frequently enriched by each work's interdependence with other texts and the way they cast light on each other. Thus, critics use an *intertextual approach* in interpreting meaning. Sometimes intertextuality is right there on the surface, as it is in Susan Ludvigson's "Inventing My Parents." The author imagines her parents in lively intellectual chat about modernist writers Ernest Hemingway, Sinclair Lewis, Kay Boyle, and F. Scott Fitzgerald, and her father quotes by heart from the seventeenth-century poet John Donne. If you investigate these writers and their devotees, you will understand much about why Ludvigson wrote a charming, lighthearted response to the painting *Nighthawks*, which usually evokes feelings of isolation and hopelessness in its viewers (see page 549). You can create an intertextual approach even when it is not explicit, by noticing relationships among literary pieces. For example, the subject of *work* is common to the poems "What I Wouldn't Do," "Digging," "Richard Cory," and "My Mother Sews Blouses." Through comparing and contrasting what *work* means in each poem, you could write an essay of intertextual criticism.

Where Do You Stand?

As you read our brief summaries of critical approaches, you probably recognized the ones that you most regularly use when you think and write about literature. You may find it illuminating to try out some different approaches, especially when your usual tools are not working. You may also find it mind-expanding to look up work by other critics who share your favorite stance, learning from them how to use it more consciously and effectively. You can begin by reading an example of a formalist interpretation of Robert Hayden's "Those Winter Sundays" that we have reprinted on pages 520–24 or by examining the critical interpretations in the Casebook on "Where Are You Going, Where Have You Been?" on pages 221–23.

GLOSSARY
Literary and Rhetorical Terms

Allegory A form of symbolism in which ideas or abstract qualities are represented as characters or events in a story, novel, or play. For example, in the medieval drama *Everyman*, Fellowship, Kindred, and Goods, the friends of the title character, will not accompany him on his end-of-life journey, and he must depend on Good Works, whom he has previously neglected.

Alliteration Repetition of the same consonant sounds, usually at the beginning of words:

> Should the glee—glaze—
> In Death's—stiff—stare—
> —Emily Dickinson

Allusion An indirect reference to some character or event in literature, history, or mythology that enriches the meaning of the passage. For example, the title of W. H. Auden's poem "The Unknown Citizen" is an ironic allusion to the Tomb of the Unknown Soldier.

Ambiguity Something that may be validly interpreted in more than one way; double meaning.

Analysis A method of understanding the theme and structure of a literary work by examining its component parts, resulting in a relatively complete, consistent interpretation.

Anapest *See* Meter.

Antagonist The character (or a force such as war or poverty) in a drama, poem, or work of fiction whose actions oppose those of the protagonist (hero or heroine).

Anticlimax A trivial event following immediately after significant events.

Archetype A recurring character type, plot, symbol, or theme of seemingly universal significance: the blind prophet figure, the journey to the underworld, the sea as source of life, the initiation theme.

Argument Writing that attempts to influence readers to accept an opinion or interpretation; a good argument includes a clear claim or stance, ample evidence, and sound reasoning that explains the claim and connects it to the evidence.

Assonance The repetition of similar vowel sounds within syllables:

> On desperate seas long wont to roam
> —Edgar Allan Poe

Atmosphere *See* Mood.

Audience In composition, the readers for whom a piece of writing is intended.

Ballad A narrative poem in four-line stanzas, rhyming *xaxa*, often sung or recited as a folk tale. The *x* means that those two lines do not rhyme.

Blank Verse Unrhymed iambic pentameter, the line that most closely resembles speech in English:

> When I see birches bend to left and right
> Across the lines of straighter darker trees,
> I like to think some boy's been swinging them.
> —Robert Frost

Carpe Diem Literally, seize the day, a phrase applicable to many lyric poems advocating lustful living:

> Gather ye rosebuds while ye may,
> Old time is still a-flying:
> And this same flower that smiles today
> Tomorrow will be dying.
> —Robert Herrick

Catharsis In classical tragedy, the purging of pity and fear experienced by the audience at the end of the play; a "there but for the grace of the gods go I" sense of relief.

Chorus In Greek drama, a group (often led by an individual) who comments on or interprets the action of the play.

Claim A positive statement or assertion that requires support. Claims are the backbone of any interpretation of a literary work.

Climax The point toward which the action of a plot builds as the conflicts become increasingly intense or complex; the turning point.

Coherence In good writing, the orderly, logical relationship among the many parts—the smooth moving forward of ideas through clearly related sentences. *Also see* Unity.

Comedy A play, light in tone, designed to amuse and entertain, that usually ends happily, often with a marriage.

Comparative Argument A form of argument that examines the relative strengths and weaknesses of two views or interpretations.

Complication The rising action of a plot during which the conflicts build toward the climax.

Conceit A highly imaginative, often startling, figure of speech drawing an analogy between two unlike things in an ingenious way:

> In this sad state, God's tender bowels run
> Out streams of grace....
>
> —Edward Taylor

Concrete Poetry Poems that convey meaning by the way they look on the page. Also called *shaped poetry*.

Conflict The antagonism between opposing characters or forces that causes tension or suspense in the plot.

Connotation The associations that attach themselves to many words, deeply affecting their literal meanings (e.g., *politician*, *statesman*).

Consonance Close repetition of the same consonant sounds preceded by different vowel sounds (*flesh/flash* or *breed/bread*). At the end of lines of poetry, this pattern produces half-rhyme.

Controlling Idea *See* Thesis.

Controlling Image In a short story, novel, play, or poem, an image that recurs and carries such symbolic significance that it embodies the theme of the work, as the quilts do in Walker's "Everyday Use," and as the grass does in Whitman's "Leaves of Grass."

Convention An accepted improbability in a literary work, such as the dramatic aside, in which an actor turns from the stage and addresses the audience.

Counterargument A form of argument organized as a point-by-point refutation of opposing views or interpretations.

Couplet Two rhymed lines of poetry:

> For thy sweet love remembered such wealth brings
> That then I scorn to change my state with kings.
>
> —William Shakespeare

Crisis *See* Climax.

Critical Reading and Thinking The use of analysis, inference, synthesis, and evaluation to seek the meaning beneath the surface of any text, written or visual; the process of seeing and judging implications, connections, and assumptions that might otherwise go unnoticed.

Dactyl *See* Meter.

Denotation The literal dictionary meaning of a word.

Denouement Literally, the "untying"; the resolution of the conflicts following the climax (or crisis) of a plot.

Diction Words chosen in writing or speaking.

Double Entendre A double meaning, one of which usually carries sexual suggestions, as in the country-western song about a truck driver who calls his wife long distance to say he is bringing his "big ol' engine" home to her.

Dramatic Irony *See* Irony.

Dramatic Monologue A poem consisting of a self-revealing speech delivered by one person to a silent listener; for instance, Robert Browning's "My Last Duchess."

Dramatic Point of View *See* Point of View.

Elegy A poem commemorating someone's death but usually encompassing a larger issue as well.

Empathy Literally, "feeling in"; the emotional identification that a reader or an audience feels with a character.

English Sonnet *See* Sonnet.

Epigraph A quotation at the beginning of a poem, novel, play, or essay that suggests the theme of the work.

Epilogue The concluding section of a literary work, usually a play, in which loose threads are tied together or a moral is drawn.

Epiphany A moment of insight in which something simple and commonplace is seen in a new way and, as James Joyce said, "its soul, its whatness leaps to us from the vestment of its appearance."

Episode In a narrative, a unified sequence of events; in Greek drama, the action between choruses.

Evidence Facts, details, examples, reasoning, quotations, personal experiences, and the like, which are used to develop and explain the claims in an argument or interpretation.

Explication An explanation of a literary work developed by analyzing details, images, meanings, and comparisons derived from a close reading of the text.

Exposition That part of a plot devoted to supplying background information, explaining events that happened before the current action.

Fable A story, usually using symbolic characters and settings, designed to teach a lesson.

Falling Action In classical dramatic structure, the part of a play after the climax, in which the consequences of the conflict are revealed. *Also see* Denouement.

Figurative Language Words that carry suggestive or symbolic meaning beyond the literal level.

First-Person Point of View *See* Point of View.

Flashback Part of a narrative that interrupts the chronological flow by relating events from the past.

Flat Character In contrast to a well-developed round character, a flat one is stereotyped or shallow, not seeming as complex as real people; flat characters are often created deliberately to give them a symbolic role, like Old Man Warner in "The Lottery."

Foil A character, usually a minor one, who emphasizes the qualities of another one through implied contrast between the two.

Foot A unit of poetic rhythm. *See* Meter.

Foreshadowing Early clues about what will happen later in a narrative or play.

Formal Writing The highest level of usage, in which no slang, contractions, or fragments are used.

Free Verse Poetry that does not have regular rhythm, rhyme, or standard form.

Freewriting Writing without regard to coherence or correctness, intended to relax the writer and produce ideas for further writing.

Genre A classification of literature: drama, novel, short story, poem.

Hero/Heroine The character intended to engage most fully the audience's or reader's sympathies and admiration. *Also see* Protagonist.

Hubris Unmitigated pride, often the cause of the hero's downfall in Greek tragedy.

Hyperbole A purposeful exaggeration.

Iamb *See* Meter.

Image/Imagery Passages or words that stir feelings or memories through an appeal to the senses.

Inductive Reasoning The use of known facts and specific details to arrive at a general conclusion or interpretation.

Informal Writing (or Usage) The familiar, everyday level of usage, which includes contractions and perhaps slang but precludes nonstandard grammar and punctuation.

Internal Rhyme The occurrence of similar sounds within the lines of a poem rather than just at the ends of lines:

> Too bright for our infirm delight
> —Emily Dickinson

Invention The process of generating subjects, topics, details, and plans for writing.

Irony Lack of agreement between expectation and reality.

Verbal irony involves a major discrepancy between the words spoken or written and the intended meaning. For example, Stephen Crane writes, "War is kind," but he means—and the poem shows—that war is hell.

Situational irony can stem quite literally from irony of situation. For example, in Shirley Jackson's "The Lottery," the fact that the inhabitants of a small town get together on a beautiful summer day not for a picnic but to stone one of their neighbors to death is heavily ironic. Situational irony can also involve the contrast between the hopes, aspirations, or fears of a character and the outcome of that person's actions or eventual fate. For example, in Flannery O'Connor's "Good Country People," the intellectual Hulga Joy is taken in by the uneducated Bible salesman she plans to seduce.

Dramatic irony involves the difference between what a character knows or believes and what the better-informed reader or audience knows to be true. For example, in Susan Glaspell's *Trifles* the audience knows that the evidence to establish motive for the murder is right under the noses of the law enforcement officials, but the men overlook it because they consider the suspect's "women's work" not worthy of their notice.

Issue An important point or question that has more than one view or answer and provides the basis for the claims in an argument or interpretation.

Italian Sonnet *See* Sonnet.

Jargon The specialized words and expressions belonging to certain professions, sports, hobbies, or social groups. Sometimes any tangled and incomprehensible prose is called jargon.

Juxtaposition The simultaneous presentation of two conflicting images or ideas, designed to make a point of the contrast: for example, an elaborate and well-kept church surrounded by squalorous slums.

Limited Point of View *See* Point of View.

Lyric A poem that primarily expresses emotion.

Metaphor A figure of speech that makes an imaginative comparison between two literally unlike things:

Sylvia's face was a pale star.

Metaphysical Poetry A style of poetry (usually associated with seventeenth-century poet John Donne) that boasts intellectual, complex, and even strained images (called *conceits*), which frequently link the personal and familiar to the cosmic and mysterious. *Also see* Conceit.

Meter Recurring patterns of stressed and unstressed syllables in poetry. A metrical unit is called a *foot*. There are four basic patterns of stress: an *iamb*, or *iambic foot*, which consists of an unstressed syllable followed by a stressed one *(before, return)*; a *trochee*, or *trochaic foot*, which consists of a stressed syllable followed by an unstressed one *(funny, double)*; an *anapest*, or *anapestic foot*, which consists of two unstressed syllables followed by a stressed one *(contradict)*; and a *dactyl*, or *dactylic foot*, which consists of a stressed syllable followed by two unstressed ones *(merrily, syllable)*. One common variation is the *spondee*, or *spondaic foot*, which consists of two stressed syllables *(moonshine, football)*.

Lines are classified according to the number of metrical feet they contain: *monometer* (one foot), *dimeter* (two feet), *trimeter* (three feet), *tetrameter* (four feet), *pentameter* (five feet), *hexameter* (six feet), and so on.

Metonymy A figure of speech in which the name of one thing is substituted for that of something else closely associated with it—for example, *the White House* (meaning the president or the whole executive branch), or *the pen is mightier than the sword* (meaning written words are more powerful than military force).

Mood The emotional content of a scene or setting, usually described in terms of feeling: somber, gloomy, joyful, expectant. *Also see* Tone.

Motif A pattern of identical or similar images recurring throughout a passage or entire work.

Myth A traditional story involving deities and heroes, usually expressing and inculcating the established values of a culture.

Narrative A story line in prose or verse.

Narrator The person who tells the story to the audience or reader. *Also see* Unreliable Narrator.

Objective Point of View *See* Point of View.

Ode A long, serious lyric focusing on a stated theme: "Ode on a Grecian Urn."

Omniscient Point of View *See* Point of View.

Onomatopoeia A word that sounds like what it names: *whoosh, clang, babble*.

Oxymoron A single phrase that juxtaposes opposite terms:

the lonely crowd, a roaring silence.

Parable A story designed to demonstrate a principle or lesson using symbolic characters, details, and plot lines.

Paradox An apparently contradictory statement that, upon examination, makes sense:

In my end is my beginning.
—Mary, Queen of Scots

The motto is intelligible only in the context of Christian theology, which promises renewed life after death.

Paraphrase In prose, a restatement in different words, usually briefer than the original version; in poetry, a statement of the literal meaning of the poem in everyday language.

Parody An imitation of a piece of writing, copying some features such as diction, style, and form, but changing or exaggerating other features for humorous effect.

Pentameter A line of poetry that contains five metrical feet. *See* Meter.

Persona The person created by the writer to be the speaker of the poem or story. The persona is not usually identical to the writer—for example, a personally optimistic writer could create a cynical persona to narrate a story.

Personification Giving human qualities to nonhuman things:

the passionate song of bullets and the banshee shrieks of shells
—Stephen Crane

Phallic Symbol An image shaped like the male sex organ; suggests male potency or male dominance *(towers, snakes, guns, spurs, jet planes, sleek cars)*.

Plagiarism Carelessly or deliberately presenting the words or ideas of another writer as your own; literary theft.

Plot A series of causally related events or episodes that occur in a narrative or play. *Also see* Climax, Complication, Conflict, Denouement, Falling Action, Resolution, and Rising Action.

Point of Attack The moment of the play at which the main action of the plot begins; it may occur in the first scene or after several scenes of exposition.

Point of View The angle or perspective from which a story is reported and interpreted. There are a number of points of view that authors can use.

First person—someone, often the main character, tells the story as he or she experienced it (and uses the pronoun *I*).

Omniscient—the narrator knows everything about the characters and events and can move about in time and place and into the minds of all the characters.

Limited—the story is limited to the observations, thoughts, and feelings of a single character (not identified as *I*).

Shifting—a limited view which can shift to the perspective of more than one character.

Objective or *dramatic*—the actions and conversations are presented in detail as they occur, more or less objectively, without any comment from the author or a narrator.

Unreliable—narrated from the point of view of a character unable or perhaps unwilling to give a fully accurate account.

Prewriting The process that writers use to gather ideas, consider audience, determine purpose, develop a thesis and tentative structure (plan), and generally prepare for the actual composing stage.

Primary Source The literary work under consideration by the reader.

Protagonist The main character in drama or fiction, sometimes called the hero or heroine.

Pun A verbal joke based on the similarity of sound between words that have different meanings:

> They went and *told* the sexton and the sexton *tolled* the bell.
>
> —Thomas Hood

Quatrain A four-line stanza of poetry, which can have any number of rhyme schemes.

Reasoning The process of thinking carefully about something in order to make a judgment; drawing conclusions through the use of observations and explanations.

Resolution The conclusion of the conflict in a fictional or dramatic plot. *Also see* Denouement *and* Falling Action.

Rhyme Similar or identical sounds between words, usually the end sounds in lines of verse *(brain/strain; liquor/quicker)*.

Rhythm The recurrence of stressed and unstressed syllables in a regular pattern. *Also see* Meter.

Rising Action The complication and development of the conflict leading to the climax in a plot.

Round Character A literary character with sufficient complexity to be convincing, true to life.

Sarcasm A form of *verbal irony* that presents caustic and bitter disapproval in the guise of praise. *Also see* Irony.

Satire Literary expression that uses humor and wit to attack and expose human folly and weakness. *Also see* Parody.

Secondary Source Critical material from the library or the Internet (articles, reviews, books, sections of books).

Sentimentality The attempt to produce an emotional response that exceeds the circumstances and to draw from the reader a stock response instead of a genuine emotional response.

Setting The time and place in which a story, play, or novel occurs. *Also see* Mood.

Shakespearean Sonnet *See* Sonnet.

Simile A verbal comparison in which a similarity is expressed directly, using *like* or *as*:

> houses leaning together like conspirators.
>
> —James Joyce

Also see Metaphor.

Situational Irony *See* Irony.

Soliloquy A speech in which a dramatic character reveals what is going through his or her mind by talking aloud to herself or himself. *Also see* Dramatic Monologue.

Sonnet A poem of fourteen ten-syllable lines, arranged in a pattern of rhyme schemes. The *English* or *Shakespearean sonnet* uses seven rhymes that divide the poem into three quatrains and a couplet: abab, cdcd, efef, gg. The *Italian sonnet* usually divides into an octave (eight lines) and a sestet (six lines) by using only five rhymes: abba, abba, cdecde. (The rhyme scheme of the sestet varies widely from sonnet to sonnet.)

Speaker The voice or person presenting a poem.

Spondee *See* Meter.

Standard English The language that is written and spoken by most educated persons of English-speaking countries.

Stereotype An oversimplified, commonly held image or opinion about a person, a race, or an issue.

Stilted Language Words and expressions that are too formal for the writing situation; unnatural, artificial language.

Structure The general plan, framework, or form of a piece of writing.

Style Individuality of expression, achieved in writing through the selection and arrangement of words and punctuation.

Subplot Secondary plot in a novel or play, usually reinforcing the main theme but sometimes just providing interest, excitement, or comic relief.

Summary A short, objective restatement of the important ideas in a passage or a complete document, usually without analysis, explanation, paraphrasing, or personal comment.

Symbol Something that suggests or stands for an idea, quality, or concept larger than itself: the lion is a symbol of courage; a voyage or journey can symbolize life; water suggests spirituality, dryness the lack thereof.

Synecdoche A figure of speech in which some prominent feature is used to name the whole, or vice versa—for example, *a sail in the harbor* (meaning a ship), or *call the law* (meaning call the law enforcement officers).

Synesthesia Figurative language in which two or more sense impressions are combined:

> blue uncertain stumbling buzz
> —Emily Dickinson

Syntax Sentence structure; the relationship between words and among word groups in sentences.

Theater of the Absurd A form of drama that departs markedly from the realistic representation of events on stage, attempting to show that the human predicament is anguished, meaningless, and futile.

Theme The central or dominating idea advanced by a literary work, usually containing some insight into the human condition.

Thesis The main point or position that a writer develops and supports in a composition. *Also see* Claim.

Tone The attitude a writer conveys toward his or her subject and audience. In poetry this attitude is sometimes called *voice*.

Tragedy A serious drama that relates the events in the life of a protagonist, or *tragic hero*, whose error in judgment, dictated by a *tragic flaw*, results in the hero's downfall and culminates in catastrophe. In less classical terms, any serious drama, novel, or short story that ends with the death or defeat of the main character may be called tragic.

Trochee *See* Meter.

Type Character A literary character who embodies a number of traits that are common to a particular group or class of people (a rebellious daughter, a stern father, a jealous lover); all of the characters in Valdez's *Los Vendidos* are types.

Understatement A form of ironic expression that intentionally minimizes the importance of an idea or fact.

Unity The fitting together or harmony of all elements in a piece of writing. *Also see* Coherence.

Unreliable Narrator A viewpoint character who presents a biased or erroneous report that may mislead or distort a reader's judgments about other characters and actions; sometimes the unreliable narrator may be self–deceived.

Usage The accepted or customary way of using words in speaking and writing a language.

Verbal Irony *See* Irony.

Verisimilitude The appearance of truth or believability in a literary work.

Versification The mechanics of poetic composition, including such elements as rhyme, rhythm, meter, and stanza form.

Yonic Symbol An image shaped like the female breasts, uterus, or genitalia; suggests fecundity or female sexuality *(caves, pots, rooms, apples, full-blown roses)*.

Credits

Chinua Achebe, "Dead Men's Path," copyright © 1972, 1973 by Chinua Achebe, from *Girls at War and Other Stories* by Chinua Achebe. Used by permission of Doubleday, a division of Random House, Inc., and by permission of The Wylie Agency LLC.

Sherman Alexie, "This Is What It Means to Say Phoenix, Arizona" from *The Lone Ranger and Tonto Fistfight in Heaven.* Copyright © 1993, 2005 by Sherman Alexie. Used by permission of Grove/Atlantic.

Sherwood Anderson, "Hands" from *Winesburg, Ohio,* 1919.

Matthew Arnold, "Dover Beach," 1867.

Fernando Arrabal, "Picnic on the Battlefield" from *Guernica and Other Plays* by Fernando Arrabal, translated by Barbara Wright, pp. 109–126. Copyright © 1967 by Calder & Boyars Ltd., London. Used by permission of Grove/Atlantic, Inc.

Margaret Atwood, "Happy Endings" from *Good Bones and Simple Murders* by Margaret Atwood. Copyright © 1983, 1992, 1994 by O.W. Toad Ltd. A Nan A. Talese Book. Used by permission of Doubleday, a division of Random House. Published in Canada by McClelland & Stewart Ltd. Used with permission of the publisher.

W.H. Auden, "Lullaby," copyright 1940 and 1968 by W.H. Auden; "Funeral Blues," copyright 1940 and renewed 1968 by W.H. Auden; "Musée des Beaux Arts," copyright 1940 and renewed 1968 by W.H. Auden; "The Unknown Citizen," copyright 1940 and renewed 1968 by W.H. Auden from *Collected Poems* by W.H. Auden. Used by permission of Random House, Inc.

Jimmy Santiago Baca, "There Are Black" from *Immigrants in Our Own Land.* Copyright © 1977, 1979, 1981, 1982, 1990 by Jimmy Santiago Baca. Reprinted by permission of New Directions Publishing Corp.

Toni Cade Bambara, "The Lesson," copyright © 1972 by Toni Cade Bambara, from *Gorilla, My Love* by Toni Cade Bambara. Used by permission of Random House, Inc.

Amiri Baraka, "Biography" (1969). Reprinted by permission of SLL/Sterling Lord Literistic, Inc. Copyright by Amiri Baraka.

Jan Beatty, "A Waitress's Instructions on Tipping or Get the Cash Up and Don't Waste My Time" from *Mad River.* © 1996. Reprinted by permission of the University of Pittsburgh Press.

Jeanne Marie Beaumont, "Afraid So" from *Curious Conduct.* Copyright © 2004 by Jeanne Marie Beaumont. Reprinted with permission of BOA Editions, Ltd., www.boaeditions.org.

David Bevington, Notes to "Othello" from *The Complete Works of Shakespeare,* 4th ed., by David Bevington. Copyright © 1992 HarperCollins Publishers. Reprinted by permission of Pearson Education, Inc.

George Bilgere, "Like Riding a Bicycle" from *The Good Kiss.* Copyright © 2002. Reprinted by permission of The University of Akron Press.

Christine Birdwell, "Death as a Fastball on the Outside Corner" from *Aethlon: The Journal of Sports Literature,* Vol. 8, No. 1, Fall 1990.

Elizabeth Bishop, "One Art" from *The Complete Poems 1927–1979.* Copyright © 1979, 1983 by Alice Helen Methfessel. Reprinted by permission of Farrar, Straus and Giroux, LLC.

William Blake, "London," 1794, "The Lamb," 1789, "The Tyger," 1794, "The Sick Rose," 1794.

T. Coraghessan Boyle, "The Love of My Life" from *After the Plague* by T. Coraghessan Boyle. Copyright © 2001 by T. Coraghessan Boyle. Used by permission of Viking Penguin, a division of Penguin Group (USA) Inc.

Gwendolyn Brooks, "Sadie and Maud," "We Real Cool," and "The Bean Eaters" from *Blacks* (Third World Press, 1991). Reprinted by permission of the author.

Robert Browning, "My Last Duchess," 1842.

Octavia Butler, "Speech Sounds" from *BloodChild and Other Stories.* Originally published in *Isaac Asimov's Science Fiction Magazine* (December 1983). Copyright © 1983, 1995 by Octavia E. Butler. Reprinted with permission of Seven Stories Press, www.sevenstories.com.

George Gordon Byron (Lord Byron), "She Walks in Beauty," 1814.

Hayden Carruth, "In the Long Hall" from *Scrambled Eggs & Whiskey: Poems 1991–1995.* Copyright © 1996 by Hayden Carruth. Reprinted with permission of Copper Canyon Press, www.coppercanyonpress.org.

Raymond Carver, "What We Talk About When We Talk About Love" from *What We Talk About When We Talk About Love.* Copyright © 1974, 1976, 1978, 1980, 1981 by Raymond Carver. Used by permission of Alfred A. Knopf, a division of Random House, Inc.

Kate Chopin, "Désirée's Baby," 1893, "The Story of an Hour," 1894.

Sandra Cisneros, from *The House on Mango Street.* Copyright © 1984 by Sandra Cisneros. Published by Vintage Books, a division of Random House, Inc., and in hardcover by Alfred A. Knopf in 1994. By permission of Susan Bergholz Literary Services, New York, NY and Lamy, NM. All rights reserved.

Lucille Clifton, "homage to my hips." Copyright © 1980 by Lucille Clifton. First appeared in *Two-Headed Woman,* published by The University of Massachusetts Press. Reprinted by permission of Curtis Brown, Ltd.

Judith Ortiz Cofer, "Latin Women Pray" from *Reaching for the Mainland and Selected New Poems.* Bilingual Press/Editorial Bilingüe, 1995, Tempe, Arizona. Reprinted by permission of the publisher.

Billy Collins, "Introduction to Poetry" from *The Apple That Astonished Paris.* Copyright © 1988, 1996 by Billy Collins. Used by permission of The University of Arkansas Press, www.uapress.com.

Billy Collins, "Sonnet," copyright © 2001 by Billy Collins, from *Sailing Alone Around the Room* by Billy Collins. Used by permission of Random House, Inc.

Stephen Crane, "War Is Kind," 1899.

Countee Cullen, "Incident" as published in *Color.* Copyright 1925 Harper & Bros, NY. Copyright renewed 1952 by Ida M. Cullen. Copyrights held by Amistad Research Center Tulane University. Administered by Thompson and Thompson, Brooklyn, NY. By permission.

E.E. Cummings, "in Just-." Copyright 1923, 1951, © 1991 by the Trustees for the E.E. Cummings Trust. Copyright © 1976 by George James Firmage; "next to of course god america i." Copyright 1926, 1954, © 1991 by the Trustees for the E.E. Cummings Trust. Copyright © 1985 by George James Firmage; "pity this busy monster, man-unkind." Copyright 1944, © 1972, 1991 by the Trustees for the E.E. Cummings Trust; "anyone lived in a pretty how town." Copyright 1940, © 1968, 1991 by the Trustees for the E.E. Cummings Trust. From *Complete Poems: 1904–1962* by E.E. Cummings, edited by George J. Firmage. Used by permission of Liveright Publishing Corporation.

James Dickey, "The Leap" from *Poems, 1957–1967* (Middletown, CT: Wesleyan University Press, 1967). Reprinted by permission of University Press of New England.

Emily Dickinson, "Faith Is a Fine Invention," 1860.

Emily Dickinson, "Because I could not stop for death," "He put the belt around my life," "I'm Nobody, Who are You?" "Much madness is divinest sense," "Some keep the Sabbath going to church," "Wild nights! Wild nights!" Reprinted by permission of the publishers and the Trustees of Amherst College from *The Poems of Emily Dickinson,* Thomas H. Johnson, ed., Cambridge, MA: The Belknap Press of Harvard University Press, Copyright © 1951, 1955, 1979, 1983 by the President and Fellows of Harvard College.

John Donne, "Death, Be Not Proud," "The Flea," "A Valediction: Forbidding Mourning," 1633.

Rita Dove, "Daystar" from *Thomas and Beulah,* Carnegie Mellon University Press, © 1986 by Rita Dove. Reprinted by permission of the author.

Paul Laurence Dunbar, "We Wear the Mask," 1896.

Cornelius Eady, reprinted from *The Gathering of My Name:* "The Supremes" by permission of Carnegie Mellon University Press. © 1991 by Cornelius Eady.

T.S. Eliot, "The Love Song of J. Alfred Prufrock" from *Collected Poems 1909–1950* by T.S. Eliot. Reprinted by permission of Faber and Faber Ltd.

Louise Erdrich, "Indian Boarding School: The Runaways" from *Jacklight.* © 1984 by Louise Erdrich. Reprinted with permission of The Wylie Agency.

Louise Erdrich, "The Red Convertible" pp. 1–16, from *The Red Convertible: Selected and New Stories 1978–2008* by Louise Erdrich. Copyright © 2009 by Louise Erdrich. Reprinted by permission of HarperCollins Publishers.

Martín Espada, "Bully" from *Rebellion Is the Circle of a Lover's Hands* by Martín Espada (Curbstone Press, 1990). Reprinted with permission of Curbstone Press. Distributed by Consortium.

Ruth Fainlight, "Flower Feet" from *Selected Poems,* originally appeared in *The New Yorker.* Reprinted by permission of the author.

U.A. Fanthorpe, "Not My Best Side" from *Collected Poems 1978–2003.* Peterloo Poets, 2005. Reprinted by permission of the publisher, Peterloo Poets.

William Faulkner, "A Rose for Emily," copyright 1930 and renewed 1958 by William Faulkner, from *Collected Stories of William Faulkner* by William Faulkner. Used by permission of Random House, Inc.

Karen Jackson Ford, "Do Right to Write Right: Langston Hughes's Aesthetics of Simplicity," *Twentieth Century Literature* 38.4, 1992.

Robert Frost, "Design" and "The Silken Tent" from *The Poetry of Robert Frost,* edited by Edward Connery Lathem. Copyright © 1969 by Henry Holt and Company. Copyright 1936, 1942 by Robert Frost. Copyright © 1964, 1970 by Lesley Frost Ballantine. Reprinted by arrangement with Henry Holt and Company, LLC.

Robert Frost, "Mending Wall" from *The Poetry of Robert Frost,* edited by Edward Connery Lathem. Copyright 1930, 1939, 1969 by Henry Holt and Company. Copyright 1958 by Robert Frost. Copyright 1967 by Lesley Frost Ballantine. "Birches," "Fire and Ice," and "Out, Out" from *The Poetry of Robert Frost,* edited by Edward Connery Lathem. Copyright 1916, 1923, 1969 by Henry Holt and Company. Copyright 1944, 1951 by Robert Frost. Reprinted by arrangement with Henry Holt and Company, LLC.

Dagoberto Gilb, "Love in L.A." from *The Magic of Blood.* Copyright © 1993 University of New Mexico Press. Reprinted by permission of the publisher.

Nikki Giovanni, "Dreams" from *Black Feeling, Black Talk, Black Judgment.* Copyright © 1968, 1970 by Nikki Giovanni. Reprinted by permission of HarperCollins Publishers. William Morrow.

Susan Glaspell, "Trifles," 1916, "A Jury of Her Peers," 1917.

Donald Hall, "My Son My Executioner" from *Old and New Poems.* Copyright © 1990 by Donald Hall. Reprinted by permission of Houghton Mifflin Harcourt Publishing Company. All rights reserved.

Lorraine Hansberry, *A Raisin in the Sun,* copyright 1958 by Robert Nemiroff, as an unpublished work. Copyright © 1959, 1966, 1984 by Robert Nemiroff. Copyright renewed 1986, 1987 by Robert Nemiroff. Used by permission of Random House, Inc.

Thomas Hardy, "The Convergence of the Twain," 1912, "The Ruined Maid," 1866.

Nathaniel Hawthorne, "The Birthmark," 1844.

Robert Hayden, "Those Winter Sundays." Copyright © 1966 by Robert Hayden, from *Angle of Ascent: New and Selected Poems* by Robert Hayden. Used by permission of Liveright Publishing Corporation.

Seamus Heaney, "Digging" from *Opened Ground: Selected Poems 1966–1996* by Seamus Heaney. Copyright © 1998 by Seamus Heaney. Reprinted by permission of Farrar, Straus and Giroux, LLC.

Seamus Heaney, "Digging" from *Death of a Naturalist* by Seamus Heaney. Reprinted by permission of Faber and Faber Ltd.

Ernest Hemingway, "Hills Like White Elephants." Reprinted with the permission of Scribner, a Division of Simon & Schuster, Inc., from *Men Without Women* by Ernest Hemingway. Copyright 1927 by Charles Scribner's Sons. Copyright renewed 1955 by Ernest Hemingway.

Essex Hemphill, "Commitments" from *Ceremonies: Prose and Poetry* by Essex Hemphill. Copyright © 1992 by Essex Hemphill. Used by permission of Plume, an imprint of Penguin Group (USA) Inc.

Nancy Henry, "People Who Take Care" from *Hard.* Copyright © 2003 MuscleHead Press. Reprinted by permission of MuscleHead Press.

Edward Hirsch, "Execution" from *The Night Parade.* Copyright © 1989 by Edward Hirsch. Used by permission of Alfred A. Knopf, a division of Random House, Inc.

Tony Hoagland, "The Change" from *What Narcissism Means to Me.* Copyright © 1993 by Tony Hoagland. Reprinted by permission of Graywolf Press, Saint Paul, Minnesota, www.graywolfpress.org.

Gerald Manley Hopkins, "Pied Beauty," 1877, "Spring and Fall," 1880.

A.E. Housman, "Eight O'Clock," 1922; "To An Athlete Dying Young," 1887; "Loveliest of Trees," 1896.

David Huddle, "The 'Banked Fire' of Robert Hayden's 'Those Winter Sundays'" from Robert Pak and Jay Parini, eds., *Touchstones: American Poets on a Favorite Poem.* Reprinted by permission of the author.

Langston Hughes, "Harlem (2) ["What happens to a dream deferred . . ."]," "Mother to Son," "The Negro Speaks of Rivers," "Theme for English B," "Trumpet Player," "The Weary Blues," and "Saturday Night," edited by Arnold Rampersad wih David Roessel, Assoc., from *The Collected Poems of Langston Hughes* by Langston Hughes, edited by Arnold Rampersad with David Roessel, Associate Editor. Copyright © 1994 by The Estate of Langston Hughes. Used by permission of Alfred A. Knopf, a division of Random House, Inc.

Langston Hughes, "Salvation" and excerpt from "Harlem Rent Parties" from *The Big Sea* by Langston Hughes. Copyright © 1940 by Langston Hughes. Copyright renewed 1968 by Arna Bontemps and George Houston Bass. Reprinted by permission of Hill and Wang, a division of Farrar, Straus and Giroux, LLC.

Langston Hughes, "On the Road" and "Thank You, M'am" from *Short Stories* by Langston Hughes. Copyright © 1996 by Ramona Bass and Arnold Rampersad. Reprinted by permission of Hill and Wang, a division of Farrar, Straus and Giroux, LLC.

Zora Neale Hurston, "Spunk" from *Spunk: Selected Short Stories of Zora Neale Hurston.* Originally published in *Opportunity*, 1925.

David Henry Hwang, *M. Butterfly.* Copyright © 1986, 1987, 1988 by David Henry Hwang. Used by permission of Dutton Signet, a division of Penguin Group (USA) Inc.

Henrik Ibsen, *A Doll's House*, translated and edited by R. Farquharson Sharp.

David Ives, *Sure Thing.* (Dramatists Play Service, Inc.) Reprinted by permission of the author and Dramatists Play Service, Inc.

Shirley Jackson, "The Lottery" from *The Lottery and Other Short Stories* by Shirley Jackson. Copyright © 1948, 1949 by Shirley Jackson. Copyright renewed 1976, 1977 by Laurence Hyman, Barry Hyman, Mrs. Sarah Webster, and Mrs. Joanne Schnurer. Reprinted by permission of Farrar, Straus and Giroux, LLC.

Onwuchekwa Jemie, *Langston Hughes: An Introduction to Poetry.* New York: Columbia University Press, 1976.

Ha Jin, "The Bridegroom," *Harper's Magazine*, July 1999. Copyright © 1999 by Harper's Magazine. All rights reserved. Reproduced from the July issue by special permission.

Greg Johnson, *Invisible Writer: A Biography of Joyce Carol Oates.* New York: Dutton, 1998.

Greg Johnson, *Understanding Joyce Carol Oates.* Columbia, SC: University of South Carolina Press, 1987: 101–02.

James Joyce, "Eveline," *Dubliners*, 1916.

John Keats, "Ode on a Grecian Urn," 1819.

Ron Koertge, "Cinderella's Diary" from *Fever.* Copyright © 2007 Red Hen Press. Reprinted by permission of Red Hen Press.

Yusef Komunyakaa, "Facing It" from *Dien Cai Dau.* (Wesleyan University Press, 1988). Reprinted with permission of University Press of New England.

Maxine Kumin, "Woodchucks." Copyright © 1972, 1997 by Maxine Kumin, from *Selected Poems 1960–1990* by Maxine Kumin. Used by permission of W.W. Norton & Company, Inc.

Margaret Larkin, from "A Poet for the People," *Opportunity: Journal of Negro Life*, 5 (March 1927): 84–85. Reprinted by permission of The National Urban League.

Philip Larkin, "Home Is So Sad" from *Collected Poems* by Philip Larkin. Copyright © 1988, 2003 by the Estate of Philip Larkin. Reprinted by permission of Farrar, Straus and Giroux, LLC.

Philip Larkin, "Home Is So Sad" from *The Whitsun Weddings* by Philip Larkin. Reprinted by permission of Faber and Faber Ltd.

Peg Lauber, "Six National Guardsmen Blown Up Together" from *New Orleans Suite.* Copyright © 2006. Reprinted by permission of Marsh River Editions.

Dorianne Laux, "What I Wouldn't Do" from *What We Carry.* Copyright © 1994 by Dorianne Laux. Reprinted with permission of BOA Editions, Ltd., www.boaeditions.org.

D.H. Lawrence, "The Rocking Horse-Winner," copyright 1933 by the estate of D.H. Lawrence, renewed © 1961 by Angelo Ravagli and C.M. Weekley, Executors of the Estate of Frieda Lawrence, from *Complete Short Stories of D.H. Lawrence* by D.H. Lawrence. Used by permission of Viking Penguin, a division of Penguin Group (USA) Inc.

D.H. Lawrence, "Piano,"1916.

Jay Leeming, "Man Writes Poem" from *Dynamite on a China Plate.* © 2006. Reprinted by permission of the author.

Audre Lorde, "Hanging Fire" from *The Black Unicorn* by Audre Lorde. Copyright © 1978 by Audre Lorde. Used by permission of W.W. Norton & Company, Inc.

Richard Lovelace, "To Lucasta," 1649.

Susan Ludvigson, "Inventing My Parents" from *Everything Winged Must Be Dreaming: Poems.* Copyright © 1993 by Susan Ludvigson. Reprinted by permission of Louisiana State University Press.

Christopher Marlowe, "The Passionate Shepherd to His Love," 1600.

Don Marquis, "the lesson of the moth" from *Archy and Mehitabel* by Don Marquis. Copyright 1927 by Doubleday, a division of Random House, Inc. Used by permission of Doubleday, a division of Random House, Inc.

Jane Martin, *Beauty.* Copyright © 2001. Reprinted by permission of Alexander Speer, Trustee.

Andrew Marvell, "To His Coy Mistress," 1681.

Carla J. McDonough, *Staging Masculinity: Male Identity in Contemporary American Drama.* Jefferson, NC: McFarland & Co., 1997.

Roger McGough, "40------Love" from *After the Merrymaking.* Reprinted by permission of United Agents Limited on behalf of Roger McGough. © Roger McGough 1971.

Claude McKay, "America," *Harlem Shadows,* 1922.

Edna St. Vincent Millay, "First Fig" and "Oh, Oh, You Will Be Sorry for That Word!" from *Fatal Interview,* from *Collected Poems.* Copyright © 1923, 1931, 1951, 1958 by Edna St. Vincent Millay and Norma Millay Ellis. Reprinted with the permission of Elizabeth Barnett, Literary Executor.

Rosario Morales, "The Day It Happened," *Callaloo,* 15.4 (1992), pp. 970–972. © 1992 The Johns Hopkins University Press. Reprinted with permission of The Johns Hopkins University Press.

Dan Moser, excerpt from "The Pied Piper of Tucson," *Life,* March 4, 1966. Copyright 1966, Life, Inc. Reprinted with permission. All rights reserved.

Lisel Mueller, "American Literature" from *Alive Together: New and Selected Poems.* Copyright © 1996 by Lisel Mueller. Reprinted by permission of the publisher, Louisiana State University Press.

Bharati Mukherjee, "A Father." Copyright © 1985 by Bharati Mukherjee. Originally published in *Darkness.* Reprinted by permission of the author.

Pablo Neruda, "Sweetness, Always" from *Extravagaria* by Pablo Neruda, translated by Alastair Reed. Translation copyright © 1974 by Alastair Reed. Reprinted by permission of Farrar, Straus and Giroux, LLC.

Joyce Carol Oates, "Where Are You Going, Where Have You Been?" from *The Wheel of Love and Other Stories.* Copyright © 1970 Ontario Review. Reprinted by permission of John Hawkins & Associates, Inc.

Tim O'Brien, "The Things They Carried" from *The Things They Carried.* Copyright © 1990 by Tim O'Brien. Reprinted by permission of Houghton Mifflin Harcourt Publishing Company. All rights reserved.

Flannery O'Connor, "Good Country People" from *A Good Man Is Hard to Find and Other Stories.* Copyright 1955 by Flannery O'Connor and renewed 1983 by Regina O'Connor. Reprinted by permission of Houghton Mifflin Harcourt Publishing Company.

Flannery O'Connor, "A Good Man Is Hard to Find" from *A Good Man Is Hard to Find and Other Stories.* Copyright 1953 by Flannery O'Connor and renewed 1981 by Regina O'Connor. Reprinted by permission of Houghton Mifflin Harcourt Publishing Company.

Frank O'Connor, "My Oedipus Complex" from *The Collected Stories of Frank O'Connor.* Copyright © 1981 by Harriet O'Donovan Sheehy, Executrix of the Estate of Frank O'Connor. Used by permission of Alfred A. Knopf, a division of Random House, Inc., and used by permission of The Jennifer Lyons Literary Agency as agent for the proprietor.

Dwight Okita, "In Response to Executive Order 9066" from *Crossing with the Light.* Copyright © 1992 by Dwight Okita. Reprinted by permission of the author.

Sharon Olds, "Sex Without Love" and "The Death of Marilyn Monroe" from *The Dead and the Living.* Copyright © 1987 by Sharon Olds. Used by permission of Alfred A. Knopf, a division of Random House, Inc.

Mary Oliver, "Black Snake" from *Twelve Moons* by Mary Oliver. Copyright © 1972, 1973, 1974, 1976, 1977, 1978, 1979 by Mary Oliver. Reprinted by permission of Little, Brown and Company, Inc.

Tillie Olson, "I Stand Here Ironing" from *Tell Me a Riddle.* Copyright 1956, 1957, 1960, 1961 by Tillie Olson. Reprinted by permission of Elaine Markson Literary Agency, Inc.

Daniel Orozco, "Orientation" as published in *Best American Short Stories 1995,* first appeared in *Seattle Review,* 1995. Reprinted by permission of the author.

Wilfred Owen, "Dulce et Decorum Est," 1921.

Dorothy Parker, "One Perfect Rose," copyright 1926, renewed © 1954 by Dorothy Parker, from *The Portable Dorothy Parker* by Dorothy Parker, edited by Marion Meade. Used by permission of Viking Penguin, a division of Penguin Group (USA) Inc.

Linda Pastan, "Marks." Copyright © 1978 by Linda Pastan, from *PM/AM: New and Selected Poems* by Linda Pastan. Used by permission of W.W. Norton & Company, Inc.

Octavio Paz, "The Street" from *Early Poems 1935–1955.* © 1963, 1973 by Octavio Paz and Muriel Rukeyser. Reprinted with permission of Indiana University Press.

Peter Pereira, "Reconsidering the Seven" from *What's Written on the Body.* Copyright © 2007 by Peter Pereira. Reprinted with the permission of Copper Canyon Press, www.coppercanyonpress.org.

Marge Piercy, "Barbie Doll" from *Circles on the Water.* Copyright © 1982 by Marge Piercy. Used by permission of Alfred A. Knopf, a division of Random House, Inc.

Sylvia Plath, "Mirror" from *Crossing the Water* by Sylvia Plath. Copyright © 1963 by Ted Hughes. Originally appeared in *The New Yorker.* Reprinted by permission of HarperCollins Publishers and by permission of Faber and Faber Ltd.

Edgar Allen Poe, "The Cask of Amontillado," 1846.

Katherine Anne Porter, "The Grave" from *The Leaning Tower and Other Stories.* Copyright 1944 and renewed 1972 by Katherine Anne Porter. Reprinted by permission of Houghton Mifflin Harcourt Publishing Company.

Craig Raine, "A Martian Sends a Postcard Home" from *A Martian Sends a Postcard Home.* Oxford University Press, 1979. Reprinted by permission of David Godwin Associates Ltd.

Sir Walter Raleigh, "The Nymph's Reply to the Shepherd," 1600.

Dudley Randall, "Ballad of Birmingham" from *Poem Counterpoem.* Broadside Press, 1966. Reprinted by permission of Melba Joyce Boyd, Literary Executor.

Dudley Randall, "To the Mercy Killers" from *After the Killing.* Copyright © 1973. Reprinted by permission.

"Aunt Jennifer's Tigers," copyright © 2002, 1951 by Adrienne Rich and "Living in Sin," copyright © 2002, 1955 by Adrienne Rich, from *The Fact of a Doorframe: Selected Poems 1950–2001* by Adrienne Rich. Used by permission of the author and W.W. Norton & Company, Inc.

Frank Rich, "Theater: Family Ties in Wilson's *Fences*," *New York Times,* March 27, 1987.

Alberto Ríos, "In Second Grade Miss Lee I Promised Never to Forget You and I Never Did" from *The Smallest Muscle in the Human Body.* Copyright © 2002 by Albert Rios. Reprinted with permission of Copper Canyon Press, www.coppercanyonpress.org.

Edwin Arlington Robinson, "Richard Cory," 1896.

Theodore Roethke, "My Papa's Waltz," copyright 1942 by Hearst Magazines, Inc., "I Knew a Woman," copyright 1954 by Theodore Roethke, from *Collected Poems of Theodore Roethke* by Theodore Roethke. Used by permission of Doubleday, a division of Random House, Inc.

Larry Rubin, "Oates's 'Where Are You Going, Where Have You Been,'" *Explicator,* 42, pp. 57–59, 1984. Reprinted with permission of the Helen Dwight Reid Educational Foundation. Published by Heldref Publications, 1319 Eighteenth St., NW, Washington, DC 20036–1802. Copyright © 1984.

Kay Ryan, "Turtle" from *Flamingo Watching.* © 1994 by Kay Ryan. Used by permission of Copper Beach Press.

Carl Sandburg, "Chicago" and "Fog" from *Chicago Poems.* Copyright 1916 by Holt, Rinehart, and Winston and renewed 1944 by Carl Sandburg. Reprinted by permission of Houghton Mifflin Harcourt Publishing Company.

Carl Sandburg, "Grass" from *Cornhuskers.* Copyright 1918 by Holt, Rinehart, and Winston and renewed 1946 by Carl Sandurg. Reprinted by permission of Houghton Mifflin Harcourt Publishing Company.

May Sarton, "AIDS" from *The Silence Now: New and Uncollected Earlier Poems* by May Sarton. Copyright © 1988 by May Sarton. Used by permission of W.W. Norton & Company, Inc.

David Sedaris, "Nuit of the Living Dead" from *Dress Your Family in Corduroy and Denim* by David Sedaris. Copyright © 2004 by David Sedaris. By permission of Little, Brown & Company.

Anne Sexton, "The Starry Night" from *All My Pretty Ones.* Copyright © 1962 by Anne Sexton, renewed 1990 by Linda G. Sexton. Reprinted by permission of Houghton Mifflin Harcourt Publishing Company. All rights reserved.

Anne Sexton, "You All Know the Story of the Other Woman" from *Love Poems.* Copyright © 1967, 1968, 1969 by Anne Sexton. Reprinted by permission of Houghton Mifflin Harcourt Publishing Company. All rights reserved.

William Shakespeare, *Othello, The Moor of Venice,* 1604.

William Shakespeare, "Shall I Compare Thee to a Summer's Day?" "When in Disgrace with Fortune and Men's Eyes," "Let Me Not to the Marriage of True Minds," "That Time of year Thou Mayst in Me behold," "My Mistress' Eyes Are Nothing Like the Sun," 1609.

Karl Shapiro, "Auto Wreck" from *Collected Poems 1940–1978.* Copyright © Karl Shapiro. Used by permission of Wieser & Wieser, Inc.

Percy Bysshe Shelley, "Ozymandias," 1817.

Paul Simon, "Richard Cory." Copyright © 1966 by Paul Simon. Reprinted with permission of the publisher, Paul Simon Music.

David R. Slavitt, "Titanic" from *Big Nose.* Copyright © 1983 by David R. Slavitt. Reprinted by permission of the publisher, Louisiana State University Press.

Stevie Smith, "Not Waving But Drowning" from *Collected Poems of Stevie Smith.* Copyright © 1972 by Stevie Smith. Reprinted by permission of New Directions Publishing Corp.

Mary Ellen Snodgrass, *August Wilson: A Literary Companion.* Jefferson, NC: McFarland & Co., 2004.

W.D. Snodgrass, "Matisse: The Red Studio" from *Selected Poems 1957–87* (Soho Press, 1987). Originally appeared in *After Experience: Poems and Translations* (Harper & Row, 1968). Reprinted by permission by Kathleen Snodgrass.

Cathy Song, "Beauty and Sadness" from *Picture Bride.* Copyright © 1983, Yale University Press. Reprinted by permission of Yale University Press.

Sophocles, "Antigone" from *Three Theban Plays* by Sophocles, translated by Robert Fagles. Copyright © 1982 by Robert Fagles. Used by permission of Viking Penguin, a division of Penguin Group (USA) Inc.

Wole Soyinka, "Telephone Conversation." Copyright © 1962, 1990 by Wole Soyinka. Reprinted with permission by Melanie Jackson Agency, LLC.

Gabriel Spera, "My Ex-Husband," *Poetry,* 159: 5, February 1992. Reprinted by permission.

William Stafford, "Traveling Through the Dark" from *Stories That Could Be True.* New York: Harper & Row, 1977. Reprinted by permission of Kim Stafford.

Brent Staples, "*Fences:* No Barrier to Emotion," *The New York Times,* April 5, 1987.

John Steinbeck, "The Chrysanthemums," copyright 1937, renewed © 1965 by John Steinbeck from *The Long Valley* by John Steinbeck. Used by permission of Viking Penguin, a division of Penguin Group (USA), Inc.

Wislaw Szmborska, "End and Beginning" translated by Joseph Brodsky from *Collected Poems in English* by Joseph Brodsky. Copyright © 2000 by the Estate of Joseph Brodsky. Reprinted by permission of Farrar, Straus and Giroux, LLC.

Dylan Thomas, "Do Not Go Gentle into That Good Night," copyright 1952 by Dylan Thomas and "The Force That Through the Green Fuse Drives the Flower," copyright 1989 by New Directions Publishing Corp., from *The Poems of Dylan Thomas.* Reprinted by permission of New Directions Publishing Corp.

Mike Tierce and John Michael Crafton, excerpt from "Connie's Tambourine Man: A New Reading of Arnold Friend," *Studies in Short Fiction*, Vol. 22 (Spring 1985). Reprinted by permission.

Jean Toomer, "Reapers" from *Cane* by Jean Toomer. Copyright 1923 by Boni & Liveright, renewed 1951 by Jean Toomer. Used by permission of Liveright Publishing Corporation.

Peter Townsend, *Jazz in American Culture.* Jackson, Miss: University Press of Mississippi, 2000.

John Updike, "A & P" from *Pigeon Feathers and Other Stories.* Copyright © 1962 and renewed 1990 by John Updike. Used by permission of Alfred A. Knopf, a division of Random House, Inc.

John Updike, "Ex Basketball Player" from *Collected Poems 1953–1993.* Copyright © 1993 by John Updike. Used by permission of Alfred A. Knopf, a division of Random House, Inc.

Gina Valdes, "My Mother Sews Blouses" from *Comiendo/Eating Fire* (Colorado Springs, CO: Maize Press, 1986). Reprinted by permission of the author.

Luis Valdez. "Los Vendidos" is reprinted with permission from the publisher from *Luis Valdez—Early Works* by Luis Valdez. © 1971 Arte Público Press–University of Houston.

Alice Walker, "Everyday Use" from *In Love & Trouble: Stories of Black Women.* Copyright © 1973 by Alice Walker. Reprinted by permission of Houghton Mifflin Harcourt Publishing Company.

Edmund Waller, "Go Lovely, Rose," 1645.

Joyce Wegs, excerpt from *Journal of Narrative Technique* 5, 1975.

Eudora Welty, "Why I Live at the P.O." from *A Curtain of Green and Other Stories.* Copyright 1941 and renewed 1969 by Eudora Welty. Reprinted by permission of Houghton Mifflin Harcourt Publishing Company.

Walt Whitman, "When I Heard the Learn'd Astronomer," 1865, "A Noiseless Patient Spider," 1881, "Song of Myself," 1881.

Richard Wilbur, "Love Calls Us to the Things of This World" from *Things of This World.* Copyright 1956 and renewed 1984 by Richard Wilbur. Reprinted by permission of Houghton Mifflin Publishing Company.

William Carlos Williams, "Danse Russe" and "The Red Wheelbarrow" from *Collected Poems: Volume I, 1909–1939.* Copyright 1938 by New Directions Publishing Corp. Reprinted by permission of New Directions Publishing Corp.

August Wilson, from *Fences* by August Wilson. Copyright © 1986 by August Wilson. Used by permission of Dutton Signet, a division of Penguin Group (USA) Inc.

August Wilson/David Savran, in an interview with August Wilson, *In Their Own Words: Contemporary American Playwrights.* New York: Theatre Communications Group, 1988.

Tobias Wolff, "Hunters in the Snow" from *In the Garden of the North American Martyrs* by Tobias Wolff. Copyright © 1981 by Tobias Wolff. Reprinted by permission of HarperCollins Publishers. Ecco Press.

William Wordsworth, "The World Is Too Much with Us," 1807.

Richard Wright, excerpt from "Forerunner and Ambassador" from *The New Republic*, 103, October 1940. Copyright 1940 Richard Wright. Reprinted by permission of John Hawkins & Associates.

Richard Wright, "The Man Who Was Almost a Man" from *Eight Men* by Richard Wright. Copyright 1940, © 1961 by Richard Wright; renewed © 1989 by Ellen Wright. Introduction © 1996 by Paul Gilroy. Reprinted by permission of HarperCollins Publishers.

Thomas Wyatt, "They Flee from Me," c. 1530.

Hisaye Yamamoto, "Seventeen Syllables" from *Seventeen Syllables.* Latham, NY: Kitchen Table: Women of Color Press, 1988. Reprinted by permission.

William Butler Yeats, "The Second Coming," 1921.

William Butler Yeats, "Sailing to Byzantium." Reprinted with permission from Scribner, a Division of Simon & Schuster, Inc., from *The Collected Works of W.B. Yeats, Volume I: The Poems, Revised,* edited by Richard J. Finneran. Copyright 1928 by The Macmillan Company. Copyright renewed © 1956 by Georgie Yeats. All rights reserved.

Samuel Yellen, "Nighthawks." Reprinted from *Commentary*, November 1951, by permission. All Rights Reserved.

PHOTO CREDITS

Page 5: The Irish Architectural Archive; **p. 123:** Kyoichi Sawada/CORBIS; **p. 162:** The Newark Museum/Art Resource; **p. 223:** Picture Desk, Inc./Kobal Collection; **p. 323:** Loomis Dean Getty Images/Time Life Pictures; **p. 360:** Alamy Images; **p. 416:** Picture Desk, Inc./Kobal Collection; **p. 490:** Esbin/Anderson Omni-Photo Communications, Inc.; **p. 506:** Getty Images Inc./Stone Allstock; **p. 527:** Art Resource/The New York Public Library; **p. 531:** Art Kane; **p. 628:** Heloisa Passos/Getty Images; **p. 636:** Getty Images, Inc./AFP; **p. 639:** Cleve Bryant/PhotoEdit Inc.; **p. 648:** National Labor Committee; **p. 658:** Fred Mullane/CORBIS; **p. 660:** Frank Driggs Getty Images Inc./Hulton Archive Photos; **p. 676:** Hulton/Getty Images, Inc.; **p. 688:** Imperial War Museum, London; **p. 694:** Alan Schein Photography, Inc./CORBIS; **p. 696:** Dorothea Lange/CORBIS; **p. 723:** AP Wide World Photos; **p. 777:** Ron Scherl/The Image Works; **p. 823:** Ron Scherl/The Image Works; **p. 1023:** Photofest; **p. 1076:** Peter Stranks/Disney ABC Television Group; **p. 1096:** Derek Howard.

Index of Authors, Titles, and First Lines of Poems

Note: First lines are set in roman type; all titles are italicized

Subject Index